## Summary of the Audit Process

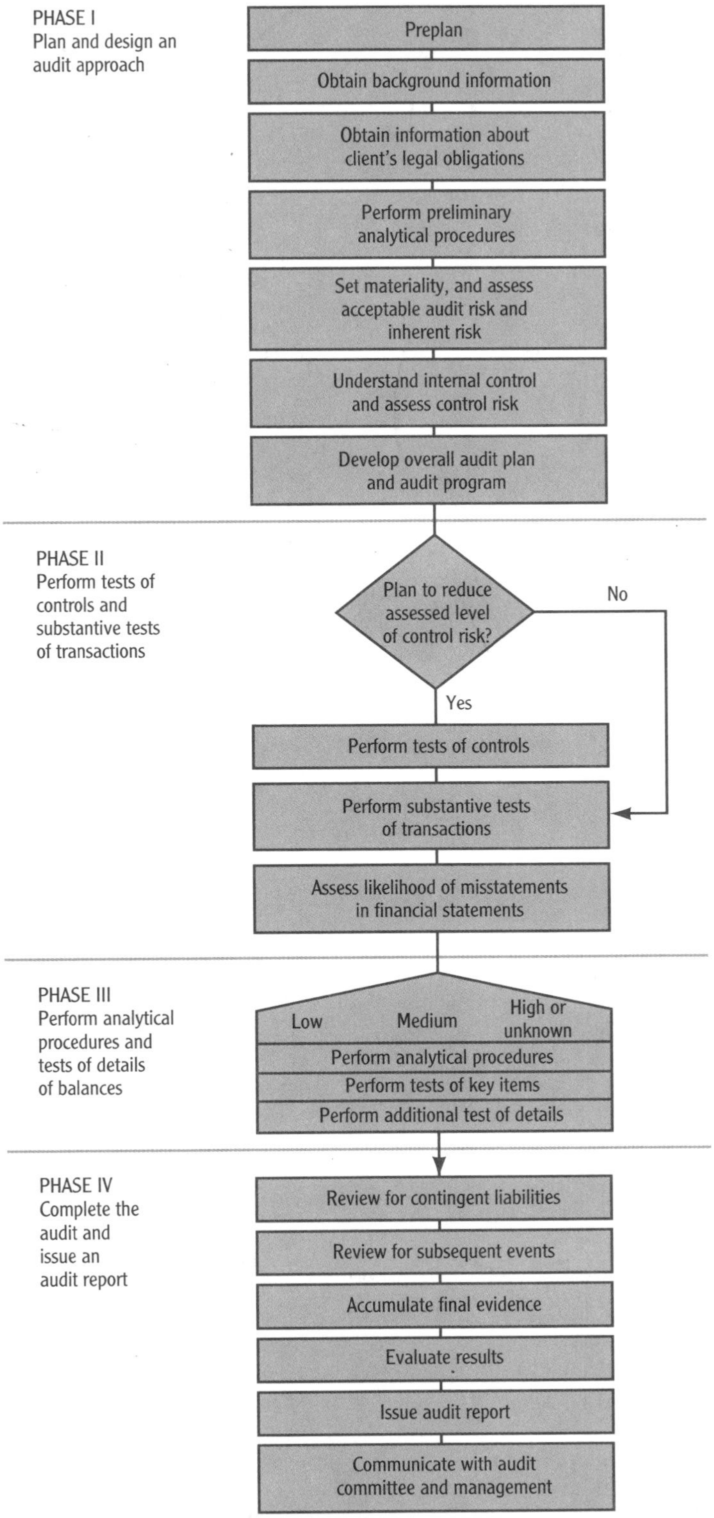

# AUDITING

## Prentice Hall Series in Accounting

***Charles T. Horngren, Consulting Editor***

AUDITING: AN INTEGRATED APPROACH, 7/E
Arens/Loebbecke

ADVANCED ACCOUNTING, 6/E
Beams

KOHLER'S DICTIONARY FOR ACCOUNTANTS, 6/E
Cooper/Ijiri

FINANICAL STATEMENT ANALYSIS, 2/E
Foster

GOVERNMENTAL AND NONPROFIT ACCOUNTING: THEORY AND PRACTICE, 5/E
Freeman/Shoulders

FINANCIAL ACCOUNTING, 2/E
Harrison/Horngren

CASES IN FINANCIAL REPORTING
Hirst/McAnally

COST ACCOUNTING: A MANAGERIAL EMPHASIS, 9/E
Horngren/Foster/Datar

ACCOUNTING, 3/E
Horngren/Harrison/Robinson

PRINCIPLES OF FINANCIAL AND MANAGEMENT ACCOUNTING: A CORPORATE APPROACH
Horngren/Harrison/Robinson

PRINCIPLES OF FINANCIAL AND MANAGEMENT ACCOUNTING: A SOLE PROPRIETORSHIP APPROACH
Horngren/Harrison/Robinson

INTRODUCTION TO FINANCIAL ACCOUNTING, 6/E
Horngren/Sundem/Elliott

INTRODUCTION TO MANAGEMENT ACCOUNTING, 10/E
Horngren/Sundem/Stratton

INTRODUCTION TO FINANCIAL ACCOUNTING
Jones /Price/Werner/Doran

BUDGETING: PROFIT PLANNING AND CONTROL 5/E
Welsch/Hilton, Gordon

# AUDITING
## An Integrated Approach
### Seventh Edition

**Alvin A. Arens**
*Price Waterhouse*
*Auditing Professor*
*Michigan State University*

**James K. Loebbecke**
*Kenneth A. Sorensen*
*Peat Marwick Professor of Accounting*
*University of Utah*

Prentice Hall, Upper Saddle River, New Jersey 07458

*Acquisitions Editor:* Annie Todd
*Executive Editor:* P.J. Boardman
*Associate Editor:* Natacha St. Hill
*Editorial Assistant:* Elaine Oyzon-Mast
*Editor-in-Chief:* Richard Wohl
*Production Coordinator:* David Cotugno
*Managing Editor:* Katherine Evancie
*Manufacturing Buyer:* Alana Zdinak
*Senior Manufacturing Supervisor:* Paul Smolenski
*Manufacturing Manager:* Vincent Scelta
*Senior Designer:* Suzanne Behnke
*Interior Design:* Dorothy Bungert
*Cover Design:* Suzanne Behnke
*Composition:* TSI Graphics
*Cover Art:* Marjory Dressler
*Marketing Manager:* Deborah Hoffman Emry



Printed in the United States of America

10 9 8 7 6 5 4 3

ISBN 0-13-649385-8

Prentice-Hall International (UK) Limited, *London*
Prentice-Hall of Australia Pty. Limited, *Sydney*
Prentice-Hall Canada Inc., *Toronto*
Prentice-Hall Hispanoamericana, S.A., *Mexico*
Prentice-Hall of India Private Limited, *New Delhi*
Prentice-Hall of Japan, Inc., *Tokyo*
Simon & Schuster Asia Pte. Ltd., *Singapore*
Editora Prentice-Hall do Brasil, Ltda., *Rio de Janeiro*

# CONTENTS

Preface xv

**PART 1 THE AUDITING PROFESSION**

*1* **The Auditing Profession 1**

LEARNING OBJECTIVES 1
Nature of Auditing 2
Distinction between Auditing and Accounting 4
Types of Audits 4
Types of Auditors 6
Economic Demand for Auditing 7
Certified Public Accountant 10
Certified Public Accounting Firms 11
Activities of CPA Firms 13
Structure of CPA Firms 14
AICPA 15
Ways CPAs Are Encouraged to Perform Effectively 17
Generally Accepted Auditing Standards 17
Statements on Auditing Standards 18
Quality Control 21
Securities and Exchange Commission 24
ESSENTIAL TERMS 25
REVIEW QUESTIONS 26
MULTIPLE CHOICE QUESTIONS FROM CPA EXAMINATIONS 27
DISCUSSION QUESTIONS AND PROBLEMS 29

*2* **Audit Reports 35**

LEARNING OBJECTIVES 35
Standard Unqualified Audit Report 37
Categories of Audit Reports 39
Unqualified Audit Report with Explanatory Paragraph or Modified Wording 40
Conditions Requiring a Departure from an Unqualified Audit Report 44
Audit Reports Other than Unqualified 45
Materiality 45
Discussion of Conditions Requiring a Departure 48
More than One Condition Requiring a Departure or Modification 53

Number of Paragraphs in the Report 53
Negative Assurances 53
Auditor's Decision Process for Audit Reports 54
ESSENTIAL TERMS 55
REVIEW QUESTIONS 55
MULTIPLE CHOICE QUESTIONS FROM CPA EXAMINATIONS 56
DISCUSSION QUESTIONS AND PROBLEMS 57
CASE 64

3 **Professional Ethics 67**

LEARNING OBJECTIVES 67
What Are Ethics? 68
Ethics in Business 70
Ethical Dilemmas 71
Special Need for Ethical Conduct in Professions 74
Ways CPAs Are Encouraged to Conduct Themselves Professionally 75
Code of Professional Conduct 75
Independence 80
Integrity and Objectivity 86
Technical Standards 86
Confidentiality 87
Contingent Fees 89
Discreditable Acts 89
Advertising and Solicitation 90
Commissions and Referral Fees 91
Form of Organization and Name 92
Enforcement 93
ESSENTIAL TERMS 94
REVIEW QUESTIONS 94
MULTIPLE CHOICE QUESTIONS FROM CPA EXAMINATIONS 95
DISCUSSION QUESTIONS AND PROBLEMS 96
CASES 99

4 **Legal Liability 105**

LEARNING OBJECTIVES 105
Changed Legal Environment 106
Distinction among Business Failure, Audit Failure, and Audit Risk 107
Legal Concepts Affecting Liability 109
Definitions of Legal Terms 110
Liability to Clients 111
Liability to Third Parties under Common Law 113
Civil Liability under the Federal Securities Laws 116
Criminal Liability 121

The Profession's Response to Legal Liability 123
The Individual CPA's Response to Legal Liability 124
SUMMARY 125
ESSENTIAL TERMS 126
REVIEW QUESTIONS 127
MULTIPLE CHOICE QUESTIONS FROM CPA EXAMINATIONS 128
DISCUSSION QUESTIONS AND PROBLEMS 130
CASES 134

**PART 2 THE AUDITING PROCESS**

**5 Audit Responsibilities and Objectives 137**

LEARNING OBJECTIVES 137
Objective of Conducting an Audit of Financial Statements 142
Management's Responsibilities 142
Auditor's Responsibilities 142
Financial Statement Cycles 148
Setting Audit Objectives 151
Transaction-Related Audit Objectives 153
Balance-Related Audit Objectives 154
How Audit Objectives Are Met 157
SUMMARY 160
ESSENTIAL TERMS 160
REVIEW QUESTIONS 161
MULTIPLE CHOICE QUESTIONS FROM CPA EXAMINATIONS 162
DISCUSSION QUESTIONS AND PROBLEMS 163
CASE 175

**6 Audit Evidence 177**

LEARNING OBJECTIVES 177
Nature of Evidence 178
Audit Evidence Decisions 179
Persuasiveness of Evidence 180
Types of Audit Evidence 183
Terms Used in Audit Procedures 189
Analytical Procedures 190
Purposes and Timing of Analytical Procedures 191
Five Types of Analytical Procedures 193
Using Statistical Techniques and Computer Software 196
Appendix A: Common Financial Ratios 198
Short-Term Debt-Paying Ability 198
Short-Term Liquidity 199
Ability to Meet Long-Term Debt Obligations and Preferred Dividends 200
Operating and Performance Ratios 200

Illustration 202
Essential Terms 203
Review Questions 204
Multiple Choice Questions from CPA Examinations 205
Discussion Questions and Problems 206
Case 214

7 **Audit Planning and Documentation 217**
Learning Objectives 217
Planning 218
Preplan the Audit 220
Obtain Background Information 223
Obtain Information about Client's Legal Obligations 225
Perform Preliminary Analytical Procedures 227
Summary of the Purposes of Audit Planning 227
Working Papers 229
Summary of Working Papers 236
Essential Terms 236
Review Questions 237
Multiple Choice Questions from CPA Examinations 238
Discussion Questions and Problems 241
Case 245

8 **Materiality and Risk 247**
Learning Objectives 247
Materiality 248
Set Preliminary Judgment about Materiality 249
Allocate Preliminary Judgment about Materiality to Segments (Tolerable Misstatement) 252
Estimate Misstatement and Compare 254
Risk 255
Inherent Risk 261
Other Materiality and Risk Considerations 265
Evaluating Results 268
Summary 271
Essential Terms 272
Review Questions 272
Multiple Choice Questions from CPA Examinations 274
Discussion Questions and Problems 275
Cases 282

9 **The Study of Internal Control and Assessment of Control Risk 289**
Learning Objectives 289
Client and Auditor Concerns 290

Key Concepts 293
Method of Data Processing 294
Components of Internal Control 294
The Control Environment 294
Risk Assessment 296
Control Activities 296
Information and Communication 300
Monitoring 300
Overview of Obtaining an Understanding of Internal Control and Assessing Control Risk 301
Procedures to Obtain an Understanding 307
Assess Control Risk 310
Tests of Controls 313
ESSENTIAL TERMS 316
REVIEW QUESTIONS 317
MULTIPLE CHOICE QUESTIONS FROM CPA EXAMINATIONS 318
DISCUSSION QUESTIONS AND PROBLEMS 320
CASE 324
INTEGRATED CASE APPLICATION 324

**10** **Overall Audit Plan and Audit Program 329**

LEARNING OBJECTIVES 329
Types of Tests 330
Relationship Between Tests and Evidence 335
Evidence Mix 337
Design of the Audit Program 339
Summary of the Audit Process 346
ESSENTIAL TERMS 350
REVIEW QUESTIONS 350
MULTIPLE CHOICE QUESTIONS FROM CPA EXAMINATIONS 352
DISCUSSION QUESTIONS AND PROBLEMS 354
CASES 359

**PART 3 APPLICATION OF THE AUDITING PROCESS TO THE SALES AND COLLECTION CYCLE**

**11** **Audit of the Sales and Collection Cycle: Tests of Controls and Substantive Tests of Transactions 363**

LEARNING OBJECTIVES 363
Nature of the Sales and Collection Cycle 365
Business Functions in the Cycle and Related Documents and Records 365
Methodology for Designing Tests of Controls and Substantive Tests of Transactions for Sales 369
Sales Returns and Allowances 377

Internal Controls, Tests of Controls, and Substantive Tests of Transactions for Cash Receipts 378
Audit Tests for Uncollectible Accounts 380
Additional Internal Controls Over Account Balances 380
Effect of Results of Tests of Controls and Substantive Tests of Transactions 381
Case Illustration—Hillsburg Hardware, Part I 382
ESSENTIAL TERMS 390
REVIEW QUESTIONS 391
MULTIPLE CHOICE QUESTIONS FROM CPA EXAMINATIONS 392
DISCUSSION QUESTIONS AND PROBLEMS 393
CASE 400
INTEGRATED CASE APPLICATION 401

## 12 Audit Sampling for Tests of Controls and Substantive Tests of Transactions 403

LEARNING OBJECTIVES 403
Representative Samples 404
Statistical Versus Nonstatistical Sampling 405
Nonprobabilistic Sample Selection 407
Probabilistic Sample Selection 408
Sampling for Exception Rates 411
Application of Nonstatistical Audit Sampling 412
Attributes Sampling 420
Sampling Distribution 421
Application of Attributes Sampling 422
Other Considerations 426
Case Illustration—Hillsburg Hardware, Part II 427
ESSENTIAL TERMS 434
REVIEW QUESTIONS 435
MULTIPLE CHOICE QUESTIONS FROM CPA EXAMINATIONS 436
DISCUSSION QUESTIONS AND PROBLEMS 437
CASE 442
INTEGRATED CASE APPLICATION 442

## 13 Completing the Tests in the Sales and Collection Cycle: Accounts Receivable 445

LEARNING OBJECTIVES 445
Methodology for Designing Tests of Details of Balances 446
Accounts Receivable Balance-Related Audit Objectives 447
Tests of Details of Balances 452
Confirmation of Accounts Receivable 456
Case Illustration—Hillsburg Hardware—Part III 462
ESSENTIAL TERMS 466
REVIEW QUESTIONS 467

MULTIPLE CHOICE QUESTIONS FROM CPA EXAMINATIONS 468
DISCUSSION QUESTIONS AND PROBLEMS 469
CASE 475
INTEGRATED CASE APPLICATION 476

**14 Audit Sampling for Tests of Details of Balances 483**

LEARNING OBJECTIVES 483
Comparisons of Audit Sampling for Tests of Details of Balances and for Tests of Controls and Substantive Tests of Transactions 484
Nonstatistical Sampling 485
Monetary Unit Sampling 492
Variables Sampling 503
Illustration Using Difference Estimation 508
Appendix A: Formulas for Monetary Unit Sampling 514
ESSENTIAL TERMS 516
REVIEW QUESTIONS 517
MULTIPLE CHOICE QUESTIONS FROM CPA EXAMINATIONS 518
DISCUSSION QUESTIONS AND PROBLEMS 519
CASES 524

**PART 4 AUDITING COMPLEX EDP SYSTEMS**

**15 Auditing Complex EDP Systems 527**

LEARNING OBJECTIVES 527
Complexity of EDP Systems 528
Effect of EDP on Organizations 531
EDP Controls 533
Understanding Internal Control in an EDP Environment 536
Auditing Around the Computer 536
Auditing with Use of the Computer 537
Generalized Audit Software 540
Microcomputer-Aided Auditing 545
Audit of Computer Service Centers 548
ESSENTIAL TERMS 548
REVIEW QUESTIONS 549
MULTIPLE CHOICE QUESTIONS FROM CPA EXAMINATIONS 550
DISCUSSION QUESTIONS AND PROBLEMS 551

**PART 5 APPLICATION OF THE AUDITING PROCESS TO OTHER CYCLES**

**16 Audit of the Payroll and Personnel Cycle 555**

LEARNING OBJECTIVES 555
Functions in the Cycle, Related Documents and Records, and Internal Controls 557

Tests of Controls and Substantive Tests of Transactions 560
Analytical Procedures 565
Tests of Details of Balances for Liability and Expense Accounts 565
Summary 568
ESSENTIAL TERMS 569
REVIEW QUESTIONS 569
MULTIPLE CHOICE QUESTIONS FROM CPA EXAMINATIONS 570
DISCUSSION QUESTIONS AND PROBLEMS 571
CASE 577

**17 Audit of the Acquisition and Payment Cycle: Tests of Controls, Substantive Tests of Transactions, and Accounts Payable 579**

LEARNING OBJECTIVES 579
Nature of the Cycle 580
Tests of Controls and Substantive Tests of Transactions 584
Accounts Payable 590
Summary 597
ESSENTIAL TERMS 598
REVIEW QUESTIONS 598
MULTIPLE CHOICE QUESTIONS FROM CPA EXAMINATIONS 599
DISCUSSION QUESTIONS AND PROBLEMS 600
CASES 607

**18 Completing the Tests in the Acquisition and Payment Cycle: Verification of Selected Accounts 611**

LEARNING OBJECTIVES 611
Audit of Manufacturing Equipment 613
Audit of Prepaid Expenses 620
Audit of Accrued Liabilities 624
Audit of Operations 626
ESSENTIAL TERMS 631
REVIEW QUESTIONS 631
MULTIPLE CHOICE QUESTIONS FROM CPA EXAMINATIONS 632
DISCUSSION QUESTIONS AND PROBLEMS 634
CASES 637

**19 Audit of the Inventory and Warehousing Cycle 641**

LEARNING OBJECTIVES 641
Functions in the Cycle and Internal Controls 643
Parts of the Audit of Inventory 644
Audit of Cost Accounting 646
Analytical Procedures 649

Tests of Details for Inventory 649
Physical Observation of Inventory 650
Audit of Pricing and Compilation 653
Integration of the Tests 657
ESSENTIAL TERMS 659
REVIEW QUESTIONS 659
MULTIPLE CHOICE QUESTIONS FROM CPA EXAMINATIONS 660
DISCUSSION QUESTIONS AND PROBLEMS 662
CASES 669

**20 Audit of the Capital Acquisition and Repayment Cycle 673**

LEARNING OBJECTIVES 673
Notes Payable 675
Owners' Equity 678
ESSENTIAL TERMS 687
REVIEW QUESTIONS 687
MULTIPLE CHOICE QUESTIONS FROM CPA EXAMINATIONS 688
DISCUSSION QUESTIONS AND PROBLEMS 689

**21 Audit of Cash Balances 695**

LEARNING OBJECTIVES 695
Types of Cash Accounts 696
Cash in the Bank and Transaction Cycles 697
Audit of the General Cash Account 699
Audit of the Payroll Bank Account 710
Audit of Petty Cash 710
ESSENTIAL TERMS 711
REVIEW QUESTIONS 712
MULTIPLE CHOICE QUESTIONS FROM CPA EXAMINATIONS 713
DISCUSSION QUESTIONS AND PROBLEMS 714
CASE 721

**PART 6 COMPLETING THE AUDIT AND OFFERING OTHER SERVICES**

**22 Completing the Audit 723**

LEARNING OBJECTIVES 723
Review for Contingent Liabilities and Commitments 724
Inquiry of Client's Attorneys 726
Review for Subsequent Events 729
Final Evidence Accumulation 731
Evaluate Results 733
Communicate with the Audit Committee and Management 739
Subsequent Discovery of Facts 740

ESSENTIAL TERMS 741
REVIEW QUESTIONS 742
MULTIPLE CHOICE QUESTIONS FROM CPA EXAMINATIONS 743
DISCUSSION QUESTIONS AND PROBLEMS 744
CASES 748

**23 Other Audit, Attestation Services, and Compilation Engagements 751**

LEARNING OBJECTIVES 751
Review and Compilation Services 752
Review of Interim Financial Information for Public Companies 757
Other Audits or Limited Assurance Engagements 759
Attestation Engagements 764
Prospective Financial Statements 767
Internal Control Over Financial Reporting 769
Compliance Attestation 771
Agreed-Upon Procedures Engagements 772
ESSENTIAL TERMS 774
REVIEW QUESTIONS 775
MULTIPLE CHOICE QUESTIONS FROM CPA EXAMINATIONS 776
DISCUSSION QUESTIONS AND PROBLEMS 779

**24 Internal and Governmental Financial Auditing and Operational Auditing 785**

LEARNING OBJECTIVES 785
Internal Financial Auditing 786
Governmental Financial Auditing 788
Operational Auditing 791
ESSENTIAL TERMS 801
REVIEW QUESTIONS 802
MULTIPLE CHOICE QUESTIONS FROM CPA, IIA, AND CMA EXAMINATIONS 802
CASES 805

**Index 813**

# PREFACE

## OBJECTIVES

The seventh edition of *Auditing: An Integrated Approach* contains numerous changes and revisions, but the objectives and emphasis remain essentially the same.

The book is an introduction to auditing for students who have not had significant experience in auditing. It is intended for either a one-quarter or one-semester course at the undergraduate or graduate level. The book is also appropriate for introductory professional development courses for CPA firms, internal auditors, and government auditors.

The primary emphasis in this text is on the auditor's decision-making process. We believe that the most fundamental concepts in auditing relate to determining the nature and amount of evidence the auditor should accumulate after considering the unique circumstances of each engagement. If a student of auditing understands the objectives to be accomplished in a given audit area, the circumstances of the engagement, and the decisions to be made, he or she should be able to determine the appropriate evidence to gather and how to evaluate the evidence obtained.

Thus, as the title of the book reflects, our purpose is to integrate the most important concepts of auditing as well as certain practical aspects in a logical manner to assist students in understanding audit decision making and evidence accumulation. For example, internal control is integrated into each of the chapters dealing with a particular functional area and is related to tests of controls and substantive tests of transactions; tests of controls and substantive tests of transactions are, in turn, related to the tests of details of financial statement balances for the area; and audit sampling is applied to the accumulation of audit evidence rather than treated as a separate topic.

To enhance students' understanding of the auditor's decision-making process, a new feature of the seventh edition is the addition of vignettes to each chapter. Each chapter begins with an opening vignette that describes a realistic scenario similar to one that students might encounter in audit practice. In addition, several vignettes appear throughout the chapters to provide students with practice examples, supplemental information, and technology updates related to chapter material.

## ORGANIZATION

The text is divided into six parts.

**Part 1, The Auditing Profession (Chapters 1–4)** The book begins with a description of the nature of auditing and auditing firms, the AICPA, and the SEC. In Chapter 2, there is a detailed discussion of audit reports. It emphasizes the conditions affecting the type of report the auditor must issue and the type of audit report applicable to each condition under varying levels of materiality. Chapter 3 explains ethical dilemmas, professional ethics, and the AICPA *Code of Professional Conduct.* Chapter 4 ends this part with an investigation of auditors' legal liability.

**Part 2, The Auditing Process (Chapters 5–10)** The first two of these chapters deal with auditors' and managements' responsibilities, audit objectives, and general concepts of evidence accumulation. In addition, Chapter 6 emphasizes analytical procedures as an audit tool.

Chapter 7 deals with planning the engagement and the preparation of audit working papers. Chapter 8 introduces materiality and risk, and shows their effect on the audit. The study of internal control and assessment of control risk are discussed in Chapter 9, which emphasizes a proper methodology for obtaining an understanding of the five components of internal control. Chapter 10 summarizes Chapters 5 through 9 and integrates them with the remainder of the text.

**Part 3, Application of the Auditing Process to the Sales and Collection Cycle (Chapters 11–14)** These chapters apply the concepts from Part 2 to the audit of sales, cash receipts, and the related income statement and balance sheet accounts. The appropriate audit procedures for accounts in the sales and collection cycle are related to internal control and audit objectives for tests of controls, substantive tests of transactions, and tests of details of balances. Students learn to apply audit sampling to the audit of sales, cash receipts, and accounts receivable.

In response to various instructors' comments, we have reorganized Chapters 12 and 14 on audit sampling. Each chapter now begins with a general discussion of audit sampling for tests of controls and substantive tests of transactions (Chapter 12) and tests of details of balances (Chapter 14). The next topic covered in each chapter is nonstatistical sampling. This topic has been expanded significantly in the seventh edition in response to instructors' requests. The last part of each chapter covers statistical sampling techniques.

**Part 4, Auditing Complex EDP Systems (Chapter 15)** This chapter covers understanding internal control and assessing control risk for more complex EDP systems, the audit of systems that include significant EDP applications, and auditing with or without the use of the computer. The emphasis in this chapter is on the effect of a more complex EDP system on the way an audit is conducted.

**Part 5, Application of the Auditing Process to Other Cycles (Chapters 16–21)** Each of these chapters deals with a specific transaction cycle or part of a transaction cycle in much the same manner as Chapters 11 through 14 deal with the sales and collection cycle. Each chapter in Part 5 is meant to demonstrate the relationship of internal control, tests of controls, and substantive tests of transactions for each broad category of transactions to the related balance sheet and income statement accounts. Cash in the bank is studied late in the text to demonstrate how the audit of cash balances is related to most other audit areas.

**Part 6, Completing the Audit and Offering Other Services (Chapters 22–24)** This set of chapters begins with summarizing all audit tests, reviewing working papers and other aspects of completing the audit. The remaining two chapters deal with various types of engagements and reports, other than the audit of financial statements using generally accepted accounting principles. Topics covered include review and compilation services, other audit engagements, attestation engagements, agreed-upon procedures engagements, internal financial auditing, governmental financial auditing, and operational auditing.

## SUPPLEMENTS

### Service for the Instructor

**The Prentice Hall Accounting and Taxation Hotline 1-800-227-1816** Prentice Hall's unique Accounting and Taxation Hotline is your direct link to satisfying all your adoption needs! By calling our toll-free telephone number, you can receive information on Prentice Hall's Accounting and Tax texts and supplements. The Hotline will also process your orders and keep you up-to-date on the upcoming Prentice Hall Accounting Seminars for Educators (PHASE) in your area.

## Several Supplements are Available for Faculty and/or Students' Use

**Instructor's Resource Manual** This integrated source assists the instructor in teaching the course. The features include Teaching Transparencies instructions for assignments, as well as helpful suggestions provided by the text authors on how to effectively teach each chapter. To enhance and simplify course planning, chapter Learning Objectives are integrated throughout the problem material. Identified in the problem material are **spreadsheet template related problems.** Refer to xix of the Instructions Resource Manual for alternative uses.

**Solutions Manual** This comprehensive resource provides detailed solutions to all the end-of-chapter review questions, multiple choice questions, problems, and cases.

**Test Item File—prepared by David Kerr of Texas A&M University** Completely revised for this edition, the Test Item File contains approximately 3,000 test items including true/false, multiple-choice, exercises/problems, critical thinking/essay, fill-in-the-blanks, short answer, questions adapted from CPA exams, and questions on the new chapter opening vignettes. Each test item in this effective testing tool includes a difficulty level and has been content-reviewed for clarity and checked for accuracy.

**Prentice Hall Custom Test, by Engineering Software Associates (ESA), Inc.** Available on both DOS and Windows, this easy-to-use computerized testing program is available on 3.5″ diskettes. This user-friendly program allows you to create an exam, as well as evaluate and track student results. The PH Custom Test also provides on-line testing capabilities. Test material is adapted from the Test Item File.

**A Database of PowerPoint Slides—prepared by Douglas S. Beets, Wake Forest University** A variety of PowerPoint slides are available for each chapter of the text. This computerized supplement provides the instructor with an interactive presentation that outlines the chapter material and reinforces text concepts using colorful graphics and charts. Instructors have the flexibility to customize the existing slides to meet their courses' needs.

## Supplements for the Student

**Study Guide—prepared by Dennis L. Kimmell of Akron University** For each text chapter, the Study Guide discusses the chapter objectives and summarizes its content. In addition, each chapter contains true/false, completion statements, and multiple-choice questions to reinforce text concepts and help students prepare for examinations. CPA and CIA examination questions are also provided.

**Career Paths in Accounting—CD–ROM** Winner of the New Media INVISION Gold Award in Education, this CD-ROM provides students with a dynamic, interactive job-searching tool. Included are workshops in career planning, resume writing, and interviewing skills. Students can learn the latest market trends and facts as well as the skills required to get the right job. In addition, the CD–ROM provides the student with salary information, video clips describing specific jobs, and profiles of practitioners in the field.

**The Audit: Its Environment and Application—by Gregory C. Yost** This hands-on text is designed to stimulate elements of the actual audit process, the accounting profession, the public accounting firm, and the client. Used as a stand alone or as a supplement to a traditional text, this text requires students to identify and resolve issues associated with the auditing practice. An Instructor's Guide is also available.

**The Lakeside Company: Case Studies in the Life-Cycle of an Audit prepared by John Trussel, Hood College, and Joe Ben Hoyle, University of Richmond** An efficient and effective Practice Set that guides the student through the life cycle of an audit from beginning to end. The cases are designed to create a realistic view of how an auditor organizes and carries out an audit. An Instructor's Solutions Manual is also available.

## ACKNOWLEDGMENTS

We acknowledge the American Institute of Certified Public Accountants for permission to quote extensively from statements on auditing standards, the *Code of Professional Conduct*, Accounting Principles Board Opinions, Uniform CPA Examinations, and other publications. The willingness of this major accounting organization to permit the use of its materials is a significant contribution to the book.

The continuing generous support of the Price Waterhouse Foundation is acknowledged, particularly in regard to the word processing, editing, and moral support for this text.

We especially acknowledge three faculty members who spent an extraordinary amount of time reviewing chapters and making detailed suggestions. Bob Allen, University of Utah, and Randy Elder, Syracuse University, worked closely with us on most chapters and were generous with their time and innovative ideas. Mike Groomer, Indiana University, reviewed Chapter 15 extensively and made many suggestions to improve the chapter.

We also gratefully acknowledge the contributions of the following reviewers for their suggestions and support: Sherri Anderson, Sonoma State University; Dale E. Armstrong, Oklahoma State University; Stephen K. Asare, University of Florida; Brian Ballou, Michigan State University; Mark Beasley, North Carolina State University; Stanley F. Biggs, University of Connecticut; Joseph V. Calmie, Thomas Nelson Community College; Eric Carlsen, Kean College of New Jersey; Freddie Choo, San Francisco State University; Frank Daroca, Loyola Marymount University; Barb Esteves, Michigan State University; William L. Felix, University of Arizona; Gary L. Holstrum, University of South Florida; C. Randy Howard, Montana State University; James Jiambalvo, University of Washington; David S. Kerr, Texas A & M University; Dennis Lee Kimmell, University of Akron; William R. Kinney, Jr., University of Texas; W. Robert Knechel, University of Florida; Heidi H. Meier, Cleveland State University; Alfred R. Michenzi, Loyola College in Maryland; Tad Miller, California Polytechnic State University; Lawrence C. Mohrweis, Northern Arizona University; Frederick L. Neumann, University of Illinois; Robert R. Tucker, University of Illinois at Chicago; D. Dewey Ward, Michigan State University; Robert J. Warth, Rochester Institute of Technology.

A special note of thanks is extended to Carol Borsum for her editorial and production efforts and to Mary Jo Mercer for word processing. Finally, the encouragement and support of our families are acknowledged. We thank the members of the Prentice Hall book team for their hard work and dedication including Katherine Evancie, Alana Zdinak, Paul Smolenski, Vincent Scelta, Suzanne Behnke, and Patricia Wosczyk for managing the book through the production process; Debbie Emry and Bob Prokop for their marketing efforts; and Natacha St. Hill, Elaine Oyzon-Mast, and Annie Todd for their editorial guidance.

A.A.A
J.K.L.

# AUDITING

# 1

# THE AUDITING PROFESSION

## LEARNING OBJECTIVES

Thorough study of this chapter will enable you to

- **1-1** Define and explain auditing.
- **1-2** Distinguish between auditing and accounting.
- **1-3** Describe the three primary types of audits.
- **1-4** Describe the primary types of auditors.
- **1-5** Discuss why reducing information risk is the prime economic reason behind the demand for audits.
- **1-6** Describe the requirements for being a CPA.
- **1-7** Describe the nature of CPA firms, what they do, and their structure.
- **1-8** Describe the key functions performed by the AICPA.
- **1-9** Identify ways CPAs are encouraged to perform effectively.
- **1-10** Use generally accepted auditing standards as a basis for further study.
- **1-11** Identify quality control standards and practices within the accounting profession.
- **1-12** Summarize the role of the Securities and Exchange Commission in accounting and auditing.

## AUDITING PLAYS AN IMPORTANT SOCIAL ROLE[1]

Bob Davis is the CEO of TechProducts, Inc., a publicly held computer products company. Harry Longstreet is a partner with the CPA firm that will do TechProducts' upcoming audit. They are discussing the standard engagement letter that Harry has asked Bob to sign.

**BOB** What exactly do you mean, Harry, when you say the audit can't guarantee that you'll find all errors and fraud?

**HARRY** Well, Bob, the audit process simply isn't perfect. There is a chance something can slip by, even when we do the best audit possible, which, of course, is our standard. If we tried to find everything that's wrong, the cost of the audit would be unacceptable. We focus on the areas where the risk of material errors and fraud is greatest, and when the audit is done, we'll have a very high level of assurance that we've found those.

**BOB** But not total assurance.

**HARRY** That's right, Bob, but a very high level of assurance.

**BOB** I guess the idea is that if all audits are done at a high level of assurance, the overall accuracy of financial statement information across all companies will be good enough so that the markets will work the way they're supposed to.

**HARRY** Yes. But you seem awfully concerned about this, Bob. What's the problem?

**BOB** Well, a couple of years ago two things happened that continue to bother me; in fact, one of them really shook me up. First, I heard the managing partner of one of your competitors brag about how good the quality of auditing was. He said that of the 10,000 or so audits done each year, there were only a few failures. Of course, he failed to mention that of those 10,000 audits, most of the companies didn't have anything wrong with their financial statements in the first place, so his denominator was too high. He also didn't mention that many failures aren't in the press, and those that are reported can be huge in terms of losses to lenders and investors.

The second thing was that my grandparents had invested a significant portion of their retirement funds in Western Power Bonds. You know, they were touted as an extremely safe investment, but then they went broke trying to build nuclear power plants. Eventually, there was a settlement with the utility, its auditors, and others, but my grandparents lost about 85 percent of their investment. It devastated them, and I've been kind of sour on the system, including auditors, ever since.

**HARRY** That's an awful situation Bob. I'm really sorry to hear about it.

**BOB** The real reason I'm telling you about it, Harry, is that a lot of people have invested in our company who cannot afford big losses. We're a hot item right now. Our price earnings ratio is thirty-five to one. Don't let anything slip through here, Harry. I hired you to be there for *my* investors. I don't care about all the other companies in the economy or your overall level of assurance. I want to make sure that *this* audit is done right.

**HARRY** You can count on us, Bob.

[1]Each chapter's opening vignette illustrates important auditing principles using fictitious, although realistic, situations. Any resemblance to real firms, companies, or individuals is unintended and purely coincidental.

Auditing provides many economic benefits to society. There are almost 15,000 publicly traded companies with annual audit requirements in the United States. Without financial statement audits, these companies would be unable to obtain capital through the securities markets. Many privately held companies are also required to have annual financial statement audits to obtain and maintain financing from banks and other financial institutions. In most cases, a company can obtain financing at a lower rate by having a financial statement audit performed annually. Therefore, financial statement audits reduce the cost of capital.

Auditors, including CPAs, government auditors, and internal auditors, also assist companies in improving operations and internal controls. Auditors often make suggestions to management that ultimately reduce costs by promoting operational efficiency and reducing errors and fraud. Finally, when management and other employees are aware that an audit is being performed, they are often more careful in their work and are less likely to commit fraud.

This chapter presents background information about the nature of auditing and the major influences affecting auditing activities. The first part of the chapter discusses auditing in the broad sense. It describes what auditing is, why it is needed, and the various types of audits and auditors. The remainder of the chapter focuses on audits performed for purposes of external reporting by independent certified public accountants. It discusses the nature of certified public accounting (CPA) firms, the influence of the American Institute of Certified Public Accountants (AICPA), the nature of generally accepted auditing standards and interpretations of the standards, quality control, and the role of the Securities and Exchange Commission (SEC).

## NATURE OF AUDITING

**OBJECTIVE 1-1**
**Define and explain auditing.**

Auditing is the accumulation and evaluation of evidence about information to determine and report on the degree of correspondence between the information and established criteria. Auditing should be done by a competent independent person.

This description includes several key words and phrases. Each is discussed in this section and analyzed more extensively in later chapters. For ease of understanding, the terms are discussed in a different order than they occur in the description.

### Information and Established Criteria

To do an audit, there must be information in a *verifiable form* and some standards (*criteria*) by which the auditor can evaluate the information. Information can and does take many forms. Auditors routinely perform audits of quantifiable information, including companies' financial statements and individuals' federal income tax returns. Auditors also perform audits of more subjective information, such as the effectiveness of computer systems and the efficiency of manufacturing operations.

The criteria for evaluating information also vary depending on the information being audited. For example, in the audit of historical financial statements by CPA firms, the criteria are usually generally accepted accounting principles. To illustrate, this means that in the audit of General Motors' financial statements the CPA firm determines whether General Motors' financial statements have been prepared in accordance with generally accepted accounting principles. For the audit of tax returns by the Internal Revenue Service, the criteria are found in the Internal Revenue Code. In the audit of General Motors' corporate tax return by the Internal Revenue Service, the internal revenue agent would use the Internal Revenue Code as the criteria for correctness, not generally accepted accounting principles.

For more subjective information, such as auditing the effectiveness of computer operations, it is more difficult to establish criteria. Typically, auditors and the entities being audited agree on the criteria well before the audit starts. For a computer application, the criteria might, for example, include the absence of input or output errors.

## Accumulating and Evaluating Evidence

*Evidence* is defined as any information used by the auditor to determine whether the information being audited is stated in accordance with the established criteria. Evidence takes many different forms, including oral testimony of the auditee (client), written communication with outsiders, and observations by the auditor. It is important to obtain a sufficient quality and volume of evidence to satisfy the purpose of the audit. Determining the types and amount of evidence necessary and evaluating whether the information corresponds to the established criteria is a critical part of every audit. It is the primary subject of this book.

## Competent, Independent Person

The auditor must be *qualified* to understand the criteria used and *competent* to know the types and amount of evidence to accumulate to reach the proper conclusion after the evidence has been examined. The auditor also must have an *independent mental attitude.* It does little good to have a competent person who is biased performing the evidence accumulation when unbiased information and objective thinking are needed for the judgments and decisions to be made.

Independence cannot be absolute, but it must be a goal that is worked toward, and it can be achieved to the necessary degree. For example, even though an auditor of published financial statements is paid a fee by a company, he or she is normally sufficiently independent to conduct audits that can be relied upon by users. Auditors may or may not be sufficiently independent if they are also company employees. They would normally not be sufficiently independent for auditing published financial statements, but would be for auditing the efficiency of a company's computer operations.

## Reporting

The final stage in the audit process is the *audit report,* which is the communication of the findings to users. Reports differ in nature, but in all cases they must inform readers of the degree of correspondence between information and established criteria. Reports also differ in form and can vary from the highly technical type usually associated with financial statement audits to a simple oral report in the case of an operational audit done of a small department's effectiveness.

Figure 1-1 summarizes the important ideas in the description of auditing by illustrating an audit of an individual's tax return by an internal revenue agent. The objective is to determine whether the tax return was prepared in a manner consistent with the requirements of the federal Internal Revenue Code. To accomplish the objective, the agent examines supporting records provided by the taxpayer and from other sources, such as the taxpayer's employer. After completing the audit, the internal revenue agent will issue a

**FIGURE 1-1**

**Audit of a Tax Return**

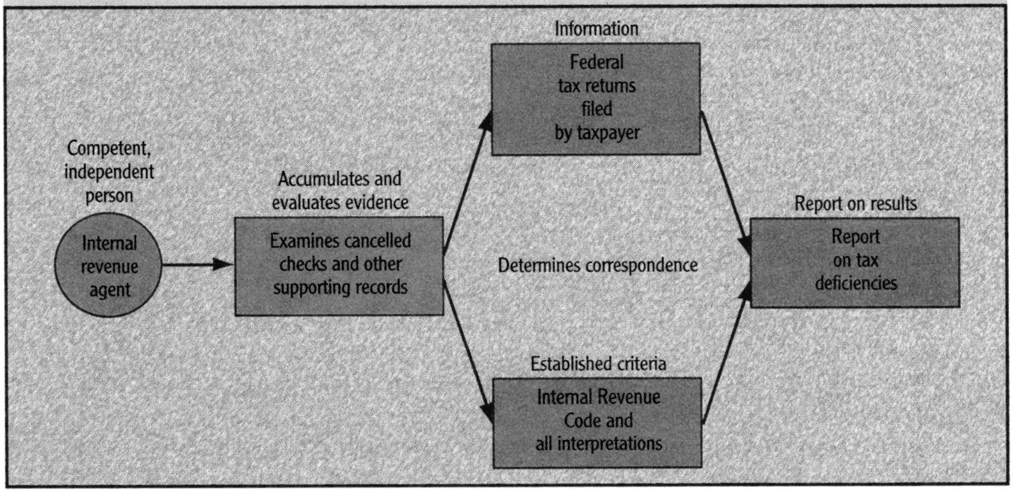

report to the taxpayer assessing additional taxes, advising that a refund is due, or stating that there is no change in the status of the tax return.

## DISTINCTION BETWEEN AUDITING AND ACCOUNTING

**OBJECTIVE 1-2**
**Distinguish between auditing and accounting.**

Many financial statement users and members of the general public confuse *auditing* with *accounting*. The confusion results because most auditing is usually concerned with accounting information, and many auditors have considerable expertise in accounting matters. The confusion is increased by giving the title "certified public accountant" to many individuals who perform audits.

*Accounting* is the recording, classifying, and summarizing of economic events in a logical manner for the purpose of providing financial information for decision making. The function of accounting is to provide certain types of quantitative information that management and others can use to make decisions. To provide relevant information, accountants must have a thorough understanding of the principles and rules that provide the basis for preparing the accounting information. In addition, accountants must develop a system to make sure that the entity's economic events are properly recorded on a timely basis and at a reasonable cost.

In *auditing* accounting data, the concern is with determining whether recorded information properly reflects the economic events that occurred during the accounting period. Because accounting rules are the criteria for evaluating whether the accounting information is properly recorded, any auditor involved with these data must also thoroughly understand those rules. In the context of the audit of financial statements, the rules are generally accepted accounting principles. Throughout this text the assumption is made that the reader has already studied generally accepted accounting principles.

In addition to understanding accounting, the auditor must possess expertise in the accumulation and interpretation of audit evidence. It is this expertise that distinguishes auditors from accountants. Determining the proper audit procedures, the number and types of items to test, and evaluating the results are problems unique to the auditor.

## TYPES OF AUDITS

**OBJECTIVE 1-3**
**Describe the three primary types of audits.**

Three types of audits are discussed in this section: financial statement audits, operational audits, and compliance audits.

### Financial Statement Audits

An *audit of financial statements* is conducted to determine whether the *overall* financial statements (the information being verified) are stated in accordance with specified criteria. Normally, the criteria are generally accepted accounting principles, although it is also common to conduct audits of financial statements prepared using the cash basis or some other basis of accounting appropriate for the organization. The financial statements most commonly included are the statement of financial position, income statement, and statement of cash flows, including accompanying footnotes.

### Operational Audits

An *operational audit* is a review of any part of an organization's operating procedures and methods for the purpose of evaluating *efficiency* and *effectiveness*. At the completion of an operational audit, recommendations to management for improving operations are normally expected. An example of an operational audit is evaluating the efficiency and accuracy of processing payroll transactions in a newly installed computer system. Another example, where most accountants would feel less qualified, is evaluating the efficiency, accuracy, and customer satisfaction in processing the distribution of letters and packages by a company such as Federal Express.

Because of the many different areas in which operational effectiveness can be evaluated, it is impossible to characterize the conduct of a typical operational audit. In one organization, the auditor might evaluate the relevancy and sufficiency of the information used by management in making decisions to acquire new fixed assets, while in a different organization the auditor might evaluate the efficiency of the paper flow in processing sales. In operational auditing, the reviews are not limited to accounting. They can include the evaluation of organization structure, computer operations, production methods, marketing, and any other area in which the auditor is qualified.

The conduct of an operational audit and the reported results are less easily defined than for either of the other two types of audits. Efficiency and effectiveness of operations are far more difficult to evaluate objectively than compliance or the presentation of financial statements in accordance with generally accepted accounting principles; and establishing criteria for evaluating the information in an operational audit is an extremely subjective matter. In this sense, operational auditing is more like management consulting than what is generally regarded as auditing. Operational auditing has increased in importance in the past decade. It is studied in greater depth in Chapter 24.

### Compliance Audits

The purpose of a *compliance audit* is to determine whether the auditee is following specific procedures, rules, or regulations set down by some higher authority. A compliance audit for a private business could include determining whether accounting personnel are following the procedures prescribed by the company controller, reviewing wage rates for compliance with minimum wage laws, or examining contractual agreements with bankers and other lenders to be sure the company is complying with legal requirements. In the audit of governmental units such as school districts, there is extensive compliance auditing due to extensive regulation by higher government authorities. In virtually every private and not-for-profit organization, there are prescribed policies, contractual agreements, and legal requirements that may call for compliance auditing.

Results of compliance audits are typically reported to someone within the organizational unit being audited rather than to a broad spectrum of users. Management, as opposed to outside users, is the primary group concerned with the extent of compliance with certain prescribed procedures and regulations. Hence, a significant portion of work of this type is done by auditors employed by the organizational units themselves. There are exceptions. When an organization wants to determine whether individuals or organizations that are obligated to follow its requirements are actually complying, the auditor is employed by the organization issuing the requirements. An example is the auditing of taxpayers for

**TABLE 1-1**

**Examples of the Three Types of Audits**

| Type of Audit | Example | Information | Established Criteria | Available Evidence |
|---|---|---|---|---|
| Financial Statement Audit | Annual Audit of General Motors' financial statements | General Motors' financial statements | Generally accepted accounting principles | Documents, records, and outside sources of evidence |
| Operational Audit | Evaluate whether the computerized payroll processing for subsidiary H is operating efficiently and effectively | Number of payroll records processed in a month, costs of the department, and number of errors made | Company standards for efficiency and effectiveness in payroll department | Error reports, payroll records, and payroll processing costs |
| Compliance Audit | Determine if bank requirements for loan continuation have been met | Company records | Loan agreement provisions | Financial statements and calculations by the auditor |

compliance with the federal tax laws, where the auditor is employed by the government to audit the taxpayers' tax returns. Compliance audits for federally funded grant programs are widely performed by CPAs. These are discussed in detail in Chapter 24.

Table 1-1 on page 5 summarizes the three types of audits and includes an example of each type and an illustration of three of the key parts of the definitions of auditing applied to each type of audit.

## TYPES OF AUDITORS

**OBJECTIVE 1-4**
**Describe the primary types of auditors.**

In this section, the four most widely known types of auditors are discussed briefly. They are certified public accounting firms, general accounting office auditors, internal revenue agents, and internal auditors.

### Certified Public Accounting Firms

Certified public accounting firms have as their primary responsibility the performance of audits of the published historical financial statements of all publicly traded companies, most other reasonably large companies, and many smaller companies and noncommercial organizations. Because of the widespread use of audited financial statements in the U.S. economy, as well as businesspersons' and other users' familiarity with these statements, it is common to use the terms *auditor* and *CPA firm* synonymously even though there are several different types of auditors. Another term frequently used to describe a CPA firm is *independent auditor*. CPA firms are discussed in greater detail shortly.

### General Accounting Office Auditors

The United States General Accounting Office (GAO) is a nonpartisan agency in the legislative branch of the federal government. The GAO, which is headed by the Comptroller General, reports to and is responsible solely to Congress. The primary responsibility of the audit staff is to perform the audit function for Congress.

Many of the GAO's audit responsibilities are the same as those of a CPA firm. Much of the financial information prepared by various government agencies is audited by the GAO before it is submitted to Congress. Since the authority for expenditures and receipts of governmental agencies is defined by law, there is considerable emphasis on compliance in these audits.

An increasing portion of the GAO's audit efforts has been devoted to evaluating the *operational efficiency and effectiveness* of various federal programs. An example is the evaluation of the computer operations of a governmental unit. The auditor can review and evaluate any aspect of the computer system, but he or she is likely to emphasize the adequacy of the equipment, the efficiency of the operations, the adequacy and usefulness of the output, and similar matters, with the objective of identifying means of providing the same services at a lower cost.

Because of the immense size of many federal agencies and the similarity of their operations, the GAO has made significant advances in recent years in developing better methods of auditing through the widespread use of highly sophisticated statistical sampling and computer auditing techniques.

In many states, experience as a GAO auditor fulfills the experience requirement for becoming a CPA. In those states, if an individual passes the CPA examination and fulfills the experience stipulations for becoming a GAO auditor, he or she may then obtain a CPA certificate.

As a result of their great responsibility for auditing the expenditures of the federal government, their use of advanced auditing concepts, their eligibility to be CPAs, and their opportunities for performing operational audits, GAO auditors are highly regarded in the auditing profession.

### Internal Revenue Agents

The Internal Revenue Service (IRS), under the direction of the Commissioner of Internal Revenue, has as its responsibility the enforcement of the *federal tax laws* as they have been defined by Congress and interpreted by the courts. A major responsibility of the IRS is to audit the returns of taxpayers to determine whether they have complied with the tax laws. The auditors who perform these examinations are referred to as internal revenue agents. These audits can be regarded as solely compliance audits.

It might seem that the audit of returns for compliance with the federal tax laws would be a simple and straightforward problem, but nothing could be further from the truth. The tax laws are highly complicated, and there are hundreds of volumes of interpretations. The tax returns being audited vary from the simple returns of individuals who work for only one employer and take the standard tax deduction to the highly complex returns of multinational corporations. There are taxation problems involving individual taxpayers, gift taxes, estate taxes, corporate taxes, trusts, and so forth. An auditor involved in any of these areas must have considerable tax knowledge and auditing skills to conduct an effective audit.

### Internal Auditors

Internal auditors are employed by individual companies to audit for management much as the GAO does for Congress. The internal audit group in some large firms can include over a hundred people and typically reports directly to the president, another high executive officer, or even the audit committee of the board of directors.

Internal auditors' responsibilities vary considerably, depending upon the employer. Some internal audit staffs consist of only one or two employees who may spend most of their time doing routine compliance auditing. Other internal audit staffs consist of numerous employees who have diverse responsibilities, including many outside the accounting area. Many internal auditors are involved in operational auditing or have expertise in evaluating computer systems.

To operate effectively, an internal auditor must be independent of the line functions in an organization, but he or she cannot be independent of the entity as long as an employer-employee relationship exists. Internal auditors provide management with valuable information for making decisions concerning effective operation of its business. Users from outside the entity are unlikely to want to rely on information verified solely by internal auditors because of their lack of independence. This lack of independence is the major difference between internal auditors and CPA firms.

## ECONOMIC DEMAND FOR AUDITING

**OBJECTIVE 1-5**
**Discuss why reducing information risk is the prime economic reason behind the demand for audits.**

Auditing services are used extensively by business, government, and other not-for-profit organizations. A brief study of the economic reasons for auditing is useful for understanding why auditing is so necessary, as well as some of the legal problems auditors face.

To illustrate the need for auditing, consider the decision of a bank manager in making a loan to a business. That decision will be based on such factors as previous financial relations with the business and the financial condition of the business as reflected by its financial statements. If the bank makes the loan, it will charge a rate of interest determined primarily by three factors:

1. *Risk-free interest rate.* This is approximately the rate the bank could earn by investing in U.S. treasury notes for the same length of time as the business loan.
2. *Business risk for the customer.* This risk reflects the possibility that the business will not be able to repay its loan because of economic or business conditions such as a recession, poor management decisions, or unexpected competition in the industry.
3. *Information risk.* This risk reflects the possibility that the information upon which the business risk decision was made was inaccurate. A likely cause of the information risk is the possibility of inaccurate financial statements.

Auditing has no effect on either the risk-free interest rate or business risk. It can have a significant effect on information risk. If the bank manager is satisfied that there is no information risk because a borrower's financial statements are audited, the risk is eliminated and the overall interest rate to the borrower can be reduced. Even if information risk cannot be totally eliminated, its reduction can have a significant effect on the borrower's ability to obtain capital at a reasonable cost. For example, assume a large company has total interest-bearing debt of approximately $10 billion. If the interest rate on that debt is reduced by only one percent, the annual savings in interest is $100 million.

## Causes of Information Risk

As society becomes more complex, there is an increased likelihood that unreliable information will be provided to decision makers. There are several reasons for this: remoteness of information, biases and motives of provider, voluminous data, and the existence of complex exchange transactions.

**Remoteness of Information** In the modern world, it is virtually impossible for a decision maker to have much firsthand knowledge about the organization with which he or she does business. Information provided by others must be relied upon. Whenever information is obtained from others, the likelihood of it being intentionally or unintentionally misstated increases.

**Biases and Motives of Provider** If information is provided by someone whose goals are inconsistent with those of the decision maker, the information may be *biased* in favor of the provider. The reason could be an honest optimism about future events or an intentional emphasis designed to influence users in a certain manner. In either case, the result is a misstatement of information. For example, in a lending decision in which the borrower provides financial statements to the lender, there is considerable likelihood that the borrower will bias the statements to increase the chance of obtaining a loan. The misstatement could be in the form of outright incorrect dollar amounts or inadequate or incomplete disclosures of information.

**Voluminous Data** As organizations become larger, so does the volume of their exchange transactions. This increases the likelihood that improperly recorded information will be included in the records—perhaps buried in a large amount of other information. For example, if a check by a large government agency in payment of a vendor's invoice is overstated by $200, there is a fairly good chance that it will not be uncovered unless the agency has instituted reasonably complex procedures to find this type of misstatement. If large numbers of minor misstatements remain undiscovered, the combined total could be significant.

**Complex Exchange Transactions** In the past few decades, exchange transactions between organizations have become increasingly complex and hence more difficult to record properly. For example, the correct accounting treatment of the acquisition of one entity by another poses relatively difficult and important accounting problems. Other examples include the proper combining and disclosure of the results of operations of subsidiaries in different industries, and the proper disclosures about derivative financial instruments under Financial Accounting Standards Board Statement No. 119 (FASB 119).

## Reducing Information Risk

Managements of businesses and the users of their financial statements may conclude that the best way to deal with information risk is simply to have it remain reasonably high. A small company may find it less expensive to pay higher interest costs than to increase the costs of reducing information risk.

For larger businesses, it is usually practical to incur costs to reduce information risk. There are three main ways to do so:

**User Verifies Information** The user may go to the business premises to examine records and obtain information about the reliability of the statements. Normally, this is impractical because of costs. In addition, it would be economically inefficient for all users to verify the information individually. Nevertheless, some users perform their own verification. For example, the Internal Revenue Service does considerable verification of businesses and individuals to determine whether tax returns filed reflect the actual tax due the federal government. Similarly, if a business intends to purchase another business, it is common for the purchaser to use a special audit team to independently verify and evaluate key information of the prospective business.

**User Shares Information Risk with Management** There is considerable legal precedent indicating that management is responsible for providing reliable information to users. If users rely on inaccurate financial statements and as a result incur a financial loss, there is a basis for a lawsuit against management.

A difficulty with sharing information risk with management is that users may not be able to collect on losses. If a company is unable to repay a loan because of bankruptcy, it is unlikely that management will have sufficient funds to repay users. Nevertheless, users do evaluate the likelihood of being able to share their information risk loss with management.

**Audited Financial Statements Are Provided** The most common way for users to obtain reliable information is to have an independent audit performed. The audited information is then used in the decision-making process on the assumption that it is reasonably complete, accurate, and unbiased.

Whenever more than one decision maker uses a certain type of information, it is usually less expensive to have someone perform the audit for all the users than to have each user verify the information individually. Since the financial statements of most companies have many users, there is considerable demand for auditing.

Typically, management engages the auditor to provide assurances to users that the financial statements are reliable. If the financial statements are ultimately determined to be incorrect, the auditor can be sued by both the users and management. Users sue on the basis that the auditor had a professional responsibility to make sure the financial information was reliable. Users are also likely to sue management. Management sues the auditor as an agent who had a responsibility to management to make sure the information was reliable. Auditors obviously have considerable legal responsibility for their work.

**CAPITAL COSTS TO SHRINK**

According to a recent article in *Accounting Today*, corporate America is paying too much for new capital, and independent auditors are part of the solution. Robert Elliott, a senior partner with KPMG Peat Marwick, believes the cost of capital could shrink significantly in the next five years due to advances in technology, streamlined regulations, and broader audit coverage.

Elliott uses a hypothetical example to illustrate his prediction. Assuming a cost of capital of 13 percent, he estimates this rate is composed of the following:

- 5.5 percent risk-free interest rate
- 3.5 percent economic risk premium (*business risk*)
- 4 percent information cost (*information risk*)

According to Elliott's example, information risk comprises approximately 30 percent of the cost of capital. Elliott believes the following factors will drastically reduce information risk in the next five to ten years:

- Technological advances, including reduction in silicon-based memory costs, will drastically decrease the cost of providing relevant and timely information to investors.
- As more companies go "on-line," the risk of investors obtaining outdated information decreases.
- New accounting and auditing standards already require better disclosures about segment operations, risks, and uncertainties. New rules may require data on nonfinancial performance and forward-looking information.
- Auditors will find more efficient ways to audit, which may provide new levels of assurance.

Elliott predicts that when and if all of the preceding factors materialize, the cost of capital in his hypothetical example could be reduced from 13 percent to 11.5 percent. The entire reduction would result from reduced information risk.

Source: Adapted from *Accounting Today*, December 11, 1995, p. 16.

In business practice, all three methods described are used to reduce information risk. As society becomes more complex, reliance on auditors to reduce information risk increases. In many cases, federal or state regulations have been passed requiring an annual audit by a CPA firm. For example, all companies filing annually with the Securities and Exchange Commission are required to have an annual audit. Similarly, in some states, every governmental unit must be periodically audited. Although not required by specific regulations, many lenders such as banks require annual audits for companies having loans outstanding to their bank over a specific amount.

## CERTIFIED PUBLIC ACCOUNTANT

**OBJECTIVE 1-6**
**Describe the requirements for being a CPA.**

Use of the title *certified public accountant* (CPA) is regulated by state law through the licensing departments of each state. Within any state, the regulations usually differ for becoming a CPA and retaining a license to practice after the designation has been initially achieved. To become a CPA, there are three requirements. These are summarized in Figure 1-2.

For a person planning to become a CPA, it is essential to know the requirements in the state where he or she plans to obtain and maintain the CPA designation. The best source of that information is the State Board of Accountancy for the state in which the person plans to be certified. It is possible to transfer the CPA designation from one state to another, but frequently additional requirements must be met for formal education, practice experience, or continuing education.

Individuals wanting more information about the CPA examination will find the booklet *Information for CPA Candidates* useful. Past CPA examinations and unofficial solutions through the November 1995 examination are also available. Both can be obtained from the AICPA, 1211 Avenue of the Americas, New York, N.Y. 10036-8775. Effective with the May 1996 examination, the AICPA will no longer publish CPA examinations and unofficial solutions.

Some of the questions and problems at the end of the chapters in this book have been taken from past CPA examinations. They are designated "AICPA" or "AICPA adapted."

Most young professionals who want to become CPAs start their careers working for a CPA firm. After they become CPAs, many leave the firm to work in industry, government, or education. These people may continue to be CPAs but often give up their right to prac-

**FIGURE 1-2**
**Three Requirements for Becoming a CPA**

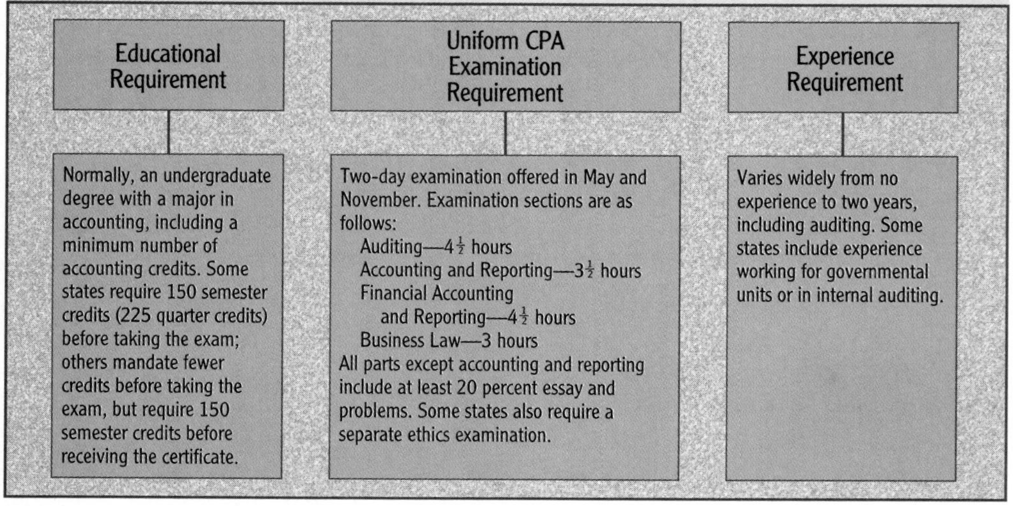

tice as independent auditors. CPAs who practice as independent auditors must meet defined continuing education and licensing requirements to maintain their right to practice in most states. It is common, therefore, for accountants to be CPAs who do not practice as independent auditors.

**CPA EXAM CHANGES ARE COMING**

The AICPA board of examiners expects that by the end of the 1990s, the Uniform CPA Examination will be administered as a computer-adaptive test, according to the board's 1994 annual report.

In such tests, a candidate's answer to a first question, or set of questions, determines the next question. The examination is variable in length depending on the candidate's answers. The strongest and the weakest candidates spend only a short time on the test; only those on the borderline between passing and failing spend the allotted time.

Benefits of such tests include increased exam security, because there are no paper copies to account for, and the ability to design questions that more closely reflect performance of skills used in practice and to offer the examination on a year-round basis. In this type of test, each candidate receives a slightly different combination of questions and may take the exam when he or she wishes at a designated professional examination site. The board expects to work with the state boards of accountancy to develop proposals on how to implement this plan.

Source: *Journal of Accountancy*, November 1994, p. 116.

## CERTIFIED PUBLIC ACCOUNTING FIRMS

**OBJECTIVE 1-7**
**Describe the nature of CPA firms, what they do, and their structure.**

Emphasis in this book is on the audit of historical financial statements by CPA firms. There are three reasons for this: a larger percentage of students who become auditors initially work for a CPA firm than for any other type of audit organization; CPA firms have more clearly defined audit responsibilities than the other major audit organizations; and there are more professional and auditing requirements for CPA firms than for the other organizations because of the need for reliance on the financial statements by external users.

In the United States, the auditing of general use financial statements of organizations other than certain governmental units is done exclusively by CPA firms. The right and responsibility for doing these audits is granted by each of the fifty states through regulation. The result of this legal franchise is a large number of firms that are authorized to do audits, and for economic reasons also provide other services to clients. Because of this impact, it is useful to understand more about CPA firms.

There are currently more than 45,000 CPA firms in the United States. The size of CPA firms ranges from one person to several thousand staff and partners. Four size categories can be used to describe CPA firms: Big Six international firms, national firms, large local and regional firms, and small local firms.

*Accounting Today* annually publishes a list of the 100 largest accounting firms. The list includes a few companies such as H&R Block Tax Services Inc., but most are CPA firms. Data for selected CPA firms is included in Table 1-2 on page 12. Observe that the smallest of the top six firms is over seven times as large as the next largest firm. Also observe that the seventy-fifth largest firm has one office and nearly $11 million in revenue.

### International Firms

The six largest CPA firms in the United States are referred to as the "Big Six" international CPA firms. Each has offices in every major U.S. city and in many cities throughout the world. As can be seen in Table 1-2, there is no major difference in size among these six firms. The smallest has international revenues exceeding $3 billion and national revenues exceeding $1.7 billion. The total number of partners and staff of the largest firm is nearly

**TABLE 1-2**

**Revenue and Other Data for the Largest CPA Firms in the U.S.**

| 1996 Size by Revenue | Firm | Net Revenue—U.S. Only (in $ millions) | Partners | Professionals | U.S. Offices | Percent of Total Revenue from Accounting and Auditing/Taxes/Management Advisory Services |
|---|---|---|---|---|---|---|
| | **Big Six** | | | | | |
| 1 | Andersen Worldwide | $3,860.2 | 1,529 | 24,606 | 91 | 32/16/52 |
| 2 | Ernst & Young | $2,974.0 | 1,864 | 14,195 | 91 | 43/22/35 |
| 3 | Deloitte & Touche | $2,570.0 | 1,477 | 11,458 | 110 | 44/20/36 |
| 4 | KPMG Peat Marwick | $2,289.0 | 1,425 | 10,700 | 124 | 45/19/36 |
| 5 | Coopers & Lybrand | $1,905.0 | 1,229 | 11,369 | 117 | 45/20/35 |
| 6 | Price Waterhouse | $1,770.0 | 957 | 10,671 | 106 | 40/24/36 |
| | **National** | | | | | |
| 7 | Grant Thornton | $240.0 | 282 | 1,734 | 48 | 46/32/22 |
| 8 | McGladrey & Pullen | $229.8 | 387 | 1,723 | 73 | 49/33/18 |
| 9 | BDO Seidman | $202.5 | 230 | 1,016 | 40 | 54/29/17 |
| | **Regional** | | | | | |
| 10 | Crowe, Chizek & Co. | $76.0 | 79 | 603 | 8 | 35/19/46 |
| 11 | Baird Kurtz & Dobson | $75.4 | 120 | 503 | 20 | 48/32/20 |
| 12 | Plante & Moran | $67.6 | 105 | 479 | 13 | 57/24/19 |
| 13 | Moss Adams | $59.0 | 85 | 396 | 16 | 44/40/16 |
| 14 | Clifton Gunderson & Co. | $57.7 | 105 | 522 | 41 | 52/35/12 |
| | **Large Local** | | | | | |
| 50 | Kennedy & Coe | $14.2 | 24 | 125 | 19 | 13/76/11 |
| 75 | Philip Rootberg & Co. | $10.7 | 16 | 59 | 1 | 62/29/9 |

Source: *Accounting Today,* March 18–April 7, 1996, pp. 17–19.

60,000 internationally and 2,000 in the New York City office alone. These six firms audit nearly all of the largest companies both in the United States and worldwide, and many of the smaller companies as well.

Prior to 1989, there were eight large CPA firms commonly referred to as the "Big Eight." In 1989, two mergers of two firms each resulted in the Big Six. There was no single reason for these mergers, but a major factor was the need for international CPA firms to serve all major international cities due to the increasing globalization of businesses. For example, if a German company has offices in Brazil, Japan, and the United States, the CPA firm doing the company's audit needs auditors in each of those countries. Each of the Big Six now has the capability to serve all major international markets.

## National Firms

Three other CPA firms in the United States are referred to as national firms because they have offices in most major cities. Table 1-2 shows that these firms are large, but considerably smaller than the Big Six. These firms perform the same services as Big Six firms and compete directly with them for clients. In addition, each is affiliated with firms in other countries and therefore has an international capability. Competitive pressures have reduced national firms from seven a few years ago to only three. Most of the others merged with Big Six Firms.

### Large Local and Regional Firms

There are only approximately 100 CPA firms with professional staffs of more than fifty people. Some have only one office and serve clients primarily within commuting distance. Others have several offices in a state or region and serve a larger radius of clients. For example, Table 1-2 shows that the largest regional firms are not dramatically smaller than the three national firms. Large local and regional firms compete for clients with other CPA firms, including international and national firms. Many of them have become affiliated with associations of CPA firms to share resources for such things as technical information and continuing education.

### Small Local Firms

More than 95 percent of all CPA firms have fewer than twenty-five professionals in their single-office firm. They perform audits and related services primarily for smaller businesses and not-for-profit entities, although some do have one or two clients with public ownership.

## ACTIVITIES OF CPA FIRMS

CPA firms perform four broad categories of services: attestation services, accounting and bookkeeping services, tax services, and management advisory services.

### Attestation Services

Attestation services are any services in which the CPA firm issues a written communication that expresses a conclusion about the reliability of a written assertion that is the responsibility of another party. There are three categories of attestation services: audits of historical financial statements, reviews of historical financial statements, and other attestation services.

**Audits** Audits of historical financial statements are the predominant type of attestation services performed by CPAs. For larger CPA firms, audits may constitute over 50 percent of total services. In the audit of historical financial statements, the responsible other party is the client that is making various assertions in the form of its published financial statements. The auditor's report expresses an opinion as to whether those financial statements are in conformity with generally accepted accounting principles. External users of financial statements look to the auditor's report as an indication of the reliability of the statements for their decision-making purposes.

**Reviews** Many nonpublic companies wish to issue financial statements to various users but do not wish to incur the cost of an audit report to accompany them. A type of attestation service that is useful in these circumstances is a review service. Whereas in an audit, the CPA firm performs an extensive examination that accumulates evidence sufficient to render a high level of assurance about the client's financial statements, in a review the evidence supports a moderate level of assurance. This is often adequate to meet users' needs and can be provided by the CPA firm at a much lower fee than a full audit.

**Other Attestation Services** There are numerous other types of attestation services. In recent years, more aggressive CPA firms have expanded their practices considerably by developing new types of these services. Just a few of the many examples of attest engagement subject matter are prospective financial statements (forecasts and projections), investment performance statistics for organizations such as mutual funds, and characteristics of computer software.

### Accounting and Bookkeeping Services

Many small clients with limited accounting staff rely upon CPA firms to prepare their financial statements. Some small clients lack the personnel or expertise to prepare even their own journals and ledgers. Thus, CPA firms perform a variety of accounting and bookkeeping services (termed *write-up work*) to meet the needs of these clients. In many cases where the financial statements are to be given to a third party, a review or even an audit is also performed. Where neither of these is done, the financial statements will be accompanied by a type of report by the CPA firm called a *compilation* report, which provides no assurance to third parties.[2]

Table 1-2 shows that attestation services and accounting and bookkeeping services account for approximately one-third to one-half of the revenue for most large CPA firms. Reviews, other attestation services, and compilations are studied in greater detail in Chapter 23.

**Tax Services** CPA firms prepare corporate and individual tax returns for both audit and nonaudit clients. In addition, estate tax, gift tax, tax planning, and other aspects of tax services are provided by most CPA firms. Tax services are now performed by almost every CPA firm, and for many small firms such services are far more important to their practice than auditing. Table 1-2 shows that revenue from taxes for larger firms ranges from 16 percent to 40 percent. Many small firms receive a much larger portion of their revenue from tax services.

**Management Advisory Services** Most CPA firms provide certain services that enable their clients to operate their businesses more effectively. These range from simple suggestions for improving the client's accounting system to advice in marketing strategies, computer installations, and actuarial benefit consulting. Many large CPA firms have departments involved exclusively in management advisory services with little interaction with the audit or tax staff. Revenue from management advisory services has increased signficantly in recent years. Table 1-2 shows that some CPA firms receive approximately half of their revenue from management advisory services.

## STRUCTURE OF CPA FIRMS

Three factors influence the organizational structure of CPA firms:

1. *The need for independence from clients.* Independence permits auditors to remain unbiased in drawing conclusions about the financial statements.
2. *The importance of a structure to encourage competence.* Competence permits auditors to conduct audits efficiently and effectively.
3. *The increased litigation risk faced by auditors.* In the last decade, several partners of CPA firms have been forced to file for personal bankruptcy because of lawsuits against their firms. Practitioners want to minimize this risk.

There are six organizational structures available to CPA firms, as discussed in the following section. All constitute the firm as a separate entity and provide the independence and competence features. The existence of a separate entity to perform audits encourages independence by avoiding an employee-employer relationship between CPA firms and their clients. A separate entity also enables a CPA firm to become sufficiently large to prevent any one client from representing a significant portion of a partner's or shareholder's total income and thereby endangering the firm's independence. Competence is encouraged by having a large number of professionals with related interests associated in one firm, which facilitates a professional attitude and makes continuing professional education more meaningful. The last four organizational structures discussed in the next section also provide some protection from litigation loss.

**Proprietorship** Only firms with one owner can operate in this form. Traditionally, all one-owner firms were organized as proprietorships, but in recent years most of them have changed to organizational forms with more limited liability because of litigation risks.

[2]As of the date of this publication, the Auditing Standards Board had an exposure draft outstanding that would permit CPAs to prepare unaudited financial statements of a nonpublic entity assembled for the entity's internal use only. *Assembly* is defined by the exposure draft to include preparing a working trial balance, assisting in adjusting the books of account, consulting on accounting matters, and preparing the financial statements.

**General Partnership** This form of organization is the same as a proprietorship, except that it applies to multiple owners. Until recently, all CPA firms were organized as general partnerships or proprietorships. Litigation risks caused the other four forms of organization described in the following section.

**General Corporation** The advantage of a corporation is that shareholders are only liable to the extent of their investment in the corporation. Most CPA firms do not organize as general corporations because they are prohibited by law from doing so in most states. State societies of CPAs and others are now lobbying to change these laws.

**Professional Corporation (PC)** A professional corporation provides professional services and is owned by one or more shareholders. Professional corporation laws and the resulting liability protection vary significantly from state to state. Professional corporation laws in some states offer personal liability protection similar to that of general corporations, whereas the protection in other states is minimal. This variation makes it difficult for a CPA firm with clients in different states to operate as a PC.

**Limited Liability Company (LLC)** An LLC combines the most favorable attributes of a general corporation and a general partnership. An LLC is structured and taxed like a general partnership, but its owners have limited personal liability similar to that of a general corporation.

The accounting profession has lobbied recently to enact LLC laws in more states. Currently, nearly all of the states have LLC laws and many of them allow accounting firms to operate as LLCs.

**Limited Liability Partnership (LLP)** An LLP is owned by one or more partners. It is structured and taxed like a general partnership, but the personal liability protection of an LLP is less than that of a general corporation or an LLC. Partners of an LLP are personally liable for the partnership's debts and obligations, their own acts, and acts of others under their supervision. Partners are not personally liable for liabilities arising from negligent acts of other partners and employees not under their supervision. It is not surprising that all of the Big Six firms and many smaller firms now operate as LLPs.

### Hierarchy of a Typical CPA Firm

The organizational hierarchy in a typical CPA firm includes partners or shareholders, managers, supervisors, seniors or in-charge auditors, and assistants, with a new employee usually starting as an assistant and spending two or three years in each classification before achieving partner status. The titles of the positions vary from firm to firm, but the structure is similar in all. When we refer in this text to the *auditor,* we mean the person performing some aspect of an audit. It is common to have one or more auditors from each level on larger engagements.

## AICPA

**OBJECTIVE 1-8**
**Describe the key functions performed by the AICPA.**

The most important influence on CPAs is exerted by their national professional organization, the American Institute of Certified Public Accountants (AICPA). The AICPA sets professional requirements for CPAs, conducts research, and publishes materials on many different subjects related to accounting, auditing, management advisory services, and taxes.

The membership of the AICPA is restricted to CPAs and currently exceeds 328,000, but not all members are practicing as independent auditors. Many formerly worked for a CPA firm but are currently in government, industry, and education. AICPA membership is not required of CPAs.

The AICPA has four major functions: establishing standards and rules, research and publications, CPA examination preparation and grading, and continuing education.

## Establishing Standards and Rules

The AICPA is empowered to set standards (guidelines) and rules that all members and other practicing CPAs must follow. The requirements are set by committees made up of AICPA members. There are four major areas in which the AICPA has authority to set standards and make rules.

1. *Auditing standards.* The Auditing Standards Board (ASB) is responsible for issuing pronouncements on auditing matters. They are referred to as Statements on Auditing Standards (SASs). The ASB and its predecessor organizations have been responsible for a considerable portion of the existing auditing literature. The SASs are examined later in this chapter and discussed throughout the text.

2. *Compilation and review standards.* The Compilation and Review Standards Committee is responsible for issuing pronouncements of the CPA's responsibilities when the CPA is associated with financial statements of privately owned companies that are not audited. They are referred to as Statements on Standards for Accounting and Review Services (SSARS). SSARS 1, issued in December 1978, supersedes preceding statements on auditing standards for unaudited financial statements. It covers two specific types of services: first, situations in which the accountant assists a client in preparing financial statements without giving any assurance about them (compilation services); second, situations in which the accountant performs inquiry and analytical procedures that provide a reasonable basis for expressing limited assurances that there are no material modifications that should be made to the statements (review services).

3. *Other attestation standards.* In 1986, the AICPA issued its *Statement on Standards for Attestation Engagements.* The purpose of that statement is twofold: First, it provides a framework to be followed by standard-setting bodies within the AICPA in developing detailed standards on specific types of attestation services. Second, it provides a framework for guidance to practitioners when no such specific standards exist. Both generally accepted auditing standards and compilation and review standards are consistent with the broader attestation standards. An example of a specific standard on other attestation services that has been issued under the broader attestation standards is the *Statement on Standards for Accountant's Services on Prospective Financial Information.* This standard is studied in Chapter 23.

4. *Code of Professional Conduct.* The AICPA Committee on Professional Ethics sets rules of conduct that CPAs are required to meet. These rules apply to all services performed by CPAs and provide a framework for the technical standards. The rules and their relationships to ethical conduct are the subject of Chapter 3.

## Research and Publications

The AICPA supports research by its own research staff and provides grants to others. It also publishes a variety of materials, including journals such as *The Journal of Accountancy,* industry audit guides for several industries, periodic updates of the *Codification of Statements on Auditing Standards,* and the *Code of Professional Conduct.*

## CPA Examination

The AICPA is responsible for both writing and grading the CPA exam. Approximately 65,000 candidates take the examination each time it is offered. The content and other information about the exam were discussed earlier.

## Continuing Education

The extensive and ever-changing body of knowledge in accounting, auditing, management advisory services, and taxes is such that continuous study is required for CPAs to stay current. The AICPA provides to its members a considerable number of seminars and education aids in a variety of subject matters. An example is a two-day seminar entitled "Professional and Legal Liability of the CPA."

## WAYS CPAs ARE ENCOURAGED TO PERFORM EFFECTIVELY

**OBJECTIVE 1-9**
**Identify ways CPAs are encouraged to perform effectively.**

Because CPA firms play an important social role, it is essential for the management of those firms and their professional staff to conduct themselves appropriately and do high-quality audits and other services. The AICPA and other outside organizational influences have developed several mechanisms to increase the likelihood of appropriate audit quality and professional conduct. These are summarized in Figure 1-3 and discussed in the remainder of this and subsequent chapters. For example, the ability of individuals separately or together to sue CPA firms exerts considerable influence on the way practitioners perform audits. Legal liability is studied in Chapter 4. The AICPA *Code of Professional Conduct* also has a significant influence on practitioners. It is meant to provide a standard of conduct for CPAs. The AICPA code and related issues of professional conduct are examined in Chapter 3. Shaded circles indicate items discussed in this chapter.

**FIGURE 1-3**
**Ways the Profession and Society Encourage CPAs to Conduct Themselves at a High Level**

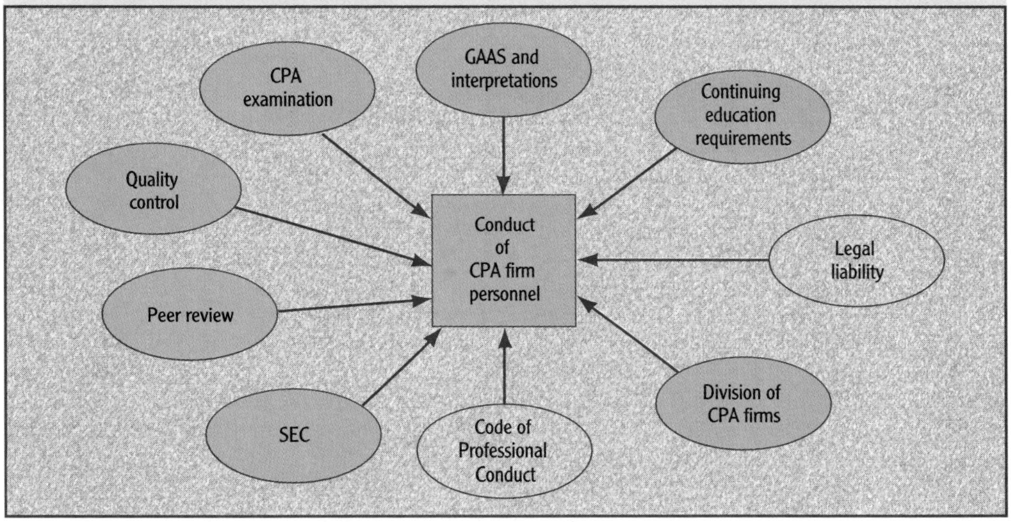


## GENERALLY ACCEPTED AUDITING STANDARDS

**OBJECTIVE 1-10**
**Use generally accepted auditing standards as a basis for further study.**

*Auditing standards* are general guidelines to aid auditors in fulfilling their professional responsibilities in the audit of historical financial statements. They include consideration of professional qualities such as competence and independence, reporting requirements, and evidence.

The broadest guidelines available are the ten *generally accepted auditing standards* (GAAS). Developed by the AICPA in 1947, they have, with minimal changes, remained the same. These standards are not sufficiently specific to provide any meaningful guide to practitioners, but they do represent a framework upon which the AICPA can provide interpretations. These ten standards are summarized in Figure 1-4 on page 19 and are stated in their entirety as follows (see page 18):

**GENERAL STANDARDS**

1. The audit is to be performed by a person or persons having adequate technical training and proficiency as an auditor.
2. In all matters relating to the assignment, an independence in mental attitude is to be maintained by the auditor or auditors.
3. Due professional care is to be exercised in the planning and performance of the audit and the preparation of the report.

**STANDARDS OF FIELD WORK**

1. The work is to be adequately planned and assistants, if any, are to be properly supervised.
2. A sufficient understanding of internal control is to be obtained to plan the audit and to determine the nature, timing, and extent of tests to be performed.
3. Sufficient competent evidential matter is to be obtained through inspection, observation, inquiries, and confirmations to afford a reasonable basis for an opinion regarding the financial statements under audit.

**STANDARDS OF REPORTING**

1. The report shall state whether the financial statements are presented in accordance with generally accepted accounting principles.
2. The report shall identify those circumstances in which such principles have not been consistently observed in the current period in relation to the preceding period.
3. Informative disclosures in the financial statements are to be regarded as reasonably adequate unless otherwise stated in the report.
4. The report shall either contain an expression of opinion regarding the financial statements, taken as a whole, or an assertion to the effect that an opinion cannot be expressed. When an overall opinion cannot be expressed, the reasons therefor should be stated. In all cases where an auditor's name is associated with financial statements, the report should contain a clear-cut indication of the character of the auditor's work, if any, and the degree of responsibility the auditor is taking.

## STATEMENTS ON AUDITING STANDARDS

The 1972 Statement on Auditing Standards No. 1 (SAS 1) and all subsequent SASs are the most authoritative references available to auditors. These statements are issued by the AICPA and are interpretations of generally accepted auditing standards. Frequently, these interpretations are referred to as auditing standards or GAAS, even though they are not one of the ten generally accepted auditing standards. This book will follow common practice and refer to the interpretations as auditing standards or SASs.

Statements on auditing standards are successors to the statements on auditing procedure of the AICPA. SAS 1 is a codification of fifty-four previous statements on auditing procedure dating from 1939 to 1972, while subsequent SASs are new pronouncements. New statements are issued whenever an auditing problem arises of sufficient importance to warrant an official interpretation by the AICPA. At this writing, SAS 82 was the last one issued and incorporated into the text materials. Readers should be alert to subsequent standards that influence auditing requirements.

All SASs are given two classification numbers: an SAS and an AU number. For example, the Statement on Auditing Standards, *The Relationship of Generally Accepted Auditing Standards to Quality Control Standards,* is SAS 25 and AU 161. The SAS number identifies the order in which it was issued in relation to other SASs; the AU number identifies its location in the AICPA codification of all SASs. For example, AUs beginning with a "2" are always interpretations of the general standards. Those beginning with a "3" are related to field work standards, and those beginning with a "4," "5," or "6" deal with reporting standards. Both classification systems are used in practice.

Generally accepted auditing standards and statements on auditing standards are regarded as *authoritative* literature because every member of the profession is required to fol-

**FIGURE 1-4**

**Summary of Generally Accepted Auditing Standards**

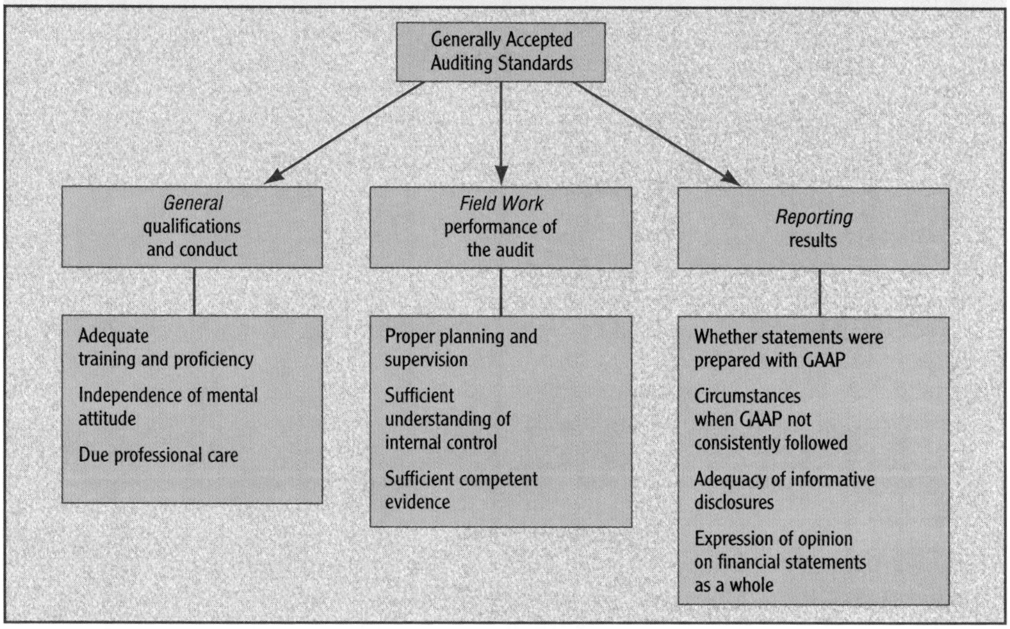


low their recommendations whenever they are applicable. They obtain their status of authoritative literature through the *Code of Professional Conduct,* Rule of Conduct 202, which is discussed in Chapter 3.

Although GAAS and the SASs are the authoritative auditing guidelines for members of the profession, they provide less direction to auditors than might be assumed. There are almost no specific audit procedures required by the standards; and there are no specific requirements for auditors' decisions, such as determining sample size, selecting sample items from the population for testing, or evaluating results. Many practitioners believe the standards should provide more clearly defined guidelines for determining the extent of evidence to be accumulated. Such specificity would eliminate some difficult audit decisions and provide a line of defense for a CPA firm charged with conducting an inadequate audit. However, highly specific requirements could turn auditing into mechanistic evidence gathering, devoid of professional judgment. From the point of view of both the profession and the users of auditing services, there is probably greater harm in defining authoritative guidelines too specifically than too broadly.

GAAS and the SASs should be looked upon by practitioners as *minimum standards* of performance rather than as maximum standards or ideals. Any professional auditor who seeks means of reducing the scope of the audit by relying only on the standards, rather than evaluating the substance of the situation, fails to satisfy the spirit of the standards. At the same time, the existence of auditing standards does not mean the auditor must always follow them blindly. If an auditor believes the requirement of a standard is impractical or impossible to perform, the auditor is justified in following an alternative course of action. Similarly, if the issue in question is immaterial in amount, it is also unnecessary to follow the standard. It is important to note, however, that the burden of justifying departures from the standards falls upon the practitioner.

When auditors desire more specific guidelines, they must turn to less authoritative sources. These include textbooks, journals, and technical publications. Materials published by the AICPA, mentioned earlier in the chapter, such as the *Journal of Accountancy* and industry audit guides, are useful in furnishing assistance on specific questions. In the remainder of this section, GAAS and their interpretations are discussed briefly. There is further study of the standards and frequent reference to the SASs throughout the text.

### Adequate Technical Training and Proficiency

The *general standards* stress the important personal qualities the auditor should possess. The first standard is normally interpreted as requiring the auditor to have formal education in auditing and accounting, adequate practical experience for the work being performed, and continuing professional education. Recent court cases clearly demonstrate that auditors must be technically qualified and experienced in those industries in which their audit clients are engaged.

In any case in which the CPA or the CPA's assistants are not qualified to perform the work, a professional obligation exists to acquire the requisite knowledge and skills, suggest someone else who is qualified to perform the work, or decline the engagement.

### Independence in Mental Attitude

The importance of independence was stressed earlier in the definition of auditing. The *Code of Professional Conduct* and the SASs stress the need for independence. CPA firms are required to follow several practices to increase the likelihood of independence of all personnel. For example, there are established procedures on larger audits whenever there is a dispute between management and the auditors. Specific methods to ensure that auditors maintain their independence are studied in Chapter 3.

### Due Professional Care

The third general standard involves *due care* in the performance of all aspects of auditing. Simply stated, this means that the auditor is a professional responsible for fulfilling his or her duties diligently and carefully. As an illustration, due care includes consideration of the completeness of the working papers, the sufficiency of the audit evidence, and the appropriateness of the audit report. As a professional, the auditor must avoid negligence and bad faith, but the auditor is not expected to make perfect judgments in every instance.

### Adequate Planning and Supervision

The *field work standards* concern evidence accumulation and other activities during the actual conduct of the audit in the field. The first standard deals with ascertaining that the engagement is sufficiently planned to ensure an adequate audit and proper supervision of assistants. Supervision is essential in auditing because a considerable portion of the field work is done by less experienced staff members.

### Understand the Client's Internal Control

One of the most widely accepted concepts in the theory and practice of auditing is the importance of the client's system of internal control to generate reliable financial information. If the auditor is convinced that the client has an excellent system of internal control, one that includes adequate internal controls for providing reliable data and for safeguarding assets and records, the amount of audit evidence to be accumulated can be significantly less than where there is one that is not adequate. In some instances internal control may be so inadequate as to preclude conducting an effective audit.

### Sufficient Competent Evidence

The decisions as to how much and what types of evidence to accumulate for a given set of circumstances are ones requiring professional judgment. A major portion of this book is concerned with the study of evidence accumulation and the circumstances affecting the amount and types needed.

### Four Reporting Standards

The four *reporting standards* require the auditor to prepare a report on the financial statements taken as a whole, including informative disclosures. The reporting standards require that the report state whether the statements are presented in accordance with generally accepted accounting principles and also identify any circumstances in which generally accepted accounting principles have not been consistently applied in the current year compared to the previous one.

## QUALITY CONTROL

**OBJECTIVE 1-11**
**Identify quality control standards and practices within the accounting profession.**

In 1978, the AICPA established the Quality Control Standards Committee and gave it responsibility to help CPA firms develop and implement quality control standards. For a CPA firm, quality control comprises the methods used to make sure that the firm meets its professional responsibilities to clients. These methods include the organizational structure of the CPA firm and procedures the firm establishes. For example, a CPA firm might have an organizational structure that assures the technical review of every engagement by a partner who has expertise in the client's industry.

Quality control is closely related to, but distinct from, GAAS. A CPA firm must make sure that generally accepted auditing standards are followed on every audit. Quality controls are the procedures used by the CPA firm that help it meet those standards consistently on every engagement. Quality controls are therefore established for the entire CPA firm, whereas GAAS are applicable to individual engagements.

SAS 25 (AU 161) requires a CPA firm to establish quality control policies and procedures. The standard recognizes that a quality control system can provide only reasonable assurance, not a guarantee, that GAAS are followed.

### Elements of Quality Control

The AICPA has not set specific quality control procedures for CPA firms. Procedures should depend on such things as the size of the firm, the number of practice offices, and the nature of the practice. For example, the quality control procedures of a 150-office international firm with many complex multinational clients should differ considerably from those of a five-person firm specializing in small audits in one or two industries.

The Quality Control Standards Committee identified nine elements of quality control that firms should consider in setting up their own policies and procedures. In May of 1996, the Auditing Standards Board reduced these nine elements to five, effective January 1, 1997. The five elements of quality control are listed in Table 1-3 (page 22) with a brief description of the requirement for each element and an example of a quality control procedure that a firm might use to satisfy the requirement.

### Division of CPA Firms

The AICPA has established a division for CPA firms and created two sections, the SEC Practice Section and the Private Companies Practice Section. The intent was to improve the quality of practice by CPA firms consistent with AICPA quality control standards. It represents an attempt at self-regulation and is intended to be responsive to the SEC and other critics of the profession. Each practice section has membership requirements and the authority to impose sanctions for noncompliance by members. A firm can choose to belong to one section, both sections, or neither. However, if a CPA firm audits one or more publicly held companies, it is required to belong to the SEC Practice Section. (The only exception is if no member of the CPA firm is a member of the AICPA, which is rare.)

The two sections have caused considerable controversy in the profession. Some members feel the change was needed to improve self-regulation. Others believe it establishes two classes of CPAs and implies a lower performance quality for firms that are not members of the SEC Practice Section.

The following are requirements for belonging to the SEC Practice Section (the first three are requirements of the Private Companies Practice Section as well and are considered by many to be the most critical requirements):

- *Adherence to quality control standards.* The CPA firm must agree to, and adhere to, the quality control standards set forth in the preceding section.
- *Mandatory peer review.* Each firm must have a periodic review of its quality controls and auditing and accounting practices by another qualified CPA firm.
- *Continuing education.* Every professional in the firm is required to have 120 hours of continuing professional education in every three-year period.

**TABLE 1-3**

**Five Elements of Quality Control**

| Element | Summary of Requirements | Example of a Procedure |
|---|---|---|
| Independence, integrity, and objectivity | All personnel on engagements should maintain independence in fact and in appearance, perform all professional responsibilities with integrity, and maintain objectivity in performing their professional responsibilities. | Each partner and employee must answer an "independence questionnaire" annually, dealing with such things as stock ownership and membership on boards of directors. |
| Personnel management | Policies and procedures should be established to provide the firm with reasonable assurance that<br>• All new personnel should be qualified to perform their work competently.<br>• Work is assigned to personnel who have adequate technical training and proficiency.<br>• All personnel should participate in continuing professional education and professional development activities that enable them to fulfill their assigned responsibilities.<br>• Personnel selected for advancement have the qualifications necessary for the fulfillment of their assigned responsibilities. | Each professional must be evaluated on every engagement using the firm's individual engagement evaluation report. |
| Acceptance and continuation of clients and engagements | Policies and procedures should be established for deciding whether to accept or continue a client relationship. These policies and procedures should minimize the risk of associating with a client whose management lacks integrity. The firm should also only undertake engagements that can be completed with professional competence. | A client evaluation form, dealing with such matters as predecessor auditor comments and evaluation of management, must be prepared for every new client before acceptance. |
| Engagement performance | Policies and procedures should exist to make sure that the work performed by engagement personnel meets applicable professional standards, regulatory requirements, and the firm's standards of quality. | The firm's director of accounting and auditing is available for consultation and must approve all engagements before their completion. |
| Monitoring | Policies and procedures should exist to make sure that the other four quality control elements are being effectively applied. | The quality control partner must test the quality control procedures at least annually to make sure the firm is in compliance. |

- *Partner rotation.* The assignment of a new audit partner to be in charge of each SEC engagement is required if another audit partner has been in charge of the engagement for a period of seven consecutive years. The incumbent partner is prohibited from returning to in-charge status on the engagement for a minimum of two years. Very small firms may be exempted from this requirement.
- *Concurring partner review.* All audits of publicly held companies must have a review by a partner other than the engagement partner, who must concur with the audit report before it can be issued.
- *Proscription of certain services.* The CPA firm must refrain from performing certain types of management advisory services for audit clients that are publicly held. These services include psychological testing, public opinion polls, merger and acquisition assistance for a finder's fee, executive recruitment, and actuarial services to insurance companies.

- *Reporting on disagreements.* An auditor is required to report to the audit committee or board of directors of each SEC audit client on the nature of major disagreements with management about accounting, disclosure, or auditing matters.
- *Reporting on management advisory services performed.* An auditor is required to report to the audit committee or board of directors of each SEC audit client the types of management advisory services performed for the client during the audit year, and the total fees for such services received.

The AICPA has also set up a special committee (Professional Oversight Board) to establish policies and solutions for the regulation of the SEC Practice Section. The members of the committee are highly respected individuals from business and the professions, mostly in fields other than accounting. This board has the potential for significantly influencing the practice of public accounting.

## Peer Review

Peer review is the review, by CPAs, of a CPA firm's compliance with its quality control system. The purpose of peer review is to determine and report whether the CPA firm being reviewed has developed adequate policies and procedures for the five elements of quality control and follows them in practice. Unless a firm has a peer review, all members of the CPA firm lose their eligibility for AICPA membership.

CPA firms that are members of the SEC Practice Section (SECPS) or Private Companies Practice Section (PCPS) must be reviewed at least once every three years. Peer reviews of SECPS member firms are administered under the peer review program of the Public Oversight Board. Peer reviews of PCPS member firms are administered through the state CPA societies under the overall direction of the AICPA peer review board. Typically, the review is done by a CPA firm selected by the firm being reviewed. Another option is to request the AICPA or state society to send a review team. After the review is completed, the reviewers issue a report stating their conclusions and recommendations. Only firms

**FIGURE 1-5**

**Relationship among GAAS, Quality Control, Division of CPA Firms, and Peer Review**

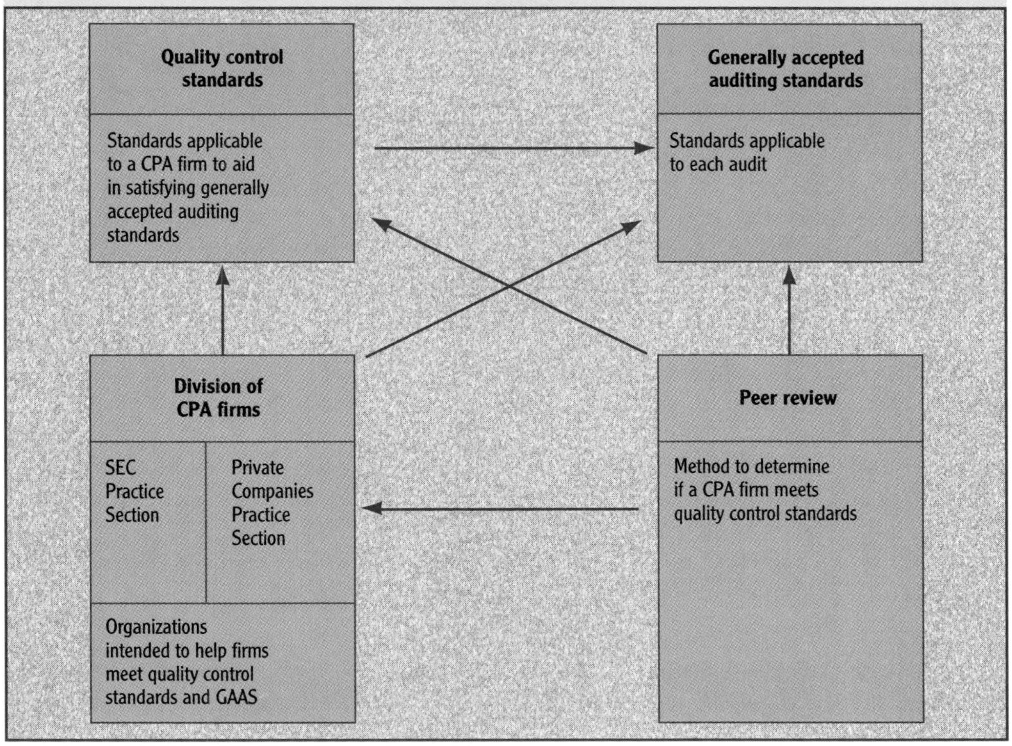

satisfactorily passing an SECPS or PCPS peer review can be members of the two practice sections. Approximately 1,200 firms are enrolled in the SECPS peer review program, while 7,300 PCPS member firms participate in the AICPA peer review program.

AICPA member firms who are not members of the SECPS or PCPS are also required to have peer reviews every three years (formerly called *quality reviews*). This type of peer review has the same objective as a peer review of an SECPS or PCPS member, but it is typically less extensive in the review of the implementation of the firm's quality control system. These peer reviews are also administered through the state CPA societies under the overall direction of the AICPA peer review board. Currently, approximately 32,000 firms are enrolled in this part of the AICPA peer review program.

Peer reviews can be beneficial to the profession and individual firms. By helping firms meet quality control standards, the profession gains from improved practitioner performance and higher-quality audits. A firm having a peer review can also gain if it improves the firm's practice and thereby enhances its reputation and effectiveness and reduces the likelihood of lawsuits. Of course, these reviews are costly. There is always a trade-off between cost and benefit. Figure 1-5 (page 23) summarizes the relationship among GAAS, quality control, division of CPA firms, and peer review.

## SECURITIES AND EXCHANGE COMMISSION

**OBJECTIVE 1-12**

**Summarize the role of the Securities and Exchange Commission in accounting and auditing.**

The overall purpose of the Securities and Exchange Commission (SEC), an agency of the federal government, is to assist in providing investors with reliable information upon which to make investment decisions. To this end, the Securities Act of 1933 requires most companies planning to issue *new securities* to the public to submit a registration statement to the SEC for approval. The Securities Exchange Act of 1934 provides additional protection by requiring the same companies and others to file detailed annual reports with the commission. The commission examines these statements for completeness and adequacy before permitting the company to sell its securities through the securities exchanges.

Although the SEC requires considerable information that is not of direct interest to CPAs, the securities acts of 1933 and 1934 require financial statements, accompanied by the opinion of an independent public accountant, as part of a registration statement and subsequent reports.

Of special interest to auditors are several specific reports that are subject to the reporting provisions of the securities acts. The most important of these are

- *Forms S-1 to S-16.* These forms must be completed and registered with the SEC whenever a company plans to issue new securities to the public. The S-1 form is the general form when there is no specifically prescribed form. The others are specialized forms. For example, S-10 is for restrictions of landholders' royalty interests in gas and oil. All S forms apply to the Securities Act of 1933.
- *Form 8-K.* This report is filed at the end of any month in which significant events have occurred that are of interest to public investors. Such events include the acquisition or sale of a subsidiary, a change in officers or directors, an addition of a new product line, or a change in auditors.
- *Form 10-K.* This report must be filed annually within 90 days after the close of each fiscal year. Extensive detailed financial information is contained in this report, including audited financial statements.
- *Form 10-Q.* This report must be filed quarterly for all publicly held companies. It contains certain financial information and requires audit involvement whenever there is a change in accounting principles.

Since large CPA firms usually have clients that must file one or more of these reports each year, and the rules and regulations affecting filings with the SEC are extremely complex, most CPA firms have specialists who spend a large portion of their time making sure that their clients satisfy all SEC requirements.

The SEC has considerable influence in setting generally accepted accounting principles and disclosure requirements for financial statements as a result of its authority for specifying reporting requirements considered necessary for fair disclosure to investors. The Accounting Principles Board followed the practice of working closely with the SEC, and the Financial Accounting Standards Board (FASB) has continued that tradition. In addition, the SEC has power to establish rules for any CPA associated with audited financial statements submitted to the commission. Even though the commission has taken the position that accounting principles and auditing standards should be set by the profession, the SEC's attitude is generally considered in any major change proposed by the FASB or the Auditing Standards Board.

The SEC requirements of greatest interest to CPAs are set forth in the commission's Regulation S-X, Accounting Series Releases, and Accounting and Auditing Enforcement Releases. These publications constitute important regulations, as well as decisions and opinions on accounting and auditing issues affecting any CPA dealing with publicly held companies. Some of the major influences the SEC has had on auditors in the past few decades are discussed in the text under the topics of independence, legal liability, and audit reporting.

## ESSENTIAL TERMS

**Accounting**—the recording, classifying, and summarizing of economic events in a logical manner for the purpose of providing financial information for decision making

**AICPA**—American Institute of Certified Public Accountants, a voluntary organization of CPAs that sets professional requirements, conducts research, and publishes materials relevant to accounting, auditing, management advisory services, and taxes

**Attestation**—a written communication regarding the reliability of another party's written assertion

**Auditing**—the accumulation and evaluation of evidence about information to determine and report on the degree of correspondence between the information and established criteria

**Audit report**—the communication of audit findings to users

**Certified public accountant**—a person who has met state regulatory requirements, including passing the uniform CPA exam and has thus been certified. A CPA may have as his or her primary responsibility the performance of the audit function on published historical financial statements of commercial and noncommercial financial entities.

**Compliance audit**—(1) a review of an organization's financial records performed to determine whether the organization is following specific procedures, rules, or regulations set down by some higher authority; (2) an audit performed to determine whether an entity that receives financial assistance from the federal government has complied with specific laws and regulations

**Division of CPA firms**—a division of the AICPA established for CPA firms and consisting of two sections: the SEC Practice Section and the Private Companies Practice Section. The division was established to improve the quality of practice by CPA firms consistent with AICPA quality control standards.

**Evidence**—any information used by the auditor to determine whether the information being audited is stated in accordance with established criteria

**Financial statement audit**—an audit conducted to determine whether the overall financial statements of an entity are stated in accordance with specified criteria (usually GAAP)

**General accounting office auditor**—an auditor working for the United States General Accounting Office (GAO). The GAO reports to, and is responsible solely to, Congress.

**Generally accepted auditing standards (GAAS)**—ten auditing standards, developed by the AICPA, consisting of general standards, standards of field work, and standards of reporting, along with interpretations. Often called auditing standards.

**Independent auditor**—a certified public accountant or accounting firm that performs audits of commercial and noncommercial financial entities

**Information risk**—the risk that information upon which a business decision is made is inaccurate

**Internal auditor**—an auditor employed by a company to audit for the company's board of directors and management

**Internal revenue agent**—an auditor who works for the Internal Revenue Service (IRS) and conducts examinations of taxpayers' returns

**Operational audit**—a review of any part of an organization's operating procedures and methods for the purpose of evaluating efficiency and effectiveness

**Peer review**—the review by CPAs of a CPA firm's compliance with its quality control system

**Quality control**—methods used by a CPA firm to make sure that the firm meets its professional responsibilities

**Securities and Exchange Commission (SEC)**—a federal agency that oversees the orderly conduct of the securities markets; the SEC assists in providing investors in public corporations with reliable information upon which to make investment decisions

**Statements on Auditing Standards**—pronouncements issued by the AICPA to interpret generally accepted auditing standards

## REVIEW QUESTIONS

**1-1 (Objective 1-1)** Explain what is meant by determining the degree of correspondence between information and established criteria. What are the information and established criteria for the audit of Jones Company's tax return by an internal revenue agent? What are they for the audit of Jones Company's financial statements by a CPA firm?

**1-2 (Objectives 1-1, 1-4)** Describe the nature of the evidence the internal revenue agent will use in the audit of Jones Company's tax return.

**1-3 (Objective 1-2)** In the conduct of audits of financial statements it would be a serious breach of responsibility if the auditor did not thoroughly understand accounting. However, many competent accountants do not have an understanding of the auditing process. What causes this difference?

**1-4 (Objective 1-3)** What are the differences and similarities in audits of financial statements, compliance audits, and operational audits?

**1-5 (Objectives 1-3, 1-4)** List five examples of specific operational audits that could be conducted by an internal auditor in a manufacturing company.

**1-6 (Objective 1-4)** What are the major differences in the scope of the audit responsibilities for CPAs, GAO auditors, IRS agents, and internal auditors?

**1-7 (Objective 1-5)** Discuss the major factors in today's society that have made the need for independent audits much greater than it was fifty years ago.

**1-8 (Objective 1-5)** Distinguish among the following three risks: risk-free interest rate, business risk, and information risk. Which one or ones does the auditor reduce by performing an audit?

**1-9 (Objective 1-5)** Identify the major causes of information risk and identify the three main ways information risk can be reduced. What are the advantages and disadvantages of each?

**1-10 (Objective 1-6)** Identify the four parts of the Uniform CPA Examination.

**1-11 (Objective 1-7)** State the four major types of services CPAs perform, and explain each.

**1-12 (Objectives 1-7, 1-9, 1-11)** What major characteristics of the organization and conduct of CPA firms permit them to fulfill their social function competently and independently?

**1-13 (Objective 1-8)** What roles are played by the American Institute of Certified Public Accountants for its members?

**1-14 (Objective 1-8)** What are the purposes of the AICPA *Standards for Attestation Engagements?*

**1-15 (Objective 1-10)** Distinguish between generally accepted auditing standards and generally accepted accounting principles, and give two examples of each.

**1-16 (Objective 1-10)** The first standard of field work requires the performance of the audit by a person or persons having adequate technical training and proficiency as an auditor. What are the various ways in which auditors can fulfill the requirement of the standard?

**1-17 (Objective 1-10)** Generally accepted auditing standards have been criticized by different sources for failing to provide useful guidelines for conducting an audit. The critics believe the standards should be more specific to enable practitioners to improve the quality of their performance. As the standards are now stated, some critics believe that they provide little more than an excuse to conduct inadequate audits. Evaluate this criticism of the 10 generally accepted auditing standards.

**1-18 (Objective 1-11)** What is meant by the term *quality control* as it relates to a CPA firm?

**1-19 (Objective 1-11)** The following is an example of a CPA firm's quality control procedure requirement: "Any person being considered for employment by the firm must have completed a basic auditing course and have been interviewed and approved by an audit partner of the firm before he or she can be hired for the audit staff." Which element of quality control does this procedure affect and what is the purpose of the requirement?

**1-20 (Objective 1-11)** State what is meant by the term *mandatory peer review*. What are the implications for the profession?

**1-21 (Objective 1-11)** What are the two sections of practice to which CPA firms may belong? State the arguments for and against these sections.

**1-22 (Objective 1-12)** Describe the role of the Securities and Exchange Commission in society and discuss its relationship with and influence on the practice of auditing.

## MULTIPLE CHOICE QUESTIONS FROM CPA EXAMINATIONS

**1-23 (Objectives 1-1, 1-5, 1-10)** The following questions deal with audits by CPA firms. Choose the best response.

a. Which of the following *best* describes why an independent auditor is asked to express an opinion on the fair presentation of financial statements?
   (1) It is difficult to prepare financial statements that fairly present a company's financial position, operations, and cash flows without the expertise of an independent auditor.
   (2) It is management's responsibility to seek available independent aid in the appraisal of the financial information shown in its financial statements.
   (3) The opinion of an independent party is needed because a company may *not* be objective with respect to its own financial statements.
   (4) It is a customary courtesy that all stockholders of a company receive an independent report on management's stewardship of the affairs of the business.

b. Independent auditing can *best* be described as
   (1) a branch of accounting.
   (2) a discipline that attests to the results of accounting and other functional operations and data.
   (3) a professional activity that measures and communicates financial and business data.
   (4) a regulatory function that prevents the issuance of improper financial information.

c. Rogers & Co. CPAs' policies require that all members of the audit staff submit weekly time reports to the audit manager, who then prepares a weekly summary work report regarding variance from budget for Rogers' review. This provides written evidence of Rogers & Co.'s professional concern regarding compliance with which of the following generally accepted auditing standards?

(1) Quality control. (3) Adequate review.
(2) Due professional care. (4) Adequate planning.

**1-24 (Objectives 1-3, 1-4)** The following questions deal with types of audits and auditors. Choose the best response.

a. Operational audits generally have been conducted by internal auditors and governmental audit agencies but may be performed by certified public accountants. A primary purpose of an operational audit is to provide
   (1) a means of assurance that internal accounting controls are functioning as planned.
   (2) a measure of management performance in meeting organizational goals.
   (3) the results of internal examinations of financial and accounting matters to a company's top-level management.
   (4) aid to the independent auditor, who is conducting the audit of the financial statements.

b. In comparison to the external auditor, an internal auditor is more likely to be concerned with
   (1) internal administrative control. (3) operational auditing.
   (2) cost accounting procedures. (4) internal control.

c. Which of the following *best* describes the operational audit?
   (1) It requires the constant review by internal auditors of the administrative controls as they relate to the operations of the company.
   (2) It concentrates on implementing financial and accounting control in a newly organized company.
   (3) It attempts and is designed to verify the fair presentation of a company's results of operations.
   (4) It concentrates on seeking out aspects of operations in which waste should be reduced by the introduction of controls.

d. Compliance auditing often extends beyond audits leading to the expression of opinion on the fairness of financial presentation and includes audits of efficiency, economy, effectiveness, as well as
   (1) accuracy. (3) adherence to specific rules or procedures.
   (2) evaluation. (4) internal control.

**1-25 (Objective 1-10)** The following questions deal with generally accepted auditing standards. Choose the best response.

a. The first general standard, which states in part that the audit is to be performed by a person or persons having adequate technical training, requires that an auditor have
   (1) education and experience in the field of auditing.
   (2) ability in the planning and supervision of the audit work.
   (3) proficiency in business and financial matters.
   (4) knowledge in the areas of financial accounting.

b. Which of the following *best* describes what is meant by generally accepted auditing standards?
   (1) Acts to be performed by the auditor.
   (2) Measures of the quality of the auditor's performance.
   (3) Procedures to be used to gather evidence to support financial statements.
   (4) Audit objectives generally determined on audit engagements.

c. The general group of the generally accepted auditing standards includes a requirement that
   (1) field work be adequately planned and supervised.
   (2) the auditor's report state whether or not the financial statements conform to generally accepted accounting principles.

(3) due professional care be exercised by the auditor.
(4) informative disclosures in the financial statements be reasonably adequate.

d. What is the general character of the three generally accepted auditing standards classified as standards of field work?
(1) The competence, independence, and professional care of persons performing the audit.
(2) Criteria for the content of the auditor's report on financial statements and related footnote disclosures.
(3) The criteria of audit planning and evidence gathering.
(4) The need to maintain an independence in mental attitude in all matters pertaining to the audit.

## DISCUSSION QUESTIONS AND PROBLEMS

**1-26 (Objective 1-1)** Fred Oatly is the loan officer of the National Bank of Dallas. National has a loan of $260,000 outstanding to Regional Delivery Service, a company specializing in delivering products of all types on behalf of smaller companies. National's collateral on the loan consists of 35 small delivery trucks with an average original cost of $17,000.

Oatly is concerned about the collectibility of the outstanding loan and whether the trucks still exist. He therefore engages Susan Virms, CPA, to count the trucks, using registration information held by Oatly. She was engaged because she spends most of her time auditing used automobile and truck dealerships and has extensive specialized knowledge about used trucks. Oatly requests that Virms issue a report stating:

1. Which of the 35 trucks is parked in Regional's parking lot on the night of June 30, 1996.
2. Whether all of the trucks are owned by Regional Delivery Service.
3. The condition of each truck, using the guidelines of poor, good, and excellent.
4. The fair market value of each truck, using the current "blue book" for trucks, which states the approximate wholesale prices of all used truck models, and also using the poor, good, and excellent condition guidelines.

### Required

a. For each of the following parts of the definition of auditing, state which part of the preceding narrative fits the definition:
(1) Information.
(2) Established criteria.
(3) Accumulating and evaluating evidence.
(4) Competent, independent person.
(5) Report of results.

b. Identify the greatest difficulties Virms is likely to have doing this audit.

**1-27 (Objective 1-4)** Five college seniors with majors in accounting are discussing alternative career plans. The first senior plans to become an internal revenue agent because his primary interest is income taxes. He believes the background in tax auditing will provide him with better exposure to income taxes than will any other available career choice. The second senior has decided to go to work for a CPA firm for at least five years, possibly as a permanent career. She feels the variety of experience in auditing and related fields offers a better alternative than any other available choice. The third senior has decided upon a career in internal auditing with a large industrial company because of the many different aspects of the organization with which internal auditors become involved. The fourth senior plans to become an auditor for the GAO because she believes that this career will provide excellent experience in computer auditing techniques. A fifth senior plans to pursue some aspect of auditing as a career but has not decided upon the type of organization to enter. He is especially interested in an opportunity to continue to grow professionally, but meaningful and interesting employment is also an important consideration.

### Required

a. What are the major advantages and disadvantages of each of the four types of auditing careers?

b. What other types of auditing careers are available to those who are qualified?

**1-28 (Objectives 1-3, 1-4)** In the normal course of performing their responsibilities, auditors frequently conduct audits or reviews of the following:

1. Federal income tax returns of an officer of the corporation to determine whether he or she has included all taxable income in his/her return.
2. Disbursements of a branch of the federal government for a special research project to determine whether it would have been possible to accomplish the same research results at a lower cost to the taxpayers.
3. Computer operations of a corporation to evaluate whether the computer center is being operated as efficiently as possible.
4. Annual statements for the use of management.
5. Operations of the Internal Revenue Service to determine whether the internal revenue agents are using their time efficiently in conducting audits.
6. Statements for bankers and other creditors when the client is too small to have an audit staff.
7. Financial statements of a branch of the federal government to make sure that the statements present fairly the actual disbursements made during a period of time.
8. Federal income tax returns of a corporation to determine whether the tax laws have been followed.
9. Financial statements for use by stockholders when there is an internal audit staff.
10. A bond indenture agreement to make sure a company is following all requirements of the contract.
11. The computer operations of a large corporation to evaluate whether the internal controls are likely to prevent misstatements in accounting and operating data.
12. Disbursements of a branch of the federal government for a special research project to determine whether the expenditures were consistent with the legislative bill that authorized the project.

### Required

a. For each of the 12 examples, state the most likely type of auditor (CPA, GAO, IRS, or internal).

b. In each example, state the type of audit (audit of financial statements, operational audit, or compliance audit).

**1-29 (Objectives 1-3, 1-4)** A large conglomerate is considering acquiring a medium-sized manufacturing company in a closely related industry. A major consideration by the management of the conglomerate in deciding whether to pursue the merger is the operational efficiency of the company. Management has decided to obtain a detailed report based on an intensive investigation of the operational efficiency of the sales department, production department, and research and development department.

### Required

a. Whom should the conglomerate engage to conduct the operational audit?

b. What major problems are the auditors likely to encounter in conducting the investigation and writing the report?

**1-30 (Objective 1-4)** Consumers Union is a nonprofit organization that provides information and counsel on consumer goods and services. A major part of its function is the testing of different brands of consumer products that are purchased on the open market and then reporting the results of the tests in *Consumer Reports,* a monthly publication. Examples of the types of products it tests are middle-sized automobiles, residential dehumidifiers, canned tuna, and boys' jeans.

## Required

a. Compare the concept of information risk introduced in the chapter with the information risk problem faced by a buyer of an automobile.

b. Compare the four causes of information risk faced by users of financial statements as discussed in the chapter with those faced by a buyer of an automobile.

c. Compare the three ways users of financial statements can reduce information risk with those available to a buyer of an automobile.

d. In what ways are the services provided by Consumers Union similar to audit services, and in what ways do they differ?

**1-31 (Objective 1-11)** The following comments summarize the beliefs of some practitioners about quality control and peer review.

> Quality control and peer review are quasi-governmental methods of regulating the profession. There are two effects of such regulation. First, it gives a competitive advantage to national CPA firms because they already need formal structures to administer their complex organizations. Quality control requirements do not significantly affect their structure. Smaller firms now need a more costly organizational structure, which has proven unnecessary because of existing partner involvement on engagements. The major advantage smaller CPA firms have traditionally had is a simple and efficient organizational structure. Now that advantage has been eliminated because of quality control requirements. Second, quality control and peer review are not needed to regulate the profession. The first four elements of quality control have always existed, at least informally, for quality firms. Three things already provide sufficient assurance that informal quality control elements are followed without peer review. They are competitive pressures to do quality work, legal liability for inadequate performance, and a code of professional conduct requiring that CPA firms follow generally accepted auditing standards.

## Required

a. State the pros and cons of those comments.

b. Evaluate whether quality control requirements and peer reviews are worth their cost.

**1-32 (Objective 1-11)** For each of the following procedures taken from the quality control manual of a medium-sized regional CPA firm, identify the applicable element of quality control from Table 1-3 on page 22.

## Required

a. Appropriate accounting and auditing research requires adequate technical reference library facilities. Each practice office must maintain minimal facilities including industry audit guides to help assure an awareness of problems unique to specific industries. In addition, a more extensive library is maintained in the office of the director of accounting and auditing.

b. Each audit engagement of the firm is directed by a partner and, in most instances, a manager of the firm. On every engagement, an attempt is made to maintain continuity of at least a portion of the personnel.

c. When prospective employees are interviewed by campus recruiters and are deemed to possess the potential for employment, they will be further screened by a practice office interview pursuant to the firm procedure for practice office visitation.

Practice office partners make the final hiring decisions pursuant to the guidelines established by the director of personnel.

d. At all stages of any engagement, an effort is made to involve professional staff at appropriate levels in the accounting and auditing decisions. Various approvals of the manager or senior accountant are obtained throughout the audit.

e. No employee will have any direct or indirect financial interest, association, or relationship (for example, a close relative serving a client in a decision-making capacity) not otherwise disclosed, that might be adverse to the firm's best interest.

f. Each office of the firm shall be visited on at least an annual basis by review persons selected by the director of accounting and auditing. Procedures to be undertaken by the reviewers are illustrated by the office review program.

g. Existing clients of the firm are reviewed on a continuing basis by the engagement partner. Termination may result if circumstances indicate there is reason to question the integrity of management or our independence, or if accounting and auditing differences of opinion cannot be reconciled. Doubts concerning whether the client–auditor relationship should be continued must be promptly discussed with the director of accounting and auditing.

h. Individual partners submit the nominations of those persons whom they wish to be considered for partner. To become a partner, an individual must have exhibited a high degree of technical competence, must possess integrity, motivation, and judgment, and must have a desire to help the firm progress through the efficient dispatch of the job responsibilities to which he or she is assigned.

i. Through our continuing employee evaluation and counseling program, and through the quality control review procedures as established by the firm, educational needs are reviewed and formal staff training programs modified to accommodate changing needs. At the conclusion of practice office reviews, apparent accounting and auditing deficiencies are summarized and reported to the firm's director of personnel.

**1-33 (Objectives 1-10, 1-12)** The Mobile Home Manufacturing Company is audited by Rossi and Montgomery, CPAs. Mobile Home has decided to issue stock to the public and wants Rossi and Montgomery to perform all the audit work necessary to satisfy the requirements for filing with the SEC. The CPA firm has never had a client go public before.

## Required

a. What are the ethical implications of Rossi and Montgomery's accepting the engagement?

b. List the additional problems confronting the auditors when they file with the SEC as compared with dealing with a regular audit client.

**1-34 (Objective 1-10)** Ray, the owner of a small company, asked Holmes, CPA, to conduct an audit of the company's records. Ray told Holmes that an audit was to be completed in time to submit audited financial statements to a bank as part of a loan application. Holmes immediately accepted the engagement and agreed to provide an auditor's report within three weeks. Ray agreed to pay Holmes a fixed fee plus a bonus if the loan was granted.

Holmes hired two accounting students to conduct the audit and spent several hours telling them exactly what to do. Holmes told the students not to spend time reviewing the controls but instead to concentrate on proving the mathematical accuracy of the ledger accounts, and summarizing the data in the accounting records that support Ray's financial statements. The students followed Holmes's instructions and after two weeks gave Holmes the financial statements, which did not include footnotes. Holmes reviewed the statements and prepared an unqualified auditor's report. The report did not refer to generally accepted accounting principles nor to the consistent application of such principles.

## Required

Briefly describe each of the generally accepted auditing standards and indicate how the action(s) of Holmes resulted in a failure to comply with each standard.

Organize your answer as follows:*

| BRIEF DESCRIPTION OF GAAS | HOLMES' ACTIONS RESULTING IN FAILURE TO COMPLY WITH GAAS |
|---|---|

*AICPA adapted

# 2

# AUDIT REPORTS

## LEARNING OBJECTIVES

Thorough study of this chapter will enable you to

**2-1** Describe the nature of and need for the auditor's report.

**2-2** Specify the conditions that justify issuing the standard unqualified audit report, and describe the report.

**2-3** Identify the four categories of audit reports.

**2-4** Describe the five circumstances when an unqualified report with an explanatory paragraph or modified wording is appropriate.

**2-5** List the three conditions requiring a departure from an unqualified audit report.

**2-6** Identify the three types of audit reports that can be issued when an unqualified opinion is not justified.

**2-7** Explain how materiality affects audit reporting decisions.

**2-8** Draft appropriately modified audit reports under a variety of circumstances.

**2-9** Describe the process for deciding the appropriate audit report.

## THE AUDIT REPORT WAS TIMELY, BUT AT WHAT COST?

In 1987, Halvorson & Co., CPAs became the auditor for Machinetron, Inc., a company that manufactured high-precision, computer-operated lathes. Machinetron had been started by Al Trent, a man considered to be a fine engineer as well as an astute businessperson. Trent felt that he was ready to take Machinetron public, and he engaged Halvorson to conduct the upcoming audit and assist in the preparation of the registration statement for a securities offering.

Because Machinetron's machines were large and complex, they were expensive. Although the number of sales per year were few, the high sales prices resulted in large revenues. In addition, individual sales often transpired over a long period of time and Trent negotiated many of the sales personally. Due to these facts, improper recording of just one or two machines could represent a material misstatement of the financial statements.

The engagement partner in charge of the Machinetron audit was Bob Lehman, who had significant experience in auditing manufacturing companies. He realized the risks associated with a growing company, including testing the existence of recorded sales at year-end. For that reason, he insisted that the staff obtain confirmations of the receivables associated with all sales occurring during the months just before year-end.

In addition to his responsibilities on the Machinetron engagement, Lehman was overburdened with work for two other clients. He conducted his review of the Machinetron working papers on the same day that Trent wanted to make the Company's registration statement effective. In reviewing the confirmation working papers, Lehman saw that a major receivable for a sale occurring at year-end was supported by a telegram rather than by a conventional confirmation reply. Apparently, relations were "touchy" with this customer, and Trent discouraged the staff from talking directly with the customer about the confirmation. Finally, this telegram arrived. Given that the machine had been shipped (although not yet paid for), the staff felt the sale was supported.

At the end of the day, a meeting was called at Machinetron's office. It was attended by Lehman, Trent, a representative of the Company's underwriting firm, and the Company's attorney. When Trent asked Lehman if there were any problems with the audit, Lehman mentioned the telegram confirmation. He said he felt his firm needed to obtain a better form of confirmation. At this news, Trent blew his stack. After a few moments, Machinetron's lawyer stepped in and got Trent to calm down. He offered to write Halvorson & Co. a letter stating that in his opinion, a telegram had legal substance as a valid confirmation reply. Lehman, feeling under tremendous pressure, accepted this proposal and the registration went ahead.

Six months later, Machinetron issued a public statement indicating that its revenues reported for the previous fiscal year and the first two quarters of the current fiscal year were overstated due to improperly recorded sales, including the sale supported by the telegram confirmation. Lawsuits and an SEC investigation followed, during which it was discovered that the subject telegram was sent by Trent, not the customer. Halvorson suffered significant damages, and Bob Lehman was subsequently forbidden to practice before the SEC. He ultimately left public accounting.

**OBJECTIVE 2-1**
**Describe the nature of and need for the auditor's report.**

Reports are essential to the audit or other attestation process because they inform users what the auditor did and the conclusions reached. From the user's perspective, the report is considered the primary product of the attestation process.

Professional Standards require that a report be issued whenever a CPA firm is associated with financial statements.[1] Association exists, for example, even if a CPA firm only assists a client in preparing financial statements but does not do an audit. In that case, either a compilation or a review report, but certainly not an audit report, would be appropriate. An audit report is appropriate only when an audit is conducted.

CPA firms issue a wide variety of audit or other attestation reports, depending on the circumstances. There are four primary categories of attestation reports, which are shown in Table 2-1. Because of the complexity of the wide variety of reporting requirements, only the basics can be covered in a fundamentals of auditing text. This chapter covers only reports on basic historical financial statements prepared on the basis of generally accepted accounting principles. Reporting topics dealing with the other three categories of reports included in Table 2-1 are discussed in Chapter 23.

The requirements for issuing audit reports are derived from the four generally accepted auditing standards for reporting, included on page 18. The last standard is especially important because it requires an expression of an opinion about the overall financial statements or a specific statement that an overall opinion is not possible, along with the reasons for not expressing an opinion. The standard also requires a clear-cut statement by the auditor of the nature of the audit and the degree to which the auditor limits his or her responsibility. Approximately half of the SASs involve reporting requirements. Given the importance of auditors' reports as a communication device, that is not surprising.

The profession recognizes the need for uniformity in reporting as a means of avoiding confusion. Users would have considerable difficulty interpreting the meaning of an auditor's report if each were an original creation. The professional standards, therefore, have defined and enumerated the types of audit reports that should be included with financial statements. The wording of audit reports is reasonably uniform, but different audit reports are appropriate for different circumstances.

**TABLE 2-1**

**Four Primary Categories of Audit or Other Attestation Reports**

| Type of Report | Example | Source of Authoritative Support |
|---|---|---|
| Audit report based on an audit of historical financial statements prepared in accordance with generally accepted accounting principles | Audit report for the audit of General Mills' financial statements | Auditing Standards |
| Special audit report based on audits of certain accounts, agreed-upon audit procedures, or a basis of accounting other than generally accepted accounting principles | Special audit report for the audit of Ron's Shoe Store's ending balance in inventory | Auditing Standards |
| Attestation report based on performing an attestation engagement | Attestation report for the attestation of General Mills' forecasted financial statements | Attestation Standards |
| Report based on performing a review engagement | Review report for the review of Ron's Shoe Store's quarterly financial statements | Accounting and Review Services Standards for nonpublic companies; Auditing Standards for public companies |

[1]As described in the footnote on page 14, as of the date of this publication, the Auditing Standards Board had an outstanding exposure draft that would permit CPAs to prepare unaudited financial statements of a nonpublic entity assembled for the entity's internal use only.

The audit report is the final step in the entire audit process. The reason for studying it now, rather than later, is to permit reference to different audit reports as evidence accumulation is studied throughout the text. After you understand the form and content of the final product of the audit, evidence accumulation concepts are more meaningful.

## STANDARD UNQUALIFIED AUDIT REPORT

The most common type of audit report is the *standard unqualified audit report.* It is used for more than 90 percent of all audit reports. The standard unqualified report is used when the following conditions have been met:

### Conditions for Standard Unqualified Report

**OBJECTIVE 2-2**
**Specify the conditions that justify issuing the standard unqualified audit report, and describe the report.**

1. All statements—balance sheet, income statement, statement of retained earnings, and statement of cash flows—are included in the financial statements.
2. The three general standards have been followed in all respects on the engagement.
3. Sufficient evidence has been accumulated and the auditor has conducted the engagement in a manner that enables him or her to conclude that the three standards of field work have been met.
4. The financial statements are presented in accordance with generally accepted accounting principles. This also means that adequate disclosures have been included in the footnotes and other parts of the financial statements.
5. There are no circumstances requiring the addition of an explanatory paragraph or modification of the wording of the report.

When these conditions are met, the standard audit report, as shown in Figure 2-1 (page 38), is issued. Different auditors may vary the wording slightly in standard reports, but the meaning will be the same. Notice that the report in Figure 2-1 is on comparative financial statements; therefore, a report on both years' statements is needed.

### Parts of Standard Unqualified Audit Report

Regardless of the auditor, the following seven parts of the audit report remain the same. These seven parts are labeled in bold letters in Figure 2-1.

*1. Report title.* Auditing standards require that the report be titled and that the title include the word *independent.* For example, appropriate titles would be "independent auditor's report," "report of independent auditor," or "independent accountant's opinion." The requirement that the title include the word "independent" is intended to convey to users that the audit was unbiased in all aspects.

*2. Audit report address.* The report is usually addressed to the company, its stockholders, or the board of directors. In recent years, it has become customary to address the report to the stockholders, to indicate that the auditor is independent of the company and the board of directors.

*3. Introductory paragraph.* The first paragraph of the report does three things: First, it makes the simple statement that the CPA firm has done an *audit.* This is intended to distinguish the report from a compilation or review report. The scope paragraph (see part 4) clarifies what is meant by an audit.

Second, it lists the financial statements that were audited, including the balance sheet dates and the accounting periods for the income statement and statement of cash flows. The wording of the financial statements in the report should be identical to those used by management on the financial statements.

Third, the introductory paragraph states that the statements are the responsibility of management and that the auditor's responsibility is to express an opinion on the statements based on an audit. The purpose of these statements is to communicate that management is responsible for selecting the appropriate generally accepted accounting principles and making the measurement decisions and disclosures in applying those principles, and to clarify the respective roles of management and the auditor.

**FIGURE 2-1**

**Standard Unqualified Report on Comparative Statements**

| | |
|---|---|
| | ANDERSON and ZINDER, P.C.<br>Certified Public Accountants<br>Suite 100<br>Park Plaza East<br>Denver, Colorado 80110<br>303/359-0800 |
| **Report Title** | Independent Auditor's Report |
| **Address** | To the Stockholders<br>General Ring Corporation |
| **Introductory Paragragh (Factual Statement)** | We have audited the accompanying balance sheets of General Ring Corporation as of December 31, 1997 and 1996, and the related statements of income, retained earnings, and cash flows for the years then ended. These financial statements are the responsibility of the Company's management. Our responsibility is to express an opinion on these financial statements based on our audits. |
| **Scope Paragraph (Factual Statement)** | We conducted our audits in accordance with generally accepted auditing standards. Those standards require that we plan and perform the audit to obtain reasonable assurance about whether the financial statements are free of material misstatement. An audit includes examining, on a test basis, evidence supporting the amounts and disclosures in the financial statements. An audit also includes assessing the accounting principles used and significant estimates made by management, as well as evaluating the overall financial statement presentation. We believe that our audits provide a reasonable basis for our opinion. |
| **Opinion Paragraph (Conclusions)** | In our opinion, the financial statements referred to above present fairly, in all material respects, the financial position of General Ring Corporation as of December 31, 1997 and 1996 and the results of its operations and its cash flows for the years then ended in conformity with generally accepted accounting principles. |
| **Name of CPA Firm** | ANDERSON AND ZINDER, P.C., CPAs |
| **Audit Report Date(Date Audit Field Work Is Completed)** | March 5, 1998 |

*4. Scope paragraph.* The scope paragraph is a factual statement about what the auditor did in the audit. This paragraph first states that the auditor followed generally accepted auditing standards. The remainder briefly describes important aspects of an audit.

The scope paragraph states that the audit is designed to obtain *reasonable assurance* about whether the statements are free of *material* misstatement. The inclusion of the word *material* conveys that auditors are responsible only to search for significant misstatements, not minor misstatements that do not affect users' decisions. The use of the term *reasonable assurance* is intended to indicate that an audit cannot be expected to completely eliminate the possibility that a material misstatement will exist in the financial statements. In other words, an audit provides a high level of assurance, but it is not a guarantee.

The remainder of the scope paragraph discusses the audit evidence accumulated and states that the auditor believes that the evidence accumulated was appropriate for the circumstances to express the opinion presented. The words *test basis* indicate that sampling was used rather than an audit of every transaction and amount on the statements. Whereas the introductory paragraph of the report states that management is responsible for the preparation and content of the financial statements, the scope paragraph states that the auditor evaluates the appropriateness of those accounting principles, estimates, and financial statement disclosures and presentations given.

*5. Opinion paragraph.* The final paragraph in the standard report states the auditor's conclusions based on the results of the audit. This part of the report is so important that frequently the entire audit report is referred to simply as the *auditor's opinion.* The opinion paragraph is stated as an opinion rather than as a statement of absolute fact or a guarantee. The intent is to indicate that the conclusions are based on professional judgment. Using the terminology of Chapter 1, the phrase "in our opinion" indicates that there may be some information risk associated with the financial statements, even though the statements have been audited.

The opinion paragraph is directly related to the first and fourth generally accepted auditing reporting standards listed on page 18. The auditor is required to state an opinion about the financial statements taken as a whole, including a conclusion about whether the company followed generally accepted accounting principles.

One of the controversial parts of the auditor's report is the meaning of the term *present fairly.* Does this mean that if generally accepted accounting principles are followed, the financial statements are presented fairly, or something more? Occasionally, the courts have concluded that auditors are responsible for looking beyond generally accepted accounting principles to determine whether users might be misled, even if those principles are followed. Most auditors believe that financial statements are "presented fairly" when the statements are in accordance with generally accepted accounting principles, but that it is also necessary to examine the substance of transactions and balances for possible misinformation.

*6. Name of CPA Firm.* The name identifies the CPA firm or practitioner that performed the audit. Typically, the firm's name is used, since the entire CPA firm has the legal and professional responsibility to make certain that the quality of the audit meets professional standards.

*7. Audit report date.* The appropriate date for the report is the one on which the auditor has completed the most important auditing procedures in the field. This date is important to users because it indicates the last day of the auditor's responsibility for the review of significant events that occurred after the date of the financial statements. For example, if the balance sheet is dated December 31, 1996, and the audit report is dated March 6, 1997, this indicates that the auditor has searched for material unrecorded transactions and events that occurred up to March 6, 1997.

## CATEGORIES OF AUDIT REPORTS

**OBJECTIVE 2-3**
**Identify the four categories of audit reports.**

Most knowledgeable users of financial statements read the auditor's report. When they observe that the report consists of three standard paragraphs, they conclude that the five conditions listed on page 37 have been met. Such a report provides users comfort that information risk has been reduced to a reasonable level.

A deviation from the standard unqualified report will cause knowledgeable users of financial statements to recognize that the auditor intends to communicate additional or limiting information. In extreme cases, the auditor may conclude that the financial statements are materially misstated, but usually the cause of the deviation is far less significant. Nevertheless, the information must have potential relevance to users or the auditor wouldn't include it.

The categorization of audit reports in Figure 2-2 on page 40 is used throughout the remainder of the chapter. The departures from a standard unqualified report are considered increasingly severe as one goes down the figure. Stated differently, a disclaimer or adverse opinion is normally far more important to users than an unqualified report with an explanatory paragraph or modified wording.

**FIGURE 2-2**

**Four Categories of Audit Reports**

| | |
|---|---|
| Standard Unqualified | The five conditions stated on page 37 have been met. |
| Unqualified with Explanatory Paragraph or Modified Wording | A complete audit took place with satisfactory results and financial statements that are fairly presented, but the auditor believes that it is important or required to provide additional information. |
| Qualified | The auditor concludes that the overall financial statements are fairly presented, but the scope of the audit has been materially restricted or generally accepted accounting principles were not followed in preparing the financial statements. |
| Adverse or Disclaimer | The auditor concludes that the financial statements are not fairly presented (adverse) or he or she is not able to form an opinion as to whether the financial statements are fairly presented (disclaimer). |

## UNQUALIFIED AUDIT REPORT WITH EXPLANATORY PARAGRAPH OR MODIFIED WORDING

**OBJECTIVE 2-4**

**Describe the five circumstances when an unqualified report with an explanatory paragraph or modified wording is appropriate.**

In certain situations, an unqualified audit report is issued, but the wording deviates from the standard unqualified report. It is important to distinguish between these reports and the qualified, adverse, and disclaimer reports which are discussed in a later section. The *unqualified report with explanatory paragraph or modified wording* meets the criteria of a complete audit with satisfactory results and financial statements that are fairly presented, but the auditor believes it is important, or is required, to provide additional information. In a *qualified, adverse, or disclaimer report*, the auditor either has not performed a satisfactory audit or is not satisfied that the financial statements are fairly presented.

The following are the most important causes of the addition of an explanatory paragraph or a modification in the wording of the unqualified standard report:

- Lack of consistent application of generally accepted accounting principles
- Substantial doubt about going concern
- Auditor agrees with a departure from promulgated accounting principles
- Emphasis of a matter
- Reports involving other auditors

The first four reports all require an explanatory paragraph. In each case, the three standard report paragraphs are included without modification and there is a separate explanatory paragraph.

Only reports involving the use of other auditors use a modified wording report. This report contains three paragraphs and all three paragraphs are modified.

### Lack of Consistent Application of GAAP

The second reporting standard requires the auditor to call attention to circumstances in which accounting principles have not been consistently observed in the current period in relation to the preceding period. Generally accepted accounting principles require that changes in accounting principles, or their method of application, be to a preferable principle and that the nature and impact of the change be adequately disclosed. When such changes occur, the auditor should modify the report by adding an explanatory paragraph after the opinion paragraph that discusses the nature of the change and points the reader to the footnote that discusses the change. Figure 2-3 presents such an explanatory paragraph.

**FIGURE 2-3**

**Explanatory Paragraph Because of Change in Accounting Principle**

**INDEPENDENT AUDITOR'S REPORT**

(Same introductory, scope, and opinion paragraphs as the standard report)

As discussed in Note 8 to the financial statements, the Company changed its method of computing depreciation in 1996.

**Fourth Paragraph—Explanatory Paragraph**

It is implicit in the explanatory paragraph in Figure 2-3 that the auditor concurs with the appropriateness of the change in accounting principles. If the auditor does not so concur, the change is considered a violation of generally accepted accounting principles, and his or her opinion must be qualified as discussed in the next section.

**Consistency versus Comparability** The auditor must be able to distinguish between changes that affect consistency and those that may affect comparability but do not affect consistency. The following are examples of changes that affect consistency and, therefore, require an explanatory paragraph if they are material:

1. Changes in accounting principles, such as a change from FIFO to LIFO inventory valuation
2. Changes in reporting entities, such as the inclusion of an additional company in combined financial statements
3. Corrections of errors involving principles, by changing from an accounting principle that is not generally acceptable to one that is generally acceptable, including correction of the resulting error

Changes that affect comparability but not consistency, and therefore need not be included in the audit report, include the following:

1. Changes in an estimate, such as a decrease in the life of an asset for depreciation purposes
2. Error corrections not involving principles, such as a previous year's mathematical error
3. Variations in format and presentation of financial information
4. Changes because of substantially different transactions or events, such as new endeavors in research and development or the sale of a subsidiary

Items that materially affect the comparability of financial statements generally require disclosure in the footnotes. A qualified audit report for inadequate disclosure may be required if the client refuses to properly disclose the items.

## Substantial Doubt about Going Concern

Even though the purpose of an audit is not to evaluate the financial health of the business, the auditor has a responsibility to evaluate whether the company is likely to continue as a going concern. SAS 59 (AU 341) addresses this problem under the heading *The Auditor's Consideration of an Entity's Ability to Continue as a Going Concern.* For example, the existence of one or more of the following factors causes uncertainty about the ability of a company to continue as a going concern:

1. Significant recurring operating losses or working capital deficiencies
2. Inability of the company to pay its obligations as they come due
3. Loss of major customers, the occurrence of uninsured catastrophes such as an earthquake or flood, or unusual labor difficulties

4. Legal proceedings, legislation, or similar matters that have occurred that might jeopardize the entity's ability to operate

The auditor's concern in such situations is the possibility that the client may not be able to continue its operations or meet its obligations for a reasonable period of time. For this purpose, a reasonable period of time is considered not to exceed one year from the date of the financial statements being audited.

When the auditor concludes that there is substantial doubt about the entity's ability to continue as a going concern, an unqualified opinion with an explanatory paragraph is required, regardless of the disclosures in the financial statements. Figure 2-4 provides an example in which there is substantial doubt about going concern.

**FIGURE 2-4**

**Explanatory Paragraph Because of Substantial Doubt about Going Concern**

**INDEPENDENT AUDITOR'S REPORT**

(Same introductory, scope, and opinion paragraphs as the standard report)

**Fourth Paragraph—Explanatory Paragraph**

The accompanying financial statements have been prepared assuming that Fairfax Company will continue as a going concern. As discussed in Note 11 to the financial statements, Fairfax Company has suffered recurring losses from operations and has a net capital deficiency that raise substantial doubt about the company's ability to continue as a going concern. Management's plans in regard to these matters are also described in Note 11. The financial statements do not include any adjustments that might result from the outcome of this uncertainty.

SAS 59 permits, but does not require, a disclaimer of opinion when there is substantial doubt about going concern. (Disclaimers are discussed in a later section.) The criteria for issuing a disclaimer of opinion instead of adding an explanatory paragraph are not stated in the standards and this type of opinion is rarely issued in practice. An example for which a disclaimer might be issued is when a regulatory agency, such as the Environmental Protection Agency, is considering a severe sanction against a company and, if the proceedings are adverse, the company will be forced to liquidate.

## Auditor Agrees with a Departure from a Promulgated Principle

As discussed in a later section (pages 51–52), Rule 203 of the AICPA *Code of Professional Conduct* states that in unusual situations a departure from an accounting principle promulgated by a body designated by the AICPA to establish accounting principles may not require a qualified or adverse opinion. However, to justify an unqualified opinion, the auditor must be satisfied and must state and explain, in a separate paragraph or paragraphs in the audit report, that to have adhered to the principle would have produced a misleading result in that situation.

## Emphasis of a Matter

Under certain circumstances, the CPA may wish to emphasize specific matters regarding the financial statements even though he or she intends to express an unqualified opinion. Normally, such explanatory information should be included in a separate paragraph in the report. The following are examples of explanatory information the auditor may feel should be expressed: the existence of significant related party transactions, important events occurring subsequent to the balance sheet date, and the description of accounting matters affecting the comparability of the financial statements with those of the preceding year.

## Reports Involving Other Auditors

When the CPA relies upon a different CPA firm to perform part of the audit, which is common when the client has several widespread branches or subdivisions, the principal CPA firm has three alternatives. Only the second is an unqualified report with modified wording.

**1. Make no reference in the audit report** When no reference is made to the other auditor, a standard unqualified opinion is given unless other circumstances require a departure. This approach is typically followed when the other auditor audited an immaterial portion of the statements, the other auditor is well-known or closely supervised by the principal auditor, or the principal auditor has thoroughly reviewed the other auditor's work. The other auditor is still responsible for his or her own report and work in the event of a lawsuit or SEC action.

**2. Make reference in the report (modified wording report)** This type of report is referred to as a *shared opinion or report.* A shared unqualified report is appropriate when it is impractical to review the work of the other auditor or when the portion of the financial statements audited by the other CPA is material in relation to the whole. An example of a shared report that should not be construed as a qualification is shown in Figure 2-5. Notice that the report *does not* include a separate paragraph that discusses the shared responsibility, but does so in the introductory paragraph, and refers to the other auditor in the scope and opinion paragraphs. Notice also that the portions of the financial statements audited by the other auditor are stated as absolute amounts.

**3. Qualify the opinion** The principal auditor may conclude that a qualified opinion is required. A qualified opinion or disclaimer, depending on materiality, is required if the principal auditor is not willing to assume any responsibility for the work of the other

**FIGURE 2-5**

**Unqualified Shared Report**

**INDEPENDENT AUDITOR'S REPORT**

Stockholders and Board of Directors
Washington Felp, Midland, Texas

We have audited the accompanying consolidated balance sheets of Washington Felp as of July 31, 1997 and 1996, and the related consolidated statements of income, retained earnings, and cash flows for the years then ended. These financial statements are the responsibility of the Company's management. Our responsibility is to express an opinion on these financial statements based on our audits. We did not audit the financial statements of Stewart Pane and Lighting, a consolidated subsidiary in which the Company had an equity interest of 84% as of July 31, 1997, which statements reflect total assets of $2,420,000 and $2,237,000 as of July 31, 1997 and 1996, respectively, and total revenues of $3,458,000 and $3,121,000 for the years then ended. Those statements were audited by other auditors whose report has been furnished to us, and our opinion, insofar as it relates to the amounts included for Stewart Pane and Lighting, is based solely on the report of the other auditors.

**Introductory Paragraph—Modified Wording**

We conducted our audits in accordance with generally accepted auditing standards. Those standards require that we plan and perform the audit to obtain reasonable assurance about whether the financial statements are free of material misstatement. An audit includes examining, on a test basis, evidence supporting the amounts and disclosures in the financial statements. An audit also includes assessing the accounting principles used and significant estimates made by management, as well as evaluating the overall financial statement presentation. We believe that our audits and the report of other auditors provide a reasonable basis for our opinion.

**Scope Paragraph—Modified Wording**

In our opinion, based on our audits and the report of other auditors, the consolidated financial statements referred to above present fairly, in all material respects, the financial position of Washington Felp as of July 31, 1997 and 1996, and the results of its operations and its cash flows for the years then ended in conformity with generally accepted accounting principles.

**Opinion Paragraph—Modified Wording**

September 16, 1997
Farn, Ross, & Co.
Certified Public Accountants
Dallas, Texas

auditor. (An alternative option is for the principal auditor to extend his or her work in that portion of the audit done by the other auditor.) The principal auditor may also decide that a qualification is required in the overall report if the other auditor qualified his or her portion of the audit. Qualified opinions and disclaimers are discussed in a later section.

**Material Uncertainties**

Management often makes estimates in preparing financial statements. Usually, management has sufficient information to calculate these estimates, but sometimes it is impractical to do so. These matters are defined as uncertainties. Examples include: realizable value of a significant receivable where collectibility is questionable and income tax or litigation contingencies. The accounting for these types of estimates and uncertainties is prescribed by FASB 5, *Accounting for Contingencies* and Statement of Position 94-6, *Disclosure of Certain Significant Risks and Uncertainties.*

Prior to December of 1995, an auditor was required to add an explanatory paragraph to the audit report for material uncertainties under certain conditions. In December of 1995, the Auditing Standards Board issued SAS 79, which amended SAS 58 (AU 508) to eliminate this requirement. The Board concluded that accounting standards now provide adequate disclosure of risks and uncertainties in financial statements and that the previously required uncertainties explanatory paragraph did not communicate new information to financial statement users.

An explanatory paragraph for uncertainties is no longer required. However, if the auditor has not gathered sufficient evidence or if the financial statements do not adequately disclose the uncertainty, a departure from an unqualified opinion may be required. These are discussed in the next section.

## CONDITIONS REQUIRING A DEPARTURE FROM AN UNQUALIFIED AUDIT REPORT

**OBJECTIVE 2-5**
**List the three conditions requiring a departure from an unqualified audit report.**

It is essential that auditors and readers of audit reports understand the circumstances when an unqualified report is not appropriate and the type of audit report issued in each circumstance. In the study of audit reports that depart from an unqualified report, there are three closely related topics: the conditions requiring a departure from an unqualified opinion, the types of opinions other than unqualified, and materiality.

First, the three conditions requiring a departure are briefly summarized. Each is discussed in greater depth later in the chapter.

**Condition 1. The Scope of the Audit Has Been Restricted** When the auditor has not accumulated sufficient evidence to conclude whether financial statements are stated in accordance with GAAP, a scope restriction exists. There are two major causes of scope restrictions: restrictions imposed by the client and those caused by circumstances beyond either the client's or auditor's control. An example of a client restriction is management's refusal to permit the auditor to confirm material receivables or to physically examine inventory. An example of a restriction caused by circumstances is when the engagement is not agreed upon until after the client's year-end. It may not be possible to physically observe inventories, confirm receivables, or perform other important procedures after the balance sheet date.

**Condition 2. The Financial Statements Have Not Been Prepared in Accordance with Generally Accepted Accounting Principles** For example, if the client insists upon using replacement costs for fixed assets or values inventory at selling price rather than historical cost, a departure from the unqualified report is required. When generally accepted accounting principles are referred to in this context, consideration of the adequacy of all informative disclosures, including footnotes, is especially important.

**Condition 3. The Auditor Is Not Independent** Independence ordinarily is determined by Rule 101 of the rules of the *Code of Professional Conduct.*

## AUDIT REPORTS OTHER THAN UNQUALIFIED

**OBJECTIVE 2-6**
**Identify the three types of audit reports that can be issued when an unqualified opinion is not justified.**

Whenever any of the three conditions requiring a departure from an unqualified report exists and is material, a report other than an unqualified report must be issued. Three main types of audit reports are issued under these conditions: *qualified opinion, adverse opinion,* and *disclaimer of opinion.*

### Qualified Opinion

A qualified opinion report can result from a limitation on the scope of the audit (condition 1) or failure to follow generally accepted accounting principles (condition 2).

A qualified opinion report can be used *only when the auditor concludes that the overall financial statements are fairly stated.* A disclaimer or an adverse report must be used if the auditor believes the condition being reported upon is highly material. For this reason, the qualified opinion is considered the least severe type of departure from an unqualified report.

A qualified report can take the form of a *qualification of both the scope and the opinion* or of the *opinion alone.* A scope and opinion qualification can be issued only when the auditor has not been able to accumulate all the evidence required by generally accepted auditing standards. Therefore, this type of qualification is used when the auditor's scope has been restricted by the client or when circumstances exist that prevent the auditor from conducting a complete audit (condition 1). The use of a qualification of the opinion alone is restricted to those situations in which the financial statements are not stated in accordance with GAAP (condition 2).

Whenever an auditor issues a qualified report, he or she must use the term *except for* in the opinion paragraph. The implication is that the auditor is satisfied that the overall financial statements are correctly stated "except for" a specific aspect of them. Examples of this qualification are given later in the chapter. It is unacceptable to use the phrase *except for* with any other type of audit opinion.

### Adverse Opinion

An adverse opinion is used only when the auditor believes that the overall financial statements are so *materially misstated or misleading* that they do not present fairly the financial position or results of operations and cash flows in conformity with generally accepted accounting principles (condition 2). The adverse opinion report can arise only when the auditor has knowledge, after an adequate investigation, of the absence of conformity. This is not a common occurrence, and thus the adverse opinion is rarely employed.

### Disclaimer of Opinion

A disclaimer is issued whenever the auditor has been *unable to satisfy himself or herself* that the overall financial statements are fairly presented. The necessity for disclaiming an opinion may arise because of a *severe limitation on the scope* of the audit (condition 1), or a *nonindependent relationship* under the *Code of Professional Conduct* between the auditor and the client (condition 3). Either of these situations prevents the auditor from expressing an opinion on the financial statements as a whole. The auditor also has the option, but is not required, to issue a disclaimer of opinion for a going concern problem.

The disclaimer is distinguished from an adverse opinion in that it can arise only from a *lack of knowledge* by the auditor, whereas to express an adverse opinion the auditor must have knowledge that the financial statements are not fairly stated. Both disclaimers and adverse opinions are used only when the condition is highly material.

## MATERIALITY

**OBJECTIVE 2-7**
**Explain how materiality affects audit reporting decisions.**

Materiality is an essential consideration in determining the appropriate type of report for a given set of circumstances. For example, if a misstatement is immaterial relative to the financial statements of the entity for the current period and is not expected to have a material effect in future periods, it is appropriate to issue an unqualified report. A common instance is the immediate expensing of office supplies rather than carrying the unused portion in inventory because the amount is insignificant.

The situation is totally different when the amounts are of such significance that the financial statements are materially affected as a whole. In these circumstances it is necessary to issue a *disclaimer of opinion* or an *adverse opinion*, depending on the nature of the misstatement. In other situations, of lesser materiality, a qualified opinion is appropriate.

**Definition**

The common definition of materiality as it applies to accounting and, therefore, to audit reporting is

> A misstatement in the financial statements can be considered material if knowledge of the misstatement would affect a decision of a reasonable user of the statements.

In applying this definition, three levels of materiality are used for determining the type of opinion to issue.

**Amounts Are Immaterial** When a misstatement in the financial statements exists but is unlikely to affect the decisions of a reasonable user, it is considered to be immaterial. An unqualified opinion is therefore appropriate. For example, assume that management recorded unexpired insurance as an asset in the previous year and decides to expense it in the current year to reduce record-keeping costs. Management has failed to follow GAAP (condition 2), but if the amounts are small, the misstatement would be immaterial, and a standard unqualified audit report would be appropriate.

**Amounts Are Material but Do Not Overshadow the Financial Statements as a Whole** The second level of materiality exists when a misstatement in the financial statements would affect a user's decision, but the overall statements are still fairly stated, and therefore useful. For example, knowledge of a large misstatement in fixed assets might affect a user's willingness to loan money to a company if the assets were the collateral. A misstatement of inventory does not mean that cash, accounts receivable, and other elements of the financial statements, or the financial statements as a whole, are materially incorrect.

To make materiality decisions when a condition requiring a departure from an unqualified report exists, the auditor must evaluate all effects on the financial statements. Assume that the auditor is unable to satisfy himself or herself whether inventory is fairly stated (condition 1) in deciding on the appropriate type of opinion. Because of the effect of a misstatement in inventory on other accounts and on totals in the statements, the auditor needs to consider the materiality of the combined effect on inventory, total current assets, total working capital, total assets, income taxes, income taxes payable, total current liabilities, cost of goods sold, net income before taxes, and net income after taxes.

When the auditor concludes that a misstatement is material but does not overshadow the financial statements as a whole, a qualified opinion (using "except for") is appropriate.

**Amounts Are So Material or So Pervasive That Overall Fairness of the Statements Is in Question** The highest level of materiality exists when users are likely to make incorrect decisions if they rely on the overall financial statements. To return to the previous example, if inventory is the largest balance on the financial statements, a large misstatement would probably be so material that the auditor's report should indicate the financial statements taken as a whole cannot be considered fairly stated. When the highest level of materiality exists, the auditor must issue either a disclaimer of opinion or an adverse opinion depending on which conditions exist.

When determining whether an exception is highly material, the extent to which the exception affects different parts of the financial statements must be considered. This is referred to as *pervasiveness.* A misclassification between cash and accounts receivable affects only those two accounts and is therefore not pervasive. On the other hand, failure to record a material sale is highly pervasive because it affects sales, accounts receivable, income tax expense, accrued income taxes, and retained earnings, which in turn affect current assets, total assets, current liabilities, total liabilities, owners' equity, gross margin, and operating income.

As misstatements become more pervasive, the likelihood of issuing an adverse opinion rather than a qualified opinion increases. For example, suppose the auditor decides a misclassification between cash and accounts receivable should result in a qualified opinion because it is material; the failure to record a sale of the same dollar amount may result in an adverse opinion because of pervasiveness.

Regardless of the amount involved, a disclaimer of opinion must be issued if the auditor is determined to lack independence under the rules of the *Code of Professional Conduct.* This harsh requirement reflects the importance of independence to auditors. Any deviation from the independence rule is therefore considered highly material. Table 2-2 summarizes the relationship between materiality and the type of opinion to be issued.

**TABLE 2-2**

**Relationship of Materiality to Type of Opinion**

| Materiality Level | Significance in Terms of Reasonable Users' Decisions | Type of Opinion |
|---|---|---|
| Immaterial | Users' decisions are unlikely to be affected. | Unqualified |
| Material | Users' decisions are likely to be affected only if the information in question is important to the specific decisions being made. The overall financial statements are presented fairly. | Qualified |
| Highly material | Most or all users' decisions based on the financial statements are likely to be significantly affected. | Disclaimer or Adverse |

*Note:* Lack of independence requires a disclaimer regardless of materiality.

## Materiality Decisions

In concept, the effect of materiality on the type of opinion to issue is straightforward. In application, deciding upon actual materiality in a given situation is a difficult judgment. There are no simple, well-defined guidelines that enable auditors to decide when something is immaterial, material, or highly material.

There are differences in applying materiality for deciding whether failure to follow GAAP is material compared to deciding whether a scope limitation is material. A discussion follows for making materiality decisions in these two situations.

**Materiality Decisions—Non-GAAP Condition** When a client has failed to follow GAAP, the audit report will be unqualified, qualified opinion only, or adverse, depending on the materiality of the departure. Several aspects of materiality must be considered.

***Dollar Amounts Compared with a Base*** The primary concern in measuring materiality when a client has failed to follow GAAP is usually the total dollar misstatement in the accounts involved, compared with some base. A $10,000 misstatement might be material for a small company, but not for a larger one. Misstatements must, therefore, be compared with some measurement base before a decision can be made about the materiality of the failure to follow GAAP. Common bases include net income, total assets, current assets, and working capital.

For example, assume that the auditor believes there is a $100,000 overstatement of inventory because of the client's failure to follow GAAP. Also assume recorded inventory of $1,000,000, current assets of $3,000,000, and net income before taxes of $2,000,000. In this case, the auditor must evaluate the materiality of a misstatement of inventory of 10 percent, current assets of 3.3 percent, and net income before taxes of 5 percent.

To evaluate overall materiality, the auditor must also combine all unadjusted misstatements and judge whether there may be individually immaterial misstatements that, when combined, significantly affect the statements. In the inventory example above, assume the auditor believes there is also an overstatement of $150,000 in accounts receivable. The total effect on current assets is now 8.3 percent ($250,000 divided by $3,000,000) and on net income before taxes is 12.5 percent ($250,000 divided by $2,000,000).

When comparing potential misstatements with a base, the auditor must carefully consider all accounts affected by a misstatement (pervasiveness). It is, for example, important not to overlook the effect of an understatement of inventory on cost of goods sold, income before taxes, income tax expense, and accrued income taxes payable.

***Measurability*** The dollar amount of some misstatements cannot be accurately measured. For example, a client's unwillingness to disclose an existing lawsuit or the acquisition of a new company subsequent to the balance sheet date is difficult, if not impossible, to measure in terms of dollar amounts. The materiality question the auditor must evaluate in such situations is the effect on statement users of the failure to make the disclosure.

***Nature of the Item*** The decision of a user may also be affected by the kind of misstatement in the statement. The following may affect the user's decision and, therefore, the auditor's opinion in a different way than most misstatements.

1. Transactions are illegal or fraudulent.
2. An item may materially affect some future period even though it is immaterial when only the current period is considered.
3. An item has a "psychic" effect (for example, small profit versus small loss or cash balance versus overdraft).
4. An item may be important in terms of possible consequences arising from contractual obligations (for example, the effect of failure to comply with a debt restriction may result in a material loan being called).

**Materiality Decisions—Scope Limitations Condition** When there is a scope limitation in an audit, the audit report will be unqualified, qualified scope and opinion, or disclaimer, depending on the materiality of the scope limitation. The auditor will consider the same three factors included in the previous discussion about materiality decisions for failure to follow GAAP, but they will be considered differently. The size of *potential* misstatements, rather than known misstatements, is important in determining whether an unqualified report, a qualified report, or a disclaimer of opinion is appropriate for a scope limitation. For example, if recorded accounts payable of $400,000 was not audited, the auditor must evaluate the potential misstatement in accounts payable and decide how materially the financial statements could be affected. The pervasiveness of these potential misstatements must also be considered.

It is typically more difficult to evaluate the materiality of potential misstatements resulting from a scope limitation than for failure to follow GAAP. Misstatements resulting from failure to follow GAAP are known. Those resulting from scope limitations must usually be subjectively measured in terms of potential or likely misstatements. For example, a recorded accounts payable of $400,000 might be understated by more than a million dollars, which may affect several totals, including gross margin, net earnings, and total assets.

## DISCUSSION OF CONDITIONS REQUIRING A DEPARTURE

**OBJECTIVE 2-8**
**Draft appropriately modified audit reports under a variety of circumstances.**

You should now understand the relationships among the conditions requiring a departure from an unqualified report, the major types of reports other than unqualified, and the three levels of materiality. This part of the chapter examines the conditions requiring a departure from an unqualified report in greater detail and shows examples of reports.

## Auditor's Scope Has Been Restricted

There are two major categories of scope restrictions: those caused by a client and those caused by conditions beyond the control of either the client or the auditor. The effect on the auditor's report is the same for either, but the interpretation of materiality is likely to be different. Whenever there is a scope restriction, the appropriate response is to issue an unqualified report, a qualification of scope and opinion, or a disclaimer of opinion, depending on materiality.

For client-imposed restrictions, the auditor should be concerned about the possibility that management is trying to prevent discovery of misstated information. In such cases, the AICPA has encouraged a disclaimer of opinion whenever materiality is in question. When restrictions are due to conditions beyond the client's control, a qualification of scope and opinion is more likely.

Two restrictions occasionally imposed by clients on the auditor's scope relate to the observation of physical inventory and the confirmation of accounts receivable, but other restrictions may also occur. Reasons for client-imposed scope restrictions may be a desire to save audit fees and, in the case of confirming receivables, to prevent possible conflicts between the client and customer when amounts differ. A qualified or disclaimer of opinion resulting from a client restriction requires a qualifying paragraph to describe the restriction. In the case of disclaimer, the scope paragraph is excluded from the report in its entirety.

The most common case in which conditions beyond the client's and auditor's control cause a scope restriction is an engagement agreed upon after the client's balance sheet date. The confirmation of accounts receivable, physical examination of inventory, and other important procedures may not be possible under those circumstances. When the auditor cannot perform procedures he or she considers desirable but can be satisfied with alternative procedures that the information being verified is fairly stated, an unqualified report is appropriate. If alternative procedures cannot be performed, a scope qualification and, depending on the materiality, either an opinion qualification or a disclaimer of opinion is necessary.

For example, the report in Figure 2-6 would be appropriate for an audit in which the amounts were material but not pervasive, and the auditor could not obtain audited financial statements supporting an investment in a foreign affiliate and could not satisfy himself or herself by alternate procedures. The entire introductory paragraph and bulk of the second paragraph are omitted because they use standard wording.

**FIGURE 2-6**

**Qualified Scope and Opinion Report Due to Scope Restriction**

**INDEPENDENT AUDITOR'S REPORT**

(Same introductory paragraph as standard report)

Except as discussed in the following paragraph, we conducted our audit . . . (remainder is the same as the scope paragraph in the standard report)

**Scope Paragraph—Qualified**

We were unable to obtain audited financial statements supporting the Company's investment in a foreign affiliate stated at $475,000, or its equity in earnings of that affiliate of $365,000, which is included in net income, as described in Note X to the financial statements. Because of the nature of the Company's records, we were unable to satisfy ourselves as to the carrying value of the investment or the equity in its earnings by means of other auditing procedures.

**Third Paragraph—Added**

In our opinion, except for the effects of such adjustments, if any, as might have been determined to be necessary had we been able to examine evidence regarding the foreign affiliate investment and earnings, the financial statements referred to above present fairly, in all material respects, the financial position of Laughlin Corporation as of December 31, 1997, and the results of its operations and its cash flows for the year then ended in conformity with generally accepted accounting principles.

**Opinion Paragraph—Qualified**

When the amounts are so material that a disclaimer of opinion rather than a qualified is required, the auditor uses only three paragraphs. The first (introductory) paragraph is modified slightly to say "We were engaged to audit. . . ." The second paragraph is the same as the third paragraph in Figure 2-6. The scope paragraph is deleted and the final (opinion) paragraph is changed to a disclaimer. The reason for deleting the scope paragraph is to avoid stating anything that might lead readers to believe that other parts of the financial statements were audited and therefore might be fairly stated. Figure 2-7 shows the audit report assuming the auditor had concluded that the facts in Figure 2-6 required a disclaimer rather than a qualified opinion.

**FIGURE 2-7**

**Disclaimer of Opinion Due to Scope Restriction**

**INDEPENDENT AUDITOR'S REPORT**

**Introductory Paragraph—Modification of Standard Report**

We were engaged to audit . . . (remainder is the same as the introductory paragraph in the standard report)

**Second Paragraph—Added**

(Same wording as that used for the third paragraph in Figure 2-6)

**Opinion Paragraph—Disclaimer**

Since we were unable to obtain audited financial statements supporting the Company's investment in a foreign affiliate and we were unable to satisfy ourselves as to the carrying value of the investment or the equity in its earnings by means of other auditing procedures, the scope of our work was not sufficient to enable us to express, and we do not express, an opinion on these financial statements.

*Note:* In a disclaimer due to a scope restriction, the scope paragraph is omitted entirely.

## Statements Are Not in Conformity with GAAP

When the auditor knows that the financial statements may be misleading because they were not prepared in conformity with generally accepted accounting principles, he or she must issue a qualified or an adverse opinion, depending on the materiality of the item in question. The opinion must clearly state the nature of the deviation from accepted principles and the amount of the misstatement, if it is known. Figure 2-8 shows an example of a qualified opinion when a client did not capitalize leases as required by GAAP. The first and second paragraphs are omitted because they include standard wording.

When the amounts are so material or pervasive that an adverse opinion is required, the scope would still be unqualified, and the qualifying paragraph could remain the same, but the opinion paragraph might be as shown in Figure 2-9.

**FIGURE 2-8**

**Qualified Opinion Report Due to Non-GAAP**

**INDEPENDENT AUDITOR'S REPORT**

(Same introductory and scope paragraphs as the standard report)

**Third Paragraph—Added**

The Company has excluded from property and debt in the accompanying balance sheet certain lease obligations that, in our opinion, should be capitalized in order to conform with generally accepted accounting principles. If these lease obligations were capitalized, property would be increased by $4,600,000, long-term debt by $4,200,000, and retained earnings by $400,000 as of December 31, 1997, and net income and earnings per share would be increased by $400,000 and $1.75, respectively, for the year then ended.

**Opinion Paragraph—Qualified**

In our opinion, except for the effects of not capitalizing lease obligations, as discussed in the preceding paragraph, the financial statements referred to above present fairly, in all material respects, the financial position of Ajax, Inc., as of December 31, 1997, and the results of its operations and its cash flows for the year then ended in conformity with generally accepted accounting principles.

**FIGURE 2-9**

**Adverse Opinion Due to Non-GAAP**

**INDEPENDENT AUDITOR'S REPORT**

(Same introductory and scope paragraphs as the standard report)

(Same third paragraph as that used for the third paragraph in Figure 2-8)

**Third Paragraph—Added**

In our opinion, because of the effects of the matters discussed in the preceding paragraph, the financial statements referred to above do not present fairly, in conformity with generally accepted accounting principles, the financial position of Ajax Company as of December 31, 1997, or the results of its operations and its cash flows for the year then ended.

**Opinion Paragraph—Adverse**

**FIGURE 2-10**

**Qualified Opinion Due to Inadequate Disclosure**

**INDEPENDENT AUDITOR'S REPORT**

(Same introductory and scope paragraphs as the standard report)

On January 15, 1996, the company issued debentures in the amount of $3,600,000 for the purpose of financing plant expansion.The debenture agreement restricts the payment of future cash dividends to earnings after December 31, 1996. In our opinion, disclosure of this information is required to conform with generally accepted accounting principles.

**Third Paragraph—Added**

In our opinion, except for the omission of the information discussed in the preceding paragraph, the financial statements referred to above present fairly . . . (remainder is the same as the opinion in the standard report)

**Opinion Paragraph—Qualified**

When the client fails to include information that is necessary for the fair presentation of financial statements in the body of the statements or in the related footnotes, it is the responsibility of the auditor to present the information in the audit report and to issue a qualified or an adverse opinion. It is common to put this type of qualification in an added paragraph (the scope paragraph will remain unqualified) and to refer to the added paragraph in the opinion paragraph. Figure 2-10 shows an example of an audit report in which the auditor considered the financial statement disclosure inadequate.

**Rule 203 Reports** Determining whether statements are in accordance with generally accepted accounting principles can be difficult. Rule 203, from the *Code of Professional Conduct*, permits a departure from accounting research bulletins, Accounting Principles Board opinions, and FASB statements when the auditor believes that adherence to these would result in misleading statements.

> **Rule 203—Accounting Principles** A member shall not (1) express an opinion or state affirmatively that financial statements or other financial data of any entity are presented in conformity with generally accepted accounting principles or (2) state that he or she is not aware of any material modifications that should be made to such statements or data in order for them to be in conformity with generally accepted accounting principles, if such statements or data contain any departure from an accounting principle promulgated by bodies designated by Council to establish such principles that has a material effect on the statements or data taken as a whole. If, however, the statements or data contain such a departure and the member can demonstrate that due to unusual circumstances the financial statements or data would otherwise have been misleading, the member can comply with the rule by describing the departure, its approximate effects, if practicable, and the reasons why compliance with the principle would result in a misleading statement.

When the auditor decides that adherence to generally accepted accounting principles would result in misleading statements, there should be a complete explanation in a third paragraph. The paragraph should fully explain the departure and why generally accepted accounting principles would have resulted in misleading statements. The opinion paragraph should then be unqualified except for the reference to the third paragraph. As discussed earlier in the chapter, this is referred to as an unqualified audit report with an explanatory paragraph.

**Lack of Statement of Cash Flows** The client's unwillingness to include a statement of cash flows is specifically addressed in SAS 58 (AU 508). When the statement is omitted, there must be a third paragraph stating the omission and an "except for" opinion qualification.

## Auditor Is Not Independent

If the auditor has not fulfilled the independence requirements specified by the *Code of Professional Conduct*, a disclaimer of opinion is required even though all the audit procedures considered necessary in the circumstances were performed. The wording in Figure 2-11 is recommended when the auditor is not independent.

The lack of independence overrides any other scope limitations. Therefore, no other reason for disclaiming an opinion should be cited. There should be no mention in the report of the performance of any audit procedures. It is an example of a one-paragraph audit report.

**FIGURE 2-11**

**Disclaimer Due to Lack of Independence**

We are not independent with respect to XYZ Company, and the accompanying balance sheet as of December 31, 1997, and the related statements of income, retained earnings, and cash flows for the year then ended were not audited by us. Accordingly, we do not express an opinion on them.

*Note:* When the auditor lacks independence, no report title is included.

**Summary of Departure From Unqualified Reports** A summary of the types of audit reports and their use with the three conditions requiring a departure from an unqualified report is shown in Table 2-3.

**TABLE 2-3**

**Audit Report for Each Condition Requiring a Departure from an Unqualified Report at Different Levels of Materiality**

| | Level of Materiality | | |
|---|---|---|---|
| **Condition Requiring a Departure** | **Immaterial** | **Material, but Does Not Overshadow Financial Statements as a Whole** | **So Material that Overall Fairness Is in Question** |
| Scope restricted by client or conditions | Unqualified report | Qualified scope, additional paragraph, and qualified opinion (except for) | Disclaimer of opinion |
| Financial statements not prepared in accordance with GAAP* | Unqualified report | Additional paragraph and qualified opinion (except for) | Adverse opinion |
| The auditor is not independent | | Disclaimer of opinion (regardless of materiality) | |

*If the auditor can demonstrate that GAAP would be misleading, a report with modified wording would be appropriate.

## MORE THAN ONE CONDITION REQUIRING A DEPARTURE OR MODIFICATION

Frequently, auditors encounter situations involving more than one of the conditions requiring a departure from an unqualified report or modification of the standard unqualified report. In these circumstances, the auditor should modify his or her opinion for each condition unless one has the effect of neutralizing the others. For example, if there is a scope limitation and a situation in which the auditor was not independent, the scope limitation should not be revealed. In the following situations more than one modification should be included in the report:

- The auditor is not independent and the auditor knows that the company has not followed generally accepted accounting principles.
- There is a scope limitation and there is substantial doubt about the company's ability to continue as a going concern.
- A review service engagement has been performed and the reviewer knows that the statements do not conform to generally accepted accounting principles.
- There is a substantial doubt about the company's ability to continue as a going concern, and information about the causes of the uncertainties is not adequately disclosed in a footnote.
- There is a deviation in the statements' preparation in accordance with generally accepted accounting principles, and another accounting principle was applied on a basis that was not consistent with that of the preceding year.

## NUMBER OF PARAGRAPHS IN THE REPORT

The number of paragraphs in the auditor's reports is perceived by many readers as an important "signal" as to whether the financial statements are correct, or whether there is some exception that requires their attention. This is because a three-paragraph report ordinarily indicates there are no exceptions in the audit. More than three paragraphs indicates some type of qualification or required explanation.

When a qualified or adverse opinion is issued, an additional paragraph is inserted between the scope and opinion paragraph to explain the nature of the qualification that affects the opinion. For example, the additional paragraph in Figure 2-6 on page 49 explains the nature of a scope limitation. The opinion is qualified in the last paragraph. There are other examples of this type of report in Chapter 23.

When an unqualified opinion with an explanatory paragraph or modified wording is used, there is normally a fourth paragraph. Figure 2-3 on page 41 is an example of such a paragraph. An exception is an unqualified shared report for reports involving other auditors. Figure 2-5 on page 43 is an example of that type of report.

There is only one situation in which a three-paragraph report is other than unqualified. That is a disclaimer of opinion. For most disclaimers, the second paragraph of the standard report is omitted and replaced with other wording, and the opinion paragraph is the disclaimer. (See Figure 2-7, page 50.) For a disclaimer for lack of independence, a one-paragraph report is issued. (See Figure 2-11, page 52.)

## NEGATIVE ASSURANCES

It is inappropriate to include in the audit report any additional comments that counterbalance the auditor's opinion. For example, the use of such terminology as "However, nothing came to our attention that would lead us to question the fairness of the presentations" as a part of a disclaimer of opinion is inappropriate and a violation of the standards of reporting. Statements of this kind, which are referred to as *negative assurances*, tend to confuse readers about the nature of the audit and the degree of responsibility being assumed.

The use of negative assurances with certain types of engagements is appropriate, but not for audits of historical financial statements. These other types of engagements are considered in Chapter 23.

## AUDITOR'S DECISION PROCESS FOR AUDIT REPORTS

**OBJECTIVE 2-9**
**Describe the process for deciding the appropriate audit report.**

Auditors use a well-defined process for deciding the appropriate audit report in a given set of circumstances. There are four steps to the process.

**Determine Whether Any Condition Exists Requiring a Departure from a Standard Unqualified Report** The most important of these conditions are identified in Table 2-4. Auditors identify these conditions as they perform the audit and include information about any condition in the working papers as discussion items for audit reporting. If none of these conditions exist, which is the case in the great majority of all audits, the auditor issues a standard unqualified audit report.

**TABLE 2-4**
**Audit Report for Each Condition Requiring a Departure from a Standard Unqualified Report at Different Levels of Materiality**

| Condition Requiring an Unqualified Report with Modified Wording or Explanatory Paragraph | Level of Materiality: Immaterial | Level of Materiality: Material |
|---|---|---|
| Accounting principles not consistently applied* | Unqualified | Unqualified report, explanatory paragraph |
| Substantial doubt about going concern† | Unqualified | Unqualified report, explanatory paragraph |
| Justified departure from GAAP or other accounting principle | Unqualified | Unqualified report, explanatory paragraph |
| Emphasis of a matter | Unqualified | Unqualified report, explanatory paragraph |
| Use of another auditor | Unqualified | Unqualified report, modified wording |

| Condition Requiring a Departure from Unqualified Report | Level of Materiality: Immaterial | Material, But Does Not Overshadow Financial Statements as a Whole | So Material That Overall Fairness Is in Question |
|---|---|---|---|
| Scope restricted by client or conditions | Unqualified | Qualified scope, additional paragraph, and qualified opinion (except for) | Disclaimer |
| Financial statements not prepared in accordance with GAAP‡ | Unqualified | Additional paragraph and qualified opinion (except for) | Adverse |
| The auditor is not independent | | Disclaimer, regardless of materiality | |

*If auditor does not concur with the appropriateness of the change, the condition is considered a violation of GAAP.
†Auditor has the option of issuing a disclaimer of opinion.
‡If the auditor can demonstrate that GAAP would be misleading, a report with modified wording would be appropriate.

**Decide the Materiality for Each Condition** When a condition requiring a departure from a standard unqualified opinion exists, the auditor evaluates the potential effect on the financial statements. For departures from generally accepted accounting principles or scope restrictions, the auditor must decide among immaterial, material, and highly material. All other conditions, except for lack of auditor independence, require only a distinction between immaterial and material. The materiality decision is a difficult one, requiring considerable judgment. For example, assume that there is a scope limitation in auditing inventory. It is difficult to assess the potential misstatement of an account that the auditor does not audit.

**Decide the Appropriate Type of Report for the Condition, Given the Materiality Level** After making the first two decisions, it is easy to decide the appropriate type of opinion by using a decision aid. An example of such an aid is Table 2-4. For example, assume that the auditor concludes that there is a departure from generally accepted accounting principles and it is material, but not highly material. Table 2-4 shows that the appropriate audit report is a qualified opinion with an additional paragraph discussing the departure. The introductory and scope paragraphs will be included using standard wording.

**Write the Audit Report** Most CPA firms have audit report manuals that include precise wording for different circumstances to help the auditor write the audit report. Also, one or more partners in most CPA firms have special expertise in writing audit reports. These partners typically write or review all audit reports before they are issued.

## ESSENTIAL TERMS

**Adverse opinion**—a report issued when the auditor believes the financial statements are so materially misstated or misleading as a whole that they do not present fairly the entity's financial position or the results of its operations and cash flows in conformity with generally accepted accounting principles

**Disclaimer of opinion**—a report issued when the auditor has not been able to become satisfied that the overall financial statements are fairly presented

**Material misstatement**—a misstatement in the financial statements, knowledge of which would affect a decision of a reasonable user of the statements

**Qualified opinion**—a report issued when the auditor believes that the overall financial statements are fairly stated but that either the scope of the audit was limited or the financial data indicated a failure to follow generally accepted accounting principles

**Standard unqualified audit report**—the report a CPA issues when all auditing conditions have been met, no significant misstatements have been discovered and left uncorrected, and it is the auditor's opinion that the financial statements are fairly stated in accordance with generally accepted accounting principles

## REVIEW QUESTIONS

**2-1 (Objective 2-1)** Explain why auditors' reports are important to users of financial statements.

**2-2 (Objective 2-2)** What five circumstances are required for a standard unqualified report to be issued?

**2-3 (Objective 2-2)** List the seven parts of an unqualified audit report and explain the meaning of each part. How do the parts compare with those found in a qualified report?

**2-4 (Objective 2-2)** What are the purposes of the scope paragraph in the auditor's report? Identify the most important information included in the scope paragraph.

**2-5 (Objective 2-2)** What are the purposes of the opinion paragraph in the auditor's report? Identify the most important information included in the opinion paragraph.

**2-6 (Objective 2-2)** On February 17, 1997, a CPA completed the field work on the financial statements for the Buckheizer Corporation for the year ended December 31, 1996. The audit is satisfactory in all respects except for the existence of a change in accounting principles from FIFO to LIFO inventory valuation, which results in an explanatory paragraph to consistency. On February 26, the auditor completed the tax return and the pencil draft of the financial statements. The final audit report was completed, attached to the financial statements, and delivered to the client on March 7. What is the appropriate date on the auditor's report?

**2-7 (Objectives 2-4, 2-8)** What type of opinion should an auditor issue when the financial statements are not in accordance with generally accepted accounting principles because such adherence would result in misleading statements?

**2-8 (Objectives 2-3, 2-4, 2-6)** Distinguish between an unqualified report with an explanatory paragraph or modified wording and a qualified report. Give examples when an explanatory paragraph or modified wording should be used in an unqualified opinion.

**2-9 (Objective 2-4)** Describe what is meant by reports involving the use of other auditors. What are the three options available to the principal auditor and when should each be used?

**2-10 (Objective 2-4)** The client has restated the prior-year statements due to a change from LIFO to FIFO. How should this be reflected in the auditor's report?

**2-11 (Objective 2-4)** Distinguish between changes that affect consistency and those that may affect comparability but do not affect consistency. Give an example of each.

**2-12 (Objective 2-5)** List the three conditions requiring a departure from an unqualified opinion and give one specific example of each of those conditions.

**2-13 (Objectives 2-3, 2-6)** Distinguish between a qualified opinion, an adverse opinion, and a disclaimer of opinion and explain the circumstances under which each is appropriate.

**2-14 (Objective 2-7)** Define *materiality* as it is used in audit reporting. What conditions will affect the auditor's determination of materiality?

**2-15(Objective 2-7)** Explain how materiality differs for failure to follow GAAP and lack of independence.

**2-16 (Objective 2-8)** How does the auditor's opinion differ between scope limitations caused by client restrictions and limitations resulting from conditions beyond the client's control? Under which of these two would the auditor be most likely to issue a disclaimer of opinion? Explain.

**2-17 (Objective 2-6)** Distinguish between a report qualified as to opinion only and one with both a scope and opinion qualification.

**2-18 (Objectives 2-7, 2-8)** Identify the three alternative opinions that may be appropriate when the client's financial statements are not in accordance with GAAP. Under what circumstance is each appropriate?

**2-19 (Objectives 2-6, 2-8)** Discuss why the AICPA has such strict requirements on audit opinions when the auditor is not independent.

**2-20 (Objective 2-8)** When an auditor discovers more than one condition that requires departure from or modification of the standard unqualified report, what should the auditor's report include?

## MULTIPLE CHOICE QUESTIONS FROM CPA EXAMINATIONS

**2-21 (Objectives 2-2, 2-3, 2-4)** The following questions concern unqualified audit reports. Choose the best response.

a. An auditor's unqualified report
   (1) implies only that items disclosed in the financial statements and footnotes are properly presented and takes no position on the adequacy of disclosure.

(2) implies that disclosure is adequate in the financial statements and footnotes.
(3) explicitly states that disclosure is adequate in the financial statements and footnotes.
(4) explicitly states that all material items have been disclosed in conformity with generally accepted accounting principles.

b. The date of the CPA's opinion on the financial statements of his or her client should be the date of the
(1) closing of the client's books.
(2) receipt of the client's letter of representation.
(3) completion of all important audit procedures.
(4) submission of the report to the client.

c. If a principal auditor decides that he or she will refer in his report to the audit of another auditor, he or she is required to disclose the
(1) name of the other auditor.
(2) nature of his inquiry into the other auditor's professional standing and extent of his review of the other auditor's work.
(3) portion of the financial statements audited by the other auditor.
(4) reasons why he or she is unwilling to assume responsibility for the other auditor's work.

**2-22 (Objectives 2-3, 2-6, 2-7, 2-8)** The following questions concern audit reports other than unqualified audit reports with standard wording. Choose the best response.

a. A CPA will issue an adverse auditor's opinion if
(1) the scope of his or her audit is limited by the client.
(2) his or her exception to the fairness of presentation is so material that an "except for" opinion is not justified.
(3) he or she did not perform sufficient auditing procedures to form an opinion on the financial statements taken as a whole.
(4) major uncertainties exist concerning the company's future.

b. An auditor will express an "except for" opinion if
(1) the client refuses to provide for a probable federal income tax deficiency that is highly material.
(2) there is a high degree of uncertainty associated with the client company's future.
(3) he or she did not perform procedures sufficient to form an opinion on the consistency of application of generally accepted accounting principles.
(4) he or she is basing his or her opinion in part upon work done by another auditor.

c. Under which of the following sets of circumstances should an auditor issue a qualified opinion?
(1) The financial statements contain a departure from generally accepted accounting principles, the effect of which is material.
(2) The principal auditor decides to make reference to the report of another auditor who audited a subsidiary.
(3) There has been a material change between periods in the method of the application of accounting principles.
(4) There are significant uncertainties affecting the financial statements.

## DISCUSSION QUESTIONS AND PROBLEMS

**2-23 (Objective 2-2)** A careful reading of an unqualified report indicates several important phrases. Explain why each of the following phrases or clauses is used rather than the alternative provided.

a. "In our opinion, the financial statements present fairly" rather than "The financial statements present fairly."

b. "We conducted our audit in accordance with generally accepted auditing standards" rather than "Our audit was performed to detect material misstatements in the financial statements."

c. "The financial statements referred to above present fairly in all material respects the financial position" rather than "The financial statements mentioned above are correctly stated."

d. "In conformity with generally accepted accounting principles" rather than "are properly stated to represent the true economic conditions."

e. "Brown & Phillips, CPAs (firm name)," rather than "James E. Brown, CPA (individual partner's name)."

2-24 **(Objectives 2-2, 2-4, 2-7, 2-8)** Roscoe, CPA, has completed the audit of the financial statements of Excelsior Corporation as of and for the year ended December 31, 1997. Roscoe also audited and reported on the Excelsior financial statements for the prior year. Roscoe drafted the following report for 1997.

> We have audited the balance sheet and statements of income and retained earnings of Excelsior Corporation as of December 31, 1997. We conducted our audit in accordance with generally accepted accounting standards. Those standards require that we plan and perform the audit to obtain reasonable assurance about whether the financial statements are free of misstatement.
>
> We believe that our audits provide a reasonable basis for our opinion.
>
> In our opinion, the financial statements referred to above present fairly the financial position of X Company as of December 31, 1997, and the results of its operations for the year then ended in conformity with generally accepted auditing standards, applied on a basis consistent with those of the preceding year.
>
> Roscoe, CPA
> (Signed)

**Other Information**

- Excelsior is presenting comparative financial statements.
- Excelsior does not wish to present a statement of cash flows for either year.
- During 1997 Excelsior changed its method of accounting for long-term construction contracts and properly reflected the effect of the change in the current year's financial statements and restated the prior year's statements. Roscoe is satisfied with Excelsior's justification for making the change. The change is discussed in footnote 12.
- Roscoe was unable to perform normal accounts receivable confirmation procedures, but alternate procedures were used to satisfy Roscoe as to the existence of the receivables.
- Excelsior Corporation is the defendant in a litigation, the outcome of which is highly uncertain. If the case is settled in favor of the plaintiff, Excelsior will be required to pay a substantial amount of cash, which might require the sale of certain fixed assets. The litigation and the possible effects have been properly disclosed in footnote 11.
- Excelsior issued debentures on January 31, 1996, in the amount of $10,000,000. The funds obtained from the issuance were used to finance the expansion of plant facilities. The debenture agreement restricts the payment of future cash dividends to earnings after December 31, 2001. Excelsior declined to disclose this essential data in the footnotes to the financial statements.

## Required

a. Identify and explain any items included in "Other Information" that need not be part of the auditor's report.

b. Explain the deficiencies in Roscoe's report as drafted.*

*AICPA adapted

**2-25** (**Objectives 2-4, 2-5, 2-6, 2-7, 2-8, 2-9**) For the following independent situations, assume that you are the audit partner on the engagement:

1. During your audit of Debold Batteries, you conclude that there is a possibility that inventory is materially overstated. The client refuses to allow you to expand the scope of your audit sufficiently to verify whether the balance is actually misstated.
2. You are auditing Woodcolt Linen Services for the first time. Woodcolt has been in business for several years but has never had an audit before. After the audit is completed, you conclude that the current year balance sheet is stated correctly in accordance with GAAP. The client did not authorize you to do test work for any of the previous years.
3. You were engaged to audit the Cutter Steel Company's financial statements after the close of the corporation's fiscal year. Because you were not engaged until after the balance sheet date, you were not able to physically observe inventory, which is highly material. On the completion of your audit, you are satisfied that Cutter's financial statements are presented fairly, including inventory about which you were able to satisfy yourself by the use of alternative audit procedures.
4. Four weeks after the year-end date, a major customer of Prince Construction Co. declared bankruptcy. Because the customer had confirmed the balance due to Prince at the balance sheet date, management refuses to charge off the account or otherwise disclose the information. The receivable represents approximately 10 percent of accounts receivable and 20 percent of net earnings before taxes.
5. You complete the audit of Johnson Department Store, and in your opinion, the financial statements are fairly presented. On the last day of the field work, you discover that one of your supervisors assigned to the audit had a material investment in Johnson.
6. Auto Delivery Company has a fleet of several delivery trucks. In the past, Auto Delivery had followed the policy of purchasing all equipment. In the current year they decided to lease the trucks. The method of accounting for the trucks is therefore changed to lease capitalization. This change in policy is fully disclosed in footnotes.

## Required

a. For each situation, identify which of the conditions requiring a modification of or a deviation from an unqualified standard report is applicable.

b. State the level of materiality as immaterial, material, or highly material. If you cannot decide the level of materiality, state the additional information needed to make a decision.

c. Given your answers in parts a and b, state the type of audit report that should be issued. If you have not decided on one level of materiality in part b, state the appropriate report for each alternative materiality level.

**2-26** (**Objectives 2-4, 2-5, 2-6, 2-7, 2-8, 2-9**) For the following independent situations, assume that you are the audit partner on the engagement:

1. Kieko Corporation has prepared financial statements but has decided to exclude the statement of cash flows. Management explains to you that the users of their financial statements find this statement confusing and prefer not to have it included.
2. Jet Stream Airlines has been audited by your firm for ten years. In the past three years their financial condition has steadily declined. In the current year, for the first time, the current ratio is below 2.1, which is the minimum requirement specified in Jet Stream's major loan agreement. You now have reservations about the ability of Jet Stream to continue in operation for the next year.
3. Approximately 20 percent of the audit of Fur Farms, Inc., was performed by a different CPA firm, selected by you. You have reviewed their working papers and believe they did an excellent job on their portion of the audit. Nevertheless, you are unwilling to take *complete* responsibility for their work.
4. The controller of Fair City Hotels Co. will not allow you to confirm the receivable balance from two of its major customers. The amount of the receivable is material in

relation to Fair City's financial statements. You are unable to satisfy yourself as to the receivable balance by alternative procedures.

5. In the last three months of the current year, Oil Refining Company decided to change direction and go significantly into the oil drilling business. Management recognizes that this business is exceptionally risky and could jeopardize the success of its existing refining business, but there are significant potential rewards. During the short period of operation in drilling, the company has had three dry wells and no successes. The facts are adequately disclosed in footnotes.
6. Your client, Auto Rental Company, has changed from straight line to sum-of-the-years'–digits depreciation. The effect on this year's income is immaterial, but the effect in future years is likely to be material. The facts are adequately disclosed in footnotes.

**Required**

For each situation, do the following:

a. For each situation, identify which of the conditions requiring a modification of or a deviation from an unqualified standard report is applicable.

b. State the level of materiality as immaterial, material, or highly material. If you cannot decide the level of materiality, state the additional information needed to make a decision.

c. Given your answers in parts a and b, state the appropriate audit report from the following alternatives (if you have not decided on one level of materiality in part b, state the appropriate report for each alternative materiality level):
(1) Unqualified—standard wording.
(2) Unqualified—explanatory paragraph.
(3) Unqualified—modified wording.
(4) Qualified opinion only—except for.
(5) Qualified scope and opinion.
(6) Disclaimer.
(7) Adverse.

**2-27 (Objectives 2-4, 2-5, 2-6, 2-7, 2-8, 2-9)** The following are independent situations for which you will recommend an appropriate audit report:

1. Subsequent to the date of the financial statements as part of his postbalance sheet date audit procedures, a CPA learned of heavy damage to one of a client's two plants due to a recent fire; the loss will not be reimbursed by insurance. The newspapers described the event in detail. The financial statements and appended notes as prepared by the client did not disclose the loss caused by the fire.
2. A CPA is engaged in the audit of the financial statements of a large manufacturing company with branch offices in many widely separated cities. The CPA was not able to count the substantial undeposited cash receipts at the close of business on the last day of the fiscal year at all branch offices.

   As an alternative to this auditing procedure used to verify the accurate cutoff of cash receipts, the CPA observed that deposits in transit as shown on the year-end bank reconciliation appeared as credits on the bank statement on the first business day of the new year. He was satisfied as to the cutoff of cash receipts by the use of the alternative procedure.
3. On January 2, 1997, the Retail Auto Parts Company received a notice from its primary supplier that effective immediately, all wholesale prices would be increased 10 percent. On the basis of the notice, Retail Auto Parts revalued its December 31, 1996, inventory to reflect the higher costs. The inventory constituted a material proportion of total assets; however, the effect of the revaluation was material to current assets but not to total assets or net income. The increase in valuation is adequately disclosed in the footnotes.
4. During 1997, the research staff of Scientific Research Corporation devoted its entire efforts toward developing a new pollution-control device. All costs that could be attrib-

uted directly to the project were accounted for as deferred charges and classified on the balance sheet at December 31, 1997, as a noncurrent asset. In the course of his audit of the corporation's 1997 financial statements, Anthony, CPA, found persuasive evidence that the research conducted to date would probably result in a marketable product. The deferred research charges are significantly material in relation to both income and total assets.

5. For the past five years a CPA has audited the financial statements of a manufacturing company. During this period, the audit scope was limited by the client as to the observation of the annual physical inventory. Since the CPA considered the inventories to be of material amount and he was not able to satisfy himself by other auditing procedures, he was not able to express an unqualified opinion on the financial statements in each of the five years.

   The CPA was allowed to observe physical inventories for the current year ended December 31, 1997, because the client's banker would no longer accept the audit reports. In the interest of economy, the client requested the CPA to not extend his audit procedures to the inventory as of January 1, 1997.
6. During the course of his audit of the financial statements of a corporation for the purpose of expressing an opinion on the statements, a CPA is refused permission to inspect the minute books. The corporation secretary instead offers to give the CPA a certified copy of all resolutions and actions involving accounting matters.
7. A CPA has completed his audit of the financial statements of a bus company for the year ended December 31, 1997. Prior to 1997, the company had been depreciating its buses over a 10-year period. During 1997, the company determined that a more realistic estimated life for its buses was 12 years and computed the 1997 depreciation on the basis of the revised estimate. The CPA has satisfied himself that the 12-year life is reasonable.

   The company has adequately disclosed the change in estimated useful lives of its buses and the effect of the change on 1997 income in a note to the financial statements.

### Required

a. For each situation, identify which of the conditions requiring a deviation from or modification of an unqualified standard report is applicable.

b. State the level of materiality as immaterial, material, or highly material. If you cannot decide the level of materiality, state the additional information needed to make a decision.

c. Given your answers in parts a and b, state the appropriate audit report from the following alternatives (if you have not decided on one level of materiality in part b, state the appropriate report for each alternative materiality level):
   (1) Unqualified—standard wording.
   (2) Unqualified—explanatory paragraph.
   (3) Unqualified—modified wording.
   (4) Qualified opinion only—except for.
   (5) Qualified scope and opinion.
   (6) Disclaimer.
   (7) Adverse.*

**2-28 (Objective 2-4)** Various types of "accounting changes" can affect the second reporting standard of the generally accepted auditing standards. This standard reads, "The report shall identify those circumstances in which such principles have not been consistently observed in the current period in relation to the preceding period."

Assume that the following list describes changes that have a material effect on a client's financial statements for the current year.

1. A change from the completed-contract method to the percentage-of-completion method of accounting for long-term construction contracts.
2. A change in the estimated useful life of previously recorded fixed assets based on newly acquired information.

*AICPA adapted

3. Correction of a mathematical error in inventory pricing made in a prior period.
4. A change from prime costing to full absorption costing for inventory valuation.
5. A change from presentation of statements of individual companies to presentation of consolidated statements.
6. A change from deferring and amortizing preproduction costs to recording such costs as an expense when incurred because future benefits of the costs have become doubtful. The new accounting method was adopted in recognition of the change in estimated future benefits.
7. A change to including the employer share of FICA taxes as "retirement benefits" on the income statement from including it with "other taxes."
8. A change from the FIFO method of inventory pricing to the LIFO method of inventory pricing.

## Required

Identify the type of change described in each item above, and state whether any modification is required in the auditor's report *as it relates to the second standard of reporting.* Organize your answer sheet as shown below. For example, a change from the LIFO method of inventory pricing to the FIFO method of inventory pricing would appear as shown.

Assume that each item is material.*

| Item No. | Type of Change | Should Auditor's Report be Modified? |
|---|---|---|
| Example | An accounting change from one generally accepted accounting principle to another generally accepted accounting principle. | Yes |

**2-29 (Objective 2-4)** The following is the first paragraph of an audit report of a publicly held company, modified for the most current audit reporting standards.

REPORT OF INDEPENDENT, CERTIFIED PUBLIC ACCOUNTANTS

To The Board of Directors and Stockholders, Farmers Group, Inc.

We have audited the consolidated balance sheets of Farmers Group, Inc., as of December 31, 1997 and 1996, and the related consolidated statements of income, stockholders' equity, and cash flows for each of the three years ended December 31, 1997. These financial statements are the responsibility of Farmers Group, Inc.'s management. Our responsibility is to express an opinion on these financial statements based on our audits. We did not audit the financial statements of Farmers New World Life Insurance Company, The Ohio State Life Insurance Company, and Investors Guaranty Life Insurance Company as of December 31, 1997 and 1996, and the related combined statements of income, stockholders' equity, and cash flows for each of the three years in the period ended December 31, 1997, which statements reflect assets constituting $26.2 million in 1997 and $26.2 million in 1996, and net income of $3.92 million, $2.43 million, and $1.68 million in 1997, 1996, and 1995, respectively, of the related consolidated totals. These statements were audited by other auditors whose report has been furnished to us, and our opinion, insofar as it relates to the amounts included for the above named three companies, is based solely on the report of the other auditors.

*AICPA adapted.

## Required

a. Should the audit opinion in this case be unqualified, qualified, a disclaimer, or adverse?

b. Assuming that the audit was completed on March 9, 1998, write the opinion paragraph for this audit report.

**2-30 (Objective 2-8)** The following is an audit report, except for the opinion paragraph, of Tri-Nation Coin Investments.

INDEPENDENT AUDITOR'S REPORT

To the Board of Directors and Stockholders, Tri-Nation Coin Investments, Philadelphia, Pennsylvania

We have audited the accompanying consolidated balance sheet of Tri-Nation Coin Investments and subsidiaries as of July 31, 1997, and the related statements of income, stockholders' equity, and cash flows for the year then ended and the related schedules listed in the accompanying index. These financial statements are the responsibility of the Company's management. Our responsibility is to express an opinion on these financial statements based on our audits.

The company had significant deficiencies in internal control including the lack of detailed records and certain supporting data which were not available for our audit. Therefore, we were not able to obtain sufficient evidence in order to form an opinion on the accompanying financial statements including whether the inventory at July 31, 1997 ($670,490) was stated at lower of cost or market, or whether the deferred subscription revenue ($90,260) is an adequate estimate for the applicable liability, as discussed in Notes 5 and 12, respectively.

## Required

Write the auditor's opinion to accompany this portion of the audit report. Where is the opinion located in this audit report?

**2-31 (Objectives 2-5, 2-6, 2-7, 2-8)** The following two paragraphs were taken from the California First Bank audit report, modified for changes in current reporting standards.

INDEPENDENT ACCOUNTANT'S REPORT

To the Shareholders and Board of Directors of California First Bank

We have audited the accompanying consolidated balance sheets of California First Bank (a California chartered state bank, and a 76.5% owned subsidiary of The Bank of Tokyo, Ltd.) and subsidiaries as of December 31, 1996 and 1995, and the related consolidated statements of income, changes in shareholders' equity, and cash flows for each of the three years in the period ended December 31, 1996. These financial statements are the responsibility of the Company's management. Our responsibility is to express an opinion on these financial statements based on our audits.

As explained in Note 2 to the financial statements, the Bank has charged goodwill and certain other intangible assets acquired in two separate acquisitions directly to shareholders' equity. Under generally accepted accounting principles, these intangibles should have been recorded as assets and amortized to income over future periods.

## Required

a. Which condition requiring a departure from an unqualified opinion exists for the portion of the foregoing report?

b. Should the opinion be unqualified, qualified, disclaimer, or adverse?

c. Assuming a standard wording scope paragraph, write the opinion paragraph for this audit situation.

**2-32 (Objectives 2-2, 2-4)** The following tentative auditor's report was drafted by a staff accountant and submitted to a partner in the accounting firm of Better & Best, CPAs:

AUDIT REPORT

To the Audit Committee of American Widgets, Inc.

We have examined the consolidated balance sheets of American Widgets, Inc., and subsidiaries as of December 31, 1996 and 1995, and the related consolidated statements of income, retained earnings, and cash flows for the years then ended. These financial statements are the responsibility of the Company's management. Our responsibility is to express an opinion on these financial statements based on our audits.

Our audits were made in accordance with generally accepted auditing standards as we considered necessary in the circumstances. Other auditors audited the financial statements of certain subsidiaries and have furnished us with reports thereon containing no exceptions. Our opinion expressed herein, insofar as it relates to the amounts included for those subsidiaries, is based solely upon the reports of the other auditors.

As fully discussed in Note 7 to the financial statements, in 1996, the company extended the use of the last-in, first-out (LIFO) method of accounting to include all inventories. In examining inventories, we engaged Dr. Irwin Same (Nobel Prize winner 1994) to test check the technical requirements and specifications of certain items of equipment manufactured by the company.

In our opinion, the financial statements referred to above present fairly the financial position of American Widgets, Inc., as of December 31, 1996, and the results of operations for the years then ended, in conformity with generally accepted accounting principles.

To be signed by
Better & Best, CPAs

March 1, 1997

## Required

Identify deficiencies in the staff accountant's tentative report that constitute departures from the generally accepted standards of reporting.*

## CASE

**2-33 (Objective 2-2, 2-5, 2-6, 2-8)** Following are the auditor's report and the complete financial statements of the Young Manufacturing Corporation for the year ended January 31, 1997. The audit was conducted by John Smith, an individual practitioner who has audited the corporation's financial statements and has reported on them for many years.

## Required

List and discuss the deficiencies of the auditor's report prepared by John Smith. Your discussion should include justifications that the matters you cited are deficiencies. (Do not check the additions in the statements. Assume that the additions are correct.)*

*AICPA adapted

To: Mr. Paul Young, President
Young Manufacturing Corporation

January 31, 1997

I have audited the balance sheet of the Young Manufacturing Corporation and the related statements of income and retained earnings.

These statements present fairly the financial position and results of operations in conformity with generally accepted principles of accounting applied on a consistent basis. My audit was made in accordance with generally accepted auditing standards and, accordingly, included such tests of the accounting records and such other auditing procedures as I considered necessary in the circumstances.

(Signed) John Smith

**YOUNG MANUFACTURING CORPORATION**
**Statements of Condition January 31, 1997 and 1996**

| | **1997** | **1996** |
|---|---|---|
| *Assets* | | |
| Current assets: | | |
| Cash | $ 43,822 | $ 51,862 |
| Accounts receivable, pledged—less allowances for doubtful accounts of $3,800 in 1997 and $3,000 in 1996 (see note) | 65,298 | 46,922 |
| Inventories, pledged—at average cost, not in excess of replacement cost | 148,910 | 118,264 |
| Other current assets | 6,280 | 5,192 |
| Total current assets | 264,310 | 222,240 |
| Fixed assets: | | |
| Land—at cost | 38,900 | 62,300 |
| Buildings—at cost, less accumulated depreciation of $50,800 in 1997 and $53,400 in 1996 | 174,400 | 150,200 |
| Machinery and equipment—at cost, less accumulated depreciation of $30,500 in 1997 and $25,640 in 1996 | 98,540 | 78,560 |
| Total fixed assets | 311,840 | 291,060 |
| Total assets | $576,150 | $513,300 |
| *Liabilities and Stockholders' Equity* | | |
| Current liabilities: | | |
| Accounts payable | $ 27,926 | $ 48,161 |
| Other liabilities | 68,743 | 64,513 |
| Current portion of long-term mortgage payable | 3,600 | 3,600 |
| Income taxes payable | 46,840 | 30,866 |
| Total current liabilities | 147,109 | 147,140 |
| Long-term liabilities: | | |
| Mortgage payable | 90,400 | 94,000 |
| Total liabilities | 237,509 | 241,140 |
| Stockholders' equity: | | |
| Capital stock, par value $100, 1,000 shares authorized, issued and outstanding | 100,000 | 100,000 |
| Retained earnings | 238,641 | 172,160 |
| Total stockholders' equity | 338,641 | 272,160 |
| Total liabilities and stockholders' equity | $576,150 | $513,300 |

YOUNG MANUFACTURING CORPORATION
**Income Statements for the Years Ended January 31, 1997 and 1996**

| | **1997** | **1996** |
|---|---|---|
| Income: | | |
| Sales | $884,932 | $682,131 |
| Other income | 3,872 | 2,851 |
| Total | 888,804 | 684,982 |
| Costs and expenses: | | |
| Costs of goods sold | 463,570 | 353,842 |
| Selling expenses | 241,698 | 201,986 |
| Administrative expenses | 72,154 | 66,582 |
| Provision for income taxes | 45,876 | 19,940 |
| Other expenses | 12,582 | 13,649 |
| Total | 835,880 | 655,999 |
| Net income | $ 52,924 | $ 28,983 |

# 3

# PROFESSIONAL ETHICS

## LEARNING OBJECTIVES

Thorough study of this chapter will enable you to

**3-1** Distinguish ethical from unethical behavior in personal, professional, and business contexts.

**3-2** Identify ethical dilemmas and describe how they can be addressed.

**3-3** Describe the ethical concerns specific to the accounting profession.

**3-4** Explain the purpose and content of the AICPA *Code of Professional Conduct.*

**3-5** Discuss independence as it applies to the AICPA *Code.*

**3-6** Discuss integrity and objectivity as they apply to the AICPA *Code.*

**3-7** Discuss the AICPA *Code* rules on technical standards.

**3-8** Discuss the AICPA *Code* rules on confidentiality and contingent fees.

**3-9** Explain the AICPA *Code* rule on discreditable acts.

**3-10** Explain the AICPA *Code* rules on advertising, solicitation, commissions, and referral fees.

**3-11** Explain the acceptable forms of organization of CPA firms.

**3-12** Describe the enforcement mechanisms for the rules of conduct.

## YOU NEVER REALLY KNOW WHAT YOUR ETHICS ARE UNTIL THEY'RE PUT TO THE TEST

Lorina Carroll had heard some real winners in her day, but this was a new one. She was the administrative manager for the Milwaukee office of Bjornson, Johnson, Halberg & Smith. One of her functions was to review time sheets and expense reports. Standing in front of her was Donald Ransom. Donald was a second-year staff auditor assigned to work on the Belltrain, Inc. audit, and had spent the last two weeks doing work in Belltrain's plant in Des Moines, Iowa. When Lorina reviewed Ransom's expenses, she saw a charge for hotel expenses, at $67.00 a night, but there was no hotel bill attached.

When Lorina called Ransom to ask for a copy of the bill, he said he'd lost it. The same day, she overheard two other staff members talking about their trip to Des Moines, and Ransom and his expenses. She talked to one of them in confidence and was told that Ransom had an aunt and uncle in Des Moines, and that he stayed with them rather than in the hotel with the other staff.

Lorina called Ransom into her office and confronted him with what she had heard. She asked him if he had paid his aunt and uncle for their hospitality, to which he replied, "No." Ransom looked surprised that this would be such a big deal. As he explained to Lorina, "I put the same amount on my expense report that I would have spent if I had stayed at the hotel. Staying with my aunt and uncle was my choice and the client is no worse off, so I just figured I was entitled to keep the money myself. I thought resourcefulness was something the firm encouraged. I feel like I'm being bawled out for a little creative thinking here."

Ethics is a topic that is receiving a great deal of attention throughout our society today. This attention is an indication of both the importance of ethical behavior to maintaining a civil society, and a significant number of notable instances of unethical behavior. The authors believe that ethical behavior is the backbone of the practice of public accounting and deserving of serious study by all accounting students. This chapter is intended to motivate such study. It begins with a definition and discussion of ethics at a general level, talks about ethical dilemmas and how they can be approached, and ends with a discussion of ethics in the accounting profession with a focus on the AICPA *Code of Professional Conduct.*

## WHAT ARE ETHICS?

**OBJECTIVE 3-1**
**Distinguish ethical from unethical behavior in personal, professional, and business contexts.**

*Ethics* can be defined broadly as a set of moral principles or values. Each of us has such a set of values, although we may or may not have considered them explicitly. Philosophers, religious organizations, and other groups have defined in various ways ideal sets of moral principles or values. Examples of prescribed sets of moral principles or values at the implementation level include laws and regulations, church doctrine, codes of business ethics for professional groups such as CPAs, and codes of conduct within individual organizations.

An example of a prescribed set of principles that was developed by the Josephson Institute for the Advancement of Ethics is included in Figure 3-1. The Josephson Institute was established as a not-for-profit foundation to encourage ethical conduct of professionals in the fields of government, law, medicine, business, accounting, and journalism.

It is common for people to differ in their moral principles or values. For example, a person might examine the Josephson Institute's ethical principles and conclude that several principles should not be included. Even if two people agree on the ethical principles that determine ethical behavior, it is unlikely that they will agree on the relative importance of each principle. These differences result from all of our life experiences. Parents, teachers, friends, and employers are known to influence our values, but so do television, team sports, life successes and failures, and thousands of other experiences.

### Need for Ethics

Ethical behavior is necessary for a society to function in an orderly manner. It can be argued that ethics is the glue that holds a society together. Imagine, for example, what would happen if we couldn't depend on the people we deal with to be honest. If parents, teachers, employers, siblings, co-workers, and friends all consistently lied, it would be almost impossible for effective communication to occur.

The need for ethics in society is sufficiently important that many commonly held ethical values are incorporated into laws. For example, laws dealing with driving while intoxicated and selling drugs concern responsible citizenship and respect for others. Similarly, if a company sells a defective product, it can be held accountable if harmed parties choose to sue through the legal system.

A considerable portion of the ethical values of a society cannot be incorporated into law because of the judgmental nature of certain values. Looking again at Figure 3-1 at the honesty principle, it is practical to have laws that deal with cheating, stealing, lying, or deceiving others. It is far more difficult to establish meaningful laws that deal with many aspects of principles such as integrity, loyalty, and pursuit of excellence. That does not imply that these principles are less important for an orderly society.

### Why People Act Unethically

Most people define unethical behavior as conduct that differs from what they believe would have been appropriate given the circumstances. Each of us decides for ourselves what we consider unethical behavior, both for ourselves and others. It is important to understand what causes people to act in a manner that we decide is unethical.

There are two primary reasons why people act unethically: the person's ethical standards are different from those of society as a whole, or the person chooses to act selfishly. In many instances, both reasons exist.

**FIGURE 3-1**

**Illustrative Prescribed Ethical Principles**

The following list of ethical principles incorporates the characteristics and values that most people associate with ethical behavior.

**Honesty** Be truthful, sincere, forthright, straightforward, frank, candid; do not cheat, steal, lie, deceive, or act deviously.

**Integrity** Be principled, honorable, upright, courageous, and act on convictions; do not be two-faced, or unscrupulous, or adopt an end-justifies-the-means philosophy that ignores principle.

**Promise Keeping** Be worthy of trust, keep promises, fulfill commitments, abide by the spirit as well as the letter of an agreement; do not interpret agreements in an unreasonably technical or legalistic manner in order to rationalize noncompliance or create excuses and justifications for breaking commitments.

**Loyalty (Fidelity)** Be faithful and loyal to family, friends, employers, clients, and country; do not use or disclose information learned in confidence; in a professional context, safeguard the ability to make independent professional judgments by scrupulously avoiding undue influences and conflicts of interest.

**Fairness** Be fair and open-minded, be willing to admit error and, where appropriate, change positions and beliefs, demonstrate a commitment to justice, the equal treatment of individuals, and tolerance for and acceptance of diversity; do not overreach or take undue advantage of another's mistakes or adversities.

**Caring for Others** Be caring, kind, and compassionate; share, be giving, be of service to others; help those in need and avoid harming others.

**Respect for Others** Demonstrate respect for human dignity, privacy, and the right to self-determination of all people; be courteous, prompt, and decent; provide others with the information they need to make informed decisions about their own lives; do not patronize, embarrass, or demean.

**Responsible Citizenship** Obey just laws; if a law is unjust, openly protest it; exercise all democratic rights and privileges responsibly by participation (voting and expressing informed views), social consciousness, and public service; when in a position of leadership or authority, openly respect and honor democratic processes of decision making, avoid unnecessary secrecy or concealment of information, and assure that others have all the information they need to make intelligent choices and exercise their rights.

**Pursuit of Excellence** Pursue excellence in all matters; in meeting your personal and professional responsibilities, be diligent, reliable, industrious, and committed; perform all tasks to the best of your ability, develop and maintain a high degree of competence, be well informed and well prepared; do not be content with mediocrity; do not "win at any cost."

**Accountability** Be accountable, accept responsibility for decisions, for the foreseeable consequences of actions and inactions, and for setting an example for others. Parents, teachers, employers, many professionals, and public officials have a special obligation to lead by example, to safeguard and advance the integrity and reputation of their families, companies, professions, and the government itself; an ethically sensitive individual avoids even the appearance of impropriety, and takes whatever actions are necessary to correct or prevent inappropriate conduct of others.

**Person's Ethical Standards Differ from General Society** Extreme examples of people whose behavior violates almost everyone's ethical standards are drug dealers, bank robbers, and larcenists. Most people who commit such acts feel no remorse when they are apprehended, because their ethical standards differ from those of society as a whole.

There are also many far less extreme examples when others violate our ethical values. When people cheat on their tax returns, treat other people with hostility, lie on employment applications, or perform below their competence level as employees, most of us regard that as unethical behavior. If the other person has decided that this behavior is ethical and acceptable, there is a conflict of ethical values that is unlikely to be resolved.

**The Person Chooses to Act Selfishly** The following example illustrates the difference between ethical standards that differ from general society's and acting selfishly. Person A finds a briefcase in an airport containing important papers and $1,000. He tosses the briefcase and keeps the money. He brags to his family and friends about his good fortune. Person A's values probably differ from most of society's. Person B faces the same situation but responds differently. He keeps the money but leaves the briefcase in a conspicuous place. He tells nobody and spends the money on a new wardrobe. It is likely that Person B has violated his own ethical standards, but he decided that the money was too important to pass up. He has chosen to act selfishly.

A considerable portion of unethical behavior results from selfish behavior. Watergate and other political scandals resulted from the desire for political power; cheating on tax returns and expense reports is motivated by financial greed; performing below one's competence and cheating on tests are typically due to laziness. In each case, the person knows that the behavior is inappropriate, but chooses to do it anyway because of the personal sacrifice needed to act ethically.

## ETHICS IN BUSINESS

There have been many well-publicized cases of failures by businesspersons to conduct their affairs consistently with society's ethical values. For example, recently a well-known food manufacturer admitted to intentionally mislabeling a food product for the purpose of reducing product costs. Similarly, management of several savings and loan companies have been charged with misusing company assets for personal gain and in some cases converting company assets to personal use.

There are several potential effects of these types of cases and the frequent criticisms of business in movies, television, and other media. One is to create the impression that unethical business behavior is normal behavior. Another is to conclude that management cannot conduct itself ethically and also have its business succeed financially. Finally and perhaps most important is to conclude that actions must be extreme to constitute unethical behavior. There is considerable evidence that none of these conclusions about business ethics is correct. A large number of highly successful businesses follow ethical business practices because management believes that it has a social responsibility to conduct itself ethically, and also because it is good business to do so. For example, it is socially responsible to treat employees, customers, and vendors honestly and fairly, and in the long run such actions also result in business success.

The decision of management to operate its business ethically is not a new business philosophy. For example, in the 1930s, Rotary International developed its code of ethics that is still used extensively by millions of businesspeople. It uses four questions that are called the *Four-Way Test* of ethical behavior for any ethical issue a business faces:

- Is it the truth?
- Is it fair to all concerned?
- Will it build goodwill and better friendships?
- Will it be beneficial to all concerned?

Many companies have established their own formal ethical codes of conduct for management and employees. These codes are intended to encourage all personnel to act ethically and to provide guidance as to what constitutes ethical behavior. For example, the last paragraph of the Report of Management on page 163 indicates that General Foods Corporation has a code of ethical conduct. The report also states that it is reviewed regularly to assure compliance with their ethical standards.

**ETHICS POLICIES CAN REDUCE OTHER COSTS**

According to a 1993 survey conducted by the Cost Management Group of the Institute of Management Accountants (IMA), 53 percent of the respondents believed that having a strong and comprehensive ethics policy in place reduces a company's overall cost of internal control. A company's initial investment in creating a formal ethics policy may therefore result in a significant future payback of cost reductions.

Source: *Cost Management Update,* November 1993, p. 1.

## ETHICAL DILEMMAS

**OBJECTIVE 3-2**
**Identify ethical dilemmas and describe how they can be addressed.**

An ethical dilemma is a situation a person faces in which a decision must be made about the appropriate behavior. A simple example of an ethical dilemma is finding a diamond ring, which necessitates deciding whether to attempt to find the owner or to keep it. A far more difficult ethical dilemma to resolve is the following one, taken from *Easier Said Than Done,* a publication dealing with ethical issues. It is the type of case that might be used in an ethics course:

- In Europe, a woman was near death from a special kind of cancer. There was one drug that the doctors thought might save her. It was a form of radium that a druggist in the same town had recently discovered. The drug was expensive to make, but the druggist was charging ten times what the drug cost him to make. He paid $200 for the radium and charged $2,000 for a small dose of the drug. The sick woman's husband, Heinz, went to everyone he knew to borrow the money, but he could only get together about $1,000, which is half of what it cost. He told the druggist that his wife was dying and asked him to sell it cheaper or let him pay later. But the druggist said: "No, I discovered the drug and I'm going to make money from it." So Heinz got desperate and broke into the man's store to steal the drug for his wife. Should the husband have done that?[1]

Auditors, accountants, and other businesspeople face many ethical dilemmas in their business careers. Dealing with a client who threatens to seek a new auditor unless an unqualified opinion is issued presents a serious ethical dilemma if an unqualified opinion is inappropriate. Deciding whether to confront a supervisor who has materially overstated departmental revenues as a means of receiving a larger bonus is a difficult ethical dilemma. Continuing to be a part of the management of a company that harasses and mistreats employees or treats customers dishonestly is a moral dilemma, especially if the person has a family to support and the job market is tight.

### Rationalizing Unethical Behavior

There are alternative ways to resolve ethical dilemmas, but care must be taken to avoid methods that are rationalizations of unethical behavior. The following are rationalization methods commonly employed that can easily result in unethical conduct:

**Everybody Does It** The argument that it is acceptable behavior to falsify tax returns, cheat on exams, or sell defective products is commonly based on the rationalization that everyone else is doing it and therefore it is acceptable.

**If It's Legal, It's Ethical** Using the argument that all legal behavior is ethical relies heavily on the perfection of laws. Under this philosophy, one would have no obligation to return a lost object unless the other person could prove that it was his or hers.

**Likelihood of Discovery and Consequences** This philosophy relies on evaluating the likelihood that someone else will discover the behavior. Typically, the person also assesses the severity of the penalty (consequences) if there is a discovery. An example is deciding whether to correct an unintentional overbilling to a customer when the customer has already paid the full billing. If the seller believes that the customer will detect the error and respond by not buying in the future, the seller will inform the customer now; otherwise he will wait to see if the customer complains.

### Resolving Ethical Dilemmas

In recent years, formal frameworks have been developed to help people resolve ethical dilemmas. The purpose of such a framework is in identifying the ethical issues and deciding on an appropriate course of action using the person's own values. The six-step

[1] Norman Sprinthall and Richard C. Sprinthall, "Value and Moral Development," *Easier Said Than Done,* Vol. 1, No. 1, Winter 1988, p. 17.

approach that follows is intended to be a relatively simple approach to resolving ethical dilemmas:

1. Obtain the relevant facts.
2. Identify the ethical issues from the facts.
3. Determine who is affected by the outcome of the dilemma and how each person or group is affected.
4. Identify the alternatives available to the person who must resolve the dilemma.
5. Identify the likely consequence of each alternative.
6. Decide the appropriate action.

An illustration is used to demonstrate how a person might use this six-step approach to resolve an ethical dilemma.

## Ethical Dilemma

Bryan Longview has been working six months as a staff assistant for Barton & Barton CPAs. Currently he is assigned to the audit of Reyon Manufacturing Company under the supervision of Charles Dickerson, an experienced audit senior. There are three auditors assigned to the audit, including Bryan, Charles, and a more experienced assistant, Martha Mills. During lunch on the first day, Charles says, "It will be necessary for us to work a few extra hours on our own time to make sure we come in on budget. This audit isn't very profitable anyway, and we don't want to hurt our firm by going over budget. We can accomplish this easily by coming in a half hour early, taking a short lunch break, and working an hour or so after normal quitting time. We just won't write that time down on our time report." Bryan recalls reading in the firm's policy manual that working hours and not charging for them on the time report is a violation of Barton & Barton's employment policy. He also knows that seniors are paid bonuses, instead of overtime, whereas staff are paid for overtime but get no bonuses. Later, when discussing the issue with Martha, she says, "Charles does this on all of his jobs. He is likely to be our firm's next audit manager. The partners think he's great because his jobs always come in under budget. He rewards us by giving us good engagement evaluations, especially under the cooperative attitude category. Several of the other audit seniors follow the same practice."

## Resolving the Ethical Dilemma Using the Six-Step Approach

**Relevant Facts** There are three key facts in this situation that deal with the ethical issue and how the issue will likely be resolved:

- The staff person has been informed that he will work hours without recording them as hours worked.
- Firm policy prohibits this practice.
- Another staff person has stated that this is common practice in the firm.

**Ethical Issue** The ethical issue in this situation is not difficult to identify.

- Is it ethical for Bryan to work hours and not record them as hours worked in this situation?

**Who Is Affected and How Is Each Affected?** There are typically more people affected in situations where ethical dilemmas occur than would normally be expected. The following are the key persons involved in this situation:

| *Who* | *How Affected* |
|---|---|
| Bryan | Being asked to violate firm policy.<br>Hours of work will be affected.<br>Pay will be affected.<br>Performance evaluations may be affected.<br>Attitude about firm may be affected. |
| Martha | Same as Bryan. |

| | |
|---|---|
| Charles | Success on engagement and in firm may be affected.<br>Hours of work will be affected. |
| Barton & Barton | Stated firm policy is being violated.<br>May result in underbilling clients in the current and future engagements.<br>May affect firm's ability to realistically budget engagements and bill clients.<br>May affect the firm's ability to motivate and retain employees. |
| Staff assigned to Reyon Manufacturing in the future | May result in unrealistic time budgets.<br>May result in unfavorable time performance evaluations.<br>May result in pressures to continue practice of not charging for hours worked. |
| Other staff in firm | Following the practice on this engagement may motivate others to follow the same practice on other engagements. |

**Bryan's Available Alternatives**

- Refuse to work the additional hours.
- Perform in the manner requested.
- Inform Charles that he will not work the additional hours or will charge the additional hours to the engagement.
- Talk to a manager or partner about Charles's request.
- Refuse to work on the engagement.
- Quit working for the firm.

Each of these options includes a potential consequence, the worst likely one being termination by the firm.

**Consequences of Each Alternative** In deciding the consequences of each alternative, it is essential to evaluate both the short- and long-term effects. There is a natural tendency to emphasize the short term because those consequences will occur quickly, even when the long-term consequences may be more important. For example, consider the potential consequences if Bryan decides to work the additional hours and not report them. In the short term, he will likely get good evaluations for cooperation and perhaps a salary increase. In the longer term, what will be the effect of not reporting the hours this time when other ethical conflicts arise? Consider the following similar ethical dilemmas Bryan might face in his career as he advances:

- A supervisor asks Bryan to work 3 unreported hours daily and 15 unreported hours each weekend.
- A supervisor asks Bryan to initial certain audit procedures as having been performed when they were not.
- Bryan concludes that he cannot be promoted to manager unless he persuades assistants to work hours that they do not record.
- Management informs Bryan, who is now a partner, that either the company gets an unqualified opinion for a $40,000 audit fee or the company will change auditors.
- Management informs Bryan that the audit fee will be increased $25,000 if Bryan can find a plausible way to increase earnings by $1 million.

**Appropriate Action** Only Bryan can decide the appropriate option to select in the circumstances after considering his ethical values and the likely consequences of each option. At one extreme Bryan could decide that the only relevant consequence is the potential impact on his career. Most of us would conclude that Bryan is an unethical person if he follows that course. At the other extreme, Bryan can decide to refuse to work for a firm that permits even one supervisor to violate firm policies. Many people would consider such an extreme reaction naive.

## SPECIAL NEED FOR ETHICAL CONDUCT IN PROFESSIONS

**OBJECTIVE 3-3**
**Describe the ethical concerns specific to the accounting profession.**

Our society has attached a special meaning to the term *professional.* A professional is expected to conduct him- or herself at a higher level than most other members of society. For example, when the press reports that a physician, clergyperson, U.S. senator, or CPA has been indicted for a crime, most people feel more disappointment than when the same thing happens to people who are not labeled as professionals.

The term "professional" means a responsibility for conduct that extends beyond satisfying the person's responsibilities to him- or herself and beyond the requirements of our society's laws and regulations. A CPA, as a professional, recognizes a responsibility to the public, to the client, and to fellow practitioners, including honorable behavior, even if that means personal sacrifice.

The underlying reason for a high level of professional conduct by any profession is the need for *public confidence* in the quality of service by the profession, regardless of the individual providing it. For the CPA, it is essential that the client and external financial statement users have confidence in the quality of audits and other services. If users of services do not have confidence in physicians, judges, or CPAs, the ability of those professionals to serve clients and the public effectively is diminished.

It is not practical for users to evaluate the quality of the performance of most professional services because of their *complexity.* A patient cannot be expected to evaluate whether an operation was properly performed. A financial statement user cannot be expected to evaluate audit performance. Most users have neither the competence nor the time for such an evaluation. Public confidence in the quality of professional services is enhanced when the profession encourages high standards of performance and conduct on the part of all practitioners.

In recent years increased competition has made it more difficult for CPAs and many other professionals to conduct themselves in a professional manner. Increased competition sometimes has the effect of making CPA firms more concerned about keeping clients and maintaining a reasonable profit than with providing high-quality audits for users. Because of the increased competition, many CPA firms have implemented philosophies and practices that are frequently referred to as *improved business practices.* These include such things as improved recruiting and personnel practices, better office management, and more effective advertising and other promotional methods. CPA firms are also attempting to become more efficient in doing audits in a variety of ways. For example, CPA firms are obtaining efficiency through the use of computers, effective audit planning, and careful assignment of staff.

Most people, including the authors, believe that these changes are desirable for our society's benefit as long as they do not interfere with the conduct of CPAs as professionals. A CPA firm can implement effective business practices and still conduct itself in a highly professional manner.

### Difference between CPA Firms and Other Professionals

CPA firms have a different relationship with users of financial statements than most other professionals have with the users of their services. Attorneys, for example, are typically engaged and paid by a client and have primary responsibility to be an advocate for that client. CPA firms are engaged and paid by the company issuing the financial statements, but the primary beneficiaries of the audit are statement users. Frequently the auditor doesn't know or have contact with the statement users, but has frequent meetings and ongoing relationships with client personnel.

It is essential that users regard CPA firms as competent and unbiased. If users were to believe that CPA firms do not perform a valuable service (reduce information risk), the value of CPA firms' audit and other attestation reports would be reduced, and the demand for audits would thereby also be reduced. There is, therefore, considerable incentive for CPA firms to conduct themselves at a high professional level.

## WAYS CPAS ARE ENCOURAGED TO CONDUCT THEMSELVES PROFESSIONALLY

As first discussed in Chapter 1, there are several ways in which the CPA profession and society encourage CPAs to conduct themselves appropriately and to do high-quality audits and related services. Figure 3-2 shows the most important ways. Several items already discussed include GAAS and their interpretations, the CPA examination, quality control, peer review requirements, SEC, division of CPA firms, and continuing education. The ability of individuals separately or together to sue CPA firms also exerts considerable influence on the way in which practitioners conduct themselves and audits. Legal liability is studied in Chapter 4. The AICPA *Code of Professional Conduct* also has a significant influence on practitioners. It is meant to provide a standard of conduct for CPAs. The AICPA *Code* and related issues of professional conduct are the content of the remainder of this chapter. For this reason the *Code of Professional Conduct* oval is shaded in Figure 3-2.

**FIGURE 3-2**

**Ways the Profession and Society Encourage CPAs to Conduct Themselves at a High Level**

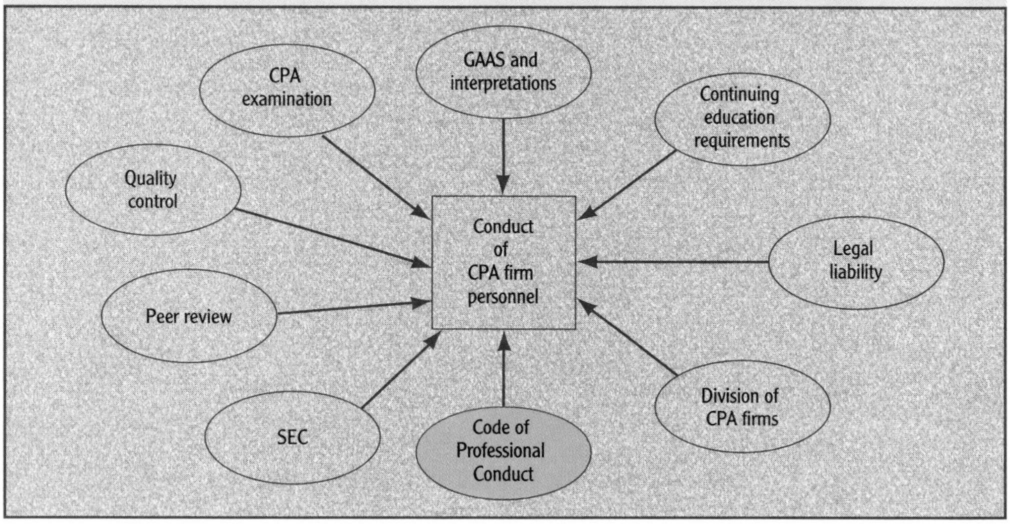


## CODE OF PROFESSIONAL CONDUCT

**OBJECTIVE 3-4**
**Explain the purpose and content of the AICPA Code of Professional Conduct.**

A code of conduct can consist of *general statements* of ideal conduct or *specific rules* that define unacceptable behavior. The advantage of general statements is the emphasis on positive activities that encourage a high level of performance. The disadvantage is the difficulty of enforcing general ideals because there are no minimum standards of behavior. The advantage of carefully defined specific rules is the enforceability of minimum behavior and performance standards. The disadvantage is the tendency of some practitioners to define the rules as maximum rather than minimum standards.

The AICPA *Code of Professional Conduct* has attempted to accomplish both the objectives of general statements of ideal conduct and of specific rules. There are four parts to the code: principles, rules of conduct, interpretations, and ethical rulings. The parts are listed in order of increasing specificity; the principles provide ideal standards of conduct, whereas ethical rulings are highly specific. The four parts are summarized in Figure 3-3 (page 76) and discussed on pages 76–79.

**FIGURE 3-3**

**Code of Professional Conduct**

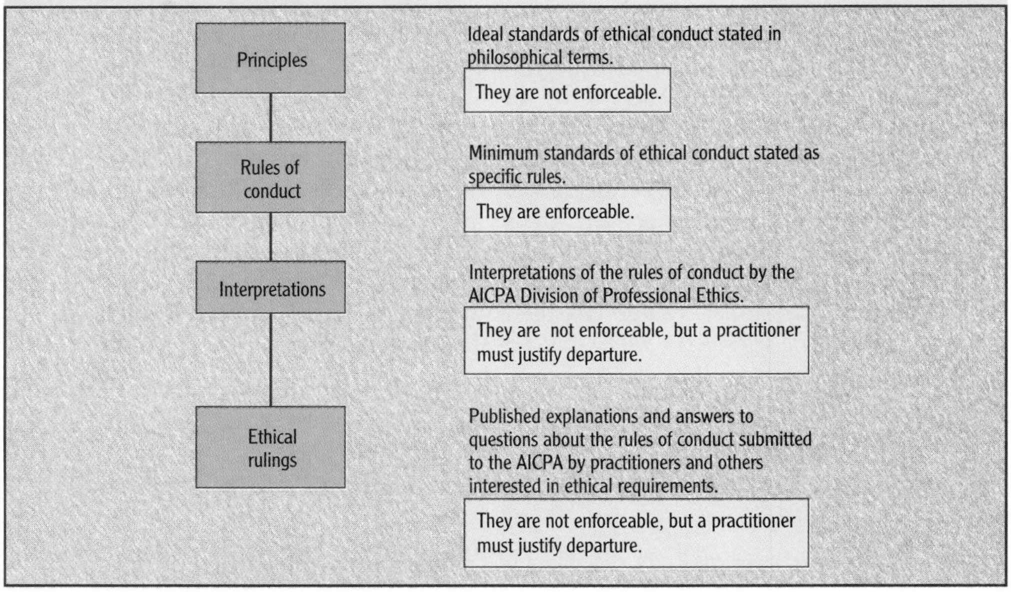


## Principles of Professional Conduct

The section of the AICPA *Code* dealing with principles of professional conduct contains a general discussion of certain characteristics required of a CPA. The principles section consists of two main parts: six ethical principles and a discussion of those principles. The ethical principles are listed as follows. Discussions throughout the chapter include ideas taken from the principles section.

**Ethical Principles**

1. **Responsibilities** In carrying out their responsibilities as professionals, members should exercise sensitive professional and moral judgments in all their activities.
2. **The Public Interest** Members should accept the obligation to act in a way that will serve the public interest, honor the public trust, and demonstrate commitment to professionalism.
3. **Integrity** To maintain and broaden public confidence, members should perform all professional responsibilities with the highest sense of integrity.
4. **Objectivity and Independence** A member should maintain objectivity and be free of conflicts of interest in discharging professional responsibilities. A member in public practice should be independent in fact and appearance when providing auditing and other attestation services.
5. **Due Care** A member should observe the profession's technical and ethical standards, strive continually to improve competence and the quality of services, and discharge professional responsibility to the best of the member's ability.
6. **Scope and Nature of Services** A member in public practice should observe the Principles of the *Code of Professional Conduct* in determining the scope and nature of services to be provided.

## Discussion of Principles

The first five of these principles are equally applicable to all members of the AICPA, regardless of whether they practice in a CPA firm, work as accountants in business or government, are involved in some other aspect of business, or are in education. One exception is the last sentence of objectivity and independence. It applies only to members in public practice, and then only when they are providing attestation services such as audits. The sixth principle, scope and nature of services, applies only to members in public practice. That principle addresses whether a practitioner should provide a certain service, such as providing personnel consulting when an audit client is hiring a controller. Providing such a service could create a loss of independence if the CPA firm recommends a controller who is hired and performs incompetently.

A careful examination of these six principles will likely lead us to conclude that they are applicable to any professional, not just CPAs. For example, physicians should exercise sensitive professional and moral judgment, act in the public interest, act with integrity, be objective and avoid conflicts of interest, follow due care, and evaluate the appropriateness of the nature of medical services provided. One difference between auditors and other professionals, as discussed earlier, is that most professionals need not be concerned about remaining independent.

## Rules of Conduct

This part of the *Code* includes the explicit rules that must be followed by every CPA in the practice of public accounting.[2] (Those individuals holding the CPA certificate but not actually practicing public accounting must follow most, but not all, of the requirements.) Because the section on rules of conduct is the only enforceable part of the code, it is stated in more precise language than the section on principles. Because of their enforceability, many practitioners refer to the rules as the AICPA *Code of Professional Conduct.*

The difference between the standards of conduct set by the *principles* and those set by the *rules of conduct* is shown in Figure 3-4. When practitioners conduct themselves at the minimum level in Figure 3-4, that does not imply unsatisfactory conduct. The profession has presumably set the standards sufficiently high to make the minimum conduct satisfactory.

At what level do practitioners conduct themselves in practice? As in any profession, the level varies among practitioners. Some operate at high levels, whereas others operate as close to the minimum level as possible. Unfortunately, some also conduct themselves below the minimum level set by the profession. It is hoped that there are few of those.

**FIGURE 3-4**

**Standards of Conduct**

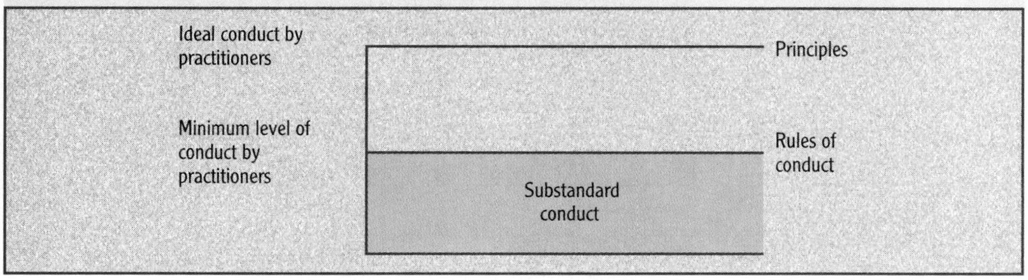


## Interpretation of Rules of Conduct

The need for published interpretations of the rules of conduct arises when there are frequent questions from practitioners about a specific rule. The Division of Professional Ethics of the AICPA prepares each interpretation based on a consensus of a committee made up principally of public accounting practitioners. Before interpretations are finalized, they are sent to a large number of key people in the profession for comment. Interpretations are not officially enforceable, but a departure from the interpretations would be difficult, if not impossible, for a practitioner to justify in a disciplinary hearing.

The interpretations are briefly summarized in Table 3-1 on page 78. The most important interpretations are discussed as a part of each section of the rules.

[2] The AICPA *Code of Professional Conduct* is applicable to every CPA who is a member of the AICPA. Each state also has rules of conduct that are required for licensing by the state. Many states follow the AICPA rules, but some have somewhat different requirements.

**TABLE 3-1**

**Summary of Rules of Conduct and Interpretations**

| RULES OF CONDUCT | | APPLICABILITY | | INTERPRETATIONS |
|---|---|---|---|---|
| **Number** | **Topic** | **All Members** | **Members in Public Practice** | |
| 101 | Independence | | x | • Transactions, interests, or relationships affecting independence<br>• Honorary directorships and trusteeships<br>• Former practitioners and firm independence<br>• Accounting services<br>• Effect of family relationships on independence<br>• Meaning of normal lending procedures, terms, and requirements<br>• The effect of actual or threatened litigation on independence<br>• Application of Rule 101 to professional personnel<br>• Effect on independence of financial interest in nonclients having investor or investee relationships with a member's client<br>• Effect on independence of relationships concerned with the financial statements of a government-reporting entity<br>• Independence and attestation engagements and SAS 75 engagements<br>• Extended audit services |
| 102 | Integrity and objectivity | x | | • Knowing that misrepresentations exist in the preparation of financial statements or records<br>• Conflicts of interest<br>• Members performing educational services<br>• Professional services involving client advocacy |
| 201 | General standards | x | | • Competence |
| 202 | Compliance with standards | x | | • Definition of the term engagement as used in Rule 201 |
| 203 | Accounting principles | x | | • Departures from established accounting principles<br>• Status of FASB interpretations |
| 301 | Confidential client information | | x | • Confidential information and technical standards<br>• Disclosure of confidential client information in certain circumstances<br>• Confidential information and the purchase, sale, or merger of a practice |
| 302 | Contingent fees | | x | • None |
| 501 | Acts discreditable | x | | • Client's records and accountant's working papers<br>• Discrimination in employment practices<br>• Failure to follow requirements of governmental bodies, commissions, or other regulatory agencies in performing attest or similar engagements<br>• Negligence in the preparation of financial statements or records<br>• Solicitation or disclosure of CPA Examination questions or answers |
| 502 | Advertising and other forms of solicitation | | x | • None |
| 503 | Commissions and referral fees | | x | • None |
| 505 | Form of organization and name | | x | • Investment in commercial accounting corporation<br>• Application of rules of conduct to members who operate a separate business |

## Ethical Rulings

Rulings are explanations by the executive committee of the professional ethics division of *specific factual circumstances.* A large number of ethical rulings are published in the expanded version of the AICPA *Code of Professional Conduct.* The following is an example (Rule 101–Independence; Ruling No. 16):

- *Question*—A member serves on the board of directors of a nonprofit social club. Would the independence of the member's firm be considered to be impaired with respect to the club?
- *Answer*—Independence of the member's firm would be considered to be impaired since the board of directors has the ultimate responsibility for the affairs of the club. The exception in the interpretations was intended primarily to cover those situations in which a member lends his or her name to some worthwhile cause without assuming important administrative or financial responsibilities.

## Applicability of the Rules of Conduct

The rules of conduct contained in the AICPA *Code of Professional Conduct* apply to all AICPA members for all services provided whether or not the member is in the practice of public accounting, unless it is specifically stated otherwise in the code. For example, when a rule is restricted to members in public practice, it is so stated in the rules. Rule 101 is an example:

**Rule 101—Independence** *A member in public practice* shall be independent in the performance of professional services as required by standards promulgated by bodies designated by Council (italics added).

Each of the rules apply to attestation services and *unless stated otherwise,* each rule also applies to all services provided by CPA firms such as taxes and management services. There are only two rules that exempt certain nonattestation services:

- Rule 101—Independence. This rule requires independence only when the AICPA has established independence requirements through its rule-setting bodies, such as the Auditing Standards Board. The AICPA requires independence only for attestation engagements. For example, a CPA firm can perform management services for a company in which the partners own stock. Of course, if the CPA firm also did an audit, that would violate the independence requirements for attestation services.
- Rule 203—Accounting Principles. This rule applies only to issuing an audit opinion or review service opinion on financial statements.

It would be a violation of the rules if someone did something on behalf of a member that would have been a violation if the member had done it. An example is a banker who puts in a newsletter that Johnson and Able CPA firm has the best tax department in the state and consistently gets large refunds for its tax clients. That is likely to create false or unjustified expectations and is a violation of Rule 502. A member is also responsible for compliance with the rules by employees, partners, and shareholders.

## Definitions

A few definitions, taken from the AICPA *Code of Professional Conduct,* must be understood to minimize misinterpretation of the rules.

**Client** Any person or entity, other than the member's employer, that engages a member or a member's firm to perform professional services.

**Firm** A form of organization permitted by state law or regulation whose characteristics conform to resolutions of Council that is engaged in the practice of public accounting, including the individual owners thereof.

**Institute** The American Institute of Certified Public Accountants.

**Member** A member, associate member, or international associate of the American Institute of Certified Public Accountants.

**Practice of Public Accounting** The practice of public accounting consists of the performance for a client, by a member or a member's firm, while holding out as CPA(s), of the professional services of accounting, tax, personal financial planning, litigation support services, and those professional services for which standards are promulgated by bodies designated by Council.

### Summary of AICPA Code of Professional Conduct

The next several sections are organized by area of ethical responsibility and related rules of conduct. Each rule of conduct is boxed, but only summaries of interpretations and a few rulings are included. Table 3-1 summarizes the rules of conduct and interpretations.

## INDEPENDENCE

**OBJECTIVE 3-5**
**Discuss independence as it applies to the AICPA *Code*.**

**Rule 101—Independence** A member in public practice shall be independent in the performance of professional services as required by standards promulgated by bodies designated by Council.

Independence in auditing means taking an *unbiased viewpoint* in the performance of audit tests, the evaluation of the results, and the issuance of the audit report. If the auditor is an advocate for the client, a banker, or anyone else, he or she cannot be considered independent. Independence must certainly be regarded as the auditor's most critical characteristic. The reason that many diverse users are willing to rely upon the CPA's reports as to the fairness of financial statements is their expectation of an unbiased viewpoint. It is not surprising that independence is included as a generally accepted auditing standard, an accounting principle, and a rule of conduct.

CPA firms are required to be independent for certain services that they provide, but not for others. The last phrase in Rule 101, "as required by standards promulgated by bodies designated by Council" is a convenient way for the AICPA to include or exclude independence requirements for different types of services. For example, the Auditing Standards Board requires that auditors of historical financial statements be independent. Rule 101 therefore applies to audits. Independence is also required for other types of attestations such as review services and audits of prospective financial statements. A CPA firm can, however, do tax returns and provide management services without being independent. Rule 101 does not apply to those types of services.

Not only is it essential for auditors to maintain an independent attitude in fulfilling their responsibilities, but it is also important that the users of financial statements have confidence in that independence. These two objectives are frequently identified as **independence in fact** and **independence in appearance.** Independence in fact exists when the auditor is actually able to maintain an unbiased attitude throughout the audit, whereas independence in appearance is the result of others' interpretations of this independence. If auditors are independent in fact, but users believe them to be advocates for the client, most of the value of the audit function will be lost.

Although it is possible to take the extreme position that anything affecting either independence in fact or in appearance must be eliminated to ensure a high level of respect in the community, it is doubtful whether this would solve as many problems as it would create. The difficulty with this position is that it is likely to significantly restrict the services offered to clients, the freedom of CPAs to practice in the traditional manner, and the ability of CPA firms to hire competent staff. At this point it will be helpful to examine some conflicts of independence that have arisen within the profession, evaluate their significance, and determine how the profession has resolved them. The profession deals with most independence issues through Interpretations of the Rules of Conduct. Observe in Table 3-1 that there are more interpretations for independence than for any of the other rules.

## Financial Interests

Interpretations of Rule 101 prohibit CPAs in public accounting from owning *any stock or other direct investment* in audit clients because it is potentially damaging to actual audit independence, and it certainly is likely to affect the users' perceptions of the auditors' independence. *Indirect investments,* such as ownership of stock in a client's company by an auditor's grandparent, are also prohibited, but *only if the amount is material* to the auditor. The ownership of stock rule is more complex than it appears at first glance. A more detailed examination of that requirement is included to aid in understanding and to show the complexity of one of the rules. There are three important distinctions in the rules as they relate to independence and stock ownership.

**Partners or Shareholders versus Nonpartners or Nonshareholders** Rule 101 applies to partners and shareholders for all clients of a CPA firm. The rule applies to nonpartners or nonshareholders only *when they are involved in the engagement* or *when the engagement is performed by staff in the same office.* For example, a staff member in a national CPA firm could own stock in a client corporation and not violate Rule 101 if he or she was never involved in the engagement, but as soon as the staff member became a partner he or she would have to dispose of the stock or the CPA firm must stop doing the audit.

Some CPA firms do not permit any ownership by staff of client's stock regardless of which office serves the client. These firms have decided to have higher requirements than the minimums set by the rules of conduct.

**Direct versus Indirect Financial Interest** Direct ownership refers to the ownership of stock or other equity shares by members or their immediate family. For example, if either a partner or the partner's spouse had a partnership interest in a company, the CPA firm would be prohibited by Rule 101 from expressing an opinion on the financial statements of that company.

Ownership is indirect when there is a close, but not a direct, ownership relationship between the auditor and the client. An example of indirect ownership occurs when a CPA firm audits a mutual fund which owns stock that an audit partner also has in his or her personal portfolio. Another example is the ownership of a stock by a member's grandparent.

**Material or Immaterial** *Materiality* affects whether ownership is a violation of Rule 101 only for *indirect* ownership. Materiality must be considered in relation to the member person's wealth and income. For example, if a mutual fund client has a large portion of its ownership in the XY Company and a firm partner has a significant amount of her personal wealth invested in XY Company, a violation of the code exists.

## Related Financial Interest Issues

Several interpretations of Rule 101 deal with specific aspects of financial relationships between CPA firm personnel and clients. These are summarized in this section.

**Former Practitioners** In most situations, the interpretations permit former partners or shareholders who left the firm due to such things as retirement or the sale of their ownership interest to have relationships with clients of the firm of the type that are normally a violation of Rule 101, without affecting a firm's independence. A violation by the firm would occur if the former partner was held out as an associate of the firm or took part in activities that are likely to cause other parties to believe the person was still active in the firm. Examples include participation in the CPA firm's business activities, the use of the CPA firm's office space when the former partner has significant influence over a client of the firm, or the receipt of benefits from the former CPA firm that are dependent on the firm's profitability.

**Normal Lending Procedures** Generally, loans between a CPA firm or its members and an audit client are prohibited because it is a financial relationship. There are several exceptions to the rule, however, including automobile loans, loans fully collateralized by cash deposits at the same financial institution, and unpaid credit card balances not exceeding $5,000 in total. It is also acceptable to accept a financial institution as a client even if members of the CPA firm have existing home mortgages, other fully collateralized secured loans, and immaterial loans with the institution. No new loans would be permitted, however. Both the restrictions and exceptions are reasonable ones, considering the trade-off between independence and the need to permit CPAs to function as business people and individuals.

**Financial Interests of Next of Kin** The financial interests of a spouse, dependent children, or relatives living with or supported by a member are ordinarily treated as if they were the financial interests of the member. For example, if the spouse of a partner of a CPA firm owned any stock in an audit client, Rule 101 would be violated. The interpretations provide two other examples in which a violation is presumed but may be offset by other circumstances such as infrequent contact or geographical separation. The first is when close kin such as nondependent children, brothers and sisters, grandparents, parents-in-law, or spouses of these kin have a significant financial interest, investment, or business relationship with an audit client of a member. The second is when any of these close kin have an important executive position such as director, chief executive, or financial officer with a client. Imagine the difficulty a CPA firm faces if it has an opportunity to accept a new audit client where the father of a young audit partner is chief executive officer and has material ownership in the potential client. Presumably, the partners of the CPA firm would discuss the matter and may contact the AICPA Ethics Division to decide whether to accept the client.

**Joint Investor or Investee Relationship with Client** Assume, for example, that a CPA firm partner owns stock in a nonaudit client, Jackson Company. Frank Company, which is an audit client, also owns stock in Jackson Company. This may be a violation of Rule 101. The interpretations prohibit the partners from owning any stock in Jackson Company or similar financial relationships if the investment in Jackson by Frank Company is material. The interpretation defines materiality for investee–investor relationships as either 5 percent of Frank's total assets or 5 percent of Frank's operating income before taxes, whichever is more restrictive. This is an illustration of an interpretation leaving little, if any, room for practitioners to make judgments.

**Director, Officer, Management, or Employee of a Company** If a CPA is a member of the board of directors or an officer of a client company, his or her ability to make independent evaluations of the fair presentation of financial statements would be affected. Even if holding one of these positions did not actually affect the auditor's independence, the frequent involvement with management and the decisions it makes is likely to affect how statement users would perceive the CPA's independence. To eliminate this possibility, interpretations prohibit the CPA from being a director or officer of an audit client company. Similarly, the auditor cannot be an underwriter, voting trustee, promoter, or trustee of a client's pension fund, or act in any other capacity of management, or be an employee of the company.

Interpretations permit members to do audits and be *honorary* directors or trustees for not-for-profit organizations, such as charitable and religious organizations, as long as the position is purely honorary. To illustrate, it is common for a partner of the CPA firm doing the audit of a city's United Fund drive to also be an honorary director, along with many other civic leaders. The CPA cannot vote or participate in any management functions.

## Litigation between CPA Firm and Client

When there is a lawsuit or intent to start a lawsuit between a CPA firm and its client, the ability of the CPA firm and client to remain objective is questionable. The interpretations regard such litigation as a violation of Rule 101 for the current audit. For example, if management sues a CPA firm claiming a deficiency in the previous audit, the CPA firm is not considered independent for the current year's audit. Similarly, if the CPA firm sues management for fraudulent financial reporting or deceit, independence is lost.

Litigation by the client related to tax or other nonaudit services, or litigation against both the client and the CPA firm by another party, would not usually impair independence. The key consideration in all such suits is the likely effect on the ability of client, management, and CPA firm personnel to remain objective and comment freely.

## Bookkeeping Services and Audits for the Same Client

If a CPA records transactions in the journals for the client, posts monthly totals to the general ledger, makes adjusting entries, and subsequently does an audit, there is some question as to whether the CPA can be independent in his or her audit role. The interpretations *permit a CPA firm to do both bookkeeping and auditing for the same client.* The AICPA's conclusion is presumably based on a comparison of the effect on independence of having both bookkeeping and auditing services performed by the same CPA firm with the additional cost of having a different CPA firm do the audit. There are three important requirements that the auditor must satisfy before it is acceptable to do bookkeeping and auditing for the client:

*1.* The client must accept full responsibility for the financial statements. The client must be sufficiently knowledgeable about the enterprise's activities and financial condition and the applicable accounting principles so that the client can reasonably accept such responsibility, including the fairness of valuation and presentation and the adequacy of disclosure. When necessary, the CPA must discuss accounting matters with the client to be sure that the client has the required degree of understanding.

*2.* The CPA must not assume the role of employee or of management conducting the operations of an enterprise. For example, the CPA shall not consummate transactions, have custody of assets, or exercise authority on behalf of the client. The client must prepare the source documents on all transactions in sufficient detail to identify clearly the nature and amount of such transactions and maintain accounting control over data processed by the CPA, such as control totals and document counts.

*3.* The CPA, in making an audit of financial statements prepared from books and records that the CPA has maintained completely or in part, must conform to generally accepted auditing standards. The fact that the CPA has processed or maintained certain records does not eliminate the need to make sufficient audit tests.

The first two requirements are often difficult to satisfy for smaller clients where the owner may have little knowledge of or interest in accounting or processing transactions.

For SEC clients, *the SEC prohibits the performance of bookkeeping services and auditing by the same CPA firm.* Most SEC clients are larger and are more likely to have an accounting staff. This prohibition, therefore, causes few difficulties.

## Engagement and Payment of Audit Fees by Management

Can an auditor be truly independent in fact and appearance if the payment of fees is dependent upon the management of the audited entity? There is probably no satisfactory answer to this question, but it does demonstrate the difficulty of obtaining an atmosphere of complete independence of auditors. The alternative to engagement of the CPA and payment of audit fees by management would probably be the use of either government or quasi-government auditors. All things considered, it is questionable whether the audit function would be performed better or more cheaply by the public sector.

## Unpaid Fees

Under Rule 101 and its rulings and interpretations, independence is considered to be impaired if billed or unbilled fees remain unpaid for professional services provided more than one year prior to the date of the report. Such unpaid fees are deemed to be a loan from the auditor to the client, and are therefore a violation of Rule 101. Unpaid fees from a client in bankruptcy do not violate Rule 101.

## Aids to Maintaining Independence

The profession and society, especially in the past decade, have been concerned about ensuring that (1) auditors maintain an unbiased attitude in performing their work (independence in fact) and (2) users perceive auditors as being independent (independence in appearance). Many of the elements shown in Figure 3-2 and other requirements or inducements encourage CPAs to maintain independence in fact and appearance. These are now briefly summarized. The most important elements have already been discussed in Chapter 1 and early in this chapter.

**Legal Liability** The penalty involved when a court concludes that a practitioner is not independent can be severe, including criminal action. The courts have certainly provided major incentives for auditors to remain independent. Legal liability is studied in the next chapter.

**Rule 101, Interpretations and Rulings** The existing rule on independence, interpretations of that rule, and rulings restrict CPAs in their financial and business relationships with clients. They are a considerable aid in maintaining independence.

**Generally Accepted Auditing Standards** The second general standard requires the auditor to maintain an independent mental attitude in all matters related to the assignment.

**AICPA Quality Control Standards** As shown in Chapter 1, one of the AICPA quality control standards requires a CPA firm to establish policies and procedures to provide reasonable assurance that all personnel are independent.

**Division of Firms** For CPA firms that choose to join the SEC Practice Division of the AICPA Division of Firms, there are several requirements involving independence. Reporting disagreements between auditors and clients, rotation of partners, restrictions on management services, and mandatory peer review are all likely to enhance independence. Although many CPA firms are not members of the SEC Division, all of the largest firms are.

**Audit Committee** An audit committee is a selected number of members of a company's board of directors whose responsibilities include helping auditors remain independent of management. Most audit committees are made up of three to five or sometimes as many as seven directors who are not a part of company management.

A typical audit committee decides such things as which CPA firm to retain and the scope of services the CPA firm is to perform. It meets periodically with the CPA firm to discuss audit progress and findings, and helps resolve conflicts between the CPA firm and management. Audit committees for larger companies are looked upon with favor by most auditors, users, and management. The requirement of an audit committee would be costly for smaller companies.

An audit committee is required for all companies listed on the New York Stock Exchange. The AICPA rules of conduct and the SEC do not require audit committees.

**Communication with Predecessor Auditors** SAS 7 (AU 315) requires a successor auditor to communicate with the previous auditor as a part of deciding whether to accept an engagement. The primary concern in this communication is information that will help the successor auditor determine whether the client management has integrity. For example, the successor auditor asks for information from the predecessor about disagreements with management, about accounting principles or audit procedures, and reasons for the change of auditors. SAS 7 requires the predecessor auditor to respond to the request by the successor.

**Shopping for Accounting Principles** Both management and representatives of management, such as investment bankers, often consult with other accountants on the application of accounting principles. Although consultation with other accountants is an appropriate practice, it can lead to a loss of independence in certain circumstances. For example, suppose one CPA firm replaces the existing auditors on the strength of accounting advice offered but later finds facts and circumstances that require the CPA firm to change its stance. It may be difficult for the new CPA firm to remain independent in such a situation. SAS 50 (AU 625) sets forth requirements that must be followed when a CPA firm is requested to provide a written or oral opinion on the application of accounting principles or the type of audit opinion that would be issued for a specific or hypothetical transaction of an audit client of another CPA firm. The purpose of the requirement is to minimize the likelihood of management following the practice commonly called "opinion shopping" and the potential threat to independence of the kind described above. Primary among the requirements is that the consulted CPA firm should communicate with the entity's existing auditors to ascertain all the available facts relevant to forming a professional judgment on the matters the firm has been requested to report on.

**Approval of Auditor by Stockholders** Although not required by the AICPA or SEC, an increasing number of companies require stockholders to approve the selection of a new CPA firm or continuation of the existing one. Stockholders are usually a more objective group than management. It is questionable, however, whether they are in a position to evaluate the performance of previous or potential auditors.

**Conclusion** Regardless of the rules set forth by the AICPA *Code of Professional Conduct*, it is essential that the CPA maintain an unbiased relationship with management and all other parties affected by the performance of the CPA's responsibilities. In every engagement, including those involving management advisory and tax services, the CPA must not subordinate his or her professional judgment to that of others. Even though pressures on the CPA's objectivity and integrity are frequent, the long-run standing of the profession in the

**TEST YOUR KNOWLEDGE OF REAL SITUATIONS**

Periodically, the *Journal of Accountancy* publishes questions on ethics topics that have been raised by AICPA members. This set deals with Rule 101—Independence.

**QUESTIONS**

1. A staff member's father owns a single unit in a condominium association, the value of which is material to his net worth. The father is not a dependent of the staff member. Is the firm's independence impaired if the staff member participates in the audit engagement of the condominium association?

   ❑ Yes ❑ No

2. A tax manager in a multi-office CPA firm owns shares of stock in a review client and has transferred them to a blind trust. If the manager is located in the office of the firm that performs the review engagement, will the firm's independence be impaired after the transfer, even if the manager does not participate in the engagement?

   ❑ Yes ❑ No

3. A partner in a CPA firm is on the board of directors of an entity during May and June 1997. If the entity wishes to engage the partner's firm to perform an audit for the year ended June 30, 1997, may the firm accept the engagement if the partner resigns from the board before the firm's acceptance of the engagement?

   ❑ Yes ❑ No

**ANSWERS**

1. Yes. 2. Yes. 3. No. The firm's independence would be considered impaired because the partner was a member of the board of directors during the period covered by the financial statements under audit.

Source: Adapted from the *Journal of Accountancy*, September 1995, p. 91.

financial community demands resisting those pressures. If the conflicts are sufficiently great to compromise the CPA's objectivity, it may be necessary for the CPA firm to resign from the engagement.

## INTEGRITY AND OBJECTIVITY

**OBJECTIVE 3-6**
**Discuss integrity and objectivity as they apply to the AICPA *Code*.**

> **Rule 102—Integrity and Objectivity** In the performance of any professional service, a member shall maintain objectivity and integrity, shall be free of conflicts of interest, and shall not knowingly misrepresent facts or subordinate his or her judgment to others.

Objectivity means impartiality in performing all services. For example, assume that an auditor believes that accounts receivable may not be collectible, but accepts management's opinion without an independent evaluation of collectibility. The auditor has subordinated his or her judgment and thereby lacks objectivity. Now assume that a CPA is preparing the tax return for a client, and as a client advocate, encourages the client to take a deduction on the returns which he or she believes is valid, but for which there is some but not complete support. This would not be a violation of either objectivity or integrity because it is acceptable for the CPA to be a client advocate in tax and management services. If the CPA encourages the client to take a deduction for which there is no support, but which has little chance of discovery by the IRS, a violation has occurred. That is a misrepresentation of the facts and therefore the integrity of the CPA has been impaired.

Freedom from conflicts of interest means the absence of relationships that might interfere with objectivity or integrity. For example, it would be inappropriate for an auditor who is also an attorney to represent a client in legal matters. The attorney is an advocate for the client, whereas the auditor must be impartial.

An interpretation of Rule 102 states that apparent conflicts of interest may not be a violation of the rules of conduct if the information is disclosed to the member's client or employer. For example, if a partner of a CPA firm recommends that a client have its insurance coverage evaluated by an insurance agency that is owned by the partner's spouse, a conflict of interest may appear to exist. No violation of Rule 102 would occur if the partner informed the client's management of the relationship and management proceeded with the evaluation with that knowledge. The interpretation makes it clear that the independence requirements under Rule 101 cannot be eliminated by these disclosures.

## TECHNICAL STANDARDS

**OBJECTIVE 3-7**
**Discuss the AICPA *Code* rules on technical standards.**

> **Rule 201—General Standards** A member shall comply with the following standards and with any interpretations thereof by bodies designated by Council.
>
> A. *Professional competence.* Undertake only those professional services that the member or the member's firm can reasonably expect to be completed with professional competence.
> B. *Due professional care.* Exercise due professional care in the performance of professional services.
> C. *Planning and supervision.* Adequately plan and supervise the performance of professional services.
> D. *Sufficient relevant data.* Obtain sufficient relevant data to afford a reasonable basis for conclusions or recommendations in relation to any professional services performed.

**Rule 202—Compliance with Standards** A member who performs auditing, review, compilation, management consulting, tax, or other professional services shall comply with standards promulgated by bodies designated by Council.

**Rule 203—Accounting Principles** A member shall not (1) express an opinion or state affirmatively that the financial statements or other financial data of any entity are presented in conformity with generally accepted accounting principles or (2) state that he or she is not aware of any material modifications that should be made to such statements or data in order for them to be in conformity with generally accepted accounting principles, if such statements or data contain any departure from an accounting principle promulgated by bodies designated by Council to establish such principles that has a material effect on the statements or data taken as a whole. If, however, the statements or data contain such a departure and the member can demonstrate that due to unusual circumstances the financial statements or data would otherwise have been misleading, the member can comply with the rule by describing the departure, its approximate effects, if practicable, and the reasons why compliance with the principle would result in a misleading statement.

The primary purpose of the requirements of Rules 201 to 203 is to provide support for the ASB and FASB and other technical standard-setting bodies. For example, notice that requirements A and B of Rule 201 are the same in substance as general auditing standards 1 and 3, and C and D of Rule 201 have the same intent as field work standards 1 and 3. The only difference is that Rule 201 is stated in terms that apply to all types of services, whereas auditing standards apply only to audits. Rule 202 makes it clear that when a practitioner violates an auditing standard, the rules of conduct are also automatically violated.

## CONFIDENTIALITY

**OBJECTIVE 3-8**
**Discuss the AICPA *Code* rules on confidentiality and contingent fees.**

**Rule 301—Confidential Client Information** A member in public practice shall not disclose any confidential client information without the specific consent of the client.

This rule shall not be construed (1) to relieve a member of his or her professional obligations under Rules 202 and 203, (2) to affect in any way the member's obligation to comply with a validly issued and enforceable subpoena or summons, or to prohibit a member's compliance with applicable laws and government regulations, (3) to prohibit review of a member's professional practice under AICPA or state CPA society or Board of Accountancy authorization, or (4) to preclude a member from initiating a complaint with, or responding to any inquiry made by, the professional ethics division or trial board of the Institute or a duly constituted investigative or disciplinary body of a state CPA society or Board of Accountancy.

Members of any of the bodies identified in (4) above and members involved with professional practice reviews identified in (3) above shall not use to their own advantage or disclose any member's confidential client information that comes to their attention in carrying out those activities. This prohibition shall not restrict members' exchange of information in connection with the investigative or disciplinary proceedings described in (4) above or the professional practice reviews described in (3) above.

### Need for Confidentiality

During an audit or other type of engagement, practitioners obtain a considerable amount of information of a confidential nature, including officers' salaries, product pricing and advertising plans, and product cost data. If auditors divulged this information to outsiders or to client employees who have been denied access to the information, their relationship with management would be seriously strained, and in extreme cases the client could be harmed. The confidentiality requirement applies to all services provided by CPA firms, including tax and management services.

Ordinarily, the CPA's working papers can be provided to someone else only with the express permission of the client. This is the case even if a CPA sells his or her practice to another CPA firm or is willing to permit a successor auditor to examine the working papers prepared for a former client. Permission is not required from the client, however, if the working papers are subpoenaed by a court or are used as part of an authorized peer review program with other CPA firms. If the working papers are subpoenaed, the client should be informed immediately. The client and its legal counsel may wish to challenge the subpoena.

## Exceptions to Confidentiality

As stated in the second paragraph of Rule 301, there are four exceptions to the confidentiality requirements. All four exceptions concern responsibilities that are more important than maintaining confidential relations with the client.

**Obligations Related to Technical Standards** Suppose that three months after an unqualified audit report was issued, the auditor discovers that the financial statements were materially misstated. When the chief executive officer is confronted, he responds that even though he agrees that the financial statements are misstated, confidentiality prevents the CPA from informing anyone. The previous example is similar to an actual legal case, *Yale Express.* Disagreements during the *Yale Express* case resulted in AU 561, which deals with auditors' responsibilities when subsequent facts show that an inappropriate audit report has been issued. (AU 561 is discussed in Chapter 22.) Exception (1) in Rule 301 makes it clear that the auditor's responsibility to discharge professional standards is greater than that for confidentiality. In such a case, a revised, correct audit report must be issued. Note, however, that the conflict seldom occurs.

**Subpoena or Summons** Legally, information is called *privileged* if legal proceedings cannot require a person to provide the information, even if there is a subpoena. Information communicated by a client to an attorney or by a patient to a physician is privileged. *Information obtained by a CPA from a client generally is not privileged.* Exception (2) of Rule 301 is therefore needed to put CPA firms in compliance with the law.

There have been considerable discussion and disagreement among CPAs, attorneys, and legislators about the need for privileged communications between CPAs and clients. Most CPAs and businesspeople dealing with CPAs support legislation protecting privileged communications. In fact, there are statutes in a number of states that provide some level of privilege to accountant-client communications. Of course, these statutes would apply only to litigation in state courts and would have no bearing on federal court suits.

**Peer Review** When a CPA or CPA firm conducts a peer review of the quality controls of another CPA firm, it is normal practice to examine several sets of working papers. If the peer review is authorized by the AICPA, state CPA society, or state Board of Accountancy, client permission to examine the working papers is not needed. Requiring permission from each client may restrict access of the peer reviewers and would be a time burden on all concerned. Naturally, the peer reviewers must keep the information obtained confidential and cannot use the information for other purposes.

**Response to Ethics Division** If a practitioner is charged with inadequate technical performance by the AICPA Ethics Division trial board under any of Rules 201 to 203, the board members are likely to want to examine working papers. Exception (4) in Rule 301 prevents a CPA firm from denying the inquirers access to working papers by saying that they are confidential information. Similarly, a CPA firm that observes substandard working papers of another CPA firm cannot use confidentiality as the reason for not initiating a complaint of substandard performance against the firm.

## CONTINGENT FEES

> **Rule 302—Contingent Fees** A member in public practice shall not
>
> (1) Perform for a contingent fee any professional services for, or receive such a fee from, a client for whom the member or member's firm performs:
> (a) an audit or review of a financial statement; or
> (b) a compilation of a financial statement when the member expects, or reasonably might expect, that a third party will use the financial statement and the member's compilation report does not disclose a lack of independence; or
> (c) an examination of prospective financial information;
>
> or
>
> (2) Prepare an original or amended tax return or claim for a tax refund for a contingent fee for any client.
>
> The prohibition in (1) above applies during the period in which the member or the member's firm is engaged to perform any of the services listed above and the period covered by any historical financial statements involved in any such listed services.
>
> Except as stated in the next sentence, a contingent fee is a fee established for the performance of any service pursuant to an arrangement in which no fee will be charged unless a specified finding or result is attained, or in which the amount of the fee is otherwise dependent upon the finding or result of such service. Solely for purposes of this rule, fees are not regarded as being contingent if fixed by courts or other public authorities, or, in tax matters, if determined based on the results of judicial proceedings or the findings of governmental agencies.
>
> A member's fees may vary depending, for example, on the complexity of services rendered.

To help CPAs maintain objectivity in conducting audits or other attestation services, basing fees on the outcome of the engagement is prohibited. For example, suppose a CPA firm was permitted to charge a fee of $5,000 if an unqualified opinion was provided, but only $2,500 if the opinion was qualified. Such an agreement may tempt a practitioner to issue the wrong opinion and would be a violation of Rule 302. It is also a violation of Rule 302 for members to prepare an original or amended tax return, or a claim for tax refunds for a contingent fee.

In late 1990 the AICPA and Federal Trade Commission reached an agreement that eliminates the restrictions on contingent fees *for nonattestation services, unless the CPA firm was also performing attestation services* for the same client. The agreement also permits the AICPA to prohibit tax return preparation on a contingent fee basis. Under the agreement, for example, it is *not a violation* for a CPA to charge fees as an expert witness determined by the amount awarded to the plaintiff or to base consulting fees on a percentage of a bond issue *if the CPA firm does not also do an audit or other attestation for the same client.*

The reason for the agreement was a contention by the Federal Trade Commission that contingent fee restrictions reduce competition and therefore are not in the public interest. After considerable negotiation, the AICPA agreed to restrict the contingent fee prohibition only to attestation services clients and for tax return preparation. The Federal Trade Commission agreed to allow the AICPA to prohibit contingent fees for attestation services and tax return preparation because of the importance of independence and objectivity.

## DISCREDITABLE ACTS

**OBJECTIVE 3-9**
**Explain the AICPA *Code* rule on discreditable acts.**

> **Rule 501—Acts Discreditable** A member shall not commit an act discreditable to the profession.

A discreditable act is not well defined in the rules or interpretations. There are three interpretations, but except for the first one, they are vague. The three interpretations can be summarized as follows (see page 90):

1. It is a discreditable act to retain a client's records after a demand is made for them. Assume, for example, that management did not pay an audit fee and the partners of the CPA firm therefore refused to return client-owned records. The partners have violated Rule 501.
2. A CPA firm cannot discriminate on the basis of race, color, religion, sex, age, or national origin.
3. If a practitioner agrees to do an audit of a governmental agency that requires audit procedures different from GAAS, both the governmental agency procedures and GAAS must be followed unless the audit report states otherwise.

Do excessive drinking, rowdy behavior, or other acts that many people would consider unprofessional constitute a discreditable act? Probably not. Determining what constitutes professional behavior continues to be the responsibility of each professional.

**Bylaws Requirements**

For guidance as to what constitutes a discreditable act, the AICPA bylaws provide clearer guidelines than the AICPA *Code of Professional Conduct.* The bylaws state that membership in the AICPA can be terminated without a hearing for judgment of conviction for any of the following four crimes: (1) a crime punishable by imprisonment for more than one year; (2) the willful failure to file any income tax return that the CPA, as an individual taxpayer, is required by law to file; (3) the filing of a false or fraudulent income tax return on the CPA's or client's behalf; or (4) the willful aiding in the preparation and presentation of a false and fraudulent income tax return of a client. Observe that three of these deal with income tax matters of the member or a client.

## ADVERTISING AND SOLICITATION

**OBJECTIVE 3-10**
**Explain the AICPA *Code* rules on advertising, solicitation, commissions, and referral fees.**

**Rule 502—Advertising and Other Forms of Solicitation** A member in public practice shall not seek to obtain clients by advertising or other forms of solicitation in a manner that is false, misleading, or deceptive. Solicitation by the use of coercion, over-reaching, or harassing conduct is prohibited.

Solicitation consists of the various means that CPA firms use to engage new clients, other than accepting new clients who approach the firm. Examples include taking prospective clients to lunch to explain the CPA's services, offering seminars on current tax law changes to potential clients, and advertisements in the Yellow Pages of a phone book. The last example is advertising, which is only one form of solicitation. Advertising is the use of various media, such as magazines and radio, to communicate favorable information about the CPA firm's services.

Until 1978, advertising in any form was prohibited. Now, solicitation or advertising that is not *false or deceptive* is acceptable. This change in the rules of conduct is similar to that for other professions. Advertising is now acceptable within most professions.

The Federal Trade Commission prohibits the AICPA from restricting its membership from advertising and other forms of solicitation. The late 1990 agreement discussed earlier *prohibits the AICPA from preventing* any of the following practices, as long as there are no falsehoods or deceptions:

- in-person solicitation of prospective clients
- self-laudatory advertising
- comparative advertising
- testimonial or endorsement advertising
- advertising that some members may believe is "undignified" or lacking in "good taste"
- using trade names, such as "Suburban Tax Services"
- offering clients a discount for referring a prospective client

### Effect on the Profession

Starting in the late 1970s, the federal government has pressured the AICPA to eliminate rules of conduct that restricted competition among CPA firms. Until then, the AICPA prohibited direct solicitation of clients, advertising, competitive bidding, contingent fees, commissions for obtaining client services, and referral fees. Now, all six of these activities are permitted for nonattestation clients and only the last three are prohibited for attestation services clients.

The effect of these changes has been an increased emphasis on marketing and more competitive pricing of services. Many CPA firms have developed sophisticated advertising for national journals read by business people and for local newspapers. It is common for CPA firms to identify potential clients being serviced by other CPA firms and make formal and informal presentations to convince management to change CPA firms. Price bidding for audits and other services is now common and often highly competitive. As a result of these changes, some companies now change auditors more often than previously to reduce audit cost. Most practitioners believe audits are less profitable than previously.

Has the quality of audits become endangered by these changes? The existing legal exposure of CPAs, peer review requirements, and the potential for interference by the SEC and government has kept audit quality high. In the opinion of the authors, the changes in the rules have caused greater competition in the profession, but not so much that high-quality, efficiently run CPA firms have been significantly harmed. However, for this to continue to be so, CPA firms need to be on guard so that increasing competitive pressures do not cause auditors to reduce quality below an acceptable level.

## COMMISSIONS AND REFERRAL FEES

**Rule 503—Commissions and Referral Fees**

(*A*) *Prohibited commissions.* A member in public practice shall not for a commission recommend or refer to a client any product or service, or for a commission recommend or refer any product or service to be supplied by a client, or receive a commission, when the member or the member's firm also performs for that client:

(a) an audit or review of a financial statement; or

(b) a compilation of a financial statement when the member expects, or reasonably might expect, that a third party will use the financial statement and the member's compilation report does not disclose a lack of independence; or

(c) an examination of prospective financial information.

This prohibition applies during the period in which the member is engaged to perform any of the services listed above and the period covered by any historical financial statements involved in such listed services.

*B.* *Disclosure of permitted commissions.* A member in public practice who is not prohibited by this rule from performing services for or receiving a commission and who is paid or expects to be paid a commission shall disclose that fact to any person or entity to whom the member recommends or refers a product or service to which the commission relates.

*C.* *Referral fees.* Any member who accepts a referral fee for recommending or referring any service of a CPA to any person or entity or who pays a referral fee to obtain a client shall disclose such acceptance or payment to the client.

The rule for commissions and referral fees means that a CPA firm does not violate AICPA Rules of Conduct if it sells such things as real estate, securities, and entire firms on a commission basis *if the transaction does not involve a client who is receiving attestation services from the same CPA firm.* This rule enables CPA firms to profit by providing many services to nonattestation services clients that were previously prohibited.

The reason for the AICPA continuing to prohibit commissions for any attestation service client is the need to assure that the CPA firm is independent. This requirement and the reasons for it are the same as those discussed under contingent fees.

The rationale for the AICPA's less restrictive enforcement of Rule 503 than formerly is the same as that discussed for contingent fees. The Federal Trade Commission contends that restrictions reduce competition and therefore are not in the public interest.

It is essential to understand that the Board of Accountancy in the state in which the firm is licensed may have more restrictive rules than the AICPA's. The CPA firm must follow the more restrictive requirements if different rules exist.

## FORM OF ORGANIZATION AND NAME

**OBJECTIVE 3-11**
**Explain the acceptable forms of organization of CPA firms.**

> **Rule 505—Form of Organization and Name** A member may practice public accounting only in a form of organization permitted by state law or regulation whose characteristics conform to resolutions of Council.
>
> A member shall not practice public accounting under a firm name that is misleading. Names of one or more past owners may be included in the firm name of a successor organization. Also, an owner surviving the death or withdrawal of all other owners may continue to practice under a name which includes the name of past owners for up to two years after becoming a sole practitioner.
>
> A firm may not designate itself as "Members of the American Institute of Certified Public Accountants" unless all of its owners are members of the Institute.

Rule 505 permits practitioners to organize in any of six forms, as long as they are permitted by state law: proprietorship, general partnership, general corporation, professional corporation (PC), limited liability company (LLC), or limited liability partnership (LLP). Each of these forms of organization was discussed in Chapter 1 (pages 14–15).

Prior to April of 1994, all owners of a CPA firm had to be CPAs who were qualified to practice. In April of 1994, the AICPA council adopted a resolution allowing non-CPA ownership of CPA firms under the following conditions:

- The CPAs must own 66-2/3 percent of the firm's financial interests and voting rights.
- A CPA must have ultimate responsibility for all of the services provided by the firm that are governed by Statements on Auditing Standards or Statements of Standards for Accounting and Review Services.
- Owners must at all times own their equity in their own right.
- The following rules apply to all non-CPA owners:

1. They must actively provide services to the firm's clients as their principal occupation.
2. They cannot hold themselves out as CPAs, but may use any title permitted by state law such as principal, owner, officer, member, or shareholder.
3. They cannot assume ultimate responsibility for any financial statement attest or compilation engagement.
4. They are not eligible for AICPA membership, but must abide by the AICPA *Code of Professional Conduct.*
5. New non-CPA owners must have a bachelor's degree. Beginning in 2010, they must also meet the AICPA 150-hour education requirement.
6. They must meet the same continuing professional education requirements as AICPA members.

A CPA firm may use any name as long as it is not misleading. Most firms use the name of one or more of the owners. It is not unusual for a firm name to include the names of five or more owners. A CPA firm can use a trade name, although this is unusual in practice. Names such as Marshall Audit Co. or Chicago Tax Specialists are permissible if they are not misleading.

## ENFORCEMENT

**OBJECTIVE 3-12**
**Describe the enforcement mechanisms for the rules of conduct.**

Failure to follow the rules of conduct can result in *expulsion* from the AICPA. This by itself would not prevent a CPA from practicing public accounting, but it would certainly be a weighty social sanction. All expulsions from the AICPA for a violation of the rules are published in the *CPA Newsletter,* a publication that is sent to all AICPA members.

In addition to the rules of conduct, the AICPA bylaws provide for automatic suspension or expulsion from the AICPA for conviction of a crime punishable by imprisonment for more than one year for various tax-related crimes.

### Action by AICPA Professional Ethics Division

The AICPA Professional Ethics Division is responsible for investigating other violations of the code and deciding disciplinary action. The division's investigations result from information obtained primarily from complaints of practitioners or other individuals, state societies of CPAs, or governmental agencies.

There are two primary levels of disciplinary action. For less serious, and probably unintentional violations, the Division limits the discipline to a requirement of remedial or corrective action. An example is the unintentional failure to make sure that a small audit client included all disclosures in its financial statements, which would violate Rule 203 of the rules of conduct. The Division would likely require the member to attend a specified number of hours of continuing education courses to improve technical competence. The second level of disciplinary action is action before the Joint Trial Board. This board has authority to *suspend or expel members from the AICPA* for various violations of professional ethics. Typically, action by the board also results in publication in the *CPA Newsletter* of the name and address of the person suspended or expelled and reasons for the action.

### Action by a State Board of Accountancy

Even more important than expulsion from the AICPA is the existence of rules of conduct, similar to the AICPA's, that have been enacted by the Board of Accountancy of each of the 50 states. Since each state grants the individual practitioner a license to practice as a CPA, a significant breach of a state Board of Accountancy's code of conduct can result in the *loss of the CPA certificate and the license to practice.* Although it happens infrequently, the loss removes the practitioner from public accounting. Most states adopt the AICPA Rules of Conduct, but several have more restrictive codes. For example, some states have retained restrictions on advertising and other forms of solicitation. In recent years, an increasing number of states have adopted more restrictive codes of conduct than the AICPA's.

**IT'S ALL A MATTER OF TRUST**

Today's business environment clearly is different from that of 20 years ago. When the AICPA and most state CPA societies changed their conduct codes in the late 1970s to permit direct uninvited solicitations of clients, CPAs found themselves in a far more competitive business climate than ever before.

Public practitioners today must be particularly concerned with the efficiency and the effectiveness of their work. One can't cut corners and hope to prosper; one can't act unprofessionally and expect to survive. Maintaining skills throughout a career, exercising due professional care, following the promulgated standards for whatever kind of work is being done and acting professionally in all endeavors are a practitioner's keys to success.

The bottom line is dedication to professional excellence. The *Code of Professional Conduct* calls for members to "observe the profession's technical and ethical standards, strive continually to improve competence and the quality of services, and discharge professional responsibility to the best of the member's ability." That's not a lofty ideal; it's what is needed to ensure public trust in the profession.

*Source:* Michael A. Pearson, "Doing the Right Thing," *Journal of Accountancy,* June 1995, p. 86.

## ESSENTIAL TERMS

**Audit committee**—selected members of a client's board of directors, whose responsibilities include helping auditors to remain independent of management

**Client information**—information communicated by a client to a professional

**Confidential client information**—client information that may not be disclosed without the specific consent of the client except under authoritative professional or legal investigation

**Ethical dilemma**—a situation in which a decision must be made about the appropriate behavior

**Ethics**—a set of moral principles or values

**Financial interest**—ownership of stock or any other direct investment by the CPA in the client

**Independence in appearance**—the auditor's ability to maintain an unbiased viewpoint *in the eyes of others*

**Independence in fact**—the auditor's ability to take an unbiased viewpoint in the performance of professional services

**Objectivity**—impartiality in performing all professional services

**Privileged information**—client information that the professional cannot be legally required to provide; information that an accountant obtains from a client is confidential but not privileged

## REVIEW QUESTIONS

**3-1 (Objective 3-4)** Explain the need for a code of professional conduct for CPAs. In which ways should the CPA's code of conduct be similar to and different from that of other professional groups, such as attorneys or dentists?

**3-2 (Objective 3-4)** List the four parts of the *Code of Professional Conduct,* and state the purpose of each.

**3-3 (Objective 3-5)** Distinguish between independence in fact and independence in appearance. State three activities that may not affect independence in fact but are likely to affect independence in appearance.

**3-4 (Objective 3-5)** Why is an auditor's independence so essential?

**3-5 (Objective 3-5)** Explain how the rules concerning stock ownership apply to partners and nonpartners. Give an example of when stock ownership would be prohibited for each.

**3-6 (Objectives 3-5, 3-7)** What is the profession's position regarding providing management advisory services for an audit client?

**3-7 (Objective 3-5)** Many people believe that a CPA cannot be truly independent when payment of fees is dependent on the management of the client. Explain two approaches that could reduce this appearance of lack of independence.

**3-8 (Objective 3-7)** After accepting an engagement, a CPA discovers that the client's industry is more technical than he realized and that he is not competent in certain areas of the operation. What are the CPA's options?

**3-9 (Objective 3-8)** Assume that an auditor makes an agreement with a client that the audit fee will be contingent upon the number of days required to complete the engagement. Is this a violation of the *Code of Professional Conduct?* What is the essence of the rule of professional ethics dealing with contingent fees, and what are the reasons for the rule?

**3-10 (Objective 3-8)** The auditor's working papers usually can be provided to someone else only with the permission of the client. Give three exceptions to this general rule.

**3-11 (Objective 3-10)** Identify and explain factors that should keep the quality of audits high even though advertising and competitive bidding are allowed.

**3-12 (Objective 3-10)** Summarize the restrictions on advertising by CPA firms in the rules of conduct and interpretations.

**3-13 (Objective 3-10)** What is the purpose of the AICPA's *Code of Professional Conduct* restriction on commissions as stated in Rule 503?

**3-14 (Objective 3-11)** State the allowable forms of organization a CPA firm may assume.

**3-15 (Objective 3-12)** Distinguish between the effect on a CPA firm's practice of enforcing the rules of conduct by the AICPA versus a state Board of Accountancy.

## MULTIPLE CHOICE QUESTIONS FROM CPA EXAMINATIONS

**3-16 (Objectives 3-8, 3-9, 3-10)** The following questions concern possible violations of the *Code of Professional Conduct.* Choose the best response.

a. Triolo, CPA, has a small public accounting practice. One of Triolo's clients desires services that Triolo cannot adequately provide. Triolo has recommended a larger CPA firm, Pinto and Company, to his client, and in return, Pinto has agreed to pay Triolo 10 percent of the fee for services rendered by Pinto for Triolo's client. Who, if anyone, is in violation of the AICPA's *Code of Professional Conduct?*
   (1) Both Triolo and Pinto
   (2) Neither Triolo nor Pinto
   (3) Only Triolo
   (4) Only Pinto

b. A CPA who is seeking to sell an accounting practice must
   (1) not allow a peer review team to look at working papers and tax returns without permission from the client prior to consummation of the sale.
   (2) not allow a prospective purchaser to look at working papers and tax returns without permission from the client.
   (3) give all working papers and tax returns to the client.
   (4) retain all working papers and tax returns for a period of time sufficient to satisfy the statute of limitations.

c. A CPA's retention of client records as a means of enforcing payment of an overdue audit fee is an action that is
   (1) not addressed by the AICPA *Code of Professional Conduct.*
   (2) acceptable if sanctioned by the state laws.
   (3) prohibited under the AICPA rules of conduct.
   (4) a violation of generally accepted auditing standards.

**3-17 (Ojective 3-5)** The following questions concern independence and the *Code of Professional Conduct* or GAAS. Choose the best response.

a. What is the meaning of the generally accepted auditing standard that requires the auditor be independent?
   (1) The auditor must be without bias with respect to the client under audit.
   (2) The auditor must adopt a critical attitude during the audit.
   (3) The auditor's sole obligation is to third parties.
   (4) The auditor may have a direct ownership interest in his client's business if it is not material.

b. The independent audit is important to readers of financial statements because it
   (1) determines the future stewardship of the management of the company whose financial statements are audited.
   (2) measures and communicates financial and business data included in financial statements.
   (3) involves the objective examination of and reporting on management-prepared statements.
   (4) reports on the accuracy of all information in the financial statements.

**3-18 (Objectives 3-8, 3-11)** The following questions concern possible violations of the AICPA *Code of Professional Conduct.* Choose the best response.

a. In which one of the following situations would a CPA be in violation of the AICPA *Code of Professional Conduct* in determining his or her audit fee?

(1) A fee based on whether the CPA's report on the client's financial statements results in the approval of a bank loan.
(2) A fee based on the outcome of a bankruptcy proceeding.
(3) A fee based on the nature of the service rendered and the CPA's expertise instead of the actual time spent on the engagement.
(4) A fee based on the fee charged by the prior auditor.

b. The AICPA *Code of Professional Conduct* states that a CPA shall not disclose any confidential information obtained in the course of a professional engagement except with the consent of his client. In which one of the situations given below would disclosure by a CPA be in violation of the code?
(1) Disclosing confidential information in order to properly discharge the CPA's responsibilities in accordance with the profession's standards.
(2) Disclosing confidential information in compliance with a subpoena issued by a court.
(3) Disclosing confidential information to another accountant interested in purchasing the CPA's practice.
(4) Disclosing confidential information during an AICPA authorized peer review.

c. Below are the names of four CPA firms and pertinent facts for each firm. Unless otherwise indicated, the individuals named are CPAs and partners, and there are no other partners. Which firm name and related facts indicate a violation of the AICPA *Code of Professional Conduct?*
(1) Green, Lawrence, and Craig, CPAs. (Craig died about five years ago; Green and Lawrence are continuing the firm.)
(2) Clay and Sharp, CPAs. (The name of Andy Randolph, CPA, a third active partner, is omitted from the firm name.)
(3) Fulton and Jackson, CPAs. (Jackson died about three years ago; Fulton is continuing the firm as a sole proprietorship.)
(4) Schneider & Co., CPAs, Inc. (The firm has ten other stockholders who are all CPAs.)

## DISCUSSION QUESTIONS AND PROBLEMS

**3-19 (Objectives 3-5, 3-6, 3-7, 3-8, 3-9)** Each of the following situations involves a possible violation of the AICPA's *Code of Professional Conduct.* For each situation, state the applicable section of the rules of conduct and whether it is a violation.

a. John Brown is a CPA, but not a partner, with three years of professional experience with Lyle and Lyle, CPAs, a one-office CPA firm. He owns 25 shares of stock in an audit client of the firm, but he does not take part in the audit of the client and the amount of stock is not material in relation to his total wealth.

b. In preparing the personal tax returns for a client, Phyllis Allen, CPA, observed that the deductions for contributions and interest were unusually large. When she asked the client for backup information to support the deductions, she was told, "Ask me no questions, and I will tell you no lies." Allen completed the return on the basis of the information acquired from the client.

c. A client requests assistance of J. Bacon, CPA, in the installation of a computer system for maintaining production records. Bacon had no experience in this type of work and no knowledge of the client's production records, so he obtained assistance from a computer consultant. The consultant is not in the practice of public accounting, but Bacon is confident of his professional skills. Because of the highly technical nature of the work, Bacon is not able to review the consultant's work.

d. Five small Chicago CPA firms have become involved in an information project by taking part in an interfirm working paper review program. Under the program, each firm designates two partners to review the working papers, including the tax returns and the financial statements of another CPA firm taking part in the program. At the end of each review, the auditors who prepared the working papers and the reviewers have a conference to discuss the strengths and weaknesses of the audit. They do not obtain the authorization from the audit client before the review takes place.

e. James Thurgood, CPA, stayed longer than he should have at the annual Christmas party of Thurgood and Thurgood, CPAs. On his way home he drove through a red light and was stopped by a policeman, who observed that he was intoxicated. In a jury trial, Thurgood was found guilty of driving under the influence of alcohol. Since this was not his first offense, he was sentenced to 30 days in jail and his driver's license was revoked for 1 year.

f. Bill Wendal, CPA, set up a casualty and fire insurance agency to complement his auditing and tax services. He does not use his own name on anything pertaining to the insurance agency and has a highly competent manager, Frank Jones, who runs it. Wendal frequently requests Jones to review the adequacy of a client's insurance with management if it seems underinsured. He feels that he provides a valuable service to clients by informing them when they are underinsured.

g. Rankin, CPA, provides tax services, management advisory services, and bookkeeping services and conducts audits for the same client. Since the firm is small, the same person frequently provides all the services.

**3-20 (Objectives 3-5, 3-8, 3-10, 3-11)** Each of the following situations involves possible violations of the AICPA's *Code of Professional Conduct.* For each situation, state whether it is a violation of the code. In those cases in which it is a violation, explain the nature of the violation and the rationale for the existing rule.

a. Ralph Williams is the partner on the audit of a nonprofit charitable organization. He is also a member of the board of directors, but this position is honorary and does not involve performing a management function.

b. Pickens and Perkins, CPAs, are incorporated to practice public accounting. The only shareholders in the corporation are existing employees of the organization, including partners, staff members who are CPAs, staff members who are not CPAs, and administrative personnel.

c. Fenn and Company, CPAs, has time available on a computer that it uses primarily for its own record keeping. Aware that the computer facilities of Delta Equipment Company, one of Fenn's audit clients, are inadequate for company needs, Fenn maintains on its computer certain routine accounting records for Delta.

d. Godette, CPA, has a law practice. Godette has recommended one of his clients to Doyle, CPA. Doyle has agreed to pay Godette 10 percent of the fee for services rendered by Doyle to Godette's client.

e. Theresa Barnes, CPA, has an audit client, Smith, Inc., which uses another CPA for management services work. Barnes sends her firm's literature covering its management services capabilities to Smith on a monthly basis, unsolicited.

f. A bank issued a notice to its depositors that it was being audited and requested them to comply with the CPA's effort to obtain a confirmation on the deposit balances. The bank printed the name and address of the CPA in the notice. The CPA has knowledge of the notice.

g. Myron Jones, CPA, is a member of a national CPA firm. His business card includes his name, the firm's name, address, and telephone number, and the word *consultant.*

h. Gutowski, a practicing CPA, has written a tax article that is being published in a professional publication. The publication wishes to inform its readers about

Gutowski's background. The information, which Gutowski has approved, includes his academic degrees, other articles he has had published in professional journals, and a statement that he is a tax expert.

i. Poust, CPA, has sold his public accounting practice, which includes bookkeeping, tax services, and auditing, to Lyons, CPA. Poust obtained permission from all audit clients for audit-related working papers before making them available to Lyons. He did not get permission before releasing tax- and management services-related working papers.

j. Murphy and Company, CPAs, is the principal auditor of the consolidated financial statements of Lowe, Inc., and subsidiaries. Lowe accounts for approximately 98 percent of consolidated assets and consolidated net income. The two subsidiaries are audited by Trotman and Company, CPAs, a firm with an excellent professional reputation. Murphy insists on auditing the two subsidiaries because he deems this necessary to warrant the expression of an opinion.*

**3-21 (Objective 3-5)** The New York Stock Exchange now requires all its member firms to have audit committees.

## Required

a. Describe an audit committee.

b. What are the typical functions performed by an audit committee?

c. Explain how an audit committee can help an auditor be more independent.

d. Some critics of audit committees believe that they bias companies in favor of larger and perhaps more expensive CPA firms. These critics contend that a primary concern of audit committee members is to reduce their exposure to legal liability. The committees will therefore recommend larger, more prestigious CPA firms even if the cost is somewhat higher, to minimize the potential criticism of selecting an unqualified firm. Evaluate these comments.

**3-22 (Objective 3-10)** The membership of the AICPA voted to eliminate Rule 401 on encroachment. In recent years there have been other changes in the *Code of Professional Conduct,* which now permits advertising, competitive bidding, and offers of employment to employees of other firms.

## Required

a. Identify the likely effects on relations between competing CPA firms and other effects on the practice of auditing resulting from these changes.

b. Identify the likely costs and benefits to audit clients and users of financial statements resulting from these changes.

c. Make a subjective judgment about whether you believe that the rule changes have been beneficial or detrimental to each of the following groups:
(1) Large CPA firms
(2) Small CPA firms
(3) Young professionals beginning their career with a CPA firm
(4) Companies obtaining audits
(5) Users of financial statements

**3-23 (Objective 3-5)** The following relate to auditors' independence:

## Required

a. Why is independence so essential for auditors?

b. Compare the importance of independence of CPAs with that of other professionals, such as attorneys.

*AICPA adapted.

c. Explain the difference between independence in appearance and in fact.

d. Assume that a partner of a CPA firm owns two shares of stock of a large audit client. The ownership is an insignificant part of his total wealth.
   (1) Has he violated the *Code of Professional Conduct?*
   (2) Explain whether the ownership is likely to affect the partner's *independence in fact.*
   (3) Explain the reason for the strict requirements about stock ownership in the rules of conduct.

e. Discuss how each of the following could affect independence in fact and independence in appearance, and evaluate the social consequence of prohibiting auditors from doing each one.
   (1) Ownership of stock in a client company
   (2) Having bookkeeping services for an audit client performed by the same person who does the audit
   (3) Recommending adjusting entries to the client's financial statements and preparing financial statements, including footnotes, for the client
   (4) Having management services for an audit client performed by individuals in a department that is separate from the audit department
   (5) Having the annual audit performed by the same audit team, except for assistants, for five years in a row
   (6) Having the annual audit performed by the same CPA firm for 10 years in a row
   (7) Having management select the CPA firm

f. Which of (1) through (7) above are prohibited by the AICPA *Code of Professional Conduct?* Which are prohibited by the SEC?

**3-24 (Objective 3-5)** Marie Janes encounters the following situations in doing the audit of a large auto dealership. Janes is not a partner.

1. The sales manager tells her that there is a sale (at a substantial discount) on new cars that is limited to long-established customers of the dealership. Because her firm has been doing the audit for several years, the sales manager has decided that Janes should also be eligible for the discount.
2. The auto dealership has an executive lunchroom that is available free to employees above a certain level. The controller informs Janes that she can also eat there any time.
3. Janes is invited to and attends the company's annual Christmas party. When presents are handed out, she is surprised to find her name included. The present has a value of approximately $200.

## Required

a. Assuming Janes accepts the offer or gift in each situation, has she violated the rules of conduct?

b. Discuss what Janes should do in each situation.

## CASES

**3-25 (Objectives 3-7, 3-8, 3-11)** Gilbert and Bradley formed a corporation called Financial Services, Inc., each partner taking 50 percent of the authorized common stock. Gilbert is a CPA and a member of the American Institute of CPAs. Bradley is a CPCU (Chartered Property Casualty Underwriter). The corporation performs auditing and tax services under Gilbert's direction and insurance services under Bradley's supervision. The opening of the corporation's office was announced by a 3-inch, two-column "card" in the local newspaper.

One of the corporation's first audit clients was the Grandtime Company. Grandtime had total assets of $600,000 and total liabilities of $270,000. In the course of his audit,

Gilbert found that Grandtime's building with a book value of $240,000 was pledged as security for a 10-year term note in the amount of $200,000. The client's statements did not mention that the building was pledged as security for the note. However, as the failure to disclose the lien did not affect either the value of the assets or the amount of the liabilities and his audit was satisfactory in all other respects, Gilbert rendered an unqualified opinion on Grandtime's financial statements. About two months after the date of his opinion, Gilbert learned that an insurance company was planning to loan Grandtime $150,000 in the form of a first mortgage note on the building. Realizing that the insurance company was unaware of the existing lien on the building, Gilbert had Bradley notify the insurance company of the fact that Grandtime's building was pledged as security for the term note.

Shortly after the events just described, Gilbert was charged with a violation of professional ethics.

### Required

Identify and discuss the ethical implications of those acts by Gilbert that were in violation of the AICPA *Code of Professional Conduct.**

**3-26 (Objectives 3-5, 3-8, 3-10)** The following are situations that may violate the *Code of Professional Conduct.* Assume, in each case, that the CPA is a partner.

1. Able, CPA, owns a substantial limited partnership interest in an apartment building. Frederick Marshall is a 100 percent owner in Marshall Marine Co. Marshall also owns a substantial interest in the same limited partnership as Able. Able does the audit of Marshall Marine Co.
2. Baker, CPA, approaches a new audit client and tells the president that he has an idea that could result in a substantial tax refund in the prior year's tax return by application of a technical provision in the tax law that the client had overlooked. Baker adds that the fee will be 50 percent of the tax refund after it has been resolved by the Internal Revenue Service. The client agrees to the proposal.
3. Contel, CPA, advertises in the local paper that his firm does the audit of 14 of the 36 largest savings and loans in the city. The advertisement also states that the average audit fee, as a percentage of total assets for the savings and loans he audits, is lower than any other CPA firm's in the city.
4. Davis, CPA, sets up a small loan company specializing in loans to business executives and small companies. Davis does not spend much time in the business because he spends full time with his CPA practice. No employees of Davis's CPA firm are involved in the small loan company.
5. Elbert, CPA, owns a material amount of stock in a mutual fund investment company, which in turn owns stock in Elbert's largest audit client. Reading the investment company's most recent financial report, Elbert is surprised to learn that the company's ownership in his client has increased dramatically.
6. Finigan, CPA, does the audit, tax return, bookkeeping, and management services work for Gilligan Construction Company. Mildred Gilligan follows the practice of calling Finigan before she makes any major business decision to determine the effect on her company's taxes and the financial statements. Finigan attends continuing education courses in the construction industry to make sure that she is technically competent and knowledgeable about the industry. Finigan normally attends board of directors meetings and accompanies Gilligan when she is seeking loans. Mildred Gilligan often jokingly introduces Finigan with this statement, "I have my three business partners—my banker, the government, and my CPA, but Finny's the only one that is on my side."

### Required

Discuss whether the facts in any of the situations indicate violations of the *Code of Professional Conduct.* If so, identify the nature of the violation(s).

*AICPA adapted.

**3-27 (Objectives 3-2, 3-6)** Barbara Whitley had great expectations about her future as she sat in her graduation ceremony in May 1996. She was about to receive her Master of Accountancy degree, and next week she would begin her career on the audit staff of Green, Thresher & Co., CPAs.

Things looked a little different to Barbara in February 1997. She was working on the audit of Delancey Fabrics, a textile manufacturer with a calendar year-end. The pressure was enormous. Everyone on the audit team was putting in 70-hour weeks and it still looked as if the audit wouldn't be done on time. Barbara was doing work in the property area, vouching additions for the year. The audit program indicated that a sample of all items over $10,000 should be selected, plus a judgmental sample of smaller items. When Barbara went to take the sample, Jack Bean, the senior, had left the client's office and couldn't answer her questions about the appropriate size of the judgmental sample. Barbara forged ahead with her own judgment and selected 50 smaller items. Her basis for doing this was that there were about 250 such items, so 50 was a reasonably good proportion of such additions.

Barbara audited the additions with the following results: the items over $10,000 contained no misstatements; however, the 50 small items contained a large number of misstatements. In fact, when Barbara projected them to all such additions, the amount seemed quite significant.

A couple of days later, Jack Bean returned to the client's office. Barbara brought her work to Jack in order to apprise him of the problems she found, and got the following response:

- My God, Barbara, why did you do this? You were only supposed to look at the items over $10,000 plus 5 or 10 little ones. You've wasted a whole day on that work, and we can't afford to spend any more time on it. I want you to throw away the schedules where you tested the last 40 small items and forget you ever did them.

When Barbara asked about the possible audit adjustment regarding the small items, none of which arose from the first 10 items, Jack responded, "Don't worry, it's not material anyway. You just forget it; it's my concern, not yours."

## Required

1. In what way is this an ethical dilemma for Barbara?
2. Use the six-step approach discussed in the book to resolve the ethical dilemma.

**3-28 (Objectives 3-1, 3-2, 3-3)** In 1992, Arnold Diaz was a bright, upcoming audit manager in the South Florida office of a national public accounting firm. He was an excellent technician and a good "people person." Arnold also was able to bring new business into the firm as the result of his contacts in the rapidly growing Hispanic business community.

Arnold was assigned a new client in 1993, XYZ Securities, Inc., a privately held broker–dealer in the secondary market for U.S. government securities. Neither Arnold nor anyone else in the South Florida office had broker–dealer audit experience. However, the AICPA and Arnold's firm had audit aids for the industry, which Arnold used to get started.

Arnold was promoted to partner in 1993. Although this was a great step forward for him (he was a new staff assistant in 1984), Arnold was also under a great deal of pressure. Upon making partner, he was required to contribute capital to the firm. He also felt he must maintain a special image with his firm, his clients, and within the Hispanic community. To accomplish this, Arnold maintained an impressive wardrobe, bought a Cadillac Seville and a small speedboat, and traded up to a nicer house. He also entertained freely. Arnold financed much of this higher living with credit cards. He had six American Express and banking cards and ran up a balance of about $40,000.

After the audit was completed and before the 1994 audit was to begin, Arnold contacted Jack Oakes, the CFO of XYZ Securities, with a question. Arnold had noticed an anomaly in the financial statements that he couldn't understand and asked Oakes for an explanation. Oakes's reply was as follows:

- Arnold, the 1993 financial statements were materially misstated and you guys just blew it. I thought you might realize this and call me, so here's my advice to you. Keep your mouth shut. We'll make up the loss we covered up last year, this year, and nobody will ever know the difference. If you blow the whistle on us, your firm will know you screwed up, and your career as the star in the office will be down the tubes.

Arnold said he'd think about this and get back to Oakes the next day. When Arnold called Oakes, he had decided to go along with him. After all, it would only be a "shift" of a loss between two adjacent years. XYZ is a private company and no one would be hurt or know the difference. In reality, only he was the person exposed to any harm in this situation, and he had to protect himself, didn't he?

When Arnold went to XYZ to plan for the 1994 audit, he asked Oakes how things were going and Oakes assured him they were fine. He then said to Oakes,

- Jack, you guys are in the money business, maybe you can give me some advice. I've run up some debts and I need to refinance them. How should I go about it?

After some discussions, Oakes volunteered a "plan." Oakes would give Arnold a check for $15,000. XYZ would request its bank to put $60,000 in an account in Arnold's name and guarantee the loan security on it. Arnold would pay back the $15,000 and have $45,000 of refinancing. Arnold thought the plan was great and obtained Oakes's check for $15,000.

During 1994 through 1996, three things happened. First, Arnold incurred more debts, and went back to the well at XYZ. By the end of 1996, he had "borrowed" a total of $125,000. Second, the company continued to lose money in various "off-the-books" investment schemes. These losses were covered up by falsifying the results of normal operations. Third, the audit team, under Arnold's leadership, "failed to find" the fraud and issued unqualified opinions.

In 1995, Oakes had a tax audit of his personal 1994 return. He asked Arnold's firm to handle it, and the job was assigned to Bob Smith, a tax manager. In reviewing Oakes's records, Smith found a $15,000 check payable from Oakes to Diaz. Smith asked to see Diaz and inquired about the check. Arnold somewhat broke down and confided in Smith about his problems. Smith responded by saying,

- Don't worry Arnold, I understand. And believe me, I'll never tell a soul.

In 1997, XYZ's continuing losses caused it to be unable to deliver nonexistent securities when requested by a customer. This led to an investigation and bankruptcy by XYZ. Losses totaled in the millions. Arnold's firm was held liable, and Arnold was found guilty of conspiracy to defraud. He is still in prison today.

### Required

1. Try to put yourself in Arnold's shoes. What would you have done (be honest with yourself now) when told of the material misstatement in mid-1994?
2. What do you think of Bob Smith's actions to help Arnold?
3. Where does one draw the line between ethical and unethical behavior?

**3-29 (Objective 3-2)** Frank Dorrance, a senior audit manager for Bright and Lorren, CPAs, has recently been informed that the firm plans to promote him to partner within the next year or two if he continues to perform at the same high-quality level as in the past. Frank excels at dealing effectively with all people, including client personnel, professional staff, partners and potential clients. He has recently built a bigger home for entertaining and has joined the city's most prestigious golf and tennis club. He is excited about his future with the firm.

Frank has recently been assigned to the audit of Machine International, a large wholesale company that ships goods throughout the world. It is one of Bright and Lorren's most prestigious clients. During the audit, Frank determines that Machine International uses a method of revenue recognition called "bill and hold" that has recently been questioned by the SEC. After considerable research, Frank concludes that the method of revenue recognition is not appropriate for Machine International. In discussing the matter with the engagement partner, she concludes that the accounting method has been used for more than 10 years by the client and is appropriate, especially considering that the client does not file with the SEC. The partner is certain the firm would lose the client if the revenue recognition method is found inappropriate. Frank argues that the revenue recognition method was appropriate in prior years, but the SEC ruling makes it inappropriate in the current year. Frank recognizes the partner's responsibility to make the final decision, but he feels strongly enough to state that he plans to follow the requirements of SAS 22 (AU 311) and include a statement in the working papers that he disagrees with the partner's decision. The partner informs Frank that she is unwilling to permit such a statement because of the potential legal implications. She is willing, however, to write a letter to Frank stating that she takes full responsibility for making the final decision if a legal dispute ever arises. She concludes by saying, "Frank, partners must act like partners, not like loose cannons trying to make life difficult for their partners. You have some growing up to do before I would feel comfortable with you as a partner."

## Required

Use the six-step approach discussed in the book to resolve the ethical dilemma.

4

# LEGAL LIABILITY

## IT TAKES THE NET PROFIT FROM MANY AUDITS TO OFFSET THE COST OF ONE LAWSUIT

Orange & Rankle, a CPA firm in San Jose, audited a small high-tech client that developed software. A significant portion of the client's capital was provided by a syndicate of 40 limited partners. The owners of these interests were knowledgeable business and professional people, including several lawyers.

Orange & Rankle audited the company for four consecutive years, from its inception, for an average annual fee of approximately $13,000. The audits were well done by competent auditors. It was clear to the firm and to others who subsequently reviewed the audits that they complied with generally accepted auditing standards in every way.

In the middle of the fifth year of the company's existence, it became apparent that the marketing plan it had developed was overly optimistic and the company was going to require additional capital or make a significant strategy change. The limited partners were polled and refused to provide the capital. The company folded its tent and filed bankruptcy. The limited partners lost their investment in the company. They subsequently filed a lawsuit against all parties involved in the enterprise, including the auditors.

Over the next several years the auditors proceeded through the process of preparing to defend themselves in the lawsuit. They went through complete discovery, hired an expert witness on auditing-related issues, filed motions, and so forth. They attempted a settlement at various times, but the plaintiffs would not agree to a reasonable amount. Finally, during the second day of trial, the plaintiffs settled for a nominal amount.

It was clear that the plaintiffs knew the auditors bore no fault, but kept them in the suit anyway. The total *out-of-pocket* cost to the audit firm was $1 million, not to mention personnel time, possible damage to their reputation, and general stress and strain. Thus, the cost of this suit, where the auditors were completely innocent, was more than seventy-five times the average annual audit fee earned from this client.

### LEARNING OBJECTIVES

Thorough study of this chapter will enable you to

- **4-1** Appreciate the litigious environment in which CPAs practice.
- **4-2** Explain why the failure of financial statement users to differentiate among business failure, audit failure, and audit risk has resulted in lawsuits.
- **4-3** Define the primary legal concepts and terms concerning accountants' liability.
- **4-4** Describe accountants' liability to clients and related defenses.
- **4-5** Describe accountants' liability to third parties under common law and related defenses.
- **4-6** Describe accountants' civil liability under the federal securities laws and related defenses.
- **4-7** Discuss the impact of the Racketeer Influenced and Corrupt Organization Act and the Foreign Corrupt Practices Act on accountants' liability.
- **4-8** Specify what constitutes criminal liability for accountants.
- **4-9** Describe what the profession and the individual CPA can do and what is being done to reduce the threat of litigation.

Legal liability and its consequent effects are considered by many CPAs to be the profession's most important problem. To put this problem in perspective, it was reported that in 1991, the six largest auditing firms incurred a combined $447 million in direct costs in the settlement and defense of lawsuits. This represented 9 percent of their U.S. accounting and auditing revenues. This was an increase from 7.7 percent in 1990, and it has since been estimated that these costs have risen to as high as 11.9 percent of comparable 1994 revenues. Further, it is estimated that the profession's aggregate liability exposure exceeds $30 billion.

Although firms have insurance to help alleviate the impact of assessed damages, the premiums are high and the policies available to the firms have large deductible amounts. The deductibles are such that the large firms are essentially self-insured for losses of many millions of dollars.

The problem of liability became more visible in 1990 when the seventh largest CPA firm, Laventhol & Horwath, filed for bankruptcy. A primary cause was the large number of suits alleging malpractice with large amounts of damages claimed that were facing the firm. A plan to liquidate the firm was approved by the court in 1992, requiring the partners of the firm to pay $48 million to avoid personal bankruptcy. A second large firm, Panell Kerr Forster, closed or sold about 90 percent of its offices and reorganized its offices as individual professional corporations in 1992. A former partner of that firm was quoted as saying that the liability was one of the reasons for this massive restructuring.

Accountants' liability also affects the profession in human terms. For example, a study completed in 1994 indicated that of partners and managers leaving the six largest auditing firms in recent years, 29 percent were influenced by the threat of litigation, and 46 percent were influenced by the effect of ongoing litigation costs on future profits.

This chapter discusses the nature of legal liability of CPAs. First, the reasons for increased litigation against CPAs are discussed. This is followed by a detailed examination of the nature of the lawsuits and the sources of potential liability. A summary of significant lawsuits involving CPAs is included. The chapter ends with a discussion of the courses of action available to the profession and individual practitioners to minimize liability while meeting society's needs.

## CHANGED LEGAL ENVIRONMENT

**OBJECTIVE 4-1**
**Appreciate the litigious environment in which CPAs practice.**

Professionals have always had a duty to provide a reasonable level of care while performing work for those they serve. Audit professionals have a responsibility under common law to fulfill implied or expressed contracts with clients. They are liable to their clients for negligence and/or breach of contract should they fail to provide the services or not exercise due care in their performance. Auditors may also be held liable under common law in certain circumstances to parties other than their clients. Although the criteria for legal actions against auditors by third parties vary by state, the most common view is that the auditor owes a duty of care to third parties who are part of a limited group of persons whose reliance is "foreseen" by the auditor. Some states, including New York, take a more restrictive view of when auditors may be liable to third parties. A few states take a far broader view, extending the duty of due care to all persons whose reliance was "foreseeable." In addition to common law, auditors may be held liable to third parties under statutory law. Both the Securities Act of 1933 and the Securities Exchange Act of 1934 contain sections that serve as a basis for actions against auditors. Finally, in rare cases auditors have also been held liable for criminal acts. A criminal conviction against an auditor can result when it is demonstrated that the auditor intended to deceive or harm others.

The four sources of auditors' legal liability identified in the previous paragraph are the main focus of this chapter. They are summarized in Figure 4-1, with an example of a potential claim from each source.

In recent years, both the number of lawsuits and size of awards to plaintiffs have significantly increased, especially for suits involving third parties under both common law and

**FIGURE 4-1**

**Four Major Sources of Auditors' Legal Liability**

| **Source of Liability** | **Example of Potential Claim** |
|---|---|
| Client—liability to client under common law | Client sues auditor for not discovering a defalcation during the audit. |
| Third party—liability to third parties under common law | Bank sues auditor for not discovering that a borrower's financial statements are partially misstated. |
| Liability under federal securities acts | Combined group of stockholders sues auditor for not discovering materially misstated financial statements. |
| Criminal liability | Federal government prosecutes auditor for knowingly issuing an incorrect audit report. |

the federal securities acts. There are no simple reasons for this increase, but the following are major factors:

- The growing awareness of the responsibilities of public accountants by users of financial statements.
- An increased consciousness on the part of the Securities and Exchange Commission (SEC) regarding its responsibility for protecting investors' interests.
- The greater complexity of auditing and accounting due to such factors as the increasing size of business, the globalization of business, and the intricacies of business operations.
- Society's acceptance of lawsuits by injured parties against anyone who might be able to provide compensation, regardless of who was at fault, coupled with the joint and several liability doctrine. This is frequently called the *deep-pocket* concept of liability.
- Large civil court judgments against CPA firms in a few cases, which have encouraged attorneys to provide legal services on a contingent-fee basis. This arrangement offers the injured party a potential gain when the suit is successful, but minimal loss when it is unsuccessful.
- The willingness of many CPA firms to settle their legal problems out of court in an attempt to avoid costly legal fees and adverse publicity rather than resolving them through the judicial process.
- The difficulty courts have in understanding and interpreting technical accounting and auditing matters.

Increasing litigation costs for accountants and others caused great concern in Congress and in society in general during this period of increasing and more costly litigation. It was recognized that all members of society bear these costs. As a result, legislation was introduced to attempt to control litigation costs, both by discouraging nonmeritorious lawsuits and by bringing damages more in line with relative fault. In January 1996, a law was passed bringing significant relief to accountants in the area of federal securities litigation. Nevertheless, accountants' liability is still onerous and a major consideration in the conduct of a CPA firm's professional practice.

## DISTINCTION AMONG BUSINESS FAILURE, AUDIT FAILURE, AND AUDIT RISK

Many accounting and legal professionals believe that a major cause of lawsuits against CPA firms is the lack of understanding by financial statement users of the difference between a *business* failure and an *audit* failure and between an *audit failure* and *audit risk*. These terms

**OBJECTIVE 4-2**

**Explain why the failure of financial statement users to differentiate among business failure, audit failure, and audit risk has resulted in lawsuits.**

are first defined, then followed by a discussion of how misunderstanding the differences often results in lawsuits against auditors.

**Business Failure** This occurs when a business is unable to repay its lenders, or meet the expectations of its investors, because of economic or business conditions, such as a recession, poor management decisions, or unexpected competition in the industry. The extreme case of business failure is filing for bankruptcy. As stated in Chapter 1, there is always some risk that a business will fail.

**Audit Failure** This occurs when the auditor issues an erroneous audit opinion as the result of an underlying failure to comply with the requirements of generally accepted auditing standards. For example, the auditor may have assigned unqualified assistants to perform audit tasks and because of their lack of competence, they failed to find material misstatements that qualified auditors would have discovered.

**Audit Risk** The risk that the auditor will conclude that the financial statements are fairly stated and an unqualified opinion can therefore be issued when, in fact, they are materially misstated. As will be shown in subsequent chapters, auditing cannot be expected to uncover all material financial statement misstatements. Auditing is limited by sampling, and certain misstatements and well-concealed frauds are extremely difficult to detect; therefore, there is always some risk that the audit will not uncover a material misstatement even when the auditor has complied with generally accepted auditing standards.

Most accounting professionals agree that in most cases when an audit has failed to uncover material misstatements, and the wrong type of audit opinion is issued, a legitimate question may be raised whether the auditor exercised due care. If the auditor failed to use due care in the conduct of the audit, then there is an audit failure. In such cases, the law often allows parties who suffered losses as a result of the auditor's breach of a duty of care owed to them to recover some or all of the losses proximately caused by the audit failure. It is difficult in practice to determine when the auditor has failed to use due care because of the complexity of auditing. It is also difficult to determine who has a right to expect the benefits of an audit because of legal traditions. Nevertheless, an auditor's failure to follow due care often may be expected to result in liability and, where appropriate, damages against the CPA firm.

The difficulty arises when there has been a business failure, but not an audit failure. For example, when a company goes bankrupt or cannot pay its debts, it is common for statement users to claim that there was an audit failure, especially when the most recently issued auditor's opinion indicates that the financial statements were fairly stated. Even worse, if there is a business failure and the financial statements are later determined to have been misstated, users may claim that the auditor was negligent even if the audit was conducted in accordance with generally accepted auditing standards. This conflict between statement users and auditors often arises because of what is referred to as the *expectation gap* between users and auditors. Most auditors believe that the conduct of the audit in accordance with generally accepted auditing standards is all that can be expected of auditors. Many users believe that auditors guarantee the accuracy of financial statements, and some users even believe that the auditor guarantees the financial viability of the business. Fortunately for the profession, courts continue to support the auditor's view. Unfortunately, the expectation gap often results in unwarranted lawsuits. Perhaps the profession has a responsibility to educate statement users about the role of auditors and the difference between business risk, audit failure, and audit risk. Realistically, however, auditors must recognize that, in part, the claims of audit failure may also result from the hope of those who suffer a business loss to recover from any source, regardless of who is at fault.

## LEGAL CONCEPTS AFFECTING LIABILITY

**OBJECTIVE 4-3**
**Define the primary legal concepts and terms concerning accountants' liability.**

The CPA is responsible for every aspect of his or her public accounting work, including auditing, taxes, management advisory services, and accounting and bookkeeping services. For example, if a CPA negligently failed to properly prepare and file a client's tax return, the CPA can be held liable for any penalties and interest that the client was required to pay plus the tax preparation fee charged. In some states, the court can also assess punitive damages.

Most of the major lawsuits against CPA firms have dealt with audited or unaudited financial statements. The discussion in this chapter is restricted primarily to those two aspects of public accounting. The areas of liability in auditing can be classified as (1) liability to clients, (2) liability to third parties under common law, (3) liability to third parties under statutory law, and (4) criminal liability. Several legal concepts apply to all these types of lawsuits against CPAs. These are the *prudent person concept, liability for the acts of others,* and the *lack of privileged communication.*

### Prudent Person Concept

There is agreement within the profession and the courts that the auditor is not a guarantor or insurer of financial statements. The auditor is only expected to conduct the audit with due care. Even then, the auditor cannot be expected to be perfect.

The standard of due care to which the auditor is expected to be held is often referred to as the *prudent person concept.* It is expressed in *Cooley on Torts* as follows:

- Every man who offers his service to another and is employed assumes the duty to exercise in the employment such skill as he possesses with reasonable care and diligence. In all these employments where peculiar skill is prerequisite, if one offers his service, he is understood as holding himself out to the public as possessing the degree of skill commonly possessed by others in the same employment, and, if his pretentions are unfounded, he commits a species of fraud upon every man who employs him in reliance on his public profession. But no man, whether skilled or unskilled, undertakes that the task he assumes shall be performed successfully, and without fault or error. *He undertakes for good faith and integrity, but not for infallibility,* and he is liable to his employer for negligence, bad faith, or dishonesty, but not for losses consequent upon pure errors of judgment.

### Liability for the Acts of Others

Generally, the partners, or shareholders in the case of a professional corporation, are jointly liable for the civil actions against any owner. However, if the firm operates as a limited liability partnership (LLP), a limited liability company (LLC), a general corporation, or a professional corporation with limited liability, the liability for one owner's actions does not extend to another owner's *personal* assets, unless the other owner was directly involved in the actions of the owner causing the liability. Of course, the firm's assets are all subject to the damages that arise.

The partners may also be liable for the work of others on whom they rely under the laws of agency. The three groups an auditor is most likely to rely on are *employees, other CPA firms* engaged to do part of the work, and *specialists* called upon to provide technical information. For example, if an employee performs improperly in doing an audit, the partners can be held liable for the employee's performance.

### Lack of Privileged Communication

CPAs do not have the right under common law to withhold information from the courts on the grounds that the information is privileged. As stated in Chapter 3, information in an auditor's working papers can be subpoenaed by a court. Confidential discussions between the client and auditor cannot be withheld from the courts.

A number of states have statutes that permit privileged communication between the client and auditor. Even then, the intent at the time of the communication must have been for the communication to remain confidential. A CPA can refuse to testify in a state with privileged communications statutes. The privilege does not extend to federal courts.

## DEFINITIONS OF LEGAL TERMS

The material in the rest of the chapter can be covered more effectively if the most common legal terms affecting CPAs' liability are understood.

### Negligence and Fraud

The first four terms deal with the degree of fault for which an auditor may be exposed to liability. The distinctions are useful for discussing the application of the law to various types of lawsuits against auditors because they affect the outcome of many suits.

**Ordinary Negligence** Absence of reasonable care that can be expected of a person in a set of circumstances. When negligence of an auditor is being evaluated, it is in terms of what other competent auditors would have done in the same situation.

**Gross Negligence** Lack of even slight care, tantamount to reckless behavior, that can be expected of a person. Some states do not distinguish between ordinary and gross negligence.

**Constructive Fraud** Existence of extreme or unusual negligence even though there was no intent to deceive or do harm. Constructive fraud is also termed *recklessness.* Recklessness in the case of an auditor has been defined by the Federal Court of Appeals as meaning that the auditor has expressed an opinion on financial statements despite lacking a genuine belief that the auditor had the information on which he or she could predicate such an opinion. Thus, if the auditor knew he or she had not done an adequate audit, but still issued an opinion, the auditor could be found reckless, even though he or she had no intention of deceiving statement users.

**Fraud** Occurs when a misstatement is made and there is both the knowledge of its falsity and the intent to deceive.

### Contract Law

**Breach of Contract** Failure of one or both parties in a contract to fulfill the requirements of the contract. An example is the failure of a CPA firm to deliver a tax return on the agreed-upon date. Parties who have a relationship that is established by a contract are said to have *privity of contract.*

Typically, CPA firms and clients sign an *engagement letter* to formalize their agreement about the services to be provided, fees, and timing. There can be privity of contract without a written agreement, but an engagement letter defines the contract more clearly.

**Third-Party Beneficiary** A third party who does not have privity of contract but is known to the contracting parties and is intended to have certain rights and benefits under the contract. A common example is a bank that has a large loan outstanding at the balance sheet date and requires an audit as a part of its loan agreement. The naming of a third party in an engagement letter often establishes that party as a third-party beneficiary.

### Common and Statutory Law

**Common Law** Laws that have been developed through court decisions rather than through government statutes. An example is an auditor's negligence related to a failure to discover material misstatements in financial statements that were relied on by a bank in issuing a loan.

**Statutory Law** Laws that have been passed by the U.S. Congress and other governmental units. The securities acts of 1933 and 1934 are important statutory laws affecting auditors.

### Assessed Proportion of Liability

**Joint and Several Liability** The assessment against a defendant of the full loss suffered by a plaintiff regardless of the extent to which other parties shared in the wrongdoing. For example, if management intentionally misstates financial statements, an auditor can be assessed the entire loss to shareholders if the company is bankrupt and management is unable to pay.

**Separate and Proportionate Liability** The assessment against a defendant of that portion of the damage caused by the defendant's negligence. For example, if the courts determine that an auditor's negligence in conducting an audit was the cause of 30 percent of a loss to a defendant, only 30 percent of the aggregate damage would be assessed to the CPA firm.

The distinction between joint and several liability and separate and proportionate liability is an extremely significant one, as the amounts will vary greatly between these two bases for assessing damages. Generally, these damage approaches apply in cases of liability to third parties under common law and under the federal securities laws. Where lawsuits are filed in state court, the state laws will determine which approach to damages applies. Where lawsuits are brought under the federal securities laws, the separate and proportionate approach will apply except where it can be shown that the CPA defendant has actual knowledge of fraud or has participated in fraud, in which case joint and several liability would apply. It should be noted that under the federal statutes, the amount of damages under separate and proportionate liability can be increased to 150 percent of the amount determined to be proportionate to the CPA's degree of fault, where the main defendant is insolvent.

## LIABILITY TO CLIENTS

**OBJECTIVE 4-4**
**Describe accountants' liability to clients and related defenses.**

The most frequent source of lawsuits against CPAs is from clients. The suits vary widely, including such claims as failure to complete a nonaudit engagement on the agreed-upon date, inappropriate withdrawal from an audit, failure to discover a defalcation (theft of assets), and breaching the confidentiality requirements of CPAs. Typically the amount of these lawsuits is relatively small, and they do not receive the publicity often given to other types of suits. The *Fund of Funds* case is a notable exception, where the court awarded the company $80 million in a suit against a CPA firm for breach of confidentiality requirements.

A typical lawsuit involves a claim that the auditor did not discover an employee defalcation as a result of negligence in the conduct of the audit. The lawsuit can be for breach of contract, a tort action for negligence, or both. Tort actions can be based on ordinary negligence, gross negligence, or fraud. Tort actions are common because the amounts recoverable under them are normally larger than under breach of contract.

The principal issue in cases involving alleged negligence is usually the level of care required. Although it is generally agreed that nobody is perfect, not even a professional, in most instances any significant error or mistake in judgment will create at least a presumption of negligence that the professional will have to rebut. In the auditing environment, failure to meet generally accepted auditing standards is often conclusive evidence of negligence. A typical example of an audit case raising the question of negligent performance by a CPA firm is the case of *Cenco Incorporated* v. *Seidman & Seidman.* The case involved alleged negligence by the auditor in failing to find a fraud. It is included as an illustrative case in Figure 4-2 on the following page. The reader should remember from the study of generally accepted auditing standards in Chapter 1 that determining whether there is a violation is a highly subjective matter.

The question of level of care becomes more difficult in the environment of an unaudited review or compilation of financial statements in which there are fewer accepted standards to evaluate performance. A widely known example of a lawsuit dealing with the failure to uncover fraud in unaudited financial statements is the *1136 Tenants* case, summarized in Figure 4-3 on the following page.

**FIGURE 4-2**

***Cenco Incorporated* v. *Seidman & Seidman* (1982)—Liability to Clients**

Between 1970 and 1975 Cenco's managerial employees, ultimately including top management, were involved in a massive fraud to inflate the value of the company's inventory. This in turn enabled the company to borrow money at a lower interest rate and to obtain higher fire insurance settlements than were proper. After the fraud was discovered by an employee of Cenco and reported to the SEC, a class action suit was filed by stockholders against Cenco, its management, and its auditors. The CPA firm settled out of court on the class action suit by paying $3.5 million.

By now, new management was operating Cenco. They brought a second suit against the CPA firm on behalf of Cenco for breach of contract, professional negligence, and fraud. The primary defense used by the CPA firm was that a diligent attempt was made on the part of the auditors to follow up any indications of fraud, but the combined efforts of a large number of Cenco's management prevented them from uncovering the fraud. The CPA firm argued that the wrongdoings of management were a valid defense against the charges.

The Seventh Circuit Court of Appeals concluded that the CPA firm was not responsible in this case. The wrongdoings of Cenco's management were considered an appropriate defense against the charges of breach of contract, negligence, and fraud, even though the management no longer worked for the company. Considering management's involvement, the CPA firm was not considered negligent.

**FIGURE 4-3**

***1136 Tenants* v. *Max Rothenberg and Company* (1967)—Liability to Clients**

The *1136 Tenants* case was a civil case concerning a CPA's failure to uncover fraud as a part of unaudited financial statements. The tenants recovered approximately $235,000.

A CPA firm was engaged by a real estate management agent for $600 per year to prepare financial statements, a tax return, and a schedule showing the apportionment of real estate taxes for the 1136 Tenants Corporation, a cooperative apartment house. The statements were sent periodically to the tenants. The statements included the words "unaudited" and there was a cover letter stating that "The statement was prepared from the books and records of the corporation and no independent verifications were taken thereon."

During the period of the engagement, from 1963 to 1965, the manager of the management firm embezzled significant funds from the tenants of the cooperative. The tenants sued the CPA firm for negligence and breach of contract for failure to find the fraud.

There were two central issues in the case. Was the CPA firm engaged to do an audit instead of only write-up work, and was there negligence on the part of the CPA firm? The court answered yes on both counts. The reasoning for the court's conclusion that an audit had taken place was the performance of "some audit procedures" by the CPA firm, including the preparation of a worksheet entitled "missing invoices." Had the CPA followed up on these, the fraud would likely have been uncovered. Most important, the court concluded that even if the engagement had not been considered an audit, the CPA had a duty to follow up on any potential significant exceptions uncovered during an engagement.

Two developments resulted from the *1136 Tenants* case and similar lawsuits concerning unaudited financial statements:

- Engagement letters between the client and CPA firm have been strongly recommended by the AICPA for all engagements, but especially for unaudited engagements. The letter should clearly define the intent of the engagement, the CPA's responsibilities, and any restrictions imposed on the CPA.
- The Accounting and Review Services Committee was formed as a major committee of the AICPA to set forth guidelines for unaudited financial statements of nonpublic companies. They issued their first pronouncement in 1979. The Auditing Standards Board has eliminated all references to unaudited statements for nonpublic companies in SASs, to avoid confusion between audited and unaudited engagements.

### Auditor's Defenses Against Client Suits

The CPA firm normally uses one or a combination of four defenses when there are legal claims by clients: lack of duty to perform the service, nonnegligent performance, contributory negligence, and absence of causal connection.

**Lack of Duty** The lack of duty to perform the service means that the CPA firm claims that there was no implied or expressed contract. For example, the CPA firm might claim that misstatements were not uncovered because the firm did a review service, not an audit. A common way for a CPA firm to demonstrate a lack of duty to perform is by use of an *engagement letter.* Many litigation experts believe that a well-written engagement letter is one of the most important ways in which CPA firms can reduce the likelihood of adverse legal actions.

**Nonnegligent Performance** For nonnegligent performance in an audit, the CPA firm claims that the audit was performed in accordance with generally accepted auditing standards. Even if there were undiscovered misstatements, the auditor is not responsible if the audit was properly conducted. The prudent person concept discussed earlier establishes in law that the CPA firm is not expected to be infallible. Similarly, SAS 47 (AU 312) and SAS 82 make clear that an audit in accordance with GAAS is subject to limitations and cannot be relied upon for complete assurance that all misstatements will be found. Requiring auditors to discover all material misstatements would, in essence, make them insurers or guarantors of the accuracy of the financial statements. The courts do not require that.

**Contributory Negligence** A defense of contributory negligence exists when the client's own actions either result in the loss which is the basis for damages, or interfered with the conduct of the audit in such a way that prevented the auditor from discovering the cause of the loss. As an example of the first circumstance, suppose a client claims that a CPA firm was negligent in not uncovering an employee's theft of cash. If the CPA firm had notified the client (preferably in writing) of a weakness in internal control that would have prevented the theft, but management did not correct it, the CPA firm would have a defense of contributory negligence. As an example of the second circumstance, suppose a CPA firm failed to determine that certain accounts receivable were uncollectible, and in reviewing collectibility, were lied to and given false documents by the credit manager. In this circumstance, assuming the audit of accounts receivable was done in accordance with generally accepted auditing standards, a defense of contributory negligence would exist.

**Absence of Causal Connection** To succeed in an action against the auditor, the client must be able to show that there is a close causal connection between the auditor's breach of the standard of due care and the damages suffered by the client. For example, assume that an auditor failed to complete an audit on the agreed-upon date. The client alleges that this caused a bank not to renew an outstanding loan, which caused damages. A potential auditor defense is that the bank refused to renew the loan for other reasons, such as the weakening financial condition of the client.

## LIABILITY TO THIRD PARTIES UNDER COMMON LAW

**OBJECTIVE 4-5**
**Describe accountants' liability to third parties under common law and related defenses.**

A CPA firm may be liable to third parties if a loss was incurred by the claimant due to reliance on misleading financial statements. Third parties include actual and potential stockholders, vendors, bankers and other creditors, employees, and customers. A typical suit might occur when a bank is unable to collect a major loan from an insolvent customer. The bank can claim that misleading audited financial statements were relied upon in making the loan, and that the CPA firm should be held responsible because it failed to perform the audit with due care.

### *Ultramares* Doctrine

The leading precedent-setting auditing case in third-party liability is a 1931 case, *Ultramares Corporation* v. *Touche.* It established the traditional common law approach known as the *Ultramares* doctrine. The case is summarized in Figure 4-4 on page 114.

**FIGURE 4-4**

***Ultramares Corporation* v. *Touche* (1931)—Liability to Third Parties**

> The creditors of an insolvent corporation (Ultramares) relied on the audited financials and subsequently sued the accountants, alleging that they were guilty of negligence and fraudulent misrepresentation. The accounts receivable had been falsified by adding to approximately $650,000 in accounts receivable another item of over $700,000. The creditors alleged that careful investigation would have shown the $700,000 to be fraudulent. The accounts payable contained similar discrepancies.
>
> The court held that the accountants had been negligent but ruled that accountants would not be liable to third parties for honest blunders beyond the bounds of the original contract unless they were primary beneficiaries. The court held that only one who enters into a contract with an accountant for services can sue if those services are rendered negligently.
>
> The court went on, however, to order a new trial on the issue of fraudulent misstatement. The form of certificate then used said, "We further certify that subject to provisions for federal taxes on income the said statement in our opinion presents a true and correct view of the financial condition." The court pointed out that to make such a representation if one did not have an honest belief in its truth would be *fraudulent misrepresentation.*

The key aspect of the *Ultramares* doctrine is that ordinary negligence is insufficient for liability to third parties, because of the lack of *privity of contract* between the third party and the auditor, unless the third party is a *primary beneficiary*. In this context, a primary beneficiary is one about whom the auditor was informed prior to conducting the audit (*known third party*). In addition, *Ultramares* also held that if there had been fraud or gross negligence, the auditor could be held liable to more general third parties.

## Foreseen Users

In recent years, many courts have broadened the *Ultramares* doctrine to allow recovery by third parties in more circumstances than previously by introducing the concept of *foreseen users*. Generally, a foreseen user is a member of a limited class of users whom the auditor is aware will rely on the financial statements. For example, a bank that has loans outstanding to a client at the balance sheet date may be a foreseen user. Under this concept, a foreseen user would be treated the same as a known third party.

Although the concept of foreseen users may seem straightforward, its application is not, and has developed differently in different jurisdictions. At present three approaches have emerged: the *Credit Alliance* approach, the *Restatement of Torts* approach, and the *Reasonably Foreseeable User* approach.

**Credit Alliance** *Credit Alliance* v. *Arthur Andersen & Co.* (1986) was a case in New York in which a lender brought suit against the auditor of one of its borrowers, alleging that it relied on the financial statements of the borrower, who was in default, in granting the loan. The New York State Court of Appeals reversed a lower court's decision that prevented the defendant auditor from using absence of privity as a defense. In so doing, the appellate court upheld the basic concept of privity established by *Ultramares*, and stated that to be liable (1) an auditor must know and intend that his or her work product would be used by the plaintiff third party for a specific purpose, and (2) the knowledge and intent must be evidenced by the auditor's conduct. At present, eleven states (Arkansas, California, Idaho, Illinois, Kansas, Montana, Nebraska, New Jersey, New York, Pennsylvania, and Utah) follow some variation of this approach.

**Restatement of Torts** The approach followed by the most states is to apply the rule cited in the *Restatement of Torts*, an authoritative compendium of legal principles. The *Restatement Rule* is that foreseen users must be members of a *reasonably limited and identifiable group of users* that have relied on the CPA's work, such as creditors, even though those persons were

**FIGURE 4-5**

***Rusch Factors* v. *Levin* (1968)—Liability to Third Parties**

> The plaintiff, a lender, asked the defendant auditor to audit the financial statements of a company seeking a loan. The auditor issued an unqualified opinion on the financial statements indicating that the company was solvent when, in fact, it was insolvent. The plaintiff went forward with the loan, suffered a subsequent loss, and sued the auditor for recovery.
>
> The auditor's defense in the case was based on the absence of privity on the part of Rusch Factors. The court found in favor of this plaintiff. Whereas the court could have found in favor of Rusch Factors under *Ultramares* in that it was a primary beneficiary, it chose to rely on the *Restatement of Torts,* stating that the auditor should be liable for ordinary negligence in audits where the financial statements are relied upon by *actually foreseen and limited classes of persons.*

not specifically known to the CPA at the time the work was done. A leading case supporting the application of this rule is *Rusch Factors* v. *Levin,* presented in Figure 4-5.

**Foreseeable User** The broadest interpretation of the rights of third-party beneficiaries is to use the concept of *foreseeable users.* Under this concept, any users that the auditor should have reasonably been able to foresee as being likely users of financial statements have the same rights as those with privity of contract. These users are often referred to as an unlimited class. Whereas a significant number of states have followed this approach in the past, there are now only two that use it, Mississippi and Wisconsin.

Although there has been confusion caused by differing views of liability to third parties under common law, the movement is clearly away from the foreseeable user approach, and thus from three approaches to two. And there may be some movement from the *Restatement of Torts* approach toward *Credit Alliance.* For example, in New Jersey, where the foreseeable user approach had been followed by the courts, the legislature recently adopted a strict privity standard. And in *Bily* v. *Arthur Young* (1992), the California Supreme Court reversed a lower court decision against Arthur Young, clearly upholding the *Restatement* doctrine. In its decision, the Court stated that "an auditor owes no general duty of care regarding the conduct of an audit to persons other than the client," and reasoned that the potential liability to auditors under the foreseeable user doctrine would be distinctly out of proportion to fault.

## Auditor Defenses Against Third-Party Suits

Three of the four defenses available to auditors in suits by clients are also available in third-party lawsuits. Contributory negligence is ordinarily not available, because a third party is not in a position to contribute to misstated financial statements.

The preferred defense in third-party suits is nonnegligent performance. If the auditor conducted the audit in accordance with GAAS, the other defenses are unnecessary. On the other hand, nonnegligent performance is difficult to demonstrate to a court, especially if it is a jury trial and the jury is made up of lay people.

A lack of duty defense in third-party suits contends lack of privity of contract. The extent to which privity of contract is an appropriate defense and the nature of their defense depends heavily on the judicial jurisdiction. As we have shown, for example, there would be significant differences between New York, Florida, and Wisconsin in the nature of this defense.

Absence of causal connection in third-party suits often means nonreliance on the financial statements by the user. For example, assume that the auditor can demonstrate that a lender relied upon an ongoing banking relationship with a customer, rather than the financial statements, in making a loan. The fact that the auditor was negligent in the conduct of the audit would not be relevant in that situation. Of course, it is difficult to prove nonreliance on the financial statements. And, losses can be caused by other factors, such as market behavior.

## CIVIL LIABILITY UNDER THE FEDERAL SECURITIES LAWS

**OBJECTIVE 4-6**
**Describe accountants' civil liability under the federal securities laws and related defenses.**

Although there has been some growth in actions brought against accountants by their clients and third parties under common law, the greatest growth in CPA liability litigation has been under the federal securities laws.

The emphasis on federal remedies has resulted primarily from the recently expanded availability of class action litigation and the relative ease of obtaining massive recovery from defendants. In addition, several sections of the securities laws impose rather strict liability standards on CPAs. Federal courts are often likely to favor plaintiffs in lawsuits in which there are strict standards. However, this may change in light of recent tort reform legislation.

### Securities Act of 1933

The Securities Act of 1933 deals with the information in registration statements and prospectuses. It concerns only the reporting requirements for companies issuing new securities. The only parties who can recover from auditors under the 1933 act are original purchasers of securities. The amount of the potential recovery is the original purchase price less the value of the securities at the time of the suit. If the securities have been sold, users can recover the amount of the loss incurred.

The Securities Act of 1933 imposes an unusual burden on the auditor. Section 11 of the 1933 act defines the rights of third parties and auditors. These are summarized as follows:

- Any third party who purchased securities described in the registration statement may sue the auditor for material misrepresentations or omissions in audited financial statements included in the registration statement.
- The third-party user does not have the burden of proof that he or she relied on the financial statements or that the auditor was negligent or fraudulent in doing the audit. The user must only prove that the audited financial statements contained a material misrepresentation or omission.
- The auditor has the burden of demonstrating as a defense that (1) an adequate audit (i.e., "reasonable investigation") was conducted in the circumstances or (2) all or a portion of the plaintiff's loss was caused by factors other than the misleading financial statements. The 1933 act is the only common or statutory law where the burden of proof is on the defendant.

Furthermore, the auditor has responsibility for making sure that the financial statements were fairly stated beyond the date of issuance, up to the date the registration statement became effective, which could be several months later. For example, assume that the audit report date for December 31, 1996 financial statements is February 10, 1997, but the registration statement is dated November 1, 1997. In a typical audit, the auditor must review transactions through the audit report date, February 10, 1997. In statements filed under the 1933 act, the auditor is responsible to review transactions through the registration statement date, November 1, 1997.

Although the burden may appear harsh to auditors, there have been few cases tried under the 1933 act. The most significant one is *Escott* v. *Bar Chris Construction Corporation* (1968). Because of its effect on audit standards and the auditing profession, a summary of this case appears in Figure 4-6.

### Securities Exchange Act of 1934

The liability of auditors under the Securities Exchange Act of 1934 frequently centers on the audited financial statements issued to the public in annual reports or submitted to the SEC as a part of annual 10-K reports.

Every company with securities traded on national and over-the-counter exchanges is required to submit audited statements annually. Obviously, a much larger number of statements fall under the 1934 act than under the 1933 act.

**FIGURE 4-6**

***Escott et al.* v. *Bar Chris Construction Corporation* (1968)—Securities Act of 1933**

Bar Chris filed a registration statement in 1961 for the issuance of convertible subordinated debentures. They were thereby subject to the Securities Act of 1933. Approximately 17 months later Bar Chris filed for bankruptcy. The purchasers of the debentures filed suit against the CPA firm under the 1933 act.

There are several issues involved in the case, including the appropriateness of the percentage-of-completion method of accounting and other related accounting issues, the materiality of the misstatements, and the adequacy of the audit work performed.

The court ruled that the percentage-of-completion method of accounting was appropriate in the circumstances. It concluded that other accounting methods, such as the handling of a sale and subsequent leaseback of a bowling alley and the classification of a cash advance for a subsidiary, were improperly handled.

Materiality was also a significant issue in the case. Bar Chris is one of the few cases in the history of the profession that directly addressed the question of materiality. Earnings per share was misstated by about 15 percent, but the court surprisingly held that the amount was immaterial. There was a significant increase in earnings in the current year of over 25 percent that may have accounted for the court's conclusion. At the same time, the court concluded that the balance sheet was materially misstated when the current ratio was stated at 1.9 to 1 rather than 1.6 to 1, a 16 percent difference.

The most significant issue of the case, especially to audit staff personnel, was the matter of the review for events subsequent to the balance sheet, called an S-1 review for registration statements. The courts concluded that the CPA firm's written audit program was in conformity with generally accepted auditing standards in existence at that time. However, they were highly critical of the auditor conducting the review, who was inexperienced in audits of construction companies, for the failure to appropriately follow up on answers by management. The following is an important part of the court's opinion in the case:

- Accountants should not be held to a higher standard than that recognized in their profession. I do not do so here. Richard's review did not come up to that written standard. He did not take the steps which the CPA firm's written program prescribed. He did not spend an adequate amount of time on a task of this magnitude. *Most important of all, he was too easily satisfied with glib answers to his inquiries.* This is not to say that he should have made a complete audit. But there were enough danger signals in the materials which he did examine to require some further investigation on his part.... It is not always sufficient merely to ask questions. [Italics were added and the name used in the case was changed.]

The CPA firm was found liable in the case on the grounds that they had not established due diligence required under the 1933 securities act.

Two significant results occurred directly due to this case:

- Statements on Auditing Standards were changed to require greater emphasis on procedures that the auditor must perform regarding subsequent events, SAS 1 (AU 560). This change is a good example of the effect that the SEC has on the audits of all companies.
- A greater emphasis began to be placed on the importance of the audit staff understanding the client's business and industry.

In addition to annual audited financial statements, there is potential legal exposure to auditors for quarterly (10-Q), monthly (8-K), or other reporting information. The auditor is frequently involved in reviewing the information in these other reports; therefore, there may be legal responsibility. However, few cases have involved auditors for reports other than annual reports.

**Rule 10b-5 of the Securities Exchange Act of 1934**

The principal focus on CPA liability litigation under the 1934 act has been Rule 10b-5, a section of the federal Securities Exchange Act of 1934, which appears in the rules and regulations of the Securities and Exchange Commission. Rule 10b-5 states:

- It shall be unlawful for any person directly or indirectly, by the use of any means or instrumentality of interstate commerce, or of the mails or of any facility of any national securities exchange, (a) to employ any device, scheme, or artifice to defraud, (b) to make any untrue statement of a material fact or omit to state a material fact necessary in order to make the statements made, in the light of the circumstances under which they were made, not misleading, or (c) to engage in any act, practice, or course of business which operates or would operate as a fraud or deceit upon any person in connection with the purchase or sale of any security.

Section 10 and Rule 10b-5 are often referred to as the antifraud provisions of the 1934 Act, as they were designed primarily to thwart the commission of fraud by persons selling securities. Numerous federal court decisions have clarified that Rule 10b-5 applies not only to direct sellers, but also to accountants, underwriters, and others. Generally, accountants can be held liable under Section 10 and Rule 10b-5 if they intentionally or recklessly misrepresent information intended for third-party use.

In 1976, in *Hochfelder* v. *Ernst & Ernst*, a leading securities law case as well as CPA liabilities case, the U.S. Supreme Court ruled that knowledge and intent to deceive are required before CPAs could be held liable for violation of Rule 10b-5. A summary of *Hochfelder* is included in Figure 4-7.

Many auditors believed the *Hochfelder* case would significantly reduce auditors' exposure to liability. However, suits have subsequently been brought under Rule 10b-5. In earlier suits, the knowledge and deceit standard was more easily met by plaintiffs in cases in which the auditor knew all the relevant facts but made poor judgments. In such a situation, the courts emphasized that the CPAs had requisite knowledge. The *Solitron Devices* case,

**FIGURE 4-7**

***Hochfelder* v. *Ernst & Ernst* (1976)—Securities Exchange Act of 1934**

The case involved the auditor's responsibility for detecting fraud perpetrated by the president of the client firm. Lestor Nay, the president of First Securities Co. of Chicago, fraudulently convinced certain customers to invest funds in escrow accounts that he represented would yield a high return. There were no escrow accounts. Nay converted the customers' funds to his own use.

The transactions were not in the usual form of dealings between First Securities and its customers. First, all correspondence with customers was made solely with Nay. Second, checks of the customers were drawn payable to Nay and because of a *mail rule* that Nay imposed, such mail was opened only by him. Third, the escrow accounts were not reflected on the books of First Securities, nor in filings with the SEC, nor in connection with customers' other investment accounts. The fraud was uncovered at the time of Nay's suicide.

Respondent customers originally sued in district court for damages against Ernst & Ernst as aiders and abettors under section 10b-5. They alleged that Ernst & Ernst failed to conduct a proper audit that should have led them to discover the "mail rule" and the fraud. No allegations were made as to Ernst & Ernst's fraudulent and intentional conduct. The action was based solely on a claim that Ernst & Ernst failed to conduct a proper audit. The district court dismissed the action, but did not resolve the issue of whether or not a cause of action could be based merely on allegations of negligence.

The court of appeals reversed the district court. The appeals court held that one who breaches a duty of inquiry and disclosure owed another is liable in damages for aiding and abetting a third party's violation of Rule 10b-5 if the fraud would have been discovered or prevented had the breach not occurred. The court reasoned that Ernst & Ernst had a common law and statutory duty of inquiry into the adequacy of First Securities' internal control system because it had contracted to audit First Securities and to prepare for filing with the commission the annual report of its financial condition.

The U.S. Supreme Court reversed the court of appeals, concluding that the interpretation of Rule 10b-5 required the "intent to deceive, manipulate or defraud." Justice Powell wrote in the Court's opinion that:

- When a statute speaks so specifically in terms of manipulation and deception, and of implementing devices and contrivances—the commonly understood terminology of intentional wrongdoing—and when its history reflects no more expansive intent, we are quite unwilling to extend the scope of the statute to negligent conduct.

The Court pointed out that in certain areas of the law, recklessness is considered to be a form of intentional conduct for purposes of imposing liability. This left open the possibility that reckless behavior may be sufficient for liability under Rule 10b-5.

**FIGURE 4-8**

***Howard Sirota* v. *Solitron Devices, Inc.* (1982)—Securities Exchange Act of 1934**

Solitron was a manufacturer of electronic devices, with its stock issued on the American Stock Exchange. It was involved in government contracts that subjected it to assessments on excess profits as determined by the Renegotiations Board. When the board determined that profits were excessive, management admitted that profits had been intentionally overstated to aid in acquiring new companies. It was subsequently shown in court, through an audit by another CPA firm, that earnings had been materially overstated by more than 30 percent in two different years, by overstating inventory.

A jury trial found the auditor responsible for reckless behavior in the conduct of the audit. The trial judge overturned the jury verdict on the grounds that the CPA firm could not be held liable for damages under Rule 10b-5 unless there was proof that the CPA firm *had actual knowledge* of the misstatement. Reckless behavior was not sufficient for damages.

On appeal, the Second Circuit Court of Appeals concluded that there had been sufficient evidence for the jury to conclude that the CPA firm had knowledge of the fraud. It therefore overturned the trial judge's findings and affirmed the original jury's guilty verdict.

The court of appeals also stated that proof of recklessness may meet the requirement of intent in Rule 10b-5, but that it need not address whether there was sufficient recklessness in this case because the CPA firm had knowledge of the misstatement.

described in Figure 4-8, is an example of that reasoning. However, in two more recent suits, *Worlds of Wonder* and *Software Toolworks*, two key Ninth Circuit decisions stated that questioning judgments isn't proof of fraud. This view appears now to be winning in the courts.

Another line of reasoning that has received some judicial support has been to adopt the Supreme Court's requirements of fraud and hold that recklessness constitutes a constructive fraud and therefore is actionable under Rule 10b-5. *McLean* v. *Alexander* is a leading case involving allegations of recklessness. It is summarized in Figure 4-9. Even if no intentional misrepresentation or recklessness were evident in the financial statements, lawyers have argued that if the CPA knew that the audit was in less than full compliance

**FIGURE 4-9**

***McLean* v. *Alexander* (1979)—Securities Exchange Act of 1934**

This is a case in which CPA defendants were found liable by a lower court under Rule 10b-5 and were also found liable for common law fraud, even though there was no evidence that the accountant knew the financial statements to be incorrect or intended to mislead anyone. The lower court was, however, overruled by a higher court.

The case was brought by a businessman and investor who had purchased all the stock of a speculative company, relying on glowing reports of sales. The financial statements included accounts receivable that apparently were based on sales of sixteen laser devices that the company manufactured. In fact, all sixteen sales were guaranteed or consignment sales rather than true sales. Although the sixteen sales in the aggregate did not have a material effect on the financial statements in terms of pure numbers, the plaintiff allegedly relied on the accounts receivable as an indication of the business ability of the company.

The auditors did not receive confirmations that they had mailed on these accounts. When pressed by the client to complete the audit, the auditors brought up this problem. The auditors subsequently received two telegram confirmations of purchase orders rather than of accounts receivable. The auditors made no attempt to investigate further and did not find out that, in fact, one of the telegrams was fraudulent.

There were other indications of discrepancies in these accounts that the auditors did not follow up. The lower court held that the information that the auditors obtained during the course of the audit, but did not follow up on, was the kind of information that should have been disclosed. The lower court held that failure to disclose that information constituted reckless disregard for the truth.

The appellate court ruled that the auditors were at most guilty of negligence, but not of bad-faith recklessness. They held the CPAs not liable under Rule 10b-5 and Delaware common law fraud.

with all the requirements of generally accepted auditing standards, the audit opinion stating that generally accepted auditing standards were complied with is in itself fraudulent and, therefore, actionable.

It is clear from the previous discussion that Rule 10b-5 continues to be a basis for lawsuits against auditors, even though *Hochfelder* has limited the liability somewhat.

### Auditor Defenses—1934 Act

The same three defenses available to auditors in common law suits by third parties are also available for suits under the 1934 Act. These are nonnegligent performance, lack of duty, and absence of causal connection.

As discussed in this section, the use of the lack of duty defense in response to actions under Rule 10b-5 has had varying degrees of success, depending upon the jurisdiction. In the *Hochfelder* case, that defense was successful. In other cases negligent or reckless behavior resulted in liability. Continued court interpretations are likely to clarify this unresolved issue.

### SEC Sanctions

Closely related to auditors' liability is the SEC's authority to sanction. The SEC has the power in certain circumstances to sanction or suspend practitioners from doing audits for SEC companies. Rule 2(e) of the SEC's *Rules of Practice* says:

- The commission may deny, temporarily or permanently, the privilege of appearing or practicing before it in any way to any person who is found by the commission . . . (1) not to possess the requisite qualifications to represent others, or (2) to be lacking in character or integrity or to have engaged in unethical or improper professional conduct.

The SEC has temporarily suspended a number of individual CPAs from doing any audits of SEC clients in recent years. It has similarly prohibited a number of CPA firms from accepting any new SEC clients for a period, such as six months. At times, the SEC has required an extensive review of a major CPA firm's practices by another CPA firm. In some cases, individual CPAs and their firms have been required to participate in continuing education programs and to make changes in their practice. Sanctions such as these are published by the SEC and are often reported in the business press, making them a significant embarrassment to those involved.

### Racketeer Influenced and Corrupt Organization Act

**OBJECTIVE 4-7**
**Discuss the impact of the Racketeer Influenced and Corrupt Organization Act and the Foreign Corrupt Practices Act on accountants' liability.**

In 1970, Congress passed legislation aimed at preventing organized crime from invading legitimate business enterprises. One of the elements of that legislation is the Racketeer Influenced and Corrupt Organization Act, or RICO. That act allows an injured party to seek treble (triple) damages and recovery of legal fees in cases where it can be demonstrated that the defendant was engaged in a "pattern of racketeering activity." The statute states that a pattern of racketeering activity means at least two acts of racketeering activity within a 10-year period. In interpreting these requirements, the courts have generally focused on the continuity and relatedness of the acts to determine whether a pattern exists. Prior to 1993, the case law applying RICO to accountants was mixed. Some courts made it clear that a complaint must allege extensive participation by the auditor in the enterprise's affairs beyond conducting an annual audit, while others held that the issuance of a materially false audit report would constitute an act of racketeering activity. Legislation has been considered by the U.S. Congress to clarify the applicability of the act. However, from the auditor's point of view, the issue was essentially resolved by the United States Supreme Court. In a 1993 decision, the court ruled that outside professionals such as accountants who don't help run corrupt businesses can't be sued under the provisions of RICO.

### Foreign Corrupt Practices Act of 1977

Another significant congressional action affecting both CPA firms and their clients was the passage of the Foreign Corrupt Practices Act of 1977. The act makes it illegal to offer a bribe to an official of a foreign country for the purpose of exerting influence and obtaining or retaining business. The prohibition against payments to foreign officials is applicable to all U.S. domestic firms, regardless of whether they are publicly or privately held, and to foreign companies filing with the SEC.

Apart from the bribery provisions that affect all companies, the law also requires SEC registrants under the Securities Exchange Act of 1934 to meet additional requirements. These include the maintenance of reasonably complete and accurate records and an adequate system of internal control. The law significantly affects all SEC companies, but the unanswered question to the profession at this time is how it affects auditors.

The act may affect auditors through their responsibility to review and evaluate systems of internal control as a part of doing the audit. Most auditors believe that they are not currently required to do a review of internal control thorough enough to judge whether their clients meet the requirements of the Foreign Corrupt Practices Act.

To date, there have been no legal cases affecting auditors' legal responsibilities under the Foreign Corrupt Practices Act. But there is considerable disagreement about auditors' responsibilities under the law. There is likely to be ongoing discussion, and perhaps litigation, to resolve the issue.

## CRIMINAL LIABILITY

**OBJECTIVE 4-8**
**Specify what constitutes criminal liability for accountants.**

It is possible for CPAs to be found guilty for criminal action under both federal and state laws. The most likely statutes to be used under state law are the Uniform Securities Acts, which are similar to parts of the SEC rules. The 1933 and 1934 securities acts, as well as the Federal Mail Fraud Statute and the Federal False Statements Statute, are the most relevant federal laws affecting auditors. All make it a criminal offense to defraud another person through *knowingly being involved* with false financial statements.

Unfortunately, there have been several criminal cases of notoriety involving CPAs. Although these are not great in absolute number, they have the effect of damaging the integrity of the profession, and reducing the profession's ability to attract and retain outstanding people. On the positive side, criminal actions encourage practitioners to use extreme care and exercise good faith in their activities.

The leading case of criminal action against CPAs is *United States* v. *Simon*, which occurred in 1969. That case is summarized in Figure 4-10 on page 122. Simon has been followed by three additional major criminal cases. In *United States* v. *Natelli* (1975), two auditors were convicted of criminal liability under the 1934 Act for certifying financial statements of National Student Marketing Corporation that contained inadequate disclosures pertaining to accounts receivable.

In *United States* v. *Weiner* (1975), three auditors were convicted of securities fraud in connection with their audit of Equity Funding Corporation of America. Equity Funding was a financial conglomerate whose financial statements had been overstated through a massive fraud by management. The fraud was so extensive and the audit work so poor that the court concluded that the auditors must have been aware of the fraud and were therefore guilty of knowing complicity.

In *ESM Government Securities* v. *Alexander Grant & Co.* (1986), it was revealed by management to the partner in charge of the audit of ESM that the previous year's audited financial statements contained a material misstatement. Rather than complying with professional and firm standards in such circumstances, the partner agreed to say nothing in the hope that management would work its way out of the problem during the current year. Instead, the situation worsened, eventually to the point where losses exceeded $300 million. The partner was convicted of criminal charges for his role in sustaining the fraud and is now serving a 12-year prison term.

**FIGURE 4-10**

***United States* v. *Simon* (1969)—Criminal Liability**

The case was a criminal one concerning three auditors prosecuted for filing false statements with a government agency and violation of the 1934 Securities Exchange Act. The CPA firm had already settled out of court for civil liability issues for over $2 million after the audit client, Continental Vending Corporation, filed for bankruptcy.

The main issue of the trial was the reporting of transactions between Continental and its affiliate, Valley Commercial Corporation. Before the audit was complete, the auditors had learned that Valley was not in a position to repay its debt, and it was accordingly arranged that collateral would be posted. The president of Continental Vending, Roth, and members of his family transferred their equity in certain securities to Continental's counsel, as trustee to secure Roth's debt to Valley and Valley's debt to Continental. Note 2 included with the financial statements read as follows:

- The amount receivable from Valley Commercial Corp. (an affiliated company of which Mr. Harold Roth is an officer, director, and stockholder) bears interest at 12 percent a year. Such amount, less the balance of the notes payable to that company, is secured by the assignment to the Company of Valley's equity in certain marketable securities. As of February 15, 1963, the amount of such equity at current market quotations exceeded the net amount receivable.

The government contended that this note was inadequate and should have disclosed that the amount receivable from Valley was uncollectible at September 30, 1962, since Valley had loaned approximately the same amount to Roth, who was unable to pay. The note should also have stated that approximately 80 percent of the securities Roth had pledged was stock and convertible debentures of Continental Vending. The defendants called eight expert independent accountants as witnesses. They testified generally that, except for the misstatement with respect to netting, the treatment of the Valley receivable in note 2 was in no way inconsistent with generally accepted accounting principles or generally accepted auditing standards. Specifically, they testified that neither generally accepted accounting principles nor generally accepted auditing standards required disclosure of the makeup of the collateral or of the increase in the receivables after the closing date of the balance sheet, although three of the eight stated that in light of hindsight they would have preferred that the makeup of the collateral be disclosed. The witnesses also testified that the disclosure of the Roth borrowings from Valley was not required, and seven of the eight were of the opinion that such disclosure would be inappropriate.

The defendants asked for two instructions which, in substance, would have told the jury that a defendant could be found guilty only if, according to generally accepted accounting principles, the statements as a whole did not fairly present the financial condition of Continental at September 30, 1962, and then only if this departure from accepted standards was due to willful disregard of those standards with knowledge of the falsity of the statements and an intent to deceive.

The judge declined to give those instructions and instead said that the critical test was whether the *statements were fairly presented and, if not, whether the defendants had acted in good faith.* Proof of compliance with generally accepted standards was "evidence which may be very persuasive but not necessarily conclusive that he acted in good faith, and that the facts as certified were not materially false or misleading."

The appeals court upheld the earlier conviction of the three auditors with the comment that even without satisfactory showing of motive, "the government produced sufficient evidence of criminal intent. Its burden was not to show that the defendants were wicked men . . . but rather that they had certified a statement knowing it to be false."

The effect on the three men was significant. The total fine was $17,000, but far more important, they lost their CPA certificates under Rule 501 of the *Code of Professional Conduct* (acts discreditable) and were forced to leave the profession. They were ultimately pardoned by President Nixon.

Several critical lessons can be learned from these four cases:

- An investigation of the integrity of management is an important part of deciding on the acceptability of clients and the extent of work to perform. SAS 7 (AU 315) gives guidance to auditors in investigating new clients.
- The auditor can be found criminally guilty in the conduct of an audit even if the person's background indicates integrity in his or her personal and professional life. The criminal liability can extend to partners and staff.

- Independence in appearance and fact by all individuals on the engagement is essential, especially in a defense involving criminal actions. SAS 1 (AU 220) requires a firm to implement policies to help assure independence in fact and in appearance.
- Transactions with related parties require special scrutiny because of the potential for misstatement. SAS 45 (AU 334) gives guidance in auditing related party transactions.
- Generally accepted accounting principles cannot be relied upon exclusively in deciding whether financial statements are fairly presented. The substance of the statements, considering all facts, is required. The SEC preferability requirement provides guidelines in selecting accounting principles.
- Good documentation may be just as important in the auditor's defense of criminal charges as in a civil suit.
- The potential consequences of the auditor knowingly committing a wrongful act are so severe that it is unlikely that the potential benefits could ever justify the actions.

## THE PROFESSION'S RESPONSE TO LEGAL LIABILITY

**OBJECTIVE 4-9**
**Describe what the profession and the individual CPA can do and what is being done to reduce the threat of litigation.**

There are a number of things the AICPA and the profession as a whole can do to reduce the practitioner's exposure to lawsuits. The AICPA's division of firms into SEC practice and private practice sections is one positive step in recognizing additional responsibility that the public demands of professionals. Some of the others are discussed briefly.

1. *Research in auditing.* Continued research is important in finding better ways to do such things as uncover unintentional material misstatements or fraud, communicate audit results to statement users, and make sure that auditors are independent. Significant research already takes place through the AICPA, CPA firms, and universities.

2. *Standard and rule setting.* The AICPA must constantly set standards and revise them to meet the changing needs of auditing. New statements on auditing standards, revisions of the *Code of Professional Conduct*, and other pronouncements must be issued as society's needs change and as new technology arises from experience and research.

3. *Set requirements to protect auditors.* The AICPA can help protect its members by setting certain requirements that better practitioners already follow. Naturally, these requirements should not be in conflict with meeting users' needs. An example of an auditor-set standard is the SAS 19 (AU 333) requirement of a written letter of representation from management in all audits.

4. *Establish peer review requirements.* The periodic examination of a firm's practices and procedures is a way to educate practitioners and identify firms not meeting the standards of the profession.

5. *Oppose lawsuits.* It is important that CPA firms continue to oppose unwarranted lawsuits even if, in the short run, the costs of winning are greater than the costs of settling. The AICPA has aided practitioners in fighting an unwarranted expansion of legal liability for accountants by filing briefs as "a friend of the court" known as *amicus curiae* briefs.

6. *Education of users.* It is important to educate investors and others who read financial statements as to the meaning of the auditor's opinion and the extent and nature of the auditor's work. Users must be educated to understand that auditors do not test 100 percent of all records and do not guarantee the accuracy of the financial records or the future prosperity of the company. It is also important to educate users to understand that accounting and auditing are arts, not sciences, and that perfection and precision are not achievable.

7. *Sanction members for improper conduct and performance.* One characteristic of a profession is its responsibility for policing its own membership. The AICPA has made progress toward dealing with the problems of inadequate CPA performance, but more rigorous review of alleged failures is still needed.

*8. Lobby for changes in laws.* 1996 brought with it a major victory in the accounting profession's long efforts to obtain changes in federal laws concerning accountants' liability. As indicated at the beginning of this chapter, a federal law was passed that significantly reduced potential damages in securities-related litigation. This law was the culmination of many years of effort by the Coalition to Eliminate Abusive Securities Suits, formed by the Big Six accounting firms and 180 industrial and commercial companies. The focus of their efforts was to have separate and proportionate liability replace joint and several liability, to require that plaintiffs pay a prevailing defendant's legal fees if the court determines that the lawsuit was without merit, and to allow accounting firms to practice in different organizational forms, including limited liability organizations. They were successful in regards to the first and last of these objectives. Now that this battle has been won, the profession will undoubtedly turn its attention to those states that have statutes that it believes are unfair to practicing professionals. Given the changes in federal law, it should be easier to obtain changes at the state level than it has been in the past.

## THE INDIVIDUAL CPA'S RESPONSE TO LEGAL LIABILITY

Practicing auditors may also take specific action to minimize their liability. Most of this book deals with that subject. A summary of several of these practices is included at this point.

*1. Deal only with clients possessing integrity.* There is an increased likelihood of having legal problems when a client lacks integrity in dealing with customers, employees, units of government, and others. A CPA firm needs procedures to evaluate the integrity of clients and should dissociate itself from clients found lacking.

*2. Hire qualified personnel and train and supervise them properly.* A considerable portion of most audits is done by young professionals with relatively little experience. Given the high degree of risk CPA firms have in doing audits, it is important that these young professionals be qualified and well trained. Supervision of their work by experienced and qualified professionals is also essential.

*3. Follow the standards of the profession.* A firm must implement procedures to make sure that all firm members understand and follow the SASs, FASB opinions, rules of conduct, and other professional guidelines.

*4. Maintain independence.* Independence is more than merely financial. Independence in fact requires an attitude of responsibility separate from the client's interest. Much litigation has arisen from a too willing acceptance by an auditor of a client's representation or of a client's pressures. The auditor must maintain an attitude of *healthy skepticism.*

*5. Understand the client's business.* The lack of knowledge of industry practices and client operations has been a major factor in auditors failing to uncover misstatements in several cases. It is important that the audit team be educated in these areas.

*6. Perform quality audits.* Quality audits require that auditors obtain appropriate evidence and make appropriate judgments about the evidence. It is essential, for example, that the auditor evaluate a client's internal controls and modify the evidence to reflect the findings. Improved auditing reduces the likelihood of misstatements and the likelihood of lawsuits.

*7. Document the work properly.* The preparation of good working papers helps the auditor organize and perform quality audits. Quality working papers are essential if an auditor has to defend an audit in court.

*8. Obtain an engagement letter and a representation letter.* These two letters are essential in defining the respective obligations of the client and the auditor. They are helpful especially in lawsuits between the client and auditor, but also in third-party lawsuits.

*9. Maintain confidential relations.* Auditors are under an ethical and sometimes legal obligation not to disclose client matters to outsiders.

*10. Carry adequate insurance.* It is essential for a CPA firm to have adequate insurance protection in the event of a lawsuit. Although insurance rates have risen considerably in the past few years as a result of increasing litigation, professional liability insurance is still available for all CPAs.

*11. Seek legal counsel.* Whenever serious problems occur during an audit, a CPA would be wise to consult experienced counsel. In the event of a potential or actual lawsuit, the auditor should immediately seek an experienced attorney.

*12. Choose a form of organization with limited liability.* As discussed in Chapter 1, many CPA firms now operate as professional corporations, limited liability companies, or limited liability partnerships in order to provide some personal liability protection to owners.

**WHAT LIMITED PERSONAL LIABILITY WILL AND WILL NOT DO**

In recent years, new forms of organization have become available to CPA firms to limit the personal liability of their owners. Here is a summary of exactly what limiting owner's personal liability will and will not do:

Limiting owner's personal liability will

- Give owners and their families the relative security of knowing that a firm's bankruptcy will not carry the risk of personal bankruptcy.
- Introduce equity into an inequitable situation by giving CPA firm owners at least some of the liability protection afforded other business owners and professionals.
- Help ensure the future viability of the profession by eliminating one factor from the "no" column under the question: "Should I enter or continue in public accounting?"

Limiting owner's personal liability will *not*

- Reduce CPA firms' responsibility for their quality of performance.
- Protect CPA firms from bankruptcy resulting from a liability system that produces unpredictable and excessive damage awards.
- Completely eliminate liability as a serious disadvantage in attracting the most competent aspiring accountants.
- End the accounting profession's liability crisis.

*Source:* Gilbert Simonetti, Jr., and Andrea R. Andrews, "A Profession at Risk/A System in Jeopardy," *Journal of Accountancy,* April 1994, p. 49.

## SUMMARY

The auditing profession has been under a great deal of attack in recent years not only in court but also at the Securities and Exchange Commission and in congressional committee proceedings and reports. Demands for increased regulation and increased legal liability are heard frequently. The profession is struggling to respond constructively to these pressures.

The determination of the extent to which auditors should be legally responsible for the reliability of financial statements is relevant to both the profession and society. Clearly, the existence of legal responsibility is an important deterrent to the inadequate and even dishonest activities of some auditors.

No reasonable CPA would want to eliminate the profession's legal responsibility for fraudulent or incompetent performance. It is certainly in the profession's self-interest to maintain public trust in the competent performance of the auditing function.

However, it is unreasonable for auditors to be held legally responsible for every misstatement in financial statements. The auditor cannot serve as the insurer or guarantor of financial statement accuracy or business health. The audit costs to society that would be required to achieve such high levels of assurance would exceed the benefits. Moreover, even with increased audit costs, well-planned frauds would not necessarily be discovered, nor errors of judgment eliminated.

It is necessary for the profession and society to determine a reasonable trade-off between the degree of responsibility the auditor should take for fair presentation and the audit cost to society. CPAs, Congress, the SEC, and the courts will all have a major influence in shaping the final solution.

**LESSONS LEARNED FROM AUDITOR LITIGATION**

In considering the advisability of the laws being considered in reform of accountants' liability, it is useful to consider actual experiences with past accountants' litigation. Accordingly, a review was conducted of twenty-three cases of alleged audit failure with which I have been involved as a litigation consultant and expert witness. Of these twenty-three cases, six were clearly without merit and should not have been brought on equitable grounds. Of the seventeen that were with merit, thirteen did, in fact, represent a real audit failure. In considering the nature of the failure in each case, it was observed that the evidence that would lead the auditor to identify the misstatement that existed was usually there. In other words, the problem was not any inadequacy in the audit process as presented by professional standards; it was *a lack of professional skepticism* on the part of the auditor. The auditor had evidence in his or her possession that indicated the problem, but did not see it as such.

*Source:* Presentation by James K. Loebbecke at the Forum on Responsibilities and Liabilities of Accountants and Auditors, United Nations Conference on Trade and Development, March 16, 1995.

## ESSENTIAL TERMS

**Absence of causal connection**—an auditor's legal defense under which the auditor contends that the damages claimed by the client were not brought about by any act of the auditor

**Audit failure**—a situation in which the auditor issues an erroneous audit opinion as the result of an underlying failure to comply with the requirements of generally accepted auditing standards

**Audit risk**—the risk that the auditor will conclude that the financial statements are fairly stated and an unqualified opinion can therefore be issued when, in fact, they are materially misstated

**Business failure**—the situation when a business is unable to repay its lenders, or meet the expectations of its investors, because of economic or business conditions

**Contributory negligence**—an auditor's legal defense under which the auditor claims that the client failed to perform certain obligations and that it is the client's failure to perform those obligations that brought about the claimed damages

**Criminal liability for auditors**—defrauding a person through knowing involvement with false financial statements

**Defalcation**—theft of assets

**Foreign Corrupt Practices Act of 1977**—a federal statute that makes it illegal to offer a bribe to an official of a foreign country for the purpose of exerting influence and obtaining or retaining business, and that requires U.S. companies to maintain reasonably complete and accurate records and an adequate system of internal control

**Foreseeable user**—an unlimited class of users that the auditor should have reasonably been able to foresee as being likely users of financial statements

**Foreseen user**—a member of a limited class of users whom the auditor is aware will rely on the financial statements

**Lack of duty to perform**—an auditor's legal defense under which the auditor claims that no contract existed with the client; therefore no duty existed to perform the disputed service

**Legal liability**—the professional's obligation under the law to provide a reasonable level of care while performing work for those he or she serves

**Nonnegligent performance**—an auditor's legal defense under which the auditor claims that the audit was performed in accordance with generally accepted auditing standards

**Prudent person concept**—the legal concept that a person has a duty to exercise reasonable care and diligence in the performance of his or her obligations to another

**Racketeer Influenced and Corrupt Organization Act (RICO)**—a 1970 federal statute designed to discourage fraud, extortion, and other racketeering activities, under which an injured party may recover treble damages and legal fees. A 1993 Supreme Court ruling ruled that CPA firms are ordinarily exempt from this statute.

**Securities Act of 1933**—a federal statute dealing with companies that register and sell securities to the public; under the statute, third parties who are original purchasers of securities may recover damages from the auditor if the financial statements are misstated unless the auditor proves that the audit was adequate or that the third party's loss was caused by factors other than misleading financial statements

**Securities Exchange Act of 1934**—a federal statute dealing with companies that trade securities on national and over-the-counter exchanges. Auditors are involved because the annual reporting requirements include audited financial statements.

***Ultramares* doctrine**—a common-law approach to third-party liability, established in 1931 in the case of *Ultramares Corporation* v. *Touche*, in which ordinary negligence is insufficient for liability to third parties, because of the lack of *privity of contract* between the third party and the auditor, unless the third party is a *primary beneficiary*

## REVIEW QUESTIONS

**4-1 (Objective 4-1)** State several factors that have affected the incidence of lawsuits against CPAs in recent years.

**4-2 (Objective 4-1)** Lawsuits against CPA firms have increased dramatically in the past decade. State your opinion of the positive and negative effects of the increased litigation on CPAs and on society as a whole.

**4-3 (Objective 4-2)** Distinguish between business failure and audit risk. Why is business risk a concern to auditors?

**4-4 (Objective 4-3)** How does the *prudent person concept* affect the liability of the auditor?

**4-5 (Objective 4-3)** Distinguish between "fraud" and "constructive fraud."

**4-6 (Objectives 4-1, 4-9)** Discuss why many CPA firms have willingly settled lawsuits out of court. What are the implications to the profession?

**4-7 (Objective 4-4)** A common type of lawsuit against CPAs is for the failure to detect a defalcation. State the auditor's responsibility for such discovery. Give authoritative support for your answer.

**4-8 (Objectives 4-3, 4-4)** What is meant by "contributory negligence"? Under what conditions will this likely be a successful defense?

**4-9 (Objective 4-4)** What are the purposes of a letter of representation and an engagement letter?

**4-10 (Objectives 4-4, 4-5)** Compare and contrast traditional auditors' legal responsibilities to clients and third-party users under common law. How has that law changed in recent years?

**4-11 (Objective 4-5)** Is the auditor's liability affected if the third party was unknown rather than known? Explain.

**4-12 (Objective 4-6)** Contrast the auditor's liability under the Securities Act of 1933 with that under the Securities Exchange Act of 1934.

**4-13 (Objectives 4-4, 4-5, 4-6, 4-8)** Distinguish between the auditor's potential liability to the client, liability to third parties under common law, civil liability under the securities laws, and criminal liability. Describe one situation for each type of liability in which the auditor could be held legally responsible.

**4-14 (Objective 4-6)** What sanctions does the SEC have against a CPA firm?

**4-15 (Objective 4-9)** In what ways can the profession positively respond and reduce liability in auditing?

## MULTIPLE CHOICE QUESTIONS FROM CPA EXAMINATIONS

**4-16 (Objectives 4-4, 4-5)** The following questions concern CPA firms' liability under common law. Choose the best response.

a. Sharp, CPA, was engaged by Peters & Sons, a partnership, to give an opinion on the financial statements that were to be submitted to several prospective partners as part of a planned expansion of the firm. Sharp's fee was fixed on a per diem basis. After a period of intensive work, Sharp completed about half of the necessary field work. Then, due to unanticipated demands upon his time by other clients, Sharp was forced to abandon the work. The planned expansion of the firm failed to materialize because the prospective partners lost interest when the audit report was not promptly available. Sharp offered to complete the task at a later date. This offer was refused. Peters & Sons suffered damages of $4,000 as a result. Under the circumstances, what is the probable outcome of a lawsuit between Sharp and Peters & Sons?
   (1) Sharp will be compensated for the reasonable value of the services actually performed.
   (2) Peters & Sons will recover damages for breach of contract.
   (3) Peters & Sons will recover both punitive damages and damages for breach of contract.
   (4) Neither Sharp nor Peters & Sons will recover against the other.

b. Magnus Enterprises engaged a CPA firm to perform the annual audit of its financial statements. Which of the following is a correct statement with respect to the CPA firm's liability to Magnus for negligence?
   (1) Such liability cannot be varied by agreement of the parties.
   (2) The CPA firm will be liable for any fraudulent scheme it does not detect.
   (3) The CPA firm will not be liable if it can show that it exercised the ordinary care and skill of a reasonable person in the conduct of its own affairs.
   (4) The CPA firm must not only exercise reasonable care in what it does, but also must possess at least that degree of accounting knowledge and skill expected of a CPA.

c. Martin Corporation orally engaged Humm & Dawson to audit its year-end financial statements. The engagement was to be completed within two months after the close of Martin's fiscal year for a fixed fee of $15,000. Under these circumstances what obligation is assumed by Humm & Dawson?
   (1) None, because the contract is unenforceable since it is not in writing.
   (2) An implied promise to exercise reasonable standards of competence and care.
   (3) An implied obligation to take extraordinary steps to discover all defalcations.
   (4) The obligation of an insurer of its work, which is liable without fault.

d. If a CPA firm is being sued for common law fraud by a third party based upon materially false financial statements, which of the following is the best defense the accountants could assert?
   (1) Lack of privity.
   (2) Nonnegligent performance.
   (3) A disclaimer contained in the engagement letter.
   (4) Contributory negligence on the part of the client.

**4-17 (Objectives 4-5, 4-6, 4-8)** The following questions deal with important cases in accountants' liability. Choose the best response.

a. The most significant aspect of the *Continental Vending* (*United States* v. *Simon*) case was that it
   (1) created a more general awareness of the auditor's exposure to criminal prosecution.
   (2) extended the auditor's responsibility for financial statements of subsidiaries.
   (3) extended the auditor's responsibility for events after the end of the audit period.
   (4) defined the auditor's common-law responsibilities to third parties.

b. The *1136 Tenants* case was important chiefly because of its emphasis upon the legal liability of the CPA when associated with
   (1) an SEC engagement.
   (2) unaudited financial statements.
   (3) an audit resulting in a disclaimer of opinion.
   (4) letters for underwriters.

**4-18 (Objective 4-6)** The following questions deal with liability under the 1933 and 1934 Securities Acts. Choose the best response.

a. Major, Major, & Sharpe, CPAs, are the auditors of MacLain Industries. In connection with the public offering of $10 million of MacLain securities, Major expressed an unqualified opinion as to the financial statements. Subsequent to the offering, certain misstatements were revealed. Major has been sued by the purchasers of the stock offered pursuant to the registration statement that included the financial statements audited by Major. In the ensuing lawsuit by the MacLain investors, Major will be able to avoid liability if
   (1) the misstatements were caused primarily by MacLain.
   (2) it can be shown that at least some of the investors did *not* actually read the audited financial statements.
   (3) it can prove due diligence in the audit of the financial statements of MacLain.
   (4) MacLain had expressly assumed any liability in connection with the public offering.

b. Donalds & Company, CPAs, audited the financial statements included in the annual report submitted by Markum Securities, Inc., to the Securities and Exchange Commission. The audit was improper in several respects. Markum is now insolvent and unable to satisfy the claims of its customers. The customers have instituted legal action against Donalds based upon Section 10b and Rule 10b-5 of the Securities Exchange Act of 1934. Which of the following is likely to be Donalds's best defense?
   (1) They did *not* intentionally certify false financial statements.
   (2) Section 10b does *not* apply to them.
   (3) They were *not* in privity of contract with the creditors.
   (4) Their engagement letter specifically disclaimed any liability to any party which resulted from Markum's fraudulent conduct.

c. Josephs & Paul is a growing medium-sized partnership of CPAs. One of the firm's major clients is considering offering its stock to the public. This will be the firm's first client to go public. Which of the following is true with respect to this engagement?
   (1) If the client is a service corporation, the Securities Act of 1933 will not apply.
   (2) If the client is not going to be listed on an organized exchange, the Securities Exchange Act of 1934 will not apply.
   (3) The Securities Act of 1933 imposes important additional potential liability on Josephs & Paul.
   (4) As long as Josephs & Paul engages exclusively in intrastate business, the federal securities laws will not apply.

## DISCUSSION QUESTIONS AND PROBLEMS

**4-19 (Objectives 4-4, 4-5)** Verna Cosden & Co., a medium-sized CPA firm, was engaged to audit Joslin Supply Company. Several staff were involved in the audit, all of whom had attended the firm's in-house training program in effective auditing methods. Throughout the audit, Cosden spent most of her time in the field planning the audit, supervising the staff, and reviewing their work.

A significant part of the audit entailed verifying the physical count, cost, and summarization of inventory. Inventory was highly significant to the financial statements and Cosden knew the inventory was pledged as collateral for a large loan to East City National Bank. In reviewing Joslin's inventory count procedures, Cosden told the president she believed the method of counting inventory at different locations on different days was highly undesirable. The president stated that it was impractical to count all inventory on the same day because of personnel shortages and customer preference. After considerable discussion Cosden agreed to permit the practice if the president would sign a statement that no other method was practical. The CPA firm had at least one person at each site to audit the inventory count procedures and actual count. There were more than forty locations.

Eighteen months later Cosden found out that the worst had happened. Management below the president's level had conspired to materially overstate inventory, as a means of covering up obsolete inventory and inventory losses due to mismanagement. The misstatement occurred by physically transporting inventory at night to other locations after it had been counted in a given location. The accounting records were inadequate to uncover these illegal transfers.

Both Joslin Supply Company and East City National Bank sued Verna Cosden & Co.

### Required

Answer the following questions, setting forth reasons for any conclusions stated:

a. What defense should Cosden & Co. use in the suit by Joslin?

b. What defense should Cosden & Co. use in the suit by East City National Bank?

c. Is Cosden likely to be successful in her defenses?

d. Would the issues or outcome be significantly different if the suit was brought under the Securities Exchange Act of 1934?

**4-20 (Objective 4-5)** The CPA firm of Bigelow, Barton, and Brown was expanding rapidly. Consequently, it hired several junior accountants, including a man named Small. The partners of the firm eventually became dissatisfied with Small's production and warned him they would be forced to discharge him unless his output increased significantly.

At that time, Small was engaged in audits of several clients. He decided that to avoid being fired, he would reduce or omit some of the standard auditing procedures listed in audit programs prepared by the partners. One of the CPA firm's clients, Newell Corporation, was in serious financial difficulty and had adjusted several of the accounts being audited by Small to appear financially sound. Small prepared fictitious working papers in his home at night to support purported completion of auditing procedures assigned to him, although he in fact did not examine the adjusting entries. The CPA firm rendered an unqualified opinion on Newell's financial statements, which were grossly misstated. Several creditors, relying on the audited financial statements, subsequently extended large sums of money to Newell Corporation.

### Required

Would the CPA firm be liable to the creditors who extended the money because of their reliance on the erroneous financial statements if Newell Corporation should fail to pay them? Explain.*

*AICPA adapted.

**4-21 (Objectives 4-3, 4-5)** Watts and Williams, a firm of certified public accountants, audited the accounts of Sampson Skins, Inc., a corporation that imports and deals in fine furs. Upon completion of the audit, the auditors supplied Sampson Skins with twenty copies of the certified balance sheet. The firm knew in a general way that Sampson Skins wanted that number of copies of the auditor's report to furnish to banks and other potential lenders.

The balance sheet in question was misstated by approximately $800,000. Instead of having a $600,000 net worth, the corporation was insolvent. The management of Sampson Skins had doctored the books to avoid bankruptcy. The assets had been overstated by $500,000 of fictitious and nonexisting accounts receivable and $300,000 of nonexisting skins listed as inventory when in fact Sampson Skins had only empty boxes. The audit failed to detect these fraudulent entries. Martinson, relying on the certified balance sheet, loaned Sampson Skins $200,000. He seeks to recover his loss from Watts and Williams.

## Required

State whether each of the following is true or false and give your reasons:

a. If Martinson alleges and proves negligence on the part of Watts and Williams, he will be able to recover his loss.

b. If Martinson alleges and proves constructive fraud (that is, gross negligence on the part of Watts and Williams) he will be able to recover his loss.

c. Martinson does not have a contract with Watts and Williams.

d. Unless actual fraud on the part of Watts and Williams could be shown, Martinson could not recover.

e. Martinson is a third-party beneficiary of the contract Watts and Williams made with Sampson Skins.*

**4-22 (Objective 4-4, 4-5, 4-8)** Donald Sharpe recently joined the CPA firm of Spark, Watts, and Wilcox. He quickly established a reputation for thoroughness and a steadfast dedication to following prescribed auditing procedures to the letter. On his third audit for the firm, Sharpe examined the underlying documentation of 200 disbursements as a test of acquisitions, receiving, vouchers payable, and cash disbursement procedures. In the process he found twelve disbursements for the acquisition of materials with no receiving reports in the documentation. He noted the exceptions in his working papers and called them to the attention of the in-charge accountant. Relying on prior experience with the client, the in-charge accountant disregarded Sharpe's comments, and nothing further was done about the exceptions.

Subsequently, it was learned that one of the client's purchasing agents and a member of its accounting department were engaged in a fraudulent scheme whereby they diverted the receipt of materials to a public warehouse while sending the invoices to the client. When the client discovered the fraud, the conspirators had obtained approximately $70,000, $50,000 of which was recovered after the completion of the audit.

## Required

Discuss the legal implications and liabilities to Spark, Watts, and Wilcox as a result of the facts just described.*

**4-23 (Objectives 4-3, 4-4, 4-5)** In confirming accounts receivable on December 31, 1997, the auditor found fifteen discrepancies between the customer's records and the recorded amounts in the accounts receivable master file. A copy of all confirmations that had exceptions was turned over to the company controller to investigate the reason for the difference. He, in turn, had the bookkeeper perform the analysis. The bookkeeper analyzed each exception, determined its cause, and prepared an elaborate working paper explaining each

*AICPA adapted.

difference. Most of the differences in the bookkeeper's report indicated that the exceptions were caused by timing differences in the client's and customer's records. The auditor reviewed the working paper and concluded that there were no material exceptions in accounts receivable.

Two years subsequent to the audit, it was determined that the bookkeeper had stolen thousands of dollars in the past three years by taking cash and overstating accounts receivable. In a lawsuit by the client against the CPA, an examination of the auditor's December 31, 1997 accounts receivable working papers, which were subpoenaed by the court, indicated that one of the explanations in the bookkeeper's analysis of the exceptions was fictitious. The analysis stated the exception was caused by a sales allowance granted to the customer for defective merchandise the day before the end of the year. The difference was actually caused by the bookkeeper's theft.

### Required

a. What are the legal issues involved in this situation? What should the auditor use as a defense in the event that he is sued?

b. What was the CPA's deficiency in conducting the audit of accounts receivable?

**4-24 (Objectives 4-4, 4-5, 4-8)** Smith, CPA, is the auditor for Juniper Manufacturing Corporation, a privately owned company that has a June 30 fiscal year. Juniper arranged for a substantial bank loan that was dependent on the bank's receiving, by September 30, audited financial statements that showed a current ratio of at least 2 to 1. On September 25, just before the audit report was to be issued, Smith received an anonymous letter on Juniper's stationery indicating that a five-year lease by Juniper, as lessee, of a factory building accounted for in the financial statements as an operating lease was, in fact, a capital lease. The letter stated that there was a secret written agreement with the lessor modifying the lease and creating a capital lease.

Smith confronted the president of Juniper, who admitted that a secret agreement existed but said it was necessary to treat the lease as an operating lease to meet the current ratio requirement of the pending loan and that nobody would ever discover the secret agreement with the lessor. The president said that if Smith did not issue his report by September 30, Juniper would sue Smith for substantial damages that would result from not getting the loan. Under this pressure and because the working papers contained a copy of the five-year lease agreement that supported the operating lease treatment, Smith issued his report with an unqualified opinion on September 29.

In spite of the fact that the loan was received, Juniper went bankrupt within two years. The bank is suing Smith to recover its losses on the loan and the lessor is suing Smith to recover uncollected rents.

### Required

Answer the following questions, setting forth reasons for any conclusions stated:

a. Is Smith liable to the bank?

b. Is Smith liable to the lessor?

c. Is there potential for criminal action against Smith?*

**4-25 (Objective 4-4)** Ward & East, CPAs, were the auditors of Southern Development, Inc., a real estate company that owned several shopping centers. It was Southern's practice to let each shopping center manager negotiate that center's leases; they felt that such an arrangement resulted in much better leases because a local person did the negotiating.

Two of the center managers were killed in a plane accident returning home from a company meeting at the head office in Phoenix. In both cases, the new managers appointed

*AICPA adapted.

to take their places discovered kickback schemes in operation; the managers had negotiated lower rents than normal in return for kickbacks from the tenants.

Southern brought in a new CPA firm, Jasper & Co., to investigate the extent of the fraud at those two locations and the possibility of similar frauds at other centers. Jasper & Co. completed their investigation and found that four locations were involved quite independently of each other and that the total loss over five years was over $1,000,000.

Southern sued Ward & East for negligence for $1,000,000 plus interest.

### Required

What defense would Ward & East use? What would they have to prove?

**4-26 (Objective 4-6)** Gordon & Groton, CPAs, were the auditors of Bank & Company, a brokerage firm and member of a national stock exchange. Gordon & Groton audited and reported on the financial statements of Bank, which were filed with the Securities and Exchange Commission.

Several of Bank's customers were swindled by a fraudulent scheme perpetrated by Bank's president, who owned 90 percent of the voting stock of the company. The facts establish that Gordon & Groton were negligent but not reckless or grossly negligent in the conduct of the audit, and neither participated in the fraudulent scheme or knew of its existence.

The customers are suing Gordon & Groton under the antifraud provisions of Section 10(b) and Rule 10b-5 of the Securities Exchange Act of 1934 for aiding and abetting the fraudulent scheme of the president. The customers' suit for fraud is predicated exclusively on the nonfeasance of the auditors in failing to conduct a proper audit, thereby failing to discover the fraudulent scheme.

### Required

Answer the following questions, setting forth reasons for any conclusions stated:

a. What is the probable outcome of the lawsuit?

b. What other theory of liability might the customers have asserted?*

**4-27 (Objective 4-5)** Sarah Robertson, CPA, had been the auditor of Majestic Co. for several years. As she and her staff prepared for the audit for the year ended December 31, 1996, Herb Majestic told her that he needed a large bank loan to "tide him over" until sales picked up as expected in late 1997.

In the course of the audit Robertson discovered that the financial situation at Majestic was worse than Majestic had revealed and that the company was technically bankrupt. She discussed the situation with Majestic, who pointed out that the bank loan would "be his solution"—he was sure he would get it as long as the financial statements didn't look too bad.

Robertson stated that she believed the statements would have to include a going concern note. Majestic said that such a note really wasn't needed because the bank loan was so certain and that inclusion of such a note would certainly cause the management of the bank to change its mind about the loan.

Robertson finally acquiesced and the audited statements were issued without the note. The company received the loan, but things didn't improve as Majestic thought they would and the company filed for bankruptcy in August 1997.

The bank sued Sarah Robertson for fraud.

### Required

Indicate whether or not you think the bank would succeed. Support your answer.

*AICPA adapted.

**4-28 (Objectives 4-5, 4-6)** *Part 1.* Whitlow & Company is a brokerage firm registered under the Securities Exchange Act of 1934. The act requires such a brokerage firm to file audited financial statements with the SEC annually. Mitchell & Moss, Whitlow's CPAs, performed the annual audit for the year ended December 31, 1996, and rendered an unqualified opinion, which was filed with the SEC along with Whitlow's financial statements. During 1996, Charles, the president of Whitlow & Company, engaged in a huge embezzlement scheme that eventually bankrupted the firm. As a result substantial losses were suffered by customers and shareholders of Whitlow & Company, including Thaxton, who had recently purchased several shares of stock of Whitlow & Company after reviewing the company's 1996 audit report. Mitchell & Moss's audit was deficient; if they had complied with generally accepted auditing standards, the embezzlement would have been discovered. However, Mitchell & Moss had no knowledge of the embezzlement, nor could their conduct be categorized as reckless.

## Required

Answer the following questions, setting forth reasons for any conclusions stated:

a. What liability to Thaxton, if any, does Mitchell & Moss have under the Securities Exchange Act of 1934?

b. What theory or theories of liability, if any, are available to Whitlow & Company's customers and shareholders under common law?

*Part 2.* Jackson is a sophisticated investor. As such, she was initially a member of a small group that was going to participate in a private placement of $1 million of common stock of Clarion Corporation. Numerous meetings were held among management and the investor group. Detailed financial and other information was supplied to the participants. Upon the eve of completion of the placement, it was aborted when one major investor withdrew. Clarion then decided to offer $2.5 million of Clarion common stock to the public pursuant to the registration requirements of the Securities Act of 1933. Jackson subscribed to $300,000 of the Clarion public stock offering. Nine months later, Clarion's earnings dropped significantly and as a result the stock dropped 20 percent beneath the offering price. In addition, the Dow Jones Industrial Average was down 10 percent from the time of the offering.

Jackson has sold her shares at a loss of $60,000 and seeks to hold all parties liable who participated in the public offering, including Clarion's CPA firm of Allen, Dunn, and Rose. Although the audit was performed in conformity with generally accepted auditing standards, there were some relatively minor misstatements. The financial statements of Clarion Corporation, which were part of the registration statement, contained minor misleading facts. It is believed by Clarion and Allen, Dunn, and Rose that Jackson's asserted claim is without merit.

## Required

Answer the following questions, setting forth reasons for any conclusions stated:

a. If Jackson sues under the Securities Act of 1933, what will be the basis of her claim?

b. What are the probable defenses that might be asserted by Allen, Dunn, and Rose in light of these facts?*

**4-29 (Objectives 4-3, 4-5)** Western Leasing Incorporated (WSI) was a leasing company headquartered in San Diego that leased equipment to construction companies, restaurants, gas stations, and medical and dental practices. WSI grew rapidly during the 1980s and by the mid-1990s had a portfolio of over $100 million of gross lease receivables. WSI obtained its financing from its primary banker, First National Bank. The line of credit obtained by

*AICPA adapted.

First National was secured by WSI's lease receivables. In order to maintain its credit line, WSI was required to maintain positive earnings and a positive net worth, and to provide First National with annual audited financial statements. WSI engaged the accounting firm of Sinclair & Lewis as its auditors. Through the year ended December 31, 1995, Sinclair & Lewis had audited WSI for ten consecutive years. Each audit had resulted in an unqualified opinion.

In June of 1996, WSI's president, Wally Vernon, became seriously ill and was forced to take sudden retirement. The Maxwell family, who owned all of the stock of WSI but were not actively involved in management other than holding two seats on the board, hired a consultant to consider Vernon's replacement. The consultant advised the Maxwells that first, an outsider should be brought in as the new CEO, and second, that he perceived that there were serious problems at WSI.

As its next step, the Maxwells hired Bob Riddell as WSI's new CEO. Riddell promptly informed the Maxwells that he believed there were a number of serious problems at WSI, including the quality of the lease portfolio. He requested that Sinclair & Lewis be brought in to do a June 30 special audit. This was done and, to Sinclair & Lewis and the Maxwell's unpleasant surprise, it was discovered that WSI's lease receivable loss reserves were understated by approximately $16 million. This amount resulted in a violation of the company's lending agreement. This default eventually resulted in WSI's filing for bankruptcy, with eventual losses to the Maxwells in excess of $10 million. The Maxwells sued Sinclair & Lewis for breach of contract, claiming that they failed to properly conduct their audits of WSI, for at least the period 1990 through 1995, the period during which, the Maxwells and Riddell concluded, Vernon and other management personnel made misrepresentations to Sinclair & Lewis about the condition of many leases, misrepresentations that Sinclair & Lewis failed to find.

During the discovery portion of the litigation, the Maxwells' attorney deposed Harold Raines, the Sinclair & Lewis manager on the WSI audit. The following questions and answers are excerpted from that deposition.

Q. How long were you associated with the WSI audit, Mr. Raines?

A. Ever since we did it. I started as staff auditor on the job and worked my way up to manager.

Q. Have you ever been to a training program on auditing leasing companies?

A. No sir, WSI was so small, I guess the partners in our firm didn't think it was necessary. Besides, when you get right down to it, all audits are about the same. I don't think there is anything special about a leasing company audit.

Q. Have you ever read the AICPA Industry Audit Guide for Commercial Finance Companies?

A. I may have; I don't recall.

Q. What were the higher risk areas in the audit?

A. I'm not sure that I looked at it that way. We have a standard audit program where we try to do the appropriate things in all areas of the audit. Saying that one area is riskier than another doesn't make sense.

Q. How did you audit the lease loss reserve account?

A. We did several things:

- We asked for and received a delinquency list that showed all leases past due.
- We tested the completeness of the list by pulling a sample of lease cards and seeing that those we selected were on the delinquency list if they were overdue.
- We discussed the large delinquent leases with Mr. Vernon and obtained his estimate of the potential losses. We added those up and compared them to the loss reserve balance to judge its reasonableness.

Q. When you added the potential losses for December 31, 1995, what did they total in relation to the balance in the loss reserve account?

A. They were significantly less than the reserve account balance. As I recall, the reserve account balance was about $3 million and the sum of the potential losses was only about $2.7 million.

Q. And you believe that indicates that the overall loss reserve was adequate to cover all losses?

A. Well, yes. But more important, WSI thought it was. They said so in their representations letter to us that we obtained at the end of the audit.

Q. As I understand it, in the closing conference for the audit, Mr. Vernon told you that ABC Manufacturing, one of their largest customers, had filed bankruptcy at about year end, yet that lease wasn't on the delinquency list. Didn't that cause you concern that the delinquency list might not be complete?

A. No, not really. After all, Mr. Vernon volunteered the information. Also, when I weighed ten years of good experience with Mr. Vernon against that one incident, I certainly felt he was as trustworthy as ever.

## Required

a. Analyze Raines's responses to the questions posed in terms of possible violations by Sinclair & Lewis of generally accepted auditing standards.

b. Assuming Sinclair & Lewis did fail to comply with generally accepted auditing standards in its audit of WSI, what should its responsibility be for damages relative to the responsibility of the other parties involved?

# 5

# AUDIT RESPONSIBILITIES AND OBJECTIVES

## LEARNING OBJECTIVES

Thorough study of this chapter will enable you to

- **5-1** Know the objective of conducting an audit of financial statements.
- **5-2** Describe management's responsibilities in preparing financial statements.
- **5-3** Describe the auditor's responsibilities to verify financial statements and discover material errors, fraud, and illegal acts.
- **5-4** Describe the financial-statement-cycles approach to segmenting the audit.
- **5-5** Describe why the auditor obtains assurance by auditing classes of transactions and ending balances in accounts.
- **5-6** Identify the five categories of management assertions about financial information.
- **5-7** Identify the six general transaction-related audit objectives, explain their purpose, and relate them to management assertions.
- **5-8** Identify the nine general balance-related audit objectives, explain their purpose, and relate them to management assertions.
- **5-9** Describe the process by which audit objectives are met, and use it as a basis for further study.

## WHERE WERE THE AUDITORS?

Barry Minkow was a true "whiz kid." He started his own business as a teenager, and by the time he was in his early twenties, he was the chief executive officer of ZZZZ Best Company, a high-flying carpet cleaning company specializing in insurance restoration contracts. Minkow started the company in 1982, at the age of sixteen, operating out of his garage. In 1984 the company earned less than $200,000, but was experiencing incredible growth. Minkow took the company public in 1986, and in 1987, the company had sales of $50 million and earnings of over $5 million. The market value of Minkow's stock in ZZZZ Best exceeded $100 million.

As it turned out, Minkow's genius lay not in business, but in deception. Instead of being a solid operation company, ZZZZ Best was an illusion. There were no large restoration jobs and no real revenues and profits; they were only on paper and supported by an effective network of methods to deceive shareholders, the SEC, and the reputable professionals who served the company, including its auditors. Many, including members of Congress asked, "How could this happen? Where were the auditors?"

When ZZZZ Best first started to grow, Minkow ran into the common problem of needing credit. He devised a scheme to conspire with an insurance claims adjuster to confirm over the telephone to banks and other creditors the validity of Minkow's alleged insurance restoration contracts. When ZZZZ Best had its first audit, for the fiscal year ended April 30, 1986, this conspiracy had grown to the point where the adjuster ran a captive company whose job it was to generate fake contracts for ZZZZ Best. The company's auditor confirmed the existing restoration contracts with the adjuster—all part of the conspiracy.

ZZZZ Best decided in 1987, at the request of their investment banker, to engage a "Big Eight" firm to do its audit. Although the engaged firm resigned from the ZZZZ Best audit before they issued their report, they completed a number of auditing procedures. Among these were visits to the sites of major restoration projects. The underlying contracts were bogus, of course, but the sites appeared to be real. To deceive the auditors, Minkow devised ways of finding actual buildings undergoing construction and convincing the auditors that the construction was under ZZZZ Best's contract. In one case he leased a partially completed building and hired subcontractors to perform work on the site, all for the sake of a visit by the auditors.

As incredible as the ZZZZ Best story may seem, when asked about it, most knowledgeable observers would answer: "It's not the first time, and it won't be the last." It is also not the last time people will ask, "Where were the auditors?"

The study of evidence accumulation begins with this chapter. It is necessary first to understand the objectives of an audit and the way the auditor approaches accumulating evidence. Those are the most important topics covered in this chapter. Figure 5-1 summarizes the five topics that provide keys to understanding evidence accumulation; these are the steps used to develop audit objectives.

Figure 5-2 presents the December 31, 1996 financial statements of Hillsburg Hardware Company. The adjusted trial balance from which the financial statements were prepared is included in Figure 5-3 (page 141). These financial statements will be used as a frame of reference for subsequent discussion. Footnotes and the statement of cash flows have been excluded to keep the discussion as simple as practical. Assume that Ross and Co., CPAs, audited the December 31, 1995 financial statements and are also doing the 1996 audit.

**FIGURE 5-1**

**Steps to Develop Audit Objectives**

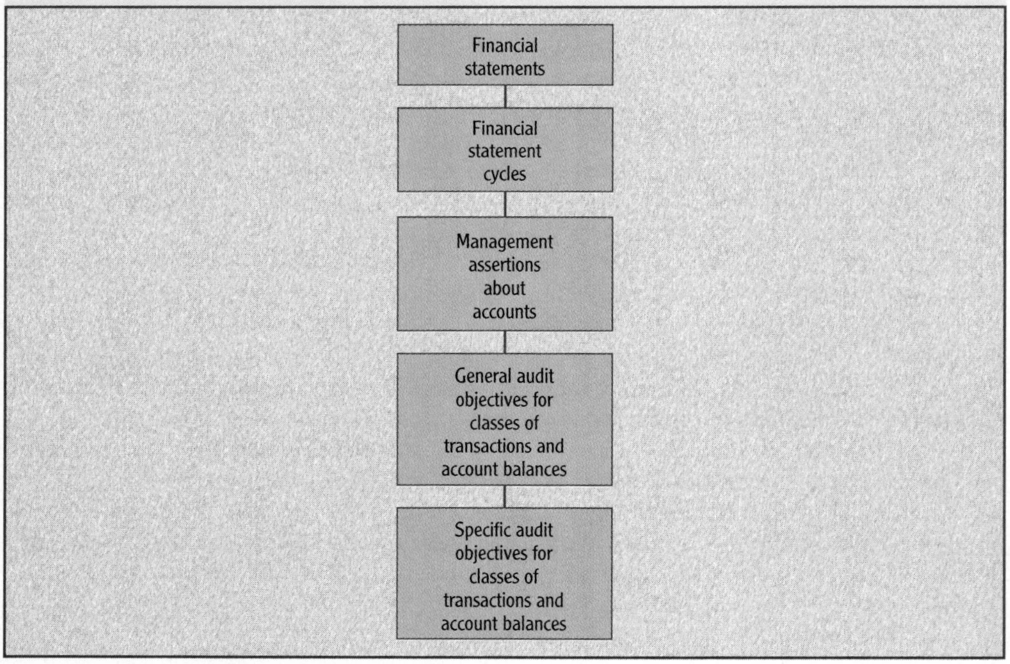

**FIGURE 5-4**

**Coca-Cola Bottling Co. Consolidated's Report of Management**

**REPORT OF MANAGEMENT**

The management of Coca-Cola Bottling Co. Consolidated is responsible for the preparation and integrity of the consolidated financial statements of the Company. The financial statements and notes have been prepared by the Company in accordance with generally accepted accounting principles and, in the judgment of management, present fairly the Company's financial position and results of operations. The financial information contained elsewhere in this annual report is consistent with that in the financial statements. The financial statements and other financial information in this annual report include amounts that are based on management's best estimates and judgments and give due consideration to materiality.

The Company maintains a system of internal accounting controls to provide reasonable assurance that assets are safeguarded and that transactions are executed in accordance with management's authorization and recorded properly to permit the preparation of financial statements in accordance with generally accepted accounting principles.

The Internal Audit Department of the Company reviews, evaluates, monitors and makes recommendations on both administrative and accounting controls, and acts as an integral, but independent part of the system of internal controls.

The Company's independent accountants were engaged to perform an audit of the consolidated financial statements. This audit provides an objective outside review of management's responsibility to report operating results and financial condition. Working with the Company's internal auditors, they review and perform tests, as appropriate, of the data included in the financial statements.

The Board of Directors discharges its responsibility for the Company's financial statements primarily through its Audit Committee. The Audit Committee meets periodically with the independent accountants, internal auditors and management. Both the independent accountants and internal auditors have direct access to the Audit Committee to discuss the scope and results of their work, the adequacy of internal accounting controls, and the quality of financial reporting.

James L. Moore, Jr.
President and Chief Operating Officer

David V. Singer
Vice President and Chief Financial Officer

This paragraph and the related discussion in the standards includes several important terms and phrases.

**Material Versus Immaterial Misstatements** Misstatements are usually considered material if the combined uncorrected errors and fraud in the financial statements would likely have changed or influenced the decisions of a reasonable person using the statements. Although it is extremely difficult to quantify a measure of materiality, auditors are responsible for obtaining reasonable assurance that this materiality threshold has been satisfied. It would be extremely costly (and probably impossible) for auditors to have responsibility for finding all immaterial errors and fraud.

**Reasonable Assurance** Assurance is a measure of the level of certainty that the auditor has obtained at the completion of the audit. Reasonable assurance is not defined in the literature, but it is presumably less than certainty or absolute assurance and more than a low level of assurance.

The concept of reasonable, but not absolute, assurance indicates that the auditor is not an insurer or guarantor of the correctness of the financial statements. If the auditor were responsible for making certain that all the assertions in the statements were correct, evidence requirements and the resulting cost of the audit function would increase to such an extent that audits would not be economically practical. The auditor's best defense when material misstatements are not uncovered in the audit is that the audit was conducted in accordance with generally accepted auditing standards.

**Errors Versus Fraud** SAS 82 (AU 316) distinguishes between two types of misstatements: *errors* and *fraud*. Either type of misstatement can be material or immaterial. An error is an *unintentional* misstatement of the financial statements, whereas fraud is *intentional*. Two examples of errors are a mistake in extending prices times quantity on a sales invoice and overlooking older raw materials in determining the lower of cost or market for inventory.

For fraud, there is a distinction between *misappropriation of assets*, often called defalcation or employee fraud, and *fraudulent financial reporting*, often called management fraud. An example of misappropriation of assets is a clerk taking cash at the time a sale is made and not entering the sale in the cash register. An example of fraudulent financial reporting is the intentional overstatement of sales near the balance sheet date to increase reported earnings.

**Professional Skepticism** SAS 1 (AU 230) requires that an audit be designed to provide reasonable assurance of detecting *both* material errors and fraud in the financial statements. To accomplish this, the audit must be planned and performed with an *attitude of professional skepticism* in all aspects of the engagement. Professional skepticism is an attitude that includes a questioning mind and a critical assessment of audit evidence. The auditor should not assume that management is dishonest, but the possibility of dishonesty must be considered.

## Auditor's Responsibilities for Detecting Material Errors

Auditors spend a great portion of their time planning and performing audits to detect the unintentional mistakes made by management and employees. Auditors find a variety of errors resulting from such things as mistakes in calculation, omissions, misunderstanding and misapplication of accounting standards, and incorrect summarizations and descriptions. Most of the remainder of the book deals with how the auditor plans and performs audits for detecting both errors and fraud.

## Auditor's Responsibilities for Detecting Material Fraud

Auditing standards make no distinction between the auditor's responsibilities for searching for errors and fraud, whether from fraudulent financial reporting or misappropriation of assets. For both errors and fraud, the auditor must obtain reasonable assurance about whether the statements are free of material misstatements.

The standards also recognize that it is frequently more difficult to detect fraud than errors because management or the employees perpetrating the fraud *attempt to conceal the*

**AUDITING STANDARDS BOARD ISSUES SAS 82, *CONSIDERATION OF FRAUD IN A FINANCIAL STATEMENT AUDIT***

The Auditing Standards Board and its predecessor organizations have repeatedly addressed the difficult problem of stating the auditor's responsibility for detecting fraud in audits. In 1997, the Board issued a new standard, SAS 82, *Consideration of Fraud in a Financial Statement Audit.* This lengthy standard addresses many significant fraud-related issues, including the following especially important ones.

The standard does not change the auditor's responsibility that previously existed for finding fraud in audits. The standard continues to "require the auditor to plan and perform the audit to obtain reasonable assurance about whether the financial statements are free of material misstatement, whether caused by error or fraud." The standard does change the guidance to auditors in what they should do to meet their responsibilities. Following are the five areas in which guidance is provided:

- Requires the auditor to specifically assess and document whether there is a heightened risk of fraud in each audit.
- Provides categories of fraud risk factors that should be considered in the auditor's assessment.
- Provides guidance about how the auditor should respond when there is a heightened risk of fraud.
- Provides guidance on the evaluation of audit test results as they relate to the risk of fraud.
- Provides guidance regarding the communication about fraud to management, the audit committee, and others.

*fraud*. The difficulty of detection does not change the auditor's responsibility to properly plan and perform the audit.

An important part of planning every audit is to assess the risk of errors and fraud. Risk assessment for both errors and fraud is discussed in detail in Chapter 8. The discussion that follows deals only with the risk assessment requirements for fraud outlined in SAS 82.

In making a risk assessment for fraud, it is useful to keep in mind that fraud typically includes two characteristics. The auditor's risk assessment for fraud focuses on both of these two characteristics, which are:

- *Pressure or incentive to commit the fraud.* Frequently this pressure is a desire for direct financial gain in the case of misappropriation of assets, or an indirect gain in the case of fraudulent financial reporting. The gain in the second case may be, for example, an increase in the market value of company shares held by management.
- *Perceived opportunity to commit the fraud.* Even though there is an incentive to commit fraud, it is unlikely to occur unless the individual or individuals involved believe they can do so without being detected.

**Fraud Resulting from Fraudulent Financial Reporting Versus Misappropriation of Assets** There is an important difference between fraudulent financial reporting and misappropriation of assets. Fraudulent financial reporting harms users by providing incorrect financial statement information for their decision making. When assets are misappropriated, stockholders, creditors, and others are harmed because assets are no longer available to their rightful owners. Both types of fraud are potentially harmful to users.

Typically, fraudulent financial reporting is committed by management, sometimes without the knowledge of employees. Management is in a position to make accounting and reporting decisions without employees' knowledge. An example is the decision to omit an important footnote about pending litigation.

Usually, but not always, theft of assets is perpetrated by employees and not by management, and the amounts are often immaterial. There are, however, well-known examples of extremely material misappropriation of assets by employees and management.

An important concept for misappropriation of assets is the distinction between the theft of assets and misstatements arising from the theft of assets. To illustrate, following are three situations involving the theft of assets:

1. Assets were taken and the theft was covered by overstating assets. The misstatements have not been discovered.
2. Assets were taken and the theft was covered by understating revenues or overstating expenses. The misstatements have not been discovered.
3. Assets were taken, but the misappropriation was discovered. The income statement and related footnotes clearly describe the misappropriations.

In all three situations, there has been a misappropriation of assets, but the financial statements are misstated only in situations 1 and 2. In situation 1, the balance sheet is misstated, whereas in situation 2, revenues or expenses are misstated.

## Assessing Risks of Fraud

An important part of SAS 82 is the requirement that auditors specifically assess the risk of material misstatement due to fraud. The risk factors for fraudulent financial reporting are different than those for misappropriation of assets because the nature of the fraud is different.

For fraudulent financial reporting, three categories of risk factors are identified in SAS 82. For each category, the standard includes examples of these risk factors to provide guidance to practitioners. The three categories of risk factors and examples for each category are included in Table 5-1 (page 146).

The risk factors that auditors assess for misappropriation of assets are somewhat different than those for fraudulent financial reporting. The two categories of risk factors for misappropriation of assets and examples for each category are shown in Table 5-2 (page 146).

**TABLE 5–1**

**The Three SAS 82 Categories of Risk Factors for Fraudulent Financial Reporting and Three Examples of Each**

| CATEGORY 1<br>Management's Characteristics and Influence over the Control Environment | CATEGORY 2<br>Industry Conditions | CATEGORY 3<br>Operating Characteristics and Financial Stability |
|---|---|---|
| These pertain to management's abilities, pressures, style, and attitude relating to internal control and the financial reporting process. | These involve the economic and regulatory environment in which the entity operates. | These pertain to the nature and complexity of the entity and its transactions, financial condition, and profitability. |
| Examples of Risk Factors<br>• A motivation for management to engage in fraudulent financial reporting, such as an excessive interest by management to maintain or increase the entity's stock price or earnings trend through the use of unusually aggressive accounting practices.<br>• A failure by management to display and communicate an appropriate attitude regarding internal control and the financial reporting process, such as domination of management by a single person or small group without compensating controls.<br>• High turnover of senior management, counsel, or board members. | Examples of Risk Factors<br>• New accounting, statutory, or regulatory requirements that could impair the financial stability or profitability of the entity.<br>• Declining industry with increasing business failures and significant declines in customer demand.<br>• Rapid changes in the industry, such as high vulnerability to rapidly changing technology or rapid product obsolescence. | Examples of Risk Factors<br>• Significant pressure to obtain additional capital necessary to stay competitive considering the financial position of the entity.<br>• Significant, unusual, or highly complex transactions, especially those close to year-end, that pose difficult "substance over form" questions.<br>• Overly complex organizational structure involving numerous or unusual legal entities, managerial lines of authority, or contractual arrangements without apparent business purpose. |

For both fraudulent financial reporting and misappropriation of assets, the auditor must also:

- Make inquiries of management about their assessment of the likelihood of fraud.
- Evaluate the risk of fraud as the audit proceeds. Frequently, the auditor's perception of the likelihood of fraud changes as he or she performs audit procedures and makes inquiries of management throughout the audit. For example, important missing documents or records may affect the auditor's assessment of the likelihood of fraud.

**TABLE 5-2**

**The Two SAS 82 Categories of Risk Factors for Misappropriation of Assets and Three Examples of Each**

| CATEGORY 1<br>Susceptibility of Assets to Misappropriation | CATEGORY 2<br>Controls |
|---|---|
| These pertain to the nature of an entity's assets and the degree to which they are subject to theft. | These involve the lack of controls designed to prevent or detect misappropriations of assets. |
| Examples of Risk Factors<br>• Large amounts of cash on hand or processed.<br>• Easily convertible assets, such as bearer bonds, diamonds, or computer chips.<br>• Fixed asset characteristics, such as small size, marketability, or lack of ownership identification. | Examples of Risk Factors<br>• Lack of appropriate management oversight, such as inadequate supervision or monitoring of remote locations.<br>• Inadequate record keeping with respect to assets susceptible to misappropriation.<br>• Lack of timely and appropriate documentation for transactions, such as credits for merchandise returns. |

**Evaluating Risk Factors and Modifying Evidence or Taking Other Action** After the auditor has identified risk factors indicating a higher than normal potential for fraud, the auditor must decide the potential for fraud and what to do about it. These decisions are complex and require considerable professional judgment. SAS 82 provides guidance to help the auditor make these decisions. In concept, the process is the same for errors, fraudulent financial reporting, and misappropriation of assets. The specific effects will, of course, depend on the circumstances. This evaluation process is studied in Chapter 8 through the end of this book.

## Auditor's Responsibilities for Discovering Illegal Acts

Illegal acts are defined in SAS 54 (AU 317) as violations of laws or government regulations *other than fraud.* Two examples of illegal acts are a violation of federal tax laws and a violation of the federal environmental protection laws.

**Direct-Effect Illegal Acts** Certain violations of laws and regulations have a direct financial effect on specific account balances in the financial statements. For example, a violation of federal tax laws directly affects income tax expense and income taxes payable. The auditor's responsibilities under SAS 54 for these direct-effect illegal acts is the same as for errors and fraud. On each audit, therefore, the auditor will normally evaluate whether or not there is evidence available to indicate material violations of federal or state tax laws. This might be done by discussions with client personnel and examination of reports issued by the Internal Revenue Service after they have completed an examination of the client's tax return.

**Indirect-Effect Illegal Acts** Most illegal acts affect the financial statements only indirectly. For example, if the company violates environmental protection laws, there is an effect on the financial statements only if there is a fine or sanction. This is called an indirect-effect illegal act. Other examples of illegal acts that are likely to have only an indirect effect are violations of insider securities trading regulations, civil rights laws, and federal employee safety requirements.

Auditing standards clearly state that the auditor provides *no assurance* that indirect-effect illegal acts will be detected. Auditors lack legal expertise, and the frequent indirect relationship between illegal acts and the financial statements makes it impractical for auditors to assume responsibility for discovering those illegal acts.

There are three levels of responsibility that the auditor has for finding and reporting illegal acts.

**Evidence Accumulation When There Is No Reason to Believe Indirect-Effect Illegal Acts Exist** Many audit procedures normally performed on audits to search for errors and fraud may also uncover illegal acts. Examples include reading the minutes of the board of directors and inquiring of the client's attorneys about litigation. The auditor should also inquire of management about policies they have established to prevent illegal acts and whether management knows of any laws or regulations that the company has violated. Other than these procedures, the auditor should not search for indirect-effect illegal acts unless there is reason to believe they may exist.

**Evidence Accumulation and Other Actions When There Is Reason to Believe Direct- or Indirect-Effect Illegal Acts May Exist** The auditor may find indications of possible illegal acts in a variety of ways. For example, the minutes may indicate that an investigation by a government agency is in process or the auditor may have identified unusually large payments to consultants or government officials.

When the auditor believes that an illegal act may have occurred, it is necessary to take several actions: First, the auditor should inquire of management at a level above those likely to be involved in the potential illegal act. Second, the auditor should consult with the client's legal counsel or other specialist who is knowledgeable about the potential illegal act. Third, the auditor should consider accumulating additional evidence to determine if there actually is an illegal act. All three of these actions are intended to provide the auditor information about whether the suspected illegal act actually exists.

**Actions When the Auditor Knows of an Illegal Act** The first course of action when an illegal act has been identified is to consider the effects on the financial statements, including the adequacy of disclosures. These effects may be complex and difficult to resolve. For example, a violation of civil rights laws could involve significant fines, but it could also result in the loss of customers or key employees that could materially affect future revenues and expenses. If the auditor concludes that the disclosures relative to an illegal act are inadequate, the auditor should modify the audit report accordingly.

The auditor should also consider the effect of such illegal acts on its relationship with management. If management knew of the illegal act and failed to inform the auditor, it is questionable whether management can be believed in other discussions.

The auditor should communicate with the audit committee or others of equivalent authority to make sure that they know of the illegal act. If the client either refuses to accept the auditor's modified report or fails to take appropriate remedial action concerning the illegal act, the auditor may find it necessary to withdraw from the engagement. If the client is publicly held, the auditor must also report the matter directly to the SEC. Such decisions are complex and normally involve consultation by the auditor with the auditor's legal counsel.

## FINANCIAL STATEMENT CYCLES

**OBJECTIVE 5-4**
**Describe the financial-statement-cycles approach to segmenting the audit.**

Audits are performed by dividing the financial statements into smaller segments or components. The division makes the audit more manageable and aids in the assignment of tasks to different members of the audit team. For example, most auditors treat fixed assets and notes payable as different segments. Each segment is audited separately but not completely independently. (For example, the audit of fixed assets may reveal an unrecorded note payable.) After the audit of each segment is completed, including interrelationships with other segments, the results are combined. A conclusion can then be reached about the financial statements taken as a whole.

There are different ways of segmenting an audit. Referring to the financial statements in Figure 5-2, one obvious approach would be to treat every account balance on the statements as a separate segment. Segmenting that way is usually inefficient. It would result in the independent audit of such closely related accounts as inventory and cost of goods sold.

### Cycle Approach to Segmenting an Audit

A more common way to divide an audit is to keep closely related types (or classes) of transactions and account balances in the same segment. This is called the *cycle approach.* For example, sales, sales returns, cash receipts, and charge-offs of uncollectible accounts are the four classes of transactions that cause accounts receivable to increase and decrease. They are therefore all part of the sales and collection cycle. Similarly, payroll transactions and accrued payroll are a part of the payroll and personnel cycle.

The logic of using the cycle approach can be seen by thinking about the way transactions are recorded in journals and summarized in the general ledger and financial statements. Figure 5-5 on the following page shows that flow. To the extent that it is practical, the cycle approach combines transactions recorded in different journals with the general ledger balances that result from those transactions.

The cycles used in this text are shown in Table 5-3 on page 150. The journals associated with each cycle for Hillsburg Hardware Co. as well as the 1996 financial statement accounts are included.

The following observations expand the information contained in Table 5-3:

- All general ledger accounts and journals for Hillsburg Hardware Co. are included at least once. For a different company, the number and titles of journals and general ledger accounts would differ, but all would be included.
- Some journals and general ledger accounts are included in more than one cycle. When that occurs, it means that the journal is used to record transactions from more than one cycle and indicates a tie-in between the cycles. The most important general ledger

**FIGURE 5-5**

**Transaction Flow from Journals to Financial Statements**

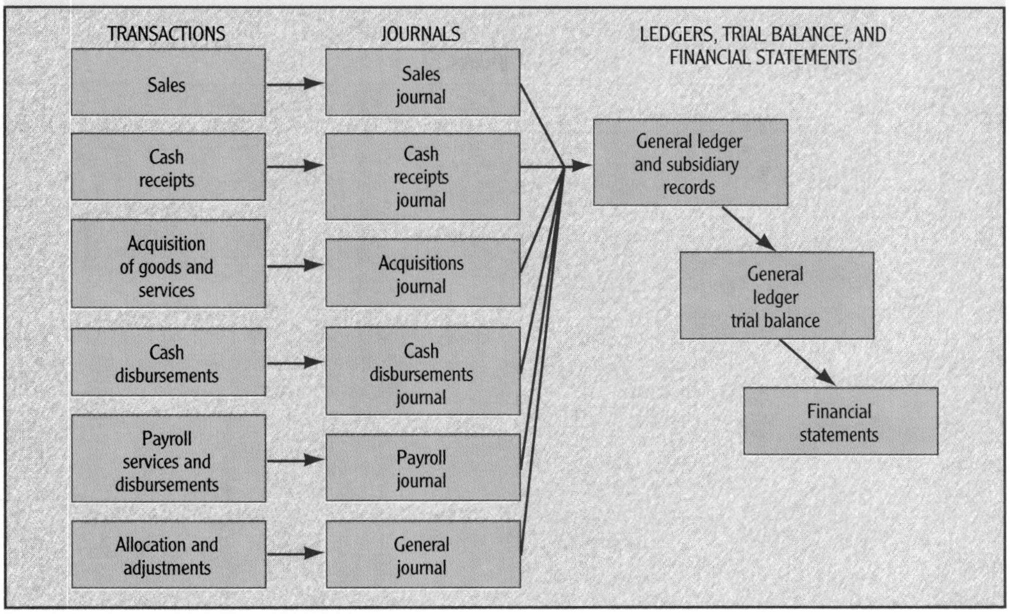


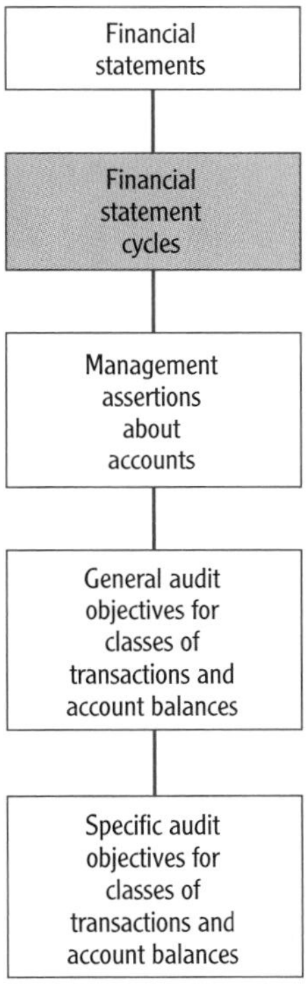


account included in and affecting several cycles is general cash (cash in bank). General cash connects most cycles.

- The capital acquisition and repayment cycle is closely related to the acquisition and payment cycle. The same three journals are used to record transactions for both cycles, and the transactions are similar. There are two reasons for treating capital acquisition and repayment separately from the acquisition of goods and services. First, the transactions are related to financing a company rather than to its operations. Second, most capital acquisition and repayment cycle accounts involve few transactions, but each is often highly material and therefore should be audited extensively. Considering both reasons, it is more convenient to separate the two cycles.
- The inventory and warehousing cycle is closely related to all other cycles, especially for a manufacturing company. The cost of inventory includes raw materials (acquisition and payment cycle), direct labor (payroll and personnel cycle), and manufacturing overhead (acquisition and payment and payroll and personnel cycles). The sale of finished goods involves the sales and collection cycle. Because inventory is material for most manufacturing companies, it is common to borrow money using inventory as security. In those cases, the capital acquisition and repayment cycle is also related to inventory and warehousing.

## Relationships Among Cycles

Figure 5-6 on page 151 illustrates the relationships of the cycles. In addition to the five cycles, general cash is also shown. Each cycle is studied in detail in later chapters.

Figure 5-6 shows that cycles have no beginning or end except at the origin and final disposition of a company. A company begins by obtaining capital, usually in the form of cash. In a manufacturing company, cash is used to acquire raw materials, fixed assets, and related goods and services to produce inventory (acquisition and payment cycle). Cash is also used to acquire labor for the same reason (payroll and personnel cycle). Acquisition and payment and payroll and personnel are similar in nature, but the functions are sufficiently different to justify separate cycles. The combined result of these two cycles is inventory (inventory and warehousing cycle). At a subsequent point, the inventory is sold and billings and collections result (sales and collection cycle). The cash generated is used to pay

**TABLE 5-3**

**Cycles Applied to Hillsburg Hardware Co.**

| | | General Ledger Account Included in the Cycle (See Figure 5-3) | |
|---|---|---|---|
| **Cycle** | **Journals Included in the Cycle (See Figure 5-5)** | **Balance Sheet** | **Income Statement** |
| Sales and collection | Sales journal<br>Cash receipts journal<br>General journal | Cash in bank<br>Trade accounts receivable<br>Other accounts receivable<br>Allowance for uncollectible accounts | Sales<br>Sales returns and allowances<br>Bad debt expense |
| Acquisition and payment | Acquisitions journal<br>Cash disbursements journal<br>General journal | Cash in bank<br>Inventories<br>Prepaid expenses<br>Land<br>Buildings<br>Delivery equipment<br>Furniture and fixtures<br>Accumulated depreciation<br>Trade accounts payable<br>Other accrued payables<br>Estimated income tax<br>Deferred tax | Advertising[S]<br>Travel and entertainment[S]<br>Sales meetings and training[S]<br>Sales and promotional literature[S]<br>Miscellaneous sales expense[S]<br>Travel and entertainment[A]<br>Stationery and supplies[A]<br>Postage[A]<br>Telephone and telegraph[A]<br>Dues and memberships[A]<br>Taxes[A]<br>Depreciation—office building and equipment[A]<br>Rent[A]<br>Legal fees and retainers[A]<br>Auditing[A]<br>Insurance[A]<br>Office repairs and maintenance expense[A]<br>Miscellaneous office expense[A]<br>Miscellaneous general expense[A]<br>Gain on sale of assets<br>Income taxes |
| Payroll and personnel | Payroll journal<br>General journal | Cash in bank<br>Accrued payroll<br>Accrued payroll taxes | Salaries and commissions[S]<br>Sales payroll taxes[S]<br>Executive and office salaries[A]<br>Administrative payroll taxes[A] |
| Inventory and warehousing | Acquisitions journal<br>Sales journal<br>General journal | Inventories | Cost of goods sold |
| Capital acquisition and repayment | Acquisitions journal<br>Cash disbursements journal<br>General journal | Cash in bank<br>Notes payable<br>Long-term notes payable<br>Accrued interest<br>Capital stock<br>Capital in excess of par value<br>Retained earnings<br>Dividends<br>Dividends payable | Interest expense |

S = Selling expense
A = General and administrative expense

dividends and interest and to start the cycles again. The cycles interrelate in much the same way in a service company, where there will be no inventory, but there may be unbilled receivables.

Transaction cycles are of major importance in the conduct of the audit. For the most part, auditors treat each cycle separately during the audit. Although care should be taken to interrelate different cycles at different times, the auditor must treat the cycles somewhat independently in order to manage complex audits effectively.

**FIGURE 5-6**

**Relationships Among Transaction Cycles**

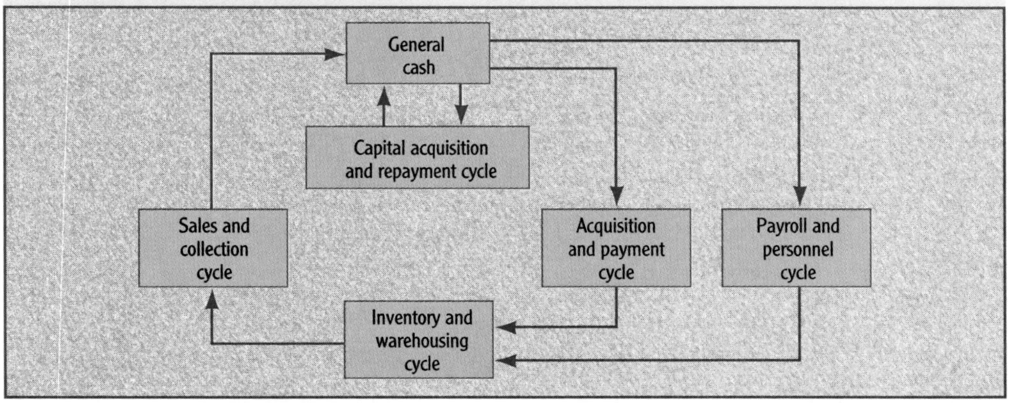


## SETTING AUDIT OBJECTIVES

**OBJECTIVE 5-5**

**Describe why the auditor obtains assurance by auditing classes of transactions and ending balances in accounts.**

Auditors conduct audits consistently with the cycle approach by performing audit tests of the transactions making up ending balances and also by performing audit tests of the account balances themselves. Figure 5-7 illustrates this important concept by showing the four classes of transactions that determine the ending balance in accounts receivable. Assume that the beginning balance of $96 was audited in the prior year and is therefore considered reliable. If the auditor could be completely sure that each of the four classes of transactions was correctly stated, the auditor could also be sure that the ending balance of $166 was correctly stated. But it may be impractical for the auditor to obtain complete assurance about the correctness of each class of transactions resulting in less than complete assurance about the ending balance in accounts receivable. In such a case, overall assurance can be increased by auditing the ending balance of accounts receivable. Auditors have found that, generally, the most efficient way to conduct audits is to *obtain some combination of assurance for each class of transactions and for the ending balance in the related account.*

**FIGURE 5-7**

**Balances and Transactions Affecting Those Balances for Accounts Receivable**

| Accounts Receivable | | | |
|---|---|---|---|
| Beginning balance | $ 96 | | |
| Sales | $660 | $590 | Cash receipts |
| | | 0 | Sales returns and allowances |
| | | 0 | Charge-off of uncollectible accounts |
| Ending balance | $166 | | |

For any given class of transactions, there are several audit objectives that must be met before the auditor can conclude that the total is fairly stated. They are called *transaction-related audit objectives* in the remainder of this book. For example, there are specific sales transaction-related audit objectives and specific sales returns and allowances transaction-related audit objectives.

Similarly, there are several audit objectives that must be met for each account balance. They are called *balance-related audit objectives.* For example, there are specific accounts receivable balance-related audit objectives and specific accounts payable balance-related audit objectives. It will be shown later that the transaction-related and balance-related audit objectives are somewhat different but closely related. Throughout the remainder of this text, the term *audit objectives* refers to both transaction-related and balance-related audit objectives.

Before examining audit objectives in more detail, it is necessary to understand management assertions. These are studied next.

## Management Assertions

**OBJECTIVE 5-6**
**Identify the five categories of management assertions about financial information.**

Assertions are implied or expressed representations by management about classes of transactions and the related accounts in the financial statements. As an illustration, the management of Hillsburg Hardware Co. asserts that cash of $41,000 (see Figure 5-2) was present in the company's bank accounts or on the premises as of the balance sheet date. Unless otherwise disclosed in the financial statements, management also asserts that the cash was unrestricted and available for normal use. Similar assertions exist for each asset, liability, owners' equity, revenue, and expense item in the financial statements. These assertions apply to both classes of transactions and account balances.

Management assertions are directly related to generally accepted accounting principles. These assertions are part of the *criteria that management uses to record and disclose accounting information in financial statements.* Return to the definition of auditing at the beginning of Chapter 1. It states, in part, that auditing is a comparison of information (financial statements) to established criteria (assertions established according to generally accepted accounting principles). Auditors must therefore understand the assertions to do adequate audits.

SAS 31 (AU 326) classifies assertions into five broad categories:

1. Existence or occurrence
2. Completeness
3. Valuation or allocation
4. Rights and obligations
5. Presentation and disclosure

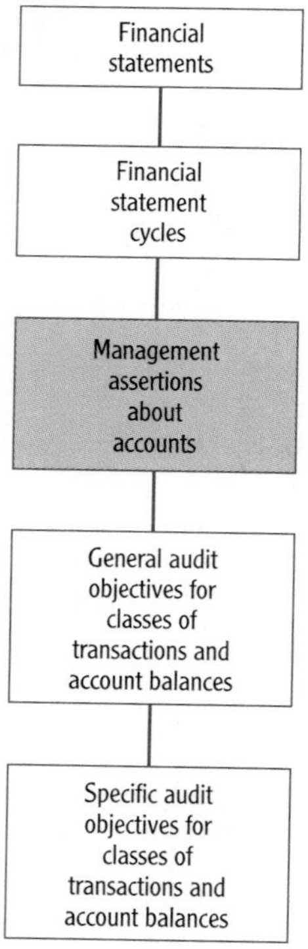


**Assertions about Existence or Occurrence** Assertions about existence deal with whether assets, obligations, and equities included in the balance sheet actually existed on the balance sheet date. Assertions about occurrence concern whether recorded transactions included in the financial statements actually occurred during the accounting period. For example, management asserts that merchandise inventory included in the balance sheet exists and is available for sale at the balance sheet date. Similarly, management asserts that recorded sales transactions represent exchanges of goods or services that actually took place.

**Assertions about Completeness** These management assertions state that all transactions and accounts that should be presented in the financial statements are included. For example, management asserts that all sales of goods and services are recorded and included in the financial statements. Similarly, management asserts that notes payable in the balance sheet include all such obligations of the entity.

The completeness assertion deals with matters opposite from those of the existence or occurrence assertion. The completeness assertion is concerned with the possibility of omitting items from the financial statements that should have been included, whereas the existence or occurrence assertion is concerned with inclusion of amounts that should not have been included.

Thus, recording a sale that did not take place would be a violation of the occurrence assertion, whereas the failure to record a sale that did occur would be a violation of the completeness assertion.

**Assertions about Valuation or Allocation** These assertions deal with whether asset, liability, equity, revenue, and expense accounts have been included in the financial statements at appropriate amounts. For example, management asserts that property is recorded at historical cost and that such cost is systematically allocated to appropriate accounting periods through depreciation. Similarly, management asserts that trade accounts receivable included in the balance sheet are stated at net realizable value.

**Assertions about Rights and Obligations** These management assertions deal with whether assets are the rights of the entity and liabilities are the obligations of the entity at a given date. For example, management asserts that assets are owned by the company or that amounts capitalized for leases in the balance sheet represent the cost of the entity's rights to leased property and that the corresponding lease liability represents an obligation of the entity.

**Assertions about Presentation and Disclosure** These assertions deal with whether components of the financial statements are properly combined or separated, described, and disclosed. For example, management asserts that obligations classified as long-term liabilities in the balance sheet will not mature within one year. Similarly, management asserts that amounts presented as extraordinary items in the income statement are properly classified and described.

## TRANSACTION-RELATED AUDIT OBJECTIVES

**OBJECTIVE 5-7**
**Identify the six general transaction-related audit objectives, explain their purpose, and relate them to management assertions.**

The auditor's transaction-related audit objectives follow and are closely related to management assertions. That is not surprising, since the auditor's primary responsibility is to determine whether management assertions about financial statements are justified.

These transaction-related audit objectives are intended to provide a *framework* to help the auditor accumulate sufficient competent evidence required by the third standard of field work and decide the proper evidence to accumulate for classes of transactions given the circumstances of the engagement. The objectives remain the same from audit to audit, but the evidence varies, depending on the circumstances.

A distinction must be made between *general transaction-related audit objectives* and *specific transaction-related audit objectives* for each class of transactions. The general transaction-related audit objectives discussed here are applicable to every class of transactions but are stated in broad terms. Specific transaction-related audit objectives are also applied to each class of transactions but are stated in terms tailored to a class of transactions such as sales transactions. Once you know the general transaction-related audit objectives, they can be used to develop specific transaction-related audit objectives for each class of transactions being audited. The six general transaction-related audit objectives are discussed next.

### General Transaction-Related Audit Objectives

**Existence—Recorded Transactions Exist** This objective deals with whether recorded transactions have actually occurred. Inclusion of a sale in the sales journal when no sale occurred violates the existence objective. This objective is the auditor's counterpart to the management assertion of existence or occurrence.

**Completeness—Existing Transactions Are Recorded** This objective deals with whether all transactions that should be included in the journals have actually been included. Failure to include a sale in the sales journal and general ledger when a sale occurred violates the completeness objective. The objective is the counterpart to the management assertion of completeness.

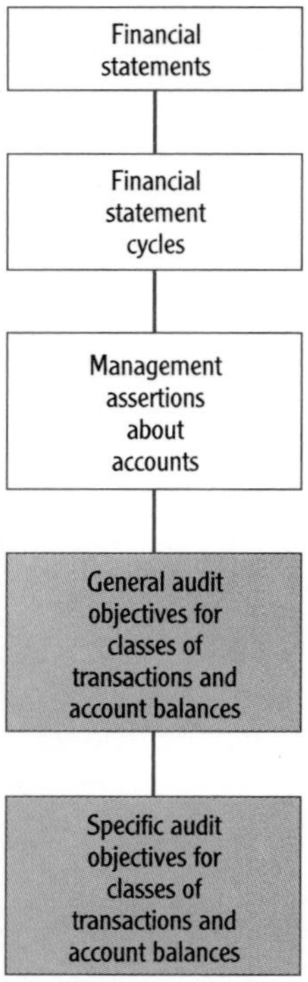


The existence and completeness objectives emphasize opposite audit concerns; existence deals with potential overstatement and completeness with unrecorded transactions (understatement).

**Accuracy—Recorded Transactions Are Stated at the Correct Amounts** This objective deals with the accuracy of information for accounting transactions. For sales transactions, there would be a violation of the accuracy objective if the quantity of goods shipped was different from the quantity billed, the wrong selling price was used for billing, extension or adding errors occurred in billing, or the wrong amount was included in the sales journal. Accuracy is one part of the valuation or allocation assertion.

**Classification—Transactions Included in the Client's Journals Are Properly Classified** Examples of misclassifications for sales are including cash sales as credit sales, recording a sale of operating fixed assets as revenue, and misclassifying commercial sales as residential sales. Classification is also a part of the valuation or allocation assertion.

**Timing—Transactions Are Recorded on the Correct Dates** A timing error occurs if transactions are not recorded on the dates the transactions took place. A sales transaction, for example, should be recorded on the date of shipment. Timing is also a part of the valuation or allocation assertion.

**Posting and Summarization—Recorded Transactions Are Properly Included in the Master Files and Are Correctly Summarized** This objective deals with the accuracy of the transfer of information from recorded transactions in journals to subsidy records and the general ledger. For example, if a sales transaction is recorded in the wrong customer's record or at the wrong amount in the master file, it is a violation of this objective. Posting and summarization is also a part of the valuation or allocation assertion.

### Specific Transaction-Related Audit Objectives

The general transaction-related audit objectives must be applied to each material type (class) of transaction in the audit. Such transactions typically include sales, cash receipts, acquisitions of goods and services, payroll, and so on. Table 5-4 on page 155 summarizes the six transaction-related audit objectives. It includes the general form of the objectives, the application of the objectives to sales transactions, and the assertions. Notice that only three assertions are associated with transaction-related audit objectives. This shows that two of the assertions are not satisfied by performing tests of controls and substantive tests of transactions.

## BALANCE-RELATED AUDIT OBJECTIVES

**OBJECTIVE 5-8**
**Identify the nine general balance-related audit objectives, explain their purpose, and relate them to management assertions.**

Balance-related audit objectives are similar to the transaction-related audit objectives just discussed. They also follow from management assertions and they provide a framework to help the auditor accumulate sufficient competent evidence. There are also both general and specific balance-related audit objectives.

There are two differences between balance-related and transaction-related audit objectives. First, as the terms imply, balance-related audit objectives are applied to account balances, whereas transaction-related audit objectives are applied to classes of transactions such as sales transactions and cash disbursements transactions. Because of the way audits are done, balance-related audit objectives are almost *always* applied to the ending balance in balance sheet accounts, such as accounts receivable, inventory, and notes payable. Second, there are more audit objectives for account balances than for classes of transactions. There are nine balance-related audit objectives compared to six transaction-related audit objectives.

**TABLE 5-4**

**Transaction-Related Audit Objectives and Management Assertions for Sales Transactions**

| Management Assertions | General Transaction-Related Audit Objectives | Specific Sales Transaction-Related Audit Objectives |
|---|---|---|
| Existence or occurrence | Existence | Recorded sales are for shipments made to nonfictitious customers. |
| Completeness | Completeness | Existing sales transactions are recorded. |
| Valuation or allocation | Accuracy | Recorded sales are for the amount of goods shipped and are correctly billed and recorded. |
| | Classification | Sales transactions are properly classified. |
| | Timing | Sales are recorded on the correct dates. |
| | Posting and summarization | Sales transactions are properly included in the master file and are correctly summarized. |
| Rights and obligations | N/A | N/A |
| Presentation and disclosure | N/A | N/A |

When using the balance-related audit objectives as a framework for auditing balance sheet account balances, the auditor accumulates evidence to verify detail that supports the account balance, rather than verifying the account balance itself. For example, in auditing accounts receivable, the auditor obtains a listing of the accounts receivable master file from the client that agrees to the general ledger balance (see page 452 for an illustration). The accounts receivable balance-related audit objectives are applied to the customer accounts in that listing.

Following is a brief discussion of the nine general balance-related audit objectives. Throughout the discussion, there is reference to a supporting schedule, which refers to a client-provided working paper such as the accounts receivable listing just described.

## General Balance-Related Audit Objectives

**Existence—Amounts Included Exist** This objective deals with whether the amounts included in the financial statements should actually be included. For example, inclusion of an account receivable from a customer in the accounts receivable trial balance when there is no receivable from that customer violates the existence objective. This objective is the auditor's counterpart to the management assertion of existence or occurrence.

**Completeness—Existing Amounts Are Included** This objective deals with whether all amounts that should be included have actually been included. Failure to include an account receivable from a customer in the accounts receivable trial balance when a receivable exists violates the completeness objective. This objective is the counterpart to the management assertion of completeness.

The existence and completeness objectives emphasize opposite audit concerns; existence deals with potential overstatement and completeness with unrecorded transactions and amounts (understatement).

**Accuracy—Amounts Included Are Stated at the Correct Amounts** The accuracy objective refers to amounts being included at the correct arithmetic amount. An inventory item on a client's inventory listing could be wrong because the number of units of inventory on hand was misstated, the unit price was wrong, or the total was incorrectly extended. Each of these violates the accuracy objective. Accuracy is one part of the valuation or allocation assertion.

**Classification—Amounts Included in the Client's Listing Are Properly Classified** Classification involves determining whether items on a client's listing are included in the correct accounts. For example, on the accounts receivable listing, receivables must be separated into short-term and long-term, and amounts due from affiliates, officers, and directors must be classified separately from amounts due from customers. Classification is also a part of the valuation or allocation assertion.

**Cutoff—Transactions Near the Balance Sheet Date Are Recorded in the Proper Period** In testing for cutoff, the objective is to determine whether transactions are recorded in the proper period. The transactions that are most likely to be misstated are those recorded near the end of the accounting period. It is proper to think of cutoff tests as a part of verifying either the balance sheet accounts or the related transactions, but for convenience auditors usually perform them as a part of auditing balance sheet accounts. Cutoff is also a part of the valuation or allocation assertion.

**Detail Tie-in—Details in the Account Balance Agree with Related Master File Amounts, Foot to the Total in the Account Balance, and Agree with the Total in the General Ledger** Account balances on financial statements are supported by details in master files and schedules prepared by clients. The detail tie-in objective is concerned that the details on lists are accurately prepared, correctly added, and agree with the general ledger. For example, individual accounts receivable on a listing of accounts receivable should be the same in the accounts receivable master file and the total should equal the general ledger control account. Detail tie-in is also a part of the valuation or allocation assertion.

**Realizable Value—Assets Are Included at the Amounts Estimated to Be Realized** This objective concerns whether an account balance has been reduced for declines from historical cost to net realizable value. Examples when the objective applies are considering the adequacy of the allowance for uncollectible accounts receivable and write-downs of inventory for obsolescence. The objective applies only to asset accounts and is also a part of the valuation or allocation assertion.

**Rights and Obligations** In addition to existing, most assets must be owned before it is acceptable to include them in the financial statements. Similarly, liabilities must belong to the entity. Rights are always associated with assets and obligations with liabilities. This objective is the auditor's counterpart to the management assertion of rights and obligations.

**Presentation and Disclosure—Account Balances and Related Disclosure Requirements Are Properly Presented in the Financial Statements** In fulfilling the presentation and disclosure objective, the auditor tests to make certain that all balance sheet and income statement accounts and related information are correctly set forth in the financial statements and properly described in the body and footnotes of the statements. This objective has its counterpart in the management assertion of presentation and disclosure.

Presentation and disclosure is closely related to, but distinct from, classification. Accounting information for balance-related audit objectives is correctly classified if all information on a detailed schedule supporting an account balance is summarized in the appropriate accounts. The information is correctly disclosed if those account balances and related footnote information are properly combined, described, and presented in the financial statements. For example, if a long-term note receivable is included on an accounts receivable listing, there is a violation of the classification objective. If the long-term note receivable is correctly classified, but combined with accounts receivable on the financial statements, there is a violation of the presentation and disclosure objective.

## Specific Balance-Related Audit Objectives

After the general balance-related audit objectives are understood, specific balance-related audit objectives for each account balance on the financial statements can be developed. There should be at least one specific balance-related audit objective for each general balance-related audit objective unless the auditor believes that the general balance-related audit objective is not relevant or is unimportant in the circumstances. There may be more than one specific balance-related audit objective for a general balance-related audit objective. For example, specific balance-related audit objectives for rights and obligations of the inventory of Hillsburg Hardware Co. could include (1) the company has title to all inventory items listed and (2) inventories are not pledged as collateral unless it is disclosed.

### Relationships Among Management Assertions and Balance-Related Audit Objectives

The reason there are more general balance-related audit objectives than management assertions is to provide additional guidance to auditors in deciding what evidence to accumulate. Table 5-5 illustrates this by showing the relationships among management assertions, the general balance-related audit objectives, and specific balance-related audit objectives as applied to inventory for Hillsburg Hardware Co.

**TABLE 5-5**

**Hillsburg Hardware Co.: Management Assertions and Balance-Related Audit Objectives Applied to Inventory**

| Management Assertions | General Balance-Related Audit Objectives | Specific Balance-Related Audit Objectives Applied to Inventory |
|---|---|---|
| Existence or occurrence | Existence | All recorded inventory exists at the balance sheet date. |
| Completeness | Completeness | All existing inventory has been counted and included in inventory summary. |
| Valuation or allocation | Accuracy | Inventory quantities agree with items physically on hand.<br>Prices used to value inventories are materially correct.<br>Extensions of price times quantity are correct and details are correctly added. |
| | Classification | Inventory items are properly classified as to raw materials, work in process, and finished goods. |
| | Cutoff | Purchase cutoff at year-end is proper.<br>Sales cutoff at year-end is proper. |
| | Detail tie-in | Total of inventory items agrees with general ledger. |
| | Realizable value | Inventories have been written down where net realizable value is impaired. |
| Rights and obligations | Rights and obligations | The company has title to all inventory items listed.<br>Inventories are not pledged as collateral. |
| Presentation and disclosure | Presentation and disclosure | Major categories of inventories and their bases of valuation are disclosed.<br>The pledge or assignment of any inventories is disclosed. |

## HOW AUDIT OBJECTIVES ARE MET

**OBJECTIVE 5-9**
**Describe the process by which audit objectives are met, and use it as a basis for further study.**

The auditor must obtain sufficient competent audit evidence to support all management assertions in the financial statements. As stated earlier, this is done by accumulating evidence in support of some appropriate combination of transaction-related audit objectives and balance-related audit objectives. A comparison of Tables 5-2 and 5-3 shows a significant overlap between the two types of audit objectives. The only assertions that must be addressed through balance-related audit objectives, rather than some combination of balance- and transaction-related audit objectives, are rights and obligations and presentation and disclosure.

The auditor plans the appropriate combination of audit objectives and the evidence that must be accumulated to meet them by following an audit process. An audit process is a well-defined methodology for organizing an audit to ensure that the evidence gathered is both sufficient and competent, and that all appropriate audit objectives are both specified and met. The audit process described in this text has four specific phases. These are shown in Figure 5-8. An expanded summary of the audit process is presented in Figure 10-10. The remainder of this chapter provides a brief introduction to each of the four phases.

## Plan and Design an Audit Approach (Phase I)

For any given audit, there are many ways in which an auditor can accumulate evidence to meet the overall audit objectives. Two overriding considerations affect the approach the auditor selects: *sufficient competent evidence must be accumulated to meet the auditor's professional responsibility*, and *the cost of accumulating the evidence should be minimized.* The first consideration is the more important, but cost minimization is necessary if CPA firms are to be competitive and profitable. If there were no concern for controlling costs, evidence decision making would be easy. Auditors would keep adding evidence, without concern for efficiency, until they were sufficiently certain that there were no material misstatements.

Concern for sufficient competent evidence and cost control necessitates planning the engagement. The plan should result in an effective audit approach at reasonable cost. Planning and designing an audit approach can be broken down into several parts. Two are addressed briefly here. Others are discussed in later chapters.

**Obtaining Knowledge of the Client's Business** To interpret adequately the meaning of information obtained throughout the audit, an *understanding of the client's business and industry* is essential. Unique aspects of different businesses are reflected in the financial statements. An audit of a life insurance company could not be performed with due care without an understanding of the unique characteristics of that business. Imagine attempting to audit a client in the bridge construction industry without understanding the construction business and the percentage-of-completion method of accounting. A reasonable understanding of the client's business and industry is required by SAS 22 (AU 311).

**FIGURE 5-8**

**Four Phases of an Audit**

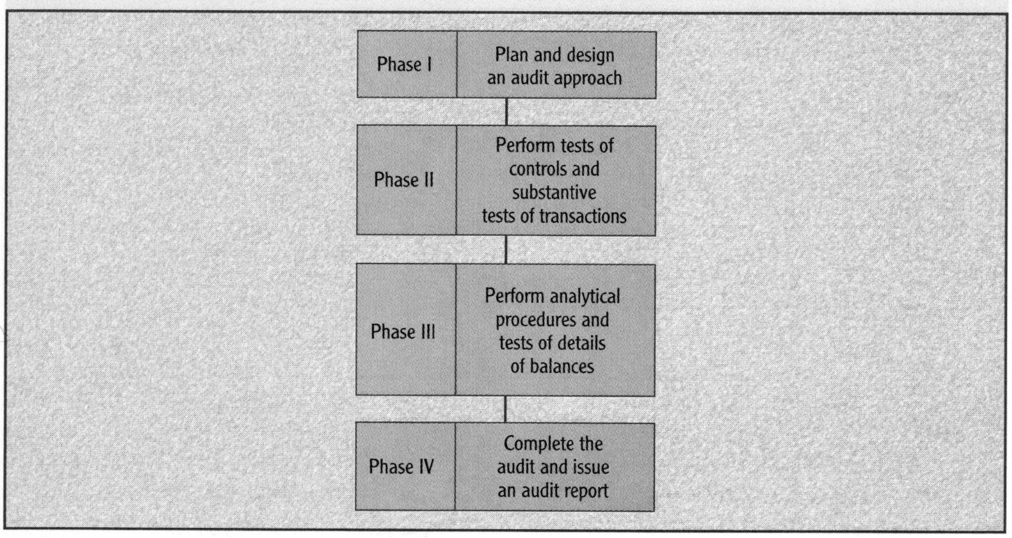

**Understanding Internal Control and Assessing Control Risk** It was pointed out in Chapter 1 that the ability of the client's internal controls to generate reliable financial information and safeguard assets and records is one of the most important and widely accepted concepts in the theory and practice of auditing. If the client has excellent internal controls, *control risk* will be low and the amount of audit evidence to be accumulated can be significantly less than for internal controls that are not adequate.

To adequately plan the appropriate audit evidence, generally accepted auditing standards *require* the auditor to gain an understanding of internal control. This understanding is obtained by reviewing organization charts and procedural manuals, by discussions with client personnel, by completing internal control questionnaires and flowcharts, and by observing client activities.

After gaining an understanding of internal control, the auditor is in a position to evaluate how effective it should be in preventing and detecting errors and fraud. This evaluation involves identifying specific controls that reduce the likelihood that errors and fraud will occur and not be detected and corrected on a timely basis. This process is referred to as *assessing control risk.*

## Perform Tests of Controls and Substantive Tests of Transactions (Phase II)

Where the auditor has reduced assessed control risk based on the identification of controls, he or she may then reduce the extent to which the accuracy of the financial statement information directly related to those controls must be supported through the accumulation of evidence. However, to justify reducing planned assessed control risk, the auditor must test the effectiveness of the controls. The procedures involved in this type of testing are commonly referred to as *tests of controls.* For example, assume that the client's internal controls require the verification by an independent clerk of all unit selling prices on sales before sales invoices are mailed to customers. This control is directly related to the accuracy transaction-related audit objective for sales. One possible test of the effectiveness of this control is for the auditor to examine a sample of the clerk's initials that he or she was required to put on each duplicate sales invoice after verifying the unit selling price.

Auditors also evaluate the client's recording of transactions by verifying the dollar amounts of transactions. This is referred to as substantive tests of transactions. An example is for the auditor to compare the unit selling price on a duplicate sales invoice with the approved price list as a test of the accuracy objective for sales transactions. Like the test of control in the previous paragraph, this test satisfies the accuracy transaction-related audit objective for sales. Frequently, auditors perform tests of controls and substantive tests of transactions at the same time.

## Perform Analytical Procedures and Tests of Details of Balances (Phase III)

There are two general categories of phase III procedures: analytical procedures and tests of details of balances. Analytical procedures tests are those that assess the overall reasonableness of transactions and balances. An example of an analytical procedure that would provide some assurance for the accuracy objective for both sales transactions (transaction-related audit objective) and accounts receivable (balance-related audit objective) is to examine sales transactions in the sales journal for unusually large amounts and to compare total monthly sales to prior years. If a company is consistently using incorrect sales prices, significant differences are likely.

Tests of details of balances are specific procedures intended to test for monetary misstatements in the balances in the financial statements. An example related to the accuracy objective for accounts receivable (balance-related audit objective) is direct written communication with the client's customers. Tests of details of ending balances are essential to the conduct of the audit, because most of the evidence is obtained from a source independent of the client and therefore considered to be of high quality.

There is a close relationship among the general review of the client's circumstances, results of understanding internal control and assessing control risk, analytical procedures, and the tests of details of the financial statement account balances. If the auditor has obtained a reasonable level of assurance for any given audit objective through performing tests of controls, substantive tests of transactions, and analytical procedures, the tests of details for that objective can be significantly reduced. In most instances, however, some tests of details of significant financial statement account balances are necessary.

### Complete the Audit and Issue an Audit Report (Phase IV)

After the auditor has completed all the procedures for each audit objective and for each financial statement account, it is necessary to combine the information obtained to reach an *overall conclusion* as to whether the financial statements are fairly presented. This is a highly subjective process that relies heavily on the auditor's professional judgment. In practice, the auditor continuously combines the information obtained as he or she proceeds through the audit. The final combination is a summation at the completion of the engagement. When the audit is completed, the CPA must issue an audit report to accompany the client's published financial statements. The report must meet well-defined technical requirements that are affected by the scope of the audit and the nature of the findings. These reports have already been studied in Chapter 2.

## SUMMARY

This chapter discusses the objectives of the audit and the way the auditor subdivides an audit to result in specific audit objectives. The auditor then accumulates evidence to obtain assurance that each audit objective has been satisfied. The illustration on meeting the accuracy objectives for sales transactions and accounts receivable shows that the auditor can obtain assurance by accumulating evidence using tests of controls, substantive tests of transactions, analytical procedures, and tests of details of balances. In some audits there is more emphasis on certain of these tests such as analytical procedures and tests of controls, whereas on others there is emphasis on substantive tests of transactions and tests of details of balances. We will study the circumstances under which it is appropriate to emphasize each of these four types of tests in later chapters.

## ESSENTIAL TERMS

**Analytical procedures**—use of comparisons and relationships to determine whether account balances or other data appear reasonable

**Balance-related audit objectives**—nine audit objectives that must be met before the auditor can conclude that any given account balance is fairly stated. The general balance-related audit objectives are existence, completeness, accuracy, classification, cutoff, detail tie-in, realizable value, rights and obligations, and presentation and disclosure.

**Cycle approach**—a method of dividing an audit by keeping closely related types of transactions and account balances in the same segment

**Error**—an unintentional misstatement of the financial statements

**Fraud**—an intentional misstatement of the financial statements

**Fraudulent financial reporting**—intentional misstatements or omissions of amounts or disclosures in financial statements to deceive users

**Illegal acts**—violations of laws or government regulations other than fraud

**Management assertions**—implied or expressed representations by management about classes of transactions and related accounts in the financial statements

**Misappropriation of assets (defalcation)**—a fraud involving the theft of an entity's assets

**Specific audit objectives**—transaction-related or balance-related audit objectives for each class of transactions and account balance

**Substantive tests of transactions**—an auditor's tests for monetary misstatements for a class of transactions

**Tests of controls**—audit procedures to test the effectiveness of control policies and procedures in support of a reduced assessed control risk

**Tests of details of balances**—an auditor's tests for monetary misstatements in the details of balance sheet and income statement accounts

**Transaction-related audit objectives**—six audit objectives that must be met before the auditor can conclude that the total for any given class of transactions is fairly stated. The general transaction-related audit objectives are existence, completeness, accuracy, classification, timing, and posting and summarization.

## REVIEW QUESTIONS

**5-1 (Objective 5-1)** State the objective of the ordinary audit of financial statements. In general terms, how do auditors meet that objective?

**5-2 (Objectives 5-2, 5-3)** Distinguish between management's and the auditor's responsibility for the financial statements being audited.

**5-3 (Objective 5-3)** Distinguish between the terms *errors* and *fraud*. What is the auditor's responsibility for finding each?

**5-4 (Objective 5-3)** Distinguish between fraudulent financial reporting and misappropriation of assets. Discuss the likely difference between these two types of fraud on the fair presentation of financial statements.

**5-5 (Objective 5-3)** "It is well accepted in auditing that throughout the conduct of the ordinary audit, it is essential to obtain large amounts of information from management and to rely heavily on management's judgments. After all, the financial statements are management's representations, and the primary responsibility for their fair presentation rests with management, not the auditor. For example, it is extremely difficult, if not impossible, for the auditor to evaluate the obsolescence of inventory as well as management can in a highly complex business. Similarly, the collectibility of accounts receivable and the continued usefulness of machinery and equipment is heavily dependent on management's willingness to provide truthful responses to questions." Reconcile the auditor's responsibility for discovering material misrepresentations by management with these comments.

**5-6 (Objective 5-3)** List two major considerations that are useful in predicting the likelihood of fraudulent financial reporting in an audit. For each of the considerations, state two things that the auditor can do to evaluate its significance in the engagement.

**5-7 (Objective 5-4)** Describe what is meant by the cycle approach to auditing. What are the advantages of dividing the audit into different cycles?

**5-8 (Objective 5-4)** Identify the cycle to which each of the following general ledger accounts would ordinarily be assigned: sales, accounts payable, retained earnings, accounts receivable, inventory, and repairs and maintenance.

**5-9 (Objectives 5-4, 5-5)** Why are sales, sales returns and allowances, bad debts, cash discounts, accounts receivable, and allowance for uncollectible accounts all included in the same cycle?

**5-10 (Objective 5-6)** Define what is meant by a management assertion about financial statements. Identify the five broad categories of management assertions.

**5-11 (Objectives 5-6, 5-7)** Distinguish between the general audit objectives and management assertions. Why are the general audit objectives more useful to auditors?

**5-12 (Objective 5-7)** An acquisition of a repair service by a construction company is recorded on the wrong date. Which transaction-related audit objective has been violated? Which transaction-related audit objective has been violated if the acquisition had been capitalized as a fixed asset rather than expensed?

**5-13 (Objective 5-8)** Distinguish between the existence and completeness balance-related audit objectives. State the effect on the financial statements (overstatement or understatement) of a violation of each in the audit of accounts receivable.

**5-14 (Objectives 5-7, 5-8)** What are specific audit objectives? Explain their relationship to the general audit objectives.

**5-15 (Objectives 5-6, 5-8)** Identify the management assertion and general balance-related audit objective for the specific balance-related audit objective: All recorded fixed assets exist at the balance sheet date.

**5-16 (Objectives 5-6, 5-8)** Explain how management assertions, general balance-related audit objectives, and specific balance-related audit objectives are developed for an account balance such as accounts receivable.

**5-17 (Objective 5-9)** Identify the four phases of the audit. What is the relationship of the four phases to the objective of the audit of financial statements?

## MULTIPLE CHOICE QUESTIONS FROM CPA EXAMINATIONS

**5-18 (Objective 5-1)** The following questions concern the reasons auditors do audits. Choose the best response.

a. Which of the following *best* describes the reason why an independent auditor reports on financial statements?
   (1) A misappropriation of assets may exist, and it is more likely to be detected by independent auditors.
   (2) Different interests may exist between the company preparing the statements and the persons using the statements.
   (3) A misstatement of account balances may exist and is generally corrected as the result of the independent auditor's work.
   (4) Poorly designed internal controls may be in existence.

b. An independent audit aids in the communication of economic data because the audit
   (1) confirms the accuracy of management's financial representations.
   (2) lends credibility to the financial statements.
   (3) guarantees that financial data are fairly presented.
   (4) assures the readers of financial statements that any fraudulent activity has been corrected.

c. The major reason an independent auditor gathers audit evidence is to
   (1) form an opinion on the financial statements.
   (2) detect fraud.
   (3) evaluate management.
   (4) assess control risk.

**5-19 (Objective 5-3)** The following questions deal with errors and fraud. Choose the best response.

a. An independent auditor has the responsibility to design the audit to provide reasonable assurance of detecting errors and fraud that might have a material effect on the financial statements. Which of the following, if material, would be a fraud as defined in *Codification of Statements on Auditing Standards?*
   (1) Misappropriation of an asset or groups of assets.
   (2) Clerical mistakes in the accounting data underlying the financial statements.
   (3) Mistakes in the application of accounting principles.
   (4) Misinterpretation of facts that existed when the financial statements were prepared.

b. Although the discovery of misappropriation of assets is not the objective of the CPA's ordinary audit engagement, the CPA most likely would be responsible for the detection of this fraud if it is material and he or she failed to detect it due to
   (1) management's failure to disclose an unrecorded transaction. The documents pertaining to the transaction are kept in a confidential file.
   (2) management's description of internal control.
   (3) management's misstatement of the value of an inventory of precious gems.
   (4) the amount of fidelity bond coverage for certain employees not being compatible with the amount of potential defalcation that might be committed.

c. If an independent audit leading to an opinion on financial statements causes the auditor to believe that *material* errors or fraud exist, the auditor should
   (1) consider the implications and discuss the matter with appropriate levels of management.
   (2) make the investigation necessary to determine whether the errors or fraud have in fact occurred.
   (3) request that management investigate to determine whether the errors or fraud have in fact occurred.
   (4) consider whether the errors or fraud were the result of a failure by employees to comply with existing internal controls.

**5-20 (Objectives 5-2, 5-3)** The following are miscellaneous questions from Chapter 5. Choose the best response.

a. To emphasize auditor independence from management, many corporations follow the practice of
   (1) appointing a partner of the CPA firm conducting the audit to the corporation's audit committee.
   (2) establishing a policy of discouraging social contact between employees of the corporation and the staff of the independent auditor.
   (3) requesting that a representative of the independent auditor be on hand at the annual stockholders' meeting.
   (4) having the independent auditor report to an audit committee of outside members of the board of directors.

b. The audit client's board of directors and audit committee refused to take any action with respect to an immaterial illegal act that was brought to their attention by the auditor. Because of their failure to act, the auditor withdrew from the engagement. The auditor's decision to withdraw was primarily due to doubts concerning
   (1) inadequate financial statement disclosures.
   (2) compliance with the Foreign Corrupt Practices Act of 1977.
   (3) scope limitations resulting from their inaction.
   (4) reliance on management's representations.

c. The primary responsibility for the adequacy of disclosure in the financial statements and footnotes rests with the
   (1) partner assigned to the engagement.
   (2) auditor in charge of field work.
   (3) staff member who drafts the statements and footnotes.
   (4) client.

## DISCUSSION QUESTIONS AND PROBLEMS

**5-21 (Objectives 5-2, 5-3)** The following two reports are taken from the same page of a published annual report. (The first two paragraphs of a standard unqualified report have been omitted.)

REPORT OF MANAGEMENT

The management of General Foods Corporation is responsible for the preparation and integrity of the consolidated financial statements of the corporation. The financial statements have been prepared in accordance with generally accepted accounting principles using management's estimates and judgments where necessary. The financial information contained elsewhere in this annual report is consistent with that in the financial statements.

General Foods maintains a system of internal accounting controls designed to provide reasonable assurance that assets are safeguarded against loss or unauthorized use and that financial records are adequate and can be relied upon to produce financial statements in accordance with generally accepted accounting principles. The concept of reasonable assurance is based on the recognition that the cost of maintaining our system of internal accounting controls should not exceed benefits expected to be derived from the system. The system is supported by comprehensive written policies and guidelines, and is continuously reviewed and augmented by our internal audit program.

Price Waterhouse, independent accountants, are retained to audit General Foods' financial statements. Their audit is conducted in accordance with generally accepted auditing standards and provides an independent assessment that helps assure fair presentation of the corporation's financial position, results of operations, and cash flows.

The Audit Committee of the Board of Directors is composed entirely of outside directors. The committee meets periodically with management, internal auditors, and the independent accountants. These meetings include discussions of internal accounting control and the quality of financial reporting. Financial management as well as the internal auditors and the independent accountants have full and free access to the Audit Committee.

The management of your company recognizes its responsibility to conduct General Foods' business in accordance with high ethical standards. This responsibility is reflected in key policy statements that address, among other things, potentially conflicting outside business interests of company employees and the proper conduct of domestic and international business activities. Ongoing communications and review programs are designed to help ensure compliance with these policies.

Chairman and Chief Executive

Senior Vice President and Chief Financial Officer

REPORT OF INDEPENDENT ACCOUNTANTS—PRICE WATERHOUSE

153 East 53rd Street
New York, N.Y. 10022
May 11, 1996

To the Board of Directors and Stockholders of General Foods Corporation:

(First two paragraphs of standard unqualified report have been omitted.)

In our opinion, the financial statements referred to above present fairly, in all material respects, the financial position of General Foods Corporation as of April 3, 1996 and March 28, 1995, and the results of its operations and cash flows for the years then ended in conformity with generally accepted accounting principles.

As discussed in Notes 1 and 12 to the financial statements, the Company changed its method of accounting for foreign currency translation in 1996.

Price Waterhouse

## Required

a. What are the purposes of the two reports and who was responsible for writing each?
b. What information does the report of management provide to users of financial statements?
c. Explain the purpose of the audit committee as described in the fourth paragraph of management's report. What is the relevance of the phrase "composed entirely of outside directors"?
d. Is the audit report a standard wording unqualified, qualified—except for, or something else? Explain your answer.
e. How long after the balance sheet date did the CPA firm complete the audit field work?

**5-22 (Objectives 5-1, 5-3)** Frequently, questions have been raised "regarding the responsibility of the independent auditor for the discovery of fraud (including misappropriation of assets and fraudulent financial reporting), and concerning the proper course of conduct of the independent auditor when his or her audit discloses specific circumstances that arouse suspicion as to the existence of fraud."

## Required

a. What are (1) the function and (2) the responsibilities of the independent auditor in the audit of financial statements? Discuss fully, but in this part do not include fraud in the discussion.

b. What are the responsibilities of the independent auditor for the detection of fraud? Discuss fully.

c. What is the independent auditor's proper course of conduct when his or her audit discloses specific circumstances that arouse his or her suspicion as to the existence of fraud?*

**5-23 (Objectives 5-2, 5-3)** A competent auditor has done a conscientious job of conducting an audit, but because of a clever fraud by management, a material fraud is included in the financial statements. The fraud, which is an overstatement of inventory, took place over several years, and it covered up the fact that the company's financial position was rapidly declining. The fraud was accidentally discovered in the latest audit by an unusually capable audit senior, and the SEC was immediately informed. Subsequent investigation indicated that the company was actually near bankruptcy, and the value of the stock dropped from $26 per share to $1 in less than one month. Among the losing stockholders were pension funds, university endowment funds, retired couples, and widows. The individuals responsible for perpetrating the fraud were also bankrupt.

After making an extensive investigation of the audit performance in previous years, the SEC was satisfied that the auditor had done a high-quality audit and had followed generally accepted auditing standards in every respect. The commission concluded that it would be unreasonable to expect auditors to uncover this type of fraud.

## Required

State your opinion as to who should bear the loss of the fraudulent financial reporting. Include in your discussion a list of potential bearers of the loss, and state why you believe they should or should not bear the loss.

**5-24 (Objective 5-4)** The following are the classes of transactions and the titles of the journals used for Phillips Equipment Rental Co.

| Classes of Transactions | Titles of Journals |
|---|---|
| Purchase returns | Cash receipts journal |
| Rental revenue | Cash disbursements journal |
| Charge-off of uncollectible accounts | Acquisitions journal |
| Acquisition of goods and services (except payroll) | Revenue journal |
| Rental allowances | Payroll journal |
| Adjusting entries (for payroll) | Adjustments journal |
| Payroll service and payments | |
| Cash disbursements (except payroll) | |
| Cash receipts | |

*AICPA adapted.

## Required

a. Identify one financial statement balance that is likely to be affected by each of the nine classes of transactions.

b. For each class of transactions, identify the journal that is likely to be used to record the transactions.

c. Identify the transaction cycle that is likely to be affected by each of the nine classes of transactions.

d. Explain how total rental revenue, as cited on the financial statements of Phillips Equipment Rental Co., is accumulated in journals and is summarized on the financial statements. Assume that there are several adjusting entries for rental revenue at the balance sheet date.

**5-25 (Objective 5-4)** The following general ledger accounts are included in the trial balance for an audit client, Jones Wholesale Stationery Store.

Income tax expense
Income tax payable
Accounts receivable
Advertising expense
Traveling expense
Accounts payable
Bonds payable
Common stock
Unexpired insurance
Furniture and equipment
Cash
Notes receivable—trade
Purchases
Sales salaries expense
Accumulated depreciation of furniture and equipment
Notes payable
Allowance for doubtful accounts
Inventory
Property tax expense
Interest expense
Depreciation expense—furniture and equipment
Retained earnings
Sales
Salaries, office and general
Telephone and telegraph expense
Bad debt expense
Insurance expense
Interest receivable
Interest income
Accrued sales salaries
Rent expense
Prepaid interest expense
Property tax payable

## Required

a. Identify the accounts in the trial balance that are likely to be included in each transaction cycle. Some accounts will be included in more than one cycle. Use the format on the following page.

| Cycle | Balance Sheet Accounts | Income Statement Accounts |
|---|---|---|
| Sales and collection | | |
| Acquisition and payment | | |
| Payroll and personnel | | |
| Inventory and warehousing | | |
| Capital acquisition and repayment | | |

b. How would the general ledger accounts in the trial balance probably differ if the company were a retail store rather than a wholesale company? How would they differ for a hospital or a government unit?

**5-26 (Objective 5-4)** The following is the detailed chart of accounts for the Southwest Metal Furniture Manufacturing Company.

**BALANCE SHEET ACCOUNTS (100–299)**

**Assets (100–199)**

**Current Assets (100–129)**

| | |
|---|---|
| 101 | Cash in bank |
| 102 | Payroll cash |
| 103 | Petty cash |
| 106 | Notes receivable—trade |
| 109 | Accounts receivable |
| 109.1 | Allowance for doubtful accounts |
| 115 | Finished goods |
| 116 | Work in process |
| 117 | Materials |
| 120 | Prepaid property tax |
| 121 | Prepaid insurance |
| 122 | Miscellaneous prepaid items |

**Property, Plant, and Equipment (130–159)**

| | |
|---|---|
| 130 | Land |
| 132 | Buildings |
| 132.1 | Accumulated depreciation—buildings |
| 135 | Machinery and equipment—factory |
| 135.1 | Accumulated depreciation—machinery and equipment—factory |
| 143 | Automobiles |
| 143.1 | Accumulated depreciation—automobiles |
| 146 | Office furniture and fixtures |
| 146.1 | Accumulated depreciation—office furniture and fixtures |

**Intangible Assets (170–179)**

| | |
|---|---|
| 170 | Goodwill |
| 171 | Patents |
| 172 | Franchises, licenses, and other privileges |

**Liabilities and Capital (200–299)**

**Current Liabilities (200–219)**

| | |
|---|---|
| 201 | Notes payable |
| 203 | Accounts payable |

| | |
|---|---|
| 206 | Accrued payroll |
| 207 | Accrued interest payable |
| 208 | Accrued sales tax |
| 209 | Other accrued liabilities |
| 210 | Employees income tax payable |
| 211 | FICA tax payable |
| 212 | Federal unemployment tax payable |
| 213 | State unemployment tax payable |
| 214 | Estimated federal income tax payable |
| 215 | Estimated state income tax payable |
| 216 | Long-term debt (due within one year) |
| 218 | Dividends payable |

**Long-Term Liabilities (220–229)**

| | |
|---|---|
| 220 | Bonds payable |
| 222 | Mortgage payable |
| 224 | Other long-term debt |
| 226 | Deferred income tax payable |

**Capital (250–299)**

| | |
|---|---|
| 250 | Common stock |
| 250.1 | Treasury stock |
| 255 | Paid-in capital in excess of par |
| 260 | Retained earnings |

**INCOME STATEMENT ACCOUNTS (300–899)**

**Sales (300–349)**

| | |
|---|---|
| 301 | Sales |
| 301.1 | Sales returns |
| 301.2 | Sales allowances |
| 301.3 | Sales discounts |

**Cost of Goods Sold (350–399)**

| | |
|---|---|
| 351 | Cost of goods sold |
| 353 | Purchases |
| 353.1 | Purchase returns |
| 353.2 | Purchase allowances |
| 356 | Materials price variance |
| 357 | Materials quantity variance |
| 358 | Purchases discounts |
| 366 | Labor rate variance |
| 367 | Labor efficiency variance |
| 372 | Applied factory overhead |
| 376 | Factory overhead spending variance |
| 377 | Factory overhead idle capacity variance |
| 378 | Factory overhead efficiency variance |
| 379 | Over- or underapplied factory overhead |

**Factory Overhead (400–499)**

| | |
|---|---|
| 400 | Factory overhead control |
| 401 | Salaries—factory |
| 411 | Indirect materials |
| 412 | Indirect labor |

| | |
|---|---|
| 414 | Freight in |
| 417 | Training |
| 420 | Overtime premium |
| 422 | FICA tax |
| 423 | Federal unemployment tax |
| 424 | State unemployment tax |
| 425 | Vacation pay |
| 427 | Workmen's compensation |
| 434 | Fuel—factory |
| 436 | Light and power |
| 438 | Telephone and telegraph |
| 440 | Tools |
| 442 | Defective work |
| 450 | Insurance expense |
| 460 | Depreciation expense—buildings |
| 461 | Depreciation expense—machinery and equipment |
| 462 | Repairs and maintenance of buildings |
| 463 | Repairs and maintenance of roads |
| 464 | Repairs and maintenance of transportation facilities |
| 465 | Repairs and maintenance of machinery and equipment |
| 480 | Rent of equipment |
| 485 | Property tax |
| 486 | Amortization of patents |

**Marketing Expenses (500–599)**

| | |
|---|---|
| 500 | Marketing expenses control |
| 501 | Salaries—sales supervision |
| 503 | Salaries—salespeople |
| 504 | Salaries—clerical help |
| 507 | Sales commissions |
| 515 | Freight out |
| 522 | FICA tax |
| 523 | Federal unemployment tax |
| 524 | State unemployment tax |
| 530 | Supplies |
| 534 | Fuel |
| 536 | Light and power |
| 538 | Telephone and telegraph |
| 546 | Postage |
| 548 | Travel expenses |
| 550 | Insurance expense |
| 560 | Depreciation expense—buildings |
| 561 | Depreciation expense—automobiles |
| 562 | Repairs and maintenance of buildings |
| 565 | Advertising |
| 567 | Display materials |
| 568 | Conventions and exhibits |
| 580 | Rent of equipment |
| 585 | Property tax |

**Administrative Expenses (600–699)**

| | |
|---|---|
| 600 | Administrative expenses control |
| 601 | Salaries—administrative |
| 604 | Salaries—administrative clerical help |

| | |
|---|---|
| 620 | Overtime premium |
| 622 | FICA tax |
| 623 | Federal unemployment tax |
| 624 | State unemployment tax |
| 630 | Supplies |
| 634 | Fuel |
| 636 | Light and power |
| 638 | Telephone and telegraph |
| 646 | Postage |
| 648 | Travel expenses |
| 650 | Insurance expense |
| 660 | Depreciation expense—buildings |
| 661 | Depreciation expense—furniture and fixtures |
| 662 | Repairs and maintenance of buildings |
| 670 | Legal and accounting fees |
| 680 | Rent of equipment |
| 685 | Property tax |
| 691 | Donations |
| 693 | Uncollectible accounts expense |
| **Other Expenses (700–749)** | |
| 701 | Interest paid on notes payable |
| 703 | Interest paid on mortgage |
| 707 | Interest paid on bonds |
| **Other Income (800–849)** | |
| 801 | Income from investments |
| 816 | Interest earned |
| 817 | Rental income |
| 818 | Miscellaneous income |
| **Income Deductions (890–899)** | |
| 890 | Federal income tax |
| 891 | State income tax |

## Required

a. Explain the differences among a chart of accounts, a general ledger trial balance, and financial statements. What are the relationships among them?

b. What are the reasons for and benefits of associating general ledger trial balance accounts with transaction cycles?

c. For each account in the chart of accounts, identify the transaction cycle to which the account pertains. Some accounts belong to more than one cycle.

5-27 **(Objective 5-4)** Following are the detailed financial statements titles for Marshall Town Electronics. Their business primarily includes repairing and selling parts for radios, televisions, and video games.

**Marshall Town Electronics**
**Balance Sheet**
**December 31, 1996**

**Assets**

Current assets
  Cash

Accounts receivable
Less: Allowance for doubtful accounts
Notes receivable
Inventories—at average cost
Supplies on hand
Prepaid expenses
Total current assets

Long-term investments
Securities at cost (market value $62,000)

Property, plant, and equipment
Land—at cost
Buildings—at cost
Less: Accumulated depreciation
Total property, plant, and equipment

Intangible assets
Goodwill
Total assets

**Liabilities and Stockholders' Equity**

Current liabilities
Notes payable to banks
Accounts payable
Accrued interest on notes payable
Accrued federal income taxes
Accrued salaries, wages, and other expenses
Deposits received from customers
Total current liabilities

Long-term debt
Twenty-year 8 percent debentures, due January 1, 1998
Total liabilities

Stockholders' equity
Preferred stock, 9 percent, cumulative
Authorized and outstanding, 10,000 shares of $20 par value
Common
Authorized, 200,000 shares of $200 par value; issued and outstanding, 100,000 shares
Additional paid-in capital
Earnings retained in the business
Appropriated
Unappropriated
Total stockholders' equity
Total liabilities and stockholders' equity

**Marshall Town Electronics**
**Income Statement**
**for the Year Ended December 31, 1996**

Sales
Revenues
Less: Sales discounts
Sales returns and allowances
Net sales

Cost of goods sold
  Parts inventory, January 1, 1996
  Purchases of parts
  Less: Purchase discounts
      Net purchases
  Freight and transportation-in
  Total parts available for sale
  Less: Merchandise inventory, December 31, 1996
      Cost of goods sold
  Gross profit on sales

Operating expenses
  Selling expenses
    Sales salaries and commissions
    Sales office salaries
    Travel and entertainment
    Advertising expense
    Freight and transportation-out
    Shipping supplies and expense
    Postage and stationery
    Depreciation of sales equipment
    Telephone and telegraph
  Administrative expenses
    Officers' salaries
    Office salaries
    Legal and professional services
    Utilities expense
    Insurance expense
    Depreciation of building
    Depreciation of office equipment
    Stationery, supplies, and postage
    Miscellaneous office expenses
      Income from operations

Other income
  Rental income

Other expense
  Interest on bonds and notes
    Income before taxes

Income taxes
  Net income for the year
  Earnings per share

## Required

Identify the accounts in the detailed financial statements that are likely to be included in each transaction cycle. Some accounts will be included in more than one cycle. Use the format shown below.

| Cycle | Balance Sheet Accounts | Income Statement Accounts |
|---|---|---|
| Sales and collection | | |
| Acquisition and payment | | |
| Payroll and personnel | | |
| Inventory and warehousing | | |
| Capital acquisition and repayment | | |

evidence from the perspective of a scientist doing an experiment, an attorney prosecuting an accused thief, and an auditor of financial statements. There are six bases of comparison. Note the similarities and differences among the three professions.

## AUDIT EVIDENCE DECISIONS

**OBJECTIVE 6-2**
**Describe the four audit evidence decisions that the auditor must make to create an audit program.**

A major decision facing every auditor is determining the appropriate *types and amount of evidence* to accumulate to be satisfied that the components of the client's financial statements and the overall statements are fairly stated. This judgment is important because of the prohibitive cost of examining and evaluating all available evidence. For example, in an audit of financial statements of most organizations, it is impossible for the CPA to examine all cancelled checks, vendors' invoices, customer orders, payroll time cards, and the many other types of documents and records.

The auditor's *decisions* on evidence accumulation can be broken into the following four subdecisions:

1. Which audit procedures to use
2. What sample size to select for a given procedure
3. Which items to select from the population
4. When to perform the procedures

### Audit Procedures

An *audit procedure* is the detailed instruction for the collection of a type of audit evidence that is to be obtained at some time during the audit. For example, evidence such as physical inventory counts, comparisons of cancelled checks with cash disbursements, journal entries, and shipping document details is collected using audit procedures.

In designing audit procedures, it is common to spell them out in sufficiently specific terms to permit their use as instructions during the audit. For example, the following is an audit procedure for the verification of cash disbursements:

- Obtain the cash disbursements journal and compare the payor name, amount, and date on the cancelled check with the cash disbursements journal.

Several commonly used audit procedure terms are defined and illustrated with examples later in this chapter.

### Sample Size

Once an audit procedure is selected, it is possible to vary the sample size from one to all the items in the population being tested. In the audit procedure above, suppose there are 6,600 checks recorded in the cash disbursements journal. The auditor might select a sample size of 200 checks for comparison with the cash disbursements journal. The decision of how many items to test must be made by the auditor for each audit procedure. The sample size for any given procedure is likely to vary from audit to audit.

### Items to Select

After the sample size has been determined for an audit procedure, it is still necessary to decide which items in the population to test. If the auditor decides, for example, to select 200 cancelled checks from a population of 6,600 for comparison with the cash disbursements journal, several different methods can be used to select the specific checks to be examined. The auditor could (1) select a week and examine the first 200 checks, (2) select the 200 checks with the largest amounts, (3) select the checks randomly, or (4) select those checks that the auditor thinks are most likely to be in error. Or a combination of these methods could be used.

### Timing

An audit of financial statements usually covers a period such as a year, and an audit is usually not completed until several weeks or months after the end of the period. The timing of audit procedures can therefore vary from early in the accounting period to long after it has ended. In the audit of financial statements, the client normally wants the audit completed one to three months after year-end.

Audit procedures often incorporate sample size, items to select, and timing into the procedure. The following is a modification of the audit procedure previously used to include all four audit evidence decisions. (Italics identify the timing, items to select, and sample size decisions).

- Obtain the *October* cash disbursements journal and compare the payee name, amount, and date on the cancelled check with the cash disbursements journal for a *randomly selected sample of forty* check numbers.

### Audit Program

The detailed instructions for the entire collection of evidence for an audit area or an entire audit is called an *audit program.* The audit program always includes a list of the audit procedures. It usually also includes sample sizes, items to select, and the timing of the tests. Normally, there is an audit program for each component of the audit. Therefore, there will be an audit program for accounts receivable, for sales, and so on. An example of an audit program that includes audit procedures, sample size, items to select, and timing is given on page 345 in Table 10-4. The right side of the audit program also includes the balance-related audit objectives for each procedure, as studied in Chapter 5.

## PERSUASIVENESS OF EVIDENCE

**OBJECTIVE 6-3**
**Explain the third standard of field work and discuss its relationship to the four determinants of the persuasiveness of evidence.**

The third standard of field work requires the auditor to accumulate *sufficient competent evidence to support the opinion issued.* Because of the nature of audit evidence and the cost considerations of doing an audit, it is unlikely that the auditor will be completely convinced that the opinion is correct. However, the auditor must be persuaded that his or her opinion is correct with a high level of assurance. By combining all evidence from the entire audit, the auditor is able to decide when he or she is sufficiently persuaded to issue an audit report.

The four determinants of the persuasiveness of evidence are *relevance, competence, sufficiency,* and *timeliness.* Notice that the second and third determinants are taken directly from the third standard of field work.

### Relevance

Evidence must *pertain to or be relevant to the audit objective* that the auditor is testing before it can be persuasive. For example, assume that the auditor is concerned that a client is failing to bill customers for shipments (completeness objective). If the auditor selected a sample of duplicate sales invoices and traced each to related shipping documents, the evidence would *not be relevant* for the completeness objective. A relevant procedure would be to trace a sample of shipping documents to related duplicate sales invoices to determine if each had been billed.

Relevance can be considered only in terms of specific audit objectives. Evidence may be relevant to one audit objective but not to a different one. In the previous example, when the auditor traced from the duplicate sales invoices to related shipping documents, the evidence was relevant to the existence objective. Most evidence is relevant to more than one, but not all, audit objectives.

### Competence

Competence refers to the degree to which evidence can be considered believable or worthy of trust. If evidence is considered highly competent, it is a great help in persuading the auditor that financial statements are fairly stated. For example, if an auditor counted the inventory, that evidence would be more competent than if management gave the auditor its own figures. Most auditors, as well as the authors of this text, use the term *reliability of evidence* as being synonymous with competence.

Competence of evidence deals only with the audit procedures selected. Competence cannot be improved by selecting a larger sample size or different population items. It can only be improved by selecting audit procedures that contain a higher quality of one or more of the following five characteristics of competent evidence.

**Independence of Provider** Evidence obtained from a source outside the entity is more reliable than that obtained within. For example, external evidence such as communications from banks, attorneys, or customers is generally regarded as more reliable than answers obtained from inquiries of the client. Similarly, documents that originate from outside the client's organization are considered more reliable than are those that originate within the company and have never left the client's organization. An example of the former is an insurance policy and the latter a purchase requisition.

**Effectiveness of Client's Internal Controls** When a client's internal controls are effective, evidence obtained is more reliable than when they are weak. For example, if internal controls over sales and billing are effective, the auditor could obtain more competent evidence from sales invoices and shipping documents than if the controls were inadequate.

**Auditor's Direct Knowledge** Evidence obtained directly by the auditor through physical examination, observation, computation, and inspection is more competent than information obtained indirectly. For example, if the auditor calculates the gross margin as a percentage of sales and compares it with previous periods, the evidence would be more reliable than if the auditor relied on the calculations of the controller.

**Qualifications of Individuals Providing the Information** Although the source of information is independent, the evidence will not be reliable unless the individual providing it is qualified to do so. For this reason, communications from attorneys and bank confirmations are typically more highly regarded than accounts receivable confirmations from persons not familiar with the business world. Also, evidence obtained directly by the auditor may not be reliable if he or she lacks the qualifications to evaluate the evidence. For example, examination of an inventory of diamonds by an auditor not trained to distinguish between diamonds and glass would not provide reliable evidence of the existence of diamonds.

**Degree of Objectivity** Objective evidence is more reliable than evidence that requires considerable judgment to determine whether it is correct. Examples of objective evidence include confirmation of accounts receivable and bank balances, the physical count of securities and cash, and adding (footing) a list of accounts payable to determine if it agrees with the balance in the general ledger. Examples of subjective evidence include a letter written by a client's attorney discussing the likely outcome of outstanding lawsuits against the client, observation of obsolescence of inventory during physical examination, and inquiries of the credit manager about the collectibility of noncurrent accounts receivable. In evaluating the reliability of subjective evidence, the qualifications of the person providing the evidence are important.

## Sufficiency

The *quantity* of evidence obtained determines its sufficiency. Quantity is measured primarily by the sample size the auditor selects. For a given audit procedure, the evidence obtained from a sample of 200 would ordinarily be more sufficient than from a sample of 100.

There are several factors that determine the appropriate sample size in audits. The two most important ones are the auditor's expectation of misstatements and the effectiveness of the client's internal controls. To illustrate, assume in the audit of Jones Computer Parts Co. that the auditor concludes that there is a high likelihood of obsolete inventory due to the nature of the client's industry. The auditor would sample more inventory items for obsolescence in an audit such as this than one where the likelihood of obsolescence was low. Similarly, if the auditor concludes that a client has effective rather than ineffective internal controls over recording fixed assets, a smaller sample size in the audit of acquisitions of fixed assets is warranted. Expectation of misstatements and internal controls and their effect on sample size are critical topics in this book and are studied in depth in subsequent chapters, starting with Chapter 8.

In addition to sample size, the individual items tested affect the sufficiency of evidence. Samples containing population items with large dollar values, items with a high likelihood of misstatement, and items that are representative of the population are usually considered sufficient. In contrast, most auditors would usually consider samples insufficient that contain only the largest dollar items from the population unless these items make up a large portion of the total population amount.

### Timeliness

The timeliness of audit evidence can refer either to when it is accumulated or to the period covered by the audit. Evidence is usually more persuasive for balance sheet accounts when it is obtained as close to the balance sheet date as possible. For example, the auditor's count of marketable securities on the balance sheet date would be more persuasive than a count two months earlier. For income statement accounts, evidence is more persuasive if there is a sample from the entire period under audit rather than from only a part of the period. For example, a random sample of sales transactions for the entire year would be more persuasive than a sample from only the first six months.

### Combined Effect

The persuasiveness of evidence can be evaluated only after considering the combination of relevance, competence, sufficiency, and timeliness. A large sample of highly competent evidence is not persuasive unless it is relevant to the audit objective being tested. A large sample of evidence that is neither competent nor timely is also not persuasive. Similarly, a small sample of only one or two pieces of relevant, competent, and timely evidence also lacks persuasiveness. The auditor must evaluate the degree to which all four qualities have been met in deciding persuasiveness.

There are direct relationships among the four evidence decisions and the four qualities that determine the persuasiveness of evidence. Table 6-2 shows those relationships.

To illustrate the relationships shown in Table 6-2, assume an auditor is verifying inventory that is a major item in the financial statements. Generally accepted auditing standards require that the auditor be reasonably persuaded that inventory is not materially misstated. The auditor must therefore obtain a sufficient amount of relevant, competent, and timely evidence about inventory. This means deciding which procedures to use for auditing inventory to satisfy the relevance and competency requirements, as well as determining the appropriate sample size and items to select from the population to satisfy the sufficiency requirement. Finally, the auditor must determine timing of these procedures. The combination of these four evidence decisions must result in sufficiently persuasive evidence to satisfy the auditor that inventory is materially correct. The audit program section for inventory will reflect these decisions. In practice, the auditor applies the four evidence decisions to specific audit objectives in deciding sufficient competent evidence.

**TABLE 6-2**

**Relationships Among Evidence Decisions and Persuasiveness**

| Audit Evidence Decisions | Qualities Affecting Persuasiveness of Evidence |
|---|---|
| Audit procedures | Relevance<br>Competence<br>  Independence of provider<br>  Effectiveness of internal controls<br>  Auditor's direct knowledge<br>  Qualifications of provider<br>  Objectivity of evidence |
| Sample size and items to select | Sufficiency<br>  Adequate sample size<br>  Selecting appropriate population items |
| Timing | Timeliness<br>  When procedures are performed<br>  Portion of period audited |

## Persuasiveness and Cost

In making decisions about evidence for a given audit, both persuasiveness and cost must be considered. It is rare when only one type of evidence is available for verifying information. The persuasiveness and cost of all alternatives should be considered before selecting the best type or types. The auditor's goal is to obtain a sufficient amount of timely, reliable evidence that is relevant to the information being verified, and to do so at the lowest possible total cost.

# TYPES OF AUDIT EVIDENCE

**OBJECTIVE 6-4**
**Identify and describe the seven types of evidence used in auditing.**

In deciding which audit procedures to use, there are seven broad categories of evidence from which the auditor can choose. These categories, referred to as *types of evidence*, are listed below and defined and discussed in this section.

- Physical examination
- Confirmation
- Documentation
- Observation
- Inquiries of the client
- Reperformance
- Analytical procedures

Before beginning the study of types of evidence, it is useful to show the relationships among auditing standards, which were studied in Chapter 1, types of evidence, and the four evidence decisions discussed earlier in this chapter. These relationships are shown in Figure 6-1.

**FIGURE 6-1**

**Relationships Among Auditing Standards, Types of Evidence, and the Four Audit Evidence Decisions**

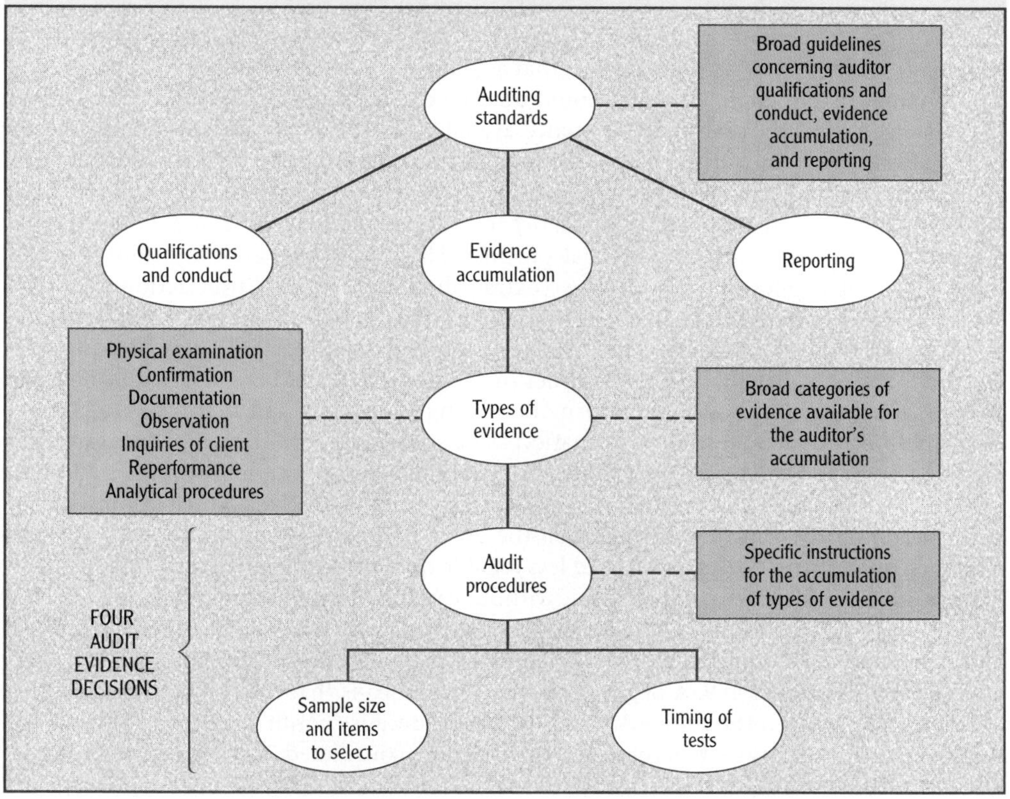

Notice that the standards are general, whereas audit procedures are specific. Types of evidence are broader than procedures and narrower than the standards. Every audit procedure obtains one or more types of evidence.

## Physical Examination

*Physical examination* is the inspection or count by the auditor of a *tangible asset.* This type of evidence is most often associated with inventory and cash, but it is also applicable to the verification of securities, notes receivable, and tangible fixed assets. The distinction between the physical examination of assets, such as marketable securities and cash, and the examination of documents, such as cancelled checks and sales documents, is important for auditing purposes. If the object being examined, such as a sales invoice, has no inherent value, the evidence is called *documentation.* For example, before a check is signed, it is a document; after it is signed, it becomes an asset; and when it is cancelled, it becomes a document again. Technically, physical examination of the check can only occur while the check is an asset.

Physical examination, which is a direct means of verifying that an asset actually exists, is regarded as one of the most reliable and useful types of audit evidence. Generally, physical examination is an objective means of ascertaining both the quantity and the description of the asset. In some cases, it is also a useful method for evaluating an asset's condition or quality. However, physical examination is not sufficient evidence to verify that existing assets are owned by the client, and in many cases the auditor is not qualified to judge qualitative factors such as obsolescence or authenticity. Also, proper valuation for financial statement purposes usually cannot be determined by physical examination.

## Confirmation

*Confirmation* describes the *receipt* of a *written or oral response* from an *independent third party* verifying the accuracy of information that was *requested by the auditor.* Because confirmations come from sources independent of the client, they are a highly regarded and often used type of evidence. However, confirmations are relatively costly to obtain and may cause some inconvenience to those asked to supply them. Therefore, they are not used in every instance in which they are applicable. Because of the high reliability of confirmations, auditors typically obtain written responses rather than oral ones whenever it is practical. Written confirmations are easier for supervisors to review, and they provide better support if it is necessary to demonstrate that a confirmation was received.

Whether or not confirmations should be used depends on the reliability needs of the situation as well as the alternative evidence available. Traditionally, confirmations are seldom used in the audit of fixed asset additions because these can be verified adequately by documentation and physical examination. Similarly, confirmations are ordinarily not used to verify individual transactions between organizations, such as sales transactions, because the auditor can use documents for that purpose. Naturally, there are exceptions. Assume the auditor determines that there are two extraordinarily large sales transactions recorded three days before year-end. Confirmation of these two transactions may be appropriate.

SAS 67 (AU 330) identifies three common types of confirmations used by auditors. They are described briefly here in the order of their reliability and are discussed further in chapters dealing with the specific information being confirmed. The first type is a positive confirmation with a request for information to be supplied by the recipient. An example is included on page 596. A positive confirmation means that the recipient is requested to return the confirmation in all circumstances. The second is a positive confirmation with the information to be confirmed included on the form. An example is included on page 458. This type of confirmation is considered less reliable than the first one, because the recipient may sign the confirmation and return it without carefully examining the information. Research shows that the response rate for the first type is lower, because it requires more effort by the recipient to complete the form. The third type is a negative confirmation. An example is included on page 459. A negative confirmation means that the recipient is requested to respond only when the information is incorrect. Because confirmations are considered significant evidence only when returned, negatives are considered less competent than positive confirmations.

**TABLE 6-3**

**Information Frequently Confirmed**

| Information | Source |
|---|---|
| **Assets** | |
| Cash in bank | Bank |
| Accounts receivable | Customer |
| Notes receivable | Maker |
| Owned inventory out on consignment | Consignee |
| Inventory held in public warehouses | Public warehouse |
| Cash surrender value of life insurance | Insurance company |
| **Liabilities** | |
| Accounts payable | Creditor |
| Notes payable | Lender |
| Advances from customers | Customer |
| Mortgages payable | Mortgagor |
| Bonds payable | Bondholder |
| **Owners' Equity** | |
| Shares outstanding | Registrar and transfer agent |
| **Other Information** | |
| Insurance coverage | Insurance company |
| Contingent liabilities | Bank, lender, and others |
| Bond indenture agreements | Bondholder |
| Collateral held by creditors | Creditor |

Whenever practical and reasonable, the confirmation of a sample of accounts receivable is *required* of CPAs. This requirement, imposed by SAS 67, exists because accounts receivable usually represent a significant balance on the financial statements, and confirmations are a highly reliable type of evidence. The circumstances where confirmation of accounts receivable is not necessary are discussed in Chapter 13.

Although confirmation is not required for any account other than accounts receivable, this type of evidence is useful in verifying many types of information. The major types of information that are frequently confirmed, along with the source of the confirmation, are indicated in Table 6-3.

To be considered reliable evidence, confirmations must be controlled by the auditor from the time they are prepared until they are returned. If the client controls the preparation of the confirmation, does the mailing, or receives the responses, the auditor has lost control and with it independence; thus the reliability of the evidence is reduced.

## Documentation

*Documentation* is the auditor's examination of the *client's documents and records* to substantiate the information that is or should be included in the financial statements. The documents examined by the auditor are the records used by the client to provide information for conducting its business in an organized manner. Since each transaction in the client's organization is normally supported by at least one document, there is a large volume of this type of evidence available. For example, the client normally retains a customer order, a shipping document, and a duplicate sales invoice for each sales transaction. These same documents are useful evidence for verification by the auditor of the accuracy of the client's records for sales transactions. Documentation is a form of evidence widely used in every audit because it is usually readily available to the auditor at a relatively low cost. Sometimes it is the only reasonable type of evidence available.

Documents can be conveniently classified as internal and external. An *internal document* is one that has been prepared and used within the client's organization and is retained without ever going to an outside party such as a customer or a vendor. Examples of internal documents include duplicate sales invoices, employees' time reports, and inventory receiving reports. An *external document* is one that has been in the hands of someone outside the client's organization who is a party to the transaction being documented, but which is either currently in the hands of the client or readily accessible. In some cases, external documents originate outside the client's organization and end up in the hands of the client. Examples of this type of external document are vendors' invoices, cancelled notes payable, and insurance policies. Other documents, such as cancelled checks, originate with the client, go to an outsider, and are finally returned to the client.

The primary determinant of the auditor's willingness to accept a document as reliable evidence is whether it is internal or external, and when internal, whether it was created and processed under conditions of good internal control. Internal documents created and processed under conditions of weak internal control may not constitute reliable evidence.

Since external documents have been in the hands of both the client and another party to the transaction, there is some indication that both members are in agreement about the information and the conditions stated on the document. Therefore, external documents are regarded as more reliable evidence than internal ones. Some external documents have exceptional reliability because they are prepared with considerable care and, frequently, have been reviewed by attorneys or other qualified experts. Examples include title papers to property such as land, insurance policies, indenture agreements, and contracts.

When auditors use documentation to support recorded transactions or amounts, it is often referred to as *vouching.* To vouch recorded acquisition transactions, the auditor might, for example, trace from the acquisitions journal to supporting vendors' invoices and receiving reports and thereby satisfy the existence objective. If the auditor traces from receiving reports to the acquisitions journal to satisfy the completeness objective, it would not be appropriate to call it vouching.

**EVIDENCE AVAILABLE TO AUDITORS IS CHANGING**

The Auditing Standards Board issued an exposure draft to amend SAS 31 in 1996 that recognizes changes in evidence available to auditors.[1] Following is a proposed new paragraph:

> In certain environments, some of the accounting data and corroborating evidential matter is available only in electronic form. Source documents such as purchase orders, bills of lading, invoices, and checks are replaced with electronic messages. For example, entities may use Electronic Data Interchange (EDI) or image processing systems. In EDI, the entity and its customers or suppliers use communication links to transact business electronically. Purchase, shipping, billing, cash receipt and cash disbursement transactions are often consummated entirely by exchange of electronic messages between the parties. In image processing systems, documents are scanned and converted into electronic images to facilitate storage and reference; and the source documents may not be retained after conversion. Certain electronic evidence may exist at a certain point in time. However, such evidence may not be retrievable after a specified period of time if files are changed and if backup files do not exist. Therefore, the auditor should consider the time during which information exists or is available in determining the nature, timing, and extent of his or her substantive tests.

[1]The Auditing Standards Board sends exposure drafts of all proposed SASs or amendments to interested parties for their comments. The comments are used to evaluate and revise the draft before issuing a final SAS or amendment.

## Observation

*Observation* is the use of the senses to assess certain activities. Throughout the audit there are many opportunities to exercise sight, hearing, touch, and smell to evaluate a wide range of things. For example, the auditor may tour the plant to obtain a general impression of the client's facilities, observe whether equipment is rusty to evaluate whether it is obsolete, and watch individuals perform accounting tasks to determine whether the person assigned a responsibility is performing it. Observation is rarely sufficient by itself. It is necessary to follow up initial impressions with other kinds of corroborative evidence. Nevertheless, observation is useful in most parts of the audit.

## Inquiries of the Client

*Inquiry* is the obtaining of *written* or *oral* information from the client in response to questions from the auditor. Although considerable evidence is obtained from the client through inquiry, it usually cannot be regarded as conclusive because it is not from an independent source and may be biased in the client's favor. Therefore, when the auditor obtains evidence through inquiry, it is normally necessary to obtain further corroborating evidence through other procedures. As an illustration, when the auditor wants to obtain information about the client's method of recording and controlling accounting transactions, he or she usually begins by asking the client how the internal controls operate. Later, the auditor performs audit tests using documentation and observation to determine if the transactions are recorded and authorized in the manner stated.

## Reperformance

As the word implies, *reperformance* involves rechecking a sample of the computations and transfers of information made by the client during the period under audit. Rechecking of computations consists of testing the client's arithmetical accuracy. It includes such procedures as extending sales invoices and inventory, adding journals and subsidiary records, and checking the calculation of depreciation expense and prepaid expenses. Rechecking of transfers of information consists of tracing amounts to be confident that when the same information is included in more than one place, it is recorded at the same amount each time. For example, the auditor normally makes limited tests to ascertain that the information in the sales journal has been included for the proper customer and at the correct amount in the subsidiary accounts receivable records and is accurately summarized in the general ledger.

## Analytical Procedures

*Analytical procedures* use comparisons and relationships to determine whether account balances or other data appear reasonable. An example is comparing the gross margin percent in the current year with the preceding year's. For certain immaterial accounts, analytical procedures may be the only evidence needed. For other accounts, other types of evidence may be reduced when analytical procedures indicate that an account balance appears reasonable. In some cases, analytical procedures are also used to isolate accounts or transactions that should be investigated more extensively to help in deciding whether additional verification is needed. An example is comparison of the current period's total repair expense with previous years' and investigation of the difference, if it is significant, to determine the cause of the increase or decrease.

The Auditing Standards Board has concluded that analytical procedures are so important that they are *required during the planning and completion phases on all audits.* For certain audit objectives or small account balances, analytical procedures alone may be sufficient evidence. In most cases, however, additional evidence beyond analytical procedures is also necessary to satisfy the requirement for sufficient competent evidence.

Because analytical procedures are an important part of planning audits, performing tests of each cycle, and completing audits, their use is studied more extensively at the end of this chapter and in most remaining chapters of this book.

## Reliability of Types of Evidence

The criteria discussed earlier in the chapter for determining the reliability of evidence are related to the seven types of evidence in Table 6-4 on page 188. Several observations are apparent from a study of Table 6-4.

**TABLE 6-4**

**Reliability of Types of Evidence**

| | Criteria to Determine Reliability | | | | |
|---|---|---|---|---|---|
| **Type of Evidence** | **Independence of Provider** | **Effectiveness of Client's Internal Control** | **Auditor's Direct Knowledge** | **Qualifications of Provider** | **Objectivity of Evidence** |
| Physical examination | High (auditor does) | Varies | High | Normally high (auditor does) | High |
| Confirmation | High | Not applicable | Low | Varies—usually high | High |
| Documentation | Varies—external more independent than internal | Varies | Low | Varies | High |
| Observation | High (auditor does) | Varies | High | Normally high (auditor does) | Medium |
| Inquiries of client | Low (client provides) | Not applicable | Low | Varies | Varies—low to high |
| Reperformance | High (auditor does) | Varies | High | High (auditor does) | High |
| Analytical procedures | High/Low (auditor does/client responds) | Varies | Low | Normally high (auditor does/client responds) | Varies—usually low |

First, the effectiveness of the client's internal controls has a significant impact on the reliability of most types of evidence. For example, internal documentation from a company with effective internal control is more reliable because the documents are more likely to be accurate. Similarly, analytical procedures will not be competent evidence if the controls that produced the data provide inaccurate information.

Second, both physical examination and reperformance are likely to be highly reliable if the internal controls are effective, but their use differs considerably. These two types of evidence effectively illustrate that equally reliable evidence may be completely different.

Third, a specific type of evidence is rarely sufficient by itself to provide competent evidence to satisfy any audit objective. It is apparent from examining Table 6-4 that observation, inquiries of client, and analytical procedures are examples of this.

## Cost of Types of Evidence

The two most expensive types of evidence are physical examination and confirmation. Physical examination is costly because it normally requires the auditor's presence when the client is counting the asset, often on the balance sheet date. For example, physical examination of inventory can result in several auditors traveling to widely separated geographical locations. Confirmation is costly because the auditor must follow careful procedures in the confirmation preparation, mailing, and receipt, and in the follow-up of nonresponses and exceptions.

Documentation and analytical procedures are moderately costly. If client personnel locate documents for the auditor and organize them for convenient use, documentation usually has a fairly low cost. When auditors must find those documents themselves, documentation can be extremely costly. Even under ideal circumstances, information and data on documents are sometimes complex and require interpretation and analysis. For example, it is usually time-consuming to read and evaluate a client's contracts, lease agreements, and minutes of the board of directors meetings. Analytical procedures require the auditor to decide which analytical procedures to use, make the calculations, and evaluate the results. Doing so often takes considerable time.

The three least expensive types of evidence are observation, inquiries of the client, and reperformance. Observation is normally done concurrently with other audit procedures. An auditor can easily observe whether client personnel are following appropriate inventory counting procedures at the same time he or she counts a sample of inventory (physical examination). Inquiries of clients are done extensively on every audit and normally have a low cost. Certain inquiries may be costly, such as obtaining written statements from the client documenting discussions throughout the audit. Reperformance is usually low cost, because it involves simple calculations and tracing that can be done at the auditor's convenience. Often, the auditor's computer software is used to perform many of these tests.

### Application of Types of Evidence to the Four Evidence Decisions

An application of three types of evidence to the four evidence decisions for one balance-related audit objective is shown in Table 6-5. First, examine column 3 in Table 5-5 on page 157. These are the balance-related audit objectives for the audit of inventory for Hillsburg Hardware Co. The overall objective is to obtain persuasive evidence (relevant, sufficient, competent, and timely), at minimum cost, that inventory is materially correct. The auditor must therefore decide which audit procedures to use to satisfy each balance-related audit objective, what the sample size should be for each procedure, which items from the population to include in the sample, and when to perform each procedure.

One balance-related audit objective from Table 5-5 is selected for further study: inventory quantities agree with items physically on hand. Several types of evidence are available to satisfy this objective. Table 6-5 lists three types of evidence and gives examples of the four evidence decisions for each type.

**TABLE 6-5**

**Types of Evidence and Four Evidence Decisions for a Balance-Related Audit Objective for Inventory***

| | Evidence Decisions | | | |
|---|---|---|---|---|
| **Type of Evidence** | **Audit Procedure** | **Sample Size** | **Items to Select** | **Timing** |
| Observation | Observe client's personnel counting inventory to determine whether they are properly following instructions | All count teams | Not applicable | Balance sheet date |
| Physical examination | Count a sample of inventory and compare quantity and description to client's counts | 120 items | 40 items with large dollar value, plus 80 randomly selected | Balance sheet date |
| Documentation | Compare quantity on client's perpetual records to quantity on client's counts | 70 items | 30 items with large dollar value, plus 40 randomly selected | Balance sheet date |

*Balance-related audit objective: Inventory quantities agree with items physically on hand.

## TERMS USED IN AUDIT PROCEDURES

**OBJECTIVE 6-5**
**Define terms commonly used in audit procedures.**

Audit procedures are the detailed steps, usually written in the form of instructions, for the accumulation of the seven types of audit evidence. They should be sufficiently clear to enable members of the audit team to understand what is to be done.

Several different terms are commonly used to describe audit procedures. These are presented and defined in Table 6-6 on the following page. To help you understand each term, an illustrative audit procedure and the type of evidence that it is associated with are shown.

**TABLE 6-6**

**Terms, Audit Procedures, and Types of Evidence**

| Term and Definition | Illustrative Audit Procedure | Type of Evidence |
|---|---|---|
| *Examine*—A reasonably detailed study of a document or record to determine specific facts about it. | *Examine* a sample of vendors' invoices to determine whether the goods or services received are reasonable and of the type normally used by the client's business. | Documentation |
| *Scan*—A less detailed examination of a document or record to determine if there is something unusual warranting further investigation. | *Scan* the sales journal, looking for large and unusual transactions. | Analytical procedures |
| *Read*—An examination of written information to determine facts pertinent to the audit. | *Read* the minutes of a board of directors' meeting and summarize all information that is pertinent to the financial statements in a working paper. | Documentation |
| *Compute*—A calculation done by the auditor independent of the client. | *Compute* the inventory turnover ratios and compare to previous years as a test of inventory obsolescence. | Analytical procedures |
| *Recompute*—A calculation done to determine whether a client's calculation is correct. | *Recompute* the unit sales price times the number of units for a sample of duplicate sales invoices and compare the totals to the calculations. | Reperformance |
| *Foot*—Addition of a column of numbers to determine if the total is the same as the client's. | *Foot* the sales journal for a one-month period and compare all totals to the general ledger. | Reperformance |
| *Trace*—An instruction normally associated with documentation or reperformance. The instruction should state what the auditor is tracing and where it is being traced from and to. Frequently, an audit procedure that includes the term *trace* will also include a second instruction, such as *compare* or *recalculate.* | *Trace* a sample of sales transactions from the sales journal to sales invoices and *compare* customer name, date, and the total dollar value of the sale.<br>*Trace* postings from the sales journal to the general ledger accounts. | Documentation<br>Reperformance |
| *Compare*—A comparison of information in two different locations. The instruction should state which information is being compared in as much detail as practical. | Select a sample of sales invoices and *compare* the unit selling price as stated on the invoice to the list of unit selling prices authorized by management. | Documentation |
| *Count*—A determination of assets on hand at a given time. This term should be associated only with the type of evidence defined as physical examination. | *Count* petty cash on hand at the balance sheet date. | Physical examination |
| *Observe*—The act of observation should be associated with the type of evidence defined as observation. | *Observe* whether the two inventory count teams independently count and record inventory costs. | Observation |
| *Inquire*—The act of inquiry should be associated with the type of evidence defined as inquiry. | *Inquire* of management whether there is any obsolete inventory on hand at the balance sheet date. | Inquiries of client |

## ANALYTICAL PROCEDURES

**OBJECTIVE 6-6**
**Discuss the purposes of analytical procedures.**

Analytical procedures (analytical tests) are defined by SAS 56 (AU 329) as *evaluations of financial information made by a study of plausible relationships among financial and nonfinancial data…involving comparisons of recorded amounts to expectations developed by the auditor.* This definition is more formal than the description of analytical procedures used earlier in the chapter, but they say essentially the same thing. The emphasis in the SAS 56 definition is on expectations developed by the auditor. For example, the auditor might compare current year recorded commissions expense to total recorded sales multiplied by the average commission rate as a test of the overall reasonableness of recorded commissions. For this analytical procedure to be relevant and reliable, the auditor has likely concluded that recorded sales are correctly stated, all sales earn a commission, and there is an average actual commission rate that is readily determinable.

The rest of the chapter focuses on the purposes of analytical procedures, the appropriate timing of their use, the five major types of analytical procedures used by practitioners, and using statistical techniques and computer software for more effective application of analytical procedures. Appendix A includes common financial ratios and discusses their interpretation.

## PURPOSES AND TIMING OF ANALYTICAL PROCEDURES

The most important reasons for using analytical procedures are discussed in this section. As a part of that discussion, the appropriate timing is also examined.

### Understanding the Client's Industry and Business

In the next chapter, there is a discussion of the need to obtain knowledge about the client's industry and business. Analytical procedures are one of the techniques commonly used in obtaining that knowledge.

Generally, an auditor considers knowledge and experience about a client company obtained in prior years as a starting point for planning the audit for the current year. By conducting analytical procedures where the current year's unaudited information is compared to prior years' audited information, changes are highlighted. These changes can represent important trends or specific events, all of which will influence audit planning. For example, a decline in gross margin percentages over time may indicate increasing competition in the company's market area, and the need to consider inventory pricing more carefully during the audit. Similarly, an increase in the balance in fixed assets may indicate a significant acquisition that must be reviewed.

### Assessment of the Entity's Ability to Continue as a Going Concern

Analytical procedures are often useful as an indication that the client company is encountering severe financial difficulty. The likelihood of financial failure must be considered by the auditor in the assessment of audit-related risks (discussed further in Chapter 8) as well as in connection with management's use of the going concern assumption in preparing the financial statements. Certain analytical procedures can be helpful in that regard. For example, if a higher than normal ratio of long-term debt to net worth is combined with a lower than average ratio of profits to total assets, a relatively high risk of financial failure may be indicated. Not only would such conditions affect the audit plan, they may indicate that substantial doubt exists about the entity's ability to continue as a going concern, which would require a report modification, as discussed in Chapter 2.

### Indication of the Presence of Possible Misstatements in the Financial Statements

Significant unexpected differences between the current year's unaudited financial data and other data used in comparisons are commonly referred to as *unusual fluctuations.* Unusual fluctuations occur when significant differences are not expected but do exist, or when significant differences are expected but do not exist. In either case, one of the possible reasons for an unusual fluctuation is the presence of an accounting misstatement. Thus, if the unusual fluctuation is large, the auditor must determine the reason for it and must be satisfied that the cause is a valid economic event and not a misstatement. For example, in comparing the ratio of the allowance for uncollectible accounts receivable to gross accounts receivable with that of the previous year, suppose that the ratio had decreased while, at the same time, accounts receivable turnover also decreased. The combination of these two pieces of information would indicate a possible understatement of the allowance. This aspect of analytical procedures is often referred to as *attention directing,* because it results in more detailed procedures in the specific audit areas where misstatements might be found.

### Reduction of Detailed Audit Tests

When an analytical procedure reveals no unusual fluctuations, the implication is that the possibility of a material misstatement is minimized. In that case, the analytical procedure constitutes substantive evidence in support of the fair statement of the related account balances, and it is possible to perform fewer detailed tests in connection with those accounts. For example, if analytical procedures results of a small account balance such as prepaid

prepaid insurance are favorable, no detailed tests may be necessary. In other cases, certain audit procedures can be eliminated, sample sizes can be reduced, or the timing of the procedures can be moved farther away from the balance sheet date.

Analytical procedures are usually inexpensive compared with tests of details. Most auditors therefore prefer to replace tests of details with analytical procedures whenever possible. To illustrate, it may be far less expensive to calculate and review sales and accounts receivable ratios than to confirm accounts receivable. If it is possible to reduce or replace confirmations by doing analytical procedures, considerable cost savings can occur.

The extent to which analytical procedures provide useful substantive evidence depends on their reliability in the circumstances. For some audit objectives and in some circumstances, they may be the most effective procedure to apply. These audit objectives might include proper classification of transactions, completeness of recording transactions, and accuracy of management's judgments and estimates in certain areas, such as the allowance for uncollectible accounts. For other audit objectives and circumstances, analytical procedures may be considered attention directing at best, and not relied on for gathering substantive evidence. An example is determining the existence of sales transactions. The factors that determine when analytical procedures are effective are discussed in a later section of the chapter.

**Timing**

Analytical procedures may be performed at any of three times during an engagement. Some analytical procedures are *required* to be performed in the *planning phase* to assist in determining the nature, extent, and timing of work to be performed. Performance of ana-

**FIGURE 6-2**

**Timing and Purposes of Analytical Procedures**

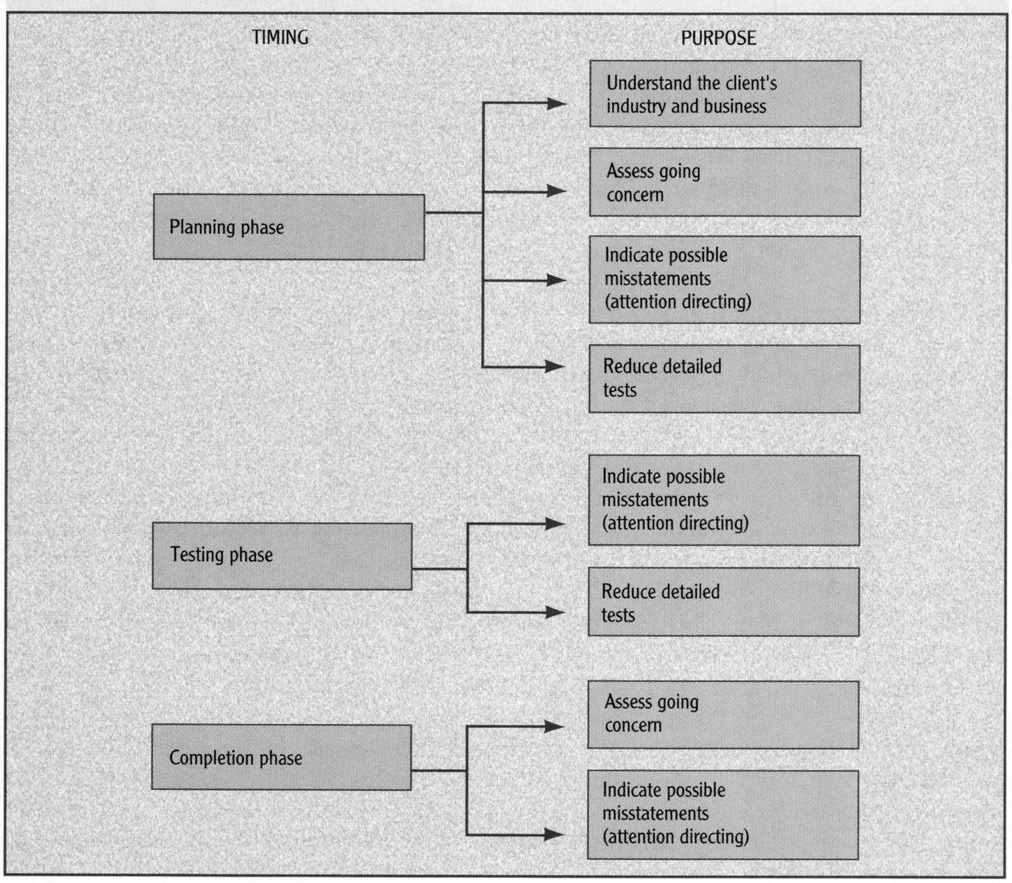

**FIGURE 6-3**

**Hillsburg Hardware Overall Tests of Interest Expense December 31, 1996**

Hillsburg Hardware Co.
Overall Test of Interest Expense
12/31/96

Schedule N-3 Date
Prepared by JM 3/6/97
Approved by JW 3/12/97

| | | | | |
|---|---|---|---|---|
| Interest expense per general ledger | | | | 120,432 ① |
| Computation of estimate: | | | | |
| Short-term loans: | | | | |
| Balance outstanding at month-end: ② | | | | |
| Jan. | 147,500 | | | |
| Feb. | 159,200 | | | |
| Mar. | 170,600 | | | |
| Apr. | 170,800 | | | |
| May | 130,200 | | | |
| June | 93,700 | | | |
| July | 70,000 | | | |
| Aug. | –0– | | | |
| Sept. | –0– | | | |
| Oct. | 42,700 | | | |
| Nov. | 126,300 | | | |
| Dec. | 209,000 | | | |
| Total | 1,320,000 | | | |
| Average (÷12) | 110,000 | @ 12.5% ③ | 13,750 | |
| Long-term loans: | | | | |
| Beginning balance | 1,326,000 ② | | | |
| Ending balance | 1,206,000 ② | | | |
| | 2,532,000 | | | |
| Average (÷2) | 1,266,000 | @ 8.5% ④ | 107,610 | |
| Estimated total interest expense | | | | 121,360 |
| Differences | | | | (928) ⑤ |

Legend and Comments

① Agrees with general ledger and working trial balance.
② Obtained from general ledger.
③ Estimated based on examination of several notes throughout the year with rates ranging from 12% to 13%.
④ Agrees with permanent file schedule of long-term debt.
⑤ Difference not significant. Indicates that interest expense per books is reasonable.

(regressing) the total to other relevant information. For example, the auditor might conclude that total selling expenses should be related to total sales, the previous year's selling expenses, and the number of salespeople. The auditor would then use regression analysis to statistically determine an estimated value of selling expenses for comparison with recorded values. Regression and other statistical methods commonly used for analytical procedures can be found in several advanced texts dealing with statistical sampling techniques for auditing.

**OBJECTIVE 6-8**
**Explain the benefits of using statistical techniques and computer software for analytical procedures.**

**Auditor's Computer Software**

Microcomputer-based audit software can be used to do extensive analytical procedures as a by-product of other audit testing. In the past several years, many CPA firms have begun to use computer software as a tool for doing more efficient and effective audits (see Chapter 15 for a more thorough study). One feature common to all such software is the ability to input the client's general ledger into the auditor's computer system. Adjusting entries and financial statements are thereby computerized to save time. The general ledger information for the client is saved and carried forward in the auditor's computerized data file year after year. The existence of current and previous years' general ledger information on the auditor's computer files permits extensive and inexpensive computerized analytical calculations. The analytical information can also be shown in different forms such as graphs and charts to help interpret the data.

A major benefit of computerized analytical procedures is the ease of updating the calculations when adjusting entries to the client's statements are made. If there are several adjusting entries to the clients' records, the analytical procedures calculations can be quickly revised. For example, a change in inventory and cost of goods sold affects a large number of ratios. All affected ratios would be revised at almost no cost with microcomputer software.

## APPENDIX A: COMMON FINANCIAL RATIOS

Auditors' analytical procedures often include the use of general financial ratios during planning and final review of the audited financial statements. These are useful for understanding the most recent events and financial status of the business, and for viewing the statements from the perspective of a user. The general financial analysis may be effective for identifying possible problem areas for additional analysis and audit testing, as well as business problem areas for which the auditor can provide other assistance. This appendix presents a number of widely used general financial ratios.

## SHORT-TERM DEBT-PAYING ABILITY

$$\text{Current ratio} = \frac{\text{current assets}}{\text{current liabilities}}$$

$$\text{Quick ratio} = \frac{\text{cash} + \text{marketable securities} + \text{net accounts receivable}}{\text{current liabilities}}$$

$$\text{Cash ratio} = \frac{\text{cash} + \text{marketable securities}}{\text{current liabilities}}$$

Many companies follow an operating cycle whereby production inputs are obtained and converted into finished goods, and then sold and converted into cash. This requires an investment in working capital; that is, funds are needed to finance inventories and accounts receivable. A majority of these funds come from trade creditors, and the balance will arise from initial capitalization, bank borrowings, and positive net cash flow from operations.

At any given time, the company will attain a net working capital position. This is the excess of current assets over current liabilities, and is also measured by the current ratio. Presumably, if net working capital is positive (that is, the current ratio is greater than 1.0), the company has sufficient available assets to pay its immediate debts; the greater the excess (the larger the ratio), the better able the company is in this regard. Thus, companies with a comfortable net working capital position are considered preferred customers by their bankers and trade creditors and are given favorable treatment. Companies with inadequate net working capital will be in danger of not being able to obtain credit.

However, this is a somewhat simplistic view. The current assets of companies will differ in terms of both valuation and liquidity, and these aspects will affect a company's ability to meet its current obligations. One way to examine this problem is to restrict the analysis to the most available and objective current assets. Thus, the quick ratio eliminates inventories from the computation and the cash ratio further eliminates accounts receivable. Usually, if the cash ratio is greater than 1.0, the company has excellent short-term debt-paying ability. In some cases it is appropriate to state marketable securities at market value rather than cost in computing these ratios.

## SHORT-TERM LIQUIDITY

If a company does not have sufficient cash and cashlike items to meet its obligations, the key to its debt-paying ability will be the length of time it takes the company to convert less liquid current assets into cash. This is measured by the short-term liquidity ratios.

The two turnover ratios—accounts receivable and inventory—are especially useful to auditors. Trends in the accounts receivable turnover ratio are frequently used in assessing the reasonableness of the allowance for uncollectible accounts. Trends in the inventory turnover ratio are used in identifying a potential inventory obsolescence problem.

$$\text{Average accounts receivable turnover} = \frac{\text{net sales}}{\text{average gross receivables}}$$

$$\text{Average days to collect} = \frac{\text{average gross receivables} \times 360}{\text{net sales}}$$

$$\text{Average inventory turnover} = \frac{\text{cost of goods sold}}{\text{average inventory}}$$

$$\text{Average days to sell} = \frac{\text{average inventory} \times 360}{\text{cost of goods sold}}$$

$$\text{Average days to convert inventory to cash} = \text{average days to sell} + \text{average days to collect}$$

When the short-term liquidity ratios (and the current ratio) are used to examine a company's performance over time or to compare performance among companies, differences in inventory accounting methods, fiscal year-ends, and cash–credit sales mix can have a significant effect. With regard to inventories, many companies have adopted the LIFO method. This can cause inventory values to differ significantly from FIFO values. When companies with different valuation methods are being compared, the company's LIFO value inventory can be adjusted to FIFO to obtain a better comparison.

When companies have different fiscal year-ends, such that one is on a natural business year and the other is not, the simple average gross receivables and inventory figures for the former will be lower. This will tend to cause the natural business year company to appear more liquid than it really is. If this is a problem, an averaging computation with quarterly data can be used.

Finally, the use of net sales per the financial statements in the receivables liquidity ratios can be a problem when a significant portion of sales is for cash. This will be somewhat mitigated when the proportions are fairly constant among periods or companies for which comparisons are being made.

## ABILITY TO MEET LONG-TERM DEBT OBLIGATIONS AND PREFERRED DIVIDENDS

$$\text{Debt to equity ratio} = \frac{\text{total liabilities}}{\text{total equity}}$$

$$\text{Tangible net assets to equity ratio} = \frac{\text{total equity} - \text{intangible assets}}{\text{total equity}}$$

$$\text{Times interest earned} = \frac{\text{operating income}}{\text{interest expense}}$$

$$\text{Times interest and preferred dividends earned} = \frac{\text{operating income}}{\text{Interest expense} + (\text{preferred dividends}/1 - \text{tax rate})}$$

A company's long-run solvency depends on the success of its operations and on its ability to raise capital for expansion or even survival over periods of temporary difficulty. From another point of view, common shareholders will benefit from the leverage obtained from borrowed capital that earns a positive net return.

A key measure in evaluating this long-term structure and capacity is the debt-to-equity ratio. If this ratio is too high, it may indicate that the company has used up its borrowing capacity and has no cushion for future events. If it is too low, it may mean that available leverage is not being used to the owner's benefit. If the ratio is trending up, it may mean that earnings are too low to support the needs of the enterprise. And if it is trending down, it may mean that the company is doing well and setting the stage for future expansion.

The tangible net assets-to-equity ratio indicates the current quality of the company's equity by removing assets such as goodwill whose realization is wholly dependent on future operations. This ratio can be used to interpret better the debt-to-equity ratio.

Lenders are generally concerned about a company's ability to meet interest payments as well as its ability to repay principal amounts. The latter will be appraised by evaluating the company's long-term prospects as well as its net asset position. The realizable value of assets will be important in this regard and may involve specific assets that collateralize the debt.

The ability to make interest payments is more a function of the company's ability to generate positive cash flows from operations in the short run, as well as over time. Thus, times interest earned shows how comfortably the company should be able to make interest (and preferred dividend) payments, assuming that earnings trends are stable.

## OPERATING AND PERFORMANCE RATIOS

The key to remedying many financial ills is to improve operations. All creditors and investors, therefore, are interested in the results of operations of a business enterprise, and it is not surprising that a number of operating and performance ratios are in use. The most widely used operating and performance ratio is earnings per share, which is an integral part of the basic financial statements for most companies. Several additional ratios can be calculated and will give further insights into operations.

The first of these is the efficiency ratio. This shows the relative volume of business generated from the company's operating asset base. In other words, it shows whether sufficient revenues are being generated to justify the assets employed. When the efficiency ratio is low, there is an indication that additional volume should be sought before more assets are obtained. When the ratio is high, it may be an indication that assets are reaching the end of their useful lives and an investment in additional assets will soon be necessary.

The second ratio is the profit margin ratio. This shows the portion of sales that exceeds cost (both variable and fixed). When there is weakness in this ratio, it is generally an indication that either (1) gross margins (revenues in excess of variable costs) are too low or (2) volume is too low with respect to fixed costs.

$$\text{Efficiency ratio} = \frac{\text{net sales}}{\text{tangible operating assets}}$$

$$\text{Profit margin ratio} = \frac{\text{operating income}}{\text{net sales}}$$

$$\text{Profitability ratio} = \frac{\text{operating income}}{\text{tangible operating assets}}$$

$$\text{Return on total assets ratio} = \frac{\text{income before interest + taxes}}{\text{total assets}}$$

$$\text{Return on common equity ratio} = \frac{\text{income before taxes} - (\text{preferred dividends}/1 - \text{tax rate})}{\text{common equity}}$$

Leverage ratios (computed separately for each source of capital other than common equity, for example, short-term debt, long-term debt, deferred taxes) =

$$\frac{(\text{RTA} \times \text{amount of source}) - \text{cost attributable to source}}{\text{common equity}}$$

$$\text{Book value per common share} = \frac{\text{common equity}}{\text{common shares}}$$

Two ratios that indicate the adequacy of earnings relative to the asset base are the profitability ratio and the return on total assets ratio. In effect, these ratios show the efficiency and profit margin ratios combined.

An important perspective on the earnings of the company is what kind of return is provided to the owners. This is reflected in the return (before taxes) on common equity. If this ratio is below prevailing long-term interest rates or returns on alternative investments, owners will perceive that they should convert the company's assets to some other use, or perhaps liquidate, unless return can be improved.

An interesting supplemental analysis is provided through leverage analysis. Here, the proportionate share of assets for each source of capital is multiplied times the company's return on total assets. This determines the return on each source of capital. The result is compared to the cost of each source of capital (for example, interest expense), and a net contribution by capital source is derived. If this amount is positive for a capital source, it may be an indication that additional capital should be sought. If the leverage is negative from a capital source, recapitalization alternatives and/or earnings improvements should be investigated. It is also helpful to use this leverage analysis when considering the debt-to-equity ratio.

The final operating and performance ratio is book value per common share. This shows the combined effect of equity transactions over time.

The use of operating and performance ratios is subject to the same accounting inconsistencies mentioned for the liquidity ratios previously identified. The usefulness of these ratios in making comparisons over time or among companies may be affected by the classification of operating versus nonoperating items, inventory methods, depreciation methods, amortization of goodwill, research and development costs, and off-balance-sheet financing.

## ILLUSTRATION

Computation of the various ratios is illustrated using the financial statements of Hillsburg Hardware Co. introduced in Chapter 5 (pp. 139–140).

Simplifying assumptions:

1. Assumes that average receivables and inventories for the year are not significantly different from the year-end balances.
2. Assumes that there is no preferred stock and the tax rate is 34 percent.
3. Assumes that there are 250,000 common shares with a market value of \$12 per share.

$$\text{Current ratio} = \frac{2{,}550}{659} = 3.9$$

$$\text{Quick ratio} = \frac{41 + 948 + 47}{659} = 1.6$$

$$\text{Cash ratio} = \frac{41}{659} = .06$$

$$\text{Accounts receivable turnover} = \frac{7{,}154}{948 + 62} = 7.1$$

$$\text{Days to collect} = \frac{(948 + 62) \times 360}{7{,}154} = 50.8 \text{ days}$$

$$\text{Inventory turnover} = \frac{5{,}162}{1{,}493} = 3.5$$

$$\text{Days to sell} = \frac{1{,}493 \times 360}{5{,}162} = 104.1 \text{ days}$$

$$\text{Days to convert to cash} = 50.8 + 104.1 = 154.9 \text{ days}$$

$$\text{Debt to equity} = \frac{1{,}284 + 659}{1{,}124} = 1.7$$

$$\text{Tangible net assets to equity} = \frac{1{,}124}{1{,}124} = 1.0$$

$$\text{Times interest earned} = \frac{369}{120} = 3.1$$

$$\text{Times interest and preferred dividends earned} = \frac{369}{120 + (0/1 - .34)} = 3.1$$

$$\text{Efficiency ratio} = \frac{7{,}154}{3{,}067} = 2.3$$

$$\text{Profit margin ratio} = \frac{369}{7{,}154} = .05$$

$$\text{Profitability ratio} = \frac{369}{3{,}067} = .12$$

$$\text{Return on total assets} = \frac{369 + 36}{3{,}067} = .13$$

$$\text{Return on common equity} = \frac{285 - (0/1 - .34)}{1{,}124} = .25$$

Leverage ratios:

$$\text{Current liabilities} = \frac{(.13 \times 659) - 0}{1{,}124} = .08$$

$$\text{Notes payable} = \frac{(.13 \times 1{,}206) - 120}{1{,}124} = .03$$

$$\text{Book value per common share} = \frac{1{,}124}{250} = 4.50$$

## ESSENTIAL TERMS

**Analytical procedures**—use of comparisons and relationships to determine whether account balances or other data appear reasonable

**Audit procedure**—detailed instruction for the collection of a type of audit evidence

**Audit program**—detailed instructions for the entire collection of evidence for an audit area or an entire audit. The audit program always includes audit procedures and may also include sample sizes, items to select, and timing of the tests.

**Budgets**—written records of the client's expectations for the period; a comparison of budgets with actual results may indicate whether or not misstatements are likely

**Competence of evidence**—the degree to which evidence can be considered believable or worthy of trust; evidence is competent when it is obtained from (1) an independent provider; (2) a client with effective internal controls; (3) the auditor's direct knowledge; (4) qualified providers such as law firms and banks; and (5) objective sources

**Confirmation**—the auditor's receipt of a written or oral response from an independent third party verifying the accuracy of information requested

**Documentation**—the auditor's examination of the client's documents and records to substantiate the information that is or should be included in the financial statements

**External document**—a document, such as a vendor's invoice, that has been used by an outside party to the transaction being documented, and that the client now has or can easily obtain

**Inquiry of the client**—the obtaining of written or oral information from the client in response to specific questions during the audit

**Internal document**—a document, such as an employee time report, that is prepared and used within the client's organization

**Observation**—the use of the senses to assess certain activities

**Persuasiveness of evidence**—the degree to which the auditor is convinced that the evidence supports the audit opinion. The four determinants of persuasiveness are the relevance, competence, sufficiency, and timeliness of the evidence.

**Physical examination**—the auditor's inspection or count of a tangible asset

**Relevance of evidence**—the pertinence of the evidence to the audit objective being tested

**Reliability**—see *competence of evidence*

**Reperformance**—the rechecking of a sample of the computations and transfers of information made by the client during the period under audit

**Sufficiency of evidence**—the quantity of evidence; appropriate sample size

**Timeliness**—the timing of audit evidence in relation to the period covered by the audit

**Unusual fluctuations**—significant unexpected differences indicated by analytical procedures between the current year's unaudited financial data and other data used in comparisons

**Vouching**—the use of documentation to support recorded transactions or amounts

## REVIEW QUESTIONS

**6-1 (Objective 6-1)** Discuss the similarities and differences between evidence in a legal case and evidence in an audit of financial statements.

**6-2 (Objective 6-2)** List the four major evidence decisions that must be made on every audit.

**6-3 (Objective 6-2)** Describe what is meant by an audit procedure. Why is it important for audit procedures to be carefully worded?

**6-4 (Objective 6-2)** Describe what is meant by an audit program for accounts receivable. What four things should be included in an audit program?

**6-5 (Objective 6-3)** State the third standard of field work. Explain the meaning of each of the major phrases of the standard.

**6-6 (Objective 6-3)** Explain why the auditor can only be persuaded with a reasonable level of assurance, rather than convinced, that the financial statements are correct.

**6-7 (Objective 6-3)** Identify the four factors that determine the persuasiveness of evidence. How are these four factors related to audit procedures, sample size, items to select, and timing?

**6-8 (Objective 6-3)** Identify the five characteristics that determine the competence of evidence. For each characteristic, provide one example of a type of evidence that is likely to be competent.

**6-9 (Objective 6-4)** List the seven types of audit evidence included in this chapter and give two examples of each.

**6-10 (Objective 6-4)** What are the four characteristics of the definition of a confirmation? Distinguish between a confirmation and external documentation.

**6-11 (Objective 6-4)** Distinguish between internal documentation and external documentation as audit evidence and give three examples of each.

**6-12 (Objectives 6-4, 6-6)** Explain the importance of analytical procedures as evidence in determining the fair presentation of the financial statements.

**6-13 (Objectives 6-4, 6-6)** Identify the most important reasons for performing analytical procedures.

**6-14 (Objectives 6-6, 6-7)** Your client, Harper Company, has a contractual commitment as a part of a bond indenture to maintain a current ratio of 2.0. If the ratio falls below that level on the balance sheet date, the entire bond becomes payable immediately. In the current year, the client's financial statements show that the ratio has dropped from 2.6 to 2.05 over the past year. How should this situation affect your audit plan?

**6-15 (Objective 6-6)** Distinguish between attention-directing analytical procedures and those intended to eliminate or reduce detailed substantive procedures.

**6-16 (Objective 6-6)** Explain why the statement "Analytical procedures are essential in every part of an audit, but these tests are rarely sufficient by themselves for any audit area" is correct or incorrect.

**6-17 (Objective 6-7)** Gale Gordon, CPA, has found ratio and trend analysis relatively useless as a tool in conducting audits. For several engagements he computed the industry ratios included in publications by Robert Morris Associates and compared them with industry standards. For most engagements the client's business was significantly different from the industry data in the publication and the client would automatically explain away any discrepancies by attributing them to the unique nature of its operations. In cases in which the client had more than one branch in different industries, Gordon found the ratio analysis no help at all. How could Gordon improve the quality of his analytical procedures?

**6-18 (Objective 6-7)** At the completion of every audit, Roger Morris, CPA, calculates a large number of ratios and trends for comparison with industry averages and prior-year calculations. He believes the calculations are worth the relatively small cost of doing them because they provide him with an excellent overview of the client's operations. If the ratios are out of line, Morris discusses the reasons with the client and frequently makes suggestions on how to bring the ratio back in line in the future. In some cases, these discussions with management have been the basis for management services engagements. Discuss the major strengths and shortcomings in Morris's use of ratio and trend analysis.

**6-19 (Objective 6-7)** It is imperative that the auditor follow up on all material differences discovered through analytical procedures. What factors will affect such investigations?

## MULTIPLE CHOICE QUESTIONS FROM CPA EXAMINATIONS

**6-20 (Objectives 6-3, 6-4)** The following questions concern competence and persuasiveness of evidence. Choose the best response.

a. Which of the following types of documentary evidence should the auditor consider to be the most reliable?
   (1) A sales invoice issued by the client and supported by a delivery receipt from an outside trucker.
   (2) Confirmation of an account payable balance mailed by and returned directly to the auditor.
   (3) A check, issued by the company and bearing the payee's endorsement, that is included with the bank statements mailed directly to the auditor.
   (4) A working paper prepared by the client's controller and reviewed by the client's treasurer.

b. The most reliable type of audit evidence that an auditor can obtain is
   (1) physical examination by the auditor.
   (2) calculations by the auditor from company records.
   (3) confirmations received directly from third parties.
   (4) external documents.

c. Audit evidence can come in different forms with different degrees of persuasiveness. Which of the following is the *least* persuasive type of evidence?
   (1) Vendor's invoice.
   (2) Bank statement obtained from the client.
   (3) Computations made by the auditor.
   (4) Prenumbered sales invoices.

d. Which of the following is the *least* persuasive documentation in support of an auditor's opinion?
   (1) Schedules of details of physical inventory counts conducted by the client.
   (2) Notation of inferences drawn from ratios and trends.
   (3) Notation of appraisers' conclusions documented in the auditor's working papers.
   (4) Lists of negative confirmation requests for which *no* response was received by the auditor.

**6-21 (Objectives 6-4, 6-6, 6-7)** The following questions deal with analytical procedures. Choose the best response.

a. Analytical procedures are
   (1) statistical tests of financial information designed to identify areas requiring intensive investigation.
   (2) analytical procedures of financial information made by a computer.
   (3) substantive tests of financial information made by a study and comparison of relationships among data.
   (4) diagnostic tests of financial information that may *not* be classified as evidential matter.

b. Significant unexpected fluctuations identified by analytical procedures will usually necessitate a(n)
   (1) consistency qualification.
   (2) understanding of the client's internal control.
   (3) explanation in the representation letter.
   (4) auditor investigation.

c. Which of the following situations has the best chance of being detected when a CPA compares 1997 revenues and expenses with the prior year and investigates all changes exceeding a fixed percentage?
   (1) An increase in property tax rates has not been recognized in the company's 1997 accrual.
   (2) The cashier began lapping accounts receivable in 1997.
   (3) Because of worsening economic conditions, the 1997 provision for uncollectible accounts was inadequate.
   (4) The company changed its capitalization policy for small tools in 1997.

d. Your analytical procedures and other tests of the Dey Company reveal that the firm's poor financial condition makes it unlikely that it will survive as a going concern. Assuming that the financial statements have otherwise been prepared in accordance with generally accepted accounting principles, what disclosure should you make of the company's precarious financial position?
   (1) You should issue a qualified opinion and, in a paragraph between the scope and opinion paragraphs of your report, direct the reader's attention to the poor financial condition of the company.
   (2) You should insist that a note to the financial statements clearly indicates that the company appears to be on the verge of bankruptcy.
   (3) You need not insist on any specific disclosure, since the company's poor financial condition is clearly indicated by the financial statements themselves.
   (4) You should make sure there is adequate disclosure and appropriately modify your report because the company does not appear to have the ability to continue as a going concern.

## DISCUSSION QUESTIONS AND PROBLEMS

**6-22 (Objective 6-4)** The following are examples of documentation typically obtained by auditors:

1. Vendors' invoices
2. General ledgers
3. Bank statements
4. Cancelled payroll checks
5. Payroll time cards
6. Purchase requisitions
7. Receiving reports (documents prepared when merchandise is received)
8. Minutes of the board of directors
9. Remittance advices
10. Signed W-4s (Employees' Withholding Exemption Certificates)
11. Signed lease agreements
12. Duplicate copies of bills of lading
13. Subsidiary accounts receivable records
14. Cancelled notes payable
15. Duplicate sales invoices
16. Articles of incorporation
17. Title insurance policies for real estate
18. Notes receivable

## Required

a. Classify each of the preceding items according to type of documentation: (1) internal or (2) external.

b. Explain why external evidence is more reliable than internal evidence.

**6-23 (Objective 6-4)** The following are examples of audit procedures:

1. Review the accounts receivable with the credit manager to evaluate their collectibility.
2. Stand by the payroll time clock to determine whether any employee "punches in" more than one time.
3. Count inventory items and record the amount in the audit working papers.
4. Obtain a letter from the client's attorney addressed to the CPA firm stating that the attorney is not aware of any existing lawsuits.
5. Extend the cost of inventory times the quantity on an inventory listing to test whether it is accurate.
6. Obtain a letter from an insurance company to the CPA firm stating the amount of the fire insurance coverage on building and equipment.
7. Examine an insurance policy stating the amount of the fire insurance coverage on buildings and equipment.
8. Calculate the ratio of cost of goods sold to sales as a test of overall reasonableness of gross margin relative to the preceding year.
9. Obtain information about internal control by requesting the client to fill out a questionnaire.
10. Trace the total on the cash disbursements journal to the general ledger.
11. Watch employees count inventory to determine whether company procedures are being followed.
12. Examine a piece of equipment to make sure that a major acquisition was actually received and is in operation.
13. Calculate the ratio of sales commissions expense to sales as a test of sales commissions.
14. Examine corporate minutes to determine the authorization of the issue of bonds.
15. Obtain a letter from management stating that there are no unrecorded liabilities.
16. Review the total of repairs and maintenance for each month to determine whether any month's total was unusually large.
17. Compare a duplicate sales invoice with the sales journal for customer name and amount.
18. Add the sales journal entries to determine whether they were correctly totaled.
19. Make a petty cash count to make sure that the amount of the petty cash fund is intact.
20. Obtain a written statement from a bank stating that the client has $15,671 on deposit and liabilities of $50,000 on a demand note.

## Required

Classify each of the preceding items according to the seven types of audit evidence: (1) physical examination, (2) confirmation, (3) documentation, (4) observation, (5) inquiries of the client, (6) reperformance, and (7) analytical procedures.

**6-24 (Objective 6-4)** List two examples of audit evidence the auditor can use in support of each of the following:

a. Recorded amount of entries in the acquisitions journal

b. Physical existence of inventory

c. Accuracy of accounts receivable

d. Ownership of fixed assets

e. Liability for accounts payable

f. Obsolescence of inventory

g. Existence of petty cash

**6-25 (Objectives 6-4, 6-6)** Seven different types of evidence were discussed. The following questions concern the reliability of that evidence:

a. Explain why confirmations are normally more reliable evidence than inquiries of the client.

b. Describe a situation in which confirmation would be considered highly reliable and another in which it would not be reliable.

c. Under what circumstances is the physical observation of inventory considered relatively unreliable evidence?

d. Explain why reperformance tests are highly reliable, but of relatively limited use.

e. Give three examples of relatively reliable documentation and three examples of less reliable documentation. What characteristics distinguish the two?

f. Give several examples in which the qualifications of the respondent or the qualifications of the auditor affect the reliability of the evidence.

g. Explain why analytical procedures are important evidence even though they are relatively unreliable by themselves.

**6-26 (Objectives 6-3, 6-4, 6-7)** In an audit of financial statements, an auditor must judge the competence of the audit evidence obtained.

## Required

a. In the course of his or her audit, the auditor asks many questions of client officers and employees.
   (1) Describe the factors the auditor should consider in evaluating oral evidence provided by client officers and employees.
   (2) Discuss the competence and limitations of oral evidence.

b. An audit may include computation of various balance sheet and operating ratios for comparison with previous years and industry averages. Discuss the competence and limitations of ratio analysis.*

**6-27 (Objective 6-4)** As auditor of the Star Manufacturing Company, you have obtained

a. a trial balance taken from the books of Star one month prior to year-end:

| | DR. (CR.) |
|---|---|
| Cash in bank | $87,000 |
| Trade accounts receivable | 345,000 |
| Notes receivable | 125,000 |
| Inventories | 317,000 |
| Land | 66,000 |
| Buildings, net | 350,000 |
| Furniture, fixtures, and equipment, net | 325,000 |
| Trade accounts payable | (235,000) |
| Mortgages payable | (400,000) |
| Capital stock | (300,000) |
| Retained earnings | (510,000) |
| Sales | (3,130,000) |
| Cost of sales | 2,300,000 |
| General and administrative expenses | 622,000 |
| Legal and professional fees | 3,000 |
| Interest expense | 35,000 |

b. There are no inventories consigned either in or out.

c. All notes receivable are due from outsiders and held by Star.

*AICPA adapted

## Required

Which accounts should be confirmed with outside sources? Briefly describe from whom they should be confirmed and the information that should be confirmed. Organize your answer in the following format:*

| Account Name | From Whom Confirmed | Information to Be Confirmed |
|---|---|---|

6-28 **(Objectives 6-4, 6-5)** The following audit procedures were performed in the audit of inventory to satisfy specific balance-related audit objectives as discussed in Chapter 5. The audit procedures assume that the auditor has obtained the inventory count sheets that list the client's inventory. The general balance-related audit objectives from Chapter 5 are also included.

**Audit Procedures**

1. Test extend unit prices times quantity on the inventory list, test foot the list and compare the total to the general ledger.
2. Trace selected quantities from the inventory list to the physical inventory to make sure that it exists and the quantities are the same.
3. Question operating personnel about the possibility of obsolete or slow-moving inventory.
4. Select a sample of quantities of inventory in the factory warehouse and trace each item to the inventory count sheets to determine if it has been included and if the quantity and description are correct.
5. Compare the quantities on hand and unit prices on this year's inventory count sheets with those in the preceding year as a test for large differences.
6. Examine sales invoices and contracts with customers to determine if any goods are out on consignment with customers. Similarly, examine vendors' invoices and contracts with vendors to determine if any goods on the inventory listing are owned by vendors.
7. Send letters directly to third parties who hold the client's inventory and request that they respond directly to us.

**General Balance-Related Audit Objectives**

Existence
Completeness
Accuracy
Classification
Cutoff
Detail tie-in
Realizable value
Rights and obligations
Presentation and disclosure

## Required

a. Identify the type of audit evidence used for each audit procedure.
b. Identify the general balance-related audit objective or objectives satisfied by each audit procedure.

6-29 **(Objectives 6-4, 6-5)** Audit procedures differ from, but are related to, types of evidence. The following questions relate to types of evidence and audit procedures.

*AICPA adapted

## Required

a. What is an audit procedure?

b. Why should audit procedures be specific and carefully written?

c. For each of the following types of evidence, carefully write one audit procedure for the audit of accounts receivable.

| Type of Evidence | Audit Procedure |
|---|---|
| (1) Confirmation | |
| (2) Documentation | |
| (3) Inquiries of the client | |
| (4) Reperformance | |
| (5) Analytical procedures | |

**6-30 (Objectives 6-3, 6-4, 6-5)** The following are nine situations, each containing two means of accumulating evidence.

1. Confirm accounts receivable with business organizations versus confirming receivables with consumers.
2. Physically examine 3-inch steel plates versus examining electronic parts.
3. Examine duplicate sales invoices when several competent people are checking each other's work versus examining documents prepared by a competent person in a one-person staff.
4. Physically examine inventory of parts for the number of units on hand versus examining them for the likelihood of inventory being obsolete.
5. Discuss the likelihood and amount of loss in a lawsuit against the client with client's in-house legal counsel versus discussion with the CPA firm's own legal counsel.
6. Confirm a bank balance versus confirming the oil and gas reserves with a geologist specializing in oil and gas.
7. Confirm a bank balance versus examining the client's bank statements.
8. Physically count the client's inventory held by an independent party versus confirming the count with an independent party.
9. Physically count the client's inventory versus obtaining a count from the company president.

## Required

a. Identify the five factors that determine the competence of evidence.

b. For each of the nine situations, state whether the first or second type of evidence is more reliable.

c. For each situation, state which of the five factors affected the competence of the evidence.

**6-31 (Objectives 6-4, 6-5)** Following are 10 audit procedures with words missing and a list of several terms commonly used in audit procedures.

**Audit Procedures**

1. ______________ whether the accounts receivable bookkeeper is prohibited from handling cash.
2. ______________ the ratio of cost of goods sold to sales and compare the ratio to previous years.
3. ______________ the sales journal and ______________ the total to the general ledger.
4. ______________ the sales journal, looking for large and unusual transactions requiring investigation.
5. ______________ of management whether all accounting employees are required to take annual vacations.

6. _______________ the balance in the bank account directly with the East State Bank.
7. _______________ all marketable securities as of the balance sheet date to determine whether they equal the total on the client's list.
8. _______________ a sample of duplicate sales invoices to determine if the controller's approval is included and _______________ each duplicate sales invoice to the sales journal for agreement of name and amount.
9. _______________ the unit selling price times quantity on the duplicate sales invoice and compare the total to the amount on the duplicate sales invoice.
10. _______________ the agreement between Johnson Wholesale Company and the client to determine if the shipment is a sale or a consignment.

**Terms**

a. Examine
b. Scan
c. Read
d. Compute
e. Recompute
f. Foot
g. Trace
h. Compare
i. Count
j. Observe
k. Inquire
l. Confirm

## Required

a. For each of the 12 blanks in procedures 1 through 10, identify the most appropriate term. No term can be used more than once.

b. For each of procedures 1 through 10, identify the type of evidence that is being used.

**6-32 (Objectives 6-4, 6-6)** In auditing the financial statements of a manufacturing company that were prepared by electronic data processing equipment, the CPA has found that the traditional audit trail has been obscured. As a result, the CPA may place increased emphasis on analytical procedures of the data under audit. These tests, which are also applied in auditing visibly posted accounting records, include the computation of ratios that are compared with prior year ratios or with industrywide norms. Examples of analytical procedures are the computation of the rate of inventory turnover and the computation of the number of days in receivables.

## Required

a. Discuss the advantages to the CPA of the use of analytical procedures in an audit.

b. In addition to the computations given above, list ratios that an auditor may compute during an audit on balance sheet accounts and related income accounts. For each ratio listed, name the two (or more) accounts used in its computation.

c. When an auditor discovers that there has been a significant change in a ratio when compared with the preceding year's, he or she considers the possible reasons for the change. Give the possible reasons for the following significant changes in ratios:
   (1) The rate of inventory turnover (ratio of cost of sales and average inventory) has decreased from the preceding year's rate.
   (2) The number of days' sales in receivables (ratio of average daily accounts receivable and sales) has increased over the prior year.*

*AICPA adapted

**6-33 (Objective 6-7)** Your comparison of the gross margin percentage for Jones Drugs for the years 1994 through 1997 indicates a significant decline. This is shown by the following information:

| | **1997** | **1996** | **1995** | **1994** |
|---|---|---|---|---|
| Sales (thousands) | $14,211 | $12,916 | $11,462 | $10,351 |
| CGS (thousands) | 9,223 | 8,266 | 7,313 | 6,573 |
| Gross margin | $4,988 | $4,650 | $4,149 | $3,778 |
| Percentage | 35.1 | 36.0 | 36.2 | 36.5 |

A discussion with Marilyn Adams, the controller, brings to light two possible explanations. She informs you that the industry gross profit percentage in the retail drug industry declined fairly steadily for three years, which accounts for part of the decline. A second factor was the declining percentage of the total volume resulting from the pharmacy part of the business. The pharmacy sales represent the most profitable portion of the business, yet the competition from discount drugstores prevents it from expanding as fast as the nondrug items such as magazines, candy, and many other items sold. Adams feels strongly that these two factors are the cause of the decline.

The following additional information is obtained from independent sources and the client's records as a means of investigating the controller's explanations:

| | **Jones Drugs ($ in thousands)** | | | | **Industry Gross Profit Percentage for Retailers of Drugs and Related Products** |
|---|---|---|---|---|---|
| | **Drug Sales** | **Nondrug Sales** | **Drug Cost of Goods Sold** | **Nondrug Cost of Goods Sold** | |
| 1997 | $5,126 | $9,085 | $3,045 | $6,178 | 32.7 |
| 1996 | 5,051 | 7,865 | 2,919 | 5,347 | 32.9 |
| 1995 | 4,821 | 6,641 | 2,791 | 4,522 | 33.0 |
| 1994 | 4,619 | 5,732 | 2,665 | 3,908 | 33.2 |

## Required

a. Evaluate the explanation provided by Adams. Show calculations to support your conclusions.

b. Which specific aspects of the client's financial statements require intensive investigation in this audit?

**6-34 (Objective 6-7)** In the audit of the Worldwide Wholesale Company, you performed extensive ratio and trend analysis. No material exceptions were discovered except for the following:

1. Commission expense as a percentage of sales has stayed constant for several years but has increased significantly in the current year. Commission rates have not changed.
2. The rate of inventory turnover has steadily decreased for four years.
3. Inventory as a percentage of current assets has steadily increased for four years.
4. The number of days' sales in accounts receivable has steadily increased for three years.
5. Allowance for uncollectible accounts as a percentage of accounts receivable has steadily decreased for three years.
6. The absolute amounts of depreciation expense and depreciation expense as a percentage of gross fixed assets are significantly smaller than in the preceding year.

## Required

a. Evaluate the potential significance of each of the exceptions above for the fair presentation of financial statements.

b. State the follow-up procedures you would use to determine the possibility of material misstatements.

**6-35 (Objective 6-7)** As part of the analytical procedures of Mahogany Products, Inc., you perform calculations of the following ratios:

| | Industry Averages | | Mahogany Products | |
|---|---|---|---|---|
| **Ratio** | **1997** | **1996** | **1997** | **1996** |
| 1. Current ratio | 3.30 | 3.80 | 2.20 | 2.60 |
| 2. Days to collect receivables | 87.00 | 93.00 | 67.00 | 60.00 |
| 3. Days to sell inventory | 126.00 | 121.00 | 93.00 | 89.00 |
| 4. Purchases divided by accounts payable | 11.70 | 11.60 | 8.50 | 8.60 |
| 5. Inventory divided by current assets | .56 | .51 | .49 | .48 |
| 6. Operating income divided by tangible assets | .08 | .06 | .14 | .12 |
| 7. Operating income divided by net sales | .06 | .06 | .04 | .04 |
| 8. Gross margin percentage | .21 | .27 | .21 | .19 |
| 9. Earnings per share | $14.27 | $13.91 | $2.09 | $1.93 |

## Required

For each of the preceding ratios:

a. State whether there is a need to investigate the results further and, if so, the reason for further investigation.

b. State the approach you would use in the investigation.

c. Explain how the operations of Mahogany Products appear to differ from those of the industry.

**6-36 (Objective 6-7)** Below and on page 214 are the auditor's calculations of several key ratios for Cragston Star Products. The primary purpose of this information is to assess the risk of financial failure, but any other relevant conclusions are also desirable.

| Ratio | 1997 | 1996 | 1995 | 1994 | 1993 |
|---|---|---|---|---|---|
| Current ratio | 2.08 | 2.26 | 2.51 | 2.43 | 2.50 |
| Quick ratio | .97 | 1.34 | 1.82 | 1.76 | 1.64 |
| Earnings before taxes divided by interest expense | 3.50 | 3.20 | 4.10 | 5.30 | 7.10 |
| Accounts receivable turnover | 4.20 | 5.50 | 4.10 | 5.40 | 5.60 |
| Days to collect receivables | 108.20 | 83.10 | 105.20 | 80.60 | 71.60 |
| Inventory turnover | 2.03 | 1.84 | 2.68 | 3.34 | 3.36 |
| Days to sell inventory | 172.60 | 195.10 | 133.90 | 107.80 | 108.30 |
| Net sales divided by tangible assets | .68 | .64 | .73 | .69 | .67 |

| Ratio | 1997 | 1996 | 1995 | 1994 | 1993 |
|---|---|---|---|---|---|
| Operating income divided by net sales | .13 | .14 | .16 | .15 | .14 |
| Operating income divided by tangible assets | .09 | .09 | .12 | .10 | .09 |
| Net income divided by common equity | .05 | .06 | .10 | .10 | .11 |
| Earnings per share | $4.30 | $4.26 | $4.49 | $4.26 | $4.14 |

### Required

a. What major conclusions can be drawn from this information about the company's future?

b. What additional information would be helpful in your assessment of this company's financial condition?

c. Based on the ratios above, which aspects of the company do you believe should receive special emphasis in the audit?

## CASE

**6-37 (Objectives 6-7, 6-8)** Solomon is a highly successful, closely held Boston, Massachusetts, company that manufactures and assembles automobile specialty parts that are sold in auto parts stores in the East. Sales and profits have expanded rapidly in the past few years, and the prospects for future years are every bit as encouraging. In fact, the Solomon brothers are currently considering either selling out to a large company or going public to obtain additional capital.

The company originated in 1960 when Frank Solomon decided to manufacture tooled parts. In 1975 the company changed over to the auto parts business. Fortunately, it has never been necessary to expand the facilities, but space problems have recently become severe and expanded facilities will be necessary. Land and building costs in Boston are currently extremely inflated.

Management has always relied on you for help in its problems because the treasurer is sales oriented and has little background in the controllership function. Salaries of all officers have been fairly modest in order to reinvest earnings in future growth. In fact the company is oriented toward long-run wealth of the brothers more than toward short-run profit. The brothers have all of their personal wealth invested in the firm.

A major reason for the success of Solomon has been the small but excellent sales force. The sales policy is to sell to small auto shops at high prices. This policy is responsible for fairly high credit losses, but the profit margin is high and the results have been highly successful. The firm has every intention of continuing this policy in the future.

Your firm has been auditing Solomon since 1970, and you have been on the job for the past three years. The client has excellent internal controls and has always been cooperative. In recent years the client has attempted to keep net income at a high level because of borrowing needs and future sellout possibilities. Overall, the client has always been pleasant to deal with and willing to help in any way possible. There have never been any major audit adjustments, and an unqualified opinion has always been issued.

In the current year you have completed the tests of the sales and collection area. The tests of controls and substantive tests of transactions for sales and sales returns and allowances were excellent, and an extensive confirmation yielded no material misstatements. You have carefully reviewed the cutoff for sales and for sales returns and allowances and find these to be excellent. All recorded bad debts appear reasonable, and a review of the aged trial balance indicates that conditions seem about the same as in past years.

## Required

a. Evaluate the information in the case to provide assistance to management for improved operation of its business. Prepare the supporting analysis using an electronic spreadsheet program (instructor option).

b. Do you agree that sales, accounts receivable, and allowance for doubtful accounts are probably correctly stated? Show calculations to support your conclusion.

| | 12-31-97 (Current Year) | 12-31-96 | 12-31-95 | 12-31-94 |
|---|---|---|---|---|
| **Balance Sheet** | | | | |
| Cash | $ 49,615 | $ 39,453 | $ 51,811 | $ 48,291 |
| Accounts receivable | 2,366,938 | 2,094,052 | 1,756,321 | 1,351,470 |
| Allowance for doubtful accounts | (250,000) | (240,000) | (220,000) | (200,000) |
| Inventory | 2,771,833 | 2,585,820 | 2,146,389 | 1,650,959 |
| Current assets | 4,938,386 | 4,479,325 | 3,734,521 | 2,850,720 |
| Fixed assets | 3,760,531 | 3,744,590 | 3,498,930 | 3,132,133 |
| Total assets | $8,698,917 | $8,223,915 | $7,233,451 | $5,982,853 |
| Current liabilities | $2,253,422 | $2,286,433 | $1,951,830 | $1,625,811 |
| Long-term liabilities | 4,711,073 | 4,525,310 | 4,191,699 | 3,550,481 |
| Owners' equity | 1,734,422 | 1,412,172 | 1,089,922 | 806,561 |
| Total liabilities and owners' equity | $8,698,917 | $8,223,915 | $7,233,451 | $5,982,853 |
| **Income Statement Information** | | | | |
| Sales | $6,740,652 | $6,165,411 | $5,313,752 | $4,251,837 |
| Sales returns and allowances | (207,831) | (186,354) | (158,367) | (121,821) |
| Sales discounts allowed | (74,147) | (63,655) | (52,183) | (42,451) |
| Bad debts | (248,839) | (245,625) | (216,151) | (196,521) |
| Net sales | $6,209,835 | $5,669,777 | $4,887,051 | $3,891,044 |
| Gross margin | $1,415,926 | $1,360,911 | $1,230,640 | $1,062,543 |
| Net income after taxes | $335,166 | $322,250 | $283,361 | $257,829 |
| **Aged Accounts Receivable** | | | | |
| 0–30 days | $ 942,086 | $ 881,232 | $ 808,569 | $ 674,014 |
| 31–60 days | 792,742 | 697,308 | 561,429 | 407,271 |
| 61–120 days | 452,258 | 368,929 | 280,962 | 202,634 |
| >120 days | 179,852 | 146,583 | 105,361 | 67,551 |
| Total | $2,366,938 | $2,094,052 | $1,756,321 | $1,351,470 |

# 7

# AUDIT PLANNING AND DOCUMENTATION

## LEARNING OBJECTIVES

Thorough study of this chapter will enable you to

- **7-1** Discuss why adequate audit planning is essential.
- **7-2** Apply the steps involved in preplanning the audit.
- **7-3** Know appropriate background information to obtain about an audit client.
- **7-4** Know appropriate information to obtain about an audit client's legal obligations.
- **7-5** Discuss the nature and purposes of preliminary analytical procedures.
- **7-6** Explain the purposes of audit working papers.
- **7-7** Discuss and apply the concepts behind the preparation and organization of audit working papers.

## AN AUDITOR WHO DOESN'T UNDERSTAND A CLIENT'S BUSINESS TAKES A GREAT RISK

Art Berger, of Sensdorf, Berger & Co., CPAs, got an opportunity to break into the health care market when his physician, Dr. Gary Nettles, approached him about auditing Brookside Health Associates, a new health maintenance organization (HMO) that Gary and his associates had started. Brookside's main thrust was to market health plans to commercial entities, charge a monthly membership fee per employee, and provide medical services to those members. The monthly membership fee was set annually as part of the contracting process with the participating entities, and was expected to be competitive while being sufficient to recover costs.

When Brookside was formed, its owners hired Michael Sullivan to be the chief financial officer. Michael had been with the university in a financial position. Just prior to the end of Brookside's first fiscal year, Art met with Michael to plan Brookside's initial audit. Neither Art nor Michael had any direct experience with an HMO (nor did anyone else in Sensdorf, Berger), but they both read articles and other literature about the subject. In fact, Art obtained two copies of the AICPA Healthcare Audit Guide and gave one to Michael.

A specific area of focus at the planning meeting was how to estimate the liability for medical services rendered but for which no documentation had been received by the HMO. This liability is called "incurred but not recorded" (IBNR) and was new to both Art and Michael. Art agreed to investigate how to calculate this and get back to Michael.

Art's approach was to contact a friend of his who audited an HMO in another state. His friend, who only had one HMO client, sent Art a copy of some working papers that included a formula for estimating the IBNR liability. The formula was based on historical data and made sense to Art. He gave the formula to Michael, who applied it using the twelve months of data available from the initial year of operations. During the audit, Sensdorf, Berger determined the formula was applied accurately.

Shortly after the completion of Brookside's second year of operations, Michael Sullivan had some personal problems that required him to move to another city. Brookside's administrative manager was actually relieved about this because he had lost some confidence in Michael. He was concerned that, although the financial statements showed favorable results, cash flows were not as expected. He replaced Michael with Bart Chemers, primarily because Bart had previously worked for an HMO.

When Bart saw how IBNR was estimated, he questioned the formula used and made an in-depth investigation of the situation. He determined that the formula was significantly underestimating the IBNR liability, that the liability was materially understated in the previously audited financial statements, and that as a result, the rates negotiated in contracts with participants were much lower than they should have been. This finding led to a change in auditors and a sizable monetary settlement by Sensdorf, Berger.

This chapter introduces the topic of planning an audit and designing an audit approach, and discusses four major parts of the planning process. You can see how planning fits into the overall audit by examining Figure 5-8 on page 158. This chapter also deals with the study of auditors' working papers to document what the auditor did and the auditor's conclusions.

## PLANNING

**OBJECTIVE 7-1**
**Discuss why adequate audit planning is essential.**

The first generally accepted auditing standard of field work requires adequate planning.

> The work is to be adequately planned and assistants, if any, are to be properly supervised.

There are three main reasons why the auditor should properly plan engagements: to enable the auditor to obtain sufficient competent evidence for the circumstances, to help keep audit costs reasonable, and to avoid misunderstandings with the client. Obtaining sufficient competent evidence is essential if the CPA firm is to minimize legal liability and maintain a good reputation in the business community. Keeping costs reasonable helps the firm remain competitive and thereby retain or expand its client base, assuming the firm has a reputation for doing high-quality work. Avoiding misunderstandings with the client is important for good client relations and for facilitating high-quality work at reasonable cost. For example, suppose that the auditor informs the client that the audit will be completed before June 30 but is unable to finish it until August because of inadequate scheduling of staff. The client is likely to be upset with the CPA firm and may even sue for breach of contract.

Figure 7-1 presents the seven major parts of audit planning: preplan, obtain background information about the client, obtain information about the client's legal obligations, perform preliminary analytical procedures, assess materiality and risk, understand internal control and assess control risk, and develop an overall audit plan and audit program. Each of the first six parts is intended to help the auditor develop the last part, an effective and efficient overall audit plan and audit program. The first four parts of the planning phase of an audit are studied in this chapter. The last three are studied separately in each of the next three chapters.

Before beginning the discussion of the first four parts of the planning phase, it is useful to briefly introduce two risk terms that are discussed in depth in the next chapter: acceptable audit risk and inherent risk. These two risks have a significant effect on the conduct and cost of audits. Much of the early planning on audits deals with obtaining information to help auditors assess these risks.

*Acceptable audit risk* is a measure of how willing the auditor is to accept that the financial statements may be materially misstated after the audit is completed and an unqualified opinion has been issued. When the auditor decides on a lower acceptable audit risk, it means that the auditor wants to be more certain that the financial statements are *not* materially misstated. Zero risk would be certainty, and a 100 percent risk would be complete uncertainty.

When the auditor decides that a lower acceptable audit risk on an audit is appropriate, there are three potential effects:

- More evidence is required to increase audit assurance that there are no material misstatements. It is difficult to implement increased evidence accumulation because acceptable audit risk applies to the entire audit. It is expensive and often impractical to increase evidence in every part of an audit.

**FIGURE 7-1**

**Planning an Audit and Designing an Audit Approach**

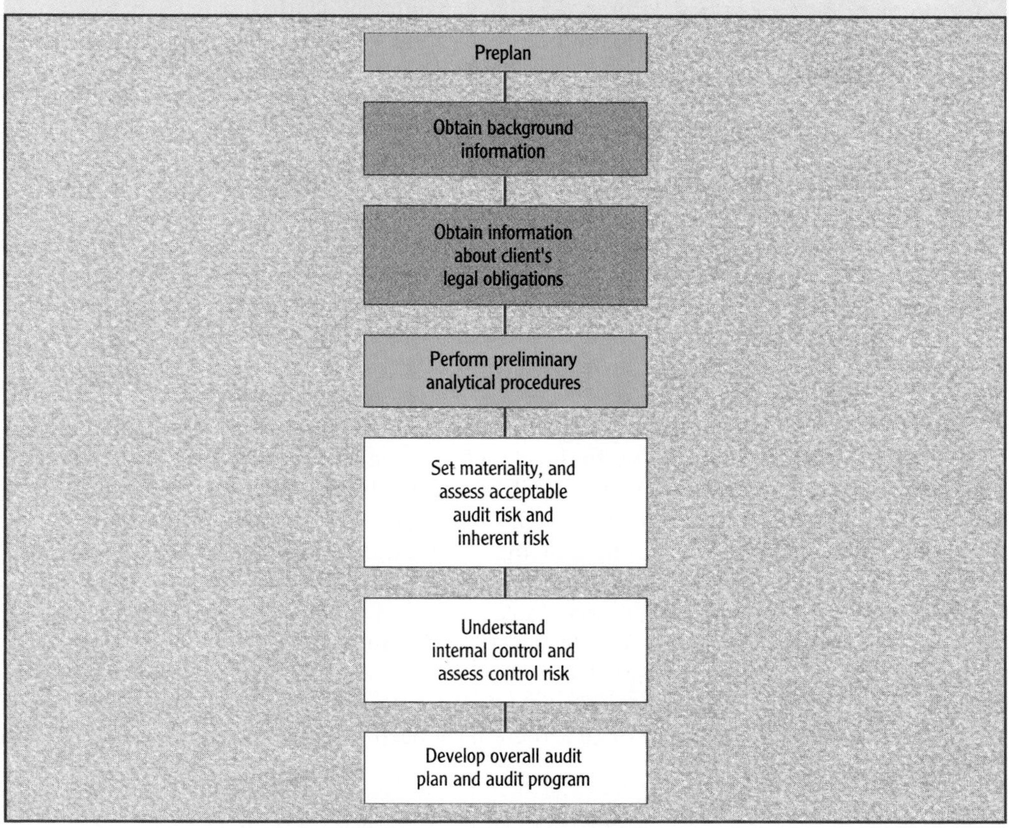


- The engagement may require more experienced staff. CPA firms should staff all engagements with qualified staff, but for low acceptable audit risk clients, special care is appropriate in staffing.
- The engagement will be reviewed more carefully than usual. CPA firms need to be sure that the working papers and other matters on all audits are adequately reviewed. When acceptable audit risk is low, there is often more extensive review, including a review by personnel who were not assigned to the engagement.

*Inherent risk* is a measure of the auditor's assessment of the likelihood that there are material misstatements in a segment before considering the effectiveness of internal control. If, for example, the auditor concludes that there is a high likelihood of material misstatement in an account such as accounts receivable, the auditor would conclude that inherent risk for accounts receivable is high.

When the auditor concludes that there is a high inherent risk for an account or a class of transactions, the same three potential effects are appropriate as for the lower acceptable audit risk. However, it is easier and more common to implement increased evidence accumulation for inherent risk than for acceptable audit risk because inherent risk can usually be isolated to one or two accounts. For example, if inherent risk is high only for accounts receivable, the auditor can restrict the evidence expansion to the audit of accounts receivable.

## PREPLAN THE AUDIT

**OBJECTIVE 7-2**
**Apply the steps involved in preplanning the audit.**

Most preplanning takes place early in the engagement, frequently in the client's office, to the extent that it is practical. Preplanning involves the following steps: decide whether to accept or continue doing the audit for the client, identify the client's reasons for the audit, obtain an engagement letter, and select staff for the engagement.

### Client Acceptance and Continuance

Even though obtaining and retaining clients is not easy in a competitive profession such as public accounting, a CPA firm must use care in deciding which clients are acceptable. The firm's legal and professional responsibilities are such that clients who lack integrity or argue constantly about the proper conduct of the audit and fees can cause more problems than they are worth. Some CPA firms now refuse any clients in certain high-risk industries such as savings and loans, health, and casualty insurance companies, and may even discontinue auditing existing clients in those industries.

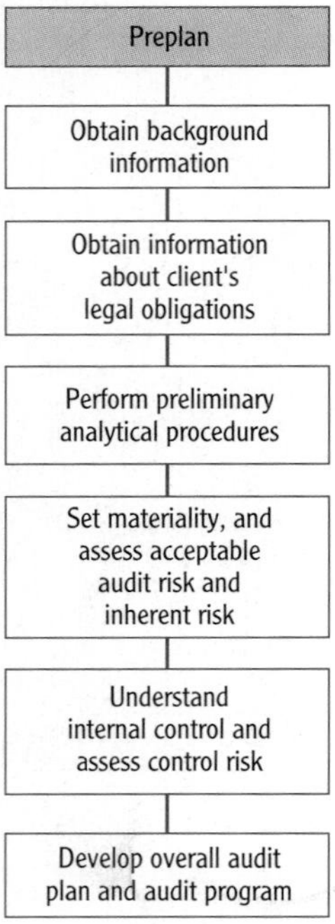


**New Client Investigation** Before accepting a new client, most CPA firms investigate the company to determine its acceptability. To the extent possible, the prospective client's standing in the business community, financial stability, and relations with its previous CPA firm should be evaluated. For example, many CPA firms use considerable caution in accepting new clients in newly formed, rapidly growing businesses. Many of these businesses fail financially and expose the CPA firm to significant potential liability.

For prospective clients that have previously been audited by another CPA firm, the new (successor) auditor is *required* by SAS 7 (AU 315) to communicate with the predecessor auditor. The purpose of the requirement is to help the successor auditor evaluate whether to accept the engagement. The communication may, for example, inform the successor auditor that the client lacks integrity or that there have been disputes over accounting principles, audit procedures, or fees.

The burden of initiating the communication rests with the successor auditor. The predecessor auditor is required to respond to the request for information. However, because of the confidentiality requirement in the *Code of Professional Conduct,* the predecessor auditor must obtain permission from the client before the communication can be made. In the event that there are legal problems or disputes between the client and the predecessor, the latter's response can be limited to stating that no information will be provided. The successor should seriously consider the desirability of accepting a prospective engagement, without considerable other investigation, if a client will not permit the communication or the predecessor will not provide a comprehensive response.

Even when a prospective client has been audited by another CPA firm, other investigations are often made. Sources of information include local attorneys, other CPAs, banks, and other businesses. In some cases, the auditor may hire a professional investigator to obtain information about the reputation and background of the key members of management. More extensive investigation is appropriate when there has been no previous auditor, when a predecessor auditor will not provide the desired information, or if any indication of problems arises from the communication.

**Continuing Clients** Many CPA firms evaluate existing clients annually to determine whether there are reasons for not continuing to do the audit. Previous conflicts over such things as the appropriate scope of the audit, the type of opinion to issue, or fees may cause the auditor to discontinue association. The auditor may also determine that the client lacks integrity and therefore should no longer be a client. If there is a lawsuit against a CPA firm by the client or a suit against the client by the CPA firm, the firm cannot do the audit. Similarly, if there are unpaid fees for services performed more than a year previously, the CPA firm cannot do the current year audit. To do an audit in either of these circumstances violates the AICPA *Code of Professional Conduct* on independence.

Even if none of the previously discussed conditions exist, the CPA firm may decide not to continue doing audits for a client because of excessive risk. For example, a CPA firm might decide that there is considerable risk of a regulatory conflict between a governmental agency and a client which could result in financial failure of the client and ultimately lawsuits against the CPA firm. Even if the engagement is profitable, the risk may exceed the short-term benefits of doing the audit.

Investigation of new clients and reevaluation of existing ones is an essential part of deciding acceptable audit risk. Assume a potential client in a reasonably risky industry, where management has a reputation of integrity, but is also known to take aggressive financial risks. If the CPA firm decides that acceptable audit risk is extremely low, it may choose not to accept the engagement. If the CPA firm concludes that acceptable audit risk is low but the client is still acceptable, it is likely to affect the fee proposed to the client. Audits with a low acceptable audit risk will normally result in higher audit costs, which should be reflected in higher audit fees.

### Identify Client's Reasons for Audit

Two major factors affecting acceptable audit risk are the likely statement users and their intended uses of the statements. It will be shown in Chapter 8 that the auditor is likely to accumulate more evidence when the statements are to be used extensively. This is often the case for publicly held companies, those with extensive indebtedness, and companies that are to be sold in the near future.

The most likely uses of the statements can be determined from previous experience with the client and discussion with management. Throughout the engagement the auditor may get additional information as to why the client is having an audit and the likely uses of the financial statements. This information may affect the auditor's assessment of acceptable audit risk.

### Obtain an Engagement Letter

A clear understanding of the terms of the engagement should exist between the client and the CPA firm. The terms should be in writing to minimize misunderstandings. This is the purpose of an engagement letter.

The engagement letter is an agreement between the CPA firm and the client for the conduct of the audit and related services. It should specify whether the auditor will perform an audit, a review, or a compilation, plus any other services such as tax returns or management advisory services. It should also state any restrictions to be imposed on the auditor's work, deadlines for completing the audit, assistance to be provided by the client's personnel in obtaining records and documents, and schedules to be prepared for the auditor. It often includes an agreement on fees. The engagement letter is also a means of informing the client that the auditor cannot guarantee that all acts of fraud will be discovered.

The engagement letter does not affect the CPA firm's responsibility to external users of audited financial statements, but it can affect legal responsibilities to the client. For example, if the client sued the CPA firm for failing to find a material misstatement, one defense a CPA firm could use would be a signed engagement letter stating that a review service, rather than an audit, was agreed upon.

Engagement letter information is important in planning the audit principally because it affects the timing of the tests and the total amount of time the audit and other services will take. If the deadline for submitting the audit report is soon after the balance sheet date, a significant portion of the audit must be done before the end of the year. When the auditor is preparing tax returns and a management letter, or if client assistance is not available, arrangements must be made to extend the amount of time for the engagement. Client-imposed restrictions on the audit could affect the procedures performed and possibly even the type of audit opinion issued. An example of an engagement letter for the audit of Hillsburg Hardware Co. is given in Figure 7-2 on page 223. The financial statements for Hillsburg Hardware Co. are included on pages 139 and 140.

**"BIG ACCOUNTING FIRMS WEED OUT RISKY CLIENTS"**

In a recent *Wall Street Journal* article, Lee Berton discussed the impact of extensive lawsuits against CPAs by their clients on the firms' willingness to accept or continue auditing risky clients. Excerpts from the article follow:

> Big accounting firms say they have begun dropping risky audit clients to lower their risk of lawsuits for allegedly faulty audits. New companies, which have a particularly high chance of failure, are affected most, because almost nothing triggers lawsuits against accountants faster than company failures.
>
> But established companies are getting the ax, too. KPMG Peat Marwick, the fourth-biggest U.S. accounting firm, is currently dropping fifty to one hundred audit clients annually, up from only zero to twenty five years ago, says Robert W. Lambert, the firm's new director of risk management. "When a client we audit goes bust," he says, "it costs us a bundle in court if we're sued by investors, whether we win or lose the case."
>
> Mr. Lambert says that legal costs were "staggering" for a lawsuit filed in a federal court in Texas alleging a faulty review of a bank's books by Peat. The bank was taken over by the federal government in 1992 after big losses. The jury ruled in Peat's favor in 1993, but the firm had to spend $7 million to defend itself "even though the fee for the job was only $15,000," Mr. Lambert says. "We just can't afford to take on risky audit clients anymore."
>
> Lawrence Weinbach, managing partner of Arthur Andersen & Co., another leading accounting firm, says his organization has either dropped or declined to audit more than 100 companies over the past two years. "When the company has a risky profile and its stock price is volatile, we're just not going to jump in and do the audit and invite a lawsuit," says Mr. Weinbach.
>
> . . . "No risky client can pay us enough money to defend ourselves after the client develops problems," asserts J. Michael Cook, chairman of Deloitte & Touche, the third biggest U.S. accounting firm. "We must reduce our legal risks to remain viable."

*Source:* Excerpted from an article by Lee Berton, "Big Accounting Firms Weed Out Risky Clients," *Wall Street Journal,* June 26, 1995, p. B1.

## Select Staff for the Engagement

Assigning the appropriate staff to the engagement is important to meet generally accepted auditing standards and to promote audit efficiency. The first general standard states:

> The audit is to be performed by a person or persons having adequate technical training and proficiency as an auditor.

Staff must, therefore, be assigned with that standard in mind. On larger engagements, there are likely to be one or more partners and staff at several experience levels doing the audit. Specialists in such technical areas as statistical sampling and computer auditing may also be assigned. On smaller audits there may be only one or two staff members.

A major consideration affecting staffing is the need for continuity from year to year. An inexperienced staff assistant is likely to become the most experienced nonpartner on the engagement within a few years. Continuity helps the CPA firm maintain familiarity with the technical requirements and closer interpersonal relations with client personnel.

Another consideration is that the persons assigned be familiar with the client's industry. This is discussed shortly.

To illustrate the importance of assigning appropriate staff to engagements, consider a computer manufacturing client with extensive inventory of computers and computer parts. Inherent risk for inventory has been assessed as high. It is essential for the staff person doing the inventory portion of the audit to be experienced in auditing inventory. In addition, he or she should have a good understanding of the computer manufacturing industry.

**FIGURE 7-2**

**Engagement Letter**

BERGER AND ANTHONY, CPAs
Gary, Indiana 46405

Mr. Rick Chulick, President
Hillsburg Hardware Co.
2146 Willow St.
Gary, Indiana 46405

June 14, 1996

Dear Mr. Chulick:

This letter confirms our arrangements for the audit of Hillsburg Hardware Co. for the year ended 12-31-96.

The purpose of our engagement is to audit the company's financial statements for the year ended 12-31-96 and evaluate the fairness of presentation of the statements in conformity with generally accepted accounting principles.

Our audit will be conducted in accordance with generally accepted auditing standards and, accordingly, will include consideration of the Company's internal control to the extent we believe necessary to determine the nature, timing, and extent of our audit procedures. This consideration will not entail a detailed study of internal control to the extent that would be required if the audit was intended to provide assurances thereon. However, any significant matters relating to internal control noted during our audit will be communicated to you, along with our comments and suggestions for improvement.

We direct your attention to the fact that management has the responsibility for establishing and maintaining the Company's internal control. Effective internal control reduces the likelihood that errors, fraud, and illegal acts will occur and remain undetected; however, it does not eliminate that possibility. Similarly, while we cannot guaranty that our audit will detect all errors, fraud, and illegal acts that might be present, we will design our audit to provide reasonable assurance of detecting such instances that would have a material effect on the financial statements.

The timing of our audit will be scheduled for performance and completion as follows:

| | **Begin** | **Complete** |
|---|---|---|
| Preliminary tests | 9-11-96 | 9-24-96 |
| Internal control letter | | 10-3-96 |
| Year-end closing | 2-3-97 | 2-18-97 |
| Delivery of report and tax return | | 3-10-97 |

Assistance to be supplied by your personnel, including the preparation of schedules and analyses of accounts, is described on a separate attachment. Timely completion of this work will facilitate the conclusion of our audit.

Our fees will be billed as work progresses and are based on the amount of time required at various levels of responsibility, plus actual out-of-pocket expenses (travel, typing, telephone, etc.). Invoices are payable upon presentation. We will notify you immediately of any circumstances we encounter which could significantly affect our initial estimate of total fees of $21,000.

If the foregoing is in accordance with your understanding, please sign and return to us the duplicate copy of this letter.

We very much appreciate the opportunity to serve you and trust that our association will be a long and pleasant one.

Yours very truly,

*Joe Anthony*

Joe Anthony
Partner

Accepted:

By: *Rick Chulick*
Date: 6-21-96

## OBTAIN BACKGROUND INFORMATION

An extensive understanding of the client's business and industry and knowledge about the company's operations are essential for doing an adequate audit. Most of this information is obtained at the client's premises, especially for a new client.

**OBJECTIVE 7-3**
**Know appropriate background information to obtain about an audit client.**

## Obtain Knowledge of Client's Industry and Business

There are three primary reasons for obtaining a good understanding of the client's industry. First, many industries have unique accounting requirements that the auditor must understand to evaluate whether the client's financial statements are in accordance with generally accepted accounting principles. For example, if an auditor is doing an audit of a city, the auditor must understand governmental accounting requirements. There are also unique accounting requirements for construction companies, railroads, not-for-profit organizations, financial institutions, and many other organizations.

Second, the auditor can often identify risks in the industry that may affect the auditor's assessment of acceptable audit risk, or even whether auditing companies in the industry is advisable. As stated earlier, certain industries are more risky than others, such as the savings and loan and health insurance industries.

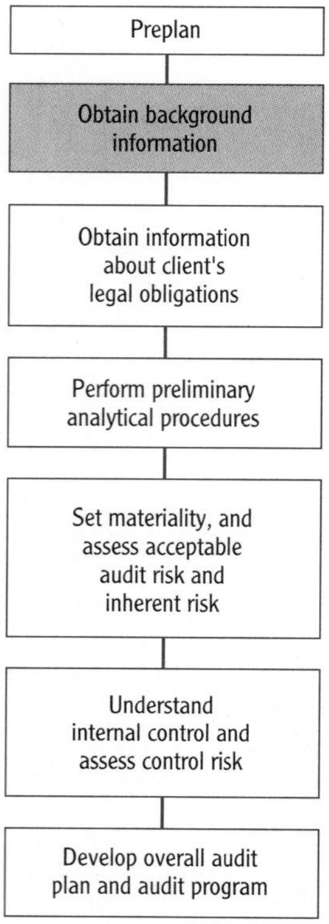


Finally, there are inherent risks that are typically common to all clients in certain industries. Understanding those risks aids the auditor in identifying the client's inherent risks. Examples include potential inventory obsolescence inherent risk in the fashion clothes industry, accounts receivable collection inherent risk in the consumer loan industry, and reserve for loss inherent risk in the casualty insurance industry.

Knowledge of the client's industry can be obtained in different ways. These include discussions with the auditor who was responsible for the engagement in previous years and auditors currently on similar engagements, as well as conferences with the client's personnel. There are AICPA industry audit guides, textbooks, and technical magazines available for the auditor to study in most major industries. Some auditors follow the practice of subscribing to specialized journals for those industries to which they devote a large amount of time. Considerable knowledge can also be obtained by participating actively in industry associations and training programs.

Knowledge about the client's business that differentiates it from other companies in its industry is also needed. That knowledge will help the auditor more effectively assess acceptable audit risk and inherent risk, and will also be useful in designing analytical procedures.

Companies filing with the SEC are required under FASB 14 to disclose segment information for different lines of business in the financial statements. SAS 21 (AU 435) provides guidelines for auditing the segment information. Auditors must have sufficient knowledge of a company's business to enable them to evaluate whether there are segments requiring separate disclosure. Since SAS 21 requires audit testing of the segment information, it is important for the auditor to identify the segments early.

The auditor's *permanent files* frequently include the history of the company, a list of the major lines of business, and a record of the most important accounting policies in previous years. Study of this information and discussions with the client's personnel aid in understanding the business.

**MANY CPA FIRMS REORGANIZE TO FOCUS ON INDUSTRIES**

A high level of knowledge of a client's industry and business is so critical to conducting quality audits and providing value-added tax and consulting services that many CPA firms have reorganized to focus on industry lines. For example, KPMG Peat Marwick has reorganized their entire practice around the following lines of business: Financial Services; Health Care and Life Sciences; Manufacturing, Retailing and Distribution; Information, Communications and Entertainment; and Public Services. Reorganizing along industry lines may help CPA firms such as KPMG Peat Marwick better understand their clients' businesses and provide additional value-added services.

## Tour the Plant and Offices

A *tour of the client's facilities* is helpful in obtaining a better understanding of the client's business and operations because it provides an opportunity to observe operations firsthand and to meet key personnel. The actual viewing of the physical facilities aids in understanding physical safeguards over assets and in interpreting accounting data by providing a frame of reference in which to visualize such assets as inventory in process and factory equipment. A knowledge of the physical layout also facilitates getting answers to questions later in the audit. The tour may also help the auditor identify inherent risks. For example, if the auditor observes unused equipment and potentially unsalable inventory, it will affect the assessment of inherent risks for equipment and inventory. Discussions with nonaccounting employees during the tour and throughout the audit are useful in maintaining a broad perspective.

### Identify Related Parties

Transactions with related parties are important to auditors because they will be *disclosed in the financial statements* if they are material. Generally accepted accounting principles require disclosure of the nature of the related party relationship; a description of transactions, including dollar amounts; and amounts due from and to related parties. Most auditors assess inherent risk as high for related parties and related party transactions, both because of the accounting disclosure requirements and the lack of independence between the parties involved in the transactions.

A *related party* is defined in SAS 45 (AU 334) as an affiliated company, a principal owner of the client company, or any other party with which the client deals where one of the parties can influence the management or operating policies of the other. A *related party transaction* is any transaction between the client and a related party. Common examples include sales or purchase transactions between a parent company and its subsidiary, exchanges of equipment between two companies owned by the same person, and loans to officers. A less common example is the exercise of significant management influence on an audit client by its most important customer.

Because material related party transactions must be disclosed, it is important that all related parties be *identified and included in the permanent files* early in the engagement. Finding undisclosed related party transactions is thereby enhanced. Common ways of identifying related parties include inquiry of management, review of SEC filings, and examination of stockholders' listings to identify principal stockholders.

### Evaluate Need for Outside Specialists

When the auditor encounters situations requiring specialized knowledge, it may be necessary to consult a specialist. SAS 73 (AU 336) establishes the requirements for selecting specialists and reviewing their work. Examples include using a diamond expert in evaluating the replacement cost of diamonds and an actuary for determining the appropriateness of the recorded value of insurance loss reserves. Another common use of specialists is consulting with attorneys on the legal interpretation of contracts and titles. In the previously discussed example of a large inventory of computers and computer parts, the CPA firm may decide to engage a specialist if no one within the firm is qualified to evaluate whether the inventory is obsolete.

The auditor should have a sufficient understanding of the client's business to recognize the need for a specialist. The auditor should evaluate the specialist's professional qualifications and understand the objectives and scope of the specialist's work. The auditor should also consider the specialist's relationship to the client, including circumstances that might impair the specialist's objectivity.

## OBTAIN INFORMATION ABOUT CLIENT'S LEGAL OBLIGATIONS

**OBJECTIVE 7-4**
**Know appropriate information to obtain about an audit client's legal obligations.**

Three closely related types of legal documents and records should be examined early in the engagement: corporate charter and bylaws, minutes of board of directors' and stockholders' meetings, and contracts. Some information, such as contracts, must be disclosed in the financial statements. Other information, such as authorizations in the board of directors' minutes, is useful in other parts of the audit. Early knowledge of these legal documents and records enables auditors to interpret related evidence throughout the engagement and to make sure there is proper disclosure in the financial statements.

## Corporate Charter and Bylaws

The *corporate charter* is granted by the state in which the company is incorporated and is the legal document necessary for recognizing a corporation as a separate entity. It includes the exact name of the corporation, the date of incorporation, the kinds and amounts of capital stock the corporation is authorized to issue, and the types of business activities the corporation is authorized to conduct. In specifying the kinds of capital stock, there is also included such information as the voting rights of each class of stock, par or stated value of the stock, preferences and conditions necessary for dividends, and prior rights in liquidation.

The *bylaws* include the rules and procedures adopted by the stockholders of the corporation. They specify such things as the fiscal year of the corporation, the frequency of stockholder meetings, the method of voting for directors, and the duties and powers of the corporate officers.

The auditor must understand the requirements of the corporate charter and the bylaws in order to determine whether the financial statements are properly presented. The correct disclosure of the stockholders' equity, including the proper payment of dividends, depends heavily on these requirements.

## Minutes of Meetings

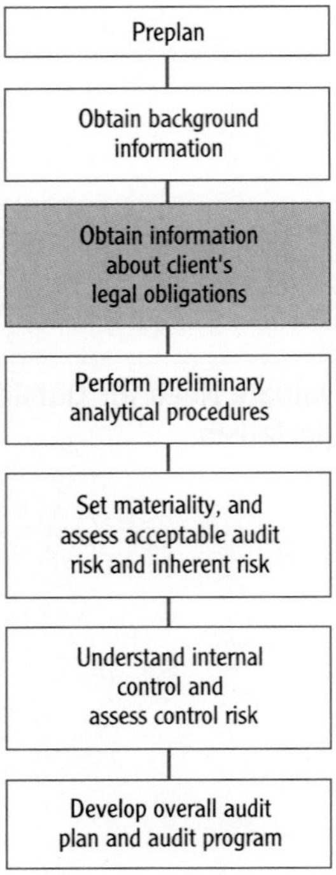


The *corporate minutes* are the official record of the meetings of the board of directors and stockholders. They include summaries of the most important topics discussed at these meetings and the decisions made by the directors and stockholders. The auditor should read the minutes to obtain information that is relevant to performing the audit. There are two categories of relevant information in minutes: authorizations and discussions by the board of directors affecting inherent risk.

Common authorizations in the minutes include compensation of officers, new contracts and agreements, acquisitions of property, loans, and dividend payments. While reading the minutes, the auditor should identify relevant authorizations and include the information in the working papers by making an abstract of the minutes or by obtaining a copy and underlining significant portions. Some time before the audit is completed, there must be a follow-up of this information to be sure that management has complied with actions taken by the stockholders and the board of directors. As an illustration, the authorized compensation of officers should be traced to each individual officer's payroll record as a test of whether the correct total compensation was paid. Similarly, the auditor should compare the authorizations of loans with notes payable to make certain that these liabilities are recorded.

Information included in the minutes affecting the auditor's assessment of inherent risk is likely to involve more general discussions. To illustrate, assume that the minutes state that the board of directors discussed two topics: changes in its industry that affect the usefulness of existing machinery and equipment, and a possible lawsuit by the Environmental Protection Agency for chemical seepage at a plant in Pennsylvania. The first discussion is likely to affect the inherent risk of obsolete equipment and the second one the inherent risk of an illegal act.

## Contracts

Clients become involved in different types of contracts that are of interest to the auditor. These can include such diverse items as long-term notes and bonds payable, stock options, pension plans, contracts with vendors for future delivery of supplies, government contracts for completion and delivery of manufactured products, royalty agreements, union contracts, and leases.

Most contracts are of primary interest in individual parts of the audit and, in practice, receive special attention during the different phases of the detailed tests. For example, the provisions of a pension plan would receive substantial emphasis as a part of the audit of the unfunded liability for pensions. The auditor should review and abstract the documents early in the engagement to gain a better perspective of the organization and to become familiar with potential problem areas. Later these documents can be examined more carefully as a part of the tests of individual audit areas.

The existence of contracts often affects the auditor's assessed inherent risks. To illustrate, assume that the auditor determines early in the audit that the client has signed several sales contracts with severe nonperformance clauses committing the company to deliver specified quantities of its product at agreed-upon prices during the current and next five years. The inherent risks for total sales, liabilities for penalties, and sales commitment disclosures are likely to be assessed as high in this situation.

## PERFORM PRELIMINARY ANALYTICAL PROCEDURES

**OBJECTIVE 7-5**
**Discuss the nature and purposes of preliminary analytical procedures.**

Chapter 6 discussed the timing of analytical procedures and the four purposes of performing them. Doing analytical procedures during the planning phase is an essential part of conducting both efficient and effective audits. For a brief review, you should examine the four purposes of analytical procedures on pages 191 and 192 and especially Figure 6-2 on page 192.

Instead of restating the importance of analytical procedures during the planning phase, one example of analytical procedures typically done during planning is provided for each of the four purposes shown in Table 7-1.

**TABLE 7-1**
**Examples of Analytical Procedures Performed during Planning**

| Purpose | Analytical Procedure Performed during the Planning Phase |
|---|---|
| Understanding the client's industry and business | Calculate key ratios for the client's business and compare them to industry averages. |
| Assess going concern | Calculate the debt to equity ratio and compare it to previous years and successful companies in the industry. |
| Indicate possible misstatements | Compare repair and maintenance expense to prior years, looking for large fluctuations. |
| Reduce detailed tests | Compare prepaid expenses and related expense accounts to prior years. |

## SUMMARY OF THE PURPOSES OF AUDIT PLANNING

There are several purposes of the planning procedures discussed in this section. A major purpose is to provide information to aid the auditor in assessing acceptable audit risk and inherent risk. These assessments will affect the auditor's client acceptance or continuation decision, the proposed audit fee, and the auditor's evidence decisions. A second purpose is to obtain information that requires follow-up during the audit. Doing so is one step in obtaining sufficient competent evidence. Examples include identifying approvals in the minutes of such items as dividends and officers' salaries, and searching for the names of related parties to help the auditor determine if related party transactions exist. Other purposes include staffing the engagement, and obtaining an engagement letter. Figure 7-3 on the following page summarizes the four major parts of audit planning discussed in this section and the key components of each part, with a brief illustration of how a CPA firm applied each component to a continuing client, Hillsburg Hardware Co.

**FIGURE 7-3**

**Key Parts of Planning: Preplan, Obtain Background Information, Obtain Information about Client's Legal Obligations, and Perform Preliminary Analytical Procedures Applied to Hillsburg Hardware Co.**

| MAJOR PART OF PLANNING | SUBPARTS OF PLANNING | APPLICATION TO HILLSBURG HARDWARE CO. |
|---|---|---|
| Preplan | New client acceptance and continuance | Hillsburg is a continuing audit client. No circumstances were identified in the continuation review to cause discontinuance. |
| | Identify client's reasons for audit | There are two primary reasons. Audit is required by bank due to large notes payable outstanding and management desires an audit for the assurance it provides. |
| | Obtain an engagement letter | (See Figure 7-2, page 223) Obtained prior to starting field work. |
| | Staff the engagement | Partner—Joe Anthony<br>Senior—Fran Moore<br>Assistant—One person to be named later |
| Obtain background information | Obtain knowledge of client's industry and business | Fran Moore discussed with Chulick and updated permanent files. |
| | Tour the plant and offices | Done by Fran Moore and assistant on the first day of field work. Fran made notes of significant observations for later follow-up. |
| | Identify related parties | Fran Moore reviewed information in permanent file with owner and chief accountant and updated file. |
| | Evaluate need for outside specialists | Due to noncomplexity of the audit, no specialists are considered necessary. |
| Obtain information about client's legal obligations | Corporate charter and bylaws | Fran Moore discussed with owner and chief accountant. There were no changes. |
| | Minutes of meetings | Fran Moore read all minutes. She had a copy made for the working papers and identified items requiring follow-up during the audit and two inherent risks. |
| | Contracts | Fran Moore briefly reviewed all continuing contracts for changes and summarized all new contracts that were relevant to the audit. |
| Perform preliminary analytical procedures | | Fran Moore compared 12-31-96 unaudited balances to the prior year. She calculated key ratios and compared them to prior years and industry averages. All significant differences were identified for follow-up. |

**WILL IT STAND UP IN COURT?**

Rhonda McMillan had been the in-charge auditor on the audit of Blaine Construction Company in 1990. Now she is sitting here, in 1996, in a room full of attorneys who are asking her questions about the 1990 audit. Blaine was sold to another company in 1991 at a purchase price that was based primarily on the 1990 audited financial statements. Several of the large construction contracts showed a profit in 1990 using the percentage of completion method, but ultimately resulted in large losses for the buyer. Since Rhonda's firm audited the 1990 financial statements, the buyer is trying to make the case that Rhonda's firm failed in their audit of contract costs and revenues.

The buyer's attorney is taking Rhonda's deposition and is asking her about the audit work she did on contracts. Referring to the working papers, his examination goes something like this:

ATTORNEY Do you recognize this exhibit, and if you do, would you please identify it for us?

RHONDA Yes, this is the summary of contracts in progress at the end of 1990.

ATTORNEY Did you prepare this document?

RHONDA I believe the client prepared it, but I audited it. My initials are right here in the upper right-hand corner.

ATTORNEY When did you do this audit work?

RHONDA I'm not sure, I forgot to date this one. But it must have been about the second week in March, because that's when we did the field work.

ATTORNEY Now I'd like to turn your attention to this tick mark next to the Baldwin contract. You see where it shows Baldwin, and then the red sort of cross-like mark?

RHONDA Yes.

ATTORNEY In the explanation for that mark it says: "Discussed status of job with Elton Burgess. Job is going according to schedule and he believes that the expected profit will be earned." Now my question is, Ms. McMillan, what exactly was the nature and content of your discussion with Mr. Burgess?

RHONDA Other than what is in the explanation to this tick mark, I have no idea. I mean, this all took place five years ago. I only worked on the engagement that one year, and I can hardly even remember that.

## WORKING PAPERS

**OBJECTIVE 7-6**
**Explain the purposes of audit working papers.**

According to SAS 41 (AU 339), working papers are the *records kept by the auditor of the procedures applied, the tests performed, the information obtained, and the pertinent conclusions reached in the engagement.* Working papers should include all the information the auditor considers necessary to conduct the audit adequately and to provide support for the audit report.

### Purposes of Working Papers

The overall objective of working papers is to aid the auditor in providing reasonable assurance that an adequate audit was conducted in accordance with generally accepted auditing standards. More specifically, the working papers, as they pertain to the current year's audit, provide a basis for planning the audit, a record of the evidence accumulated and the results of the tests, data for determining the proper type of audit report, and a basis for review by supervisors and partners.

**Basis for Planning the Audit** If the auditor is to plan the current year's audit adequately, the necessary reference information must be available in the working papers. The papers include such diverse planning information as descriptive information about internal control, a time budget for individual audit areas, the audit program, and the results of the preceding year's audit.

**Record of the Evidence Accumulated and the Results of the Tests** The working papers are the primary means of documenting that an adequate audit was conducted in accordance with GAAS. If the need arises, the auditor must be able to demonstrate to regulatory agencies and courts that the audit was well planned and adequately supervised, the evidence accumulated was competent, sufficient, and timely, and the audit report was proper, considering the results of the audit.

**Data for Deciding the Proper Type of Audit Report** The working papers provide an important source of information to assist the auditor in deciding the appropriate audit report to issue in a given set of circumstances. The data in the papers are useful for evaluating the adequacy of audit scope and the fairness of the financial statements. In addition, the working papers contain information needed for the preparation of the financial statements.

**Basis for Review by Supervisors and Partners** The working papers are the primary frame of reference used by supervisory personnel to evaluate whether sufficient competent evidence was accumulated to justify the audit report.

In addition to the purposes directly related to the audit report, the working papers have other uses. They often serve as the basis for preparing tax returns, filings with the SEC, and other reports. They are a source of information for issuing communications to the audit committee and management concerning various matters such as internal control weaknesses or operations recommendations. Working papers are also a useful frame of reference for training personnel and as an aid in planning and coordinating subsequent audits.

## Contents and Organization

**OBJECTIVE 7-7**
**Discuss and apply the concepts behind the preparation and organization of audit working papers.**

Each CPA firm establishes its own approach to preparing and organizing working papers, and the beginning auditor must adopt his or her firm's approach. The emphasis in this text is on the general concepts common to all working papers.

Figure 7-4 illustrates the contents and organization of a typical set of papers. They contain virtually everything involved in the audit. There is a definite logic to the type of working papers prepared for an audit and the way they are arranged in the files, even though different firms may follow somewhat different approaches. In the figure, the working papers start with more general information, such as corporate data in the permanent files, and end with the financial statements and audit report. In between are the working papers supporting the auditor's tests.

## Permanent Files

Permanent files are intended to contain data of a *historical or continuing nature* pertinent to the current audit. These files provide a convenient source of information about the audit that is of continuing interest from year to year. The permanent files typically include the following:

- *Extracts or copies of such company documents of continuing importance as the articles of incorporation, bylaws, bond indentures, and contracts.* The contracts are pension plans, leases, stock options, and so on. Each of these documents is of significance to the auditor for as many years as it is in effect.
- *Analyses, from previous years, of accounts that have continuing importance to the auditor.* These include accounts such as long-term debt, stockholders' equity accounts, goodwill, and fixed assets. Having this information in the permanent files enables the auditor to concentrate on analyzing only the changes in the current year's balance while retaining the results of previous years' audits in a form accessible for review.

**FIGURE 7-4**

**Working Paper Contents and Organization**

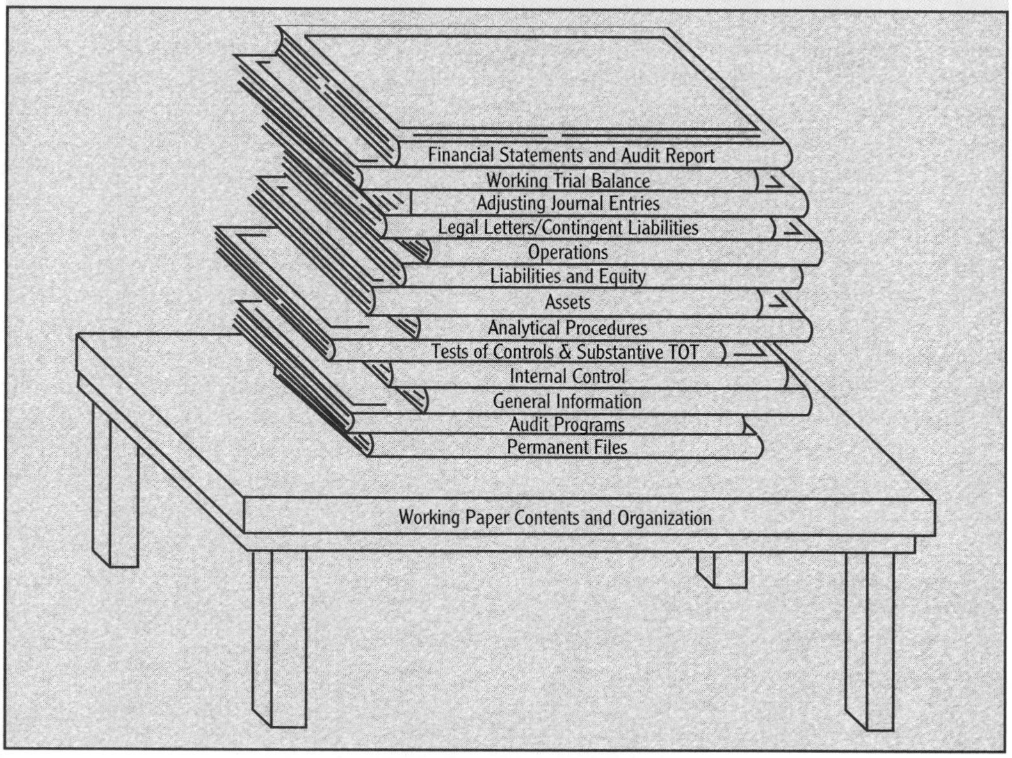


- *Information related to the understanding of internal control and assessment of control risk.* This includes organization charts, flowcharts, questionnaires, and other internal control information, including enumeration of controls and weaknesses in the system.
- *The results of analytical procedures from previous years' audits.* Among these data are ratios and percentages computed by the auditor, and the total balance or the balance by month for selected accounts. This information is useful in helping the auditor decide whether there are unusual changes in the current year's account balances that should be investigated more extensively.

Analytical procedures and the understanding of internal control and assessment of control risk are included in the current period working papers rather than in the permanent file by many CPA firms.

## Current Files

The current files include all working papers applicable to the year under audit. There is one set of permanent files for the client and a set of current files for each year's audit. The types of information included in the current file are briefly discussed in the sections that follow.

**Audit Program** The *audit program* is ordinarily maintained in a separate file to improve the coordination and integration of all parts of the audit, although some firms also include a copy of each section with that section's working papers. As the audit progresses, each auditor initials the program for the audit procedures performed and indicates the date of completion. The inclusion in the working papers of a well-designed audit program completed in a conscientious manner is evidence of a high-quality audit.

**General Information** Some working papers include current period information that is of a general nature rather than designed to support specific financial statement amounts. This includes such items as audit planning memos, abstracts or copies of minutes of the board of directors' meetings, abstracts of contracts or agreements not included in the permanent files, notes on discussions with the client, working paper review comments, and general conclusions. Documentation of the assessment of control risk may also be included.

**Working Trial Balance** Since the basis for preparing the financial statements is the general ledger, the amounts included in that record are the focal point of the audit. As early as possible after the balance sheet date, the auditor obtains or prepares a listing of the general ledger accounts and their year-end balances. This schedule is the working trial balance.

The technique used by many firms is to have the auditor's working trial balance in the same format as the financial statements. Each line item on the trial balance is supported by a *lead schedule,* containing the detailed accounts from the general ledger making up the line item total. Each detailed account on the lead schedule is, in turn, supported by appropriate schedules supporting the audit work performed and the conclusions reached. As an example, the relationship between cash as it is stated on the financial statements, the working trial balance, the lead schedule for cash, and the supporting working papers is presented in Figure 7-5. As the figure indicates, cash on the financial statements is the same as on the working trial balance and the total of the detail on the cash lead schedule. Initially, figures for the lead schedule were taken from the general ledger. The audit work performed resulted in an adjustment to cash that would be evidenced in the detail schedules and reflected on the lead schedule, the working trial balance, and the financial statements.

**FIGURE 7-5**

**Relationship of Working Papers to Financial Statements**

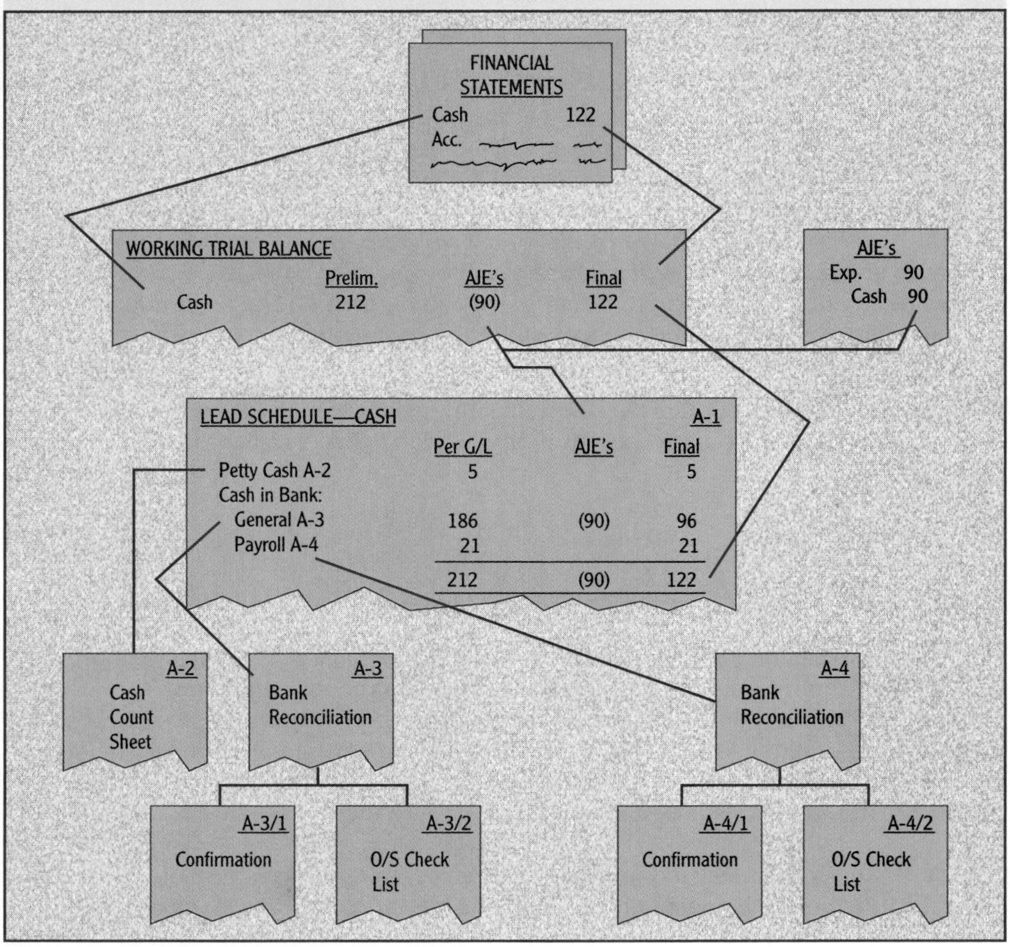

**Adjusting and Reclassification Entries** When the auditor discovers material misstatements in the accounting records, the financial statements must be corrected. For example, if the client failed to properly reduce inventory for obsolete raw materials, an adjusting entry can be made by the auditor to reflect the realizable value of the inventory. Even though adjusting entries discovered in the audit are typically prepared by the auditor, they must be approved by the client, because management has primary responsibility for the fair presentation of the statements. Figure 7-5 illustrates an adjustment of the general cash account for $90.

Reclassification entries are frequently made in the statements to present accounting information properly, even when the general ledger balances are correct. A common example is the reclassification for financial statement purposes of material credit balances in accounts receivable to accounts payable. Because the balance in accounts receivable on the general ledger reflects the accounts receivable properly from the point of view of operating the company on a day-to-day basis, the reclassification entry is not included in the client's general ledger.

Only those adjusting and reclassification entries that significantly affect the fair presentation of financial statements must be made. The determination of when a misstatement should be adjusted is based on *materiality.* The auditor should keep in mind that several immaterial misstatements that are not adjusted could result in a material overall misstatement when they are combined. It is common for auditors to summarize all entries that have not been recorded on a separate working paper as a means of determining their cumulative effect.

**Supporting Schedules** The largest portion of working papers includes the detailed schedules prepared by the client or the auditors in support of specific amounts on the financial statements. Many different types of schedules are used. Use of the appropriate type for a given aspect of the audit is necessary to document the adequacy of the audit and to fulfill the other objectives of working papers. Following are the major types of supporting schedules:

- *Analysis.* An analysis is designed to show the *activity in a general ledger account* during the entire period under audit, tying together the beginning and ending balances. This type of schedule is normally used for accounts such as marketable securities, notes receivable, allowance for doubtful accounts, property, plant, and equipment, long-term debt, and for all equity accounts. The common characteristic of these accounts is the significance of the activity in the account during the year. In most cases, the working papers for analysis have cross-references to other working papers.
- *Trial balance or list.* This type of schedule consists of the *details that make up a year-end balance* of a general ledger account. It differs from an analysis in that it includes only those items constituting the end-of-the-period balance. Common examples include trial balances or lists in support of trade accounts receivable, trade accounts payable, repair and maintenance expense, legal expense, and miscellaneous income. An example is included in Figure 7-6 on page 235.
- *Reconciliation of amounts.* A reconciliation *supports a specific amount* and is normally expected to tie the amount recorded in the client's records to another source of information. Examples include the reconciliation of bank balances with bank statements, the reconciliation of subsidiary accounts receivable balances with confirmations from customers, and the reconciliation of accounts payable balances with vendors' statements. An example is included on page 702.
- *Tests of reasonableness.* A test of reasonableness schedule, as the name implies, contains information that enables the auditor to evaluate whether the client's balance appears to include a misstatement considering the circumstances in the engagement. Frequently, auditors test depreciation expense, the provision for federal income taxes, and the allowance for doubtful accounts by tests of reasonableness. These tests are primarily analytical procedures.

- *Summary of procedures.* Another type of schedule *summarizes the results* of a specific audit procedure performed. Examples are the summary of the results of accounts receivable confirmation and the summary of inventory observations.
- *Examination of supporting documents.* A number of special-purpose schedules are designed to *show detailed tests performed,* such as examination of documents during tests of controls and substantive tests of transactions or cutoffs. These schedules show no totals, and they do not tie in to the general ledger because they document only the tests performed and the results found. The schedules must, however, state a definite positive or negative conclusion about the objective of the test.
- *Informational.* This type of schedule contains information as opposed to audit evidence. These schedules include information for tax returns and SEC Form 10-K data, and data such as time budgets and the client's working hours, which are helpful in administration of the engagement.
- *Outside documentation.* Much of the content of the working papers consists of the outside documentation gathered by auditors, such as confirmation replies and copies of client agreements. Although not "schedules" in the real sense, these are indexed and interfiled, and procedures are indicated on them in the same manner as on the other schedules.

## Preparation of Working Papers

The proper preparation of schedules to document the audit evidence accumulated, the results found, and the conclusions reached is an important part of the audit. The auditor must recognize the circumstances requiring the need for a schedule and the appropriate design of schedules to be included in the files. Although the design depends on the objectives involved, working papers should possess certain characteristics:

- Each working paper should be properly identified with such information as the client's name, the period covered, a description of the contents, the initials of the preparer, the date of preparation, and an index code.
- Working papers should be indexed and cross-referenced to aid in organizing and filing. One type of indexing is illustrated in Figure 7-5. The lead schedule for cash has been indexed as A-1, and the individual general ledger accounts making up the total cash on the financial statements are indexed as A-2 through A-4. The final indexing is for the schedules supporting A-3 and A-4.
- Completed working papers must clearly indicate the audit work performed. This is accomplished in three ways: by a written statement in the form of a memorandum, by initialing the audit procedures in the audit program, and by notations directly on the working paper schedules. Notations on working papers are accomplished by the use of *tick marks,* which are *symbols* written adjacent to the detail on the body of the schedule. These notations must be clearly explained at the bottom of the working paper.
- Each working paper should include sufficient information to fulfill the objectives for which it was designed. If the auditor is to prepare working papers properly, the auditor must be aware of his or her goals. For example, if a working paper is designed to list the detail and show the verification of support of a balance sheet account, such as prepaid insurance, it is essential that the detail on the working paper reconcile with the trial balance.
- The conclusions that were reached about the segment of the audit under consideration should be plainly stated.

The common characteristics of proper working paper preparation are indicated in Figure 7-6.

**FIGURE 7-6**

**Common Characteristics of Proper Working Papers**

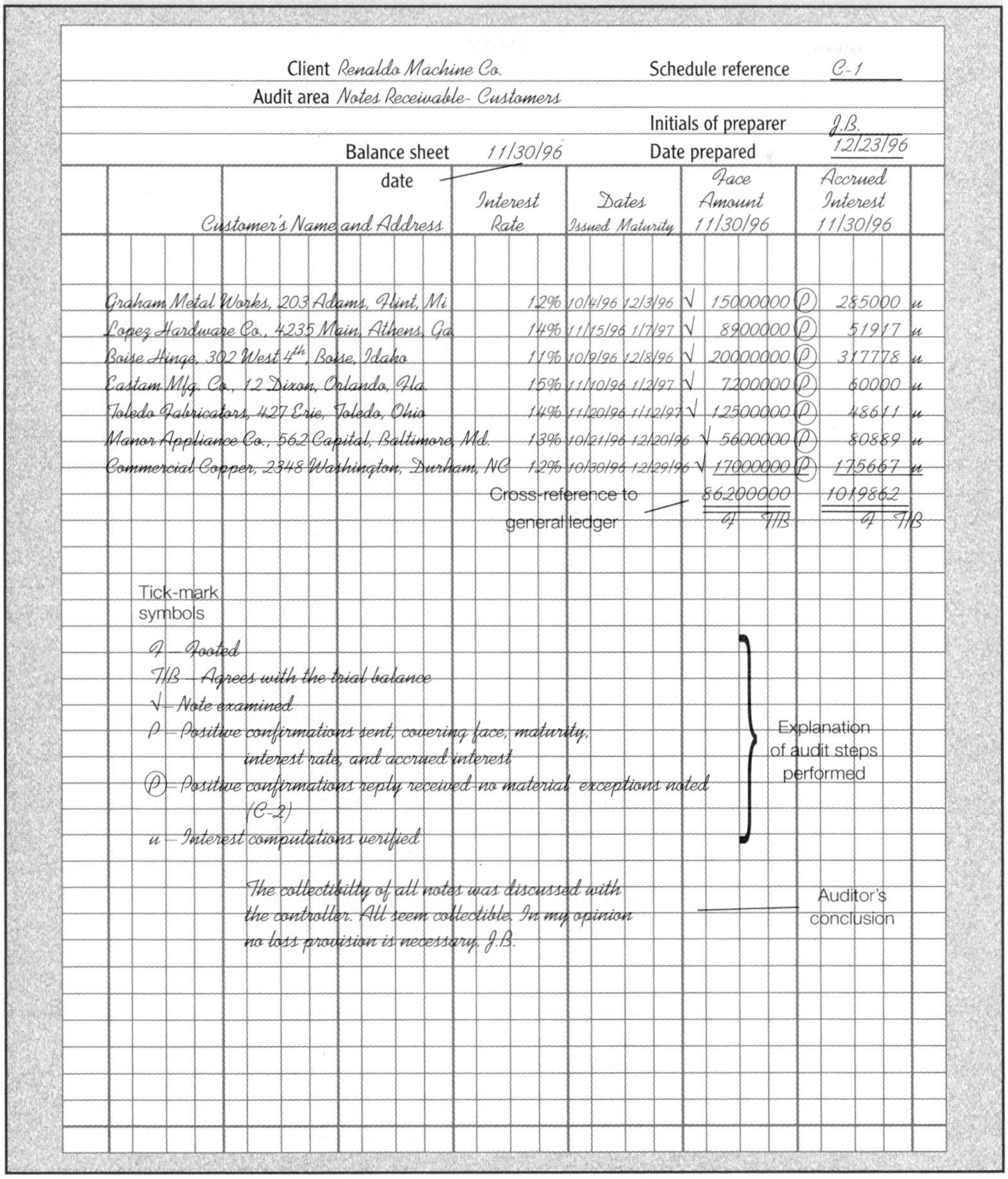

Client *Renaldo Machine Co.* Schedule reference *C-1*

Audit area *Notes Receivable- Customers*

Initials of preparer *J.B.*

Balance sheet date *11/30/96* Date prepared *12/23/96*

| Customer's Name and Address | Interest Rate | Dates Issued | Dates Maturity | | Face Amount 11/30/96 | | Accrued Interest 11/30/96 | |
|---|---|---|---|---|---|---|---|---|
| Graham Metal Works, 203 Adams, Flint, Mi | 12% | 10/4/96 | 12/3/96 | √ | 15000000 | Ⓟ | 285000 | u |
| Lopez Hardware Co., 4235 Main, Athens, Ga | 14% | 11/15/96 | 1/7/97 | √ | 8900000 | Ⓟ | 51917 | u |
| Boise Hinge, 302 West 4th, Boise, Idaho | 11% | 10/9/96 | 12/8/96 | √ | 20000000 | Ⓟ | 317778 | u |
| Eastam Mfg. Co., 12 Dixon, Orlando, Fla. | 15% | 11/10/96 | 1/2/97 | √ | 7200000 | Ⓟ | 60000 | u |
| Toledo Fabricators, 427 Erie, Toledo, Ohio | 14% | 11/20/96 | 1/12/97 | √ | 12500000 | Ⓟ | 48611 | u |
| Manor Appliance Co., 562 Capital, Baltimore, Md. | 13% | 10/21/96 | 12/20/96 | √ | 5600000 | Ⓟ | 80889 | u |
| Commercial Copper, 2348 Washington, Durham, NC | 12% | 10/30/96 | 12/29/96 | √ | 17000000 | Ⓟ | 175667 | u |
| | | | | | 86200000 | | 1019862 | |
| | | | | | F T/B | | F T/B | |

Cross-reference to general ledger

Tick-mark symbols

F — Footed
T/B — Agrees with the trial balance
√ — Note examined
P — Positive confirmations sent, covering face, maturity, interest rate, and accrued interest
Ⓟ — Positive confirmations reply received-no material exceptions noted (C-2)
u — Interest computations verified

Explanation of audit steps performed

*The collectibility of all notes was discussed with the controller. All seem collectible. In my opinion no loss provision is necessary. J.B.*

Auditor's conclusion

---

Many CPA firms use their own computers to produce some or all of their working papers. Most large firms develop their own software. Smaller firms usually buy commercial working paper software. An example of such software is ACE (Automated Client Engagement). Using ACE, an auditor can prepare a trial balance, lead schedules, supporting working papers, and financial statements, as well as perform ratio analysis. Tick marks and other items, such as reviewer notes, can be entered directly on the computer screen. In addition, data can be imported from and exported to other applications. Examples include downloading a client's general ledger into ACE and exporting tax information to a commercial tax preparation package.

**CPA FIRMS USE COMPUTER-AUTOMATED WORKING PAPERS**

**Ownership of Working Papers**

The working papers prepared during the engagement, including those prepared by the client for the auditor, are the *property of the auditor.* The only time anyone else, including the client, has a legal right to examine the papers is when they are subpoenaed by a court as legal evidence. At the completion of the engagement, working papers are retained on the CPA's premises for future reference. Many firms follow the practice of microfilming the working papers after several years to reduce storage costs.

**Confidentiality of Working Papers**

The need to maintain a confidential relationship with the client is expressed in Rule 301 of the *Code of Professional Conduct,* which states

- A member shall not disclose any confidential information obtained in the course of a professional engagement except with the consent of the client.

During the course of the audit, auditors obtain a considerable amount of information of a confidential nature, including officer salaries, product pricing and advertising plans, and product cost data. If auditors divulged this information to outsiders or to client employees who have been denied access, their relationship with management would be seriously strained. Furthermore, having access to the working papers would give employees an opportunity to alter information on them. For these reasons, care must be taken to protect the working papers at all times.

Ordinarily, the working papers can be provided to someone else only with the express permission of the client. This is the case even if a CPA sells his or her practice to another CPA firm. Permission is not required from the client, however, if the working papers are subpoenaed by a court or are used as part of an AICPA or state society approved peer review program with other CPA firms.

## SUMMARY OF WORKING PAPERS

Working papers are an essential part of every audit for effectively planning the audit, providing a record of the evidence accumulated and the results of the tests, deciding the proper type of audit report, and reviewing the work of assistants. CPA firms establish their own policies and approaches for working paper preparation to make sure that these objectives are met. High-quality CPA firms make sure that working papers are properly prepared and are appropriate for the circumstances in the audit.

**THE BURDEN OF PROOF**

Jury studies conducted by a professional liability insurance company in California show jurors consider CPAs experts in documentation. Therefore, when practitioners are faced with a liability suit and have fallen short of that expectation, they are likely to be judged negligent. On the other hand, even an informal note documenting a brief telephone conversation can sway a jury in the CPA's favor. Legally, the burden of proof rests with the plaintiff, but as a practical matter, the burden to document falls on the CPA.

*Source:* Excerpted from an article by Ric Rosario, "Making Documentation Pay Off," *Journal of Accountancy,* February 1995, p. 70.

## ESSENTIAL TERMS

**Acceptable audit risk**—a measure of how willing the auditor is to accept that the financial statements may be materially misstated after the audit is completed and an unqualified opinion has been issued

**Analysis working paper**—a supporting schedule that shows the activity in a general ledger account during the entire period under audit

**Bylaws**—the rules and procedures adopted by a corporation's stockholders, including the corporation's fiscal year and the duties and powers of its officers

**Corporate charter**—a legal document granted by the state in which a company is incorporated that recognizes a corporation as a separate entity. It includes the name of the corporation, the date of incorporation, capital stock the corporation is authorized to issue, and the types of business activities the corporation is authorized to conduct.

**Corporate minutes**—the official record of the meetings of a corporation's board of directors and stockholders, in which corporate issues such as the declaration of dividends and the approval of contracts are documented

**Current files**—all working papers applicable to the year under audit

**Engagement letter**—an agreement between the CPA firm and the client as to the terms of the engagement for the conduct of the audit and related services

**Inherent risk**—a measure of the auditor's assessment of the likelihood that there are material misstatements in a segment before considering the effectiveness of internal control

**Lead schedule**—a working paper that contains the detailed accounts from the general ledger making up a line item total in the working trial balance

**Permanent files**—auditors' working papers that contain data of a *historical or continuing nature* pertinent to the current audit such as copies of articles of incorporation, bylaws, bond indentures, and contracts

**Preplanning the audit**—involves deciding whether to accept or continue doing the audit for the client, identifying the client's reasons for the audit, obtaining an engagement letter, and selecting staff for the engagement

**Reconciliation of amounts working paper**—a schedule that supports a specific amount; it normally ties the amount recorded in the client's records to another source of information, such as a bank statement or a confirmation

**Related party**—affiliated company, principal owner of the client company, or any other party with which the client deals where one of the parties can influence the management or operating policies of the other

**Related party transaction**—any transaction between the client and a related party

**Supporting schedule working paper**—a detailed schedule prepared by the client or the auditor in support of a specific amount on the financial statements

**Trial balance or list working paper**—a supporting schedule of the details that make up the year-end balance of a general ledger account

**Working papers**—the records kept by the auditor of the procedures applied, the tests performed, the information obtained, and the pertinent conclusions reached in the engagement

**Working trial balance**—a listing of the general ledger accounts and their year-end balances

## REVIEW QUESTIONS

**7-1 (Objective 7-1)** What benefits does the auditor derive from planning audits?

**7-2 (Objective 7-1)** Identify the seven major steps in planning audits.

**7-3 (Objective 7-2)** What are the responsibilities of the successor and predecessor auditors when a company is changing auditors?

**7-4 (Objective 7-2)** What factors should an auditor consider prior to accepting an engagement? Explain.

**7-5 (Objective 7-2)** What is the purpose of an engagement letter? What subjects should be covered in such a letter?

**7-6 (Objective 7-3)** List the four types of information the auditor should obtain or review as a part of gaining background information for the audit, and provide one specific example of how the information will be useful in conducting an audit.

**7-7 (Objective 7-3)** When a CPA has accepted an engagement from a new client who is a manufacturer, it is customary for the CPA to tour the client's plant facilities. Discuss the ways in which the CPA's observations made during the course of the plant tour will be of help as he or she plans and conducts the audit.

**7-8 (Objective 7-3)** An auditor often tries to acquire background knowledge of the client's industry as an aid to his or her audit work. How does the acquisition of this knowledge aid the auditor in distinguishing between obsolete and current inventory?

**7-9 (Objective 7-3)** Define what is meant by a related party. What are the auditor's responsibilities for related parties and related party transactions?

**7-10 (Objective 7-6)** Jennifer Bailey is an experienced senior auditor who is in charge of several important audits for a medium-sized firm. Her philosophy of conducting audits is to ignore all previous years' and permanent working papers until near the end of the audit as a means of keeping from prejudicing herself. She believes that this enables her to perform the audit in a more independent manner because it eliminates the tendency of simply doing the same things in the current audit that were done on previous audits. Near the end of the audit Bailey reviews the working papers from the preceding year, evaluates the significance of any items she has overlooked, and modifies her evidence if she considers it necessary. Evaluate Bailey's approach to conducting an audit.

**7-11 (Objective 7-4)** Your firm has performed the audit of the Rogers Company for several years and you have been assigned the audit responsibility for the current audit. How would your review of the corporate charter and bylaws for this audit differ from that of the audit of a client who was audited by a different CPA firm in the preceding year?

**7-12 (Objective 7-4)** For the audit of Radline Manufacturing Company, the audit partner asks you to carefully read the new mortgage contract with the First National Bank and abstract all pertinent information. List the information in a mortgage that is likely to be relevant to the auditor.

**7-13 (Objective 7-4)** Identify two types of information in the client's minutes of the board of directors' meetings that are likely to be relevant to the auditor. Explain why it is important to read the minutes early in the engagement.

**7-14 (Objective 7-6)** List the purposes of working papers and explain why each purpose is important.

**7-15 (Objective 7-7)** Explain why it is important for working papers to include each of the following: identification of the name of the client, period covered, description of the contents, initials of the preparer, date of the preparation, and an index code.

**7-16 (Objective 7-7)** Define what is meant by a permanent file of working papers, and list several types of information typically included. Why does the auditor not include the contents of the permanent file with the current year's working papers?

**7-17 (Objective 7-7)** Distinguish between the following types of current period supporting schedules and state the purpose of each: analysis, trial balance, and tests of reasonableness.

**7-18 (Objective 7-7)** Why is it essential that the auditor not leave questions or exceptions in the working papers without an adequate explanation?

**7-19 (Objective 7-7)** Define what is meant by a tick mark. What is its purpose?

**7-20 (Objective 7-7)** Who owns the working papers? Under what circumstances can they be used by other people?

**7-21 (Objective 7-7)** A CPA sells his auditing practice to another CPA firm and includes all working papers as a part of the purchase price. Under what circumstances is this a violation of the *Code of Professional Conduct?*

## MULTIPLE CHOICE QUESTIONS FROM CPA EXAMINATIONS

**7-22 (Objectives 7-1, 7-3)** The following questions concern the planning of the engagement. Select the best response.

a. Which of the following is an effective audit planning procedure that helps prevent misunderstandings and inefficient use of audit personnel?
   (1) Arrange to make copies, for inclusion in the working papers, of those client-supporting documents examined by the auditor.
   (2) Arrange to provide the client with copies of the audit programs to be used during the audit.

(3) Arrange a preliminary conference with the client to discuss audit objectives, fees, timing, and other information.
(4) Arrange to have the auditor prepare and post any necessary adjusting or reclassification entries prior to final closing.

b. An auditor is planning an audit engagement for a new client in a business with which he is unfamiliar. Which of the following would be the most useful source of information during the preliminary planning stage, when the auditor is trying to obtain a general understanding of audit problems that might be encountered?
(1) Client manuals of accounts and charts of accounts.
(2) AICPA Industry Audit Guides.
(3) Prior-year working papers of the predecessor auditor.
(4) Latest annual and interim financial statements issued by the client.

c. The independent auditor should acquire an understanding of a client's internal audit function to determine whether the work of internal auditors will be a factor in determining the nature, timing, and extent of the independent auditor's procedures. The work performed by internal auditors might be such a factor when the internal auditor's work includes
(1) verification of the mathematical accuracy of invoices.
(2) review of administrative practices to improve efficiency and achieve management objectives.
(3) study and evaluation of internal control.
(4) preparation of internal financial reports for management purposes.

**7-23 (Objective 7-2)** The following questions pertain to the predecessor/successor auditor relationship. Choose the best response.

a. When approached to perform an audit for the first time, the CPA should make inquiries of the predecessor auditor. This is a necessary procedure because the predecessor may be able to provide the successor with information that will assist the successor in determining
(1) whether the predecessor's work should be used.
(2) whether the company follows the policy of rotating its auditors.
(3) whether in the predecessor's opinion internal control of the company has been satisfactory.
(4) whether the engagement should be accepted.

b. Hawkins requested permission to communicate with the predecessor auditor and review certain portions of the predecessor's working papers. The prospective client's refusal to permit this will bear directly on Hawkins' decision concerning the
(1) adequacy of the preplanned audit program.
(2) ability to establish consistency in application of accounting principles between years.
(3) apparent scope limitation.
(4) integrity of management.

c. What is the responsibility of a successor auditor with respect to communicating with the predecessor auditor in connection with a prospective new audit client?
(1) The successor auditor has *no* responsibility to contact the predecessor auditor.
(2) The successor auditor should obtain permission from the prospective client to contact the predecessor auditor.
(3) The successor auditor should contact the predecessor regardless of whether the prospective client authorizes contact.
(4) The successor auditor need *not* contact the predecessor if the successor is aware of all available relevant facts.

**7-24 (Objectives 7-6, 7-7)** The following questions concern working papers. Choose the best response.

a. Which of the following is *not* a primary purpose of audit working papers?

(1) To coordinate the audit.
(2) To assist in preparation of the audit report.
(3) To support the financial statements.
(4) To provide evidence of the audit work performed.

b. Audit working papers are used to record the results of the auditor's evidence-gathering procedures. When preparing working papers, the auditor should remember that working papers should be
(1) kept on the client's premises so that the client can have access to them for reference purposes.
(2) the primary support for the financial statements being audited.
(3) considered as a part of the client's accounting records that are retained by the auditor.
(4) designed to meet the circumstances and the auditor's needs on each engagement.

c. Which of the following eliminates voluminous details from the auditor's working trial balance by classifying and summarizing similar or related items?
(1) Account analyses
(2) Supporting schedules
(3) Control accounts
(4) Lead schedules

d. During an audit engagement, pertinent data are compiled and included in the audit working papers. The working papers primarily are considered to be
(1) a client-owned record of conclusions reached by the auditors who performed the engagement.
(2) evidence supporting financial statements.
(3) support for the auditor's representations as to compliance with generally accepted auditing standards.
(4) a record to be used as a basis for the following year's engagement.

e. Although the quantity, type, and content of working papers will vary with the circumstances, the working papers generally would include the
(1) copies of those client records examined by the auditor during the course of the engagement.
(2) evaluation of the efficiency and competence of the audit staff assistants by the partner responsible for the audit.
(3) auditor's comments concerning the efficiency and competence of client management personnel.
(4) auditing procedures followed and the testing performed in obtaining evidential matter.

**7-25 (Objective 7-5)** The following questions concern the use of analytical procedures during the planning phase of an audit. Select the best response.

a. Analytical procedures used in planning an audit should focus on identifying
(1) material weaknesses of internal control.
(2) the predictability of financial data from individual transactions.
(3) the various assertions that are embodied in the financial statements.
(4) areas that may represent specific risks relevant to the audit.

b. A basic premise underlying the application of analytical procedures is that
(1) the study of financial ratios is an acceptable alternative to the investigation of unusual fluctuations.
(2) statistical tests of financial information may lead to the discovery of material misstatements in the financial statements.
(3) plausible relationships among data may reasonably be expected to exist and continue in the absence of known conditions to the contrary.
(4) these procedures *cannot* replace tests of controls, substantive transactions, and tests of details of balances.

**7-26 (Objectives 7-2, 7-3, 7-4)** In late spring you are advised of a new assignment as in-charge accountant of your CPA firm's recurring annual audit of a major client, the Lancer Company. You are given the engagement letter for the audit covering the current calendar year and a list of personnel assigned to this engagement. It is your responsibility to plan and supervise the field work for the engagement.

## Required

Discuss the necessary preparation and planning for the Lancer Company annual audit *prior* to beginning field work at the client's office. In your discussion include the sources you should consult, the type of information you should seek, the preliminary plans and preparation you should make for the field work, and any actions you should take relative to the staff assigned to the engagement.*

**7-27 (Objective 7-3)** Generally accepted accounting principles set certain requirements for disclosure of related parties and related party transactions. Similarly, the SASs set requirements for the audit of related parties and related party transactions. For this problem you are expected to research appropriate SFASs and SASs.

## Required

a. Define *related party* as used for generally accepted accounting principles and explain the disclosure requirements for related parties and related party transactions.

b. Explain why disclosure of related party transactions is relevant information for decision makers.

c. List the most important related parties who are likely to be involved in related party transactions.

d. List several different types of related party transactions that could take place in a company.

e. Discuss ways the auditor can determine the existence of related parties and related party transactions.

f. For each type of related party transaction, discuss different ways the auditor can evaluate whether they are recorded on an arm's-length basis, assuming that the auditor knows the transactions exist.

g. Assume that you know the material related party transactions occurred and were transacted at significantly less favorable terms than ordinarily occur when business is done with independent parties. The client refuses to disclose these facts in the financial statements. What are your responsibilities?

**7-28 (Objective 7-4)** The minutes of the board of directors of the Marygold Catalog Company for the year ended December 31, 1996 were provided to you.

MEETING OF FEBRUARY 16, 1996

Ruth Jackson, chairman of the board, called the meeting to order at 4:00 p.m. The following directors were in attendance:

| | |
|---|---|
| John Aronson | Licorine Phillips |
| Fred Brick | Lucille Renolds |
| Oron Carlson | J. T. Smith |
| Homer Jackson | Raymond Werd |
| Ruth Jackson | Ronald Wilder |

The minutes of the meeting of October 11, 1995 were read and approved.

*AICPA adapted.

Homer Jackson, president, discussed the new marketing plan for wider distribution of catalogs in the southwestern U.S. market. He made a motion for approval of increased expenditures of approximately $50,000 for distribution costs that was seconded by Wilder and unanimously passed.

The unresolved dispute with the Internal Revenue Service over the tax treatment of leased office buildings was discussed with Cecil Makay, attorney. In Mr. Makay's opinion, the matter would not be resolved for several months and may result in an unfavorable settlement.

J. T. Smith moved that the computer equipment that was no longer being used in the Kingston office, because of new equipment acquired in 1995, be donated to the Kingston vocational school for use in their repair and training program. John Aronson seconded the motion and it unanimously passed.

Annual cash dividends were unanimously approved as being payable April 30, 1996, for stockholders of record April 15, 1996, as follows:

Class A common—$10 per share
Class B common—$5 per share

Officers' bonuses for the year ended December 31, 1995 were approved for payment March 1, 1996, as follows:

| | |
|---|---|
| Homer Jackson—President | $26,000 |
| Lucille Renolds—Vice president | 12,000 |
| Ronald Wilder—Controller | 12,000 |
| Fred Brick—Secretary-treasurer | 9,000 |

Meeting adjourned 6:30 p.m.

*Fred Brick, Secretary*

---

MEETING OF SEPTEMBER 15, 1996

Ruth Jackson, chairman of the board, called the meeting to order at 4:00 p.m. The following directors were in attendance:

| | |
|---|---|
| John Aronson | Licorine Phillips |
| Fred Brick | Lucille Renolds |
| Oron Carlson | J. T. Smith |
| Homer Jackson | Raymond Werd |
| Ruth Jackson | Ronald Wilder |

The minutes of the meeting of February 16, 1996 were read and approved.

Homer Jackson, president, discussed the improved sales and financial condition for 1996. He was pleased with the results of the catalog distribution and cost control for the company. No action was taken.

The nominations for officers were made as follows:

| | |
|---|---|
| President | —Homer Jackson |
| Vice president | —Lucille Renolds |
| Controller | —Ronald Wilder |
| Secretary-treasurer | —Fred Brick |

The nominees were elected by unanimous voice vote.

Salary increases of 6 percent, exclusive of bonuses, were recommended for all officers for 1997. Homer Jackson moved that such salary increases be approved, seconded by J. T. Smith and unanimously approved.

| | SALARY | |
|---|---|---|
| | 1996 | 1997 |
| Homer Jackson, President | $90,000 | $95,000 |
| Lucille Renolds, Vice president | 60,000 | 63,600 |
| Ronald Wilder, Controller | 60,000 | 63,600 |
| Fred Brick, Secretary-treasurer | 40,000 | 42,000 |

Ronald Wilder moved that the company consider adopting a pension/profit-sharing plan for all employees as a way to provide greater incentive for employees to stay with the company. Considerable discussion ensued. It was agreed without adoption that Wilder should discuss the legal and tax implications with attorney Cecil Makay and a CPA firm reputed to be knowledgeable about pension and profit-sharing plans, Able and Better, CPAs.

Ronald Wilder discussed expenditure of $58,000 for acquisition of a new computer for the Kingston office to replace equipment that was purchased in 1995 and has proven ineffective. A settlement has been tentatively reached to return the equipment for a refund of $21,000. Wilder moved that both transactions be approved, seconded by Jackson, and unanimously adopted.

Fred Brick moved that a loan of $36,000, from the Kingston Federal Bank and Trust, be approved. The interest is floating at 2 percent above prime. The collateral is to be the new computer equipment being installed in the Kingston office. A checking account, with a minimum balance of $2,000 at all times until the loan is repaid, must be opened and maintained if the loan is granted. Seconded by Phillips and unanimously approved.

Lucille Renolds, chair of the audit committee, moved that the CPA firm of Moss and Lawson be selected again for the company's annual audit and related tax work for the year ended December 31, 1996. Seconded by Aronson and unanimously approved.

Meeting adjourned 6:40 p.m.

*Fred Brick, Secretary*

## Required

a. How do you, as the auditor, know that all minutes have been made available to you?

b. Read the minutes of the meetings of February 16 and September 15. Use the following format to list and explain information that is relevant for the 1996 audit:

| Information Relevant to 1996 Audit | Audit Action Required |
|---|---|
| 1. | |
| 2. | |

c. Read the minutes of the meeting of February 16, 1996. Did any of that information pertain to the December 31, 1995 audit? Explain what the auditor should have done during the December 31, 1995 audit with respect to 1996 minutes.

**7-29 (Objectives 7-4, 7-5)** You are engaged in the annual audit of the financial statements of Maulack Company, a medium-sized wholesale company that manufactures light fixtures. The company has twenty-five stockholders. During your review of the minutes you observe that the president's salary has been increased substantially over the preceding year by action of the board of directors. His present salary is much greater than salaries paid to presidents of companies of comparable size and is clearly excessive. You determine that the method of computing the president's salary was changed for the year under audit. In previous years, the president's salary was consistently based on sales. In the latest year, however, his salary was based on net income before income taxes. The Maulack company is in a cyclical industry and would have had an extremely profitable year except that the increase in the president's salary siphoned off much of the income that would have accrued to the stockholders. The president is a substantial stockholder.

## Required

a. What is the implication of this condition on the fair presentation of the financial statements?

b. Discuss your responsibility for disclosing this situation.

c. Discuss the effect, if any, that the situation has on your auditor's opinion as to
   (1) the fairness of the presentation of the financial statements.
   (2) the consistency of the application of accounting principles.*

**7-30 (Objectives 7-6, 7-7)** The preparation of working papers is an integral part of a CPA's audit of financial statements. On a recurring engagement, a CPA reviews audit programs and working papers from the prior audit while planning the current audit to determine their usefulness for the current engagement.

## Required

a. What are the purposes or functions of audit working papers?

b. What records may be included in audit working papers?

c. What factors affect the CPA's judgment of the type and content of the working papers for an engagement?*

**7-31 (Objectives 7-6, 7-7)** Do the following with regard to the working paper for the ABC Company shown below.

a. List the deficiencies in the working paper.

b. For each deficiency, state how the working paper could be improved.

c. Prepare an improved working paper, using an electronic spreadsheet software program. Include an indication of the audit work done as well as the analysis of the client data. (Instructor's option.)

**ABC Company, Inc.**
**A/C # 110 - Notes Receivable**
**12-31-96**

| | | Date |
|---|---|---|
| **Schedule** | N-1 | |
| **Prepared by** | JD | 1-21-97 |
| **Approved by** | PP | 2-15-97 |

| | APEX CO. | | AJAX, INC. | | J.J. CO. | | P. SMITH | | MARTIN-PETERSON | | TENT CO. | | TOTALS | |
|---|---|---|---|---|---|---|---|---|---|---|---|---|---|---|
| Date made | 6/15/95 | | 11/21/95 | | 11/1/95 | | 7/26/96 | | 5/12/95 | | 9/3/96 | | | |
| Date due | 6/15/97 | | Demand | | $200/mo. | | $1,000/mo. | | Demand | | $400/mo. | | | |
| Paid to date | None | | Paid | | 12/31/96 | | 9/30/96 | | Paid | | 11/30/96 | | | |
| Face amount | $5,000 | x | $3,591 | x | $13,180 | x | $25,000 | x | $2,100 | x | $12,000 | x | | |
| Interest rate | 5% | | 5% | | 5% | | 5% | | 5% | | 6% | | | |
| Value of security | None | | None | | $24,000 | | $50,000 | | None | | $10,000 | | | |
| **Note Receivable:** | | | | | | | | | | | | | | |
| Beg. balance 12/31/95 | $4,000 | py | $3,591 | py | $12,780 | py | $0 | | $2,100 | py | $0 | | | |
| Additions | | | | | | | 25,000 | | | | 12,000 | | | |
| Payments | (1,000) | x | (3,591) | x | (2,400) | x | (5,000) | x | (2,100) | x | (1,600) | x | | |
| End. balance 12/31/96 | $3,000 | | $0 | | $10,380 | | $20,000 | | $0 | | $10,400 | | | |
| Current | $3,000 | | — | | $2,400 | | $12,000 | | — | | $4,800 | | $22,200 | tb |
| Long-term | — | | — | | 7,980 | | 8,000 | | — | | 5,600 | | 21,580 | tb |
| Total end. balance | $3,000 | @ | $0 | | $10,380 | @ | $20,000 | @ | $0 | | $10,400 | @ | $43,780 | tb |
| **Interest Receivable:** | | | | | | | | | | | | | | |
| Beg. balance 12/31/95 | $104 | py | $0 | py | $24 | py | $0 | | $0 | py | $0 | | $128 | |
| Interest earned | 175 | x | 102 | x | 577 | x | 468 | x | 105 | x | 162 | x | 1,589 | # |
| Interest received | 0 | | (102) | x | (601) | x | (200) | x | (105) | x | (108) | x | (1,116) | |
| End. balance 12/31/96 | $279 | | $0 | | $0 | | $268 | | $0 | | $54 | | $601 | a/r |

| | |
|---|---|
| x | Tested |
| py | Agrees with prior year's working papers. |
| tb | Agrees with working trial balance. |
| # | Agrees with miscellaneous income analysis in operations w/p. |
| a/r | Agrees with A/R lead schedule. |

*AICPA adapted

FIGURE 8-1

**Steps in Applying Materiality**

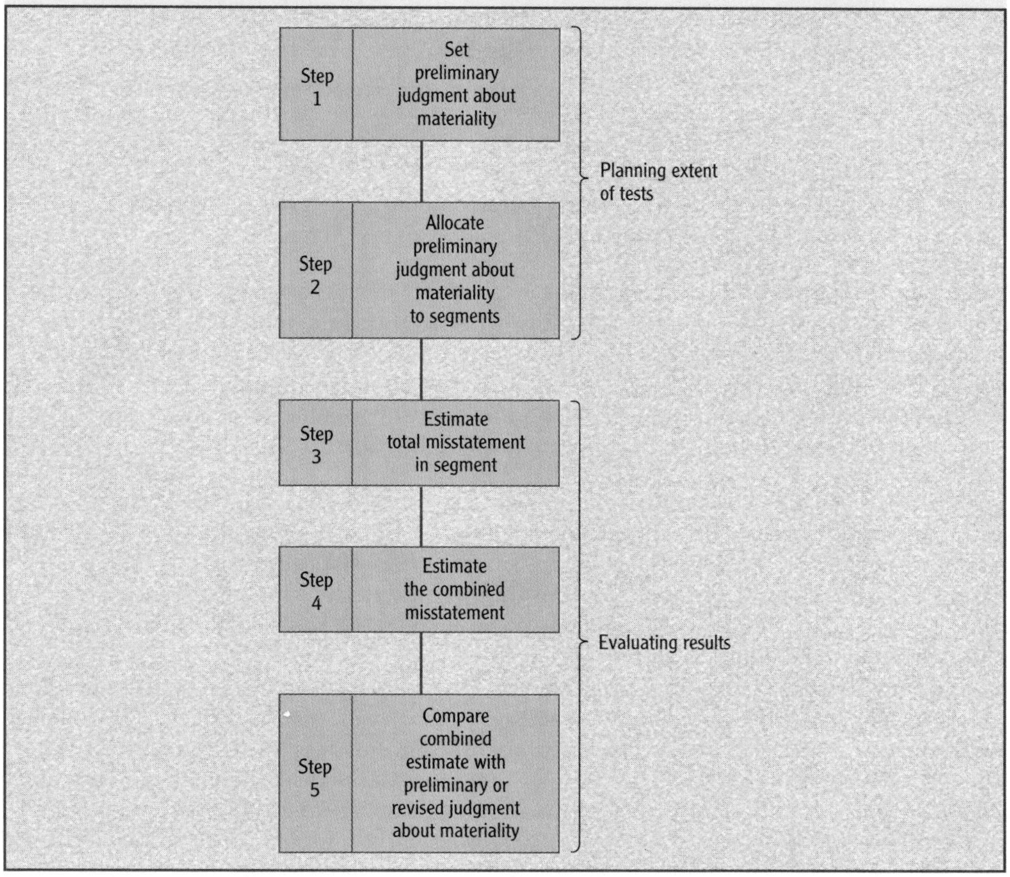


## SET PRELIMINARY JUDGMENT ABOUT MATERIALITY

**OBJECTIVE 8-2**

**Make a preliminary judgment about what amounts to consider material.**

Ideally, an auditor decides early in the audit the combined amount of misstatements in the financial statements that would be considered material. SAS 47 (AU 312) defines the amount as the *preliminary judgment about materiality.* This judgment need not be quantified but often is. It is called a preliminary judgment about materiality because it is a professional judgment and may change during the engagement if circumstances change.

The preliminary judgment about materiality (step 1 in Figure 8-1) is thus the maximum amount by which the auditor believes the statements could be misstated and still *not* affect the decisions of reasonable users. (Conceptually, this would be an amount that is $1 less than materiality as defined by the FASB. Preliminary materiality is defined in this manner as a convenience in application.) This judgment is one of the most important decisions the auditor makes. It requires considerable professional judgment.

The reason for setting a preliminary judgment about materiality is to help the auditor plan the appropriate evidence to accumulate. If the auditor sets a low dollar amount, more evidence is required than for a high amount. Examine again the financial statements of Hillsburg Hardware Co. on pages 139–140. What do you think is the combined amount of misstatements that would affect decisions of reasonable users? Do you believe that a $100 misstatement would affect users' decisions? If so, the amount of evidence required for the audit is likely to be beyond that for which the management of Hillsburg Hardware would be willing to pay. Do you believe that a $1 million misstatement would be material? Most experienced auditors would say that amount is far too large as a combined materiality amount in these circumstances.

The auditor will frequently change the preliminary judgment about materiality during the audit. Whenever that is done, the new judgment is called a revised judgment about materiality. Reasons for using a revised judgment can include a change in one of the factors used to determine the preliminary judgment or a decision by the auditor that the preliminary judgment was too large or too small.

## Factors Affecting Judgment

Several factors affect setting a preliminary judgment about materiality for a given set of financial statements. The most important of these are discussed below.

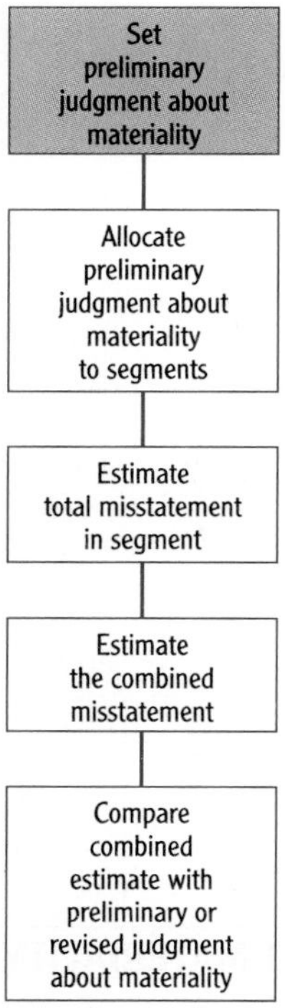


**Materiality Is a Relative Rather Than an Absolute Concept** A misstatement of a given magnitude might be material for a small company, whereas the same dollar misstatement could be immaterial for a large one. For example, a total misstatement of $1 million would be extremely material for Hillsburg Hardware Co., but it would be immaterial for a company such as IBM. Hence, it is not possible to establish any dollar-value guidelines for a preliminary judgment about materiality applicable to all audit clients.

**Bases Are Needed for Evaluating Materiality** Since materiality is relative, it is necessary to have bases for establishing whether misstatements are material. *Net income before taxes* is normally the most important base for deciding what is material, because it is regarded as a critical item of information for users. It also is important to learn whether the misstatements could materially affect the reasonableness of other possible bases such as current assets, total assets, current liabilities, and owners' equity.

Assume that for a given company, an auditor decided that a misstatement of income before taxes of $100,000 or more would be material, but a misstatement of $250,000 or more would be material for current assets. It would be inappropriate for the auditor to use a preliminary judgment about materiality of $250,000 for both income before taxes and current assets. The auditor must therefore plan to find all misstatements affecting income before taxes that exceed the preliminary judgment about materiality of $100,000. Since most misstatements affect both the income statement and balance sheet, the auditor will not be greatly concerned about the possibility of misstatement of current assets exceeding $250,000, and will use a materiality level of $100,000 for most tests. However, some misstatements, such as misclassifying a long-term asset as a current one, affect only the balance sheet. The auditor will therefore also need to plan the audit with the $250,000 preliminary judgment about materiality for certain tests of current assets.

**Qualitative Factors Also Affect Materiality** Certain types of misstatements are likely to be more important to users than others, even if the dollar amounts are the same. For example:

- Amounts involving fraud are usually considered more important than unintentional errors of equal dollar amounts, because fraud reflects on the honesty and reliability of the management or other personnel involved. To illustrate, most users would consider an intentional misstatement of inventory as being more important than clerical errors in inventory of the same dollar amount.
- Misstatements that are otherwise minor may be material if there are possible consequences arising from contractual obligations. An example is when net working capital included in the financial statements is only a few hundred dollars more than the required minimum in a loan agreement. If the correct net working capital were less than the required minimum putting the loan in default, the current and noncurrent liability classifications would be materially affected.
- Misstatements that are otherwise immaterial may be material if they affect a trend in earnings. For example, if reported income has increased 3 percent annually for the past five years, but income for the current year has declined 1 percent, that change of trend may be material. Similarly, a misstatement that would cause a loss to be reported as a profit would be of concern.

## Illustrative Guidelines

The FASB and AICPA are currently unwilling to provide specific materiality guidelines to practitioners. The concern is that such guidelines might be applied without considering all the complexities that should affect the auditor's final decision.

To show the application of materiality, illustrative guidelines are provided. They are intended only to help you better understand the concept of applying materiality in practice. The guidelines are stated in Figure 8-2 in the form of a policy guideline for a CPA firm.

**FIGURE 8-2**

**Illustrative Materiality Guidelines**

BERGER AND ANTHONY, CPAs
Gary, Indiana 46405
219/916-6900

*POLICY STATEMENT*
*No. 32 IC*
*Title: Materiality Guidelines*

Charles G. Berger
Joe Anthony

Professional judgment is to be used at all times in setting and applying materiality guidelines. As a general guideline the following policies are to be applied:

1. The combined total of misstatements in the financial statements exceeding 10 percent is normally considered material. A combined total of less than 5 percent is presumed to be immaterial in the absence of qualitative factors. Combined misstatements between 5 percent and 10 percent require the greatest amount of professional judgment to determine their materiality.
2. The 5 percent to 10 percent must be measured in relation to the appropriate base. Many times there is more than one base to which misstatements should be compared. The following guides are recommended in selecting the appropriate base:
   a. *Income statement.* Combined misstatements in the income statement should ordinarily be measured at 5 percent to 10 percent of operating income before taxes. A guideline of 5 percent to 10 percent may be inappropriate in a year in which income is unusually large or small. When operating income in a given year is not considered representative, it is desirable to substitute as a base a more representative income measure. For example, average operating income for a three-year period may be used as the base.
   b. *Balance sheet.* Combined misstatements in the balance sheet should originally be evaluated for current assets, current liabilities, and total assets. For current assets and current liabilities, the guidelines should be between 5 percent and 10 percent, applied in the same way as for the income statement. For total assets the guidelines should be between 3 percent and 6 percent, applied in the same way as for the income statement.
3. Qualitative factors should be carefully evaluated on all audits. In many instances they are more important than the guidelines applied to the income statement and balance sheet. The intended uses of the financial statements and the nature of the information in the statements, including footnotes, must be carefully evaluated.

## Application to Hillsburg Hardware

Using the illustrative guidelines for Berger and Anthony, CPAs, it is now possible to decide on a preliminary judgment about materiality for Hillsburg Hardware Co. The guidelines are:

| | Preliminary Judgment about Materiality | | | |
|---|---|---|---|---|
| | Minimum | | Maximum | |
| | Percentage | Dollar Amount | Percentage | Dollar Amount |
| Earnings from operations | 5 | $ 19,000 | 10 | $ 37,000 |
| Current assets | 5 | 128,000 | 10 | 255,000 |
| Total assets | 3 | 92,000 | 6 | 184,000 |
| Current liabilities | 5 | 33,000 | 10 | 66,000 |

If the auditor for Hillsburg Hardware decides that the general guidelines are reasonable, the first step is to evaluate whether any qualitative factors significantly affect the materiality judgment. If not, the auditor must decide that if combined misstatements of operating income before taxes were less than $19,000, the statements would be considered fairly stated. If the combined misstatements exceeded $37,000, the statements would not be considered fairly stated. If the misstatements were between $19,000 and $37,000, a more careful consideration of all facts would be required. The auditor then applies the same process to the other three bases.

## ALLOCATE PRELIMINARY JUDGMENT ABOUT MATERIALITY TO SEGMENTS (TOLERABLE MISSTATEMENT)

**OBJECTIVE 8-3**
**Allocate preliminary materiality to segments of the audit during planning.**

Allocating the preliminary judgment about materiality to segments (step 2 in Figure 8-1) is necessary because evidence is accumulated by segments rather than for the financial statements as a whole. If auditors have a preliminary judgment about materiality for each segment, it helps them decide the appropriate audit evidence to accumulate. For example, an auditor is likely to accumulate more evidence for an accounts receivable balance of $1,000,000 when a misstatement of $50,000 in accounts receivable is considered material than if $300,000 were material.

Most practitioners allocate materiality to balance sheet rather than income statement accounts. Most income statement misstatements have an equal effect on the balance sheet because of the double-entry bookkeeping system. Therefore, the auditor can allocate materiality to either income statement or balance sheet accounts. Since there are fewer balance sheet than income statement accounts in most audits, and most audit procedures focus on balance sheet accounts, allocating materiality to balance sheet accounts is the most appropriate alternative.

When auditors allocate the preliminary judgment about materiality to account balances, the materiality allocated to any given account balance is referred to in SAS 39 (AU 350) as *tolerable misstatement*. For example, if an auditor decides to allocate $100,000 of a total preliminary judgment about materiality of $200,000 to accounts receivable, tolerable misstatement for accounts receivable is $100,000. This means that the auditor is willing to consider accounts receivable fairly stated if it is misstated by $100,000 or less.

There are three major difficulties in allocating materiality to balance sheet accounts (segments): auditors expect certain accounts to have more misstatements than others, both overstatements and understatements must be considered, and relative audit costs affect the allocation. All three of these difficulties are considered in the allocation in Figure 8-3.

### Allocation Illustrated

Figure 8-3 illustrates the allocation approach followed by the senior, Fran Moore, for the audit of Hillsburg Hardware Co. It summarizes the balance sheet from page 139, combining certain accounts, and shows the allocation of total materiality of $37,000 (10 percent of earnings from operations). The allocation approach followed by Moore for Hillsburg Hardware Co. is to use judgment in the allocation, subject to two arbitrary requirements established by Berger and Anthony, CPAs: tolerable misstatement for any account cannot exceed 60 percent of the preliminary judgment (60 percent of $37,000 = $22,000), and the sum of all tolerable misstatements cannot exceed twice the preliminary judgment about materiality (2 × $37,000 = $74,000).

The reason for the first requirement is to keep the auditor from allocating all of total materiality to one account. If, for example, all of the preliminary judgment of $37,000 is allocated to trade accounts receivable, a $37,000 misstatement in that account would be acceptable. However, it may not be acceptable to have such a large misstatement in one account, and even if it is acceptable, it would not allow for any misstatements in other accounts.

**FIGURE 8-3**

**Tolerable Misstatement Allocated to Hillsburg Hardware Co.**

| | Balance 12-31-96 (in Thousands) | Tolerable Misstatement (in Thousands) | |
|---|---|---|---|
| Cash | $ 41 | $ 1 (a) | |
| Trade accounts receivable | 948 | 22 (b) | |
| Inventories | 1,493 | 22 (b) | |
| Other current assets | 68 | 5 (c) | |
| Property, plant, and equipment | 517 | 4 (d) | |
| Total assets | $3,067 | | |
| Trade accounts payable | $ 236 | 9 (e) | |
| Notes payable—total | 1,415 | 0 (a) | |
| Accrued payroll and payroll tax | 73 | 5 (c) | |
| Accrued interest and dividends payable | 102 | 0 (a) | |
| Other liabilities | 117 | 6 (c) | |
| Capital stock and capital in excess of par | 425 | 0 (a) | |
| Retained earnings | 699 | NA (f) | |
| Total liabilities and equity | $3,067 | $74 | (2 × $37) |

NA = not applicable

(a) Zero or small tolerable misstatement because account can be completely audited at low cost and no misstatements are expected.

(b) Large tolerable misstatement because account is large and requires extensive sampling to audit the account.

(c) Large tolerable misstatement as a percent of account because account can be verified at extremely low cost, probably with analytical procedures, if tolerable misstatement is large.

(d) Small tolerable misstatement as a percent of account balance because most of the balance is in land and buildings, which is unchanged from the prior year and need not be audited.

(e) Moderately large tolerable misstatement because a relatively large number of misstatements are expected.

(f) Not applicable—retained earnings is a residual account which is affected by the net amount of the misstatements in the other accounts.

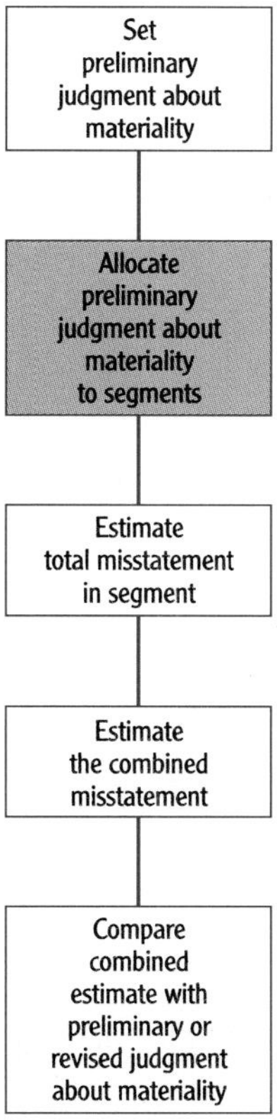


There are two reasons for permitting the sum of the tolerable misstatement to exceed overall materiality. First, it is unlikely that all accounts will be misstated by the full amount of tolerable misstatement. If, for example, other current assets have a tolerable misstatement of $5,000, but no misstatements are found in auditing those accounts, it means that the auditor, after the fact, could have allocated zero or a small tolerable misstatement to other current assets. It is common for auditors to find fewer misstatements than tolerable misstatement. Second, some accounts are likely to be overstated while others are likely to be understated, resulting in a net amount that is likely to be less than overall materiality.

Notice in the allocation that the auditor is concerned about the combined effect on operating income of the misstatement of each balance sheet account. An overstatement of an asset account will therefore have the same effect on the income statement as an understatement of a liability account. In contrast, a misclassification in the balance sheet, such as a classification of a note payable as an account payable, will have no effect on operating income. The materiality of items not affecting the income statement must be considered separately.

Figure 8-3 also includes the rationale that Fran Moore followed in deciding tolerable misstatement for each account. For example, she concluded that it was unnecessary to assign any tolerable misstatement to notes payable, even though it is as large as inventories. If she had assigned $11,000 to each of those two accounts, more evidence would have been required in inventories, but the confirmation of the balance in notes payable would still have been required. It was therefore more efficient to allocate $22,000 to inventories and none to notes payable. Similarly, she allocated $5,000 to other current assets and accrued payroll and payroll tax, both of which are large compared to the recorded account balance. Moore did so because she believes that these accounts can be verified within $5,000 by using only analytical procedures, which are low cost. If tolerable misstatement were set lower, she would have to use more costly audit procedures such as documentation and confirmation.

In practice it is often difficult to predict in advance which accounts are most likely to be misstated, and whether misstatements are likely to be overstatements or understatements. Similarly, the relative costs of auditing different account balances often cannot be determined. It is therefore a difficult professional judgment to allocate the preliminary judgment about materiality to accounts. Accordingly, many accounting firms have developed rigorous guidelines and sophisticated statistical methods for doing so.

To summarize, the purpose of allocating the preliminary judgment about materiality to balance sheet accounts is to help the auditor decide the appropriate evidence to accumulate for each. An aim of the allocation should be to minimize audit costs. Regardless of how the allocation is done, when the auditor has completed the audit, he or she must be confident that the combined misstatements in all accounts are less than or equal to the preliminary (or revised) judgment about materiality.

## ESTIMATE MISSTATEMENT AND COMPARE

**OBJECTIVE 8-4**

**Use materiality to evaluate audit findings.**

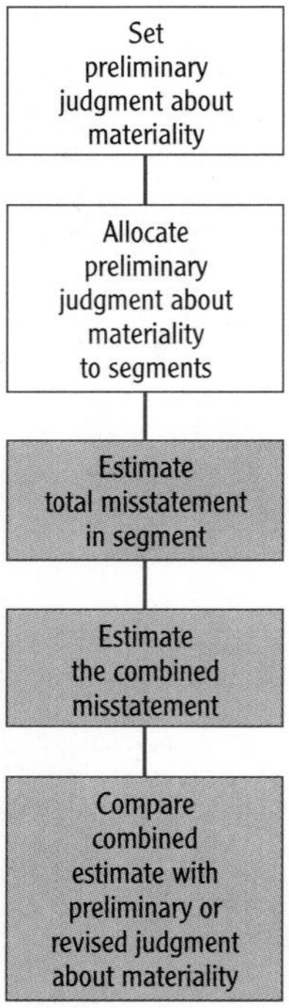


The first two steps in applying materiality involve planning, whereas the last three (steps 3, 4, and 5 in Figure 8-1) result from performing audit tests. The last three steps are discussed in greater detail in later chapters; this section only shows their relationship to the first two.

When the auditor performs audit procedures for each segment of the audit, a worksheet is kept of all misstatements found. For example, assume that the auditor finds six client misstatements in a sample of 200 in testing inventory costs. These misstatements are used to estimate the *total* misstatements in inventory (step 3). The total is referred to as an estimate or often a "projection" because only a sample, rather than the entire population, was audited. Estimation of projected misstatement is required by SAS 39 (AU 350). The projected misstatement amounts for each account are combined on the worksheet (step 4), and then the combined misstatement is compared to materiality (step 5).

Figure 8-4 is used to illustrate the last three steps in applying materiality. For simplicity, only three accounts are included. The estimated misstatements are calculated based on actual audit tests. Assume, for example, that in auditing inventory, the auditor found $3,500 of net overstatement amounts in a sample of $50,000 of the total population of $450,000. One way to calculate the estimate of the misstatements is to make a direct projection from the sample to the population and add an estimate for sampling error. The calculation of the direct projection is:

$$\frac{\text{Net misstatements in the sample (\$3,500)}}{\text{Total sampled (\$50,000)}} \times \begin{array}{c}\text{Total recorded}\\ \text{population}\\ \text{value (\$450,000)}\end{array} = \begin{array}{c}\text{Direct projection}\\ \text{estimate (\$31,500)}\end{array}$$

The direct projection for accounts receivable of $12,000 is not illustrated.

The estimate for sampling error results because the auditor has sampled only a portion of the population (this is discussed in detail in Chapters 12 and 14). In this simplified example, the estimate for sampling error is assumed to be 50 percent of the direct projection of the misstatement amounts for the accounts where sampling was used (accounts receivable and inventory).

In combining the misstatements in Figure 8-4, observe that the direct projection misstatements for the three accounts add to $43,500. The total sampling error, however, is less than the sum of the individual sampling errors. This is because sampling error represents the maximum misstatement in account details not audited. It is unlikely that this maxi-

**FIGURE 8-4**

**Illustration of Comparison of Estimated Total Misstatement to Preliminary Judgment about Materiality**

| | | Estimated Misstatement Amount | | |
|---|---|---|---|---|
| **Account** | **Tolerable Misstatement** | **Direct Projection** | **Sampling Error** | **Total** |
| Cash | $ 4,000 | $ 0 | $ NA | $ 0 |
| Accounts receivable | 20,000 | 12,000 | 6,000 | 18,000 |
| Inventory | 36,000 | 31,500 | 15,750 | 47,250 |
| Total estimated misstatement amount | | $43,500 | $16,800 | $60,300 |
| Preliminary judgment about materiality | $50,000 | | | |

NA = not applicable; Cash audited 100 percent.

mum misstatement amount would exist in all accounts subjected to sampling. Thus, sampling methodology provides for determining a combined sampling error that takes this into consideration. Again, this is discussed in detail in Chapters 12 and 14.

Figure 8-4 shows that total estimated misstatement of $60,300 exceeds the preliminary judgment about materiality of $50,000. Furthermore, the major area of difficulty is inventory, where estimated misstatement of $47,250 is significantly greater than tolerable misstatement of $36,000. Because the estimated combined misstatement exceeds the preliminary judgment, the financial statements are not acceptable. The auditor can either determine whether the estimated misstatement actually exceeds $50,000 by performing additional audit procedures or require the client to make an adjustment for estimated misstatements. If additional audit procedures are performed, they would be concentrated in the inventory area.

If the estimated net overstatement amount for inventory had been $28,000 ($18,000 plus $10,000 sampling error), the auditor probably would not need to expand audit tests, as it would have met both the tests of tolerable misstatement ($36,000) and the preliminary judgment about materiality ($18,000 + $28,000 = $46,000 < $50,000). In fact, there would be some leeway with that amount because the results of cash and accounts receivable procedures indicate that those accounts are well within their tolerable misstatement limits. If the auditor were to approach the audit of the accounts in a sequential manner, the findings of the audit of the earlier accounts can be used to revise the tolerable misstatement established for other accounts. For example, in the illustration, if the auditor had audited cash and accounts receivable before inventories, tolerable misstatement for inventories could be increased.

## RISK

**OBJECTIVE 8-5**
**Define risk in auditing.**

*Risk* in auditing means that the auditor accepts some level of uncertainty in performing the audit function. The auditor recognizes, for example, that there is uncertainty about the competence of evidence, uncertainty about the effectiveness of a client's internal controls, and uncertainty as to whether the financial statements are fairly stated when the audit is completed.

An effective auditor recognizes that risks exist and deals with those risks in an appropriate manner. Most risks auditors encounter are difficult to measure and require careful thought to respond to appropriately. For example, assume the auditor determines that the client's industry is undergoing significant technological changes which affect both the client and the client's customers. This change may affect the obsolescence of the client's inventory, collectibility of accounts receivable, and perhaps even the ability of the client's business to continue. Responding to these risks properly is critical to achieving a high-quality audit.

The remainder of this chapter deals mostly with the risks that affect planning the engagement to determine the appropriate evidence to accumulate by applying the AICPA's audit risk model. It concludes by showing the relationship between risk and materiality.

## Illustration Concerning Risks and Evidence

Before discussing the audit risk model, an illustration for a hypothetical company is provided in Figure 8-5 as a frame of reference for the discussion. The illustration first shows that there are differences among cycles in the frequency and size of expected misstatements (A). For example, there are almost no misstatements expected in payroll and personnel, but many in inventory and warehousing. The reason may be that the payroll transactions are highly routine, whereas there may be considerable complexities in recording inventory. Similarly, internal control is believed to differ in effectiveness among the five cycles (B). For

**FIGURE 8-5**

**Illustration of Differing Evidence Among Cycles**

| | | **Sales and Collection Cycle** | **Acquisition and Payment Cycle** | **Payroll and Personnel Cycle** | **Inventory and Warehousing Cycle** | **Capital Acquisition and Repayment Cycle** |
|---|---|---|---|---|---|---|
| A | Auditor's assessment of expectation of material misstatement before considering internal control (inherent risk) | Expect some misstatements (medium) | Expect many misstatements (high) | Expect few misstatements (low) | Expect many misstatements (high) | Expect few misstatements (low) |
| B | Auditor's assessment of effectiveness of internal controls to prevent or detect material misstatements (control risk) | Medium effectiveness (medium) | High effectiveness (low) | High effectiveness (low) | Low effectiveness (high) | Medium effectiveness (medium) |
| C | Auditor's willingness to permit material misstatements to exist after completing the audit (acceptable audit risk) | Low willingness (low) | Low willingness (low) | Low willingness (low) | Low willingness (low) | Low willingness (low) |
| D | Extent of evidence the auditor plans to accumulate (planned detection risk) | Medium level (medium) | Medium level (medium) | Low level (high) | High level (low) | Medium level (medium) |

example, internal controls in payroll and personnel are considered highly effective, whereas those in inventory and warehousing are considered ineffective. Finally, the auditor has decided on a low willingness that material misstatements exist after the audit is complete for all five cycles (C). It is common for auditors to want an equally low likelihood of misstatements for each cycle after the audit is finished to permit the issuance of an unqualified opinion.

The previous considerations (A, B, C) affect the auditor's decision about the appropriate extent of evidence to accumulate (D). For example, because the auditor expects few misstatements in payroll and personnel (A) and internal controls are effective (B), the auditor plans for less evidence (D) than for inventory and warehousing. Notice that the auditor has the same level of willingness to accept material misstatements after the audit is finished for all five cycles, but a different extent of evidence is needed for various cycles. The difference is caused by differences in the auditor's expectations of misstatements and assessment of internal control.

## Audit Risk Model for Planning

**OBJECTIVE 8-6**
**Describe the audit risk model and its components.**

The primary way that auditors deal with risk in planning audit evidence is through the application of the audit risk model. The source of the audit risk model is the professional literature in SAS 39 (AU 350) on audit sampling and SAS 47 (AU 312) on materiality and risk. A thorough understanding of the model is essential to effective audit planning and to the study of the remaining chapters of this book.

The audit risk model is used primarily for planning purposes in deciding how much evidence to accumulate in each cycle. It is usually stated as follows:

$$PDR = \frac{AAR}{IR \times CR}$$

where:

$$PDR = \text{planned detection risk}$$
$$AAR = \text{acceptable audit risk}$$
$$IR = \text{inherent risk}$$
$$CR = \text{control risk}$$

A numerical example is provided for discussion, even though it is not practical in practice to measure as precisely as these numbers imply. The numbers used are for the inventory and warehousing cycle in Figure 8-5.

$$IR = 100\%$$
$$CR = 100\%$$
$$AAR = 5\%$$
$$PDR = \frac{.05}{1.0 \times 1.0} = .05 \text{ or } 5\%$$

## Planned Detection Risk

*Planned detection risk* is a measure of the risk that audit evidence for a segment will fail to detect misstatements exceeding a tolerable amount, should such misstatements exist. There are two key points about planned detection risk: first, it is dependent on the other three factors in the model. Planned detection risk will change only if the auditor changes one of the other factors. Second, it determines the amount of substantive evidence that the auditor plans to accumulate, inversely with the size of planned detection risk. If planned detection risk is reduced, the auditor needs to accumulate more evidence to achieve the reduced planned risk. For example, in Figure 8-5 (D) planned detection risk is low for inventory and warehousing, which causes planned evidence to be high. The opposite is true for payroll and personnel.

The planned detection risk of .05 in the numerical example above means the auditor plans to accumulate evidence until the risk of misstatements exceeding tolerable misstatement is reduced to 5 percent. If control risk had been .50 instead of 1.0, planned detection risk would be .10 and planned evidence could therefore be reduced.

## Inherent Risk

As stated in Chapter 7, *inherent risk* is a measure of the auditor's assessment of the likelihood that there are material misstatements (errors or fraud) in a segment before considering the effectiveness of internal control. Inherent risk is the susceptibility of the financial statements to material misstatement, assuming no internal controls. If the auditor concludes that there is a high likelihood of misstatement, ignoring internal controls, the auditor would conclude that inherent risk is high. Internal controls are ignored in setting inherent risk because they are considered separately in the audit risk model as control risk. In Figure 8-5 inherent risk (A) has been assessed high for inventory and warehousing and lower for payroll and personnel and capital acquisition and repayment. The assessment was likely based on discussions with management, knowledge of the company, and results in prior year audits.

The relationship of inherent risk to planned detection risk and planned evidence is that inherent risk is inversely related to planned detection risk and directly related to evidence. Inherent risk for inventory and warehousing in Figure 8-5 is high, and in the numerical example 1.0, which will result in a lower planned detection risk and more planned evidence than would be necessary had inherent risk been lower. Inherent risk is examined in greater detail later in the chapter.

In addition to increasing audit evidence for a higher inherent risk in a given audit area, it is also common to assign more experienced staff to that area and review the completed working papers more thoroughly. For example, if inherent risk for inventory obsolescence is extremely high, it makes sense for the CPA firm to have an experienced staff person perform more extensive tests for inventory obsolescence and to have the audit results more carefully reviewed.

## Control Risk

*Control risk* is a measure of the auditor's assessment of the likelihood that misstatements exceeding a tolerable amount in a segment will not be prevented or detected by the client's internal controls. Control risk represents (1) an assessment of whether a client's internal controls are effective for preventing or detecting misstatements, and (2) the auditor's intention to make that assessment at a level below the maximum (100 percent) as part of the audit plan. For example, assume that the auditor concludes that internal controls are completely ineffective to prevent or detect misstatements. That is the likely conclusion for inventory and warehousing in Figure 8-5 (B). The auditor would therefore assign a high, perhaps 100 percent, risk factor to control risk. The more effective the internal controls, the lower the risk factor that *could* be assigned to control risk.

As with inherent risk, the relationship between control risk and planned detection risk is inverse, whereas the relationship between control risk and substantive evidence is direct. For example, if the auditor concludes that internal controls are effective, planned detection risk can be increased and evidence therefore decreased. The auditor can increase planned detection risk when controls are effective because effective internal controls reduce the likelihood of misstatements in the financial statements.

Before auditors can set control risk less than 100 percent, they must do three things: obtain an understanding of internal control, evaluate how well it should function based on the understanding, and test the internal controls for effectiveness. The first of these is the *understanding* requirement that relates to all audits. The latter two are the *assessment of control risk* steps that are required when the auditor *chooses* to assess control risk below maximum.

Understanding internal control, assessing control risk, and their impact on evidence requirements are so important that the entire next chapter is devoted to that topic. However, it should be noted here that if the auditor elects not to assess control risk below maximum, control risk must be set at 100 percent regardless of the actual effectiveness of the underlying controls. Use of the audit risk model in this circumstance then causes the auditor to control acceptable audit risk entirely through a low level of planned detection risk (assuming that inherent risk is high).

## Acceptable Audit Risk

As stated in Chapter 7, *acceptable audit risk* is a measure of how willing the auditor is to accept that the financial statements may be materially misstated after the audit is completed and an unqualified opinion has been issued. When the auditor decides on a lower acceptable audit risk, it means the auditor wants to be more certain that the financial statements are *not* materially misstated. Zero risk would be certainty, and a 100 percent risk would be complete uncertainty. Complete assurance (zero risk) of the accuracy of the financial statements is not economically practical. It has already been established in Chapter 5 that the auditor cannot guarantee the complete absence of material misstatements.

Frequently auditors refer to the terms *audit assurance, overall assurance,* or *level of assurance* instead of acceptable audit risk. Audit assurance or any of the equivalent terms is the complement of acceptable audit risk, that is, one minus acceptable audit risk. For example, acceptable audit risk of 2 percent is the same as audit assurance of 98 percent.

The concept of acceptable audit risk can be more easily understood by thinking in terms of a large number of audits, say, 10,000. What portion of these audits could include material misstatements without having an adverse effect on society? Certainly, the portion would be below 10 percent. It is probably much closer to 1 or one-half of 1 percent or perhaps even one-tenth of 1 percent. If an auditor believes that the appropriate percentage is 1 percent, then acceptable audit risk should be set at 1 percent, or perhaps lower, based on the specific circumstances.

Using the audit risk model, there is a direct relationship between acceptable audit risk and planned detection risk, and an inverse relationship between acceptable audit risk and planned evidence. For example, if the auditor decides to reduce acceptable audit risk, planned detection risk is thereby reduced and planned evidence must be increased. As stated in Chapter 7, auditors also often assign more experienced staff or review the working papers more extensively for a client with lower acceptable audit risk.

## Changing Acceptable Audit Risk for Business Risk

**OBJECTIVE 8-7**
**Consider the impact of business risk on acceptable audit risk.**

*Business risk* is the risk that the auditor or audit firm will suffer harm because of a client relationship, even though the audit report rendered for the client was correct. For example, if a client declares bankruptcy after an audit is completed, the likelihood of a lawsuit against the CPA firm is reasonably high even if the quality of the audit was good.

There is a difference of opinion among auditors as to whether business risk should be considered in planning the audit. Opponents of modifying evidence for business risk contend that auditors do not provide different levels of assurance audit opinions and, therefore, should not provide more or less assurance because of business risk. Proponents contend that it is appropriate for auditors to accumulate additional evidence, assign more experienced personnel, and review the audit more thoroughly on audits where legal exposure is high, as long as the assurance level is not decreased below a reasonably high level when there is low business risk.

When auditors modify evidence for business risk, it is done by control of acceptable audit risk. The authors believe that a reasonably low acceptable audit risk is always desirable, but in some circumstances an even lower risk is needed because of business risk factors. Research has indicated that several factors affect business risk and therefore acceptable audit risk. Only three of those are discussed here: the degree to which external users rely on the statements, the likelihood that a client will have financial difficulties after the audit report is issued, and the integrity of management.

**The Degree to Which External Users Rely on the Statements** When external users place heavy reliance on the financial statements, it is appropriate that acceptable audit risk be decreased. When the statements are heavily relied on, a great social harm could result if a significant misstatement were to remain undetected in the financial statements. The cost of additional evidence can be more easily justified when the loss to users from material misstatements is substantial. Several factors are good indicators of the degree to which statements are relied on by external users:

- *Client's size.* Generally speaking, the larger a client's operations, the more widely the statements will be used. The client's size, measured by total assets or total revenues, will have an effect on the acceptable audit risk.
- *Distribution of ownership.* The statements of publicly held corporations are normally relied on by many more users than those of closely held corporations. For these companies, the interested parties include the SEC, financial analysts, and the general public.
- *Nature and amount of liabilities.* When statements include a large amount of liabilities, they are more likely to be used extensively by actual and potential creditors than when there are few liabilities.

**The Likelihood That a Client Will Have Financial Difficulties after the Audit Report Is Issued** If a client is forced to file for bankruptcy or suffers a significant loss after completion of the audit, there is a greater chance of the auditor's being required to defend the quality of the audit than if the client were under no financial strain. There is a natural tendency for those who lose money in a bankruptcy or because of a stock price reversal to file suit against the auditor. This can result from the honest belief that the auditor failed to conduct an adequate audit or from the users' desire to recover part of their loss regardless of the adequacy of the audit work.

In situations in which the auditor believes the chance of financial failure or loss is high, and there is a corresponding increase in business risk for the auditor, acceptable audit risk should be reduced. If a subsequent challenge does occur, the auditor will then be in a better position to defend the audit results successfully. The total audit evidence and costs will increase, but this is justifiable because of the additional risk of lawsuits that the auditor faces.

It is difficult for an auditor to predict financial failure before it occurs, but certain factors are good indicators of its increased probability:

- *Liquidity position.* If a client is constantly short of cash and working capital, it indicates a future problem in paying bills. The auditor must assess the likelihood and significance of a steadily declining liquidity position.
- *Profits (losses) in previous years.* When a company has rapidly declining profits or increasing losses for several years, the auditor should recognize the future solvency problems that the client is likely to encounter. It is also important to consider the changing profits relative to the balance remaining in retained earnings.
- *Method of financing growth.* The more a client relies on debt as a means of financing, the greater the risk of financial difficulty if the client's operations become less successful. It is also important to evaluate whether fixed assets are being financed with short-term or long-term loans. Large amounts of required cash outflows during a short period of time can force a company into bankruptcy.
- *Nature of the client's operations.* Certain types of businesses are inherently riskier than others. For example, other things being equal, there is a much greater likelihood of bankruptcy of a stockbroker than of a utility.
- *Competence of management.* Competent management is constantly alert for potential financial difficulties and modifies its operating methods to minimize the effects of short-run problems. The ability of management must be assessed as a part of the evaluation of the likelihood of bankruptcy.

**The Auditor's Evaluation of Management's Integrity** As discussed in Chapter 7 as a part of new client investigation and continuing client evaluation, if a client has questionable integrity, the auditor is likely to assess acceptable audit risk lower. Companies with low integrity often conduct their business affairs in a manner that results in conflicts with their stockholders, regulators, and customers. These conflicts in turn often reflect on the users' perceived quality of the audit and can result in lawsuits and other disagreements. An obvious example of a situation where management's integrity is questionable is prior criminal convictions of key management personnel. Other examples of questionable integrity might include frequent disagreements with previous auditors, the Internal Revenue Service, and the SEC. Frequent turnover of key financial and internal audit personnel and ongoing conflicts with labor unions and employees may also indicate integrity problems.

### Assessing Acceptable Audit Risk

To assess acceptable audit risk, the auditor must first assess each of the factors affecting acceptable audit risk. Table 8-1 illustrates the methods used by auditors to assess each of the three factors already discussed. It is easy to see after examining Table 8-1 that the assessment of each of the factors is highly subjective, which means that the overall assessment is also highly subjective. A typical evaluation of acceptable audit risk is high, medium, or low, where a low acceptable audit risk assessment means a "risky" client requiring more extensive evidence, assignment of more experienced personnel, and/or a more extensive review of working papers. As the audit progresses, additional information about the client is obtained and acceptable audit risk may be modified.

**TABLE 8-1**

**Methods Practitioners Use to Assess Acceptable Audit Risk**

| Factors | Methods Used by Practitioners to Assess Acceptable Audit Risk |
|---|---|
| External users' reliance on financial statements | • Examine the financial statements, including footnotes.<br>• Read minutes of board of directors meetings to determine future plans.<br>• Examine 10K form for a publicly held company.<br>• Discuss financing plans with management. |
| Likelihood of financial difficulties | • Analyze the financial statements for financial difficulties using ratios and other analytical procedures.<br>• Examine historical and projected cash flow statements for the nature of cash inflows and outflows. |
| Management integrity | Follow the procedures discussed in Chapter 7 for client acceptance and continuance. |

**ASSESSING ACCEPTABLE AUDIT RISK IN PRACTICE**

Henry Rinsk, of Links, Rinsk and Rodman, CPAs, is the partner responsible for the audit of Hungry Food Restaurants, a chain of nine Midwestern family restaurants. The firm has audited Hungry Food for ten years and has always found management competent, cooperative, and easy to deal with. Hungry Food is family-owned with a business succession plan in place; it is profitable, liquid, and has little debt. Management has a reputation in the community for high integrity and good relationships with employees, customers, and suppliers.

After meeting with the other partners as part of the firm's annual client continuation meeting, Henry recommends that acceptable audit risk for Hungry Food be assessed at high. For Links, Rinsk and Rodman, this means no expansion of evidence, a "standard" review of working papers, and a "standard" assignment of personnel to the engagement.

## INHERENT RISK

The inclusion of inherent risk in the audit risk model is one of the most important concepts in auditing. It implies that auditors should attempt to predict where misstatements are most and least likely in the financial statement segments. This information affects

**OBJECTIVE 8-8**
**Consider the impact of several factors on the assessment of inherent risk.**

the total amount of evidence that the auditor is required to accumulate and influences how the auditor's efforts to gather the evidence are allocated among the segments of the audit.

There is always some risk that the client has made misstatements that are individually or collectively large enough to make the financial statements misleading. The misstatements can be intentional or unintentional, and they can affect the dollar balance in accounts or disclosure. Inherent risk can be low in some instances and extremely high in others.

The audit risk model shows the close relationship between inherent and control risks. For example, an inherent risk of 40 percent and a control risk of 60 percent affect planned detection risk and planned evidence the same as an inherent risk of 60 percent and a control risk of 40 percent. In both cases, multiplying IR by CR results in a denominator in the audit risk model of 24 percent. The combination of inherent risk and control risk can be thought of as the *expectation of misstatements after considering the effect of internal control.* Inherent risk is the expectation of misstatements before considering the effect of internal control.

At the start of the audit, there is not much that can be done about changing inherent risk. Instead, the auditor must *assess the factors* that make up the risk and *modify audit evidence* to take them into consideration. The auditor should consider several major factors when assessing inherent risk:

- Nature of the client's business
- Factors related to misstatements arising from fraudulent financial reporting
- Results of previous audits
- Initial versus repeat engagement
- Related parties
- Nonroutine transactions
- Judgment required to correctly record account balances and transactions
- Susceptibility of assets to misappropriation
- Makeup of the population

## Nature of the Client's Business

Inherent risk for certain accounts is affected by the nature of the client's business. For example, there is a greater likelihood of obsolete inventory for an electronics manufacturer than for a steel fabricator. Inherent risk is most likely to vary from business to business for accounts such as inventory, accounts and loans receivable, and property, plant, and equipment. The nature of the client's business should have little or no effect on inherent risk for accounts such as cash, notes, and mortgages payable. Information gained while obtaining knowledge about the client's industry and business, as discussed in Chapter 7, is useful for assessing this factor.

**AICPA *INDUSTRY AUDIT RISK ALERTS* FOR SPECIALIZED INDUSTRIES**

Many companies operate in specialized industries that have unique economic, regulatory, and accounting issues. In an effort to provide auditors with current guidance on assessing inherent risks for clients in specialized industries, the AICPA has developed a series of *Industry Audit Risk Alerts.* Some of the industries covered by the publications are banks and savings institutions, construction contractors, health care providers, not-for-profit organizations, public utilities, and real estate. The AICPA issues new or revised risk alerts whenever they conclude that auditors should be aware of recent economic, regulatory, or technical developments for companies in specific industries.

### Factors Related to Misstatements Arising from Fraudulent Financial Reporting

There was a discussion in Chapter 5 of the auditor's responsibilities under SAS 82 to assess the risk of fraud arising from fraudulent financial reporting and misappropriation of assets. The three categories of risk factors for fraudulent financial reporting are summarized in Table 5-1, page 138, including examples. These three categories are:

- Management's characteristics and influence over the control environment
- Industry conditions
- Operating characteristics and financial stability

It is difficult in concept and practice to separate these three categories of factors into acceptable audit risk, inherent risk, or control risk. For example, management that lacks integrity and is motivated to misstate financial statements (management characteristics) is one of the factors in acceptable audit risk, but it also increases the likelihood of misstatement, which is an inherent risk. Similarly, it will be shown in Chapter 9 that several of the risk factors influencing management characteristics are a part of the control environment. An example is the attitude, actions, and policies that reflect the overall attitudes of top management about integrity, ethical values, and commitment to competence.

To satisfy the requirements of SAS 82, it is more important for the auditor to assess the risks and to respond to them than it is to identify them as acceptable audit risk, inherent risk, or control risk.

### Results of Previous Audits

Misstatements found in the previous year's audit have a high likelihood of occurring again in the current year's audit. This is because many types of misstatements are systemic in nature, and organizations are often slow in making changes to eliminate them. Therefore, an auditor would be negligent if the results of the preceding year's audit were ignored during the development of the current year's audit program. For example, if the auditor found a significant number of misstatements in pricing inventory, inherent risk would likely be high, and extensive testing would have to be done in the current audit as a means of determining whether the deficiency in the client's system had been corrected. If, however, the auditor has found no misstatements for the past several years in conducting tests of an audit area, the auditor is justified in reducing inherent risk, provided that changes in relevant circumstances have not occurred.

### Initial Versus Repeat Engagement

Auditors gain experience and knowledge about the likelihood of misstatements after auditing a client for several years. The lack of previous years' audit results would cause most auditors to use a larger inherent risk for initial audits than for repeat engagements in which no material misstatements had been found. Most auditors set a high inherent risk in the first year of an audit and reduce it in subsequent years as they gain experience.

### Related Parties

Transactions between parent and subsidiary companies and those between management and the corporate entity are examples of related-party transactions as defined by FASB 57. Because these transactions do not occur between two independent parties dealing at "arm's length," a greater likelihood exists that they might be misstated, causing an increase in inherent risk. Determining the existence of related parties was discussed in Chapter 7.

### Nonroutine Transactions

Transactions that are unusual for the client are more likely to be incorrectly recorded by the client than routine transactions because the client lacks experience in recording them. Examples include fire losses, major property acquisitions, and lease agreements. Knowledge of the client's business and review of minutes of meetings, as discussed in Chapter 7, are useful to learn about nonroutine transactions.

### Judgment Required to Correctly Record Account Balances and Transactions

Many account balances require estimates and a great deal of management judgment. Examples are allowance for uncollectible accounts receivable, obsolete inventory, liability for warranty payments, and bank loan loss reserves. Similarly, transactions for major repairs or partial replacement of assets are examples where considerable judgment is needed to correctly record the information.

### Susceptibility of Assets to Misappropriation

The auditor should be concerned about the risk of possible defalcation in situations where it is relatively easy to convert company assets to personal use. Such is the case when currency, marketable securities, or highly marketable inventory are not closely controlled. When the likelihood of defalcation is high, inherent risk is increased.

### Makeup of the Population

The individual items making up the total population also frequently affect the auditor's expectation of material misstatement. For example, most auditors would use a higher inherent risk for accounts receivable where most accounts are significantly overdue than where most accounts are current. Transactions with affiliated companies, amounts due from officers, cash disbursements made payable to cash, and accounts receivable outstanding for several months are examples of situations requiring a higher inherent risk and therefore greater investigation, because there is usually a greater likelihood of misstatement than for more typical transactions.

### Assessing Inherent Risk

The auditor must evaluate the information affecting inherent risk and decide on an appropriate inherent risk factor for each cycle, account, and many times for each audit objective. Some factors, such as the integrity of management, will affect many or perhaps all cycles, whereas others, such as nonroutine transactions, will affect only specific accounts or audit objectives. Although the profession has not established standards or guidelines for setting inherent risk, the authors believe that auditors are generally conservative in making such assessments. Most auditors would probably set inherent risk at well above 50 percent, even in the best of circumstances, and at 100 percent when there is any reasonable possibility of significant misstatements. For example, assume that in the audit of inventory the auditor notes that (1) a large number of misstatements were found in the previous year and (2) inventory turnover has slowed in the current year. Many auditors would probably set inherent risk at a relatively high level (some would use 100 percent) for each audit objective for inventory in this situation.

### Obtain Information to Assess Inherent Risk

Auditors begin their assessments of inherent risk during the planning phase and update the assessments throughout the audit. A considerable portion of Chapter 7 dealt with information that is relevant to inherent risk assessment during the planning phase. For example, the discussion of obtaining knowledge about the client's business and industry, touring the client's plant and offices, and identifying related parties all pertain directly to inherent risk assessment. As the auditor performs the wide variety of tests on an audit, additional information is obtained that often affects the original assessment.

### Summary of Risks

**OBJECTIVE 8-9**
**Discuss the relationships among the components of risk.**

Figure 8-6 summarizes the factors that determine each of the risks, the effect of the three component risks on the determination of planned detection risk, and the relationship of all four risks to planned audit evidence. "D" in the figure indicates a direct relationship between a component risk and planned detection risk or planned evidence. "I" indicates an inverse relationship. For example, an increase in acceptable audit risk results in an increase in planned detection risk (D) and a decrease in planned audit evidence (I). Compare Figure 8-6 to Figure 8-5 on page 256 and observe that these two figures include the same concepts. In addition to affecting planned audit evidence, acceptable audit risk can also affect the selection of personnel assigned to the audit and the extent of the review of the completed audit.

**FIGURE 8-6**

**Relationship of Factors Influencing Risks to Risks and Risks to Planned Evidence**

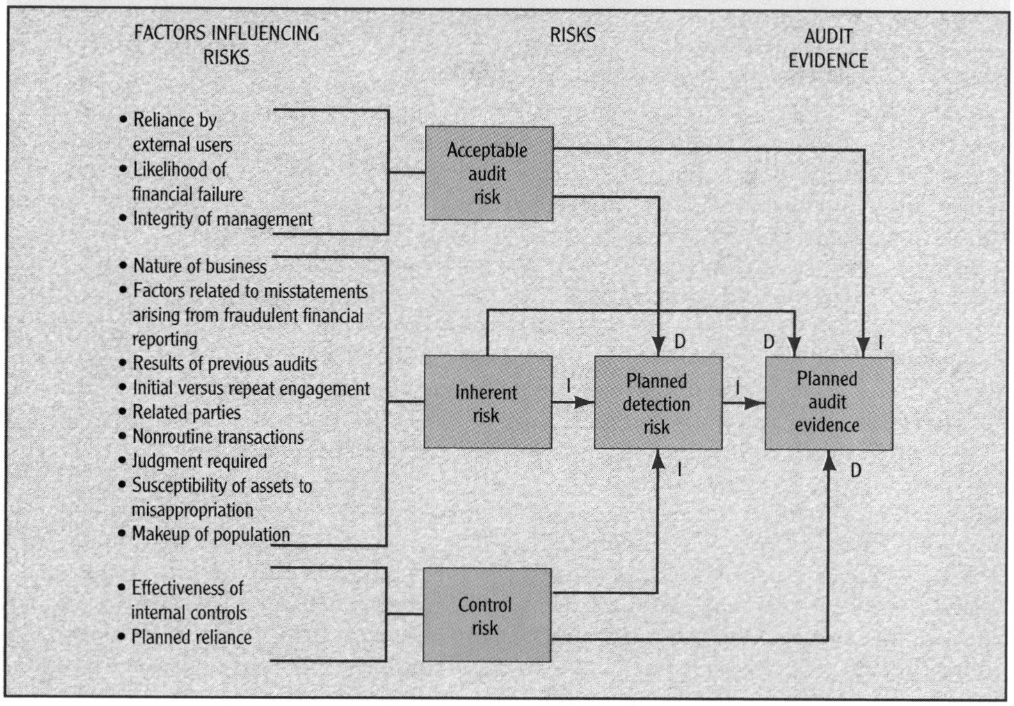


## OTHER MATERIALITY AND RISK CONSIDERATIONS

### Audit Risk for Segments

**OBJECTIVE 8-10**
**Discuss risk for segments and measurement difficulties.**

Both control risk and inherent risk are typically set for each cycle, each account, and often even each audit objective, not for the overall audit, and are likely to vary from cycle to cycle, account to account, and objective to objective on the same audit. Internal controls may be more effective for inventory-related accounts than for those related to fixed assets. Control risk would therefore also be different for different accounts depending on the effectiveness of the controls. Factors affecting inherent risk, such as susceptibility to defalcation and routineness of the transactions, are also likely to differ from account to account. For that reason, it is normal to have inherent risk vary for different accounts in the same audit unless there is some strong overriding factor of concern, such as management integrity.

Acceptable audit risk is ordinarily set by the auditor during planning and held constant for each major cycle and account. Auditors normally use the same acceptable audit risk for each segment because the factors affecting acceptable audit risk are related to the entire audit, not individual accounts. For example, the extent to which financial statements are relied on for external users' decisions is usually related to the overall financial statements, not just one or two accounts.

In some cases, however, a *lower* acceptable audit risk may be more appropriate for one account than for others. In the previous example, even though the auditor decided to use a medium acceptable audit risk for the audit as a whole, the auditor might decide to reduce acceptable audit risk to low for inventory if inventory is used as collateral for a short-term loan.

Some auditors use the same acceptable audit risk for each segment as overall acceptable audit risk, whereas others use a higher acceptable audit risk for each segment. The argument for using a higher acceptable audit risk for each segment is the effect of the interactions of the various accounts and transactions making up the financial statements and the synergy of multiple tests. Stated differently, if all individual segments of the audit are completed at an acceptable audit risk of a given level, the auditor can be assured that the audit risk for the financial statements as a whole will be lower. Other auditors use the same acceptable audit risk for segments as overall acceptable audit risk because of the difficulties of measurement. The latter approach is followed in the illustrations in this and subsequent chapters, but either approach is acceptable.

Because control risk and inherent risk vary from cycle to cycle, account to account, or objective to objective, planned detection risk and required audit evidence will also vary. This conclusion should not be surprising. The circumstances of each engagement are different, and the extent of evidence needed will depend on the unique circumstances. For example, inventory might require extensive testing on an engagement due to weak internal controls and concern about obsolescence due to technological changes in the industry. On the same engagement, accounts receivable may require little testing because of effective internal controls, fast collection of receivables, excellent relationships between the client and customers, and good audit results in previous years. Similarly, for a given audit of inventory, an auditor may assess that there is a higher inherent risk of a realizable value misstatement because of the higher potential for obsolescence, but a low inherent risk of a classification misstatement because there is only purchased inventory.

## Relating Tolerable Misstatement and Risks to Balance-Related Audit Objectives

Although it is common in practice to assess inherent and control risks for each balance-related audit objective, it is not common to allocate materiality to objectives. Auditors are able to effectively associate most risks with different objectives. It is reasonably easy to determine the relationship between a risk and one or two objectives. For example, obsolescence in inventory would be unlikely to affect any objective other than realizable value. It is more difficult to decide how much of the materiality allocated to a given account should in turn be allocated to one or two objectives. Most auditors do not attempt to do so.

## Measurement Limitations

One major limitation in the application of the audit risk model is the difficulty of measuring the components of the model. In spite of the auditor's best efforts in planning, the assessments of acceptable audit risk, inherent risk, and control risk and therefore planned detection risk are highly subjective and are approximations of reality at best. Imagine, for example, attempting to precisely assess inherent risk by determining the impact of factors such as the misstatements discovered in prior years' audits and technology changes in the client's industry.

To offset this measurement problem, many auditors use broad and subjective measurement terms, such as "low," "medium," and "high." Table 8-2 shows how auditors can use the information to decide on the appropriate amount of evidence to accumulate. For example, in situation 1, the auditor has decided to accept a high audit risk for an account or objec-

**TABLE 8-2**

**Relationships of Risk to Evidence**

| Situation | Acceptable Audit Risk | Inherent Risk | Control Risk | Planned Detection Risk | Amount of Evidence Required |
|---|---|---|---|---|---|
| 1 | High | Low | Low | High | Low |
| 2 | Low | Low | Low | Medium | Medium |
| 3 | Low | High | High | Low | High |
| 4 | Medium | Medium | Medium | Medium | Medium |
| 5 | High | Low | Medium | Medium | Medium |

tive. The auditor has concluded that there is a low risk of misstatement in the financial statements and that internal controls are effective. Therefore, a high planned detection risk is appropriate. As a result, a low level of evidence is needed. Situation 3 is at the opposite extreme. If both inherent and control risks are high, and the auditor wants a low audit risk, considerable evidence is required. The other three situations fall between the two extremes.

It is equally difficult to measure the amount of evidence implied by a given planned detection risk. A typical audit program that is intended to reduce detection risk to the planned level is a combination of several audit procedures, each using a different type of evidence which is applied to different audit objectives. Auditor's measurement methods are too imprecise to permit an accurate quantitative measure of the combined evidence. Instead, auditors subjectively evaluate whether sufficient evidence has been planned to satisfy a planned detection risk of low, medium, or high. Presumably, measurement methods are sufficient to permit an auditor to know that more evidence is needed to satisfy a low planned detection risk than for medium or high. Considerable professional judgment is needed to decide how much more.

In applying the audit risk model, auditors are concerned about both over- and underauditing, but most auditors are more concerned about the latter. Underauditing exposes the CPA firm to legal liability and loss of professional reputation.

Because of the concern to avoid underauditing, auditors typically assess risks conservatively. For example, an auditor might not assess either control risk or inherent risk below .5 even when the likelihood of misstatement is low. In these audits, a low risk might be .5, medium .8, and high 1.0, if the risks are quantified.

## Tests of Details of Balances Evidence Planning Worksheet

Practicing auditors develop various types of worksheets to aid in relating the considerations affecting audit evidence to the appropriate evidence to accumulate. One such worksheet is included in Figure 8-7 on page 268 for the audit of accounts receivable for Hillsburg Hardware Co. The nine balance-related audit objectives introduced in Chapter 5 are included in the columns at the top of the worksheet. Rows one and two are acceptable audit risk and inherent risk, which were studied in this chapter. Tolerable misstatement is included at the bottom of the worksheet. The engagement in-charge, Fran Moore, made the following decisions in the audit of Hillsburg Hardware Co.:

- *Tolerable misstatement.* The preliminary judgment about materiality was set at \$37,000 (10 percent of earnings from operations of \$369,000). She allocated \$22,000 to the audit of accounts receivable (see page 253).
- *Acceptable audit risk.* Fran assessed acceptable audit risk as high because of the good financial condition of the company, high management integrity, and the relatively few users of the financial statements.
- *Inherent risk.* Fran assessed inherent risk as low for all balance-related audit objectives except realizable value. In past years, there have been audit adjustments to the allowance for uncollectible accounts because it was found to be understated.

Planned detection risk would be approximately the same for each balance-related audit objective in the audit of accounts receivable for Hillsburg Hardware Co. if the only three factors the auditor needs to consider are acceptable audit risk, inherent risk, and tolerable misstatement. The evidence planning worksheet shows that other factors must be considered before making the final evidence decisions. These are studied in subsequent chapters and will be integrated into the evidence planning worksheet at that time.

## Relationship of Risk and Materiality and Audit Evidence

**OBJECTIVE 8-11**

**Discuss how materiality and risk are related and integrated into the audit process.**

The concepts of materiality and risk in auditing are closely related and inseparable. Risk is a measure of uncertainty, whereas materiality is a measure of magnitude or size. Taken together they measure the uncertainty of amounts of a given magnitude. For example, the statement that the auditor plans to accumulate evidence such that there is only a 5 percent risk (acceptable audit risk) of failing to uncover misstatements exceeding tolerable misstatements of \$25,000 (materiality) is a precise and meaningful statement. If the statement eliminates either the risk or materiality portion, it would be meaningless. A 5 percent risk

**FIGURE 8-7**

**Evidence Planning Worksheet to Decide Tests of Details of Balances for Hillsburg Hardware Co.—Accounts Receivable**

| | Detail tie-in | Existence | Completeness | Accuracy | Classification | Cutoff | Realizable value | Rights | Presentation and disclosure |
|---|---|---|---|---|---|---|---|---|---|
| Acceptable audit risk | high | high | high | high | high | high | high | high | high |
| Inherent risk | low | low | low | low | low | low | medium | low | low |
| Control risk—Sales | | | | | | | | | |
| Control risk—Cash receipts | | | | | | | | | |
| Control risk—Additional controls | | | | | | | | | |
| Substantive tests of transactions—Sales | | | | | | | | | |
| Substantive tests of transactions—Cash receipts | | | | | | | | | |
| Analytical procedures | | | | | | | | | |
| Planned detection risk for tests of details of balances | | | | | | | | | |
| Planned audit evidence for tests of details of balances | | | | | | | | | |

Tolerable misstatement $22,000

without a specific materiality measure could imply that a $100 or $1 million misstatement is acceptable. A $25,000 overstatement without a specific risk could imply that a 1 percent or 80 percent risk is acceptable.

The relationships between tolerable misstatement and the four risks to planned audit evidence are shown in Figure 8-8. This figure expands Figure 8-6 to include tolerable misstatement. Observe that tolerable misstatement does not affect any of the four risks and the risks have no effect on tolerable misstatement, but together they determine the planned evidence.

## EVALUATING RESULTS

After the auditor plans the engagement and accumulates audit evidence, results can also be stated in terms of the evaluation version of the audit risk model. There is a brief discussion of these results in this chapter on planning only to provide a more complete discussion of the audit risk model. Audit results are studied more extensively in later chapters.

**FIGURE 8-8**

**Relationship of Tolerable Misstatement and Risks to Planned Evidence**

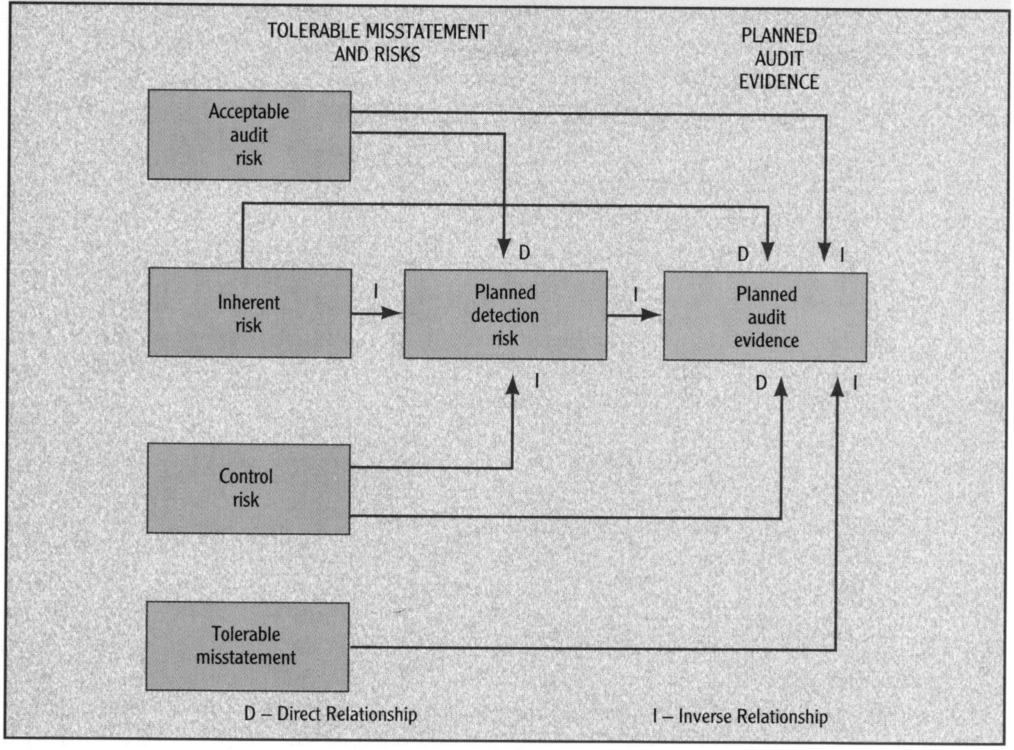


The audit risk model for evaluating audit results is stated in SAS 47 as:

$$AcAR = IR \times CR \times AcDR$$

where:

***AcAR* = *Achieved audit risk*** A measure of the risk the auditor has taken that an account in the financial statements is materially misstated after the auditor has accumulated audit evidence.

***IR* = *Inherent risk*** It is the same inherent risk factor discussed in planning unless it has been revised as a result of new information.

***CR* = *Control risk*** It is also the same control risk discussed previously unless it has been revised during the audit.

***AcDR* = *Achieved detection risk*** A measure of the risk that audit evidence for a segment did not detect misstatements exceeding a tolerable amount, if such misstatements existed. The auditor can reduce achieved detection risk only by accumulating substantive evidence.

Research subsequent to the issuance of SAS 47 has shown that it is *not appropriate to use this evaluation formula* in the way it is stated in SAS 47. The research indicates that using the formula can result in an understatement of achieved audit risk.

Even though it is not appropriate to use the formula to calculate achieved audit risk, the relationships in the formula are valid and should be used in practice. The formula shows that there are three ways to reduce achieved audit risk to an acceptable level:

- *Reduce inherent risk.* Because inherent risk is assessed by the auditor based on the client's circumstances, this assessment is done during planning and is typically not changed unless new facts are uncovered as the audit progresses.

- *Reduce control risk.* Assessed control risk is affected by the client's internal controls and the auditor's tests of those controls. Auditors can reduce control risk by more extensive tests of controls if the client has effective controls.
- *Reduce achieved detection risk by increasing substantive audit tests.* Auditors reduce achieved detection risk by accumulating evidence using analytical procedures, substantive tests of transactions, and tests of details of balances. Additional audit procedures, assuming that they are effective, and larger sample sizes both reduce achieved detection risk.

Subjectively combining these three factors to achieve an acceptably low audit risk requires considerable professional judgment. Some firms develop sophisticated approaches to help their auditors make those judgments, while other firms leave those decisions to each audit team.

Figure 8-9 graphically shows both the planning and evaluating results versions of the audit risk model. The right side of the figure shows that accumulating more substantive evidence reduces achieved detection risk. A lower achieved detection risk along with lower inherent and control risk reduce achieved audit risk.

## Revising Risks and Evidence

As already stated, the audit risk model is primarily a *planning* model, and is therefore of limited use in evaluating results. Great care must be used in revising the risk factors when the actual results are not as favorable as planned.

No difficulties occur when the auditor accumulates planned evidence and concludes that the assessment of each of the risks was reasonable or better than originally thought. The auditor will conclude that sufficient competent evidence has been collected for that account or cycle.

Special care must be exercised when the auditor decides, on the basis of accumulated evidence, that the original assessment of control risk or inherent risk was understated or acceptable audit risk was overstated. In such a circumstance, the auditor should follow a two-step approach. First, the auditor must revise the original assessment of the appropriate

**FIGURE 8-9**

**Audit Risk Models for Planning Evidence and Evaluating Results**

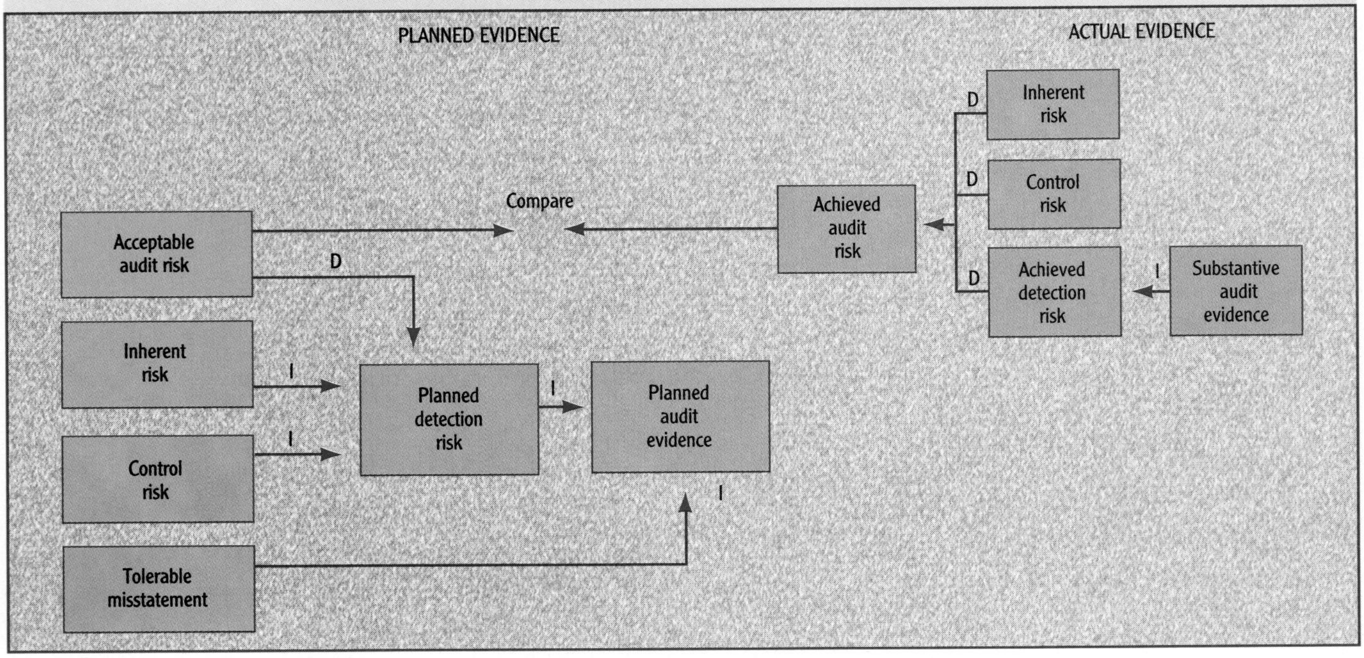

risk. It would violate due care to leave the original assessment unchanged if the auditor knows it is inappropriate. Second, the auditor should consider the effect of the revision on evidence requirements, *without use of the audit risk model.* Research in auditing has shown that if a revised risk is used in the audit risk model to determine a revised planned detection risk, there is a danger of not increasing the evidence sufficiently. Instead, the auditor should carefully evaluate the implications of the revision of the risk and modify evidence appropriately, outside of the audit risk model. An example is used to illustrate revision of a factor in the audit risk model. Assume that the auditor confirms accounts receivable and, based on the misstatements found, concludes that the original control risk assessment as low was inappropriate. The auditor should revise the estimate of control risk upward and carefully consider the effect of the revision on the additional evidence needed in the sales and collection cycle. That should be done without recalculating planned detection risk.

## SUMMARY

This chapter discussed the effects of materiality and relevant risks on audit planning. The purpose of using materiality and risks is to help the auditor accumulate sufficient competent evidence in the most efficient way possible. Figure 8-10 shows the effect of materiality and the most important risks discussed in this chapter on the evidence decisions discussed in Chapter 6.

**FIGURE 8-10**

**Relationship of Materiality, Risks, and Available Evidence to Audit Planning**

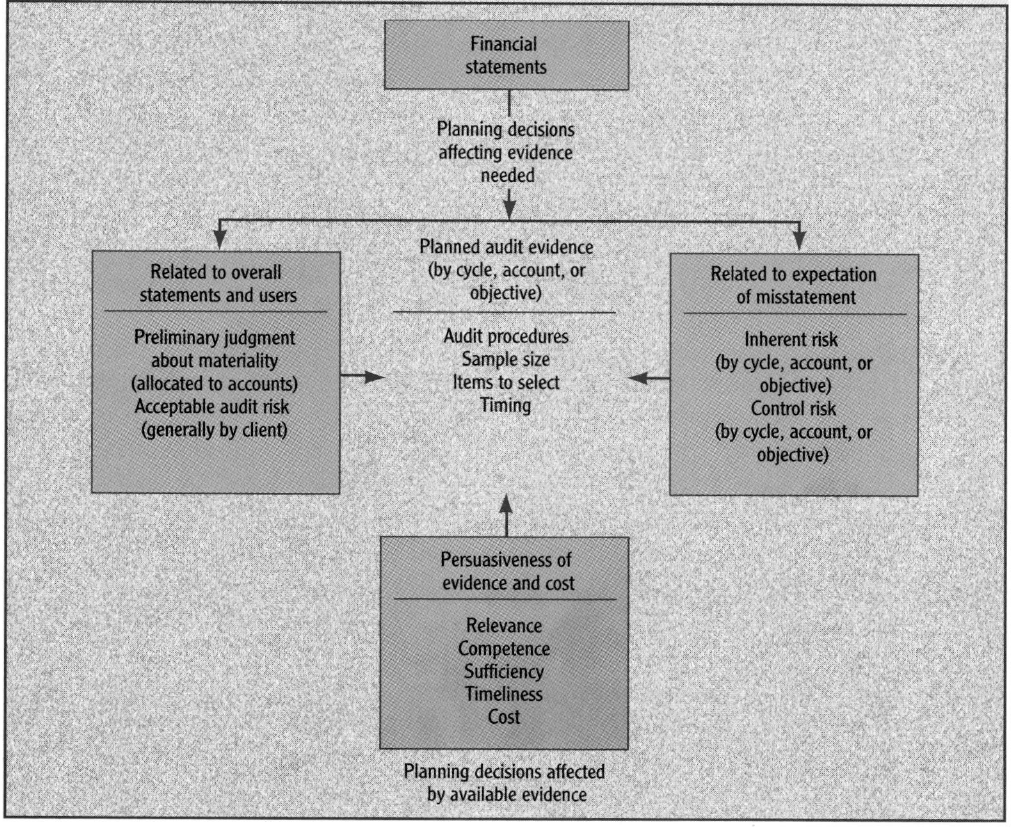

## ESSENTIAL TERMS

**Acceptable audit risk**—a measure of how willing the auditor is to accept that the financial statements may be materially misstated after the audit is completed and an unqualified audit opinion has been issued; see also *audit assurance*

**Allocation of preliminary judgment about materiality**—the process of assigning to each balance sheet account the misstatement amount to be considered material based on the auditor's preliminary judgment

**Audit assurance**—a complement to *acceptable audit risk*; an acceptable audit risk of 2 percent is the same as audit assurance of 98 percent; also called *overall assurance* and *level of assurance*

**Audit risk model**—a formal model reflecting the relationships between acceptable audit risk (AAR), inherent risk (IR), control risk (CR), and planned detection risk (PDR); $PDR = AAR/(IR \times CR)$

**Business risk**—risk that the auditor or audit firm will suffer harm because of a client relationship, even though the audit report rendered for the client was correct

**Control risk**—a measure of the auditor's assessment of the likelihood that misstatements exceeding a tolerable amount in a segment will not be prevented or detected by the client's internal controls

**Direct projection method of estimating misstatement**—net misstatements in the sample, divided by the total sampled, multiplied by the total recorded population value

**Inherent risk**—a measure of the auditor's assessment of the likelihood that there are material misstatements in a segment before considering the effectiveness of internal control

**Materiality**—the magnitude of an omission or misstatement of accounting information that, in the light of surrounding circumstances, makes it *probable* that the judgment of a reasonable person relying on the information would have been changed or influenced by the omission or misstatement

**Planned detection risk (PDR)**—a measure of the risk that audit evidence for a segment will fail to detect misstatements exceeding a tolerable amount, should such misstatements exist; $PDR = AAR/(IR \times CR)$

**Preliminary judgment about materiality**—the maximum amount by which the auditor believes that the statements could be misstated and still *not* affect the decisions of reasonable users; used in audit planning

**Revised judgment about materiality**—a change in the auditor's preliminary judgment made when the auditor determines that the preliminary judgment was too large or too small

**Risk**—the acceptance by auditors that there is some level of uncertainty in performing the audit function

**Sampling error**—results because the auditor has sampled only a portion of the population

**Tolerable misstatement**—the materiality allocated to any given account balance; used in audit planning

## REVIEW QUESTIONS

**8-1 (Objective 8-1)** Chapter 7 introduced the seven parts of the planning phase of an audit. Which part is the evaluation of materiality and risk?

**8-2 (Objective 8-1)** Define the meaning of the term *materiality* as it is used in accounting and auditing. What is the relationship between materiality and the phrase *obtain reasonable assurance* used in the auditor's report?

**8-3 (Objectives 8-1, 8-2)** Explain why materiality is important but difficult to apply in practice.

**8-4 (Objective 8-2)** What is meant by setting a preliminary judgment about materiality? Identify the most important factors affecting the preliminary judgment.

**8-5 (Objective 8-2)** What is meant by using bases for setting a preliminary judgment about materiality? How would those bases differ for the audit of a manufacturing company and a government unit such as a school district?

**8-6 (Objective 8-2)** Assume that Rosanne Madden, CPA, is using 5 percent of net income before taxes, current assets, or current liabilities as her major guidelines for evaluating materiality. What qualitative factors should she also consider in deciding whether misstatements may be material?

**8-7 (Objectives 8-2, 8-3)** Distinguish between the terms *tolerable misstatement* and *preliminary judgment about materiality*. How are they related to each other?

**8-8 (Objective 8-3)** Assume a company with the following balance sheet accounts:

| Account | Amount |
|---|---|
| Cash | $10,000 |
| Fixed assets | 60,000 |
| | $70,000 |
| Long-term loans | $30,000 |
| M. Johnson, proprietor | 40,000 |
| | $70,000 |

You are concerned only about overstatements of owner's equity. Set tolerable misstatement for the three relevant accounts such that the preliminary judgment about materiality does not exceed $5,000. Justify your answer.

**8-9 (Objective 8-4)** Explain what is meant by making an estimate of the total misstatement in a segment and in the overall financial statements. Why is it important to make these estimates? What is done with them?

**8-10 (Objective 8-2)** How would the conduct of an audit of a medium-sized company be affected by the company's being a small part of a large conglomerate as compared with its being a separate entity?

**8-11 (Objective 8-6)** Define the audit risk model and explain each term in the model.

**8-12 (Objective 8-6)** What is meant by planned detection risk? What is the effect on the amount of evidence the auditor must accumulate when planned detection risk is increased from medium to high?

**8-13 (Objective 8-6)** Explain the causes of an increased or decreased planned detection risk.

**8-14 (Objectives 8-6, 8-8)** Define what is meant by inherent risk. Identify four factors that make for *high* inherent risk in audits.

**8-15 (Objective 8-8)** Explain why inherent risk is set for segments rather than for the overall audit. What is the effect on the amount of evidence the auditor must accumulate when inherent risk is increased from medium to high for a segment? Compare your answer with the one for 8-12.

**8-16 (Objective 8-8)** Explain the effect of extensive misstatements found in the prior year's audit on inherent risk, planned detection risk, and planned audit evidence.

**8-17 (Objectives 8-6, 8-7)** Explain what is meant by the term *acceptable audit risk*. What is its relevance to evidence accumulation?

**8-18 (Objective 8-7)** Explain the relationship between acceptable audit risk and the legal liability of auditors.

**8-19 (Objective 8-7)** State the three categories of factors that affect acceptable audit risk and list the factors that the auditor can use to indicate the degree to which each category exists.

**8-20 (Objective 8-10)** Auditors have not been successful in measuring the components of the audit risk model. How is it possible to use the model in a meaningful way without a precise way of measuring the risk?

**8-21 (Objective 8-11)** Explain the circumstances when the auditor should revise the components of the audit risk model and the effect of the revisions on planned detection risk and planned evidence.

## MULTIPLE CHOICE QUESTIONS FROM CPA EXAMINATIONS

**8-22 (Objectives 8-1, 8-2)** The following questions deal with materiality. Choose the best response.

a. Which one of the following statements is correct concerning the concept of materiality?
   (1) Materiality is determined by reference to guidelines established by the AICPA.
   (2) Materiality depends only on the dollar amount of an item relative to other items in the financial statements.
   (3) Materiality depends on the nature of an item rather than the dollar amount.
   (4) Materiality is a matter of professional judgment.

b. The concept of materiality will be least important to the CPA in determining the
   (1) scope of the audit of specific accounts.
   (2) specific transactions that should be reviewed.
   (3) effects of audit exceptions upon the opinion.
   (4) effects of the CPA's direct financial interest in a client upon his or her independence.

**8-23 (Objectives 8-1, 8-6, 8-8)** The following questions concern materiality and risk. Choose the best response.

a. Edison Corporation has a few large accounts receivable that total $1,400,000. Victor Corporation has a great number of small accounts receivable that also total $1,400,000. The importance of a misstatement in any one account is, therefore, greater for Edison than for Victor. This is an example of the auditor's concept of
   (1) materiality.
   (2) comparative analysis.
   (3) reasonable assurance.
   (4) relative risk.

b. Which of the following elements ultimately determines the specific auditing procedures that are necessary in the circumstances to afford a reasonable basis for an opinion?
   (1) Auditor judgment
   (2) Materiality
   (3) Inherent risk
   (4) Reasonable assurance

c. Which of the following *best* describes the element of inherent risk that underlies the application of generally accepted auditing standards, specifically the standards of field work and reporting?
   (1) Cash audit work may have to be carried out in a more conclusive manner than inventory audit work.
   (2) Intercompany transactions are usually subject to less detailed scrutiny than arm's-length transactions with outside parties.
   (3) Inventories may require more attention by the auditor on an engagement for a merchandising enterprise than on an engagement for a public utility.
   (4) The scope of the audit need *not* be expanded if misstatements that arouse suspicion of fraud are of relatively insignificant amounts.

**8-24 (Objectives 8-1, 8-2, 8-5, 8-6, 8-8)** The following questions deal with materiality and risk. Choose the best response.

a. Which of the following statements is **not** correct about materiality?
   (1) The concept of materiality recognizes that some matters are important for fair presentation of financial statements in conformity with GAAP, while other matters are **not** important.
   (2) An auditor considers materiality for planning purposes in terms of the largest aggregate level of misstatements that could be material to any one of the financial statements.
   (3) Materiality judgments are made in light of surrounding circumstances and necessarily involve both quantitative and qualitative judgments.

(4) An auditor's consideration of materiality is influenced by the auditor's perception of the needs of a reasonable person who will rely on the financial statements.

b. Inherent risk and control risk differ from planned detection risk in that they
   (1) arise from the misapplication of auditing procedures.
   (2) may be assessed in either quantitative or nonquantitative terms.
   (3) exist independently of the financial statement audit.
   (4) can be changed at the auditor's discretion.

c. In considering materiality for planning purposes, an auditor believes that misstatements aggregating $10,000 would have a material effect on an entity's income statement, but that misstatements would have to aggregate $20,000 to materially affect the balance sheet. Ordinarily, it would be appropriate to design auditing procedures that would be expected to detect misstatements that aggregate.
   (1) $10,000 (3) $20,000
   (2) $15,000 (4) $30,000

## DISCUSSION QUESTIONS AND PROBLEMS

**8-25 (Objectives 8-2, 8-3, 8-4)** You are evaluating audit results for current assets in the audit of Quicky Plumbing Co. You set the preliminary judgment about materiality for current assets at $12,500 for overstatements and at $20,000 for understatements. The preliminary and actual estimates are shown below.

| | Tolerable Misstatement | | Estimate of Total Misstatement | |
|---|---|---|---|---|
| **Account** | **Overstatements** | **Understatements** | **Overstatements** | **Understatements** |
| Cash | $ 2,000 | $ 3,000 | $ 2,000 | $ 0 |
| Accounts receivable | 12,000 | 18,000 | 4,000 | 19,000 |
| Inventory | 8,000 | 14,000 | 3,000 | 10,000 |
| Prepaid expenses | 3,000 | 5,000 | 2,000 | 1,000 |
| Total | $25,000 | $40,000 | $11,000 | $30,000 |

## Required

a. Justify a lower preliminary judgment about materiality for overstatement than understatement in this situation.

b. Explain why the totals of the tolerable misstatements exceed the preliminary judgments about materiality for both understatements and overstatements.

c. Explain how it is possible that three of the estimates of total misstatement have both an overstatement and an understatement.

d. Assume that you are not concerned whether the estimate of misstatement exceeds tolerable misstatement for individual accounts if the total estimate is less than the preliminary judgment.
   (1) Given the audit results, should you be more concerned about the existence of material overstatements or understatements at this point in the audit of Quicky Plumbing Co.?
   (2) Which account or accounts would you be most concerned about in (1)? Explain.

e. Assume that the estimate of total overstatement amount for each account is less than tolerable misstatement, but the total overstatement estimate exceeds the preliminary judgment of materiality.
   (1) Explain why this would occur.
   (2) Explain what the auditor should do.

**8-26 (Objectives 8-2, 8-3, 8-4)** Below and on page 277 are statements of earnings and financial position for General Foods Corporation.

## Required

a. Use professional judgment in deciding on the preliminary judgment about materiality for earnings, current assets, current liabilities, and total assets. Your conclusions should be stated in terms of percentages and dollars.

b. Assume that you define *materiality* for this audit as a combined misstatement of earnings from continuing operations before income taxes of 5 percent. Also assume that you believe there is an equal likelihood of a misstatement of every account in the financial statements and each misstatement is likely to result in an overstatement of earnings. Allocate materiality to these financial statements as you consider appropriate.

c. Now, assume that you have decided to allocate 75 percent of your preliminary judgment to accounts receivable, inventories, and accounts payable because you believe all other accounts have a low inherent and control risk. How does this affect evidence accumulation on the audit?

d. Assume that you complete the audit and conclude that your preliminary judgment about materiality for current assets, current liabilities, and total assets has been met. The actual estimate of misstatements in *earnings* exceeds your preliminary judgment. What should you do?

**Consolidated Statements of Earnings**
**General Foods Corporation and Subsidiaries**

| | For the 53 Weeks Ended April 3, 1997* | For the 52 Weeks Ended March 28, 1996 | March 29, 1995 |
|---|---|---|---|
| **Revenue** | | | |
| Net sales | $8,351,149 | $6,601,255 | $5,959,587 |
| Other income | 59,675 | 43,186 | 52,418 |
| | 8,410,824 | 6,644,441 | 6,012,005 |
| **Costs and expenses** | | | |
| Cost of sales | 5,197,375 | 4,005,548 | 3,675,369 |
| Marketing, general, and administrative expenses | 2,590,080 | 2,119,590 | 1,828,169 |
| Provision for loss on restructured operations | 64,100 | — | — |
| Interest expense | 141,662 | 46,737 | 38,546 |
| | 7,993,217 | 6,171,875 | 5,542,084 |
| **Earnings from continuing operations before income taxes** | 417,607 | 472,566 | 469,921 |
| **Income taxes** | (196,700) | (217,200) | (214,100) |
| **Earnings from continuing operations** | 220,907 | 255,366 | 255,821 |
| **Provision for loss on discontinued operations, net of income taxes** | (20,700) | — | — |
| **Net earnings** | $ 200,207 | $ 255,366 | $ 255,821 |

*All dollar amounts are expressed in thousands.

**Consolidated Statements of Financial Position**
**General Foods Corporation and Subsidiaries**

| **Assets** | **April 3, 1997*** | **March 28, 1996** |
|---|---|---|
| **Current assets** | | |
| Cash | $ 39,683 | $ 37,566 |
| Temporary investments, including time deposits of $65,361 in 1997 and $181,589 in 1996 (at cost, which approximates market) | 123,421 | 271,639 |
| Receivables, less allowances of $16,808 in 1997 and $17,616 in 1996 | 899,752 | 759,001 |
| Inventories | | |
| Finished product | 680,974 | 550,407 |
| Raw materials and supplies | 443,175 | 353,795 |
| | 1,124,149 | 904,202 |
| Deferred income tax benefits | 9,633 | 10,468 |
| Prepaid expenses | 57,468 | 35,911 |
| **Current assets** | **2,254,106** | **2,018,787** |
| **Land, buildings, and equipment, at cost, less accumulated depreciation** | **1,393,902** | **1,004,455** |
| **Investments in affiliated companies and sundry assets** | **112,938** | **83,455** |
| **Goodwill and other intangible assets** | **99,791** | **23,145** |
| **Total** | **$3,860,737** | **$3,129,842** |

| **Liabilities and Stockholders' Equity** | | |
|---|---|---|
| **Current liabilities** | | |
| Notes payable | $ 280,238 | $ 113,411 |
| Current portion of long-term debt | 64,594 | 12,336 |
| Accounts and drafts payable | 359,511 | 380,395 |
| Accrued salaries, wages, and vacations | 112,200 | 63,557 |
| Accrued income taxes | 76,479 | 89,151 |
| Other accrued liabilities | 321,871 | 269,672 |
| **Current liabilities** | **1,214,893** | **928,522** |
| **Long-term debt** | **730,987** | **390,687** |
| **Other noncurrent liabilities** | **146,687** | **80,586** |
| **Deferred income taxes** | **142,344** | **119,715** |
| **Stockholders' equity** | | |
| Common stock issued, 51,017,755 shares in 1997 and 50,992,410 in 1996 | 51,018 | 50,992 |
| Additional paid-in capital | 149,177 | 148,584 |
| Cumulative foreign currency translation adjustment | (76,572) | — |
| Retained earnings | 1,554,170 | 1,462,723 |
| Common stock held in treasury, at cost, 1,566,598 shares | (51,967) | (51,967) |
| **Stockholders' equity** | **1,625,826** | **1,610,332** |
| **Total** | **$3,860,737** | **$3,129,842** |

* All dollar amounts are expressed in thousands.

**8-27 (Objectives 8-2, 8-3, 8-4, 8-6, 8-7, 8-8, 8-11)** The following are concepts discussed in Chapter 8:

1. Preliminary judgment about materiality
2. Estimate of the combined misstatements
3. Acceptable audit risk
4. Tolerable misstatement
5. Inherent risk
6. Estimated total misstatement in a segment
7. Control risk
8. Planned detection risk

**Required**

a. Identify which items are *audit planning decisions* requiring professional judgment.

b. Identify which items are *audit conclusions* resulting from application of audit procedures and requiring professional judgment.

c. Under what circumstances is it acceptable to change those items in part a, after the audit is started? Which items can be changed after the audit is 95 percent completed?

**8-28 (Objectives 8-6, 8-7)** Describe what is meant by acceptable audit risk. Explain why each of the following statements is true:

a. A CPA firm should attempt to achieve the same audit risk for all audit clients when circumstances are similar.

b. A CPA firm should decrease acceptable audit risk for audit clients when external users rely heavily on the statements.

c. A CPA firm should decrease acceptable audit risk for audit clients when there is a reasonably high likelihood of a client's filing bankruptcy.

d. Different CPA firms should attempt to achieve reasonably similar audit risks for clients with similar circumstances.

**8-29 (Objectives 8-5, 8-6, 8-7, 8-8, 8-9)** State whether each of the following statements is true or false, and give your reasons:

a. The audit evidence accumulated for every client should be approximately the same, regardless of the circumstances.

b. If acceptable audit risk is the same for two different clients, the audit evidence for the two clients should be approximately the same.

c. If acceptable audit risk, inherent risk, and control risk are approximately the same for two different clients, the audit evidence for the two clients should be approximately the same.

**8-30 (Objectives 8-6, 8-7, 8-8)** The following questions deal with the use of the audit risk model.

a. Assume that the auditor is doing a first-year municipal audit of Redwood City, Missouri, and concludes that the internal controls are not likely to be effective.
   (1) Explain why the auditor is likely to set both inherent and control risks at 100 percent for most segments.
   (2) Assuming (1), explain the relationship of acceptable audit risk to planned detection risk.
   (3) Assuming (1), explain the effect of planned detection risk on evidence accumulation compared with its effect if planned detection risk were larger.

b. Assume that the auditor is doing the third-year municipal audit of Redwood City, Missouri, and concludes that internal controls are effective and inherent risk is low.
   (1) Explain why the auditor is likely to set inherent and control risks for material segments at a higher level than, say, 40 percent, even when the two risks are low.
   (2) For the audit of fixed asset accounts, assume inherent and control risks of 50 percent each, and an acceptable audit risk of 5 percent. Calculate planned detection risk.
   (3) For (2), explain the effect of planned detection risk on evidence accumulation compared with its effect if planned detection risk were smaller.

c. Assume that the auditor is doing the fifth-year municipal audit of Redwood City, Missouri, and concludes that acceptable audit risk can be set high, and inherent and control risks should be set low.
   (1) What circumstances would result in these conclusions?
   (2) For the audit of repairs and maintenance, inherent and control risk are set at 20 percent each. Acceptable audit risk is 5 percent. Calculate planned detection risk.
   (3) How much evidence should be accumulated in this situation?

**8-31 (Objective 8-6)** Following are six situations that involve the audit risk model as it is used for planning audit evidence requirements. Numbers are used only to help you understand the relationships among factors in the risk model.

| | Situation | | | | | |
|---|---|---|---|---|---|---|
| **Risk** | **1** | **2** | **3** | **4** | **5** | **6** |
| Acceptable audit risk | 5% | 5% | 5% | 5% | 1% | 1% |
| Inherent risk | 100% | 40% | 60% | 20% | 100% | 40% |
| Control risk | 100% | 60% | 40% | 30% | 100% | 60% |
| Planned detection risk | — | — | — | — | — | — |

## Required

a. Explain what each of the four risks mean.

b. Calculate planned detection risk for each situation.

c. Using your knowledge of the relationships among the foregoing factors, state the effect on planned detection risk (increase or decrease) of changing each of the following factors while the other two remain constant.
   (1) A decrease in acceptable audit risk
   (2) A decrease in control risk
   (3) A decrease in inherent risk
   (4) An increase in control risk and a decrease in inherent risk of the same amount

d. Which situation requires the greatest amount of evidence and which requires the least?

**8-32 (Objectives 8-6, 8-9, 8-10)** Following are six situations that involve the audit risk model as it is used for planning audit evidence requirements in the audit of inventory.

| | Situation | | | | | |
|---|---|---|---|---|---|---|
| **Risk** | **1** | **2** | **3** | **4** | **5** | **6** |
| Acceptable audit risk | High | High | Low | Low | High | Medium |
| Inherent risk | Low | High | High | Low | Medium | Medium |
| Control risk | Low | Low | High | High | Medium | Medium |
| Planned detection risk | — | — | — | — | — | — |
| Planned evidence | — | — | — | — | — | — |

## Required

a. Explain what low, medium, and high mean for each of the four risks and planned evidence.

b. Fill in the blanks for planned detection risk and planned evidence using the terms *low, medium,* or *high.*

c. Using your knowledge of the relationships among the foregoing factors, state the effect on planned evidence (increase or decrease) of changing each of the following five factors, while the other three remain constant.
   (1) An increase in acceptable audit risk
   (2) An increase in control risk
   (3) An increase in planned detection risk
   (4) An increase in inherent risk
   (5) An increase in inherent risk and a decrease in control risk of the same amount

**8-33 (Objectives 8-6, 8-9, 8-11)** Using the audit risk model, state the effect on control risk, inherent risk, acceptable audit risk, and planned evidence for each of the following independent events. In each of the events a to j, circle one letter for each of the three independent variables and planned evidence: I = increase, D = decrease, N = no effect, and C = cannot determine from the information provided.

a. The client's management materially increased long-term contractual debt:

| | | | |
|---|---|---|---|
| Control risk | I D N C | Acceptable audit risk | I D N C |
| Inherent risk | I D N C | Planned evidence | I D N C |

b. The company changed from a privately held company to a publicly held company:

| | | | |
|---|---|---|---|
| Control risk | I D N C | Acceptable audit risk | I D N C |
| Inherent risk | I D N C | Planned evidence | I D N C |

c. The auditor decided to set assessed control risk below maximum (it was previously assessed at maximum):

| | | | |
|---|---|---|---|
| Control risk | I D N C | Acceptable audit risk | I D N C |
| Inherent risk | I D N C | Planned evidence | I D N C |

d. The account balance increased materially from the preceding year without apparent reason:

| | | | |
|---|---|---|---|
| Control risk | I D N C | Acceptable audit risk | I D N C |
| Inherent risk | I D N C | Planned evidence | I D N C |

e. You determined through the planning phase that working capital, debt to equity ratio, and other indicators of financial condition had improved during the past year:

| | | | |
|---|---|---|---|
| Control risk | I D N C | Acceptable audit risk | I D N C |
| Inherent risk | I D N C | Planned evidence | I D N C |

f. This is the second year of the engagement and there were few misstatements found in the previous year's audit. The auditor also decided to increase reliance on internal control:

| | | | |
|---|---|---|---|
| Control risk | I D N C | Acceptable audit risk | I D N C |
| Inherent risk | I D N C | Planned evidence | I D N C |

g. About halfway through the audit, you discover that the client is constructing its own building during idle periods, using factory personnel. This is the first time the client has done this, and it is being done at your recommendation:

| | | | |
|---|---|---|---|
| Control risk | I D N C | Acceptable audit risk | I D N C |
| Inherent risk | I D N C | Planned evidence | I D N C |

h. In discussions with management, you conclude that management is planning to sell the business in the next few months. Because of the planned changes, several key accounting personnel quit several months ago for alternative employment. You also observe that the gross margin percent has significantly increased compared with that of the preceding year:

| | | | |
|---|---|---|---|
| Control risk | I D N C | Acceptable audit risk | I D N C |
| Inherent risk | I D N C | Planned evidence | I D N C |

i. There has been a change in several key management personnel. You believe that management is somewhat lacking in personal integrity, compared with the previous management. You believe it is still appropriate to do the audit:

| | | | |
|---|---|---|---|
| Control risk | I D N C | Acceptable audit risk | I D N C |
| Inherent risk | I D N C | Planned evidence | I D N C |

j. In auditing inventory, you obtain an understanding of internal control and perform tests of controls. You find it significantly improved compared with that of the preceding year. You also observe that due to technology changes in the industry, the client's inventory may be somewhat obsolete:

Control risk I D N C Acceptable audit risk I D N C

Inherent risk I D N C Planned evidence I D N C

**8-34 (Objectives 8-6, 8-7, 8-8, 8-9)** In the audit of Whirland Chemical Company, a large publicly traded company, you have been assigned the responsibility for obtaining background information for the audit. Your firm is auditing the client for the first time in the current year as a result of a dispute between Whirland and the previous auditor over the proper valuation of work-in-process inventory and the inclusion in sales of inventory that has not been delivered but has for practical purposes been completed and sold.

Whirland Chemical has been highly successful in its field in the past two decades, primarily because of many successful mergers negotiated by Bert Randolph, the president and chairman of the board. Even though the industry as a whole has suffered dramatic setbacks in recent years, Whirland continues to prosper, as evidenced by its constantly increasing earnings and growth. Only in the last two years have the company's profits turned downward. Randolph has a reputation for having been able to hire an aggressive group of young executives by the use of relatively low salaries combined with an unusually generous profit-sharing plan.

A major difficulty you face in the new audit is the lack of highly sophisticated accounting records for a company the size of Whirland. Randolph believes that profits come primarily from intelligent and aggressive action based on forecasts, not by relying on historical data that come after the fact. Most of the forecast data are generated by the sales and production department rather than by the accounting department. The personnel in the accounting department do seem competent but somewhat overworked and underpaid relative to other employees. One of the recent changes that will potentially improve the record keeping is the installation of sophisticated computer equipment. All the accounting records are not computerized yet, but such major areas as inventory and sales are included in the new system. Most of the computer time is being reserved for production and marketing because these areas are more essential to operations than the record-keeping function.

The first six months' financial statements for the current year include a profit of approximately only 10 percent less than the first six months of the preceding year, which is somewhat surprising, considering the reduced volume and the disposal of a segment of the business, Mercury Supply Co. The disposal of this segment was considered necessary because it had become increasingly unprofitable over the past four years. At the time of its acquisition from Roger Randolph, who is a brother of Bert Randolph, the company was highly profitable and it was considered a highly desirable purchase. The major customer of Mercury Supply Co. was the Mercury Corporation, which is owned by Roger Randolph. Gradually the market for its products declined as the Mercury Corporation began diversifying and phasing out its primary products in favor of more profitable business. Even though Mercury Corporation is no longer buying from Mercury Supply Company, it compensates for it by buying a large volume of other products from Whirland Chemical.

The only major difficulty Whirland faces right now, according to financial analysts, is underfinancing. There is an excessive amount of current debt and long-term debt because of the depressed capital markets. Management is reluctant to obtain equity capital at this point because the increased number of shares would decrease the earnings per share even more than 10 percent. At the present time, Randolph is negotiating with several cash-rich companies in the hope of being able to merge with them as a means of overcoming the capital problems.

### Required

a. List the major concerns you should have in the audit of Whirland Company and explain why they are potential problems.

b. State the appropriate approach to investigating the significance of each item you listed in a.

## CASES

8-35 **(Objectives 8-3, 8-6, 8-7, 8-8, 8-11)** The purpose of this case is to give you practice in and an appreciation for the value of analytical procedures. This case involves preliminary analytical procedures of a publicly held company using information available from the annual report, Form 10-K, and information from partners. Data for several years' financial statements are presented for you to analyze; you are then asked to interpret the analyses from differing points of view. The data and supplemental information are presented in Exhibits I through V, which follow. The specific requirements for the case are as follows.

**Background Information**

ABC Company is a large retail chain. In recent years it has had as many as 1,100 stores and operated with 80,000 employees. Stores vary in size, but many are full-time department stores carrying both hard and soft goods.

ABC has financed its growth over the years with both equity capital and debt. The stock of ABC is widely traded and of great interest to observers on Wall Street.

Exhibits I and II provide you with a comparative balance sheet and income statement for ABC for the most recent eight years. Exhibit III presents certain additional information that is important. Exhibit IV provides a limited awareness of industry information. Exhibit V provides additional facts and events for the company.

### Required

a. Identify any factors that would affect acceptable audit risk, inherent risk, or tolerable misstatement in the audit of ABC Company.

b. Prepare a general financial analysis of the financial statements of ABC Company. Use appropriate ratios and trends. These should focus on such methods as short-term debt-paying ability, liquidity, long-term debt-paying ability, and operating performance. Prepare the analysis, using a computer with appropriate financial analysis software (instructor option).

c. Interpret the analysis or analyses prepared from the viewpoint of each of the following:
(1) Present auditor
(2) Prospective auditor
(3) Potential stockholder (securities analysts)
(4) Stockholder
(5) Banker
(6) Supplier
(7) Bondholder

d. Consider the various problems the company is having as developed in parts a and c. Indicate the appropriate ways an auditor might adjust his or her audit to deal with each problem identified.

The following are some additional miscellaneous facts about the company:

1. An aggressive expansion program has been occurring. Well-managed chains normally take three to four years to generate a profit from new stores. In 1997, 50 percent of ABC's stores were new.
2. There is a shift in credit policy from coupon-type credit to revolving charge accounts. Credit policies are somewhat lax.
3. High interest rates are occurring at a time when borrowing needs are significant.
4. An inflation is coinciding with a recession.
5. The company is having difficulties in carving out a place for itself in the retailing industry. It had been a blue-collar store for budget-minded value seekers. It has begun to buy better quality clothing, furnishings, and appliances to compete with JC Penney and Sears.
6. To decrease inventory levels, prices were slashed by 50 percent during the Christmas season.

**EXHIBIT I**

**ABC Company Consolidated Balance Sheet (in thousands)**

| | Year Ended December 31, | | | | | | | |
|---|---|---|---|---|---|---|---|---|
| **Assets** | **1997** | **1996** | **1995** | **1994** | **1993** | **1992** | **1991** | **1990** |
| Cash | $ 45,951 | $ 30,943 | $ 49,851 | $ 34,009 | $ 32,977 | $ 25,639 | $ 25,141 | $ 39,040 |
| Accounts receivable, gross | 597,382 | 547,323 | 481,446 | 424,178 | 381,757 | 324,358 | 282,647 | 237,068 |
| Allowance for doubtful accounts | 18,067 | 15,770 | 15,750 | 15,527 | 15,270 | 13,074 | 11,307 | 9,383 |
| Accounts receivable, net | 579,315 | 531,553 | 465,696 | 408,651 | 366,487 | 311,284 | 271,340 | 227,685 |
| Inventories | 450,637 | 399,533 | 298,676 | 260,492 | 222,128 | 208,623 | 183,722 | 174,631 |
| Other current assets | 26,782 | 17,846 | 17,006 | 16,031 | 11,546 | 9,844 | 7,462 | 7,967 |
| Total current assets | 1,102,685 | 979,875 | 831,229 | 719,183 | 633,138 | 555,390 | 487,665 | 449,323 |
| Property, plant, and equipment, net | 100,984 | 91,420 | 77,173 | 61,832 | 55,311 | 49,931 | 47,579 | 48,076 |
| Noncurrent, nonoperating assets | 49,313 | 39,402 | 36,268 | 26,613 | 24,121 | 21,629 | 19,986 | 17,847 |
| Total assets | $1,252,982 | $1,110,697 | $ 944,670 | $ 807,628 | $ 712,570 | $ 626,950 | $ 555,230 | $ 515,246 |
| **Liabilities and Stockholders' Equity** | | | | | | | | |
| Total current liabilities | $ 690,062 | $ 633,067 | $ 475,576 | $ 459,000 | $ 372,493 | $ 290,118 | $ 244,383 | $ 225,403 |
| Long-term debt | 220,336 | 126,672 | 128,432 | 32,301 | 35,402 | 43,251 | 62,622 | 70,000 |
| Other long-term liabilities | 18,844 | 16,620 | 14,917 | 14,291 | 13,986 | 13,460 | 12,409 | 11,983 |
| Preferred stock | 7,465 | 8,600 | 9,053 | 9,600 | 11,450 | 13,250 | 14,750 | 15,000 |
| Common equity | 316,275 | 325,738 | 316,692 | 292,436 | 279,239 | 266,871 | 221,066 | 192,860 |
| Total liabilities and stockholders' equity | $1,252,982 | $1,110,697 | $ 944,670 | $ 807,628 | $ 712,570 | $ 626,950 | $ 555,230 | $ 515,246 |

**EXHIBIT II**

**ABC Company Consolidated Income Statement (in thousands)**

| | Year Ended December 31, | | | | | | | |
|---|---|---|---|---|---|---|---|---|
| | 1997 | 1996 | 1995 | 1994 | 1993 | 1992 | 1991 | 1990 |
| Net sales | $1,853,773 | $1,648,540 | $1,378,251 | $1,259,116 | $1,214,666 | $1,099,025 | $ 982,244 | $ 923,047 |
| Cost of goods sold | 1,181,711 | 1,036,140 | 856,259 | 780,669 | 762,975 | 696,031 | 627,860 | 588,405 |
| Gross margin | 672,062 | 612,400 | 521,992 | 478,447 | 451,691 | 402,994 | 354,384 | 334,642 |
| Operating expenses, less depreciation | 605,934 | 519,368 | 438,218 | 382,671 | 352,353 | 314,129 | 280,150 | 264,090 |
| Depreciation | 13,579 | 12,004 | 10,577 | 9,619 | 8,972 | 8,388 | 8,203 | 7,524 |
| Operating income | 52,549 | 81,028 | 73,197 | 86,157 | 90,366 | 80,477 | 66,031 | 63,028 |
| Other (income) expense | (6,679) | (5,702) | (4,034) | (4,313) | (3,556) | (2,918) | (4,069) | (2,404) |
| Interest expense | 50,012 | 20,525 | 15,519 | 18,093 | 14,113 | 8,932 | 10,887 | 8,954 |
| Income before special items | 9,216 | 66,205 | 61,712 | 72,377 | 79,809 | 74,463 | 59,213 | 56,478 |
| Taxes on income before extraordinary items | 786 | 23,417 | 26,500 | 32,800 | 38,000 | 36,280 | 26,650 | 25,200 |
| Net income before extraordinary items | $ 8,430 | $ 42,788 | $ 35,212 | $ 39,577 | $ 41,809 | $ 38,183 | $ 32,563 | $ 31,278 |

**EXHIBIT III**

**ABC Company Additional Information (in thousands)**

| | Year Ended December 31, | | | | | | | |
|---|---|---|---|---|---|---|---|---|
| | 1997 | 1996 | 1995 | 1994 | 1993 | 1992 | 1991 | 1990 |
| Common dividends | $ 20,807 | $ 20,829 | $ 20,794 | $ 20,426 | $ 19,280 | $ 17,160 | $ 13,804 | $ 13,528 |
| Preferred dividends | 335 | 293 | 346 | 395 | 457 | 526 | 563 | 563 |
| Capital expenditures | 23,143 | 26,251 | 25,918 | 16,141 | 14,357 | 10,626 | 7,763 | 15,257 |
| Common shares outstanding at end of year | 14,072 | 13,993 | 14,168 | 13,829 | 13,874 | 13,421 | 12,953 | 12,509 |
| Market value excess, marketable securities | — | — | — | — | — | — | — | — |
| Amount of intangibles included in nonoperating assets | — | — | — | — | — | — | — | — |
| Interest attributable to debt in current liabilities | 39,775 | 22,232 | 13,551 | 14,046 | 10,382 | — | — | — |

## EXHIBIT IV

### Industry Data 1997

| Dun & Bradstreet Industry Averages: | | |
|---|---|---|
| Current assets/current debt | 2.09 | times |
| Net profit/net sales | 1.61 | percent |
| Net profit/tangible net worth | 11.36 | percent |
| Net profit/net working capital | 12.50 | percent |
| Net sales/tangible net worth | 5.72 | times |
| Net sales/net working capital | 6.88 | times |
| Net sales/inventory | 4.9 | times |
| Fixed assets/tangible net worth | 32.3 | percent |
| Current debt/tangible net worth | 77.5 | percent |
| Total debt/tangible net worth | 129.7 | percent |
| Inventory/net working capital | 139.8 | percent |
| Current debt/inventory | 67.2 | percent |
| Funded debts/net working capital | 39.2 | percent |

## EXHIBIT V

### ABC Company Additional Facts and Events

| Date | Events |
|---|---|
| 12/6/06 | Arthur B. Carter opened 25¢ store in Lynn, Mass. During the next two decades five similar stores were opened in the northeast. |
| 1928 | Stock offered to public. |
| 1940 | Limitation of 25¢ merchandise removed and product line expanded. |
| 1941 | First stores opened in suburban areas. Previously had only downtown stores. |
| 1953 | Chain had 500 stores. |
| 1963 | Chain expanded to 1,050 stores, one-half in the suburbs. |
| 1966 | Arthur B. Carter retired. |
| 1969 | Twenty-eight stores opened in October, fifteen in one day. During the next five years, the company opened 410 large stores, closed 307 smaller stores, and enlarged 36 successful stores. |
| 9/26/97 | Nationwide group of banks agree to $600 million short-term loan despite significant earnings decline. Dividend omitted. |
| 11/7/97 | Agreement signed to accept MasterCharge and BankAmericard as alternatives to costly in-house financing. |
| 12/9/97 | Stock price at 2, down from 1993 high of 70 ⅝. Capitalization comprised of $600 million debt, and $202 million equity.<br>Standard & Poor's downgrades ABC Company paper. Banks ease restrictive covenants (especially work ing capital and net worth requirements) in loan agreements and defer payment of amounts due. |

**8-36 (Objectives 8-2, 8-3, 8-6, 8-7, 8-8)** Pamela Albright is the manager of the audit of Stanton Enterprises, a public company that manufactures formed steel subassemblies for other manufacturers. Albright is planning the 1996 audit and is considering an appropriate amount for planning materiality, what tolerable misstatement should be allocated to the financial statement accounts, and the appropriate inherent risks. Summary financial statement information is shown in Exhibit I. Additional relevant planning information is summarized below:

1. Stanton has been a client for four years and Albright's firm has always had a good relationship with the Company. Management and the accounting people have always been cooperative, honest, and have had a positive attitude about the audit and financial reporting. No material misstatements were found in the prior year's audit. Albright's firm has monitored the relationship carefully, because when the audit was obtained, Leonard Stanton, the CEO, had the reputation of being a "high-flyer" and had been through bankruptcy at an earlier time in his career.
2. Stanton runs the Company in an autocratic way, primarily because of a somewhat controlling personality. He believes that it is his job to make all the tough decisions. He delegates responsibility to others, but is not always willing to delegate a commensurate amount of authority.
3. The industry in which Stanton participates has been in a favorable cycle the past few years and that trend is continuing in the current year. Industry profits are reasonably favorable and there are no competitive or other apparent threats on the horizon.
4. Internal controls for Stanton are evaluated as reasonably effective for all cycles, but not unusually strong. Although Stanton supports the idea of control, Albright has been disappointed that management has continually rejected Albright's recommendation to establish an internal audit function.
5. Stanton has a contract with its employees that if earnings before taxes, interest expense, and pension cost exceeds $7.8 million for the year, an additional contribution must be made to the pension fund equal to 5 percent of the excess.

## Required:

a. You are to play the role of Pamela Albright in the 12-31-96 audit of Stanton Enterprises. Make a preliminary judgment of materiality and allocate tolerable misstatement to financial statement accounts. Prepare a working paper showing your calculations.

b. Make an acceptable audit risk decision for the current year as high, medium, or low, and support your answer.

c. Perform analytical procedures for Stanton Enterprises that will help you identify accounts that may require additional evidence in the current year's audit. Document the analytical procedures you perform and your conclusions.

d. The evidence planning worksheet to decide tests of details of balances for Stanton's accounts receivable is shown in Exhibit II. Use the information in the case and your conclusions in parts a–c to complete the following rows of the evidence planning worksheet: Acceptable audit risk, Inherent risk, and Analytical procedures. Also fill in tolerable misstatement for accounts receivable at the bottom of the worksheet. Make any assumptions you believe are reasonable and appropriate and document them.

**EXHIBIT I**

**Stanton Enterprises**
**Summary Financial Statements**

**Balance Sheet**

| | Preliminary 12-31-96 | Audited 12-31-95 |
|---|---|---|
| Cash | $ 243,689 | $ 133,981 |
| Trade accounts receivable | 3,544,009 | 2,224,921 |
| Allowance for uncollectible accounts | (120,000) | (215,000) |
| Inventories | 4,520,902 | 3,888,400 |
| Prepaid expenses | 29,500 | 24,700 |
| Total current assets | 8,218,100 | 6,057,002 |
| Property, plant and equipment: | | |
| At cost | 12,945,255 | 9,922,534 |
| Less accumulated depreciation | (4,382,990) | (3,775,911) |
| | 8,562,265 | 6,146,623 |
| Goodwill | 1,200,000 | 345,000 |
| Total assets | $17,980,365 | $12,548,625 |
| Accounts payable | $ 2,141,552 | $ 2,526,789 |
| Bank loan payable | 150,000 | — |
| Accrued liabilities | 723,600 | 598,020 |
| Federal income taxes payable | 1,200,000 | 1,759,000 |
| Current portion of long-term debt | 240,000 | 240,000 |
| Total current liabilities | 4,455,152 | 5,123,809 |
| Long-term debt | 960,000 | 1,200,000 |
| Stockholders' equity: | | |
| Common stock | 1,250,000 | 1,000,000 |
| Additional paid-in capital | 2,469,921 | 1,333,801 |
| Retained earnings | 8,845,292 | 3,891,015 |
| Total stockholders' equity | 12,565,213 | 6,224,816 |
| Total liabilities and stockholders' equity | $17,980,365 | $12,548,625 |

**Combined Statement of Income and Retained Earnings**

| | Preliminary 12-31-96 | Audited 12-31-95 |
|---|---|---|
| Sales | $43,994,931 | $32,258,015 |
| Cost of goods sold | 24,197,212 | 19,032,229 |
| Gross profit | 19,797,719 | 13,225,786 |
| Selling, general, and administrative expenses | 10,592,221 | 8,900,432 |
| Pension cost | 1,117,845 | 865,030 |
| Interest expense | 83,376 | 104,220 |
| | 11,793,442 | 9,869,682 |
| Income before taxes | 8,004,277 | 3,356,104 |
| Income tax expense | 1,800,000 | 1,141,000 |
| Net income | 6,204,277 | 2,215,104 |
| Beginning retained earnings | 3,891,015 | 2,675,911 |
| | 10,095,292 | 4,891,015 |
| Dividends declared | (1,250,000) | (1,000,000) |
| Ending retained earnings | $ 8,845,292 | $ 3,891,015 |

**EXHIBIT II**

## Stanton Enterprises
## Evidence Planning Worksheet to Decide Tests of Details of Balances for Accounts Receivable

| | Detail tie-in | Existence | Completeness | Accuracy | Classification | Cutoff | Realizable value | Rights | Presentation and disclosure |
|---|---|---|---|---|---|---|---|---|---|
| Acceptable audit risk | | | | | | | | | |
| Inherent risk | | | | | | | | | |
| Control risk—Sales | | | | | | | | | |
| Control risk—Cash receipts | | | | | | | | | |
| Control risk—Additional controls | | | | | | | | | |
| Substantive tests of transactions—Sales | | | | | | | | | |
| Substantive tests of transactions—Cash receipts | | | | | | | | | |
| Analytical procedures | | | | | | | | | |
| Planned detection risk for tests of details of balances | | | | | | | | | |
| Planned audit evidence for tests of details of balances | | | | | | | | | |

Tolerable misstatement ______

# 9

# THE STUDY OF INTERNAL CONTROL AND ASSESSMENT OF CONTROL RISK

## LEARNING OBJECTIVES

Thorough study of this chapter will enable you to

- **9-1** Discuss the nature of internal control and its importance to both management and the auditor.
- **9-2** Describe the three key concepts in the study of internal control.
- **9-3** Identify the five components of internal control, and discuss their characteristics.
- **9-4** Describe the requirements of understanding internal control and assessing control risk.
- **9-5** Know how to obtain an understanding of internal control.
- **9-6** Know how to assess control risk for each major type of transaction.
- **9-7** Understand the process of designing and performing tests of controls as a basis for further study.

## GOOD INTERNAL CONTROLS PREVENT MORE DEFALCATIONS THAN GOOD AUDITORS FIND

When Able & Co. issued their audit report on the Foundation for Youth Bible Studies (FYBS), they included a qualification that is common for such charities. The qualification explained that the auditors could only verify those revenues that were actually recorded on the organization's books. Because many contributions came in the form of cash and were received from many sources, there was no way to know what the total contributions should be.

Shortly after its tenth consecutive audit of FYBS, Able was informed that FYBS's general ledger accountant was found to have embezzled $2 million during the past four years. FYBS wanted to know how this could have occurred without Able discovering it. Able responded that he would have to know how the fraud was carried out to answer the question.

After an extensive investigation and criminal trial against FYBS's general ledger accountant, the following facts came to light: The FYBS's camp facility was in a different state than its home office. Funds were collected from campers and taken to a local bank by an independent person for transmittal to the home office. The funds were given to the bank in exchange for a cashier's check that was sent to the general ledger accountant who, in turn, sent it to the home office cash receipts clerk. She also recorded the revenue using the information on the cashier's check and related documentation. Because the funds were never deposited into the local FYBS bank account, there was no external record established. To perpetrate the fraud, the accountant periodically deposited one of the checks in an account that she controlled, with a name and endorsement "FYBS—Special Account." Obviously, she did not record the revenue for these defalcations.

When the auditors conducted their review of internal controls at FYBS, they regularly interviewed employees about how the system functioned. During the course of those discussions, they were never told about the procedure for transmitting funds from the camp. It is not clear that anyone in the home office, other than the embezzler, was aware of it. Given the disclaimer in the audit report and the conduct of their audit, Able & Co. wasn't held responsible for the loss. They helped FYBS implement new controls to prevent a similar occurrence, but nevertheless, FYBS changed auditors.

Chapter 9 is the third chapter dealing with planning the audit and designing an audit approach. The subject of internal control is sufficiently important in the audit process to merit a separate generally accepted auditing standard:

> **A sufficient understanding of internal control is to be obtained to plan the audit and to determine the nature, timing, and extent of tests to be performed.**

The shaded part of the chart included in the margin below shows where obtaining an understanding of internal control and assessing control risk fit into planning the audit. The study of internal control, assessment of control risk, and related evidence gathering are major components in the audit risk model studied in Chapter 8. Control risk is CR in the audit risk model. It was shown in Chapter 8 that planned audit evidence can be reduced when there are effective internal controls. This chapter shows why and how this can be done.

To understand how internal control is used in the risk model, knowledge of key internal control concepts is needed. Accordingly, this chapter focuses on the meaning and objectives of internal control from both the client's and the auditor's point of view, the components of internal control, and the auditor's methodology for fulfilling the requirements of the second standard of field work. Professional guidance in considering internal control is found in SAS 55 (as amended by SAS 78, AU 319). Many practitioners consider it to be the most complex auditing standard in the literature.

## CLIENT AND AUDITOR CONCERNS

**OBJECTIVE 9-1**
**Discuss the nature of internal control and its importance to both management and the auditor.**

In designing a system for control, management is likely to have some of the same concerns auditors have in evaluating the system, as well as additional or different concerns. This section examines the concerns of both clients and auditors.

### Client Concerns

The reason a company establishes a system for control is to help meet its own goals. The system consists of many specific *policies and procedures* designed to provide management with reasonable assurance that the goals and objectives it believes important to the entity will be met. These policies and procedures are often called *controls,* and collectively they comprise the entity's *internal control.*

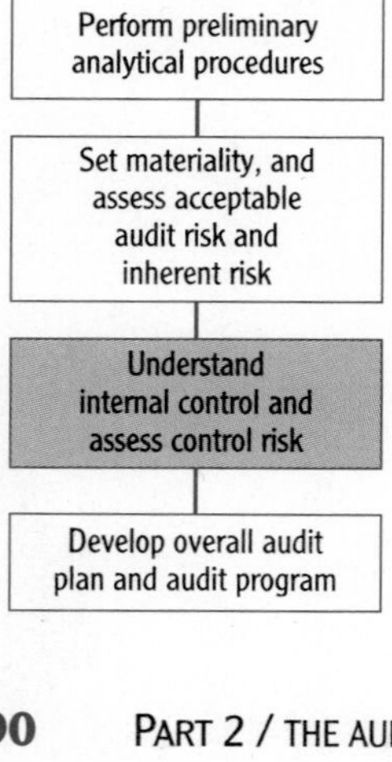


In 1992, a significant study on internal control titled *Internal Control—Integrated Framework* was published. It was sponsored by the Committee of Sponsoring Organizations of the Treadway Commission, a group of several accounting organizations. The study is often referred to as the *COSO Report.* In December 1995, the Auditing Standards Board issued SAS 78 (AU 319), which amended SAS 55 to adopt the definition and description of internal control contained in the *COSO Report.* The client concerns discussed in this section are taken primarily from SAS 78 and the *COSO Report.*

Control systems must be *cost beneficial.* The controls adopted are selected by comparing the costs to the organization to the benefits expected. One benefit to management, but certainly not the most important, is the reduced cost of an audit when the auditor evaluates internal control as good or excellent and assesses control risk as low.

Management typically has the following three concerns, or broad objectives, in designing an effective control system.

**Reliability of Financial Reporting** As discussed in Chapter 5, management is responsible for preparing financial statements for investors, creditors, and other users. Management has both a legal and professional responsibility to be sure that the information is fairly prepared in accordance with reporting requirements such as generally accepted accounting principles.

**Efficiency and Effectiveness of Operations** Controls within an organization are meant to encourage efficient and effective use of its resources, including personnel, to optimize the company's goals. An important part of these controls is accurate information for internal decision making. A variety of information is used for making critical business decisions. For example, the price to charge for products is based in part on information about the cost of making the products.

Another important part of effectiveness and efficiency is safeguarding assets and records. The physical assets of a company can be stolen, misused, or accidentally destroyed unless they are protected by adequate controls. The same is true of nonphysical assets such as accounts receivable, important documents (confidential government contracts), and records (general ledger and journals). Safeguarding certain assets and records has become increasingly important since the advent of computer systems. Large amounts of information stored on computer media such as magnetic tape can be destroyed if care is not taken to protect them. Safeguarding of accounting records also affects the reliability of financial reporting.

**Compliance with Applicable Laws and Regulations** There are many laws and regulations that organizations are required to follow. Some are only indirectly related to accounting. Examples include environmental protection and civil rights laws. Others are closely related to accounting. Examples include income tax regulations and fraud.

One important law affecting all companies subject to the Securities and Exchange Act of 1934 is the Foreign Corrupt Practices Act of 1977. This law requires that a company maintain "proper record-keeping systems." These have not been defined by the 1977 law, which amended the securities acts, but they include a sufficient system to enable the preparation of reliable external financial statements and to prevent off-the-books slush funds and payment of bribes.

## Auditor Concerns

As discussed on page 290, the study of internal control and the resulting assessment of control risk are important to auditors and are specifically included as a generally accepted auditing standard.

**Reliability of Financial Reporting** To comply with the second standard of field work, the auditor is interested primarily in controls that relate to the first of management's internal control concerns: reliability of financial reporting. This is the area that directly impacts the financial statements and their related assertions, and therefore impacts the auditor's objective of determining that the financial statements are fairly stated. The financial statements are not likely to correctly reflect generally accepted accounting principles if the controls affecting the reliability of financial reporting are inadequate. On the other hand, the statements can be fairly stated even if the company's controls do not promote efficiency and effectiveness in its operations.

As stated in Chapter 5, auditors have significant responsibility for the discovery of material fraudulent financial reporting and misappropriation of assets (fraud) and direct-effects illegal acts. Auditors are therefore also concerned with a client's controls over the safeguarding of assets and compliance with applicable laws and regulations if they affect the fairness of the financial statements.

It has already been stated that auditors should emphasize controls concerned with the reliability of data for *external reporting purposes,* but controls affecting internal management information, such as budgets and internal performance reports, should not be completely ignored. These types of information are often important sources of evidence in helping the auditor decide whether the financial statements are fairly presented. If the controls over these internal reports are considered inadequate, the value of the reports as evidence diminishes.

**Emphasis on Controls over Classes of Transactions** The primary emphasis by auditors is on controls over classes of transactions rather than account balances. The reason is that the

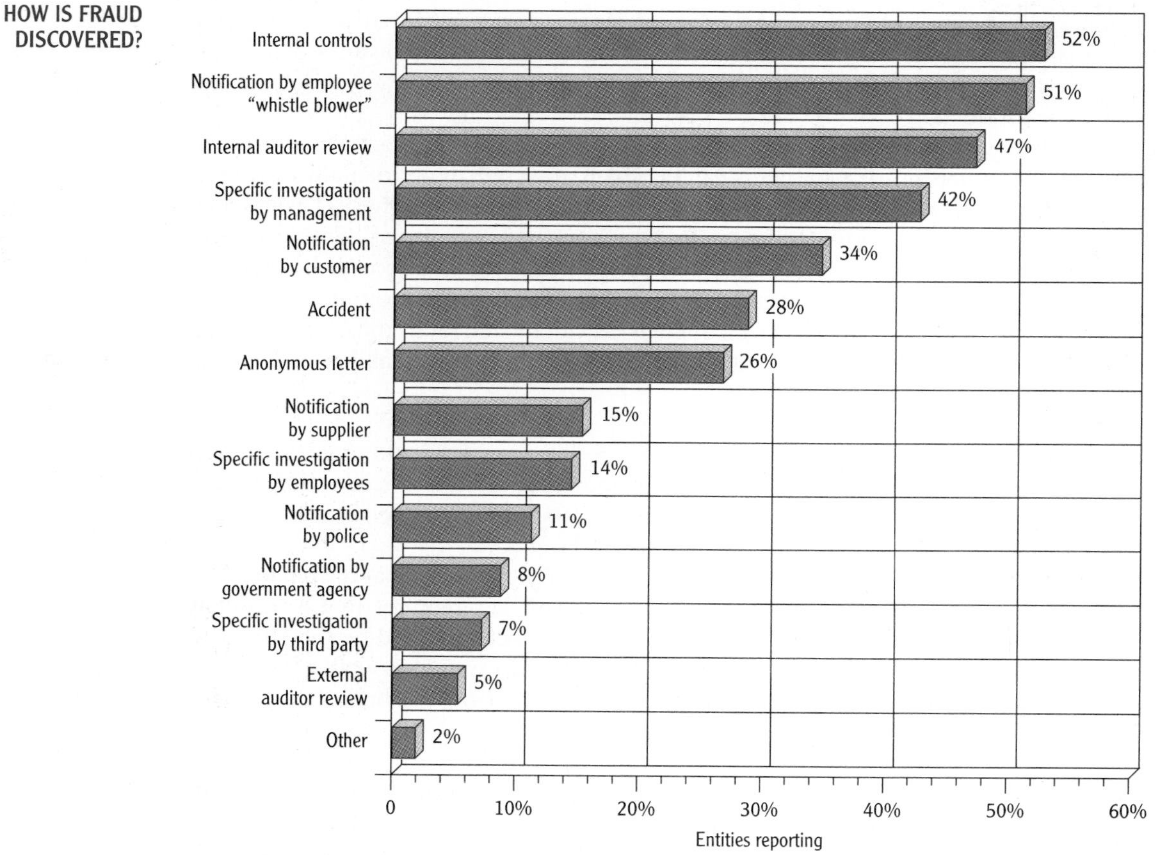


Note: Multiple responses given.

*Source:* KPMG Peat Marwick survey of 3000 large and midsized U.S. companies, "Combating Fraud: Know the Facts," *Journal of Accounting*, September 1995, p. 20.

accuracy of the output of the accounting system (account balances) is heavily dependent upon the accuracy of the inputs and processing (transactions). For example, if products sold, units shipped, or unit selling prices are wrong in billing customers for sales, both sales and accounts receivable will be misstated. If controls are adequate to make sure billings, cash receipts, sales returns and allowances, and charge-offs are correct, the ending balance in accounts receivable is likely to be correct.

In the study of internal control and assessment of control risk, therefore, auditors are primarily concerned with the transaction-related audit objectives discussed in Chapter 5. These objectives were discussed in detail on pages 152–153. Table 9-1 illustrates the development of transaction-related audit objectives for sales transactions.

During the study of internal control and assessment of control risk, the auditor does not, however, ignore internal controls over account balances. For example, transaction-related audit objectives typically have no effect on three balance-related audit objectives: realizable value, rights and obligations, and presentation and disclosure. The auditor is likely to make a separate evaluation as to whether management has implemented internal controls for each of these three balance-related audit objectives.

**TABLE 9-1**

**Sales Transaction-Related Audit Objectives**

| Transaction-Related Audit Objectives—General Form | Sales Transaction-Related Audit Objectives |
|---|---|
| Recorded transactions exist (existence) | Recorded sales are for shipments made to existing customers |
| Existing transactions are recorded (completeness) | Existing sales transactions are recorded |
| Recorded transactions are stated at the correct amounts (accuracy) | Recorded sales are for the amount of goods shipped and are correctly billed and recorded |
| Transactions are properly classified (classification) | Sales transactions are properly classified |
| Transactions are recorded on the correct dates (timing) | Sales are recorded on the correct dates |
| Recorded transactions are properly included in the master files and correctly summarized (posting and summarization) | Sales transactions are properly included in the master files and are correctly summarized |

## KEY CONCEPTS

**OBJECTIVE 9-2**
**Describe the three key concepts in the study of internal control.**

There are three key concepts that underlie the study of internal control and assessment of control risk.

### Management's Responsibility

Management, not the auditor, must establish and maintain the entity's controls. This concept is consistent with the requirement that management, not the auditor, is responsible for the preparation of financial statements in accordance with generally accepted accounting principles.

### Reasonable Assurance

A company should develop internal controls that provide reasonable, but not absolute, assurance that the financial statements are fairly stated. Internal controls are developed by management after considering both the costs and benefits of the controls. Management is often unwilling to implement an ideal system because the costs may be too high. For example, it is unreasonable to expect management of a small company to hire several additional accounting personnel to bring about a small improvement in the reliability of accounting data. It is often less expensive to have auditors do more extensive auditing than to incur higher internal control costs.*

### Inherent Limitations

Internal controls can never be regarded as completely effective, regardless of the care followed in their design and implementation. Even if systems personnel could design an ideal system, its effectiveness depends on the competency and dependability of the people using it. For example, assume that a procedure for counting inventory is carefully developed and requires two employees to count independently. If neither of the employees understands the instructions or if both are careless in doing the counts, the count of inventory is likely to be wrong. Even if the count is right, management might override the procedure and instruct an employee to increase the count of quantities in order to improve reported earnings. Similarly, the employees might decide to overstate the counts intentionally to cover up a theft of inventory by one or both of them. An act of two or more employees to steal assets or misstate records is called *collusion.*

*Because the Foreign Corrupt Practices Act requires public companies to have an effective accounting system, public companies must evaluate whether their records meet legal requirements even if it is less expensive to have auditors uncover misstatements.

Because of these inherent limitations of controls and because auditors cannot have more than reasonable assurance of their effectiveness, there is almost always some level of control risk greater than zero. Therefore, even with the most effectively designed internal controls, the auditor must obtain audit evidence beyond testing the controls for every material financial statement account.

## METHOD OF DATA PROCESSING

The control concepts discussed in this chapter apply to all accounting systems regardless of complexity. There are major differences between a simple computerized accounting system using purchased software for a small service company and a complex EDP system for an international manufacturing business. Nevertheless, the transaction-related audit objectives are the same and the methodology discussed in this chapter is applicable to both.

For simplicity, most illustrations in this chapter apply to simple computerized systems. Unique considerations in more advanced EDP systems are studied in Chapter 15.

## COMPONENTS OF INTERNAL CONTROL

**OBJECTIVE 9-3**
**Identify the five components of internal control, and discuss their characteristics.**

Internal control includes five categories of controls that management designs and implements to provide reasonable assurance that management's control objectives will be met. These are called the *components of internal control* and are (1) the control environment, (2) risk assessment, (3) control activities, (4) information and communication, and (5) monitoring. These five components are summarized in Figure 9-1.

**FIGURE 9-1**
**Five Components of Internal Control**

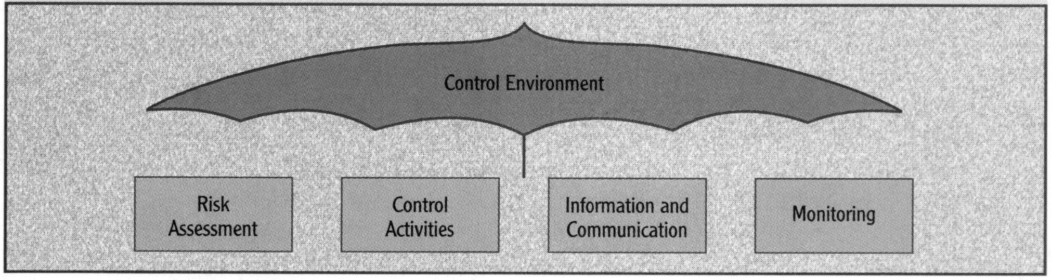


Figure 9-1 shows that the control environment is the umbrella for the other four components. Without an effective control environment, the other four components are unlikely to result in effective internal controls, regardless of their quality.

As discussed above, the categories contain many controls. The auditor is concerned primarily with those designed to prevent or detect material misstatements in the financial statements. Those aspects will be the focus of the remainder of the chapter.

## THE CONTROL ENVIRONMENT

The essence of an effectively controlled organization lies in the attitude of its management. If top management believes that control is important, others in the organization will sense that and respond by conscientiously observing the controls established. On the other hand,

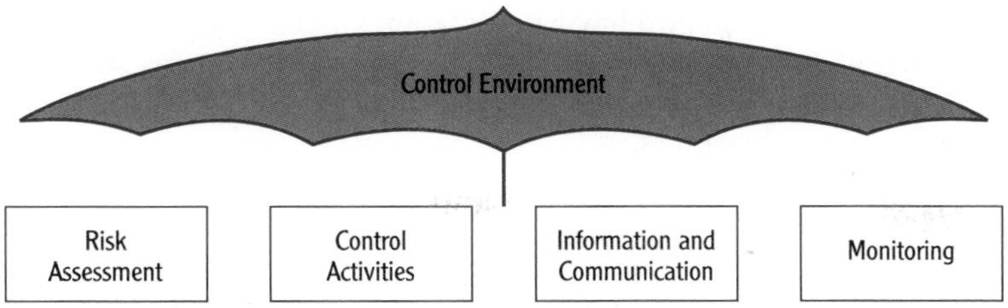


if it is clear to members of the organization that control is not an important concern to top management, and is given lip service rather than meaningful support, it is almost certain that management's control objectives will not be effectively achieved.

The *control environment* consists of the actions, policies, and procedures that reflect the overall attitudes of top management, directors, and owners of an entity about control and its importance to the entity. For the purpose of understanding and assessing the control environment, the following are the most important subcomponents the auditor should consider.

**Integrity and Ethical Values** Integrity and ethical values are the product of the entity's ethical and behavioral standards and how they are communicated and reinforced in practice. They include management's actions to remove or reduce incentives and temptations that might prompt personnel to engage in dishonest, illegal, or unethical acts. They also include the communication of entity values and behavioral standards to personnel through policy statements and codes of conduct and by example.

**Commitment to Competence** Competence is the knowledge and skills necessary to accomplish tasks that define the individual's job. Commitment to competence includes management's consideration of the competence levels for specific jobs and how those levels translate into requisite skills and knowledge.

**Board of Directors or Audit Committee Participation** An effective board of directors is independent of management and its members are involved in and scrutinize management's activities. As stated in Chapter 3, all public companies traded on the New York Stock Exchange are required to have an audit committee composed of outside directors. Many other companies also have audit committees. The audit committee is usually charged with oversight responsibility for the entity's financial reporting process and must maintain ongoing communication with both external and internal auditors. This allows the auditors and directors to discuss matters that might relate to such things as the integrity or actions of management.

**Management's Philosophy and Operating Style** Management, through its activities, provides clear signals to employees about the importance of control. For example, does management take significant risks, or are they risk averse? Are profit plans and budget data set as "best possible" plans or "most likely" targets? Can management be described as "fat and bureaucratic," "lean and mean," dominated by one or a few individuals, or is it "just right"? Understanding these and similar aspects of management's philosophy and operating style gives the auditor a sense of its attitude about control.

**Organizational Structure** The entity's organizational structure defines the lines of responsibility and authority that exist. By understanding the client's organizational structure, the auditor can learn the management and functional elements of the business and perceive how controls are carried out.

**Assignment of Authority and Responsibility** In addition to the informal aspects of communication already mentioned, formal methods of communication about authority and responsibility and similar control-related matters are equally important. These might include such methods as memoranda from top management about the importance of control and control-related matters, formal organizational and operating plans, and employee job descriptions and related policies.

**Human Resource Policies and Practices** The most important aspect of internal control is personnel. If employees are competent and trustworthy, other controls can be absent and reliable financial statements will still result. Honest, efficient people are able to perform at a high level even when there are few other controls to support them. Even if there are numerous other controls, incompetent or dishonest people can reduce the system to a shambles. Even though personnel may be competent and trustworthy, people have certain innate shortcomings. They can, for example, become bored or dissatisfied, personal problems can disrupt their performance, or their goals may change.

Because of the importance of competent, trustworthy personnel in providing effective control, the methods by which persons are hired, evaluated, trained, promoted, and compensated are an important part of the internal control structure.

## RISK ASSESSMENT

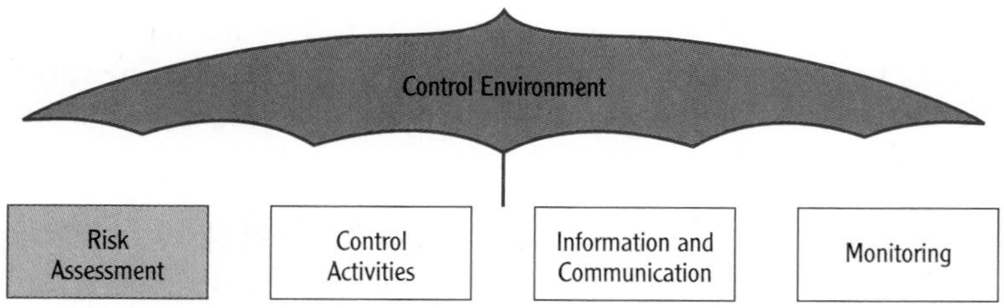


Risk assessment for financial reporting is *management's* identification and analysis of risks relevant to the preparation of financial statements in conformity with generally accepted accounting principles. For example, if a company frequently sells products at a price below inventory cost because of rapid technology changes, it is essential for the company to incorporate adequate controls to overcome the risk of overstating inventory.

Management's risk assessment differs from, but is closely related to, the auditor's risk assessment discussed in Chapter 8. Management assesses risks as a part of designing and operating internal controls to minimize errors and fraud. Auditors assess risks to decide the evidence needed in the audit. If management effectively assesses and responds to risks, the auditor will typically accumulate less evidence than when management fails to identify or respond to significant risks.

## CONTROL ACTIVITIES

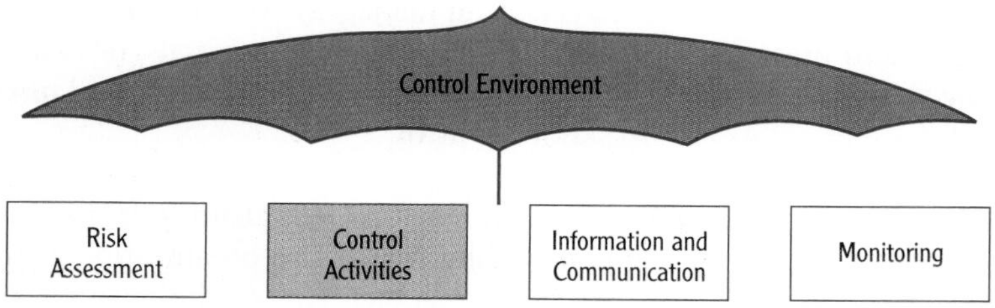


Control activities are the policies and procedures, in addition to those included in the other four components, that help ensure that necessary actions are taken to address risks in the achievement of the entity's objectives. There are potentially many such control activities in any entity. However, they generally fall into the following five categories discussed in this section:

- Adequate separation of duties
- Proper authorization of transactions and activities
- Adequate documents and records
- Physical control over assets and records
- Independent checks on performance

SAS 78 and the *COSO Report* identify slightly different categories of control activities, but the concepts are consistent with the five categories discussed below.

## Adequate Separation of Duties

Four general guidelines for separation of duties to prevent both fraud and errors are of special significance to auditors.

**Separation of the Custody of Assets from Accounting** The reason for not permitting the person who has temporary or permanent custody of an asset to account for that asset is to protect the firm against defalcation. When one person performs both functions, there is an excessive risk of that person's disposing of the asset for personal gain and adjusting the records to relieve himself or herself of responsibility. If the cashier, for example, receives cash and is responsible for data entry for cash receipts and sales, it is possible for the cashier to take the cash received from a customer and adjust the customer's account by failing to record a sale or by recording a fictitious credit to the account.

**Separation of the Authorization of Transactions from the Custody of Related Assets** If possible, it is desirable to prevent persons who authorize transactions from having control over the related asset. For example, the same person should not authorize the payment of a vendor's invoice and also sign the check in payment of the bill. The authorization of a transaction and the handling of the related asset by the same person increase the possibility of defalcation within the organization.

**Separation of Operational Responsibility from Record-Keeping Responsibility** If each department or division in an organization were responsible for preparing its own records and reports, there would be a tendency to bias the results to improve its reported performance. In order to ensure unbiased information, record keeping is typically included in a separate department under the controller.

**Separation of Duties within EDP** To the extent practical, it is desirable to separate the major functions within EDP. Ideally, the following should all be separated.

- *Systems analyst* The systems analyst is responsible for the general design of the system. The analyst sets the objectives of the overall system and the specific design of applications.
- *Programmer* Based on the individual objectives specified by the systems analyst, the programmer develops special flowcharts for the application, prepares computer instructions, tests the program, and documents the results. It is important that the programmer not have access to input data or computer operation, since understanding of the program can easily be used for personal benefit.
- *Computer operator* The computer operator is responsible for running data through the system in conjunction with the computer program. Ideally, the operator should be prevented from having sufficient knowledge of the program to modify it immediately before or during its use.
- *Librarian* The librarian is responsible for maintaining the computer programs, transaction files, and other important computer records. The librarian provides a means of important physical control over these records and releases them only to authorized personnel.

- *Data control group* The function of the data control group is to test the effectiveness and efficiency of all aspects of the system. This includes the application of various controls, the quality of the input, and the reasonableness of the output. Inasmuch as control group personnel perform internal verification, the importance of their independence is obvious.

Naturally, the extent of separation of duties depends heavily on the size of the organization. In many small companies it is not practical to segregate the duties to the extent suggested. In these cases, audit evidence may require modification.

### Proper Authorization of Transactions and Activities

Every transaction must be properly authorized if controls are to be satisfactory. If any person in an organization could acquire or expend assets at will, complete chaos would result. Authorization can be either *general* or *specific*. General authorization means that management establishes policies for the organization to follow. Subordinates are instructed to implement these general authorizations by approving all transactions within the limits set by the policy. Examples of general authorization are the issuance of fixed price lists for the sale of products, credit limits for customers, and fixed reorder points for making acquisitions.

Specific authorization has to do with individual transactions. Management is often unwilling to establish a general policy of authorization for some transactions. Instead, it prefers to make authorizations on a case-by-case basis. An example is the authorization of a sales transaction by the sales manager for a used-car company.

There is also a distinction between authorization and approval. Authorization is a policy decision for either a general class of transactions or specific transactions. Approval is the implementation of management's general authorization decisions. For example, assume that management sets a policy authorizing the ordering of inventory when there is less than a three-week supply on hand. That is a general authorization. When a department orders inventory, the clerk responsible for maintaining the perpetual record approves the order to indicate that the authorization policy has been met.

### Adequate Documents and Records

*Documents* and *records* are the physical objects upon which transactions are entered and summarized. They include such diverse items as sales invoices, purchase orders, subsidiary records, sales journals, and employee time cards. In a computerized accounting system, many of these documents and records are maintained in the form of computer files until they are printed out for specific purposes. Both documents of original entry and records upon which transactions are entered are important, but the inadequacy of documents normally causes greater control problems.

Documents perform the function of transmitting information throughout the client's organization and between different organizations. The documents must be adequate to provide reasonable assurance that all assets are properly controlled and all transactions correctly recorded. For example, if the receiving department fills out a receiving report when material is obtained, the accounts payable department can verify the quantity and description on the vendor's invoice by comparing it with the information on the receiving report.

Certain relevant principles dictate the proper design and use of documents and records. Documents and records should be

- Prenumbered consecutively to facilitate control over missing documents, and as an aid in locating documents when they are needed at a later date (significantly affects the transaction-related audit objective of completeness).
- Prepared at the time a transaction takes place, or as soon thereafter as possible. When there is a longer time interval, records are less credible and the chance for misstatement is increased (affects the transaction-related audit objective of timing).
- Sufficiently simple to ensure that they are clearly understood.
- Designed for multiple use whenever possible, to minimize the number of different forms. For example, a properly designed and used shipping document can be the basis for releasing goods from storage to the shipping department, informing billing of the

quantity of goods to bill to the customer and the appropriate billing date, and updating the perpetual inventory records.

- Constructed in a manner that encourages correct preparation. This can be done by providing a degree of internal check within the form or record. For example, a document might include instructions for proper routing, blank spaces for authorizations and approvals, and designated column spaces for numerical data.

When data for the preparation of documents are entered into the computer, the effective design of the computer input screens is an important control mechanism.

**Chart of Accounts** A control closely related to documents and records is the *chart of accounts*, which classifies transactions into individual balance sheet and income statement accounts. The chart of accounts is an important control because it provides the framework for determining the information presented to management and other financial statement users. The chart of accounts is helpful in preventing classification errors if it accurately and precisely describes which type of transactions should be in each account.

**Systems Manuals** The procedures for proper record keeping should be spelled out in systems manuals to encourage consistent application. The manuals should provide sufficient information to facilitate adequate record keeping and the maintenance of proper control over assets. Larger companies with reasonably complex computer systems will also maintain a standards manual pertaining to the EDP system.

## Physical Control over Assets and Records

It is essential to adequate internal control to protect assets and records. If assets are left unprotected, they can be stolen. If records are not adequately protected, they can be stolen, damaged, or lost. In the event of such an occurrence, the accounting process as well as normal operations could be seriously disrupted. When a company is highly computerized, it is especially important to protect its computer equipment, programs, and data files. The equipment and programs are expensive and essential to operations. The data files are the records of the company, and if damaged, could be costly, or even impossible, to reconstruct.

The most important type of protective measure for safeguarding assets and records is the use of physical precautions. An example is the use of storerooms for inventory to guard against pilferage. When the storeroom is under the control of a competent employee, there is also further assurance that obsolescence is minimized. Fireproof safes and safety deposit vaults for the protection of assets such as currency and securities are other important physical safeguards.

There are three categories of controls related to safeguarding EDP equipment, programs, and data files. As with other types of assets, *physical controls* are used to protect the computer facilities. Examples are locks on doors to the computer room and terminals, adequate storage space for software and data files to protect them from loss, and proper fire-extinguishing systems. *Access controls* deal with ensuring that only authorized people can use the equipment and have access to software and data files. An example is an on-line access password system. *Backup and recovery procedures* are steps an organization can take in the event of a loss of equipment, programs, or data. For example, a backup copy of programs and critical data files stored in a safe remote location is a common backup control.

## Independent Checks on Performance

The last category of control procedures is the careful and continuous review of the other four, often referred to as independent checks or internal verification. The need for independent checks arises because internal control tends to change over time unless there is a mechanism for frequent review. Personnel are likely to forget or intentionally fail to follow procedures, or become careless unless someone observes and evaluates their performance. In addition, both fraudulent and unintentional misstatements are possible, regardless of the quality of the controls.

An essential characteristic of the persons performing internal verification procedures is independence from the individuals originally responsible for preparing the data. The least expensive means of internal verification is the separation of duties in the manner previously discussed. For example, when the bank reconciliation is performed by a person independent of the accounting records and handling of cash, there is an opportunity for verification without incurring significant additional costs.

Computerized accounting systems can be designed so that many internal verification procedures can be automated as part of the system.

## INFORMATION AND COMMUNICATION

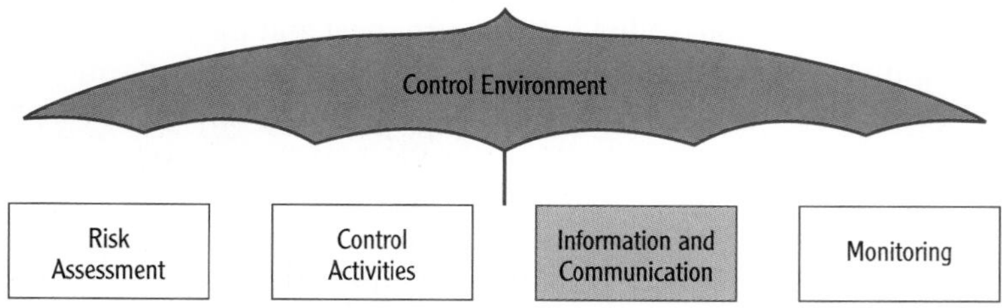


The purpose of an entity's accounting information and communication system is to identify, assemble, classify, analyze, record, and report the entity's transactions, and to maintain accountability for the related assets. An accounting information and communication system has several subcomponents, typically made up of classes of transactions such as sales, sales returns, collections, acquisitions, and so on. For each class of transactions, the accounting system must satisfy all of the six transaction-related audit objectives identified earlier in the chapter (page 293). For example, the sales accounting system should be designed to assure that all shipments of goods by a company are correctly recorded as sales (completeness and accuracy objectives) and reflected in the financial statements in the proper period (timing objective). The system must also avoid duplicate recording of sales and recording a sale if a shipment did not occur (existence objective).

For a small company with active involvement by the owner, a simple computerized accounting system involving primarily one honest competent accountant may provide an adequate accounting information system. A larger company requires a more complex system that includes carefully defined responsibilities and written procedures.

## MONITORING

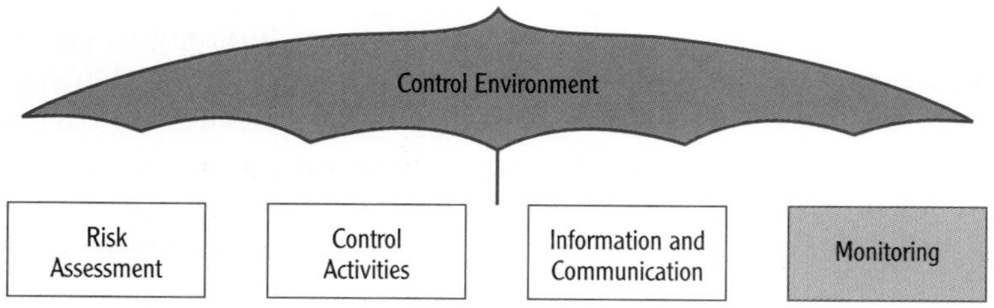


Monitoring activities deal with ongoing or periodic assessment of the quality of internal control performance by management to determine that controls are operating as intended and that they are modified as appropriate for changes in conditions. Information for assessment and modification comes from a variety of sources including studies of existing internal controls, internal auditor reports, exception reporting on control activities, reports by regulators such as bank regulatory agencies, feedback from operating personnel, and complaints from customers about billing charges.

### Internal Audit Function

For many companies, especially larger ones, an internal audit department is essential to effective monitoring. For an internal audit function to be effective, it is essential that the internal audit staff be independent of both the operating and accounting departments, and that it report directly to a high level of authority within the organization, either top management or the audit committee of the board of directors.

In addition to its role in monitoring an entity's internal controls, an adequate internal audit staff can contribute to reduced external audit costs by providing direct assistance to the external auditor. SAS 65 (AU 322) defines the way internal auditors affect the external auditor's evidence accumulation. If the external auditor obtains evidence that supports the competence, integrity, and objectivity of internal auditors, the external auditor can rely on the internal auditor's work in a number of ways.

### Size of Business and Internal Control

The size of a company has a significant effect on the nature of internal control and the specific controls. Obviously, it is more difficult to establish adequate separation of duties in a small company. It would also be unreasonable to expect a small firm to have internal auditors. However, if the various subcomponents of internal control are examined, it becomes apparent that most are applicable to both large and small companies. Even though it may not be common to formalize policies in manuals, it is certainly possible for a small company to have competent, trustworthy personnel with clear lines of authority; proper procedures for authorization, execution, and recording of transactions; adequate documents, records, and reports; physical controls over assets and records; and, to a limited degree, independent checks on performance.

A major control available in a small company is the knowledge and concern of the top operating person, who is frequently an owner-manager. A personal interest in the organization and a close relationship with the personnel makes careful evaluation of the competence of the employees and the effectiveness of the overall system possible. For example, internal control can be significantly strengthened if the owner conscientiously performs such duties as signing all checks after carefully reviewing supporting documents, reviewing bank reconciliations, examining accounts receivable statements sent to customers, approving credit, examining all correspondence from customers and vendors, and approving bad debts.

### Summary of Internal Control

The five components of internal control discussed in the preceding sections are summarized in Figure 9-2 on page 302.

## OVERVIEW OF OBTAINING AN UNDERSTANDING OF INTERNAL CONTROL AND ASSESSING CONTROL RISK

**OBJECTIVE 9-4**
**Describe the requirements of understanding internal control and assessing control risk.**

The remainder of the chapter deals with how auditors obtain information about internal control, and use that information as a basis for audit planning. To help understand how the auditor accomplishes this, an overview of the relevant parts of obtaining an understanding of internal control, assessing control risk, and relating the results to tests of financial statement balances is shown in summary form below and in more detail in Figure 9-3 (page 303). The process described by Figure 9-3 is discussed first. The remainder of the chapter deals with ways that practitioners implement the first three parts.

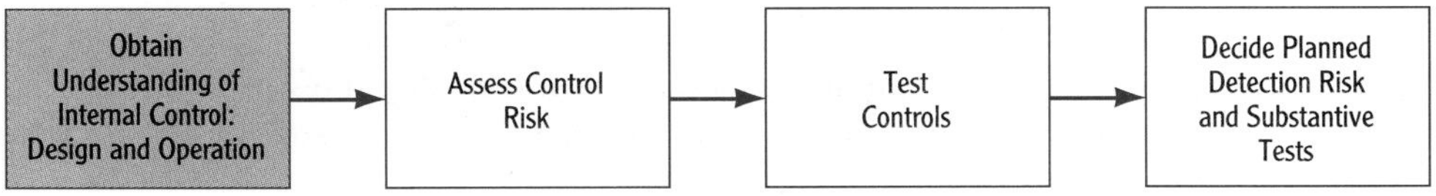

**FIGURE 9-2**

**Components of Internal Control**

| | **Internal Control** | |
|---|---|---|
| **Components** | **Description of Component** | **Further Subdivision (if applicable)** |
| Control environment | Actions, policies, and procedures that reflect the overall attitude of top management, directors, and owners of an entity about control and its importance | Subcomponents of the control environment<br>• integrity and ethical values<br>• commitment to competence<br>• board of directors or audit committee participation<br>• management's philosophy and operating style<br>• organizational structure<br>• assignment of authority and responsibility<br>• human resource policies and practices |
| Risk assessment | Management's identification and analysis of risks relevant to the preparation of financial statements in accordance with GAAP | Management assertions that must be satisfied<br>• existence or occurrence<br>• completeness<br>• valuation or allocation<br>• rights and obligations<br>• presentation and disclosure |
| Control activities | Policies and procedures that management has established to meet its objectives for financial reporting | Categories of control activities<br>• adequate separation of duties<br>• proper authorization of transactions and activities<br>• adequate documents and records<br>• physical control over assets and records<br>• independent checks on performance |
| Information and communication | Methods used to identify, assemble, classify, record, and report an entity's transactions and to maintain accountability for related assets | Transaction-related audit objectives that must be satisfied<br>• existence<br>• completeness<br>• accuracy<br>• classification<br>• timing<br>• posting and summarization |
| Monitoring | Management's ongoing and periodic assessment of the quality of internal control performance to determine if controls are operating as intended and modified when needed | Not applicable |

## Reasons for Understanding Internal Control Sufficient to Plan the Audit

SAS 55 (as amended by SAS 78, AU 319) *requires the auditor to obtain an understanding of internal control for every audit.* The extent of that understanding must, at a minimum, be sufficient to adequately plan the audit, in terms of four specific planning matters.

**Auditability** The auditor must obtain information about the integrity of management and the nature and extent of the accounting records to be satisfied that sufficient, competent evidence is available to support the financial statement balances.

**FIGURE 9-3**

**Overview of Understanding Internal Control and Assessing Control Risk**

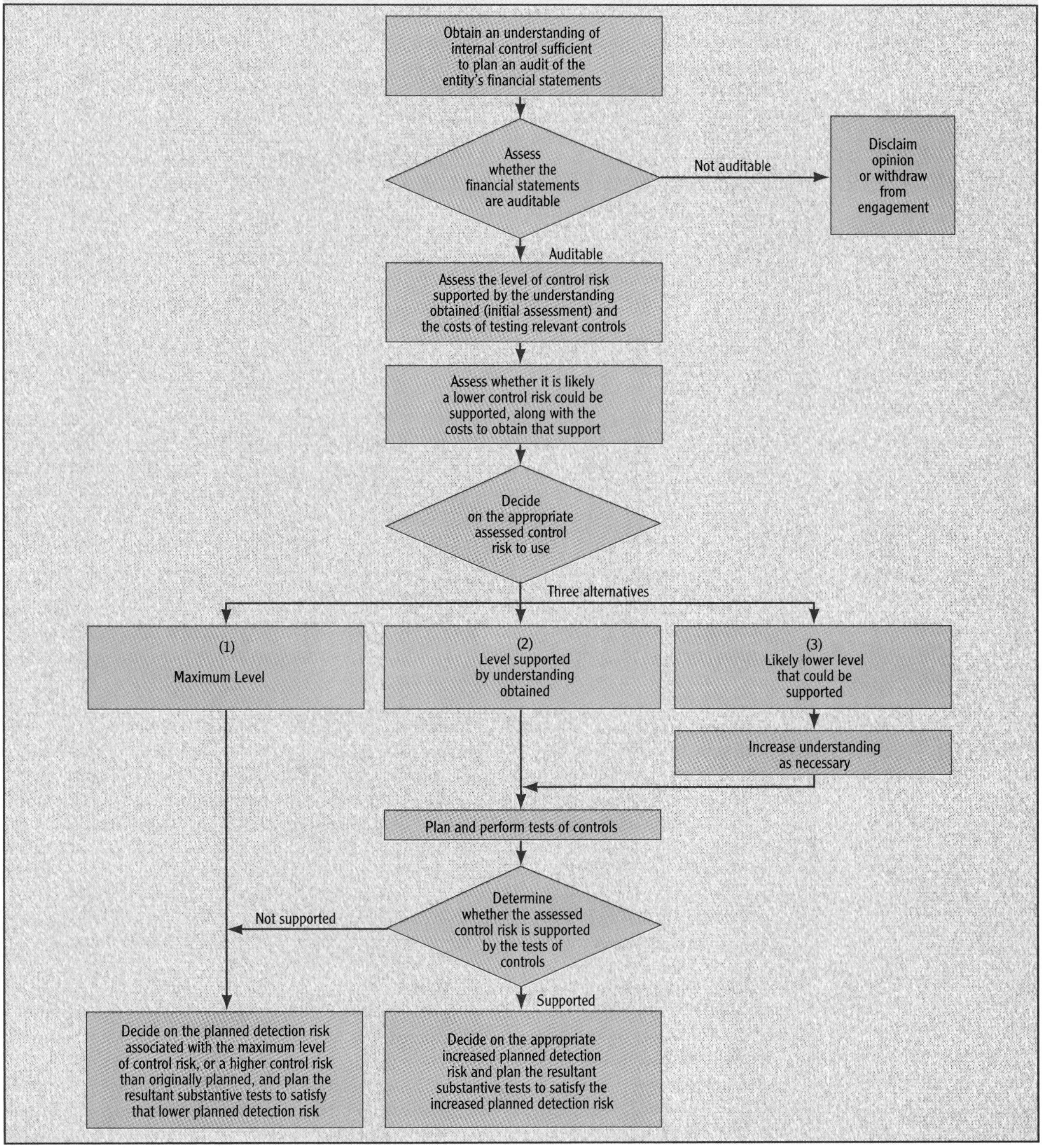

**Potential Material Misstatements** The understanding should allow the auditor to identify the types of potential errors and fraud that might affect the financial statements, and to assess the risk that such misstatements might occur in amounts that are material to the financial statements.

**Detection Risk** Control risk in the planning form of the audit risk model directly affects planned detection risk for each audit objective [PDR = AAR ÷ (IR × CR)]. Information about internal control is used to assess control risk for each objective, which in turn affects planned detection risk and planned audit evidence.

**Design of Tests** The information obtained should allow the auditor to design effective tests of the financial statement balances. Such tests include tests for monetary correctness of both transactions and balances, and analytical procedures. These are discussed in more detail in Chapter 10.

## Understanding Internal Control for Design and Operation

Each of the five components of internal control must be studied and understood. In obtaining that understanding, the auditor should consider two aspects: (1) the *design* of the various controls within each component and (2) whether they have been placed in *operation.*

**Understanding the Control Environment** Information is obtained about the control environment for each of the subcomponents discussed earlier in the chapter. The auditor then uses the understanding as a basis for assessing management's and the directors' attitude and awareness about the importance of control. For example, the auditor might determine the nature of a client's budgeting system as a part of understanding the design of the control environment. The operation of the budgeting system might then be evaluated in part by inquiry of budgeting personnel to determine budgeting procedures and follow-up of differences between budget and actual. The auditor might also examine client schedules comparing actual results to budgets.

**Understanding Risk Assessment** The auditor obtains knowledge about management's risk assessment process by determining how management identifies risks relevant to financial reporting, evaluating their significance and likelihood of occurrence, and deciding the actions needed to address the risks. Questionnaires and discussions with management are the most common ways to obtain this understanding.

**Understanding the Control Activities** Auditors obtain an understanding of the control environment and risk assessment in a similar manner for most audits, but obtaining an understanding of control activities varies considerably. For smaller clients, it is common to identify few or even no control activities because controls are often ineffective due to limited personnel. In that case, the auditor sets a high assessed control risk. For clients with extensive controls where the auditor believes controls are likely to be excellent, it is often appropriate to identify many controls during the understanding phase. In other audits, the auditor may identify a limited number of controls during this phase and then identify additional controls later in the process. The extent to which controls are identified is a matter of audit judgment. A methodology for identifying controls is studied later in the chapter.

**Understanding Information and Communication** To understand the design of the accounting information system, the auditor determines (1) the major classes of transactions of the entity; (2) how those transactions are initiated; (3) what accounting records exist and their nature; (4) how transactions are processed from initiation to completion, including the extent and nature of computer use; and (5) the nature and details of the financial reporting process followed. Typically, this is accomplished and documented by a *narrative description* of the system or by *flowcharting.* (These are described later in the chapter.) The operation of the accounting information system is often determined by tracing one or a few transactions through the system (called a *transaction walk-through*).

**Understanding Monitoring** The most important knowledge the auditor needs about monitoring is the major types of monitoring activities a company uses and how these activities are used to modify internal controls when necessary. Discussion with management is the most common way to obtain this understanding.

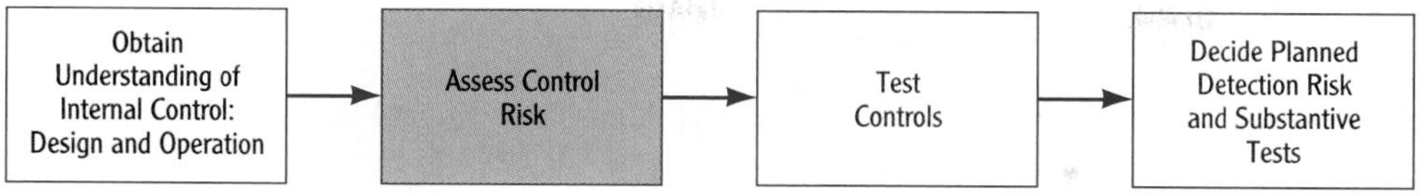


## Assessments and Decisions

Once an understanding of internal control sufficient for audit planning is obtained, four specific assessments must be made. As shown in Figure 9-3, these also require the auditor to make certain decisions.

**Assess Whether the Financial Statements Are Auditable** The first assessment is whether the entity is auditable. Two primary factors determine auditability: the integrity of management and the adequacy of accounting records. Many audit procedures rely to some extent on the representations of management. For example, it is difficult for the auditor to evaluate whether inventory is obsolete without an honest assessment by management. If management lacks integrity, management may provide false representations, causing the auditor to rely on unreliable evidence.

The accounting records serve as a direct source of audit evidence for most audit objectives. If the accounting records are deficient, necessary audit evidence may not be available. For example, if the client has not kept duplicate sales invoices and vendors' invoices, it would normally not be possible to do an audit. Unless the auditor can identify an alternative source of reliable evidence, or unless appropriate records can be constructed for the auditor's use, the only recourse may be to consider the entity unauditable.

When it is concluded that the entity is not auditable, the auditor discusses the circumstances with the client (usually at the highest level) and either withdraws from the engagement or issues a disclaimer form of audit report.

**Determine Assessed Control Risk Supported by the Understanding Obtained** After obtaining an understanding of internal control, the auditor makes an initial assessment of control risk. Control risk is a measure of the auditor's expectation that internal controls *will neither prevent material misstatements* from occurring, *nor detect and correct them* if they have occurred.

The initial assessment is made for each transaction-related audit objective for each major type of transaction. For example, the auditor makes an assessment of the existence objective for sales and a separate assessment for the completeness objective. There are different ways to express this expectation. Some auditors use a subjective expression such as high, moderate, or low. Others use numerical probabilities such as 1.0, .6, or .2.

The initial assessment usually starts with consideration of the control environment. If the attitude of management is that control is unimportant, it is doubtful that detailed control procedures will be reliable. The best course of action in that case is to assume that control risk for all transaction-related audit objectives is at the maximum (such as high or 1.0). On the other hand, if management's attitude is positive, the auditor then considers the specific policies and procedures within the subcomponents of the control environment and those of the four other components of internal control. The controls within all five components are used as a basis for an assessment below the maximum.

There are two important considerations about the initial assessment: First, the auditor does not have to make the initial assessment in a formal, detailed manner. In many audits, such as audits of smaller companies, the auditor assumes that the control risk is at the maximum whether or not it actually is. The auditor's reason for taking this approach is that he or she has concluded that it is more economical to more extensively audit the financial statement balances.

Second, even though the auditor believes control risk is low, assessed control risk is limited to that level supported by the evidence obtained. For example, suppose that the auditor believes that control risk for unrecorded sales is low, but has gathered little evidence in support of controls for the completeness transaction-related audit objective. The auditor's assessment of control risk for unrecorded sales must either be moderate or high. It could be low only if additional evidence was obtained in support of the pertinent controls.

**Assess Whether It Is Likely That a Lower Assessed Control Risk Could Be Supported** When the auditor believes that actual control risk may be significantly lower than the initial assessment, he or she may decide to support a lower assessed control risk. The most likely case where this occurs is when the auditor has identified a limited number of controls during the understanding phase. Based on the results of the initial assessment, the auditor now believes that additional controls can be identified and tested to further reduce assessed control risk.

**Decide on the Appropriate Assessed Control Risk** After the auditor completes the initial assessment and considers whether a lower assessed control risk is likely, he or she is in a position to decide which assessed control risk should be used: either a level already supported in the initial assessment, or a lower level. The decision as to which level to use is essentially an economic one, recognizing the trade-off between the costs of testing relevant controls and the costs of substantive tests that would be avoided by reducing assessed control risk. Assume, for example, that for the existence and accuracy transaction-related audit objectives for sales, the auditor believes that the cost of confirming accounts receivable could be reduced by $5,000 by incurring $2,000 to support a lower assessed control risk. It would be cost effective to incur the $2,000 additional cost.

## Tests of Controls

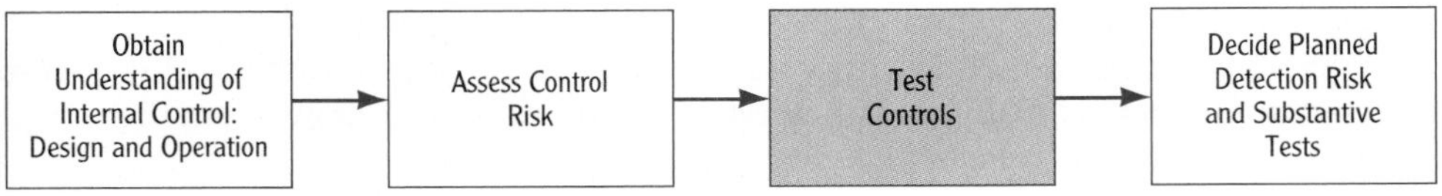


Assessing control risk requires the auditor to consider the design of controls to evaluate whether they should be effective in meeting transaction-related audit objectives. Some evidence will have been gathered in support of the design of the controls, as well as evidence that they have been placed in operation, during the understanding phase. In order to use specific controls as a basis for reducing assessed control risk, however, specific evidence must be obtained about their *effectiveness* throughout all, or at least most, of the period under audit. The procedures to gather evidence about design and placement in operation during the understanding phase are termed *procedures to obtain an understanding*. The procedures to test effectiveness of controls in support of a reduced assessed control risk are called *tests of controls*. Both are discussed in more detail later in the chapter.

Where the results of tests of controls support the design of controls as expected, the auditor proceeds to use the same assessed control risk. If, however, the tests of controls indicate that the controls did not operate effectively, the assessed control risk must be reconsidered. For example, the tests may indicate that the application of a control was curtailed midway through the year, or that the person applying it made frequent misstatements. In such situations, a higher assessed control risk would be used, unless additional controls for the same transaction-related audit objectives could be identified and found effective.

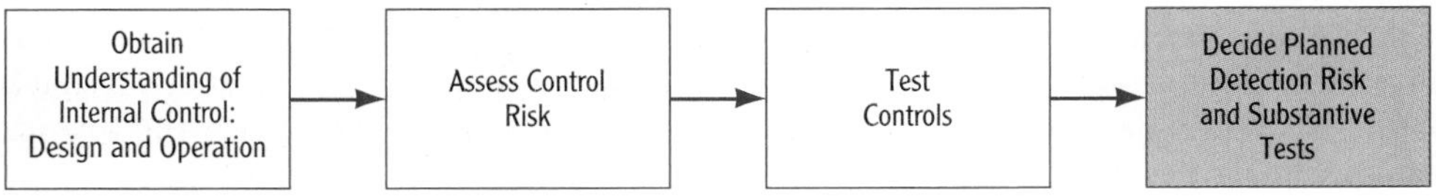

### Planned Detection Risk and Substantive Tests

The result of the preceding steps is the assessed control risk for each transaction-related audit objective, for each of the entity's major transaction types. Where assessed control risk is below the maximum, it will be supported by specific tests of controls. These assessments are then related to the balance-related audit objectives for the accounts affected by the major transaction types. The appropriate level of detection risk for each balance-related audit objective is then determined using the audit risk model. The relationship of transaction-related audit objectives to balance-related audit objectives and the selection and design of audit procedures for substantive tests of financial statement balances are discussed and illustrated in Chapter 10.

## PROCEDURES TO OBTAIN AN UNDERSTANDING

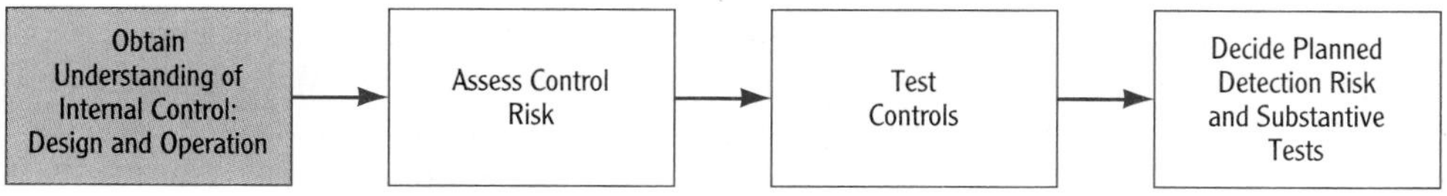


**OBJECTIVE 9-5**
**Know how to obtain an understanding of internal control.**

In practice, the study of internal control and assessment of control risk varies considerably from client to client. For smaller clients, many auditors obtain only a level of understanding sufficient to assess whether the statements are auditable, evaluate the control environment for management's attitude, and determine the adequacy of the client's accounting system. Often, for efficiency, internal controls are ignored, control risk is assumed to be maximum, and detection risk is therefore low.

For many larger clients, especially for repeat engagements, the auditor sets a low assessed control risk for most parts of the audit before the audit starts. A common approach is to (1) obtain an understanding of the control environment, risk assessment procedures, accounting information and communication system, and monitoring methods at a fairly detailed level, (2) identify specific controls that will reduce control risk and make an assessment of control risk, and (3) test the controls for effectiveness. The auditor can conclude that control risk is low only after all three steps are completed. The three steps discussed above are now explained in more detail to illustrate further how the study of a client's internal control structure and assessment of control risk are done.

### Procedures to Determine Design and Placement in Operation

The auditor's task in obtaining an understanding of internal control is to find out about the components of internal control, to see that they have been placed in operation, and to document the information obtained in a useful manner. The following are procedures to determine the design and placement in operation.

**Update and Evaluate Auditor's Previous Experience with the Entity** Most audits of a company are done annually by the same CPA firm. Except for initial engagements, the auditor begins the audit with a great deal of information about the client's internal controls developed in prior years. Because systems and controls usually don't change frequently, this information can be updated and carried forward to the current year's audit.

**Make Inquiries of Client Personnel** A logical starting place for updating information carried forward from the previous audit, or for obtaining information initially, is with appropriate client personnel. Inquiries of client personnel at the management, supervisory, and staff level will usually be conducted as part of obtaining an understanding of internal control.

**Read Client's Policy and Systems Manuals** To design, implement, and maintain internal controls, an entity must have extensive documentation of its own. This includes policy manuals and documents (such as a corporate code of conduct) and systems manuals and documents (such as an accounting manual and an organization chart). This information is read by the auditor and discussed with company personnel to assure that it is properly interpreted and understood.

**Examine Documents and Records** The five components of internal control all involve the creation of many documents and records. These will have been presented to some degree in the policy and systems manuals. By examining actual, completed documents and records, the auditor can bring the contents of the manuals to life and better understand them. Examination of the documents and records also provides evidence that the control policies and procedures have been placed in operation.

**Observe Entity Activities and Operations** In addition to examining completed documents and records, the auditor can observe client personnel in the process of preparing them and carrying out their normal accounting and control activities. This further enhances understanding and knowledge that controls have been placed in operation.

Observation, documentation, and inquiry can be conveniently and effectively combined in the form of the transaction walk-through mentioned earlier. With that procedure, the auditor selects one or a few documents for the initiation of a transaction type and traces it (them) through the entire accounting process. At each stage of processing, inquiries are made and current activities are observed, in addition to examining completed documentation for the transaction or transactions selected.

## Documentation of the Understanding

Three commonly used methods of documenting the understanding of internal control are narratives, flowcharts, and internal control questionnaires. These may be used separately or in combination, as discussed below.

**Narrative** A narrative is a written description of a client's internal controls. A proper narrative of an accounting system and related controls includes four characteristics:

- The origin of every document and record in the system. For example, the description should state where customer orders come from and how sales invoices arise.
- All processing that takes place. For example, if sales amounts are determined by a computer program that multiplies quantities shipped by stored standard prices, that should be described.
- The disposition of every document and record in the system. The filing of documents, sending them to customers, or destroying them should be shown.
- An indication of the controls relevant to the assessment of control risk. These typically include separation of duties (such as separating recording cash from handling cash); authorizations and approvals (such as credit approvals); and internal verification (such as comparison of unit selling price to sales contracts).

**Flowchart** An internal control flowchart is a symbolic, diagrammatic representation of the client's documents and their sequential flow in the organization. An adequate flowchart includes the same four characteristics identified above for narratives.

Flowcharting is advantageous primarily because it can provide a concise overview of the client's system which is useful to the auditor as an analytical tool in evaluation. A well-prepared flowchart aids in identifying inadequacies by facilitating a clear understanding of how the system operates. For most uses, it is superior to narratives as a method of communicating the characteristics of a system, especially to show adequate separation of duties. It is easier to follow a diagram than to read a description. It is also usually easier to update a flowchart than a narrative.

It would be unusual to use both a narrative and a flowchart to describe the same system, since both are intended to describe the flow of documents and records in an accounting system. Sometimes a combination of a narrative and flowchart is used. The decision to use one or the other or a combination of the two is dependent on two factors: relative ease of understanding by current- and subsequent-year auditors and relative cost of preparation.

**Internal Control Questionnaire** An internal control questionnaire asks a series of questions about the controls in each audit area as a means of indicating to the auditor aspects of internal control that may be inadequate. In most instances, it is designed to require a "yes" or a "no" response, with "no" responses indicating potential internal control deficiencies.

The primary advantage of using a questionnaire is the ability to thoroughly cover each audit area reasonably quickly at the beginning of the audit. The primary disadvantage is that individual parts of the client's systems are examined without providing an overall view. In addition, a standard questionnaire is often inapplicable to some audit clients, especially smaller ones.

Figure 9-4 illustrates part of an internal control questionnaire for the sales and collection cycle of Hillsburg Hardware Co. The questionnaire is also designed for use with the six

**FIGURE 9-4**

**Partial Internal Control Questionnaire for Sales**

Client *Hillsburg Hardware Co* Audit Date *12/31/96*

Auditor *MSW* Date Completed *9/30/96* Reviewed by *FR* Date Completed *10/1/96*

| Objective (shaded) and Question | Answer Yes | No | N/A | Remarks |
|---|---|---|---|---|
| **Sales** | | | | |
| **A. Recorded sales are for shipments actually made to existing customers.** | | | | *Pam Dilley examines underlying documentation.* |
| 1. Is the recording of sales supported by authorized shipping documents and approved customer orders? | ✓ | | | |
| 2. Is customers' credit approved by a responsible official? | ✓ | | | *By Chulick, the president* |
| 3. Is a prenumbered written shipping order required for any merchandise to leave the premises? | ✓ | | | |
| **B. Existing sales transactions are recorded.** | | | | |
| 1. Is a record of shipments maintained? | ✓ | | | |
| 2. Is the shipping document controlled from the office in a manner that helps assure that all shipments are billed? | ✓ | | | |
| 3. Are shipping documents prenumbered and accounted for? | ✓ | | | |
| 4. Are sales invoices prenumbered and accounted for? | | ✓ | | *Prenumbered but not accounted for. Additional substantive testing required.* |
| **C. Recorded sales are for the amount of goods shipped and are correctly billed and recorded.** | | | | |
| 1. Is there independent comparison of the quantity on the shipping documents to the sales invoices? | ✓ | | | *By Pam Dilley, controlled by Chulick* |
| 2. Is an authorized price list used? | ✓ | | | |
| 3. Are monthly statements sent to customers? | ✓ | | | |
| **D. Recorded sales transactions are properly classified.** | | | | *All sales are on account and there is only one sales account.* |
| 1. Is there independent comparison of recorded sales to the chart of accounts? | | | ✓ | |
| **E. Sales are recorded on the correct dates.** | | | | *There is a weakness in the system and additional substantive testing required.* |
| 1. Is there independent comparison of dates on shipping documents to dates recorded? | | ✓ | | |
| **F. Sales transactions are properly included in the master files and correctly summarized.** | | | | |
| 1. Are journals independently footed and traced to the general ledger and printout of master file? | | ✓ | | *Examined for reasonableness by Chulick.* |
| 2. Is there a comparison of customer names on shipping documents to posting in the printout of the master file? | ✓ | | | *By Pam Dilley* |

transaction-related audit objectives. Notice that each objective (A through F) is a transaction-related audit objective as it applies to sales transactions (see shaded portions). The same is true for all other audit areas.

We believe the use of both questionnaires and flowcharts is highly desirable for understanding the client's system. Flowcharts provide an overview of the system, and questionnaires are useful checklists to remind the auditor of many different types of controls that should exist. When properly used, a combination of these two approaches should provide the auditor with an excellent description of the system.

It is often desirable to use the client's narratives or flowcharts and have the client fill out the internal control questionnaire. When understandable and reliable narratives, flowcharts, and questionnaires are not available from a client, which is frequently the case, the auditor must prepare them.

## ASSESS CONTROL RISK

**OBJECTIVE 9-6**
**Know how to assess control risk for each major type of transaction.**

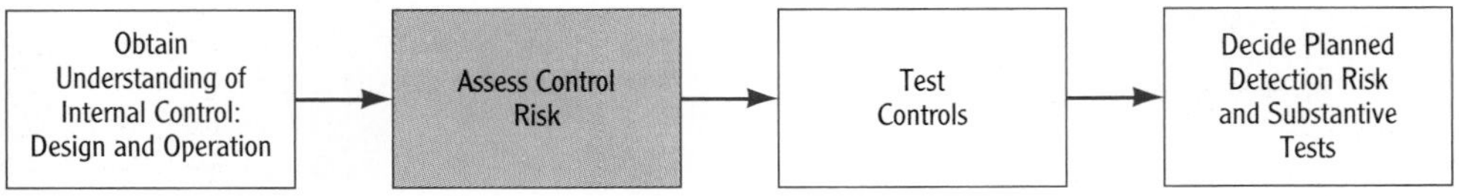


Once the auditor has obtained descriptive information and evidence in support of the design and operation of internal control, an assessment of control risk by transaction-related audit objective can be made. This is normally done separately for each major type of transaction in each transaction cycle. For example, in the sales and collection cycle, the types of transactions usually involve sales, sales returns and allowances, cash receipts, and the provision for and write-off of uncollectible accounts.

### Identify Transaction-Related Audit Objectives

The first step in the assessment is to identify the transaction-related audit objectives to which the assessment applies. This is done by applying the transaction-related audit objectives introduced earlier, which are stated in general form, to each major type of transaction for the entity.

### Identify Specific Controls

The next step is to identify the specific controls that contribute to accomplishing each transaction-related audit objective. The auditor identifies pertinent controls by proceeding through the descriptive information about the client's system. Those policies, procedures, and activities that in his or her judgment provide control over the transaction involved are identified. In doing this, it is often helpful to refer back to the types of controls that *might* exist, and ask if they *do* exist. For example: Is there adequate separation of duties and how is it achieved? Are the documents used well designed? Are prenumbered documents properly accounted for?

In making this analysis, it is not necessary to consider *every* control. The auditor should identify and include those controls that are expected to have the greatest impact on meeting the transaction-related audit objectives. These are often termed *key controls.* The reason for including only key controls is that they will be sufficient to achieve the transaction-related audit objectives and should provide audit efficiency.

### Identify and Evaluate Weaknesses

*Weaknesses* are defined as the *absence of adequate controls,* which increases the risk of misstatements existing in the financial statements. If, in the judgment of the auditor, there are inadequate controls to satisfy one of the transaction-related audit objectives, expectation of such a misstatement occurring increases. For example, if no internal verification of the accuracy of payroll transactions is taking place, the auditor may conclude that there is a weakness in internal control.

A four-step approach can be used for identifying significant weaknesses.

**Identify Existing Controls** Because weaknesses are the absence of adequate controls, the auditor must first know which controls exist. The methods for identifying existing controls have already been discussed.

**Identify the Absence of Key Controls** Internal control questionnaires, narratives, and flowcharts are useful to identify areas in which key controls are lacking and the likelihood of misstatements is thereby increased. Where control risk is assessed as moderate or high, there is usually an absence of controls.

**Determine Potential Material Misstatements That Could Result** This step is intended to identify specific misstatements that are likely to result because of the absence of controls. The importance of a weakness is proportionate to the magnitude of the misstatements that are likely to result from it.

**Consider the Possibility of Compensating Controls** A compensating control is one elsewhere in the system that offsets a weakness. A common example in a smaller company is active involvement of the owner. When a compensating control exists, the weakness is no longer a concern because the potential for misstatement has been sufficiently reduced.

Figure 9-5 shows the documentation of weaknesses for the sales and collection cycle of Airtight Machine Company. The effect on audit evidence column shows the effect of the weakness on the auditor's planned audit program.

**FIGURE 9-5**

**Weaknesses in Internal Control**

Client *Airtight Machine Co.* Schedule *P-3*

Weaknesses in Internal Control Prepared by *JR*

Cycle *Sales and Collection* Period *12/31/96*

| Weakness | Compensating Control | Potential Misstatement | Materiality | Effect on Audit Evidence |
|---|---|---|---|---|
| *1. The accounts receivable clerk approves credit memos and has access to cash.* | *The owner reviews all credit memos after they are recorded. He knows all customers.* | *N/A* | *N/A* | *N/A* |
| *2. There is no internal verification of the key entry of customer number, quantities, and related information for sales invoices and credit memos.** | *None* | *Clerical errors in billings to customers, posting to master file and account classification.* | *Potentially material* | *Increase substantive tests of transactions for sales to 125 transactions.* |

*Included in the reportable conditions letter.

## The Control Risk Matrix

Many auditors use a *control risk matrix* to assist in the control-risk-assessment process. Most controls affect more than one transaction-related audit objective, and often several different controls affect a given transaction-related audit objective. These complexities make a control risk matrix a useful way to help assess control risk. The control risk matrix is used to assist in identifying both controls and weaknesses, and in assessing control risk.

Figure 9-6 illustrates the use of a control risk matrix for sales transactions of Airtight Machine Company. In constructing the matrix, the transaction-related audit objectives for sales were listed as column headings, and pertinent controls that were identified were listed as headings for the rows. In addition, where significant weaknesses were identified, they were also entered as row headings below the listing of key controls. The body of the matrix

**FIGURE 9-6**

**Control Risk Matrix for Sales Transactions—Airtight Machine Company**

| | | SALES TRANSACTION-RELATED AUDIT OBJECTIVES | | | | | |
|---|---|---|---|---|---|---|---|
| | INTERNAL CONTROL | *Recorded sales are for shipments made to existing customers (existence)* | *Existing sales transactions are recorded (completeness)* | *Recorded sales are for the amount of goods shipped and are correctly billed and recorded (accuracy)* | *Recorded sales are properly classified (classification)* | *Sales are recorded on the correct dates (timing)* | *Sales transactions are properly included in the accounts receivable master file and correctly summarized (posting and summarization)* |
| ILLUSTRATIVE KEY CONTROLS | Credit is approved before shipment occurs | C | | | | | |
| | Sales are supported by authorized shipping documents and approved customer orders, which are attached to the duplicate sales invoice | C | | | | | |
| | Separation of duties among billing, recording sales, and handling cash receipts | C | C | | | | C |
| | An approved price list is used to determine unit selling prices | | | C | | | |
| | Shipping documents are forwarded to billing daily and billed the subsequent day | | C | | | C | |
| | Shipping documents and duplicate sales invoice numbers are accounted for weekly and traced to the sales journal | | C | | | C | |
| | Shipping documents are batched daily by quantity shipped | C | C | C | | C | C |
| | Statements are mailed to all customers each month | C | | C | | | C |
| | There is an adequate chart of accounts | | | | C | | |
| | Sales journal is reviewed monthly for reasonableness of total and compared to the general ledger for sales and sales returns | | | | | | C |
| WEAKNESSES | Lack of internal verification of the key entry of customer number, quantities, and related information for sales invoices and credit memos | | | W | W | | W |
| | Assessed control risk | low | low | mod | mod | low | mod |

C = The control partially or fully satisfies the sales transaction-related audit objective.
W = Weakness identified in Figure 9-5.

was then used to show how the controls contribute to the accomplishment of the transaction-related audit objectives, and how weaknesses impact the objectives. In this illustration, a *C* was entered in each cell where a control partially or fully satisfied an objective, and a *W* was entered to show the impact of the weaknesses.

### Assess Control Risk

Once controls and weaknesses have been identified and related to transaction-related audit objectives, there can be an assessment of control risk. Again, the control risk matrix is a useful tool for that purpose. Referring to Figure 9-6, the auditor assessed control risk for Airtight's sales by reviewing each column for pertinent controls and weaknesses, and asking: "What is the likelihood that a material misstatement of the type to be controlled would not be prevented or detected and corrected by these controls, and what is the impact of the weaknesses?" If the likelihood is high, then control risk is high, and so forth.

Once a preliminary assessment of control risk is made for sales and cash receipts, the auditor can complete the three control risk rows of the evidence planning worksheet that was introduced in Chapter 8 on page 268. If tests of controls results do not support the preliminary assessment of control risk, the auditor must modify the worksheet accordingly. Alternatively, the auditor can wait until tests of controls are done to complete the three control risk rows of the worksheet. An evidence planning worksheet for Hillsburg Hardware with the three rows for control risk completed is illustrated in Figure 12-9 on page 434.

### Communicate Reportable Conditions and Related Matters

During the course of obtaining an understanding of internal control and assessing control risk, auditors obtain information that is of interest to the audit committee in fulfilling its responsibilities. Generally, such information concerns significant deficiencies in the design or operation of internal control. Such matters are termed *reportable conditions* in SAS 60 (AU 325).

**Audit Committee Communications** Reportable conditions should be communicated to the audit committee as a part of every audit. If the client does not have an audit committee, then the communication should go to the person or persons in the organization who have overall responsibility for internal control, such as the board of directors or the owner-manager.

The form of communication would normally be a letter, although oral communication, documented in the working papers, is also allowable under professional standards. An illustrative reportable conditions letter is shown in Figure 9-7 on page 314.

**Management Letters** In addition to reportable conditions, auditors often observe less significant internal control related matters, as well as opportunities for the client to make operational improvements. These types of matters should also be communicated to the client. The form of communication is often a separate letter for that purpose, called a management letter.

## TESTS OF CONTROLS

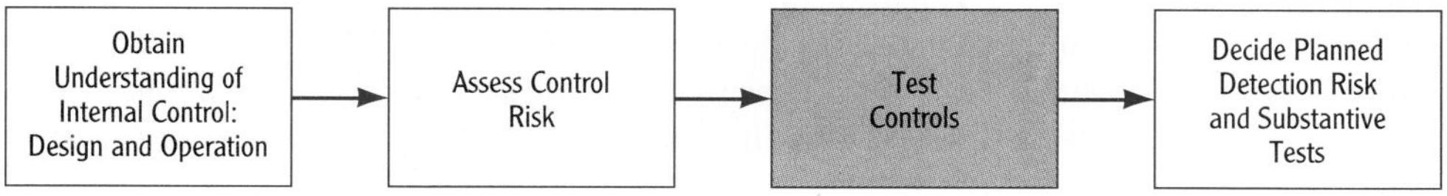


**OBJECTIVE 9-7**
**Understand the process of designing and performing tests of controls as a basis for further study.**

The controls the auditor has identified in the assessment as reducing control risk (the key controls) must be supported by tests of controls to make sure that they have been operating effectively throughout all or most of the audit period. For example, in Figure 9-6, each key control that the auditor intends to rely on must be supported by sufficient tests of controls.

**FIGURE 9-7**

**Reportable Conditions Letter**

**JOHNSON AND SEYGROVES**
**Certified Public Accountants**
**2016 Village Boulevard**
**Troy, Michigan 48801**

February 12, 1997

Board of Directors
Airtight Machine Company
1729 Athens Street
Troy, MI 48801

Gentlemen:

In planning and performing our audit of the financial statements of Airtight Machine Company for the year ended December 31, 1996, we considered its internal control in order to determine our auditing procedures for the purpose of expressing our opinion on the financial statements and not to provide assurance on internal control. However, we noted certain matters involving internal control and its operation that we consider to be a reportable condition under standards established by the American Institute of Certified Public Accountants. Reportable conditions involve matters coming to our attention relating to significant deficiencies in the design or operation of internal control that, in our judgment, could adversely affect the organization's ability to record, process, summarize, and report financial data consistent with the assertions of management in the financial statements.

The matter noted is that there is a lack of independent verification of the key entry of the customer's name, product number, and quantity shipped on sales invoices and credit memos. As a consequence, errors in these activities could occur and remain uncorrected, adversely affecting both recorded net sales and accounts receivable. This deficiency is significant because of the large size of the average sale of Airtight Machine Company.

This report is intended solely for the information and use of the board of directors, management, and others in Airtight Machine Company.

*Very truly yours,*

*Johnson and Seygroves*

*Johnson and Seygroves, CPAs*

## Procedures for Tests of Controls

Four types of procedures are used to support the operation of internal controls. They are as follows:

**Make Inquiries of Appropriate Client Personnel** Although inquiry is not generally a strong source of evidence about the effective operation of controls, it is an appropriate form of evidence. For example, the auditor may determine that unauthorized personnel are not allowed access to computer files by making inquiries of the person who controls the computer library.

**Examine Documents, Records, and Reports** Many controls leave a clear trail of documentary evidence. Suppose, for example, that when a customer order is received, it is used to create a customer sales order, which is approved for credit. (See the first and second key controls in Figure 9-6.) The customer order is attached to the sales order as authorization for further processing. The auditor examines the documents to make sure that they are complete and properly matched, and that required signatures or initials are present.

**Observe Control-Related Activities** Other types of control-related activities do *not* leave an evidential trail. For example, separation of duties relies on specific persons performing specific tasks, and there is typically no documentation of the separate performance. (See the third key control in Figure 9-6.) For controls that leave no documentary evidence, the auditor generally observes them being applied.

**Reperform Client Procedures** There are also control-related activities for which there are related documents and records, but their content is insufficient for the auditor's purpose of assessing whether controls are operating effectively. For example, assume that prices on sales invoices are to be verified to a standard price list by client personnel as an internal verification procedure, but no indication of performance is entered on the sales invoices. (See the fourth key control in Figure 9-6.) In these cases, it is common for the auditor to actually reperform the control activity to see whether the proper results were obtained. For this example, the auditor can reperform the procedure by tracing the sales prices to the authorized price list in effect at the date of the transaction. If no misstatements are found, the auditor can conclude that the procedure is operating as intended.

## Extent of Procedures

The extent to which tests of controls are applied depends on the desired assessed control risk. If the auditor wants a lower assessed control risk, more extensive tests of controls are applied, both in terms of the number of controls tested and the extent of the tests for each control. For example, if the auditor wants to use a low assessed control risk, a larger sample size for documentation, observation, and reperformance procedures should be applied.

**Reliance on Evidence from Prior Year's Audit** If evidence was obtained in the prior year's audit that indicates that a key control was operating effectively, and the auditor determines that it is still in place, the extent of the tests of that control may be reduced to some extent in the current year. For example, in such circumstances, the auditor might use a reduced sample size in testing a control that leaves documentary evidence, or certain tests might be rotated among areas across two or more years.

**Testing Less Than the Entire Audit Period** Ideally, tests of controls should be applied to transactions and controls for the entire period under audit. However, it is not always practical to do so. Where less than the entire period is tested, the auditor should determine whether changes in controls occurred in the period not tested and obtain evidential matter about the nature and extent of any changes.

## Relationship of Tests of Controls to Procedures to Obtain an Understanding

You will notice that there is a significant overlap between tests of controls and procedures to obtain an understanding. Both include inquiry, documentation, and observation. There are two primary differences in the application of these common procedures between phases. First, in obtaining an understanding, the procedures are applied to all the controls identified as part of the understanding of internal control. Tests of controls, on the other hand, are applied only where the assessed control risk is below the maximum, and then only to the key controls.

Second, procedures to obtain an understanding are performed only on one or a few transactions or, in the case of observations, at a single point in time. Tests of controls are performed on larger samples of transactions (perhaps 20 to 100), and often observations are made at more than one point in time.

For key controls, tests of controls other than reperformance are essentially an *extension* of related procedures to obtain an understanding. For that reason, when auditors plan at the outset to obtain a low assessed control risk, they will combine both types of procedures and perform them simultaneously.

Figure 9-8 illustrates this concept in more detail. Where only the required minimum study of internal control is planned, the auditor will conduct a transaction walk-through. In so doing, the auditor determines that the audit documentation is complete and accurate, and observes that the control-related activities described are in operation.

When the control risk is assessed below maximum, not only is a transaction walk-through performed, but a larger sample of documents is examined for indications of the effectiveness of the operation of controls. (The determination of appropriate sample size is discussed in Chapters 12 and 14.) Similarly, when observations are made, they will be more extensive and often at several points in time. Also, the auditors will do reperformance for some controls.

**FIGURE 9-8**

**Relationship of Assessed Control Risk and Extent of Procedures**

| | **Assessed Control Risk** | |
|---|---|---|
| **Type of Procedure** | **High Level: Obtaining an Understanding Only** | **Lower Level: Tests of Controls** |
| Inquiry | Yes—extensive | Yes—some |
| Documentation | Yes—with transaction walk-through | Yes—using sampling |
| Observation | Yes—with transaction walk-through | Yes—at multiple times |
| Reperformance | No | Yes—using sampling |

## ESSENTIAL TERMS

**Assessed control risk**—a measure of the auditor's expectation that internal controls will neither prevent material misstatements from occurring, nor detect and correct them if they have occurred; control risk is assessed for each transaction-related audit objective in a cycle or class of transactions

**Chart of accounts**—a listing of all the entity's accounts, which classifies transactions into individual balance sheet and income statement accounts

**Collusion**—a cooperative effort among employees to defraud a business of cash, inventory, or other assets

**Control activities**—policies and procedures, in addition to those included in the other four components, that help ensure that necessary actions are taken to address risks in the achievement of the entity's objectives. They include (1) adequate separation of duties, (2) proper authorization of transactions and activities, (3) adequate documents and records, (4) physical control over assets and records, and (5) independent checks on performance.

**Control environment**—the actions, policies, and procedures that reflect the overall attitudes of top management, directors, and owners of an entity about control and its importance to the entity

**Control risk**—see *assessed control risk*

**Control risk matrix**—a methodology used to help the auditor assess control risk by matching key internal controls and internal control weaknesses with transaction-related audit objectives

**Electronic data processing (EDP)**—computerized management and use of information

**Flowchart**—a diagrammatic representation of the client's documents and records, and the sequence in which they are processed

**General authorization**—companywide policies for the approval of all transactions within stated limits

**Independent checks**—internal control activities designed for the continuous internal verification of other controls

**Information and communication**—the set of manual and/or computerized procedures that identifies, assembles, classifies, analyzes, records, and reports an entity's transactions and maintains accountability for the related assets

**Internal control**—a process designed to provide reasonable assurance regarding the achievement of management's objectives in the following categories: (1) reliability of financial reporting, (2) effectiveness and efficiency of operations, and (3) compliance with applicable laws and regulations

**Internal control questionnaire**—a series of questions about the controls in each audit area used as a means of indicating to the auditor aspects of internal control that may be inadequate

**Internal control weakness**—the absence of adequate controls; an internal control weakness increases the risk of misstatements in the financial statements

**Management letter**—the auditor's written communications to management to point out weaknesses in internal control, other than reportable conditions, and possibilities for operational improvements

**Monitoring**—management's ongoing and periodic assessment of the quality of internal control performance to determine that controls are operating as intended and modified when needed

**Narrative**—a written description of a client's internal controls, including the origin, processing, and disposition of documents and records, and the relevant control procedures

**Procedures to obtain an understanding**—procedures used by the auditor to gather evidence about the design and placement in operation of specific controls

**Reportable conditions**—significant deficiencies in the design or operation of internal control

**Risk assessment**—management's identification and analysis of risks relevant to the preparation of financial statements in accordance with generally accepted accounting principles

**Separation of duties**—segregation of the following activities in an organization: custody of assets, accounting, authorization, and operational responsibility

**Specific authorization**—case-by-case approval of transactions not covered by companywide policies

**Tests of controls**—audit procedures to test the effectiveness of controls in support of a reduced assessed control risk

**Transaction-related audit objectives**—six audit objectives that must be met before the auditor can conclude that the total for any given class of transactions is fairly stated. The general transaction-related audit objectives are existence, completeness, accuracy, classification, timing, and posting and summarization.

**Transaction walk-through**—the tracing of selected transactions through the accounting system

## REVIEW QUESTIONS

**9-1 (Objective 9-1)** Chapter 7 introduced the seven parts of the planning phase of audits. Which part is understanding internal control and assessing control risk? What parts precede and follow that understanding and assessing?

**9-2 (Objective 9-1)** Compare management's concerns about internal control with those of the auditor.

**9-3 (Objective 9-1)** Frequently, management is more concerned about internal controls that promote operational efficiency than about those that result in reliable financial data. How can the independent auditor persuade management to devote more attention to controls affecting the reliability of accounting information when management has this attitude?

**9-4 (Objectives 9-1, 9-6)** State the six transaction-related audit objectives.

**9-5 (Objective 9-3)** What is meant by the control environment? What are the factors the auditor must evaluate to understand it?

**9-6 (Objective 9-3)** What is the relationship among the five components of internal control?

**9-7 (Objective 9-3)** List the five categories of control activities and provide one specific illustration of a control in the sales area for each control activity.

**9-8 (Objective 9-3)** The separation of operational responsibility from record keeping is meant to prevent different types of misstatements than the separation of the custody of assets from accounting. Explain the difference in the purposes of these two types of separation of duties.

**9-9 (Objective 9-3)** Distinguish between general and specific authorization of transactions and give one example of each type.

**9-10 (Objective 9-3)** For each of the following, give an example of a physical control the client can use to protect the asset or record:

1. Petty cash
2. Cash received by retail clerks
3. Accounts receivable records
4. Raw material inventory
5. Perishable tools
6. Manufacturing equipment
7. Marketable securities

**9-11 (Objective 9-3)** Explain what is meant by independent checks on performance and give five specific examples.

**9-12 (Objectives 9-4, 9-5)** Distinguish between obtaining an understanding of internal control and assessing control risk. Also explain the methodology the auditor uses for each of them.

**9-13 (Objective 9-6)** Define what is meant by a control and a weakness in internal control. Give two examples of each in the sales and collection cycle.

**9-14 (Objectives 9-3, 9-6)** Frank James, a highly competent employee of Brinkwater Sales Corporation, had been responsible for accounting-related matters for two decades. His devotion to the firm and his duties had always been exceptional, and over the years he had been given increased responsibility. Both the president of Brinkwater and the partner of an independent CPA firm in charge of the audit were shocked and dismayed to discover that James had embezzled more than $500,000 over a 10-year period by not recording billings in the sales journal and subsequently diverting the cash receipts. What major factors permitted the defalcation to take place?

**9-15 (Objectives 9-4, 9-5)** Jeanne Maier, CPA, believes that it is appropriate to obtain an understanding of internal control about halfway through the audit, after she is familiar with the client's operations and the way the system actually works. She has found through experience that filling out internal control questionnaires and flowcharts early in the engagement is not beneficial because the system rarely functions the way it is supposed to. Later in the engagement, the auditor can prepare flowcharts and questionnaires with relative ease because of the knowledge already obtained on the audit. Evaluate her approach.

**9-16 (Objective 9-5)** Distinguish between the objectives of an internal control questionnaire and the objectives of a flowchart for documenting information about a client's internal control structure. State the advantages and disadvantages of each of these two methods.

**9-17 (Objective 9-6)** Explain what is meant by *reportable conditions* as they relate to internal control. What should the auditor do with reportable conditions?

**9-18 (Objective 9-6)** Examine the control risk matrix in Figure 9-6, page 312. Explain the purpose of the matrix. Also explain the meaning and effect of an assessment of control risk of low compared to one of medium.

**9-19 (Objectives 9-4, 9-7)** Explain what is meant by tests of controls. Write one examination of documents test of control and one reperformance test of control for the following internal control: hours on time cards are re-added by an independent payroll clerk and initialed to indicate performance.

## MULTIPLE CHOICE QUESTIONS FROM CPA EXAMINATIONS

**9-20 (Objectives 9-1, 9-2, 9-4)** The following are general questions about internal control. Choose the best response.

a. When considering internal control, an auditor must be aware of the concept of reasonable assurance which recognizes that the

(1) employment of competent personnel provides assurance that management's control objectives will be achieved.
(2) establishment and maintenance of internal control is an important responsibility of the management and *not* of the auditor.
(3) cost of internal control should *not* exceed the benefits expected to be derived therefrom.
(4) separation of incompatible functions is necessary to ascertain that the internal control is effective.

b. When an auditor issues an unqualified opinion, it is implied that the
(1) entity has *not* violated provisions of the Foreign Corrupt Practices Act.
(2) likelihood of fraud is minimal.
(3) financial records are sufficiently reliable to permit the preparation of financial statements.
(4) entity's internal control is in conformity with criteria established by its audit committee.

c. The Foreign Corrupt Practices Act requires that
(1) auditors engaged to audit the financial statements of publicly held companies report all illegal payments to the SEC.
(2) publicly held companies establish independent audit committees to monitor the effectiveness of their internal controls.
(3) U.S. firms doing business abroad report sizable payments to non-U.S. citizens to the Justice Department.
(4) publicly held companies devise and maintain adequate internal control.

d. What is the independent auditor's principal purpose for obtaining an understanding of internal control and assessing control risk?
(1) To comply with generally accepted accounting principles.
(2) To obtain a measure of assurance of management's efficiency.
(3) To maintain a state of independence in mental attitude during the audit.
(4) To determine the nature, timing, and extent of subsequent audit work.

**9-21 (Objective 9-6)** The following questions deal with weaknesses of internal control. Choose the best response.

a. In general, a material internal control weakness may be defined as a condition under which material misstatements would ordinarily *not* be detected within a timely period by
(1) an auditor during the normal obtaining of an understanding of internal control and assessment of control risk.
(2) a controller when reconciling accounts in the general ledger.
(3) employees in the normal course of performing their assigned functions.
(4) the chief financial officer when reviewing interim financial statements.

b. Which of the following statements with respect to required auditor communication of reportable conditions is correct?
(1) Such communication is required to be in writing.
(2) Such communication must include a description of all weaknesses.
(3) Such communication is the principal reason for testing and evaluating internal controls.
(4) Such communication is incidental to the auditor's understanding of internal control and assessment of control risk.

c. The auditor who becomes aware of a reportable condition is required to communicate this to the
(1) audit committee.
(2) senior management and board of directors.
(3) board of directors and internal auditors.
(4) internal auditors and senior management.

**9-22 (Objective 9-6)** The following questions deal with assessing control risk. Choose the best response.

a. The ultimate purpose of assessing control risk is to contribute to the auditor's evaluation of the
   (1) factors that raise doubts about the auditability of the financial statements.
   (2) operating effectiveness of internal controls.
   (3) risk that material misstatements exist in the financial statements.
   (4) possibility that the nature and extent of substantive tests may be reduced.

b. An auditor uses assessed control risk to
   (1) evaluate the effectiveness of the entity's internal controls.
   (2) identify transactions and account balances where inherent risk is at the maximum.
   (3) indicate whether materiality thresholds for planning and evaluation purposes are sufficiently high.
   (4) determine the acceptable level of detection risk for financial statement assertions.

c. On the basis of audit evidence gathered and evaluated, an auditor decides to increase assessed control risk from that originally planned. To achieve an audit risk level (AcAR) that is substantially the same as the planned audit risk level (AAR), the auditor would
   (1) increase inherent risk.
   (2) increase materiality levels.
   (3) decrease substantive testing.
   (4) decrease planned detection risk.

## DISCUSSION QUESTIONS AND PROBLEMS

**9-23 (Objectives 9-3, 9-6, 9-7)** Each of the following internal controls has been taken from a standard internal control questionnaire used by a CPA firm for assessing control risk in the payroll and personnel cycle.

1. Approval of department head or foreman on time cards is required prior to preparing payroll.
2. All prenumbered time cards are accounted for before beginning data entry for preparation of checks.
3. Persons preparing the payroll do not perform other payroll duties (time-keeping, distribution of checks) or have access to other payroll data or cash.
4. Clerical operations in payroll are double-checked before payment is made.
5. All voided and spoiled payroll checks are properly mutilated and retained.
6. Personnel requires an investigation of an employment application from new employees. Investigation includes checking employee's background, former employers, and references.
7. Written termination notices, with properly documented reasons for termination, and approval of an appropriate official are required.
8. All checks not distributed to employees are returned to the treasurer for safekeeping.

### Required

a. For each internal control, identify the type(s) of control activities to which it applies (such as adequate documents and records or physical control over assets and records).

b. For each internal control, identify the transaction-related audit objective(s) to which it applies.

c. For each internal control, identify a specific misstatement that is likely to be prevented if the control exists and is effective.

d. For each control, list a specific misstatement that could result from the absence of the control.

e. For each control, identify one audit test that the auditor could use to uncover misstatements resulting from the absence of the control.

**9-24 (Objectives 9-3, 9-6)** The following are misstatements that have occurred in Fresh Foods Grocery Store, a retail and wholesale grocery company.

1. The incorrect price was used on sales invoices for billing shipments to customers because the wrong price was entered into the computer file.
2. A vendor's invoice was paid twice for the same shipment. The second payment arose because the vendor sent a duplicate copy of the original two weeks after the payment was due.
3. Employees in the receiving department took sides of beef for their personal use. When a shipment of meat was received, the receiving department filled out a receiving report and forwarded it to the accounting department for the amount of goods actually received. At that time, two sides of beef were put in an employee's pickup truck rather than in the storage freezer.
4. During the physical count of inventory of the retail grocery, one counter wrote down the wrong description of several products and miscounted the quantity.
5. A salesperson sold an entire carload of lamb at a price below cost because she did not know the cost of lamb had increased in the past week.
6. On the last day of the year, a truckload of beef was set aside for shipment but was not shipped. Because it was still on hand the inventory was counted. The shipping document was dated the last day of the year, so it was also included as a current-year sale.

## Required

a. For each misstatement, identify one or more types of controls that were absent.

b. For each misstatement, identify the transaction-related audit objectives that have not been met.

c. For each misstatement, suggest a control to correct the deficiency.

**9-25 (Objective 9-3)** The division of the following duties is meant to provide the best possible controls for the Meridian Paint Company, a small wholesale store.

†1. Assemble supporting documents for general and payroll cash disbursements.
†2. Sign general cash disbursement checks.
†3. Input information to prepare checks for signature, record checks in the cash disbursements journal, and update the appropriate master files.
†4. Mail checks to suppliers and deliver checks to employees.
5. Cancel supporting documents to prevent their reuse.
†6. Approve credit for customers.
†7. Input shipping and billing information to bill customers, record invoices in the sales journal, and update the accounts receivable master file.
†8. Open the mail and prepare a prelisting of cash receipts.
†9. Enter cash receipts data to prepare the cash receipts journal and update the accounts receivable master file.
†10. Prepare daily cash deposits.
†11. Deliver daily cash deposits to the bank.
†12. Assemble the payroll time cards and input the data to prepare payroll checks and update the payroll journal and payroll master files.
†13. Sign payroll checks.
14. Update the general ledger at the end of each month and review all accounts for unexpected balances.

15. Reconcile the accounts receivable master file with the control account and review accounts outstanding more than 90 days.
16. Prepare monthly statements for customers by printing the accounts receivable master file; then mail the statements to customers.
17. Reconcile the monthly statements from vendors with the accounts payable master file.
18. Reconcile the bank account.

### Required

You are to divide the accounting-related duties 1 through 18 among Robert Smith, James Cooper, and Bill Miller. All of the responsibilities marked with a dagger are assumed to take about the same amount of time and must be divided equally between Smith and Cooper. Both employees are equally competent. Miller, who is president of the company, is not willing to perform any functions designated by a dagger and will only perform a maximum of two of the other functions.*

**9-26 (Objectives 9-1, 9-2, 9-3, 9-6)** Recently, while eating lunch with your family at a local cafeteria, you observe a practice that is somewhat unusual. As you reach the end of the cafeteria line, an adding machine operator asks how many persons are in your party. He then totals the food purchases on the trays for all of your family and writes the number of persons included in the group on the adding machine tape. He hands you the tape and asks you to pay when you finish eating. Near the end of the meal, you decide you want a piece of pie and coffee so you return to the line, select your food, and again go through the line. The adding machine operator goes through the same procedures, but this time he staples the second tape to the original and returns it to you.

When you leave the cafeteria, you hand the stapled adding machine tapes to the cash register operator, who totals the two tapes, takes your money, and puts the tapes on a spindle.

### Required

a. What internal controls has the cafeteria instituted for its operations?
b. How can the manager of the cafeteria evaluate the effectiveness of the controls?
c. How do these controls differ from those used by most cafeterias?
d. What are the costs and benefits of the cafeteria's system?

**9-27 (Objectives 9-2, 9-4, 9-5)** Lew Pherson and Vera Collier are friends who are employed by different CPA firms. One day during lunch they are discussing the importance of internal control in determining the amount of audit evidence required for an engagement. Pherson expresses the view that internal control must be carefully evaluated in all companies, regardless of their size, in a similar manner. His CPA firm requires a standard internal control questionnaire on every audit as well as a flowchart of every transaction area. In addition, he says the firm requires a careful evaluation of the system and a modification in the evidence accumulated based on the controls and weaknesses in the system.

Collier responds by saying she believes that internal control cannot be adequate in many of the small companies she audits, therefore, she simply ignores internal control and acts under the assumption of inadequate controls. She goes on to say, "Why should I spend a lot of time obtaining an understanding of internal control and assessing control risk when I know it has all kinds of weaknesses before I start? I would rather spend the time it takes to fill out all those forms in testing whether the statements are correct."

### Required

a. Express in general terms the most important difference between the nature of the potential controls available for large and small companies.
b. Criticize the positions taken by Pherson and Collier, and express your own opinion

*AICPA adapted

about the similarities and differences that should exist in understanding internal control and assessing control risk for different-sized companies.

**9-28 (Objective 9-6)** The following are partial descriptions of internal controls for companies engaged in the manufacturing business:

1. When Mr. Clark orders materials for his machine-rebuilding plant, he sends a duplicate purchase order to the receiving department. During the delivery of materials, Mr. Smith, the receiving clerk, records the receipt of shipment on this purchase order. After recording, Mr. Smith sends the purchase order to the accounting department, where it is used to record materials purchased and accounts payable. The materials are transported to the storage area by forklifts. The additional purchased quantities are recorded on storage records.
2. Every day hundreds of employees clock in using time cards at Generous Motors Corporation. The timekeepers collect these cards once a week and deliver them to the computer department. There the data on these time cards are entered into the computer. The information entered into the computer is used in the preparation of the labor cost distribution records, the payroll journal, and the payroll checks. The treasurer, Mrs. Webber, compares the payroll journal with the payroll checks, signs the checks, and returns them to Mr. Strode, the supervisor of the computer department. The payroll checks are distributed to the employees by Mr. Strode.
3. The smallest branch of Connor Cosmetics in South Bend employs Mary Cooper, the branch manager, and her sales assistant, Janet Hendrix. The branch uses a bank account in South Bend to pay expenses. The account is kept in the name of "Connor Cosmetics—Special Account." To pay expenses, checks must be signed by Mary Cooper or by the treasurer of Connor Cosmetics, John Winters. Cooper receives the cancelled checks and bank statements. She reconciles the branch account herself and files cancelled checks and bank statements in her records. She also periodically prepares reports of cash disbursements and sends them to the home office.

## Required

a. List the weaknesses in internal control for each of the above. To identify the weaknesses, use the methodology that was discussed in the chapter.

b. For each weakness, state the type of misstatement(s) that is (are) likely to result. Be as specific as possible.

c. How would you improve internal controls for each of the three companies?*

**9-29 (Objective 9-6)** The Art Appreciation Society operates a museum for the benefit and enjoyment of the community.

When the museum is open to the public, two clerks who are positioned at the entrance collect a $5.00 admission fee from each nonmember patron. Members of the Art Appreciation Society are permitted to enter free of charge upon presentation of their membership cards.

At the end of each day, one of the clerks delivers the proceeds to the treasurer. The treasurer counts the cash in the presence of the clerk and places it in a safe. Each Friday afternoon the treasurer and one of the clerks deliver all cash held in the safe to the bank, and receive an authenticated deposit slip that provides the basis for the weekly entry in the accounting records.

The Art Appreciation Society board of directors has identified a need to improve its internal controls over cash admission fees. The board has determined that the cost of installing turnstiles, sales booths, or otherwise altering the physical layout of the museum will greatly exceed any benefits.

However, the board has agreed that the sale of admission tickets must be an integral part of its improvement efforts.

Smith has been asked by the board of directors of the Art Appreciation Society to review the internal control over cash admission fees and provide suggestions for improvements.

*AICPA adapted

## Required

Indicate weaknesses in the existing internal controls over cash admission fees that Smith should identify, and recommend one improvement for each of the weaknesses identified. To identify the weaknesses, use the methodology that was discussed in the chapter. Organize the answer as indicated in the following illustrative example:*

| Weakness | Recommendation |
|---|---|
| 1. There is no basis for establishing the documentation of the number of paying patrons. | 1. Prenumbered admission tickets should be issued upon payment of the admission fee. |

**9-30 (Objective 9-6)** Anthony, CPA, prepared the flowchart on page 325, which portrays the raw materials purchasing function of one of Anthony's clients, Medium-Sized Manufacturing Company, from the preparation of initial documents through the vouching of invoices for payment in accounts payable. Assume that all documents are prenumbered.

## Required

Identify the weaknesses of internal control that can be determined from the flowchart. Use the methodology discussed in the chapter. Include internal control weaknesses resulting from activities performed or not performed.*

# CASE

**9-31 (Objective 9-6)** The following is the description of sales and cash receipts for the Lady's Fashion Fair, a retail store dealing in expensive women's clothing. Sales are for cash or credit, using the store's own billing rather than credit cards.

Each salesclerk has her own sales book with prenumbered, three-copy, multicolored sales slips attached, but perforated. Only a central cash register is used. It is operated by the store supervisor, who has been employed for 10 years by Alice Olson, the store owner. The cash register is at the store entrance to control theft of clothes.

Salesclerks prepare the sales invoices in triplicate. The original and the second copy are given to the cashier. The third copy is retained by the salesclerk in the sales book. When the sale is for cash, the customer pays the salesclerk, who marks all three copies "paid"and presents the money to the cashier with the invoice copies.

All clothing is put into boxes or packages by the supervisor after comparing the clothing to the description on the invoice and the price on the sales tag. She also rechecks the clerk's calculations. Any corrections are approved by the salesclerk. The clerk changes her sales book at that time.

A credit sale is approved by the supervisor from an approved credit list after the salesclerk prepares the three-part invoice. Next, the supervisor enters the sale in her cash register as a credit or cash sale. The second copy of the invoice, which has been validated by the cash register, is given to the customer.

At the end of the day, the supervisor recaps the sales and cash and compares the totals to the cash register tape. The supervisor deposits the cash at the end of each day in the bank's lock box. The cashier's copies of the invoices are sent to the accounts receivable clerk along with a summary of the day's receipts. The bank mails the deposit slip directly to the accounts receivable clerk.

*AICPA adapted

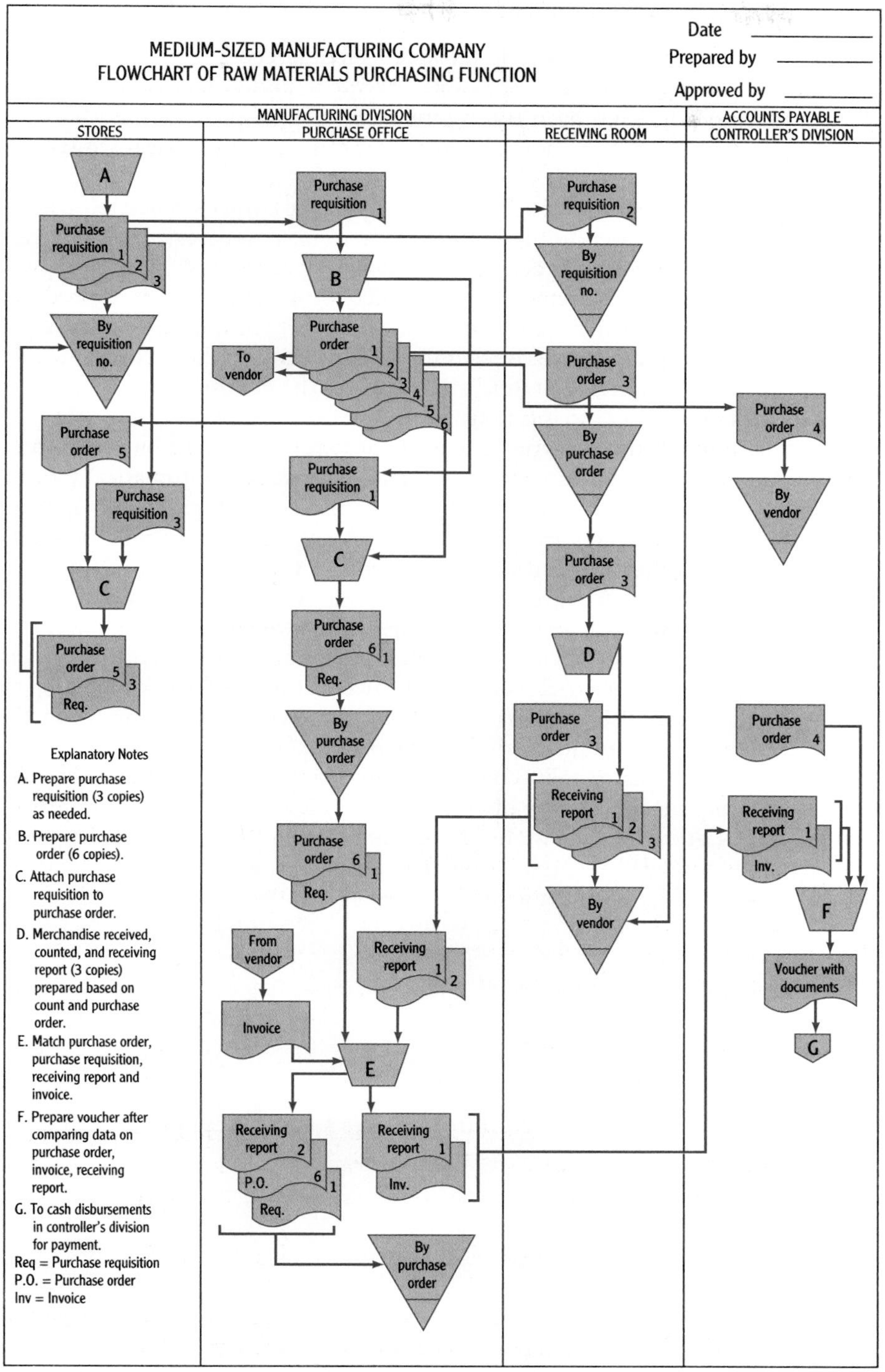
MEDIUM-SIZED MANUFACTURING COMPANY
FLOWCHART OF RAW MATERIALS PURCHASING FUNCTION
Date
Prepared by
Approved by
MANUFACTURING DIVISION
STORES
PURCHASE OFFICE
RECEIVING ROOM
ACCOUNTS PAYABLE
CONTROLLER'S DIVISION
A
Purchase requisition 1 2 3
By requisition no.
Purchase order 5
Purchase requisition 3
C
Purchase order 5 3
Req.
Purchase requisition 1
B
Purchase order 1 2 3 4 5 6
To vendor
Purchase requisition 1
C
Purchase order 6 1
Req.
By purchase order
Purchase order 6 1
Req.
From vendor
Invoice
Receiving report 1 2
E
Receiving report 2
P.O. 6 1
Req.
Receiving report 1
Inv.
By purchase order
Purchase requisition 2
By requisition no.
Purchase order 3
By purchase order
Purchase order 3
D
Purchase order 3
Receiving report 1 2 3
By vendor
Purchase order 4
By vendor
Purchase order 4
Receiving report 1
Inv.
F
Voucher with documents
G
Explanatory Notes
A. Prepare purchase requisition (3 copies) as needed.
B. Prepare purchase order (6 copies).
C. Attach purchase requisition to purchase order.
D. Merchandise received, counted, and receiving report (3 copies) prepared based on count and purchase order.
E. Match purchase order, purchase requisition, receiving report and invoice.
F. Prepare voucher after comparing data on purchase order, invoice, receiving report.
G. To cash disbursements in controller's division for payment.
Req = Purchase requisition
P.O. = Purchase order
Inv = Invoice

Each clerk summarizes her sales each day on a daily summary form, which is used in part to calculate employees' sales commissions. Marge, the accountant who is prohibited from handling cash, receives the supervisor's summary and the clerk's daily summary form. Daily, she puts all sales invoice information into the firm's computer, which provides a complete printout of all input and summaries. The accounting summary includes sales by salesclerk, cash sales, credit sales, and total sales. Marge compares this output to the supervisor's and salesclerks' summaries and reconciles all differences.

The computer updates accounts receivable, inventory, and general ledger master files. After the update procedure has been run on the computer, Marge's assistant files all sales invoices by customer number. A list of the invoice numbers in numerical sequence is included in the sales printout.

The mail is opened each morning by a secretary in the owner's office. All correspondence and complaints are given to the owner. The secretary prepares a prelist of cash receipts. He totals the list, prepares a deposit slip, and deposits the cash daily. A copy of the prelist, the deposit slip, and all remittances returned with the cash receipts are given to Marge. She uses this list and the remittances to record cash receipts and update accounts receivable, again by computer. She reconciles the total receipts on the prelist to the deposit slip and to her printout. At the same time, she compares the deposit slip received from the bank for cash sales to the cash receipts journal.

Marge prepares a weekly aged trial balance of accounts receivable by use of the computer. A separate listing of all unpaid bills over 60 days is also automatically prepared. These are given to Mrs. Olson, who acts as her own credit collector. She also approves all charge-offs of uncollectible items and forwards the list to Marge, who writes them off.

Each month Marge prepares and mails statements to customers. Complaints and disagreements from customers are directed to Mrs. Olson, who resolves them and informs Marge in writing of any write-downs or misstatements that require correction.

The computer system also automatically totals the journals and posts the totals to the general ledger. A general ledger trial balance is printed out from which Marge prepares financial statements. Marge also prepares a monthly bank reconciliation and reconciles the general ledger to the aged accounts receivable trial balance.

Because of the importance of inventory control, Marge prints out the inventory perpetual totals monthly, on the last day of each month. Salesclerks count all inventory after store hours on the last day of each month for comparison to the perpetuals. An inventory shortages report is provided to Mrs. Olson. The perpetuals are adjusted by Marge after Mrs. Olson has approved the adjustments.

### Required

a. For each sales transaction-related audit objective, identify one or more existing controls.

b. For each cash receipts transaction-related audit objective, identify one or more existing controls.

c. Identify weaknesses of internal control for sales and cash receipts.

## INTEGRATED CASE APPLICATION

9-32 (Objective 9-6) **ABC AUDIT—PART I** This case study is presented in four parts. Each part deals with the material in the chapter in which that part appears. However, the parts are connected in such a way that in completing all four, you will gain a better understanding of how the parts of the audit are interrelated and integrated by the audit process. The parts appear in the following locations:

Part I—Understand internal control and assess control risk for the acquisition and payment cycle, Chapter 9, pages 326–328.

Part II—Design tests of controls and substantive tests of transactions, Chapter 11, pages 401–402.

Part III—Determine sample sizes using audit sampling and evaluate results, Chapter 12, pages 442–443.

Part IV—Evaluation of the results of analytical procedures and tests of details of balances, Chapter 13, pages 476–481.

### Background Information

ABC Company is a medium-sized manufacturing company with a December 31 year-end. You have been assigned the responsibility of auditing the acquisition and payment cycle and one related balance sheet account, accounts payable. The general approach to be taken will be to reduce assessed control risk to a low level, if possible, for the two main types of transactions affecting accounts payable: acquisitions and cash disbursements. The following are furnished as background information:

Figure 9-9—A summary of key information from the audit of the acquisition and payment cycle and accounts payable in the prior year's audit.

Figure 9-10—A flowchart description of the accounting system and internal controls for the acquisition and payment cycle.

**FIGURE 9-9**

**Information for Audit of Accounts Payable—Previous Year**

| | |
|---|---|
| Accounts payable, 12-31-96 | |
| Number of accounts | 52 |
| Total accounts payable | $163,892.27 |
| Range of individual balances | $27.83–$14,819.62 |
| Tolerable misstatement for accounts payable | $6,500 |
| Transactions, 1996 | |
| Acquisitions: | |
| Number of acquisitions | 3,800 |
| Total acquisitions | $2,933,812 |
| Cash disbursements: | |
| Number of disbursements | 2,600 |
| Total cash disbursements | $3,017,112 |
| Results of audit procedures—tests of controls and substantive tests of transactions for acquisitions (sample size of 100): | |
| Purchase order not approved | 2 |
| Purchase quantities, prices, and/or extensions not correct | 1 |
| Transactions charged to wrong general ledger account | 1 |
| Transactions recorded in wrong period | 1 |
| No other exceptions | |
| Results of audit procedures—cash disbursements (sample size of 100): | |
| Cash disbursement recorded in wrong period | 1 |
| No other exceptions | |
| Results of audit procedures—accounts payable | |
| 20 percent of vendors' balances were verified; combined net understatement amounts were projected to the population as follows: | |
| Three cutoff misstatements | $4,873.28 |
| One difference in amounts due to disputes and discounts | $1,103.12 |
| No adjustment was necessary, since the total projected misstatement was not material. | |

### Part I

The purpose of Part I is to obtain an understanding of internal control and assess control risk for ABC Company's acquisitions and cash disbursement transactions.

## Required

Study Figures 9-9 and 9-10 to gain an understanding of ABC's internal control for the acquisition and payment cycle. Assess control risk as high, medium, or low on an objective-by-objective basis for the acquisition and payment cycle's internal controls, considering both internal controls and weaknesses. You should use a matrix similar to the one in Figure 9-6, page 312, for the assessment. There should be one matrix for acquisitions and a separate one for cash disbursements. The source of the internal controls and weaknesses is the information in Figure 9-10.

**FIGURE 9-10**

**ABC Company—Acquisition and Payment Cycle**

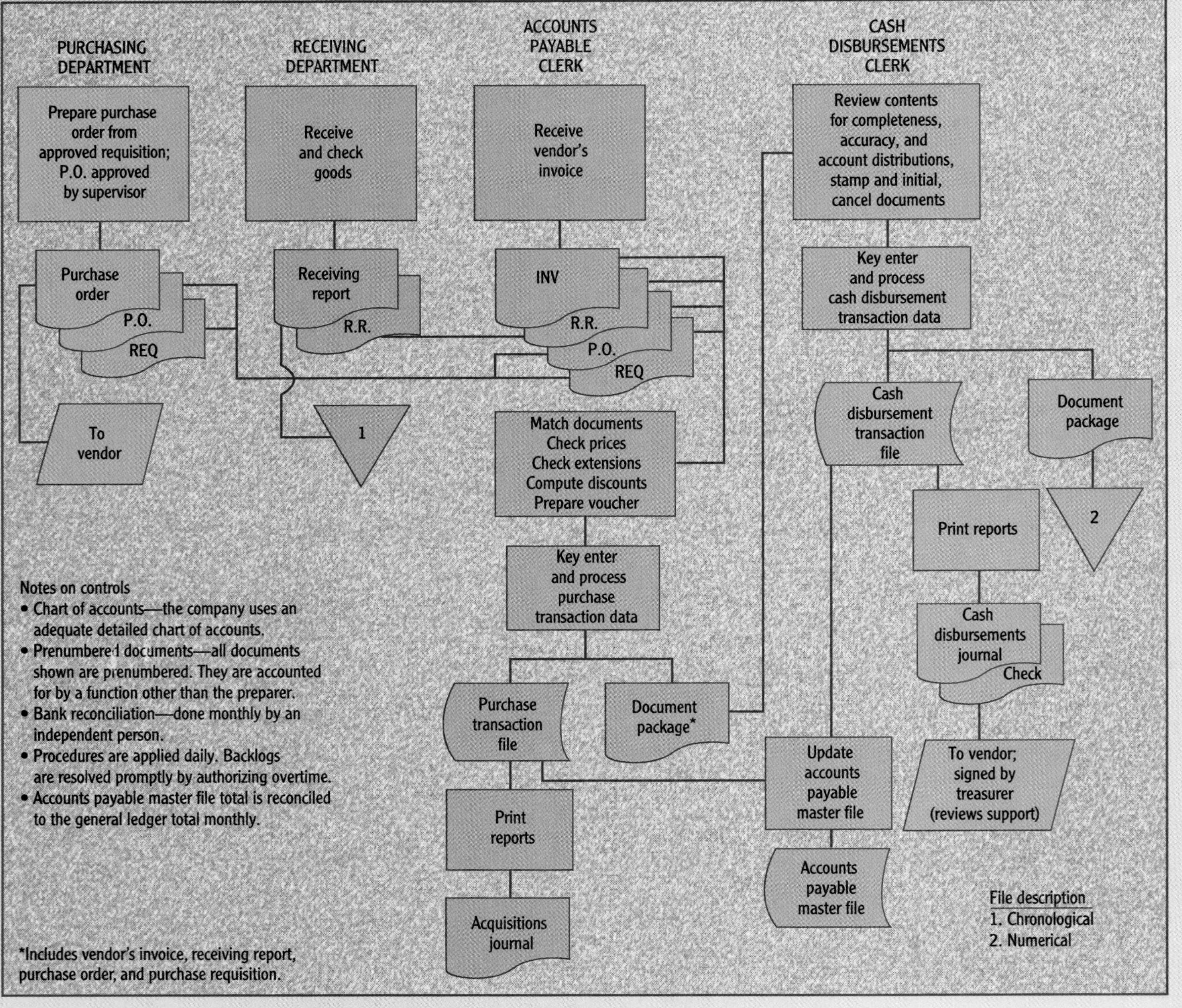


Notes on controls
- Chart of accounts—the company uses an adequate detailed chart of accounts.
- Prenumbered documents—all documents shown are prenumbered. They are accounted for by a function other than the preparer.
- Bank reconciliation—done monthly by an independent person.
- Procedures are applied daily. Backlogs are resolved promptly by authorizing overtime.
- Accounts payable master file total is reconciled to the general ledger total monthly.

*Includes vendor's invoice, receiving report, purchase order, and purchase requisition.

# 10

# OVERALL AUDIT PLAN AND AUDIT PROGRAM

## LEARNING OBJECTIVES

Thorough study of this chapter will enable you to

**10-1** Describe the five types of audit tests used to determine whether financial statements are fairly stated.

**10-2** Discuss the relative costs of each type of test, the relationships between types of tests and types of evidence, and the relationships among types of tests.

**10-3** Understand the meaning of evidence mix and how it should be varied in different circumstances.

**10-4** Know the methodology for the design of an audit program.

**10-5** Understand the relationship of transaction-related audit objectives to balance-related audit objectives.

**10-6** Integrate the four phases of the audit process.

## HOW MUCH AND WHAT KIND OF TESTING WILL GET THE JOB DONE?

Terry Holland and Al Baker have known each other for years, and it seems like the debate they are having has been going on that long as well. Terry is a partner in the Southern California office of a national accounting firm. Al is an auditing professor at a nearby university. They get together once a month faithfully for lunch, and the conversation always gets around to auditing theory versus practice. Following is their most recent conversation:

PROFESSOR AL A shortcoming of GAAS is that it offers too many choices of approaches. An auditor can do an audit with virtually no testing of detailed transactions by relying on observation, inquiry, analytical procedures, and tests of details of balances involving only large items. In a highly competitive market like we have now, I am concerned that firms will take the lowest cost approach instead of being concerned enough about quality. There is already evidence that this is happening by CPA firms shifting away from large sample sizes.

PARTNER TERRY Auditors must understand internal control on all audits and where control risk is reduced below the maximum, some tests of controls and substantive tests of transactions are always done to support that reduction. Detailed cutoff tests are always performed and it is appropriate to concentrate on larger items in tests of details of balances. We only take this efficient approach on the clients that don't present any real risks. Where risks are high, we pull out all the stops and do a lot of detailed testing.

PROFESSOR AL That sounds fine, but there are certain things that only detailed testing will find. I'm thinking specifically about misappropriation of assets. I'm sure your clients expect you to find it, but analytical procedures and tests of large items at year-end won't get that job done. What about that?

PARTNER TERRY Well, Al, our clients also tell us they want our opinion on their financial statements at as low a cost as possible. If we went looking for misappropriation of assets in every audit, our costs would go through the roof. And I'll tell you, the best way for the client to deal with fraud is to have good controls. We focus our attention on giving them good recommendations for improving their controls. It's "value-added" and they appreciate that.

PROFESSOR AL I'm not convinced. I'm sure your clients would appreciate it a lot more if you actually found that John Bookkeeper was dipping his fingers into the till, but I'm also concerned about the reduction in testing to search for errors as well as fraud. Some of my former students were telling me at "meet-the-firms night" last week that some of the tests of account balances they're doing involve samples of less than ten items. Aren't you worried about that?

PARTNER TERRY That does happen, Al, but only under very carefully controlled circumstances. As you know, we use monetary unit sampling. When controls are good, analytical procedures don't indicate problems, and the tests are spread across all the major asset accounts, the sample sizes for any individual account will seem very small. But remember, if we find just one exception in any of the sample items, we'll expand our tests.

PROFESSOR AL I understand that, Terry, but you know, it seems to me you guys are taking the requirements of GAAS and figuring out how to audit so efficiently that you're not allowing any slack in the process. I think you're creeping more and more toward being an insurer rather than an assurer of the financial statements.

PARTNER TERRY What do you mean, Al? I don't understand your theory at all.

PROFESSOR AL Well, you guys are counting on most of your clients not having misstated financial statements, doing minimal audit work at relatively high fees, and then banking on the fact that you'll be able to absorb the cost of any damages you suffer from bad audit opinions.

PARTNER TERRY Oh come on, Al, sitting in this ivory tower of yours has turned you into a cynic. I hope you don't talk to your students this way. Auditors do a terrific job and there are lots of incentives for high quality. We want people to come into the profession with a positive attitude. Let's talk about something else. Say, I believe it's your turn to pay.

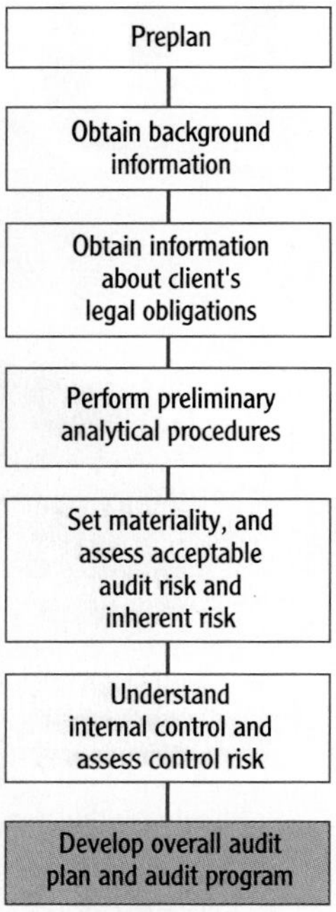


The first six steps in the planning process are primarily for the purpose of helping the auditor develop an effective and efficient audit plan and audit program. As was indicated in Chapter 6, the audit program includes a listing of all of the audit procedures to be used to gather sufficient, competent evidence. The related details for each procedure regarding sample size, the items to select, and the timing of the tests are also included.

The most important consideration in developing the audit plan and audit program is the planning form of the audit risk model:

$$PDR = \frac{AAR}{IR \times CR}$$

where

$PDR$ = planned detection risk

$AAR$ = acceptable audit risk

$IR$ = inherent risk

$CR$ = control risk

In previous chapters, each of the independent variables (*AAR, IR, CR*) has been discussed. In this chapter the relationship between these three variables and the dependent variable (*PDR*) is studied.

In this chapter, the audit plan and audit program are discussed in terms of five types of audit tests. First, the nature of each type of test is defined and discussed. Next, the relative emphasis on the different types of tests that result from differing audit plans is studied. The chapter ends with a summary of the audit process as developed in this and the previous five chapters.

## TYPES OF TESTS

**OBJECTIVE 10-1**
**Describe the five types of audit tests used to determine whether financial statements are fairly stated.**

Auditors use five types of tests to determine whether financial statements are fairly stated: *procedures to obtain an understanding of internal control, tests of controls, substantive tests of transactions, analytical procedures,* and *tests of details of balances.* The first two types of tests are performed to reduce assessed control risk, whereas the last three are all substantive tests. Substantive tests are used to reduce planned detection risk. All audit procedures fall into one, and sometimes more than one, of these five categories.

### Procedures to Obtain an Understanding of Internal Control

The methodology and procedures used to obtain an understanding of internal control were studied in Chapter 9. During this phase of an audit, the auditor must focus attention on both the *design* and the *operation* of aspects of internal control to the extent necessary to effectively plan the rest of the audit. A critical point made in Chapter 9 was the requirement to support the understanding obtained with evidence. The purpose of the procedures is to obtain an understanding and provide evidence to support that understanding. Five types of audit procedures that relate to the auditor's understanding of internal control were identified in Chapter 9:

- Update and evaluate the auditor's previous experience with the entity.
- Make inquiries of client personnel.
- Read clients' policy and systems manuals.
- Examine documents and records.
- Observe entity activities and operations.

## Tests of Controls

A major use of the auditor's understanding of internal control is to assess control risk for each transaction-related audit objective. Examples are assessing the accuracy objective for sales transactions as low and the existence objective as moderate. Where the auditor believes control policies and procedures are effectively designed, and where it is efficient to do so, he or she will elect to assess control risk at a level that reflects that evaluation. In making this risk assessment, however, assessed control risk must be limited to the level supported by evidence. The procedures used to obtain such evidence are called tests of controls.

Tests of controls are performed to determine the effectiveness of both the design and operations of specific internal controls. These tests include the following types of procedures:

- Make inquiries of appropriate client personnel.
- Examine documents, records, and reports.
- Observe control-related activities.
- Reperform client procedures.

The first two procedures are the same as those used to obtain an understanding of internal control. Thus, performing tests of controls can be thought of as a continuation of the audit procedures used to obtain the understanding of internal control. The main difference is that with tests of controls, the objective is more specific and the tests are more extensive. For example, if the client's budgeting process is to be used as a basis for assessing a low level of risk that expenditures are misclassified, in addition to the procedures described in the example given for obtaining an understanding, the auditor might also select a recent budget report, trace its contents to source records, prove its mathematical accuracy, examine all variance reports and memos that flow from it, talk to responsible personnel about the follow-up actions they took, and examine documentation in support of those actions. In effect, when the auditor decides to assess control risk below the maximum for any transaction-related audit objective, the procedures used to obtain an understanding of internal control are combined with the tests of controls. The amount of additional evidence required for tests of controls depends on the extent of evidence obtained in gaining the understanding.

To illustrate typical tests of controls, it is useful to return to the control risk matrix for Airtight Machine Company in Figure 9-6 (page 312). For each of the ten controls included in Figure 9-6, Table 10-1 (page 332) identifies a test of control that might be performed to test its effectiveness. Notice that no test of control is performed for the weakness in Figure 9-6. It would make no sense to determine if the absence of a control is being adequately performed.

## Substantive Tests of Transactions

A *substantive test* is a procedure designed to test for dollar misstatements directly affecting the correctness of financial statement balances. Such misstatements (often termed *monetary misstatements*) are a clear indication of the misstatement of the accounts. There are three types of substantive tests: substantive tests of transactions, analytical procedures, and tests of details of balances.

The purpose of *substantive tests of transactions* is to determine whether all six transaction-related audit objectives have been satisfied for each class of transactions. For example, the auditor performs substantive tests of transactions to test whether recorded transactions exist and existing transactions are recorded. The auditor also performs these tests to determine if recorded sales transactions are accurately recorded, recorded in the appropriate time period, correctly classified, and are accurately summarized and posted to the general ledger and master files. If the auditor is confident that transactions were correctly recorded in the journals and correctly posted, he or she can be confident that general ledger totals are correct.

The effect of performing substantive tests of transactions is illustrated in Figure 10-1 on page 333. For simplicity, two assumptions are made. First, only sales and cash receipts transactions and three general ledger balances make up the sales and collection cycle. Second, the beginning balances in cash ($47) and accounts receivable ($96) were audited in

**TABLE 10-1**

**Illustration of Tests of Controls**

| Illustrative Key Controls | Typical Tests of Controls |
|---|---|
| Credit is approved before shipment occurs. | Examine a page of customer orders to determine the existence of authorized initials indicating credit approval (documentation). |
| Sales are supported by authorized shipping documents and approved customer orders, which are attached to the duplicate sales invoice. | Examine a sample of duplicate sales invoices to determine that each one is supported by an attached authorized shipping document and approved customer order (documentation). |
| Separation of duties between billing, recording sales, and handling cash receipts. | Observe whether personnel responsible for handling cash have no accounting responsibilities and inquire as to their duties (observation and inquiry). |
| An approved price list is used to determine unit selling prices. | Observe whether a price list is used when invoices are prepared and compare the price list with a list of current selling prices (observation and documentation). |
| Shipping documents are forwarded to billing daily and billed the subsequent day. | Observe whether shipping documents are forwarded daily to billing and observe when they are billed (observation). |
| Shipping documents and duplicate sales invoice numbers are accounted for weekly and traced to the sales journal. | Account for a sequence of duplicate sales invoices and shipping documents and trace each to the sales journal (documentation and reperformance). |
| Shipping documents are batched daily by quantity shipped. | Examine a sample of daily batches, re-add the shipping quantities, and trace totals to reconciliation with input reports (reperformance). |
| Statements are mailed to all customers each month. | Observe whether statements are mailed for a month and inquire about whose responsibility it is (observation and inquiry). |
| There is an adequate chart of accounts. | Examine a sample of sales invoices to determine whether each one has an account number and that the account number is correct (documentation and reperformance). |
| The sales journal is reviewed monthly for reasonableness of total and compared to the general ledger for sales and sales returns. | Re-add the sales journal for one month and trace the total to the general ledger (reperformance). |

the previous year and are considered correct. If the auditor verifies that sales ($660) and cash receipt ($590) transactions were correctly recorded in the journals and posted in the general ledger, he or she can conclude that the ending balance in accounts receivable ($166) and sales ($660) are correct. [Cash disbursements ($563) will have to be audited before the auditor can reach a conclusion about the balance in cash in bank.] The auditor verifies the recording and summarizing of transactions by performing substantive tests of transactions. In this example, there is one set of tests for sales and another for cash receipts.

Tests of controls can be performed separately from all other tests, but, for efficiency, they are frequently done at the same time as substantive tests of transactions. For example, tests of controls involving documentation and reperformance usually are applied to the same transactions tested for monetary misstatements. In fact, reperformance always simultaneously provides evidence about both controls and monetary correctness. In the remainder of this book, it is assumed that tests of controls and substantive tests of transactions are done at the same time.

**FIGURE 10-1**

**Relationship of Transactions to Journals and General Ledger**

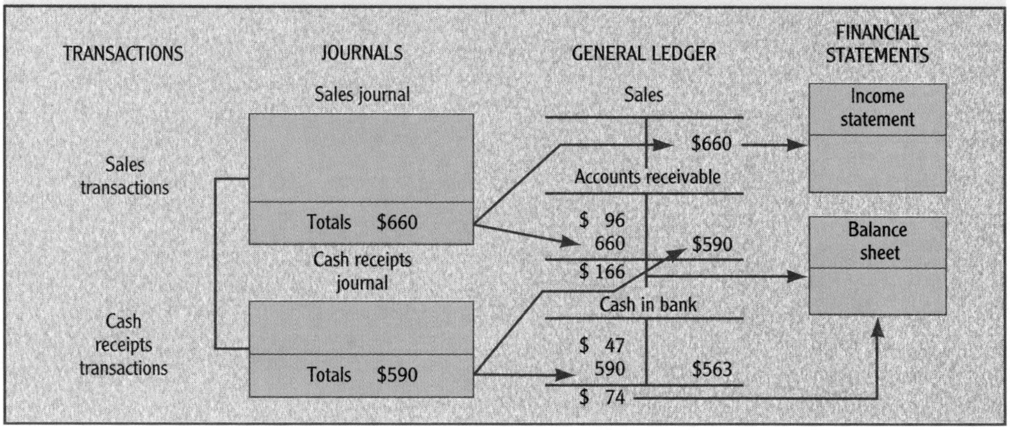


## Analytical Procedures

As discussed in Chapter 6, *analytical procedures* involve comparisons of recorded amounts to expectations developed by the auditor. They often involve the calculation of ratios by the auditor for comparison with the previous years' ratios and other related data. For example, in Figure 10-1 the auditor could compare sales, cash receipts, and accounts receivable in the current year to amounts in previous years and calculate the gross margin percentage for comparison to previous years.

There are four purposes of analytical procedures, all of which were discussed in Chapter 6: understand the client's business, assess the entity's ability to continue as a going concern, indicate the presence of possible misstatements in the financial statements, and reduce detailed audit tests. All of these, but especially the last two, help the auditor decide the extent of other audit tests. To illustrate, if analytical procedures indicate that there may be misstatements, more extensive investigation may be needed. An example is an unexpected change in the current year's gross margin percentage compared to the previous year's. Other tests may be needed to determine if there is a misstatement in sales or cost of goods sold that caused the change. On the other hand, if no material differences are found using analytical procedures and the auditor concludes that differences should not have occurred, other tests may be reduced. The SASs state that analytical procedures can be used as substantive tests.

## Tests of Details of Balances

*Tests of details of balances* focus on the ending general ledger balances for both balance sheet and income statement accounts, but the primary emphasis in most tests of details of balances is on the balance sheet. Examples include confirmation of customer balances for accounts receivable, physical examination of inventory, and examination of vendor's statements for accounts payable. These tests of ending balances are essential because the evidence is usually obtained from a source independent of the client and, thus, is considered to be highly reliable.

Examine Figure 10-1 to see the role of tests of details of balances in the audit. There are three general ledger accounts in the figure: sales, accounts receivable, and cash in bank. Detailed tests of the balances in these accounts will be performed. These include audit procedures such as confirmation of account receivable balances, sales cutoff tests, and review of bank account reconciliations. The extent of these tests depends on the results of tests of controls, substantive tests of transactions, and analytical procedures for these accounts.

Tests of details of balances have the objective of establishing the monetary correctness of the accounts they relate to and, therefore, are substantive tests. For example, confirmations test for monetary misstatements and are therefore substantive. Similarly, counts of inventory and cash on hand are also substantive tests.

**FIGURE 10-2**

**Types of Audit Tests and the Audit Risk Model**

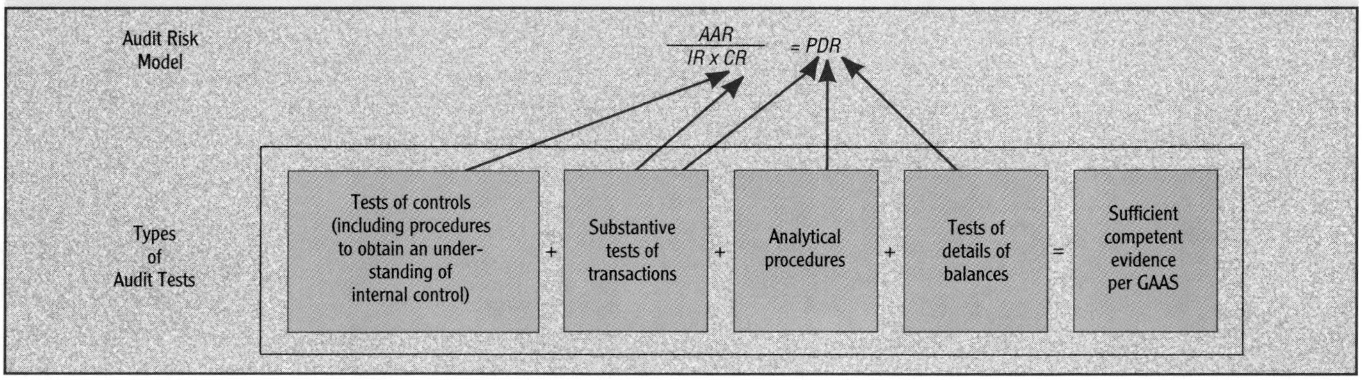


## Summary of Types of Tests

Figure 10-2 summarizes the types of audit tests. Procedures to obtain an understanding of internal control and tests of controls are combined in Figure 10-2 because they are essentially the same. Relating the information in Figure 10-2 to that in Figure 10-1, we see that substantive tests of transactions emphasize the verification of transactions recorded in the journals and then posted in the general ledger, analytical procedures emphasize the overall reasonableness of transactions and the general ledger balances, and tests of details of balances emphasize the ending balances in the general ledger. Procedures to obtain an understanding of internal control and tests of controls are concerned with evaluating whether controls are sufficiently effective to justify reducing control risk and thereby reducing substantive audit tests.

Figure 10-2 also shows the relationships of the types of tests to the audit risk model. Observe that all five types of tests are used to satisfy sufficient competent evidence requirements. Also observe that procedures to obtain an understanding and tests of controls reduce control risk, whereas the three substantive tests are used to satisfy planned detection risk.

Figure 10-3 shows how the five types of tests are used to obtain assurance in the audit of one account, accounts receivable. The totals in the account are taken from Figure 10-1, page 333. It is apparent from examining Figure 10-3 that the auditor obtained a higher

**FIGURE 10-3**

**Types of Audit Tests and Audit Assurance for Accounts Receivable**

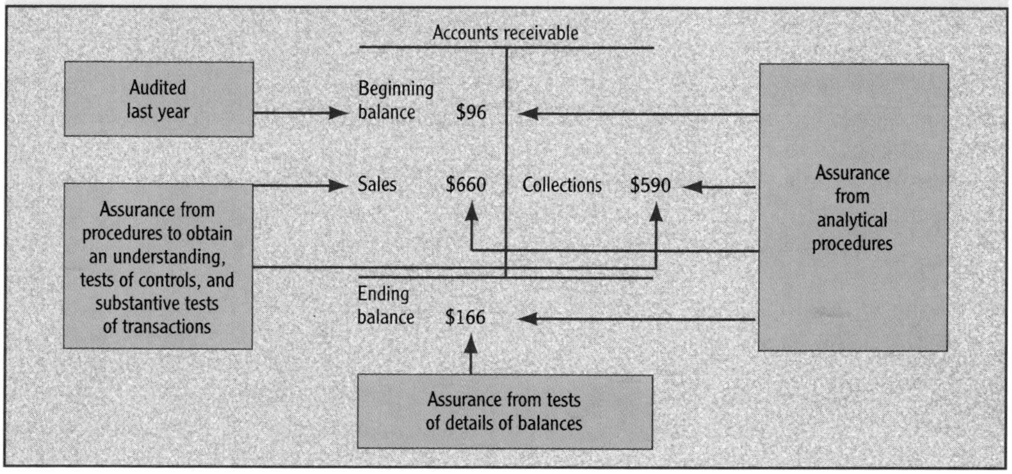

overall assurance for accounts receivable than the assurance obtained from any one test. The auditor can increase overall assurance by increasing the assurance obtained from any of the tests.

## RELATIONSHIP BETWEEN TESTS AND EVIDENCE

**OBJECTIVE 10-2**

**Discuss the relative costs of each type of test, the relationships between types of tests and types of evidence, and the relationships among types of tests.**

Only certain types of evidence (confirmation, documentation, and so forth) are obtained through each of the five types of tests. Table 10-2 summarizes the relationship between types of tests and types of evidence. Several observations about Table 10-2 follow:

- Procedures to obtain an understanding of internal control and tests of controls involve only observation, documentation, inquiry, and reperformance. Substantive tests of transactions involve only the last three of these types of evidence.
- More types of evidence are obtained by using tests of details of balances than by using any other type of test. Only tests of details of balances involve confirmation and physical examination.
- Inquiries of clients are made with every type of test.
- Documentation and reperformance are used for every type of test except analytical procedures.

**TABLE 10-2**

**Relationship Between Types of Tests and Evidence**

| Type of Test | Type of Evidence | | | | | | |
|---|---|---|---|---|---|---|---|
| | Physical Examination | Confirmation | Documentation | Observation | Inquiries of the Client | Reperformance | Analytical Procedures |
| Procedures to obtain an understanding of internal control | | | ✓ | ✓ | ✓ | ✓ | |
| Tests of controls | | | ✓ | ✓ | ✓ | ✓ | |
| Substantive tests of transactions | | | ✓ | | ✓ | ✓ | |
| Analytical procedures | | | | | ✓ | | ✓ |
| Tests of details of balances | ✓ | ✓ | ✓ | | ✓ | ✓ | |

### Relative Costs

The types of tests are listed in order of increasing cost as follows:

- Analytical procedures
- Procedures to obtain an understanding of internal control and tests of controls
- Substantive tests of transactions
- Tests of details of balances

The reason analytical procedures are least costly is the relative ease of making calculations and comparisons. Often, considerable information about potential misstatements can be obtained by simply comparing two or three numbers. Frequently auditors calculate these ratios using computer software at almost no cost.

Tests of controls are also low in cost because the auditor is making inquiries and observations and examining such things as initials on documents and outward indications of other controls. Frequently, tests of controls can be done on a large number of items in a few minutes.

Substantive tests of transactions are more expensive than tests of controls that do not include reperformance because recalculations and tracings are often required.

Tests of details of balances are almost always considerably more costly than any of the other types of procedures. It is costly to send confirmations and to count assets. Because of the high cost of details of balances, auditors usually try to plan the audit to minimize their use.

Naturally, the cost of each type of evidence varies in different situations. For example, the cost of an auditor's test-counting inventory (a substantive test of the details of the inventory balance) frequently depends on the nature and dollar value of the inventory, its location, and the number of different items.

### Relationship between Tests of Controls and Substantive Tests

To understand better the nature of tests of controls and substantive tests, an examination of how they differ is useful. An exception in a test of control is only an *indication* of the likelihood of misstatements affecting the dollar value of the financial statements, whereas an exception in a substantive test *is* a financial statement misstatement. Exceptions in tests of controls are often referred to as *control test deviations.* Thus, control test deviations are significant only if they occur with sufficient frequency to cause the auditor to believe there may be material dollar misstatements in the statements. Substantive tests should then be performed to determine whether dollar misstatements have actually occurred.

As an illustration, assume that the client's controls require an independent clerk to verify the quantity, price, and extension of each sales invoice, after which the clerk must initial the duplicate invoice to indicate performance. A test of control audit procedure would be to examine a sample of duplicate sales invoices for the initials of the person who verified the quantitative data. If there are a significant number of documents without a signature, the auditor should follow up with substantive tests. This can be done by extending the tests of the duplicate sales invoices to include verifying prices, extensions, and footings (substantive tests of transactions) or by increasing the sample size for the confirmation of accounts receivable (substantive test of details of balances). Of course, even though the control is not operating effectively, the invoices may still be correct. This will be the case if the person originally preparing the sales invoices did a conscientious and competent job. Similarly, even if there is an initial, there may be monetary misstatements due to initialing without performance or careless performance of the internal control procedure. For these reasons, many auditors prefer to include reperformance as part of the original tests of controls. Others prefer to reperform, in the form of a substantive test, only when there is indication of the need to do so.

### Trade-off between Tests of Controls and Substantive Tests

As explained in Chapter 9, there is a trade-off between tests of controls and substantive tests. The auditor makes a decision during planning whether to assess control risk below the maximum. Tests of controls must be performed to determine whether the assessed control risk is supported. If it is, planned detection risk in the audit risk model is increased, and planned substantive tests can therefore be reduced. Figure 10-4 shows the relationship between substantive tests and control risk assessment (including tests of controls) at differing levels of internal control effectiveness.

The shaded area in Figure 10-4 is the maximum assurance obtainable from control risk assessment and tests of controls. For example, at any point to the left of point *A*, assessed control risk is 1.0 because the auditor evaluates internal controls as ineffective. Any point to the right of point *B* results in no further reduction of control risk because the CPA firm has established a minimum assessed control risk it will permit.

After the auditor decides the effectiveness of the client's internal controls, it is appropriate to select any point within the shaded area of Figure 10-4 consistent with the assessed

**FIGURE 10-4**

**Audit Assurance from Substantive Tests and Tests of Controls at Different Levels of Internal Control Effectiveness**

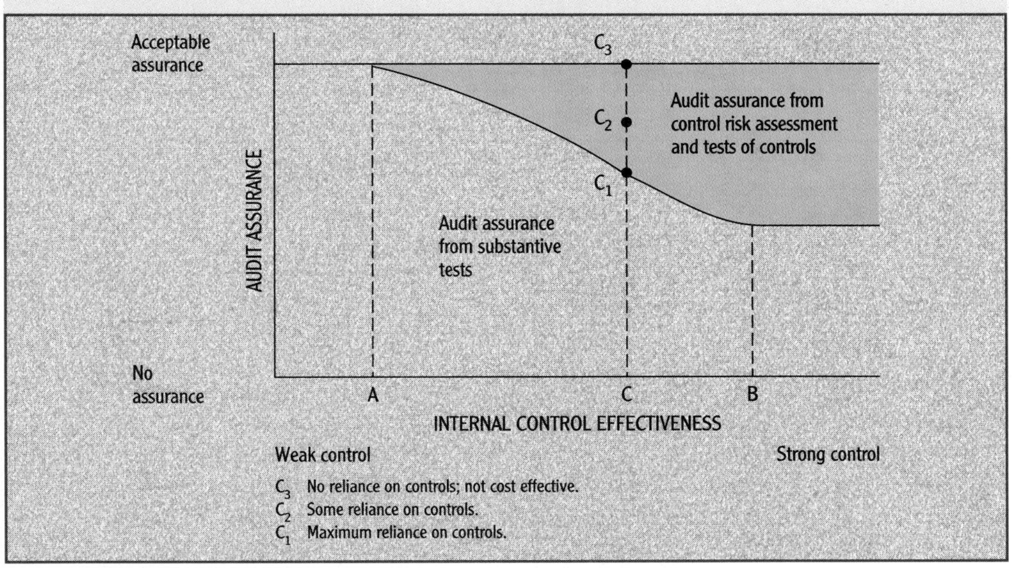


control risk the auditor decides to support. To illustrate, assume that the auditor contends that internal control effectiveness is at point *C*. Tests of controls at the $C_1$ level would provide the minimum control risk, given the internal controls. The auditor could choose to perform no tests of controls (point $C_3$) which would support a control risk of 1.0. Any point between the two, such as $C_2$, would also be appropriate. If $C_2$ is selected, the audit assurance from tests of controls is $C_3$–$C_2$ and from substantive tests is $C$–$C_2$. The auditor will likely select $C_1$, $C_2$, or $C_3$ based upon the relative cost of tests of controls and substantive tests.

## EVIDENCE MIX

**OBJECTIVE 10-3**
**Understand the meaning of evidence mix and how it should be varied in different circumstances.**

There are significant variations in the extent to which the five types of tests can be used in different audits for differing levels of internal control effectiveness and inherent risk. There can also be variations from cycle to cycle within a given audit. The combination of the five types of tests used for any given cycle is often referred to as the *evidence mix.* Table 10-3 on page 338 shows the evidence mix for four different audits. In each case, assume that sufficient competent evidence was accumulated. An analysis of each audit follows.

**Analysis of Audit 1** This client is a large company with sophisticated internal controls and low inherent risk. The auditor, therefore, performs extensive tests of controls and relies heavily on the client's internal controls to reduce substantive tests. Extensive analytical procedures are also performed to reduce other substantive tests. Substantive tests of transactions and tests of details of balances are, therefore, minimized. Because of the emphasis on tests of controls and analytical procedures, this audit can be done inexpensively.

**Analysis of Audit 2** This company is medium sized, with some controls and a few inherent risks. The auditor has, therefore, decided to do a medium amount of testing for all types of tests except analytical procedures, which will be done extensively. There will be more extensive testing done where there are specific inherent risks.

**TABLE 10-3**

**Variations in Evidence Mix**

| | Procedures to Obtain an Understanding of Internal Control | Tests of Controls | Substantive Tests of Transactions | Analytical Procedures | Tests of Details of Balances |
|---|---|---|---|---|---|
| Audit 1 | E | E | S | E | S |
| Audit 2 | M | M | M | E | M |
| Audit 3 | M | N | E | M | E |
| Audit 4 | M | M | E | E | E |

E = extensive amount of testing; M = medium amount of testing; S = small amount of testing; N = no testing.

**Analysis of Audit 3** This company is medium sized, but has few effective controls and significant inherent risks. Management has decided that it is not cost effective to have better internal controls. No tests of controls are done because reliance on internal controls is inappropriate when controls are insufficient. The emphasis is on tests of details of balances and substantive tests of transactions, but analytical procedures are also done. The reason for limiting analytical procedures is the auditor's expectations of misstatements in the account balances. The cost of the audit is likely to be relatively high because of the amount of detailed substantive testing.

**Analysis of Audit 4** The original plan on this audit was to follow the approach used in Audit 2. However, the auditor found extensive control test deviations and significant errors while performing substantive tests of transactions and analytical procedures. The auditor, therefore, concluded that the internal controls were not effective. Extensive tests of details of balances are performed to offset the unacceptable results of the other tests. The costs of this audit are higher because tests of controls and substantive tests of transactions were performed but could not be used to reduce tests of details of balances.

**CAN THE AUDITOR ALWAYS LIMIT EVIDENCE TO SUBSTANTIVE TESTS?**

The Auditing Standards Board issued an exposure draft to amend SAS 31 in 1996 that may affect the auditor's assessment of control risk.[1] Following is one of the proposed new paragraphs:

> In certain engagement environments where significant information is transmitted, processed, maintained or accessed electronically, the auditor may determine that it is not practical or possible to reduce detection risk to an acceptable level by performing only substantive tests for one or more financial statement assertions. For example, the potential for improper initiation or alteration of information to occur and not be detected may be greater when information is produced, maintained or accessible only in electronic form. In such circumstances, the auditor should consider performing tests of controls to support an assessed level of control risk below the maximum for certain assertions, such as completeness or occurrence.

[1]The Auditing Standards Board sends exposure drafts of all proposed SASs or amendments to interested parties for their comments. The comments are used to evaluate and revise the draft before issuing a final SAS or amendment.

## DESIGN OF THE AUDIT PROGRAM

**OBJECTIVE 10-4**
**Know the methodology for the design of an audit program.**

The audit program for most audits is designed in three parts: tests of controls and substantive tests of transactions, analytical procedures, and tests of details of balances. There will likely be a separate set of subaudit programs for each transaction cycle. An example in the sales and collection cycle might be tests of controls and substantive tests of transactions audit programs for sales and cash receipts; an analytical procedures audit program for the entire cycle; and tests of details of balances audit programs for cash, accounts receivable, bad debt expense, allowance for uncollectible accounts, and miscellaneous accounts receivable.

### Tests of Controls and Substantive Tests of Transactions

The tests of controls and substantive tests of transactions audit program normally includes a descriptive section documenting the understanding obtained about internal control. It is also likely to include a description of the procedures performed to obtain an understanding of internal control and assessed control risk. Both of these affect the tests of controls and substantive tests of transactions audit program. The methodology to design these tests is shown in Figure 10-5. The first three steps in the figure were described in Chapter 9. The audit procedures include both tests of controls and substantive tests of transactions and vary depending on assessed control risk. When controls are effective and assessed control risk is low, there will be heavy emphasis on tests of controls. Some substantive tests of transactions will also be included. If control risk is assessed at 1.0, only substantive tests of transactions will be used. The procedures already performed in obtaining an understanding of internal control will affect both tests of controls and substantive tests of transactions.

**Audit Procedures** The approach to designing tests of controls and substantive tests of transactions emphasizes satisfying the transaction-related audit objectives developed in Chapter 5. A four-step approach is followed when the auditor plans to reduce assessed control risk.

**FIGURE 10-5**
**Methodology for Designing Tests of Controls and Substantive Tests of Transactions**

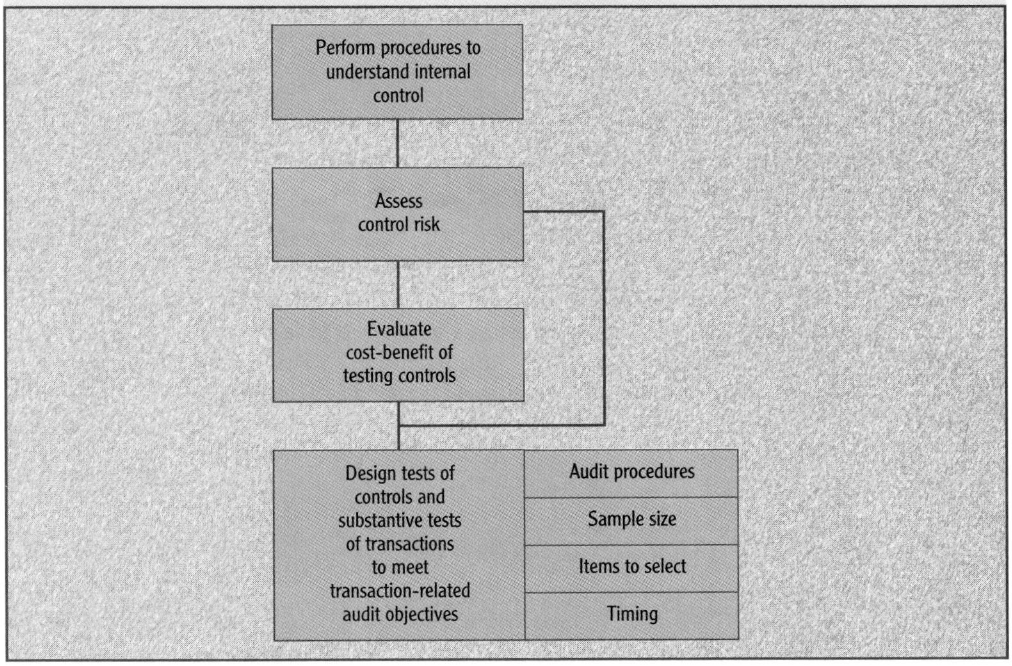

1. Apply the transaction-related audit objectives to the class of transactions being tested, such as sales.
2. Identify specific controls that should reduce control risk for each transaction-related audit objective.
3. For all internal controls to which reduction in control risk is attributed (key controls), develop appropriate tests of controls.
4. For the potential types of misstatements related to each transaction-related audit objective, design appropriate substantive tests of transactions, considering weaknesses in internal control and expected results of the tests of controls in step 3.

This four-step approach to designing tests of controls and substantive tests of transactions is summarized in Figure 10-6. The approach is illustrated in several chapters in the text. For example, see Table 11-2 on page 370 for an application four-step procedure for the audit of sales transactions. Each of the steps corresponds to a column in Table 11-2.

## Analytical Procedures

Because they are relatively inexpensive, many auditors perform extensive analytical procedures on all audits. As stated in Chapter 6, analytical procedures are performed at three different stages of the audit: in the planning stage to help the auditor decide the other

**FIGURE 10-6**

**Four-Step Approach to Designing Tests of Controls and Substantive Tests of Transactions**

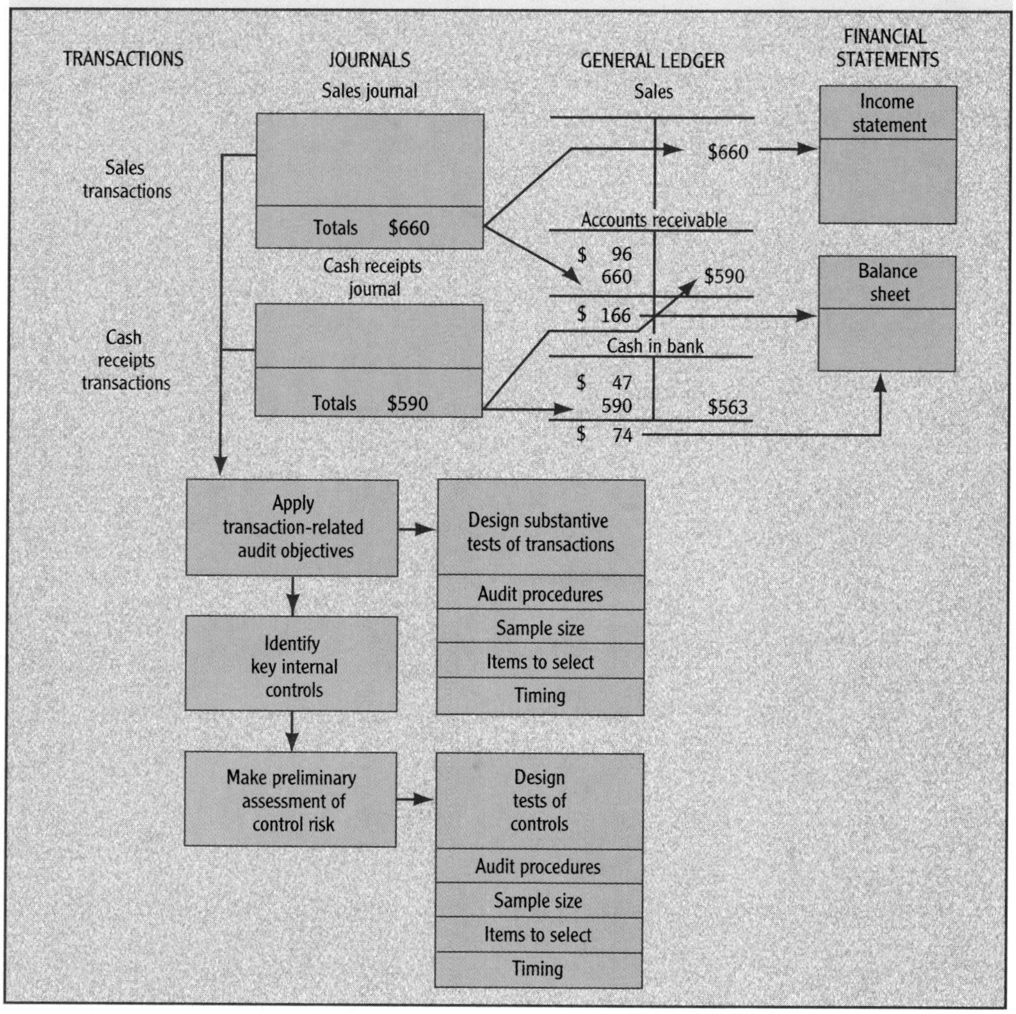

evidence needed to satisfy acceptable audit risk; during the audit in conjunction with tests of controls, substantive tests of transactions, and tests of details of balances; and near the end of the audit as a final test of reasonableness. Auditing standards require the auditor to perform analytical procedures during the planning and completion phases, but those done in conjunction with the other tests are optional.

Choosing the appropriate analytical procedures requires the auditor to use professional judgment. The appropriate use of analytical procedures and illustrative ratios are included in Chapter 6. There are also examples in several subsequent chapters. For example, page 450 illustrates several analytical procedures for the audit of accounts receivable.

## Tests of Details of Balances

The methodology for designing tests of details of balances is oriented to the balance-related audit objectives developed in Chapter 5 (pages 154–156). For example, if the auditor is verifying accounts receivable, the planned tests must be sufficient to satisfy each of the balance-related audit objectives. In planning tests of details of balances to satisfy these objectives, many auditors follow a methodology such as the one shown in Figure 10-7 for accounts receivable. The design of these tests is normally the most difficult part of the entire planning process. Designing such procedures is subjective and requires considerable professional judgment.

A discussion of the key decisions in designing tests of details of balances as shown in Figure 10-7 follows.

**Set Materiality and Assess Acceptable Audit Risk and Inherent Risk for Accounts Receivable** Setting the preliminary judgment about materiality for the audit as a whole and allocating the total to account balances (tolerable misstatement) are auditor decisions that were discussed

**FIGURE 10-7**

**Methodology for Designing Tests of Details of Financial Statement Balances—Accounts Receivable**

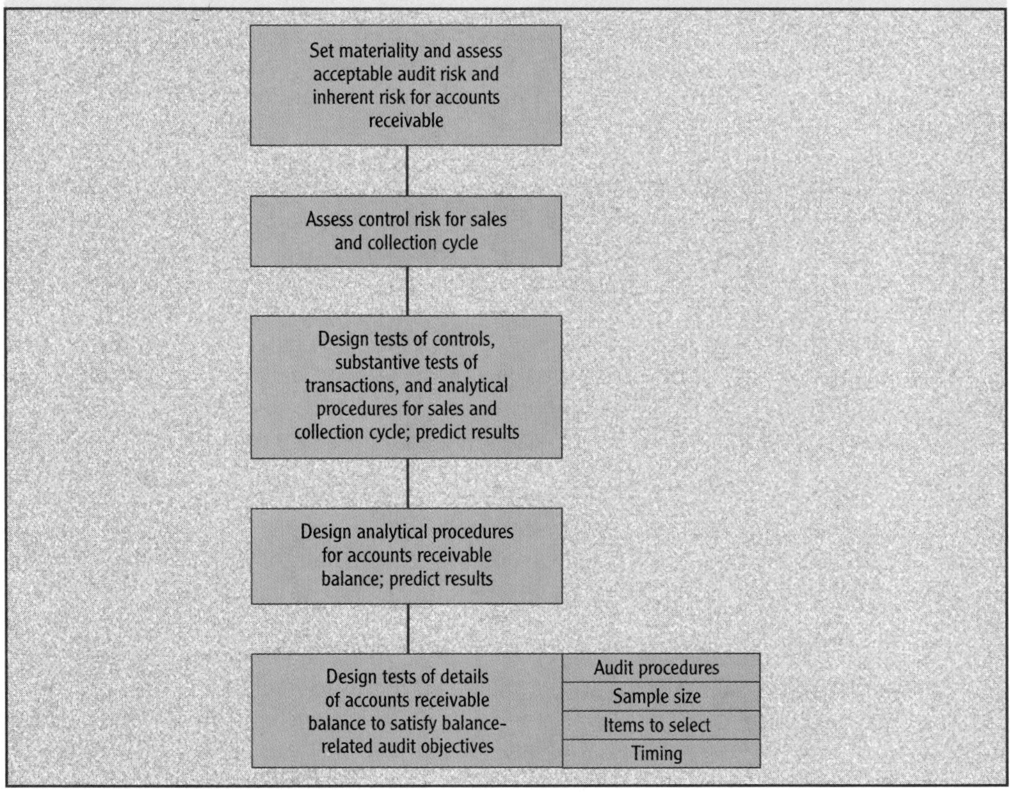

in Chapter 8. After the preliminary judgment about materiality is made, tolerable misstatement is set for each significant balance. A lower tolerable misstatement would result in more testing of details than a higher amount. Some auditors may allocate tolerable misstatement to individual balance-related audit objectives, but most do not.

As discussed in Chapter 8, acceptable audit risk is normally decided for the audit as a whole, rather than by cycle. An exception might be when the auditor believes that a misstatement of a specific account such as accounts receivable would negatively affect users more than the same size misstatement of any other account. For example, if accounts receivable is pledged to a bank as security on a loan, acceptable audit risk may be set lower for the sales and collection cycle than for other cycles.

Inherent risk is assessed by identifying any aspect of the client's history, environment, or operations that indicates a high likelihood of misstatement in the current year's financial statements. Considerations affecting inherent risk that were discussed in Chapter 8 applied to accounts receivable include make-up of accounts receivable, nature of the client's business, initial engagement, and so on. An account balance for which inherent risk has been assessed as high would result in more evidence accumulation than for an account with low inherent risk.

Inherent risk also can be extended to individual balance-related audit objectives. For example, because of adverse economic conditions in the client's industry, the auditor may conclude that there is a high risk of uncollectible accounts receivable (realizable value objective). Inherent risk could still be low for all other objectives.

**Assess Control Risk** Control risk is evaluated in the manner discussed in Chapter 9 and in earlier parts of this chapter. That methodology would be applied to both sales and cash receipts in the audit of accounts receivable. Effective controls reduce control risk and therefore the evidence required for substantive tests of transactions and tests of details of balances; inadequate controls increase the substantive evidence needed.

**Design Tests of Controls, Substantive Tests of Transactions, and Analytical Procedures and Predict Results** The methodology for designing tests of controls and substantive tests of transactions and analytical procedures was discussed earlier in this section and will be illustrated in subsequent chapters. The tests are designed with the expectation that certain results will be obtained. These predicted results affect the design of tests of details of balances as discussed below.

**Design Tests of Details of Balances to Satisfy Balance-Related Audit Objectives** The planned tests of details of balances include audit procedures, sample size, items to select, and timing. Procedures must be selected and designed for each account and each balance-related audit objective within each account. The balance-related audit objectives for accounts receivable are shown on page 447.

A difficulty the auditor faces in designing tests of details of balances is the need to predict the outcome of the tests of controls, substantive tests of transactions, and analytical procedures before they are performed. This is necessary because the auditor should design tests of details of balances during the planning phase, but the appropriate design depends on the outcome of the other tests. In planning tests of details of balances, the auditor usually predicts that there will be few or no exceptions in tests of controls, substantive tests of transactions, and analytical procedures, unless there are reasons to believe otherwise. If the results of the tests of controls, substantive tests of transactions, and analytical procedures are *not* consistent with the predictions, the tests of details of balances will need to be changed as the audit progresses.

The discussion about the approach to designing tests of details of balances applied to accounts receivable is summarized in Figure 10-8. The unshaded portion of the upper part of the figure is the financial information being audited. The light shading in the lower left is the design of tests of controls and substantive tests of transactions as discussed in Figure 10-6. The figure shows that the tests of controls and substantive tests of transac-

**FIGURE 10-8**

**Approach to Designing Tests of Details of Balances**

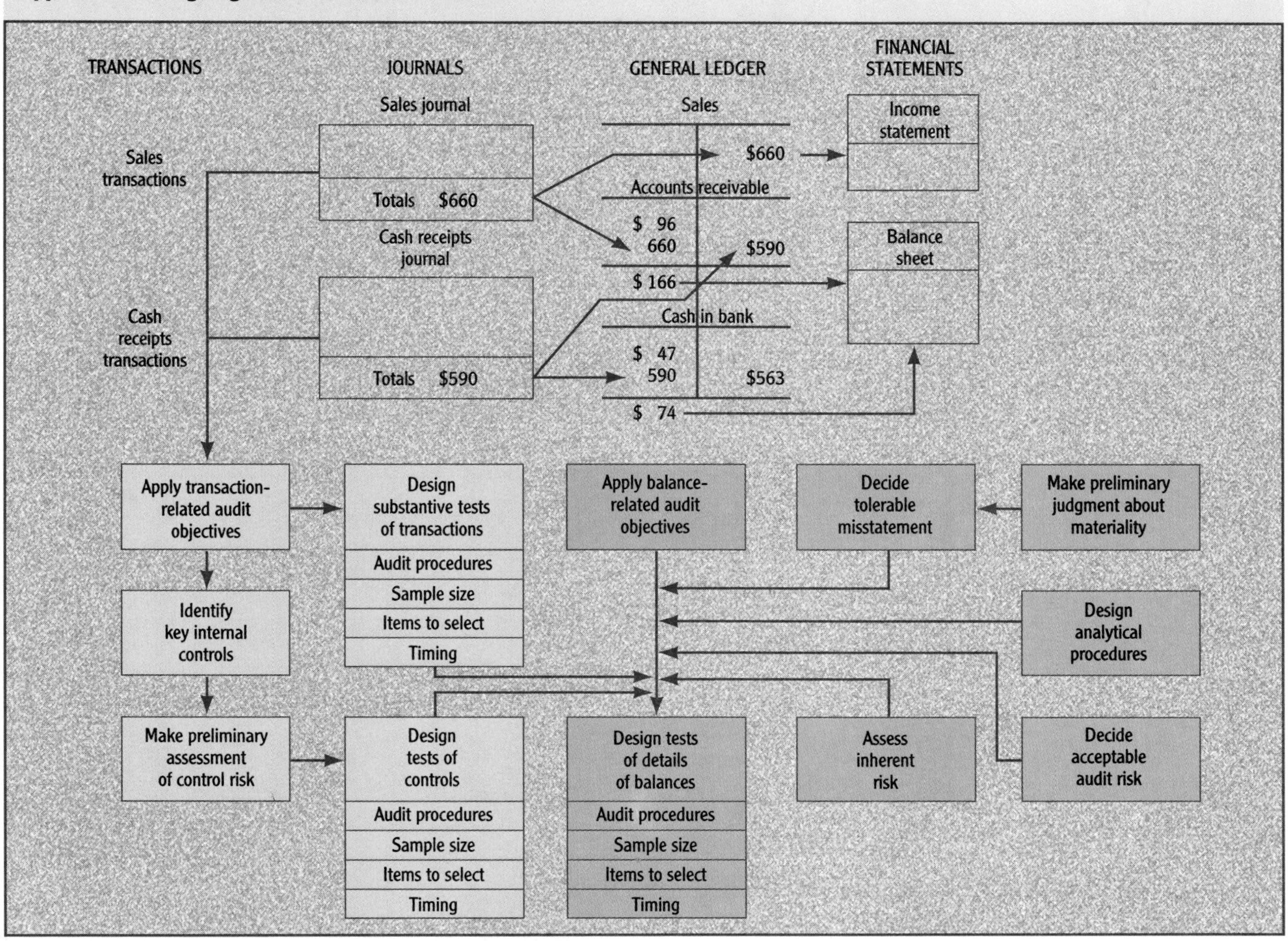


tions affect the design of the tests of details of balances. The darker shading in the lower right portion shows the design of tests of details of balances and the factors affecting that decision.

One of the most difficult parts of auditing is properly applying the factors that affect tests of details of balances. Each of the factors is subjective, requiring considerable professional judgment. The impact of each factor on tests of details of balances is equally subjective. For example, if inherent risk is reduced from medium to low, there is agreement that tests of details of balances can be reduced. Deciding the specific effect on audit procedures, sample size, timing, and items to select is a difficult decision.

## Level of Disaggregation of Planning Activities

The various planning activities discussed in Chapters 5 through 10 are applied at different levels of disaggregation, depending on the nature of the activity. Figure 10-9 on page 344 shows the primary planning activities and the levels of disaggregation normally applied. These levels of disaggregation range from the overall audit to the balance-related audit objective for each account. For example, when the auditor obtains background information about the client's business and industry, it pertains to the overall audit. As the audit progresses, the information will first be used in assessing acceptable audit risk and assessing inherent risk and later is likely to affect tests of details of balances.

**FIGURE 10-9**

**Disaggregation Level to Which Planning Activities Are Applied**

| PLANNING ACTIVITY | LEVEL OF DISAGGREGATION: Overall Audit | Cycle | Account | Transaction-Related Audit Objective | Balance-Related Audit Objective |
|---|---|---|---|---|---|
| Preplan audit | P | | | | |
| Obtain background information | P | | | | |
| Obtain information about client's legal obligations | P | | | | |
| Understand internal control | | | | | |
| Control environment | P | | | | |
| Risk assessment | | P | | | |
| Control activities | | P | | | |
| Information and communication | | P | | | |
| Monitoring | | P | | | |
| Identify key internal controls | | | | P | |
| Identify internal control weaknesses | | | | P | |
| Design tests of controls | | | | P | |
| Design substantive tests of transactions | | | | P | |
| Assess control risk | | | | P | |
| Assess inherent risk | | | P | | |
| Assess acceptable audit risk | P | | | | |
| Set preliminary judgment about materiality | P | | | | |
| Set tolerable misstatement | | | P | | |
| Design analytical procedures | | | P | | |
| Design tests of details of balances | | | | | P |

P = Primary level to which planning activity is applied.

## Illustrative Audit Program

Table 10-4 shows the tests of details of balances segment of an audit program for accounts receivable. The format used relates the audit procedures to the balance-related audit objectives. Notice that most procedures satisfy more than one objective. Also, more than one audit procedure is used for each objective. Audit procedures can be added or deleted as the auditor considers necessary. Sample size, items to select, and timing can also be changed for most procedures.

The audit program in Table 10-4 was developed after consideration of all the factors affecting tests of details of balances and is based on several assumptions about inherent risk, control risk, and the results of tests of controls, substantive tests of transactions, and analytical procedures. As indicated, if those assumptions are materially incorrect, the planned audit program will require revision. For example, analytical procedures could

**TABLE 10-4**

**Tests of Details of Balances Audit Program for Accounts Receivable**

| Sample Size | Items to Select | Timing* | Tests of Details of Balances Audit Procedures | Accounts Receivable Balance-Related Audit Objectives | | | | | | | | |
|---|---|---|---|---|---|---|---|---|---|---|---|---|
| | | | | Detail tie-in | Existence | Completeness | Accuracy | Classification | Cutoff | Realizable value | Rights | Presentation and disclosure |
| Trace 20 items; foot 2 pages and all subtotals | Random | I | 1. Obtain an aged list of receivables: trace accounts to the master file, foot schedule, and trace to general ledger. | x | | | | | | | | |
| All | All | Y | 2. Obtain an analysis of the allowance for doubtful accounts and bad debt expense: test accuracy, examine authorization for write-offs, and trace to general ledger. | x | x | x | x | | | x | | |
| 100 | 30 largest 70 random | I | 3. Obtain direct confirmation of accounts receivable and perform alternative procedures for nonresponses. | | x | x | x | x | x | | x | |
| NA | NA | Y | 4. Review accounts receivable control account for the period. Investigate the nature of, and review support for, any large or unusual entries or any entries not arising from normal journal sources. Also investigate any significant increases or decreases in sales toward year-end. | | x | | x | x | x | | x | x |
| All | All | Y | 5. Review receivables for any that have been assigned or discounted. | | | | | | | | x | x |
| NA | NA | Y | 6. Investigate collectibility of account balances. | | | | | | | x | | |
| All | All | Y | 7. Review lists of balances for amounts due from related parties or employees, credit balances, and unusual items, as well as notes receivable due after one year. | | x | | | x | | | | x |
| 30 transactions for sales and cash receipts; 10 for credit memos | 50% before and 50% after year-end | Y | 8. Determine that proper cutoff procedures were applied at the balance sheet date to ensure that sales, cash receipts, and credit memos have been recorded in the correct period. | | | | | | x | | | |

*I = Interim; Y = Year-end; NA = Not applicable.

indicate potential misstatements for several balance-related audit objectives, tests of controls results could indicate weak internal controls, or new facts could cause the auditor to change inherent risk.

**AUDIT PROGRAMS USED IN PRACTICE**

Most large CPA firms develop their own standard audit programs, while smaller firms often purchase similar audit programs from outside organizations. Standard audit programs are normally computerized and can easily be modified to meet the circumstances of individual audit engagements. One example of standard audit programs available for purchase is the AICPA's *Audit Program Generator (APG). APG* contains audit programs, as well as general and industry-specific checklists that auditors can use and modify for individual engagements.

Standard audit programs, whether developed internally or purchased from an outside organization, can dramatically increase audit efficiency if they are used properly. They should *not* be used, however, as a substitute for an auditor's professional judgment. Because each audit is different, it is usually necessary to add, modify, or delete steps within a standard audit program in order to accumulate sufficient and competent evidence.

### Relationship of Transaction-Related Audit Objectives to Balance-Related Audit Objectives

**OBJECTIVE 10-5**
**Understand the relationship of transaction-related audit objectives to balance-related audit objectives.**

It has already been shown that tests of details of balances must be designed to satisfy balance-related audit objectives for each account and the extent of these tests can be reduced when transaction-related audit objectives have been satisfied by tests of controls or substantive tests of transactions. It is, therefore, important to understand how each transaction-related audit objective relates to each balance-related audit objective. A general presentation of these relationships is shown in Table 10-5. The major implication of Table 10-5 is that even when all transaction-related audit objectives are met, the auditor will still rely primarily on substantive tests of balances to meet the following balance-related audit objectives: realizable value, rights and obligations, and presentation and disclosure. Some substantive tests of balances are also likely for the other balance-related audit objectives, depending on the results of the tests of controls and substantive tests of transactions.

The relationship of transaction-related audit objectives to balance-related audit objectives is shown in greater detail in Figure 13-3, page 449. That figure shows how transaction-related audit objectives for sales and cash receipts affect accounts receivable balance-related audit objectives. Notice in Figure 13-3 that the existence transaction-related audit objective for sales affects the existence balance-related audit objective for accounts receivable, whereas the existence transaction-related audit objective for cash receipts affects the completeness balance-related audit objective for accounts receivable. The reason is that sales increase accounts receivable, whereas cash receipts decrease accounts receivable.

## SUMMARY OF THE AUDIT PROCESS

**OBJECTIVE 10-6**
**Integrate the four phases of the audit process.**

The four phases of an audit were introduced at the end of Chapter 5. Considerable portions of Chapters 6 through 10 have discussed the different aspects of the process. Figure 10-10 (page 348) shows the four phases for the entire audit process. Table 10-6 (page 349) shows the timing of the tests in each phase for an audit with a December 31 balance sheet date.

### Phase I: Plan and Design an Audit Approach

Chapters 6 through 10 have emphasized various aspects of planning the audit. At the end of phase I, the auditor should have a well-defined audit plan and a specific audit program for the entire audit.

**TABLE 10-5**

**Relationship of Transaction-Related Audit Objectives to Balance-Related Audit Objectives**

| Transaction-Related Audit Objective | Balance-Related Audit Objective | Nature of Relationship | Explanation |
|---|---|---|---|
| Existence | Existence or completeness | Direct | There is a direct relationship of the existence transaction-related audit objective to the existence balance-related audit objective if a class of transactions increases the related account balance (e.g., sales transactions increase accounts receivable). There is a direct relationship of the existence transaction-related audit objective to the completeness balance-related audit objective if a class of transactions decreases the related account balance (e.g., cash receipts transactions decrease accounts receivable). |
| Completeness | Completeness or existence | Direct | See comments above for existence objective. |
| Accuracy | Accuracy | Direct | — |
| Classification | Classification | Direct | — |
| Timing | Cutoff | Direct | — |
| Posting and summarization | Detail tie-in | Direct | — |
| | Realizable value | None | Few internal controls over realizable value are related to classes of transactions. |
| | Rights and obligations | None | Few internal controls over rights and obligations are related to classes of transactions. |
| | Presentation and disclosure | None | Internal controls provide little assurance that proper presentations and disclosures will be made and there are no relevant substantive tests of transactions. |

Information obtained during preplanning, obtaining background information, obtaining information about the client's legal obligations, and performing preliminary analytical procedures (first four boxes in Figure 10-10) is used primarily to assess inherent risk and acceptable audit risk. Assessments of materiality, acceptable audit risk, inherent risk, and control risk are used to develop an overall audit plan and audit program.

## Phase II: Perform Tests of Controls and Substantive Tests of Transactions

Performance of the tests of controls and substantive tests of transactions occurs during this phase. The objectives of phase II are to (1) obtain evidence in support of the specific controls that contribute to the auditor's assessed control risk (that is, where it is reduced below the maximum) and (2) to obtain evidence in support of the monetary correctness of transactions. The former objective is met by performing tests of controls, and the latter by performing substantive tests of transactions. Many of both types of tests are conducted simultaneously on the same transactions. When controls are not considered effective, or when control deviations are discovered, substantive tests can be expanded in this phase or in phase III.

Since the results of tests of controls and substantive tests of transactions are a major determinant of the extent of tests of details of balances, they are often performed two or three months before the balance sheet date. This helps the auditor plan for contingencies, revise the audit program for unexpected results, and complete the audit as soon as possible after the balance sheet date.

**FIGURE 10-10**

**Summary of the Audit Process**

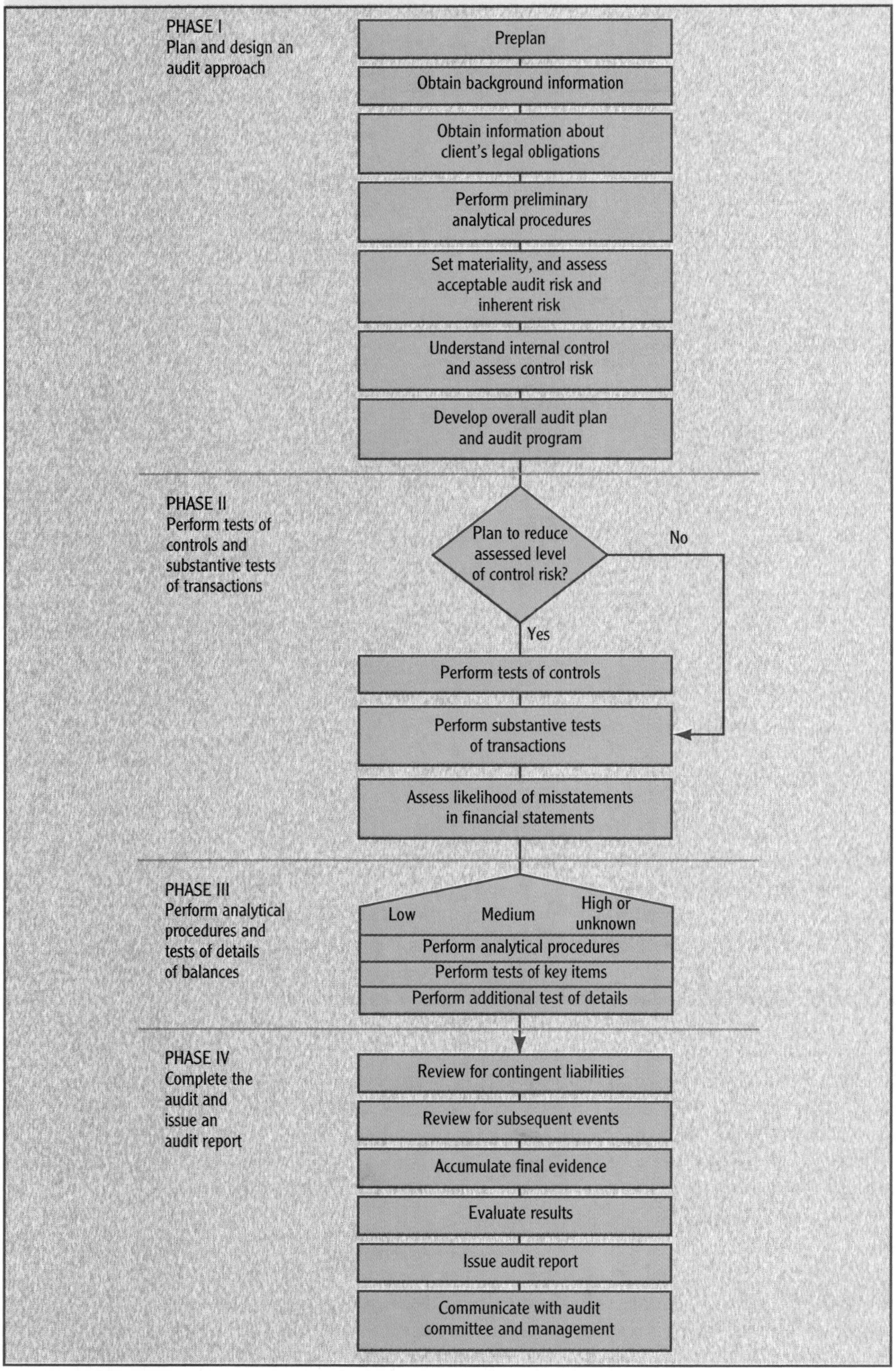

**TABLE 10-6**
**Timing of Tests**

| | | | |
|---|---|---|---|
| Phase I | Plan and design audit approach. Update understanding of internal control. Update audit program. Perform preliminary analytical procedures. | 8-30-96 | |
| Phase II | Perform tests of controls and substantive tests of transactions for first 9 months of the year. | 9-30-96 | |
| Phase III | Confirm accounts receivable. Observe inventory. | 10-31-96 | |
| | Count cash. Perform cutoff tests. Request various other confirmations. | 12-31-96 | Balance sheet date |
| | Perform analytical procedures, complete tests of controls and substantive tests of transactions, and complete most tests of details of balances. | 1-7-97 | Books closed |
| Phase IV | Summarize results, review for contingent liabilities, review for subsequent events, accumulate final evidence including analytical procedures, and finalize audit. | 3-8-97 | Last date of field work |
| | Issue audit report. | 3-15-97 | |

## Phase III: Perform Analytical Procedures and Tests of Details of Balances

The objective of phase III is to obtain sufficient additional evidence to determine whether the ending balances and footnotes in financial statements are fairly stated. The nature and extent of the work will depend heavily on the findings of the two previous phases.

There are two general categories of phase III procedures: analytical procedures and tests of details of balances. Analytical procedures are those that assess the overall reasonableness of transactions and balances. Tests of details of balances are specific procedures intended to test for monetary misstatements in the balances in the financial statements. Certain key transactions and amounts are so important that each one must be audited. Other items can be sampled.

Table 10-6 shows analytical procedures being done both before and after the balance sheet date. Because of their low cost, it is common to use analytical procedures whenever they are relevant. They are frequently done early with preliminary data prior to year-end as a means of planning and directing other audit tests to specific areas. But the greatest benefit from calculating ratios and making comparisons occurs after the client has finished preparing its financial statements. Ideally, these analytical procedures are done before tests of details of balances so that they can then be used to determine how extensively to test balances. They are also used as a part of performing tests of balances and during the completion phase of the audit.

Table 10-6 also shows that tests of details of balances are normally done last. On some audits, all are done after the balance sheet date. When clients want to issue statements soon after the balance sheet date, however, the more time-consuming tests of details of balances will be done at interim dates prior to year-end with additional work being done to "bring up" the audited interim-date balances to year-end. Substantive tests of balances performed before year-end provide less assurance and are not normally done unless internal controls are effective.

## Phase IV: Complete the Audit and Issue an Audit Report

After the first three phases are completed, it is necessary to accumulate some additional evidence for the financial statements, summarize the results, issue the audit report, and perform other forms of communication. This phase has several parts.

**Review for Contingent Liabilities** Contingent liabilities are potential liabilities that must be disclosed in the client's footnotes. Auditors must make sure that the disclosure is adequate. A considerable portion of the search for contingent liabilities is done during the first three phases, but additional testing is done during phase IV. Contingent liabilities are studied in Chapter 22.

**Review for Subsequent Events** Occasionally, events occurring subsequent to the balance sheet date but before the issuance of the financial statements and auditor's report will have an effect on the information presented in the financial statements. Specific review procedures are designed to bring to the auditor's attention any subsequent events that may require recognition in the financial statements. Review for subsequent events is also studied in Chapter 22.

**Accumulate Final Evidence** In addition to the evidence obtained for each cycle during phases I and II and for each account during phase III, it is also necessary to gather evidence for the financial statements as a whole during the completion phase. This evidence includes performing final analytical procedures, evaluating the going concern assumption, obtaining a client representation letter, and reading information in the annual report to make sure that it is consistent with the financial statements.

**Issue Audit Report** The type of audit report issued depends on the evidence accumulated and the audit findings. The appropriate reports for differing circumstances were studied in Chapter 2.

**Communicate with Audit Committee and Management** The auditor is required to communicate reportable conditions to the audit committee or senior management. The SASs also require the auditor to communicate certain other matters to the audit committee or a similarly designated body upon completion of the audit or sooner. Although not required, auditors often also make suggestions to management to improve business performance.

## ESSENTIAL TERMS

**Analytical procedures**—use of comparisons and relationships to determine whether account balances or other data appear reasonable

**Audit evidence mix**—the combination of the five types of tests to obtain sufficient competent evidence for a cycle. There are likely to be variations in the mix from cycle to cycle depending on the circumstances of the audit.

**Phases of the audit process**—the four aspects of a complete audit: (1) plan and design an audit approach, (2) perform tests of controls and substantive tests of transactions, (3) perform analytical procedures and tests of details of balances, and (4) complete the audit and issue the audit report

**Procedures to obtain an understanding**—procedures used by the auditor to gather evidence about the design and placement in operation of specific controls

**Substantive tests of transactions**—audit procedures testing for monetary misstatements to determine whether the six transaction-related audit objectives have been satisfied for each class of transactions

**Tests of controls**—audit procedures to test the effectiveness of controls in support of a reduced assessed control risk

**Tests of details of balances**—audit procedures testing for monetary misstatements to determine whether the nine balance-related audit objectives have been satisfied for each significant account balance

**Types of tests**—the five categories of audit tests auditors use to determine whether financial statements are fairly stated: procedures to obtain an understanding of internal control, tests of controls, substantive tests of transactions, analytical procedures, and tests of details of balances

## REVIEW QUESTIONS

**10-1 (Objective 10-1)** What are the five types of tests auditors use to determine whether financial statements are fairly stated? Identify which tests are performed to reduce control risk and which tests are performed to reduce planned detection risk.

**10-2 (Objective 10-1)** What is the purpose of tests of controls? Identify specific accounts on the financial statements that are affected by performing tests of controls for the acquisition and payment cycle.

**10-3 (Objective 10-1)** Distinguish between a test of control and a substantive test of transactions. Give two examples of each.

**10-4 (Objectives 10-1, 10-4)** State a test of control audit procedure to test the effectiveness of the following control: approved wage rates are used in calculating employees' earnings. State a substantive test of transactions audit procedure to determine whether approved wage rates are actually used in calculating employees' earnings.

**10-5 (Objective 10-1)** A considerable portion of the tests of controls and substantive tests of transactions are performed simultaneously as a matter of audit convenience. But the substantive tests of transactions procedures and sample size are, in part, dependent upon the results of the tests of controls. How can the auditor resolve this apparent inconsistency?

**10-6 (Objectives 10-2, 10-3)** Evaluate the following statement: "Tests of sales and cash receipts transactions are such an essential part of every audit that I like to perform them as near the end of the audit as possible. By that time I have a fairly good understanding of the client's business and its internal controls because confirmations, cutoff tests, and other procedures have already been completed."

**10-7 (Objectives 10-1, 10-2)** Explain how the calculation and comparison to previous years of the gross margin percentage and the ratio of accounts receivable to sales is related to the confirmation of accounts receivable and other tests of the accuracy of accounts receivable.

**10-8 (Objective 10-1)** Distinguish between substantive tests of transactions and tests of details of balances. Give one example of each for the acquisition and payment cycle.

**10-9 (Objective 10-3)** Assume that the client's internal controls over the recording and classifying of fixed asset additions are considered weak because the individual responsible for recording new acquisitions has inadequate technical training and limited experience in accounting. How would this situation affect the evidence you should accumulate in auditing fixed assets as compared with another audit in which the controls are excellent? Be as specific as possible.

**10-10 (Objective 10-2)** For each of the seven types of evidence discussed in Chapter 6, identify whether it is applicable for procedures to obtain an understanding of internal control, tests of controls, substantive tests of transactions, analytical procedures, and tests of details of balances.

**10-11 (Objective 10-2)** Rank the following types of tests from most costly to least costly: analytical procedures, tests of details of balances, procedures to obtain an understanding of the internal control structure and tests of controls, and substantive tests of transactions.

**10-12 (Objective 10-2)** In Figure 10-4, explain the difference among $C_3$, $C_2$, and $C_1$. Explain the circumstances under which it would be a good decision to obtain audit assurance from substantive tests at part $C_1$. Do the same for parts $C_2$ and $C_3$.

**10-13 (Objective 10-2)** The following are three decision factors related to assessed control risk: effectiveness of internal controls, cost-effectiveness of a reduced assessed control risk, and results of tests of controls. Identify the combination of conditions for these three factors that is required before reduced substantive testing is permitted.

**10-14 (Objective 10-3)** Table 10-3 illustrates variations in the emphasis on different types of audit tests. What are the benefits to the auditor of identifying the best mix of tests?

**10-15 (Objective 10-4)** State the four-step approach to designing tests of controls and substantive tests of transactions.

**10-16 (Objective 10-4)** Explain the relationship between the methodology for designing tests of controls and substantive tests of transactions in Figure 10-5 to the methodology for designing tests of details of balances in Figure 10-7.

**10-17 (Objective 10-4)** Why is it desirable to design tests of details of balances before performing tests of controls and substantive tests of transactions? State the assumptions that the auditor must make in doing that. What does the auditor do if the assumptions are wrong?

**10-18 (Objective 10-4)** Explain the relationship between tolerable misstatement, inherent risk, and control risk to planned tests of details of balances.

**10-19 (Objective 10-4)** List the nine balance-related audit objectives in the verification of the ending balance in inventory, and provide one useful audit procedure for each of the objectives.

**10-20 (Objective 10-6)** Why do auditors frequently consider it desirable to perform audit tests throughout the year rather than wait until year-end? List several examples of evidence that can be accumulated prior to year-end.

## MULTIPLE CHOICE QUESTIONS FROM CPA EXAMINATIONS

**10-21 (Objective 10-1)** The following questions concern types of audit tests. Choose the best response.

a. The auditor looks for an indication on duplicate sales invoices to see if the invoices have been verified. This is an example of
   (1) a test of details of balances.
   (2) a test of control.
   (3) a substantive test of transactions.
   (4) both a test of control and a substantive test of transactions.

b. Analytical procedures may be classified as being primarily
   (1) tests of controls.
   (2) substantive tests.
   (3) tests of ratios.
   (4) tests of details of balances.

c. Failure to detect material dollar misstatements in the financial statements is a risk that the auditor mitigates primarily by
   (1) performing substantive tests.
   (2) performing tests of controls.
   (3) evaluating internal control.
   (4) obtaining a client representation letter.

d. Before reducing assessed control risk, the auditor obtains reasonable assurance that the internal control procedures are in use and operating as planned. The auditor obtains this assurance by performing
   (1) tests of details of balances.
   (2) substantive tests of transaction.
   (3) tests of controls.
   (4) tests of trends and ratios.

e. The auditor faces a risk that the audit will not detect material misstatements that occur in the accounting process. In regard to minimizing this risk, the auditor relies primarily on
   (1) substantive tests.
   (2) tests of controls.
   (3) internal control.
   (4) statistical analysis.

**10-22 (Objective 10-1)** The following questions deal with tests of controls. Choose the best response.

a. Which of the following statements about tests of controls is most accurate?
   (1) Auditing procedures cannot concurrently provide both evidence of the effectiveness of internal control procedures and evidence required for substantive tests.
   (2) Tests of controls include observations of the proper segregation of duties that ordinarily may be limited to the normal audit period.
   (3) Tests of controls should be based upon proper application of an appropriate statistical sampling plan.
   (4) Tests of controls ordinarily should be performed as of the balance sheet date or during the period subsequent to that date.

b. Which of the following would be *least* likely to be included in an auditor's tests of controls?
   (1) Documentation.
   (2) Observation.
   (3) Inquiry.
   (4) Confirmation.

c. The two phases of the auditor's involvement with internal control are sometimes referred to as "understanding and assessment" and "tests of controls." In the tests of controls phase, the auditor attempts to
   (1) obtain a reasonable degree of assurance that the client's controls are in use and are operating as planned.
   (2) obtain sufficient, competent evidential matter to afford a reasonable basis for the auditor's opinion.
   (3) obtain assurances that informative disclosures in the financial statements are reasonably adequate.
   (4) obtain knowledge and understanding of the client's prescribed procedures and methods.

d. Which of the following is ordinarily considered a test of control audit procedure?
   (1) Send confirmation letters to banks.
   (2) Count and list cash on hand.
   (3) Examine signatures on checks.
   (4) Obtain or prepare reconciliations of bank accounts as of the balance sheet date.

**10-23 (Objectives 10-4, 10-6)** The following questions concern the sequence and timing of audit tests. Choose the best response.

a. A conceptually logical approach to the auditor's evaluation of internal control consists of the following four steps:
   I. Determine the internal controls that should prevent or detect errors and fraud.
   II. Identify weaknesses to determine their effect on the nature, timing, or extent of auditing procedures to be applied and suggestions to be made to the client.
   III. Determine whether the necessary procedures are prescribed and are being followed satisfactorily.
   IV. Consider the types of errors and fraud that could occur.

   What should be the order in which these four steps are performed?
   (1) I, II, III, and IV.
   (2) I, III, IV, and II.
   (3) III, IV, I, and II.
   (4) IV, I, III, and II.

b. The sequence of steps in gathering evidence as the basis of the auditor's opinion is:
   (1) substantive tests, assessment of control risk, and tests of controls.
   (2) assessment of control risk, substantive tests, and tests of controls.
   (3) assessment of control risk, tests of controls, and substantive tests.
   (4) tests of controls, assessment of control risk, and substantive tests.

c. Which of the following procedures is *least* likely to be performed before the balance sheet date?
   (1) Observation of inventory.
   (2) Assessment of control risk for cash disbursements.
   (3) Search for unrecorded liabilities.
   (4) Confirmation of receivables.

## DISCUSSION QUESTIONS AND PROBLEMS

**10-24 (Objectives 10-1, 10-2)** The following are eleven audit procedures taken from an audit program:

1. Foot the accounts payable trial balance and compare the total with the general ledger.
2. Examine vendors' invoices to verify the ending balance in accounts payable.
3. Compare the balance in payroll tax expense with previous years. The comparison takes the increase in payroll tax rates into account.
4. Discuss the duties of the cash disbursements clerk with him and observe whether he has responsibility for handling cash or preparing the bank reconciliation.
5. Confirm accounts payable balances directly with vendors.
6. Account for a sequence of checks in the cash disbursements journal to determine whether any have been omitted.
7. Examine the internal auditor's initials on monthly bank reconciliations as an indication of whether they have been reviewed.
8. Examine vendors' invoices and other documentation in support of recorded transactions in the acquisitions journal.
9. Multiply the commission rate by total sales and compare the result with commission expense.
10. Examine vendors' invoices and other supporting documents to determine whether large amounts in the repair and maintenance account should be capitalized.
11. Examine the initials on vendors' invoices that indicate internal verification of pricing, extending, and footing by a clerk.

### Required

a. Indicate whether each procedure is a test of control, substantive test of transactions, analytical procedure, or a test of details of balances.

b. Identify the type of evidence for each procedure.

**10-25 (Objectives 10-1, 10-2, 10-5)** The following are audit procedures from different transaction cycles:

1. Foot and cross-foot the cash disbursements journal and trace the balance to the general ledger.
2. Select a sample of entries in the acquisitions journal and trace each one to a related vendor's invoice to determine if one exists.
3. Compute inventory turnover for each major product and compare with previous years.
4. Confirm a sample of notes payable balances, interest rates, and collateral with lenders.
5. Foot the accounts payable trial balance and compare the balance with the general ledger.
6. Examine documentation for acquisition transactions before and after the balance sheet date to determine whether they are recorded in the proper period.
7. Observe whether cash is prelisted daily at the time it is received by the president's secretary.
8. Inquire of the credit manager whether each account receivable on the aged trial balance is collectible.

## Required

a. For each audit procedure, identify the transaction cycle being audited.

b. For each audit procedure, identify the type of evidence.

c. For each audit procedure, identify whether it is a test of control or a substantive test.

d. For each substantive audit procedure, identify whether it is a substantive test of transactions, a test of details of balances, or an analytical procedure.

e. For each test of control or substantive test of transactions procedure, identify the transaction-related audit objective or objectives being satisfied.

f. For each test of details of balances procedure, identify the balance-related audit objective or objectives being satisfied.

**10-26 (Objective 10-1)** For each of the following controls, identify whether the control leaves an audit trail. Also identify a test of control audit procedure the auditor can use to test the effectiveness of the control.

a. An accounting clerk accounts for all shipping documents on a monthly basis.

b. Bank reconciliations are prepared by the controller, who does not have access to cash receipts.

c. As employees check in daily by using time clocks, a supervisor observes to make certain that no individual "punches in" more than one time card.

d. Vendors' invoices are approved by the controller after she examines the purchase order and receiving report attached to each invoice.

e. The cashier, who has no access to accounting records, prepares the deposit slip and delivers the deposit directly to the bank on a daily basis.

f. An accounting clerk verifies the price, extensions, and footings of all sales invoices in excess of $300 and initials the duplicate sales invoice when he has completed the procedure.

g. All mail is opened and cash is prelisted daily by the president's secretary, who has no other responsibility for handling assets or recording accounting data.

**10-27 (Objectives 10-1, 10-4, 10-5)** The following are independent internal controls commonly found in the acquisition and payment cycle. Each control is to be considered independently.

1. At the end of each month an accounting clerk accounts for all prenumbered receiving reports (documents evidencing the receipt of goods) issued during the month, and he traces each one to the related vendor's invoice and acquisitions journal entry. The clerk's tests do not include testing quantity or description of the merchandise received.
2. The cash disbursements clerk is prohibited from handling cash. The bank account is reconciled by another person even though the clerk has sufficient expertise and time to do it.
3. Before a check is prepared to pay for acquisitions by the accounts payable department, the related purchase order and receiving report are attached to the vendor's invoice being paid. A clerk compares the quantity on the invoice with the receiving report and purchase order, compares the price with the purchase order, recomputes the extensions, re-adds the total, and examines the account number indicated on the invoice to determine whether it is properly classified. He indicates his performance of these procedures by initialing the invoice.
4. Before a check is signed by the controller, she examines the supporting documentation accompanying the check. At that time she initials each vendor's invoice to indicate her approval.
5. After the controller signs the checks, her secretary writes the check number and the date the check was issued on each of the supporting documents to prevent their reuse.

## Required

a. For each of the internal controls, state the transaction-related audit objective(s) the control is meant to fulfill.

b. For each control, list one test of control the auditor could perform to test the effectiveness of the control.

c. For each control, list one substantive test the auditor could perform to determine whether financial misstatements are actually taking place.

**10-28 (Objectives 10-1, 10-4, 10-5)** The following internal controls for the acquisition and payment cycle were selected from a standard internal control questionnaire.

1. Vendors' invoices are recalculated prior to payment.
2. Approved price lists are used for acquisitions.
3. Prenumbered receiving reports are prepared as support for acquisitions and numerically accounted for.
4. Dates on receiving reports are compared with vendors' invoices before entry into the acquisitions journal.
5. The accounts payable master file is updated, balanced, and reconciled to the general ledger monthly.
6. Account classifications are reviewed by someone other than the preparer.
7. All checks are signed by the owner or manager.
8. The check signer compares data on supporting documents with checks.
9. All supporting documents are cancelled after the checks are signed.
10. Checks are mailed by the owner or manager or a person under her supervision after signing.

## Required

a. For each control, identify which element of the five categories of control activities is applicable (separation of duties, proper authorization, adequate documents or records, physical control over assets and records, or independent checks on performance).

b. For each control, state which transaction-related audit objective or objectives is applicable.

c. For each control, write an audit procedure that could be used to test the control for effectiveness.

d. For each control, identify a likely misstatement, assuming that the control does not exist or is not functioning.

e. For each likely misstatement, identify a substantive audit procedure to determine if the misstatement exists.

**10-29 (Objectives 10-4, 10-6)** Jennifer Schaefer, CPA, follows the philosophy of performing interim tests of controls and substantive tests of transactions on every December 31 audit as a means of keeping overtime to a minimum. Typically, the interim tests are performed some time between August and November.

## Required

a. Evaluate her decision to perform interim tests of controls and substantive tests of transactions.

b. Under what circumstances is it acceptable for her to perform *no additional* tests of controls and substantive tests of transactions work as a part of the year-end audit tests?

c. If she decides to perform no additional testing, what is the effect on other tests she performs during the remainder of the engagement?

**10-30 (Objectives 10-3, 10-4)** Following are several decisions that the auditor must make in an audit. Letters indicate alternative conclusions that could be made:

| Decisions | Alternative Conclusions |
|---|---|
| 1. Determine whether it is cost effective to perform tests of control | A. It is cost effective<br>B. It is not cost effective |
| 2. Perform substantive tests of details of balances | C. Perform reduced tests<br>D. Perform expanded tests |
| 3. Assess control risk | E. Controls are effective<br>F. Controls are not effective |
| 4. Perform tests of controls | G. Controls are effective<br>H. Controls are not effective |

## Required

a. Identify the sequence in which the auditor should make decisions 1–4 above.

b. For the audit of the sales and collection cycle and accounts receivable, an auditor reached the following conclusions: A, D, E, H. Put the letters in the appropriate sequence and evaluate whether the auditor's logic was reasonable. Explain your answer.

c. For the audit of inventory and related inventory cost records, an auditor reached the following conclusions: B, C, E, G. Put the letters in the appropriate sequence and evaluate whether the auditor used good professional judgment. Explain your answer.

d. For the audit of property, plant, and equipment and related acquisition records, an auditor reached the following conclusions: A, C, F, G. Put the letters in the appropriate sequence and evaluate whether the auditor used good professional judgment. Explain your answer.

e. For the audit of payroll expenses and related liabilities, an auditor recorded the following conclusions: D, F. Put the letters in the appropriate sequence and evaluate whether the auditor used good professional judgment. Explain your answer.

**10-31 (Objective 10-3)** The following are three situations in which the auditor is required to develop an audit strategy:

1. The client has inventory at approximately fifty locations in a three-state region. The inventory is difficult to count and can be observed only by traveling by automobile. The internal controls over acquisitions, cash disbursements, and perpetual records are considered effective. This is the fifth year that you have done the audit, and audit results in past years have always been excellent. The client is in excellent financial condition and is privately held.
2. This is the first year of an audit of a medium-sized company that is considering selling its business because of severe underfinancing. A review of the acquisition and payment cycle indicates that controls over cash disbursements are excellent, but controls over acquisitions cannot be considered effective. The client lacks receiving reports and a policy as to the proper timing to record acquisitions. When you review the general ledger, you observe that there are many large adjusting entries to correct accounts payable.
3. You are doing the audit of a small loan company with extensive receivables from customers. Controls over granting loans, collections, and loans outstanding are considered effective, and there is extensive follow-up of all outstanding loans weekly. You have recommended a computer system for the past two years, but management believes the cost is too great, given their low profitability. Collections are an ongoing problem because many of the customers have severe financial problems. Because of adverse economic conditions, loans receivable have significantly increased and collections are less than normal. In previous years, you have had relatively few adjusting entries.

### Required

a. For audit 1, recommend an evidence mix for the five types of tests for the audit of inventory and cost of goods sold. Justify your answer. Include in your recommendations both tests of controls and substantive tests.

b. For audit 2, recommend an evidence mix for the audit of the acquisition and payment cycle including accounts payable. Justify your answer.

c. For audit 3, recommend an evidence mix for the audit of outstanding loans. Justify your answer.

**10-32 (Objectives 10-1, 10-4)** Brad Jackson was assigned to the audit of a client that had not been audited by any CPA firm in the preceding year. In conducting the audit, he did no testing of the beginning balance of accounts receivable, inventory, or accounts payable on the grounds that the audit report is being limited to the ending balance sheet, the income statement, and the statement of cash flows. No comparative financial statements are to be issued.

### Required

a. Explain the error in Jackson's reasoning.

b. Suggest an approach that Jackson can follow in verifying the beginning balance in accounts receivable.

c. Why does the same problem not exist in the verification of beginning balances on continuing audit engagements?

**10-33 (Objective 10-3)** Kim Bryan, a new staff auditor, is confused by the inconsistency of the three audit partners she has been assigned to on her first three audit engagements. On the first engagement, she spent a considerable amount of time in the audit of cash disbursements by examining cancelled checks and supporting documentation, but almost no testing was spent in the verification of fixed assets. On the second engagement, a different partner had her do less intensive tests in the cash disbursements area and take smaller sample sizes than in the first audit even though the company was much larger. On her most recent engagement under a third audit partner, there was a thorough test of cash disbursement transactions, far beyond that of the other two audits, and an extensive verification of fixed assets. In fact, this partner insisted on a complete physical examination of all fixed assets recorded on the books. The total audit time on the most recent audit was longer than that of either of the first two audits in spite of the smaller size of the company. Bryan's conclusion is that the amount of evidence to accumulate depends on the audit partner in charge of the engagement.

### Required

a. State several factors that could explain the difference in the amount of evidence accumulated in each of the three audit engagements as well as the total time spent.

b. What could the audit partners have done to help Bryan understand the difference in the audit emphasis on the three audits?

c. Explain how these three audits are useful in developing Bryan's professional judgment. How could the quality of her judgment have been improved on the audits?

**10-34 (Objectives 10-4, 10-6)** The following are parts of a typical audit for a company with a fiscal year-end of July 31.

1. Confirm accounts payable.
2. Do tests of controls and substantive tests of transactions for the acquisition and payment and payroll and personnel cycles.
3. Do other tests of details of balances for accounts payable.
4. Do tests for review of subsequent events.
5. Preplan the audit.
6. Issue the audit report.

7. Understand internal control and assess control risk.
8. Do analytical procedures for accounts payable.
9. Set acceptable audit risk and decide preliminary judgment about materiality and tolerable misstatement.

## Required

a. Put parts 1 through 9 of the audit in the sequential order in which you would expect them to be performed in a typical audit.

b. Identify those parts that would frequently be done before July 31.

## CASES

**10-35 (Objectives 10-3, 10-4)** Gale Brewer, CPA, has been the partner in charge of the audit of Merkle Manufacturing Company, a client listed on the Midwest Stock Exchange, for 13 years. Merkle has had excellent growth and profits in the past decade, primarily as a result of the excellent leadership provided by Bill Merkle and other competent executives. Brewer has always enjoyed a close relationship with the company and prides himself on having made several constructive comments over the years that have aided in the success of the firm. Several times in the past few years, Brewer's CPA firm has considered rotating a different audit team on the engagement, but this has been strongly resisted by both Brewer and Merkle.

For the first few years of the audit, internal controls were inadequate and the accounting personnel had inadequate qualifications for their responsibilities. Extensive audit evidence was required during the audit, and numerous adjusting entries were necessary. However, because of Brewer's constant prodding, internal controls improved gradually and competent personnel were hired. In recent years, there were normally no audit adjustments required, and the extent of the evidence accumulation was gradually reduced. During the past three years, Brewer was able to devote less time to the audit because of the relative ease of conducting the audit and the cooperation obtained throughout the engagement.

In the current year's audit, Brewer decided that the total time budget for the engagement should be kept approximately the same as in recent years. The senior in charge of the audit, Phil Warren, was new on the job and highly competent, and he had the reputation of being able to cut time off the budget. The fact that Merkle had recently acquired a new division through merger would probably add to the time, but Warren's efficiency would probably compensate for it.

The interim tests of control took somewhat longer than expected because of the use of several new assistants, a change in the accounting system to computerize the inventory and other accounting records, a change in accounting personnel, and the existence of a few more errors in the tests of the system. Neither Brewer nor Warren was concerned about the budget deficit, however, because they could easily make up the difference at year-end.

At year-end, Warren assigned the responsibility for inventory to an assistant who also had not been on the audit before but was competent and extremely fast at his work. Even though the total value of inventory increased, he reduced the size of the sample from that of other years because there had been few errors in the preceding year. He found several items in the sample that were overstated due to errors in pricing and obsolescence, but the combination of all of the errors in the sample was immaterial. He completed the tests in 25 percent less time than the preceding year. The entire audit was completed on schedule and in slightly less time than the preceding year. There were only a few adjusting entries for the year, and only two of them were material. Brewer was extremely pleased with the results and wrote a special letter to Warren and the inventory assistant complimenting them on the audit.

Six months later Brewer received a telephone call from Merkle and was informed that the company was in serious financial trouble. Subsequent investigation revealed that the inventory had been significantly overstated. The major cause of the misstatement was the inclusion of obsolete items in inventory (especially in the new division), errors in pricing due to the new computer system, and the inclusion of nonexistent inventory in the final inventory listing. The new controller had intentionally overstated the inventory to compensate for the reduction in sales volume from the preceding year.

## Required

a. List the major deficiencies in the audit and state why they took place.

b. What things should have been apparent to Brewer in the conduct of the audit?

c. If Brewer's firm is sued by stockholders or creditors, what is the likely outcome?

**10-36 (Objectives 10-3, 10-4)** McClain Plastics has been an audit client of Belcor, Rich, Smith & Barnes, CPAs (BRS&B) for several years. McClain Plastics was started by Evers McClain, who owns 51 percent of the Company's stock. The balance is owned by about 200 stockholders who are investors with no operational responsibilities. McClain Plastics makes products that have plastic as their primary material. Some are made to order, but most products are made for inventory. An example of a McClain–manufactured product is a plastic chair pad that is used in a carpeted office. Another is a plastic bushing that is used with certain fastener systems.

McClain has grown from a small two-product company, when they first engaged BRS&B, to a successful diverse company. At the time Randall Sessions of BRS&B became manager of the audit, annual sales had grown to $20 million and profits to $1.9 million. Historically, the Company presented no unusual audit problems, and BRS&B had issued an unqualified opinion every year.

The audit approach BRS&B always used on the audit of McClain Plastics was a "substantive" audit approach. Under this approach, the in-charge auditor obtained an understanding of internal control, but control risk was assumed to be at the maximum (100 percent). Extensive analytical procedures were done on the income statement and unusual fluctuations were investigated. Detailed audit procedures emphasized balance sheet accounts. The theory was that if the balance sheet accounts were correct at year-end, and had been audited as of the beginning of the year, then retained earnings and the income statement must be correct.

### Part I

In evaluating the audit approach for McClain for the current year's audit, Sessions believed that a substantive approach was certainly within the bounds of generally accepted auditing standards, but was really only appropriate for the audits of small companies. In his judgment, McClain Plastics, with sales of $20 million and 46 employees, had reached the size where it was not economical, and probably not wise, to concentrate all the tests on the balance sheet. Therefore, he designed an audit program that emphasized identifying internal controls in all major transaction cycles and included tests of controls. The intended economic benefit of this "reducing control risk" approach was that the time spent testing controls would be more than offset by reduced tests of details of the balance sheet accounts.

In planning tests of inventories, Sessions used the *Audit Risk Model* included in the Statements on Auditing Standards to determine the number of inventory items BRS&B would test at year-end. Because of the number of different products, features, sizes, and colors, McClain's inventory consisted of 2,450 different items. These were maintained on a perpetual inventory management system that used a relational data base.

In using the Audit Risk Model for inventories, Sessions believed that an audit risk of 5 percent was acceptable. He assessed inherent risk as high (100 percent) because inventory, by its nature, is subject to many types of misstatements. Based on his understanding of the relevant transaction cycles, Sessions believed that internal controls were good. He therefore assessed control risk as low (50 percent), prior to performing tests of controls. Sessions also planned to use analytical procedures for tests of inventory. These planned tests included comparing gross profit margins by month and reviewing for slow-moving items. Sessions felt these tests would provide assurance of 40 percent. Substantive tests of details would include tests of inventory quantities, costs, and net realizable values at an interim date two months prior to year-end. Cutoff tests would be done at year-end. Inquiries and analytical procedures would be relied on for assurance about events between the interim audit date and fiscal year-end.

## Required

a. Decide which of the following would likely be done under both a "reducing control risk" approach and a "substantive" approach:
   (1) Assess acceptable audit risk
   (2) Assess inherent risk
   (3) Obtain an understanding of internal control
   (4) Assess control risk at less than 100%
   (5) Perform analytical procedures
   (6) Assess planned detection risk

b. What advantages does the "reducing control risk" approach Sessions plans to use have over the "substantive" approach previously used in the audit of McClain Plastics?

c. What advantages does the "substantive" approach have over the "reducing control risk" approach?

**Part II**

The engagement partner agreed with Sessions's recommended approach. In planning the audit evidence for detailed inventory tests, the Audit Risk Model was applied with the following results:

$$TDR = \frac{AAR}{IR \times CR \times APR}$$

where,

$$TDR = \text{test of details risk}$$

$$AAR = \text{acceptable audit risk}$$

$$IR = \text{inherent risk}$$

$$CR = \text{control risk}$$

$$APR = \text{analytical procedures risk}$$

Therefore, using Sessions's assessments and judgments as described previously,

$$TDR = \frac{.05}{1.0 \times .5 \times .6}$$

$$TDR = .17$$

## Required

a. Explain what .17 means in this audit.

b. Calculate *TDR* assuming that Sessions had assessed control risk at 100% and all other risks as they are stated.

c. Explain the effect of your answer in requirement b on the planned audit procedures and sample size in the audit of inventory compared with the .17 calculated by Sessions.

**Part III**

Although the planning went well, the actual testing yielded some surprises. When conducting tests of controls over acquisitions and additions to the perpetual inventory, the staff person performing the tests found that the exception rates for several important controls were significantly higher than expected. As a result, the staff person considered internal control weak, supporting an 80 percent control risk rather than the 50 percent level used. Accordingly, the staff person "reworked" the audit risk model as follows:

$$TDR = \frac{.05}{1.0 \times .8 \times .6}$$

$$TDR = .10$$

A 10 percent test of details risk still seemed to the staff person to be in the "moderate" range, so he recommended no increase in planned sample size for substantive tests.

## Required

Do you agree with the staff person's revised judgments about the effect of tests of controls on planned substantive tests? Explain the nature and basis of any disagreement.

# 11

# AUDIT OF THE SALES AND COLLECTION CYCLE: TESTS OF CONTROLS AND SUBSTANTIVE TESTS OF TRANSACTIONS

## LEARNING OBJECTIVES

Thorough study of this chapter will enable you to

**11-1** Identify the classes of transactions and accounts in the sales and collection cycle.

**11-2** Describe the business functions and the related documents and records in the sales and collection cycle.

**11-3** Determine the client's internal controls over sales transactions, design and perform tests of the controls and substantive tests of transactions, and assess related control risk.

**11-4** Apply the methodology for controls over sales transactions to controls over sales returns and allowances.

**11-5** Determine the client's internal controls over cash receipts transactions, design and perform tests of the controls and substantive tests of transactions, and assess related control risk.

**11-6** Apply the methodology for controls over the sales and collection cycle to write-offs of uncollectible accounts receivable.

**11-7** Develop an integrated audit plan for the sales and collection cycle.

## THE CHOICE IS SIMPLE—RELY ON INTERNAL CONTROL OR RESIGN

City Finance is the largest client managed out of the Pittsburgh office of a Big Six firm. It is a financial services conglomerate with almost a thousand offices in the United States and Canada, as well as correspondent offices overseas. The company's records contain over a million accounts receivable and process millions of transactions a year.

The company's computer center is in a large environmentally–controlled room containing several large mainframe computers and a great deal of ancillary equipment. There are two complete on-line systems, one serving as a backup for the other, as systems failure would preclude operations in all of the company's branches.

The company has an unusual system of checks and balances where branch office transaction records are reconciled to data processing controls daily, which, in turn, are reconciled to outside bank account records monthly. Whenever this massive reconciliation exercise indicates a significant out-of-balance condition, special procedures are initiated to resolve the problem as quickly as possible. There is a large internal audit staff that oversees any special investigative efforts that are required.

Because City Finance is a public company, it must file its report on Form 10-K with the Securities and Exchange Commission within 90 days after its fiscal year-end. In addition, the company likes to announce annual earnings and issue its annual report as soon after year-end as reasonably feasible. Under these circumstances, there is always a great deal of pressure on the CPA firm to complete the audit expeditiously.

A standard audit planning question is: "How much shall we rely on internal control?" In the case of the City Finance audit, there is only one possible answer: as much as we can. Otherwise, how could the audit possibly be completed to meet the reporting deadlines, let alone control audit cost to a reasonable level? Accordingly, the CPA firm conducts the audit with significant reliance on data processing controls, reconciliation processes, and internal audit procedures. They test these controls extensively and perform many of their substantive procedures prior to year-end. In all honesty, if City Finance did not have excellent internal controls, the CPA firm would admit that an audit of the company just couldn't be done.

**OBJECTIVE 11-1**

**Identify the classes of transactions and accounts in the sales and collection cycle.**

The overall objective in the audit of the sales and collection cycle is to evaluate whether the account balances affected by the cycle are fairly presented in accordance with generally accepted accounting principles. The following are typical accounts included in the sales and collection cycle:

- Sales
- Sales returns and allowances
- Bad debt expense
- Cash discounts taken
- Trade accounts receivable
- Allowance for uncollectible accounts
- Cash in the bank (debits from cash receipts)

For example, look at the adjusted trial balance for Hillsburg Hardware Co. on page 141. Accounts on the trial balance affected by the sales and collection cycle are identified by the letter *S* in the left margin. Each of the above accounts is included, except cash discounts taken. For other audits the names and the nature of the accounts may vary, of course, depending on the industry and client involved. There are differences in account titles for a service industry, a retail company, and an insurance company, but the key concepts are the same. To provide a frame of reference for understanding the material in this chapter, a wholesale merchandising company is assumed.

A brief summary of the way accounting information flows through the various accounts in the sales and collection cycle is illustrated in Figure 11-1 by the use of T-accounts. This figure shows that there are five classes of transactions included in the sales and collection cycle:

- Sales (cash and sales on account)
- Cash receipts
- Sales returns and allowances

**FIGURE 11-1**

**Accounts in the Sales and Collection Cycle**

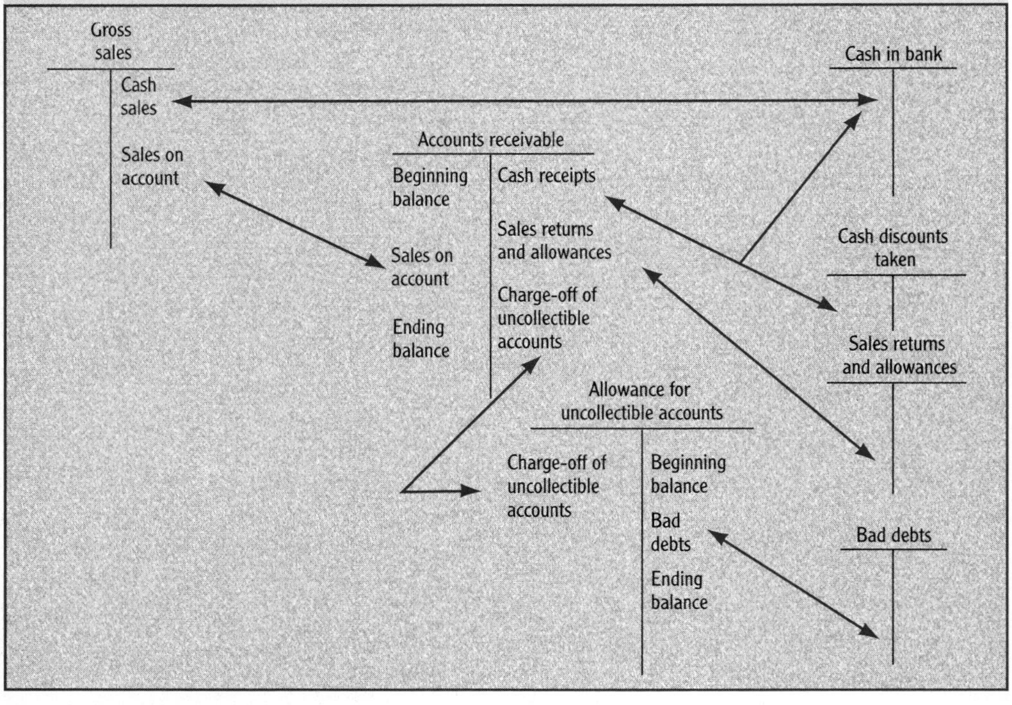

- Charge-off of uncollectible accounts
- Bad debt expense

Figure 11-1 also shows that with the exception of cash sales, every transaction and amount ultimately is included in two balance sheet accounts, accounts receivable or allowance for uncollectible accounts. For simplicity, assume that the same internal controls exist for both cash and credit sales.

For the most part, the audit of the sales and collection cycle can be performed independently of the audit of other cycles and subjectively combined with the other parts of the audit as the evidence accumulation process proceeds. Auditors must keep in mind that the concept of materiality requires them to consider the combination of misstatements in all parts of the audit before making a final judgment on the fair presentation in the financial statements. This is done by stopping at various times throughout the engagement and integrating the parts of the audit.

The types of audit tests discussed in Chapter 10, and shown in Figure 10-2 on page 334, are all used extensively in the audit of the sales and collection cycle. Tests of controls are used primarily to test the effectiveness of internal controls over the five classes of transactions in the cycle. Substantive tests of transactions are used both to test the effectiveness of internal controls and to test the dollar amounts of these same five classes of transactions. Analytical procedures are used to test the relationships among the account balances in the cycle, both to each other and to prior years' balances. Tests of details of balances are used to verify ending account balances, primarily accounts receivable. Tests of controls and substantive tests of transactions are studied in this chapter.

## NATURE OF THE SALES AND COLLECTION CYCLE

The sales and collection cycle involves the decisions and processes necessary for the transfer of the ownership of goods and services to customers after they are made available for sale. It begins with a request by a customer and ends with the conversion of material or service into an account receivable, and ultimately into cash.

The cycle includes several classes of transactions, accounts, and business functions, as well as a number of documents and records. These are shown in Table 11-1 on page 366.

## BUSINESS FUNCTIONS IN THE CYCLE AND RELATED DOCUMENTS AND RECORDS

**OBJECTIVE 11-2**
**Describe the business functions and the related documents and records in the sales and collection cycle.**

The business functions for a cycle are the key activities that an organization must complete to execute and record business transactions. Column three of Table 11-1 identifies the eight business functions in a typical sales and collection cycle. An understanding of these business functions for the sales and collection cycle is useful for understanding how an audit of the cycle is conducted. Students often also find it difficult to envision which documents exist in any given audit area and how they flow through the client's organization. The business functions for the sales and collection cycle and the most common documents used in each function are examined in this section.

### Processing Customer Orders

The request for goods by a customer is the starting point for the entire cycle. Legally, it is an offer to buy goods under specified terms. The receipt of a customer order often results in the immediate creation of a sales order.

**Customer Order** A request for merchandise by a customer. It may be received by telephone, letter, a printed form that has been sent to prospective and existing customers, through salespeople, or in other ways.

**TABLE 11-1**

**Classes of Transactions, Accounts, Business Functions, and Related Documents and Records for the Sales and Collection Cycle**

| Classes of Transactions | Accounts | Business Functions | Documents and Records |
|---|---|---|---|
| Sales | Sales<br>Accounts receivable | Processing customer orders | Customer order<br>Sales order |
| | | Granting credit | Customer order or sales order |
| | | Shipping goods | Shipping document |
| | | Billing customers and recording sales | Sales invoice<br>Sales journal<br>Summary sales report<br>Accounts receivable master file<br>Accounts receivable trial balance<br>Monthly statements |
| Cash receipts | Cash in bank (debits from cash receipts)<br>Accounts receivable | Processing and recording cash receipts | Remittance advice<br>Prelisting of cash receipts<br>Cash receipts journal |
| Sales returns and allowances | Sales returns and allowances<br>Accounts receivable | Processing and recording sales returns and allowances | Credit memo<br>Sales returns and allowances journal |
| Charge-off of uncollectible accounts | Accounts receivable<br>Allowance for uncollectible accounts | Charging off uncollectible accounts receivable | Uncollectible account authorization form |
| Bad debt expense | Bad debt expense<br>Allowance for uncollectible accounts | Providing for bad debts | Not applicable |

**Sales Order** A document for communicating the description, quantity, and related information for goods ordered by a customer. This is frequently used to indicate credit approval and authorization for shipment.

## Granting Credit

Before goods are shipped, a properly authorized person must *approve credit* to the customer for sales on account. Weak practices in credit approval frequently result in excessive bad debts and accounts receivable that may be uncollectible. For most firms, an indication of credit approval on the sales order is the approval to ship the goods.

## Shipping Goods

This critical function is the first point in the cycle where company assets are given up. Most companies recognize sales when goods are shipped. A shipping document is prepared at the time of shipment; this can be done automatically by the computer based on sales order information. The shipping document, which is frequently a multicopy bill of lading, is essential to the proper billing of shipments to customers. Companies that maintain perpetual inventory records also update them based upon shipping information.

**Shipping Document** A document prepared to initiate shipment of the goods, indicating the description of the merchandise, the quantity shipped, and other relevant data. The original is sent to the customer and one or more copies are retained. It is also used as a signal to bill the customer. One type of shipping document is a *bill of lading,* which is a written contract between the carrier and seller of the receipt and shipment of goods. Often bills of lading include only the number of boxes or pounds shipped, rather than complete details of quantity and description. Throughout the text, we assume that complete details are included on bills of lading. The computer operator informs the computer by a key entry that the goods described on the shipping document have been shipped.

## Billing Customers and Recording Sales

Since the billing of customers is the means by which the customer is informed of the amount due for the goods, it must be done correctly and on a timely basis. The most important aspects of billing are making sure that all shipments made have been billed, that no shipment has been billed more than once, and that each one is billed for the proper amount. Billing at the proper amount is dependent on charging the customer for the quantity shipped at the authorized price. The authorized price includes consideration for freight charges, insurance, and terms of payments.

In most systems, billing of the customer includes preparation of a multicopy sales invoice and simultaneous updating of the sales transactions file, accounts receivable master file, and general ledger master file for sales and accounts receivable. This information is used to generate the sales journal and, along with cash receipts and miscellaneous credits, allows preparation of the accounts receivable trial balance.

**Sales Invoice** A document indicating the description and quantity of goods sold, the price including freight, insurance, terms, and other relevant data. Typically, it is automatically prepared by the computer after the customer number, quantity, destination of goods shipped, and sales terms are entered. The sales invoice is the method of indicating to the customer the amount of a sale and due date of a payment. The original is sent to the customer and one or more copies are retained.

**Sales Journal** A journal for recording sales transactions. A detailed sales journal includes each sales transaction. It usually indicates gross sales for different classifications, such as product lines, the entry to accounts receivable, and miscellaneous debits and credits. The sales journal can also include sales returns and allowances transactions. This journal is generated for any time period from the sales transactions included in the computer files.

**Summary Sales Report** A computer generated document that summarizes sales for a period. The report typically includes information analyzed by key components such as salesperson, product, and territory.

**Accounts Receivable Master File** A file for recording individual sales, cash receipts, and sales returns allowances for each customer and maintaining customer account balances. The master file is updated from the sales, sales returns and allowances, and cash receipts computer transaction files. The total of the individual account balances in the master file equals the total balance of accounts receivable in the general ledger. A printout of the accounts receivable master file shows, by customer, the beginning balance in accounts receivable, each sales transaction, sales returns and allowances, cash receipts, and the ending balance. Whenever the term *master file* is used in this book, it refers to either the computer file or a printout of that file. It is also sometimes called the accounts receivable subsidiary ledger or subledger.

**Accounts Receivable Trial Balance** A listing of the amount owed by each customer at a point in time. This is prepared directly from the accounts receivable master file. It is most often an *aged* trial balance, showing how old the accounts receivable components of each customer's balance are as of the report date.

**Monthly Statement** A document sent to each customer indicating the beginning balance of accounts receivable, the amount and date of each sale, cash payments received, credit memos issued, and the ending balance due. It is, in essence, a copy of the customer's portion of the accounts receivable master file.

## Processing and Recording Cash Receipts

The preceding four functions are necessary for getting the goods into the hands of customers, properly billing them, and reflecting the information in the accounting records. The result of these four functions is sales transactions. The remaining four functions involve the collection and recording of cash, sales returns and allowances, charge-off of uncollectible accounts, and providing for bad debt expense.

Processing and recording cash receipts includes receiving, depositing, and recording cash. Cash includes both currency and checks. The most important concern is the possibility of theft. Theft can occur before receipts are entered in the records or later. The most important consideration in the handling of cash receipts is that all cash must be deposited in the bank at the proper amount on a timely basis and recorded in the cash receipts transaction file, which is used to prepare the cash receipts journal and update the accounts receivable and general ledger master files. Remittance advices are important for this purpose.

**Remittance Advice** A document that accompanies the sales invoice mailed to the customer and can be returned to the seller with the cash payment. It is used to indicate the customer name, the sales invoice number, and the amount of the invoice when the payment is received. If the customer fails to include the remittance advice with his or her payment, it is common for the person opening the mail to prepare one at that time. A remittance advice is used to permit the immediate deposit of cash and to improve control over the custody of assets.

**Prelisting of Cash Receipts** A list prepared by an independent person (someone without access to cash and who has no responsibility for recording sales or accounts receivable) when cash is received. It is used to verify whether cash received was recorded and deposited at the correct amounts and on a timely basis.

**Cash Receipts Journal** A journal for recording cash receipts from collections, cash sales, and all other cash receipts. It indicates total cash received, the credit to accounts receivable at the gross amount of the original sale, trade and cash discounts taken, and other debits and credits. The daily entries in the cash receipts journal are supported by remittance advices. The journal is generated for any time period from the cash receipts transactions included in the computer files.

## Processing and Recording Sales Returns and Allowances

When a customer is dissatisfied with the goods, the seller frequently accepts the return of the goods or grants a reduction in the charges. The company normally prepares a receiving report for the returned goods and returns them to storage. Returns and allowances must be correctly and promptly recorded in the sales returns and allowances transaction file and the accounts receivable master file. *Credit memos* are normally issued for returns and allowances to aid in maintaining control and to facilitate record keeping.

**Credit Memo** A document indicating a reduction in the amount due from a customer because of returned goods or an allowance granted. It often takes the same general form as a sales invoice, but it supports reductions in accounts receivable rather than increases.

**Sales Returns and Allowances Journal** A journal for recording sales returns and allowances. It performs the same function as the sales journal. Many companies record these transactions in the sales journal rather than in a separate journal.

## Charging Off Uncollectible Accounts Receivable

Regardless of the diligence of credit departments, it is not unusual if some customers do not pay their bills. When the company concludes that an amount is no longer collectible, it must be charged off. Typically, this occurs after a customer files bankruptcy or the account is turned over to a collection agency. Proper accounting requires an adjustment for these uncollectible accounts.

**Uncollectible Account Authorization Form** A document used internally, indicating authority to write an account receivable off as uncollectible.

## Providing for Bad Debts

The provision for bad debts must be sufficient to allow for the current period sales that the company will be unable to collect in the future. For most companies the provision represents a residual, resulting from management's end-of-period adjustment of the allowance for uncollectible accounts.

## METHODOLOGY FOR DESIGNING TESTS OF CONTROLS AND SUBSTANTIVE TESTS OF TRANSACTIONS FOR SALES

**OBJECTIVE 11-3**
**Determine the client's internal controls over sales transactions, design and perform tests of the controls and substantive tests of transactions, and assess related control risk.**

The methodology for obtaining an understanding of internal control and designing tests of controls and substantive tests of transactions for sales is shown in Figure 11-2. That methodology was studied in general terms in Chapters 9 and 10. It is applied specifically to sales in this section. The bottom box in Figure 11-2 shows the four evidence decisions the auditor must make. This section deals with deciding the appropriate audit procedures. For the timing decision, the tests are usually performed at an interim date if internal controls are effective, but they can also be done after the balance sheet date. Decisions on the appropriate sample size and the items to select are studied in Chapter 12.

Figure 11-2 is supported by Table 11-2 (page 370), which summarizes the application of the methodology in the figure. Table 11-2 lists the specific transaction-related audit objectives for sales along with related key controls, tests of those controls, and substantive tests of transactions for the objectives. Table 11-2 is referred to frequently throughout the section.

### Understand Internal Control—Sales

Chapter 9 discussed how auditors obtain an understanding of internal control. A typical approach for sales is to study the clients' flowcharts, prepare an internal control questionnaire, and perform walk-through tests of sales. Figures 11-5 (page 382) and 11-6 (page 383) include an organization chart and a flowchart for the Hillsburg Hardware Co. that are used to demonstrate the design of tests of controls and substantive tests of transactions audit procedures.

**FIGURE 11-2**

**Methodology for Designing Tests of Controls and Substantive Tests of Transactions for Sales**

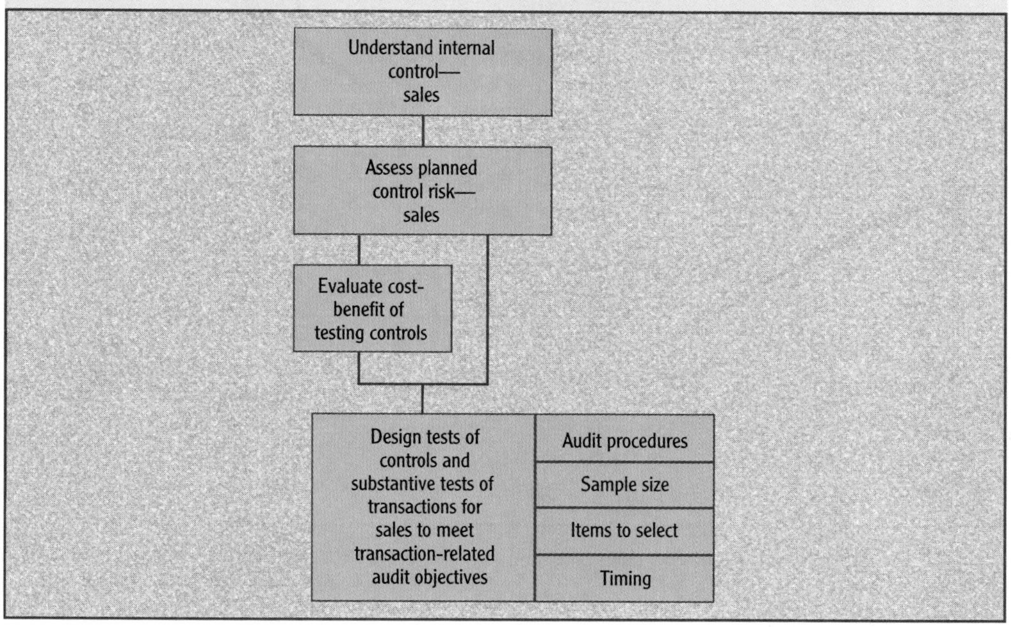

**TABLE 11-2**

## Summary of Transaction-Related Audit Objectives, Key Controls, Tests of Controls, and Substantive Tests of Transactions for Sales

| Transaction-Related Audit Objective | Key Internal Control | Common Test of Control | Common Substantive Tests of Transactions |
|---|---|---|---|
| Recorded sales are for shipments actually made to existing customers (existence). | Recording of sales is supported by authorized shipping documents and approved customer orders.<br>Credit is authorized before shipment takes place.<br>Sales invoices are prenumbered and properly accounted for.<br>Only customer numbers existing in the computer data files are accepted when they are entered.<br>Monthly statements are sent to customers; complaints receive independent follow-up. | Examine copies of sales invoices for supporting bills of lading and customers' orders.<br>Examine customer order for credit approval.<br>Account for integrity of numerical sequence of sales invoices.<br>Examine printouts of transactions rejected by the computer as having nonexistent customer numbers.†<br>Observe whether statements are mailed and examine customer correspondence files. | Review the sales journal, general ledger, and accounts receivable master file or trial balance for large or unusual items.*<br>Trace sales journal entries to copies of sales orders, sales invoices, and shipping documents.<br>Trace shipping documents to entry of shipments in perpetual inventory records.<br>Trace credit entries in accounts receivable master file to existing source. |
| Existing sales transactions are recorded (completeness). | Shipping documents are prenumbered and accounted for.<br>Sales invoices are prenumbered and accounted for. | Account for integrity of numerical sequence of shipping documents.<br>Account for integrity of numerical sequence of sales invoices. | Trace shipping documents to resultant sales invoices and entry into sales journal and accounts receivable master file. |
| Recorded sales are for the amount of goods shipped and are correctly billed and recorded (accuracy). | Determination of prices, terms, freight, and discounts is properly authorized.<br>Internal verification of invoice preparation.<br>Approved unit selling prices are entered into the computer and used for all sales.<br>Batch totals are compared with computer summary reports. | Examine copies of sales invoices for proper authorization.<br>Examine indication of internal verification on affected documents.<br>Examine approved computer printout of unit selling prices.†<br>Examine file of batch totals for initials of data control clerk; compare totals to summary reports.† | Recompute information on sales invoices.<br>Trace entries in sales journal to sales invoices.<br>Trace details on sales invoices to shipping documents, approved price lists, and customers' orders. |
| Sales transactions are properly classified (classification). | Use of adequate chart of accounts.<br>Internal review and verification. | Review chart of accounts for adequacy.<br>Examine indication of internal verification on affected documents. | Examine documents supporting sales transactions for proper classification. |
| Sales are recorded on the correct dates (timing). | Procedures requiring billing and recording of sales on a daily basis as close to time of occurrence as possible.<br>Internal verification. | Examine documents for unbilled shipments and unrecorded sales.<br>Examine indication of internal verification on affected documents. | Compare dates of recorded sales transactions with dates on shipping records. |
| Sales transactions are properly included in the accounts receivable master file and are correctly summarized (posting and summarization). | Regular monthly statements to customers.<br>Internal verification of accounts receivable master file contents.<br>Comparison of accounts receivable master file or trial balance totals with general ledger balance. | Observe whether statements are mailed.<br>Examine indication of internal verification.<br>Examine initials on general ledger account indicating comparison. | Foot journals and trace postings to general ledger and accounts receivable master file. |

*This analytical procedure can also apply to other transaction-related audit objectives, including completeness, accuracy, and timing.
†This control would be tested on many audits by using the computer.

## Assess Planned Control Risk—Sales

The auditor uses the information obtained in understanding internal control to assess control risk. There are four essential steps to this assessment, all of which were discussed in Chapter 9.

- First, the auditor needs a framework for assessing control risk. The framework for all classes of transactions is the six transaction-related audit objectives. For sales, these are shown for Hillsburg Hardware in Figure 11-7 on page 384. These six objectives are the same for every audit of sales.
- Second, the auditor must identify the key internal controls and weaknesses for sales. These are also shown on page 384. The controls and weaknesses will be different for every audit.
- After identifying the controls and weaknesses, the auditor associates them with the objectives. This is also shown on page 384 with *W*'s and *C*'s in appropriate columns.
- Finally, the auditor assesses control risk for each objective by evaluating the controls and weaknesses for each objective. This step is a critical one because it affects the auditor's decisions about both tests of controls and substantive tests. It is a highly subjective decision. The bottom of page 384 shows the auditor's conclusions for Hillsburg Hardware.

The section that follows discusses the key control activities (see pages 296–300) for sales. A knowledge of these control activities is important for identifying the key controls and weaknesses for sales, which is the second step in assessing control risk.

**Adequate Separation of Duties** Proper separation of duties is useful to prevent various types of misstatements, both intentional and unintentional. To prevent fraud, it is important that anyone responsible for inputting sales and cash receipts transaction information into the computer be denied access to cash. It is also desirable to separate the credit-granting functions from the sales function, since credit checks are intended to offset the natural tendency of sales personnel to optimize volume even at the expense of high bad debt write-offs. It is equally desirable that personnel responsible for doing internal comparisons are independent of those entering the original data. For example, comparison of batch control totals to summary reports and comparison of accounts receivable master file totals to the general ledger balance should be done by someone independent of those who input sales and cash receipt transactions.

**Proper Authorization** The auditor is concerned about authorization at *three key points:* credit must be properly authorized before a sale takes place; goods should be shipped only after proper authorization; and prices, including base terms, freight, and discounts, must be authorized. The first two controls are meant to prevent the loss of company assets by shipping to fictitious customers or those who will fail to pay for the goods. Price authorization is meant to make sure that the sale is billed at the price set by company policy.

**Adequate Documents and Records** Since each company has a unique system of originating, processing, and recording transactions, it may be difficult to evaluate whether its procedures are designed for maximum control; nevertheless, adequate record-keeping procedures must exist before most of the transaction-related audit objectives can be met. Some companies, for example, automatically prepare a multicopy prenumbered sales invoice at the time a customer order is received. Copies of this document are used to approve credit, authorize shipment, record the number of units shipped, and bill customers. Under this system, there is almost no chance of the failure to bill a customer if all invoices are accounted for periodically. Under a different system, in which the sales invoice is prepared only after a shipment has been made, the likelihood of failure to bill a customer is high unless some compensating control exists.

**Prenumbered Documents** An important characteristic of documents for sales is the use of prenumbering, which is meant to prevent both the *failure* to bill or record sales and the occurrence of *duplicate* billings and recordings. Of course, it does not do much good to have prenumbered documents unless they are properly accounted for. An example of the use of this control is the filing, by a billing clerk, of a copy of all shipping documents in sequential order after each shipment is billed, with someone else periodically accounting for all numbers and investigating the reason for any missing documents. Another example is to program the computer to prepare a listing of unused numbers at month's end with follow-up by appropriate personnel.

**Mailing of Monthly Statements** The mailing of monthly statements by someone who has no responsibility for handling cash or preparing the sales and accounts receivable records is a useful control because it encourages a response from customers if the balance is improperly stated. For maximum effectiveness, all disagreements about the balance in the account should be directed to a designated official who has no responsibility for handling cash or recording sales or accounts receivable.

**Internal Verification Procedures** The use of independent persons for checking the processing and recording of sales transactions is essential for fulfilling each of the six transaction-related audit objectives. Examples of these procedures include accounting for the numerical sequence of prenumbered documents, checking the accuracy of document preparation, and reviewing reports for unusual or incorrect items.

## Evaluate Cost-Benefit of Testing Controls

After the auditor has identified the key internal controls and weaknesses and assessed control risk, it is appropriate to decide whether substantive tests will be reduced sufficiently to justify the cost of performing tests of controls. Whenever it is practical, auditors make this decision before completing a matrix such as the one illustrated in Figure 11-7 on page 384. It makes little sense to incur the cost of identifying controls and assessing control risk below the maximum if there will be no reduction of substantive tests.

## Design Tests of Controls for Sales

For each control the auditor plans to rely on to reduce assessed control risk, he or she must design one or more tests of controls to verify its effectiveness. In most audits it is relatively easy to determine the nature of the test of the control from the nature of the control. For example, if the internal control is to initial customer orders after they have been approved for credit, the test of control is to examine the customer order for a proper initial.

Column three in Table 11-2 (page 370) shows one test of control for each key internal control in column two. For example, the first key internal control is "recording of sales is supported by authorized shipping documents and approved customer orders." The test of control is "examine copies of sales invoices for supporting bills of lading and customers' orders." For this test, it is important for the auditor to start with sales invoices and examine documents in support of the sales invoices rather than going in the opposite direction. If the auditor traced from shipping documents to sales invoices, it would be a test of completeness. Direction of tests is discussed further on page 374.

A common test of control for sales is to account for a sequence of various types of documents, such as duplicate sales invoices selected from the sales journal, watching for omitted and duplicate numbers or invoices outside the normal sequence. This test simultaneously provides evidence of both the existence and completeness objectives.

For example, assume that the auditor selects sales invoices #18100 to #18199. The completeness objective will be partially satisfied if all 100 sales invoices are recorded. The existence objective will be satisfied if there is no duplicate recording of any of the invoice numbers.

The appropriate tests of controls for separation of duties are ordinarily restricted to the auditor's observations of activities and discussions with personnel. For example, it is possible to observe whether the billing clerk has access to cash when opening incoming mail or depositing cash. It is usually also necessary to ask personnel what their responsibilities are and if there are any circumstances where their responsibilities are different from the normal policy. For example, the employee responsible for billing customers may state that he or she does not have access to cash. Future discussion may bring out that when the cashier is on vacation, that person takes over the cashier's duties.

Several of the tests of controls in Table 11-2 can be performed using the computer. For example, one of the key internal controls to prevent fraudulent transactions is to include a list of existing customer numbers in the computer files. If a nonexistent customer number is entered into the computer, it is rejected. A test of control is for the auditor to attempt to enter nonexistent customer numbers into the computer to make sure that the computer control is in operation. Tests of controls where the auditor uses the computer are studied in Chapter 15. For this chapter, all tests of controls are performed manually.

## Design Substantive Tests of Transactions for Sales

In deciding on substantive tests of transactions, some procedures are commonly employed on every audit regardless of the circumstances, whereas others are dependent on the adequacy of the controls and the results of the tests of controls. In Table 11-2, the substantive tests of transactions in column four are related to the transaction-related audit objectives in the first column and are designed to determine whether any monetary misstatements for that objective exist in the transaction. The audit procedures used are affected by the internal controls and tests of controls for that objective. Materiality, results of the prior year, and the other factors discussed in Chapter 8 also affect the procedures used. Some of the audit procedures employed when internal controls are inadequate are discussed in a later section.

Determining the proper substantive tests of transactions procedures for sales is relatively difficult because they vary considerably depending on the circumstances. In subsequent paragraphs, the procedures frequently *not* performed are emphasized, since they are the ones requiring an audit decision. The substantive tests of transactions procedures are discussed in the order of the sales transaction-related audit objectives in Table 11-2. It should be noted that some procedures fulfill more than one objective.

**Recorded Sales Exist** For this objective, the auditor is concerned with the possibility of *three types of misstatements:* sales being included in the journals for which no shipment was made, sales recorded more than once, and shipments being made to nonexistent customers and recorded as sales. The first two types of misstatements can be intentional or unintentional. The last type is always intentional. As might be imagined, the inclusion of fraudulent sales is rare. The potential consequences are significant because they lead to an overstatement of assets and income.

There is an important difference between finding intentional and unintentional overstatements of sales. An unintentional overstatement normally also results in a clear overstatement of accounts receivable, which can often be easily found through confirmation procedures. For fraud, the perpetrator will attempt to conceal the overstatement, making it more difficult for auditors to find. Substantive tests of transactions may be necessary to discover overstated sales in these circumstances.

The appropriate substantive tests of transactions for testing the existence objective depend on where the auditor believes the misstatements are likely to take place. Many auditors do substantive tests of transactions for the existence objective only if they believe that a control weakness exists; therefore the nature of the tests depends on the nature of the potential misstatement as follows:

***Recorded Sale For Which There Was No Shipment*** The auditor can trace from selected entries in the sales journal to make sure that related copies of the shipping and other supporting documents exist. If the auditor is concerned about the possibility of a fictitious duplicate copy of a shipping document, it may be necessary to trace the amounts to the perpetual inventory records as a test of whether inventory was reduced.

***Sale Recorded More than Once*** Duplicate sales can be determined by reviewing a numerically sorted list of recorded sales transactions for duplicate numbers.

***Shipment Made to Nonexistent Customers*** This type of fraud normally occurs only when the person recording sales is also in a position to authorize shipments. When internal controls are weak, it is difficult to detect fictitious shipments.

Another effective approach to detecting the three types of misstatements of sales transactions discussed previously is to trace the *credit* in the accounts receivable master file to its source. If the receivable was actually collected in cash or the goods were returned, there must originally have been a sale. If the credit was for a bad debt charge-off or a credit memo, or if the account was still unpaid at the time of the audit, intensive follow-up by examining shipping and customer order documents is required, since each of these could indicate an inappropriate sales transaction.

It should be kept in mind that *the ordinary audit is not primarily intended to detect fraud* unless the effect on the financial statements is material. The preceding substantive tests of transactions should be necessary only if the auditor is concerned about the occurrence of fraud due to inadequate controls.

**Existing Sales Transactions Are Recorded** In many audits, no substantive tests of transactions are made for the completeness objective on the grounds that overstatements of assets and income are a greater concern in the audit of sales transactions than their understatement. If there are inadequate controls, which is likely if the client does no independent internal tracing from shipping documents to the sales journal, substantive tests are necessary.

An effective procedure to test for unbilled shipments is to trace selected shipping documents from a file in the shipping department to related duplicate sales invoices and the sales journal. To conduct a meaningful test using this procedure, the auditor must be confident that all shipping documents are included in the file. This can be done by accounting for a numerical sequence of the documents.

***Direction of Tests*** It is important that auditors understand the difference between tracing from source documents to the journals and tracing from the journals back to supporting documents. The former is a test for *omitted transactions* (completeness objective), whereas the latter is a test for *nonexistent transactions* (existence objective).

In testing for the existence objective, the starting point is the journal. A sample of invoice numbers is selected *from* the journal and traced *to* duplicate sales invoices, shipping documents, and customer orders. In testing for the completeness objective, the likely starting point is the shipping document. A sample of shipping documents is selected and traced *to* duplicate sales invoices and the sales journal as a test of omissions.

When designing audit procedures for the existence and completeness objectives, the starting point for tracing the document is essential. This is referred to as the *direction of tests.* For example, if the auditor is concerned about the existence objective but traces in the wrong direction (from shipping documents to the journals), a serious audit deficiency exists. The direction of tests is illustrated in Figure 11-3.

**FIGURE 11-3**

**Direction of Tests for Sales**

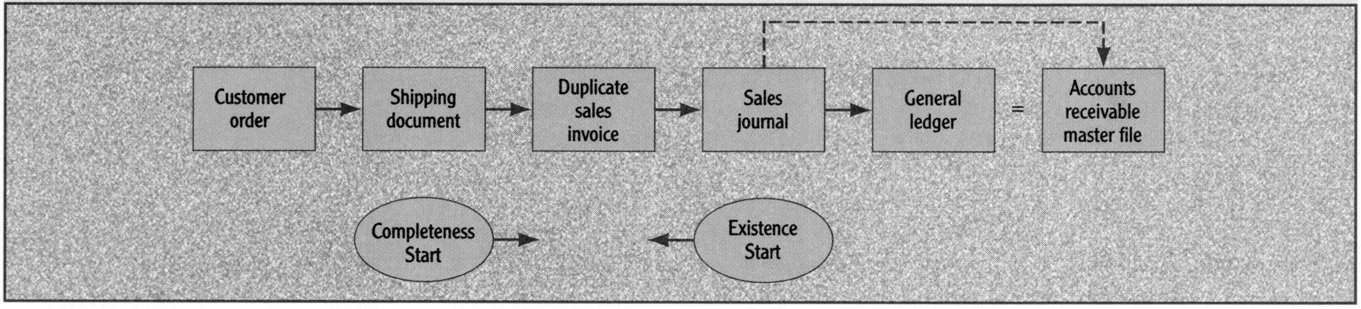

In testing for the other four transaction-related audit objectives, the direction of tests is usually not relevant. For example, the accuracy of sales transactions can be tested by tracing from a duplicate sales invoice to a shipping document or vice versa.

**Sales Are Accurately Recorded** The accurate recording of sales transactions concerns shipping the amount of goods ordered, accurately billing for the amount of goods shipped, and accurately recording the amount billed in the accounting records. Substantive tests to make sure that each of these aspects of accuracy is correct are ordinarily conducted in every audit.

Typical substantive tests of transactions include recomputing information in the accounting records to verify whether it is proper. A common approach is to start with entries in the sales journal and compare the total of selected transactions with accounts receivable master file entries and duplicate sales invoices. Prices on the duplicate sales invoices are normally compared with an approved price list, extensions and footings are recomputed, and the details listed on the invoices are compared with shipping records for description, quantity, and customer identification. Frequently, customer orders and sales orders are also examined for the same information.

The comparison of tests of controls and substantive tests of transactions for the accuracy objective is a good example of how audit time can be saved when effective internal controls exist. It is obvious that the test of control for this objective takes almost no time because it involves examining only an initial or other evidence of internal verification. Since the sample size for substantive tests of transactions can be reduced if this control is effective, a significant savings will result from performing the test of control due to its lower cost.

**Recorded Sales Are Properly Classified** Charging the correct general ledger account is less of a problem in sales than in some other transaction cycles, but it is still of some concern. When there are cash and credit sales, it is important not to debit accounts receivable for a cash sale, or to credit sales for collection of a receivable. It is also important not to classify sales of operating assets, such as buildings, as sales. For those companies using more than one sales classification, such as companies issuing segmented earnings statements, proper classification is essential.

It is common to test sales for proper classification as part of testing for accuracy. The auditor examines supporting documents to determine the proper classification of a given transaction and compares this with the actual account to which it is charged.

**Sales Are Recorded on the Correct Dates** It is important that sales be billed and recorded as soon after shipment takes place as possible to prevent the unintentional omission of transactions from the records and to make sure that sales are recorded in the proper period. At the same time that substantive tests of transactions procedures for accuracy are being performed, it is common to compare the date on selected bills of lading or other shipping documents with the date on related duplicate sales invoices, the sales journal, and the accounts receivable master file. Significant differences indicate a potential cutoff problem.

**Sales Transactions Are Properly Included in the Master File and Correctly Summarized** The proper inclusion of all sales transactions in the accounts receivable master file is essential because the accuracy of these records affects the client's ability to collect outstanding receivables. Similarly, the sales journal must be correctly totaled and posted to the general ledger if the financial statements are to be correct. In most audits, it is common to perform some clerical accuracy tests such as footing the journals and tracing the totals and details to the general ledger and the master file to check whether there are intentional or unintentional misstatements in the processing of sales transactions. The extent of such tests is affected by the quality of the internal controls. Tracing from the sales journal to the master file is typically done as a part of fulfilling other transaction-related audit objectives, but footing the sales journal and tracing the totals to the general ledger is done as a separate procedure.

The distinction between posting and summarization and other transaction-related audit objectives is that posting and summarization includes footing journals, master file records, and ledgers and tracing from one to the other among those three. Whenever footing and comparisons are restricted to these three records, the process is posting and summarization. In contrast, accuracy involves comparing documents with each other or with journals and master file records. To illustrate, comparing a duplicate sales invoice with either the sales journal or master file entry is an accuracy objective procedure. Tracing an entry from the sales journal to the master file is a posting and summarization procedure.

## Summary of Methodology for Sales

Figure 11-2 and Table 11-2 provide summaries of the previous discussion. Figure 11-2 (page 369) shows the methodology for designing tests of controls and substantive tests of transactions for sales. Table 11-2 (page 370) combines the four parts of the previous discussion.

**Transaction-Related Audit Objectives (Column 1)** The transaction-related audit objectives included in the table are derived from the framework developed in Chapters 5 and 9. Although certain internal controls satisfy more than one objective, it is desirable to consider each objective separately to facilitate a better assessment of control risk.

**Key Internal Controls (Column 2)** The internal controls for sales are designed to achieve the six transaction-related audit objectives discussed in Chapters 5 and 9. If the controls necessary to satisfy any one of the objectives are inadequate, the likelihood of misstatements related to that objective is increased, regardless of the controls for the other objectives. The methodology for determining existing controls was studied in Chapter 9.

The source of the controls in column 2 is the controls from a control risk matrix such as the one illustrated on page 384. A control will be included in more than one row in Table 11-2, if there is more than one *C* for that control on the control risk matrix.

**Tests of Controls (Column 3)** For each internal control in column 2, the auditor designs a test of control to verify its effectiveness. Observe that the tests of controls in Table 11-2 relate directly to the internal controls. For each control there should be at least one test of control.

**Substantive Tests of Transactions (Column 4)** The purpose of these tests is to determine whether there are monetary misstatements in sales transactions. In Table 11-2, the substantive tests of transactions are related to the objectives in the first column.

It is essential to understand the relationships among the columns in Table 11-2. The first column includes the six transaction-related audit objectives. The general objectives are the same for any class of transactions, but the specific objectives vary for sales, cash receipts, or any other classes of transactions. Column two lists one or more illustrative internal controls *for each transaction-related audit objective.* It is essential that any given control be related to one or more specific objective(s). Next, each common test of control in column three relates *to a given internal control.* A test of control has no meaning unless it tests a specific control. The table contains at least one test of control in column three for each internal control in column two. Finally, the common substantive tests of transactions in the table's last column are evidence to support *a specific transaction-related audit objective* in column one. The substantive tests of transactions are not directly related to the key control or test of control columns, but the extent of substantive tests of transactions depends, in part, on which key controls exist and on results of the tests of controls.

## Design and Performance Format Audit Procedures

The information presented in Table 11-2 is intended to help auditors *design audit programs* that satisfy the transaction-related audit objectives in a given set of circumstances. If certain objectives are important in a given audit or when the controls are different for different clients, the methodology helps the auditor design an effective and efficient audit program.

After the appropriate audit procedures for a given set of circumstances have been designed, they must be performed. It is likely to be inefficient to do the audit procedures as they are stated in the design format of Table 11-2. In converting from a design to a performance format, procedures are combined. This will

- Eliminate duplicate procedures.
- Make sure that when a given document is examined, all procedures to be performed on that document are done at that time.
- Enable the auditor to do the procedures in the most effective order. For example, by footing the journal and reviewing the journal for unusual items first, the auditor gains a better perspective in doing the detailed tests.

The process of converting from a design to a performance format is illustrated for the Hillsburg Hardware case application at the end of the chapter. The design format is shown on pages 386–388. The performance format is on page 389.

## SALES RETURNS AND ALLOWANCES

**OBJECTIVE 11-4**
**Apply the methodology for controls over sales transactions to controls over sales returns and allowances.**

The transaction-related audit objectives and the client's methods of controlling misstatements are essentially the same for processing credit memos as those described for sales, with two important differences. The first relates to *materiality.* In many instances sales returns and allowances are so immaterial that they can be ignored in the audit altogether. The second major difference relates to *emphasis on objectives.* For sales returns and allowances, the primary emphasis is normally on testing the existence of recorded transactions as a means of uncovering any diversion of cash from the collection of accounts receivable that has been covered up by a fictitious sales return or allowance.

Although the emphasis for the audit of sales returns and allowances is often on testing the existence of recorded transactions, the *completeness* objective cannot be ignored. Unrecorded sales returns and allowances can be material and can be used by a company's management to overstate net income.

Naturally, the other objectives should not be ignored. But because the objectives and methodology for auditing sales returns and allowances are essentially the same as for sales, we will not include a detailed study of the area. The reader should be able to apply the same logic to arrive at suitable controls, tests of controls, and substantive tests of transactions to verify the amounts.

**SALES CAN BE RETURNED (AND COME BACK TO HAUNT YOU)**

Don Sheelen sought to aggressively increase the market share of Regina Co. in the competitive vacuum cleaner market following its initial public offering in 1985. However, new products that were rushed to market without adequate testing suffered from a high defect rate. By 1987, the company was being flooded with product returns. In the third quarter of 1987 alone, more than 40,000 vacuums were returned in one product line, representing 16 percent of sales.

To protect earnings and the company's stock price, Sheelen conspired with his chief financial officer to not record the sales returns, which by now were so substantial that they had to be stored in a separate warehouse. Under Sheelen's and the CFO's direction, Regina employees altered the company's computer system so that the returns were not recorded on Regina's books. When the fraud unraveled in 1988, the company was forced to declare bankruptcy. Sheelen pleaded guilty to one count of mail and securities fraud and was fined $25,000 and sentenced to one year in a minimum security correctional facility.

*Sources:* John A. Byrne, "How Don Sheelen Made a Mess that Regina Couldn't Clean Up," *Business Week,* February 12, 1990, pp. 46–50. Michael C. Knapp, *Contemporary Auditing: Issues and Cases.* West Publishing, New York, 1993, pp. 79–85.

## INTERNAL CONTROLS, TESTS OF CONTROLS, AND SUBSTANTIVE TESTS OF TRANSACTIONS FOR CASH RECEIPTS

**OBJECTIVE 11-5**

**Determine the client's internal controls over cash receipts transactions, design and perform tests of the controls and substantive tests of transactions, and assess related control risk.**

The same methodology used for designing tests of controls and substantive tests of transactions for sales is used for cash receipts. Similarly, cash receipts tests of controls and substantive tests of transactions audit procedures are developed around the same framework used for sales; that is, given the transaction-related audit objectives, key internal controls for each objective are determined, tests of control are developed for each control, and substantive tests of transactions for the monetary misstatements related to each objective are developed. As in all other audit areas, the tests of controls depend on the controls the auditor has identified to reduce assessed control risk after consideration of the tests of controls and the other considerations in the audit.

Key internal controls, common tests of controls, and common substantive tests of transactions to satisfy each of the transaction-related audit objectives for cash receipts are listed in Table 11-3. Since this summary follows the same format as the previous one for sales, no further explanation of its meaning is necessary.

The detailed discussion of the internal controls, tests of controls, and substantive tests of transactions that was included for the audit of sales is not included for cash receipts. Instead, the audit procedures that are most likely to be misunderstood are explained in more detail.

An essential part of the auditor's responsibility in auditing cash receipts is identification of weaknesses in internal control that increase the likelihood of fraud. In expanding on Table 11-3, the emphasis will be on those audit procedures that are designed primarily for the discovery of fraud. Those procedures that are not discussed are omitted only because their purpose and the methodology for applying them should be apparent from their description.

### Determine Whether Cash Received Was Recorded

The most difficult type of cash defalcation for the auditor to detect is that which occurs *before the cash is recorded* in the cash receipts journal or other cash listing, especially if the sale and cash receipt are recorded simultaneously. For example, if a grocery store clerk takes cash and intentionally fails to register the receipt of cash on the cash register, it is extremely difficult to discover the theft. To prevent this type of fraud, internal controls such as those included in the second objective in Table 11-3 are implemented by many companies. The type of control will, of course, depend on the type of business. For example, the controls for a retail store in which the cash is received by the same person who sells the merchandise and rings up the cash receipts should be different from the controls for a company in which all receipts are received through the mail several weeks after the sales have taken place.

It is normal practice to trace from *prenumbered remittance advices* or *prelists of cash receipts* to the cash receipts journal and subsidiary accounts receivable records as a substantive test of the recording of actual cash received. This test will be effective only if a cash register tape or some other prelisting was prepared at the time cash was received.

### Prepare Proof of Cash Receipts

A useful audit procedure to test whether all recorded cash receipts have been deposited in the bank account is a proof of cash receipts. In this test the total cash receipts recorded in the cash receipts journal for a given period, such as a month, are reconciled with the actual deposits made to the bank during the same period. There may be a difference in the two due to deposits in transit and other items, but the amounts can be reconciled and compared. The procedure is not useful in discovering cash receipts that have not been recorded in the journals or time lags in making deposits, but it can help uncover recorded cash receipts that have not been deposited, unrecorded deposits, unrecorded loans, bank loans deposited directly into the bank account, and similar misstatements. A proof of cash receipts and cash disbursements is illustrated in Chapter 21 on page 708. This somewhat time-consuming procedure is ordinarily used only when the controls are weak. In rare instances in which controls are extremely weak the period covered by the proof of cash receipts may be the entire year.

**TABLE 11-3**

**Summary of Transaction-Related Audit Objectives, Key Controls, Tests of Controls, and Substantive Tests of Transactions for Cash Receipts**

| Transaction-Related Audit Objective | Key Internal Control | Common Test of Control | Common Substantive Tests of Transactions |
|---|---|---|---|
| Recorded cash receipts are for funds actually received by the company (existence). | Separation of duties between handling cash and record keeping.<br>Independent reconciliation of bank accounts. | Observe separation of duties.<br>Observe independent reconciliation of bank accounts. | Review the cash receipts journal, general ledger, and accounts receivable master file or trial balance for large and unusual amounts.*<br>Trace from cash receipts journal to bank statements.<br>Proof of cash receipts. |
| Cash received is recorded in the cash receipts journal (completeness). | Separation of duties between handling cash and record keeping.<br>Use of remittance advices or a prelisting of cash.<br>Immediate endorsement of incoming checks.<br>Internal verification of the recording of cash receipts.<br>Regular monthly statements to customers. | Discussion with personnel and observation.<br>Account for numerical sequence or examine prelisting.<br>Observe immediate endorsement of incoming checks.<br>Examine indication of internal verification.<br>Observe whether monthly statements are being sent to customers. | Trace from remittances or prelisting to cash receipts journal. |
| Cash receipts are deposited and recorded at the amounts received (accuracy). | Same as previous objective.<br>Approval of cash discounts.<br>Regular reconciliation of bank accounts.<br>Batch totals are compared with computer summary reports. | Same as previous objective.<br>Examine remittance advices for proper approval.<br>Review monthly bank reconciliations.<br>Examine file of batch totals for initials of data control clerk; compare totals to summary reports. | Proof of cash receipts.<br>Examine remittance advices and sales invoices to determine whether discounts allowed are consistent with company policy. |
| Cash receipts transactions are properly classified (classification). | Use of adequate chart of accounts.<br>Internal review and verification. | Review chart of accounts.<br>Examine indication of internal verification. | Examine documents supporting cash receipts for proper classification. |
| Cash receipts are recorded on the correct dates (timing). | Procedure requiring recording of cash receipts on a daily basis.<br>Internal verification. | Observe unrecorded cash at any point of time.<br>Examine indication of internal verification. | Compare dates of deposits with dates in the cash receipts journal and prelisting of cash receipts. |
| Cash receipts are properly included in the accounts receivable master file and are correctly summarized (posting and summarization). | Regular monthly statements to customers.<br>Internal verification of accounts receivable master file contents.<br>Comparison of accounts receivable master file or trial balance totals with general ledger balance. | Observe whether statements are mailed.<br>Examine indication of internal verification.<br>Examine initials on general ledger account indicating comparison. | Foot journals and trace postings to general ledger and accounts receivable master file. |

*This analytical procedure can also apply to other transaction-related audit objectives, including completeness, accuracy, and timing.

### Test to Discover Lapping of Accounts Receivable

Lapping of accounts receivable, which is a common type of defalcation, is the postponement of entries for the collection of receivables to *conceal an existing cash shortage.* The defalcation is perpetrated by a person who handles cash receipts and then enters them into the computer system. He or she defers recording the cash receipts from one customer and covers the shortages with receipts of another. These in turn are covered from the receipts of a third customer a few days later. The employee must continue to cover the shortage through repeated lapping, replace the stolen money, or find another way to conceal the shortage.

This defalcation can be easily prevented by separation of duties. It can be detected by comparing the name, amount, and dates shown on remittance advices with cash receipts journal entries and related duplicate deposit slips. Since the procedure is relatively time consuming, it is ordinarily performed only when there is specific concern with defalcation because of a weakness in internal control.

## AUDIT TESTS FOR UNCOLLECTIBLE ACCOUNTS

**OBJECTIVE 11-6**
**Apply the methodology for controls over the sales and collection cycle to write-offs of uncollectible accounts receivable.**

Existence of recorded write-offs is the most important transaction-related audit objective that the auditor should keep in mind in the verification of the write-off of individual uncollectible accounts. A major concern in testing accounts charged off as uncollectible is the possibility of the client covering up a defalcation by charging off accounts receivable that have already been collected. The major control for preventing this type of misstatement is proper authorization of the write-off of uncollectible accounts by a designated level of management only after a thorough investigation of the reason the customer has not paid.

Normally, verification of the accounts charged off takes relatively little time. A typical procedure is the examination of approvals by the appropriate persons. For a sample of accounts charged off, it is also usually necessary for the auditor to examine correspondence in the client's files establishing their uncollectibility. In some cases the auditor will also examine credit reports such as those provided by Dun & Bradstreet. After the auditor has concluded that the accounts charged off by general journal entries are proper, selected items should be traced to the accounts receivable master file as a test of the records.

## ADDITIONAL INTERNAL CONTROLS OVER ACCOUNT BALANCES

The preceding discussion emphasized internal controls, tests of controls, and substantive tests of transactions for the five classes of transactions that affect account balances in the sales and collection cycle. If the internal controls for these classes of transactions are determined to be effective and the related substantive tests of transactions support the conclusions, the likelihood of misstatements in the financial statements is reduced.

In addition, there may be internal controls directly related to account balances that have not been identified or tested as a part of tests of controls or substantive tests of transactions. For the sales and collection cycle, these are most likely to affect three balance-related audit objectives: realizable value, rights and obligations, and presentation and disclosure.

Realizable value is an essential balance-related audit objective for accounts receivable because collectibility of receivables is often a major financial statement item, and has been an issue in a number of accountants' liability cases. It is, therefore, common for inherent risk to be high for the realizable value objective.

Several controls are common for the realizable value objective. One that has already been discussed is credit approval by an appropriate person. A second is the preparation of a periodic aged accounts receivable trial balance for review and follow-up by appropriate management personnel. A third control is a policy of charging off uncollectible accounts when they are no longer likely to be collected.

Rights and obligations and presentation and disclosure are rarely a significant problem for accounts receivable. Therefore, competent accounting personnel are typically sufficient controls for these two balance-related audit objectives.

## EFFECT OF RESULTS OF TESTS OF CONTROLS AND SUBSTANTIVE TESTS OF TRANSACTIONS

The results of the tests of controls and substantive tests of transactions will have a significant effect on the remainder of the audit, especially on the substantive tests of details of balances. The parts of the audit most affected by the tests of controls and substantive tests of transactions for the sales and collection cycle are the balances in *accounts receivable, cash, bad debt expense,* and *allowance for doubtful accounts.* Furthermore, if the results of the tests are unsatisfactory, it is necessary to do additional substantive testing for the propriety of sales, sales returns and allowances, charge-off of uncollectible accounts, and processing of cash receipts.

At the completion of the tests of controls and substantive tests of transactions, it is essential to *analyze each exception* to determine its cause and the implication of the exception on assessed control risk, which may affect the supported detection risk and thereby the remaining substantive tests. The methodology and implications of exceptions analysis are explained more fully in Chapter 12.

The most significant effect of the results of the tests of controls and substantive tests of transactions in the sales and collection cycle is on the confirmation of accounts receivable. The type of confirmation, the size of the sample, and the timing of the test are all affected. The effect of the tests on accounts receivable, bad debt expense, and allowance for uncollectible accounts is considered in Chapter 13.

Figure 11-4 illustrates the major accounts in the sales and collection cycle and the types of audit tests used to audit these accounts. This figure also shows how the audit risk model discussed in Chapter 8 relates to the audit of the sales and collection cycle.

**FIGURE 11-4**

**Types of Audit Tests for the Sales and Collection Cycle (see Figure 11-1 on page 364 for accounts)**

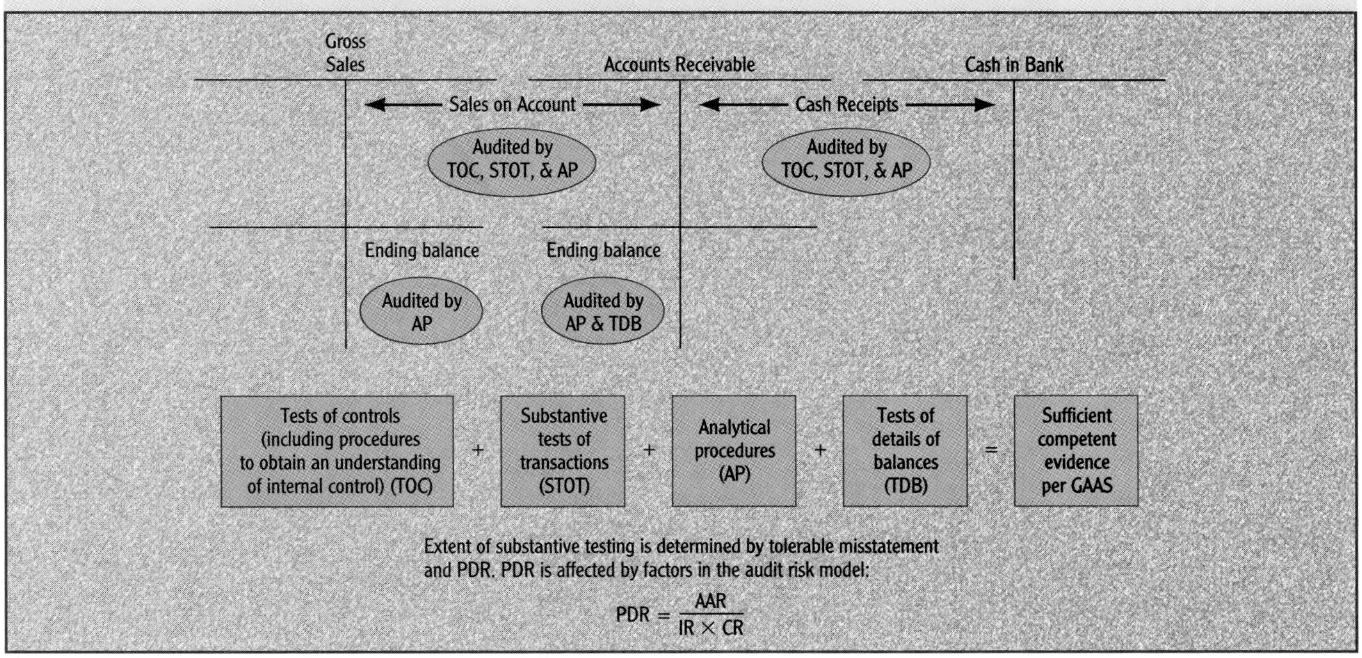

## CASE ILLUSTRATION—HILLSBURG HARDWARE, PART I

**OBJECTIVE 11-7**

**Develop an integrated audit plan for the sales and collection cycle.**

The concepts for testing the sales and collection cycle presented in this chapter are now illustrated for Hillsburg Hardware Co. The company's financial statements and the general ledger trial balance were shown in Chapter 5. Additional information was included in other chapters. A study of this case is intended to illustrate a methodology for designing audit procedures and integrating different parts of the audit.

Hillsburg Hardware Co. is a small wholesale distributor of hardware to independent, high-quality hardware stores in the southeastern part of the United States. This is the fourth year of the audit of this client, and there have never been any significant misstatements discovered in the tests. During the current year, a major change has occurred. The chief accountant left the firm and has been replaced by Erma Swanson. There has also been some turnover of other accounting personnel.

The overall assessment by management is that the accounting personnel are reasonably competent and highly trustworthy. The president, Rick Chulick, has been the chief operating officer for approximately 10 years. He is regarded as a highly competent, honest individual who does a conscientious job. The following information is provided from the auditor's files:

- *The organization chart and flowchart of internal control prepared for the audit.* This information is included in Figures 11-5 and 11-6. Sales returns and allowances for this client are too immaterial to include in the flowchart or to verify in the audit.
- *Internal controls and weaknesses, and assessment of control risk for sales and cash receipts.* An appropriate approach to identifying and documenting internal controls and weaknesses and assessing control risk is included for sales in Figure 11-7 (page 384) and for cash receipts in Figure 11-8 (page 385). There are several things the auditor, Fran Moore, did to complete each matrix. First, she identified internal controls from flowcharts, internal control questionnaires, and discussions with client personnel. Only flowcharts are available in the Hillsburg case. Second, she identified weaknesses using the same sources. Third, she decided which transaction-related audit objectives are affected by the internal controls and weaknesses. Finally, she assessed control risk using the information obtained in the preceding three steps. The use of the objective-by-objective matrix in Figures 11-7 and 11-8 is primarily to help Fran Moore effectively assess control risk.

**FIGURE 11-5**

**Hillsburg Hardware Organization Chart: Personnel**

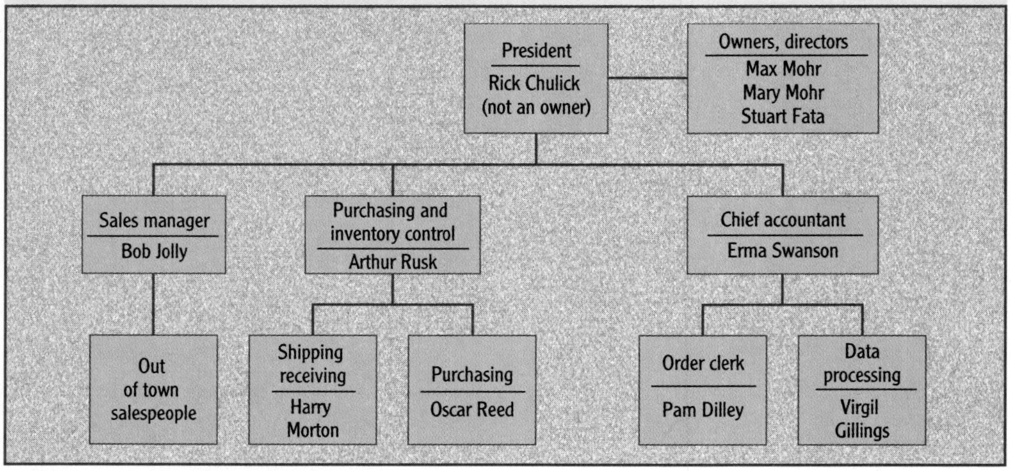

## FIGURE 11-6

### Hillsburg Hardware—Flowchart of Sales and Cash Receipts

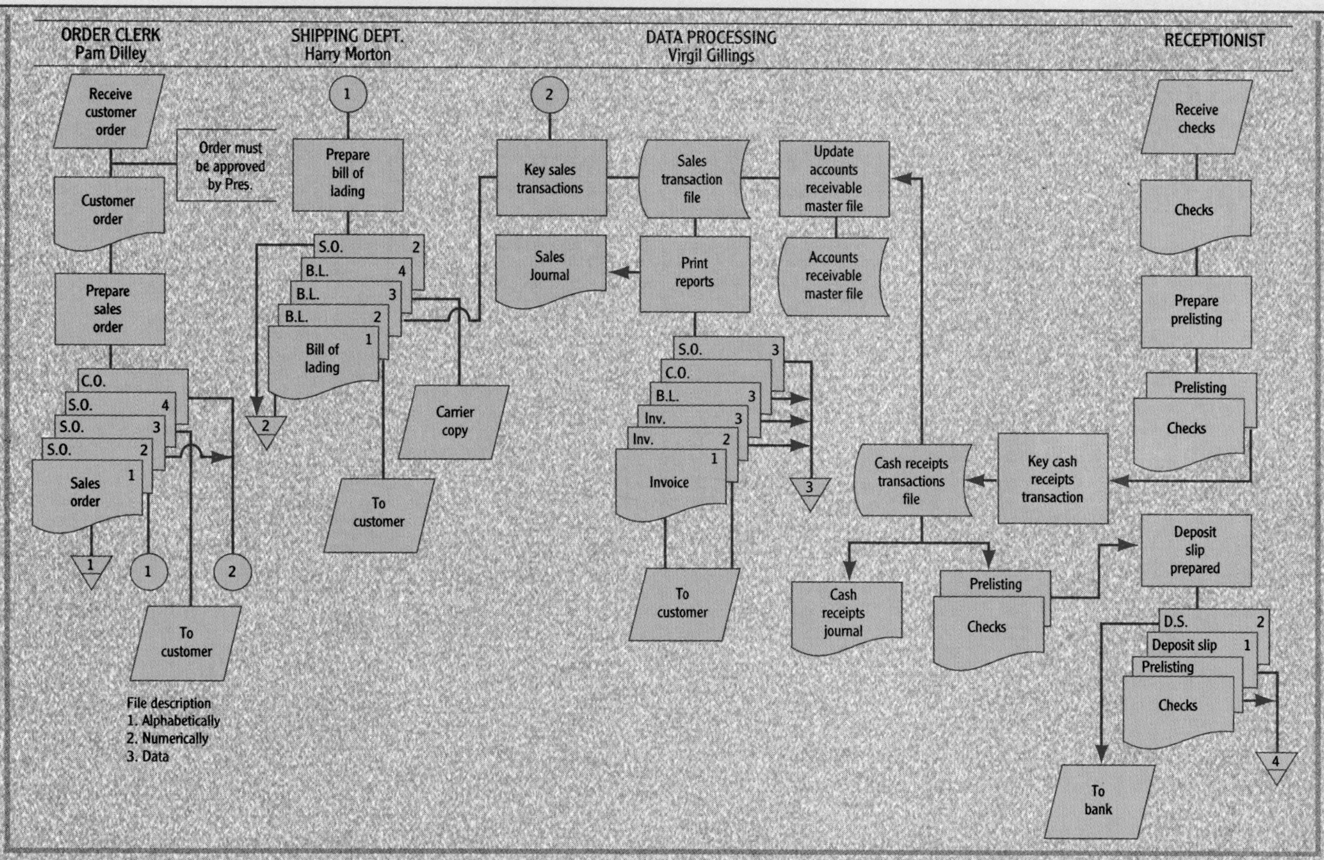


**NOTES**

1. All correspondence is sent to the president.
2. All sales order numbers are accounted for weekly by the chief accountant.
3. All bills of lading numbers are accounted for weekly by the chief accountant.
4. Sales amount recorded on sales invoice is based on standard price list. It is stored in a computer data file and can only be changed with authorization of the chief accountant.
5. Duplicate sales invoice is compared with bill of lading daily by Pam Dilley for descriptions and quantities and the sales invoice is reviewed for reasonableness of the extensions and footing. She initials a copy of the invoice before the original is mailed to the customer.
6. Sales are batched daily by Pam Dilley. The batch totals are compared to the sales journal weekly.
7. Statements are sent to customers monthly.
8. Accounts receivable master file total is compared with general ledger by the chief accountant on a monthly basis.
9. Unpaid invoices are filed separately from paid invoices.
10. The receptionist stamps incoming checks with a restrictive endorsement immediately upon receipt.
11. There are no cash sales.
12. Deposits are made at least weekly.
13. Cash receipts are batched daily by the receptionist. The batch totals are compared to the cash receipts journal weekly.
14. The bank account is reconciled by the chief accountant on a monthly basis.
15. All bad debt expense and charge-off of bad debts are approved by the president after being initiated by the chief accountant.
16. Financial statements are printed monthly by the chief accountant and reviewed by the president.
17. All errors are reviewed daily by the chief accountant immediately after the updating run. Corrections are made the same day.

- *Tests of control for each internal control.* The tests of controls for sales are included in the third column of Table 11-4 (page 386) and for cash receipts in the same column in Table 11-5 (page 387). The source of the internal controls is Figure 11-7 for sales and Figure 11-8 for cash receipts. Fran decided the appropriate tests for each control.
- *Substantive tests of transactions for each transaction-related audit objective.* The substantive tests of transactions are included in the last column of sales (Table 11-4) and cash receipts (Table 11-5). Fran decided the appropriate substantive tests of transactions for each objective after considering assessed control risk, planned tests of controls, and weaknesses of internal control for that objective.

**FIGURE 11-7**

**Control Risk Matrix for Hillsburg Hardware Co.—Sales**

| | INTERNAL CONTROL | SALES TRANSACTION-RELATED AUDIT OBJECTIVES: Recorded sales are for shipments actually made to nonfictitious customers (existence) | Existing sales transactions are recorded (completeness) | Recorded sales are for the amount of goods shipped and are correctly billed and recorded (accuracy) | Sales transactions are properly classified (classification) | Sales are recorded on the correct dates (timing) | Sales transactions are properly included in the accounts receivable master file and correctly summarized (posting and summarization) |
|---|---|---|---|---|---|---|---|
| CONTROLS | Dilley examines documents before bill is sent to customer (C1) | C | | C | | | |
| | Credit is approved by the president before shipment (C2) | C | | | | | |
| | Bills of lading are accounted for weekly by the accountant to make sure that they are billed (C3) | | C | | | | |
| | Batch totals are compared with computer summary reports (C4) | C | C | C | | | |
| | Accountant compares accounts receivable master file total with general ledger account (C5) | | | | | | C |
| | Monthly statements are sent to customers (C6) | C | | C | | | C |
| WEAKNESSES | Lack of internal verification for the possibility of sales invoices being recorded more than once (W1) | W | | | | | |
| | Lack of control to test for timely recording (W2) | | | | | W | |
| | Lack of internal verification that sales invoices are included in the sales journal (W3) | | W | | | | |
| | Assessed control risk | Medium | Medium | Low | Low * | High | Low |

* Since there are no cash sales, classification is not a problem.
C = Control
W = Weakness

**FIGURE 11-8**

**Control Risk Matrix for Hillsburg Hardware Co.—Cash Receipts**

| | INTERNAL CONTROL | Recorded cash receipts are for funds actually received by the company (existence) | Cash received is recorded in the cash receipts journal (completeness) | Cash receipts are deposited at the amount received (accuracy) | Cash receipts transactions are properly classified (classification) | Cash receipts are recorded on the correct dates (timing) | Cash receipts are properly included in the accounts receivable master file and are correctly summarized (posting and summarization) |
|---|---|---|---|---|---|---|---|
| | | CASH RECEIPTS TRANSACTION-RELATED AUDIT OBJECTIVES | | | | | |
| CONTROLS | Accountant reconciles bank account (C1) | C | | C | | | |
| | Checks are stamped with a restrictive endorsement (C2) | | C | | | | |
| | Statements are sent to customers monthly (C3) | | C | C | | | |
| | Batch totals are compared with computer summary reports (C4) | C | C | C | | | |
| | Accountant compares accounts receivable master file total with general ledger account (C5) | | | | | | C |
| WEAKNESSES | Prelisting of cash is not used to verify recorded cash receipts (W1) | | W | | | | |
| | Receptionist handles cash after it is returned from cash receipts (W2) | | W | | | | |
| | Data processor has access to cash receipts and maintains accounts receivable records (W3) | | W | | | | |
| | Cash receipts are not deposited daily (W4) | | | | | W | |
| | Lack of internal verification of classification of cash receipts (W5) | | | | W | | |
| | Assessed control risk | Low | High | Low | High | High | Medium |

C = Control
W = Weakness

Notice that the use of the objective-by-objective format in Tables 11-4 and 11-5 is to help Fran more effectively decide the appropriate substantive tests of transactions. She could have decided tests of controls as easily by selecting tests of controls for each internal control included in Figures 11-7 and 11-8.

- *Tests of controls and substantive tests of transactions audit program in a performance format.* The tests of controls and substantive tests of transactions in Table 11-4 and Table 11-5 are combined into one audit program in Figure 11-9 on page 389.

**TABLE 11-4**

**Internal Controls, Tests of Controls, and Substantive Tests of Transactions for Hillsburg Hardware Co.—Sales* (Design Format)**

| Transaction-Related Audit Objective | Existing Control† | Test of Control | Weakness | Substantive Tests of Transactions |
|---|---|---|---|---|
| Recorded sales are for shipments actually made to existing customers | Dilley examines documents before bill is sent to customer (C1)<br><br>Credit is approved by the president before shipment (C2)<br>Batch totals are compared with computer summary reports (C4)<br>Monthly statements are sent to customers (C6) | Account for a sequence of sales invoices in the sales journal (11)<br>Examine underlying documents for indication of internal verification by Pam Dilley (12b)<br>Examine customer order for credit approval by Rick Chulick (12e)<br>Examine file of batch totals for initials of data control clerk (8)<br>Observe whether monthly statements are mailed (6) | Lack of internal verification for the possibility of sales invoices being recorded more than once (W1) | Review journals and master file for unusual transactions and amounts (1)<br>Trace recorded sales from the sales journal to the file of supporting documents, which includes a duplicate sales invoice, bill of lading, sales order, and customer order (13) |
| Existing sales transactions are recorded | Bills of lading are accounted for weekly by the accountant to make sure that they are billed (C3)<br>Batch totals are compared with computer summary reports (C4) | Account for a sequence of shipping documents (9)<br><br>Examine file of batch totals for initials of data control clerk (8) | Lack of internal verification that sales invoices are included in the sales journal (W3) | Trace selected shipping documents to the sales journal to be sure that each one has been included (10) |
| Recorded sales are for the amount of goods shipped and are correctly billed and recorded | Dilley examines documents before bill is sent to customer (C1)<br><br>Credit is approved by president before shipments (C2)<br>Batch totals are compared with computer summary reports (C4)<br>Monthly statements are sent to customers (C6) | Examine underlying documents for indication of internal verification by Dilley (12b)<br>Examine customer order for credit approval by Chulick (12e)<br>Examine file of batch totals for initials of data control clerk (8)<br>Observe whether monthly statements are mailed (6) | | Trace selected duplicate sales invoice numbers from the sales journal to: (12)<br>a. Duplicate sales invoice, and check for the total amount recorded in journal, date, customer name, and account classification. Check the pricing, extensions, and footings (12b)<br>b. Bill of lading and test for customer name, product description, quantity, and date (12c)<br>c. Duplicate sales order and test for customer name, product description, quantity, and date (12d)<br>d. Customer order and test for customer name, product description, quantity, and date (12e) |

*[continued]*

**TABLE 11-4**

**Internal Controls, Tests of Controls, and Substantive Tests of Transactions for Hillsburg Hardware Co.—Sales* (Design Format)**
*[continued]*

| Transaction-Related Audit Objective | Existing Control† | Test of Control | Weakness | Substantive Tests of Transactions |
|---|---|---|---|---|
| Sales transactions are properly classified | None | | | Examine duplicate sales invoice for proper account classification (12b) |
| Sales are recorded on the correct dates | None | | Lack of control for test of timely recording (W2) | Compare dates on the bill of lading, duplicate sales invoice, and sales journal (14) |
| Sales transactions are properly included in the accounts receivable master file and are correctly summarized | Accountant compares accounts receivable master file total with general ledger account (C5)<br>Monthly statements are sent to customers (C6) | Observe whether accountant compares master file total with general ledger account (7)<br>Observe whether monthly statements are mailed (6) | | Trace selected duplicate sales invoice numbers from the sales journal to the accounts receivable master file, and test for amount, date, and invoice number (12a)<br>Foot and crossfoot the sales journal and trace the totals to the general ledger (3) |

*The procedures are summarized into a performance format in Figure 11-9. The number in parentheses after each test of control and substantive test of transactions refers to an audit procedure in Figure 11-9.
†Only the primary (key) control(s) for each transaction-related audit objective is (are) shown. Most objectives are also affected by one or more additional controls.

**TABLE 11-5**

**Internal Controls, Tests of Controls, and Substantive Tests of Transactions for Hillsburg Hardware Co.—Cash Receipts* (Design Format)**

| Transaction-Related Audit Objective | Existing Control† | Test of Control | Weakness | Substantive Tests of Transactions |
|---|---|---|---|---|
| Recorded cash receipts are for funds actually received by the company | Accountant reconciles bank account (C1)<br>Batch totals are compared with computer summary reports (C4) | Observe whether accountant reconciles the bank account (4)<br>Examine file of batch totals for initials of data control clerk (8) | | Review the journals and master file for unusual transactions and amounts (1)<br>Review the master file for miscellaneous credits (2)<br>Prepare a proof of cash receipts (18)<br>Trace cash receipt entries from the cash receipts journal to the bank statement, testing for dates and amounts of deposits (19) |

*[continued]*

**TABLE 11-5**

**Internal Controls, Tests of Controls, and Substantive Tests of Transactions for Hillsburg Hardware Co.—Cash Receipts* (Design Format)** *[continued]*

| Transaction-Related Audit Objective | Existing Control† | Test of Control | Weakness | Substantive Tests of Transactions |
|---|---|---|---|---|
| Cash received is recorded in the cash receipts journal | Checks are stamped with a restrictive endorsement (C2)<br>Statements are sent to customers monthly (C3)<br>Batch totals are compared with computer summary reports (C4) | Observe whether a restrictive endorsement is used on cash receipts (5)<br>Observe whether monthly statements are mailed (6)<br>Examine file of batch totals for initials of data control clerk (8) | Prelisting of cash is not used to verify recorded cash receipts (W1)<br>Receptionist handles cash after it is returned from cash receipts (W2)<br>Data processor has access to cash receipts and maintains accounts receivable records (W3) | Obtain the prelisting of cash receipts, and trace amounts to the cash receipts journal, testing for names, amounts, and dates (15)<br>Compare the prelisting of cash receipts with the duplicate deposit slip, testing for names, amounts, and dates (16) |
| Cash receipts are deposited and recorded at the amounts received | Accountant reconciles bank account (C1)<br>Statements are sent to customers monthly (C3)<br>Batch totals are compared with computer summary reports (C4) | Observe whether accountant reconciles the bank account (4)<br>Observe whether monthly statements are mailed (6)<br>Examine file of batch totals for initials of data control clerk (8) | | The procedures for the existence objective also fulfill this objective |
| Cash receipts transactions are properly classified | None | | Lack of internal verification of classification of cash receipts (W5) | Examine prelisting for proper account classification (17) |
| Cash receipts are recorded on the correct dates | None | | Cash receipts are not deposited daily (W4) | Trace the total from the cash receipts journal to the bank statement, testing for a delay in deposit (16) |
| Cash receipts are properly included in the accounts receivable master file and are correctly summarized | Accountant compares accounts receivable master file total with general ledger account (C5) | Observe whether accountant compares master file total with general ledger account (7) | | Trace selected entries from the cash receipts journal to entries in the accounts receivable master file, and test for dates and amounts (20)<br>Trace selected credits from the accounts receivable master file to the cash receipts journal and test for dates and amounts (21)<br>Foot and crossfoot the cash receipts journal and trace totals to the general ledger (3) |

*The procedures are summarized into a performance format in Figure 11-9. The number in parentheses after each test of control and substantive test of transactions refers to an audit procedure in Figure 11-9.
†Only the primary (key) control(s) for each transaction-related audit objective is (are) shown. Most objectives are also affected by one or more additional controls.

The cross-referencing of the numbers in parentheses shows that no procedures have been added to or deleted from Tables 11-4 and 11-5, and the wording is unchanged. The reasons that Fran prepared the performance format audit program were to eliminate audit procedures that were included more than once in Tables 11-4 and 11-5 and to include them in an order that permits audit assistants to complete the

**FIGURE 11-9**

**Audit Program for Tests of Controls and Substantive Tests of Transactions for Hillsburg Hardware Co. (Performance Format)**

**HILLSBURG HARDWARE CO.**
**Tests of Controls and Substantive Tests of Transactions Audit Procedures for Sales and Cash Receipts**
**(Sample size and the items in the sample are not included)**

**General**

1. Review journals and master file for unusual transactions and amounts.
2. Review the master file for miscellaneous credits.
3. Foot and crossfoot the sales and cash receipts journals, and trace the totals to the general ledger.
4. Observe whether accountant reconciles the bank account.
5. Observe whether a restrictive endorsement is used on cash receipts.
6. Observe whether monthly statements are mailed.
7. Observe whether accountant compares master file total with general ledger account.
8. Examine file of batch totals for initials of data control clerk.

**Shipment of Goods**

9. Account for a sequence of shipping documents.
10. Trace selected shipping documents to the sales journal to be sure that each one has been included.

**Billing of Customers and Recording the Sales in the Records**

11. Account for a sequence of sales invoices in the sales journal.
12. Trace selected duplicate sales invoice numbers from the sales journal to:
    a. accounts receivable master file and test for amount, date, and invoice number.
    b. duplicate sales invoice and check for the total amount recorded in the journal, date, customer name, and account classification. Check the pricing, extensions, and footings. Examine underlying documents for indication of internal verification by Pam Dilley.
    c. bill of lading and test for customer name, product description, quantity, and date.
    d. duplicate sales order and test for customer name, product description, quantity, date, and indication of internal verification by Pam Dilley.
    e. customer order and test for customer name, product description, quantity, date, and credit approval of Rick Chulick.
13. Trace recorded sales from the sales journal to the file of supporting documents, which includes a duplicate sales invoice, bill of lading, sales order, and customer order.
14. Compare dates on the bill of lading, duplicate sales invoice, and sales journal.

**Processing Cash Receipts and Recording the Amounts in the Records**

15. Obtain the prelisting of cash receipts, and trace amounts to the cash receipts journal, testing for names, amounts, and dates.
16. Compare the prelisting of cash receipts with the duplicate deposit slip, testing for names, amounts, and dates. Trace the total from the cash receipts journal to the bank statement, testing for a delay in deposit.
17. Examine prelisting for proper account classification.
18. Prepare a proof of cash receipts.
19. Trace cash receipt entries from the cash receipts journal to the bank statement, testing for dates and amounts of deposits.
20. Trace selected entries from the cash receipts journal to entries in the accounts receivable master file and test for dates and amounts.
21. Trace selected credits from the accounts receivable master file to the cash receipts journal and test for dates and amounts.

procedures as efficiently as possible. Sample size and the items for inclusion in the sample are not included here, but they are considered in an extension of the case in Chapter 12.

- *Update the evidence planning worksheet.* After completing tests of controls and substantive tests of transactions, the auditor should complete rows three through seven of the evidence planning worksheet. The evidence planning worksheet for Hillsburg Hardware is shown in Figure 12-9 on page 434. Recall from Chapter 9 that the control risk rows could have been completed before the tests of controls were done, and then modified if the test results were not satisfactory.

After the tests of controls and substantive tests of transactions have been performed, it will be essential to *analyze each test of control and substantive test of transaction exception* to determine its cause and the implication of the exception on assessed control risk, which may affect the supported detection risk and thereby the remaining substantive tests. The methodology and implications of exceptions analysis are explained more fully in Chapter 12.

The most significant effect of the results of the tests of controls and substantive tests of transactions in the sales and collection cycle is on the confirmation of accounts receivable. The type of confirmation, the size of the sample, and the timing of the test are all affected by the results of both tests of controls and substantive tests of transactions. The effect of the tests on accounts receivable, bad debt expense, and allowance for uncollectible accounts is considered in Chapter 13.

## ESSENTIAL TERMS

In addition to these terms, see pages 365 to 369 for descriptions of the key documents and records used in the sales and collection cycle.

**Business functions for the sales and collection cycle**—the key activities that an organization must complete to execute and record business transactions for sales, cash receipts, sales returns and allowances, charge-off of uncollectible accounts, and bad debts

**Classes of transactions in the sales and collection cycle**—the categories of transactions for the sales and collection cycle in a typical company: sales, cash receipts, sales returns and allowances, charge-off of uncollectible accounts, and bad debt expense

**Design format audit program**—the audit procedures resulting from the auditor's decisions about the appropriate audit procedures for each audit objective; this audit program is used to prepare a performance format audit program

**Lapping of accounts receivable**—the postponement of entries for the collection of receivables to *conceal an existing cash shortage;* a common type of defalcation

**Performance format audit program**—the audit procedures for a class of transactions organized in the format they will be performed; this audit program is prepared from a design format audit program

**Proof of cash receipts**—an audit procedure to test whether all recorded cash receipts have been deposited in the bank account by reconciling the total cash receipts recorded in the cash receipts journal for a given period with the actual deposits made to the bank

**Sales and collection cycle**—involves the decisions and processes necessary for the transfer of the ownership of goods and services to customers after they are made available for sale. It begins with a request by a customer and ends with the conversion of material or service into an account receivable, and ultimately into cash.

**Substantive tests of transactions in the sales and collection cycle**—audit procedures testing for monetary misstatements to determine whether the six transaction-related audit objectives have been satisfied for each class of transactions in the sales and collection cycle

**Tests of controls in the sales and collection cycle**—audit procedures performed to determine the effectiveness of both the design and operations of specific internal controls

**Transaction-related audit objectives in the sales and collection cycle**—the six objectives that the auditor must satisfy for each class of transactions in the sales and collection cycle

## REVIEW QUESTIONS

**11-1 (Objective 11-2)** Describe the nature of the following documents and records and explain their use in the sales and collection cycle: bill of lading, sales invoice, credit memo, remittance advice, monthly statement to customers.

**11-2 (Objective 11-2)** Explain the importance of proper credit approval for sales. What effect do adequate controls in the credit function have on the auditor's evidence accumulation?

**11-3 (Objective 11-2)** Distinguish between bad debt expense and the charge-off of uncollectible accounts. Explain why they are audited in completely different ways.

**11-4 (Objective 11-3)** List the transaction-related audit objectives for the verification of sales transactions. For each objective, state one internal control that the client can use to reduce the likelihood of misstatements.

**11-5 (Objective 11-3)** State one test of control and one substantive test of transactions that the auditor can use to verify the following sales transaction-related audit objective: Recorded sales are stated at the proper amount.

**11-6 (Objective 11-3)** List the most important duties that should be segregated in the sales and collection cycle. Explain why it is desirable that each duty be segregated.

**11-7 (Objective 11-3)** Explain how prenumbered shipping documents and sales invoices can be useful controls for preventing misstatements in sales.

**11-8 (Objective 11-3)** What three types of authorizations are commonly used as internal controls for sales? For each authorization, state a substantive test that the auditor could use to verify whether the control was effective in preventing misstatements.

**11-9 (Objective 11-3)** Explain the purpose of footing and crossfooting the sales journal and tracing the totals to the general ledger.

**11-10 (Objective 11-4)** What is the difference between the auditor's approach in verifying sales returns and allowances and that for sales? Explain the reasons for the difference.

**11-11 (Objective 11-5)** Explain why auditors usually emphasize the detection of fraud in the audit of cash. Is this consistent or inconsistent with the auditor's responsibility in the audit? Explain.

**11-12 (Objective 11-5)** List the transaction-related audit objectives for the verification of cash receipts. For each objective, state one internal control that the client can use to reduce the likelihood of misstatements.

**11-13 (Objective 11-5)** List several audit procedures that the auditor can use to determine whether all cash received was recorded.

**11-14 (Objective 11-5)** Explain what is meant by *proof of cash receipts* and state its purpose.

**11-15 (Objective 11-5)** Explain what is meant by *lapping,* and discuss how the auditor can uncover it. Under what circumstances should the auditor make a special effort to uncover lapping?

**11-16 (Objective 11-6)** What audit procedures are most likely to be used to verify accounts receivable charged off as uncollectible? State the purpose of each of these procedures.

**11-17 (Objective 11-7)** State the relationship between the confirmation of accounts receivable and the results of the tests of controls and substantive tests of transactions.

**11-18 (Objectives 11-3, 11-5)** Under what circumstances is it acceptable to perform tests of controls and substantive tests of transactions for sales and cash receipts at an interim date?

**11-19 (Objective 11-3)** Diane Smith, CPA, performed tests of controls and substantive tests of transactions for sales for the month of March in an audit of the financial statements for the year ended December 31, 1996. Based on the excellent results of both the tests of controls and the substantive tests of transactions, she decided to significantly reduce her substantive tests of details of balances at year-end. Evaluate this decision.

## MULTIPLE CHOICE QUESTIONS FROM CPA EXAMINATIONS

**11-20 (Objectives 11-3, 11-4)** The following questions deal with internal controls in the sales and collection cycle. Choose the best response.

a. For effective internal control, the EDP billing function should be performed by the
   (1) accounting department.
   (2) sales department.
   (3) shipping department.
   (4) credit and collection department.

b. A company policy should clearly indicate that defective merchandise returned by customers is to be delivered to the
   (1) sales clerk.
   (2) receiving clerk.
   (3) inventory control clerk.
   (4) accounts receivable clerk.

c. For good internal control, the credit manager should be responsible to the
   (1) sales manager.
   (2) customer service manager.
   (3) controller.
   (4) treasurer.

d. For good internal control, the EDP billing department should be under the direction of the
   (1) controller.
   (2) credit manager.
   (3) sales manager.
   (4) treasurer.

**11-21 (Objectives 11-3, 11-4)** For each of the following types of misstatements (parts a through d), select the control that should have prevented the misstatement:

a. A manufacturing company received a substantial sales return in the last month of the year, but the credit memorandum for the return was not prepared until after the auditors had completed their field work. The returned merchandise was included in the physical inventory.
   (1) Aged trial balance of accounts receivable is prepared.
   (2) Credit memoranda are prenumbered and all numbers are accounted for.
   (3) A reconciliation of the trial balance of customers' accounts with the general ledger control is prepared periodically.
   (4) Receiving reports are prepared for all materials received and such reports are accounted for on a regular basis.

b. The sales manager credited a salesman, Jack Smith, with sales that were actually "house account" sales. Later, Smith divided his excess sales commissions with the sales manager.
   (1) The summary sales entries are checked periodically by persons independent of sales functions.
   (2) Sales orders are reviewed and approved by persons independent of the sales department.
   (3) The internal auditor compares the sales commission statements with the cash disbursements record.
   (4) Sales orders are prenumbered, and all numbers are accounted for.

c. A sales invoice for $5,200 was computed correctly but, by mistake, was key entered as $2,500 to the sales journal and to the accounts receivable master file. The customer remitted only $2,500, the amount on his monthly statement.
   (1) Prelistings and predetermined totals are used to control postings.

(2) Sales invoice serial numbers, prices, discounts, extensions, and footings are independently checked.
(3) The customers' monthly statements are verified and mailed by a responsible person other than the bookkeeper who prepared them.
(4) Unauthorized remittance deductions made by customers or other matters in dispute are investigated promptly by a person independent of the accounts receivable function.

d. Copies of sales invoices show different unit prices for apparently identical items.
(1) All sales invoices are checked as to all details after their preparation.
(2) Differences reported by customers are satisfactorily investigated.
(3) Statistical sales data are compiled and reconciled with recorded sales.
(4) All sales invoices are compared with the customers' purchase orders.

**11-22 (Objectives 11-1, 11-3)** The following questions deal with audit evidence for the sales and collection cycle. Choose the best response.

a. Auditors sometimes use comparison of ratios as audit evidence. For example, an unexplained decrease in the ratio of gross profit to sales may suggest which of the following possibilities?
(1) Unrecorded acquisitions.
(2) Unrecorded sales.
(3) Merchandise acquisitions being charged to selling and general expense.
(4) Fictitious sales.

b. An auditor is performing substantive tests of transactions for sales. One step is to trace a sample of debit entries from the accounts receivable master file back to the supporting duplicate sales invoices. What would the auditor intend to establish by this step?
(1) Sales invoices represent existing sales.
(2) All sales have been recorded.
(3) All sales invoices have been properly posted to customer accounts.
(4) Debit entries in the accounts receivable master file are properly supported by sales invoices.

c. To verify that all sales transactions have been recorded, a substantive test of transactions should be completed on a representative sample drawn from
(1) entries in the sales journal.
(2) the billing clerk's file of sales orders.
(3) a file of duplicate copies of sales invoices for which all prenumbered forms in the series have been accounted.
(4) the shipping clerk's file of duplicate copies of bills of lading.

d. A CPA is auditing the financial statements of a small telephone company and wishes to test whether customers are being billed. One procedure that he or she might use is to
(1) check a sample of listings in the telephone directory to the billing control.
(2) trace a sample of postings from the billing control to the subsidiary accounts receivable records.
(3) balance the accounts receivable master files to the general ledger control account.
(4) confirm a representative number of accounts receivable.

## DISCUSSION QUESTIONS AND PROBLEMS

**11-23 (Objectives 11-3, 11-4, 11-5, 11-7)** Items 1 through 8 are selected questions of the type generally found in internal control questionnaires used by auditors to obtain an understanding of internal control in the sales and collection cycle. In using the questionnaire for a client, a "yes" response to a question indicates a possible internal control, whereas a "no" indicates a potential weakness.

1. Are sales invoices independently compared with customers' orders for prices, quantities, extensions, and footings?
2. Are sales orders, invoices, and credit memoranda issued and filed in numerical sequence and are the sequences accounted for periodically?
3. Are the selling function and cash register functions independent of the cash receipts, shipping, delivery, and billing functions?
4. Are all C.O.D., scrap, equipment, and cash sales accounted for in the same manner as charge sales and is the record keeping independent of the collection procedure?
5. Is the collection function independent of and does it constitute a check on billing and recording sales?
6. Are accounts receivable master files balanced regularly to control accounts by an employee independent of billing functions?
7. Are cash receipts entered in books of original entry by persons independent of the mail-opening and receipts-listing functions?
8. Are receipts deposited intact daily on a timely basis?

**Required**

a. For each of the questions above, state the transaction-related audit objectives being fulfilled if the control is in effect.

b. For each control, list a test of control to test its effectiveness.

c. For each of the questions above, identify the nature of the potential financial misstatements.

d. For each of the potential misstatements in part c, list a substantive audit procedure to determine whether a material misstatement exists.

11-24 (Objectives 11-3, 11-5, 11-7) The following misstatements are included in the accounting records of the Joyce Manufacturing Company:

1. A sales invoice was misadded by $1,000 due to a key entry mistake.
2. A material sale was unintentionally recorded for the second time on the last day of the year. The sale had originally been recorded two days earlier.
3. Cash paid on accounts receivable was stolen by the mail clerk when the mail was opened.
4. Cash paid on accounts receivable that had been prelisted by a secretary was stolen by the bookkeeper who records cash receipts and accounts receivable. He failed to record the transactions.
5. A shipment to a customer was not billed because of the loss of the bill of lading.
6. Merchandise was shipped to a customer, but no bill of lading was prepared. Since billings are prepared from bills of lading, the customer was not billed.
7. A sale to a residential customer was unintentionally classified as a commercial sale.

**Required**

a. Identify whether each misstatement is an error or a fraud.

b. For each misstatement, state a control that should have prevented it from occurring on a continuing basis.

c. For each misstatement, state a substantive audit procedure that could uncover it.

11-25 (Objectives 11-3, 11-4, 11-5) The following are commonly performed tests of controls and substantive tests of transactions audit procedures in the sales and collection cycle:

1. Examine sales returns for approval by an authorized official.
2. Account for a sequence of shipping documents and examine each one to make sure that a duplicate sales invoice is attached.
3. Account for a sequence of sales invoices and examine each one to make sure that a duplicate copy of the shipping document is attached.

4. Compare the quantity and description of items on shipping documents with the related duplicate sales invoices.
5. Trace recorded sales in the sales journal to the related accounts receivable master file and compare the customer name, date, and amount for each one.
6. Review the prelisting in the cash receipts book to determine whether cash is prelisted on a daily basis.
7. Reconcile the recorded cash receipts on the prelisting with the cash receipts journal and the bank statement for a one-month period.

## Required

a. Identify whether each audit procedure is a test of control or a substantive test of transactions.

b. State which of the six transaction-related audit objectives each of the audit procedures fulfills.

c. Identify the type of evidence used for each audit procedure, such as confirmation and observation.

**11-26 (Objectives 11-3, 11-7)** The following are selected transaction-related audit objectives and audit procedures for sales transactions:

### Transaction-Related Audit Objectives

1. Recorded sales exist.
2. Existing sales are recorded.
3. Sales transactions are properly included in the accounts receivable master file and are correctly summarized.

### Procedures

1. Trace a sample of shipping documents to related duplicate sales invoices and the sales journal to make sure that the shipment was billed.
2. Examine a sample of duplicate sales invoices to determine if each one has a shipping document attached.
3. Examine the sales journal for a sample of sales transactions to determine if each one has a tick mark in the margin indicating that it has been compared to the accounts receivable master file for customer name, date, and amount.
4. Examine a sample of shipping documents to determine if each one has a duplicate sales invoice number written on the bottom left corner.
5. Trace a sample of debit entries in the accounts receivable master file to the sales journal to determine if the date, customer name, and amount are the same.
6. Trace a sample of duplicate sales invoices to related shipping documents filed in the shipping department to make sure that a shipment was made.

## Required

a. For each objective, identify at least one specific misstatement that could occur.

b. Describe the differences between the purposes of the first and second objectives.

c. For each audit procedure, identify it as a test of control or substantive test of transactions. (There are three of each.)

d. For each objective, identify one test of control and one substantive test of transactions.

e. For each test of control, state the internal control that is being tested. Also, identify or describe a misstatement that the client is trying to prevent by use of the control.

**11-27 (Objectives 11-2, 11-3)** The following sales procedures were encountered during the annual audit of Marvel Wholesale Distributing Company.

Customer orders are received by the sales order department. A clerk computes the approximate dollar amount of the order and sends it to the credit department for approval. Credit approval is stamped on the order and sent to the accounting department. A computer is then used to generate two copies of a sales invoice. The order is filed in the customer order file.

The customer copy of the sales invoice is held in a pending file awaiting notification that the order was shipped. The shipping copy of the sales invoice is routed through the warehouse, and the shipping department has authority for the respective departments to release and ship the merchandise. Shipping department personnel pack the order and manually prepare a three-copy bill of lading: the original copy is mailed to the customer, the second copy is sent with the shipment, and the other is filed in sequence in the bill of lading file. The sales invoice shipping copy is sent to the accounting department with any changes resulting from lack of available merchandise.

A clerk in accounting matches the received sales invoice shipping copy with the sales invoice customer copy from the pending file. Quantities on the two invoices are compared and prices are compared on an approved price list. The customer copy is then mailed to the customer, and the shipping copy is sent to the data processing department.

The data processing clerk in accounting enters the sales invoice data onto the computer, which is used to prepare the sales journal and update the accounts receivable master file. She files the shipping copy in the sales invoice file in numerical sequence.

a. In order to determine whether the internal controls operated effectively to minimize instances of failure to post invoices to customers' accounts receivable master file, the auditor would select a sample of transactions from the population represented by the
   (1) customer order file.
   (2) bill of lading file.
   (3) customers' accounts receivable master file.
   (4) sales invoice file.

b. In order to determine whether the internal controls operated effectively to minimize instances of failure to invoice a shipment, the auditor would select a sample of transactions from the population represented by the
   (1) customer order file.
   (2) bill of lading file.
   (3) customers' accounts receivable master file.
   (4) sales invoice file.

c. In order to gather audit evidence that uncollected items in customers' accounts represented existing trade receivables, the auditor would select a sample of items from the population represented by the
   (1) customer order file.
   (2) bill of lading file.
   (3) customers' accounts receivable master file.
   (4) sales invoice file.*

**11-28 (Objectives 11-3, 11-5)** The following are common audit procedures for tests of sales and cash receipts.

1. Compare the quantity and description of items on duplicate sales invoices with related shipping documents.
2. Trace recorded cash receipts in the accounts receivable master file to the cash receipts journal and compare the customer name, date, and amount of each one.
3. Examine duplicate sales invoices for an indication that unit selling prices were compared to the approved price list.

*AICPA adapted.

4. Examine duplicate sales invoices to determine whether the account classification for sales has been included on the document.
5. Examine the sales journal for related party transactions, notes receivable, and other unusual items.
6. Select a sample of customer orders and trace the document to related shipping documents, vendors' invoices, and the accounts receivable master file for comparison of name, date, and amount.
7. Perform a proof of cash receipts.
8. Examine a sample of remittance advices for approval of cash discounts.
9. Account for a numerical sequence of remittance advices and determine if there is a cross-reference mark for each one, indicating that it has been recorded in the cash receipts journal.

## Required

a. Identify whether each audit procedure is a test of control or substantive test of transactions.

b. State which transaction-related audit objective(s) each of the audit procedures fulfills.

c. For each test of control in part a, state a substantive test that could be used to determine whether there was a monetary misstatement.

**11-29 (Objective 11-5)** Appliances Repair and Service Company bills all customers rather than collecting in cash when services are provided. All mail is opened by Tom Gyders, treasurer. Gyders, a CPA, is the most qualified person in the company who is in the office daily. He can, therefore, solve problems and respond to customers' needs quickly. Upon receipt of cash, he immediately prepares a listing of the cash and a duplicate deposit slip. Cash is deposited daily. Gyders uses the listing to enter the financial transactions in the computerized accounting records. He also contacts customers about uncollected accounts receivable. Because he is so knowledgeable about the business and each customer, he grants credit, authorizes all sales allowances, and charges off uncollectible accounts. The owner is extremely pleased with the efficiency of the company. He can run the business without spending much time there because of Gyders' effectiveness.

Imagine the owner's surprise when he discovers that Gyders has committed a major theft of the company's cash receipts. He did so by not recording sales, recording improper credits to recorded accounts receivable, and overstating receivables.

## Required

a. Given that cash was prelisted, went only to the treasurer, and was deposited daily, what internal control deficiency permitted the fraud?

b. What are the benefits of a prelisting of cash? Who should prepare the prelisting and what duties should that person *not* perform?

c. Assume that an appropriate person, as discussed in part b, prepares a prelisting of cash. What is to prevent that person from taking the cash after it is prelisted, but before it is deposited?

d. Who should deposit the cash, given your answer to part b?

**11-30 (Objective 11-5)** The receptionist at Jones Supply Co. prelists cash before making daily deposits. He gives the data processing clerk remittance advices, which she uses to enter the cash receipts transactions onto the computerized accounting records. Monthly, the controller prepares a proof of cash receipts, and prints out a copy of the cash receipts journal and compares it to the prelisting.

## Required

a. Define a proof of cash receipts and state its purpose.

b. For the following errors or fraud, state whether it is (i) likely to be uncovered by a proof of cash receipts, (ii) likely to be uncovered by a comparison of the prelisting to the cash receipts journal, (iii) likely to be uncovered by either a proof of cash receipts or a comparison of the prelisting to the cash receipts journal, or (iv) not likely to be uncovered by either a proof of cash receipts or a comparison of the prelisting to the cash receipts journal.

1. Cash was prelisted and correctly inputted to the computerized accounting records, but the bank credited the wrong amount to Jones's bank account.
2. The receptionist unintentionally failed to give the data processing clerk two remittance advices for which the cash had been prelisted.
3. The receptionist unintentionally threw away an unopened envelope that included a check and remittance advice.
4. The data processing clerk made a transposition error in entering the transaction into the computerized accounting records (she recorded a receipt as $4,621 rather than $6,421).
5. The data processing clerk recorded the cash received at the correct amount, but credited the wrong customer's account.
6. The receptionist listed the cash receipts, but afterward withheld a check for his own use and did not forward the remittance advice to the data processing clerk.

c. For those questions in part b that you answered (iv), identify an audit procedure that is likely to uncover the misstatement.

**11-31 (Objective 11-5)** You have been asked by the board of trustees of a local church to review its accounting procedures. As part of this review you have prepared the following comments about the collections made at weekly services and record keeping for members' pledges and contributions:

1. The church's board of trustees has delegated responsibility for financial management and audit of the financial records to the finance committee. This group prepares the annual budget and approves major cash disbursements but is not involved in collections or record keeping. No audit has been considered necessary in recent years because the same trusted employee has kept church records and served as financial secretary for 15 years.
2. The collection at the weekly service is taken by a team of ushers. The head usher counts the collection in the church office following each service. He then places the collection and a notation of the amount in the church safe. Next morning the financial secretary opens the safe and recounts the collection. He withholds about $100 to meet cash expenditures during the coming week and deposits the remainder intact. In order to facilitate the deposit, members who contribute by check are asked to draw their checks to cash.
3. At their request a few members are furnished prenumbered predated envelopes in which to insert their weekly contributions. The head usher removes the cash from the envelopes to be counted with the loose cash included in the collection and discards the envelopes. No record is maintained of issuance or return of the envelopes, and the envelope system is not encouraged.
4. Each member is asked to prepare a contribution pledge card annually. The pledge is regarded as a moral commitment by the member to contribute a stated weekly amount. Based on the amounts shown on the pledge cards, the financial secretary furnishes a letter to members, upon request, to support the tax deductibility of their contributions.

## Required

Identify the weaknesses and recommend improvements in procedures for collections made at weekly services and record keeping for members' pledges and contributions.

Use the methodology for identifying weaknesses that was discussed in Chapter 9. Organize your answer sheets as follows:*

| Weakness | Recommended Improvement |
|---|---|

**11-32 (Objectives 11-3, 11-5)** The customer billing and cash receipts functions of the Robinson Company, a small paint manufacturer, are attended to by a receptionist, an accounts receivable clerk, and a cashier who also serves as a secretary. The company's paint products are sold to wholesalers and retail stores.

The following describes all the procedures performed by the employees of the Robinson Company pertaining to customer billings and cash receipts:

1. The mail is opened by the receptionist, who gives the customers' purchase orders to the accounts receivable clerk. Fifteen to twenty orders are received each day. Under instructions to expedite the shipment of orders, the accounts receivable clerk at once prepares a five-copy sales invoice form that is distributed as follows:
   (a) Copy 1 is the customer billing copy and is held by the accounts receivable clerk until notice of shipment is received.
   (b) Copy 2 is the accounts receivable department copy and is held for the ultimate updating of the accounting records.
   (c) Copies 3 and 4 are sent to the shipping department.
   (d) Copy 5 is sent to the storeroom as authority for the release of goods to the shipping department.
2. After the paint order has been moved from the storeroom to the shipping department, the shipping department prepares the bills of lading and labels the cartons. Sales invoice copy 4 is inserted in a carton as a packing slip. After the trucker has picked up the shipment, the customer's copy of the bill of lading and copy 3, on which are noted any undershipments, are returned to the accounts receivable clerk. The company does not "back order" in the event of undershipments; customers are expected to reorder the merchandise. The Robinson Company's copy of the bill of lading is filed by the shipping department.
3. When copy 3 and the customer's copy of the bill of lading are received by the accounts receivable clerk, copies 1 and 2 are completed by numbering them and inserting quantities shipped, unit prices, extensions, discounts, and totals. Copies 2 and 3 are stapled together.
4. The accounts receivable clerk then enters the sales transactions into the computerized accounting records from copy 2. Only the quantities, prices, discounts, and accounts are entered, as the computer computes extensions and totals. These extensions and totals are then compared to copy 1. The accounts receivable clerk then mails copy 1 and the copy of the bill of lading to the customer. Copy 2 is then filed, along with staple attached copy 3, in numerical order.
5. Since the Robinson Company is short of cash, the deposit of cash receipts is also expedited. The receptionist turns over all mail receipts and related correspondence to the accounts receivable clerk, who examines the checks and determines that the accompanying vouchers or correspondence contain enough detail to permit the entering of the transactions into the computer. The accounts receivable clerk then endorses the checks and gives them to the cashier, who prepares the daily deposit. No currency is received in the mail, and no paint is sold over the counter at the factory.
6. The accounts receivable clerk uses the vouchers or correspondence that accompanied the checks to enter the transactions onto the computerized accounting records. The accounts receivable clerk is the one who corresponds with customers about unauthorized deductions for discounts, freight or advertising allowances, returns, and so forth, and prepares the appropriate credit memos. Disputed items of large amounts are

*AICPA adapted.

turned over to the sales manager for settlement. Each month the accounts receivable clerk prints out a trial balance of accounts receivable and compares the total with the general ledger control accounts for accounts receivable.

### Required

a. Identify the internal control weaknesses in the Robinson Company's procedures related to customer billings and cash receipts and the accounting for these transactions. Use the methodology for identifying weaknesses that was discussed in Chapter 9.

b. For each weakness, identify the error or fraud that could result.

c. For each weakness, list one substantive audit procedure for testing the significance of the potential misstatement.*

## CASE

11-33 (Objectives 11-3, 11-7) The Meyers Pharmaceutical Company, a drug manufacturer, has the following internal controls for billing and recording accounts receivable:

1. An incoming customer's purchase order is received in the order department by a clerk who prepares a prenumbered company sales order form in which is inserted the pertinent information, such as the customer's name and address, customer's account number, quantity, and items ordered. After the sales order form has been prepared, the customer's purchase order is stapled to it.
2. The sales order form is then passed to the credit department for credit approval. Rough approximations of the billing values of the orders are made in the credit department for those accounts on which credit limitations are imposed. After investigation, approval of credit is noted on the form.
3. Next, the sales order form is passed to the billing department, where a clerk uses a computer to generate the customer's invoice. It automatically cross-multiplies the number of items with the unit price, and adds the extended amounts for the total amount of the invoice. The billing clerk determines the unit prices for the items from a list of billing prices.

   The computer automatically accumulates daily totals of customer account numbers and invoice amounts to provide "hash" totals and control amounts. These totals, which are inserted in a daily record book, serve as predetermined batch totals for verification of inputs into the computerized accounting records.

   The billing is done on prenumbered, continuous, carbon-interleaved forms having the following designations:

   (a) Customer's copy.
   (b) Sales department copy, for information purposes.
   (c) File copy.
   (d) Shipping department copy, which serves as a shipping order. Bills of lading are also prepared as carbon copy by-products of the invoicing procedure.
4. The shipping department copy of the invoice and the bills of lading are then sent to the shipping department. After the order has been shipped, copies of the bill of lading are returned to the billing department. The shipping department copy of the invoice is filed in the shipping department.
5. In the billing department one copy of the bill of lading is attached to the customer's copy of the invoice, and both are mailed to the customer. The other copy of the bill of lading, together with the sales order form, is then stapled to the invoice file copy and filed in invoice numerical order.

*AICPA adapted.

6. As the computer is generating invoices, it is also storing the transactions on disk. This disk is then used to update the computerized accounting records. This update procedure is run daily and a summary report is generated. Hard copy output of all journals and ledgers is prepared.
7. Periodically, an internal auditor traces a sample of sales orders all the way through the system to the journals and ledgers, testing both the procedures and dollar amounts. The procedures include comparing control totals with output, recalculating invoices and refooting journals, and tracing totals to the master file and general ledger.

### Required

a. Flowchart the billing function as a means of understanding the system.

b. List the internal controls over sales for each of the six transaction-related audit objectives.

c. For each control, list a useful test of control to verify the effectiveness of the control.

d. For each transaction-related audit objective for sales, list appropriate substantive tests of transactions audit procedures, considering internal controls.

e. Combine the audit procedures from parts c and d into an efficient audit program for sales.

## INTEGRATED CASE APPLICATION

11-34 (Objective 11-7) **ABC AUDIT—PART II** In Part I of this case study (pages 326–328), you obtained an understanding of internal control and made an initial assessment of control risk for each transaction-related audit objective for acquisition and cash disbursement transactions. The purpose of Part II is to continue the assessment of control risk by deciding the appropriate tests of controls and substantive tests of transactions.

Assume that in Part I it was determined that the key internal controls are the following:

1. Segregation of the purchasing, receiving, and cash disbursement functions
2. Review of supportive documents and signing of checks by an independent, authorized person
3. Use of prenumbered checks, properly accounted for
4. Use of prenumbered purchase orders, properly accounted for
5. Use of prenumbered document package, properly accounted for
6. Internal verification of document package prior to preparation of checks
7. Independent monthly reconciliation of bank statement

For requirements a and b, you should follow a format similar to the one illustrated for sales in Table 11-2, page 370. You should prepare one matrix for acquisitions and a separate one for cash disbursements. Observe that the first column in each matrix should include the same information as the top row in the worksheet you prepared for Problem 9-32. Also, the key internal controls include only those seven from above, and the tests of controls include only those you developed in requirement a. The substantive tests of transactions procedures should be designed based on an assumption that the results of the tests of controls will be favorable.

### Required

a. Design tests of control audit procedures that will provide appropriate evidence for each of these controls. Do not include more than two tests of control for each internal control.

b. Although controls appear to be well designed and test of control deviations are not expected, last year's results indicate that misstatements may still exist. Therefore, you decide to perform substantive tests of transactions for acquisitions and cash disbursements. Design substantive tests of transactions for each transaction-related audit objective. Do not include more than two substantive tests of transactions for any objective. Use Tables 11-4 on pages 386 and 387 and 11-5 on pages 387 and 388 as frames of reference.

c. Combine the tests of controls and substantive tests of transactions designed in requirements a and b into a performance format. Include both tests of acquisitions and cash disbursements in the same audit program. Use Figure 11-9 on page 389 as a frame of reference for preparing the performance format audit program.

# 12

# AUDIT SAMPLING FOR TESTS OF CONTROLS AND SUBSTANTIVE TESTS OF TRANSACTIONS

## LEARNING OBJECTIVES

Thorough study of this chapter will enable you to

12-1 Explain the concept of representative sampling.

12-2 Distinguish between statistical and nonstatistical sampling.

12-3 Select representative samples.

12-4 Define and describe audit sampling for exception rates.

12-5 Use nonstatistical sampling in tests of controls and substantive tests of transactions.

12-6 Define and describe attributes sampling and a sampling distribution.

12-7 Use attributes sampling in tests of controls and substantive tests of transactions.

12-8 Apply sampling concepts and methodology to the audit plan for the sales and collection cycle.

## IF YOU ARE NOT GOING TO BELIEVE IT, DON'T USE IT

Brooks & Company, CPAs, uses random samples in performing audit tests whenever possible. They believe that this gives them the best chance of getting representative samples of their clients' accounting information. In the audit of Sensational Products, a random sample of thirty inventory items was taken from a population of 1,800 items in doing a test of unit and total costs. Only one of the thirty items was in error, but it was large. In investigating the error, Harold Davis, the audit staff person doing the test, was told by Sensational's controller that the error occurred while the regular inventory clerk was on vacation and was really only an "isolated error."

Harold knew that generally accepted auditing standards require that errors in random samples be projected to the entire population. In this case, such a projection would involve multiplying the error found by a factor of 60 (1,800 divided by 30). This would result in an audit adjustment or additional audit work. Harold knew that the client would not be happy about this, as the adjustment would reduce an already "strained" net income figure and additional auditing would increase the audit fee. If the error was, in fact, an isolated one, it would not be significant enough to require an audit adjustment.

Harold decided to look at the situation in terms of the probability of the error being an isolated example. He calculated the chance to be about only one in sixty of including an isolated error in a sample of thirty from a population of 1,800. He then looked at accepting the client's representation about the uniqueness of the error as a bet. If he accepted the representation and didn't do the projection and act on it, he was in effect betting his career in a situation where the odds were sixty to one against him. It didn't take Harold long to recognize the wisdom of the professional standards and conclude that the projection should be done.

SAS 39 defines audit sampling as:

> The application of an audit procedure to less than 100 percent of the items within an audit balance or class of transactions for the purpose of evaluating some characteristics of the balance or class.

"Application of an audit procedure" in this definition means dealing with three aspects of audit sampling: (1) plan the sample, (2) select the sample and perform the tests, and (3) evaluate the results. As the chapter title implies, this chapter discusses the use of audit sampling for tests of controls and substantive tests of transactions. The sales and collection cycle is used as a frame of reference for discussing these concepts, but the concepts apply to any cycle. Chapter 14 will deal with using audit sampling for tests of details of balances. Figure 12-1, which uses the same information as Figure 10-2 on page 334, shows how audit sampling is related to the types of audit tests.

**FIGURE 12-1**

**How Audit Sampling Is Related to the Types of Audit Tests**

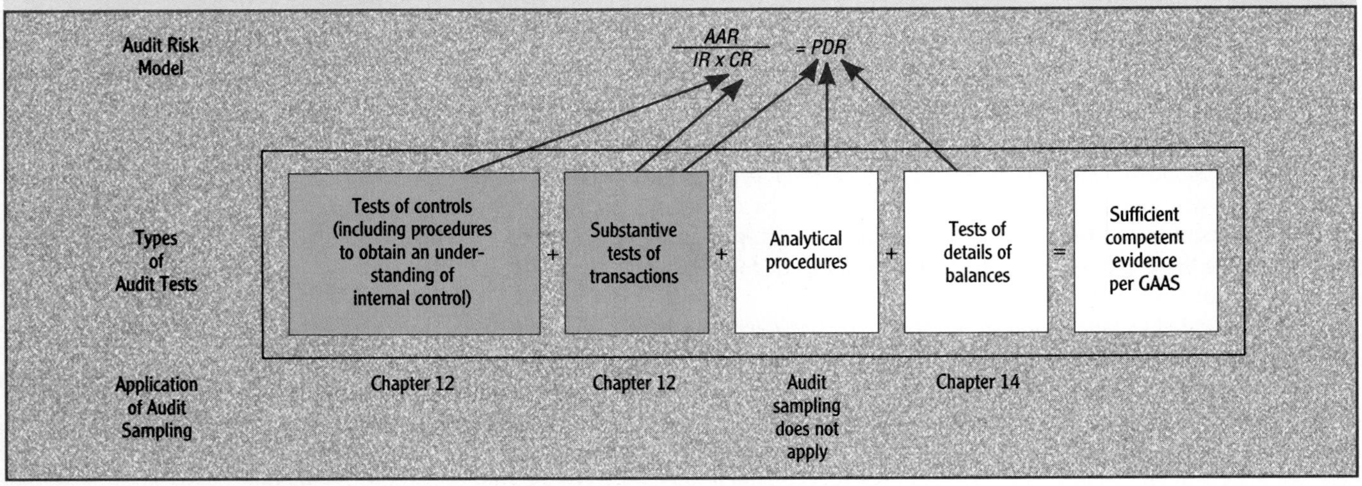


Chapter 12 is directly related to Chapter 11 in that first the auditor must decide the tests of controls and substantive tests of transactions audit procedures he or she plans to perform before applying audit sampling. Four topics are discussed at the beginning of the chapter as background knowledge about applying audit sampling to tests of controls and substantive tests of transactions: representative samples, statistical versus nonstatistical sampling, nonprobabilistic sample selection and probabilistic sample selection. Next, the use of nonstatistical sampling is applied to tests of controls and substantive tests of transactions followed by applying a statistical sampling method, attributes sampling.

## REPRESENTATIVE SAMPLES

**OBJECTIVE 12-1**
**Explain the concept of representative sampling.**

Whenever an auditor selects a sample from a population, the objective is to obtain a *representative* one. A representative sample is one in which the characteristics in the sample of audit interest are approximately the same as those of the population. This means that the sampled items are similar to the items not sampled. For example, assume that a client's internal controls require a clerk to attach a shipping document to every duplicate sales invoice, but the procedure is not followed, exactly 3 percent of the time. If the auditor selects a sample of 100 duplicate sales invoices and finds three missing, the sample is highly representative. If two or four such items are found in the sample, the sample is reasonably representative. If no or many missing items are found, the sample is *non-representative.*

In practice, auditors do not know whether a sample is representative, even after all testing is complete. Auditors can, however, increase the likelihood of a sample being representative by using care in its design, selection, and evaluation. Two things can cause a sample result to be nonrepresentative: nonsampling error and sampling error. The risk of these occurring is termed *nonsampling risk* and *sampling risk.* Both of these can be controlled.

Nonsampling risk (nonsampling error) occurs when audit tests do not uncover existing exceptions in the sample. In the previous example in which three shipping documents were not attached to duplicate sales invoices, if the auditor concluded that no exceptions existed, there is a nonsampling error.

The two causes of nonsampling error are the auditor's failure to recognize exceptions and inappropriate or ineffective audit procedures. An auditor might fail to recognize an exception because of exhaustion, boredom, or lack of understanding of what to look for. An ineffective audit procedure for the exceptions in question would be to examine a sample of shipping documents and determine if each is attached to a set of duplicate sales invoices, rather than to examine a sample of duplicate sales invoices. In this case, the auditor has done the test in the wrong direction by starting with the shipping document instead of the duplicate sales invoice. Careful design of audit procedures, proper instruction, supervision, and review are ways to control nonsampling risk.

Sampling risk (sampling error) is an inherent part of sampling that results from testing less than the entire population. Even with zero nonsampling error, there is always a chance that a sample is not reasonably representative. For example, if a population has a 3 percent exception rate, the auditor could select a sample of 100 items containing no or many exceptions.

There are two ways to control sampling risk: adjust sample size and use an appropriate method of selecting sample items from the population. Increasing sample size will reduce sampling risk, and vice versa. At the extreme, a sample of all the items of a population will have a zero sampling risk. Using an appropriate sampling method will reasonably ensure representativeness. This does not eliminate or even reduce sampling risk, but it does allow the auditor to measure the risk associated with a given sample size in a reliable manner.

## STATISTICAL VERSUS NONSTATISTICAL SAMPLING

**OBJECTIVE 12-2**
**Distinguish between statistical and nonstatistical sampling.**

Audit sampling methods can be divided into two broad categories: statistical and nonstatistical. These categories have important similarities and differences. They are similar in that they both involve the three steps identified in the introduction: (1) plan the sample, (2) select the sample and perform the tests, and (3) evaluate the results. The purpose of planning the sample is to make sure that the audit tests are performed in a manner that provides the desired sampling risk and minimizes the likelihood of nonsampling error. Selecting the sample involves deciding how to select sample items from the population. Performing the tests is the examination of documents and doing other audit procedures. Evaluating the results involves drawing conclusions based on the audit tests. To illustrate, assume that an auditor selects a sample of 100 duplicate sales invoices from a population, tests each to determine if a shipping document is attached, and determines that there are three exceptions. Deciding that a sample size of 100 is needed is a part of planning the sample.

Deciding which 100 items to select from the population is a sample selection problem. Doing the audit procedure for each of the 100 items and determining that there were three exceptions constitutes performing the tests. Reaching conclusions about the likely exception rate in the total population when there is a sample exception rate of 3 percent is evaluating the results.

Statistical sampling differs from nonstatistical sampling in that, through the application of mathematical rules, it allows the quantification (measurement) of sampling risk in planning the sample (Step 1) and evaluating the results (Step 3). (You may remember calculating a statistical result at a 95 percent confidence level in a statistics course. The 95 percent confidence level provides a 5 percent sampling risk.) The quantification of sampling risk is appropriate only when selecting the sample (Step 2) is done by using a *probabilistic* sample, which is discussed shortly.

In nonstatistical sampling, the auditor does not quantify sampling risk. Instead, the auditor selects those sample items that he or she believes will provide the most useful information in the circumstances (that is, *nonprobabilistic* samples are *chosen*), and conclusions are reached about populations on a judgmental basis. For that reason, the selection of nonprobabilistic samples is often termed *judgmental sampling.*

It is equally acceptable under professional standards for auditors to use either statistical or nonstatistical sampling methods. However, it is essential that either method be applied with due care. All steps of the process must be followed carefully. When statistical sampling is used, the sample must be a probabilistic one, and appropriate statistical evaluation methods must be used with the sample results to make the sampling risk computations.

It is also acceptable to make nonstatistical evaluations by using probabilistic selection, but many practitioners prefer not to do so. They believe that statistical measurement of sampling risk is inherent in those samples, and should not be ignored. It is *never* acceptable, however, to evaluate a nonprobabilistic sample as if it were a statistical sample. A summary of the relationship of probabilistic and nonprobabilistic selection to statistical and nonstatistical evaluation is shown in Table 12-1.

**TABLE 12-1**

**Relationship of Methods of Selecting Samples to Evaluating Results**

| | Method of Evaluating Results | |
|---|---|---|
| **Method of Selecting Sample** | **Statistical** | **Nonstatistical** |
| Probabilistic | Preferable to use statistical | Acceptable to use nonstatistical |
| Nonprobabilistic | Not acceptable to use statistical | Mandatory to use nonstatistical |

There are three types of sample selection methods commonly associated with nonstatistical audit sampling and four types of sample selection methods commonly associated with statistical audit sampling. These are listed below and discussed in the following sections.

Nonprobabilistic (judgmental) sample selection methods:

- Directed sample selection
- Block sample selection
- Haphazard sample selection

Probabilistic sample selection methods:

- Simple random sample selection
- Systematic sample selection
- Probability proportional to size sample selection
- Stratified sample selection

## NONPROBABILISTIC SAMPLE SELECTION

Nonprobabilistic sample selection methods are those that do not meet the technical requirements for probabilistic sample selection. Since these methods are not based on strict mathematical probabilities, the representativeness of the sample may be difficult to determine. The information content of the sample, including its representativeness, will be based on the knowledge and skill of the auditor in applying his or her judgment in the circumstances.

### Directed Sample Selection

Directed sample selection is the selection of each item in the sample based on some judgmental criteria established by the auditor. The auditor does not rely on equal chances of selection, but, rather, deliberately selects items according to the criteria. These criteria may relate to representativeness, or they may not. Commonly used criteria are the following.

**Items Most Likely to Contain Misstatements** Frequently, auditors are able to identify which population items are most likely to be misstated. Examples are receivables outstanding for a long time, purchases from and sales to officers and affiliated companies, and unusually large or complex transactions. These kinds of items can be efficiently investigated by the auditor, and the results can be applied to the population on a judgmental basis. The reasoning underlying the evaluation of such samples is often that, if none of the items selected contain misstatements, then it is highly unlikely that a material misstatement exists in the population.

**Items Containing Selected Population Characteristics** The auditor may be able to describe the various types and sources of items that make up the population and design the sample to be representative by selecting one or more items of each type. For example, a sample of cash disbursements might include some from each month, each bank account or location, and each major type of acquisition.

**Large Dollar Coverage** A sample can often be selected to cover such a large portion of total population dollars that the risk of drawing an improper conclusion by not examining small items is not a concern. This is a practical approach on many audits, especially smaller ones. There are also statistical methods that are intended to accomplish the same effect.

### Block Sample Selection

A block sample is the selection of several items in sequence. Once the first item in the block is selected, the remainder of the block is chosen automatically. One example of a block sample is the selection of a sequence of 100 sales transactions from the sales journal for the third week of March. A total sample of 100 could also be selected by taking five blocks of twenty items each, ten blocks of ten, or fifty blocks of two.

It is ordinarily acceptable to use block samples only if a reasonable number of blocks is used. If few blocks are used, the probability of obtaining a nonrepresentative sample is too great, considering the possibility of such things as employee turnover, changes in the accounting system, and the seasonal nature of many businesses.

### Haphazard Sample Selection

When the auditor goes through a population and selects items for the sample without regard to their size, source, or other distinguishing characteristics, he or she is attempting to select without bias. This is called a *haphazard sample.*

The most serious shortcoming of haphazard sample selection is the difficulty of remaining completely unbiased in the selection. Because of the auditor's training and "cultural bias," certain population items are more likely than others to be included in the sample.

Although haphazard and block sample selection appear to be less logical than directed sample selection, they are often useful as audit tools and should not be ignored. In some situations, the cost of more complex sample selection methods outweighs the benefits obtained from using them. For example, assume that the auditor wants to trace credits from the accounts receivable master files to the cash receipts journal and other authorized sources as a test for fictitious credits in the master files. A haphazard or block approach is simpler and much less costly than other selection methods in this situation, and would be employed by many auditors.

## PROBABILISTIC SAMPLE SELECTION

**OBJECTIVE 12-3**
**Select representative samples.**

As previously indicated, to measure sampling risk, statistical sampling requires a probabilistic sample. There are four methods commonly used by auditors to obtain probabilistic samples: simple random sample selection, systematic sample selection, probability proportional to size sample selection, and stratified sample selection.

### Simple Random Sample Selection

A simple random sample is one in which every possible combination of elements in the population has an equal chance of constituting the sample. Simple random sampling is used to sample populations that are not segmented for audit purposes. For example, the auditor may wish to sample the client's cash disbursements for the year. A simple random sample of sixty items contained in the cash disbursements journal might be selected for that purpose. Appropriate auditing procedures would be applied to the sixty items selected, and conclusions would be drawn and applied to all cash disbursement transactions recorded for the year.

**Random Number Tables** When a simple random sample is obtained, a method must be used that ensures that all items in the population have an equal chance of selection. Suppose that in the above example there were a total of 12,000 cash disbursement transactions for the year. A simple random sample of one transaction would be such that each of the 12,000 transactions would have an equal chance of being selected. This would be done by obtaining a *random number* between 1 and 12,000. If the number were 3,895, the auditor would select and test the 3,895th cash disbursement transaction recorded in the cash disbursements journal.

Random numbers are a series of digits that have equal probabilities of occurring over long runs and which have no discernable pattern. An example of a commonly used random number table is the *Table of 105,000 Random Decimal Digits*, published by the Interstate Commerce Commission. A page from that table appears in Table 12-2. This table has numbered rows and columns, with five digits in each column. This format is convenient for reading the table and documenting the portion of the table used. The presentation of the digits as five-digit numbers is purely arbitrary.

It is easy, but time-consuming, to select samples using a random number table. For example, assume that the auditor is selecting a sample of 100 sales invoices from a file of prenumbered sales invoices beginning with document number 3272 and ending with 8825. Since the invoices use four digits, it is necessary to use four digits in the random number table. Assuming the first four digits of each five-digit set were used, and the arbitrary starting point in the random number table in Table 12-2 is item 1009, column 2, then reading down, the first invoice for inclusion in the sample is 3646. The next usable number is 6186 since the next three numbers are all outside the population range.

**Computer Generation of Random Numbers** It is useful to understand the use of random number tables as a means of understanding the concept of selecting simple random samples. However, most random samples obtained by auditors are obtained by using computers. There are three main types: electronic spreadsheet programs, random number generators, and generalized audit software programs.

The advantages of using computer programs in selecting random samples are time savings, reduced likelihood of auditor error in selecting the numbers, and automatic docu-

**TABLE 12-2**

**Random Number Table**

| | Column | | | | | | | |
|---|---|---|---|---|---|---|---|---|
| **Row** | **(1)** | **(2)** | **(3)** | **(4)** | **(5)** | **(6)** | **(7)** | **(8)** |
| **1000** | 37039 | 97547 | 64673 | 31546 | 99314 | 66854 | 97855 | 99965 |
| **1001** | 25145 | 84834 | 23009 | 51584 | 66754 | 77785 | 52357 | 25532 |
| **1002** | 98433 | 54725 | 18864 | 65866 | 76918 | 78825 | 58210 | 76835 |
| **1003** | 97965 | 68548 | 81545 | 82933 | 93545 | 85959 | 63282 | 61454 |
| **1004** | 78049 | 67830 | 14624 | 17563 | 25697 | 07734 | 48243 | 94318 |
| **1005** | 50203 | 25658 | 91478 | 08509 | 23308 | 48130 | 65047 | 77873 |
| **1006** | 40059 | 67825 | 18934 | 64998 | 49807 | 71126 | 77818 | 56893 |
| **1007** | 84350 | 67241 | 54031 | 34535 | 04093 | 35062 | 58163 | 14205 |
| **1008** | 30954 | 51637 | 91500 | 48722 | 60988 | 60029 | 60873 | 37423 |
| **1009** | 86723 | 36464 | 98305 | 08009 | 00666 | 29255 | 18514 | 49158 |
| **1010** | 50188 | 22554 | 86160 | 92250 | 14021 | 65859 | 16237 | 72296 |
| **1011** | 50014 | 00463 | 13906 | 35936 | 71761 | 95755 | 87002 | 71667 |
| **1012** | 66023 | 21428 | 14742 | 94874 | 23308 | 58533 | 26507 | 11208 |
| **1013** | 04458 | 61862 | 63119 | 09541 | 01715 | 87901 | 91260 | 03079 |
| **1014** | 57510 | 36314 | 30452 | 09712 | 37714 | 95482 | 30507 | 68475 |
| **1015** | 43373 | 58939 | 95848 | 28288 | 60341 | 52174 | 11879 | 18115 |
| **1016** | 61500 | 12763 | 64433 | 02268 | 57905 | 72347 | 49498 | 21871 |
| **1017** | 78938 | 71312 | 99705 | 71546 | 42274 | 23915 | 38405 | 18779 |
| **1018** | 64257 | 93218 | 35793 | 43671 | 64055 | 88729 | 11168 | 60260 |
| **1019** | 56864 | 21554 | 70445 | 24841 | 04779 | 56774 | 96129 | 73594 |
| **1020** | 35314 | 29631 | 06937 | 54545 | 04470 | 75463 | 77112 | 77126 |
| **1021** | 40704 | 48823 | 65963 | 39359 | 12717 | 56201 | 22811 | 24863 |
| **1022** | 07318 | 44623 | 02843 | 33299 | 59872 | 86774 | 06926 | 12672 |
| **1023** | 94550 | 23299 | 45557 | 07923 | 75126 | 00808 | 01312 | 46689 |
| **1024** | 34348 | 81191 | 21027 | 77087 | 10909 | 03676 | 97723 | 34469 |
| **1025** | 92277 | 57115 | 50789 | 68111 | 75305 | 53289 | 39751 | 45760 |
| **1026** | 56093 | 58302 | 52236 | 64756 | 50273 | 61566 | 61962 | 93280 |
| **1027** | 16623 | 17849 | 96701 | 94971 | 94758 | 08845 | 32260 | 59823 |
| **1028** | 50848 | 93982 | 66451 | 32143 | 05441 | 10399 | 17775 | 74169 |
| **1029** | 48006 | 58200 | 58367 | 66577 | 68583 | 21108 | 41361 | 20732 |
| **1030** | 56640 | 27890 | 28825 | 96509 | 21363 | 53657 | 60119 | 75385 |

mentation. To illustrate computer generation of random numbers, Figure 12-2 on page 410 shows a printout from a random number generation program. In the application illustrated, the auditor wishes to sample thirty items from a population of documents numbered from 14067 to 16559. The program requires only input parameters by the auditor for a sample to be selected. It possesses great flexibility in the formatting of the numbers. For example, the program can generate random dates or ranges of sets of numbers (such as page and line numbers). It also provides output in both sorted and selection orders.

***Replacement versus Nonreplacement Sampling*** Random numbers may be obtained with replacement or without replacement. In *replacement sampling*, an element in the population can be included in the sample more than once, whereas in nonreplacement sampling, an element can be included only once. If the random number corresponding to an element is selected more than once in nonreplacement sampling, it is not included in the sample a second time. Although both selection approaches are consistent with sound statistical theory, auditors rarely use replacement sampling.

**FIGURE 12-2**

**Random Selection by Use of a Computer**

```
_RUN (TRC900) SAMGEN
THIS PROGRAM GENERATES UP TO 1,000 SINGLE OR SETTED
    RANDOM NUMBERS.
FILE OPTION-YES OR NO? NO
QUIK OPTION-YES OR NO? NO
******** D A T A   I N P U T ********

(1) INPUT THE QUANTITY OF RANDOM
    NUMBERS TO BE GENERATED? 30
(2) ARE THE NUMBERS FORMATTED
    INTO SETS - YES OR NO? NO
(3) INPUT THE QUANTITY OF DIGITS IN
    THE LARGEST NUMBER? 5
(4) INPUT THE NUMBER OF RANGES
    OF VALUES TO BE GENERATED
    (MAX = 50)? 1
(5) FOR EACH OF THE 1 RANGES INPUT
    THE LOWER (L) AND UPPER (U) LIMITS.
    SEPARATE SETS, IF ANY,
    WITH A HYPHEN (-).
(6) PRINT SELECTION-INPUT 1 FOR
    NUMERICAL ORDER, 2 FOR SELECTION
    ORDER OR 3 FOR BOTH? 3
(7) DO YOU WANT TO CHANGE ANY
    INPUTS-YES OR NO? NO
    ***INPUT COMPLETE-DATA
    CHECK WILL BEGIN***********
(8) DO YOU WANT A LISTING OF RANGES
    SELECTED BEFORE DATA CHECK
    CONTINUES-YES OR NO? NO
(9) TOTAL COUNTED ITEMS=2493
    REASONABLE-YES OR NO? YES

RANGE
-----
1 - L? 14067
    U? 16559

****DATA CHECK COMPLETE****
**RANDOM NUMBER GENERATION
WILL BEGIN**************

****GENERATION COMPLETE****
```

| RANDOM NUMBERS-SELECTION ORDER | RANDOM NUMBERS-NUMERICAL ORDER: SEQUENCE SELECTED | RANDOM NUMBERS-NUMERICAL ORDER: RANDOM NUMBERS |
|---|---|---|
| 16258 | 14 | 14090 |
| 15472 | 30 | 14134 |
| 16159 | 17 | 14199 |
| 15223 | 21 | 14224 |
| 15390 | 11 | 14249 |
| 15470 | 18 | 14273 |
| 15592 | 9 | 14297 |
| 14916 | 25 | 14431 |
| 14297 | 23 | 14682 |
| 15063 | 19 | 14775 |
| 14249 | 8 | 14916 |
| 16241 | 10 | 15063 |
| 15701 | 15 | 15100 |
| 14090 | 4 | 15223 |
| 15100 | 22 | 15308 |
| 16473 | 5 | 15390 |
| 14199 | 6 | 15470 |
| 14273 | 2 | 15472 |
| 14775 | 7 | 15592 |
| 15608 | 20 | 15608 |
| 14224 | 29 | 15674 |
| 15308 | 13 | 15701 |
| 14682 | 24 | 15742 |
| 15742 | 28 | 15900 |
| 14431 | 26 | 16017 |
| 16017 | 3 | 16159 |
| 16225 | 27 | 16225 |
| 15900 | 12 | 16241 |
| 15674 | 1 | 16258 |
| 14134 | 16 | 16473 |

```
***SORTING***                  ****RUN FINISHED****
                               ANOTHER RUN-YES OR NO? NO
```

### Systematic Sample Selection

In systematic selection (also known as systematic sampling), the auditor calculates an *interval* and then methodically selects the items for the sample based on the size of the interval. The interval is determined by dividing the population size by the number of sample items desired. For example, if a population of sales invoices ranges from 652 to 3151 and the desired sample size is 125, the interval is 20 [(3,151 – 651)/125]. The auditor must now select a random number between 0 and 19 to determine the starting point for the sample. If the randomly selected number is 9, the first item in the sample is invoice number 661 (652 + 9). The remaining 124 items are 681 (661 + 20), 701 (681 + 20), and so on through item 3141.

The advantage of systematic selection is its ease of use. In most populations a systematic sample can be drawn quickly, the approach automatically puts the numbers in sequence, and it is easy to develop the appropriate documentation.

A major problem with systematic selection is the possibility of bias. Because of the way systematic selection works, once the first item in the sample is selected, all other items are chosen automatically. This causes no problem if the characteristic of interest, such as a possible control deviation, is distributed randomly throughout the population; however, in some cases characteristics of interest may not be randomly distributed. For example, if a control deviation occurred at a certain time of the month or with certain types of documents, a systematic sample could have a higher likelihood of failing to be representative than a simple random sample. It is important, therefore, when systematic selection is used, to consider possible patterns in the population data that could cause sample bias.

### Probability Proportional to Size and Stratified Sample Selection

There are many situations in auditing where it is advantageous to select samples that emphasize population items that have larger recorded amounts. There are two ways to obtain such samples. The first is to take a sample where the probability of selecting any individual population item is proportional to its recorded amount. This method is known as sampling with *probability proportional to size* (PPS). The second way of emphasizing larger items in the population is to divide the population into subpopulations by size and take larger samples of the larger subpopulations. This is called *stratified sampling.* The first of these methods is evaluated using *monetary unit sampling* and the second using *variables sampling.* These selection methods and their related evaluation methods are discussed in Chapter 14.

## SAMPLING FOR EXCEPTION RATES

**OBJECTIVE 12-4**
**Define and describe audit sampling for exception rates.**

Audit sampling for tests of controls and substantive tests of transactions is used to estimate the *proportion* of items in a population containing a characteristic or *attribute* of interest. This proportion is called the *occurrence rate* or *exception rate* and is the ratio of the items containing the specific attribute to the total number of population items. The occurrence rate is usually expressed as a percentage. For example, an auditor might conclude that the exception rate for the internal verification of sales invoices is approximately 3 percent, meaning that invoices are not properly verified 3 percent of the time.

Auditors are interested in the occurrence of the following types of exceptions in populations of accounting data: (1) deviations from client's established controls, (2) monetary misstatements in populations of transaction data, and (3) monetary misstatements in populations of account balance details. Knowing the occurrence rate of such exceptions is particularly helpful for the first two types of exceptions, which relate to transactions. Therefore, auditors make extensive use of audit sampling that measures the occurrence or exception rate in performing tests of controls and substantive tests of transactions. With the third type of exception, the auditor usually needs to estimate the total dollar amount of the exceptions, because a judgment must be made about whether the exceptions are material. When the auditor wants to know the total amount of a misstatement, he or she will use methods that measure dollars, not the exception or occurrence rate. This topic is studied in Chapter 14.

The exception rate in a sample is intended to be an estimate of the exception rate in the entire population. It means that for a given sample, the sample exception rate is the auditor's "best estimate" of the population exception rate. The term *exception* should be understood to refer to both deviations from prescribed controls and situations where amounts are not monetarily correct, whether due to an unintentional accounting error or any other cause. The term *deviation* refers to the specific type of exception of a deviation from prescribed controls.

Assume, for example, that the auditor wants to determine the percentage of duplicate sales invoices that do not have shipping documents attached. There is an actual, but unknown, percentage of missing shipping documents. The auditor will obtain a sample of duplicate sales invoices and determine what percentage of the invoices do not have shipping documents attached. The auditor will conclude that the sample exception rate is the best estimate of the population exception rate.

Since it is based on a sample, however, there is a significant likelihood that the sample exception rate and the actual population exception rate differ. This difference is called *sampling error.* The auditor is concerned with the estimate of the sampling error and the reliability of that estimate, called *sampling risk.* Assume that the auditor determines that there is a 3 percent sample exception rate and a sampling error of 1 percent with a sampling risk of 10 percent. The auditor can now state an interval estimate of the population exception rate as between 2 percent and 4 percent (3 percent ± 1) at a 10 percent risk of being wrong (and a 90 percent chance of being right).

In using audit sampling in auditing for exception rates, the auditor is primarily interested in knowing the *most* the exception rate might be. Thus, the auditor focuses on the *upper limit* of the interval estimate. That limit is termed the *estimated* or *computed upper exception rate* (CUER) in tests of controls and substantive tests of transactions. In the above example, the auditor might conclude that the CUER for missing shipping documents is 4 percent at a 10 percent sampling risk. This means that the auditor concludes that the exception rate in the population is no greater than 4 percent with a 10 percent risk of the exception rate exceeding 4 percent. Once the CUER is determined, the auditor can consider it in the context of the specific audit objectives. For example, in testing for missing shipping documents, the auditor must determine whether a 4 percent exception rate indicates an acceptable control risk.

## APPLICATION OF NONSTATISTICAL AUDIT SAMPLING

**OBJECTIVE 12-5**
**Use nonstatistical sampling in tests of controls and substantive tests of transactions.**

We will now examine the application of nonstatistical audit sampling in testing transactions for control deviations and monetary misstatements. Before doing so, the terminology from SAS 39 (AU 350) and other terminology should be reviewed. These are summarized in Table 12-3.

Audit sampling is applied to tests of controls and substantive tests of transactions through a set of fourteen well-defined steps. The steps are divided into three sections: plan the sample, select the sample and perform the audit procedures, and evaluate the results. It is important to follow these steps carefully as a means of assuring that both the auditing and the sampling aspects of the process are properly applied. The steps provide an outline of the discussion that follows.

### *Plan the Sample*

1. State the objectives of the audit test.
2. Decide if audit sampling applies.
3. Define attributes and exception conditions.

**TABLE 12-3**

**Terms Used in Audit Sampling**

| Term | Definition |
|---|---|
| **Terms Related to Planning** | |
| Characteristic or attribute | The characteristic being tested in the application |
| Acceptable risk of assessing control risk too low (ARACR) | The risk that the auditor is willing to take of accepting a control as effective or a rate of monetary misstatements as tolerable, when the true population exception rate is greater than the tolerable exception rate |
| Tolerable exception rate (TER) | Exception rate that the auditor will permit in the population and still be willing to use the assessed control risk and/or the amount of monetary misstatements in the transactions established during planning |
| Estimated population exception rate (EPER) | Exception rate that the auditor expects to find in the population before testing begins |
| Initial sample size | Sample size decided after considering the above factors in planning |
| **Terms Related to Evaluating Results** | |
| Exception | Exception from the attribute in a sample item |
| Sample exception rate (SER) | Number of exceptions in the sample divided by the sample size |
| Computed upper exception rate (CUER) | The highest estimated exception rate in the population at a given ARACR |

4. Define the population.
5. Define the sampling unit.
6. Specify tolerable exception rate.
7. Specify acceptable risk of assessing control risk too low.
8. Estimate the population exception rate.
9. Determine the initial sample size.

*Select the Sample and Perform the Audit Procedures*

10. Select the sample.
11. Perform the audit procedures.

*Evaluate the Results*

12. Generalize from the sample to the population.
13. Analyze exceptions.
14. Decide the acceptability of the population.

### State the Objectives of the Audit Test

The overall objectives of the test must be stated in terms of the transaction cycle being tested. Typically, the overall objective of tests of controls and substantive tests of transactions is to test the application of controls and to determine whether the transactions contain monetary misstatements.

In the tests of the sales and collection cycle, the overall objective is usually to test the effectiveness of internal controls for sales or cash receipts. The objectives of the audit test are normally decided as a part of designing the audit program, which was discussed for the sales and collection cycle in Chapter 11.

### Decide If Audit Sampling Applies

Audit sampling applies whenever the auditor plans to reach conclusions about a population based on a sample. The auditor should examine the audit program and decide those audit procedures for which audit sampling applies. Assume the following partial audit program.

1. Review sales transactions for large and unusual amounts (analytical procedure).
2. Observe whether the duties of the accounts receivable clerk are separate from handling cash (test of control).

3. Examine a sample of duplicate sales invoices for
   a. credit approval by the credit manager (test of control).
   b. existence of an attached shipping document (test of control).
   c. inclusion of a chart of accounts number (test of control).
4. Select a sample of shipping documents and trace each to related duplicate sales invoices for existence (test of control).
5. Compare the quantity on each duplicate sales invoice with the quantity on related shipping documents (substantive test of transactions).

Audit sampling is inappropriate for the first two procedures in this audit program. The first is an analytical procedure for which sampling is inappropriate. The second is an observation procedure for which no documentation exists to perform audit sampling. Audit sampling can be used for the remaining three procedures.

### Define Attributes and Exception Conditions

Whenever audit sampling is used, the auditor must carefully define the characteristics (attributes) being tested and the exception conditions. Unless a precise statement of what constitutes an attribute is made in advance, the staff person who performs the audit procedure will have no guidelines for identifying exceptions.

Attributes of interest and exception conditions come directly from the audit procedures for which the auditor has decided to use audit sampling. Table 12-4 shows five attributes of interest and exception conditions for each of the attributes from audit procedures three through five mentioned previously. Each of the five attributes will be verified for every item selected for the sample. The absence of the attribute for any sample item will be an exception for that attribute.

**TABLE 12-4**
**Attributes Defined**

| Attribute | Exception Condition |
|---|---|
| 1. The duplicate sales invoice is approved for credit. (Procedure 3a) | Lack of initials indicating credit approval. |
| 2. A copy of the shipping document is attached to the duplicate sales invoice. (Procedure 3b) | Shipping document not attached to duplicate sales invoice. |
| 3. The account number charged is included on the duplicate sales invoice. (Procedure 3c) | Account number not included on duplicate sales invoice. |
| 4. A duplicate sales invoice exists for each shipping document. (Procedure 4) | Duplicate sales invoice does not exist for shipping document. |
| 5. The quantity on the sales invoice is the same as on the shipping document. (Procedure 5) | Quantity different on shipping document and duplicate sales invoice. |

### Define the Population

The population represents the body of data about which the auditor wishes to generalize. The auditor can define the population to include whatever data are desired, but he or she must sample from the entire population as it has been defined. The auditor may generalize *only* about that population which has been sampled. For example, in performing tests of controls and substantive tests of sales transactions, the auditor generally defines the population as all recorded sales for the year. If the auditor samples from only one month's transactions, it is invalid to draw conclusions about the invoices for the entire year.

It is important that the auditor carefully define the population in advance, consistent with the objectives of the audit tests. Furthermore, in some cases it may be necessary to define more than one population for a given set of audit procedures. For example, if the auditor intends to trace from sales invoices to shipping documents (attribute 2 in Table 12-4) and from shipping documents to duplicate sales invoices (attributes 4 and 5 in Table 12-4), there are two populations (one population of shipping documents and another of duplicate sales invoices). It is also important to test the population for completeness and detail tie-in before a sample is selected to ensure that all population items will be properly subjected to sample selection.

### Define the Sampling Unit

The major consideration in defining the sampling unit is to make it consistent with the objectives of the audit tests. Thus, the definition of the population and the planned audit procedures usually dictate the appropriate sampling unit. For example, if the auditor wants to determine how frequently the client fails to fill a customer's order, the sampling unit must be defined as the customer's order. If, however, the objective is to determine whether the proper quantity of the goods described on the customer's order is correctly shipped and billed, it is possible to define the sampling unit as the customer's order, the shipping document, or the duplicate sales invoice.

In Table 12-4, the appropriate sample unit for attribute 2 is the duplicate sales invoice. For attribute 4 the appropriate sampling unit is the shipping document. Either the duplicate sales invoice or the shipping document is appropriate for attributes 1, 3, and 5. For example, the auditor can define the sampling unit as the shipping document, trace it to the duplicate sales invoice for attribute 4, and examine the invoice for attributes 1, 3, and 5. It is impossible, however, to test for attribute 2 if the sampling unit is the shipping document. The auditor could also define the sampling unit as the duplicate sales invoice, examine the invoice for attributes 1 and 3, determine if a shipping document is attached (attribute 2), and perform the test for attribute 5. It is impossible, however, to test for attribute 4 if the sampling unit is the duplicate sales invoice.

### Specify Tolerable Exception Rate

Establishing the tolerable exception rate (TER) requires *professional judgment* on the part of the auditor. TER represents the exception rate that the auditor will permit in the population and still be willing to use the assessed control risk and/or the amount of monetary misstatements in the transactions established during planning. For example, assume that the auditor decides that TER for attribute 1 in Table 12-4 is 6 percent. That means that the auditor has decided that even if 6 percent of the duplicate sales invoices are not approved for credit, the credit approval control is still effective in terms of the assessed control risk included in the audit plan.

TER is the result of an auditor's judgment. The suitable TER is a question of materiality and is therefore affected by both the definition and the importance of the attribute in the audit plan.

TER has a significant impact on sample size. A larger sample size is needed for a low TER than for a high TER. For example, a larger sample is required for a TER of 4 percent for attribute 1 in the previous example than for a TER of 6 percent.

### Specify Acceptable Risk of Assessing Control Risk Too Low

Whenever a sample is taken, there is a risk that the quantitative conclusions about the population will be incorrect. This is always true unless 100 percent of the population is tested. As has already been stated, this is the case with both nonstatistical and statistical sampling.

For audit sampling in tests of controls and substantive tests of transactions, that risk is called the *acceptable risk of assessing control risk too low* (ARACR). ARACR is the risk that the auditor is willing to take of accepting a control as effective (or a rate of monetary misstatements as tolerable) when the true population exception rate is greater than TER. To illustrate, assume that TER is 6 percent, ARACR is 10 percent, and the true population exception rate is 8 percent. The control in this case is not acceptable because the true exception rate of 8 percent exceeds TER. The auditor, of course, does not know the true population exception rate. The ARACR of 10 percent means that the auditor is willing to take a 10 percent risk of concluding that the control is effective after all testing is completed, even when it is ineffective. If the auditor finds the control effective in this illustration, he or she will have overrelied on the system of internal control (used a lower assessed control risk than justified). ARACR is the auditor's measure of sampling risk.

In choosing the appropriate ARACR in a situation, the auditor must use his or her best judgment. Since ARACR is a measure of the risk that the auditor is willing to take, the main consideration is the extent to which the auditor plans to reduce assessed control risk as a basis for the extent of tests of details of balances. The lower the assessed control risk, the lower will be the ARACR chosen and the planned extent of tests of details of balances. Referring to Figure 9-3 (page 303), the most common situation where audit sampling would be used for tests of controls and substantive tests of transactions is when the auditor decides to assess control risk at a lower level than can be supported by understanding internal control (alternative 3). If the auditor decides to assess control risk at maximum (alternative 1), tests of controls are not performed. If control risk is assessed at the level supported by understanding internal control (alternative 2), tests of controls are often restricted to inquiry and transaction walk-through tests.

For nonstatistical sampling, it is common for auditors to use ARACR of high, medium, or low instead of a percentage. A low ARACR implies that the tests of controls are important and would correspond to a low assessed control risk and reduced substantive tests of details of balances.

The auditor can establish different TER and ARACR levels for different attributes of an audit test. For example, it is common for auditors to use higher TER and ARACR levels for tests of credit approval than for tests of the existence of duplicate sales invoices and bills of lading. This is because the exceptions for the latter are likely to have a more direct impact on the correctness of the financial statements than the former.

Tables 12-5 and 12-6 present illustrative guidelines for establishing TER and ARACR. The guidelines should not be interpreted as representing broad professional standards; however, they are typical of the types of guidelines CPA firms issue to their staff.

## Estimate the Population Exception Rate

An *advance estimate* of the population exception rate (EPER) should be made to plan the appropriate sample size. If the EPER is low, a relatively small sample size will satisfy the auditor's tolerable exception rate. This is because a less precise estimate is required. In other words, to be more precise, an estimate of the population exception rate must be based on more data, that is, a larger sample.

It is common to use the results of the preceding year's audit to make this estimate. If prior year results are not available, or if they are considered unreliable, the auditor can take a small *preliminary sample* of the current year's population for this purpose. It is not critical that the estimate be precise because the current year's sample exception rate is ultimately used to estimate the population characteristics.

Note that if a preliminary sample is used, it can be included in the ultimate sample, as long as appropriate sample selection procedures are followed. For example, assume that an auditor takes a preliminary sample of thirty items to estimate the EPER that considers the

**TABLE 12-5**

**Guidelines for ARACR and TER for Nonstatistical Sampling: Tests of Controls**

| Factor | Judgment | Guideline |
|---|---|---|
| Assessed control risk. Consider:<br>Nature, extent, and timing of substantive tests (extensive planned substantive tests relate to higher assessed control risk and vice versa)<br>Quality of evidence available for tests of controls (a lower quality of evidence available results in a higher assessed control risk and vice versa). | • Lowest assessed control risk<br>• Moderate assessed control risk<br>• Higher assessed control risk<br>• 100% assessed control risk | • ARACR of low<br>• ARACR of medium<br>• ARACR of high<br>• ARACR is not applicable |
| Significance of the transactions and related account balances that the internal controls are intended to affect. | • Highly significant balances<br>• Significant balances<br>• Less significant balances | • TER of 4%<br>• TER of 5%<br>• TER of 6% |

*Note:* The guidelines should recognize that there may be variations in ARACRs based on audit considerations. The guidelines above are the most conservative that should be followed.

**TABLE 12-6**

**Guidelines for ARACR and TER for Nonstatistical Sampling: Substantive Tests of Transactions**

| Planned Reduction in Substantive Tests of Details of Balances | Results of Understanding Internal Control and Tests of Controls | ARACR for Substantive Tests of Transactions (in Percentage) | TER For Substantive Tests of Transactions |
|---|---|---|---|
| Large | Excellent[1]<br>Good<br>Not good | High<br>Medium<br>Low | Percent or amount based on materiality considerations for related accounts |
| Moderate | Excellent[1]<br>Good<br>Not good | High<br>Medium<br>Medium–Low | Percent or amount based on materiality considerations for related accounts |
| Small[2] | Excellent[1]<br>Good<br>Not good | High<br>Medium–High<br>Medium | Percent or amount based on materiality considerations for related accounts |

*Notes:* The guidelines should also recognize that there may be variations in ARACRs based on audit considerations. The guidelines above are the most conservative that should be followed.

1. In this situation both internal control and evidence about it are good. Substantive tests of transactions are least likely to be performed in this situation.
2. In this situation little emphasis is being placed on internal controls. Neither tests of controls nor substantive tests of transactions are likely in this situation.

entire population. Later, if the auditor decides that a total sample size of 100 is needed, only seventy additional items will need to be properly selected and tested.

## Determine the Initial Sample Size

Four factors determine the initial sample size for audit sampling: population size, TER, ARACR, and EPER. Population size is not nearly as significant a factor as the others and typically can be ignored.

An important characteristic of nonstatistical sampling compared to statistical methods is the need to decide the sample size using professional judgment for nonstatistical methods rather than by calculation using a statistical formula. Once the three major factors affecting sample size have been determined, it is possible for the auditor to decide an initial sample size.

The initial sample size is called that because the exceptions in the actual sample must be evaluated before it is possible to know whether the sample is sufficiently large to achieve the objectives of the tests.

**Sensitivity of Sample Size to a Change in the Factors** To properly understand the concepts underlying sampling in auditing, it is helpful to understand the effect of changing any of the four factors that determine sample size while the other factors are held constant. Table 12-7 on page 418 illustrates the effect of increasing each of the four factors; a decrease will have the opposite effect.

A combination of two factors has the greatest effect on sample size: TER minus EPER. The difference is the *precision* of the planned sample estimate. A smaller precision, which is called a more precise estimate, requires a larger sample.

## Select the Sample

After the auditor has computed the initial sample size for the audit sampling application, he or she must choose the items in the population to be included in the sample. The sample can be chosen by using any of the probabilistic or nonprobabilistic methods discussed earlier in the chapter.

## Perform the Audit Procedures

The auditor performs the audit procedures by examining each item in the sample to determine whether it is consistent with the definition of the attribute and maintains a record of all the exceptions found. When audit procedures have been completed for a sampling

**TABLE 12-7**

**Effect on Sample Size of Changing Factors**

| Type of Change | Effect on Initial Sample Size |
|---|---|
| Increase acceptable risk of assessing control risk too low | Decrease |
| Increase tolerable exception rate | Decrease |
| Increase estimated population exception rate | Increase |
| Increase population size | Increase (minor effect) |

application, there will be a sample size and number of exceptions for each attribute. Using the example from Table 12-4 on page 414, there may be a sample size of 125 and 2 exceptions for attribute 1, a sample size of 150 and 3 exceptions for attribute 2, and so on.

## Generalize from the Sample to the Population

The *sample exception rate* (SER) can be easily calculated from the actual sample results. SER equals the actual number of exceptions divided by the actual sample size. Continuing the example in the previous paragraph, attribute 1 from Table 12-4 has an SER of 1.6 percent (2 ÷ 125) and attribute 2 has an SER of 2 percent (3 ÷ 150).

It is improper for the auditor to conclude that the population exception rate is exactly the same as the sample exception rate; the chance that they are exactly the same is too small. For nonstatistical methods, there are two ways to generalize from the sample to the population.

*1.* Add an estimate of sampling error to SER to arrive at a computed upper exception rate (CUER) for a given acceptable risk of assessing control risk too low. It is extremely difficult for auditors to make sampling error estimates using nonstatistical sampling because of the judgment required to do so; therefore, this approach is generally not used.

*2.* Subtract the sample exception rate from the tolerable exception rate, which is calculated sampling error (TER – SER = calculated sampling error), and evaluate whether calculated sampling error is sufficiently large to indicate the true population exception rate is acceptable. Most auditors using nonstatistical sampling follow this approach. For example, if an auditor takes a sample of 100 items for an attribute and finds no exceptions (SER = 0), and TER is 5 percent, calculated sampling error is 5 percent (TER of 5 percent – SER of 0 = 5%). On the other hand, if there had been four exceptions, calculated sampling error would have been 1 percent (TER of 5 percent – SER of 4 percent). It is much more likely that the true population exception rate is less than or equal to the tolerable exception rate in the first case than in the second one. Therefore, most auditors would probably find the population acceptable based on the first sample result, and not acceptable based on the second.

In addition, the auditor's consideration of whether sampling error is sufficiently large will depend on sample size. For example, if the sample size in the above example had been only twenty items, the auditor would have been much less confident that finding no exceptions was an indication that the true population exception rate does not exceed TER, than where no exceptions were found in a sample of 100 items.

Note that under this approach, the auditor does not make an estimate of the computed upper exception rate.

## Analyze Exceptions

In addition to determining the SER for each attribute and evaluating whether the true but unknown exception rate is likely to exceed the tolerable exception rate, it is necessary to analyze individual exceptions to determine the breakdown in the internal controls that caused them. Exceptions could be caused by carelessness of employees, misunderstood instructions, intentional failure to perform procedures, or many other factors. The nature of an exception and its cause have a significant effect on the qualitative evaluation of the system. For example, if all the exceptions in the tests of internal verification of sales invoices occurred while the person normally responsible for performing the tests was on vacation, this would affect the auditor's evaluation of the internal controls and the subsequent investigation.

## Decide the Acceptability of the Population

It was shown under generalizing from the sample to the population that most auditors subtract SER fiom TER when they use nonstatistical sampling and evaluate whether the difference, which is calculated sampling error, is sufficiently large. If the auditor concludes that the difference is sufficiently large, the control being tested can be used to reduce assessed control risk as planned, provided a careful analysis of the cause of exceptions does not indicate the possibility of other significant problems with internal controls.

When the auditor concludes that TER – SER is too small to conclude that the population is acceptable, the auditor must take specific action. Four courses of action can be followed.

**Revise TER or ARACR** This alternative should be followed only when the auditor has concluded that the original specifications were too conservative. Relaxing either TER or ARACR may be difficult to defend if the auditor is ever subject to review by a court or a commission. If these requirements are changed, it should be done on the basis of careful thought.

**Expand the Sample Size** An increase in the sample size has the effect of decreasing the sampling error if the actual sample exception rate does not increase. Of course, SER may also increase or decrease if additional items are selected.

**Revise Assessed Control Risk** If the results of the tests of controls and substantive tests of transactions do not support the planned assessed control risk, the auditor should revise assessed control risk upward. The effect of the revision is likely to increase tests of details of balances. For example, if tests of controls of internal verification procedures for verifying prices, extensions, and quantities on sales invoices indicate that those procedures are not being followed, the auditor should increase tests of the accuracy of sales transactions. This is most likely to be done through tests of accounts receivable.

The decision whether to increase sample size until sampling error is sufficiently small or to revise assessed control risk must be made on the basis of cost versus benefit. If the sample is not expanded, it is necessary to revise assessed control risk upward and therefore perform additional substantive tests. The cost of additional tests of controls must be compared with that of additional substantive tests. If an expanded sample still continues to produce unacceptable results, additional substantive tests will still be necessary.

If the original test performed is to test transactions for monetary misstatements and an exception rate higher than that assumed is indicated, the response would generally be the same as for tests of controls.

**Write a Letter to Management** This action is desirable, in combination with one of the other three above, regardless of the nature of the exceptions. When the auditor determines that the internal controls are not operating effectively, management should be informed.

In some instances, it may be acceptable to limit the action to writing a letter to management when TER minus SER is too small. This occurs if the auditor has no intention of reducing the assessed control risk or has already carried out sufficient procedures to his or her own satisfaction as a part of substantive tests of transactions.

## Summary of Nonstatistical Sampling Steps

Figure 12-3 on page 420 summarizes the steps used in nonstatistical sampling. It is apparent from the figure that planning is an essential part of using sampling. The purposes of planning are to make sure that the audit procedures are properly applied and that the sample size

**FIGURE 12-3**

**Summary of Audit Sampling Steps**

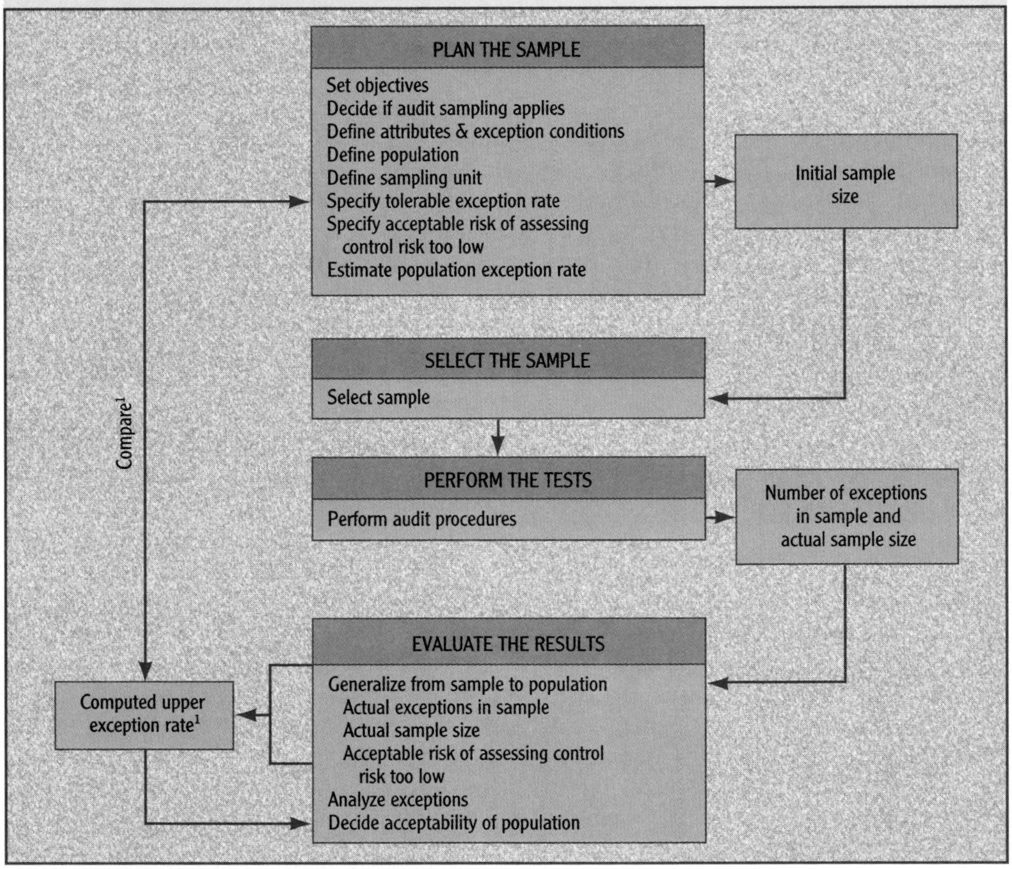


[1]Many auditors using nonstatistical methods calculate tolerable exception rate minus sample exception rate and evaluate whether the difference is sufficiently large.

is appropriate for the circumstances. Sample selection is also important and must be done with care to avoid nonsampling errors. Performing the audit procedures must be done carefully to correctly determine the number of exceptions in the sample. It is the most time-consuming part of audit sampling. Evaluating the results includes calculating sampling error (TER – SER) and determining its sufficiency, doing the judgmental analysis of the exceptions, and finally, deciding the acceptability of the population.

## ATTRIBUTES SAMPLING

**OBJECTIVE 12-6**
**Define and describe attributes sampling and a sampling distribution.**

The statistical sampling method most commonly used for tests of controls and substantive tests of transactions is *attributes sampling.* Whenever attributes sampling is used in this text, it refers to attributes statistical sampling. Both attributes sampling and nonstatistical sampling have attributes, which are the characteristics being tested for in the population, but attributes sampling is a statistical method.

There are far more similarities than differences in applying attributes sampling instead of nonstatistical sampling to tests of controls and substantive tests of transactions. All fourteen steps discussed are used for both approaches, and the terminology is essentially the same. The important differences are the calculation of planned sample sizes using tables developed from statistical probability distributions and the calculation of estimated upper exception rates using similar tables. The quantification of these calculations is an extremely important difference to those auditors who prefer statistical to nonstatistical sampling. Before applying attributes sampling using the same fourteen steps already discussed, sampling distributions are discussed.

## SAMPLING DISTRIBUTION

Statistical inferences are based on *sampling distributions.* A sampling distribution is a frequency distribution of the results of all possible samples of a specified size that could be obtained from a population containing some specific parameters. The existence of a sampling distribution allows the auditor to make probability statements about the likely degree of representativeness of any sample that is a member of that distribution.

Attributes sampling is based on the *binomial distribution.* The binomial distribution is a distribution of all possible samples where the items in the population each have one of two possible states, for example, yes/no, black/white, or control deviation/no control deviation.

Assume that a population of sales invoices exists, 5 percent of which have no shipping documents attached as required by the client's internal controls. If the auditor takes a sample of fifty sales invoices, how many will he or she find that have no shipping documents? The sample could contain no exceptions, or it might contain six or seven. A binomial-based sampling distribution would tell us the probability of each possible number of exceptions occurring. The sampling distribution for the example population is shown in Table 12-8. This distribution shows that, with a sample of fifty items from a very large population with an exception rate of 5 percent, the likelihood of obtaining a sample with at least one exception is 92.31 percent (1 – .0769). (Since the probability of no exceptions is 7.69%, the probability of more than 0 is 92.31%.)

**TABLE 12-8**

**Probability of Each Exception Rate—5% Population Exception Rate and Sample Size of 50**

| Number of Exceptions | Percentage of Exception | Probability | Cumulative Probability |
|---|---|---|---|
| 0 | 0 | .0769 | .0769 |
| 1 | 2 | .2025 | .2794 |
| 2 | 4 | .2611 | .5405 |
| 3 | 6 | .2199 | .7604 |
| 4 | 8 | .1360 | .8964 |
| 5 | 10 | .0656 | .9620 |
| 6 | 12 | .0260 | .9880 |
| 7 | 14 | .0120 | 1.0000 |

There is a unique sampling distribution for each population exception rate and sample size. The distribution for a sample size of 100 from a population with a 5 percent exception rate is different from the previous one, as is the distribution for a sample of fifty from a population with a 3 percent exception rate.

In actual audit situations, auditors do not take repeated samples from known populations. They take one sample from an unknown population and get a specific number of exceptions in that sample. But knowledge about sampling distributions enables auditors to make statistical statements about the population. For example, if the auditor selects a sample of fifty sales invoices to test for attached shipping documents and finds one exception, the auditor could examine the probability table in Table 12-8 and know there is a 20.25 percent probability that the sample came from a population with a 5 percent exception rate, and a 79.75 percent (1 – .2025) probability that the sample was taken from a population having some other exception rate. It is also possible to state by examining the cumulative probabilities column in Table 12-8 that there is a 27.94 percent probability that the sample came from a population with *more* than a 5 percent exception rate, and a 72.06 percent (1 – .2794) probability that the sample was taken from a population having an exception rate of 5 percent or less. Since it is similarly possible to calculate the probability distributions for other population exception rates, these can be examined in the aggregate to draw more specific statistical conclusions about the unknown population being sampled. These sampling distributions are the basis for the tables used by auditors for attributes sampling.

## APPLICATION OF ATTRIBUTES SAMPLING

**OBJECTIVE 12-7**
**Use attributes sampling in tests of controls and substantive tests of transactions.**

As already stated, the fourteen steps discussed for nonstatistical sampling are equally applicable to attributes sampling. This section will focus on the differences between the two.

### *Plan the Sample*

1. *State the objects of the audit test.* Same for attributes and nonstatistical sampling.
2. *Decide if audit sampling applies.* Same for attributes and nonstatistical sampling.
3. *Define attributes and exception conditions.* Same for attributes and nonstatistical sampling.
4. *Define the population.* Same for attributes and nonstatistical sampling.
5. *Define the sampling unit.* Same for attributes and nonstatistical sampling.
6. *Specify tolerable exception rate.* Same for attributes and nonstatistical sampling.
7. *Specify acceptable risk of assessing control risk too low.*

The concepts of specifying this risk are the same for both statistical and nonstatistical sampling, but the method of quantification is usually different. For nonstatistical sampling, most auditors use low, medium, or high acceptable risk whereas auditors using attributes sampling assign a specific amount such as 10 percent or 5 percent risk. The reason for the difference is the need to quantify risk when auditors plan to determine sample size and evaluate results statistically.

8. *Estimate the population exception rate.* Same for attributes and nonstatistical sampling.
9. *Determine the initial sample size.*

Four factors determine the initial sample size for both statistical and nonstatistical sampling: population size, TER, ARACR, and EPER. The difference is that special computer programs or tables developed from statistical formulas are used to determine the sample size for attributes sampling. Tables are used to illustrate determining the sample size. Determining binomial probabilities using computers is not discussed because the software required is complex.

The two tables that make up Table 12-9 are taken from the AICPA *Audit Sampling Guide.* They are the same, except that the first one is for a 5 percent ARACR and the second one a 10 percent ARACR. These tables are "one-sided tables," which means that they represent the *upper* exception rate for a given ARACR.

**Use of the Tables** Use of the tables to determine initial sample size involves four steps:

1. Select the table corresponding to the ARACR.
2. Locate the TER at the top of the table.
3. Locate the EPER in the far left column.
4. Read down the appropriate TER column until it intersects with the appropriate EPER row. The number at the intersection is the initial sample size.

**TABLE 12-9**

**Determining Sample Size for Attributes Sampling**

**5 PERCENT ARACR**

| Estimated Population Exception Rate (in Percentage) | Tolerable Exception Rate (in Percentage) 2 | 3 | 4 | 5 | 6 | 7 | 8 | 9 | 10 | 15 | 20 |
|---|---|---|---|---|---|---|---|---|---|---|---|
| 0.00 | 149 | 99 | 74 | 59 | 49 | 42 | 36 | 32 | 29 | 19 | 14 |
| 0.25 | 236 | 157 | 117 | 93 | 78 | 66 | 58 | 51 | 46 | 30 | 22 |
| 0.50 | * | 157 | 117 | 93 | 78 | 66 | 58 | 51 | 46 | 30 | 22 |
| 0.75 | * | 208 | 117 | 93 | 78 | 66 | 58 | 51 | 46 | 30 | 22 |
| 1.00 | * | * | 156 | 93 | 78 | 66 | 58 | 51 | 46 | 30 | 22 |
| 1.25 | * | * | 156 | 124 | 78 | 66 | 58 | 51 | 46 | 30 | 22 |
| 1.50 | * | * | 192 | 124 | 103 | 66 | 58 | 51 | 46 | 30 | 22 |
| 1.75 | * | * | 227 | 153 | 103 | 88 | 77 | 51 | 46 | 30 | 22 |
| 2.00 | * | * | * | 181 | 127 | 88 | 77 | 68 | 46 | 30 | 22 |
| 2.25 | * | * | * | 208 | 127 | 88 | 77 | 68 | 61 | 30 | 22 |
| 2.50 | * | * | * | * | 150 | 109 | 77 | 68 | 61 | 30 | 22 |
| 2.75 | * | * | * | * | 173 | 109 | 95 | 68 | 61 | 30 | 22 |
| 3.00 | * | * | * | * | 195 | 129 | 95 | 84 | 61 | 30 | 22 |
| 3.25 | * | * | * | * | * | 148 | 112 | 84 | 61 | 30 | 22 |
| 3.50 | * | * | * | * | * | 167 | 112 | 84 | 76 | 40 | 22 |
| 3.75 | * | * | * | * | * | 185 | 129 | 100 | 76 | 40 | 22 |
| 4.00 | * | * | * | * | * | * | 146 | 100 | 89 | 40 | 22 |
| 5.00 | * | * | * | * | * | * | * | 158 | 116 | 40 | 30 |
| 6.00 | * | * | * | * | * | * | * | * | 179 | 50 | 30 |
| 7.00 | * | * | * | * | * | * | * | * | * | 68 | 37 |

**10 PERCENT ARACR**

| Estimated Population Exception Rate (in Percentage) | 2 | 3 | 4 | 5 | 6 | 7 | 8 | 9 | 10 | 15 | 20 |
|---|---|---|---|---|---|---|---|---|---|---|---|
| 0.00 | 114 | 76 | 57 | 45 | 38 | 32 | 28 | 25 | 22 | 15 | 11 |
| 0.25 | 194 | 129 | 96 | 77 | 64 | 55 | 48 | 42 | 38 | 25 | 18 |
| 0.50 | 194 | 129 | 96 | 77 | 64 | 55 | 48 | 42 | 38 | 25 | 18 |
| 0.75 | 265 | 129 | 96 | 77 | 64 | 55 | 48 | 42 | 38 | 25 | 18 |
| 1.00 | * | 176 | 96 | 77 | 64 | 55 | 48 | 42 | 38 | 25 | 18 |
| 1.25 | * | 221 | 132 | 77 | 64 | 55 | 48 | 42 | 38 | 25 | 18 |
| 1.50 | * | * | 132 | 105 | 64 | 55 | 48 | 42 | 38 | 25 | 18 |
| 1.75 | * | * | 166 | 105 | 88 | 55 | 48 | 42 | 38 | 25 | 18 |
| 2.00 | * | * | 198 | 132 | 88 | 75 | 48 | 42 | 38 | 25 | 18 |
| 2.25 | * | * | * | 132 | 88 | 75 | 65 | 42 | 38 | 25 | 18 |
| 2.50 | * | * | * | 158 | 110 | 75 | 65 | 58 | 38 | 25 | 18 |
| 2.75 | * | * | * | 209 | 132 | 94 | 65 | 58 | 52 | 25 | 18 |
| 3.00 | * | * | * | * | 132 | 94 | 65 | 58 | 52 | 25 | 18 |
| 3.25 | * | * | * | * | 153 | 113 | 82 | 58 | 52 | 25 | 18 |
| 3.50 | * | * | * | * | 194 | 113 | 82 | 73 | 52 | 25 | 18 |
| 3.75 | * | * | * | * | * | 131 | 98 | 73 | 52 | 25 | 18 |
| 4.00 | * | * | * | * | * | 149 | 98 | 73 | 65 | 25 | 18 |
| 4.50 | * | * | * | * | * | 218 | 130 | 87 | 65 | 34 | 18 |
| 5.00 | * | * | * | * | * | * | 160 | 115 | 78 | 34 | 18 |
| 5.50 | * | * | * | * | * | * | * | 142 | 103 | 34 | 18 |
| 6.00 | * | * | * | * | * | * | * | 182 | 116 | 45 | 25 |
| 7.00 | * | * | * | * | * | * | * | * | 199 | 52 | 25 |
| 7.50 | * | * | * | * | * | * | * | * | * | 52 | 25 |
| 8.00 | * | * | * | * | * | * | * | * | * | 60 | 25 |
| 8.50 | * | * | * | * | * | * | * | * | * | 68 | 32 |

*Sample is too large to be cost effective for most audit applications.

*Notes:* 1. This table assumes a large population. 2. Sample sizes are the same in certain columns even when estimated population exception rates differ, because of the method of constructing the tables. Sample sizes are calculated for attributes sampling by using the expected number of exceptions in the population, but auditors can deal more conveniently with estimated population exception rates. For example, in the 15 percent column for tolerable exception rate, at an ARACR of 5 percent, initial sample size for most EPERs is 30. One exception, divided by a sample size of 30, is 3.3 percent. Therefore, for all EPERs greater than zero, but less than 3.3 percent, initial sample size is the same.

To illustrate, assume that an auditor is willing to reduce assessed control risk for credit approval if the rate of missing credit approvals in the population (attribute 1 in Table 12-4) does not exceed 6 percent (TER), at a 5 percent ARACR. On the basis of past experience, EPER is set at 2 percent. Use the 5 percent ARACR table; locate the 6 percent TER column; read down to where the column intersects with the 2 percent EPER row. The initial sample size is determined to be 127.

Is 127 a large enough sample size for this audit? It is not possible to say until after the tests have been performed. If the actual exception rate in the sample turns out to be greater than 2 percent, the auditor will be unsure of the effectiveness of the internal controls. The reasons for this will become apparent as we proceed.

**Effect of Population Size** In the preceding discussion, the size of the population was ignored in determining the initial sample size. It may seem strange to some readers, but statistical theory proves that in most types of populations to which attributes sampling applies, the population size is a minor consideration in determining sample size. This is true because representativeness is ensured by the sample selection process more than by sample size. Once a sample is obtained that includes a good cross section of items, additional items are not needed. Because most auditors use attributes sampling for reasonably large populations, the reduction of sample size for smaller populations is ignored here.

*Select the Sample and Perform the Audit Procedures*

10. *Select the sample.* The only difference in sample selection for statistical and nonstatistical sampling is the requirement that probabilistic methods must be used for statistical sampling. Either simple random or systematic sampling is used for attributes sampling.
11. *Perform the audit procedures.* Same for attributes and nonstatistical sampling.

*Evaluate the Results*

12. *Generalize from the sample to the population.* For attributes sampling, the auditor calculates an upper precision limit (CUER) at a specified ARACR, again using special computer programs or tables developed from statistical formulas. To illustrate the calculations, tables such as the one for a 5 percent ARACR in Table 12-10 are used. These tables are consistent with those used to determine the initial sample size, but are in a form more convenient for sample evaluation.

**Use of the Tables** Use of tables to compute CUER involves four steps:

1. Select the table corresponding to the ARACR. This ARACR should be the same as the ARACR used for determining the initial sample size.
2. Locate the actual number of exceptions found in the audit tests at the top of the table.
3. Locate the actual sample size in the far left column.
4. Read down the appropriate actual number of exceptions column until it intersects with the appropriate sample size row. The number at the intersection is the CUER.

To illustrate the use of the evaluation table, assume an actual sample size of 125 and 2 exceptions in attribute 1. Using an ARACR of 5 percent, CUER equals 4.9 percent. Stated another way, the result is that the CUER for attribute 1 is 4.9 percent at a 5 percent ARACR. Does this mean that if 100 percent of the population were tested, the true exception rate would be 4.9 percent? No, the true exception rate is unknown. The result means that if the auditor concludes that the true exception rate does not exceed 4.9 percent, there is a 95 percent chance that the conclusion is right and a 5 percent chance that it is wrong.

It is possible to have a sample size that is not equal to those provided for in the attributes sampling evaluation tables. When this occurs, it is common to interpolate.

**TABLE 12-10**

**Evaluating Sample Results Using Attributes Sampling**

**5 PERCENT ARACR**

| Sample Size | Actual Number of Exceptions Found | | | | | | | | | | |
|---|---|---|---|---|---|---|---|---|---|---|---|
| | 0 | 1 | 2 | 3 | 4 | 5 | 6 | 7 | 8 | 9 | 10 |
| 25 | 11.3 | 17.6 | * | * | * | * | * | * | * | * | * |
| 30 | 9.5 | 14.9 | 19.5 | * | * | * | * | * | * | * | * |
| 35 | 8.2 | 12.9 | 16.9 | * | * | * | * | * | * | * | * |
| 40 | 7.2 | 11.3 | 14.9 | 18.3 | * | * | * | * | * | * | * |
| 45 | 6.4 | 10.1 | 13.3 | 16.3 | 19.2 | * | * | * | * | * | * |
| 50 | 5.8 | 9.1 | 12.1 | 14.8 | 17.4 | 19.9 | * | * | * | * | * |
| 55 | 5.3 | 8.3 | 11.0 | 13.5 | 15.9 | 18.1 | * | * | * | * | * |
| 60 | 4.9 | 7.7 | 10.1 | 12.4 | 14.6 | 16.7 | 18.8 | * | * | * | * |
| 65 | 4.5 | 7.1 | 9.4 | 11.5 | 13.5 | 15.5 | 17.4 | 19.3 | * | * | * |
| 70 | 4.2 | 6.6 | 8.7 | 10.7 | 12.6 | 14.4 | 16.2 | 18.0 | 19.7 | * | * |
| 75 | 3.9 | 6.2 | 8.2 | 10.0 | 11.8 | 13.5 | 15.2 | 16.9 | 18.4 | 20.0 | * |
| 80 | 3.7 | 5.8 | 7.7 | 9.4 | 11.1 | 12.7 | 14.3 | 15.8 | 17.3 | 18.8 | * |
| 90 | 3.3 | 5.2 | 6.8 | 8.4 | 9.9 | 11.3 | 12.7 | 14.1 | 15.5 | 16.8 | 18.1 |
| 100 | 3.0 | 4.7 | 6.2 | 7.6 | 8.9 | 10.2 | 11.5 | 12.7 | 14.0 | 15.2 | 16.4 |
| 125 | 2.4 | 3.7 | 4.9 | 6.1 | 7.2 | 8.2 | 9.3 | 10.3 | 11.3 | 12.2 | 13.2 |
| 150 | 2.0 | 3.1 | 4.1 | 5.1 | 6.0 | 6.9 | 7.7 | 8.6 | 9.4 | 10.2 | 11.0 |
| 200 | 1.5 | 2.3 | 3.1 | 3.8 | 4.5 | 5.2 | 5.8 | 6.5 | 7.1 | 7.7 | 8.3 |

**10 PERCENT ARACR**

| Sample Size | Actual Number of Exceptions Found | | | | | | | | | | |
|---|---|---|---|---|---|---|---|---|---|---|---|
| | 0 | 1 | 2 | 3 | 4 | 5 | 6 | 7 | 8 | 9 | 10 |
| 20 | 10.9 | 18.1 | * | * | * | * | * | * | * | * | * |
| 25 | 8.8 | 14.7 | 19.9 | * | * | * | * | * | * | * | * |
| 30 | 7.4 | 12.4 | 16.8 | * | * | * | * | * | * | * | * |
| 35 | 6.4 | 10.7 | 14.5 | 18.1 | * | * | * | * | * | * | * |
| 40 | 5.6 | 9.4 | 12.8 | 15.9 | 19.0 | * | * | * | * | * | * |
| 45 | 5.0 | 8.4 | 11.4 | 14.2 | 17.0 | 19.6 | * | * | * | * | * |
| 50 | 4.5 | 7.6 | 10.3 | 12.9 | 15.4 | 17.8 | * | * | * | * | * |
| 55 | 4.1 | 6.9 | 9.4 | 11.7 | 14.0 | 16.2 | 18.4 | * | * | * | * |
| 60 | 3.8 | 6.3 | 8.6 | 10.8 | 12.9 | 14.9 | 16.9 | 18.8 | * | * | * |
| 70 | 3.2 | 5.4 | 7.4 | 9.3 | 11.1 | 12.8 | 14.6 | 16.2 | 17.9 | 19.5 | * |
| 80 | 2.8 | 4.8 | 6.5 | 8.3 | 9.7 | 11.3 | 12.8 | 14.3 | 15.7 | 17.2 | 18.6 |
| 90 | 2.5 | 4.3 | 5.8 | 7.3 | 8.7 | 10.1 | 11.4 | 12.7 | 14.0 | 15.3 | 16.6 |
| 100 | 2.3 | 3.8 | 5.2 | 6.6 | 7.8 | 9.1 | 10.3 | 11.5 | 12.7 | 13.8 | 15.0 |
| 120 | 1.9 | 3.2 | 4.4 | 5.5 | 6.6 | 7.6 | 8.6 | 9.6 | 10.6 | 11.6 | 12.5 |
| 160 | 1.4 | 2.4 | 3.3 | 4.1 | 4.9 | 5.7 | 6.5 | 7.2 | 8.0 | 8.7 | 9.5 |
| 200 | 1.1 | 1.9 | 2.6 | 3.3 | 4.0 | 4.6 | 5.2 | 5.8 | 6.4 | 7.0 | 7.6 |

*Over 20 percent.

*Note:* This table presents computed upper exception rates as percentages. Table assumes a large population.

These tables assume a very large (infinite) population size which results in a more conservative CUER than for smaller populations. Because the effect of population size on sample size is typically very small, it is ignored.

13. *Analyze exceptions.* Same for attributes and nonstatistical sampling.
14. *Decide the acceptability of the population.*

The methodology for deciding the acceptability of the population is essentially the same for attributes and nonstatistical sampling. For attributes sampling, the auditor compares CUER to TER for each attribute.

Before the population can be considered acceptable, the CUER determined on the basis of the actual sample results must be *less than or equal to* TER when both are based on ARACR. In the example just given, in which the auditor has specified that he or she would accept a 6 percent population exception rate at a 5 percent ARACR and the CUER was 4.9 percent, the requirements of the sample have been met. In this case the control being tested can be used to reduce assessed control risk as planned, provided a careful analysis of the cause of exceptions does not indicate the possibility of a significant problem in an aspect of the control not previously considered.

When the CUER is greater than the TER, it is necessary to take specific action. The four courses of action discussed for nonstatistical sampling are equally applicable to attributes sampling.

## OTHER CONSIDERATIONS

For the sake of greater continuity, in the preceding discussion we bypassed three important aspects of using sampling that are now discussed.

### Random Selection Versus Statistical Measurement

Auditors often do not understand the distinction between random (probabilistic) selection and statistical measurement. It should now be clear that random selection is a part of statistical sampling but is not, by itself, statistical measurement. To have statistical measurement, it is necessary to generalize mathematically from the sample to the population.

It is acceptable to use random selection procedures without drawing statistical conclusions, but this practice is questionable if a reasonably large sample size has been selected. Whenever the auditor takes a random sample, regardless of the basis for determining its size, there is a *statistical measurement inherent in the sample.* Since there is little or no cost involved in computing the upper exception rate, we believe that should be done whenever possible. It would, of course, be inappropriate to draw a statistical conclusion unless the sample were randomly selected.

### Adequate Documentation

It is important that the auditor retain adequate records of the procedures performed, the methods used to select the sample and perform the tests, the results found in the tests, and the conclusions drawn. This is necessary as a means of evaluating the combined results of all tests and as a basis for defending the audit if the need arises. Documentation is equally important for statistical or nonstatistical sampling. An example of the type of documentation commonly found in practice is included in the case illustration for Hillsburg Hardware at the end of the chapter.

### Need for Professional Judgment

A criticism occasionally leveled against statistical sampling is that it reduces the use of professional judgment. A comparison of the fourteen steps discussed in this chapter for nonstatistical and attributes sampling shows how unwarranted this criticism is. For proper application of attributes sampling, it is necessary to use professional judgment in most of the steps. For example, selection of the initial sample size depends primarily on the TER, ARACR, and EPER. Choosing the first two requires the exercise of high-level professional judgment; the latter requires a careful estimate. Similarly, the final evaluation of the adequacy of the entire application of attributes sampling, including the adequacy of the sample size, must also be based on high-level professional judgment.

## CASE ILLUSTRATION—HILLSBURG HARDWARE, PART II

**OBJECTIVE 12-8**
**Apply sampling concepts and methodology to the audit plan for the sales and collection cycle.**

To illustrate the concepts discussed in this chapter, the Hillsburg Hardware Co. case from Chapter 11 is extended to include determination of sample size, selection of items for testing, and the conclusions drawn on the basis of the results of the tests using attributes sampling (see page 389). The only parts of the tests of the sales and collection cycle included here are tests of credit approval, shipment of goods, billing of customers, and recording the amounts in the records. It should be kept in mind that the procedures for Hillsburg Hardware Co. were developed specifically for that client and would probably not be applicable for a different audit. The audit procedures for these tests are repeated in Table 12-11 along with comments to indicate the relationship of each procedure to attributes sampling.

**TABLE 12-11**
**Audit Procedures**

| Procedure | Comment |
|---|---|
| **Shipment of Goods** | |
| 9. Account for a sequence of shipping documents. | It is possible to do this by selecting a random sample and accounting for all shipping documents selected. This requires a separate set of random numbers, since the sampling unit is different from that used for the other tests. |
| 10. Trace selected shipping documents to the sales journal to be sure that each one has been included. | No exceptions are expected, and a 6 percent TER is considered acceptable at an ARACR of 10 percent. A sample size of 38 is selected. The shipping documents are traced to the sales journal. This is done for all 38 items. There are no exceptions for either test. The results are considered acceptable. There is no further information about this portion of the tests in this illustration. |
| **Billing of Customers and Recording the Sales in the Records** | |
| 11. Account for a sequence of sales invoices in the sales journal. | The audit procedures for billing and recording sales (procedures 11 to 14) are the only ones tested by using attributes sampling for this case illustration. The attributes sampling data sheet includes each of these procedures as attributes. For audit procedure 11, a random sample of sales invoices is a test of the sequence of sales invoices. |
| 12. Trace selected duplicate sales invoice numbers from the sales journal to<br>a. accounts receivable master file and test for amount, date, and invoice number.<br>b. duplicate sales invoice and check for the total amount recorded in the journal, date, customer name, and account classification. Check the pricing, extensions, and footings. Examine underlying documents for indication of internal verification by Pam Dilley.<br>c. bill of lading and test for customer name, product description, quantity, and date.<br>d. duplicate sales order and test for customer name, product description, quantity, date, and indication of internal verification by Pam Dilley.<br>e. customer order and test for customer name, product description, quantity, date, and credit approval by Rick Chulick. | |
| 13. Trace recorded sales from the sales journal to the file of supporting documents, which includes a duplicate sales invoice, bill of lading, sales order, and customer order. | |
| 14. Compare dates on the bill of lading, duplicate sales invoice, and sales journal. | |

*Note:* Random selection and statistical sampling are not applicable for the eight general audit procedures in Figure 11-9. Advanced statistical techniques, such as regression analysis, could be applicable for analysis of the results of analytical procedures. Random selection could be used for procedure 3.

In applying attributes sampling to the procedures for Hillsburg Hardware Co. (see Figure 11-9 on page 389), there are only two functions for which attributes sampling is being used: shipment of goods and billing of customers. Emphasis is placed on the billing of customers in the illustration because the duplicate sales invoice is the sampling unit for most of the audit procedures. In order to concentrate on the attributes sampling applications for the billing function, comments about the shipping function are restricted to those shown adjacent to the list of audit procedures in the table. The reader should recognize, however, that the attributes sampling methodology followed for the shipping function would be essentially the same as the methodology illustrated for the billing function in the remainder of the case.

### Objectives, Deciding If Audit Sampling Applies, Population, and Sampling Unit

Most auditors use some type of preprinted form to document each attributes sampling application. An example of a commonly used form is given in Figure 12-4. The top part of the form includes a definition of the objective, the population, and the sampling unit.

The note on the bottom of Table 12-11, page 427, indicates that audit sampling does not apply to audit procedures 1 through 8 in Figure 11-9. Audit sampling can be applied to audit procedures 9 through 14.

### Define the Attributes of Interest

The attributes used in this application are taken directly from the audit program. The procedures that can be used as attributes for a specific application of attributes sampling depend on the definition of the sampling unit. In this case, all the procedures in the billing function can be included. The nine attributes used for this case are listed in Figure 12-4.

The definition of the attribute is a critical part of attributes sampling. The decision as to which attributes to combine and which ones to keep separate is the most important aspect of the definition. If all possible types of attributes, such as customer name, date, price, and quantity, are separated for each procedure, the large number of attributes makes the problem unmanageable. However, if all the procedures are combined into one or two attributes, greatly dissimilar exceptions are evaluated together. Somewhere in between is a reasonable compromise.

### Establish TER, ARACR, EPER, and Determine Initial Sample Size

The TER for each attribute is decided on the basis of the auditor's judgment of what exception rate is material. The failure to record a sales invoice would be highly significant, especially considering this system; therefore, as indicated in Figure 12-4, the lowest TER (3 percent) is chosen for attribute 1. The incorrect billing of the customer represents potentially significant misstatements, but no misstatement is likely to be for the full amount of the invoice. As a result, a 4 percent TER is chosen for each of the attributes directly related to the billing of shipments and recording the amounts in the records. The last four attributes have higher TERs, since they are of less importance for the audit.

An ARACR of 10 percent is decided on because the potential for reducing assessed control risk is limited even if the internal controls tested are proven effective, due to several internal control weaknesses.

The estimated population exception rate is based on previous years' results, modified upward slightly due to the change in personnel. Initial sample size for each attribute is determined from Table 12-9 on the basis of the above considerations. This information is summarized for all attributes in Figure 12-4. For convenience in selection and evaluation, the auditor decided to select a sample of seventy-five for attribute 1, one hundred for attributes 2 through 5, sixty-five for attributes 6 and 9, and fifty for the other two.

### Select the Sample

The random selection for the case is straightforward except for the need for different sample sizes for different attributes. This problem can be overcome by selecting a random sample of fifty for use on all nine attributes followed by another sample of fifteen for all attributes except seven and eight, an additional ten for attribute 1, and twenty-five more for attributes 2 through 5. The documentation for the selection of the first fifty numbers is illustrated in Figure 12-5 on page 430.

**FIGURE 12-4**

**Attributes Sampling Data Sheet: Attributes**

Client *Hillsburg Hardware* Year end *12/31/96*

Audit Area *Tests of Controls and Substantive Tests of Transactions—Billing Function* Pop. size *5,764*

Define the objective(s) *Examine duplicate sales invoices and related documents to determine if the system has functioned as intended and as described in the audit program.*

Define the population precisely (including stratification, if any) *Sales invoices for the period 1/1/96 to 12/31/96. First invoice number = 3689. Last invoice number = 9452.*

Define the sampling unit, organization of population items, and random selection procedures *Sales invoice number, recorded in the sales journal sequentially; random number table.*

| Description of attributes | Planned Audit | | | | Actual Results | | | |
|---|---|---|---|---|---|---|---|---|
| | EPER | TER | ARACR | Initial sample size | Sample size | Number of exceptions | Sample exception rate | CUER |
| *1. Existence of the sales invoice number in the sales journal. (Procedure 11)* | *0* | *3* | *10* | *76* | | | | |
| *2. Amount and other data in the master file agree with sales journal entry. (Procedure 12a)* | *1* | *4* | *10* | *96* | | | | |
| *3. Amount and other data on the sales invoice agree with the sales journal entry. (Procedure 12b)* | *1* | *4* | *10* | *96* | | | | |
| *4. Evidence that pricing, extensions, and footings are checked (initials and correct amount). (Procedure 12b)* | *1* | *4* | *10* | *96* | | | | |
| *5. Quantity and other data on the bill of lading agree with the duplicate sales invoice and sales journal. (Procedures 12c and 14)* | *1* | *4* | *10* | *96* | | | | |
| *6. Quantity and other data on the sales order agree with the duplicate sales invoice. (Procedure 12d)* | *1* | *6* | *10* | *64* | | | | |
| *7. Quantity and other data on the customer order agree with the duplicate sales invoice. (Procedure 12e)* | *2* | *8* | *10* | *48* | | | | |
| *8. Credit is approved by Rick Chulick. (Procedure 12e)* | *2* | *8* | *10* | *48* | | | | |
| *9. The file of supporting documents includes a duplicate sales invoice, bill of lading, sales order, and customer order. (Procedure 13)* | *1* | *6* | *10* | *64* | | | | |

Intended use of sampling results:

1. Effect on Audit Plan:

2. Recommendations to Management:

**Perform the Audit Procedures and Generalize to the Population**

The audit procedures that are included in the audit program and summarized in the attributes sampling data sheet must be carefully performed for every item in the sample. As a means of documenting the tests and providing information for review, it is common to include a worksheet of the results. Some auditors prefer to include a worksheet containing a listing of all items in the sample; others prefer to limit the documentation to identifying the exceptions. This latter approach is followed in Figure 12-6 on page 431.

At the completion of the testing, the exceptions are tabulated to determine the number of exceptions in the sample for each attribute. This enables the auditor to compute the

**FIGURE 12-5**

**Random Sample for Testing Sales**

*Hillsburg Hardware*
*Random Sample for Testing Sales*

| | (1) | (2) | (3) | (4) | (5) | (6) |
|---|---|---|---|---|---|---|
| 1086 | 77339 | 64605 | *4* 82583 | *18* 85011 | 00955 | *49* 84348 |
| 1087 | 61714 | 57933 | *5* 37342 | 26000 | *32* 93611 | *50* 93346 |
| 1088 | 15232 | 48027 | 15832 | *19* 62924 | 11509 | 95853 ↑ *End* |
| 1089 | 41447 | 34275 | 10779 | *20* 83515 | *33* 63899 | 30932 |
| 1090 | 23244 | 43524 | 16382 | *21* 36940 | *34* 73581 | 76780 |
| 1091 | 53460 | 83542 | 25224 | *22* 70378 | *35* 49604 | 14609 |
| 1092 | 53442 | 16897 | *6* 61578 | 05032 | *36* 81825 | 76822 |
| 1093 | 55543 | 19096 | 04130 | 23104 | *37* 60534 | 44842 |
| 1094 | 18185 | 63329 | 02340 | *23* 63111 | *38* 41768 | 74409 |
| 1095 | 02372 | 45690 | *7* 38595 | 23121 | *39* 73818 | 74454 |
| 1096 | 51715 | 35492 | *8* 61371 | *24* 87132 | *40* 81585 | 55439 |
| 1097 | 24717 | 16785 | *9* 42786 | *25* 86585 | 21858 | 39489 |
| 1098 | 78002 | 32604 | *10* 87295 | *26* 93702 | 99438 | 68184 |
| 1099 | 35995 | 08275 | *11* 62405 | *27* 43313 | 03249 | 74135 |
| 1100 | 29152 | 86922 | 31508 | *28* 42703 | *41* 59638 | 31226 |
| 1101 | 84192 | *Start* ↓ 90150 | 02904 | 26835 | 17174 | 42301 |
| 1102 | 21791 | 24764 | *12* 53674 | 30093 | *42* 45134 | 24073 |
| 1103 | 63501 | 05040 | *13* 71881 | 17759 | *43* 91881 | 69614 |
| 1104 | 07149 | *1* 69285 | *14* 55481 | 24889 | *44* 67061 | 06631 |
| 1105 | 59443 | 98962 | *15* 74778 | 96920 | *45* 65620 | 36794 |
| 1106 | 39059 | *2* 58021 | 28485 | *29* 43052 | 99001 | 44400 |
| 1107 | 73176 | *3* 58913 | 22638 | *30* 69769 | 21102 | 72292 |
| 1108 | 11851 | 09065 | 96033 | 02752 | *46* 58232 | 56504 |
| 1109 | 37515 | 25668 | *16* 55785 | *31* 66463 | *47* 52758 | 67588 |
| 1110 | 45324 | 00016 | *17* 46818 | 04373 | *48* 75360 | 87519 |

*Population = 3689 to 9452*
*Correspondence — First 4 digits in table.*
*Route — Read down to end of column, start at top of the next column.*
*Sample size — 50, represented by sequential numbers 1 to 50.*

sample exception rate and determine the CUER from the tables. This information is summarized in Figures 12-7 and 12-8 (pages 432 and 433).

## Exception Analysis

The final part of the application consists of analyzing the exceptions to determine their cause and drawing conclusions about each attribute tested. For every attribute for which CUER exceeds TER, it is essential that some conclusion concerning follow-up action be reached and documented. The exception analysis and conclusions reached are illustrated in Figure 12-8 and summarized at the bottom of the data sheet in Figure 12-7.

## Update the Evidence Planning Worksheet

After completing tests of controls and substantive tests of transactions, the auditor should complete rows three through seven of the evidence planning worksheet. This worksheet is illustrated for Hillsburg Hardware in Figure 12-9 on page 434.

## FIGURE 12-6

### Inspection of Sample Items for Attributes

*Hillsburg Hardware*

INSPECTION OF SAMPLE ITEMS FOR ATTRIBUTES
DECEMBER 31, 1996

Prepared by *MSW*
Date *2/3/97*

| Identity of Item Selected | Attributes | | | | | | | | X = Exception | | |
|---|---|---|---|---|---|---|---|---|---|---|---|
| Invoice no. | 1 | 2 | 3 | 4 | 5 | 6 | 7 | 8 | 9 | 10 | 11 |
| 3694 | | | | | X | | | | | | |
| 3859 | | | | X | | | | X | | | |
| 3990 | | | | X | | | | | | | |
| 4071 | | X | | X | | | | | | | |
| 4270 | | | | | | | | X | | | |
| 4222 | | | | | X | | | | | | |
| 4331 | | | | | | | | X | | | |
| 4513 | | | | X | X | | | | | | |
| 4681 | | | | | | X | | X | | | |
| 4859 | | | | X | | | | | | | |
| 5367 | | | | | | | | X | | | |
| 5578 | | | | | | | | X | | | |
| 5802 | | | | | | | | X | | | |
| 5823 | | | | | | | | X | | | |
| 5963 | | | | | | | | X | | | |
| 6157 | | X | | X | | | | | | | |
| 6229 | | | | X | | | | | | | |
| 6311 | | | | | | | | X | | | |
| 7188 | | | | | X | | | | | | |
| 7536 | | | | X | | | | | | | |
| 8351 | | | | | | | | X | | | |
| 8517 | | | | X | | | | | | | |
| 8713 | | | | | | | | X | | | |
| 9445 | | | | X | | | | | | | |
| No. Exceptions | 0 | 2 | 0 | 10 | 4 | 1 | 0 | 12 | 0 | | |
| Sample Size | 75 | 100 | 100 | 100 | 100 | 65 | 50 | 50 | 65 | | |

**FIGURE 12-7**

**Attributes Sampling Data Sheet: Attributes**

Client *Hillsburg Hardware* Year end *12/31/96*

Audit Area *Tests of Controls and Substantive Tests of Transactions—Billing Function* Pop. size *5,764*

Define the objective(s) *Examine duplicate sales invoices and related documents to determine if the system has functioned as intended and as described in the audit program*

Define the population precisely (including stratification, if any) *Sales invoices for the period 1/1/96 to 12/31/96. First invoice number = 3689. Last invoice number = 9452.*

Define the sampling unit, organization of population items, and random selection procedures *Sales invoice number, recorded in the sales journal sequentially; random number table.*

| Description of attributes | Planned Audit | | | | Actual Results | | | |
|---|---|---|---|---|---|---|---|---|
| | EPER | TER | ARACR | Initial sample size | Sample size | Number of exceptions | Sample exception rate | CUER |
| *1. Existence of the sales invoice number in the sales journal. (Procedure 11)* | *0* | *3* | *10* | *76* | *75* | *0* | *0* | *3.0* |
| *2. Amount and other data in the master file agree with sales journal entry. (Procedure 12a)* | *1* | *4* | *10* | *96* | *100* | *2* | *2* | *5.2* |
| *3. Amount and other data on the sales invoice agree with the sales journal entry. (Procedure 12b)* | *1* | *4* | *10* | *96* | *100* | *0* | *0* | *2.3* |
| *4. Evidence that pricing extensions and footings are checked (initials and correct amount). (Procedure 12b)* | *1* | *4* | *10* | *96* | *100* | *10* | *10* | *15.0* |
| *5. Quantity and other data on the bill of lading agree with the duplicate sales invoice and sales journal. (Procedures 12c and 14)* | *1* | *4* | *10* | *96* | *100* | *4* | *4* | *7.8* |
| *6. Quantity and other data on the sales order agree with the duplicate sales invoice. (Procedure 12d)* | *1* | *6* | *10* | *64* | *65* | *1* | *1.5* | *5.9* |
| *7. Quantity and other data on the customer order agree with the duplicate sales invoice. (Procedure 12e)* | *2* | *8* | *10* | *48* | *50* | *0* | *0* | *4.5* |
| *8. Credit is approved by Rick Chulick. (Procedure 12e)* | *2* | *8* | *10* | *48* | *50* | *12* | *24* | *>20* |
| *9. The file of supporting documents includes a duplicate sales invoice, bill of lading, sales order and customer order. (Procedure 13)* | *1* | *6* | *10* | *64* | *65* | *0* | *0* | *3.5* |

Intended use of sampling results:

1. Effect on Audit Plan: *Controls tested through attributes 1, 3, 6, 7, and 9 can be relied upon as illustrated on working paper 7-6. Additional emphasis is needed in confirmation, allowance for uncollectible accounts, cutoff tests, and price tests due to results of tests for attributes 2, 4, 5 and 8.*

2. Recommendations to Management *Each of the exceptions should be discussed with management. Specific recommendations are needed to correct the internal verification of sales invoices and to improve the approach to credit approvals.*

**FIGURE 12-8**

**Analysis of Exceptions**

*Hillsburg Hardware*
ANALYSIS OF EXCEPTIONS
December 31, 1996

Prepared by *MSW*
Date *2/3/97*

| Attribute | Number of exceptions | Nature of exceptions | Effect on the audit and other comments |
|---|---|---|---|
| 2 | 2 | *Both errors were posted to the wrong account and were still outstanding after several months. The amounts were for \$125.00 and \$393.00.* | *Because the upper exception rate is greater than TER, additional substantive work is needed. Perform expanded confirmation procedures and review older uncollected balances thoroughly.* |
| 4 | 10 | *In 6 cases there were no initials for internal verification.<br>In 2 cases the wrong price was used but the errors were under \$10 in each case.<br>In 1 case there was a pricing error of \$1,000.<br>In 1 case freight was not charged.<br>(Three of the last 4 exceptions had initials for internal verification.)* | *As a result, have independent client personnel recheck a random sample of 500 duplicate sales invoices under our control. Also, expand the confirmation of accounts receivable.* |
| 5 | 4 | *In each case the date on the duplicate sales invoice was several days later than the shipping date.* | *Do extensive tests of the sales cutoff by comparing recorded sales to the shipping documents.* |
| 6 | 1 | *Just 106 items were shipped and billed though the sales order was for 112 items. The reason for the difference was an error in the perpetual inventory master file. The perpetuals indicated that 112 items were on hand, when there were actually 106. The system does not backorder for undershipments smaller than 25%.* | *No expansion of tests of controls or substantive tests. The system appears to be working effectively.* |
| 8 | 12 | *Credit was not approved. Four of these were for new customers. Discussed with Chulick, who stated his busy schedule did not permit approving all sales.* | *Expand the year-end procedures extensively in evaluating allowance for uncollectible accounts. This includes scheduling of cash receipts subsequent to year-end and for all outstanding accounts receivable.* |

**FIGURE 12-9**

**Evidence Planning Worksheet to Decide Tests of Details of Balances for Hillsburg Hardware Co.—Accounts Receivable**

| | Detail tie-in | Existence | Completeness | Accuracy | Classification | Cutoff | Realizable value | Rights | Presentation and disclosure |
|---|---|---|---|---|---|---|---|---|---|
| Acceptable audit risk | high | high | high | high | high | high | high | high | high |
| Inherent risk | low | low | low | low | low | low | medium | low | low |
| Control risk — Sales | low | medium | medium | high | low | high | high | not applicable | not applicable |
| Control risk — Cash receipts | medium | high | low | low | high | high | not applicable | not applicable | not applicable |
| Control risk — Additional controls | none | none | none | none | none | none | none | low | low |
| Substantive tests of transactions — Sales | good results | good results | good results | fair results | good results | unacceptable results | not applicable | not applicable | not applicable |
| Substantive tests of transactions — Cash receipts | good results | good results | good results | good results | good results | good results | not applicable | not applicable | not applicable |
| Analytical procedures | | | | | | | | | |
| Planned detection risk for tests of details of balances | | | | | | | | | |
| Planned audit evidence for tests of details of balances | | | | | | | | | |

Tolerable misstatement $22,000

## ESSENTIAL TERMS

**Acceptable risk of assessing control risk too low (ARACR)**—the risk that the auditor is willing to take of accepting a control as effective or a rate of monetary misstatements as tolerable, when the true population exception rate is greater than the tolerable exception rate

**Attribute**—the characteristic being tested for in the population

**Attributes sampling**—a statistical, probabilistic method of sample evaluation that results in an estimate of the proportion of items in a population containing a characteristic or attribute of interest

**Block sampling**—a nonprobabilistic method of sample selection in which items are selected in measured sequences

**Computed upper exception rate (CUER)**—the upper limit of probable population exception rate; the highest exception rate in the population at a given ARACR

**Confidence level**—statement of probability

**Directed sample selection**—a nonprobabilistic method of sample selection in which each item in the sample is selected based on some judgmental criteria established by the auditor

**Estimated population exception rate (EPER)**—exception rate the auditor expects to find in the population before testing begins

**Exception rate**—the percentage of items in a population that include exceptions in prescribed controls or monetary correctness

**Haphazard selection**—a nonprobabilistic method of sample selection in which items are chosen without regard to their size, source, or other distinguishing characteristics

**Initial sample size**—sample size determined by professional judgment (nonstatistical sampling) or by statistical tables (attributes sampling)

**Judgmental sampling**—use of professional judgment rather than probabilistic methods to select sample items for audit tests

**Nonprobabilistic sample selection**—a method of sample selection in which the auditor uses professional judgment to select items from the population

**Nonsampling risk**—the chance of exception when audit tests do not uncover existing exceptions in the sample; nonsampling risk (nonsampling error) is caused by failure to recognize exceptions and by inappropriate or ineffective audit procedures

**Nonstatistical sampling**—the auditor's use of professional judgment to select sample items, estimate the population values, and estimate sampling risk

**Occurrence rate**—the ratio of items in a population that contain a specific attribute to the total number of population items

**Probabilistic sample selection**—a method of sample selection in which it is possible to define the set of all possible samples, every possible sample has a known probability of being selected, and the sample is selected by a random process

**Random number table**—a listing of independent random digits conveniently arranged in tabular form to facilitate the selection of random numbers with multiple digits

**Random sample**—a sample in which every possible combination of elements in the population has an equal chance of constituting the sample

**Representative sample**—a sample whose characteristics are the same as those of the population

**Sample exception rate (SER)**—number of exceptions in the sample divided by the sample size

**Sampling distribution**—a frequency distribution of the results of all possible samples of a specified size that could be obtained from a population containing some specific parameters

**Sampling risk**—the chance of exception inherent in tests of less than the entire population; sampling risk may be reduced by using an increased sample size and using an appropriate method of selecting sample items from the population

**Statistical sampling**—the use of mathematical measurement techniques to calculate formal statistical results and quantify sampling risk

**Systematic selection**—a probabilistic method of sampling in which the auditor calculates an interval (the population size divided by the number of sample items desired), and selects the items for the sample based on the size of the interval and a randomly selected number between zero and the sample size

**Tolerable exception rate (TER)**—the exception rate that the auditor will permit in the population and still be willing to use the assessed control risk and/or the amount of monetary misstatements in the transactions established during planning

## REVIEW QUESTIONS

**12-1 (Objective 12-1)** State what is meant by a representative sample and explain its importance in sampling audit populations.

**12-2 (Objective 12-2)** Explain the major difference between statistical and nonstatistical sampling. What are the three main parts of statistical and nonstatistical methods?

**12-3 (Objective 12-3)** Explain the difference between "replacement sampling" and "nonreplacement sampling." Which method do auditors usually follow? Why?

**12-4 (Objective 12-3)** Explain what is meant by a random number table. Describe how an auditor would select thirty-five random numbers from a population of 1,750 items by using a random number table.

**12-5 (Objective 12-3)** Describe systematic sample selection and explain how an auditor would select thirty-five numbers from a population of 1,750 items using this approach. What are the advantages and disadvantages of systematic sample selection?

**12-6 (Objective 12-4)** What is the purpose of using nonstatistical sampling for tests of controls and substantive tests of transactions?

**12-7 (Objective 12-2)** Explain what is meant by block sample selection and describe how an auditor could obtain five blocks of twenty sales invoices from a sales journal.

**12-8 (Objective 12-5)** Define each of the following terms:

a. Acceptable risk of assessing control risk too low (ARACR)
b. Computed upper exception rate (CUER)
c. Estimated population exception rate (EPER)
d. Sample exception rate (SER)
e. Tolerable exception rate (TER)

**12-9 (Objective 12-5)** Describe what is meant by a sampling unit. Explain why the sampling unit for verifying the existence of recorded sales differs from the sampling unit for testing for the possibility of omitted sales.

**12-10 (Objective 12-5)** Distinguish between the TER and the CUER. How is each determined?

**12-11 (Objective 12-1)** Distinguish between a sampling error and a nonsampling error. How can each be reduced?

**12-12 (Objective 12-4)** What is meant by an attribute in sampling for tests of controls and substantive tests of transactions? What is the source of the attributes that the auditor selects?

**12-13 (Objective 12-4)** Explain the difference between an attribute and an exception condition. State the exception condition for the audit procedure: the duplicate sales invoice has been initialed indicating the performance of internal verification.

**12-14 (Objective 12-5)** Identify the factors an auditor uses to decide the appropriate TER. Compare the sample size for a TER of 6 percent with that of 3 percent, all other factors being equal.

**12-15 (Objective 12-5)** Identify the factors an auditor uses to decide the appropriate ARACR. Compare the sample size for an ARACR of 10 percent with that of 5 percent, all other factors being equal.

**12-16 (Objective 12-5)** State the relationship between the following:

a. ARACR and sample size
b. Population size and sample size
c. TER and sample size
d. EPER and sample size

**12-17 (Objective 12-7)** Assume that the auditor has selected 100 sales invoices from a population of 100,000 to test for an indication of internal verification of pricing and extensions. Determine the CUER at a 5 percent ARACR if three exceptions existed in the sample using attributes sampling. Explain the meaning of the statistical results in auditing terms.

**12-18 (Objective 12-5)** Explain what is meant by analysis of exceptions and discuss its importance.

**12-19 (Objective 12-5)** When the CUER exceeds the TER, what courses of action are available to the auditor? Under what circumstances should each of these be followed?

**12-20 (Objectives 12-2, 12-3)** Distinguish between random selection and statistical measurement. State the circumstances under which one can be used without the other.

**12-21 (Objective 12-7)** List the major decisions that the auditor must make in using attributes sampling. State the most important considerations involved in making each decision.

## MULTIPLE CHOICE QUESTIONS FROM CPA EXAMINATIONS

**12-22 (Objective 12-7)** The following items apply to random sampling from large populations for attributes sampling. Select the most appropriate response for each question.

a. If all other factors specified in a sampling plan remain constant, changing the ARACR from 10 percent to 5 percent would cause the required sample size to
   (1) increase.
   (2) remain the same.
   (3) decrease.
   (4) become indeterminate.

b. If all other factors specified in a sampling plan remain constant, changing the TER from 8 percent to 12 percent would cause the required sample size to
(1) increase. (3) decrease.
(2) remain the same. (4) become indeterminate.

**12-23 (Objective 12-7)** The following items apply to random sampling from large populations using attributes sampling. Select the best response.

a. In a random sample of 1,000 records, an auditor determines that the SER is 2 percent. The auditor can state that the exception rate in the population is
(1) not more than 3 percent. (3) probably about 2 percent.
(2) not less than 2 percent. (4) not less than 1 percent.

b. From a random sample of items listed from a client's inventory count, an auditor estimates with a 10 percent ARACR that the CUER is between 4 percent and 6 percent. The auditor's major concern is that there is one chance in twenty that the true exception rate in the population is
(1) more than 6 percent (3) more than 4 percent.
(2) less than 6 percent. (4) less than 4 percent.

c. If, from a random sample, an auditor can state with a 5 percent ARACR that the exception rate in the population does not exceed 20 percent, he or she can state that the exception rate does not exceed 25 percent with
(1) 5 percent risk.
(2) risk greater than 5 percent.
(3) risk less than 5 percent.
(4) This cannot be determined from the information provided.

d. If an auditor wishes to select a random sample that must have a 10 percent ARACR and a TER of 10 percent, the size of the sample he or she must select will decrease as the estimate of the
(1) population exception rate increases. (3) population size increases.
(2) population exception rate decreases. (4) ARACR increases.

## DISCUSSION QUESTIONS AND PROBLEMS

**12-24 (Objective 12-3)**

a. In each of the following independent problems, design an unbiased random sampling plan, using the random number table in Table 12-2. The plan should include defining the sampling unit, establishing a numbering system for the population, and establishing a correspondence between the random number table and the population. After the plan has been designed, select from the random number table the first five sample items for each problem. Use a starting point of item 1009, column 1, for each problem. Read down the table, using the leftmost digits in the column. When you reach the last item in a column, start at the top of the next column.
(1) Prenumbered sales invoices in a sales journal where the lowest invoice number is 1 and the highest is 6211.
(2) Prenumbered bills of lading where the lowest document number is 21926 and the highest is 28511.
(3) Accounts receivable on ten pages with sixty lines per page except the last page, which has only thirty-six full lines. Each line has a customer name and an amount receivable.
(4) Prenumbered invoices in a sales journal where each month starts over with number 1. (Invoices for each month are designated by the month and document number.) There is a maximum of twenty pages per month with a total of 185 pages for the year. All pages have seventy-five invoices except for the last page for each month.

b. Write a computer program using electronic spreadsheet software, or use an available random number generator, to obtain the above samples with the computer (instructor option).

**12-25 (Objective 12-3)** You desire a random sample of eighty sales invoices for the examination of supporting documents. The invoices range from numbers 1 to 9500 for the period January 1 through December 31. There are 128 pages of sales invoices numbered 1 through 128. Each page has seventy-five lines, but the last page in each month sometimes has a few less.

## Required

a. Design four different methods of selecting random numbers from the above population, using a random number table or systematic sample selection.

b. Which method do you consider the most desirable? Why?

**12-26 (Objectives 12-3, 12-5, 12-7)** Lenter Supply Company is a medium-sized distributor of wholesale hardware supplies in the central Ohio area. It has been a client of yours for several years and has instituted excellent internal controls for sales at your recommendation.

In providing control over shipments, the client has prenumbered "warehouse removal slips" that are used for every sale. It is company policy never to remove goods from the warehouse without an authorized warehouse removal slip. After shipment, two copies of the warehouse removal slip are sent to billing for the computerized preparation of a sales invoice. One copy is stapled to the duplicate copy of a prenumbered sales invoice, and the other copy is filed numerically. In some cases more than one warehouse removal slip is used for billing one sales invoice. The smallest warehouse removal slip number for the year is 14682 and the largest is 37521. The smallest sales invoice number is 47821 and the largest is 68507.

In the audit of sales, one of the major concerns is the effectiveness of the controls in making sure that all shipments are billed. You have decided to use audit sampling in testing internal controls.

## Required

a. State an effective audit procedure for testing whether shipments have been billed. What is the sampling unit for the audit procedure?

b. Assuming that you expect no exceptions in the sample but are willing to accept a TER of 3 percent, at a 10 percent ARACR, what is the appropriate sample size for the audit test? You may complete this requirement using nonstatistical sampling or attributes sampling.

c. Design a random selection plan for selecting the sample from the population, using the random number table. Select the first ten sample items from Table 12-2. Use a starting point of item 1013, column 3.

d. Your supervisor suggests the possibility of performing other sales tests with the same sample as a means of efficiently using your audit time. List two other audit procedures that could conveniently be performed using the same sample and state the purpose of each of the procedures.

e. Is it desirable to test the existence of sales with the random sample you have designed in part c? Why?

**12-27 (Objective 12-7)** The following is a partial audit program for the audit of cash receipts.

1. Review the cash receipts journal for large and unusual transactions.
2. Trace entries from the prelisting of cash receipts to the cash receipts journal to determine if each is recorded.
3. Compare customer name, date, and amount on the prelisting with the cash receipts journal.
4. Examine the related remittance advice for entries selected from the prelisting to determine if cash discounts were approved.
5. Trace entries from the prelisting to the deposit slip to determine if each has been deposited.

**Required**

a. Identify which audit procedures could be tested by using attributes sampling.

b. What is the appropriate sampling unit for the tests in part a?

c. List the attributes for testing in part a.

d. Assume an ARACR of 5 percent and a TER of 8 percent for tests of controls and 6 percent for substantive tests of transactions. The EPER for tests of controls is 2 percent, and for substantive tests of transactions it is 1 percent. What is the initial sample size for each attribute?

**12-28 (Objectives 12-5, 12-7)** The following questions concern the determination of the proper sample size in audit sampling using the following table:

| | 1 | 2 | 3 | 4 | 5 | 6 | 7 |
|---|---|---|---|---|---|---|---|
| ARACR (in percentage) | 10 | 5 | 5 | 5 | 10 | 10 | 5 |
| TER | 6 | 6 | 5 | 6 | 20 | 20 | 2 |
| EPER (in percentage) | 2 | 2 | 2 | 2 | 8 | 2 | 0 |
| Population size | 1,000 | 100,000 | 6,000 | 1,000 | 500 | 500 | 1,000,000 |

**Required**

a. For each of the columns number 1 through 7, decide the initial sample size using nonstatistical methods.

b. For each of the columns numbered 1 through 7, determine the initial sample size needed to satisfy the auditor's requirements using attributes sampling from the appropriate part of Table 12-9.

c. Using your understanding of the relationship between the following factors and sample size, state the effect on the initial sample size (increase or decrease) of changing each of the following factors while the other three are held constant:
(1) An increase in ARACR
(2) An increase in the TER
(3) An increase in the EPER
(4) An increase in the population size

d. Explain why there is such a large difference in the sample sizes for columns 3 and 6.

e. Compare your answers in part c with the results you determined in part a (nonstatistical sampling) or part b (attributes sampling). Which of the four factors appears to have the greatest effect on the initial sample size? Which one appears to have the least effect?

f. Why is the sample size referred to as the initial sample size?

**12-29 (Objectives 12-5, 12-7)** The questions below relate to determining the CUER in audit sampling for tests of controls, using the following table:

| | 1 | 2 | 3 | 4 | 5 | 6 | 7 | 8 |
|---|---|---|---|---|---|---|---|---|
| ARACR (in percentage) | 10 | 5 | 5 | 5 | 5 | 5 | 5 | 5 |
| Population size | 5,000 | 5,000 | 5,000 | 50,000 | 500 | 900 | 5,000 | 500 |
| Sample size | 200 | 200 | 50 | 200 | 100 | 100 | 100 | 25 |
| Number of exceptions | 4 | 4 | 1 | 4 | 2 | 10 | 0 | 0 |

**Required**

a. For each of the columns 1 through 8, estimate CUER using nonstatistical sampling.

b. For each of the columns 1 through 8, determine CUER using attributes sampling from the appropriate table.

c. Using your understanding of the relationship between the four factors above and the CUER, state the effect on the CUER (increase or decrease) of changing each of the following factors while the other three are held constant:
   (1) A decrease in the ARACR
   (2) A decrease in the population size
   (3) A decrease in the sample size
   (4) A decrease in the number of exceptions in the sample

d. Compare your answers in part c with the results you determined in part a (nonstatistical sampling) or part b (attributes sampling). Which of the factors appears to have the greatest effect on the CUER? Which one appears to have the least effect?

e. Why is it necessary to compare the CUER with the TER?

**12-30 (Objective 12-7)** The following are auditor judgments and attributes sampling results for six populations. Assume large population sizes.

| | 1 | 2 | 3 | 4 | 5 | 6 |
|---|---|---|---|---|---|---|
| EPER (in percentage) | 2 | 0 | 3 | 1 | 1 | 8 |
| TER (in percentage) | 6 | 3 | 8 | 5 | 20 | 15 |
| ARACR (in percentage) | 5 | 5 | 10 | 5 | 10 | 10 |
| Actual sample size | 100 | 100 | 60 | 100 | 20 | 60 |
| Actual number of exceptions in the sample | 2 | 0 | 1 | 4 | 1 | 8 |

## Required

a. For each population, did the auditor select a smaller sample size than is indicated by using attributes sampling tables for determining sample size? Evaluate selecting either a larger or smaller size than those determined in the tables.

b. Calculate the SER and CUER for each population.

c. For which of the six populations should the sample results be considered unacceptable? What options are available to the auditor?

d. Why is analysis of the exceptions necessary even when the populations are considered acceptable?

e. For the following terms, identify which is an audit decision, a nonstatistical estimate made by the auditor, a sample result, and a statistical conclusion about the population:
   (1) EPER
   (2) TER
   (3) ARACR
   (4) Actual sample size
   (5) Actual number of exceptions in the sample
   (6) SER
   (7) CUER

**12-31 (Objective 12-5)** For the audit of the financial statements of Mercury Fifo Company, Stella Mason, CPA, has decided to apply nonstatistical audit sampling in the tests of controls and substantive tests of transactions for sales transactions. Based on her knowledge of Mercury's operations in the area of sales, she decides that the EPER is likely to be 3 percent and that she is willing to accept a 5 percent risk that the true population exception rate is not greater than 6 percent. Given this information, Mason selects a random sample of 150 sales invoices from the 5,000 written during the year and examines them for exceptions. She notes the exceptions on page 441 in her working papers. There is no other documentation.

| Invoice No. | Comment |
|---|---|
| 5028 | Sales invoice was originally footed incorrectly but was corrected by client before the bill was sent out. |
| 6791 | Voided sales invoice examined by auditor. |
| 6810 | Shipping document for a sale of merchandise could not be located. |
| 7364 | Sales invoice for $2,875 has not been collected and is six months past due. |
| 7625 | Client unable to locate the duplicate sales invoice. |
| 8431 | Invoice was dated three days later than the date entered in the sales journal. |
| 8528 | Customer order is not attached to the duplicate sales invoice. |
| 8566 | Billing is for $100 less than it should be due to an unintentional pricing error. No indication of internal verification is included on the invoice. |
| 8780 | Client unable to locate the duplicate sales invoice. |
| 9169 | Credit not authorized, but the sale was for only $7.65. |
| 9974 | Lack of indication of internal verification of price extensions and postings of sales invoice. |

## Required

a. Which of the preceding should be defined as an exception?

b. Explain why it is inappropriate to set a single acceptable TER and EPER for the combined exceptions.

c. For each attribute in the population that is tested, calculate SER assuming a 5 percent ARACR for each attribute. (You must decide which attributes should be combined, which should be kept separate, and which exceptions are actual exceptions before you can calculate SER.)

d. Calculate TER – SER for each attribute and evaluate whether sampling error is sufficiently large given the 5% ARACR. Assume TER is 6% for each attribute.

e. State the appropriate analysis of exceptions for each of the exceptions in the sample.

**12-32 (Objectives 12-5, 12-7)** In performing tests of controls and substantive tests of transactions of sales for the Oakland Hardware Company, Ben Frentz, CPA, is concerned with the internal verification of pricing, extensions, and footings of sales invoices and the accuracy of the calculations. In testing sales using audit sampling, a separate attribute is used for the test of control (the existence of internal verification) and the substantive test of transactions (the accuracy of calculation). Since internal controls are considered good, Frentz uses a 10 percent ARACR, a zero EPER, and a 5 percent TER for both attributes; therefore, the initial sample size is forty-five items, which Ben rounded up to fifty.

In conducting the tests, the auditor finds three sample items for which there was no indication of internal verification on the sales invoice, but no sales invoices tested in the sample had a financial misstatement. You may complete the following requirements using either a nonstatistical sampling or an attributes sampling approach.

## Required

a. Estimate or determine the CUER for both the attributes, assuming a population of 5,000 sales invoices.

b. Decide whether the control is acceptable and whether the substance of the transaction is acceptable.

c. Discuss the most desirable course of action that the auditor should follow in deciding the effect of the CUER exceeding the TER.

d. Which type of exception analysis is appropriate in this case?

## CASE

12-33 (Objectives 12-4, 12-5, 12-7, 12-8) For the audit of Carbald Supply Company, Carole Wever, CPA, is conducting a test of sales for nine months of the year ended December 31, 1996. Included among her audit procedures are the following:

1. Foot and crossfoot the sales journal and trace the balance to the general ledger.
2. Review all sales transactions for reasonableness.
3. Select a sample of recorded sales from the sales journal and trace the customer name and amounts to duplicate sales invoices and the related shipping document.
4. Select a sample of shipping document numbers and perform the following tests:
   (a) Trace the shipping document to the related duplicate sales invoice.
   (b) Examine the duplicate sales invoice to determine whether copies of the shipping document, shipping order, and customer order are attached.
   (c) Examine the shipping order for an authorized credit approval.
   (d) Examine the duplicate sales invoice for an indication of internal verification of quantity, price, extensions, footings, and tracing the balance to the accounts receivable master file.
   (e) Compare the price on the duplicate sales invoice with the approved price list and the quantity with the shipping document.
   (f) Trace the balance in the duplicate sales invoice to the sales journal and accounts receivable master file for customer name, amount, and date.

### Required

a. For which of these procedures could audit sampling for exceptions be conveniently used?

b. Considering the audit procedures Wever developed, what is the most appropriate sampling unit for conducting most of the audit sampling tests?

c. Set up a sampling data sheet using attributes or nonstatistical sampling. For all tests of controls, assume a TER rate of 5 percent and an EPER of 1 percent. For all substantive tests of transactions, use a 4 percent TER and a 0 percent EPER. Use a 10 percent ARACR for all tests.

## INTEGRATED CASE APPLICATION

12-34 (Objectives 12-3, 12-5, 12-7, 12-8) **ABC AUDIT—PART III** In Part II of the ABC Integrated Application Case audit application, a tests of controls and substantive tests of transactions audit program was designed for acquisitions and cash disbursements. In Part III, sample sizes will be determined by using nonstatistical or attributes sampling, and the results of the tests will be evaluated.

a. Use the performance format audit program you prepared for acquisitions and cash disbursements from Problem 11-34 to prepare a sampling data sheet. Use Figure 12-4 on page 429 as a frame of reference for preparing the data sheet. Complete all parts of the data sheet except those parts that are blank in Figure 12-4. Use the following additional information to complete this requirement:
   (1) Prepare only one sampling data sheet.
   (2) Decide the appropriate sampling unit and select all audit procedures that are appropriate for that sampling unit from the performance format audit program you prepared in Problem 11-34.

(3) Use judgment in deciding EPER, TER, and ARACR for each attribute. Assume that assessed control risk is low for each procedure.

b. Design a random sample plan using a table of random numbers or an electronic spreadsheet (instructor option) for the attribute with the largest sample size in requirement a. Select the first ten random numbers, using Table 12-2, page 409, or the spreadsheet. Document the design and ten numbers selected, using appropriate documentation.

c. Assume that you performed all audit procedures included in Problem 11-34 using the sample sizes in requirement a. The only exceptions found when you performed the tests were one missing indication of internal verification on a vendor's invoice, one acquisition of inventory transaction recorded for $200 more than the amount stated in the vendor s invoice (the vendor was also overpaid by $200), and one vendor invoice recorded as an acquisition 18 days after the receipt of the goods. Complete the sampling data sheet prepared in part a. Use Figure 12-7 on page 432 as a frame of reference for completing the data sheet.

d. (Instructor Option) Develop the sampling data sheet, using an electronic spreadsheet.

# 13

# COMPLETING THE TESTS IN THE SALES AND COLLECTION CYCLE: ACCOUNTS RECEIVABLE

## LEARNING OBJECTIVES

Thorough study of this chapter will enable you to

**13-1** Describe the methodology for designing tests of details of balances using the audit risk model.

**13-2** Know the nine accounts receivable balance-related audit objectives.

**13-3** Design and perform analytical procedures for accounts in the sales and collection cycle.

**13-4** Design and perform tests of details of balances for accounts receivable for each balance-related audit objective.

**13-5** Obtain and evaluate accounts receivable confirmations.

**13-6** Design audit procedures for the audit of accounts receivable, using an evidence planning worksheet as a guide.

## WHEN MORE ISN'T BETTER

On Susan Jackson's first audit assignment, she is asked to handle the confirmation of accounts receivable. She is excited because it was one of the areas in her auditing class that she felt confident she understood. The audit client is a retailer with a large number of customer accounts. In previous years, Susan's firm confirmed these accounts using negative confirmations. Last year, 200 negative confirmations were sent. Confirmations were sent one month prior to year-end. Those that were returned showed only timing differences; none represented a misstatement in the client's books.

The tentative audit plan for the current year is to do about the same as the prior year. Before the current year's planned confirmation date, Susan performs a review of internal controls over sales and cash receipts transactions. She discovers that a new system for sales transactions has been implemented, but the client is having considerable problems getting it to work properly. There are a significant number of misstatements in recording sales during the past few months. Susan's tests of controls and substantive tests of sales transactions also identify similar misstatements.

When Susan takes her findings to her supervisor and asks him what to do, he responds, "No problem, Susan. Just send 300 confirmation requests instead of the usual 200. And be sure you get a good random sample so we can get a good projection of the results." Susan is seriously bothered by this instruction. She recalls that negative confirmation requests aren't considered to be good evidence when there are weak controls. Because customers are asked to respond only when there are differences, the auditor cannot be confident of the correct value for each misstatement in the sample. If this is so, then the results of using negative confirmations will be misleading even if a request is sent to *every* account. Susan concludes that expanding the sample size is the wrong solution. When Susan talks with her supervisor about her point of view, this time he responds, "You are absolutely right. I spoke too quickly. We need to sit down and think about a better strategy to find out if accounts receivable is materially misstated, probably using positive confirmations."

Chapter 13 is concerned with using analytical procedures and tests of details of balances for the accounts in the sales and collection cycle to reduce planned detection risk to a sufficiently low level. The accounts included in the sales and collection cycle for a typical company are shown in Figure 11-1 on page 364. Figure 11-4 on page 381 illustrates the relationships among the major accounts, the types of audit tests, and the audit risk model.

Analytical procedures are used to reduce planned detection risk for all accounts in the cycle. Tests of details of balances focus on balance sheet accounts, which include accounts receivable, allowance for uncollectible accounts, and cash in bank for the sales and collection cycle. Because of its interaction with all other cycles, cash in bank is treated separately in Chapter 21. This chapter, therefore, emphasizes the audit of accounts receivable and allowance for uncollectible accounts, using analytical procedures and tests of details of balances. Figure 13-1 shows the relationship between these two types of tests and planned detection risk, using the audit risk model.

To help the reader maintain perspective, refer to Figure 10-10 on page 348. Tests of controls and substantive tests of transactions for the sales and collection cycle, which were studied in Chapters 11 and 12, are done in phase II of the audit process. Tests of details of balances for the sales and collection cycle, which are studied here, are done in phase III.

**FIGURE 13-1**

**Relationship Between Analytical Procedures and Tests of Details of Balances to Planned Detection Risk**

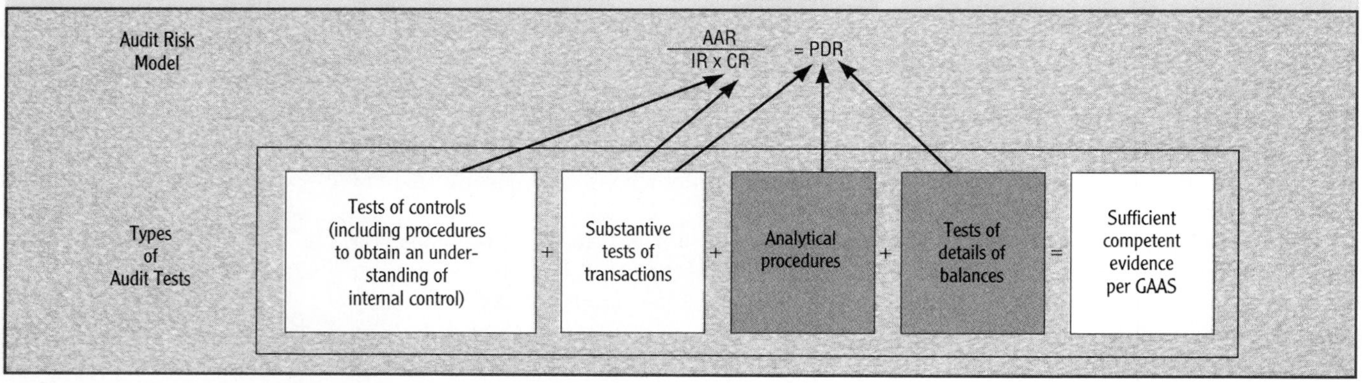


## METHODOLOGY FOR DESIGNING TESTS OF DETAILS OF BALANCES

**OBJECTIVE 13-1**
**Describe the methodology for designing tests of details of balances using the audit risk model.**

Figure 13-2 shows the methodology that auditors follow in deciding the appropriate tests of details of balances for accounts receivable. The methodology was introduced in Chapter 10 and is now applied to the audit of accounts receivable. This methodology integrates both the audit risk model and the types of audit tests that are shown in Figure 13-1.

Deciding the appropriate tests of details of balances evidence is complicated, because it must be decided on an objective-by-objective basis and there are several interactions that affect the evidence decision. For example, the auditor must consider inherent risk, which may differ by objective and results of substantive tests of sales and cash receipts, which also may vary by objective.

To help auditors manage the decision-making process for the appropriate tests of details of balances, auditors often use an evidence planning worksheet. This worksheet was first introduced in Figure 8-7 (page 268) and further amplified in Figure 12-9 (page 434). The completed evidence planning worksheet is included as Figure 13-7 on page 464. This worksheet is directly related to the methodology in Figure 13-2. Both figures are discussed as we proceed.

**FIGURE 13-2**

**Methodology for Designing Tests of Details of Balances for Accounts Receivable**

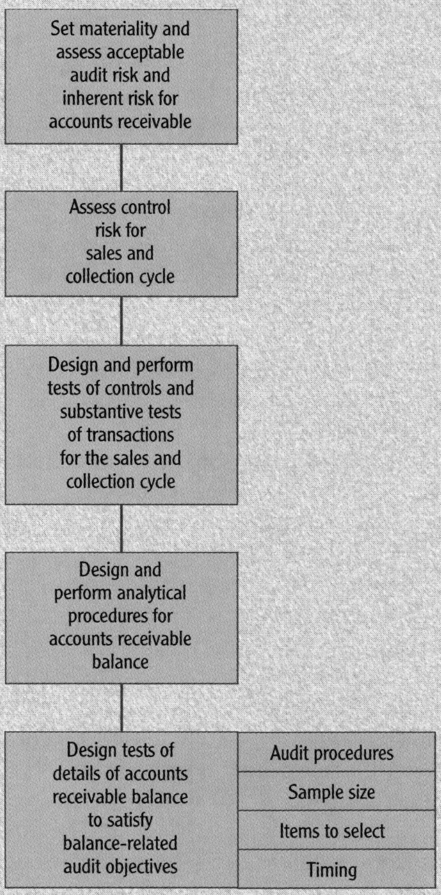


**Materiality Considerations**

Accounts receivable is typically one of the most material accounts in the financial statements for companies that sell on credit. Even if the accounts receivable balance is not large, the transactions in the sales and collection cycle that affect the balance in accounts receivable are almost certain to be highly significant.

**Inherent Risk Considerations**

For most audits, inherent risk for accounts receivable is moderate or low except for two objectives: accounts receivable is stated at realizable value and sales and sales returns and allowances cutoff is correct. It is difficult, because of the judgments involved, for clients to evaluate realizable value and correctly adjust the allowance for uncollectible accounts. It is relatively easy for clients to intentionally misstate the allowance account because of the difficulty of the judgments. Similarly, it is common for clients to intentionally or unintentionally misstate cutoff.

**Control Risk Considerations**

Internal controls over sales and cash receipts and the related accounts receivable are at least reasonably effective for most companies because management is concerned with keeping accurate records as a means to good relations with customers. Auditors are often especially concerned with three aspects of internal controls: controls that prevent or detect defalcations, controls over cutoff, and controls related to the allowance for uncollectible accounts, such as aging of accounts receivable.

## ACCOUNTS RECEIVABLE BALANCE-RELATED AUDIT OBJECTIVES

**OBJECTIVE 13-2**
**Know the nine accounts receivable balance-related audit objectives.**

The nine general balance-related audit objectives are the same for every account balance and are applied to accounts receivable as accounts receivable balance-related audit objectives. The general objectives were first introduced in Chapter 5. These nine objectives applied to accounts receivable are:[1]

- Accounts receivable in the aged trial balance agree with related master file amounts, and the total is correctly added and agrees with the general ledger (Detail tie-in).
- Recorded accounts receivable exist (Existence).
- Existing accounts receivable are included (Completeness).
- Accounts receivable are accurate (Accuracy).
- Accounts receivable are properly classified (Classification).
- Cutoff for accounts receivable is correct (Cutoff).
- Accounts receivable is stated at realizable value (Realizable value).
- The client has rights to accounts receivable (Rights).
- Accounts receivable presentation and disclosures are proper (Presentation and disclosure).

[1]Detail tie-in is included as the first objective here, compared with being objective six in Chapter 5, because tests for detail tie-in are normally done first.

The columns in the evidence planning worksheet in Figure 13-7 (page 464) include the balance-related audit objectives. The auditor uses the factors in the rows to aid in assessing planned detection risk for accounts receivable, by objective. All of these factors are decided during audit planning. They were studied in Chapters 8 through 12.

## Set Materiality and Assess Acceptable Audit Risk and Inherent Risk

Setting materiality starts with the auditor deciding the preliminary judgment about materiality for the entire financial statements. It also includes allocating the preliminary judgment amount to each significant balance sheet account, including accounts receivable. This allocation is called *setting tolerable misstatement.* Figure 13-7 shows that tolerable misstatement of $22,000 for accounts receivable in the Hillsburg Hardware audit is not allocated to each objective by including the amount on the bottom of the evidence planning worksheet.

Acceptable audit risk is assessed for the financial statements as a whole and is not usually allocated to various accounts or objectives. Figure 13-7 shows an acceptable audit risk of high for every objective, which will permit a higher planned detection risk for accounts receivable than if acceptable audit risk were low.

Inherent risk is assessed for each objective for an account such as accounts receivable. It was assessed at low for all objectives except realizable value for Hillsburg Hardware.

## Assess Control Risk for the Sales and Collection Cycle

The methodology for assessing control risk was studied in general in Chapter 9 and applied to sales and cash receipts transactions in Chapters 11 and 12. The framework used to identify control activities and internal control weaknesses was a control risk matrix. An example is included on page 384.

The internal controls studied in Chapter 11 relate specifically to transaction-related audit objectives for classes of transactions. The two primary classes of transactions in the sales and collection cycle are sales and cash receipts.

The auditor must relate control risk for transaction-related audit objectives to balance-related audit objectives in deciding planned detection risk and planned evidence for tests of details of balances. For the most part, the relationship is straightforward. Figure 13-3 shows the relationship for the two primary classes of transactions in the sales and collection cycle. For example, assume that the auditor concluded that control risk for both sales and cash receipts transactions is low for the accuracy transaction-related audit objective. The auditor can, therefore, conclude that controls for the accuracy balance-related audit objective for accounts receivable are effective because the only transactions that affect accounts receivable are sales and cash receipts. Of course, if sales returns and allowances and charge-off of uncollectible accounts receivable are significant, assessed control risk must also be considered for these two classes of transactions.

Two aspects of the relationships in Figure 13-3 deserve special mention:

- For sales, the existence transaction-related audit objective affects the existence balance-related audit objective, but for cash receipts the existence transaction–related audit objective affects the completeness balance-related audit objective. A similar relationship exists for the completeness transaction-related audit objective. The reason for this somewhat surprising conclusion is that an increase of sales increases accounts receivable, but an increase of cash receipts decreases accounts receivable. For example, recording a sale that did not occur violates the existence transaction-related audit objective and existence balance-related audit objective (both overstatements). Recording a cash receipt that did not occur violates the existence transaction-related audit objective, but it violates the completeness balance-related audit objective for accounts receivable, because a receivable that is still outstanding is no longer included in the records.
- Three accounts receivable balance-related audit objectives are not affected by assessed control risk for classes of transactions. These are realizable value, rights, and presentation and disclosure. When the auditor wants to reduce assessed control risk below the maximum for these three objectives, separate controls are identified and tested. This was discussed in Chapter 9.

**FIGURE 13-3**

**Relationship Between Transaction-Related and Balance-Related Audit Objectives for the Sales and Collection Cycle**

| | | ACCOUNTS RECEIVABLE BALANCE-RELATED AUDIT OBJECTIVES | | | | | | | | |
|---|---|---|---|---|---|---|---|---|---|---|
| CLASS OF TRANSACTIONS | TRANSACTION-RELATED AUDIT OBJECTIVES | Detail tie-in | Existence | Completeness | Accuracy | Classification | Cutoff | Realizable value | Rights | Presentation and disclosure |
| Sales | Existence | | X | | | | | | | |
| | Completeness | | | X | | | | | | |
| | Accuracy | | | | X | | | | | |
| | Classification | | | | | X | | | | |
| | Timing | | | | | | X | | | |
| | Posting and summarization | X | | | | | | | | |
| Cash receipts | Existence | | | X | | | | | | |
| | Completeness | | X | | | | | | | |
| | Accuracy | | | | X | | | | | |
| | Classification | | | | | X | | | | |
| | Timing | | | | | | X | | | |
| | Posting and summarization | X | | | | | | | | |

Figure 13-7 on page 464 includes three rows for assessed control risk: one for sales, one for cash receipts, and one for additional controls related to the accounts receivable balance. The source of each control risk for sales and cash receipts is the control risk matrix, assuming that the tests of controls results supported the original assessment. The auditor makes a separate assessment of control risk for objectives related only to the accounts receivable balance.

## Design and Perform Tests of Controls and Substantive Tests of Transactions

Chapters 11 and 12 dealt with deciding audit procedures and sample size for tests of controls and substantive tests of transactions and evaluating the results of those tests. The results of the tests of controls determine whether assessed control risk for sales and cash receipts needs to be revised. The results of the substantive tests of transactions are used to determine the extent to which planned detection risk is satisfied for each accounts receivable balance-related audit objective. The evidence planning worksheet in Figure 13-7 shows three rows for control risk and two for substantive tests of transactions, one for sales, and the other for cash receipts.

## Design and Perform Analytical Procedures

As discussed in Chapter 6, analytical procedures are often done during three phases of the audit: during planning, when performing detailed tests in phase III, and as a part of completing the audit. Those done during planning and when performing detailed tests are discussed in this chapter.

**OBJECTIVE 13-3**
**Design and perform analytical procedures for accounts in the sales and collection cycle.**

Most analytical procedures are done after the balance sheet date, but before tests of details of balances. It makes little sense to perform extensive analytical procedures before the client has recorded all transactions for the year and finalized the financial statements.

Table 13-1 presents examples of the major types of ratios and comparisons for the sales and collection cycle and potential misstatements that may be indicated by the analytical procedures. It is important to observe in the "possible misstatement" column that both balance sheet and income statement accounts are affected. For example, when the auditor performs analytical procedures for sales, evidence is being obtained about both sales and accounts receivable.

**TABLE 13-1**
**Analytical Procedures for the Sales and Collection Cycle**

| Analytical Procedure | Possible Misstatement |
|---|---|
| Compare gross margin percentage with previous years (by product line). | Overstatement or understatement of sales and accounts receivable. |
| Compare sales by month (by product line) over time. | Overstatement or understatement of sales and accounts receivable. |
| Compare sales returns and allowances as a percentage of gross sales with previous years (by product line). | Overstatement or understatement of sales returns and allowances and accounts receivable. |
| Compare individual customer balances over a stated amount with previous years. | Misstatements in accounts receivable and related income statement accounts. |
| Compare bad debt expense as a percentage of gross sales with previous years. | Uncollectible accounts receivable that have not been provided for. |
| Compare number of days that accounts receivable are outstanding with previous years. | Overstatement or understatement of allowance for uncollectible accounts and bad debt expense. |
| Compare aging categories as a percentage of accounts receivable with previous years. | Overstatement or understatement of allowance for uncollectible accounts and bad debt expense. |
| Compare allowance for uncollectible accounts as a percentage of accounts receivable with previous years. | Overstatement or understatement of allowance for uncollectible accounts and bad debt expense. |

In addition to the analytical procedures in Table 13-1, there should also be a review of accounts receivable for large and unusual amounts. Individual receivables that deserve special attention are large balances, accounts that have been outstanding for a long time, receivables from affiliated companies, officers, directors, and other related parties, and credit balances. The auditor should review the listing of accounts (aged trial balance) at the balance sheet date to determine which accounts should be investigated further.

The auditor's conclusion about analytical procedures for the sales and collection cycle is incorporated into the third row from the bottom on the evidence planning worksheet in Figure 13-7. Analytical procedures are substantive tests and therefore reduce the extent to which the auditor needs to test details of balances, if the analytical procedures' results are favorable.

## Design Tests of Details of Accounts Receivable

The appropriate tests of details of balances depend upon the factors incorporated into the evidence planning worksheet in Figure 13-7. The second row from the bottom shows planned detection risk for each accounts receivable balance-related audit objective. Planned detection risk for each objective is an auditor decision, decided by subjectively combining the conclusions reached about each of the factors listed above that row.

Combining the factors that determine planned detection risk is complex because the measurement for each factor is imprecise and the appropriate weight to be given each

PRACTICE APPLICATION OF ANALYTICAL PROCEDURES FOR GROSS MARGIN

Ron Stopps, CPA, is the auditor for Great Western Lumber Company, a wholesale wood milling company. Ron calculates the gross margin by three product lines and obtains industry information from published data as follows:

| | 1996 Gross Margin Percent | | 1995 Gross Margin Percent | | 1994 Gross Margin Percent | |
|---|---|---|---|---|---|---|
| | Great Western | Industry | Great Western | Industry | Great Western | Industry |
| Hardwood | 36.3 | 32.4 | 36.4 | 32.5 | 36.0 | 32.3 |
| Softwood | 23.9 | 22.0 | 20.3 | 22.1 | 20.5 | 22.3 |
| Plywood | 40.3 | 50.1 | 44.2 | 54.3 | 45.4 | 55.6 |

In discussing the results, the controller states that Great Western has always had a higher gross margin on hardwood products than the industry because they focus on the markets where they are able to sell at higher prices instead of emphasizing volume. The opposite is true of plywood where they have a reasonably small number of customers, each of which demands lower prices because of high volume. The controller states that competitive forces have caused reductions in plywood gross margin for both the industry and Great Western in 1995 and 1996. Great Western has traditionally had a somewhat lower gross margin for softwood than the industry until 1996, when gross margin went up significantly due to aggressive selling.

Stopps observed that most of what the controller said was reasonable given the facts. Hardwood gross margin for the industry was stable and approximately 3.5 to 4 percent lower than Great Western's every year. Industry gross margin for plywood has declined annually but is about 10 percent higher than Great Western's. Industry gross margin for softwood has been stable for the three years, but Great Western's has increased by a fairly large amount.

The change in Great Western's softwood gross margin from 20.3 percent to 23.9 percent is a concern to Stopps, so he goes through a three-step procedure:

1. Calculate the potential misstatement and evaluate the materiality of that amount. He calculates 23.9% – 20.3% × softwood sales and concludes the amount is potentially material.
2. Identify potential causes of the change.
   - Overstatement of sales
   - Overstatement of inventory (understatement of cost of goods sold)
   - Understatement of purchases (understatement of cost of goods sold)
   - Good results of aggressive selling
3. Indicate in the working papers a concern for the potential overstatement of sales and inventory, and understatement of purchases of softwood. This may require an expansion of other substantive audit tests.

factor is highly judgmental. On the other hand, the relationship between each factor and planned detection risk is well established. For example, the auditor knows that a high inherent risk or control risk decreases planned detection risk and increases planned substantive tests, whereas good results of substantive tests of transactions increases planned detection risk and decreases other planned substantive tests.

The bottom row in Figure 13-7 shows the planned audit evidence for tests of details of balances for accounts receivable, by objective. As discussed in Chapters 8 and 10, planned audit evidence is the complement of planned detection risk.

The conclusion that planned audit evidence for a given objective is high, medium, or low is implemented by the auditor deciding the appropriate audit procedures, sample size, items to select, and timing. The remainder of this chapter discusses the audit procedures and timing decisions. Chapter 14 deals with sample size and selecting items from the population for testing.

## TESTS OF DETAILS OF BALANCES

**OBJECTIVE 13-4**
**Design and perform tests of details of balances for accounts receivable for each balance-related audit objective.**

Tests of details of balances for all cycles are directed to balance sheet accounts, but income statement accounts are not ignored because they are verified as a byproduct of the balance sheet tests. For example, if the auditor confirms accounts receivable balances and finds overstatements due to mistakes in billing customers, there are overstatements of both accounts receivable and sales.

*Confirmation of accounts receivable* is the most important test of details of accounts receivable. Confirmation is discussed briefly in studying the appropriate tests for each of the balance-related audit objectives, then separately in more detail.

The discussion of tests of details of balances for accounts receivable that follows assumes that the auditor has completed an evidence planning worksheet similar to the one in Figure 13-7 and has decided planned detection risk for tests of details for each balance-related audit objective. The audit procedures selected and their sample size will depend heavily upon whether planned evidence for a given objective is low, medium, or high. The discussion focuses on accounts receivable balance-related audit objectives.

### Accounts Receivable Are Correctly Added and Agree with the Master File and the General Ledger

Most tests of accounts receivable and the allowance for uncollectible accounts are based on the *aged trial balance.* An aged trial balance is a listing of the balances in the accounts receivable master file at the balance sheet date. It includes the individual customer balances outstanding and a breakdown of each balance by the time passed between the date of sale and the balance sheet date. An illustration of a typical aged trial balance, in this case for Hillsburg Hardware Co., is given in Figure 13-4. Notice that the total is the same as accounts receivable on the general ledger trial balance on page 141.

Testing the information on the aged trial balance for detail tie-in is a necessary audit procedure. It is ordinarily done before any other tests to assure the auditor that the population being tested agrees with the general ledger and accounts receivable master file. The total column and the columns depicting the aging must be test footed, and the total on the trial balance compared to the general ledger. In addition, a sample of individual balances should be traced to supporting documents such as duplicate sales invoices to verify the customer's name, balance, and proper aging. The extent of the testing for detail tie-in depends

**FIGURE 13-4**

**Aged Trial Balance for Hillsburg Hardware Co.**

Hillsburg Hardware Co.
Accounts Receivable
Aged Trial Balance
12/31/96

Schedule
Prepared by Client — Date 1/5/97
Approved by

| Account Number | Customer | Balance 12/31/96 | Aging, Based on Invoice Date: 0-30 days | 31-60 days | 61-90 days | 91-120 days | over 120 |
|---|---|---|---|---|---|---|---|
| 01011 | Adams Supply | 7,329 | 4,511 | 2,818 | | | |
| 01044 | Argonaut, Inc. | 1,542 | 1,542 | | | | |
| 01100 | Atwater Brothers | 10,519 | 10,519 | | | | |
| 01191 | Beekman Bearings | 4,176 | 3,676 | | 500 | | |
| 01270 | Brown and Phillips | 3,000 | | | | 3,000 | |
| 01301 | Christopher Plumbing | 789 | | | | | 789 |
| 09733 | Travelers Equipment | 2,976 | 2,976 | | | | |
| 09742 | Underhill Parts and Maintenance | 8,963 | 8,963 | | | | |
| 09810 | UJW Co. | 5,111 | 1,811 | 1,700 | 1,600 | | |
| 09907 | Zephyr Plastics | 14,300 | 9,300 | 5,000 | | | |
| | | 1,009,800 | 785,856 | 128,466 | 55,432 | 34,446 | 5,600 |

on the number of accounts involved, the degree to which the master file has been tested as a part of tests of controls and substantive tests of transactions, and the extent to which the schedule has been verified by an internal auditor or other independent person before it is given to the auditor.

### Recorded Accounts Receivable Exist

The most important test of details of balances for determining the existence of recorded accounts receivable is the confirmation of customers' balances. When customers do not respond to confirmations, auditors also examine supporting documents to verify the shipment of goods and evidence of subsequent cash receipts to determine whether the accounts were collected. Normally, auditors do not examine shipping documents or evidence of subsequent cash receipts for any account in the sample that is confirmed, but these documents are used extensively as alternative evidence for nonresponses.

### Existing Accounts Receivable Are Included

It is difficult to test for account balances omitted from the aged trial balance except by relying on the self-balancing nature of the accounts receivable master file. For example, if the client accidentally excluded an account receivable from the trial balance, the only likely way it would be discovered is by footing the accounts receivable trial balance and reconciling the balance with the control account in the general ledger.

If all sales to a customer are omitted from the sales journal, the understatement of accounts receivable is almost impossible to uncover by tests of details of balances. For example, auditors rarely send accounts receivable confirmations to customers with zero balances, in part because research shows that customers are unlikely to respond to requests that indicate their balances are understated. The understatement of sales and accounts receivable is best uncovered by substantive tests of transactions for shipments made but not recorded (completeness objective for tests of sales transactions) and by analytical procedures.

### Accounts Receivable Are Accurate

Confirmation of accounts selected from the trial balance is the most common test of details of balances for the accuracy of accounts receivable. When customers do not respond to confirmation requests, auditors examine supporting documents, in the same way as described for the existence objective. Tests of the debits and credits to individual customers' balances are done by examining supporting documentation for shipments and cash receipts.

### Accounts Receivable Are Properly Classified

It is normally relatively easy to evaluate the classification of accounts receivable by reviewing the aged trial balance for material receivables from affiliates, officers, directors, or other related parties. If notes receivable or accounts that should not be classified as a current asset are included with the regular accounts, these should also be segregated. Finally, if credit balances in accounts receivable are significant, it is appropriate to reclassify them as accounts payable.

There is a close relationship between the classification objective as discussed here and the presentation and disclosure objective. Classification concerns determining whether the client has correctly separated different classifications of accounts receivable. Presentation and disclosure concerns making sure that the classifications are properly presented. For example, under the classification objective, the auditor determines if receivables from related parties have been separated on the aged trial balance. Under the presentation and disclosure objective, the auditor determines if related party transactions are correctly shown in the financial statements.

### Cutoff for Accounts Receivable Is Correct

Cutoff misstatements can occur for *sales, sales returns and allowances,* and *cash receipts.* They take place when current period transactions are recorded in the subsequent period or subsequent period transactions are recorded in the current period.

The objective of cutoff tests is the same regardless of the type of transaction, but the procedures vary. The objective is to verify whether transactions near the end of the accounting period are recorded in the proper period. The cutoff objective is one of the most important in the cycle because misstatements in cutoff can significantly affect current period income. For example, the intentional or unintentional inclusion of several large, subsequent period sales in the current period or the exclusion of several current period sales returns and allowances can materially overstate net earnings.

In determining the reasonableness of cutoff, a threefold approach is needed: first, decide on the appropriate *criteria for cutoff;* second, evaluate whether the client has established *adequate procedures* to ensure a reasonable cutoff; and third, *test* whether a reasonable cutoff was obtained.

**Sales Cutoff** The criterion used by most merchandising and manufacturing clients for determining when a sale takes place is the *shipment of goods,* but some companies record invoices at the time title passes. The passage of title can take place before shipment (as in the case of custom-manufactured goods), at the time of shipment, or subsequent to shipment. For the correct measurement of current period income, the method must be in accordance with generally accepted accounting principles and consistently applied.

The most important part of evaluating the client's method of obtaining a reliable cutoff is to determine the procedures in use. When a client issues prenumbered shipping documents sequentially, it is usually a simple matter to evaluate and test cutoff. Moreover, the segregation of duties between the shipping and the billing function also enhances the likelihood of recording transactions in the proper period. However, if shipments are made by company truck, if the shipping records are unnumbered, and if shipping and billing department personnel are not independent of each other, it may be difficult, if not impossible, to be assured of an accurate cutoff.

When the client's internal controls are adequate, the cutoff can usually be verified by obtaining the shipping document number for the last shipment made at the end of the period and comparing this number with current and subsequent period recorded sales. As an illustration, assume that the shipping document number for the last shipment in the current period is 1489. All recorded sales before the end of the period should bear a shipping document number preceding number 1490. There should also be no sales recorded in the subsequent period for a shipment with a bill of lading numbered 1489 or lower. This can easily be tested by comparing recorded sales with the related shipping documents for the last few days of the current period and the first few days of the subsequent period.

**Sales Returns and Allowances Cutoff** Generally accepted accounting principles require that sales returns and allowances be *matched with related sales* if the amounts are material. For example, if current period shipments are returned in the subsequent period, the proper treatment is to include the sales return in the current period. (The returned goods would be treated as current period inventory.) For most companies, however, sales returns and allowances are recorded in the *accounting period in which they occur,* under the assumption of approximately equal, offsetting amounts at the beginning and end of each accounting period. This is acceptable as long as the amounts are not significant.

When the auditor is confident that the client records all sales returns and allowances promptly, the cutoff tests are simple and straightforward. The auditor can examine supporting documentation for a sample of sales returns and allowances recorded during several weeks subsequent to the closing date to determine the date of the original sale. If the amounts recorded in the subsequent period are significantly different from unrecorded returns and allowances at the beginning of the period under audit, an adjustment must be considered. If the internal controls for recording sales returns and allowances are evaluated as ineffective, a larger sample is needed to verify cutoff.

**Cash Receipts Cutoff** For most audits a proper cash receipts cutoff is *less important* than either the sales or the sales returns and allowances cutoff, because the improper cutoff of cash affects only the cash and the accounts receivable balances, not earnings. Nevertheless, if the misstatement is material, it could affect the fair presentation of these accounts, especially when cash is a small or negative balance.

It is easy to test for a cash receipts cutoff misstatement (frequently referred to as *holding the cash receipts book open*) by tracing recorded cash receipts to subsequent period bank deposits on the bank statement. If there is a delay of several days, this could indicate a cutoff misstatement.

The confirmation of accounts receivable may also be relied on to some degree to uncover cutoff misstatements for sales, sales returns and allowances, and cash receipts, especially when there is a long interval between the date the transaction took place and the recording date. However, when the interval is only a few days, mail delivery delays may cause confusion of cutoff misstatements with normal timing differences. For example, if a customer mails and records a check to a client for payment of an unpaid account on December 30 and the client receives and records the amount on January 2, the records of the two organizations will be different on December 31. This is not a cutoff misstatement, but a *timing difference* due to the delivery time. It may be difficult for the auditor to evaluate whether a cutoff misstatement or a timing difference occurred when a confirmation reply is the source of information. This type of situation requires additional investigation, such as inspection of underlying documents.

### Accounts Receivable Is Stated at Realizable Value

Tests of the *realizable value* objective are for the purpose of evaluating the account, *allowance for uncollectible accounts.* Generally accepted accounting principles require that accounts receivable be stated at the amount that will ultimately be collected, which is gross accounts receivable less the allowance. The client's estimate of the total amount that is uncollectible is represented by the allowance for uncollectible accounts. Although it is not possible to predict the future precisely, it is necessary for the auditor to evaluate whether the allowance is reasonable, considering all available facts.

The starting point for the evaluation of the allowance for uncollectible accounts is to review the results of the tests of controls that are concerned with the client's credit policy. If the client's credit policy has remained unchanged and the results of the tests of credit policy and credit approval are consistent with those of the preceding year, the change in the balance in the allowance for uncollectible accounts should reflect only changes in economic conditions and sales volume. However, if the client's credit policy or the degree to which it correctly functions has significantly changed, great care must be taken to consider the effects of these changes as well.

A common way to evaluate the adequacy of the allowance is to carefully examine the noncurrent accounts on the aged trial balance to determine which ones have not been paid subsequent to the balance sheet date. The size and age of unpaid balances can then be compared with similar information from previous years to evaluate whether the amount of noncurrent receivables is increasing or decreasing over time. The examination of credit files, discussions with the credit manager, and review of the client's correspondence file may also provide insights into the collectibility of the accounts. These procedures are especially important if a few large balances are noncurrent and are not being paid on a regular basis.

There are two pitfalls in evaluating the allowance by reviewing individual noncurrent balances on the aged trial balance. First, the current accounts are ignored in establishing the adequacy of the allowance, even though some of these amounts will undoubtedly become uncollectible. Second, it is difficult to compare the results of the current year with those of previous years on such an unstructured basis. If the accounts are becoming progressively uncollectible over a period of several years, this fact could be overlooked. A way to avoid these difficulties is to establish the history of bad debt charge-offs over a period of time as a frame of reference for evaluating the current year's allowance. As an example, if historically a certain percentage of the total of each age category becomes uncollectible, it is relatively easy to compute whether the allowance is properly stated. If 2 percent of current accounts, 10 percent of 30- to 90-day accounts, and 35 percent of all balances over 90 days ultimately become uncollectible, these percentages can easily be applied to the current year's aged trial balance totals, and the result can be compared with the balance in the allowance account. Of course, the auditor has to be careful to modify the calculations for changed conditions.

**Bad Debt Expense** After the auditor is satisfied with the allowance for uncollectible accounts, it is easy to verify bad debt expense. Assume that (1) the beginning balance in the allowance account was verified as a part of the previous audit, (2) the uncollectible accounts charged off were verified as a part of the substantive tests of transactions, and (3) the ending balance in the allowance account has been verified by various means. Then bad debt expense is simply a residual balance that can be verified by a reperformance test.

**The Client Has Rights to Accounts Receivable**

The client's rights to accounts receivable ordinarily cause no audit problems because the receivables usually belong to the client, but in some cases a portion of the receivables may have been pledged as collateral, assigned to someone else, factored, or sold at discount. Normally, the client's customers are not aware of the existence of such matters; therefore, the confirmation of receivables will not bring it to light. A review of the minutes, discussions with the client, confirmation with banks, and the examination of correspondence files are usually sufficient to uncover instances in which the client has limited rights to receivables.

**Accounts Receivable Presentation and Disclosures Are Proper**

In addition to testing for the proper statement of the dollar amount in the general ledger, the auditor must also determine that information about the account balance resulting from the sales and collection cycle is properly presented and disclosed in the financial statements. The auditor must decide whether the client has properly combined amounts and disclosed related party information in the statements. To evaluate the adequacy of the presentation and disclosure, the auditor must have a thorough understanding of generally accepted accounting principles and presentation and disclosure requirements.

An important part of the evaluation involves deciding whether material amounts requiring separate disclosure have actually been separated in the statements. For example, receivables from officers and affiliated companies must be segregated from accounts receivable from customers if the amounts are material. Similarly, under SEC requirements, it is necessary to disclose sales and assets for different business segments separately. The proper aggregation of general ledger balances in the financial statements also requires combining account balances that are not relevant for external users of the statements. If all accounts included in the general ledger were disclosed separately on the statements, most statement users would be more confused than enlightened.

As a part of proper presentation and disclosure, the auditor is also required to evaluate the adequacy of the *footnotes.* One of the major lawsuits in the history of the profession, the *Continental Vending* case, revolved primarily around the adequacy of the footnote disclosure of a major receivable from an affiliated company. The required footnote disclosure includes information about the pledging, discounting, factoring, assignment of accounts receivable, and amounts due from related parties. Of course, in order to evaluate the adequacy of these disclosures, it is first necessary to know of their existence and to have complete information about their nature. This is generally obtained in other parts of the audit, as discussed in the previous section.

## CONFIRMATION OF ACCOUNTS RECEIVABLE

**OBJECTIVE 13-5**
**Obtain and evaluate accounts receivable confirmations.**

One of the most important audit procedures is the *confirmation of accounts receivable.* The primary purpose of accounts receivable confirmation is to satisfy the *existence, accuracy,* and *cutoff* objectives.

**AICPA Requirements**

Two major audit procedures are formally required by the AICPA: the *confirmation of accounts receivable* and the *physical examination of inventory.* These requirements are a direct result of the 1938 landmark legal case, *McKesson and Robbins,* in which a massive fraud involving fictitious accounts receivable and inventory was not uncovered in the audit. There was ample support to demonstrate that the confirmation of receivables and the physical observation of inventory would have brought the fraud to light, but at that time neither of these procedures was normally performed. Because of a strong reaction in the financial community, the membership of the AICPA voted in 1939 to require these two procedures whenever an unqualified report is issued.

Later, the standard for confirmations was modified by SAS 67 (AU 330) to the present requirement that permits an unqualified report even when accounts receivable are not confirmed in any of three circumstances: (1) accounts receivable are immaterial, (2) the auditor considers confirmations ineffective evidence because response rates will likely be inadequate or unreliable, or (3) the combined level of inherent risk and control risk is low and other substantive evidence can be accumulated to provide sufficient evidence. If the auditor decides not to confirm accounts receivable, the justification for doing so must be documented in the working papers. This change in requirements, especially the third consideration, is likely to reduce the use of confirmations in practice. If a client has effective internal controls and low inherent risk for the sales and collection cycle, the auditor should often be able to satisfy the evidence requirements by tests of controls, substantive tests of transactions, and analytical procedures.

Although the remaining sections in this chapter refer specifically to the confirmation of accounts receivable from customers, the concepts apply equally to other receivables such as notes receivable, amounts due from officers, and employee advances.

## Confirmation Decisions

In performing confirmation procedures, the auditor must decide the type of confirmation to use, timing of the procedures, sample size, and individual items to select. Each of these is discussed, along with the factors affecting the decision.

**Type of Confirmation** Two common types of confirmations are used for confirming accounts receivable: *positive* and *negative.* A *positive* confirmation is a communication addressed to the debtor requesting him or her to confirm directly whether the balance as stated on the confirmation request is correct or incorrect. Figure 13-5 (page 458) illustrates a positive confirmation in the audit of Hillsburg Hardware Co. Notice that this confirmation is for one of the largest accounts on the aged trial balance in Figure 13-4 on page 452. A second type of positive confirmation, often called a *blank confirmation form,* does not state the amount on the confirmation but requests the recipient to fill in the balance or furnish other information. Because blank forms require the recipient to determine the information requested before signing and returning the confirmation, they are considered more reliable than confirmations that include the information. Research shows, however, that response rates are usually lower for blank confirmation forms.

A *negative* confirmation is also addressed to the debtor, but requests a response only when the debtor disagrees with the stated amount. Figure 13-6 (page 459) illustrates a negative confirmation in the audit of Hillsburg Hardware Co. that has been attached to a customer's monthly statement with a gummed label.

A positive confirmation is *more reliable* evidence because the auditor can perform follow-up procedures if a response is not received from the debtor. With a negative confirmation, failure to reply must be regarded as a correct response, even though the debtor may have ignored the confirmation request.

Offsetting the reliability disadvantage, negative confirmations are *less expensive* to send than positive confirmations, and thus more can be distributed for the same total cost. Negative confirmations cost less because there are no second requests and no follow-up of nonresponses.

The determination of which type of confirmation to use is an auditor's decision, and it should be based on the facts in the audit. SAS 67 states that it is acceptable to use negative confirmations only when all of the following circumstances are present:

- Accounts receivable is made up of a large number of small accounts.
- Combined assessed control risk and inherent risk is low. The combined risk is unlikely to be low if either internal controls are ineffective or there is a high expectation of misstatements. For example, if prior years' audits indicate that there are often

**FIGURE 13-5**

**Positive Confirmation**

**HILLSBURG HARDWARE CO.**
**Gary, Indiana**

January 5, 1997

Atwater Brothers
19 South Main Street
Middleton, Ohio 36947

Gentlemen:

In connection with an audit of our financial statements, please confirm directly to our auditors

BERGER & ANTHONY, CPAs
Gary, Indiana

the correctness of the balance of your account with us as of December 31, 1996, as shown below.

This is not a request for payment; please do not send your remittance to our auditors. Your prompt attention to this request will be appreciated. An envelope is enclosed for your reply.

Erma Swanson
*Erma Swanson, Chief Accountant*
*No.* 3

*BERGER & ANTHONY, CPAs*
*Gary, Indiana*

The balance receivable from us of $10,519 as of December 31, 1996, is correct except as noted below:

____________________________________

Date __________ By __________

disputed or inaccurate accounts receivable, negative confirmations would be inappropriate.

- There is no reason to believe that the recipients of the confirmations are unlikely to give them consideration. For example, if the response rate to positive confirmations in prior years was extremely high or if there are high response rates on audits of similar clients, it is likely that recipients will give confirmations reasonable consideration.

Typically, when negative confirmations are used, the auditor puts considerable emphasis on the effectiveness of internal controls, substantive tests of transactions, and analytical procedures as evidence of the fairness of accounts receivable, and assumes that the large majority of the recipients will provide a conscientious reading and response to the confirmation request. Negative confirmations are often used for audits of hospitals, retail stores, banks, and other industries in which the receivables are due from the general public.

It is also common to use a combination of negative and positive confirmations by sending the latter to accounts with large balances and the former to those with small balances.

**FIGURE 13-6**

**Negative Confirmation**

**AUDITOR'S ACCOUNT CONFIRMATION**

Please examine this statement carefully. If it does NOT agree with your records, please report any exceptions directly to our auditors

*BERGER & ANTHONY, CPAs*
*Gary, Indiana*

who are conducting an audit of our financial statements. An addressed envelope is enclosed for your convenience in replying.

*Do not send your remittance to our auditors.*

The discussion of confirmations to this point shows that there is a continuum for the type of confirmation decision, starting with using no confirmation in some circumstances, to using only negatives, to using both negatives and positives, to using only positives. The primary factors affecting the decision are the materiality of total accounts receivable, the number and size of individual accounts, control risk, inherent risk, the effectiveness of confirmations as audit evidence, and the availability of other audit evidence.

**Timing** The most reliable evidence from confirmations is obtained when they are sent as close to the balance sheet date as possible, as opposed to confirming the accounts several months before year-end. This permits the auditor to directly test the accounts receivable balance on the financial statements without making any inferences about the transactions taking place between the confirmation date and the balance sheet date. However, as a means of completing the audit on a timely basis, it is frequently necessary to confirm the accounts at an interim date. This is permissible if internal controls are adequate and can provide reasonable assurance that sales, cash receipts, and other credits are properly recorded between the date of the confirmation and the end of the accounting period. Other factors the auditor is likely to consider in making the decision are the materiality of accounts receivable and the auditor's exposure to lawsuits because of the possibility of client bankruptcy and similar risks.

If the decision is made to confirm accounts receivable prior to year-end, it may be necessary to test the transactions occurring between the confirmation date and the balance sheet date by examining such internal documents as duplicate sales invoices, shipping documents, and evidence of cash receipts, in addition to performing analytical procedures of the intervening period.

**Sample Size** The major factors affecting sample size for confirming accounts receivable fall into several categories and include the following:

- Tolerable misstatement
- Inherent risk (relative size of total accounts receivable, number of accounts, prior year results, and expected misstatements)
- Control risk
- Achieved detection risk from other substantive tests (extent and results of substantive tests of transactions, analytical procedures, and other tests of details)
- Type of confirmation (negatives normally require a larger sample size)

Most of these factors are the same ones discussed in Chapter 8 for materiality and the various risks. A discussion of these factors in the context of audit sampling is given in Chapter 14.

**Selection of the Items for Testing** Some type of *stratification* is desirable with most confirmations. A typical approach to stratification is to consider both the dollar size of individual accounts and the length of time an account has been outstanding as a basis for selecting the balances for confirmation. In most audits, the emphasis should be on confirming larger and older balances, since these are most likely to include a significant misstatement. But it is also important to sample some items from every material segment of the population. In many cases, the auditor selects all accounts above a certain dollar amount and selects a random sample from the remainder.

## Maintaining Control

After the items for confirmation have been selected, the auditor must maintain control of the confirmations until they are returned from the customer. When the client assists by preparing the confirmations, enclosing them in envelopes, or putting stamps on the envelopes, close supervision by the auditor is required. A return address must be included on all envelopes to make sure that undelivered mail is received by the CPA firm. Similarly, self-addressed return envelopes accompanying the confirmations must be addressed for delivery to the CPA firm's office. It is even important to mail the confirmations *outside* the client's office. All these steps are necessary to ensure independent communication between the auditor and the customer.

## Follow-up on Nonresponses

It is inappropriate to regard confirmations mailed but not returned by customers as significant audit evidence. For example, nonresponses to positive confirmations do not provide audit evidence. Similarly, for negative confirmations, the auditor should not conclude that the recipient received the confirmation request and verified the information requested. Negative confirmations do, however, provide some evidence of the existence assertion.

When positive confirmations are used, SAS 67 requires follow-up procedures for confirmations not returned by the customer. It is common to send second and sometimes even third requests for confirmations. Even with these efforts, some customers do not return the confirmation, so it is necessary to follow up with *alternative procedures.* The objective of alternative procedures is to determine by a means other than confirmation whether the nonconfirmed account existed and was properly stated at the confirmation date. For any positive confirmation not returned, the following documentation can be examined to verify the existence and accuracy of individual sales transactions making up the ending balance in accounts receivable.

**Subsequent Cash Receipts** Evidence of the receipt of cash subsequent to the confirmation date includes examining remittance advices, entries in the cash receipts records, or perhaps even subsequent credits in the accounts receivable master file. On the one hand, the examination of evidence of subsequent cash receipts is a highly useful alternative procedure because it is reasonable to assume that a customer would not make a payment unless it was an existing receivable. On the other hand, the fact of payment does not establish whether there was an obligation on the date of the confirmation. In addition, care should be taken to match each unpaid sales transaction with evidence of its payment as a test for disputes or disagreements over individual outstanding invoices.

**Duplicate Sales Invoices** These are useful in verifying the actual issuance of a sales invoice and the actual date of the billing.

**Shipping Documents** These are important in establishing whether the shipment was actually made and as a test of cutoff.

**Correspondence with the Client** Usually, the auditor does not need to review correspondence as a part of alternative procedures, but correspondence can be used to disclose disputed and questionable receivables not uncovered by other means.

The extent and nature of the alternative procedures depend primarily upon the materiality of the nonresponses, the types of misstatements discovered in the confirmed responses, the subsequent cash receipts from the nonresponses, and the auditor's conclusions about internal control. It is normally desirable to account for all unconfirmed balances with alternative procedures even if the amounts are small, as a means of properly generalizing from the sample to the population. Another acceptable approach is to assume that nonresponses are 100% overstatement amounts.

**THE BOOKS ARE BURNING**

The Regina Co., a manufacturer of vacuum cleaners, overstated income by failing to record sales returns. This fraud in sales returns was not sufficient to allow the company to meet its earning targets, so the company generated 200 fictitious sales invoices totaling $5.4 million at the end of the June 30, 1988 fiscal year.

Although auditors usually test sales cutoff and confirm accounts receivable, these fictitious sales were cleverly disguised. The bogus invoices were prepared in the same amounts as other existing sales transactions and they were prepared only for large customers who were unlikely to respond to accounts receivable confirmation requests. The CFO also made sure that the fraudulent invoices were not sent to Regina's regular customers and were concealed from members of the accounting staff who were not involved in the scheme.

The auditors' alternative procedures failed to detect the scheme, most likely because the amounts on the fraudulent invoices matched existing sales invoices. The audit firm defended itself by saying, "If you're a good book-cooker, it's almost impossible to detect."

*Sources:* 1. John A. Byrne, "How Don Sheelen Made a Mess that Regina Couldn't Clean Up," *Business Week*, February 12, 1990, pp. 46–50.
2. Michael C. Knapp, *Contemporary Auditing: Issues and Cases.* West Publishing, New York, pp. 79–85.

## Analysis of Differences

When the confirmation requests are returned by the customer, it is necessary to determine the reason for any reported differences. In many cases, they are caused by timing differences between the client's and the customer's records. It is important to distinguish between these and *exceptions,* which represent misstatements of the accounts receivable balance. The most commonly reported types of differences in confirmations follow.

**Payment Has Already Been Made** Reported differences typically arise when the customer has made a payment prior to confirmation date, but the client has not received the payment in time for recording before the confirmation date. Such instances should be carefully investigated to determine the possibility of a cash receipts cutoff misstatement, lapping, or a theft of cash.

**Goods Have Not Been Received** These differences typically result because the client records the sale at the date of shipment and the customer records the acquisition when the goods are received. The time that the goods are in transit is frequently the cause of differences reported on confirmations. These should be investigated to determine the possibility of the customer not receiving the goods at all or the existence of a cutoff misstatement on the client's records.

**The Goods Have Been Returned** The client's failure to record a credit memo could result from timing differences or the improper recording of sales returns and allowances. Like other differences, these must be investigated.

**Clerical Errors and Disputed Amounts** The most likely types of reported differences in a client's records are when the customer states that there is an error in the price charged for the goods, the goods are damaged, the proper quantity of goods was not received, and so forth. These differences must be investigated to determine whether the client is in error and what the amount of the error is.

In most instances the auditor will ask the client to reconcile the difference and, if necessary, will communicate with the customer to resolve any disagreements. Naturally, the auditor must carefully verify the client's conclusions on each significant difference.

## Drawing Conclusions

When all differences have been resolved, including those discovered in performing alternative procedures, it is important to *reevaluate internal control.* Each client misstatement must be analyzed to determine whether it was consistent or inconsistent with the original assessed level of control risk. If a significant number of misstatements take place that are inconsistent with the assessment of control risk, it is necessary to revise the assessment and consider the effect of the revision on the audit.

It is also necessary to generalize from the sample to the entire population of accounts receivable. Even though the sum of the misstatements in the sample may not significantly affect the financial statements, the auditor must consider whether the population is likely to be materially misstated. This conclusion can be arrived at by using statistical sampling techniques or on a nonstatistical basis. Projection of misstatements was discussed in Chapter 8 and is further explained in Chapter 14.

The auditor should always evaluate the *qualitative* nature of the misstatements found in the sample, regardless of the dollar amount of the projected misstatement. Even if the projected misstatement is less than tolerable misstatement for accounts receivable, the misstatements found in a sample can be symptomatic of a more serious problem.

The final decision about accounts receivable and sales is whether sufficient evidence has been obtained through tests of controls and substantive tests of transactions, analytical procedures, cutoff procedures, confirmation, and other substantive tests to justify drawing conclusions about the correctness of the stated balance.

**TECHNOLOGY UPDATE**

In an article in *The CPA Journal,* Michael J. Fischer and John P. McAllister outline two types of new audit technologies:

- Type 1—technologies that automate existing, established procedures
- Type 2—technologies that introduce new approaches to auditing

The authors provide examples of how each of the two types of new audit technologies can be used to improve efficiency in the audit of accounts receivable.

*Using Type 1 Technology.* Use computer-assisted audit techniques to automate portions of the accounts receivable confirmation process. *Illustration:* A computer program is used to (1) read the client's accounts receivable master file, (2) select accounts for confirmation using specified criteria, and (3) prepare the confirmations using information in the master file.

*Using Type 2 Technology. Illustration*: A multiple-regression-based computer model is used to predict the year-end balance in accounts receivable. This prediction is then compared to the client's actual year-end balance. If the balance is reasonable, the auditor may be able to reduce conventional types of year-end testing, including confirmation.

The authors believe that substantial cost reductions can result from using either type of technology, but auditors must carefully plan and manage the technology so that it is used properly and efficiently.

*Source:* Michael J. Fischer and John P. McAllister, "Enhancing Audit Efficiency with New Technologies," *The CPA Journal,* November 1993, pp. 58–59.

## CASE ILLUSTRATION—HILLSBURG HARDWARE, PART III

**OBJECTIVE 13-6**
**Design audit procedures for the audit of accounts receivable, using an evidence planning worksheet as a guide.**

The Hillsburg Hardware Co. case illustration from Chapters 11 and 12 continues here to include the determination of the tests of details of balances audit procedures in the sales and collection cycle. Table 13-2 includes comparative trial balance information for the sales and collection cycle for Hillsburg Hardware Co. Some of that information is used to illustrate several analytical procedures in Table 13-3. None of the analytical procedures

**TABLE 13-2**

**Comparative Information for Hillsburg Hardware Co.—Sales and Collection Cycle**

| | Amount (in thousands) | | |
|---|---|---|---|
| | **12-31-96** | **12-31-95** | **12-31-94** |
| Sales | $7,216 | $6,321 | $5,937 |
| Sales returns and allowances | 62 | 57 | 50 |
| Gross margin | 1,992 | 1,738 | 1,621 |
| Accounts receivable | 1,010 | 898 | 825 |
| Allowance for uncollectible accounts | 62 | 77 | 69 |
| Bad debt expense | 166 | 164 | 142 |
| Total current assets | 2,550 | 2,239 | 2,099 |
| Total assets | 3,067 | 3,301 | 3,057 |
| Net earnings before taxes | 285 | 436 | 397 |
| Number of accounts receivable | 258 | 221 | 209 |
| Number of accounts receivable with balances over $5,000 | 37 | 32 | 30 |

indicated potential misstatements except the ratio of the allowance of uncollectible accounts to accounts receivable. The explanation at the bottom of Table 13-3 comments on the potential misstatement.

Fran Moore prepared the evidence planning worksheet in Figure 13-7 on page 464 as an aid to help her decide the extent of planned tests of details of balances. The source of each of the rows are as follows:

- *Tolerable misstatement.* The preliminary judgment of materiality was set at $37,000 (10 percent of earnings from operations of $369,000). She allocated $22,000 to the audit of accounts receivable (see page 253).
- *Acceptable audit risk.* Fran assessed acceptable audit risk as high because of the good financial condition of the company, its financial stability, and the relatively few users of the financial statements.
- *Inherent risk.* Fran assessed inherent risk as low for all objectives except realizable value. In past years, there have been audit adjustments to the allowance for uncollectible accounts because it was found to be understated.

**TABLE 13-3**

**Analytical Procedures for Hillsburg Hardware Co.—Sales and Collection Cycle**

| | **12-31-96** | **12-31-95** | **12-31-94** |
|---|---|---|---|
| Gross margin percent | 27.6% | 27.5% | 27.3% |
| Sales returns and allowances/gross sales | .9% | .9% | .8% |
| Bad debt expense/net sales | 2.3% | 2.6% | 2.4% |
| Allowance for uncollectible accounts/ accounts receivable | 6.1% | 8.6% | 8.4% |
| Number of days receivables outstanding | 50.8 | 51.6 | 50.5 |
| Net accounts receivable/total current assets | 37.2% | 36.7% | 36.0% |

Comment: Allowance as a percentage of accounts receivable has declined from 8.4% to 6.1%. Number of days receivable outstanding and economic conditions do not justify this change. Potential misstatement is approximately $23,000 ($1,010,000 × .084 – .061), which is greater than tolerable misstatement.

**FIGURE 13-7**

**Evidence Planning Worksheet to Decide Tests of Details of Balances for Hillsburg Hardware Co.—Accounts Receivable**

| | Detail tie-in | Existence | Completeness | Accuracy | Classification | Cutoff | Realizable value | Rights | Presentation and disclosure |
|---|---|---|---|---|---|---|---|---|---|
| Acceptable audit risk | high | high | high | high | high | high | high | high | high |
| Inherent risk | low | low | low | low | low | low | medium | low | low |
| Control risk—Sales | low | medium | medium | high | low | high | high | not applicable | not applicable |
| Control risk—Cash receipts | medium | high | low | low | high | high | not applicable | not applicable | not applicable |
| Control risk—Additional controls | none | none | none | none | none | none | none | low | low |
| Substantive tests of transactions—Sales | good results | good results | good results | good results | good results | unacceptable results | not applicable | not applicable | not applicable |
| Substantive tests of transactions—Cash receipts | good results | good results | good results | good results | good results | good results | not applicable | not applicable | not applicable |
| Analytical procedures | good results | good results | good results | good results | good results | good results | unacceptable results | not applicable | not applicable |
| Planned detection risk for tests of details of balances | high | medium | high | high | high | low | low | high | high |
| Planned audit evidence for tests of details of balances | low | medium | low | low | low | high | high | low | low |

Tolerable misstatement <u>$22,000</u>

- *Control risk.* Assessed control risk for sales and cash receipts is taken from the control risk matrix for sales and cash receipts, modified by the results of the tests of controls. The control risk matrix is shown in Figures 11-7 and 11-8 on pages 384 and 385. The results of the tests of controls and substantive tests of transactions in Chapter 12 were consistent with the assessments of control risk in Chapter 11, except for the realizable value objective. The initial assessment was low, but tests of controls and substantive tests of transactions results changed the assessment to high.
- *Substantive tests of transactions results.* These results are taken from the tests illustrated in Chapter 12 in Figures 12-7 and 12-8 (pages 432–433). All results were acceptable except the realizable value and cutoff objectives for sales.
- *Analytical procedures.* See Table 13-3.
- *Planned detection risk and planned audit evidence.* These two rows are decided for each objective based on the conclusions in the other rows.

**TABLE 13-4**

**Balance-Related Audit Objectives and Audit Program for Hillsburg Hardware Co.—Sales and Collection Cycle (Design Format)**

| Balance-Related Audit Objective | Audit Procedure |
|---|---|
| Accounts receivable in the aged trial balance agree with related master file amounts, and the total is correctly added and agrees with the general ledger. (Detail tie-in) | Trace 10 accounts from the trial balance to accounts on master file. (6)<br>Foot two pages of the trial balance, and total all pages. (7)<br>Trace the balance to the general ledger. (8) |
| The accounts receivable on the aged trial balance exist. (Existence) | Confirm accounts receivable, using positive confirmations. Confirm all amounts over $5,000 and a nonstatistical sample of the remainder. (10)<br>Perform alternative procedures for all confirmations not returned on the first or second request. (11)<br>Review accounts receivable trial balance for large and unusual receivables. (1) |
| Existing accounts receivable are included in the aged trial balance. (Completeness) | Trace 5 accounts from the accounts receivable master file to the aged trial balance. (9) |
| Accounts receivable in the trial balance are accurate. (Accuracy) | Confirm accounts receivable, using positive confirmations. Confirm all amounts over $5,000 and a nonstatistical sample of the remainder. (10)<br>Perform alternative procedures for all confirmations not returned on the first or second request. (11)<br>Review accounts receivable trial balance for large and unusual receivables. (1) |
| Accounts receivable on the aged trial balance are properly classified. (Classification) | Review the receivables listed on the aged trial balance for notes and related party receivables. (3)<br>Inquire of management whether there are any related party notes or long-term receivables included in the trial balance. (4) |
| Transactions in the sales and collection cycle are recorded in the proper period. (Cutoff) | Select the last 40 sales transactions from the current year's sales journal and the first 40 from the subsequent year's and trace each to the related shipping documents, checking for the date of actual shipment and the correct recording. (14)<br>Review large sales returns and allowances after the balance sheet date to determine whether any should be included in the current period. (15) |
| Accounts receivable is stated at realizable value. (Realizable value) | Trace 10 accounts from the aging schedule to the accounts receivable master file to test for the correct aging on the trial balance. (6)<br>Foot the aging columns on the trial balance and total the pages. (7)<br>Crossfoot the aging columns. (7)<br>Discuss with the credit manager the likelihood of collecting older accounts. Examine subsequent cash receipts and the credit file on all accounts over 90 days and evaluate whether the receivables are collectible. (12)<br>Evaluate whether the allowance is adequate after performing other audit procedures for collectibility of receivables. (13) |
| The client has rights to accounts receivable on the trial balance. (Rights) | Review the minutes of the board of directors meetings for any indication of pledged or factored accounts receivable. (5)<br>Inquire of management whether any receivables are pledged or factored. (5) |
| Accounts in the sales and collection cycle and related information are properly presented and disclosed. (Presentation and disclosure) | Review the minutes of the board of directors meetings for any indication of pledged or factored accounts receivable. (5)<br>Inquire of management whether any receivables are pledged or factored. (5) |

*Note:* The procedures are summarized into a performance format in Table 13-5 on page 466. The numbers in parentheses after the procedures refer to Table 13-5.

Table 13-4 shows the tests of details audit program for accounts receivable, by objective, and for the allowance for uncollectible accounts. The audit program reflects the conclusions for planned audit evidence on the evidence planning worksheet in Figure 13-7. Table 13-5 shows the audit program in a performance format. The audit procedures are identical to those in Table 13-4 except for procedure 2, which is an analytical procedure. The numbers in parentheses are a cross reference between the two tables.

**TABLE 13-5**

**Tests of Details of Balances Audit Program for Hillsburg Hardware Co.—Sales and Collection Cycle (Performance Format)**

1. Review accounts receivable trial balance for large and unusual receivables.
2. Calculate analytical procedures indicated in carry-forward working papers (not included) and follow up on any significant changes from prior years.
3. Review the receivables listed on the aged trial balance for notes and related party receivables.
4. Inquire of management whether there are any related party, notes, or long-term receivables included in the trial balance.
5. Review the minutes of the board of directors meetings and inquire of management to determine whether any receivables are pledged or factored.
6. Trace 10 accounts from the trial balance to the accounts receivable master file for aging and the balance.
7. Foot 2 pages of the trial balance for aging columns and balance and total all pages and crossfoot the aging.
8. Trace the balance to the general ledger.
9. Trace 5 accounts from the accounts receivable master file to the aged trial balance.
10. Confirm accounts receivable, using positive confirmations. Confirm all amounts over $5,000 and a nonstatistical sample of the remainder.
11. Perform alternative procedures for all confirmations not returned on the first or second request.
12. Discuss with the credit manager the likelihood of collecting older accounts. Examine subsequent cash receipts and the credit file on all larger accounts over 90 days and evaluate whether the receivables are collectible.
13. Evaluate whether the allowance is adequate after performing other audit procedures for collectibility of receivables.
14. Select the last 40 sales transactions from the current year's sales journal and the first 40 from the subsequent year's and trace each to the related shipping documents, checking for the date of actual shipment and the correct recording.
15. Review large sales returns and allowances after the balance sheet date to determine whether any should be included in the current period.

## ESSENTIAL TERMS

**Accounts receivable balance-related audit objectives**—the nine specific audit objectives used by the auditor to decide the appropriate audit evidence for accounts receivable

**Aged trial balance**—a listing of the balances in the accounts receivable master file at the balance sheet date broken down according to the amount of time passed between the date of sale and the balance sheet date

**Alternative procedures**—the follow-up of a positive confirmation not returned by the debtor with the use of documentation evidence to determine whether the recorded receivable exists and is collectible

**Blank confirmation form**—a letter, addressed to the debtor, requesting the recipient to fill in the amount of the accounts receivable balance; it is considered a positive confirmation

**Cutoff misstatements**—misstatements that take place as a result of current period transactions being recorded in a subsequent period, or subsequent period transactions being recorded in the current period

**Evidence planning worksheet**—a working paper used to help the auditor decide whether planned audit evidence for tests of details of balances should be low, medium, or high for each balance-related audit objective

**Negative confirmation**—a letter, addressed to the debtor, requesting a response only if the recipient disagrees with the amount of the stated account balance

**Positive confirmation**—a letter, addressed to the debtor, requesting that the recipient indicate directly on the letter whether the stated account balance is correct or incorrect and, if incorrect, by what amount

**Realizable value of accounts receivable**—the amount of the outstanding balances in accounts receivable that will ultimately be collected

**Timing difference in an accounts receivable confirmation**—a reported difference in a confirmation from a debtor that is determined to be a timing difference between the client's and debtor's records and therefore not a misstatement

## REVIEW QUESTIONS

**13-1 (Objective 13-1)** Distinguish among tests of details of balances, tests of controls, and substantive tests of transactions for the sales and collection cycle. Explain how the tests of controls and substantive tests of transactions affect the tests of details of balances.

**13-2 (Objective 13-1)** Cynthia Roberts, CPA, expresses the following viewpoint: "I do not believe in performing tests of controls and substantive tests of transactions for the sales and collection cycle. As an alternative I send a lot of negative confirmations on every audit at an interim date. If I find a lot of misstatements, I analyze them to determine their cause. If internal controls are inadequate, I send positive confirmations at year-end to evaluate the amount of misstatements. If the negative confirmations result in minimal misstatements, which is often the case, I have found that the internal controls are effective without bothering to perform tests of controls and substantive tests of transactions, and the AICPA's confirmation requirement has been satisfied at the same time. In my opinion the best test of internal controls is to go directly to third parties." Evaluate her point of view.

**13-3 (Objective 13-3)** List five analytical procedures for the sales and collection cycle. For each test, describe a misstatement that could be identified.

**13-4 (Objectives 13-2, 13-4)** Identify the nine accounts receivable balance-related audit objectives. For each objective, list one audit procedure.

**13-5 (Objectives 13-2, 13-4)** Which of the nine accounts receivable balance-related audit objectives can be partially satisfied by confirmations with customers?

**13-6 (Objective 13-4)** State the purpose of footing the total column in the client's trial balance, tracing individual customer names and amounts to the accounts receivable master file, and tracing the total to the general ledger. Is it necessary to trace each amount to the master file? Why?

**13-7 (Objective 13-4)** Distinguish between accuracy tests of gross accounts receivable and tests of the realizable value of receivables.

**13-8 (Objective 13-4)** Explain why you agree or disagree with the following statement: "In most audits it is more important to test carefully the cutoff for sales than for cash receipts." Describe how you perform each type of test, assuming the existence of prenumbered documents.

**13-9 (Objective 13-5)** Evaluate the following statement: "In many audits in which accounts receivable is material, the requirement of confirming customer balances is a waste of time and would not be performed by competent auditors if it were not required by the AICPA. When internal controls are excellent and there are a large number of small receivables from customers who do not recognize the function of confirmation, it is a meaningless procedure. Examples include well-run utilities and department stores. In these situations, tests of controls and substantive tests of transactions are far more effective than confirmations."

**13-10 (Objective 13-5)** Distinguish between a positive and a negative confirmation and state the circumstances in which each should be used. Why do CPA firms frequently use a combination of positive and negative confirmations on the same audit?

**13-11 (Objective 13-5)** Under what circumstances is it acceptable to confirm accounts receivable prior to the balance sheet date?

**13-12 (Objective 13-5)** State the most important factors affecting the sample size in confirmations of accounts receivable.

**13-13 (Objective 13-5)** In Chapter 12, one of the points brought out was the need to obtain a representative sample of the population. How can this concept be reconciled with the statement in this chapter that the emphasis should be on confirming larger and older balances, since these are most likely to contain misstatements?

**13-14 (Objective 13-5)** Define what is meant by "alternative procedures" and explain their purpose. Which alternative procedures are the most reliable? Why?

**13-15 (Objective 13-5)** Explain why the analysis of differences is important in the confirmation of accounts receivable, even if the misstatements in the sample are not material.

**13-16 (Objective 13-5)** State three types of differences that might be observed in the confirmation of accounts receivable that do not constitute misstatements. For each, state an audit procedure that would verify the difference.

**13-17 (Objective 13-1)** What is the relationship of each of the following to the sales and collection cycle: flowcharts, assessing control risk, tests of controls, and tests of details of balances?

## MULTIPLE CHOICE QUESTIONS FROM CPA EXAMINATIONS

**13-18 (Objective 13-3)** The following questions concern analytical procedures in the sales and collection cycle. Choose the best response.

a. As a result of analytical procedures, the independent auditor determines that the gross profit percentage has declined from 30 percent in the preceding year to 20 percent in the current year. The auditor should
   (1) express a qualified opinion due to inability of the client company to continue as a going concern.
   (2) evaluate management's performance in causing this decline.
   (3) require footnote disclosure.
   (4) consider the possibility of a misstatement in the financial statements.

b. Once a CPA has determined that accounts receivable have increased due to slow collections in a "tight money" environment, the CPA would be likely to
   (1) increase the balance in the allowance for bad debt account.
   (2) review the going concern ramifications.
   (3) review the credit and collection policy.
   (4) expand tests of collectibility.

c. In connection with his review of key ratios, the CPA notes that Pyzi had accounts receivable equal to 30 days' sales at December 31, 1996, and to 45 days' sales at December 31, 1997. Assuming that there had been no changes in economic conditions, clientele, or sales mix, this change most likely would indicate
   (1) a steady increase in sales in 1997.
   (2) an easing of credit policies in 1997.
   (3) a decrease in accounts receivable relative to sales in 1997.
   (4) a steady decrease in sales in 1997.

**13-19 (Objective 13-5)** The following questions deal with confirmation of accounts receivable. Choose the best response.

a. In connection with his audit of the Beke Supply Company for the year ended August 31, 1996, Derek Lowe, CPA, has mailed accounts receivable confirmations to three groups as follows:

| Group Number | Type of Customer | Type of Confirmation |
|---|---|---|
| 1 | Wholesale | Positive |
| 2 | Current retail | Negative |
| 3 | Past-due retail | Positive |

The confirmation responses from each group vary from 10 percent to 90 percent. The most likely response percentages are:
(1) Group 1—90 percent, Group 2—50 percent, Group 3—10 percent
(2) Group 1—90 percent, Group 2—10 percent, Group 3—50 percent
(3) Group 1—50 percent, Group 2—90 percent, Group 3—10 percent
(4) Group 1—10 percent, Group 2—50 percent, Group 3—90 percent

b. The negative form of accounts receivable confirmation request is useful *except* when
(1) internal control surrounding accounts receivable is considered to be effective.
(2) a large number of small balances are involved.
(3) the auditor has reason to believe the persons receiving the requests are likely to give them consideration.
(4) individual account balances are relatively large.

c. Which of the following is the best argument against the use of negative confirmations of accounts receivable?
(1) The cost per response is excessively high.
(2) There is *no* way of knowing if the intended recipients received them.
(3) Recipients are likely to feel that the confirmation is a subtle request for payment.
(4) The inference drawn from receiving no reply may *not* be correct.

d. The return of a positive confirmation of accounts receivable without an exception attests to the
(1) collectibility of the receivable balance.
(2) accuracy of the receivable balance.
(3) accuracy of the aging of accounts receivable.
(4) accuracy of the allowance for uncollectible accounts.

## DISCUSSION QUESTIONS AND PROBLEMS

**13-20 (Objectives 13-2, 13-4)** The following are common tests of details of balances for the audit of accounts receivable.

1. Obtain a list of aged accounts receivable, foot the list, and trace the total to the general ledger.
2. Trace thirty-five accounts to the accounts receivable master file for name, amount, and age categories.
3. Examine and document cash receipts on accounts receivable for 20 days after the engagement date.
4. Request twenty-five positive and sixty-five negative confirmations of accounts receivable.
5. Perform alternative procedures on accounts not responding to second requests by examining subsequent cash receipts documentation and shipping reports or sales invoices.
6. Test the sales cutoff by tracing entries in the sales journal for 15 days before and after engagement date to shipping documents, if available, and/or sales invoices.
7. Determine and disclose accounts pledged, discounted, sold, assigned, or guaranteed by others.
8. Evaluate the materiality of credit balances in the aged trial balance.

## Required

For each audit procedure, identify the balance-related audit objective or objectives it partially or fully satisfies.

13-21 (**Objectives 13-2, 13-4**) The following misstatements are sometimes found in the sales and collection cycle's account balances:

1. Cash received from collections of accounts receivable in the subsequent period is recorded as current period receipts.
2. The allowance for uncollectible accounts is inadequate due to the client's failure to reflect depressed economic conditions in the allowance.
3. Several accounts receivable are in dispute due to claims of defective merchandise.
4. The pledging of accounts receivable to the bank for a loan is not disclosed in the financial statements.
5. Goods shipped and included in the current period sales were returned in the subsequent period.
6. Several accounts receivable in the accounts receivable master file are not included in the aged trial balance.
7. One account receivable in the accounts receivable master file is included on the aged trial balance twice.
8. Long-term interest-bearing notes receivable from affiliated companies are included in accounts receivable.
9. The trial balance total does not equal the amount in the general ledger.

## Required

a. For each misstatement, identify the balance-related audit objective to which it pertains.

b. For each misstatement, list an internal control that should prevent it.

c. For each misstatement, list one test of details of balances audit procedure that the auditor can use to detect it.

13-22 (**Objectives 13-2, 13-4**) The following are audit procedures in the sales and collection cycle.

1. Examine a sample of shipping documents to determine if each has a sales invoice number included on it.
2. Discuss with the sales manager whether any sales allowances have been granted after the balance sheet date that may apply to the current period.
3. Add the columns on the aged trial balance and compare the total with the general ledger.
4. Observe whether the controller makes an independent comparison of the total in the general ledger with the trial balance of accounts receivable.
5. For the month of May, count the approximate number of shipping documents filed in the shipping department, and compare the total with the number of sales transactions in the sales journal.
6. Compare the date on a sample of shipping documents throughout the year with related duplicate sales invoices and the accounts receivable master file.
7. Examine a sample of customer orders and see if each has a credit authorization.
8. Send letters directly to former customers whose accounts have been charged off as uncollectible to determine if any have actually been paid.
9. Examine the master file of accounts receivable to see if each has an indication of *C* for a regular customer, *N* for interest-bearing receivables, and *R* for related parties.
10. Compare the date on a sample of shipping documents a few days before and after the balance sheet date with related sales journal transactions.
11. Compute the ratio of allowance for uncollectible accounts divided by accounts receivable and compare with previous years.
12. Examine a sample of noncash credits in the accounts receivable master file to determine if the internal auditor has initialed each indicating internal verification.

## Required

a. For each procedure, identify the applicable type of audit evidence.

b. For each procedure, identify which of the following it is:
   (1) Test of control
   (2) Substantive test of transactions
   (3) Analytical procedure
   (4) Test of details of balances

c. For those procedures you identified as a test of control or substantive test of transactions, what transaction-related audit objective or objectives are being satisfied?

d. For those procedures you identified as a test of details of balances, what balance-related audit objective or objectives are being satisfied?

**13-23 (Objectives 13-2, 13-4)** The following are the nine balance-related audit objectives, seven tests of details of balances for accounts receivable, and seven tests of controls or substantive tests of transactions for the sales and collection cycle.

**Balance-related audit objective**

Detail tie-in
Existence
Completeness
Accuracy
Classification
Cutoff
Realizable value
Rights
Presentation and disclosure

**Test of details of balances, test of control, or substantive test of transactions audit procedure**

1. Confirm accounts receivable.
2. Review sales returns after the balance sheet date to determine if any are applicable to the current year.
3. Compare dates on shipping documents and the sales journal throughout the year.
4. Perform alternative procedures for nonresponses to confirmation.
5. Examine sales transactions for related party or employee sales recorded as regular sales.
6. Examine duplicate sales invoices for consignment sales and other shipments for which title has not passed.
7. Trace a sample of accounts from the accounts receivable master file to the aged trial balance.
8. Trace recorded sales transactions to shipping documents to determine if a document exists.
9. Examine the financial statements to determine if all related parties, notes, and pledged receivables are properly presented.
10. Examine duplicate sales invoices for initials that indicate internal verification of extensions and footings.
11. Trace a sample of shipping documents to related sales invoice entries in the sales journal.
12. Compare amounts and dates on the aged trial balance and accounts receivable master file.
13. Trace from the sales journal to the accounts receivable master file to make sure the information is the same.
14. Inquire of management whether there are notes from related parties included with trade receivables.

## Required

a. Identify which procedures are tests of details of balances, which are tests of controls, and which are substantive tests of transactions.

b. Identify one test of details and one test of control or substantive test of transactions that will partially satisfy each balance-related audit objective. (Tests of controls and substantive tests of transactions are not used for presentation and disclosure.) Each procedure must be used at least once.

**13-24 (Objective 13-4)** Niosoki Auto Parts sells new parts for foreign automobiles to auto dealers. Company policy requires that a prenumbered shipping document be issued for each sale. At the time of pickup or shipment, the shipping clerk writes the date on the shipping document. The last shipment made in the fiscal year ended August 31, 1997, was recorded on document 2167. Shipments are billed in the order that the billing clerk receives the shipping documents.

For late August and early September, shipping documents are billed on sales invoices as follows:

| Shipping Document No. | Sales Invoice No. |
|---|---|
| 2163 | 4332 |
| 2164 | 4326 |
| 2165 | 4327 |
| 2166 | 4330 |
| 2167 | 4331 |
| 2168 | 4328 |
| 2169 | 4329 |
| 2170 | 4333 |
| 2171 | 4335 |
| 2172 | 4334 |

The August and September sales journals have the following information included:

SALES JOURNAL—AUGUST 1997

| Day of Month | Sales Invoice No. | Amount of Sale |
|---|---|---|
| 30 | 4326 | $ 726.11 |
| 30 | 4329 | 1,914.30 |
| 31 | 4327 | 419.83 |
| 31 | 4328 | 620.22 |
| 31 | 4330 | 47.74 |

SALES JOURNAL—SEPTEMBER 1997

| Day of Month | Sales Invoice No. | Amount of Sale |
|---|---|---|
| 1 | 4332 | $2,641.31 |
| 1 | 4331 | 106.39 |
| 1 | 4333 | 852.06 |
| 2 | 4335 | 1,250.50 |
| 2 | 4334 | 646.58 |

## Required

a. What are the generally accepted accounting principles requirements for a correct sales cutoff?

b. Which sales invoices, if any, are recorded in the wrong accounting period, assuming a periodic inventory? Prepare an adjusting entry to correct the financial statement for the year ended August 31, 1997.

c. Assume that the shipping clerk accidentally wrote August 31 on shipping documents 2168 through 2172. Explain how that would affect the correctness of the financial statements. How would you, as an auditor, discover that error?

d. Describe, in general terms, the audit procedures you would follow in making sure that cutoff for sales is accurate at the balance sheet date.

e. Identify internal controls that would reduce the likelihood of cutoff misstatements. How would you test each control?

**13-25 (Objective 13-5)** Dodge, CPA, is auditing the financial statements of a manufacturing company with a significant amount of trade accounts receivable. Dodge is satisfied that the accounts are properly summarized and classified and that allocations, reclassifications, and valuations are made in accordance with generally accepted accounting principles. Dodge is planning to use accounts receivable confirmation requests to satisfy the third standard of field work as to trade accounts receivable.

## Required

a. Identify and describe the two forms of accounts receivable confirmation requests and indicate what factors Dodge will consider in determining when to use each.

b. Assume that Dodge has received a satisfactory response to the confirmation requests. Describe how Dodge could evaluate collectibility of the trade accounts receivable.

c. What are the implications to a CPA if during his or her audit of accounts receivable some of a client's trade customers do not respond to a request for positive confirmation of their accounts?

d. What auditing steps should a CPA perform if there is no response to a second request for a positive confirmation?*

**13-26 (Objective 13-5)** You have been assigned to the confirmation of aged accounts receivable for the Blank Paper Company audit. You have tested the aged trial balance and selected the accounts for confirming. Before the confirmation requests are mailed, the controller asks to look at the accounts you intend to confirm to determine whether he will permit you to send them.

He reviews the list and informs you that he does not want you to confirm six of the accounts on your list. Two of them are credit balances, one is a zero balance, two of the other three have a fairly small balance, and the remaining balance is highly material. The reason he gives is that he feels the confirmations will upset these customers, because "they are kind of hard to get along with." He does not want the credit balances confirmed because it may encourage the customer to ask for a refund.

In addition, the controller asks you to send an additional twenty confirmations to customers he has listed for you. He does this as a means of credit collection for "those stupid idiots who won't know the difference between a CPA and a credit collection agency."

## Required

a. Is it acceptable for the controller to review the list of accounts you intend to confirm? Discuss.

b. Discuss the appropriateness of sending the twenty additional confirmations to the customers.

*AICPA adapted.

c. Assuming that the auditor complies with all the controller's requests, what is the effect on the auditor's opinion?

**13-27 (Objective 13-5)** You have been assigned to the first audit of the Chicago Company for the year ending March 31, 1997. Accounts receivable were confirmed on December 31, 1996 and at that date the receivables consisted of approximately two hundred accounts with balances totaling $956,750. Seventy-five of these accounts with balances totaling $650,725 were selected for confirmation. All but twenty of the confirmation requests have been returned; thirty were signed without comments, fourteen had minor differences which have been cleared satisfactorily, while eleven confirmations had the following comments:

1. We are sorry, but we cannot answer your request for confirmation of our account as the PDQ Company uses an accounts payable voucher system.
2. The balance of $1,050 was paid on December 23, 1996.
3. The balance of $7,750 was paid on January 5, 1997.
4. The balance noted above has been paid.
5. We do not owe you anything at December 31, 1996, as the goods, represented by your invoice dated December 30, 1996, number 25,050, in the amount of $11,550, were received on January 5, 1997, on FOB destination terms.
6. An advance payment of $2,500 made by us in November 1996 should cover the two invoices totaling $1,350 shown on the statement attached.
7. We never received these goods.
8. We are contesting the propriety of this $12,525 charge. We think the charge is excessive.
9. Amount okay. As the goods have been shipped to us on consignment, we will remit payment upon selling the goods.
10. The $10,000, representing a deposit under a lease, will be applied against the rent due to us during 1998, the last year of the lease.
11. Your credit memo dated December 5, 1996, in the amount of $440 cancels the balance above.

## Required

What steps would you take to satisfactorily clear each of the preceding eleven comments?*

**13-28 (Objectives 13-3, 13-4, 13-5, 13-6)** You have audited the financial statements of the Heft Company for several years. Internal controls for accounts receivable are satisfactory. The Heft Company is on a calendar-year basis. An interim audit, which included confirmation of the accounts receivable, was performed on August 31 and indicated that the accounting for cash, sales, sales returns and allowances, and receivables was reliable.

The company's sales are principally to manufacturing concerns. There are about 1,500 active trade accounts receivable of which about 35 percent represent 65 percent of the total dollar amount. The accounts receivable are maintained alphabetically in a master file of accounts receivable.

Shipping document data are keyed into a computerized system that simultaneously produces a sales invoice, sales journal, and an updated accounts receivable master file.

All cash receipts are in the form of customers' checks. Information for cash receipts is obtained from the remittance advice portions of the customers' checks. The computer operator compares the remittance advices with the list of checks that was prepared by another person when the mail was received. As for sales, a cash receipts journal and updated accounts receivable master file are simultaneously prepared after the cash receipts information is entered.

Summary totals are produced monthly by the computer operations department for updating the general ledger master file accounts such as cash, sales, and accounts receivable. An aged trial balance is prepared monthly.

## Required

Prepare the additional audit procedures necessary for testing the balances in the sales and collection cycle. (Ignore bad debts and allowance for uncollectible accounts.)*

*AICPA adapted.

**13-29 (Objective 13-5)** In the confirmation of accounts receivable for the Reliable Service Company, eighty-five positive and no negative confirmations were mailed to customers. This represents 35 percent of the dollar balance of the total accounts receivable. Second requests were sent for all nonresponses, but there were still ten customers who did not respond. The decision was made to perform alternative procedures on the ten unanswered confirmation requests. An assistant is requested to conduct the alternative procedures and report to the senior auditor after he has completed his tests on two accounts. He prepared the following information for the working papers:

1. Confirmation request no. 9
   Customer name—Jolene Milling Co.
   Balance—$3,621 at December 31, 1996

| | |
|---|---|
| Subsequent cash receipts per the accounts receivable master file | January 15, 1997—$1,837 |
| | January 29, 1997—$1,263 |
| | February 6, 1997—$1,429 |

2. Confirmation request no. 26
   Customer name—Rosenthal Repair Service
   Balance—$2,500 at December 31, 1996

| | |
|---|---|
| Subsequent cash receipts per the accounts receivable master file | February 9, 1997—$500 |
| Sales invoices per the accounts receivable master file (I examined the duplicate invoice) | September 1, 1996—$4,200 |

## Required

a. If you were called upon to evaluate the adequacy of the sample size, the type of confirmation used, and the percentage of accounts confirmed, what additional information would you need?

b. Discuss the need to send second requests and perform alternative procedures for nonresponses.

c. Evaluate the adequacy of the alternative procedures used for verifying the two nonresponses.

## CASE

**13-30 (Objectives 13-1, 13-2, 13-4, 13-5, 13-6)** You are auditing the sales and collection cycle for the Smalltown Regional Hospital, a small not-for-profit hospital. The hospital has a reputation for excellent medical services and weak record keeping. The medical people have a tradition of doing all aspects of their job correctly, but due to a shortage of accounting personnel, there is not time for internal verification or careful performance. In previous years your CPA firm has found quite a few misstatements in billings, cash receipts, and accounts receivable. As in all hospitals, the two largest assets are accounts receivable and property, plant, and equipment.

The hospital has several large loans payable to local banks, and the two banks have told management that they are reluctant to extend more credit, especially considering the modern hospital that is being built in a nearby city. In the past, county taxes have made up deficits, but in the past year, the county has also been incurring deficits because of high unemployment.

In previous years, your response from patients to confirmation requests has been frustrating at best. The response rate has been extremely low, and those who did respond did not know the purpose of the confirmations or their correct outstanding balance. You have had the same experience in confirming receivables at other hospitals.

You conclude that control over cash is excellent and the likelihood of fraud is extremely small. You are less confident about unintentional errors in billing, recording sales, cash receipts, accounts receivable, and bad debts.

## Required

a. Identify the major factors affecting acceptable audit risk for this audit.

b. What inherent risks are you concerned about?

c. In this audit of the sales and collection cycle, which types of tests are you likely to emphasize?

d. For each of the following, explain whether you plan to emphasize the tests and give reasons.
   (1) Tests of controls
   (2) Substantive tests of transactions
   (3) Analytical procedures
   (4) Tests of details of balances

# INTEGRATED CASE APPLICATION

13-31 (Objectives 13-3, 13-4, 13-5, 13-6) **ABC AUDIT—PART IV** Parts I (pp. 326–328), II (pp. 401–402), and III (pp. 442–443) of this case study dealt with obtaining an understanding of internal control and assessing control risk for transactions affecting accounts payable of ABC Company. In Part IV, we begin the audit of the accounts payable balance itself by addressing analytical procedures.

Assume that your understanding of internal controls over acquisitions and cash disbursements and the related tests of controls and substantive tests of transactions support an assessment of a low control risk. Also assume that analytical procedures support the overall reasonableness of the balance. Accounts payable at December 31, 1997 are included in Figure 13-8.

## Required

a. List those relationships, ratios, and trends that you believe will provide useful information about the overall reasonableness of accounts payable.

b. Prepare an audit program in a design format for tests of details of balances for accounts payable. Before preparing the audit program, you should review the Hillsburg Hardware Case Illustration starting on page 462. You should prepare a matrix similar to the one in Figure 13-7 on page 464 for accounts payable. Assume that assessed control risk is low for all transaction-related audit objectives and analytical procedures results were satisfactory for those balance-related audit objectives where analytical procedures are relevant. The design format audit program should include audit procedures and sample size for each procedure.

c. Prepare an audit program for accounts payable in a performance format, using the audit procedures and sample sizes from part b.

d. Assume for requirement b that (1) assessed control risk had been high rather than low for each transaction-related audit objective, (2) inherent risk was high for each balance-related audit objective, and (3) analytical procedures indicated a high potential for misstatement. What would the effect have been on the audit procedures and sample sizes for part b?

e. Figure 13-9 (pages 478–479) presents six replies to the request for information from 20 vendors specified in Figure 13-10 (page 480). These are the replies for which follow-up indicates a difference between the vendor's balance and the company's records. The auditor's follow-up findings are indicated on each reply. Calculate the estimated misstatement in accounts payable based on the misstatements in accounts payable confirmation and other relevant information provided in this case. Be sure to consider likely misstatements in accounts payable not confirmed and sampling error. Prepare a worksheet similar to the one illustrated in Figure 13-11 on page 481 to aid in your analysis. The exception for Fiberchem is analyzed as an illustration. Assume that ABC took a complete physical inventory at December 31, 1997, and the auditor concluded that recorded inventory reflects all inventory on hand at the balance sheet date.

Use a computer with appropriate software to prepare this worksheet and analysis (instructor option).

f. Based on the confirmation responses and your analysis in requirement e, what are your conclusions about the fairness of the recorded balance in accounts payable for ABC Company and your assessments of control risk as low for all transaction-related audit objectives?

**FIGURE 13-8**

**ABC Company Trial Balance of Trade Accounts Payable December 31, 1997**

| | | | |
|---|---|---|---|
| Advent Sign Mfg. Co. | $ 2,500.00 | M & A Milling | 4,662.00 |
| Alder Insurance Co. | 660.00 | Midwest Electric Utility | 3,698.15 |
| American Computing Service | 1,211.00 | Midwest Gas Co. | 2,442.10 |
| Bauer and Adamson | 86.00 | Mobil Oil Co. | 11,480.00 |
| Bleyl & Sons | 1,500.00 | Monsanto Chemical | 14,622.15 |
| Central Steel Inc. | 8,753.00 | Nielsen Enterprises | 437.56 |
| Chelsea Development Co. | 1,800.00 | Norris Industries | 9,120.00 |
| Commercial Supply | 3,250.00 | Pacific Title Co. | 320.00 |
| Country Electric | 980.00 | Permaloy Manufacturing | 3,290.00 |
| Diamond Janitorial Service | 750.00 | Polein Drill and Bit | 2,870.16 |
| Dictaphone Corp. | 675.00 | Propec Inc. | 510.00 |
| Douglas Equipment | 6,425.00 | Rayno Sales and Service | 1,917.80 |
| Ellison, Robt. & Assoc. | 346.10 | Reames Construction | 4,500.00 |
| FMC Corp. | 15,819.00 | Remington Supply Co. | 9,842.10 |
| Fiberchem Inc. | 6,315.80 | Ritter Engineering Corp. | 1,200.00 |
| Fuller Travel | 943.00 | Roberts Bros. Service | 189.73 |
| GAFCO | 5,750.00 | S & S Truck Painting | 819.00 |
| Glade Specialties | 1,000.00 | Sanders, Geo. A. & Co. | 346.00 |
| Granger Supply Co. | 4,250.00 | Semco, Inc. | 50.20 |
| Hesco Services | 719.62 | Standard Oil Co. | 12,816.27 |
| Innes, Brush & Co. CPAs | 1,500.00 | Stationery Supply | 619.12 |
| J & L Plastics Corp. | 1,412.00 | Thermal Tape Co. | 123.00 |
| Judkins Co. | 2,500.00 | Todd Machinery, Inc. | 6,888.12 |
| Kazco. Mfg. Co. | 1,627.30 | Valco Sales | 1,429.00 |
| Kedman Company | 19.27 | Vermax Corp. | 284.00 |
| Koch Plumbing Contractors | 2,750.00 | Waco Electronics, Inc. | 126.33 |
| Kohler Products | 10,483.23 | Western Telephone Co. | 2,369.62 |
| Lakeshore Inc. | 1,850.00 | Williams Controls, Inc. | 1,915.00 |
| Landscape Services | 420.00 | Xerox Corp. | 3,250.00 |
| Lundberg Coatings, Inc. | 2,733.10 | Yates Supply Co. | 919.70 |
| | | Total | $192,085.53 |

Other related information:

- The vendors with the greatest volume of transactions during the year are:

| | |
|---|---|
| Central Steel Inc. | Mobil Oil Co. |
| Commercial Supply | Monsanto Chemical |
| FMC Corp. | Norris Industries |
| Fiberchem Inc. | Remington Supply Co. |
| GAFCO | Standard Oil Co. |

- Based on preliminary results, tolerable misstatement for accounts payable is $7,500.00.

**FIGURE 13-9**

**Replies to Requests for Information**

STATEMENT FROM FIBERCHEM

ABC Company
Midvale, IL

Amounts due as of December 31, 1997:

| Invoice No. | Date | Amount | Balance Due |
|---|---|---|---|
| 8312 | 11-22-97 | 2,217.92 | 2,217.92 |
| 8469 | 12-02-97 | 2,540.11 | 4,758.03 |
| 8819 | 12-18-97 | 1,557.77 | 6,315.80(1) |
| 9002 | 12-30-97 | 2,403.42(2) | 8,719.22 |

Auditor's notes:
(1) Agrees with accounts payable listing.
(2) Goods received December 31, 1997. Due to New Year's Eve shut-down, recorded on January 2, 1998.

STATEMENT FROM MOBIL OIL

ABC Company
Midvale, IL

Amounts due as of December 31, 1997:

| Invoice No. | Date | Amount | Balance Due |
|---|---|---|---|
| DX10037 | 12-02-97 | 2,870.00 | 2,870.00 |
| DX11926 | 12-09-97 | 2,870.00 | 5,740.00 |
| DX12619 | 12-16-97 | 2,870.00 | 8,610.00 |
| DX14777 | 12-23-97 | 2,870.00 | 11,480.00(1) |
| DX16908 | 12-30-97 | 2,870.00(2) | 14,350.00 |

Auditor's notes:
(1) Agrees with accounts payable listing.
(2) Goods shipped FOB ABC Company. Arrived on January 3, 1998.

STATEMENT FROM NORRIS INDUSTRIES

ABC Company
Midvale, IL

Amounts due as of December 31, 1997:

| Invoice No. | Date | Amount | Balance Due |
|---|---|---|---|
| 14896 | 12-27-97 | 9,120.00 | 9,120.00(1) |
| 15111 | 12-27-97 | 4,300.00(2) | 13,420.00 |

Auditor's notes:
(1) Agrees with accounts payable listing.
(2) Goods shipped FOB Norris Industries' plant on December 21, 1997, arrived at ABC Company on January 4, 1998.

*[continued]*

**FIGURE 13-9**

**Replies to Requests for information** *[continued]*

STATEMENT FROM REMINGTON SUPPLY

ABC Company
Midvale, IL

Amounts due as of December 31, 1997:

| Invoice No. | Date | Amount | Balance Due |
|---|---|---|---|
| 141702 | 11-11-97 | 3,712.09(2) | 3,712.09 |
| 142619 | 11-19-97 | 1,984.80(1) | 5,696.89 |
| 142811 | 12-04-97 | 2,320.00(2) | 8,016.89 |
| 143600 | 12-21-97 | 3,810.01(2) | 11,826.90 |
| 143918 | 12-26-97 | 3,707.00(3) | 15,533.90 |

Auditor's notes:
(1) Paid by ABC Company on December 28, 1997. Payment in transit at year-end.
(2) The total of these items of $9,842.10 agrees with accounts payable listing.
(3) Goods shipped FOB Remington Supply on December 26, 1997, arrived at ABC Company on January 3, 1998.

STATEMENT FROM ADVENT SIGN MFG. CO.

ABC Company
Midvale, IL

Amounts due as of December 31, 1997:

| | |
|---|---|
| First progress billing per contract | $2,500.00(1) |
| Second progress billing per contract | 1,500.00(2) |
| Total due | $4,000.00 |

Auditor's notes:
(1) Agrees with accounts payable listing.
(2) Progress payment due as of December 31, 1997, per contract for construction of new custom electric sign. Sign installed on January 15, 1998.

STATEMENT FROM FULLER TRAVEL

ABC Company
Midvale, IL

Amounts due as of December 31, 1997:

| Ticket No. | Date | Amount | Balance Due |
|---|---|---|---|
| 843 601 102 | 12-04-97 | 280.00(2) | 280.00 |
| 843 601 819 | 12-12-97 | 280.00(2) | 560.00 |
| 843 602 222 | 12-21-97 | 383.00(1) | 943.00 |
| 843 602 919 | 12-26-97 | 383.00(2) | 1,326.00 |

Auditor's notes:
(1) Ticket not used and returned for credit. Credit given on January 1998 statement.
(2) The total of these items of $943.00 agrees with accounts payable listing.

**FIGURE 13-10**

**ABC Company Sample of Accounts Payable Selection for Confirmation—December 31, 1997**

| | | |
|---|---|---|
| **High-Volume Items** | | |
| 1. | Central Steel | $ 8,753.00 |
| 2. | Commercial Supply | 3,250.00 |
| 3. | FMC | 15,819.00 |
| 4. | Fiberchem | 6,315.80 |
| 5. | GAFCO | 5,750.00 |
| 6. | Mobil Oil | 11,480.00 |
| 7. | Monsanto | 14,622.15 |
| 8. | Norris Industries | 9,120.00 |
| 9. | Remington Supply | 9,842.10 |
| 10. | Standard Oil | 12,816.27 |
| **Other Material Items** | | |
| 11. | Kohler Products | 10,483.23 |
| **Random Sample of Additional Items** | | |
| 12. | Advent Sign Mfg. Co. | 2,500.00 |
| 13. | Country Electric | 980.00 |
| 14. | Fuller Travel | 943.00 |
| 15. | J & L Plastics | 1,412.00 |
| 16. | M & A Milling | 4,662.00 |
| 17. | Permaloy Manufacturing | 3,290.00 |
| 18. | S & S Truck Painting | 819.00 |
| 19. | Todd Machinery | 6,888.12 |
| 20. | Western Telephone Co. | 2,369.62 |
| | TOTAL TESTED | $132,115.29 |

**FIGURE 13-11**

**ABC Company Analysis of Trade Accounts Payable—December 31, 1997**

| Vendor | Balance per Books | Amount Confirmed by Vendor | Difference: Books Over(Under) Amount Confirmed | Timing Difference: No Misstatement | Misstatement in Accounts Payable DR (CR) | Misstatement in Related Accounts: Balance Sheet Misstatement DR (CR) | Misstatement in Related Accounts: Income Statement Misstatement DR (CR) | Brief Explanation |
|---|---|---|---|---|---|---|---|---|
| Fiberchem | 6,315.80 | 8,719.22 | (2,403.42) | | (2,403.42) | | 2,403.42 | Unrecorded A/P: Dr Purchases Cr A/P |
| | | | | | | | | |
| | | | | | | | | |
| | | | | | | | | |
| | | | | | | | | |
| | | | | | | | | |
| | | | | | | | | |
| | | | | | | | | |
| | | | | | | | | |
| | | | | | | | | |
| | | | | | | | | |

# 14

# AUDIT SAMPLING FOR TESTS OF DETAILS OF BALANCES

## LEARNING OBJECTIVES

Thorough study of this chapter will enable you to

**14-1** Distinguish between audit sampling for tests of details of balances and for tests of controls and substantive tests of transactions.

**14-2** Apply nonstatistical sampling to tests of details of balances.

**14-3** Define and apply monetary unit sampling.

**14-4** Define and describe variables sampling.

**14-5** Apply difference estimation to tests of details of balances.

## BOTH STATISTICAL AND NONSTATISTICAL SAMPLING ARE ACCEPTABLE UNDER GAAS, BUT WHICHEVER IS USED, IT MUST BE DONE RIGHT

Bob Lake was the manager on the audit of Images, Inc., a specialty retailer that had shops around the Midwest and was expanding into Texas and Arizona. Images appealed to upscale working women and offered its own credit card featuring a number of advantages over VISA and MasterCard. Images' accounting was done centrally. Transactions were captured on-line and sales and accounts receivable files were maintained on a database in St. Louis.

Bob Lake's firm encouraged the use of statistical sampling in its practice, and provided a training program for the development of a statistical coordinator for each office. The coordinator in St. Louis, Bob's office, was Barbara Ennis. Bob believed that sales transactions and accounts receivable confirmation tests should be done using statistical sampling, and asked Barbara to help design and oversee the statistical aspects of this testing.

Barbara developed a program for the design of the sales tests and confirmation procedures that included determining sample sizes. She left the program with Bob to carry out, and said that she would be available to help evaluate the results after the tests were performed. Bob expected that the sales tests would be done relatively soon, but it would be at least two months from the time Barbara provided the program until the confirmation procedures would be completed.

Tests of controls and substantive tests of transactions for sales indicated that there were no exceptions in the sample. Bob reported this to Barbara, and she indicated that the evaluation was very straightforward. The objectives of the tests were met and no additional work was needed. She also stated that the planned confirmation procedures, including sample size, were still appropriate.

When all the confirmation replies were received or alternative procedures were completed several weeks later, Bob called Barbara to do the statistical evaluation. Much to his dismay, he found out that Barbara had left the firm, and worse, there was no statistically-trained person to take her place. When he consulted the engagement partner about this turn of events, he was told to simply "convert the statistical tests into a nonstatistical one." Bob did this by calculating the average misstatement percentage in the confirmation sample and multiplying it by the population total. The amount was large, but not material, so Bob concluded the objectives of the confirmation tests had been met.

The next year Images, Inc.'s earnings declined sharply, partially because of large write-offs of accounts receivable. The stock price dropped sharply and a class action suit was filed, naming Bob's firm among the defendants. An outside expert was brought in to review the audit work papers. The expert calculated a confidence interval of possible misstatements with the confirmation sample results that Bob had evaluated nonstatistically. Although it could be argued that the point estimate, corresponding to Bob's estimate, was not material, the upper limit of the interval was significantly above any reasonable materiality level. Bob's firm settled the suit for $3.5 million.

Both statistical and nonstatistical audit sampling are used extensively for tests of details of balances. Deciding which one to use depends primarily on the auditor's preference, experience, and knowledge about statistical sampling. Audit sampling in the audit of accounts receivable is used as the frame of reference for discussing audit sampling for tests of details of balances in this chapter, but audit sampling is also used for auditing many other accounts. Figure 14-1 shows how audit sampling is related to the types of audit tests.

**FIGURE 14-1**

**How Audit Sampling Is Related to the Types of Audit Tests**

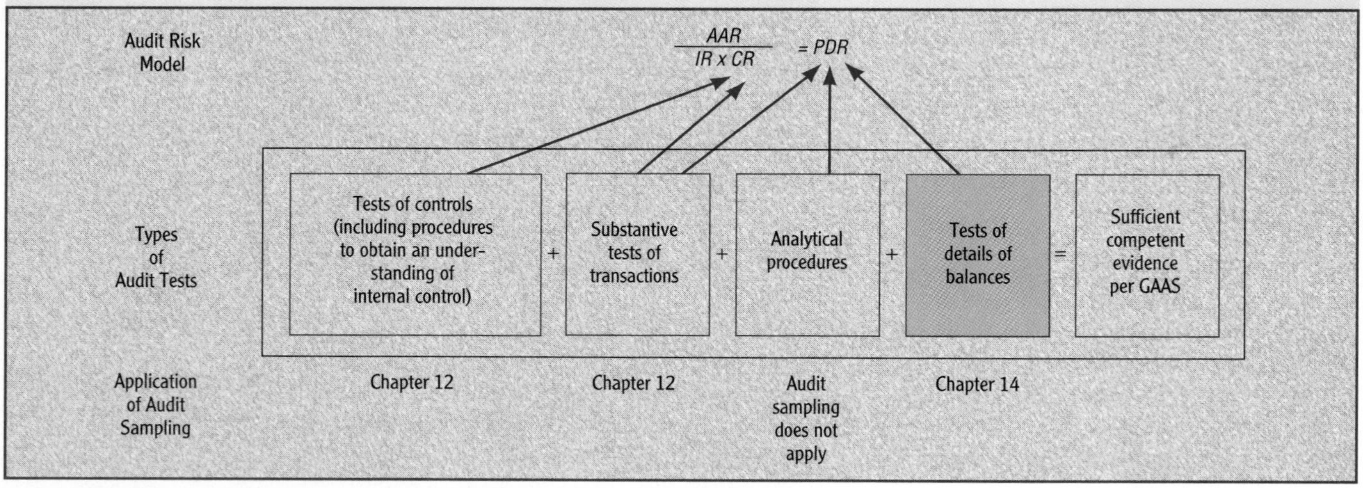


Chapter 14 is directly related to Chapters 11, 12, and 13 in that the auditor must have already decided tolerable misstatement, acceptable audit risk, inherent risk, and control risk; performed and evaluated tests of controls and substantive tests of transactions; and done analytical procedures before applying audit sampling to tests of details of balances. Stated differently, before applying audit sampling to accounts receivable, the auditor will have completed all parts of the methodology for designing tests of details of balances for accounts receivable in Figure 13-2 on page 447 except deciding sample size and items to select.

## COMPARISONS OF AUDIT SAMPLING FOR TESTS OF DETAILS OF BALANCES AND FOR TESTS OF CONTROLS AND SUBSTANTIVE TESTS OF TRANSACTIONS

**OBJECTIVE 14-1**

**Distinguish between audit sampling for tests of details of balances and for tests of controls and substantive tests of transactions.**

Most of the sampling concepts discussed in Chapter 12 for tests of controls and substantive tests of transactions apply equally to sampling for tests of details of balances. In both cases, the auditor wants to make inferences about the entire population based on a sample. Both sampling and nonsampling risks are therefore important for tests of controls, substantive tests of transactions, and tests of details of balances. In dealing with sampling risk, it is acceptable to use either nonstatistical or statistical methods for all three types of tests.

The most important differences among tests of controls, substantive tests of transactions, and tests of details of balances is in what the auditor wants to measure. In tests of controls, the concern is testing the effectiveness of internal controls using tests of controls. When an auditor performs tests of controls, the purpose is to determine if the exception rate in the population is sufficiently low to justify reducing assessed control risk to reduce substantive tests. In substantive tests of transactions, the auditor is concerned about both the effectiveness of controls and the monetary correctness of transactions in the accounting system. In tests of details of balances, the concern is determining whether the dollar amount of an account balance is materially misstated. Tests for the rate of occurrence, therefore, are seldom useful for tests of details of balances. Instead, auditors use sampling methods that provide results in *dollar* terms. There are three primary types of sampling methods used for calculating dollar misstatements in auditing: *nonstatistical sampling, monetary unit sampling,* and *variables sampling.* Each of these is examined in this chapter, starting with nonstatistical sampling.

## NONSTATISTICAL SAMPLING

**OBJECTIVE 14-2**
**Apply nonstatistical sampling to tests of details of balances.**

For both nonstatistical and statistical sampling in tests of details of balances, the fourteen steps discussed in Chapter 12 for tests of controls and substantive tests of transactions still apply. Understanding the similarities and differences in the application of audit sampling for tests of details of balances compared to those for tests of controls and substantive tests of transactions is essential. The following fourteen steps are involved, with the steps for tests of controls and substantive tests of transactions included in the right column for comparison:

| STEPS—AUDIT SAMPLING FOR TESTS OF DETAILS OF BALANCES | STEPS—AUDIT SAMPLING FOR TESTS OF CONTROLS AND SUBSTANTIVE TESTS OF TRANSACTIONS (see pages 412–413) |
|---|---|
| *Plan the Sample* | *Plan the Sample* |
| 1. State the objectives of the audit test. | 1. State the objectives of the audit test. |
| 2. Decide if audit sampling applies. | 2. Decide if audit sampling applies. |
| 3. Define misstatement conditions. | 3. Define attributes and exception conditions. |
| 4. Define the population. | 4. Define the population. |
| 5. Define the sampling unit. | 5. Define the sampling unit. |
| 6. Specify tolerable misstatement. | 6. Specify tolerable exception rate. |
| 7. Specify acceptable risk of incorrect acceptance. | 7. Specify acceptable risk of assessing control risk too low. |
| 8. Estimate misstatements in the population. | 8. Estimate the population exception rate. |
| 9. Determine the initial sample size. | 9. Determine the initial sample size. |
| *Select the Sample and Perform the Audit Procedures* | *Select the Sample and Perform the Audit Procedures* |
| 10. Select the sample. | 10. Select the sample. |
| 11. Perform the audit procedures. | 11. Perform the audit procedures. |
| *Evaluate the Results* | *Evaluate the Results* |
| 12. Generalize from the sample to the population. | 12. Generalize from the sample to the population. |
| 13. Analyze the misstatements. | 13. Analyze the exceptions. |
| 14. Decide the acceptability of the population. | 14. Decide the acceptability of the population. |

### State the Objectives of the Audit Test

When auditors sample for tests of details of balances, the objective is to determine whether the account balance being audited is fairly stated. To illustrate the nature of the sampling problem, a simple example is used. For Problem 14-27 on pages 519–520, a listing of forty accounts receivable totaling $207,295 is shown. The objective of the audit test will be to determine whether the total of $207,295 is materially misstated. Typically, materially misstated is defined in terms of tolerable misstatement.

**Decide if Audit Sampling Applies**

As stated in Chapter 12, "Audit sampling applies whenever the auditor plans to reach conclusions about a population based on a sample." While it is common to sample in many accounts, there are situations when sampling does not apply. For the population in Problem 14-27 on page 520, the auditor may decide to audit only items over $5,000 and ignore all others because the total of the smaller ones is immaterial. In this case, the auditor has not sampled. Similarly, if the auditor is verifying fixed asset additions and there are many small additions and one extremely large purchase of a building, the auditor may decide to ignore the small items entirely. Again the auditor has not sampled.

**Define Misstatement Conditions**

Audit sampling for tests of details of balances measures monetary misstatements in the population. Thus, the misstatement conditions are any conditions that represent a monetary misstatement in a sample item. In auditing accounts receivable, any client misstatement in a sample item is a misstatement.

**Define the Population**

The population is defined as the *recorded dollar population.* The auditor then evaluates whether the recorded population is overstated or understated. For example, the population of accounts receivable on page 520 consists of forty accounts totaling $207,295. Most accounting populations subject to audit would, of course, contain far more items totaling a much larger dollar amount.

**Stratified Sampling** For many populations, auditors subdivide the population into two or more subpopulations before applying audit sampling. Subdividing populations is called *stratified sampling,* where each subpopulation is a stratum. The purpose of stratification is to permit the auditor to emphasize certain population items and de-emphasize others. In most audit sampling situations, including confirming accounts receivable, auditors want to emphasize the larger recorded dollar values; therefore, stratification is typically done on the basis of the size of recorded dollar values.

Examining the population in Problem 14-27, there are different ways to stratify the population. Assume that the auditor decided to stratify as follows:

| Stratum | Stratum Criteria | Number in Population | Dollars in Population |
|---|---|---|---|
| 1 | >$10,000 | 3 | $ 88,955 |
| 2 | $ 5,000–$10,000 | 10 | 71,235 |
| 3 | < 5,000 | 27 | 47,105 |
| | | 40 | $207,295 |

**Define the Sampling Unit**

The sampling unit for nonstatistical audit sampling in tests of details of balances is almost always the item making up the account balance. For accounts receivable, it is usually the customer account name or number on the accounts receivable list.

**Specify Tolerable Misstatement**

Tolerable misstatement as it was discussed in Chapter 8 is used for determining sample size and evaluating results in nonstatistical sampling. The auditor starts with a preliminary judgment about materiality and uses that total in deciding tolerable misstatement for each account.

**Specify Acceptable Risk of Incorrect Acceptance**

For all statistical and nonstatistical sampling applications, there is a risk that the quantitative conclusions about the population will be incorrect. This is always true unless 100 percent of the population is tested.

Acceptable risk of incorrect acceptance (ARIA) is the risk that the auditor is willing to take of accepting a balance as correct when the true misstatement in the balance is greater than tolerable misstatement. ARIA is the equivalent term to acceptable risk of assessing control risk too low (ARACR) for tests of controls.

There is an inverse relationship between ARIA and required sample size. If, for example, the auditor decides to reduce ARIA from 10 percent to 5 percent, the required sample size would increase.

The primary factor affecting the auditor's decision about ARIA is assessed control risk in the audit risk model. When internal controls are effective, control risk can be reduced, permitting the auditor to increase ARIA. This, in turn, reduces the sample size required for the test of details of the related account balance.

A difficulty students often have is understanding how ARACR and ARIA affect evidence accumulation. In Chapter 10 it was shown that tests of details of balances for monetary misstatements can be reduced if internal controls are found to be effective through assessing control risk and performing tests of controls. The effects of ARACR and ARIA are consistent with that conclusion. If the auditor concludes that internal controls may be effective, control risk can be reduced. A lower control risk requires a lower ARACR in testing the controls, which in turn requires a larger sample size. If controls are found to be effective, control risk can remain low, which permits the auditor to increase ARIA (through use of the audit risk model), thereby requiring a smaller sample size in the related substantive tests of details of balances. The relationship between ARACR and ARIA is shown in Figure 14-2.

**FIGURE 14-2**

**Effect of ARACR and ARIA on Required Evidence**

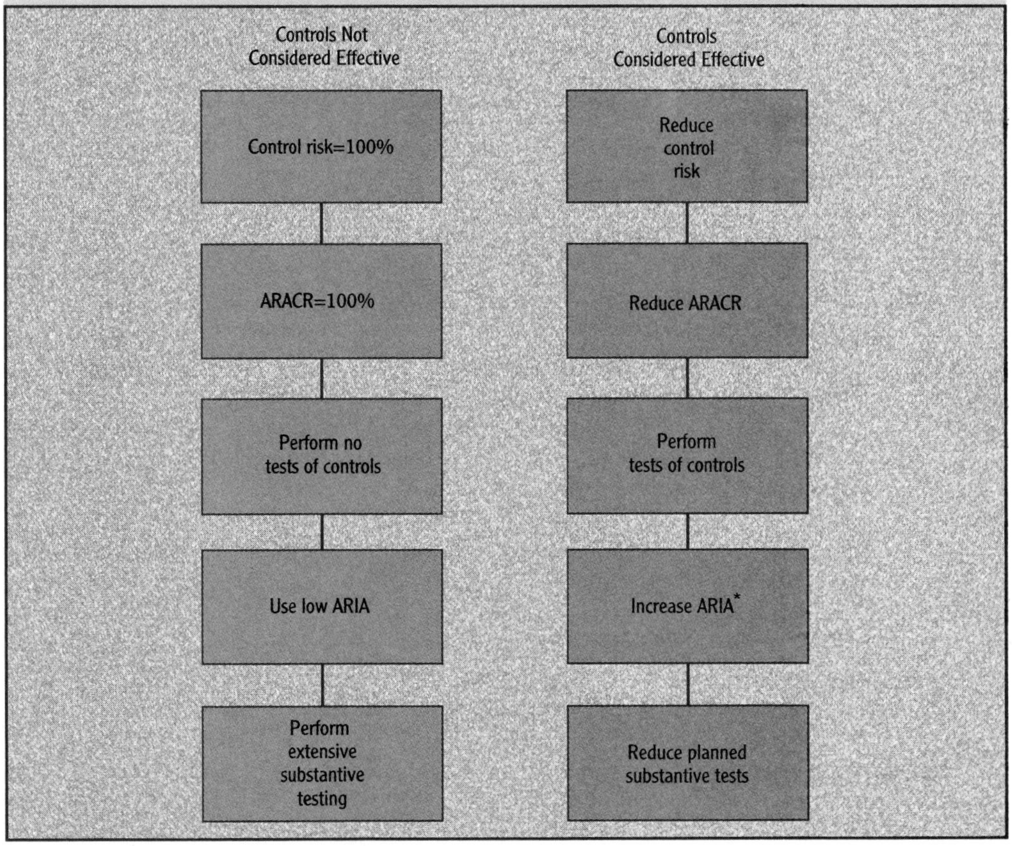


*Assumes tests of control results were satisfactory, which permits control risk to remain low.

Besides control risk, ARIA is also directly affected by acceptable audit risk and inversely by other substantive tests already performed or planned for the account balance. For example, if acceptable audit risk is reduced, ARIA should also be reduced. If analytical procedures were performed and indicate that the account balance is fairly stated, ARIA should be increased. Stated differently, the analytical procedures are evidence in support of the account balance; therefore, less evidence from the detailed test using sampling is required to achieve acceptable audit risk. The same conclusion is appropriate for the relationship among substantive tests of transactions, ARIA, and sample size for tests of details of balances. The various relationships affecting ARIA are summarized in Figure 14-3.

**FIGURE 14-3**

**Relationship among Factors Affecting ARIA, Effect on ARIA, and Required Sample Size for Audit Sampling**

| Factor Affecting ARIA | Example | Effect on ARIA | Effect on Sample Size |
|---|---|---|---|
| Effectiveness of internal controls (control risk) | Internal controls are effective (reduced control risk) | Increase | Decrease |
| Substantive tests of transactions | No exceptions were found in substantive tests of transactions | Increase | Decrease |
| Acceptable audit risk | Likelihood of bankruptcy is low (increased acceptable audit risk) | Increase | Decrease |
| Analytical procedures | Analytical procedures performed with no indications of likely misstatements | Increase | Decrease |

### Estimate Misstatements in the Population

The auditor typically makes this estimate based on prior experience with the client and by assessing inherent risk, considering the results of tests of controls, substantive tests of transactions, and analytical procedures already performed.

### Determine the Initial Sample Size

Auditors using nonstatistical sampling determine the initial sample size judgmentally considering the factors discussed so far. Figure 14-4 summarizes the primary factors that influence sample size for nonstatistical sampling and how sample size is affected.

When the auditor uses stratified sampling, the sample size must be allocated among the strata. Typically, auditors allocate a higher portion of the sample items to larger population items. For example, in the example from Problem 14-27, allocating a sample size of fifteen, the auditor might decide to select all three accounts from stratum one, and six each from strata two and three. Observe that audit sampling does not apply to stratum one because all population items are being audited.

### Select the Sample

For nonstatistical sampling, auditing standards permit the auditor to use any of the selection methods discussed in Chapter 12. It is important for the auditor to use a method that will permit meaningful conclusions about the sample results.

For stratified sampling, the auditor selects samples independently from each stratum. For example, in stratum three in the previous example, the auditor will select six sample items from the twenty-seven population items in that stratum.

### Perform the Audit Procedures

To perform the audit procedures, the auditor applies the appropriate audit procedures to each item in the sample to determine whether it is correct or contains a misstatement. For example, in the confirmation of accounts receivable the auditor will mail the sample of confirmations in the manner described in Chapter 13 and determine the amount of mis-

**FIGURE 14-4**

**Factors Influencing Sample Sizes for Tests of Details of Balances**

| Factor | Conditions Leading to Smaller Sample Size | Conditions Leading to Larger Sample Size |
|---|---|---|
| a. **Control risk (ARACR).** Affects acceptable risk of incorrect acceptance. | Low control risk. | High control risk. |
| b. **Results of other substantive tests related to the same assertion** (including analytical procedures and other relevant substantive tests). Affects acceptable risk of incorrect acceptance. | Satisfactory results in other related substantive tests. | Unsatisfactory results in other related substantive tests. |
| c. **Acceptable audit risk.** Affects acceptable risk of incorrect acceptance. | High acceptable audit risk. | Low acceptable audit risk. |
| d. **Tolerable misstatement for a specific account.** | Larger tolerable misstatement. | Smaller tolerable misstatement. |
| e. **Inherent risk.** Affects estimated misstatements in the population. | Low inherent risk. | High inherent risk. |
| f. **Expected size and frequency of misstatements.** Affects estimated misstatements in the population. | Smaller misstatements or lower frequency. | Larger misstatements or higher frequency. |
| g. **Number of items in the population.** | Almost no effect on sample size unless population is very small. | Almost no effect on sample size unless population is very small. |

statement in each account confirmed. For nonresponses, alternative procedures will be used to determine the misstatements. The auditor cannot expect meaningful results from using audit sampling unless the audit procedures are applied carefully.

Assume that the auditor sends first and second requests for confirmations and performs alternative procedures in the previous example. Assume also that the following conclusions are reached about the sample after reconciling all timing differences:

| | | Dollars Audited | | |
|---|---|---|---|---|
| **Stratum** | **Sample Size** | **Recorded Value** | **Audited Value** | **Client Misstatement** |
| 1 | 3 | $ 88,955 | $ 91,695 | $(2,740) |
| 2 | 6 | 43,995 | 43,024 | 971 |
| 3 | 6 | 13,105 | 10,947 | 2,158 |
| | 15 | $146,055 | $145,666 | $ 389 |

### Generalize from the Sample to the Population and Decide the Acceptablility of the Population

The auditor must generalize from the sample to the population by (1) projecting misstatements from the sample results to the population, and (2) considering sampling error and sampling risk (ARIA). For example, in the previous example does the auditor conclude that accounts receivable is overstated by $389? No, the auditor is interested in the *population* results, not those for the sample. It is therefore necessary to project from the sample to the population to estimate the population misstatement. The first step is to make a *point estimate* which was first shown on page 254 in Chapter 8. There are different ways to calculate the point estimate, but a common way is to assume that misstatements in the unaudited population are proportional to the misstatements in the sample. That calculation must be done for each stratum and then totaled, rather than from the total misstatements in the sample. Thus, the point estimate of the misstatement from the preceding example is determined by using a weighted-average method, as shown on the following page.

| Stratum | Client Misstatement ÷ Recorded Value of the Sample | × | Recorded Book Value for the Stratum | = | Point Estimate of Misstatement |
|---|---|---|---|---|---|
| 1 | $(2,740)/$88,955 | | $88,955 | | $(2,740) |
| 2 | $ 971 /$43,995 | | 71,235 | | 1,572 |
| 3 | $ 2,158 /$13,105 | | 47,105 | | 7,757 |
| Total | | | | | $ 6,589 |

The point estimate of the misstatement in the population is $6,589, indicating an overstatement. The point estimate, by itself, is not an adequate measure of the population misstatement, however, because of sampling error. In other words, because the estimate is based on a sample, it will be close to the true population misstatement, but it is unlikely that it is exactly the same. The auditor must consider the possibility that the true population misstatement is greater than the amount of misstatement that is tolerable in the circumstances whenever the point estimate is less than the tolerable misstatement amount. This must be done for both statistical and nonstatistical samples.

An auditor using nonstatistical sampling cannot formally measure sampling error and therefore must subjectively consider the possibility that the true population misstatement exceeds a tolerable amount. This is done by considering (1) the difference between the point estimate and tolerable misstatement, (2) the extent to which items in the population have been audited 100 percent, (3) whether misstatements tend to be offsetting or in only one direction, (4) the amounts of individual misstatements, and (5) sample size. To continue the example, suppose that tolerable misstatement is $40,000. In that case, the auditor may conclude that there is little chance, given the point estimate of $6,589, that the true population misstatement exceeds the tolerable amount.

Suppose that tolerable misstatement is $12,000, only $5,411 greater than the point estimate. In that case, other factors would be considered. For example, if the larger items in the population were audited 100 percent (as was done here), any unidentified misstatements would be restricted to smaller items. If the misstatements tend to be offsetting and are relatively small in size, the auditor may conclude that the true population misstatement is likely to be less than the tolerable amount. Also, the larger the sample size, the more confident the auditor can be that the point estimate is close to the true population value. Therefore, the auditor would be more willing to accept that the true population misstatement is less than tolerable misstatement in this example where the sample size is considered large, than where it is considered moderate or small. On the other hand, if one or more of these other conditions is different, the chance of a misstatement in excess of the tolerable amount may be judged to be high, and the recorded population unacceptable.

Even if the amount of likely misstatement is not considered material, the auditor must wait to make a final evaluation until the entire audit is completed. For example, the estimated total misstatement and estimated sampling error in accounts receivable must be combined with estimates of misstatements in all other parts of the audit to evaluate the effect of all misstatements on the financial statements as a whole.

### Analyze the Misstatements

As for sampling for tests of controls and substantive tests of transactions, an evaluation of the nature and cause of each misstatement found is essential. For example, in confirming accounts receivable, suppose that all misstatements resulted from the client's failure to record returned goods. The auditor would determine why that type of misstatement occurred so often, the implications of the misstatements on other audit areas, the potential impact on the financial statements, and its effect on company operations.

An important part of misstatement analysis is deciding whether any modification of the audit risk model is needed. If the auditor concluded that the failure to record the returns discussed in the previous paragraph resulted from a breakdown of internal controls, it might be necessary to reassess control risk. That in turn would probably cause the auditor to reduce ARIA, which would increase planned sample size. As discussed in Chapter 8, revisions of the audit risk model must be done with extreme care because the model is intended primarily for planning, not evaluating results.

## Action When a Population Is Rejected

When the auditor concludes that the misstatement in a population may be larger than tolerable misstatement after considering sampling error, the population is not considered acceptable. There are several possible courses of action.

**Take No Action Until Tests of Other Audit Areas Are Completed** Ultimately the auditor must evaluate whether the financial statements taken as a whole are materially misstated. If offsetting misstatements are found in other parts of the audit, such as in inventory, the auditor may conclude that the estimated misstatements in accounts receivable are acceptable. Of course, before the audit is finalized the auditor must evaluate whether a misstatement in one account may make the financial statements misleading even if there are offsetting misstatements.

**Perform Expanded Audit Tests in Specific Areas** If an analysis of the misstatements indicates that most of the misstatements are of a specific type, it may be desirable to restrict the additional audit effort to the problem area. For example, if an analysis of the misstatements in confirmations indicates that most of the misstatements result from failure to record sales returns, an extended search could be made of returned goods to make sure that they have been recorded. However, great care must be taken to evaluate the cause of all misstatements in the sample before a conclusion is reached about the proper emphasis in the expanded tests. There may be more than one problem area.

When a problem area is analyzed and corrected by adjusting the client's records, the sample items that led to isolating the problem area can then be shown as "correct." The point estimate can now be recalculated without the misstatements that have been "corrected." Sampling error and the acceptability of the population will also have to be reconsidered with the new facts.

**Increase the Sample Size** When the auditor increases the sample size, sampling error is reduced if the rate of misstatements in the expanded sample, their dollar amount, and their direction are similar to those in the original sample. Increasing the sample size, therefore, may satisfy the auditor's tolerable misstatement requirements.

Increasing the sample size enough to satisfy the auditor's tolerable misstatement standards is often costly, especially when the difference between tolerable misstatement and projected misstatement is small. Even if the sample size is increased, there is no assurance of a satisfactory result. If the number, amount, and direction of the misstatements in the extended sample are proportionately greater or more variable than in the original sample, the results are still likely to be unacceptable.

For tests such as accounts receivable confirmation and inventory observation, it is often difficult to increase the sample size, because of the practical problem of "reopening" those procedures once the initial work is done. By the time the auditor discovers that the sample was not large enough, several weeks have usually passed.

Despite these difficulties, sometimes the auditor must increase the sample size after the original testing is completed. It is much more common to increase sample size in audit areas other than confirmations and inventory observation, but it is occasionally necessary to do so even for these two areas. Where stratified sampling is used, increased samples usually focus on the strata containing larger amounts, unless misstatements appear to be concentrated in some other strata.

**Adjust the Account Balance** When the auditor concludes that an account balance is materially misstated, the client may be willing to adjust the book value based on the sample results. In the previous example, assume the client is willing to reduce book value by the amount of the point estimate ($6,589) to adjust for the estimate of the misstatement. The auditor's estimate of the misstatement is now zero, but it is still necessary to consider sampling error. Again, assuming a tolerable misstatement of $12,000, the auditor must now assess whether sampling error exceeds $12,000, not the $5,411 originally considered. If the auditor believes sampling error is $12,000 or less, accounts receivable is acceptable after the adjustment. If the auditor believes it is more than $12,000, adjusting the account balance is not a practical option.

**Request the Client to Correct the Population** In some cases the client's records are so inadequate that a correction of the entire population is required before the audit can be completed. For example, in accounts receivable, the client may be asked to prepare the aging schedule again if the auditor concludes that it has significant misstatements. Whenever the client changes the valuation of some items in the population, it is of course necessary to audit the results again.

**Refuse to Give an Unqualified Opinion** If the auditor believes that the recorded amount in an account is not fairly stated, it is necessary to follow at least one of the above alternatives or to qualify the audit report in an appropriate manner. If the auditor believes that there is a reasonable chance that the financial statements are materially misstated, it would be a serious breach of auditing standards to issue an unqualified opinion.

## MONETARY UNIT SAMPLING

**OBJECTIVE 14-3**
**Define and apply monetary unit sampling.**

Monetary unit sampling (MUS) is a recent innovation in statistical sampling methodology that was developed specifically for use by auditors. It is now the most commonly used statistical method of sampling for tests of details of balances. This is because it has the statistical simplicity of attributes sampling yet provides a statistical result expressed in dollars (or another appropriate currency). MUS is also referred to as *dollar unit sampling, cumulative monetary amount sampling,* and *sampling with probability proportional to size.*[1]

### Differences Between MUS and Nonstatistical Sampling

There are far more similarities than differences in using MUS and nonstatistical sampling. All fourteen of the steps must also be performed for MUS even though some are done differently. This section focuses on the differences between MUS and nonstatistical sampling and assumes that you understand the material on nonstatistical sampling in this chapter.

The following summarizes the most important differences between MUS and nonstatistical sampling. The remainder of this section discusses MUS and deals more extensively with the most important differences.

1. *The definition of the sampling unit is an individual dollar.* A critical feature of MUS is the definition of the sampling unit as an individual dollar in an account balance. The name of the statistical method, monetary unit sampling, results from this distinctive feature. For example, in the population on page 520, the sampling unit is 1 dollar and the population size is 207,295 dollars, not the 40 physical units discussed earlier.

The result of the individual dollar being the sampling unit for MUS is its automatic emphasis on physical units with larger recorded balances. Since the sample is selected on the basis of individual dollars, an account with a large balance has a greater chance of being included than an account with a small balance. For example, in accounts receivable confirmation, an account with a $5,000 balance has a 10 times greater probability of selection than one with a $500 balance, as it contains 10 times as many dollar units. As a result, there is no need to use stratified sampling with MUS. Stratification occurs automatically.

[1] The currency in many countries will be called something other than "dollars." Thus, in Mexico, for instance, one might use "Peso Unit Sampling." This is why the more universal term, *monetary* unit sampling, has been adopted. We recognize the appropriateness of this term in this text, but also refer to dollars as the sampling unit in most cases.

*2. The population size is the recorded dollar population.* For example, the population of accounts receivable on page 520 consists of 207,295 dollars which is the population size, not the 40 physical units. This definition of population size is consistent with the use of dollar units.

Because of the method of sample selection in MUS, which is discussed later, it is not possible to evaluate the likelihood of unrecorded items in the population. Assume, for example, that MUS is used to evaluate whether inventory is fairly stated. It is not possible to use MUS to evaluate whether certain inventory items exist but have not been counted. If the completeness objective is important in the audit test, and it usually is, that objective must be satisfied separately from the MUS tests.

*3. Preliminary judgment of materiality is used for each account instead of tolerable misstatement.* Another unique aspect of MUS is the use of the preliminary judgment about materiality, as discussed in Chapter 8, to directly determine the tolerable misstatement amount for the audit of each account. Other sampling techniques require the auditor to determine tolerable misstatement for each account by allocating the preliminary judgment about materiality, as illustrated on page 253. This is not required when MUS is used. For example, assume that the auditor decides that the preliminary judgment about materiality should be $60,000 for the financial statements as a whole. That materiality amount of $60,000, or a derivative of it, as discussed below, would be used as tolerable misstatement in all applications of MUS—inventory, accounts receivable, accounts payable, and so forth.

*4. Sample size is determined using a statistical formula.* The information used and the calculation of the planned sample size are shown later.

*5. A formal decision rule is used for deciding the acceptability of the population.* The decision rule used for MUS is similar to that used for nonstatistical sampling, but it is sufficiently different to merit discussion. The decision rule will be illustrated after the calculation of the misstatement bounds is shown.

*6. Sample selection is done using PPS.* Monetary unit samples are samples selected with probability proportional to size (PPS). Such samples are samples of individual dollars in the population. Auditors cannot, however, audit individual dollars. Therefore, the auditor must determine the physical unit to perform the audits tests. For example, in Table 14-1 on page 494 the auditor will take a random sample of population items between 1 and 7,376 (individual dollars). However, to perform the audit procedures, the auditor must identify the population items between 1 and 12 (physical units). If the auditor selected the random number 3014, the physical unit associated with that number is 6.

PPS samples can be obtained by using computer software, random number tables, or systematic sampling techniques. An illustration of an accounts receivable population, including cumulative totals, is provided in Table 14-1 to demonstrate using a random number table.

Assume that the auditor wants to select a PPS sample of four accounts from the population in Table 14-1. Since the sampling unit is defined as an individual dollar, the population size is 7,376, and four digits are needed from a random number table or computer program. Using the first four digits in the random number table, Table 12-2 on page 409, with a starting point of row 1002, column 4, the usable random numbers are 6,586, 1,756, 850, and 6,499. The population physical unit items that contain these random dollars are determined by reference to the cumulative total column. They are items 11 (containing dollars 6,577 through 6,980), 4 (dollars 1,699 through 2,271), 2 (dollars 358 through 1,638), and 10 (dollars 5,751 through 6,576). These will be audited, and the result for each physical unit will be applied to the random dollar it contains.

The statistical methods used to evaluate monetary unit samples permit the inclusion of a physical unit in the sample more than once. That is, in the previous example, if the random numbers had been 6,586, 1,756, 856, and 6,599, the sample items would be 11, 4, 2, and 11. Item 11 would be audited once, but would be treated as two sample items statistically, and the sample total would be four items because four monetary units were involved.

**TABLE 14-1**

**Accounts Receivable Population**

| Population Item (Physical Unit) | Recorded Amount | Cumulative Total (Dollar Unit) |
|---|---|---|
| 1 | $ 357 | $ 357 |
| 2 | 1,281 | 1,638 |
| 3 | 60 | 1,698 |
| 4 | 573 | 2,271 |
| 5 | 691 | 2,962 |
| 6 | 143 | 3,105 |
| 7 | 1,425 | 4,530 |
| 8 | 278 | 4,808 |
| 9 | 942 | 5,750 |
| 10 | 826 | 6,576 |
| 11 | 404 | 6,980 |
| 12 | 396 | 7,376 |

One problem using PPS selection is that population items with a zero recorded balance have no chance of being selected with PPS sample selection even though they could contain misstatements. Similarly, small balances that are significantly understated have little chance of being included in the sample. This problem can be overcome by doing specific audit tests for zero- and small-balance items, assuming that they are of concern.

Another problem is the inability to include negative balances, such as credit balances in accounts receivable, in the PPS (monetary unit) sample. It is possible to ignore negative balances for PPS selection and test those amounts by some other means. An alternative is to treat them as positive balances and add them to the total number of monetary units being tested; however, this complicates the evaluation process.

*7. The auditor generalizes from the sample to the population using MUS techniques.* Regardless of the sampling method selected, the auditor must generalize from the sample to the population by (1) projecting misstatements from the sample results to the population, and (2) determining the related sampling error. There are four important aspects in doing this using MUS:

- Attributes sampling tables are used to calculate the results. Tables such as the one on page 425 can be used, replacing ARACR with ARIA.
- The attributes results must be converted to dollars. MUS estimates the dollar misstatement in the population, not the percent of items in the population that are misstated. MUS accomplishes this by defining each population item as an individual dollar. Therefore, estimating the rate of population dollars that contain a misstatement is a way of estimating the total dollar misstatement.
- The auditor must make an assumption about the percentage of misstatement for each population item that is misstated. This assumption enables the auditor to use the attributes sampling tables to estimate dollar misstatements.
- The statistical results when MUS is used are referred to as misstatement bounds. These misstatement bounds are estimates of the likely maximum overstatement (upper misstatement bound) and likely maximum understatement (lower misstate-

ment bound) at a given ARIA. Both an *upper misstatement bound* and *lower misstatement bound* are calculated.

**Summary** The fourteen steps discussed for nonstatistical sampling are also applicable to monetary unit sampling, but several are applied differently because of the unique nature of MUS. The remainder of the discussion of MUS deals in more detail with generalizing from the sample to the population, a formal decision rule for deciding the acceptability of the population, and calculating the initial sample size using MUS.

## Generalizing from the Sample to the Population When No Misstatements Are Found Using MUS

Suppose that the auditor is confirming a population of accounts receivable for monetary correctness. The population totals $1,200,000, and a sample of 100 confirmations is obtained. Upon audit, no misstatements are uncovered in the sample. The auditor wants to determine the maximum amount of overstatement and understatement amounts that could exist in the population and still provide a sample with no misstatements. These are the upper misstatement bound and the lower misstatement bound, respectively. Assuming an ARIA of 5 percent, and using the attributes sampling table on page 425, both the upper and lower bounds are determined by locating the intersection of the sample size (100) and the actual number of misstatements (0) in the same manner as for attributes sampling. The CUER of 3 percent on the table represents both the upper and lower bound, *expressed as a percent.*

Thus, based on the sample results and the misstatement bounds from the table, the auditor can conclude with a 5 percent sampling risk that no more than 3 percent of the dollar units in the population are misstated. To convert this percent into *dollars,* the auditor must make an assumption about the average percent of misstatement for population dollars that contain a misstatement. This assumption significantly affects the misstatement bounds. To illustrate this, three sets of example assumptions are examined: (1) a 100 percent misstatement assumption for both overstatements and understatements; (2) a 10 percent misstatement assumption for both overstatements and understatements; and (3) a 20 percent misstatement assumption for overstatements and a 200 percent assumption for understatements.

**Assumption 1** Overstatement amounts equal 100 percent; understatement amounts equal 100 percent; misstatement bounds at a 5 percent ARIA are

$$\text{Upper misstatement bound} = \$1,200,000 \times 3\% \times 100\% = \$36,000$$

$$\text{Lower misstatement bound} = \$1,200,000 \times 3\% \times 100\% = \$36,000$$

The assumption is that, on average, those population items that are misstated are misstated by the full dollar amount of the recorded value. Since the misstatement bound is 3 percent, the dollar value of the misstatement is not likely to exceed $36,000 (3 percent of the total recorded dollar units in the population). If all the amounts are overstated, there is an overstatement of $36,000. If they are all understated, there is an understatement of $36,000.

The assumption of 100 percent misstatements is extremely conservative, especially for overstatements. Assume that the actual population exception rate is 3 percent. The following two conditions both have to exist before the $36,000 properly reflects the true overstatement amount:

1. All amounts have to be overstatements. Offsetting amounts would have reduced the amount of the overstatement.
2. All population items misstated have to be 100 percent misstated. There could not, for example, be a misstatement such as a check written for $226 that was recorded at $262. This would be only a 13.7 percent misstatement (262 – 226 = 36 overstatement; 36/262 = 13.7%).

In the calculation of the misstatement bounds of $36,000 overstatement and understatement, the auditor did not calculate a point estimate and precision amount in the manner discussed earlier in the chapter. This is because the tables used include both a point estimate and a precision amount to derive the upper exception rate. Even though the point estimate and precision amount are not calculated for MUS, they are implicit in the determination of misstatement bounds and can be determined from the tables. For example, in this illustration, the point estimate is zero and the statistical precision is $36,000.

**Assumption 2** Overstatement amounts equal 10 percent; understatement amounts equal 10 percent; misstatement bounds at a 5 percent ARIA are

Upper misstatement bound = $1,200,000 × 3% × 10% = $3,600

Lower misstatement bound = $1,200,000 × 3% × 10% = $3,600

The assumption is that, on average, those items that are misstated are misstated by no more than 10 percent. If all items were misstated in one direction, the misstatement bounds would be +$3,600 and –$3,600. The change in assumption from 100 percent to 10 percent misstatements significantly affects the misstatement bounds. The effect is in direct proportion to the magnitude of the change.

**Assumption 3** Overstatement amounts equal 20 percent; understatement amounts equal 200 percent; misstatement bounds at a 5 percent ARIA are

Upper misstatement bound = $1,200,000 × 3% × 20% = $7,200

Lower misstatement bound = $1,200,000 × 3% × 200% = $72,000

The justification for a larger percent for understatements is the potential for a larger misstatement in percentage terms. For example, an accounts receivable recorded at $20 that should have been recorded at $200 is understated by 900 percent [(200 – 20)/20], whereas one that is recorded at $200 that should have been recorded at $20 is overstated by 90 percent [(200 – 20)/200].

Items containing large understatement amounts may have a small recorded value, due to those misstatements. As a consequence, because of the mechanics of MUS, few of them will have a chance of being selected in the sample. Because of this, some auditors select an additional sample of small items to supplement the monetary unit sample whenever understatement amounts are an important audit concern.

**Appropriate Percent of Misstatement Assumption** The appropriate assumption for the overall percent of misstatement in those population items containing a misstatement is an auditor's decision. The auditor must set these percentages based on professional judgment in the circumstances. In the absence of convincing information to the contrary, most auditors believe that it is desirable to assume a 100 percent amount for both overstatements and understatements unless there are misstatements in the sample results. This approach is considered highly conservative, but it is easier to justify than any other assumption. In fact, the reason upper and lower limits are referred to as *misstatement bounds* when MUS is used, rather than maximum likely misstatement or the commonly used statistical term *confidence limit,* is because of widespread use of that conservative assumption. Unless stated otherwise, the 100 percent misstatement assumption is used in the chapter and problem materials.

## Generalizing When Misstatements Are Found

This section presents the evaluation method when there are misstatements in the sample. The same illustration is continued; the only change is the assumption about the misstatements. The sample size remains at 100 and the recorded value is still $1,200,000, but now five misstatements in the sample are assumed. The misstatements are shown in Table 14-2 on the following page.

The four aspects of generalizing from the sample to the population discussed earlier still apply, but their use is modified as follows:

- *Overstatement and understatement amounts are dealt with separately, and then combined.* First, initial upper and lower misstatement bounds are calculated separately for

**TABLE 14-2**
**Misstatements Found**

| Customer No. | Recorded Accounts Receivable Amount | Audited Accounts Receivable Amount | Misstatement | Misstatement ÷ Recorded Amount |
|---|---|---|---|---|
| 2073 | $ 6,200 | $ 6,100 | $ 100 | .016 |
| 5111 | 12,910 | 12,000 | 910 | .07 |
| 5206 | 4,322 | 4,450 | (128) | (.03) |
| 7642 | 23,000 | 22,995 | 5 | .0002 |
| 9816 | 8,947 | 2,947 | 6,000 | .671 |

overstatement and understatement amounts. Next, a point estimate of overstatements and understatements is calculated. The point estimate of understatements is used to reduce the initial upper misstatement bound, and the point estimate of overstatements is used to reduce the initial lower misstatement bound. The method and rationale for these calculations will be illustrated by using the four overstatement and one understatement amounts in Table 14-2.

- *A different misstatement assumption is made for each misstatement, including the zero misstatements.* When there were no misstatements in the sample, an assumption was required as to the average percent of misstatement for the population items misstated. The misstatement bounds were calculated showing several different assumptions. Now that misstatements have been found, sample information is available to use in determining the misstatement bounds. The misstatement assumption is still required, but it can be modified based on this actual misstatement data.

  Where misstatements are found, a 100 percent assumption for all misstatements is not only exceptionally conservative, it is inconsistent with the sample results. A common assumption in practice, and the one followed in this book, is that the actual sample misstatements are representative of the population misstatements. This assumption requires the auditor to calculate the percent that each sample item is misstated (misstatement ÷ recorded amount), and apply that percent to the population. The calculation of the percent for each misstatement is shown in the last column in Table 14-2. As will be explained shortly, a misstatement assumption is still needed for the zero misstatement portion of the computed results. For this example, a 100 percent misstatement assumption is used for the zero misstatement portion for both over– and understatement misstatement bounds.

- *The auditor must deal with layers of the computed upper exception rate (CUER) from the attributes sampling table.* The reason for doing so is that there is a different misstatement assumption for each misstatement. Layers are calculated by first determining the CUER from the table for each misstatement and then calculating each layer. Table 14-3 on page 498 shows the layers in the attributes sampling table for the example at hand. The layers were determined by reading across the table for a sample size of 100, from the 0 through 4 exception columns.
- *Misstatement assumptions must be associated with each layer.* The most common method of associating misstatement assumptions with layers is to be conservative by associating the largest dollar misstatement percents with the largest layers. Table 14-4 on page 498 shows the association. For example, the largest average misstatement was .671 for customer 9816. That misstatement is associated with the layer factor of .017, the largest layer where misstatements were found. The portion of the upper precision limit related to the zero misstatement layer has a misstatement assumption of 100

**TABLE 14-3**

**Percent Misstatement Bounds**

| Number of Misstatements | Upper Precision Limit from Table | Increase in Precision Limit Resulting from Each Misstatement (Layers) |
|---|---|---|
| 0 | .03 | .03 |
| 1 | .047 | .017 |
| 2 | .062 | .015 |
| 3 | .076 | .014 |
| 4 | .089 | .013 |

percent, which is still conservative. Table 14-4 shows the calculation of misstatement bounds before consideration of offsetting amounts. The upper misstatement bound was calculated as if there were no understatement amounts, and the lower misstatement bound was calculated as if there were no overstatement amounts.

**TABLE 14-4**

**Illustration of Calculating Initial Upper and Lower Misstatement Bounds**

| Number of Misstatements | Upper Precision Limit Portion* | Recorded Value | Unit Misstatement Assumption | Misstatement Bound Portion (Columns 2 × 3 × 4) |
|---|---|---|---|---|
| **Overstatements** | | | | |
| 0 | .030 | $1,200,000 | 1.0 | $36,000 |
| 1 | .017 | 1,200,000 | .671 | 13,688 |
| 2 | .015 | 1,200,000 | .07 | 1,260 |
| 3 | .014 | 1,200,000 | .016 | 269 |
| 4 | .013 | 1,200,000 | .0002 | 3 |
| Upper precision limit | .089 | | | |
| Initial misstatement bound | | | | $51,220 |
| **Understatements** | | | | |
| 0 | .030 | $1,200,000 | 1.0 | $36,000 |
| 1 | .017 | 1,200,000 | .03 | 612 |
| Lower precision limit | .047 | | | |
| Initial misstatement bound | | | | $36,612 |

*ARIA of 5%. Sample size of 100.

**Adjustment for Offsetting Amounts** Most MUS users believe that the approach just discussed is overly conservative when there are offsetting amounts. If an understatement amount is found, it is logical and reasonable that the bound for overstatement amounts should be lower than it would be had no understatement amounts been found, and vice versa. The adjustment of bounds for offsetting amounts is made as follows: (1) a point estimate of misstatements is made for both overstatement and understatement amounts and (2) each bound is reduced by the opposite point estimate.

The point estimate for overstatements is calculated by multiplying the average overstatement amount in the dollar units audited times the recorded value. The same approach is used for calculating the point estimate for understatements. In the example there is one understatement amount of 3 cents per dollar unit in a sample of 100. The understatement point estimate is therefore $360 (.03/100 × $1,200,000). Similarly, the overstatement point estimate is $9,086 [(.671 + .07 + .016 + .0002)/100 × $1,200,000].

Table 14-5 shows the adjustment of the bounds that follow from this procedure. The initial upper bound of $51,220 is reduced by the estimated most likely understatement amount of $360 to an adjusted bound of $50,860. The initial lower bound of $36,612 is reduced by the estimated most likely overstatement amount of $9,086 to an adjusted bound of $27,526. Thus, given the methodology and assumptions followed, the auditor concludes that there is a 5 percent risk that accounts receivable is overstated by more than $50,860, or understated by more than $27,526. It should be noted that if the misstatement assumptions are changed, the misstatement bounds will also change. The reader is advised that the method used to adjust the bounds for offsetting amounts is only one of several in current use. The method illustrated here is taken from Leslie, Teitlebaum, and Anderson.[2] All the methods in current use are reliable and somewhat conservative.

**TABLE 14-5**

**Illustration of Calculating Adjusted Misstatement Bounds**

| Number of Misstatements | Unit Misstatement Assumption | Sample Size | Recorded Population | Point Estimate | Bounds |
|---|---|---|---|---|---|
| Initial overstatement bound | | | | | $51,220 |
| Understatement amount | | | | | |
| 1 | .03 | 100 | $1,200,000 | $ 360 | (360) |
| Adjusted overstatement bound | | | | | $50,860 |
| Initial understatement bound | | | | | $36,612 |
| Overstatement amounts | | | | | |
| 1 | .671 | | | | |
| 2 | .07 | | | | |
| 3 | .016 | | | | |
| 4 | .0002 | | | | |
| Sum | .7572 | 100 | $1,200,000 | $9,086 | (9,086) |
| Adjusted understatement bound | | | | | $27,526 |

**Summary** The following seven steps summarize the calculation of the adjusted misstatement bounds for monetary unit sampling when there are offsetting amounts. The calculation of the adjusted upper misstatement bound for the four overstatement amounts in Table 14-2 is used to illustrate.

| *Steps to Calculate Adjusted Misstatement Bounds* | *Calculation for Overstatements in Tables 14-2,14-4, and 14-5* |
|---|---|
| 1. Determine misstatement for each sample item, keeping overstatements and understatements separate. | Table 14-2<br>4 overstatements |

[2]D. A. Leslie, A. D. Teitlebaum, and R. J. Anderson, *Dollar Unit Sampling: A Practical Guide for Auditors,* Toronto, Copp, Clark and Pitman, 1979.

| | |
|---|---|
| 2. Calculate misstatement per dollar unit in each sample item (misstatement/recorded amount). | Table 14-2<br>.016, .07, .0002, .671 |
| 3. Layer misstatements per dollar unit from highest to lowest, including the percent misstatement assumption for sample items not misstated. | Table 14-4<br>1.0, .671, .07, .016, .0002 |
| 4. Determine upper precision limit from attributes sampling table and calculate the percent misstatement bound for each misstatement (layer). | Table 14-4<br>Total of 8.9% for 4 misstatements; calculate 5 layers |
| 5. Calculate initial upper and lower misstatement bounds for each layer and total. | Table 14-4<br>Total of $51,220 |
| 6. Calculate point estimate for overstatements and understatements. | Table 14-5<br>$360 for understatements |
| 7. Calculate adjusted upper and lower misstatement bounds. | Table 14-5<br>$50,860 adjusted overstatement bound |

## Decide the Acceptability of the Population Using MUS

Whenever a statistical method is used, a *decision rule* is needed to decide whether the population is acceptable. The decision rule for MUS is

> If *both* the lower misstatement bound (LMB) and upper misstatement bound (UMB) fall between the understatement and overstatement tolerable misstatement amounts, *accept* the conclusion that the book value is not misstated by a material amount. Otherwise conclude that the book value is misstated by a material amount.

This decision rule is illustrated below: The auditor should conclude that both the LMB and UMB for situations 1 and 2 fall completely within both the understatement and overstatement tolerable misstatement limits. Therefore, the conclusion that the population is not misstated by a material amount is accepted. For situations 3, 4, and 5, either LMB or UMB, or both, are outside tolerable misstatements. Therefore, the population book value is rejected.

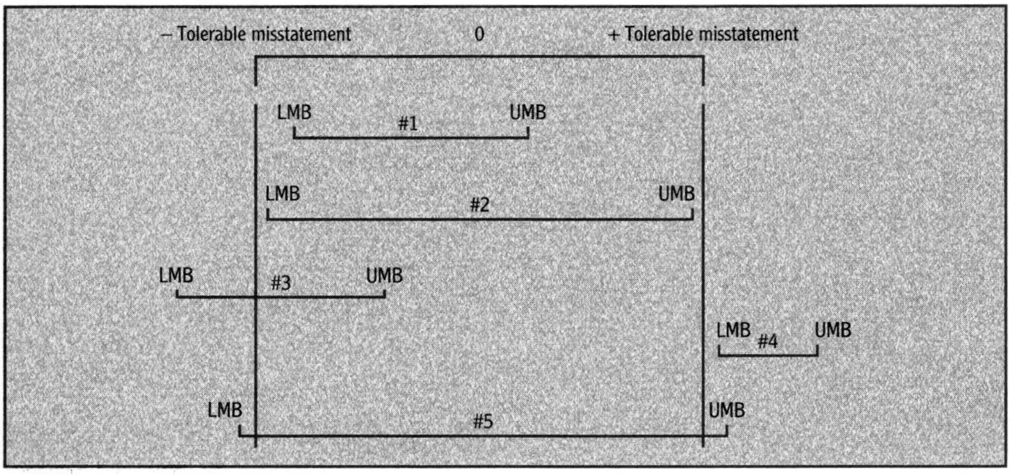

Assume in the example being used that the auditor had set a tolerable misstatement amount for accounts receivable of $40,000 (overstatement or understatement). That means the auditor will accept the recorded value if he or she concludes that accounts receivable is not overstated or understated by more than $40,000. As was previously shown, the auditor selected a sample of 100 items, found 5 misstatements, and calculated the lower bound to be $27,526 and the upper bound to be $50,860. Application of the decision rule leads the auditor to the conclusion that the population should not be accepted because the upper misstatement bound is more than tolerable misstatement of $40,000.

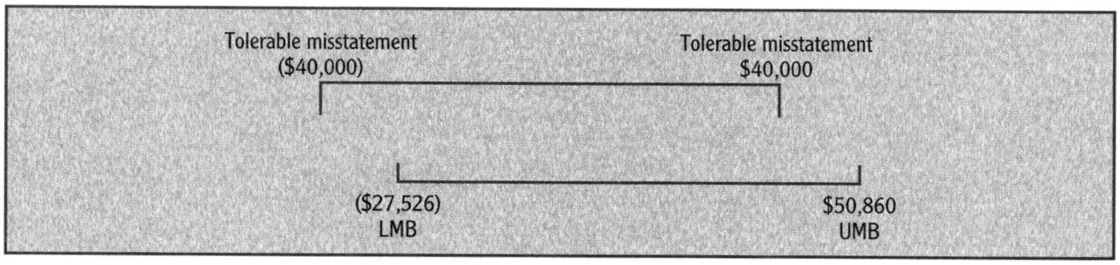


## Action When a Population Is Rejected

When one or both of the misstatement bounds lie outside the tolerable misstatement limits and the population is not considered acceptable, the auditor has several options. These are the same as for nonstatistical sampling and have already been discussed.

## Determining Sample Size Using MUS

Determining sample size was discussed earlier as one of the steps in MUS, but the method of the calculation was deferred. The topic is now covered in more depth. The method used to determine sample size for MUS is similar to that used for physical unit attributes sampling, using the attributes sampling tables. The five things that must be known or specified have already been discussed in this chapter. An example is used to illustrate determining sample size.

**Materiality** The preliminary judgment about materiality is normally the basis for the tolerable misstatement amount used. If misstatements in non-MUS tests are expected, tolerable misstatement would be materiality less those amounts. Tolerable misstatement may be different for overstatements or understatements. For this example, tolerable misstatement for both overstatements and understatements is $100,000.

**Assumption of the Average Percent of Misstatement for Population Items That Contain a Misstatement** Again there may be a separate assumption for the upper and lower bounds. This is also an auditor judgment. It should be based on the auditor's knowledge of the client and past experience, and if less than 100 percent is used, the assumption must be clearly defensible. For this example, 50 percent is used for overstatements and 100 percent for understatements.

**Acceptable Risk of Incorrect Acceptance** ARIA is an auditor judgment and is often reached with the aid of the audit risk model. It is 5 percent for this example.

**Recorded Population Value** The dollar value of the population is taken from the client's records. For this example, it is $5 million.

**Estimate the Population Exception Rate** Normally the estimate of the population exception rate for MUS is zero, as it is most appropriate to use MUS when no or only a few misstatements are expected. Where misstatements are expected, the total dollar amount of expected population misstatements is estimated and then expressed as a percent of the population recorded value. In this example, $20,000 overstatement amount is expected. This is equivalent to a .4 percent exception rate. To be conservative, a .5 percent expected exception rate is used.

These assumptions are summarized as follows:

| | |
|---|---|
| Tolerable misstatement (same for upper and lower) | $100,000 |
| Average percent of misstatement assumption, overstatements | 50% |
| Average percent of misstatement assumption, understatements | 100% |
| ARIA | 5% |
| Accounts receivable—recorded value | $5 million |
| Estimated misstatement in accounts receivable | $ 20,000 |

The sample size is calculated as follows:

| | Upper Bound | Lower Bound |
|---|---|---|
| Tolerable misstatement | 100,000 | 100,000 |
| Average percent of misstatement assumption | ÷ .50 | ÷ 1.00 |
| | 200,000 | 100,000 |
| Recorded population value | ÷ 5,000,000 | ÷ 5,000,000 |
| Tolerable exception rate | 4% | 2% |
| Estimated population exception rate (EPER) | .5% | 0 |
| Sample size from the attributes table (page 423) 5% ARACR, 4% and 2% TER, and .5% and 0 EPER | 117 | 149 |

Since only one sample is taken for both overstatements and understatements, the *larger* of the two computed sample sizes is used, in this case 149 items. In auditing the sample, finding any understatement amounts will cause the lower bound to exceed the tolerable limit, because the sample size is based on no expected misstatements. On the other hand, several overstatement amounts might be found before the tolerable limit for the upper bound is exceeded. Where the auditor is concerned about unexpectedly finding a misstatement that would cause the population to be rejected, he or she can guard against it by arbitrarily increasing sample size above the amount determined by the tables. For example, in this illustration, the auditor might use a sample size of 200 instead of 149.

**Relationship of the Audit Risk Model to Sample Size for MUS** The audit risk model for planning was shown in Chapter 8 and subsequent chapters as:

$$PDR = \frac{AAR}{IR \times CR}$$ (see pages 257–259 for description of the terms)

It was shown in Chapter 13 that the auditor reduces detection risk to the planned level by performing substantive tests of transactions, analytical procedures, and tests of details of balances. MUS is used in performing tests of details of balances. Therefore, understanding the relationship of the three independent factors in the audit risk model plus analytical procedures and substantive tests of transactions to sample size for tests of details of balances is important.

Figure 14-3 on page 488 shows that four of these five factors (control risk, substantive tests of transactions, acceptable audit risk, and analytical procedures) all affect ARIA. ARIA in turn determines the planned sample size. The other factor, inherent risk, affects the estimated population exception rate directly.

## Audit Uses of Monetary Unit Sampling

MUS is appealing to auditors for at least four reasons. First, it automatically increases the likelihood of selecting high dollar items from the population being audited. Auditors make a practice of concentrating on these items because they generally represent the greatest risk of material misstatements. Stratified sampling can also be used for this purpose, but MUS is often easier to apply.

A second advantage of MUS is that it frequently reduces the cost of doing the audit testing because several sample items are tested at once. For example, if one large item makes up 10 percent of the total recorded dollar value of the population and the sample size is 100, the PPS sample selection method is likely to result in approximately 10 percent of the sample items from that one large population item. Naturally, that item needs to be audited only once, but it counts as a sample of ten. If the item is misstated, it is also counted as ten misstatements. Larger population items may be eliminated from the sampled population by auditing them 100 percent and evaluating them separately if the auditor so desires.

Third, MUS is appealing because of its ease of application. Monetary unit samples can be evaluated by the application of simple tables. It is easy to teach and to supervise the use of MUS techniques. Firms that use MUS extensively use computer programs or special tables that streamline sample size determination and evaluation even further than shown here.

Finally, MUS provides a statistical conclusion rather than a nonstatistical one. Many auditors believe that statistical sampling aids them in making better and more defensible conclusions.

The primary disadvantage of MUS is twofold. First, the total misstatement bounds resulting when misstatements are found may be too high to be useful to the auditor. This is because these evaluation methods are inherently conservative when misstatements are found and often produce bounds far in excess of materiality. To overcome this problem, large samples may be required. Second, it may be cumbersome to select PPS samples from large populations without computer assistance.

For all these reasons, MUS is most commonly used when zero or few misstatements are expected, a dollar result is desired, and the population data are maintained on computer files.

## VARIABLES SAMPLING

**OBJECTIVE 14-4**
**Define and describe variables sampling.**

Variables sampling and nonstatistical sampling for tests of details of balances have the same objective, which is to measure the true amount of misstatement in an account balance. As with nonstatistical sampling, when it is determined that the misstatement amount exceeds the tolerable amount, the population is rejected and additional actions are taken by the auditor.

There are several sampling techniques that constitute the general class of methods called variables sampling. Those studied in this section are difference estimation, ratio estimation, and mean-per-unit estimation. These will be discussed more later.

### Differences Between Variables and Nonstatistical Sampling

There are far more similarities than differences in using variables methods and nonstatistical sampling. All fourteen of the steps discussed for nonstatistical sampling must be performed for variables methods and almost all of them are identical. This section focuses on the differences between variables and nonstatistical sampling following the assumption that you understand the material in the earlier part of this chapter on nonstatistical sampling.

To understand why and how auditors use variables sampling methods in auditing, it is important to understand sampling distributions and how they affect auditors' statistical conclusions. These are studied next.

### Sampling Distributions

Although auditors can assess the general nature of populations for the purpose of selecting the most appropriate sampling method, they do not know the mean value (average) or the distribution of the misstatement amounts or the audited values of the populations they are testing in audit engagements. The population characteristics must be *estimated* from samples. That, of course, is the purpose of the audit test. In this section there is a discussion of sampling distributions, which are essential to drawing conclusions about populations on the basis of samples using variables sampling methods.

Assume that an auditor, as an experiment, took thousands of repeated samples of equal size from a population of accounting data having a mean value of $\overline{X}$. For each sample the auditor calculates the mean value of the items in the sample as follows:

$$\overline{x} = \frac{\Sigma x_j}{n}$$

where

$\overline{x}$ = mean value of the sample items

$x_j$ = value of each individual sample item

$n$ = sample size

After calculating $\overline{x}$ for each sample, the auditor plots them into a *frequency distribution*. As long as the sample size is sufficient, the frequency distribution of the sample means will appear much like that shown in Figure 14-5.

**FIGURE 14-5**

**Frequency Distribution of Sample Means**

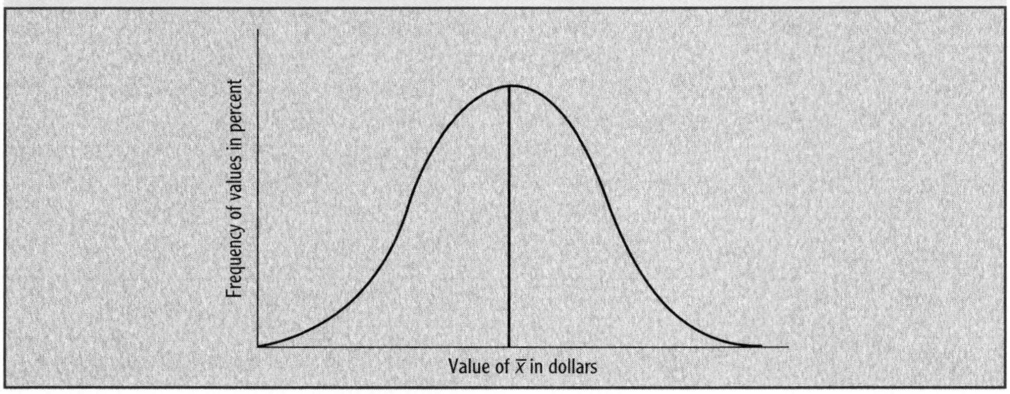


A distribution of the sample means such as this is normal and has all the characteristics of the *normal curve:* (1) the curve is symmetrical, and (2) the sample means fall within known portions of the sampling distribution around the average or mean of those means, measured by the distance along the horizontal axis in terms of *standard deviations*. Further, the mean of the sample means (the midpoint of the sampling distribution) is equal to the population mean and the standard deviation of the sampling distribution is equal to $SD/\sqrt{n}$, where SD is the population standard deviation and $n$ is the sample size.

To illustrate, assume a population with a mean of \$40 and a standard deviation of \$15 ($\overline{X}$ = \$40 and SD = \$15), from which we elected to take many random samples of 100 items each. The standard deviation of our sampling distribution would be \$1.50 ($SD/\sqrt{n} = 15/\sqrt{100} = 1.50$). The reference to "standard deviation" of the population and to "standard deviation" of the sampling distribution is often confusing. To avoid confusion, the standard deviation of the distribution of the sample means is often called the *standard error of the mean* (SE). With this information, the tabulation of the sampling distribution can be made, as shown in Table 14-6.

To summarize, three things are important about the results of the experiment of taking a large number of samples from a known population:

- The mean value of all the sample means is equal to the population mean ($\overline{X}$). A corollary is that the sample mean value ($\overline{x}$) with the highest frequency of occurrence is also equal to the population mean.

**TABLE 14-6**

**Calculated Sampling Distribution from a Population with a Known Mean and Standard Deviation**

| (1) Number of Standard Errors of the Mean (Confidence Coefficient) | (2) Value [(1) × $1.50] | (3) Range Around $\bar{X}$ [$40 ± (2)] | (4) Percent of Sample Means Included in Range |
|---|---|---|---|
| 1 | $1.50 | $38.50 – $41.50 | 68.2 |
| 2 | $3.00 | $37.00 – $43.00 | 95.4 |
| 3 | $4.50 | $35.50 – $44.50 | 99.7 |
| | | | (taken from table for normal curve) |

- The shape of the frequency distribution of the sample means is that of a normal distribution (curve), as long as the sample size is sufficiently large, *regardless of the distribution of the population.* A graphic representation of this conclusion is shown in Figure 14-6.
- The percentage of sample means between any two values of the sampling distribution is measurable. The percentage can be calculated by (1) determining the number of standard errors between any two values and (2) determining the percentage of sample means represented from a table for normal curves.

**FIGURE 14-6**

**Sampling Distribution for a Population Distribution**

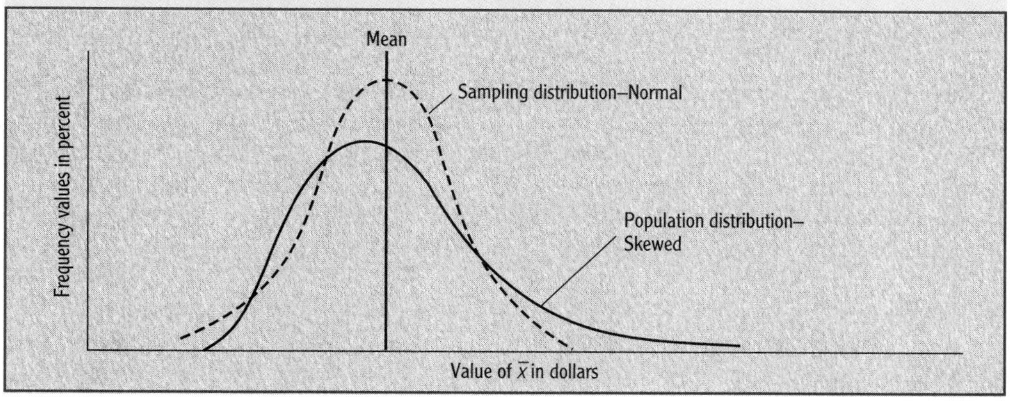


## Statistical Inference

Naturally, when the auditor samples from a population in an actual audit situation, the auditor does not know the population's characteristics and there is ordinarily only one sample taken from the population. But the *knowledge of sampling distributions* enables auditors to draw statistical conclusions (that is, to make statistical inferences) about the population. For example, assume that the auditor takes a sample from a population and calculates $\bar{x}$ as $46 and SE as $9 (the way to calculate SE will be shown later). We can now calculate a confidence interval of the population mean using the logic gained from the study of sampling distributions. It is:

$$CI_{\bar{x}} = \hat{\bar{X}} \pm Z \cdot \text{SE}$$

where

$CI_{\bar{x}}$ = confidence interval for the population mean

$$\hat{X} = \text{point estimate of the population mean}$$

$$Z = \text{confidence coefficient} \quad \begin{cases} 1 = 68.2\% \text{ confidence level} \\ 2 = 95.4\% \text{ confidence level} \\ 3 = 99.7\% \text{ confidence level} \end{cases}$$

$$\text{SE} = \text{standard error of the mean}$$

$$Z \cdot \text{SE} = \text{precision interval}$$

For the example:

$$CI_{\bar{x}} = \$46 \pm 1(\$9) = \$46 \pm \$9 \quad \text{at a 68.2\% confidence level}$$

$$CI_{\bar{x}} = \$46 \pm 2(\$9) = \$46 \pm \$18 \quad \text{at a 95.4\% confidence level}$$

$$CI_{\bar{x}} = \$46 \pm 3(\$9) = \$46 \pm \$27 \quad \text{at a 99.7\% confidence level}$$

The results can also be stated in terms of confidence limits ($CL_{\bar{x}}$). The upper confidence limit ($UCL_{\bar{x}}$) is $\hat{X} + Z \cdot \text{SE}$ ($46 + $18 = $64 at a 95 percent confidence level) and a lower confidence limit ($LCL_{\bar{x}}$) is $\hat{X} - Z \cdot \text{SE}$ ($46 – $18 = $28 at a 95 percent confidence level).

Graphically, the results are as follows:

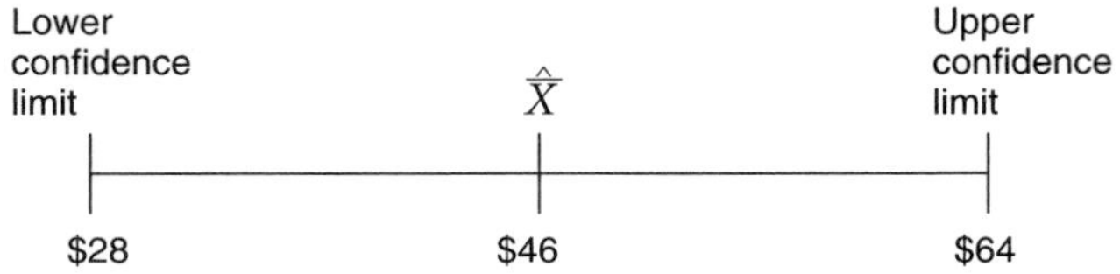


The conclusion that the auditor will draw from a confidence interval using statistical inference can be stated in different ways, but care must be taken to avoid incorrect conclusions. The auditor must remember that the true population value is always unknown. There is always a possibility that the sample is not sufficiently representative of the population to provide a sample mean and/or standard deviation reasonably close to those of the population. The auditor can say, however, that the procedure used to obtain the sample and compute the confidence interval will provide an interval that will contain the true population mean value a given percent of the time. In other words, the auditor knows the reliability of the statistical inference process that is used to draw his or her conclusions.

## Variables Methods

The statistical inference process just discussed is used for all the variables sampling methods. The main difference among the various methods is in the characteristic item and thus in the population being measured. The three variables methods are now discussed individually.

**Difference Estimation** Difference estimation is used to measure the estimated total misstatement amount in a population when there is both a recorded value and an audited value for each item in the sample. An example is to confirm a sample of accounts receivable and determine the difference (misstatement) between the client's recorded amount and the amount the auditor considers correct for each selected account. The auditor makes an estimate of the population misstatement based on the number of misstatements, average misstatement size, and individual misstatement size in the sample. The result is stated as a point estimate plus or minus a computed precision interval at a stated confidence level. For example, in the earlier discussion of sampling distributions, assume the auditor was confirming a random sample of 100 from a population of 1,000 accounts receivable and concluded that the confidence limits of the mean of the misstatement for the population was between $28 and $64 at a 95 percent confidence level. The total estimate of the population can also be easily calculated as being between $28,000 and $64,000 at a 95% confidence level (1,000 × 28 and 1,000 × 64). If the auditor's tolerable misstatement is $100,000, the population is clearly acceptable. If it is $40,000, the population is not acceptable. An extended illustration using difference estimation is shown later in the chapter.

Difference estimation frequently results in smaller sample sizes than any other method, and it is relatively easy to use. For that reason difference estimation is often the preferred variables method.

**Ratio Estimation** Ratio estimation is similar to difference estimation except that the point estimate of the population misstatement is determined by multiplying the portion of sample dollars misstated times the total recorded population book value. The calculation of confidence limits of the total misstatement can be made for ratio estimation with a calculation similar to the one shown for difference estimation. The ratio estimate results in even smaller sample sizes than difference estimation if the size of the misstatements in the population is proportionate to the recorded value of the population items. If the size of the individual misstatements is independent of the recorded value, the difference estimate results in smaller sample sizes.

**Mean-per-Unit Estimation** In mean-per-unit estimation, the auditor is concerned with the audited value rather than the misstatement amount of each item in the sample. Except for the definition of what is being measured, the mean-per-unit estimate is calculated in exactly the same manner as the difference estimate. The point estimate of the audited value is the average audited value of items in the sample times the population size. The computed precision interval is calculated on the basis of the audited value of the sample items rather than the misstatements. When the auditor has computed the upper and lower confidence limits, a decision is made about the acceptability of the population by comparing these amounts with the recorded book value.

## Stratified Statistical Methods

As discussed earlier, stratified sampling is a method of sampling in which all the elements in the total population are divided into two or more subpopulations. Each subpopulation is then independently tested. When auditors use stratified statistical sampling, the results are measured statistically. The calculations are made for each stratum. They are combined into one overall population estimate in terms of a confidence interval. Stratification is applicable to difference, ratio, and mean-per-unit estimation, but it is most commonly used with mean-per-unit estimation.

It was shown earlier that stratifying a population is not unique to statistical sampling, of course. Auditors have traditionally emphasized certain types of items when they are testing a population. For example, in confirming accounts receivable, it has been customary to place more emphasis on large accounts than on small ones. The major difference is that in statistical stratified sampling, the approach is more objective and better defined than it is under nonstatistical stratification methods.

## Sampling Risks

Acceptable risk of incorrect acceptance was discussed earlier for nonstatistical sampling. For variables sampling, acceptable risk of incorrect rejection (ARIR) is also used. The distinctions between and uses of the two risks must be understood.

**ARIA** After an audit test is performed and statistical results are calculated, the auditor must conclude either that the population is not materially misstated or that it is materially misstated. ARIA is the statistical risk that the auditor has accepted a population that is actually materially misstated. ARIA is a serious concern to auditors because there are potential legal implications in concluding that an account balance is fairly stated when it is misstated by a material amount.

An account balance can be either overstated or understated, but not both; therefore, ARIA is a one-tailed statistical test. The confidence coefficients for ARIA are therefore different from the confidence level. (Confidence level = $1 - 2 \times$ ARIA; for example, if ARIA is 10 percent, the confidence level is 80 percent.) The confidence coefficients for various ARIAs are shown in Table 14-7 (page 508) together with confidence coefficients for the confidence level and ARIR.

**TABLE 14-7**

**Confidence Coefficient for Confidence Levels, ARIAs, and ARIRs**

| Confidence Level (%) | ARIA (%) | ARIR (%) | Confidence Coefficient |
|---|---|---|---|
| 99 | .5 | 1 | 2.58 |
| 95 | 2.5 | 5 | 1.96 |
| 90 | 5 | 10 | 1.64 |
| 80 | 10 | 20 | 1.28 |
| 75 | 12.5 | 25 | 1.15 |
| 70 | 15 | 30 | 1.04 |
| 60 | 20 | 40 | .84 |
| 50 | 25 | 50 | .67 |
| 40 | 30 | 60 | .52 |
| 30 | 35 | 70 | .39 |
| 20 | 40 | 80 | .25 |
| 10 | 45 | 90 | .13 |
| 0 | 50 | 100 | .0 |

**ARIR** ARIR is the statistical risk that the auditor has concluded that a population is materially misstated when it is not. The only time that ARIR affects the auditor's actions is when an auditor concludes that a population is not fairly stated. The most likely action when the auditor finds a balance not fairly stated is to increase the sample size or perform other tests. An increased sample size will usually lead the auditor to conclude that the balance was fairly stated if the account is not materially misstated.

ARIR is important only when there is a high cost to increasing the sample size or performing other tests. ARIA is always important. Confidence coefficients for ARIR are also shown in Table 14-7.

ARIA and ARIR are summarized in Table 14-8. It may seem from Table 14-8 that the auditor should attempt to minimize ARIA and ARIR. The way to accomplish that is by increasing the sample size, thus minimizing the risks. Since that is costly, having reasonable ARIA and ARIR is a more desirable goal.

**TABLE 14-8**

**ARIA and ARIR**

| | **Actual State of the Population** | |
|---|---|---|
| **Actual Audit Decision** | **Materially Misstated** | **Not Materially Misstated** |
| Conclude that the population is materially misstated | Correct conclusion—no risk | Incorrect conclusion—risk is ARIR |
| Conclude that the population is not materially misstated | Incorrect conclusion—risk is ARIA | Correct conclusion—no risk |

## ILLUSTRATION USING DIFFERENCE ESTIMATION

**OBJECTIVE 14-5**
**Apply difference estimation to tests of details of balances.**

As previously discussed, there are several different types of variables sampling techniques that may be applicable to auditing in different circumstances. One of these, difference estimation using hypothesis testing, has been selected as a means of illustrating the concepts and methodology of variables sampling. The reason for using difference estimation is its relative simplicity. When the method is considered reliable in a given set of circumstances, it is preferred by most auditors.

In explaining difference estimation, the fourteen steps in determining whether the account balance in the audit of accounts receivable is correctly stated are illustrated. These steps correspond to the ones used for nonstatistical sampling. Positive confirmations in the audit of Hart Lumber Company are used as a frame of reference to illustrate the use of difference estimation. There are 4,000 accounts receivable listed on the aged trial balance with a recorded value of $600,000. Internal controls are considered somewhat weak and a large number of small misstatements in recorded amounts are expected in the audit. Total assets are $2,500,000 and net earnings before taxes are $400,000. Acceptable audit risk is reasonably high because of the limited users of the statements and the good financial health of Hart Lumber. Analytical procedures results indicated no significant problems.

The assumptions throughout are either that all confirmations were returned or that effective alternative procedures were carried out. Hence, the sample size is the number of positive confirmations mailed.

## Plan the Sample and Calculate the Sample Size Using Difference Estimation

The nine steps in planning the sample are almost identical for nonstatistical sampling and difference estimation. There are three important differences:

- In addition to ARIA, the auditor specifies ARIR.
- The auditor makes an advance estimate of the population standard deviation.
- The sample size is calculated using a formula.

Following are the planning steps for the audit of accounts receivable for Hart Lumber Company:

1. *State the objectives of the audit test.* To determine whether accounts receivable before consideration of the allowance for uncollectible accounts is materially misstated.

2. *Decide if audit sampling applies.* Audit sampling applies in the confirmation of the accounts receivable because of the large number of accounts receivable.

3. *Define misstatement conditions.* A client error determined in the confirmation of each account or alternative procedure.

4. *Define the population.* The population size is determined by count, as it was for attributes sampling. An accurate count is much more important in variables sampling because sample size and the computed precision limits are directly affected by population size. The population size for Hart Lumber's accounts receivable is 4,000.

5. *Define the sampling unit.* An account on the list of accounts receivable.

6. *Specify tolerable misstatement.* The amount of misstatement the auditor is willing to accept is a materiality question. The auditor decides to accept a tolerable misstatement of $21,000 in the audit of Hart Lumber's accounts receivable.

7. *Specify acceptable risk.* ***ARIA*** The risk of accepting accounts receivable as correct if it is actually misstated by more than $21,000 is affected by acceptable audit risk, results of the tests of the internal controls, analytical procedures, and the relative significance of accounts receivable in the financial statements. In Hart Lumber, an ARIA of 10 percent is used.

After the auditor specifies the tolerable misstatement and ARIA, the hypothesis can be stated. The auditor's hypothesis for the audit of accounts receivable for Hart Lumber is: accounts receivable is not misstated by more than $21,000 at an ARIA of 10 percent.

***ARIR*** The risk of rejecting accounts receivable as incorrect if it is not actually misstated by a material amount is affected by the additional cost of resampling. Since it is fairly costly to confirm receivables a second time, an ARIR of 25 percent is used. For audit tests for which it is not costly to increase the sample size, a much higher ARIR is common.

8. *Estimate misstatements in the population.* There are two parts of this estimate.

***Estimate an expected point estimate*** An advance estimate of the population point estimate is needed for difference estimation, much as the estimated population exception rate is needed for attributes sampling. The advance estimate is $1,500 (overstatement) for Hart Lumber, based on the previous year's audit tests.

***Make an advance population standard deviation estimate—variability of the population*** An advanced estimate of the variation in the misstatements in the population as measured by the population standard deviation is needed to determine the initial sample size. The calculation of the standard deviation is shown later. For Hart Lumber, it is estimated to be $20 based on the previous year's audit tests.

*9. Calculate the initial sample size.* The initial sample size for Hart Lumber can be now calculated from the following formula:

$$n = \left[\frac{SD^*(Z_A + Z_R)N}{TM - E^*}\right]^2$$

where

$n$ = initial sample size

$SD^*$ = advance estimate of the standard deviation

$Z_A$ = confidence coefficient for ARIA (see Table 14-7)

$Z_R$ = confidence coefficient for ARIR (see Table 14-7)

$N$ = population size

$TM$ = tolerable misstatement for the population (materiality)

$E^*$ = estimated point estimate of the population misstatement

Applied to Hart Lumber, this equation yields

$$n = \left[\frac{20(1.28 + 1.15)4{,}000}{21{,}000 - 1{,}500}\right]^2 = (9.97)^2 = 100$$

## Select the Sample and Perform the Procedures

The two steps in sample selection and performing the tests are the same for difference estimation and nonstatistical sampling except that the sample must be randomly selected for statistical sampling.

*10. Select the sample.* Because a random sample (other than PPS) is required, the auditor must use one of the probabilistic sample selection methods discussed in Chapter 12 to select the 100 sample items for confirmation.

*11. Perform the audit procedures.* The auditor must use care in confirming the accounts receivable and performing alternative procedures using the methods discussed in Chapter 13. For confirmations, a misstatement is the *difference* between the confirmation response and the client's balance after the reconciliation of all timing differences and customer errors. For example, if a customer returns a confirmation and states the correct balance is $887.12, and the balance in the client's records is $997.12, the difference of $110 is an overstatement amount if the auditor concludes that the client's records are incorrect. For nonresponses, the misstatements discovered by alternative procedures are treated identically to those discovered through confirmation. At the end of this step, there is a misstatement value for each item in the sample, many of which are likely to be zero. The misstatements for Hart Lumber are shown in Table 14-9.

## Evaluate the Results

*12. Generalize from the sample to the population.* In concept, nonstatistical and difference estimation do the same thing in Step 12, generalizing from the sample to the population. Both methods are measuring the likely population misstatement based on the results of the sample. Difference estimation uses statistical measurement to compute confidence limits. The four steps discussed on pages 512–513 describe the calculation of the confidence limits for Hart Lumber Company. Steps 3 through 6 in Table 14-9 illustrate the calculations.

**TABLE 14-9**

## Calculation of Confidence Limits

| Step | Statistical Formula | Illustration for Hart Lumber |
|---|---|---|
| 1. Take a random sample of size $n$. | $n$ = sample size | 100 accounts receivable are selected randomly from the aged trial balance containing 4,000 accounts. |
| 2. Determine the value of each misstatement in the sample. | | 75 accounts are confirmed by customers, and 25 accounts are verified by alternative procedures. After reconciling timing differences and customer errors, the following 12 items were determined to be client errors (understatements):<br>1. 12.75 — 7. (.87)<br>2. (69.46) — 8. 24.32<br>3. 85.28 — 9. 36.59<br>4. 100.00 — 10. (102.16)<br>5. (27.30) — 11. 54.71<br>6. 41.06 — 12. 71.56<br>Sum = 226.48 |
| 3. Compute the point estimate of the total misstatement. | $\bar{e} = \frac{\Sigma e_j}{n}$<br>$\hat{E} = N\bar{e}$ or $N\frac{\Sigma e_j}{n}$<br>where<br>$\bar{e}$ = average misstatement in the sample<br>$\Sigma$ = summation<br>$e_j$ = an individual misstatement in the sample<br>$n$ = sample size<br>$\hat{E}$ = point estimate of the total misstatement<br>$N$ = population size | $\bar{e} = \frac{226.48}{100} = 2.26$<br>$\hat{E} = 4{,}000(2.26) = \$9{,}040$<br>or<br>$\hat{E} = 4{,}000\left(\frac{226.48}{100}\right) = \$9{,}040$ |
| 4. Compute the population standard deviation of the misstatements from the sample | $SD = \sqrt{\frac{\Sigma(e_j)^2 - n(\bar{e})^2}{n-1}}$<br>where<br>SD = standard deviation<br>$e_j$ = an individual misstatement in the sample<br>$n$ = sample size<br>$\bar{e}$ = average misstatement in sample | $e_j$ (rounded to nearest dollar) — $(e_j)^2$<br>1. 13 — 169<br>2. (69) — 4,761<br>3. 85 — 7,225<br>4. 100 — 10,000<br>5. (27) — 729<br>6. 41 — 1,681<br>7. (1) — 1<br>8. 24 — 576<br>9. 37 — 1,369<br>10. (102) — 10,404<br>11. 55 — 3,025<br>12. 72 — 5,184<br>228 — 45,124<br>$SD = \sqrt{\frac{45{,}124 - 100(2.26)^2}{99}}$<br>SD = 21.2 |

*[Continued]*

**TABLE 14-9**

**Calculation of Confidence Limits** *[Continued]*

| Step | Statistical Formula | Illustration for Hart Lumber |
|---|---|---|
| 5. Compute the precision interval for the estimate of the total population misstatement at the desired confidence level. | $CPI = NZ_A \frac{SD}{\sqrt{n}} \sqrt{\frac{N-n}{N}}$<br>where<br>CPI = computed precision interval<br>$N$ = population size<br>$Z_A$ = confidence coefficient for ARIA (see Table 14-7)<br>SD = population standard deviation<br>$n$ = sample size<br>$\sqrt{\frac{N-n}{N}}$ = finite correction factor | $CPI = 4{,}000 \cdot 1.28 \cdot \frac{21.2}{\sqrt{100}} \sqrt{\frac{4{,}000 - 100}{4{,}000}}$<br>$= 4{,}000 \cdot 1.28 \cdot \frac{21.2}{10} \cdot .99$<br>$= 4{,}000 \cdot 1.28 \cdot 2.12 = \$10{,}800$ |
| 6. Compute the confidence limits at the CL desired. | $UCL = \hat{E} + CPI$<br>$LCL = \hat{E} - CPI$<br>where<br>UCL = computed upper confidence limit<br>LCL = computed lower confidence limit<br>$\hat{E}$ = point estimate of the total misstatement<br>CPI = computed precision interval at desired CL | UCL = $9,040 + $10,800 = $19,840<br>LCL = $9,040 – $10,800 = $(1,760) |

**Compute the Point Estimate of the Total Misstatement** The *point estimate* is a direct extrapolation from the misstatements in the sample to the misstatements in the population (termed *projected misstatement* in SAS 39 (AU 350)). The calculation of the point estimate for Hart Lumber is shown in Table 14-9, step 3.

It is unlikely, of course, for the actual, but unknown, misstatement to be *exactly* the same as the point estimate. It is more realistic to estimate the misstatement in terms of a confidence interval determined by the point estimate plus and minus a computed precision interval. It should be apparent at this point that the calculation of the confidence interval is an essential part of variables sampling and that the process used to develop it depends on obtaining a *representative sample.*

**Compute an Estimate of the Population Standard Deviation** The population *standard deviation* is a statistical measure of the *variability* in the values of the individual items in the population. If there is a large amount of variation in the values of population items, the standard deviation is larger than when the variation is small. For example, in the confirmation of accounts receivable, misstatements of $4, $14, and $26 have far less variation than the set $2, $275, and $812. Hence, the standard deviation is smaller in the first set.

The standard deviation has a significant effect on the computed precision interval. As might be expected, the ability to predict the value of a population is better when there is a small rather than a large amount of variation in the individual values of the population.

A reasonable estimate of the value of the population standard deviation is computed by the auditor using the standard statistical formula shown in Table 14-9, step 4. The size of the standard deviation estimate is determined solely by the characteristics of the auditor's sample results and is not affected by professional judgment.

**Compute the Precision Interval** The *precision interval* is calculated by a statistical formula. The results are a dollar measure of the inability to predict the true population misstatement because the test was based on a sample rather than on the entire population. In order for the computed precision interval to have any meaning, it must be associated with ARIA. The formula to calculate the precision interval is shown in Table 14-9, step 5.

An examination of the formula in step 5 of Table 14-9 indicates the effect of changing each factor while the other factors remain constant is as follows:

| *Type of Change* | *Effect on the Computed Precision Interval* |
|---|---|
| Increase ARIA | Decrease |
| Increase the point estimate of the misstatements | Increase |
| Increase the standard deviation | Increase |
| Increase the sample size | Decrease |

**Compute the Confidence Limits** The confidence limits, which define the confidence interval, are calculated by combining the point estimate of the total misstatements and the computed precision interval at the desired confidence level (point estimate ± computed precision interval). The formula to calculate the confidence limits is shown in Table 14-9, step 6.

The lower and upper confidence limits for Hart Lumber are ($1,760) and $19,840, respectively. There is a 10 percent statistical risk that the population is understated by more than $1,760, and the same risk that it is overstated by more than $19,840. This is because an ARIA of 10 percent is equivalent to a confidence level of 80 percent.

*13. Analyze the misstatements.* There are no differences in Step 13, analyzing misstatements, for nonstatistical and statistical methods. The auditor must evaluate misstatements to determine the cause of each misstatement and decide whether modification of the audit risk model is needed.

*14. Decide the acceptability of the population.* Whenever a statistical method is used, a decision rule is needed to decide whether the population is acceptable. The decision rule is:

> If the two-sided confidence interval for the misstatements is completely within the plus and minus tolerable misstatements, accept the hypothesis that the book value is not misstated by a material amount. Otherwise, accept the hypothesis that the book value is misstated by a material amount.

This decision rule is illustrated below: The auditor should conclude that both the LCL and UCL for situations 1 and 2 fall completely within both the understatement and overstatement tolerable misstatement limits. Therefore, the conclusion that the population is not misstated by a material amount is accepted. For situations 3, 4, and 5, either LCL or UCL, or both, are outside tolerable misstatements. Therefore, the population book value is rejected.

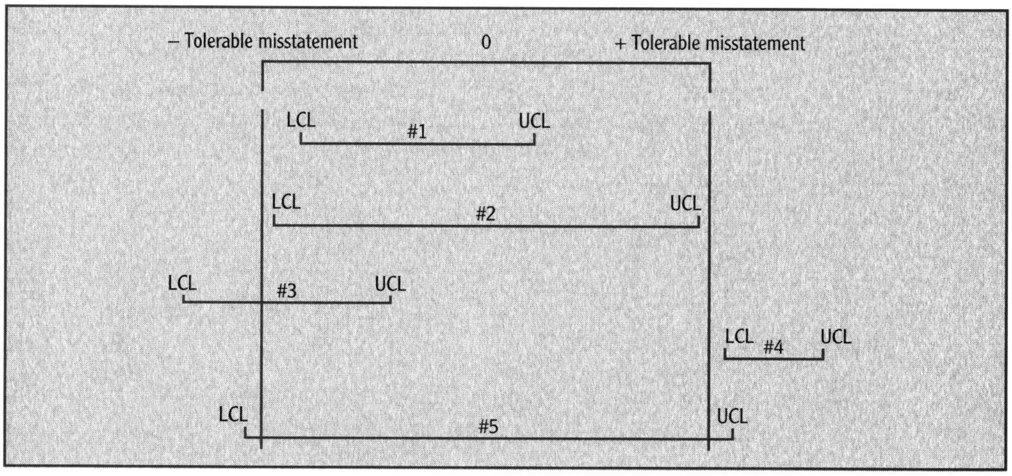

Application of the decision rule to Hart Lumber leads the auditor to the conclusion that the population should be accepted, since both confidence limits are within the tolerable misstatement range:

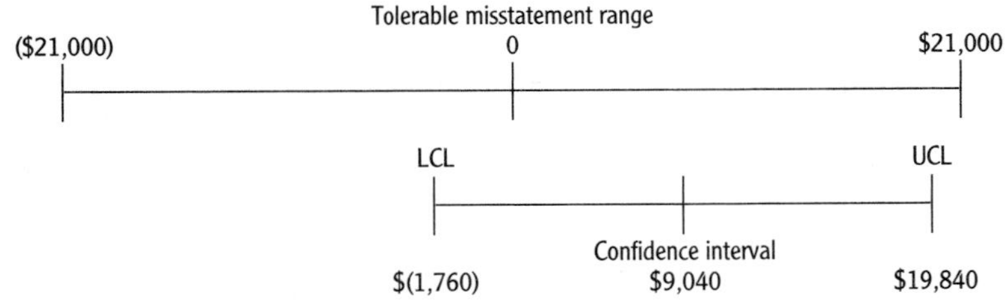


In accepting the population in this way, the auditor is taking a 10 percent chance of being wrong—that is, that the population is in fact misstated by a material amount. However, based on the auditor's planning judgments, this level of risk is appropriate.

**Analysis** Given that the actual standard deviation (21.2) was larger than the advanced estimate (20), and the actual point estimate $9,040 was larger than the advanced estimate ($1,500), it may seem surprising that the population was accepted. The reason is that the use of a reasonably small ARIR caused the sample size to be larger than if ARIR had been 100 percent. If ARIR had been 100 percent, which is common when the additional audit cost to increase the sample size is small, the required sample size would have been only 28:

$$\left[\frac{20(1.28 + 0)4{,}000}{21{,}000 - 1{,}500}\right]^2 = 28$$

Assuming a sample size of 28 and the same actual point estimate and standard deviation, the upper confidence limit would have been $29,559, and, therefore, the population book value would have been rejected. One reason that auditors use ARIR is to reduce the likelihood of needing to increase the sample size if the standard deviation or point estimate is larger than was expected.

### Action When a Hypothesis Is Rejected

When one or both of the confidence limits lie outside the tolerable misstatement range, the population is not considered acceptable. The courses of action are the same as those discussed for nonstatistical sampling, except that a better estimate of the population misstatement is practical.

For example, in the Hart Lumber case, if the confidence level had been $9,040 ± $15,800, and the client had been willing to reduce the book value by $9,040, the results would be 0 ± $15,800. The new computed lower confidence limit would be an understatement of $15,800, and the upper confidence limit a $15,800 overstatement, which are both acceptable given the tolerable misstatement of $21,000. The minimum adjustment that the auditor could make and still have the population acceptable is $3,840 [($9,040 + $15,800) – $21,000].

The client, however, may be unwilling to adjust the balance on the basis of a sample. Furthermore, if the computed precision interval exceeds tolerable misstatement, an adjustment to the books cannot be made that will satisfy the auditor. This would be the case in the previous example if tolerable misstatement was only $15,000.

## APPENDIX A: FORMULAS FOR MONETARY UNIT SAMPLING

Formulas for calculating misstatement bounds for MUS follow. Each formula is illustrated with the example that has already been shown in the text.

The following symbols are used:

$D(i)$ = maximum total population misstatement bound when $i$ misstatements are found ($D_o$ for overstatement amounts and $D_u$ for understatement amounts)

$Y$ = total population recorded dollars

$Pu(i)$ = upper precision limit from the one-sided attributes table for $i$ misstatements

$E(i)$ = amount of a dollar unit misstatement number $i$ ($E_o(i)$ for overstatement amount number $i$, and $E_u(i)$ for understatement amount number $i$)

$M$ = assumed maximum amount of misstatement in any population dollar unit ($M_o$ for overstatement amount and $M_u$ for understatement amount)

$MLE$ = estimated most likely misstatement ($MLE_o$ for overstatement amount and $MLE_u$ for understatement amount)

$\Sigma$ = summation

$n$ = sample size

**Formula Where No Misstatements Are Found**

$$D(0) = Y \cdot Pu(0) \cdot M$$

**Illustration** 100 percent misstatement assumption; 5 percent risk; sample size 100.

$$\text{Upper and lower bounds} = \$1{,}200{,}000 \times .03 \times 1 = \$36{,}000$$

**Formula Where Misstatements Are Found (Before Adjustment)**

$$D(i) = Y \cdot [Pu(0) \cdot M] + Y \cdot [Pu(1) - Pu(0)] \cdot E(1) + Y \cdot [Pu(2) - Pu(1)] \cdot E(2) + \cdots + Y \cdot [Pu(i) - Pu(i-1)] \cdot E(i)]$$

**Illustration** 100 percent misstatement assumption; four overstatement amounts and one understatement amount; misstatements are ordered from the largest dollar unit misstatement to the smallest; 5 percent risk; sample size 100. Therefore,

$$E_o(1) = .671$$

$$E_o(2) = .07$$

$$E_o(3) = .016$$

$$E_o(4) = .0002$$

$$E_u(1) = .03$$

The 5 percent risk bound for maximum total population overstatement amount (before adjustment) is:

$$\begin{aligned} D_o(4) &= [(1{,}200{,}000)(.03)(1.00)] + [(1{,}200{,}000)(.047 - .03)(.671)] \\ &\quad + [(1{,}200{,}000)(.062 - .047)(.07)] + [(1{,}200{,}000)(.076 - .062)(.016)] \\ &\quad + [(1{,}200{,}000)(.089 - .076)(.0002)] \\ &= 36{,}000 + 13{,}688 + 1{,}260 + 269 + 3 \\ &= 51{,}220 \end{aligned}$$

and the 5 percent risk bound for maximum total population understatement amount (before adjustment) is:

$$\begin{aligned} D_u(1) &= [(1{,}200{,}000)(.03)(1.00)] + [(1{,}200{,}000)(.047 - .03)(.03)] \\ &= 36{,}000 + 612 \\ &= 36{,}612 \end{aligned}$$

**Formula for Adjustment for Offsetting Amounts**

$$D_o \text{ adjusted} = D_o(i) - MLE_u$$

$$D_u \text{ adjusted} = D_u(i) - MLE_o$$

where

$$MLE = \Sigma\ E(i) \cdot \frac{Y}{n}$$

**Illustration**

$$\begin{aligned} MLE_o &= (.671 + .07 + .016 + .0002)(1{,}200{,}000/100) \\ &= (.7572)(12{,}000) \\ &= 9{,}086 \\ MLE_u &= (.03)(1{,}200{,}000/100) \\ &= (.03)(12{,}000) \\ &= 360 \\ D_o \text{ adjusted} &= 51{,}220 - 360 \\ &= 50{,}860 \\ D_u \text{ adjusted} &= 36{,}612 - 9{,}086 \\ &= 27{,}526 \end{aligned}$$

## ESSENTIAL TERMS

**Acceptable risk of incorrect acceptance (ARIA)**—the risk that the auditor is willing to take of accepting a balance as correct when the true misstatement in the balance is equal to or greater than tolerable misstatement

**Acceptable risk of incorrect rejection (ARIR)**—the risk that the auditor is willing to take of rejecting a balance as incorrect when it is not misstated by a material amount

**Difference estimation**—a method of variables sampling in which the auditor estimates the population misstatement by multiplying the average misstatement in the sample by the total number of population items and also calculates sampling risk

**Misstatement bounds**—an estimate of the largest likely overstatements and understatements in a population at a given ARIA, using monetary unit sampling

**Monetary unit sampling (MUS)**—a statistical sampling method that provides upper and lower misstatement bounds expressed in monetary amounts; also referred to as dollar unit sampling, cumulative monetary amount sampling, and sampling with probability proportional to size

**Mean-per-unit estimation**—a method of variables sampling in which the auditor estimates the audited value of a population by multiplying the average audited value of the sample times the population size and also calculates sampling risk

**Point estimate**—a method of projecting from the sample to the population to estimate the population misstatement, commonly by assuming that misstatements in the unaudited population are proportional to the misstatements found in the sample

**Probability proportion to size sample selection (PPS)**—sample selection of individual dollars in a population by the use of random or systematic sample selection

**Ratio estimation**—a method of variables sampling in which the auditor estimates the population misstatement by multiplying the portion of sample dollars misstated by the total recorded population book value and also calculates sampling risk

**Statistical inferences**—statistical conclusions that the auditor draws from sample results based on knowledge of sampling distributions

**Stratification**—a method of sampling in which all the elements in the total population are divided into two or more subpopulations that are independently tested and statistically measured

**Variables sampling**—sampling techniques that use the statistical inference process

**14-1 (Objective 14-1)** What major difference between (a) tests of controls and substantive tests of transactions and (b) tests of details of balances makes attributes sampling inappropriate for tests of details of balances?

**14-2 (Objective 14-2)** Define *stratified sampling* and explain its importance in auditing. How could an auditor obtain a stratified sample of 30 items from each of three strata in the confirmation of accounts receivable?

**14-3 (Objective 14-2)** Distinguish between the point estimate of the total misstatements and the true value of the misstatements in the population. How can each be determined?

**14-4 (Objective 14-2)** Evaluate the following statement made by an auditor: "On every aspect of the audit where it is possible, I calculate the point estimate of the misstatements and evaluate whether the amount is material. If it is, I investigate the cause and continue to test the population until I determine whether there is a serious problem. The use of statistical sampling in this manner is a valuable audit tool."

**14-5 (Objective 14-3)** Define *monetary unit sampling* and explain its importance in auditing. How does it combine the features of attributes and variables sampling?

**14-6 (Objectives 14-2, 14-3, 14-4, 14-5)** Define what is meant by *sampling risk.* Does sampling risk apply to nonstatistical sampling, MUS, attributes sampling, and variables sampling? Explain.

**14-7 (Objectives 14-1, 14-2)** What are the major differences in the fourteen steps used to do nonstatistical sampling for tests of details of balances and for tests of controls?

**14-8 (Objective 14-3)** The 2,620 inventory items described in question 14-14 are listed on 44 inventory pages with 60 lines per page. There is a total for each page. The client's data are not in machine-readable form, and the CPA firm does not have a computer terminal available. Describe how a monetary unit sample can be selected in this situation.

**14-9 (Objective 14-3)** Explain how the auditor determines tolerable misstatement for MUS.

**14-10 (Objective 14-2)** Explain what is meant by *acceptable risk of incorrect acceptance.* What are the major audit factors affecting ARIA?

**14-11 (Objective 14-4)** Evaluate the following statement made by an auditor: "I took a random sample and derived a 90 percent confidence interval of $800,000 to $900,000. That means that the true population value will be between $800,000 and $900,000, 90 percent of the time."

**14-12 (Objective 14-2)** What is the relationship between ARIA and ARACR?

**14-13 (Objective 14-3)** What is meant by the "percent of misstatement assumption" for MUS in those population items that are misstated? Why is it common to use a 100 percent misstatement assumption when it is almost certain to be highly conservative?

**14-14 (Objective 14-3)** An auditor is determining the appropriate sample size for testing inventory valuation using MUS. The population has 2,620 inventory items valued at $12,625,000. The tolerable misstatement for both understatements and overstatements is $500,000 at a 10 percent ARIA. No misstatements are expected in the population. Calculate the preliminary sample size using a 100 percent average misstatement assumption.

**14-15 (Objective 14-5)** Assume that a sample of 100 units was obtained in sampling the inventory in Question 14-14. Assume further that the following three misstatements were found:

| Misstatement | Recorded Value | Audited Value |
|---|---|---|
| 1 | $ 897.16 | $ 609.16 |
| 2 | 47.02 | 0 |
| 3 | 1,621.68 | 1,522.68 |

Calculate adjusted misstatement bounds for the population. Draw audit conclusions based on the results.

**14-16 (Objective 14-3)** Why is it difficult to determine the appropriate sample size for MUS? How should the auditor determine the proper sample size?

**14-17 (Objective 14-5)** What is meant by a decision rule using difference estimation? State the decision rule.

**14-18 (Objective 14-2)** What alternative courses of action are appropriate when a population is rejected using nonstatistical sampling for tests of details of balances? When should each option be followed?

**14-19 (Objective 14-4)** Define what is meant by the population standard deviation and explain its importance in variables sampling. What is the relationship between the population standard deviation and the required sample size?

**14-20 (Objective 14-5)** In using difference estimation, an auditor took a random sample of 100 inventory items from a large population to test for proper pricing. Several of the inventory items were misstated, but the combined net amount of the sample misstatement was not material. In addition, a review of the individual misstatements indicated that no misstatement was by itself material. As a result, the auditor did not investigate the misstatements or make a statistical evaluation. Explain why this practice is improper.

**14-21 (Objectives 14-3, 14-5)** Distinguish among difference estimation, ratio estimation, mean-per-unit estimation, and stratified mean-per-unit estimation. Give one example in which each could be used. When would MUS be preferable to any of these?

**14-22 (Objective 14-5)** An essential step in difference estimation is the comparison of each computed confidence limit with tolerable misstatement. Why is this step so important, and what should the auditor do if one of the confidence limits is larger than the tolerable misstatement?

**14-23 (Objective 14-5)** Explain why difference estimation is frequently used by auditors.

**14-24 (Objectives 14-3, 14-4)** Give an example of the use of attributes sampling, MUS, and variables sampling in the form of an audit conclusion.

## MULTIPLE CHOICE QUESTIONS FROM CPA EXAMINATIONS

**14-25 (Objective 14-2)** The following questions refer to the use of stratified sampling in auditing. For each one, select the best response.

a. Mr. Murray decides to use stratified sampling. The reason for using stratified sampling rather than unrestricted random sampling is to
   (1) reduce as much as possible the degree of variability in the overall population.
   (2) give every element in the population an equal chance of being included in the sample.
   (3) allow the person selecting the sample to use his or her own judgment in deciding which elements should be included in the sample.
   (4) reduce the required sample size from a nonhomogeneous population.

b. In an audit of financial statements, a CPA will generally find stratified sampling techniques to be most applicable to
   (1) recomputing net wage and salary payments to employees.
   (2) tracing hours worked from the payroll summary back to the individual time cards.
   (3) confirming accounts receivable for residential customers at a large electric utility.
   (4) reviewing supporting documentation for additions to plant and equipment.

c. From prior experience, a CPA is aware that cash disbursements contain a few unusually large disbursements. In using statistical sampling, the CPA's best course of action is to

(1) eliminate any unusually large cash disbursements that appear in the sample.
(2) continue to draw new samples until no unusually large cash disbursements appear in the sample.
(3) stratify the cash disbursements population so that the unusually large disbursements are reviewed separately.
(4) increase the sample size to lessen the effect of the unusually large cash disbursements.

**14-26 (Objectives 14-1, 14-2)** The following apply to audit sampling. For each one, select the best response.

a. The auditor's failure to recognize a misstatement in an amount or a control deviation is described as a
(1) statistical error. (3) standard error of the mean.
(2) sampling error. (4) nonsampling error.

b. An auditor makes separate tests of controls and substantive tests in the accounts payable area, which has good internal control. If the auditor uses audit sampling for both of these tests, the acceptable risk established for the substantive tests is normally
(1) the same as that for tests of controls.
(2) greater than that for tests of controls.
(3) less than that for tests of controls.
(4) totally independent of that for tests of controls.

c. How should an auditor determine the tolerable misstatement required in establishing an audit sampling plan?
(1) By the materiality of an allowable margin of misstatement the auditor is willing to accept.
(2) By the amount of reliance the auditor will place on the results of the sample.
(3) By reliance on a table of random numbers.
(4) By the amount of risk the auditor is willing to take that material misstatements will occur in the accounting process.

## DISCUSSION QUESTIONS AND PROBLEMS

**14-27 (Objective 14-3)** Page 520 shows the accounts receivable population for Jake's Bookbinding Company. The population is smaller than would ordinarily be the case for statistical sampling, but an entire population is useful to show how to select PPS samples.

### Required

a. Select a random PPS sample of ten items, using Table 12–2 (page 409). Use a starting point of item 1000, column 1. Take the first digit in the column to the right of the one being used to get six digits. Use only odd columns for the first five digits. Identify the physical units associated with the random numbers. (Hint: First digit translated as follows: 1 – 3 = 0; 4 – 6 = 1; 7 – 9 = 2; 0 = discard.)

b. Select a sample of ten items using systematic PPS sampling using the same concepts discussed in Chapter 12 for systematic sampling. Use a starting point of 1857. Identify the physical units associated with the sample dollars. (Hint: the interval is 207,295 ÷ 10.)

c. Which sample items will always be included in the systematic PPS sample regardless of the starting point? Will that also be true of random PPS sampling?

d. Which method is preferable in terms of ease of selection in this case?

e. Why would an auditor use MUS?

| Population Item | Recorded Amount | Population Item | Recorded Amount |
|---|---|---|---|
| 1 | $ 1,410 | 21 | $ 4,865 |
| 2 | 9,130 | 22 | 770 |
| 3 | 660 | 23 | 2,305 |
| 4 | 3,355 | 24 | 2,665 |
| 5 | 5,725 | 25 | 1,000 |
| 6 | 8,210 | 26 | 6,225 |
| 7 | 580 | 27 | 3,675 |
| 8 | 44,110 | 28 | 6,250 |
| 9 | 825 | 29 | 1,890 |
| 10 | 1,155 | 30 | 27,705 |
| 11 | 2,270 | 31 | 935 |
| 12 | 50 | 32 | 5,595 |
| 13 | 5,785 | 33 | 930 |
| 14 | 940 | 34 | 4,045 |
| 15 | 1,820 | 35 | 9,480 |
| 16 | 3,380 | 36 | 360 |
| 17 | 530 | 37 | 1,145 |
| 18 | 955 | 38 | 6,400 |
| 19 | 4,490 | 39 | 100 |
| 20 | 17,140 | 40 | 8,435 |
| | | | $207,295 |

**14-28 (Objective 14-2)** You are planning to use nonstatistical sampling to evaluate the results of accounts receivable confirmation for the Meridian Company. You have already performed tests of controls for sales, sales returns and allowances, and cash receipts, and they are considered excellent. Owing to the quality of the controls, you decide to use an acceptable risk of incorrect acceptance of 10 percent. There are 3,000 accounts receivable with a gross value of $6,800,000. An overstatement or understatement of more than $150,000 would be considered material.

## Required

a. Estimate the appropriate sample size.

b. Explain the methodology of obtaining sample items for confirmation. Your explanation should include how to select the accounts to confirm.

c. Assume that the sample size you selected for part a was 150 items. Twenty-five of the random numbers were for accounts that had already been selected by other random numbers. Evaluate whether the population is acceptable, assuming that no misstatements were found in the sample.

**14-29 (Objective 14-3)** In the audit of Price Seed Company for the year ended September 30, the auditor set a tolerable misstatement of $50,000 at an ARIA of 10 percent. A PPS sample of 100 was selected from an accounts receivable population that had a recorded balance of $1,975,000. The table on page 521 shows the differences uncovered in the confirmation process.

| Accounts Receivable per Records | Accounts Receivable per Confirmation | Follow-up Comments by Auditor |
|---|---|---|
| 1. $2,728.00 | $2,498.00 | Pricing error on two invoices. |
| 2. $5,125.00 | -0- | Customer mailed check 9/26; company received check 10/3. |
| 3. $3,890.00 | $1,190.00 | Merchandise returned 9/30 and counted in inventory; credit was issued 10/6. |
| 4. $ 791.00 | $ 815.00 | Footing error on an invoice. |
| 5. $ 548.00 | $1,037.00 | Goods were shipped 9/28; sale was recorded on 10/6. |
| 6. $3,115.00 | $3,190.00 | Pricing error on a credit memorandum. |
| 7. $1,540.00 | -0- | Goods were shipped on 9/29; customer received goods 10/3; sale was recorded on 9/30. |

## Required

a. Calculate the upper and lower misstatement bounds on the basis of the client misstatements in the sample.

b. Is the population acceptable as stated? If not, what options are available to the auditor at this point? Which option should the auditor select? Explain.

**14-30 (Objective 14-3)** You intend to use MUS as a part of the audit of several accounts for Roynpower Manufacturing Company. You have done the audit for the past several years, and there has rarely been an adjusting entry of any kind. Your audit tests of all tests of controls and substantive tests of transactions cycles were completed at an interim date, and control risk has been assessed as low. You therefore decide to use an ARIA of 10 percent and an EPER of 0 percent for all tests of details of balances. You also decide to use a 100 percent misstatement assumption for both overstatements and understatements.

You intend to use MUS in the audit of the three most material asset balance sheet account balances: accounts receivable, inventory, and marketable securities. You feel justified in using the same ARIA for each audit area because of the low assessed control risk.

The recorded balances and related information for the three accounts are as follows:

| | Recorded Value |
|---|---|
| Accounts receivable | $ 3,600,000 |
| Inventory | 4,800,000 |
| Marketable securities | 1,600,000 |
| | $10,000,000 |

Net earnings before taxes for Roynpower are $2,000,000. You decide that a combined misstatement of $100,000 is allowable for the client.

The audit approach to be followed will be to determine the total sample size needed for all three accounts. A sample will be selected from all $10 million, and the appropriate testing for a sample item will depend on whether the item is a receivable, inventory, or marketable security. The audit conclusions will pertain to the entire $10 million, and no conclusion will be made about the three individual accounts unless significant misstatements are found in the sample.

## Required

a. Evaluate the audit approach of testing all three account balances in one sample.

b. Calculate the required sample size for all three accounts.

c. Calculate the required sample size for each of the three accounts, assuming you decide that the tolerable misstatement in each account is $100,000. (Recall that tolerable misstatement equals preliminary judgment about materiality for MUS.)

d. Assume that you select the random sample using a seven-digit random number table. How would you identify which sample item in the population to audit for the number 4,627,871? What audit procedures would be performed?

e. Assume that you select a sample of 200 sample items for testing and you find one misstatement in inventory. The recorded value is $987.12, and the audit value is $887.12. Calculate the misstatement bounds for the three combined accounts and reach appropriate audit conclusions.

**14-31 (Objectives 14-2, 14-3, 14-4, 14-5)** An audit partner is developing an office training program to familiarize her professional staff with audit sampling decision models applicable to the audit of dollar-value balances. She wishes to demonstrate the relationship of sample sizes to population size and estimated population exception rate and the auditor's specifications as to tolerable misstatement and ARIA. The partner prepared the following table to show comparative population characteristics and audit specifications of the two populations.

| | **Characteristics of Population 1 Relative to Population 2** | | **Audit Specifications as to a Sample from Population 1 Relative to a Sample from Population 2** | |
|---|---|---|---|---|
| | **Size** | **Estimated Population Exception Rate** | **Tolerable Misstatement** | **ARIA** |
| Case 1 | Equal | Equal | Equal | Lower |
| Case 2 | Equal | Larger | Larger | Equal |
| Case 3 | Larger | Equal | Smaller | Higher |
| Case 4 | Smaller | Smaller | Equal | Higher |
| Case 5 | Larger | Equal | Equal | Lower |

## Required

In items (1) through (5) you are to indicate for the specific case from the table the required sample size to be selected from population 1 relative to the sample from population 2.

(1) In case 1 the required sample size from population 1 is ______________.
(2) In case 2 the required sample size from population 1 is ______________.
(3) In case 3 the required sample size from population 1 is ______________.
(4) In case 4 the required sample size from population 1 is ______________.
(5) In case 5 the required sample size from population 1 is ______________.

Your answer choice should be selected from the following responses:

a. Larger than the required sample size from population 2.

b. Equal to the required sample size from population 2.

c. Smaller than the required sample size from population 2.

d. Indeterminate relative to the required sample size from population 2.*

*AICPA adapted

**14-32 (Objective 14-5)** In auditing the valuation of inventory, the auditor, Claire Butler, decided to use difference estimation. She decided to select an unrestricted random sample of 80 inventory items from a population of 1,840 that had a book value of $175,820. Butler decided in advance that she was willing to accept a maximum misstatement in the population of $6,000 at an ARIA of 5 percent. There were eight misstatements in the sample, which were as follows:

| | Audit Value | Book Value | Sample Misstatements |
|---|---|---|---|
| | $ 812.50 | $ 740.50 | $(72.00) |
| | 12.50 | 78.20 | 65.70 |
| | 10.00 | 51.10 | 41.10 |
| | 25.40 | 61.50 | 36.10 |
| | 600.10 | 651.90 | 51.80 |
| | .12 | 0 | (.12) |
| | 51.06 | 81.06 | 30.00 |
| | 83.11 | 104.22 | 21.11 |
| Total | $1,594.79 | $1,768.48 | $173.69 |

## Required

a. Calculate the point estimate, the computed precision interval, the confidence interval, and the confidence limits for the population. Label each calculation. Use the microcomputer for this purpose (Instructor's option).

b. Should Butler accept the book value of the population? Explain.

c. What options are available to her at this point?

**14-33 (Objective 14-5)** Marjorie Jorgenson, CPA, is verifying the accuracy of outstanding accounts payable for Marygold Hardware, a large single–location retail hardware store. There are 650 vendors listed on the outstanding accounts payable list. She has eliminated from the population forty vendors that have large ending balances and will audit them separately. There are now 610 vendors.

She plans to do one of three tests for each item in the sample: examine a vendor's statement in the client's hands, obtain a confirmation when no statement is on hand, or extensively search for invoices when neither of the first two are obtained. There is no accounts payable master file available, and a large number of misstatements is expected. Marjorie has obtained facts or made audit judgments as follows:

| | | | |
|---|---|---|---|
| ARIR | 20% | ARIA | 10% |
| Tolerable misstatement | $ 45,000 | Expected misstatement | $20,000 |
| Recorded book value | $600,000 | Estimated standard deviation | $ 280 |

## Required

a. Under what circumstances is it desirable to use difference estimation in the situation described? Under what circumstances would it be undesirable?

b. Calculate the required sample size for the audit tests of accounts payable, assuming that ARIR is ignored.

c. Assume that the auditor selects exactly the sample size calculated in part b. The point estimate calculated from the sample results is $21,000 and the estimated population standard deviation is 267. Is the population fairly stated as defined by the decision rule? Explain what causes the result to be acceptable or unacceptable.

d. Calculate the required sample size for the audit tests of accounts payable, assuming that the ARIR is considered.

e. Explain the reason for the large increase of the sample size resulting from including ARIR in determining sample size.

f. Marjorie Jorgenson calculates the required sample size using the formula without consideration of ARIR. After the sample size is determined, she increases the sample size by 25 percent. Marjorie believes that this does the same thing as using ARIR without having to bother to make the calculation. Is this approach appropriate? Evaluate the desirability of the approach.

## CASES

**14-34 (Objective 14-3)** You are doing the audit of Peckinpah Tire and Parts, a wholesale auto parts company. You have decided to use monetary unit sampling (MUS) for the audit of accounts receivable and inventory. The following are the recorded balances:

| | |
|---|---|
| Accounts receivable | $12,000,000 |
| Inventory | $23,000,000 |

You have already made the following judgments:

| | |
|---|---|
| Materiality for planning purposes | $800,000 |
| Acceptable audit risk | 5% |
| Inherent risk: | |
| Accounts receivable | 80% |
| Inventory | 100% |
| Assessed control risk: | |
| Accounts receivable | 50% |
| Inventory | 80% |

Analytical procedures have been planned for inventory, but not for accounts receivable. The analytical procedures for inventory are expected to have a 60 percent chance of detecting a material misstatement should one exist.

You have concluded that it would be difficult to alter sample size for accounts receivable confirmation once confirmations are sent and replies are received. However, inventory tests could be reopened without great difficulty.

After discussions with the client, you believe that the accounts are in about the same condition this year as they were last year. Last year no misstatements were found in the confirmation of accounts receivable. Inventory tests revealed an overstatement amount of about 1 percent.

For requirements a–c, make any assumptions necessary in deciding the factors affecting sample size. If no table is available for the ARIA chosen, estimate sample size judgmentally.

### Required

a. Plan the sample size for the confirmation of accounts receivable using MUS.

b. Plan the sample size for the test of pricing of inventories using MUS.

c. Plan the combined sample size for both the confirmation of accounts receivable and the price tests of inventory using MUS.

d. [Instructor's option] Using an electronic spreadsheet, generate a list of random dollars in generation order and in ascending order, for the sample of accounts receivable items determined in part a.

**14-35 (Objectives 14-2, 14-3)** You have just completed the accounts receivable confirmation process in the audit of Danforth Paper Company, a paper supplier to retail shops and commercial users. Following are the data related to this process:

| | |
|---|---|
| Accounts receivable recorded balance | $2,760,000 |
| Number of accounts | 7,320 |
| A nonstatistical sample was taken as follows: | |
| All accounts over $10,000 (23 accounts) | $ 465,000 |
| 77 accounts under $10,000 | $ 81,500 |
| Tolerable misstatement for the confirmation test | $ 100,000 |
| Inherent and control risk are both high | |
| No relevant analytical procedures were performed | |

The following are the results of the confirmation procedures:

| | Recorded Value | Audited Value |
|---|---|---|
| Items over $10,000 | $465,000 | $432,000 |
| Items under $10,000 | 81,500 | 77,150 |
| Individual misstatements for items under $10,000: | | |
| Item 12 | 5,120 | 4,820 |
| Item 19 | 485 | 385 |
| Item 33 | 1,250 | 250 |
| Item 35 | 3,975 | 3,875 |
| Item 51 | 1,850 | 1,825 |
| Item 59 | 4,200 | 3,780 |
| Item 74 | 2,405 | 0 |

## Required

a. Evaluate the results of the nonstatistical sample. Consider both the direct implications of the misstatements found and the effect of using a sample.

b. Assume that the sample was a PPS sample. Evaluate the results using monetary unit sampling.

c. [Instructor's option] Do the above analyses using an electronic spreadsheet.

# 15

# AUDITING COMPLEX EDP SYSTEMS

## LEARNING OBJECTIVES

Thorough study of this chapter will enable you to

- **15-1** Explain how the complexities of EDP systems affect business organizations.
- **15-2** Describe EDP-related internal controls in complex systems, and their impact on evidence accumulation.
- **15-3** Know the similarities and differences in obtaining an understanding of complex and noncomplex systems of internal control.
- **15-4** Decide when it is appropriate to audit only the non-EDP internal controls to assess control risk.
- **15-5** Describe two computer auditing techniques.
- **15-6** Describe the nature, purpose, and function of generalized audit software as a computer audit tool.
- **15-7** Know the types of software available for and uses of microcomputers in auditing.
- **15-8** Discuss the special concerns of the auditor when the client's information is processed by an outside computer company.

## JUST BECAUSE THE COMPUTER DID THE WORK DOESN'T MEAN IT'S RIGHT

Foster Wellman faced a tough problem. His client, Manion's, was a department store retailer that maintained its own charge accounts. The general ledger program that maintained the accounts was new and could deliver an accounts receivable aging schedule on demand. This program was able to read and age each account receivable, compute a percentage of the amount in each aging category, and compute the balance for the allowance for doubtful accounts. Foster could easily apply the appropriate percentage to each category total, but he did not know whether the category totals were correct.

Foster discussed the problem with Rudy Rose, manager of computer systems at Manion's. Rudy indicated that he could show Foster the documentation of the pre-implementation testing of the general ledger program and articulate the controls Manion's used during the systems development process. Foster thanked Rudy, but indicated that the aging was a critical part of the audit and his firm must "prove" that Manion's computer-generated aging schedule was correct.

The solution Foster reached was inventive. He reasoned that he could obtain the program logic used in writing Manion's aging routine and then emulate it with his firm's generalized audit software. He would then run his program against the accounts receivable detail at year-end. If the results generated with his audit software were in reasonable agreement with Manion's aging schedule, this would be evidence that Manion's aging schedule was correct.

After obtaining approval from Manion's Chief Financial Officer, Foster secured an electronic copy of Manion's accounts receivable data and a file layout schedule for this data set. Using the logic Foster believed Manion's used to age the accounts receivable, he prepared a program using his firm's audit software that would read the accounts receivable data and generate an aging schedule. Foster was shocked when he compared the output from his aging schedule and that of Manion's. There was a material difference between the calculated allowance amounts from the two programs.

After Foster had gotten over the shock of finding this difference, he reasoned that the difference could be due to his program, the client's program, or both. He requested a meeting with Rudy Rose and discussed this dilemma with him, showing him the logic narratives he had used and the instructions he wrote in developing his program. Rudy agreed to assign his top systems programmer to investigate the discrepancy under Foster's direct supervision.

The result of the investigation was the discovery that programmer errors had, in fact, resulted in errors in Manion's aging the accounts receivable. The programmer in question had been engaged on a part-time basis to work on just the accounts receivable component of the revenue cycle. Furthermore, the programmer, who was no longer with Manion's, had falsified the program test documentation. Manion's then undertook a review of the program change controls to identify why this oversight occurred. This outcome caused Foster to substantially increase the amount of his substantive testing at year-end for accounts receivable.

Most organizations use electronic data processing (EDP), at least to some extent, in processing financial and accounting information. To this point, the text has described internal controls in terms of noncomplex computer-based systems. In this chapter, we discuss complex EDP systems and their effect on internal controls and on auditing.

There are several reasons for studying noncomplex systems. First, it is important that students understand noncomplex systems, inasmuch as they are used extensively in business and government. Second, we have found that students understand internal control concepts when they are studied in the less abstract context of noncomplex systems. Finally, and most important, most complex EDP-based accounting systems rely extensively on the same type of procedures for control that are used in noncomplex systems.

There is no distinction between the auditing concepts applicable to complex electronic data processing and those applicable to noncomplex systems. When computers or other aspects of EDP systems are introduced, generally accepted auditing standards and their interpretations, the *Code of Professional Conduct,* legal liability, and the concepts of evidence accumulation remain the same. However, some of the specific methods appropriate for implementing auditing concepts do change as systems become more complex.

The chapter is organized around the following topics:

- Complexity of EDP systems
- Effect of EDP on organizations
- EDP controls
- Obtain an understanding of internal control in an EDP environment
- Auditing around the computer
- Auditing with the use of a computer
- Microcomputer-aided auditing
- Audit of computer service centers

## COMPLEXITY OF EDP SYSTEMS

**OBJECTIVE 15-1**
**Explain how the complexities of EDP systems affect business organizations.**

Although most business and nonbusiness enterprises use EDP in some way, the extent of use and the characteristics of the EDP systems in use vary considerably. Before studying the effect of EDP on auditing, it is appropriate to consider the different types of EDP systems in terms of the characteristics that are significant to the auditor.

### Technical Complexity

EDP systems can be defined by their technical complexity and the extent to which they are used in an organization. In the past, technical complexity was synonymous with size. Although large systems usually are more complex, there are also many complex small systems. A better measure of complexity is the capability of a system compared with a benchmark system, which is defined as noncomplex. The characteristics of a noncomplex system are shown in Figure 15-1.

In the system shown in Figure 15-1, accounting data are stored on computer master files. They are periodically updated for transactions on a batch basis (several transactions at once, such as a batch of twenty sales transactions), and the transaction input and master file contents are periodically printed out in various reports. Usually, it is relatively easy to trace detailed transaction data from input to reports and from reports back to input. This tracing requires that data be printed, but these printouts often include considerable detail, such as individual transactions in the journals and complete details of master files.

Noncomplex systems can be made *complex* in one or a combination of the following ways (see page 529):

This is important from an audit point of view because it means that the system processes a certain type of transaction consistently correctly or consistently incorrectly. A risk, therefore, exists that erroneous processing can result in the accumulation of a great number of misstatements in a short period of time, especially if the system is not designed to recognize unusual transactions that require special handling, and the transaction trail or segregation of duties is inadequate. As a result, the emphasis in auditing more complex EDP systems for accuracy of processing is likely to be on testing for unusual transactions and for changes in the system over time rather than on testing a large sample of similar transactions.

**Unauthorized Access** Data-processing systems allow easy access to data and use of the data by those who have legitimate purposes. However, these facilities may also allow easy access for illegitimate purposes. For example, unauthorized transactions may be initiated through the computer, programs and records may be improperly changed, and confidential information may be obtained in an unauthorized manner. These are all significant risks, underlined by several sizable computer-related frauds disclosed in recent years.

**Loss of Data** When great amounts of data are centralized, there is an increased risk of their loss or destruction. The ramifications can be severe. Not only is there a problem of potentially misstated financial statements, but the organization may need to cease operations for a significant period.

### Potential for Improved Control

Despite circumstances that may increase the potential for misstatements, well-controlled EDP systems have a greater potential for reducing misstatements. This is due to the characteristic of uniformity of processing already discussed and the potential for increased management supervision. Potential for improved management supervision occurs for two reasons. First, more complex EDP systems are usually more effectively administered because it is difficult to implement and maintain an EDP system successfully without effective organization, good procedures and documentation, and effective administration. This, in turn, fosters good control. Second, EDP is typically used to provide management with more information and more effective analysis of the information than in most noncomplex systems. This expansion of information, coupled with a wide variety of analytical tools that are practical with the computer, provides management with the ability to better supervise the activities of the organization and to review and follow up on the results of these activities. This can significantly enhance overall control.

## EDP CONTROLS

**OBJECTIVE 15-2**
**Describe EDP-related internal controls in complex systems, and their impact on evidence accumulation.**

Internal controls were discussed in Chapter 9 and are therefore only summarized in this chapter.

In Chapter 9, a distinction was made among the five components of internal control. The control environment in complex EDP systems is even more critical than for less complex ones because there is greater potential for misstatements. For example, an organization with divisions in several countries, each with complex EDP, requires a sound control environment to assure that accurate accounting information is provided. Similarly, controls in such a company must be more carefully designed and more frequently evaluated than those in less complex systems. It is not surprising that almost all large companies with complex EDP systems have internal audit staffs with training in EDP.

### General and Application Controls

The types of controls in an EDP system can be conveniently classified into *general controls* and *application controls.* A general control relates to all parts of the EDP system and must therefore be evaluated early in the audit. Application controls apply to a specific use of the system, such as the processing of sales or cash receipts, and must be evaluated specifically for every audit area in which the client uses the computer where the auditor plans to reduce assessed control risk.

Figure 15-3 summarizes the four categories of general controls and three categories of application controls. It includes a specific example of each category. These categories of controls are discussed briefly in the next two sections.

**FIGURE 15-3**

**Categories for General and Application Controls**

| | **Category of Controls** | **Example of Controls** |
|---|---|---|
| General controls | Plan of organization | Separation of duties between computer programmer and operators |
| | Procedures for documenting, reviewing, and approving systems and programs | Adequate program-run instructions for operating the computer |
| | Hardware controls | Memory failure or hard-drive failure causes error messages on monitor |
| | Controls over access to equipment programs and data files | Authorized password required for computer terminal to operate |
| Application controls | Input controls | Preprocessing authorization of sales transactions |
| | Processing controls | Reasonableness test for unit selling price of a sale |
| | Output controls | Post-processing review of sales transactions by the sales department |

## General Controls

General controls include the four categories summarized in Figure 15-3. Each category is discussed briefly.

**Plan of Organization** Separation of duties in EDP systems was discussed in Chapter 9. In larger organizations, where systems are complex, the recommended separations are more likely than in smaller ones. For example, where there are several systems analysts and programmers, a separation of responsibilities is more practical.

**Procedures for Documenting, Reviewing, and Approving Systems and Programs** The purpose of this general control area is to ensure that the client adequately controls computer programs and related documentation. The primary controls are included in the design and use of systems manuals.

**Hardware Controls** Hardware controls are built into the equipment by the manufacturer to *detect equipment failure.* The independent auditor is less concerned with the adequacy of the hardware controls in the system than the organization's methods of handling the errors that the computer identifies. The hardware controls are usually carefully designed by the manufacturer to discover and report all machine failures. It is obvious, however, that unless the client's organization has made specific provision for handling machine errors, the output data will remain uncorrected.

**Controls Over Access to Equipment, Programs, and Data Files** These general controls are important for safeguarding EDP equipment and records. They were discussed in Chapter 9 as a part of physical control over assets and records.

**Importance of General Controls** Auditors usually evaluate the effectiveness of general controls before evaluating application controls. If general controls are ineffective, there may be potential for material misstatement in each computer-based accounting application. For example, suppose that there is inadequate segregation of duties such that computer operators are also programmers and have access to computer programs and data files. The auditor should be concerned about the potential for fictitious transactions or unauthorized data and omissions in accounts such as sales, purchases, and salaries. Similarly, assume that the auditor observes that there is inadequate safeguarding of data files. The auditor may conclude that there is a significant risk of loss of data because the general controls affect each application. Audit testing to satisfy the completeness objective may need to be expanded in several areas such as cash receipts, cash disbursements, and sales.

## Application Controls

Application controls are applied to input, processing, and output of an EDP application (see Figure 15-3). The difference between general and application controls is indicated in Figure 15-4. Three computer applications are shown in the figure. General controls affect all three applications, but separate application controls are developed for sales, cash receipts, and inventory. Although some application controls affect one or only a few transaction-related audit objectives, most of the procedures prevent or detect several types of misstatements in all phases of the application.

**FIGURE 15-4**

**Relationship of General Controls and Application Controls to Audit Applications**

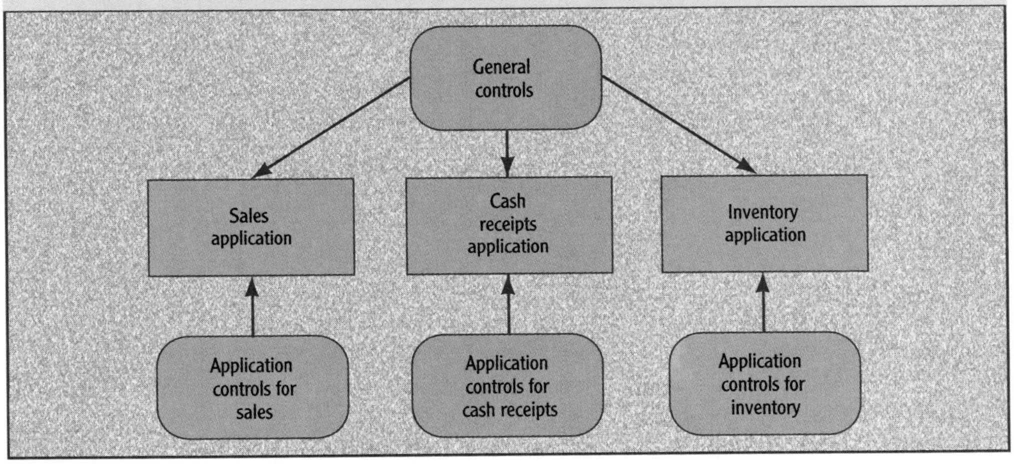


Application controls are summarized briefly here by providing a few examples of input, processing, and output controls.

**Input Controls** Controls over input are designed to assure that the information processed by the computer is valid, complete, and accurate. These controls are critical because a large portion of errors in computer systems result from input errors. Examples of input controls include proper authorization of transactions, adequate documents, key verification, and check digits.

**Processing Controls** Controls over processing are designed to assure that data input into the system is accurately processed. This means that all data entered in the computer are processed, processed only once, and processed accurately.

Most processing controls are also programmed controls, which means that the computer is programmed to do the checking. Examples include control totals, logic tests, and completeness tests.

**Output Controls** Controls over output are designed to assure that data generated by the computer are valid, accurate, and complete. Moreover, outputs should be distributed in the appropriate quantities only to authorized people. The most important output control is review of the data for reasonableness by someone who knows what the output should look like.

## UNDERSTANDING INTERNAL CONTROL IN AN EDP ENVIRONMENT

**OBJECTIVE 15-3**
**Know the similarities and differences in obtaining an understanding of complex and noncomplex systems of internal control.**

The objective of understanding internal control and assessing control risk is the same for a manual or a noncomplex or complex EDP system: to aid in determining, on the basis of the adequacy of existing internal controls, the audit evidence that should be accumulated. Similarly, the techniques for all types of systems are to obtain information about the client's internal controls, identify controls and weaknesses, initially assess control risk, and ascertain that internal controls are actually operating as planned.

A problem often arises in evaluating complex EDP systems because processing transactions usually involves more steps than in a noncomplex system, and thus opens up opportunities for misstatements. This means that there is usually a need for a greater number of internal controls in a complex EDP system. Furthermore, many controls deal with the invisible portions of the transaction trail, which often require considerable technical competence to evaluate. For these two reasons, many CPA firms use EDP specialists to evaluate internal controls when the client has a complex system.

In obtaining information about the client's internal controls, the auditor is concerned with determining the existence of EDP controls discussed in Chapter 9 and their adequacy in meeting transaction-related audit objectives. It is also necessary to evaluate the non-EDP controls discussed earlier, such as the use and control of prenumbered documents and the separation of the custody of assets from the recording function.

It is common to start the understanding of the internal controls of an EDP system by obtaining preliminary information from three major sources: *flowcharts, EDP questionnaires,* and a study of the *error listings* generated by the system. The flowcharts and questionnaires have counterparts in non-EDP systems, but an error listing is unique to EDP systems. In most cases it is desirable to use all three approaches in understanding internal control because they offer different types of information. The flowchart emphasizes the organization of the company and the flow of information throughout the system, whereas the internal control questionnaire emphasizes specific controls without relating individual controls to one another. The error listing supports both these approaches by showing the types and frequency of errors that were reported by the EDP system. Ultimately, the auditor must use the information obtained to determine the most important controls and weaknesses in the internal controls.

After obtaining an understanding of the EDP internal controls, the auditor can decide on the extent to which control risk should be reduced. In doing this, the auditor must consider all internal controls affecting each application, including non-EDP controls. Whenever the auditor concludes that control risk cannot be reduced, substantive testing must be expanded. This approach to control risk assessment is the same as that discussed in Chapters 9 through 13.

If the auditor decides that the internal controls may be effective, it is necessary to proceed with the study by obtaining an in-depth understanding of internal control and by performing tests of controls. The procedures include observing and interviewing personnel, performing other tests of controls, and investigating exceptions to controls and procedures.

As in noncomplex systems, the auditor may decide not to reduce assessed control risk in complex systems even if internal controls are adequate. This approach is followed if the auditor believes that the cost of an exhaustive study and tests of controls will exceed the savings from reduced substantive procedures. When the auditor decides not to test the controls, assessed control risk cannot be reduced.

## AUDITING AROUND THE COMPUTER

**OBJECTIVE 15-4**
**Decide when it is appropriate to audit only the non-EDP internal controls to assess control risk.**

When the auditor considers only the non-EDP controls in assessing control risk, it is commonly referred to as *auditing around* the computer. Under this approach, the auditor obtains an understanding of internal control and performs tests of controls, substantive tests of transactions, and account balance verification procedures in the same manner as in manual systems. While there is no attempt to test the client's EDP controls, the auditor may very likely use the computer to perform substantive audit procedures at year-end.

To audit around the computer, the auditor must have access to sufficient source documentation and a detailed listing of outputs in a readable form. This is possible only when all the following conditions are met:

- The source documents are available in a form readable by a human.
- The documents are filed in a manner that makes it possible to locate them for auditing purposes.
- The output is listed in sufficient detail to enable the auditor to trace individual transactions from the source documents to the output and vice versa. Put another way, the auditor must be able to trace transaction flows from the source documents forward along the audit trail to the general ledger and traverse in the opposite direction from the general ledger back to the source documents.

If any of these conditions does not exist, the auditor will have to rely on computer-oriented controls. Auditing around the computer is an acceptable and often desirable approach when the informational needs of the client's organization require it to maintain the necessary source documents and detailed output.

Complete dependence on manual controls and use of traditional techniques when conditions allow does not imply that the auditor ignores the EDP installation. The auditor continues to be responsible to obtain an understanding of internal control and to assess whether there are significant risks that may affect the financial statements. This includes both manual and EDP segments.

### Special Problems with Systems Using Microcomputers

It is now common for companies to use single or multiple microcomputers for most of their accounting system. In some companies, the processing of accounting data is done by using one or more networked microcomputers with commercial accounting software. Segregation of duties in these systems is typically weak, but there are often other effective internal controls in place. However, it is likely that the most important controls will be non-EDP in nature.

In contrast, some systems divide the accounting tasks among different users. A system might use one or more commercial packages as well as a number of applications developed in-house for the various accounting functions. There is often little control over the quality of the applications developed in-house because the persons developing the applications have little data processing knowledge. In addition, there may be little control over access to computer records or review of the processing steps performed by specific individuals. In these cases, control may be weak and the risk of misstatement high.

When microcomputers are used for the accounting functions, the auditor should be careful before deciding to rely on EDP controls, and should normally elect to rely only on non-EDP controls or take a substantive approach to the audit. When companies write their own software for accounting applications, special care is required. There is often a high risk of programming and output errors with these programs, and in such circumstances, the auditor normally audits around the computer.

## AUDITING WITH USE OF THE COMPUTER

**OBJECTIVE 15-5**
**Describe two computer auditing techniques.**

While there are a number of computer auditing techniques available to the auditor, the *test data approach* and *parallel simulation* are discussed. The *test data approach* involves processing the auditor's test data on the client's computer system, primarily as a part of the tests of controls. *Parallel simulation* involves testing the client's computer-based records primarily as a substantive procedure either at interim or at year-end.

## Test Data Approach

The objective of the test data approach is to determine whether the client's computer programs can correctly process valid and invalid transactions. To fulfill this objective, the auditor develops different types of transactions that are processed under his or her own control using the client's computer programs on the client's EDP equipment. The auditor's test data must include both *valid and invalid transactions* in order to determine whether the client's computer programs will react properly to different kinds of data. Since the auditor has complete knowledge of the misstatements that exist in the test data, it is possible for the auditor to check whether the client's system has properly processed the input. The auditor does this by examining the error listing and the details of the output resulting from the test data.

Figure 15-5 illustrates the use of the test data approach. For example, assume that an auditor wants to test the effectiveness of a computer-based control in the client's payroll system. The control being tested is called a *limit check.* The limit check in this case is a client control that disallows a payroll transaction for greater than 80 hours per week. To test this control, the auditor prepares a payroll transaction with 79, 80, and 81 hours for each sampled week and processes it through the client's system in the manner shown in Figure 15-5. If the controls are effective, the client's system should not process the transaction for 81 hours. The client's payroll error listing should report the request to pay at the 81-hour level to be in error.

Test data are helpful in evaluating the client's system of processing data and its control over errors and fraud, but several difficulties must be overcome before this approach can be used. The major concerns are discussed on the following page.

**FIGURE 15-5**

**Test Data Approach**

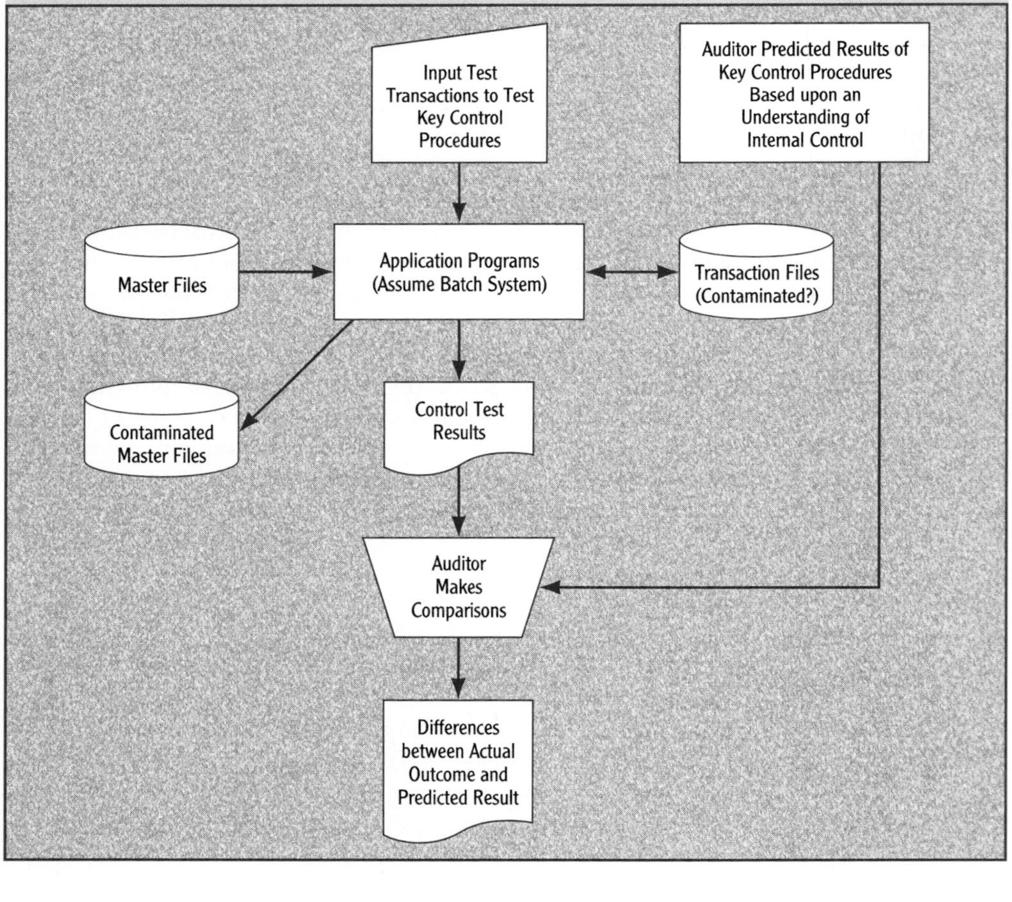

**Test Data Should Include All Relevant Conditions that the Auditor Desires to Test** The test data should test the adequacy of the key computer-based controls on which the auditor intends to rely. Because considerable competence is required in developing data to test for all relevant types of errors or fraud that could occur, the assistance of an EDP specialist is generally required.

**Program Tested by the Auditor's Test Data Must Be the Same as that Used Throughout the Year by the Client** One approach the auditor can take to ensure that this condition is met is to run the test data on a surprise basis, possibly at random times throughout the year. This approach is both costly and time consuming. A more realistic method is to rely on the client's internal controls over making changes in computer programs.

**Test Data Must Be Eliminated from the Client's Records** The elimination of test data is necessary if the program being tested is for the updating of a master file, such as the accounts receivable trial balance. It would not be proper to permit fictitious test transactions to remain permanently in a master file. Clients would obviously be upset if the auditor's test data contaminated their files or data bases. There are methods of eliminating test data, but they generally require the assistance of an EDP specialist. It should be noted that in circumstances in which elimination of test data is not possible, it is common practice for auditors to enter only invalid data. These tests are incomplete. However, they are useful for testing certain controls, for example, the extent to which invalid transactions are rejected.

## Parallel Simulation

A parallel simulation involves the auditor writing a computer program that replicates some part of a client's application system. Figure 15-6 on page 540 illustrates the use of the parallel simulation technique. For example, assume that an auditor wants to add the client's schedule of accounts receivable, which is in machine-readable form. The client's master file is processed on either the auditor's or client's computer, using the auditor's computer program. The auditor then compares the total generated by the computer with the general ledger total. Another example of a parallel simulation is the application in the vignette presented at the beginning of this chapter.

Parallel simulation and the test data approach are complementary rather than mutually exclusive, in the same way that tests of controls, substantive tests of transactions, and tests of details of balances are complementary. In the test data approach, the auditor uses test data to evaluate the ability of the client's system to handle different types of transactions. In parallel simulation, the auditor tests the output of the system for correctness. A comparison of Figures 15-5 and 15-6 illustrates this difference.

Parallel simulation is used primarily to facilitate the substantive testing of client account balances. In using this technique, there are several factors that should be noted.

**Cost** Depending on the part of the client's systems to be simulated, the cost can vary from expensive (recalculation of life insurance reserves) to inexpensive (recalculation of interest payments on savings accounts for a bank). The cost of using this technique depends on the complexity of the client's calculations and the amount of data to be processed.

**Comprehensive** Most parallel simulation applications are used to process the entire set of the relevant client data. While the parallel simulation can be designed to sample client data, this is the exception rather than the norm.

**Exception Oriented** The power of parallel simulation is its emphasis on exceptions. Revisiting Figure 15-6 shows that the auditor has both the auditor's simulated balance and the client's balance. By comparing these, the auditor can focus on those items where there are differences.

**FIGURE 15-6**

**Parallel Simulation**

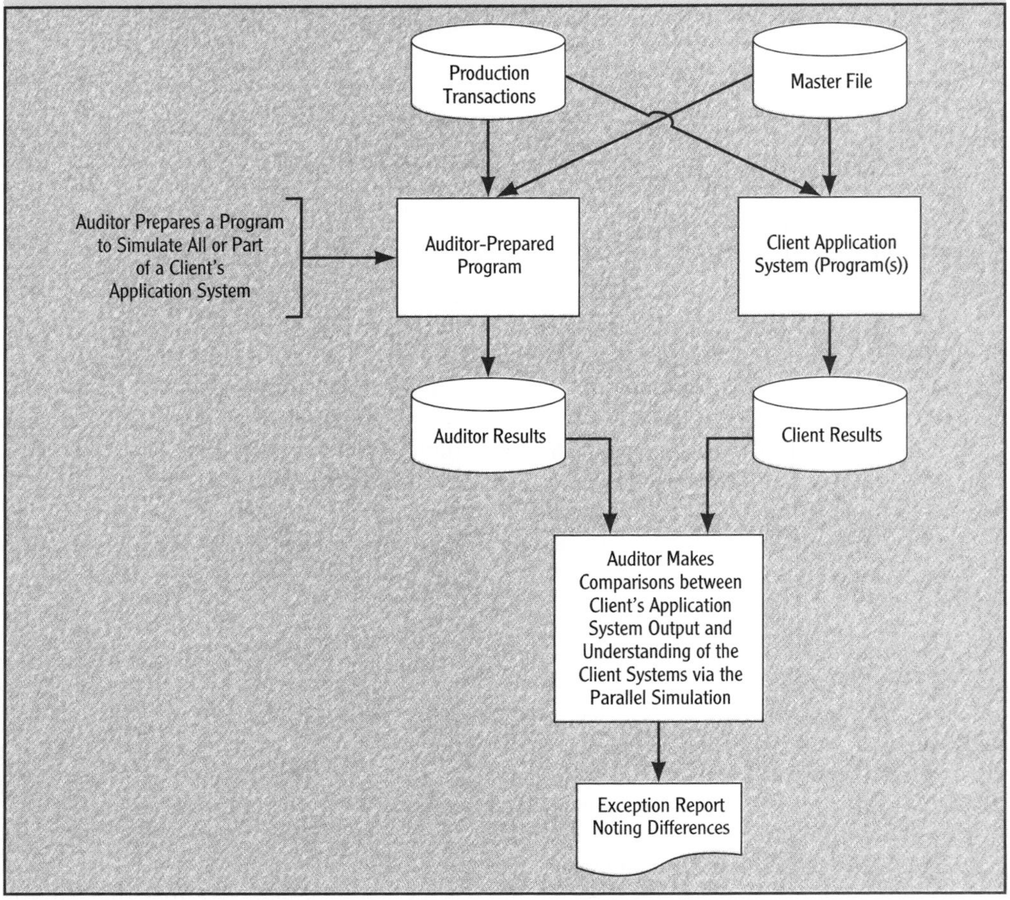


## GENERALIZED AUDIT SOFTWARE

**OBJECTIVE 15-6**
**Describe the nature, purpose, and function of generalized audit software as a computer audit tool.**

Although it is possible for auditors to write specific programs to perform the above functions, or to use existing client programs for that purpose, the most common approach is to use generalized audit software (GAS).

Generalized audit software is *an audit tool* developed by a CPA firm or other organization and used on different audits for most of the seven types of applications discussed on page 540. The generalized program consists of a series of computer programs that together perform various data processing functions. These, for the most part, can be described as data manipulations. Certain frequently used applications, such as random sampling and totaling of numeric columns, are preprogrammed and represented by commands in the software.

There are two important advantages to generalized programs. First, they are developed in such a manner that most of the audit staff can be trained to use the program even if they have little formal EDP education. Second, with generalized programs, a single program can be applied to a wide range of tasks without having to incur the cost or inconvenience of developing individualized programs. The major disadvantages of generalized computer programs are the high initial cost of their development and their relatively inefficient processing speed.

The decision whether or not to use audit software must be made by the auditor on the basis of his or her professional experience. Sometimes the auditor is forced to use the computer to perform procedures due to the inaccessibility of source documents and detailed listing of output. Even if hard-copy documents are accessible, it may be desirable to perform tests with the computer if sufficient competent evidence can be accumulated at a reduced cost.

## Using Generalized Audit Software

Since generalized audit software is used extensively in CPA firms, it is important that students of auditing understand it. An explanation of these programs in general terms is given below, followed by an illustration of their use.

Figure 15-7 illustrates the GAS process for any application. The steps are as follows:

**Objective Setting** The purpose of the test must be carefully specified in advance to achieve the desired results. The objective can be to foot a data file, select a random sample, or perform one or more of the other tasks previously described.

**Application Design** The second step consists of three parts:

- Identify and describe the client's data files and the pertinent information to which access is desired. This is necessary to extract data from the client's files.
- Design the most useful format and contents of the auditor's GAS reports.
- Develop a logical approach to extract and manipulate the data obtained from the client's records.

**Coding** The results of the application design are then coded on worksheets by the auditor in the simple GAS language. These are instructions telling the GAS what to do with the client's files to meet the specified objectives.

**Key Entry** The coded worksheets are key entered, verified by the CPA's employees, and submitted to the computer, along with the GAS and the client's data files.

**FIGURE 15-7**

**GAS Application Process**

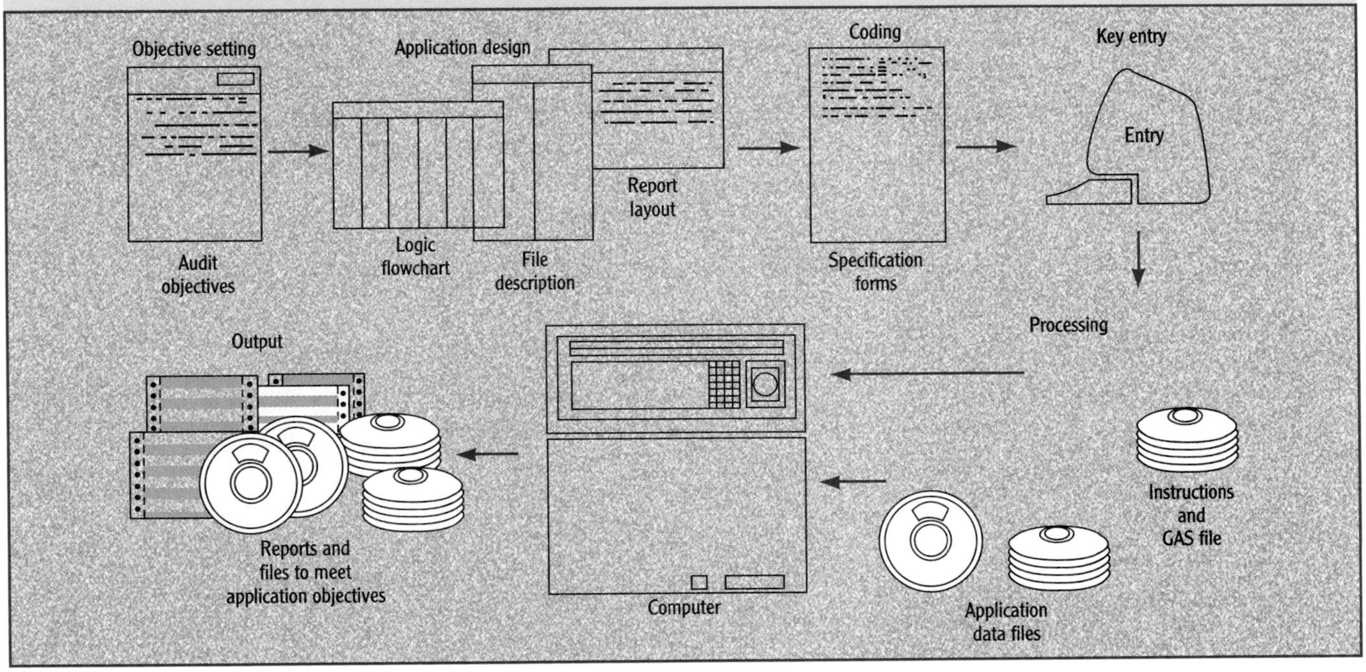

**Processing** The processing phase has two stages. In the first, the GAS directs the computer to read the data file and to copy pertinent information. The second stage involves the functions required to produce the GAS reports. At the completion of the processing, the client's data files are returned to the client and the GAS file is returned to the CPA's office. Frequently, the GAS coding instructions are retained for possible use on subsequent audits. The GAS reports are used for their intended audit purpose and retained in the working papers as documentation.

## Illustration for Accounts Receivable

The following is an illustration of a GAS application presented in terms of the preceding steps.

**Objective Setting**

1. Foot and crossfoot the accounts receivable master file and print the total and any crossfoot exceptions.
2. Determine if any balances are in excess of their credit limit and print a report of all exceptions.
3. Prepare and print an aging summary.
4. Randomly select accounts and print confirmations as follows:
   a. Positive confirmation of all accounts over $10,000 or over 90 days old.
   b. Positive confirmation of 25 percent of all accounts between $1,000 and $10,000 not over 90 days old.
   c. Negative confirmation of 5 percent of all others.
5. Print a listing of accounts selected for confirmation.
6. Select 5 percent of all accounts to trace to source documents, for a test of aging.
7. Select and print a list of accounts for collectibility follow-up that are "for special handling."

**Application Design** The client maintains accounts receivable on both a master file and a name and address file. Tables 15-1 and 15-2 list the file contents, noting whether the information was used in the application.

**TABLE 15-1**

**Accounts Receivable Master File**

| Element No. | Description of Contents | Used | Not Used |
|---|---|---|---|
| 1 | Division | X | — |
| 2 | Customer number | X | — |
| 3 | Credit limit | X | — |
| 4 | Sales personnel code | — | X |
| 5 | Cash discount percent | — | X |
| 6 | Date of last payment | X | — |
| 7 | Date of last purchase | X | — |
| 8 | Balance due | X | — |
| | Aging of balance due: | | |
| 9 | Current | X | — |
| 10 | 30 days | X | — |
| 11 | 60 days | X | — |
| 12 | 90 days | X | — |
| 13 | 6 months | X | — |
| 14 | 1 year | X | — |

**TABLE 15-2**

**Name and Address File**

| Element No. | Description of Contents | Used | Not Used |
|---|---|---|---|
| 1 | Division | X | — |
| 2 | Customer number | X | — |
| 3 | Customer name | X | — |
| 4 | Street address | X | — |
| 5 | City and state | X | — |
| 6 | Zip code | X | — |
| 7 | Shipping location code | — | X |
| 8 | Customer type | — | X |
| 9 | Risk-rating code<br>1 = no risk<br>2 = normal handling<br>3 = approval required when balance over 60 days<br>4 = special handling required for each purchase | X | — |



**Coding** The objectives of this application are met by coding the various GAS functions to process the client's data files as follows:

1. The accounts receivable master file is read and the designated information is copied. This is followed by copying the name, address, and risk information from the name and address file, using customer number as the key.
2. The copied information is subjected to the following selection criteria:
   a. Add the aging fields within each record and subtract total from balance due field. Place any difference in an aging overflow field and code the record for report 1.
   b. Foot aging and balance due fields for all records. The GAS prints such totals automatically.
   c. Compare the balance due field with the credit limit field. If the balance exceeds the limit, code the record for report 2.
   d. Compare balance due with $10,000. If greater than $10,000, code the record for positive confirmation and report 3.
   e. Compare aging fields ninety days, six months, and one year with zero. If greater than zero, code the record for positive confirmation and report 3.
   f. Compare balance due with $1,000. If greater than $1,000 and not previously coded for positive confirmation, select 25 percent at random and code for positive confirmation and report 3.
   g. Compare balance due with $1,000. If less than $1,000 and not coded for positive confirmation, select 5 percent at random and code for negative confirmation and report 4.
   h. Select 5 percent of all other accounts at random and code for report 5.
   i. Code any records with a risk rating equal to 4 and not selected for confirmation to report 6.

**Key Entry and Processing** After the codes are entered and verified, they are processed with the GAS against the accounts receivable master file and the name and address file.

**Reports** The following reports are printed:

Report 1—all accounts in which aging does not crossfoot

Report 2—all accounts in which balance is in excess of credit limit
Report 3—accounts selected for positive confirmation and collectibility follow-up
Report 4—accounts selected for negative confirmation
Report 5—accounts for test of aging, showing all aging details, including dates of last payment and purchase
Report 6—additional high-risk accounts selected for collectibility follow-up

In addition, positive and negative confirmations are printed.

## Uses of Generalized Audit Software

The auditor can potentially perform many different kinds of tests and other functions with GAS if the client's data are in machine-readable form. These include the following:

**Verifying Extensions and Footings** GAS can be used to verify the accuracy of the client's computations by calculating the information independently. Examples include recalculating sales discounts taken and employees' net pay computations, footing an accounts receivable aging schedule, and totaling the client's accounts payable trial balance.

**Examining Records for Quality, Completeness, Consistency, and Correctness** In auditing various characteristics of a manual system, the auditor routinely examines accounting records for propriety because they are visible and any inconsistencies or inaccuracies can be observed without difficulty. When auditing computer-based records, the GAS can be instructed to scan *all* records using specified criteria and to print out the exceptions. Examples include review of accounts receivable balances for amounts over the credit limit and review of payroll files for terminated employees.

**Comparing Data on Separate Files** Where records on separate files should contain compatible information, a program can be used to determine if the information agrees or to make other comparisons. For instance, changes in accounts receivable balances between two dates can be compared with details of sales and cash receipts on transaction files, and payroll details such as pay rates and withholding exemptions can be compared with personnel records.

**Summarizing or Resequencing Data and Performing Analyses** GAS can be developed to change the format and aggregate data in a variety of ways. The ability to change the form and order of data aids the auditor in preparing analyses used in audit procedures. GAS can be used to facilitate parallel simulations in order to determine the reasonableness of recorded information. Examples include verifying accounts receivable aging, preparing general ledger trial balances, summarizing inventory turnover statistics for obsolescence analysis, and resequencing inventory items by location to facilitate physical observations.

**Comparing Data Obtained through Other Audit Procedures with Company Records** Audit evidence gathered manually can be converted to machine-readable form and compared with other machine-readable data. Examples include comparing confirmation responses with the master files and comparing creditor statements with accounts payable files.

**Selecting Audit Samples** The computer can be programmed to select samples from any machine-readable data in several different ways, including at random. It is also possible to use more than one criterion for sample selection, such as a 100 percent sample of high dollar accounts receivable and random sampling of all other receivables.

**Printing Confirmation Requests** After a sample has been selected, the auditor can have the data printed on confirmation request forms. This is a useful time-saving device for the preparation of confirmations.

## MICROCOMPUTER-AIDED AUDITING

**OBJECTIVE 15-7**
**Know the types of software available for and uses of microcomputers in auditing.**

Microcomputers are now being used heavily in audit practice. These devices can support a wide range of software, including GAS, that are useful in supporting the work of the auditor.

### Types of Software

The specific tasks that the auditor performs using microcomputers depend on engagement circumstances, but a more important factor is the available software. Five types of software are frequently used by auditors: groupware, commercial general-use software, proprietary templates of commercial general-use software, special-use software, and custom programs written by the auditor.

**Groupware** One type of software being used by the "Big Six" and others is "groupware." The most notable of the groupware products is Lotus Notes. Groupware allows a number of people to work on specific applications together. As a consequence, they can coordinate their efforts and achieve productivity by organizing and sharing information as a group using electronic mail or file sharing. Since audits are normally done by teams, this seems a natural step in the evolution of microcomputer use by auditors.

**Commercial General-Use Software** A large number of software products are available for microcomputer use. Two of these, electronic spreadsheets and word processors, are useful for auditors.

An *electronic spreadsheet* is a program that presents and manipulates data in the form of a matrix of interrelated values, with columns and rows, much like an accounting worksheet and many auditors' working papers. Labels, including extended narrative information, and values are entered in the cells of the matrix, calculations are performed with the values, and all or selected results are displayed. The most popular electronic spreadsheet programs are Lotus 1-2-3, Excel, and Quattro Pro.

*Word processors* combine the capabilities of a typewriter with a microcomputer to allow the auditor to create, save, and print text in almost any form. The text is narrative but can also include numeric data in tabular form, graphics, drawings, red-lining features to support document editing in a group environment, and even sound bites. Microsoft Word and WordPerfect are among the more popular word processors.

**Templates** Predesigned formats for such things as working papers and letters can be created and saved by using both electronic spreadsheets and word processors. These are called *templates.* These templates are available for continuing use as standard formats for different engagements, or over time for the same engagement. Larger firms develop such templates centrally for distribution to each office.

**Special-Use Software** The extensive use of microcomputers by auditors has created a market for special-use software. Some *auditor's software* is developed on a commercial basis by organizations, including the AICPA and several large accounting firms. Most large CPA firms have also developed this type of software for their internal use only.

The degree of sophistication of this software varies considerably. The most popular use is for the development and maintenance of working trial balances and schedules. However, some large firms are beginning to use programs that evaluate internal controls, assist in the evaluation of client judgments and estimates, and help plan evidence accumulation. The more advanced of these programs are sophisticated, and incorporate artificial intelligence and expert-systems techniques.

**Custom Programs** Some auditors are trained and skilled in writing computer programs on a microcomputer and use that skill on audit engagements. Such programs are usually costly to develop and are typically of lower quality than good commercial or special-use software.

Most auditors develop special programs only when other software is not available for a specific task that the auditor needs to have done.

## Uses of Microcomputers

Microcomputer applications used in practice vary substantially. Typical audit uses include the following:

**Prepare Trial Balances and Lead Schedules** The microcomputer can be used to develop a working trial balance and lead schedules for the various financial statement accounts. As adjusting and reclassification journal entries are made, they are electronically posted and an updated trial balance is immediately available. When the audit work is done, the final trial balance accounts can be automatically aggregated for drafting the financial statements. If consolidated statements are needed, subtrial balances can also be combined. This type of work can be accomplished with a general ledger program or an electronic spreadsheet.

**Prepare Working Papers** Microcomputer software is ideally suited for audit working paper preparation. It is helpful where standard formats are most applicable and where there are extensive calculations. Examples include preparing working papers for proofs of cash bank balances, accounts receivable confirmation control and summarization, inventory price tests, fixed asset summaries and depreciation calculations, tax accruals, and interest computation tests.

Several large CPA firms have developed or adopted electronic working paper systems that operate in a client-server environment. These systems often use Lotus Notes as the foundation for this work. In addition to specialized templates and custom programs, these electronic working paper environments include a suite of office products, such as Microsoft Office.

The primary advantage of electronic working papers is efficiency. With a modem-equipped microcomputer, audit staff, regardless of their physical location, can use their microcomputer to create, modify, manage, and review working papers.

**Calculate Analytical Procedures** Analytical procedures are easily generated by the microcomputer. Most general ledger software can generate a variety of analytical procedures calculations and print these on demand. Electronic spreadsheets are also ideal for such analysis and allow for tailoring. Figure 15-8 illustrates the use of an electronic spreadsheet for both analytical procedures and audit working paper preparation.

**Prepare Audit Programs** The simplest form of this application is to type the audit program on a word processor and save it from one year to the next to facilitate changes and updating. A more sophisticated use is to have a special-use program that helps the auditor think through the planning considerations of the audit and select appropriate procedures from an "audit procedures data base." These are then formulated into an audit program. The underlying logic is the same as for the audit framework discussed in Chapters 10 through 13.

**Understand Internal Control** There are several types of software that assist in these tasks. First, a word processor can be used to document internal control using a narrative description. Second, internal control questionnaires can be automated both to document descriptive information and perform some evaluative steps. And, third, flowcharting software can be used to document client systems during the review of the client's internal control.

**Perform Audit Sampling** Special-use software is available to design, select, and evaluate audit samples using a variety of statistical or nonstatistical techniques. It is also possible to use an electronic spreadsheet to do the evaluation, and to write a simple program when special-use software is not available.

## FIGURE 15-8

**Ratio Analysis Using an Electronic Spreadsheet**

ABC COMPANY RATIO ANALYSIS
12/31/96

Prepared by________________
Reviewed by ________________

| 1996 Financial Data (000's omitted) | |
|---|---|
| Cash | 8558 |
| Accounts rec. – gross | 25164 |
| Allow. for D/A | -1400 |
| Inventories | 22172 |
| Other current assets | 3468 |
| Fixed assets | 115827 |
| Investments | 16167 |
| | 189956 |
| Current liabilities | 27984 |
| Long-term debt | 50201 |
| Deferred taxes | 13889 |
| Preferred stock | 18009 |
| Common equity | 79873 |
| | 189956 |
| Net sales | 150559 |
| Cost of sales | 104903 |
| Depreciation | 8183 |
| Other operating expenses | 21177 |
| Interest expense | 4253 |
| Other (income) expense | -905 |
| Taxes on income | 4290 |
| | 141901 |
| Net earnings | 8658 |
| Beg. retained earnings | 76282 |
| Preferred dividends | -2029 |
| Common dividends | -3038 |
| End. retained earnings | 79873 |
| Capital expenditures | 9553 |
| Common shares outstanding | 6075 |
| Intan. assets in investment | 4000 |
| Mkt. value of stock: | |
| Common | 70000 |
| Preferred | 20000 |

| Ratios | 1996 | 1995 | 1994 | 1993 | 1992 |
|---|---|---|---|---|---|
| Short-Term Debt Paying Ability: | | | | | |
| Current ratio | 2.07 | 2.29 | 2.24 | 2.50 | 1.91 |
| Quick ratio | 1.16 | 1.27 | 1.15 | 1.50 | 1.06 |
| Cash ratio | 0.31 | 0.31 | 0.26 | 0.30 | 0.28 |
| Short-Term Liquidity: | | | | | |
| A/R turnover | 6.01 | 5.88 | 5.24 | 5.91 | 5.81 |
| Days to collect | 60 | 61 | 69 | 61 | 62 |
| Inv. turnover | 4.91 | 4.52 | 4.23 | 5.35 | 4.79 |
| Days to sell | 73 | 80 | 85 | 67 | 75 |
| Days to convert | 133 | 141 | 154 | 128 | 137 |
| Long-Term Liquidity: | | | | | |
| Debt to equity | 0.94 | 0.98 | 0.88 | 0.82 | 0.78 |
| TNA to equity | 0.96 | 0.96 | 0.96 | 0.96 | 0.96 |
| Times int ernd | 3.83 | 3.48 | 3.78 | 5.40 | 5.17 |
| Times int + PD Ed | 2.03 | 1.70 | 1.66 | 2.28 | 2.01 |
| Operating Performance: | | | | | |
| Efficiency | 0.87 | 0.78 | 0.73 | 0.83 | 0.76 |
| Profit margin | 0.11 | 0.09 | 0.10 | 0.12 | 0.11 |
| Profitability | 0.09 | 0.07 | 0.07 | 0.10 | 0.08 |
| Return on asset | 0.09 | 0.07 | 0.06 | 0.09 | 0.08 |
| Return on Equity: | | | | | |
| Return bef tax | 0.12 | 0.08 | 0.08 | 0.12 | 0.10 |
| BV per share | 13.15 | 12.56 | 12.17 | 12.11 | 11.90 |
| Leverage from: | | | | | |
| S-T debt | 0.03 | 0.02 | 0.02 | 0.02 | 0.03 |
| L-T debt | 0.00 | 0.00 | 0.00 | 0.02 | 0.01 |
| Other liab | 0.01 | 0.01 | 0.01 | 0.01 | 0.01 |
| Pfd stock | -0.03 | -0.03 | -0.04 | -0.03 | -0.03 |

**Manage Engagements and Time Budgets** Word processors are extremely useful for the preparation of routine engagement correspondence, such as the engagement and management representation letters. Spreadsheet software with the use of a template is well suited to preparing time budgets and monitoring time spent in relation to budget. Most special-use microcomputer software includes these applications.

### Quality Control Concerns

There are special concerns when auditors use microcomputers on audits. First, much of the information about data and how they are manipulated may not be visible to the auditor or the auditor's supervisor. To check the work when it is performed and to review it after completion, special effort must be taken to document input data and computational routines. Well-designed software can provide for such documentation. A second concern is the potential for unreliable software. Widely used commercial software should have been thoroughly tested and proven reliable by the developer. However, new software and specially created software may contain "bugs" that affect their reliability. Similarly, when commercial software is used by the auditor to create computational and logic routines, auditors may make mistakes that cause the results to be in error. To protect against these situations, the auditor should consider the need to test software.

## AUDIT OF COMPUTER SERVICE CENTERS

**OBJECTIVE 15-8**
**Discuss the special concerns of the auditor when the client's information is processed by an outside computer company.**

Many clients have their data processed at an independent computer service center rather than having their own computer. This is a logical approach for a business with an excessive volume of transactions for a manual system but inadequate volume to justify the cost of implementing its own computer system.

In a computer service center operation, the client submits input data, which the service center processes for a fee and returns to the client along with the agreed-upon output. Generally, the service center is responsible for designing the computer system and providing adequate controls to ensure that the processing is reliable.

The difficulty the independent auditor faces when a computer service center is used is in determining the adequacy of the service center's internal controls. The auditor cannot automatically assume that the controls are adequate simply because it is an independent enterprise. If the client's service center application involves processing significant financial data, the auditor must consider the need to understand and test the service center's controls.

The extent of obtaining an understanding and testing of the service center should be based on the same criteria that the auditor follows in evaluating a client's own internal controls. The depth of the understanding depends on the complexity of the system and the extent to which the auditor intends to reduce assessed control risk to reduce other audit tests. If the auditor concludes that active involvement with the service center is the only way to conduct the audit, it may be necessary to obtain an extensive understanding of internal control, test it by the use of test data and other tests of controls, and use the computer to perform tests of the type discussed in the preceding sections. Extensive testing of this nature is unlikely in most audits, however, because most service center applications are reasonably simple. However, some review of the service center is usually done.

In recent years, it has become increasingly common to have *one* independent auditor obtain an understanding and test internal controls of the service center for the use of *all* customers and their independent auditors. The purpose of these independent reviews is to provide customers with a reasonable level of assurance of the adequacy of the service center's internal control and to eliminate the need for redundant audits by customers' auditors. If the service center has many customers and each requires an understanding of the service center's internal control by its own independent auditor, the inconvenience to the service center can be substantial. When the service center's independent CPA firm completes the audit of the controls and records, a special report is issued indicating the scope of the audit and the conclusions. It is then the responsibility of the customer's auditor to decide the extent to which he or she wants to rely on the service center's audit report. The professional standard for the audit of service centers is SAS 70 (AU 324).

## ESSENTIAL TERMS

**Application controls**—controls that relate to a specific use of the EDP system, such as the processing of sales or cash receipts

**Auditing around the computer**—auditing without testing the client's EDP controls; this is acceptable if the auditor has access to source documents and a detailed listing of output in a readable form

**Error listing**—a display of the actual errors that were reported by the EDP system

**General EDP controls**—controls that relate to all parts of the EDP system

**Generalized audit software** (GAS)—a computer program providing powerful data retrieval, data manipulation, and reporting capabilities specifically oriented to the needs of auditors.

**Hardware controls**—controls built into the EDP equipment by the manufacturer to detect equipment failure

**Input controls**—controls such as proper authorization of documents, adequate documentation, and check digits, designed to assure that the information processed by the computer is valid, complete, and accurate

**Microcomputer-aided auditing**—the use of microcomputers by the auditor to perform various audit functions, including generalized audit software applications, calculating analytical procedures, preparing audit working papers, and maintaining audit budgets

**Output controls**—controls, such as review of data for reasonableness, designed to assure that data generated by the computer is valid, accurate, complete, and distributed only to authorized people

**Parallel simulation**—A parallel simulation involves the auditor writing a computer program that replicates some part of a client's application system.

**Processing controls**—controls such as control totals, logic tests, and computation tests, designed to assure that data input into the system is accurately processed

**Test data approach**—a method of auditing EDP systems where the objective is to determine whether the client's computer program can correctly process valid and invalid transactions

## REVIEW QUESTIONS

**15-1 (Objective 15-1)** What are the most important factors that characterize a noncomplex EDP system? Identify the major technical factors that make EDP systems more complex.

**15-2 (Objective 15-1)** Explain how the extent to which an EDP system is used affects its complexity.

**15-3 (Objective 15-1)** Identify the major effects of EDP on organizations that use it.

**15-4 (Objective 15-1)** Define what is meant by a transaction trail and explain how the client's introduction of EDP can alter it. How does this change affect the auditor?

**15-5 (Objective 15-1)** Evaluate the following statement: "As EDP systems become more complex, the role of the traditional auditor declines. It is desirable that auditors involved with EDP systems either become competent in specialized computer concepts or use computer audit specialists on the engagement."

**15-6 (Objective 15-1)** In what ways is the potential for fraud greater in complex EDP systems than in less complex systems?

**15-7 (Objective 15-2)** Distinguish between hardware controls and application controls and explain the purpose of each.

**15-8 (Objective 15-2)** Explain why input controls are essential in an EDP system. Provide three examples.

**15-9 (Objective 15-2)** What is meant by application controls? Provide three examples of the type of misstatements they are meant to prevent.

**15-10 (Objective 15-2)** Define output controls and state their purpose. Provide an example of an output control.

**15-11 (Objective 15-2)** Explain the relationship between EDP application controls and transaction-related audit objectives.

**15-12 (Objective 15-3)** Compare the methodology of obtaining an understanding of internal control in a complex and noncomplex EDP system.

**15-13 (Objective 15-4)** Explain what is meant by "auditing around the computer." Under what circumstances is it acceptable to follow this approach?

**15-14 (Objective 15-5)** Explain what is meant by the test data approach to auditing with the computer. What are the major difficulties in using this approach?

**15-15 (Objective 15-5)** Define parallel simulation and provide an example of how a parallel simulation could be used to test a client's payroll system.

**15-16 (Objective 15-6)** Explain what is meant by generalized audit software and discuss its importance as an audit tool.

**15-17 (Objective 15-7)** What is the likely role of microcomputers as an audit tool? Identify three things that can be done with the use of microcomputers.

**15-18 (Objective 15-8)** Explain why it is unacceptable for an auditor to assume that an independent computer service center is providing reliable accounting information to an audit client. What can the auditor do to test the service center's internal controls?

## MULTIPLE CHOICE QUESTIONS FROM CPA EXAMINATIONS

**15-19 (Objectives 15-1, 15-2)** The following questions concern the characteristics of EDP systems. Choose the best response.

a. An EDP system is designed to ensure that management possesses the information it needs to carry out its functions through the integrated actions of
   (1) data gathering, analysis, and reporting functions.
   (2) a computer-based information retrieval and decision-making system.
   (3) statistical and analytical procedures functions.
   (4) production-budgeting and sales-forecasting activities.

b. Which of the following conditions would not normally cause the auditor to question whether material misstatements exist?
   (1) Bookkeeping errors are listed on an EDP-generated error listing.
   (2) Differences exist between control accounts and supporting master files.
   (3) Transactions are not supported by proper documentation.
   (4) Differences are disclosed by confirmations.

**15-20 (Objectives 15-4, 15-5, 15-6)** The following questions concern auditing EDP systems. Choose the best response.

a. Which of the following client EDP systems generally can be audited without examining or directly testing the EDP computer programs of the system?
   (1) A system that performs relatively uncomplicated processes and produces detailed output.
   (2) A system that affects a number of essential master files and produces a limited output.
   (3) A system that updates a few essential master files and produces no printed output other than final balances.
   (4) A system that performs relatively complicated processing and produces little detailed output.

b. Which of the following is true of generalized audit software programs?
   (1) They can be used only in auditing on-line computer systems.
   (2) They can be used on any computer without modification.
   (3) They each have their own characteristics that the auditor must carefully consider before using in a given audit situation.
   (4) They enable the auditor to perform all manual tests of controls procedures less expensively.

c. Assume that an auditor estimates that 10,000 checks were issued during the accounting period. If an EDP application control that performs a limit check for each check request is to be subjected to the auditor's test data approach, the sample should include
   (1) approximately 1,000 test items.
   (2) a number of test items determined by the auditor to be sufficient under the circumstances.
   (3) a number of test items determined by the auditor's reference to the appropriate sampling tables.
   (4) one transaction.

d. An auditor will use the EDP test data approach in order to gain certain assurances with respect to the

(1) input data.
(2) machine capacity.
(3) procedures contained within the program.
(4) degree of data entry accuracy.

## DISCUSSION QUESTIONS AND PROBLEMS

**15-21 (Objective 15-2)** The following are misstatements that can occur in the sales and collection cycle.

1. A customer order was filled and shipped to a former customer that had already filed bankruptcy.
2. The price of goods ordered by a customer was approved by the sales manager, but he wrote down the price for the wrong amount.
3. Several remittance advices were entered and sent to data processing. The clerk stopped for coffee, set them on a box, and failed to deliver them to the computer operator.
4. A customer number on a sales invoice was transposed and, as a result, charged to the wrong customer. By the time the error was found, the original customer was no longer in business.
5. A former computer operator, who is now a programmer, entered information for a fictitious sales return and ran it through the computer system at night. When the money came in, he took it and deposited it in his own account.
6. A computer operator picked up a computer-based data file for sales of the wrong week and processed them through the system a second time.
7. For a sale, a data entry operator erroneously failed to enter the information for the salesman's department. As a result the salesman received no commission for that sale.
8. A nonexistent part number was included in the description of goods on a shipping document. Therefore, no charge was made for those goods.

### Required

a. Identify the transaction-related audit objective(s) to which the misstatement pertains.

b. Identify one computer-based control that would have likely prevented each misstatement.

**15-22 (Objectives 15-1, 15-2, 15-3, 15-4)** You are doing the audit of Phelps College, a private school with approximately 2,500 students. With your firm's consultation, they have instituted an EDP system that separates the responsibilities of the computer operator, systems analyst, librarian, programmer, and data control group by having a different person do each function. Now, a budget reduction is necessary and one of the five people must be laid off. You are requested to give the college advice as to how the five functions could be performed with reduced personnel and minimal negative effects on internal control. The amount of time the functions take is not relevant, because all five people also perform nonaccounting functions.

### Required

a. Divide the five functions among four people in such a manner as to maintain the best possible control system.

b. Assume that economic times become worse for Phelps College and they must terminate employment of another person. Divide the five functions among three people in such a manner as to maintain the best possible internal control. Again, the amount of time each function takes should not be a consideration in your decision.

c. Assume that economic times become so severe for Phelps that only two people can be employed to perform EDP functions. Divide the five functions between two people in such a manner as to maintain the best possible control system.

d. If the five functions were performed by one person, would internal controls be so inadequate that an audit could not be performed? Discuss.

**15-23 (Objectives 15-2, 15-3, 15-4, 15-5)** The Meyers Pharmaceutical Company has the following system for billing and recording accounts receivable:

1. An incoming customer's purchase order is received in the order department by a clerk who prepares a prenumbered company sales order form on which is inserted the pertinent information, such as the customer's name and address, customer's account number, and quantity and items ordered. After the sales order form has been prepared, the customer's purchase order is stapled to it.
2. The sales order form is then passed to the credit department for credit approval. Rough approximations of the billing values of the orders are made in the credit department for those accounts on which credit limitations are imposed. After investigation, approval of credit is noted on the form.
3. Next the sales order form is passed to the billing department, where a clerk key enters the sales order information, including unit sales prices obtained from an approved price list, onto a data file. The data file is used to prepare sales invoices.

   The billing machine automatically accumulates daily totals of customer account numbers and invoice amounts to provide "hash" totals and control amounts. These totals, which are inserted in a daily record book, serve as predetermined batch totals for verification of computer inputs. The billing is done on prenumbered, continuous, carbon-interleaved forms having the following designations:
   (a) Customer's copy
   (b) Sales department copy, for information purposes
   (c) File copy
   (d) Shipping department copy, which serves as a shipping order

   Bills of lading are also prepared as carbon copy byproducts of the invoicing procedure.
4. The shipping department copy of the invoice and the bills of lading are then sent to the shipping department. After the order has been shipped, copies of the bill of lading are returned to the billing department. The shipping department copy of the invoice is filed in the shipping department.
5. In the billing department, one copy of the bill of lading is attached to the customer's copy of the invoice and both are mailed to the customer. The other copy of the bill of lading, together with the sales order form, is then stapled to the invoice file copy and filed in invoice numerical order.
6. The data file is updated for shipments that are different from those billed earlier. After these changes are made, the file is used to prepare a sales journal in sales invoice order and to update to the accounts receivable master file. Daily totals are printed to match the control totals prepared earlier. These totals are compared to the "hash" and control totals by an independent person.

## Required

a. Identify the important controls and related sales transaction-related audit objectives.

b. List the procedures that a CPA would employ in his or her audit of sales transactions to test the identified controls and the substantive aspects of the sales transactions.

**15-24 (Objective 15-6)** The following are audit procedures taken from a CPA firm's audit program for acquisitions and cash disbursements:

1. Foot the list of accounts payable and trace the balance to the general ledger.
2. Select a sample of accounts payable for confirmation, emphasizing vendors with a large balance and those that the client transacts with frequently, but include several with small and zero balances.

3. Compare all transactions recorded for four days before and after the balance sheet date with related receiving reports and vendors' invoices to determine the appropriate recording period.
4. Examine a random sample of 100 acquisition transactions to determine if each was authorized by an appropriate official and paid within the discount period to obtain the maximum cash discount.
5. Compare the total of each account payable outstanding, including zero balances, with those in the preceding year and examine vendors' statements for any total with a difference in excess of $500.
6. Compare the unit cost on a random sample of 100 vendors' invoices with catalogs or other price lists and investigate any with a difference of more than 3 percent.

### Required

a. For each audit procedure, identify whether it is a test of control, a substantive test of transactions, or a test of details of balances.

b. Explain how generalized audit software could be used, at least in part, to perform some or all of each audit procedure. Assume all information is in both machine- and nonmachine-readable form. Also, identify audit procedures or parts of procedures to which the general audit software is not likely to be applicable. Use the following format:

| Procedure | Data File or Files Needed | Kind of Test or Tests the Auditor Can Perform Using GAS | Procedure for Which GAS Is Likely to Be Inappropriate |
|---|---|---|---|

**15-25 (Objectives 15-1, 15-2, 15-3, 15-5, 15-6)** You are conducting an audit of sales for the James Department Store, a retail chain store with a computer-based sales system in which computer-based cash registers are integrated directly with accounts receivable, sales, perpetual inventory records, and sales commission expense. At the time of sale the salesclerks key-enter the following information directly into the cash register:

- Product number
- Quantity sold
- Unit selling price
- Store code number
- Salesclerk number
- Date of sale
- Cash sale or credit sale
- Customer account number for all credit sales

The total amount of the sale, including sales tax, is automatically computed by the system and indicated on the cash register's visual display. The only printed information for cash sales is the cash register receipt, which is given to the customer. For credit sales, a credit slip is prepared and one copy is retained by the clerk and submitted daily to the accounting department.

A summary of sales is printed out daily in the accounting department. The summary includes daily and monthly totals by salesclerks for each store as well as totals for each of ninety-three categories of merchandise by store. Perpetual inventory and accounts receivable records are updated daily on magnetic tape, but supporting records are limited primarily to machine-readable records.

### Required

a. What major problems does the auditor face in verifying sales and accounts receivable?

b. How can the concept of test data be employed in the audit? Explain the difficulties the auditor would have to overcome in using test data.

c. How can generalized audit software be employed in this audit? List several tests that can be conducted by using this approach.

d. The client would also like to reduce the time it takes to key-enter the information into the cash register. Suggest several ways in which this could be accomplished, considering the information now being key-entered manually.

**15-26 (Objective 15-6)** A CPA's client, Boos & Baumkirchner, Inc., is a medium-size manufacturer of products for the leisure time activities market (camping equipment, scuba gear, bows and arrows, and so forth). During the past year, a computer system was installed, and inventory records of finished goods and parts were converted to computer processing. The inventory master file is maintained on a disk. Each record of the file contains the following information:

- Item or part number
- Description
- Size
- Unit-of-measure code
- Quantity on hand
- Cost per unit
- Total value of inventory on hand at cost
- Date of last sale or usage
- Quantity used or sold this year
- Economic order quantity
- Code number of major vendor
- Code number of secondary vendor

In preparation for year-end inventory, the client has two identical sets of preprinted inventory count cards. One set is for the client's inventory counts and the other is for the CPA's use to make audit test counts. The following information has been keypunched into the cards and interpreted on their face:

- Item or part number
- Description
- Size
- Unit-of-measure code

In taking the year-end inventory, the client's personnel will write the actual counted quantity on the face of each card. When all counts are complete, the counted quantity will be keypunched into the cards. The cards will be processed against the inventory data base, and quantity-on-hand figures will be adjusted to reflect the actual count. A computer-generated edit listing will be prepared to show any missing inventory count cards and all quantity adjustments of more than $100 in value. These items will be investigated by client personnel, and all required adjustments will be made. When adjustments have been completed, the final year-end balances will be computed and posted to the general ledger.

The CPA has available generalized audit software that will run on the client's computer and can process both card and disk files.

## Required

a. In general and without regard to the facts in this case, discuss the nature of generalized audit software and list the various types and uses.

b. List and describe at least five ways generalized audit software can be used to assist in all aspects of the audit of the inventory of Boos & Baumkirchner, Inc. (For example, the software can be used to read the disk inventory master file and list items and parts with a high unit cost or total value. Such items can be included in the test counts to increase the dollar coverage of the audit verification.)*

*AICPA adapted

# 16

# AUDIT OF THE PAYROLL AND PERSONNEL CYCLE

## LEARNING OBJECTIVES

Thorough study of this chapter will enable you to

**16-1** Describe the payroll and personnel cycle and the pertinent documents and records, functions, and internal controls.

**16-2** Design and perform tests of controls and substantive tests of transactions for the payroll and personnel cycle.

**16-3** Design and perform analytical procedures for the payroll and personnel cycle.

**16-4** Design and perform tests of details of balances for accounts in the payroll and personnel cycle.

## THE STAFF AUDITOR MUST NEVER "SIMPLY FOLLOW ORDERS"

Leslie Scott graduated with a Masters of Accountancy degree from a major university and was heavily recruited by several large CPA firms. She joined the audit staff of the firm she liked best and was assigned to some of her office's better audit engagements. During her first "busy season" she was working on the audit of Sysco, Inc., a software development company. Because it was the busy season, the engagement team was working 60 to 70 hours per week.

Her immediate supervisor on the Sysco audit was Bob Stith. Bob had been with the firm three years longer than Leslie, and worked on the Sysco audit the previous year. He was supervising Leslie's work on capitalized software development costs. In preparing herself, Leslie had read FASB Statement 86, and had a good understanding of the accounting rules concerning the capitalization of such costs. She understood, for example, that costs could not be capitalized until after technological feasibility was established either through detail program design or product design and the completion of a working model, confirmed by testing.

Bob Stith drafted an audit program for capitalized software development costs. The steps were fairly general, but Bob added several oral instructions. He told Leslie to verify the payroll costs which were a significant part of the development cost and to talk to Jack Smart, Sysco's controller, about whether the projects with capitalized costs had reached the technological feasibility stage. Leslie tested the payroll costs and found no misstatements. She also made inquiries of Smart and was told that the appropriate stage was reached. Leslie documented Smart's representation in the working papers and went on to the next area assigned to her.

Later, Leslie began to have second thoughts. She understood that management's representations were a weak form of audit evidence and she was concerned about whether Jack Smart was the most knowledgeable person about the technical status of software projects. To resolve her concerns, she decided to talk to the responsible software engineers about one of the projects to confirm Smart's representations. She intended to clear this with Stith, but he was at another client's office that morning, so she proceeded on her own initiative. The engineer she talked to on the first project told her that he was almost finished with a working model, but hadn't tested it yet. She decided to inquire about another project and discovered the same thing. Leslie documented these findings on a working paper and planned to discuss the situation with Stith as soon as he returned to the job.

When Leslie (somewhat proud of herself) told Stith of her findings and showed him the working paper, he told her the following:

> Listen, Leslie, I told you just to talk to Jack. You shouldn't do procedures that you're not instructed to do. I want you to destroy this working paper and don't record the wasted time. We're under a lot of time pressure and we can't bill Sysco for procedures that aren't necessary. Jack knows what he's talking about. There's nothing wrong with the capitalized software development costs. The fact that they have working products that they're selling indicates technological feasibility was reached.

Leslie was extremely distressed with this reaction from Stith, but followed his instructions. She later talked to the audit partner about the situation during her annual counseling session. He mollified her concerns by pointing out that Stith was an experienced senior and probably had a broader perspective of the situation than she had as the staff assistant. Rather than worry, she should try and learn as much from working with the senior as she could.

The following fall, the SEC conducted an investigation of Sysco and found, among other things, that they had overstated capitalized software development costs. The SEC brought an action against both the management of Sysco and their auditors.

The payroll and personnel cycle involves the employment and payment of all employees, regardless of classification or method of determining compensation. The employees include executives on straight salary plus bonus, office workers on monthly salary with or without overtime, salespeople on a commission basis, and factory and unionized personnel paid on an hourly basis.

The cycle is important for several reasons. First, the salaries, wages, employer taxes, and other employer costs are a major expense in all companies. Second, labor is such an important consideration in the valuation of inventory in manufacturing and construction companies that the improper classification and allocation of labor can result in a material misstatement of net income. Finally, payroll is an area in which large amounts of company resources can be wasted because of inefficiency or are stolen through fraud.

The Hillsburg Hardware Co. trial balance on page 141 includes typical general ledger accounts affected by the payroll and personnel cycle. They are identified as payroll and personnel accounts by the letter *P* in the left column. In larger companies, many general ledger accounts are often affected by payroll. It is common, for example, for large companies to have fifty or more payroll expense accounts. Payroll also affects work-in-process and finished goods inventory accounts for manufacturing companies.

As with the sales and collection cycle, the audit of the payroll and personnel cycle includes obtaining an understanding of internal control, assessment of control risk, tests of controls and substantive tests of transactions, analytical procedures, and tests of details of balances. Accordingly, the first part of this chapter deals with the nature of the cycle, including its primary functions, documents and records, and internal controls. The second part includes tests of controls and substantive tests of transactions for the cycle. The third part discusses analytical procedures. Finally, the fourth part of the chapter focuses on verification by tests of details of balances of the related liability and expense accounts. These accounts include all salaries and wage expense accounts, employer payroll taxes and fringe benefits, and the liability for accrued wages, payroll taxes, and similar items connected with payroll.

There are several important differences between the payroll and personnel cycle and other cycles in a typical audit.

- *There is only one class of transactions for payroll.* Most cycles include at least two classes of transactions. For example, the sales and collection cycle includes both sales and cash receipts transactions and often sales returns and charge-off of uncollectibles. Payroll has only one class because the receipt of services from employees and the payment for those services through payroll occurs within a short time period.
- *Transactions are far more significant than related balance sheet accounts.* Payroll-related accounts such as accrued payroll and withheld taxes are usually small compared to the total amount of transactions for the year.
- *Internal controls over payroll are effective for almost all companies, even small ones.* The reasons for effective controls are harsh federal and state penalties for errors in withholding and paying payroll taxes and employee morale problems if employees are not paid or are underpaid.

Because of these three characteristics, auditors typically emphasize tests of controls, substantive tests of transactions, and analytical procedures in the audit of payroll. Tests of details of balances often take only a few minutes.

The way in which accounting information flows through the various accounts in the payroll and personnel cycle is illustrated by T-accounts in Figure 16-1. In most systems, the accrued wages and salaries account is used only at the end of an accounting period. Throughout the period, expenses are charged when the employees are actually paid rather than when the labor costs are incurred. The accruals for labor are recorded by adjusting entries at the end of the period for any earned but unpaid labor costs.

**FIGURE 16-1**

**Accounts in the Payroll and Personnel Cycle**

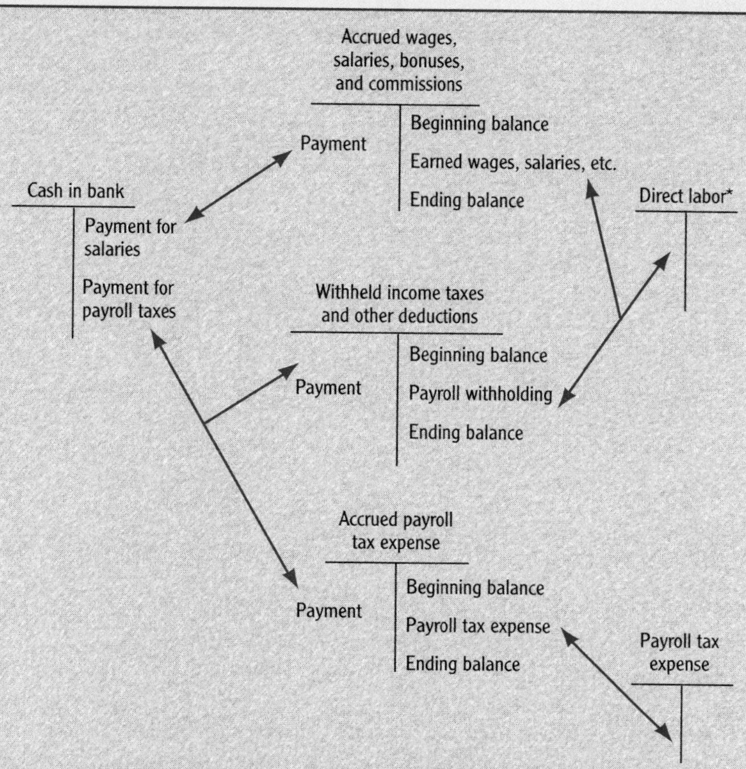


*Separate operating accounts for payroll also normally include officers' salaries and bonuses, office salaries, sales salaries and commissions, and indirect manufacturing labor. These accounts have the same relationship to accrued wages and withheld taxes and other deductions that is shown for direct labor.

## FUNCTIONS IN THE CYCLE, RELATED DOCUMENTS AND RECORDS, AND INTERNAL CONTROLS

**OBJECTIVE 16-1**

**Describe the payroll and personnel cycle and the pertinent documents and records, functions, and internal controls.**

The payroll and personnel cycle begins with the hiring of personnel and ends with payment to the employees for the services performed and to the government and other institutions for the withheld and accrued payroll taxes and benefits. In between, the cycle involves obtaining services from the employees consistent with the objectives of the company and accounting for the services in a proper manner.

Column 3 of Table 16-1 on page 558 identifies the four business functions in a typical payroll and personnel cycle. The table also shows the relationships among the business functions, classes of transactions, accounts, and documents and records. The business functions and related documents are discussed in this section. In addition, there is a discussion of key internal controls to prevent errors or fraud in providing data and to ensure the safety of assets.

### Personnel and Employment

The personnel department provides an independent source for interviewing and hiring qualified personnel. The department is also an independent source of records for the internal verification of wage information.

**TABLE 16-1**

**Classes of Transactions, Accounts, Business Functions, and Related Documents and Records for the Payroll and Personnel Cycle**

| Class of Transactions | Accounts | Business Functions | Documents and Records |
|---|---|---|---|
| Payroll | Payroll cash<br>All payroll expense accounts<br>All payroll withholding accounts<br>All payroll accrual accounts | Personnel and employment | Personnel records<br>Deduction authorization form<br>Rate authorization form |
| | | Timekeeping and payroll preparation | Time card<br>Job time ticket<br>Summary payroll report<br>Payroll journal<br>Payroll master file |
| | | Payment of payroll | Payroll check |
| | | Preparation of payroll tax returns and payment of taxes | W-2 form<br>Payroll tax returns |

**Personnel Records** Records that include such data as the date of employment, personnel investigations, rates of pay, authorized deductions, performance evaluations, and termination of employment.

**Deduction Authorization Form** A form authorizing payroll deductions, including the number of exemptions for withholding of income taxes, U.S. savings bonds, and union dues.

**Rate Authorization Form** A form authorizing the rate of pay. The source of the information is a labor contract, authorization by management, or, in the case of officers, authorization from the board of directors.

**Internal Controls** From an audit point of view, the most important internal controls in personnel involve formal methods of informing the timekeeping and payroll preparation personnel of new employees, the authorization of initial and periodic changes in pay rates, and the termination date of employees no longer working for the company. As a part of these controls, segregation of duties is extremely important. No individual with access to time cards, payroll records, or checks should also be permitted access to personnel records. A second important control is the adequate investigation of the competence and trustworthiness of new employees.

## Timekeeping and Payroll Preparation

This function is of major importance in the audit of payroll because it directly affects payroll expense for the period. It includes the preparation of time cards by employees; the summarization and calculation of gross pay, deductions, and net pay; the preparation of payroll checks; and the preparation of payroll records. There must be adequate controls to prevent misstatements in each of these activities.

**Time Card** A document indicating the time the employee started and stopped working each day and the number of hours the employee worked. For many employees, the time card is prepared automatically by time clocks. Time cards are usually submitted weekly.

**Job Time Ticket** A document indicating jobs on which a factory employee worked during a given time period. This form is used only when an employee works on different jobs or in different departments.

**Summary Payroll Report** A computer-generated document that summarizes payroll for a period in various forms. One summary is the totals debited to each general ledger account for payroll charges. These will equal gross payroll for the period. Another common summary for a manufacturing company is the totals charged to various jobs in a job cost accounting system. Similarly, commissions earned by each salesperson may be summarized.

**Payroll Journal** A journal for recording payroll checks. It typically indicates gross pay, withholdings, and net pay. The payroll journal is generated for any time period from the payroll transactions included in the computer files. The details in the journal are also included in the payroll master file. Journal totals are posted to the general ledger by the computer.

**Payroll Master File** A file for recording each payroll transaction for each employee and maintaining total employee wages paid for the year to date. The record for each employee includes gross pay for each payroll period, deductions from gross pay, net pay, check number, and date. The master file is updated from payroll computer transaction files. The total of the individual employee earnings in the master file equals the total balance of gross payroll in various general ledger accounts.

**Internal Controls** Adequate control over the time on the time cards includes the use of a time clock or other method of making certain that employees are paid for the number of hours they worked. There should also be controls to prevent anyone from checking in for several employees or submitting a fraudulent time card.

The summarization and calculation of the payroll can be controlled by well-defined policies for the payroll department, separation of duties to provide automatic cross-checks, reconciliation of payroll hours with independent production records, and independent internal verification of all important data. For example, payroll policies should require a competent, independent person to recalculate actual hours worked, review for the proper approval of all overtime, and examine time cards for erasures and alterations. Similarly, batch control totals over hours worked can be calculated from payroll time cards and compared to the actual hours processed by the computer. Finally, a printout of wage and withholding rates included in the computer files can be obtained and compared to authorized rates in the personnel files.

Controls over the preparation of payroll checks include preventing those responsible for preparing the checks from having access to time cards, signing or distributing checks, or independently verifying payroll output. In addition, the checks should be prenumbered and verified through independent bank reconciliation procedures.

When manufacturing labor affects inventory valuation, special emphasis should be put on controls to make sure labor is distributed to proper account classifications. There must also be adequate internal controls for recording job time tickets and other relevant payroll information in the cost accounting records. Independent internal verification of this information is an essential control.

**A MOBILE WORK FORCE**

In 1996, the AICPA's information technology division published a listing of the top fifteen technologies that may affect CPAs. One of these top technologies is telecommuting—an arrangement under which an employee works at a site other than the employer's central location. It is becoming increasingly common for employees to work at home in order to meet family and other personal obligations.

A company must have unique internal controls in place when employees work off-site. For example, controls should be in place to ensure that (1) recorded payments to off-site employees are for work *actually performed* (existence objective); (2) all payroll transactions involving off-site employees are recorded (completeness); and (3) payroll transactions for off-site employees are recorded on the correct dates (timing).

*Source: Journal of Accountancy,* January 1996, 25–28.

### Payment of Payroll

The actual signing and distribution of the checks must be properly handled to prevent their theft.

**Payroll Check** A check written to the employee for services performed. The check is prepared as a part of the payroll preparation function, but the authorized signature makes the check an asset. The amount of the check is the gross pay less taxes and other deductions withheld. After the check is cashed and returned to the company from the bank, it is referred to as a cancelled check. It is now common for payroll to be directly deposited into employees' bank accounts.

**Internal Controls** Controls over checks should include limiting the authorization for signing the checks to a responsible employee who does not have access to timekeeping or the preparation of the payroll, the distribution of payroll by someone who is not involved in the other payroll functions, and the immediate return of unclaimed checks for redeposit. If a check-signing machine is used to replace a manual signature, the same controls are required; in addition, the check-signing machine must be carefully controlled.

Most companies use an *imprest payroll account* to prevent the payment of unauthorized payroll transactions. An imprest payroll account is a separate payroll account in which a small balance is maintained. A check for the exact amount of each net payroll is transferred from the general account to the imprest account immediately before the distribution of the payroll. The advantages of an imprest account are that it limits the client's exposure to payroll fraud, allows the delegation of payroll check-signing duties, separates routine payroll expenditures from irregular expenditures, and facilitates cash management. It also simplifies the reconciliation of the payroll bank account if it is done at the low point in the payment cycle.

### Preparation of Payroll Tax Returns and Payment of Taxes

The timely preparation and mailing of payroll tax returns is required by federal and state payroll laws.

**W-2 Form** A form issued for each employee summarizing the earnings record for the calendar year. The information includes gross pay, income taxes withheld, and FICA withheld. The same information is also submitted to the Internal Revenue Service, and state and local tax commissions where applicable. This information is prepared from the payroll master file and is normally prepared by the computer.

**Payroll Tax Returns** Tax forms submitted to local, state, and federal units of government for the payment of withheld taxes and the employer's tax. The nature and due dates of the forms vary depending on the type of taxes. For example, federal withholding and social security payments are due weekly, monthly, or quarterly depending on the amount of withholding, and most state unemployment taxes are due quarterly. These forms are prepared from information on the payroll master file and are often prepared by the computer.

**Internal Controls** The most important control in the preparation of these returns is a well-defined set of policies that carefully indicate when each form must be filed. Most computerized payroll systems include the preparation of payroll tax returns using the information on the payroll transaction and master files. The independent verification of the output by a competent individual is an important control to prevent misstatements and potential liability for taxes and penalties.

## TESTS OF CONTROLS AND SUBSTANTIVE TESTS OF TRANSACTIONS

Figure 16-2 shows the methodology for designing tests of controls and substantive tests of transactions for the payroll and personnel cycle. It is the same methodology used in Chapter 11 for the sales and collection cycle.

**FIGURE 16-2**

**Methodology for Designing Tests of Controls and Substantive Tests of Transactions for the Payroll and Personnel Cycle**

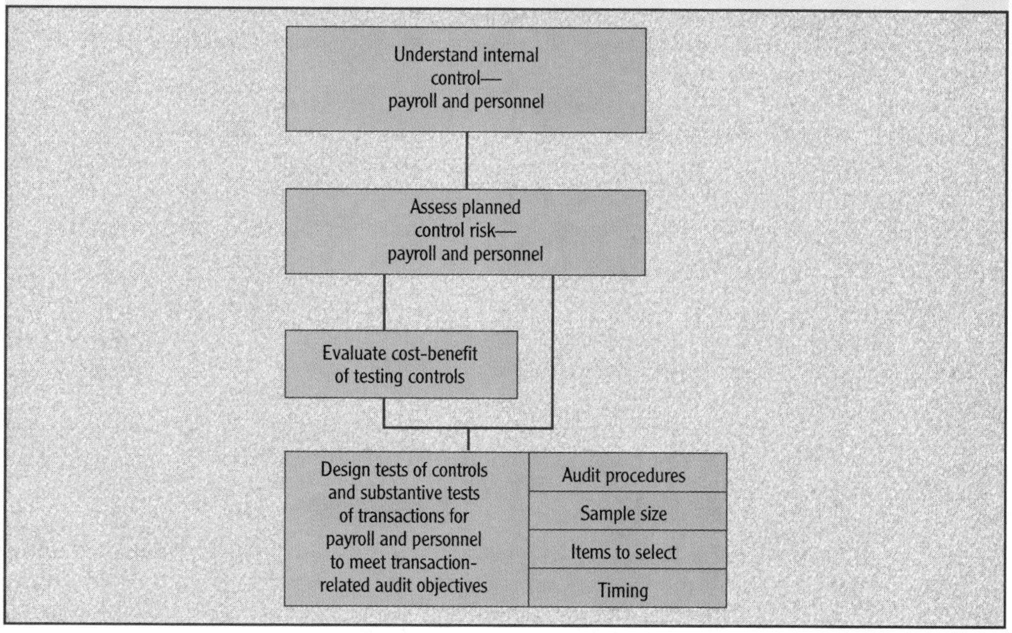


**OBJECTIVE 16-2**
**Design and perform tests of controls and substantive tests of transactions for the payroll and personnel cycle.**

Internal control for payroll is normally highly structured and well controlled, to control cash disbursed and to minimize employee complaints and dissatisfaction. It is common to use electronic data processing techniques to prepare all journals and payroll checks. In-house systems are often used, as are outside service center systems. It is usually not difficult to establish good control in the payroll and personnel cycle. For factory and office employees, there are usually a large number of relatively homogeneous, small amount transactions. There are fewer executive payroll transactions, but they are ordinarily consistent in timing, content, and amount. Because of relatively consistent payroll concerns from company to company, high-quality computer systems are available. Consequently, auditors seldom expect to find exceptions in testing payroll transactions. Occasionally control test deviations occur, but most monetary misstatements are corrected by internal verification controls or in response to employee complaints.

## Internal Controls, Tests of Controls, and Substantive Tests of Transactions

Tests of controls and substantive tests of transactions procedures are the *most important* means of verifying account balances in the payroll and personnel cycle. The emphasis on these tests is due to the lack of independent third-party evidence, such as confirmation, for verifying accrued wages, withheld income taxes, accrued payroll taxes, and other balance sheet accounts. Furthermore, in most audits the amounts in the balance sheet accounts are small and can be verified with relative ease if the auditor is confident that payroll transactions are correctly entered into the computer and payroll tax returns are properly prepared.

Even though the tests of controls and substantive tests of transactions are the most important part of testing payroll, many auditors spend little time in this area. In many audits, there is a minimal risk of material misstatements even though payroll is frequently a significant part of total expenses. There are three reasons for this: employees are likely to complain to management if they are underpaid, all payroll transactions are typically uniform and uncomplicated, and payroll transactions are extensively audited by federal and state governments for income tax withholding, social security, and unemployment taxes.

Following the same approach used in Chapter 11 for tests of sales and cash receipts transactions, the internal controls, tests of controls, and substantive tests of transactions for each transaction-related audit objective and related monetary errors and irregularities are summarized in Table 16-2. Again, the reader should recognize that

- Internal controls vary from company to company; therefore, the auditor must identify the controls and weaknesses for each organization.
- Controls the auditor intends to use for reducing assessed control risk must be tested with tests of controls.
- Substantive tests of transactions vary depending on the assessed control risk and the other considerations of the audit, such as the effect of payroll on inventory.
- Tests are not actually performed in the order given in Table 16-2. The tests of controls and substantive tests of transactions are combined where appropriate and are performed in as convenient a manner as possible, using a performance format audit program.

The purposes of the internal controls and the meaning and methodology of audit tests that can be used for payroll should be apparent from the description in Table 16-2. An extended discussion of these procedures is therefore not necessary.

## Payroll Tax Forms and Payments

Payroll taxes are an important consideration in many companies, both because the amounts are often material and because the potential liability for failure to file timely tax forms can be severe.

**Preparation of Payroll Tax Forms** As a part of understanding internal control, the auditor should review the preparation of at least one of each type of payroll tax form that the client is responsible for filing. There is a potential liability for unpaid taxes, penalty, and interest if the client fails to prepare the tax forms properly. The payroll tax forms are for such taxes as federal income and FICA withholding, state and city income withholding, and federal and state unemployment.

A detailed reconciliation of the information on the tax forms and the payroll records may be necessary when the auditor believes that there is a reasonable chance that the tax returns may be improperly prepared. Indications of potential misstatements in the returns include the payment of penalties and interest in the past for improper payments, new personnel in the payroll department who are responsible for the preparation of the returns, the lack of internal verification of the information, and the existence of serious cash flow problems for the client.

**Payment of the Payroll Taxes Withheld and Other Withholdings on a Timely Basis** It is desirable to test whether the client has fulfilled its legal obligation in submitting payments for all payroll withholdings as a part of the payroll tests even though the payments are usually made from general cash disbursements. The withholdings of concern in these tests are such items as taxes, union dues, insurance, and payroll savings. The auditor must first determine the client's requirements for submitting the payments. The requirements are determined by reference to such sources as tax laws, union contracts, and agreements with employees. After the auditor knows the requirements, it is easy to determine whether the client has paid the proper amount on a timely basis by comparing the subsequent cash disbursement with the payroll records.

## Inventory and Fraudulent Payroll Considerations

Auditors often extend their procedures considerably in the audit of payroll under the following circumstances: (1) when payroll significantly affects the valuation of inventory and (2) when the auditor is concerned about the possibility of material fraudulent payroll transactions.

**Relationship Between Payroll and Inventory Valuation** In audits in which payroll is a significant portion of inventory, a frequent occurrence for manufacturing and construction companies, the improper account classification of payroll can significantly affect asset valuation for accounts such as work in process, finished goods, or construction in process. For example,

**TABLE 16-2**

**Summary of Transaction-Related Audit Objectives, Key Controls, Tests of Controls, and Substantive Tests of Transactions for Payroll**

| Transaction-Related Audit Objective | Key Internal Control | Common Test of Control | Common Substantive Tests of Transactions |
|---|---|---|---|
| Recorded payroll payments are for work actually performed by existing employees (existence). | Time cards are approved by foremen.<br>Time clock is used to record time.<br>Adequate personnel file.<br>Authorization to work.<br>Separation of duties among personnel, timekeeping, and payroll disbursements.<br>Only employees existing in the computer data files are accepted when they are entered.<br>Authorization to issue check. | Examine the cards for indication of approvals.<br>Examine time cards.<br>Review personnel policies.<br>Examine personnel files.<br>Review organization chart, discuss with employees, and observe duties being performed.<br>Examine printouts of transactions rejected by the computer as having nonexistent employee numbers.†<br>Examine payroll records for indication of approval. | Review the payroll journal, general ledger, and payroll earnings records for large or unusual amounts.*<br>Compare cancelled checks with payroll journal for name, amount, and date.<br>Examine cancelled checks for proper endorsement.<br>Compare cancelled checks with personnel records. |
| Existing payroll transactions are recorded (completeness). | Payroll checks are prenumbered and accounted for.<br>Independent preparation of bank reconciliation. | Account for a sequence of payroll checks.<br>Discuss with employees and observe reconciliation. | Reconcile the disbursements in the payroll journal with the disbursements on the payroll bank statement.<br>Prove the bank reconciliation. |
| Recorded payroll transactions are for the amount of time actually worked and at the proper pay rate; withholdings are properly calculated (accuracy). | Internal verification of calculations and amounts.<br>Batch totals are compared with computer summary reports.<br>Authorization of wage rate, salary, or commission rate.<br>Authorization of withholdings, including amounts for insurance and payroll savings. | Examine indication of internal verification.<br>Examine file of batch totals for initials of data control clerk; compare totals to summary reports.†<br>Examine payroll records for indication of internal verification.<br>Examine authorizations in personnel file. | Recompute hours worked from time cards.<br>Compare pay rates with union contract, approval by board of directors, or other source.<br>Recompute gross pay.<br>Check withholdings by reference to tax tables and authorization forms in personnel file.<br>Recompute net pay.<br>Compare cancelled check with payroll journal for amount. |
| Payroll transactions are properly classified (classification). | Adequate chart of accounts.<br>Internal verification of classification. | Review chart of accounts.<br>Examine indication of internal verification. | Compare classification with chart of accounts or procedures manual.<br>Review time card for employee department and job ticket for job assignment, and trace through to labor distribution. |
| Payroll transactions are recorded on the correct dates (timing). | Procedures require recording transactions as soon as possible after the payroll is paid.<br>Internal verification. | Examine procedures manual and observe when recording takes place.<br>Examine indication of internal verification. | Compare date of recorded check in the payroll journal with date on cancelled checks and time cards.<br>Compare date on check with date the check cleared the bank. |
| Payroll transactions are properly included in the payroll master file and are properly summarized (posting and summarization). | Internal verification of payroll master file contents.<br>Comparison of payroll master file with payroll general ledger totals. | Examine indication of internal verification.<br>Examine initialed summary total reports indicating that comparisons have been made. | Test clerical accuracy by footing the payroll journal and tracing postings to the general ledger and the payroll master file. |

*This analytical procedure can also apply to other objectives, including completeness, accuracy, and timing.
†This control would be tested on many audits by using the computer.

the overhead charged to inventory at the balance sheet date can be overstated if the salaries of administrative personnel are inadvertently or intentionally charged to indirect manufacturing overhead. Similarly, the valuation of inventory is affected if the direct labor cost of individual employees is improperly charged to the wrong job or process. When some jobs are billed on a cost-plus basis, revenue and the valuation of inventory are both affected by charging labor to incorrect jobs.

When labor is a material factor in inventory valuation, there should be special emphasis on testing the internal controls over proper classification of payroll transactions. Consistency from period to period, which is essential for classification, can be tested by reviewing the chart of accounts and procedures manuals. It is also desirable to trace job tickets or other evidence of an employee's having worked on a job or process to the accounting records that affect inventory valuation. For example, if each employee must account for all of his or her time on a weekly basis by assigning it to individual job numbers, a useful test is to trace the recorded hours of several employees for a week to the related job-cost records to make sure each has been properly recorded. It may also be desirable to trace from the job-cost records to employee summaries as a test for nonexistent payroll charges being included in inventory.

**Tests for Nonexistent Payroll** Because auditors have significant responsibility for the detection of fraud, they must extend audit procedures when they become concerned about the possibility of material fraud. There are several ways in which employees can significantly defraud a company in the payroll area. This discussion is limited to tests for the two most common types: nonexistent employees and fraudulent hours.

The issuance of payroll checks to individuals who do not work for the company (nonexistent employees) frequently results from the continuance of an employee's check after his or her employment has been terminated. Usually, the person committing this type of defalcation is a payroll clerk, foreman, fellow employee, or perhaps the former employee. For example, under some systems a foreman could clock in daily for an employee and approve the time card at the end of the time period. If the foreman also distributes paychecks, considerable opportunity for defalcation exists.

Certain procedures can be performed on cancelled checks as a means of detecting defalcation. A procedure used on payroll audits is to compare the names on cancelled checks with time cards and other records for authorized signatures and reasonableness of the endorsements. It is also common to scan endorsements on cancelled checks for unusual or recurring second endorsements as an indication of a possible fraudulent check. The examination of checks that are recorded as voided is also desirable to make sure that they have not been fraudulently used.

A test for nonexistent employees is to trace selected transactions recorded in the payroll journal to the personnel department to determine whether the employees were actually employed during the payroll period. The endorsement on the cancelled check written out to an employee can be compared with the authorized signature on the employee's withholding authorization forms.

A procedure that tests for proper handling of terminated employees is to select several files from the personnel records for employees who were terminated in the current year to determine whether each received his or her termination pay in accordance with company policy. Continuing payments to terminated employees is tested by examining the payroll records in the subsequent period to ascertain that the employee is no longer being paid. Naturally, this procedure is not effective if the personnel department is not informed of terminations.

In some cases, the auditor may request a surprise payroll payoff. This is a procedure in which each employee must pick up and sign for his or her check in the presence of a supervisor and the auditor. Any checks that have not been claimed must be subject to an extensive investigation to determine whether an unclaimed check is fraudulent. Surprise payoff is frequently expensive and in some cases may even cause problems with a labor union, but it may be the only likely means of detecting a defalcation.

Fraudulent hours occur when an employee reports more time than was actually worked. Because of the lack of available evidence, it is usually difficult for an auditor to discover fraudulent hours. One procedure is to reconcile the total hours paid according to the payroll records with an independent record of the hours worked, such as those often maintained by production control. Similarly, it may be possible to observe an employee clocking in more than one time card under a buddy approach. However, it is ordinarily easier for the client to prevent this type of defalcation by adequate controls than for the auditor to detect it.

## ANALYTICAL PROCEDURES

**OBJECTIVE 16-3**
**Design and perform analytical procedures for the payroll and personnel cycle.**

The use of analytical procedures is as important in the payroll and personnel cycle as it is in every other cycle. Table 16-3 illustrates analytical procedures for the balance sheet and income statement accounts in the payroll and personnel cycle. Most of the relationships included in Table 16-3 are highly predictable and are therefore useful for uncovering areas in which additional investigation is desirable.

**TABLE 16-3**
**Analytical Procedures for the Payroll and Personnel Cycle**

| Analytical Procedure | Possible Misstatement |
|---|---|
| Compare payroll expense account balance with previous years (adjusted for pay rate increases and increases in volume). | Misstatement of payroll expense accounts |
| Compare direct labor as a percentage of sales with previous years. | Misstatement of direct labor and inventory |
| Compare commission expense as a percentage of sales with previous years. | Misstatement of commission expense and commission liability |
| Compare payroll tax expense as a percentage of salaries and wages with previous years (adjusted for changes in the tax rates). | Misstatement of payroll tax expense and payroll tax liability |
| Compare accrued payroll tax accounts with previous years. | Misstatement of accrued payroll taxes and payroll tax expense |

## TESTS OF DETAILS OF BALANCES FOR LIABILITY AND EXPENSE ACCOUNTS

**OBJECTIVE 16-4**
**Design and perform tests of details of balances for accounts in the payroll and personnel cycle.**

Figure 16-3 on page 566 summarizes the methodology for deciding the appropriate tests of details of balances for payroll liability accounts. The methodology is the same as that followed in Chapter 13 for accounts receivable. Normally, however, payroll-related liabilities are less material than accounts receivable; therefore, there is less inherent risk.

The verification of the liability accounts associated with payroll, often termed *accrued payroll expenses,* ordinarily is straightforward if internal controls are operating effectively. When the auditor is satisfied that payroll transactions are being properly recorded in the payroll journal and the related payroll tax forms are being accurately prepared and promptly paid, the tests of details of balances should not be time consuming.

The two major balance-related audit objectives in testing payroll liabilities are (1) accruals in the trial balance are stated at the correct amounts (accuracy) and (2) transactions in the payroll and personnel cycle are recorded in the proper period (cutoff). The primary concern in both objectives is to make sure that there are no understated or omitted accruals. The major liability accounts in the payroll and personnel cycle are now discussed.

**FIGURE 16-3**

**Methodology for Designing Tests of Details of Balances for Payroll Liabilities**

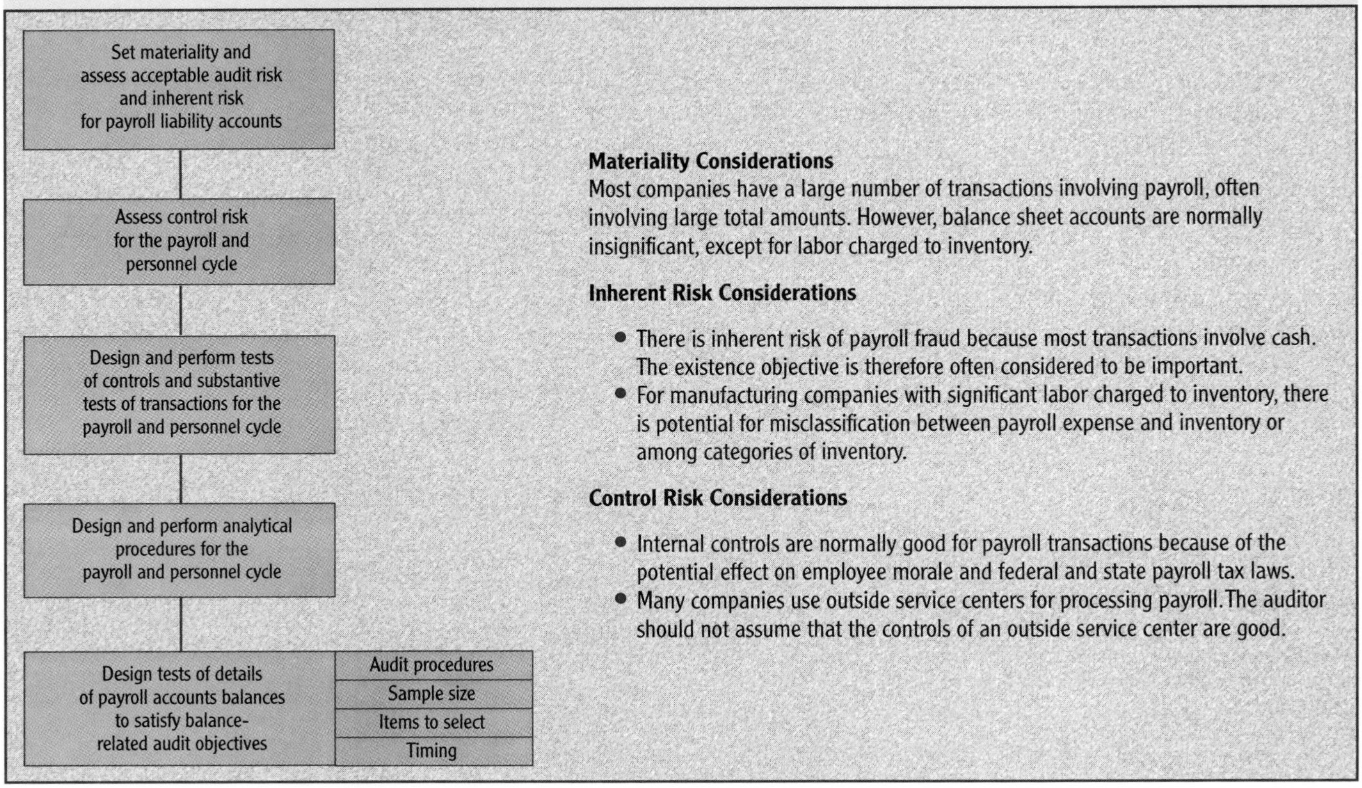


### Amounts Withheld from Employees' Pay

Payroll taxes withheld, but not yet disbursed, can be tested by comparing the balance with the payroll journal, the payroll tax form prepared in the subsequent period, and the subsequent period cash disbursements. Other withheld items such as union dues, savings bonds, and insurance can be verified in the same manner. If internal controls are operating effectively, cutoff and accuracy can easily be tested at the same time by these procedures.

### Accrued Salaries and Wages

The accrual for salaries and wages arises whenever employees are not paid for the last few days or hours of earned wages until the subsequent period. Salaried personnel usually receive all of their pay except overtime on the last day of the month, but frequently several days of wages for hourly employees are unpaid at the end of the year.

The correct cutoff and accuracy of accrued salaries and wages depends on company policy, which should be followed consistently from year to year. Some companies calculate the exact hours of pay that were earned in the current period and paid in the subsequent period, whereas others compute an approximate proportion. For example, if the subsequent payroll results from three days' employment during the current year and two days' employment during the subsequent year, the use of 60 percent of the subsequent period's gross pay as the accrual is an example of an approximation.

Once the auditor has determined the company's policy for accruing wages and knows that it is consistent with that of previous years, the appropriate audit procedure to test for cutoff and accuracy is to recalculate the client's accrual. The most likely misstatement of any significance in the balance is the failure to include the proper number of days of earned but unpaid wages.

### Accrued Commissions

The same concepts used in verifying accrued salaries and wages are applicable to accrued commissions, but the accrual is often more difficult to verify because companies frequently have several different types of agreements with salespeople and other commission employees. For example, some salespeople might be paid a commission every month and earn no salary, while others will get a monthly salary plus a commission paid quarterly. In some cases the commission varies for different products and may not be paid until several months after the end of the year. In verifying accrued commissions, it is necessary first to determine the nature of the commission agreement and then test the calculations based on the agreement. It is important to compare the method of accruing commissions with previous years for purposes of consistency. If the amounts are material, it is also common to confirm the amount that is due directly with the employees.

### Accrued Bonuses

In many companies, the year-end unpaid bonuses to officers and employees are such a major item that the failure to record them would result in a material misstatement. The verification of the recorded accrual can usually be accomplished by comparing it with the amount authorized in the minutes of the board of directors.

### Accrued Vacation Pay, Sick Pay, or Other Benefits

The consistent accrual of these liabilities relative to those of the preceding year is the most important consideration in evaluating the fairness of the amounts. The company policy for recording the liability must first be determined, followed by the recalculation of the recorded amounts. The company policy should be in accordance with FASB 43, which deals with compensated absences.

### Accrued Payroll Taxes

Payroll taxes such as FICA and state and federal unemployment taxes can be verified by examining tax forms prepared in the subsequent period to determine the amount that should have been recorded as a liability at the balance sheet date.

### Tests of Details of Balances for Expense Accounts

Several accounts in the income statement are affected by payroll transactions. The most important are officers' salaries and bonuses, office salaries, sales salaries and commissions, and direct manufacturing labor. There is frequently a further breakdown of costs by division, product, or branch. Fringe benefits such as medical insurance may also be included in the expenses.

There should be relatively little additional testing of the income statement accounts in most audits beyond the analytical procedures, tests of controls, substantive tests of transactions, and related tests of liability accounts, which have already been discussed. Extensive additional testing should be necessary only when there are weaknesses in internal control, significant misstatements are discovered in the liability tests, or major unexplained variances are found in the analytical procedures. Nevertheless, some income statement accounts are often tested in the payroll and personnel cycle. These include officers' compensation, commissions, payroll tax expense, and total payroll.

**Officers' Compensation** It is common to verify whether the total compensation of officers is the amount authorized by the board of directors, because their salaries and bonuses must be included in the SEC's 10-K report and federal income tax return. Verification of officers' compensation is also warranted because some individuals may be in a position to pay themselves more than the authorized amount. The usual audit test is to obtain the authorized salary of each officer from the minutes of the board of directors meetings and compare it with the related earnings record.

**Commissions** Commission expense can be verified with relative ease if the commission rate is the same for each type of sale and the necessary sales information is available in the accounting records. The total commission expense can be verified by multiplying the commission rate for each type of sale by the amount of sales in that category. If the desired information is not available, it may be necessary to test the annual or monthly commission payments for selected salespeople and trace those to the total commission payments. When the auditor believes it is necessary to perform these tests, they are normally done in conjunction with tests of accrued liabilities.

**Payroll Tax Expense** Payroll tax expense for the year can be tested by first reconciling the total payroll on each payroll tax form with the total payroll for the entire year. Total payroll taxes can then be recomputed by multiplying the appropriate rate by the taxable payroll. The calculation is frequently time consuming because the tax is usually applicable on only a portion of the payroll and the rate may change partway through the year if the taxpayer's financial statements are not on a calendar-year basis. On most audits, the calculation is costly and is not necessary unless analytical procedures indicate a problem that cannot be resolved through other procedures. When the auditor believes that the test is necessary, it is ordinarily done in conjunction with tests of payroll tax accruals.

**Total Payroll** A closely related test to the one for payroll taxes is the reconciliation of total payroll expense in the general ledger with the payroll tax returns and the W-2 forms. The objectives of the test are to determine whether payroll transactions were charged to a nonpayroll account or not recorded in the payroll journal at all. These objectives are certainly relevant, but it is questionable whether the procedure is useful in uncovering the type of misstatement for which it was intended. Since the payroll tax records and the payroll are both usually prepared directly from the payroll master file, the misstatements, if any, are likely to be in both records. The procedure may be worthwhile in rare situations, but it is usually not necessary to perform it. Tests of controls and substantive tests of transactions are a better means of uncovering these two types of misstatements in most audits.

## SUMMARY

Figure 16-4 illustrates the major accounts in the payroll and personnel cycle and the types of audit tests used to audit these accounts. This figure also shows how the audit risk model discussed in Chapter 8 relates to the audit of the payroll and personnel cycle.

**FIGURE 16-4**

**Types of Audit Tests for the Payroll and Personnel Cycle (see Figure 16-1 on page 557 for accounts)**

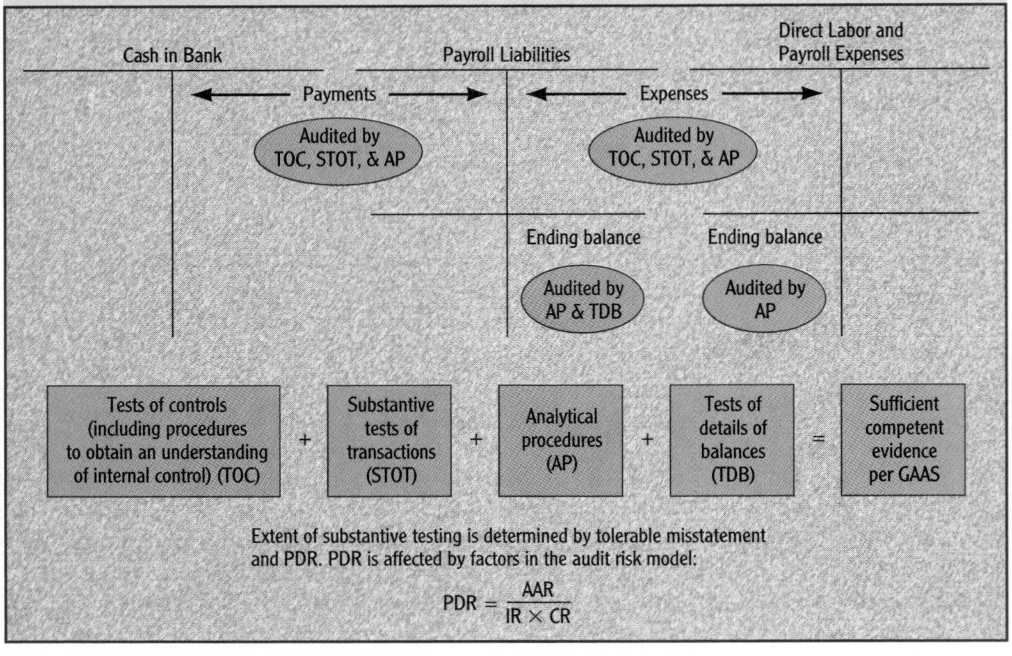

## ESSENTIAL TERMS

**Accrued payroll expenses**—the liability accounts associated with payroll; these include accounts for accrued salaries and wages, accrued commissions, accrued bonuses, accrued benefits, and accrued payroll taxes

**Imprest payroll account**—a bank account to which the exact amount of payroll for the pay period is transferred by check from the employer's general cash account

**Payroll and personnel cycle**—the transaction cycle that begins with the hiring of personnel, includes obtaining and accounting for services from the employees, and ends with payment to the employees for the services performed and to the government and other institutions for withheld and accrued payroll taxes and benefits

**Payroll master file**—a computer file for recording each payroll transaction for each employee, and maintaining total employee wages paid and related data for the year to date

**Payroll tax returns**—tax forms that the employer submits to local, state, and federal authorities for the payment of withheld taxes and the employer's tax

**Personnel records**—records that include such data as the date of employment, personnel investigations, rates of pay, authorized deductions, performance evaluations, and termination of employment

**Time card**—a document indicating the time that the employee started and stopped working each day and the number of hours worked

## REVIEW QUESTIONS

**16-1 (Objective 16-1)** Identify five general ledger accounts that are likely to be affected by the payroll and personnel cycle in most audits.

**16-2 (Objective 16-2)** Explain the relationship between the payroll and personnel cycle and inventory valuation.

**16-3 (Objective 16-2)** List five tests of controls that can be performed for the payroll and personnel cycle and state the purpose of each control being tested.

**16-4 (Objective 16-2)** Explain why the percentage of total audit time in the cycle devoted to performing tests of controls and substantive tests of transactions is usually far greater for the payroll and personnel cycle than for the sales and collection cycle.

**16-5 (Objectives 16-1, 16-2)** Evaluate the following comment by an auditor: "My job is to determine whether the payroll records are fairly stated in accordance with generally accepted accounting principles, not to find out whether they are following proper hiring and termination procedures. When I conduct an audit of payroll I keep out of the personnel department and stick to the time cards, journals, and payroll checks. I don't care whom they hire and whom they fire, as long as they properly pay the ones they have."

**16-6 (Objective 16-2)** Distinguish between the following payroll audit procedures and state the purpose of each: (1) Trace a random sample of prenumbered time cards to the related payroll checks in the payroll register and compare the hours worked with the hours paid, and (2) trace a random sample of payroll checks from the payroll register to the related time cards and compare the hours worked with the hours paid. Which of these two procedures is typically more important in the audit of payroll? Why?

**16-7 (Objective 16-4)** In auditing payroll withholding and payroll tax expense, explain why emphasis should normally be on evaluating the adequacy of the payroll tax return preparation procedures rather than the payroll tax liability. If the preparation procedures are inadequate, explain the effect this will have on the remainder of the audit.

**16-8 (Objective 16-3)** List several analytical procedures for the payroll and personnel cycle and explain the type of misstatement that might be indicated when there is a significant difference in the comparison of the current year with previous years' results for each of the tests.

**16-9 (Objective 16-2)** Explain the circumstances under which an auditor should perform audit tests primarily designed to uncover fraud in the payroll and personnel cycle. List three audit procedures that are primarily for the detection of fraud and state the type of fraud the procedure is meant to uncover.

**16-10 (Objective 16-1)** Distinguish between a payroll master file, a W-2 form, and a payroll tax return. Explain the purpose of each.

**16-11 (Objectives 16-1, 16-2)** List the supporting documents and records the auditor will examine in a typical payroll audit in which the primary objective is to detect fraud.

**16-12 (Objective 16-1)** List five types of authorizations in the payroll and personnel cycle and state the type of misstatement that is likely to occur when each authorization is lacking.

**16-13 (Objective 16-4)** Explain why it is common to verify total officers' compensation even when the tests of controls and substantive tests of transactions results in payroll are excellent. What audit procedures can be used to verify officers' compensation?

**16-14 (Objective 16-1)** Explain what is meant by an imprest payroll account. What is its purpose as a control over payroll?

**16-15 (Objective 16-2)** List several audit procedures that the auditor can use to determine whether payroll transactions are recorded at the proper amount.

**16-16 (Objective 16-2)** Explain how audit sampling can be used to test the payroll and personnel cycle.

## MULTIPLE CHOICE QUESTIONS FROM CPA EXAMINATIONS

**16-17 (Objective 16-1)** The following questions concern internal controls in the payroll and personnel cycle. Choose the best response.

a. A factory foreman at Steblecki Corporation discharged an hourly worker but did *not* notify the payroll department. The foreman then forged the worker's signature on time cards and work tickets and, when giving out the checks, diverted the payroll checks drawn from the discharged worker to his own use. The most effective procedure for preventing this activity is to
   (1) require written authorization for all employees added to or removed from the payroll.
   (2) have a paymaster who has *no* other payroll responsibility distribute the payroll checks.
   (3) have someone other than persons who prepare or distribute the payroll obtain custody of unclaimed payroll checks.
   (4) from time to time, rotate persons distributing the payroll.

b. The CPA reviews Pyzi's payroll procedures. An example of an internal control weakness is to assign to a department supervisor the responsibility for
   (1) distributing payroll checks to subordinate employees.
   (2) reviewing and approving time reports for subordinates.
   (3) interviewing applicants for subordinate positions prior to hiring by the personnel department.
   (4) initiating requests for salary adjustments for subordinate employees.

c. From the standpoint of good internal control, distributing payroll checks to employees is best handled by the
   (1) accounting department.
   (2) personnel department.
   (3) treasurer's department.
   (4) employee's departmental supervisor.

**16-18 (Objective 16-2)** The following questions concern audit testing of the payroll and personnel cycle. Choose the best response.

a. A computer operator perpetrated a theft by preparing erroneous W-2 forms. The operator's FICA withheld was overstated by $500 and the FICA withheld from all other employees was understated. Which of the following audit procedures would detect such a fraud?
   (1) Multiplication of the applicable rate by the individual's gross taxable earnings.
   (2) Using form W-4 and withholding charts to determine whether deductions authorized per pay period agree with amounts deducted per pay period.
   (3) Footing and crossfooting of the payroll register followed by tracing postings to the general ledger.
   (4) Vouching cancelled checks to federal tax form 941.
b. In the audit of which of the following types of profit-oriented enterprises would the auditor be most likely to place special emphasis on tests of controls for proper classifications of payroll transactions?
   (1) A manufacturing organization.
   (2) A retailing organization.
   (3) A wholesaling organization.
   (4) A service organization.
c. A common audit procedure in the audit of payroll transactions involves tracing selected items from the payroll journal to employee time cards that have been approved by supervisory personnel. This procedure is designed to provide evidence in support of the audit proposition that
   (1) only proper employees worked and their pay was properly computed.
   (2) jobs on which employees worked were charged with the appropriate labor cost.
   (3) internal controls over payroll disbursements are operating effectively.
   (4) all employees worked the number of hours for which their pay was computed.

## DISCUSSION QUESTIONS AND PROBLEMS

**16-19 (Objectives 16-1, 16-2)** Items 1 through 9 are selected questions typically found in internal control questionnaires used by auditors to obtain an understanding of internal control in the payroll and personnel cycle. In using the questionnaire for a client, a "yes" response to a question indicates a possible internal control, whereas a "no" indicates a potential weakness.

1. Does an appropriate official authorize initial rates of pay and any subsequent changes in rates?
2. Are written notices required documenting reasons for termination?
3. Are formal records such as time cards used for keeping time?
4. Is approval by a department head or foreman required for all time cards before they are submitted for payment?
5. Does anyone verify pay rates, overtime hours, and computations of gross payroll before payroll checks are prepared?
6. Does an adequate means exist for identifying jobs or products, such as work orders, job numbers, or some similar identification provided to employees to ensure proper coding of time records?
7. Are employees paid by checks prepared by persons independent of timekeeping?
8. Are employees required to show identification to receive paychecks?
9. Is a continuing record maintained of all unclaimed wages?

### Required

a. For each of the questions, state the transaction-related audit objective(s) being fulfilled if the control is in effect.
b. For each control, list a test of control to test its effectiveness.

c. For each of the questions, identify the nature of the potential financial misstatement(s) if the control is not in effect.

d. For each of the potential misstatements in part (c), list a substantive audit procedure for determining whether a material misstatement exists.

**16-20 (Objectives 16-1, 16-2)** Following are some of the tests of controls and substantive tests of transactions procedures frequently performed in the payroll and personnel cycle. (Each procedure is to be done on a sample basis.)

1. Reconcile the monthly payroll total for direct manufacturing labor with the labor cost distribution.
2. Examine the time card for the approval of a foreman.
3. Recompute hours on the time card and compare the total with the total hours for which the employee has been paid.
4. Compare the employee name, date, check number, and amounts on cancelled checks with the payroll journal.
5. Trace the hours from the employee time cards to job tickets to make sure that the total reconciles, and trace each job ticket to the job-cost record.
6. Account for a sequence of payroll checks in the payroll journal.
7. Select employees from the personnel file who have been terminated and determine whether their termination pay was in accordance with the union contract. As part of this procedure, examine two subsequent periods to determine whether the terminated employee is still being paid.

## Required

a. Identify whether each of the procedures is primarily a test of control or a substantive test of transactions.

b. Identify the transaction-related audit objective(s) of each of the procedures.

**16-21 (Objectives 16-1, 16-2)** The following misstatements are included in the accounting records of Lathen Manufacturing Company.

1. Direct labor was unintentionally charged to job 620 instead of job 602 by the payroll clerk when he key-entered the labor distribution sheets. Job 602 was completed and the costs were expensed in the current year, whereas job 620 was included in work-in-process.
2. Joe Block and Frank Demery take turns "punching in" for each other every few days. The absent employee comes in at noon and tells his foreman that he had car trouble or some other problem. The foreman does not know that the employee is getting paid for the time.
3. The foreman submits a fraudulent time card for a former employee each week and delivers the related payroll check to the employee's house on the way home from work. They split the amount of the paycheck.
4. Employees frequently overlook recording their hours worked on job-cost tickets as required by the system. Many of the client's contracts are on a cost-plus basis.
5. The payroll clerk prepares a check to the same nonexistent person every week when he key-enters payroll transactions in the microcomputer system, which also records the amount in the payroll journal. He submits it along with all other payroll checks for signature. When the checks are returned to him for distribution, he takes the check and deposits it in a special bank account bearing that person's name.
6. In withholding payroll taxes from employees, the computer operator deducts \$.50 extra federal income taxes from several employees each week and credits the amount to his own employee earnings record.
7. The payroll clerk manually prepares payroll checks, but frequently forgets to record one or two checks in the microcomputer-prepared payroll journal.

## Required

a. For each misstatement, state a control that should have prevented it from occurring on a continuing basis.

b. For each misstatement, state a substantive audit procedure that could uncover it.

**16-22 (Objectives 16-1, 16-2, 16-3, 16-4)** The following audit procedures are typical of those found in auditing the payroll and personnel cycle.

1. Examine evidence of double-checking payroll wage rates and calculations by an independent person.
2. Obtain a schedule of all payroll liabilities and trace to the general ledger.
3. Select a sample of twenty cancelled payroll checks and account for the numerical sequence.
4. Foot and crossfoot the payroll journal for two periods and trace totals to the general ledger.
5. For payroll liabilities, examine subsequent cash disbursements and supporting documents such as payroll tax returns, depository receipts, and tax receipts.
6. Select a sample of twenty cancelled payroll checks and trace to payroll journal entries for name, date, and amounts.
7. Compute direct labor, indirect labor, and commissions as a percentage of net sales and compare with prior years.
8. Examine owner approval of rates of pay and withholdings.
9. Compute payroll tax expense as a percentage of total wages, salaries, and commissions.
10. Discuss with management any payroll liabilities at the last engagement date that are not provided for currently.
11. Scan journals for all periods for unusual transactions to determine if they are recorded properly.
12. Select a sample of forty entries in the payroll journal and trace each to an approved time card.

## Required

a. Select the type of test for each audit procedure from the following:
   (1) Test of control
   (2) Substantive test of transactions
   (3) Analytical procedure
   (4) Test of details of balances

b. For each test of control or substantive test of transactions, identify the applicable transaction-related audit objective(s).

c. For each test of details of balances, identify the applicable balance-related audit objective(s).

**16-23 (Objectives 16-2, 16-4)** The following are steps in the methodology for designing tests of controls, substantive tests of transactions, and tests of details of balances for the payroll and personnel cycle:

1. Design tests of details of balances for the payroll and personnel cycle.
2. Evaluate risk and materiality for payroll expense and liability accounts.
3. Evaluate cost-benefit of assessing control risk as low for payroll.
4. Design and perform payroll- and personnel-related analytical procedures.
5. Identify controls and weaknesses in internal control for the payroll and personnel cycle.
6. Obtain an understanding of the payroll and personnel cycle internal controls.
7. Evaluate tests of controls and substantive tests of transactions results.
8. Design payroll and personnel cycle tests of controls and substantive tests of transactions.
9. Assess inherent risk for payroll-related accounts.

## Required

a. Identify those steps that are (1) tests of controls or substantive tests of transactions and (2) those that are tests of details of balances.

b. Put steps that are tests of controls and substantive tests of transactions in the order of their performance in most audits.

c. Put the tests of details of balances in their proper order.

**16-24 (Objective 16-3)** In comparing total payroll tax expense with the preceding year, Merlin Brendin, CPA, observed a significant increase, even though the total number of employees had increased only from 175 to 195. To investigate the difference, he selected a large sample of payroll disbursement transactions and carefully tested the withholdings for each employee in the sample by referring to federal and state tax withholding schedules. In his test he found no exceptions; therefore, he concluded that payroll tax expense was fairly stated.

## Required

a. Evaluate Brendin's approach to testing payroll tax expense.

b. Discuss a more suitable approach for determining whether payroll tax expense was properly stated in the current year.

**16-25 (Objective 16-4)** As part of the audit of McGree Plumbing and Heating, you have responsibility for testing the payroll and personnel cycle. Payroll is the largest single expense in the client's trial balance, and hourly wages make up most of the payroll total. A unique aspect of its business is the extensive overtime incurred by employees on some days. It is common for employees to work only three or four days during the week but to work long hours while they are on the job. McGree's management has found that this actually saves money, in spite of the large amount of overtime, because the union contract requires payment for all travel time. Since many of the employees' jobs require long travel times and extensive startup costs, this policy is supported by both McGree and the employees.

You have already carefully evaluated and tested the payroll and personnel cycle's internal control and concluded that it contains no significant weaknesses. Your tests included tests of the time cards, withholdings, pay rates, the filing of all required tax returns, payroll checks, and all other aspects of payroll.

As part of the year-end tests of payroll, you are responsible for verifying all accrued payroll as well as accrued and withheld payroll taxes. The accrued factory payroll includes the last six working days of the current year. The client has calculated accrued wages by taking 60 percent of the subsequent period's gross payroll and has recorded it as an adjusting entry to be reversed in the subsequent period.

## Required

List all audit procedures you would follow in verifying accrued payroll, withheld payroll taxes, and accrued payroll taxes.

**16-26 (Objective 16-2)** In the audit of Larnet Manufacturing Company, the auditor concluded that internal controls were inadequate because of the lack of segregation of duties. As a result, the decision was made to have a surprise payroll payoff one month before the client's balance sheet date. Since the auditor had never been involved in a payroll payoff, she did not know how to proceed.

## Required

a. What is the purpose of a surprise payroll payoff?

b. What other audit procedures can the auditor perform that may fulfill the same objectives?

c. Discuss the procedures that the auditor should require the client to observe when the surprise payroll payoff is taking place.

d. At the completion of the payroll payoff, there are frequently several unclaimed checks. What procedures should be followed for these?

**16-27 (Objectives 16-1, 16-2)** The Kowal Manufacturing Company employs about fifty production workers and has the following payroll procedures:

The factory foreman interviews applicants and on the basis of the interview either hires or rejects them. When the applicant is hired, he or she prepares a W-4 form (Employee's Withholding Exemption Certificate) and gives it to the foreman. The foreman writes the hourly rate of pay for the new employee in the corner of the W-4 form and then gives the form to a payroll clerk as notice that the worker has been employed. The foreman verbally advises the payroll department of rate adjustments.

A supply of blank time cards is kept in a box near the entrance to the factory. Each worker takes a time card on Monday morning, fills in his or her name, and notes in pencil his or her daily arrival and departure times. At the end of the week the workers drop the time cards in a box near the door to the factory.

On Monday morning, the completed time cards are taken from the box by a payroll clerk. One of the payroll clerks then records the payroll transactions using a microcomputer system, which records all information for the payroll journal that was calculated by the clerk and automatically updates the employees' earnings records and general ledger. Employees are automatically removed from the payroll when they fail to turn in a time card.

The payroll checks are manually signed by the chief accountant and given to the foreman. The foreman distributes the checks to the workers in the factory and arranges for the delivery of the checks to the workers who are absent. The payroll bank account is reconciled by the chief accountant, who also prepares the various quarterly and annual payroll tax reports.

## Required

a. List the most serious weaknesses in internal control and state the misstatements that are likely to result from the weaknesses. In your audit of Kowal's payroll, what will you emphasize in your audit tests? Explain.

b. List your suggestions for improving the Kowal Manufacturing Company's internal controls for the factory hiring practices and payroll procedures.*

**16-28 (Objective 16-4)** During the first-year audit of Jones Wholesale Stationery you observe that commissions amount to almost 25 percent of total sales, which is somewhat higher than in previous years. Further investigation reveals that the industry typically has larger sales commissions than Jones and that there is significant variation in rates depending on the product sold.

At the time a sale is made, the salesperson records his or her commission rate and the total amount of the commissions on the office copy of the sales invoice. When sales are entered into the microcomputer system for the recording of sales, the debit to sales commission expense and credit to accrued sales commission are also recorded. As part of recording the sales and sales commission expense, the accounts receivable clerk verifies the prices, quantities, commission rates, and all calculations on the sales invoices. Both the accounts receivable and the salespersons' commission master files are updated when the sale and sales commission are recorded. On the fifteenth day after the end of the month, the salesperson is paid for the preceding month's sales commissions.

## Required

a. Develop an audit program to verify sales commission expense, assuming that no audit tests have been conducted in any audit area to this point.

b. Develop an audit program to verify accrued sales commissions at the end of the year, assuming that the tests you designed in part a resulted in no significant misstatements.

*AICPA adapted.

**16-29 (Objective 16-1)** You are engaged to audit the financial statements of Henry Brown, a large independent contractor. All employees are paid in cash because Brown believes this arrangement reduces clerical expenses and is preferred by his employees.

During the audit you find in the petty cash fund approximately $200, of which $185 is stated to be unclaimed wages. Further investigation reveals that Brown has installed the procedure of putting any unclaimed wages in the petty cash fund so that the cash can be used for disbursements. When the claimant to the wages appears, he or she is paid from the petty cash fund. Brown contends that this procedure reduces the number of checks drawn to replenish the petty cash fund and centers the responsibility for all cash on hand in one person, inasmuch as the petty cash custodian distributes the pay envelopes.

### Required

a. Are Brown's internal controls over unclaimed wages adequate? Explain fully.

b. Because Brown insists on paying salaries in cash, what procedures would you recommend to provide better internal control over unclaimed wages?*

**16-30 (Objective 16-2)** In many companies, labor costs represent a substantial percentage of total dollars expended in any one accounting period. One of the auditor's primary means of verifying payroll transactions is by a detailed payroll test.

You are performing an annual audit of the Joplin Company, a medium-size manufacturing company. You have selected a number of hourly employees for a detailed payroll test. The worksheet outline at the bottom of this page has been prepared.

### Required

a. What factors should the auditor consider in selecting his or her sample of employees to be included in any payroll test?

b. Using the column numbers below as a reference, state the principal way(s) that the information for each heading would be verified.

c. In addition to the payroll test, the auditor employs a number of other audit procedures in the verification of payroll transactions. List five additional procedures that may be employed.*

| Column Number | Heading |
|---|---|
| 1 | Employee number |
| 2 | Employee name |
| 3 | Job classification |
| | Hours worked |
| 4 | Straight time |
| 5 | Premium time |
| 6 | Hourly rate |
| 7 | Gross earnings |
| | Deductions |
| 8 | FICA withheld |
| 9 | Medicare withheld |
| 10 | FIT withheld |
| 11 | Union dues |
| 12 | Hospitalization |
| 13 | Amount of check |
| 14 | Check number |
| 15 | Account number charged |
| 16 | Description of account |

*AICPA adapted.

**16-31 (Objective 16-2)** Roost and Briley, CPAs, are doing the audits of Leggert Lumber Co., an international wholesale lumber broker. Due to the nature of their business, payroll and telephone expense are the two largest expenses.

You are the in-charge auditor on the engagement responsible for writing the audit program for the payroll and personnel cycle. Leggert Lumber uses a computer service company to prepare weekly payroll checks, update earnings records, and prepare the weekly payroll journal for its 30 employees. The president maintains all personnel files, knows every employee extremely well, and is a full-time participant in the business.

All employees, except the president, check into the company building daily using a time clock. The president's secretary, Mary Clark, hands out the time cards daily, observes employees clocking in, collects the cards, and immediately returns them to the file. She goes through the same process when employees clock out on their way home.

At the end of each week, employees calculate their own hours. Clark rechecks those hours, and the president approves all time cards. Each Tuesday, Clark prepares a *payroll input form* for delivery to the computer service center. She files a copy of the form. The form has the following information for each employee:

| **Information** | **Source** |
|---|---|
| Employee name | Time card |
| Social security number | Employee list |
| Hourly labor rate* | Wage rate list (approved by president) |
| Regular hours | Time card |
| Overtime hours | Time card |
| Special deductions* | Special form (prepared by employee) |
| W-4 information* | W-4 form |
| Termination of employment* | President |

The service center key enters the information from the payroll input form into its computer, updates master files, and prints out payroll checks and a payroll register. The payroll register has the following headings:

| | |
|---|---|
| Employee name | FICA taxes withheld |
| Social security number | Medicare withheld |
| Regular hours | Federal taxes withheld |
| Overtime hours | State taxes withheld |
| Regular payroll dollars | Other deductions |
| Overtime payroll dollars | Net pay |
| Gross payroll | Check number |

A line is prepared for each employee and the journal is totaled.

Payroll checks and the journal are delivered to Clark, who compares the information on the journal with her payroll input form and initials the journal. She gives the checks to the president, who signs them and personally delivers them to employees.

Clark re-adds the journal and posts the totals to the ledger. Cancelled checks are mailed to the president, and he prepares a monthly bank reconciliation.

*Included on input form only for new employees, terminations, and changes.

**Required**

a. Is there any loss of documentation because of the computer service center? Explain.

b. For each transaction-related audit objective for the payroll and personnel cycle, write appropriate tests of controls and substantive tests of transactions audit procedures. Consider both controls and weaknesses in writing your program. Label each procedure as either a test of control or a substantive test of transactions.

c. Rearrange your design format audit program in part b into a performance format audit program.

d. Prepare a sampling data sheet using either nonstatistical or attributes sampling, such as the ones shown in Chapter 12, for the audit program in part b. Set ARACR and other factors required for sampling as you consider appropriate. Do not assume that you actually performed any tests.

17

# AUDIT OF THE ACQUISITION AND PAYMENT CYCLE: TESTS OF CONTROLS, SUBSTANTIVE TESTS OF TRANSACTIONS, AND ACCOUNTS PAYABLE

## LEARNING OBJECTIVES

Thorough study of this chapter will enable you to

**17-1** Describe the acquisition and payment cycle, and the pertinent documents and records, functions, and internal controls.

**17-2** Design and perform tests of controls and substantive tests of transactions for the acquisition and payment cycle, and assess related control risk.

**17-3** Discuss the nature of accounts payable, and describe the related controls.

**17-4** Design and perform analytical procedures for accounts payable.

**17-5** Design and perform tests of details for accounts payable.

**17-6** Know the importance of out-of-period liability tests for accounts payable and common tests.

**17-7** Know the relative reliability of vendors' invoices, vendors' statements, and confirmations of accounts payable.

## JUST BECAUSE IT WAS DONE THAT WAY LAST YEAR DOESN'T MEAN THAT IT'S RIGHT

When Harrison Eggers was assigned as partner on the audit of Equipment Leasing Co., his first step was to review the prior year's audit working papers. Based on his experience with leasing companies, Eggers knew that valuation of collectibility of lease receivables was a critical audit area. Accordingly, he spent significant time reviewing the work done on lease receivables.

Analytical procedures are critical in the evaluation of the allowance for uncollectible lease receivables. A schedule had been prepared and added to each year that showed a history of both lease receivables and the allowance, showing beginning balances, additions for the year, reductions, and ending balances. Ratios were developed showing relationships between the details of lease receivables and the allowance account. The carry-forward analytical procedures schedule showed trends and comparisons over time.

One key analytical procedure used to support the allowance account was the ratio of write-offs of uncollectible receivables in the current year to the balance in the allowance account at the end of the prior year. The working papers stated that the ending balance in the current year's allowance was adequate if:

- the preceding year's allowance was approximately equal to the current period write-offs (evidence that the preceding year's estimate was reasonable) and
- the current year's ratio of allowance for uncollectible lease receivables was comparable to prior years' ratios.

Eggers thought about this analysis long and hard, and the more he thought, the more it bothered him. He then studied the lease receivable data and realized that the average lease had a life of three years. This meant that for the lease portfolio, leases would become uncollectible over a three-year period, not a one-year period. Accordingly, the balance in the allowance account at a point in time should be sufficient to cover *three* years' write-offs, not just one. If his thinking was correct, Eggers realized that Equipment Leasing's allowance for uncollectible leases was materially understated at the end of the preceding year and for several prior years as well.

Not only did Eggers's findings indicate a problem with Equipment Leasing's financial statements, they implied that his firm had not used due care in their audits. He and the firm now had knowledge that had existed at the time the audits were done about the misstatements of those financial statements. The firm must now consider that knowledge in terms of the requirements of generally accepted auditing standards, specifically AU Section 561, *Subsequent Discovery of Facts Existing at the Date of the Auditor's Report.*

The third major transaction cycle discussed in this text is the acquisition of and payment for goods and services from outsiders. The acquisition of goods and services includes such items as the acquisition of raw materials, equipment, supplies, utilities, repairs and maintenance, and research and development. The cycle does not include the acquisition and payment of employees' services or the internal transfers and allocations of costs within the organization. The former are a part of the payroll and personnel cycle, and the latter are audited as part of the verification of individual assets or liabilities. The acquisition and payment cycle also excludes the acquisition and repayment of capital (interest-bearing debt and owners' equity), which are considered separately in Chapter 20.

The audit of the acquisition and payment cycle is studied in Chapters 17 and 18. In this chapter, the format for discussing internal control introduced in earlier chapters is repeated. The first part of the chapter deals with the nature of the acquisition and payment cycle, including documents and records, and its primary functions and internal controls. The second part discusses tests of controls and substantive tests of transactions for the cycle related to key internal controls. The final part covers tests of details of accounts payable, the major balance sheet account in the cycle. It emphasizes the relationship among tests of controls, substantive tests of transactions, and tests of details of balances. In Chapter 18, several other important balance sheet accounts that are a part of the acquisition and payment cycle are examined. These are manufacturing equipment, prepaid expenses, and accrued liabilities. The chapter also discusses tests of details of income statement accounts included in the acquisition and payment cycle.

The acquisition and payment cycle includes two distinct classes of transactions: acquisitions of goods and services and cash disbursements for those acquisitions. Purchases returns and allowances is also a class of transactions, but for most companies the amounts are immaterial.

There are a larger number and variety of accounts in the acquisition and payment cycle in a typical company than for any other cycle. Examine the trial balance for Hillsburg Hardware Co. on page 141. Accounts affected by the acquisition and payment cycle are identified by the letter "A" in the left column. Notice first that accounts affected by the cycle include asset, liability, expense, and miscellaneous income accounts, and second, the large number of accounts affected. It is not surprising, therefore, that it often takes more time to audit the acquisition and payment cycle than any other.

The way the accounting information flows through the various accounts in the acquisition and payment cycle is illustrated by T-accounts in Figure 17-1. To keep the illustration manageable, only the control accounts are shown for the three major categories of expenses used by most companies. For each control account, examples of the subsidiary expense accounts are also given.

Figure 17-1 shows that every transaction is either debited or credited to accounts payable. Because many companies make some acquisitions directly by check or through petty cash, the figure is an oversimplification. We assume that cash disbursement transactions are processed in the same manner as all others.

## NATURE OF THE CYCLE

**OBJECTIVE 17-1**

**Describe the acquisition and payment cycle, and the pertinent documents and records, functions, and internal controls.**

The acquisition and payment cycle involves the decisions and processes necessary for obtaining the goods and services for operating a business. The cycle typically begins with the initiation of a purchase requisition by an authorized employee who needs the goods or services and ends with payment for the benefits received. Although the discussion that follows deals with a small manufacturing company that makes tangible products for sale to third parties, the same principles apply to a service company, a government unit, or any other type of organization.

Column 3 of Table 17-1 on page 582 identifies the four business functions in a typical acquisition and payment cycle. The table shows the relationships among the classes of

**FIGURE 17-1**

**Accounts in the Acquisition and Payment Cycle**

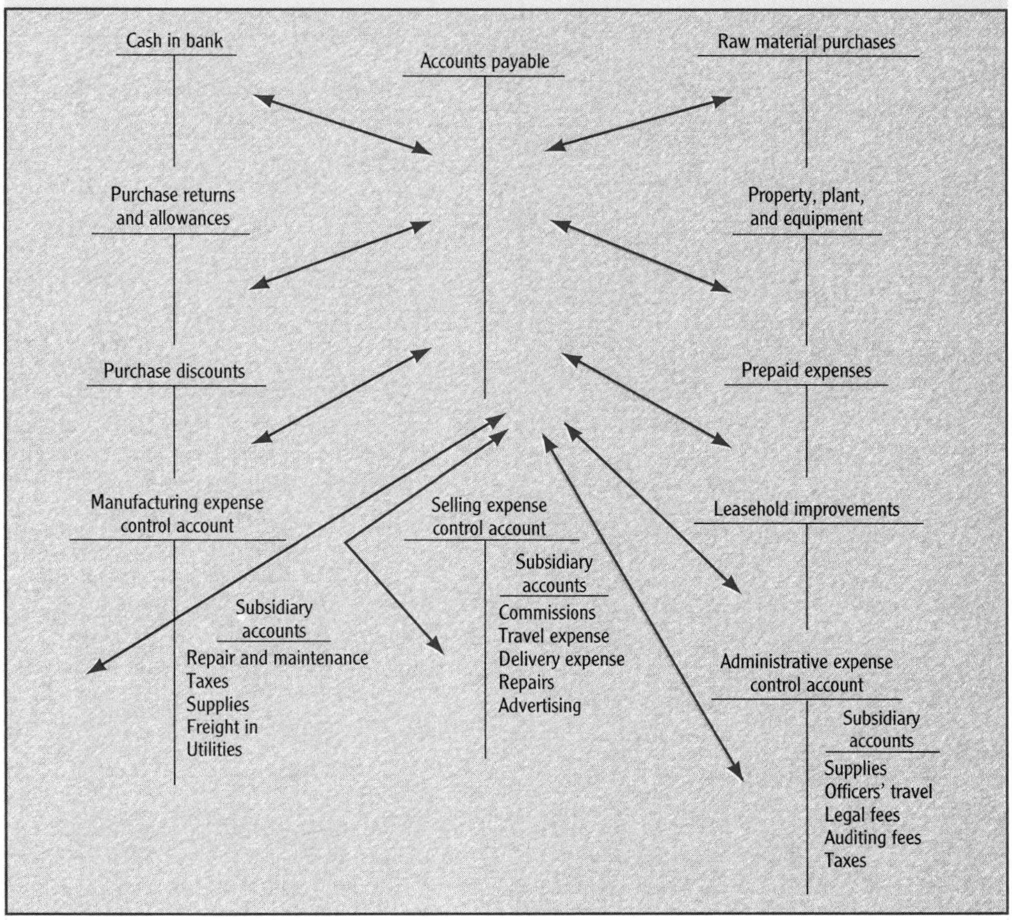


transactions, accounts, business functions, and documents and records. The business functions and related documents are discussed in this section. In addition, there is a discussion of key internal controls to prevent errors or fraud and to ensure the safety of assets.

## Processing Purchase Orders

The request for goods or services by the client's personnel is the starting point for the cycle. The exact form of the request and the required approval depend on the nature of the goods and services and company policy.

**Purchase Requisition** A request for goods and services by an authorized employee. It may take the form of a request for such acquisitions as materials by a foreman or the storeroom supervisor, outside repairs by office or factory personnel, or insurance by the vice president in charge of property and equipment.

**Purchase Order** A document identifying the description, quantity, and related information for goods and services the company intends to purchase. This document is frequently used to indicate authorization to acquire goods and services.

**Internal Controls** Proper *authorization* for acquisitions is an essential part of this function because it ensures that the goods and services acquired are for authorized company purposes and it avoids the acquisition of excessive or unnecessary items. Most companies permit general authorization for the acquisition of regular operating needs such as inventory

**TABLE 17-1**

**Classes of Transactions, Accounts, Business Functions, and Related Documents and Records for the Acquisition and Payment Cycle**

| Classes of Transactions | Accounts | Business Functions | Documents and Records |
|---|---|---|---|
| Acquisitions | Inventory<br>Property, plant, and equipment<br>Prepaid expenses<br>Leasehold improvements<br>Accounts payable<br>Manufacturing expenses<br>Selling expenses<br>Administrative expenses | Processing purchase orders | Purchase requisition<br>Purchase order |
| | | Receiving goods and services | Receiving report |
| | | Recognizing the liability | Acquisitions journal<br>Summary acquisitions report<br>Vendor's invoice<br>Debit memo<br>Voucher<br>Accounts payable master file<br>Accounts payable trial balance<br>Vendor's statement |
| Cash disbursements | Cash in bank (from cash disbursements)<br>Accounts payable<br>Purchase discounts | Processing and recording cash disbursements | Check<br>Cash disbursements journal |

at one level and acquisitions of capital assets or similar items at another. For example, acquisitions of fixed assets in excess of a specified dollar limit may require board of directors action; items acquired relatively infrequently, such as insurance policies and long-term service contracts, are approved by certain officers; supplies and services costing less than a designated amount are approved by supervisors and department heads; and some types of raw materials and supplies are reordered automatically whenever they fall to a predetermined level, often by direct communication with vendors' computers.

After an acquisition has been approved, an order to acquire the goods or services must be initiated. An order is issued to a vendor for a specified item at a certain price to be delivered at or by a designated time. The order is usually in writing and is a legal document that is an offer to buy. For most routine items, a purchase order is used to indicate the offer.

It is common for companies to establish purchasing departments to ensure an adequate quality of goods and services at a minimum price. For good internal control, the purchasing department should not be responsible for authorizing the acquisition or receiving the goods. All purchase orders should be prenumbered and should include sufficient columns and spaces to minimize the likelihood of unintentional omissions on the form when goods are ordered.

### Receiving Goods and Services

The receipt by the company of goods or services from the vendor is a critical point in the cycle because it is the point at which most companies first recognize the acquisition and related liability on their records. When goods are received, adequate control requires examination for description, quantity, timely arrival, and condition.

**Receiving Report** A document prepared at the time tangible goods are received that indicates the description of goods, the quantity received, the date received, and other relevant data. The receipt of goods and services in the normal course of business represents the date clients normally recognize the liability for an acquisition.

**Internal Controls** Most companies have the receiving department initiate a receiving report as evidence of the receipt and examination of goods. One copy is normally sent to the storeroom and another to the accounts payable department for their information needs. To prevent theft and misuse, it is important that the goods be *physically controlled* from the time of their receipt until their disposal. The personnel in the receiving department should be independent of the storeroom personnel and the accounting department. Finally, the accounting records should transfer responsibility for the goods as they are transferred from receiving to storage and from storage to manufacturing.

## Recognizing the Liability

The proper recognition of the liability for the receipt of goods and services requires *prompt and accurate* recording. The initial recording has a significant effect on the recorded financial statements and the actual cash disbursement; therefore, great care must be taken to include only existing company acquisitions at the correct amounts.

**Acquisitions Journal** A journal for recording acquisition transactions. A detailed acquisitions journal includes each acquisition transaction. It usually includes several classifications for the most significant types of acquisitions, such as the purchase of inventory, repairs and maintenance, supplies, the entry to accounts payable, and miscellaneous debits and credits. The acquisitions journal can also include acquisition returns and allowances transactions if a separate journal is not used. The acquisitions journal is generated for any time period from acquisition transactions included in the computer files. Details from the journal are posted to the accounts payable master file and journal totals are posted to the general ledger by the computer.

**Summary Acquisitions Report** A computer-generated document that summarizes acquisitions for a period. The report typically includes information analyzed by key components such as account classification, type of inventory, and division.

**Vendor's Invoice** A document that indicates such things as the description and quantity of goods and services received, price including freight, cash discount terms, and date of the billing. It is an essential document because it specifies the amount of money owed to the vendor for an acquisition.

**Debit Memo** A document indicating a reduction in the amount owed to a vendor because of returned goods or an allowance granted. It often takes the same general form as a vendor's invoice, but it supports reductions in accounts payable rather than increases.

**Voucher** A document frequently used by organizations to establish a formal means of recording and controlling acquisitions. Vouchers include a cover sheet or folder for containing documents and a package of relevant documents such as the purchase order, copy of the packing slip, receiving report, and vendor's invoice. After payment, a copy of the check is added to the voucher package.

**Accounts Payable Master File** A file for recording individual acquisitions, cash disbursements, and acquisition returns and allowances for each vendor. The master file is updated from the acquisition, returns and allowances, and cash disbursement computer transaction files. The total of the individual account balances in the master file equals the total balance of accounts payable in the general ledger. A printout of the accounts payable master file shows, by vendor, the beginning balance in accounts payable, each acquisition, acquisition returns and allowances, cash disbursements, and the ending balance. Many companies do not maintain an accounts payable master file by vendor. These companies pay on the basis of individual vendor's invoices. Therefore, the total of unpaid vendor's invoices in the master file equals total accounts payable.

**Accounts Payable Trial Balance** A listing of the amount owed to each vendor or for each invoice or voucher at a point in time. It is prepared directly from the accounts payable master file.

**Vendor's Statement** A statement prepared monthly by the vendor indicating the beginning balance, acquisitions, returns and allowances, payments to the vendor, and ending balance. These balances and activities are the vendor's representations of the transactions for the period and not the client's. Except for disputed amounts and timing differences, the client's accounts payable master file should be the same as the vendor's statement.

**Internal Controls** In some companies, the recording of the liability for acquisitions is made on the basis of the receipt of goods and services, and in other companies, it is deferred until the vendor's invoice is received. In either case, the accounts payable department typically has responsibility for verifying the propriety of acquisitions. This is done by comparing the details on the purchase order, the receiving report, and the vendor's invoice to determine that the descriptions, prices, quantities, terms, and freight on the vendor's invoice are correct. Typically, extensions, footings, and account distribution are also verified.

An important control in the accounts payable and EDP departments is to require that those personnel who record acquisitions *do not have access* to cash, marketable securities, and other assets. Adequate documents and records, proper procedures for record keeping, and independent checks on performance are also necessary controls in the accounts payable function.

### Processing and Recording Cash Disbursements

For most companies, payment is made by computer-prepared checks from information included in the acquisition transactions file at the time goods and services are received. Checks are typically prepared in a multicopy format, with the original going to the payee, one copy filed with the vendor's invoice and other supporting documents, and another filed numerically. In most cases individual checks are recorded in a cash disbursements transactions file.

**Check** The means of paying for the acquisition when payment is due. After the check is signed by an authorized person, it is an asset. Therefore, signed checks should be mailed by the signer or a person under his or her control. When cashed by the vendor and cleared by the client's bank, it is referred to as a cancelled check.

**Cash Disbursements Journal** A journal for recording cash disbursement transactions. The cash disbursements journal is generated for any time period from the cash disbursement transactions included in the computer files. Details from the journal are posted to the accounts payable master file and journal totals are posted to the general ledger by the computer.

**Internal Controls** The most important controls in the cash disbursements function include the signing of checks by an individual with proper authority, separation of responsibilities for signing the checks and performing the accounts payable function, and careful examination of the supporting documents by the check signer at the time the check is signed.

The checks should be prenumbered and printed on special paper that makes it difficult to alter the payee or amount. Care should be taken to provide physical control over blank, voided, and signed checks. It is also important to have a method of cancelling the supporting documents to prevent their reuse as support for another check at a later time. A common method is to write the check number on the supporting documents.

## TESTS OF CONTROLS AND SUBSTANTIVE TESTS OF TRANSACTIONS

**OBJECTIVE 17-2**
**Design and perform tests of controls and substantive tests of transactions for the acquisition and payment cycle, and assess related control risk.**

In a typical audit, the most time-consuming accounts to verify by tests of details of balances are accounts receivable, inventory, fixed assets, accounts payable, and expense accounts. Of these five, four are directly related to the acquisition and payment cycle. The net time saved can be dramatic if the auditor can reduce the tests of details of the accounts by using tests of controls and substantive tests of transactions to verify the effectiveness of internal controls for acquisitions and cash disbursements. It should not be surprising,

**ARE COMPANIES THROWING MONEY AWAY?**

Howard Schultz is the president of a Dallas-based accounts payable auditing firm. Mr. Schultz's firm specializes in analyzing acquisitions and cash disbursements for its clients. In an article written for the *Wall Street Journal,* Mr. Schultz states that auditors in his firm find that clients often overpay vendors. Excerpts from the article follow:

> In working with more than 1,000 companies, we have seen the same errors crop up with enough regularity to convince us that overpayments are intrinsic to the process of buying and selling. These problems usually begin with the fact that in most large companies the person or department that places the order is not the same party that pays the bill . . .
>
> Adding to the problem is the dizzying array of price promotions and special allowances that vendors offer, causing prices to fluctuate from month to month, or sometimes day to day. These marketing promotions, which may be anything from limited-time-only discounts to refund offers, turn simple invoices into complicated documents. Corporate payment clerks usually don't have time to sift through the detail to be sure that a company gets credit for all the special discounts it may be entitled to. And many vendors offer refunds and other incentives after the sale—but it's up to the buyer to request credit for them . . .

Mr. Schultz points out that companies can reduce losses from overpayments by implementing the following strategies:

- Reevaluate the purchasing and payment processes by improving communication between the marketing and finance departments.
- Be alert to the dangers of automation. Sometimes automated systems can be too complicated for clerical staff.
- Pay attention to peaks and transitional periods because companies are usually more vulnerable to errors during these times.
- Watch for patterns of overpayment, including repeated failure to take advantage of trade allowances or discounts for early payment.

*Source:* Howard Schultz, "Washing Away the Sin of Overpayment," *Wall Street Journal,* August 9, 1993, p. A.12.

therefore, that tests of controls and substantive tests of transactions for the acquisition and payment cycle receive a considerable amount of attention in well-conducted audits, especially when the client has effective internal controls.

Tests of controls and substantive tests of transactions for the acquisition and payment cycle are divided into two broad areas: *tests of acquisitions* and *tests of payments.* Acquisition tests concern three of the four functions discussed earlier in the chapter: processing purchase orders, receiving goods and services, and recognizing the liability. Tests of payments concern the fourth function, processing and recording cash disbursements.

The six transaction-related audit objectives developed in Chapters 5 and 9 are again used as the frame of reference for designing tests of controls and substantive tests of transactions for acquisition and cash disbursement transactions. For each objective, the auditor must go through the same logical process that has been discussed in previous chapters. First, the auditor must understand internal control to determine which controls exist. After the auditor has identified existing controls and weaknesses for each objective, an initial assessment of control risk can be made for each objective. At this point, the auditor must decide which controls he or she plans to test to satisfy the initial assessment of control risk. The substantive tests for monetary misstatements related to the objectives can be determined largely on the basis of this assessment and planned testing. After the auditor has developed the audit procedures for each objective, the procedures can be combined into an audit program that can be efficiently performed. Figure 17-2 on page 586 summarizes that methodology. It is the same one used in Chapter 11 for sales and cash receipts. Again, the

**FIGURE 17-2**

**Methodology for Designing Tests of Controls and Substantive Tests of Transactions for the Acquisition and Payment Cycle**

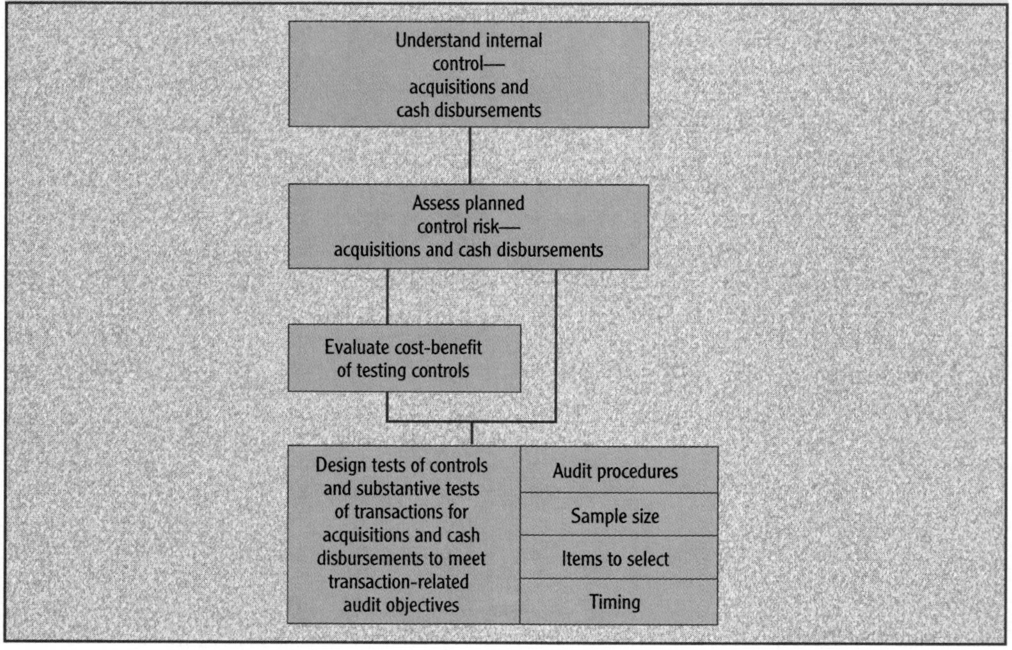


emphasis in the methodology is on determining the appropriate audit procedures, sample size, items to select, and timing.

## Verifying Acquisitions

Key internal controls, common tests of controls, and common substantive tests of transactions for each transaction-related audit objective are summarized in Table 17-2. An assumption underlying the internal controls and audit procedures is the existence of a separate acquisitions journal for recording all acquisitions.

In studying Table 17-2, it is important to relate internal controls to objectives, tests of controls to internal controls, and substantive tests of transactions to monetary misstatements that would be absent or present due to controls and weaknesses in the system. It should be kept in mind that a set of audit procedures for an audit engagement will vary with the internal controls and other circumstances.

Four of the six transaction-related audit objectives for acquisitions deserve special attention. A discussion of each of these objectives follows.

**Recorded Acquisitions Are for Goods and Services Received, Consistent with the Best Interests of the Client (Existence)** If the auditor is satisfied that the controls are adequate for this objective, tests for improper and nonexistent transactions can be greatly reduced. Adequate controls are likely to prevent the client from including as a business expense or asset those transactions that primarily benefit management or other employees rather than the entity being audited. In some instances improper transactions are obvious, such as the acquisition of unauthorized personal items by employees or the actual embezzlement of cash by recording a fraudulent acquisition in the acquisitions journal. In other instances the propriety of a transaction is more difficult to evaluate, such as the payment of officers' memberships to country clubs, expense-paid vacations to foreign countries for members of management and their families, and management-approved illegal

**TABLE 17-2**

## Summary of Transaction-Related Audit Objectives, Key Controls, Tests of Controls, and Substantive Tests of Transactions for Acquisitions

| Transaction-Related Audit Objective | Key Internal Control | Common Test of Control | Common Substantive Tests of Transactions |
|---|---|---|---|
| Recorded acquisitions are for goods and services received, consistent with the best interests of the client (existence). | Existence of purchase requisition, purchase order, receiving report, and vendor's invoice attached to the voucher.† <br> Approval of acquisitions at the proper level. <br> Cancellation of documents to prevent their reuse. <br> Internal verification of vendors' invoices, receiving reports, purchase orders, and purchase requisitions.† | Examine documents in voucher package for existence. <br> Examine indication of approval. <br> Examine indication of cancellation. <br> Examine indication of internal verification. | Review the acquisitions journal, general ledger, and accounts payable master file for large or unusual amounts.* <br> Examine underlying documents for reasonableness and authenticity (vendors' invoices, receiving reports, purchase orders, and purchase requisitions). <br> Trace inventory acquisitions to inventory master file. <br> Examine fixed assets acquired. |
| Existing acquisition transactions are recorded (completeness). | Purchase orders are prenumbered and accounted for. <br> Receiving reports are prenumbered and accounted for.† <br> Vouchers are prenumbered and accounted for. | Account for a sequence of purchase orders. <br> Account for a sequence of receiving reports. <br> Account for a sequence of vouchers. | Trace from a file of receiving reports to the acquisitions journal.† <br> Trace from a file of vendors' invoices to the acquisitions journal. |
| Recorded acquisition transactions are accurate (accuracy). | Internal verification of calculations and amounts. <br> Batch totals are compared with computer summary reports. <br> Approval of acquisitions, for prices and discounts. | Examine indication of internal verification. <br> Examine file of batch totals for initials of data control clerk; compare totals to summary reports.‡ <br> Examine indication of approval. | Compare recorded transactions in the acquisitions journal with the vendor's invoice, receiving report, and other supporting documentation.† <br> Recompute the clerical accuracy on the vendor's invoice, including discounts and freight. |
| Acquisition transactions are properly classified (classification). | Adequate chart of accounts. <br> Internal verification of classification. | Examine procedures manual and chart of accounts. <br> Examine indication of internal verification. | Compare classification with chart of accounts by reference to vendors' invoices. |
| Acquisition transactions are recorded on the correct dates (timing). | Procedures require recording transactions as soon as possible after the goods and services have been received. <br> Internal verification. | Examine procedures manual and observe whether unrecorded vendors' invoices exist. <br> Examine indication of internal verification. | Compare dates of receiving reports and vendors' invoices with dates in the acquisitions journal.† |
| Acquisition transactions are properly included in the accounts payable and inventory master files, and are properly summarized (posting and summarization). | Internal verification of accounts payable master file contents. <br> Comparison of accounts payable master file or trial balance totals with general ledger balance. | Examine indication of internal verification. <br> Examine initials on general ledger accounts indicating comparison. | Test clerical accuracy by footing the journals and tracing postings to general ledger and accounts payable and inventory master files. |

*This analytical procedure can also apply to other objectives, including completeness, accuracy, and timing.
† Receiving reports are used only for tangible goods and are therefore not used for services, such as utilities and repairs and maintenance. Frequently, vendors' invoices are the only documentation available.
‡This control would be tested on many audits by using the computer.

payments to officials of foreign countries. If the controls over improper or nonexistent transactions are inadequate, extensive examination of supporting documentation is necessary.

**Existing Acquisitions Are Recorded (Completeness)** Failure to record the acquisition of goods and services received directly affects the balance in accounts payable and may result in an overstatement of net income and owners' equity. Because of this, auditors are usually very concerned with the completeness objective. In some instances, it may be difficult to perform tests of details to determine whether there are unrecorded transactions, and the auditor must rely on controls for this purpose. In addition, since the audit of accounts payable generally takes a considerable amount of audit time, effective internal controls, properly tested, can significantly reduce audit costs.

**Acquisitions Are Accurately Recorded (Accuracy)** Since the accuracy of many asset, liability, and expense accounts depends on the correct recording of transactions in the acquisitions journal, the extent of tests of details of many balance sheet and expense accounts depends on the auditor's evaluation of the effectiveness of the internal controls over the accuracy of recorded acquisitions transactions. For example, if the auditor believes that the fixed assets are correctly recorded in the books of original entry, it is acceptable to vouch fewer current period acquisitions than if the controls are inadequate.

When a client uses perpetual inventory records, the tests of details of inventory can also be significantly reduced if the auditor believes that the perpetuals are accurate. The controls over the acquisitions included in the perpetuals are normally tested as a part of the tests of controls and substantive tests of transactions for acquisitions, and the controls over this objective play a key role in the audit. The inclusion of both quantity and unit costs in the inventory perpetual records permits a reduction in the tests of the physical count and the unit costs of inventory if the controls are operating effectively.

**Acquisitions Are Correctly Classified (Classification)** The auditor can reduce the tests of details of certain individual accounts if he or she believes that internal controls are adequate to provide reasonable assurance of correct classification in the acquisitions journal. Although all accounts are affected to some degree by effective controls over classification, the two areas most affected are current period acquisitions of fixed assets and all expense accounts, such as repairs and maintenance, utilities, and advertising. Since performing documentation tests of current period fixed asset acquisitions and expense accounts for accuracy and classification are relatively time-consuming audit procedures, the saving in audit time can be significant.

## Verifying Cash Disbursements

The same format used in Table 17-2 for acquisitions is also used in Table 17-3 for cash disbursements. The assumption underlying these controls and audit procedures is the existence of separate cash disbursements and acquisitions journals. The comments made about the methodology and process for developing audit procedures for acquisitions apply equally to cash disbursements.

Once the auditor has decided on procedures, the acquisitions and cash disbursements tests are typically performed concurrently. For example, for a transaction selected for examination from the acquisitions journal, the vendor's invoice and the receiving report are examined at the same time as the related cancelled check. Thus, the verification is done efficiently without reducing the effectiveness of the tests.

## Attributes Sampling for Tests of Controls and Substantive Tests of Transactions

Because of the importance of tests of controls and substantive tests of transactions for acquisitions and cash disbursements, the use of attributes sampling is common in this audit area. The approach is similar to that used for the tests of controls and substantive tests of transactions for sales discussed in Chapter 12. It should be noted, however, with reference to the most essential transaction-related audit objectives presented earlier, that most of the important attributes in the acquisition and payment cycle have a direct monetary effect on

**TABLE 17-3**

**Summary of Transaction-Related Audit Objectives, Key Controls, Tests of Controls, and Substantive Tests of Transactions for Cash Disbursements**

| Transaction-Related Audit Objective | Key Internal Control | Common Test of Control | Common Substantive Tests of Transactions |
|---|---|---|---|
| Recorded cash disbursements are for goods and services actually received (existence). | Adequate segregation of duties between accounts payable and custody of signed checks.<br>Examination of supporting documentation before signing of checks by an authorized person.<br>Approval of payment on supporting documents at the time checks are signed. | Discuss with personnel and observe activities.<br>Discuss with personnel and observe activities.<br>Examine indication of approval. | Review the cash disbursements journal, general ledger, and accounts payable master file for large or unusual amounts.*<br>Trace the cancelled check to the related acquisitions journal entry and examine for payee name and amount.<br>Examine cancelled check for authorized signature, proper endorsement, and cancellation by the bank.<br>Examine supporting documents as a part of the tests of acquisitions. |
| Existing cash disbursement transactions are recorded (completeness). | Checks are prenumbered and accounted for.<br>A bank reconciliation is prepared monthly by an employee independent of recording cash disbursements or custody of assets. | Account for a sequence of checks.<br>Examine bank reconciliations and observe their preparation. | Reconcile recorded cash disbursements with the cash disbursements on the bank statement (proof of cash disbursements). |
| Recorded cash disbursement transactions are accurate (accuracy). | Internal verification of calculations and amounts.<br>Monthly preparation of a bank reconciliation by an independent person. | Examine indication of internal verification.<br>Examine bank reconciliations and observe their preparation. | Compare cancelled checks with the related acquisitions journal and cash disbursements journal entries.<br>Recompute cash discounts.<br>Prepare a proof of cash disbursements. |
| Cash disbursement transactions are properly classified (classification). | Adequate chart of accounts.<br>Internal verification of classification. | Examine procedures manual and chart of accounts.<br>Examine indication of internal verification. | Compare classification with chart of accounts by reference to vendors' invoices and acquisitions journal. |
| Cash disbursement transactions are recorded on the correct dates (timing). | Procedures require recording of transactions as soon as possible after the check has been signed.<br>Internal verification. | Examine procedures manual and observe whether unrecorded checks exist.<br>Examine indication of internal verification. | Compare dates on cancelled checks with the cash disbursements journal.<br>Compare dates on cancelled checks with the bank cancellation date. |
| Cash disbursement transactions are properly included in the accounts payable master file and are properly summarized (posting and summarization). | Internal verification of accounts payable master file contents.<br>Comparison of accounts payable master file or trial balance totals with general ledger balance. | Examine indication of internal verification.<br>Examine initials on general ledger accounts indicating comparison. | Test clerical accuracy by footing journals and tracing postings to general ledger and accounts payable master file. |

*This analytical procedure can also apply to other objectives, including completeness, accuracy, and timing.

the accounts. Further, many of the types of errors and fraud that may be found represent a misstatement of earnings and are of significant concern to the auditor. For example, there may be inventory cutoff misstatements or an incorrect recording of an expense amount. Because of this, the tolerable exception rate selected by the auditor in tests of many of the attributes in this cycle is relatively low. Since the dollar amounts of individual transactions in the cycle cover a wide range, it is also common to segregate large and unusual items and to test them on a 100 percent basis.

## ACCOUNTS PAYABLE

**OBJECTIVE 17-3**
**Discuss the nature of accounts payable, and describe the related controls.**

Accounts payable are *unpaid obligations* for goods and services received in the ordinary course of business. It is sometimes difficult to distinguish between accounts payable and accrued liabilities, but it is useful to define a liability as an account payable if the total amount of the obligation is *known and owed at the balance sheet date.* The accounts payable account therefore includes obligations for the acquisition of raw materials, equipment, utilities, repairs, and many other types of goods and services that were received before the end of the year. The great majority of accounts payable can also be identified by the existence of vendors' invoices for the obligation. Accounts payable should also be distinguished from interest-bearing obligations. If an obligation includes the payment of interest, it should be recorded as a note payable, contract payable, mortgage payable, or bond payable.

The methodology for designing tests of details for accounts payable is summarized in Figure 17-3. This methodology is the same as that used for accounts receivable in Chapter 13. It is common for accounts payable to be material and thus there may be several inherent risks. Internal controls are often ineffective for accounts payable because many companies depend on the vendors to bill them and remind them of unpaid bills. Tests of details for accounts payable, therefore, often need to be extensive.

### Internal Controls

The effects of the client's internal controls on accounts payable tests can be illustrated by two examples. In the first, assume that the client has highly effective internal controls over recording and paying for acquisitions. The receipt of goods is promptly documented by prenumbered receiving reports; prenumbered vouchers are promptly and efficiently prepared and recorded in the acquisition transactions file and the accounts payable master file. Cash disbursements are also made promptly when due and immediately recorded in the cash disbursements transactions file and the accounts payable master file. On a monthly basis, individual accounts payable balances in the master file are reconciled with vendors' statements, and the total is compared with the general ledger by an independent person. Under these circumstances, the verification of accounts payable should require little audit effort once the auditor concludes that internal controls are operating effectively.

In the second example, assume that receiving reports are not used, the client defers recording acquisitions until cash disbursements are made, and, because of a weak cash position, bills are frequently paid several months after their due date. When an auditor faces such a situation, there is a high likelihood of an understatement of accounts payable; therefore, under these circumstances, extensive tests of details of accounts payable are necessary to determine whether accounts payable is properly stated on the balance sheet date.

The most important controls over accounts payable have already been discussed as part of the control and recording of acquisitions and cash disbursements. In addition to those controls, it is important to have a monthly reconciliation of vendors' statements with recorded liabilities and the accounts payable master file with the general ledger. This should be done by an independent person.

### Analytical Procedures

The use of analytical procedures is as important in the acquisition and payment cycle as it is in every other cycle. Table 17-4 on page 592 illustrates analytical procedures for the balance sheet and income statement accounts in the acquisition and payment cycle that are useful for uncovering areas in which additional investigation is desirable.

**FIGURE 17-3**

**Methodology for Designing Tests of Details of Balances for Accounts Payable**

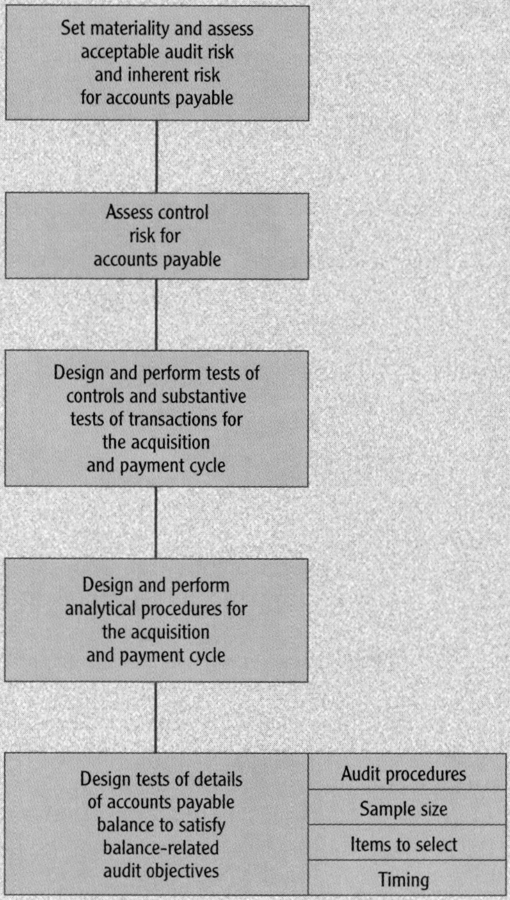


**Materiality Considerations**

Most companies have a large number of acquisition and cash disbursement transactions and one or more material balance sheet accounts such as accounts payable and property, plant, and equipment. There are also likely to be several immaterial accounts such as prepaid expenses and certain accruals.

**Inherent Risk Considerations**

Inherent risks are likely to vary widely from company to company for this cycle. Examples of potentially high inherent risk circumstances follow:

- Extensive trade-ins of property, plant, and equipment.
- Significant related party transactions.
- Purchases of goods and services for construction of buildings or equipment.

**Control Risk Considerations**

Internal controls vary widely from company to company for this cycle. Many smaller companies often lack separation of duties and other controls. Larger companies typically, but not always, have highly effective internal controls over acquisitions and cash disbursements.

**OBJECTIVE 17-4**
**Design and perform analytical procedures for accounts payable.**

One of the most important analytical procedures for uncovering misstatements of accounts payable is comparing current-year expense totals to prior years. For example, by comparing utilities expense to the prior year, the auditor may determine that the last utilities bill for the year was not recorded. Comparing expenses to prior years is an effective analytical procedure for accounts payable because expenses from year to year are typically relatively stable. Examples include rent, utilities, and other expenses billed on a regular basis.

## Balance-Related Audit Objectives for Tests of Details

**OBJECTIVE 17-5**
**Design and perform tests of details for accounts payable.**

The overall objective in the audit of accounts payable is to determine whether accounts payable is fairly stated and properly disclosed. Eight of the nine balance-related audit objectives discussed in Chapter 5 are applicable to accounts payable. Realizable value is not applicable to liabilities.

The auditor should recognize the difference in emphasis between the audit of liabilities and the audit of assets. When assets are being verified, attention is focused on making certain that the balance in the account is not overstated. The existence of recorded assets is constantly questioned and verified by confirmation, physical examination, and examination of supporting documents. The auditor should certainly not ignore the possibility of assets being understated, but the fact remains that the auditor is more concerned about the possibility of overstatement than understatement. The opposite approach is taken in veri-

**TABLE 17-4**

**Analytical Procedures for the Acquisition and Payment Cycle**

| Analytical Procedure | Possible Misstatement |
|---|---|
| Compare acquisition-related expense account balances with prior years. | Misstatement of accounts payable and expenses. |
| Review list of accounts payable for unusual, nonvendor, and interest-bearing payables. | Classification misstatement for nontrade liabilities. |
| Compare individual accounts payable with previous years. | Unrecorded or nonexistent accounts, or misstatements. |
| Calculate ratios such as purchases divided by accounts payable, and accounts payable divided by current liabilities. | Unrecorded or nonexistent accounts, or misstatements. |

fying liability balances; that is, the main focus is on the discovery of understated or omitted liabilities.

The difference in emphasis in auditing assets and liabilities results directly from the *legal liability of CPAs.* If equity investors, creditors, and other users determine subsequent to the issuance of the audited financial statements that owners' equity was materially overstated, a lawsuit against the CPA firm is fairly likely. Since an overstatement of owners' equity can arise either from an overstatement of assets or from an understatement of liabilities, it is natural for CPAs to emphasize those two types of misstatements. The probability of a successful lawsuit against a CPA for failing to discover an understatement of owners' equity is far less likely.

Nevertheless, the auditing profession must avoid too much emphasis on protecting users from overstatements of owners' equity at the expense of ignoring understatements. If assets are consistently understated and liabilities are consistently overstated for large numbers of audited companies, the decision-making value of financial statement information is likely to decline. Therefore, even though it is natural for auditors to emphasize the possibility of overstating assets and understating liabilities, uncovering the opposite types of misstatements is also a significant responsibility.

## Tests of Details of Accounts Payable

The same balance-related audit objectives that were used as a frame of reference for verifying accounts receivable in Chapter 13 are also applicable to liabilities, with three minor modifications. The most obvious difference in verifying liabilities is the nonapplicability of the realizable value objective. The second difference is in the rights and obligations objective. For assets, the auditor is concerned with the client's rights to the use and disposal of the assets. For liabilities, the auditor is concerned with the client's obligations for the payment of the liability. If the client has no obligation to pay a liability, it should not be included as a liability. The third difference was discussed above: In auditing liabilities, the emphasis is on the search for understatements rather than for overstatements.

Table 17-5 includes the balance-related audit objectives and common tests of details of balances procedures for accounts payable. The actual audit procedures will vary considerably depending on the nature of the entity, the materiality of accounts payable, the nature and effectiveness of internal controls, and inherent risk.

## Out-of-Period Liabilities Tests

Because of the emphasis on understatements in liability accounts, out-of-period liability tests are important for accounts payable. The extent of tests to uncover unrecorded accounts payable, frequently referred to as the *search for unrecorded accounts payable,* depends heavily on assessed control risk and the materiality of the potential balance in the account. The same audit procedures used to uncover unrecorded payables are applicable to the accuracy objective. The audit procedures that follow are typical tests.

**TABLE 17-5**

**Balance-Related Audit Objectives and Tests of Details of Balances for Accounts Payable**

| Balance-Related Audit Objective | Common Tests of Details of Balances Procedures | Comments |
|---|---|---|
| Accounts payable in the accounts payable list agree with related master file, and the total is correctly added and agrees with the general ledger (detail tie-in). | Foot the accounts payable list.<br>Trace the total to the general ledger.<br>Trace individual vendors' invoices to master file for names and amounts. | All pages need not ordinarily be footed.<br>Unless controls are weak, tracing to master file should be limited. |
| Accounts payable in the accounts payable list exist (existence). | Trace from accounts payable list to vendors' invoices and statements.<br>Confirm accounts payable, emphasizing large and unusual amounts. | Ordinarily receives little attention because the primary concern is with understatements. |
| Existing accounts payable are included in the accounts payable list (completeness). | Perform out-of-period liability tests (see discussion). | These are essential audit tests for accounts payable. |
| Accounts payable in the accounts payable list are accurate (accuracy). | Perform same procedures as those used for existence objective and out-of-period liability tests. | Ordinarily, the emphasis in these procedures for accuracy is understatement rather than omission. |
| Accounts payable in the accounts payable list are properly classified (classification). | Review the list and master file for related parties, notes or other interest-bearing liabilities, long-term payables, and debit balances. | Knowledge of the client's business is essential for these tests. |
| Transactions in the acquisition and payment cycle are recorded in the proper period (cutoff). | Perform out-of-period liability tests (see discussion).<br>Perform detailed tests as a part of physical observation of inventory (see discussion).<br>Test for inventory in transit (see discussion). | These are essential audit tests for accounts payable. These are referred to as *cutoff* tests. |
| The company has an obligation to pay the liabilities included in accounts payable (obligations). | Examine vendors' statements and confirm accounts payable. | Normally, not a concern in the audit of accounts payable because all accounts payable are obligations. |
| Accounts in the acquisition and payment cycle are properly presented and disclosed (presentation and disclosure). | Review statements to make sure material related parties, long-term, and interest-bearing liabilities are segregated. | Ordinarily not a problem. |

**OBJECTIVE 17-6**
**Know the importance of out-of-period liability tests for accounts payable and common tests.**

**Examine Underlying Documentation for Subsequent Cash Disbursements** The purpose of this audit procedure is to uncover cash disbursements made in the subsequent accounting period that represent liabilities at the balance sheet date. The supporting documentation is examined to determine whether a cash disbursement was for a current period obligation. For example, if inventory was received prior to the balance sheet date, it will be so indicated on the receiving report. Frequently, documentation for cash disbursements made in the subsequent period are examined for several weeks, especially when the client does not pay its bills on a timely basis. Any cash disbursement that is for a current period obligation should be traced to the accounts payable trial balance to make sure that it has been included as a liability.

**Examine Underlying Documentation for Bills Not Paid Several Weeks after the Year-End** This procedure is carried out in the same manner as the preceding one and serves the same purpose. The only difference is that it is done for unpaid obligations near the end of the audit field work rather than for obligations that have already been paid. For example, in an audit with a March 31 year-end, if the auditor examines the supporting documentation for checks paid until June 28, bills that are still unpaid at that date should be examined to determine whether they are obligations of the year ended March 31.

**Trace Receiving Reports Issued Before Year-End to Related Vendors' Invoices** All merchandise received before the year-end of the accounting period, indicated by the issuance of a receiving report, should be included as accounts payable. By tracing receiving reports issued at and before year-end to vendors' invoices and making sure that they are included in accounts payable, the auditor is testing for unrecorded obligations.

**Trace Vendors' Statements That Show a Balance Due to the Accounts Payable Trial Balance** If the client maintains a file of vendors' statements, any statement indicating a balance due can be traced to the listing to make sure that it is included as an account payable.

**Send Confirmations to Vendors with which the Client Does Business** Although the use of confirmations for accounts payable is less common than for accounts receivable, it is often used to test for vendors omitted from the accounts payable list, omitted transactions, and misstated account balances. Sending confirmations to active vendors for which a balance has not been included in the accounts payable list is a useful means of searching for omitted amounts. This type of confirmation is commonly referred to as *zero balance confirmation.* Additional discussion of confirmation of accounts payable is deferred until the end of the chapter.

## Cutoff Tests

Cutoff tests for accounts payable are intended to determine whether transactions recorded a few days before and after the balance sheet date are included in the correct period. The five audit procedures discussed in the preceding section are directly related to cutoff for acquisitions, but they emphasize understatements. For the first three procedures, it is also appropriate to examine supporting documentation as a test of overstatement of accounts payable. For example, the third procedure is to trace receiving reports issued before year-end to related vendors' invoices in order to test for unrecorded accounts payable. To test for overstatement cutoff amounts, the auditor should trace receiving reports issued *after* year-end to related invoices to make sure that they are not recorded as accounts payable (unless they are inventory in transit, which is discussed shortly).

Since most cutoff tests have already been discussed, only two aspects are expanded upon here: the examination of receiving reports and the determination of the amount of inventory in transit.

**Relationship of Cutoff to Physical Observation of Inventory** In determining that the accounts payable cutoff is correct, *it is essential that the cutoff tests be coordinated with the physical observation of inventory.* For example, assume that an inventory acquisition for $40,000 is received late in the afternoon of December 31, after the physical inventory is completed. If the acquisition is included in accounts payable and purchases, but excluded from inventory, the result is an understatement of net earnings of $40,000. Conversely, if the acquisition is excluded from both inventory and accounts payable, there is a misstatement in the balance sheet, but the income statement is correct. The only way the auditor will know which type of misstatement has occurred is to coordinate cutoff tests with the observation of inventory.

The cutoff information for acquisitions should be obtained *during the physical observation* of the inventory. At this time the auditor should review the procedures in the receiving department to determine that all inventory received was counted, and the auditor should record in his or her working papers the last receiving report number of inventory included in the physical count. During the year-end field work, the auditor should then test the accounting records for cutoff. The auditor should trace receiving report numbers to the accounts payable records to verify that they are correctly included or excluded.

For example, assume that the last receiving report number representing inventory included in the physical count was 3167. The auditor should record this document number and subsequently trace it and several preceding numbers to their related vendors' invoices and to the accounts payable list or the accounts payable master file to determine that they are all included. Similarly, accounts payable for acquisitions recorded on receiving reports with numbers larger than 3167 should be excluded from accounts payable.

When the client's physical inventory takes place before the last day of the year, it is still necessary to perform an accounts payable cutoff at the time of the physical count in the manner described in the preceding paragraph. In addition, the auditor must verify whether all acquisitions taking place between the physical count and the end of the year were added to the physical inventory and accounts payable. For example, if the client takes the physical count on December 27 for a December 31 year-end, the cutoff information is taken as of December 27. During the year-end field work, the auditor must first test to determine whether the cutoff was accurate as of December 27. After determining that the December 27 cutoff is accurate, the auditor must test whether all inventory received subsequent to the physical count, but before the balance sheet date, was added to inventory and accounts payable by the client.

**Inventory in Transit** A distinction in accounts payable must be made between acquisitions of inventory that are on an FOB *destination* basis and those that are made FOB *origin.* With the former, title passes to the buyer when it is received for inventory. Therefore, only inventory received prior to the balance sheet date should be included in inventory and accounts payable at year-end. When an acquisition is on an FOB origin basis, the inventory and related accounts payable must be recorded in the current period if shipment occurred before the balance sheet date.

Determining whether inventory has been acquired on an FOB destination or origin basis is done by examining vendors' invoices. The auditor should examine invoices for merchandise received shortly after year-end to determine if they were on an FOB origin basis. For those that were, and when the shipment dates were prior to the balance sheet date, the inventory and related accounts payable must be recorded in the current period if the amounts are material.

## Reliability of Evidence

**OBJECTIVE 17-7**
**Know the relative reliability of vendors' invoices, vendors' statements, and confirmations of accounts payable.**

In deciding upon the appropriate evidence to accumulate for verifying accounts payable, it is essential that the auditor understand the relative reliability of the three primary types of evidence ordinarily used: vendors' invoices, vendors' statements, and confirmations.

**Distinction Between Vendors' Invoices and Vendors' Statements** In verifying the amount due to a vendor, the auditor should make a distinction between vendors' invoices and vendors' statements. In examining vendors' invoices and related supporting documents, such as receiving reports and purchase orders, the auditor gets highly reliable *evidence about individual transactions.* A vendor's statement is not as desirable as invoices for verifying individual transactions because a statement includes only the total amount of the transaction. The units acquired, price, freight, and other data are not included. However, a statement has the advantage of including the ending balance according to the vendor's records. Which of these two documents is better for verifying the correct balance in accounts payable? *The vendor's statement is superior for verifying accounts payable* because it includes the ending balance. The auditor could compare existing vendors' invoices with the client's list and still not uncover missing ones, which is the primary concern in accounts payable. Which of these two documents is better for testing acquisitions in tests of controls and substantive tests of transactions? *The vendor's invoice is superior for verifying transactions* because the auditor is verifying individual transactions and the invoice shows the details of the acquisitions.

**Difference Between Vendors' Statements and Confirmations** The most important distinction between a vendor's statement and a confirmation of accounts payable is the source of the information. A vendor's statement has been prepared by an independent third party, but it is in the hands of the client at the time the auditor examines it. This provides the client with an opportunity to alter a vendor's statement or to not make certain statements available to the auditor. A confirmation of accounts payable, which normally is a request for an itemized statement sent directly to the CPA's office, provides the same information but can be regarded as more reliable. In addition, confirmations of accounts payable frequently include a request for information about notes and acceptances payable as well as consigned inventory that is owned by the vendor but stored on the client's premises. An illustration of a typical accounts payable confirmation request is given in Figure 17-4.

**FIGURE 17-4**

**Accounts Payable Confirmation Request**

**ROGER MEAD, INC.** January 15, 1997

*Jones Sales, Inc.*
*2116 Stewart Street*
*Wayneville, Kentucky 36021*

Gentlemen:

Our auditors, Murray and Rogers, CPAs, are conducting an audit of our financial statements. For this purpose, please furnish them with the following information as of December 31, 1996.

(1) Itemized statements of our accounts payable to you showing all unpaid items;
(2) A complete list of any notes and acceptances payable to you (including any which have been discounted) showing the original date, dates due, original amount, unpaid balance, collateral, and endorsers; and
(3) An itemized list of your merchandise consigned to us.

Your prompt attention to this request will be appreciated. An envelope is enclosed for your reply.

Yours truly,

*Phil Geriovini*

Phil Geriovini, President

Because of the availability of vendors' statements and vendors' invoices, which are both relatively reliable evidence because they originate from a third party, the confirmation of accounts payable is less common than confirmation of accounts receivable. If the client has adequate internal controls and vendors' statements are available for examination, confirmations are normally not sent. However, when the client's internal controls are weak, when statements are not available, or when the auditor questions the client's integrity, it is desirable to send confirmation requests to vendors. Because of the emphasis on understatements of liability accounts, the accounts confirmed should include large accounts, active accounts, accounts with a zero balance, and a representative sample of all others.

In most instances in which accounts payable are confirmed, it is done shortly after the balance sheet date. However, if assessed control risk is low, it may be possible to confirm accounts payable at an interim date as a test of the effectiveness of internal controls. Then if the confirmations indicate that the internal controls are ineffective, it is possible to design other audit procedures to test accounts payable at year-end.

When vendors' statements are examined or confirmations are received, there must be a *reconciliation* of the statement or confirmation with the accounts payable list. Frequently, differences are caused by inventory in transit, checks mailed by the client but not received by the vendor at the statement date, and delays in processing the accounting records. The reconciliation is of the same general nature as that discussed in Chapter 13 for accounts receivable. The documents typically used to reconcile the balances on the accounts payable list with the confirmations or vendors' statements include receiving reports, vendors' invoices, and cancelled checks.

### Sample Size

Sample sizes for accounts payable tests vary considerably, depending on such factors as the materiality of accounts payable, number of accounts outstanding, assessed control risk, and results of the prior year. When a client's internal controls are weak, which is not uncommon for accounts payable, almost all population items must be verified. In other situations, minimal testing is needed.

Statistical sampling is less commonly used for the audit of accounts payable than for accounts receivable. It is more difficult to define the population and determine the population size in accounts payable. Since the emphasis is on omitted accounts payable, it is essential that the population include all potential payables.

## SUMMARY

Figure 17-5 illustrates the major accounts in the acquisition and payment cycle and the types of audit tests used to audit these accounts. This figure also shows how the audit risk model discussed in Chapter 8 relates to the audit of the acquisition and payment cycle.

**FIGURE 17-5**

**Types of Audit Tests for the Acquisition and Payment Cycle (see Figure 17-1 on page 581 for accounts)**

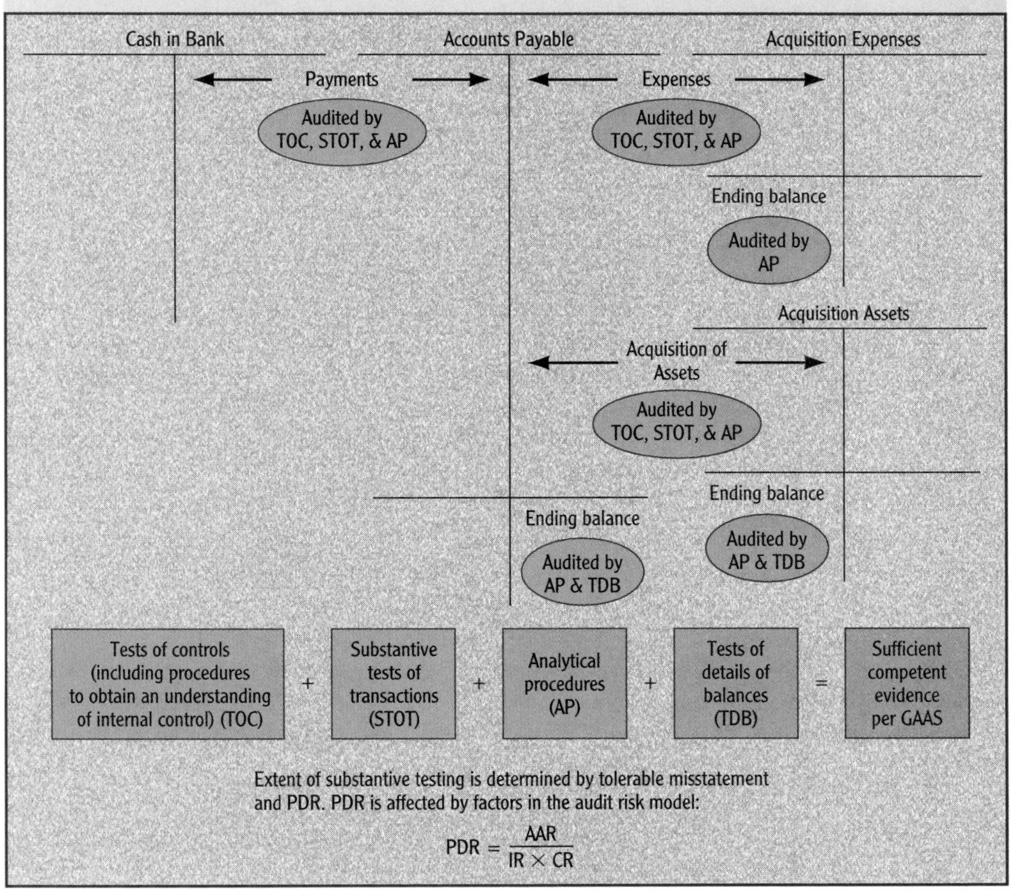

## ESSENTIAL TERMS

**Accounts payable trial balance**—a listing of the amount owed by each vendor at a point in time; prepared directly from the accounts payable master file

**Accounts payable master file**—a computer file for maintaining a record for each vendor of individual acquisitions, cash disbursements, acquisition returns and allowances, and vendor balances

**Acquisition and payment cycle**—the transaction cycle that includes the acquisition of and payment for goods and services from suppliers outside the organization

**Debit memo**—a document indicating a reduction in the amount owed to a vendor because of returned goods or an allowance granted

**FOB origin**—shipping contract in which title to the goods passes to the buyer at the time that the goods are shipped

**FOB destination**—shipping contract in which title to the goods passes to the buyer when the goods are received

**Purchase order**—a document prepared by the purchasing department indicating the description, quantity, and related information for goods and services that the company intends to purchase

**Purchase requisition**—request by an authorized employee to the purchasing department to place an order for inventory and other items used by an entity

**Receiving report**—a document prepared by the receiving department at the time tangible goods are received, indicating the description of the goods, the quantity received, the date received, and other relevant data; it is part of the documentation necessary for payment to be made

**Vendor's invoice**—a document that specifies the details of an acquisition transaction and amount of money owed to the vendor for an acquisition

**Vendor's statement**—a statement prepared monthly by the vendor, which indicates the customer's beginning balance, acquisitions, payments, and ending balance

## REVIEW QUESTIONS

**17-1 (Objective 17-1)** List five asset accounts, three liability accounts, and five expense accounts included in the acquisition and payment cycle for a typical manufacturing company.

**17-2 (Objectives 17-1, 17-2)** List one possible internal control for each of the six transaction-related audit objectives for cash disbursements. For each control, list a test of control to test its effectiveness.

**17-3 (Objectives 17-1, 17-2)** List one possible control for each of the six transaction-related audit objectives for acquisitions. For each control, list a test of control to test its effectiveness.

**17-4 (Objective 17-2)** Evaluate the following statement by an auditor concerning tests of acquisitions and cash disbursements: "In selecting the acquisitions and cash disbursements sample for testing, the best approach is to select a random month and test every transaction for the period. Using this approach enables me to thoroughly understand internal control because I have examined everything that happened during the period. As a part of the monthly test, I also test the beginning and ending bank reconciliations and prepare a proof of cash for the month. At the completion of these tests I feel I can evaluate the effectiveness of internal control."

**17-5 (Objective 17-2)** What is the importance of cash discounts to the client and how can the auditor verify whether they are being taken in accordance with company policy?

**17-6 (Objective 17-2)** What are the similarities and differences in the objectives of the following two procedures? (1) Select a random sample of receiving reports and trace them to related vendors' invoices and acquisitions journal entries, comparing the vendor's name, type of material and quantity acquired, and total amount of the acquisition. (2) Select a random sample of acquisitions journal entries and trace them to related vendors' invoices and receiving reports, comparing the vendor's name, type of material and quantity acquired, and total amount of the acquisition.

**17-7 (Objectives 17-1, 17-2)** If an audit client does not have prenumbered checks, what type of misstatement has a greater chance of occurring? Under the circumstances, what audit procedure can the auditor use to compensate for the weakness?

**17-8 (Objective 17-1)** What is meant by a voucher? Explain how its use can improve an organization's internal controls.

**17-9 (Objective 17-1)** Explain why most auditors consider the receipt of goods and services the most important point in the acquisition and payment cycle.

**17-10 (Objectives 17-1, 17-6)** Explain the relationship between tests of the acquisition and payment cycle and tests of inventory. Give specific examples of how these two types of tests affect each other.

**17-11 (Objectives 17-2, 17-3)** Explain the relationship between tests of the acquisition and payment cycle and tests of accounts payable. Give specific examples of how these two types of tests affect each other.

**17-12 (Objective 17-5)** The CPA examines all unrecorded invoices on hand as of February 29, 1997, the last day of field work. Which of the following misstatements is most likely to be uncovered by this procedure? Explain.

a. Accounts payable are overstated at December 31, 1996.

b. Accounts payable are understated at December 31, 1996.

c. Operating expenses are overstated for the twelve months ended December 31, 1996.

d. Operating expenses are overstated for the two months ended February 29, 1997.*

**17-13 (Objective 17-7)** Explain why it is common for auditors to send confirmation requests to vendors with "zero balances" on the client's accounts payable listing, but uncommon to follow the same approach in verifying accounts receivable.

**17-14 (Objectives 17-1, 17-7)** Distinguish between a vendor's invoice and a vendor's statement. Which document should ideally be used as evidence in auditing acquisition transactions and which for verifying accounts payable balances? Why?

**17-15 (Objective 17-7)** It is less common to confirm accounts payable at an interim date than accounts receivable. Explain why.

**17-16 (Objective 17-6)** In testing the cutoff of accounts payable at the balance sheet date, explain why it is important that auditors coordinate their tests with the physical observation of inventory. What can the auditor do during the physical inventory to enhance the likelihood of an accurate cutoff?

**17-17 (Objective 17-6)** Distinguish between FOB destination and FOB origin. What procedures should the auditor follow concerning acquisitions of inventory on an FOB origin basis near year-end?

## MULTIPLE CHOICE QUESTIONS FROM CPA EXAMINATIONS

**17-18 (Objective 17-1)** The following questions concern internal controls in the acquisition and payment cycle. Choose the best response.

a. Effective internal control over the purchasing of raw materials should usually include all of the following procedures *except*
   (1) systematic reporting of product changes that will affect raw materials.
   (2) determining the need for the raw materials prior to preparing the purchase order.
   (3) obtaining third-party, written quality and quantity reports prior to payment for the raw materials.
   (4) obtaining financial approval prior to making a commitment.

b. Budd, the purchasing agent of Lake Hardware Wholesalers, has a relative who owns a retail hardware store. Budd arranged for hardware to be delivered by manufacturers to the retail store on a COD basis, thereby enabling his relative to buy at Lake's wholesale prices. Budd was probably able to accomplish this because of Lake's poor internal control over

*AICPA adapted.

(1) purchase requisitions.
(2) cash receipts.
(3) perpetual inventory records.
(4) purchase orders.

c. Which of the following is an internal control that would prevent paid cash disbursement documents from being presented for payment a second time?
   (1) Unsigned checks should be prepared by individuals who are responsible for signing checks.
   (2) Cash disbursement documents should be approved by at least two responsible management officials.
   (3) The date on cash disbursement documents should be within a few days of the date that the document is presented for payment.
   (4) The official signing the check should compare the check with the documents and should deface the documents.

**17-19 (Objectives 17-5, 17-6, 17-7)** The following questions concern accumulating evidence in the acquisition and payment cycle. Choose the best response.

a. In comparing the confirmation of accounts payable with suppliers and confirmation of accounts receivable with debtors, the true statement is that
   (1) confirmation of accounts payable with suppliers is a more widely accepted auditing procedure than is confirmation of accounts receivable with debtors.
   (2) statistical sampling techniques are more widely accepted in the confirmation of accounts payable than in the confirmation of accounts receivable.
   (3) as compared with the confirmation of accounts payable, the confirmation of accounts receivable will tend to emphasize accounts with zero balances at the balance sheet date.
   (4) it is less likely that the confirmation request sent to the supplier will show the amount owed him than that the request sent to the debtor will show the amount due from him.

b. Which of the following audit procedures is best for identifying unrecorded trade accounts payable?
   (1) Examining unusual relationships between monthly accounts payable balances and recorded cash payments.
   (2) Reconciling vendors' statements to the file of receiving reports to identify items received just prior to the balance sheet date.
   (3) Reviewing cash disbursements recorded subsequent to the balance sheet date to determine whether the related payables apply to the prior period.
   (4) Investigating payables recorded just prior to and just subsequent to the balance sheet date to determine whether they are supported by receiving reports.

c. In auditing accounts payable, an auditor's procedures most likely would focus primarily on management's assertion of
   (1) existence or occurrence.
   (2) presentation and disclosure.
   (3) completeness.
   (4) valuation or allocation.

## DISCUSSION QUESTIONS AND PROBLEMS

**17-20 (Objectives 17-1, 17-2, 17-5, 17-6)** Questions 1 through 8 are typically found in questionnaires used by auditors to obtain an understanding of internal control in the acquisition and payment cycle. In using the questionnaire for a client, a "yes" response to a question indicates a possible internal control, whereas a "no" indicates a potential weakness.

1. Is the purchasing function performed by personnel who are independent of the receiving and shipping functions and the payables and disbursing functions?
2. Are all vendors' invoices routed directly to accounting from the mailroom?
3. Are all receiving reports prenumbered and the numerical sequence checked by a person independent of check preparation?
4. Are all extensions, footings, discounts, and freight terms on vendors' invoices checked for accuracy?
5. Does a responsible employee review and approve the invoice account distribution before it is recorded in the acquisitions journal?
6. Are checks recorded in the cash disbursements journal as they are prepared?
7. Are all supporting documents properly cancelled at the time the checks are signed?
8. Is the custody of checks after signature and before mailing handled by an employee independent of all payable, disbursing, cash, and general ledger functions?

## Required

a. For each of the preceding questions, state the transaction-related audit objective(s) being fulfilled if the control is in effect.

b. For each internal control, list a test of control to test its effectiveness.

c. For each of the preceding questions, identify the nature of the potential financial misstatement(s) if the control is not in effect.

d. For each of the potential misstatements in part c, list a substantive audit procedure that can be used to determine whether a material misstatement exists.

**17-21 (Objective 17-2)** Following are some of the tests of controls and substantive tests of transactions procedures frequently performed in the acquisition and payment cycle. Each is to be done on a sample basis.

1. Trace transactions recorded in the acquisitions journal to supporting documentation, comparing the vendor's name, total dollar amounts, and authorization for acquisition.
2. Account for a sequence of receiving reports and trace selected ones to related vendors' invoices and acquisitions journal entries.
3. Review supporting documents for clerical accuracy, propriety of account distribution, and reasonableness of expenditure in relation to the nature of the client's operations.
4. Examine documents in support of acquisition transactions to make sure that each transaction has an approved vendor's invoice, receiving report, and purchase order included.
5. Foot the cash disbursements journal, trace postings of the total to the general ledger, and trace postings of individual cash disbursements to the accounts payable master file.
6. Account for a numerical sequence of checks in the cash disbursements journal and examine all voided or spoiled checks for proper cancellation.
7. Prepare a proof of cash disbursements for an interim month.
8. Compare dates on cancelled checks with dates on the cash disbursements journal and the bank cancellation date.

## Required

a. State whether each procedure above is primarily a test of control or substantive test of transactions.

b. State the purpose(s) of each procedure.

**17-22 (Objectives 17-1, 17-2, 17-6)** The following misstatements are included in the accounting records of Westgate Manufacturing Company.

1. Telephone expense (account 2112) was unintentionally charged to repairs and maintenance (account 2121).
2. Acquisitions of raw materials are frequently not recorded until several weeks after the goods are received due to the failure of the receiving personnel to forward receiving

reports to accounting. When pressure from a vendor's credit department is put on Westgate's accounting department, it searches for the receiving report, records the transactions in the acquisitions journal, and pays the bill.

3. The accounts payable clerk prepares a monthly check to Story Supply Company for the amount of an invoice owed and submits the unsigned check to the treasurer for payment along with related supporting documents that have already been approved. When she receives the signed check from the treasurer, she records it as a debit to accounts payable and deposits the check in a personal bank account for a company named Story Company. A few days later she records the invoice in the acquisitions journal again, resubmits the documents and a new check to the treasurer, and sends the check to the vendor after it has been signed.
4. The amount of a check in the cash disbursements journal is recorded as $4,612.87 instead of $6,412.87.
5. The accounts payable clerk intentionally excluded from the cash disbursements journal seven larger checks written and mailed on December 26 to prevent cash in the bank from having a negative balance on the general ledger. They were recorded on January 2 of the subsequent year.
6. Each month a fraudulent receiving report is submitted to accounting by an employee in the receiving department. A few days later he sends Westgate an invoice for the quantity of goods ordered from a small company he owns and operates in the evening. A check is prepared, and the amount is paid when the receiving report and the vendor's invoice are matched by the accounts payable clerk.

### Required

a. For each misstatement, identify the transaction-related audit objective that was not met.

b. For each misstatement, state a control that should have prevented it from occurring on a continuing basis.

c. For each misstatement, state a substantive audit procedure that could uncover it.

**17-23 (Objectives 17-4, 17-5, 17-6, 17-7)** The following auditing procedures were performed in the audit of accounts payable:

1. Examine supporting documents for cash disbursements several days before and after year-end.
2. Examine the acquisitions and cash disbursements journals for the last few days of the current period and first few days of the succeeding period, looking for large or unusual transactions.
3. Trace from the general ledger trial balance and supporting working papers to determine if accounts payable, related parties, and other related assets and liabilities are properly included on the financial statements.
4. For liabilities that are payable in a foreign currency, determine the exchange rate and check calculations.
5. Discuss with the bookkeeper whether any amounts included on the accounts payable list are due to related parties, debit balances, or notes payable.
6. Obtain vendors' statements from the controller and reconcile to a listing of accounts payable.
7. Obtain vendors' statements directly from vendors and reconcile to the listing of accounts payable.
8. Obtain a list of accounts payable. Re-add and compare with the general ledger.

### Required

a. For each procedure, identify the type of audit evidence used.

b. For each procedure, use the matrix on page 603 to identify which balance-related audit objective(s) were satisfied. (Procedure 1 is completed as an illustration.)

c. Evaluate the need to have certain objectives satisfied by more than one audit procedure.

| AUDIT PROCEDURE | BALANCE-RELATED AUDIT OBJECTIVE | | | | | | | |
|---|---|---|---|---|---|---|---|---|
| | Detail tie-in | Existence | Completeness | Accuracy | Classification | Cutoff | Obligations | Presentation and disclosure |
| 1 | | | X | | | X | | |
| 2 | | | | | | | | |
| 3 | | | | | | | | |
| 4 | | | | | | | | |
| 5 | | | | | | | | |
| 6 | | | | | | | | |
| 7 | | | | | | | | |
| 8 | | | | | | | | |

**17-24 (Objectives 17-1, 17-2)** In testing cash disbursements for the Jay Klein Company, you have obtained an understanding of internal control. The controls are reasonably good, and no unusual audit problems have arisen in previous years.

Although there are not many individuals in the accounting department, there is a reasonable separation of duties in the organization. There is a separate purchasing agent who has responsibility for ordering goods and a separate receiving department for counting the goods when they are received and for preparing receiving reports. There is a separation of duties between recording acquisitions and cash disbursements, and all information is recorded in the two journals independently. The controller reviews all supporting documents before signing the checks, and he immediately mails the check to the vendor. Check copies are used for subsequent recording.

All aspects of internal control seem satisfactory to you, and you perform minimum tests of seventy-five transactions as a means of assessing control risk. In your tests you discover the following exceptions:

1. Two items in the acquisitions journal have been misclassified.
2. Three invoices had not been initialed by the controller, but there were no dollar misstatements evident in the transactions.
3. Five receiving reports were recorded in the acquisitions journal at least two weeks later than their date on the receiving report.
4. One invoice had been paid twice. The second payment was supported by a duplicate copy of the invoice. Both copies of the invoice had been marked "paid."
5. One check amount in the cash disbursements journal was for $100 less than the amount stated on the vendor's invoice.
6. One voided check was missing.
7. Two receiving reports for vendors' invoices were missing from the transaction packets. One vendor's invoice had an extension error, and the invoice had been initialed that the amount had been checked.

### Required

a. Identify whether each of 1 through 7 was a control test deviation, a monetary misstatement, or both.

b. For each exception, identify which transaction-related audit objective was not met.

c. What is the audit importance of each of these exceptions?

d. What follow-up procedures would you use to determine more about the nature of each exception?

e. How would each of these exceptions affect the balance of your audit? Be specific.

f. Identify internal controls that should have prevented each misstatement.

**17-25 (Objective 17-2)** You are the staff auditor testing the combined acquisitions and cash disbursements journal for a small audit client. The internal controls are regarded as reasonably effective, considering the number of personnel.

The in-charge auditor has decided that a sample of eighty items should be sufficient for this audit because of the excellent controls. He gives you the following instructions:

1. All transactions selected must exceed $100.
2. At least fifty of the transactions must be for acquisitions of raw material because these transactions are typically material.
3. It is not acceptable to include the same vendor in the sample more than once.
4. All vendors' invoices that cannot be located must be replaced with a new sample item.
5. Both checks and supporting documents are to be examined for the same transactions.
6. The sample must be random, after modifications for instructions 1 through 5.

### Required

a. Evaluate each of these instructions for testing acquisition and cash disbursements transactions.

b. Explain the difficulties of applying each of these instructions to attributes sampling.

**17-26 (Objectives 17-1, 17-2)** Each year near the balance sheet date, when the president of Bargon Construction, Inc., takes a three-week vacation to Hawaii, she signs several checks to pay major bills during the period she is absent. Jack Morgan, head bookkeeper for the company, uses this practice to his advantage. Morgan makes out a check to himself for the amount of a large vendor's invoice, and since there is no acquisitions journal, he records the amount in the cash disbursements journal as an acquisition from the supplier listed on the invoice. He holds the check until several weeks into the subsequent period to make sure that the auditors do not get an opportunity to examine the cancelled check. Shortly after the first of the year when the president returns, Morgan resubmits the invoice for payment and again records the check in the cash disbursements journal. At that point, he marks the invoice "paid" and files it with all other paid invoices. Morgan has been following this practice successfully for several years and feels confident that he has developed a foolproof method.

### Required

a. What is the auditor's responsibility for discovering this type of embezzlement?

b. What weaknesses exist in the client's internal control?

c. What audit procedures are likely to uncover the fraud?

**17-27 (Objective 17-6)** You were in the final stages of your audit of the financial statements of Ozine Corporation for the year ended December 31, 1996, when you were consulted by the corporation's president, who believes there is no point to your examining the 1997 acquisitions journal and testing data in support of 1997 entries. He stated that (a) bills pertaining to 1996 that were received too late to be included in the December acquisitions journal were recorded as of the year-end by the corporation by journal entry, (b) the internal auditor made tests after the year-end, and (c) he would furnish you with a letter certifying that there were no unrecorded liabilities.

### Required

a. Should a CPA's test for unrecorded liabilities be affected by the fact that the client made a journal entry to record 1996 bills that were received late? Explain.

b. Should a CPA's test for unrecorded liabilities be affected by the fact that a letter is obtained in which a responsible management official certifies that to the best of his or her knowledge all liabilities have been recorded? Explain.

c. Should a CPA's test for unrecorded liabilities be eliminated or reduced because of the internal audit tests? Explain.

d. Assume that the corporation, which handled some government contracts, had no internal auditor but that an auditor for a federal agency spent three weeks auditing the records and was just completing his work at this time. How would the CPA's unrecorded liability test be affected by the work of the auditor for a federal agency?

e. What sources in addition to the 1997 acquisitions journal should the CPA consider to locate possible unrecorded liabilities? *

**17-28 (Objectives 17-1, 17-2, 17-3, 17-5, 17-6)** Because of the small size of the company and the limited number of accounting personnel, the Dry Goods Wholesale Company initially records all acquisitions of goods and services at the time cash disbursements are made. At the end of each quarter when financial statements for internal purposes are prepared, accounts payable are recorded by adjusting journal entries. The entries are reversed at the beginning of the subsequent period. Except for the lack of an acquisitions journal, the controls over acquisitions are excellent for a small company. (There are adequate prenumbered documents for all acquisitions, proper approvals, and adequate internal verification wherever possible.)

Before the auditor arrives for the year-end audit, the bookkeeper prepares adjusting entries to record the accounts payable as of the balance sheet date. A list of all outstanding balances is prepared, by vendor, on an accounts payable listing and is given to the auditor. All vendors' invoices supporting the list are retained in a separate file for the auditor's use.

In the current year, the accounts payable balance has increased dramatically because of a severe cash shortage. (The cash shortage apparently arose from expansion of inventory and facilities rather than lack of sales.) Many accounts have remained unpaid for several months and the client is getting pressure from several vendors to pay the bills. Since the company had a relatively profitable year, management is anxious to complete the audit as early as possible so that the audited statements can be used to obtain a large bank loan.

### Required

a. Explain how the lack of an acquisitions journal will affect the auditor's tests of controls and substantive tests of transactions for acquisitions and cash disbursements.

b. What should the auditor use as a sampling unit in performing tests of acquisitions?

c. Assuming there are no misstatements discovered in the auditor's tests of controls and substantive tests of transactions for acquisitions and cash disbursements, how will that result affect the verification of accounts payable?

d. Discuss the reasonableness of the client's request for an early completion of the audit and the implications of the request from the auditor's point of view.

e. List the audit procedures that should be performed in the year-end audit of accounts payable to meet the cutoff objective.

*AICPA adapted.

f. State your opinion as to whether it is possible to conduct an adequate audit in these circumstances.

**17-29 (Objectives 17-5, 17-7)** Mincin, CPA, is the auditor of the Raleigh Corporation. Mincin is considering the audit work to be performed in the accounts payable area for the current year's engagement.

The prior year's working papers show that confirmation requests were mailed to 100 of Raleigh's 1,000 suppliers. The selected suppliers were based on Mincin's sample, which was designed to select accounts with large dollar balances. A substantial number of hours were spent by Raleigh and Mincin resolving relatively minor differences between the confirmation replies and Raleigh's accounting records. Alternative audit procedures were used for those suppliers who did not respond to the confirmation requests.

## Required

a. Identify the accounts payable balance-related audit objectives that Mincin must consider in determining the audit procedures to be followed.

b. Identify situations in which Mincin should use accounts payable confirmations and discuss whether Mincin is required to use them.

c. Discuss why the use of large dollar balances as the basis for selecting accounts payable for confirmation might not be the most effective approach and indicate what more effective procedures could be followed when selecting accounts payable for confirmation.*

**17-30 (Objective 17-7)** As part of the June 30, 1997 audit of accounts payable of Milner Products Company, the auditor sent twenty-two confirmations of accounts payable to vendors in the form of requests for statements. Four of the statements were not returned by the vendors, and five vendors reported balances different from the amounts recorded in Milner's accounts payable master file. The auditor made duplicate copies of the five vendors' statements to maintain control of the independent information and turned the originals over to the client's accounts payable clerk to reconcile the differences. Two days later the clerk returned the five statements to the auditor with the information on the following working paper.

| | | |
|---|---|---|
| Statement 1 | Balance per vendor's statement | $ 6,618.01 |
| | Payment by Milner June 30, 1997 | (4,601.01) |
| | Balance per master file | $ 2,017.00 |
| Statement 2 | Balance per vendor's statement | $ 9,618.93 |
| | Invoices not received by Milner | (2,733.18) |
| | Payment by Milner June 15, 1997 | (1,000.00) |
| | Balance per master file | $ 5,885.75 |
| Statement 3 | Balance per vendor's statement | $26,251.80 |
| | Balance per master file | (20,516.11) |
| | Difference cannot be located due to the vendor's failure to provide details of its account balance | $ 5,735.69 |
| Statement 4 | Balance per vendor's statement | $ 6,170.15 |
| | Credit memo issued by vendor on July 15, 1997 | (2,360.15) |
| | Balance per master file | $ 3,810.00 |
| Statement 5 | Balance per vendor's statement | $ 8,619.21 |
| | Payment by Milner July 3, 1997 | (3,000.00) |
| | Unlocated difference not followed up due to minor amount | 215.06 |
| | Balance per master file | $ 5,834.27 |

*AICPA adapted.

## Required

a. Evaluate the acceptability of having the client perform the reconciliations, assuming that the auditor intends to perform adequate additional tests.

b. Describe the additional tests that should be performed for each of the five statements that included differences.

c. What audit procedures should be performed for the nonresponses to the confirmation requests?

**17-31 (Objective 17-6)** The physical inventory for Ajak Manufacturing was taken on December 30, 1996, rather than December 31, because the client had to operate the plant for a special order the last day of the year. At the time of the client's physical count, you observed that acquisitions represented by receiving report number 2631 and all preceding ones were included in the physical count, whereas inventory represented by succeeding numbers was excluded. On the evening of December 31, you stopped by the plant and noted that inventory represented by receiving report numbers 2632 through 2634 was received subsequent to the physical count, but prior to the end of the year. You later noted that the final inventory on the financial statements contained only those items included in the physical count. In testing accounts payable at December 31, 1996, you obtain a schedule from the client to aid you in testing the adequacy of the cutoff. The schedule below includes the information that you have not yet resolved.

| Receiving Report Number | Amount of Vendor's Invoice | Amount Presently Included in or Excluded from Accounts Payable† | INFORMATION ON THE VENDOR'S INVOICE: Invoice Date | Shipping Date | FOB Origin or Destination |
|---|---|---|---|---|---|
| 2631 | $2,619.26 | Included | 12-30-96 | 12-30-96 | Origin |
| 2632 | $3,709.16 | Excluded | 12-26-96 | 12-15-96 | Destination |
| 2633 | $5,182.31 | Included | 12-31-96 | 12-26-96 | Origin |
| 2634 | $6,403.00 | Excluded | 12-16-96 | 12-27-96 | Destination |
| 2635 | $8,484.91 | Included | 12-28-96 | 12-31-96 | Origin |
| 2636 | $5,916.20 | Excluded | 01-03-97 | 12-31-96 | Destination |
| 2637 | $7,515.50 | Excluded | 01-05-97 | 12-26-96 | Origin |
| 2638 | $2,407.87 | Excluded | 12-31-96 | 01-03-97 | Origin |

†All entries to record inventory acquisitions are recorded by the client as a debit to purchases and a credit to accounts payable.

## Required

a. Explain the relationship between inventory and accounts payable cutoff.

b. For each of the receiving reports, state the misstatement in inventory or accounts payable, if any exists, and prepare an adjusting entry to correct the financial statements, if a misstatement exists.

c. Which of the misstatements in part b are most important? Explain.

## CASES

**PART 1**

**17-32 (Objectives 17-1, 17-2, 17-5, 17-7)** You are provided with the following information about internal control for materials acquisitions for the Johnson Machinery Company, a medium-sized firm that builds special machinery to order.

Materials purchase requisitions are first approved by the plant foreman, who then sends them to the purchasing department. A prenumbered purchase order is prepared in triplicate by one of several department employees. Employees account for all purchase order numbers. The original copy is sent to the vendor. The receiving department is sent the second copy to use for a receiving report. The third copy is kept on file in the purchasing department along with the requisition.

Delivered materials are immediately sent to the storeroom. The receiving report, which is a copy of the purchase order, is sent to the purchasing department. A copy of the receiving report is sent to the storeroom. Materials are issued to factory employees subsequent to a verbal request by one of the foremen.

When the mailroom clerk receives vendors' invoices, he forwards them to the purchasing department employee who placed the order. The invoice is compared with the purchase order on file for price and terms by the employee. The invoice quantity is compared with the receiving department's report. After checking footings, extensions, and discounts, the employee indicates approval for payment by initialing the invoice. The invoice is then forwarded to the accounting department. Vendor name, date, gross and net invoice amounts, and account distribution are key-entered into the computer system for updating the acquisitions journal and accounts payable master file, and filed by payment date due. The vendor's invoice is filed in the accounting department. The purchase order and receiving report are filed in the purchasing department.

The accounting department requisitions prenumbered checks from the cashier. They are manually prepared and then returned to the cashier, who puts them through the check-signing machine. After accounting for the sequence of numbers, the cashier sends the checks to the accounting department, where they are key-entered for recording cash disbursements and updating accounts payable. The checks are placed in envelopes and sent to the mailroom. At the end of each month, a listing of the accounts payable master file is printed and the total is compared with the general ledger balance. Any differences disclosed are investigated.

**Required**

a. Prepare a flowchart for the acquisition and payment cycle for Johnson Machinery Company.

b. List the controls in existence for each of the six transaction-related audit objectives for acquisitions.

c. For each control in part b, list one test of control audit procedure to verify its effectiveness.

d. List the most important internal control weaknesses for acquisitions and cash disbursements.

e. Design an audit program to test internal control. The program should include, but not be limited to, the tests of controls from part c and procedures to compensate for the weaknesses in part d.

**PART 2**

In confirming accounts payable at December 31, 1997, the following procedures are suggested to you for the Johnson Machinery Company.

1. Obtain a list of accounts payable at December 31, 1997, from the client and
   (a) foot the list.
   (b) compare the total with balance shown in the general ledger.
   (c) compare the amounts shown on the list with the balances in the accounts payable master file.
2. Select accounts to confirm.
   (a) Select each account with a balance payable in excess of $2,000.
   (b) Select a random sample of fifty other accounts over $100.
   (c) Indicate the accounts to be confirmed on the accounts payable list, make a copy of the list, and give it to the accounts payable clerk along with instructions to type the vendor's name, address, and balance due on confirmations.
3. Compare the confirmations with the accounts payable master file.
4. Have the client's controller sign each confirmation.

5. Have the accounts payable clerk insert the confirmations and return envelopes addressed to the CPA firm in the client's envelopes. The envelopes are also to be stamped and sealed by the clerk. This should all be done under the auditor's control.
6. Mail the confirmations.

## Required

Assume that the results of tests of controls in Part I support your preliminary assessment of control risk in the acquisition and payment cycle. Evaluate the procedures for confirming accounts payable.

**WARD PUBLISHING COMPANY—PART 1** **(SEE PAGE 610 FOR PART II AND CASE 18-31 FOR PART III)**

**17-33 (Objectives 17-2, 17-3, 17-5, 17-6)** The following tests of controls and substantive tests of transactions audit procedures for acquisitions and cash disbursements are to be used in the audit of Ward Publishing Company. You have concluded that internal control appears effective and a reduced assessed control risk is likely to be cost beneficial. Ward's active involvement in the business, good separation of duties, and a competent controller and other employees are factors affecting your opinion.

**Tests of Controls and Substantive Tests of Transactions Audit Procedures for Acquisitions and Cash Disbursements**

1. Foot and crossfoot the acquisitions and cash disbursements journals for two months and trace totals to postings in the general ledger.
2. Scan the acquisitions and cash disbursements journals for all months and investigate any unusual entries.
3. Reconcile cash disbursements per books to cash disbursements per bank statement for one month.
4. Examine evidence that the bank reconciliation is prepared by the controller.
5. Determine by observation that a check protector is in use.
6. Inquire and observe whether the accounts payable master file balances are periodically reconciled to vendors' statements by the controller.
7. Examine the log book as evidence that the numerical sequence of checks is accounted for by someone independent of the preparation function.
8. Inquire and observe that checks are mailed by D. Ward or someone under his supervision after he signs checks.
9. Examine initials indicating that the controller balances the accounts payable master file to the general ledger monthly.
10. Select a sample of entries in the cash disbursements journal, and
    a. obtain related cancelled checks and compare with entry for payee, date, and amount, and examine signature endorsement.
    b. obtain vendors' invoices, receiving reports, and purchase orders, and
       (1) examine vendors' invoices to determine that all supporting documents are attached.
       (2) determine that documents agree with the cash disbursements journal.
       (3) compare vendors' names, amounts, and dates to entries.
       (4) determine if a discount was taken when appropriate.
       (5) examine vendors' invoices for initials indicating an independent review of chart of account codings.
       (6) examine reasonableness of cash disbursements and account codings.
       (7) review invoices for approval of acquisitions by Ward.
       (8) review purchase orders and/or purchase requisitions for proper approval.
       (9) verify prices and recalculate footings and extensions on invoices.
       (10) compare quantities and descriptions on purchase orders, receiving reports, and vendors' invoices to the extent applicable.
       (11) examine vendors' invoices and receiving reports to determine that the check numbers are included and the documents are marked "paid" at the time of check signing.

c. Trace postings to the accounts payable master file for name, amount, and date.

11. Select a sample of receiving reports issued during the year and trace to vendors' invoices and entries in the acquisitions journal.

    a. Compare type of merchandise, name of vendor, date received, quantities, and amounts.

    b. If the transaction is indicated in the acquisitions journal as paid, trace check number to entry in cash disbursements journal. If unpaid, investigate reasons.

    c. Trace transactions to accounts payable master file, comparing name, amount, and date.

### Required

Prepare all parts of a sampling data sheet (such as the one on page 432) through the planned sample size for the above audit program, assuming that a line item in the cash disbursements journal is used for the sampling unit. Use either nonstatistical or attributes sampling. For all procedures for which the line item in the cash disbursements journal is not an appropriate sampling unit, assume that audit procedures were performed on a nonsampling basis. For all tests of controls, use a tolerable exception rate of 5 percent, and for all substantive tests of transactions use a rate of 6 percent. Use an ARACR of 10 percent, which is considered medium. Plan for an estimated population exception rate of 1 percent for tests of controls and 0 percent for substantive tests of transactions.

Prepare the data sheet using the microcomputer (instructor option—also applies to Part 2).

## PART 2

Assume a sample size of fifty for all procedures in Part 1, regardless of your answers in Part 1. For other procedures, assume that an adequate sample size for the circumstance was selected. The only exceptions in your audit tests for all tests of controls and substantive tests of transactions audit procedures are as follows:

1. Procedure 2—Two large transactions were identified as being unusual. Investigation determined that they were authorized acquisitions of fixed assets. They were both correctly recorded.
2. Procedure 10b(1)—A purchase order had not been attached to a vendor's invoice. The purchase order was found in a separate file and determined to be approved and appropriate.
3. Procedure 10b(5)—Six vendors' invoices were not initialed as being internally verified. Three actual misclassifications existed. The controller explained that he frequently did not review codings because of the competence of the accounting clerk doing the coding, and was surprised at the mistakes.

### Required

a. Complete the sampling data sheet from Part 1 using either nonstatistical or attributes sampling.

b. Explain the effect of the exceptions on tests of details of accounts payable. Which balance-related audit objective(s) are affected, and how do those objectives, in turn, affect the audit of accounts payable?

c. Given your tests of controls and substantive tests of transactions results, write an audit program for tests of details of balances for accounts payable. Assume:
   (1) The client provided a list of accounts payable, prepared from the master file.
   (2) Acceptable audit risk for accounts payable is high.
   (3) Inherent risk for accounts payable is low.
   (4) Analytical procedure results were excellent.

# COMPLETING THE TESTS IN THE ACQUISITION AND PAYMENT CYCLE: VERIFICATION OF SELECTED ACCOUNTS

18

## LEARNING OBJECTIVES

Thorough study of this chapter will enable you to

**18-1** Recognize the many accounts besides accounts payable that are part of the acquisition and payment cycle.

**18-2** Design and perform audit tests of manufacturing equipment and related accounts.

**18-3** Design and perform audit tests of prepaid expenses.

**18-4** Design and perform audit tests of accrued liabilities.

**18-5** Design and perform audit tests of income and expense accounts.

## PROFIT DOES NOT COME FIRST

Harry Bolemas majored in accounting and obtained a masters of professional accountancy degree. During his early years with a Big Six firm, Harry demonstrated extraordinary technical competence in both accounting and auditing. Harry advanced rapidly through the firm's hierarchy and was made a partner at the age of 31. He was given responsibility for several audit clients, but was also responsible for office technical review. As such, he became the ultimate authority at the office level for technical decisions. Harry also served as an independent review partner on audits of public companies that filed reports with the Securities and Exchange Commission.

It was as an independent review partner on Veltron Associates that Harry ran into a specific problem. The Chicago office had entered into a very competitive effort to obtain Veltron as a new client. Veltron was a clothing manufacturer with headquarters in Harry's city, but it had operations in several other countries outside of the United States. Each operation was established as a separate subsidiary and some were required to have separate audits for statutory reporting purposes in their respective countries. Harry's firm made a very aggressive bid and obtained Veltron as a client, mostly because the firm's proposal contained the lowest fees. Furthermore, the fees proposed were for three years.

After the initial excitement of getting a new client, the auditors assigned to Veltron realized they may have made an unwise commitment on audit costs. The policies and agreements the firm had for billing foreign work required it to pay foreign offices' full fees. Fairly extensive evidence was required in the foreign locations because of statutory reporting. Thus, any billing adjustments had to be made in the headquarter's work. The audit partner calculated that if all the implied write-offs were absorbed by his office, the average billing rate on the job would be only about half of the standard rate. Armed with this knowledge, the engagement partner "ordered" the staff to figure out how to reduce time for the headquarter's work in every possible way.

When Harry reviewed the finished job, he was alarmed at the low level of audit evidence. The audit was a first-year engagement, which meant that some additional risk was involved. It was also a public company. Harry believed the evidence was insufficient and more work would have to be done. When he confronted the engagement partner, the partner argued this would cause the engagement to be a financial disaster for the office, as well as present an embarrassing situation in terms of "reopening" the engagement. Harry believed the engagement partner was more concerned with how it made him look than the problems it would cause the office. Harry responded, "An audit is an audit regardless of how much it costs, and our firm must meet that standard. I will not sign the report docket documenting my review until more work is done, and I am sure your managing partner will feel the same way."

The engagement partner finally agreed with Harry and the audit scope was expanded. The firm absorbed a large billing adjustment on the Veltron engagement for three years, but did a good job. At the end of the first three years, the firm renegotiated its fee arrangement, and Veltron became a solid client for many years. Harry is still one of the most respected partners in the firm.

An important characteristic of the acquisition and payment cycle is the large number of accounts involved. These include the following:

**OBJECTIVE 18-1**
**Recognize the many accounts besides accounts payable that are part of the acquisition and payment cycle.**

- Cash in the bank
- Inventory
- Supplies
- Leases and leasehold improvements
- Land
- Buildings
- Manufacturing equipment
- Organization costs
- Patents, trademarks, and copyrights
- Commercial franchises
- Prepaid rent
- Prepaid taxes
- Prepaid insurance
- Accounts payable
- Rent payable
- Accrued professional fees
- Accrued property taxes
- Income taxes payable
- Cost of goods sold
- Rent expense
- Fines and penalties
- Property taxes
- Income tax expense
- Insurance expense
- Professional fees
- Retirement benefits
- Utilities

Since the audit procedures for many of these accounts are similar, an understanding of the appropriate methodology for each can be obtained by studying the following selected account balances:

- Cash in the bank—affected by all transaction cycles (Chapter 21)
- Inventory—represents tangible assets and is typically used up in one year (Chapter 19)
- Prepaid insurance—represents prepaid expenses (Chapter 18)
- Manufacturing equipment—represents long-lived tangible assets (Chapter 18)
- Accounts payable—represents specific liabilities for which the amount and the date of the future payment are known (Chapter 17)
- Accrued property taxes—represents estimated liabilities (Chapter 18)
- Operations accounts—include several methods of verifying all accounts in this category (Chapter 18)

The methodology for designing tests of details of balances for the above accounts is the same as that shown in Figure 17-3 on page 591 for accounts payable. Each account is a part of the acquisition and payment cycle. Therefore, the only change required in the figure is to replace accounts payable with the account being audited. For example, if the account being discussed is accrued property taxes, simply substitute accrued property taxes for accounts payable in the first, second, and last boxes in the figure.

The types of audit tests used to audit the above accounts are the same as those shown in Figure 17-5 on page 597. Figure 17-5 also illustrates how the audit risk model discussed in Chapter 8 relates to the audit of these accounts.

Property, plant, and equipment are assets that have expected lives of more than one year, are used in the business, and are not acquired for resale. The intention to use the assets as a part of the operation of the client's business and their expected life of more than one year are the significant characteristics that distinguish these assets from inventory, prepaid expenses, and investments.

Property, plant, and equipment can be classified as follows:

- Land and land improvements
- Buildings and building improvements
- Manufacturing equipment
- Furniture and fixtures
- Autos and trucks
- Leasehold improvements
- Construction of property, plant, and equipment in process

## AUDIT OF MANUFACTURING EQUIPMENT

**OBJECTIVE 18-2**
**Design and perform audit tests of manufacturing equipment and related accounts.**

In this section the audit of *manufacturing equipment* is discussed as an illustration of an appropriate approach to the audit of all property, plant, and equipment accounts. When there are significant differences in the verification of other types of property, plant, or equipment, they are briefly discussed.

### Overview of the Accounts

The accounts commonly used for manufacturing equipment are illustrated in Figure 18-1. The relationship of manufacturing equipment to the acquisition and the payment cycle is apparent by examining the debits to the asset account. Since the source of debits in the asset account is the acquisitions journal, the accounting system has already been tested for recording current period's additions to manufacturing equipment as part of the tests of the acquisition and payment cycle. Because equipment additions are infrequent and may be subject to special controls, such as board of directors approval, the auditor may decide not to rely heavily on these tests.

**FIGURE 18-1**
**Manufacturing Equipment and Related Accounts**

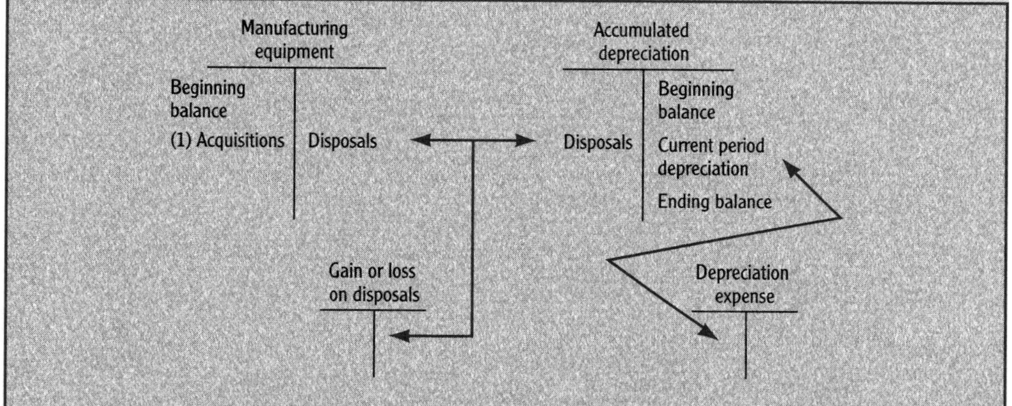


(1) Acquisitions of manufacturing equipment arise from the acquisition and payment cycle. See Figure 17-1.

The primary accounting record for manufacturing equipment and other property, plant, and equipment accounts is generally a property, or fixed asset master file. The contents of the property master file must be understood for a meaningful study of the audit of manufacturing equipment. The master file is composed of a set of records, one for each piece of equipment and other types of property owned. In turn, each record includes descriptive information, date of acquisition, original cost, current-year depreciation, and accumulated depreciation for the property. The totals for all records in the master file equal the general ledger balances for the related accounts.

The master file will also contain information about property acquired and disposed of during the year. For disposals, proceeds, gains and losses will be included.

### Auditing Manufacturing Equipment

Manufacturing equipment is normally audited differently from current asset accounts for three reasons: (1) there are usually fewer current period acquisitions of manufacturing equipment, (2) the amount of any given acquisition is often material, and (3) the equipment is likely to be kept and maintained in the accounting records for several years. Because of these differences, the emphasis in auditing manufacturing equipment is on the verification of current period acquisitions rather than on the balance in the account carried forward from the preceding year. In addition, the expected life of assets over one year requires depreciation and accumulated depreciation accounts, which are verified as a part of the audit of the assets.

Although the approach to verifying manufacturing equipment is dissimilar from that used for current assets, several other accounts are verified in much the same manner. These include patents, copyrights, catalog costs, and all property, plant, and equipment accounts.

In the audit of manufacturing equipment, it is helpful to separate the tests into the following categories:

- Analytical procedures
- Verification of current-year acquisitions
- Verification of current-year disposals
- Verification of the ending balance in the asset account
- Verification of depreciation expense
- Verification of the ending balance in accumulated depreciation

## Analytical Procedures

As in all audit areas, the nature of the analytical procedures depends on the nature of the client's operations. Table 18-1 illustrates the type of ratio and trend analysis frequently performed for manufacturing equipment.

**TABLE 18-1**

**Analytical Procedures for Manufacturing Equipment**

| Analytical Procedure | Possible Misstatement |
|---|---|
| Compare depreciation expense divided by gross manufacturing equipment cost with previous years. | Misstatement in depreciation expense and accumulated depreciation. |
| Compare accumulated depreciation divided by gross manufacturing equipment cost with previous years. | Misstatement in accumulated depreciation. |
| Compare monthly or annual repairs and maintenance, supplies expense, small tools expense, and similar accounts with previous years. | Expensing amounts that should be capital items. |
| Compare gross manufacturing cost divided by some measure of production with previous years. | Idle equipment or equipment that has been disposed of, but not written off. |

## Verification of Current-Year Acquisitions

The proper recording of current-year additions is important because of the long-term effect the assets have on the financial statements. The failure to capitalize a fixed asset, or the recording of an acquisition at the improper amount, affects the balance sheet until the firm disposes of the asset. The income statement is affected until the asset is fully depreciated.

Because of the importance of current-period acquisitions in the audit of manufacturing equipment, seven of the nine balance-related audit objectives for tests of details of balances are used as a frame of reference. (Realizable value and presentation and disclosure are discussed in connection with the verification of ending balances.)

The balance-related audit objectives and common audit tests are shown in Table 18-2. As in all other audit areas, the actual audit tests and sample size depend heavily on materiality, inherent risk, and assessed control risk. Materiality is of special importance for verifying current-year additions. They vary from immaterial amounts in some years to a large number of significant acquisitions in others. Accuracy and classification are usually the major objectives for this part of the audit.

The starting point for the verification of current-year acquisitions is normally a schedule obtained from the client of all acquisitions recorded in the general ledger during the year. A typical schedule lists each addition separately and includes the date of the acquisition, vendor, description, notation of new or used, life of the asset for depreciation purposes, depreciation method, and cost. The client obtains this information from the property master file.

**TABLE 18-2**

**Balance-Related Audit Objectives and Tests of Details of Balances for Manufacturing Equipment Additions**

| Balance-Related Audit Objective | Common Tests of Details of Balances Procedures | Comments |
|---|---|---|
| Current-year acquisitions in the acquisitions schedule agree with related master file amounts, and the total agrees with the general ledger (detail tie-in). | Foot the acquisitions schedule.<br>Trace the total to the general ledger.<br>Trace the individual acquisitions to the master file for amounts and descriptions. | These tests should be limited unless controls are weak.<br>All increases in the general ledger balance for the year should reconcile to the schedule. |
| Current-year acquisitions as listed exist (existence). | Examine vendors' invoices and receiving reports.<br>Physically examine assets. | It is uncommon to physically examine acquisitions unless controls are weak or amounts are material. |
| Existing acquisitions are recorded (completeness). | Examine vendors' invoices of closely related accounts such as repairs and maintenance to uncover items that should be manufacturing equipment.<br>Review lease and rental agreements. | This objective is one of the most important ones for manufacturing equipment. |
| Current-year acquisitions as listed are accurate (accuracy). | Examine vendors' invoices. | Extent depends on inherent risk and effectiveness of internal controls. |
| Current-year acquisitions as listed are properly classified (classification). | Examine vendors' invoices in manufacturing equipment account to uncover items that should be classified as office equipment, part of the buildings, or repairs.<br>Examine vendors' invoices of closely related accounts such as repairs to uncover items that should be manufacturing equipment.<br>Examine rent and lease expense for capitalizable leases. | The objective is closely related to tests for completeness. It is done in conjunction with that objective and tests for accuracy. |
| Current-year acquisitions are recorded in the proper period (cutoff). | Review transactions near the balance sheet date for proper period. | Usually done as a part of accounts payable cutoff tests. |
| The client has rights to current-year acquisitions (rights). | Examine vendors' invoices. | Ordinarily no problem for equipment. Property deeds, abstracts, and tax bills are frequently examined for land or major buildings. |

In studying Table 18-2, one should recognize the importance of examining vendors' invoices and related documents in verifying acquisitions of manufacturing equipment. That subject is discussed in the next section.

### Examining Supporting Documents

The most common audit test to verify additions is examining of vendors' invoices and receiving reports. Additional testing besides that which is done as a part of the tests of controls and substantive tests of transactions is frequently considered necessary because of the complexity of many equipment transactions and the materiality of the amounts. It is ordinarily unnecessary to examine supporting documentation for each addition, but it is normal to verify large and unusual transactions for the entire year as well as a representative sample of typical additions. The extent of the verification depends on the auditor's assessed control risk for acquisitions and the materiality of the additions.

**AUDIT THAT WHICH IS UNCOMFORTABLE!**

"Although this landscaping plan is expensive, the project is long overdue. I heartily approve!" wrote the president of a West Coast company in an internal memo.

One year later the internal audit department conducted a routine review of significant expenditures involving the construction, renovation, and maintenance of corporate properties. One of the disbursements selected for review was issued in connection with the relandscaping of the company's corporate headquarters.

The contractor was an established local commercial landscaping firm. Based on the disbursement vouchers and vendor invoices, project payments totaled almost $1,000,000, including $800,000 under a written contract plus $200,000 in planning, design work, and enhancements not covered under the contract. Each of 12 invoices had been approved by the vice president responsible for corporate facilities or the recently retired former president.

When the auditors went to the facilities department to get the contract, design blueprint, bidding records, and other supporting documents, the manager informed them that the relandscaping had not been administered by his department, but by the department's vice president, who had approved most of the invoices.

The vice president confirmed that:

- He had administered the project personally, with the knowledge and approval of the president.
- There was no need for bidding because of the quality and integrity of the landscaping firm, a vendor to the organization for over 20 years.

The auditors decided to probe further because the landscaping cost seemed excessive, there was no competitive bidding, and because the contract was administered by high-level executives rather than those usually administering such contracts.

The contractor initially defended his pricing as reasonable, due to adverse soil and site condition. However, after several intense meetings and discussion of possible legal action, the contractor reluctantly disclosed the true circumstances of the transaction. He was instructed by the vice president and former president to price the project so that it would also cover extensive landscaping and building renovation at each of their homes. The internal auditors' review of the contractor's records confirmed that excess charges of almost $600,000 covered the cost of a pool, hot tub, deck, marble patio, sprinkler system, fountain, dock, landscaping, and extensive building renovation at the homes of both executives.The contractor also said that the former president had contacted him during the audit to discourage cooperation.

The company went public with the audit findings, and the investigative file was turned over to the prosecutor. As a result of their no contest pleas, the two executives were convicted of obtaining money under false pretenses.Virtually all losses were recovered through successful bonding claims.

**Lessons to Be Learned**

1. All fraud is committed by those we trust.
2. Professional skepticism and acting on instinct are essential for fraud detection.
3. Audit that which is uncomfortable!
4. Even good internal controls can be circumvented.
5. Include a right-to-audit provision in all contracts.
6. Contracts that designate others to keep books and records provide opportunity to disguise improper payments.
7. Listen to "cover stories" and then follow through.
8. Don't sweep it under the carpet.

*Source:* Courtenay Thompson, "Fraud in the Executive Suite." This article was reprinted with permission from pp. 68–69 of the October 1993 issue of *Internal Auditor,* published by The Institute of Internal Auditors, Inc.

Tests for acquisitions are accomplished by comparing the charges on vendors' invoices with recorded amounts. The auditor must know the client's capitalization policies to determine whether acquisitions are recorded in accordance with generally accepted accounting principles and are treated consistently with those of the preceding year. For example, many clients automatically expense items that are less than a certain amount, such as $100. The auditor should be alert for the possibility of material transportation and installation costs, as well as the trade-in of existing equipment.

In conjunction with testing current-period additions for existence and accuracy, the auditor should also review recorded transactions for proper classification. In some cases, amounts recorded as manufacturing equipment should be classified as office equipment or as a part of the building. There is also the possibility that the client has improperly capitalized repairs, rents, or similar expenses.

The inclusion of transactions that should properly be recorded as assets in repairs and maintenance expense, lease expense, supplies, small tools, and similar accounts is a common client error. The error results from lack of understanding of generally accepted accounting principles and some clients' desire to avoid income taxes. The likelihood of these types of misclassifications should be evaluated in conjunction with obtaining an understanding of internal control in the acquisition and payment cycle. If the auditor concludes that material misstatements are likely, it may be necessary to vouch the larger amounts debited to the expense accounts. It is a common practice to do this as a regular part of the audit of the property, plant, and equipment accounts.

## Verification of Current-Year Disposals

**Internal Controls** The most important internal control over the disposal of manufacturing equipment is the existence of a formal method to inform management of the sale, trade-in, abandonment, or theft of recorded machinery and equipment. If the client fails to record disposals, the original cost of the manufacturing equipment account will be overstated indefinitely, and the net book value will be overstated until the asset is fully depreciated. Another important control to protect assets from unauthorized disposal is a provision for authorization for the sale or other disposal of manufacturing equipment. Finally, there should be adequate internal verification of recorded disposals to make sure that assets are correctly removed from the accounting records.

**Audit Tests** The two major objectives in the verification of the sale, trade-in, or abandonment of manufacturing equipment are *existing disposals are recorded* and *disposals are accurately recorded.*

The starting point for verifying disposals is the client's schedule of recorded disposals. The schedule typically includes the date when the asset was disposed of, the name of the person or firm acquiring the asset, the selling price, the original cost of the asset, the acquisition date, the accumulated depreciation of the asset, and the investment credit recapture, if any. Detail tie-in tests of the schedule are necessary, including footing the schedule, tracing the totals on the schedule to the recorded disposals in the general ledger, and tracing the cost and accumulated depreciation of the disposals to the property master file.

Because the failure to record disposals of manufacturing equipment no longer used in the business can significantly affect the financial statements, *the search for unrecorded disposals is essential.* The nature and adequacy of the controls over disposals affect the extent of the search. The following procedures are frequently used for verifying disposals:

- Review whether newly acquired assets replace existing assets.
- Analyze gains on the disposal of assets and miscellaneous income for receipts from the disposal of assets.
- Review plant modifications and changes in product line, taxes, or insurance coverage for indications of deletions of equipment.
- Make inquiries of management and production personnel about the possibility of the disposal of assets.

When an asset is sold or disposed of without having been traded in for a replacement asset, the *accuracy* of the transaction can be verified by examining the related sales invoice and property master file. The auditor should compare the cost and accumulated depreciation in the master file with the recorded entry in the general journal and recompute the gain or loss on the disposal of the asset for comparison with the accounting records.

Two areas deserve special attention in the accuracy objective. The first is the *trade-in of an asset for a replacement.* When trade-ins occur, the auditor should be sure that the new asset is properly capitalized and the replaced asset properly eliminated from the records, considering the book value of the asset traded in and the additional cost of the new asset. The second area of special concern is the disposal of assets affected by the *investment credit recapture provisions.* Since the recapture affects the current year's income tax expense and liability, the auditor must evaluate its significance. An understanding of the recapture provisions for the year the asset was acquired is necessary before the calculation can be made.

## Verification of Asset Balance

**Internal Controls** The nature of the internal controls over existing assets determines whether it is necessary to verify manufacturing equipment acquired in prior years. Important controls include the use of a master file for individual fixed assets, adequate physical controls over assets that are easily movable (such as tools and vehicles), assignment of identification numbers to each plant asset, and periodic physical count of fixed assets and their reconciliation by accounting personnel. A formal method of informing the accounting department of all disposals of fixed assets is also an important control over the balance of assets carried forward into the current year.

**Audit Tests** Usually, the auditor does not obtain a list from the client of all assets included in the ending balance of manufacturing equipment. Instead, audit tests are determined on the basis of the master file.

Typically, the first audit step concerns the detail tie-in objective: manufacturing equipment as listed in the master file agrees with the general ledger. Examining a printout of the master file that totals to the general ledger balance is ordinarily sufficient. The auditor may choose to test-foot a few pages.

After assessing control risk for the existence objective, the auditor must decide whether it is necessary to verify the existence of individual items of manufacturing equipment included in the master file. If the auditor believes there is a high likelihood of significant missing fixed assets that are still recorded on the accounting records, an appropriate procedure is to select a sample from the master file and examine the actual assets. In rare cases, the auditor may believe it is necessary that the client take a complete physical inventory of fixed assets to make sure they actually exist. If a physical inventory is taken, the auditor normally observes the count.

Ordinarily, it is unnecessary to test the accuracy or classification of fixed assets recorded in prior periods because presumably they were verified in previous audits at the time they were acquired. But the auditor should be aware that companies may occasionally have on hand manufacturing equipment that is no longer used in operations. If the amounts are material, the auditor should evaluate whether they should be written down to net realizable value (realizable value objective) or at least disclosed separately as "nonoperating equipment."

A major consideration in verifying the ending balance in fixed assets is the possibility of existing *legal encumbrances* (presentation and disclosure objective). A number of methods are available to determine if manufacturing equipment is encumbered. These include reading the terms of loan and credit agreements and mailing loan confirmation requests to banks and other lending institutions. Information with respect to encumbered assets may also be obtained through discussions with the client or letters to legal counsel. In addition, it is desirable to obtain information on possible liens by sending a form entitled *Request for Information Under the Uniform Commercial Code* to the secretary of state or other appropriate officials of the state in which the company operates.

The *proper presentation and disclosure* of manufacturing equipment in the financial statements must be carefully evaluated to make sure that generally accepted accounting principles are followed. Manufacturing equipment should include the gross cost and should ordinarily be separated from other fixed assets. Leased property should also be disclosed separately, and all liens on property must be included in the footnotes.

## Verification of Depreciation Expense

Depreciation expense is one of the few expense accounts that is not verified as a part of tests of controls and substantive tests of transactions. The recorded amounts are determined by *internal allocations* rather than by exchange transactions with outside parties. When depreciation expense is material, more tests of details of depreciation expense are required than for an account that has already been verified through tests of controls and substantive tests of transactions.

The most important objective for depreciation expense is accuracy. Two major concerns are involved in the accuracy objective: determining whether the client is following *a consistent depreciation policy* from period to period and whether the client's *calculations are correct.* In determining the former, there are four considerations: the useful life of current period acquisitions, the method of depreciation, the estimated salvage value, and the policy of depreciating assets in the year of acquisition and disposition. The client's policies can be determined by having discussions with appropriate personnel and comparing the responses with the information in the auditor's permanent files.

In deciding on the reasonableness of the useful lives assigned to newly acquired assets, the auditor must consider a number of factors: the actual physical life of the asset, the expected life (taking into account obsolescence or the company's normal policy of upgrading equipment), and established company policies on trading in equipment. Occasionally, changing circumstances may necessitate a reevaluation of the useful life of an asset. When this occurs, a change in accounting estimate rather than a change in accounting principle is involved. The effect of this on depreciation must be carefully evaluated.

A useful method of testing depreciation is to make a calculation of its overall reasonableness. The calculation is made by multiplying the undepreciated fixed assets by the depreciation rate for the year. In making these calculations, the auditor must of course make adjustments for current-year additions and disposals, assets with different lengths of life, and assets with different methods of depreciation. The calculations can be made fairly easily if the CPA firm includes in the permanent file a breakdown of the fixed assets by method of depreciation and length of life. If the overall calculations are reasonably close to the client's totals and if assessed control risk for depreciation expense is low, tests of details for depreciation can be minimized.

In many audits, it is also desirable to check the detail tie-in of a sample of depreciation calculations. This is done by recomputing depreciation expense for selected assets to determine whether the client is following a proper and consistent depreciation policy. To be relevant, the detailed calculations should be tied in to the total depreciation calculations by footing the depreciation expense on the property master file and reconciling the total with the general ledger. If the client maintains computerized depreciation and amortization records, it may be desirable to consider using the computer in testing the calculations.

## Verification of Accumulated Depreciation

The debits to accumulated depreciation are normally tested as a part of the audit of disposals of assets, whereas the credits are verified as a part of depreciation expense. If the auditor traces selected transactions to the accumulated depreciation records in the property master file as a part of these tests, little additional testing should be required.

Two objectives are usually emphasized in the audit of accumulated depreciation:

- Accumulated depreciation as stated in the property master file agrees with the general ledger. This objective can be satisfied by test-footing the accumulated depreciation or the property master file and tracing the total to the general ledger.
- Accumulated depreciation in the master file is accurate.

In some cases, the life of manufacturing equipment may be significantly reduced because of such changes as reductions in customer demands for products, unexpected physical deterioration, or a modification in operations. Because of these possibilities, it is necessary to evaluate the adequacy of the allowances for accumulated depreciation each year to make sure that the net book value exceeds the realizable value of the assets.

## AUDIT OF PREPAID EXPENSES

**OBJECTIVE 18-3**
**Design and perform audit tests of prepaid expenses.**

Prepaid expenses, deferred charges, and intangibles are assets that vary in life from several months to several years. Their inclusion as assets results more from the concept of matching expenses with revenues than from their resale or liquidation value. The following are examples:

- Prepaid rent
- Organization costs
- Prepaid taxes
- Patents
- Prepaid insurance
- Trademarks
- Deferred charges
- Copyrights

One typical difference between these assets and others, such as accounts receivable and inventory, is their immateriality in many audits. Frequently, analytical procedures are sufficient for prepaid expenses, deferred charges, and intangibles.

In this section the audit of prepaid insurance is discussed as an account representative of this group because (1) it is found in most audits—virtually every company has some type of insurance; (2) it is typical of the problems frequently encountered in the audit of this class of accounts; and (3) the auditor's responsibility for the review of insurance coverage is an additional consideration not encountered in the other accounts in this category.

### Overview of Prepaid Insurance

The accounts typically used for prepaid insurance are illustrated in Figure 18-2. The relationship between prepaid insurance and the acquisition and payment cycle is apparent in examining the debits to the asset account. Since the source of the debits in the asset account is the acquisitions journal, the payments of insurance premiums have already been partially tested by means of the tests of controls and substantive tests of acquisition and cash disbursement transactions.

**FIGURE 18-2**
**Prepaid Insurance and Related Accounts**

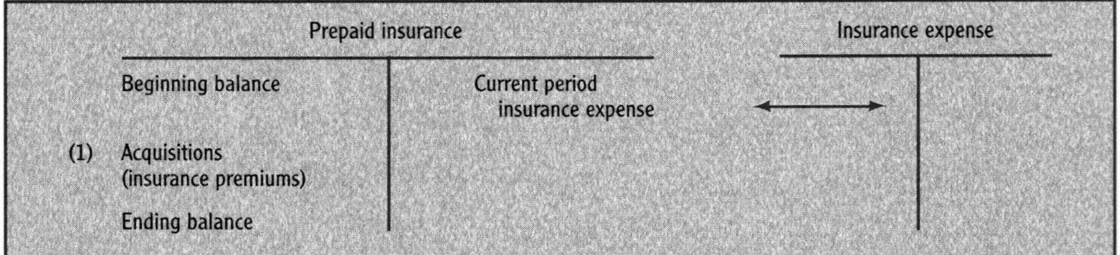


(1) Acquisitions of insurance premiums arise from the acquisition and payment cycle. This can be observed by examining Figure 17-1.

### Internal Controls

The internal controls for prepaid insurance and insurance expense can be conveniently divided into three categories: controls over the acquisition and recording of insurance, controls over the insurance register, and controls over the charge-off of insurance expense.

Controls over the acquisition and recording of insurance are a part of the acquisition and payment cycle. These should include proper authorization for new insurance policies and payment of insurance premiums consistent with the procedures discussed in that cycle.

A record of insurance policies in force and the due date of each policy *(insurance register)* is an essential control to make sure that the company has adequate insurance at all times. The control should include a provision for periodic review of the adequacy of the insurance coverage by an independent qualified person.

After they have been completed, the detailed records of the information in the prepaid insurance register should be verified by someone independent of the person preparing them. A closely related control is the use of monthly standard journal entries for insurance expense. If a significant entry is required to adjust the balance in prepaid insurance at the end of the year, it indicates a potential misstatement in the recording of the acquisition of insurance throughout the year or in the calculation of the year-end balance in prepaid insurance.

## Audit Tests

Throughout the audit of prepaid insurance and insurance expense, the auditor should keep in mind that the amount in insurance expense is a residual based on the beginning balance in prepaid insurance, the payment of premiums during the year, and the ending balance. The only verification of the balance in the expense account that is ordinarily necessary are analytical procedures and a brief test to be sure that the charges to insurance expense arose from credits to prepaid insurance. Since the payments of premiums are tested as part of the tests of controls and substantive tests of transactions and analytical procedures, the emphasis in the tests of details of balances is on prepaid insurance.

In the audit of prepaid insurance, a schedule is obtained from the client or prepared by the auditor that includes each insurance policy in force, policy number, insurance coverage for each policy, premium amount, premium period, insurance expense for the year, and prepaid insurance at the end of the year. An example of a schedule obtained from the client for the auditor's working papers is given in Figure 18-3 (pages 622–623). The auditor's tests of prepaid insurance are normally indicated on the schedule.

**Analytical Procedures** A major consideration in the audit of prepaid insurance is the frequent *immateriality* of the beginning and ending balances. Furthermore, few transactions are debited and credited to the balance during the year, most of which are small and simple to understand. Therefore, the auditor can generally spend little time verifying the balance. When the auditor plans not to verify the balance in detail, analytical procedures become increasingly important as a means of identifying potentially significant misstatements. The following are commonly performed analytical procedures of prepaid insurance and insurance expense:

- Compare total prepaid insurance and insurance expense with previous years as a test of reasonableness.
- Compute the ratio of prepaid insurance to insurance expense and compare it with previous years.
- Compare the individual insurance policy coverage on the schedule obtained from the client with the preceding year's schedule as a test of the elimination of certain policies or a change in insurance coverage.
- Compare the computed prepaid insurance balance for the current year on a policy-by-policy basis with that of the preceding year as a test of an error in calculation.
- Review the *insurance coverage* listed on the prepaid insurance schedule with an appropriate client official or insurance broker for adequacy of coverage. The auditor cannot be an expert on insurance matters, but his or her understanding of accounting and the valuation of assets is important in making certain that a company is not underinsured.

For many audits, no additional tests need be performed beyond the review for overall reasonableness unless the tests indicate a high likelihood of a significant misstatement or assessed control risk is high. The remaining audit procedures should be performed only when there is a special reason for doing so. The discussion of these tests is organized around the balance-related audit objectives for performing tests of details of asset balances. For convenience, certain objectives are combined and the order in which they are discussed is different from that previously used. Realizable value is not applicable.

**FIGURE 18-3**

**Schedule of Prepaid Insurance**

PBC

ABC Company, Inc.
Prepaid Insurance

12/31/96

Schedule 9-2 — Date
Prepared by Client/JL — 1/20/97
Approved by GG — 1/25/97

| Insurer | Policy Number | Coverage | Term |
|---|---|---|---|
| Ever-ready Casualty Co. | IBB-79016 (2) | Auto liability, collision, comprehensive, uninsured motorist-covers all autos owned and leased by the company | 6/1/95-96<br>6/1/96-97 |
| Everystate Insurance | 74-88-914 (2) | Multi peril-Headquarters and plant, including contents. | 3/15/95-96 (1)<br>3/15/96-97 (1) |
| Standard Surety Co. | 1973016 (2) | Blanket Position Bond-$25,000 | 7/1/95-96 |
| Commercial Bonding Co. | 717-639 (2) | Commercial Blanket Bond-$100,000 | 7/1/96-97 |

Reconciliation to Insurance Expense (General) Account:

| | | | |
|---|---|---|---|
| Dependable Insurance | DIC-9161 (2) | Personal property-Sales offices | 1/1/96-12/31/96 |
| Insurance Expense | | | |

(1) Policy term is 3 years, expiring 3/14/98, premium shown is annual portion. Annual premium is estimated, subject to annual review and adjustment. Premium is payable in monthly installments under terms of contract. (See work paper section CC, Contracts Payable.)

(2) Reviewed and briefed policies; details of coverage in permanent file. Blanket Position Bond replaced by Commercial Blanket Bond on expiration.

(3) Annual premium adjustment; traced to invoice and voucher

**Insurance Policies in the Prepaid Schedule Exist and Existing Policies Are Listed (Existence and Completeness)** The verification of existence and tests for omissions of the insurance policies in force can be tested in one of two ways: by referring to supporting documentation or by obtaining a confirmation of insurance information from the company's insurance agent. The first approach entails examining insurance invoices and policies in force. If these tests are performed, they should be done on a limited test basis. Sending a confirmation to the client's insurance agent is preferable because it is usually less time consuming than vouching tests, and it provides 100 percent verification. The use of confirmations for this purpose has grown rapidly in the past few years.

**The Client Has Rights to All Insurance Policies in the Prepaid Schedule (Rights)** The party who will receive the benefit if an insurance claim is filed has the rights. Ordinarily, the recipient named in the policy is the client, but when there are mortgages or other liens, the insurance claim may be payable to a creditor. The review of insurance policies for claimants other than the client is an excellent test of unrecorded liabilities and pledged assets.

| Annual Premium | Unexpired Premium 1/1/96 | Additions | Expense | Unexpired Premium 12/31/96 | |
|---|---|---|---|---|---|
| 6300 | 2625 PY | | 2625 | - | √ |
| 7000 | - | 7000 | 4083 C | 2917 | √ |
| 12600 | 2625 PY | 1800 (3) | 4425 | - | √ |
| 15100 | - | 15,100 | 11954 C | 3146 | √ |
| 1200 | 600 PY | | 600 | - | √ |
| 800 | - | 800 | 400 C | 400 | √ |
| | 5850 ΛPY | 24,700 Λ | 24087 Λ | 6463 ΛX GL | |
| 500 | | | 500 | | |
| | | | 24587 Λ GL | | |

PY *Agreed to prior year's schedule of prepaid insurance in working papers*

Λ *Footed*

X *Cross-footed*

GL *Agreed to general ledger*

C *Unearned premium confirmed by broker; confirmation filed at F-2/1.*

√ *Verified calculation*

**Prepaid Amounts on the Schedule Are Accurate and the Total Is Correctly Added and Agrees with the General Ledger (Accuracy and Detail Tie-in)** The accuracy of prepaid insurance involves verifying the total amount of the insurance premium, the length of the policy period, and the allocation of the premium to unexpired insurance. The amount of the premium for a given policy and its time period can be verified simultaneously by examining the premium invoice or the confirmation from an insurance agent. Once these two have been verified, the client's calculations of unexpired insurance can be tested by recalculation. The schedule of prepaid insurance can then be footed and the totals traced to the general ledger to complete the detail tie-in tests.

**The Insurance Expense Related to Prepaid Insurance Is Properly Classified (Classification)** The proper classification of debits to different insurance expense accounts should be reviewed as a test of the income statement. In some cases the appropriate expense account is obvious because of the type of insurance (such as insurance on a piece of equipment), but in other cases allocations are necessary. For example, fire insurance on the building may require allocation to several accounts, including manufacturing overhead. Consistency with previous years is the major consideration in evaluating classification.

**Insurance Transactions Are Recorded in the Proper Period (Cutoff)** Cutoff for insurance expense is normally not a significant problem because of the small number of policies and the immateriality of the amount. If the cutoff is checked at all, it is reviewed as a part of accounts payable cutoff tests.

**Prepaid Insurance Is Properly Presented and Disclosed (Presentation and Disclosure)** In most audits, prepaid insurance is combined with other prepaid expenses and included as a current asset. The amount is usually small and not a significant consideration to statement users.

## AUDIT OF ACCRUED LIABILITIES

**OBJECTIVE 18-4**
**Design and perform audit tests of accrued liabilities.**

Accrued liabilities are estimated unpaid obligations for services or benefits that have been received prior to the balance sheet date. Many accrued liabilities represent future obligations for unpaid services resulting from the passage of time but are not payable at the balance sheet date. For example, the benefits of property rental accrue throughout the year; therefore, at the balance sheet date a certain portion of the total rent cost that has not been paid should be accrued. If the balance sheet date and the date of the termination of the rent agreement are the same, any unpaid rent is more appropriately called rent payable than an accrued liability.

A second type of accrual is one in which the amount of the obligation must be estimated due to the uncertainty of the amount due. An illustration is the obligation for federal income taxes when there is a reasonable likelihood that the amount reported on the tax return will be changed after an audit has been conducted by the Internal Revenue Service. The following are common accrued liabilities, including payroll-related accruals discussed as a part of Chapter 16.

- Accrued officers' bonuses
- Accrued commissions
- Accrued income taxes
- Accrued interest
- Accrued payroll
- Accrued payroll taxes
- Accrued pension costs
- Accrued professional fees
- Accrued rent
- Accrued warranty costs

The verification of accrued expenses varies depending on the nature of the accrual and the circumstances of the client. For most audits, accruals take little audit time, but in some instances accounts such as accrued income taxes, warranty costs, and pension costs are material and require considerable audit effort. To illustrate, the audit of accrued property taxes is discussed in this section.

### Auditing Accrued Property Taxes

The accounts typically used by companies for accrued property taxes are illustrated in Figure 18-4. The relationship between accrued property taxes and the acquisition and payment cycle is the same as for prepaid insurance and is apparent from examining the debits to the liability account. Since the source of the debits is the cash disbursements journal, the payments of property taxes have already been partially tested by means of the tests of the acquisition and payment cycle.

As for insurance expense, the balance in property tax expense is a residual amount that results from the beginning and ending balances in accrued property taxes and the payments of property taxes. Therefore, the emphasis in the tests should be on the ending property tax liability and payments. In verifying accrued property taxes, all nine balance-related audit objectives except realizable value are relevant. But two are of special significance:

**FIGURE 18-4**

**Accrued Property Taxes and Related Accounts**

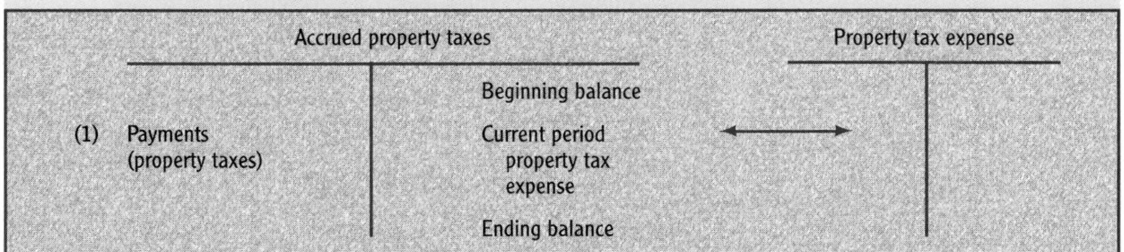


(1) Payments of property taxes arise from the acquisition and payment cycle. This can be observed by examining Figure 17-1.

1. Existing properties for which accrual of taxes is appropriate are on the accrual schedule. The failure to include properties for which taxes should be accrued would understate the liability (completeness). A material misstatement could occur, for example, if taxes on property were not paid before the balance sheet date and not included as accrued property taxes.
2. Accrued property taxes are accurately recorded. The greatest concern in accuracy is the consistent treatment of the accrual from year to year (accuracy).

The primary methods of testing for the inclusion of all accruals are (1) to perform the accrual tests in conjunction with the audit of current-year property tax payments and (2) to compare the accruals with those of previous years. In most audits there are few property tax payments, but each payment is often material, and therefore it is common to verify each one.

First, the auditor should obtain a schedule of property tax payments from the client and compare each payment with the preceding year's schedule to determine whether all payments have been included in the client-prepared schedule. It is also necessary to examine the fixed asset working papers for major additions and disposals of assets that may affect the property taxes accrual. If the client is expanding its operations, all property affected by local property tax regulations should be included in the schedule even if the first tax payment has not yet been made.

After the auditor is satisfied that all taxable property has been included in the client-prepared schedule, it is necessary to evaluate the reasonableness of the total amount of property taxes on each property being used as a basis to estimate the accrual. In some instances the total amount has already been set by the taxing authority, and it is possible to verify the total by comparing the amount on the schedule with the tax bill in the client's possession. In other instances the preceding year's total payments must be adjusted for the expected increase in property tax rates.

The auditor can verify the accrued property tax by recomputing the portion of the total tax applicable to the current year for each piece of property. The most important consideration in making this calculation is to use the same portion of each tax payment as the accrual that was used in the preceding year unless justifiable conditions exist for a change. After the accrual and property tax expense for each piece of property have been recomputed, the totals should be added and compared with the general ledger. In many cases, property taxes are charged to more than one expense account. When this happens, the auditor should test for proper classification by evaluating whether the proper amount was charged to each account.

A typical working paper showing property tax expense, accrued property taxes, and the audit procedures used to verify the balances is illustrated in Figure 18-5 (pages 626–627).

**FIGURE 18-5**

**Schedule for Property Taxes**

ABC Company, Inc.
Property Tax Worksheet
12/31/96

ABC

Schedule 9-6 Date
Prepared by Client/PC 1/15/97
Approved by GS 1/20/97

| Tax Bill No. | Area Code | Assessing Authority | Property | Assessed Value (1) | Total Tax (2) | Date Lien (3) Payable Paid (4) | Period Covered |
|---|---|---|---|---|---|---|---|
| | | West Coast Facilities | | | | | |
| 526391 | 51 | King County | Westside Warehouse | 400000 | 16000 | Jan., 1, 1996<br>Apr. 30, 1997<br>Oct. 31, 1997 | 1996 |
| 526392 | 51 | King County | Headquarters Bldg | 250000 | 10000 | Jan. 1, 1995<br>Apr. 30, 1996<br>Oct. 31, 1996 | 1995 |
| | | | | | | Jan., 1, 1996<br>Apr. 30, 1997 | 1996 |
| | | Mid-West Facilities | | | | | |
| 17923 | A | Minor County | Manufacturing Plant | 2000000 | 23000 | Jul. 1, 1995 | Jul. 1, 1995-96 |
| | | | | | 25000 | Jul. 1, 1996<br>Dec. 31, 1996 | Jul. 1, 1996-97 |

(1) Assessed valuation is defined by the laws of both states as 50% of "true and fair value."

(2) Millage rates:

King County .0400 ($40 per $1,000)

Minor County .0115 ($11.50 per $1,000) for 1995-96

.0125 ($12.50 per $1,000) for 1996-97

(3) Laws of both states establish the lien date to be the same as the assessment date; assessment date for the West Coast state is statutorily defined as January 1, and for the Midwest state as July 1.

(4) Taxes are payable as follows

West Coast state - one half no later than April 30 and the balance no later than October 31, for the preceding calendar year.

Midwest state - payable in full not later than December 31 following assessment date.

## AUDIT OF OPERATIONS

**OBJECTIVE 18-5**
**Design and perform audit tests of income and expense accounts.**

The audit of operations is meant to determine whether the income and expense accounts in the financial statements are fairly presented in accordance with generally accepted accounting principles. The auditor must be satisfied that each of the income and expense totals included in the income statement as well as net earnings is not materially misstated.

In conducting audit tests of the financial statements, the auditor must always be aware of the importance of the income statement to users of the statements. It is clear that many users rely more heavily on the income statement than on the balance sheet for making decisions. Equity investors, long-term creditors, union representatives, and frequently even short-term creditors are more interested in the ability of a firm to generate profit than in the historical cost or book value of the individual assets.

| Prepaid | | | | Accrued | | | |
|---|---|---|---|---|---|---|---|
| Beginning Balance | Additions (6) | Expense | Ending Balance | Beginning Balance | Additions (6) | Payments | Ending Balance |
| -0- | 16000 √ | 16000 | -0- | (5) -0- | 16000 √ | -0- | 16000x |
| | | | | 10000 | | 5000 # | |
| | | | | | | 5000 # | -0-x |
| -0- | 10000 √ | 10000^ | -0-x | -0- | 10000 √ | | 10000x |
| 11500 | | 11500^ | -0-x | -0- | | | -0-x |
| | 25000 | 12500^ | 12500x | -0- | 25000 √ | 25000 # | -0-x |
| 11500 \/\ PY | 51000 \/\ | 50000 \/\ | 12500x \/\ | 10000 \/\ PY | 51000 \/\ | 35000 \/\ | 26000x \/\ |

*(5) Warehouse certified complete and accepted Dec. 22, 1995 inspected and valued by County in March 1996. Per state law (note 3) assessment date and lien date statutorily set at Jan. 1, 1996.*

*(6) Liability and deferred charge are recorded by company on the lien date. The deferred charge is amortized monthly and the liability account relieved when installments are paid.*

*PY Agreed to prior year's working papers.*

*√ Agreed to county tax due notice (identified in left column).*

*^ Agreed to amortization schedule and traced to standard journal entry.*

*# Traced to cancelled check and validated receipt.*

*\/\, x Footed, cross-footed*

Considering the purposes of the statement of earnings, the following two concepts are essential in the audit of operations:

1. The matching of periodic income and expense is necessary for a proper determination of operating results.
2. The consistent application of accounting principles for different periods is necessary for comparability.

These concepts must be applied to the recording of individual transactions and to the combining of accounts in the general ledger for statement presentation.

## Approach to Auditing Operations

The audit of operations cannot be regarded as a separate part of the total audit process. A misstatement of an income statement account will almost always equally affect a balance sheet account, and vice versa. The audit of operations is so intertwined with the other parts of the audit that it is necessary to interrelate different aspects of testing operations with the different types of tests previously discussed. A brief description of these tests serves as a review of material covered in other chapters; more important, it shows the interrelationship of different parts of the audit with operations testing. The parts of the audit directly affecting operations are

- Analytical procedures
- Tests of controls and substantive tests of transactions
- Analysis of account balances
- Tests of details of balance sheet accounts
- Tests of allocations

The emphasis in this section is on the operations accounts directly related to the acquisition and payment cycle, but the same concepts apply to the operations accounts in all other cycles.

## Analytical Procedures

Analytical procedures were first discussed in Chapter 6 as a general concept and have been referred to in subsequent chapters as a part of specific audit areas. Analytical procedures should be thought of as a part of the test of the fairness of the presentation of both balance sheet and income statement accounts. A few analytical procedures and their effect on operations in the acquisition and payment cycle are shown in Table 18-3.

**TABLE 18-3**

**Analytical Procedures for Operations**

| Analytical Procedure | Possible Misstatement |
|---|---|
| Compare individual expenses with previous years. | Overstatement or understatement of a balance in an expense account. |
| Compare individual asset and liability balances with previous years. | Overstatement or understatement of a balance sheet account that would also affect an income statement account (for example, a misstatement of inventory affects cost of goods sold). |
| Compare individual expenses with budgets. | Misstatement of expenses and related balance sheet accounts. |
| Compare gross margin percentage with previous years. | Misstatement of cost of goods sold and inventory. |
| Compare inventory turnover ratio with previous years. | Misstatement of cost of goods sold and inventory. |
| Compare prepaid insurance expense with previous years. | Misstatement of insurance expense and prepaid insurance. |
| Compare commission expense divided by sales with previous years. | Misstatement of commission expense and accrued commissions. |
| Compare individual manufacturing expenses divided by total manufacturing expenses with previous years. | Misstatement of individual manufacturing expenses and related balance sheet accounts. |

## Tests of Controls and Substantive Tests of Transactions

Tests of controls and substantive tests of transactions both have the effect of simultaneously verifying balance sheet and operations accounts. For example, when an auditor concludes that internal controls are adequate to provide reasonable assurance that transactions in the acquisitions journal exist, are accurately recorded, correctly classified, and recorded in a timely manner, evidence exists as to the correctness of individual balance sheet accounts such as accounts payable and fixed assets, and income statement accounts such as advertising and repairs. Conversely, inadequate controls and misstatements discovered through tests of controls and substantive tests of transactions are an indication of the likelihood of misstatements in both the income statement and the balance sheet.

Understanding of internal control and the related tests of controls and substantive tests of transactions to determine the appropriate assessed control risk are the most important means of verifying many of the operations accounts in each of the transaction cycles. For example, if the auditor concludes after adequate tests that assessed control risk can be reduced to low, the only additional verification of operating accounts such as utilities, advertising, and purchases should be analytical procedures and cutoff tests. However, certain income and expense accounts are not verified at all by tests of controls and substantive tests of transactions, and others must be tested more extensively by other means. These are discussed as we proceed.

## Analysis of Account Balances

For some accounts, the amounts included in the operations accounts must be analyzed even though the previously mentioned tests have been performed. The meaning and methodology of analysis of accounts will be described first, followed by a discussion of when expense account analysis is appropriate.

*Expense account analysis* is the examination of underlying documentation of the individual transactions and amounts making up the total of an expense account. The underlying documents are of the same nature as those used for examining transactions as a part of tests of acquisition transactions and include invoices, receiving reports, purchase orders, and contracts. Figure 18-6 on page 630 illustrates a typical working paper showing expense analysis for legal expenses.

Thus, expense account analysis is closely related to tests of controls and substantive tests of transactions. The major difference is the degree of concentration on an individual account. Since the tests of controls and substantive tests of transactions are meant to assess the appropriate control risk, they constitute a general review that usually includes the verification of many different accounts. The analysis of expense and other operations accounts consists of the examination of the transactions in specific accounts to determine the propriety, classification, accuracy, and other specific information about each account analyzed.

Assuming satisfactory classification results are found in tests of controls and substantive tests of transactions, auditors normally restrict expense analysis to those accounts with a relatively high likelihood of material misstatement. For example, auditors often analyze repairs and maintenance expense accounts to determine if they erroneously include property, plant, and equipment transactions; rent and lease expense are analyzed to determine the need to capitalize leases; and legal expense is analyzed to determine whether there are potential contingent liabilities, disputes, illegal acts, or other legal issues that may affect the financial statements. Accounts such as utilities, travel expense, and advertising are rarely analyzed unless analytical procedures indicate high potential for material misstatement.

Frequently, expense account analysis is done as a part of the verification of the related asset. For example, it is common to analyze repairs and maintenance as a part of verifying fixed assets, rent expense as a part of verifying prepaid or accrued rent, and insurance expense as a part of testing prepaid insurance.

## Tests of Allocations

Several expense accounts that have not yet been discussed arise from the internal allocation of accounting data. These include expenses such as depreciation, depletion, and the amortization of copyrights and catalog costs. The allocation of manufacturing overhead between inventory and cost of goods sold is an example of a different type of allocation that affects the expenses.

Allocations are important because they determine whether an expenditure is an asset or a current-period expense. If the client fails to follow generally accepted accounting principles or fails to calculate the allocation properly, the financial statements can be materially misstated. The allocation of many expenses such as the depreciation of fixed assets and the amortization of copyrights is required because the life of the asset is greater than one year. The original cost of the asset is verified at the time of acquisition, but the charge-off takes place over several years. Other types of allocations directly affecting the financial

**FIGURE 18-6**

**Expense Analysis for Legal Expense**

ABC

ABC Company, Inc.
General and Administrative Expenses

12/31/96

| Schedule V-10 | Date |
| --- | --- |
| Prepared by Client/GL | 1/21/97 |
| Approved by SW | 1/28/97 |

Acct. 913-Legal Expense

| Paid to | For | Date | Amount |
| --- | --- | --- | --- |
| ② Alexander J. Schweppe | Retainer-12 months @$500 | Monthly ① | 6000 √ |
| | ABC vs. Carson - patent infringement suit | Apr. 14<br>Aug. 9 | 2800 √<br>3109 √ |
| ② Smith, Tom & Ball. | Consultation re: inquiry from Consumer Protection Bureau, State Attorney General's office | June 6<br>July 10 | 200 √<br>200 √ |
| ③ L. Marvin Hall | Assistance in collecting overdue receivable from Star Mfg. | Nov. 10 | 105 √ |
| | | | 12,414 GL<br>⋀⋀ |

① Per minutes of meeting of Board of Directors 1/10/97. Schweppe reappointed general counsel with retainer.

② Attorney's letter requested — Received 1/23/97, all matters listed are covered therein; letters filed in General Section of working papers.

③ Attorney's letter not requested. Per phone conversation with Mr. Hall, 1/21/97, he rarely represents the company, and his services have been limited to collection problems. The Star Mfg. matter was closed in October 1996, and he has not been involved in any other matters related to the company since that time.

√ Examined statement and vouchers.
⋀⋀ Footed
GL Agreed to general ledger

statements arise because the life of a short-lived asset does not expire on the balance sheet date. Examples include prepaid rent and insurance. Finally, the allocation of costs between current-period manufacturing expenses and inventory is required by generally accepted accounting principles as a means of reflecting all the costs of making a product.

Income statement accounts resulting from allocations are typically not verified as a part of tests of controls, substantive tests of transactions, or tests of details of balance sheet accounts. Analytical procedures are used extensively for verifying allocations, but frequently additional detailed testing is needed.

In auditing the allocation of expenditures such as prepaid insurance and manufacturing overhead, the two most important considerations are adherence to generally accepted accounting principles and consistency with the preceding period. The two most important audit procedures for allocations are tests for overall reasonableness using analytical procedures and recalculation of the client's results. It is common to perform these tests as a part of the audit of the related asset or liability accounts. For example, depreciation expense is usually verified as part of the audit of property, plant, and equipment; amortization of patents is tested as part of verifying new patents or the disposal of existing ones; and allocations between inventory and cost of goods sold are verified as part of the audit of inventory.

## ESSENTIAL TERMS

**Accrued liabilities**—estimated unpaid obligations for services or benefits that have been received prior to the balance sheet date; common accrued liabilities include accrued commissions, accrued income taxes, accrued payroll, and accrued rent

**Allocation**—the division of certain expenses, such as depreciation and manufacturing overhead, among several expense accounts

**Expense account analysis**—the examination of underlying documentation of individual transactions and amounts making up the total of an expense account

**Fixed asset master file**—a computer file containing records for each piece of equipment and other types of property owned; the primary accounting record for manufacturing equipment and other property, plant, and equipment accounts

**Insurance register**—a record of insurance policies in force and the due date of each policy

## REVIEW QUESTIONS

**18-1 (Objective 18-2)** Explain the relationship between substantive tests of transactions for the acquisition and payment cycle and tests of details of balances for the verification of property, plant, and equipment. Which aspects of property, plant, and equipment are directly affected by the tests of controls and substantive tests of transactions and which are not?

**18-2 (Objective 18-2)** Explain why the emphasis in auditing property, plant, and equipment is on the current-period acquisitions and disposals rather than on the balances in the account carried forward from the preceding year. Under what circumstances will the emphasis be on the balances carried forward?

**18-3 (Objective 18-2)** What is the relationship between the audit of property, plant, and equipment accounts and the audit of repair and maintenance accounts? Explain how the auditor organizes the audit to take this relationship into consideration.

**18-4 (Objective 18-2)** List and briefly state the purpose of all audit procedures that might reasonably be applied by an auditor to determine that all property, plant, and equipment retirements have been recorded on the books.

**18-5 (Objective 18-2)** In auditing depreciation expense, what major considerations should the auditor keep in mind? Explain how each can be verified.

**18-6 (Objective 18-3)** Explain the relationship between substantive tests of transactions for the acquisition and payment cycle and tests of details of balances for the verification of prepaid insurance.

**18-7 (Objective 18-3)** Explain why the audit of prepaid insurance should ordinarily take a relatively small amount of audit time if the client's assessed control risk for acquisitions is low.

**18-8 (Objective 18-3)** Distinguish between the evaluation of the adequacy of insurance coverage and the verification of prepaid insurance. Explain which is more important in a typical audit.

**18-9 (Objective 18-3)** What are the major differences between the audit of prepaid expenses and other asset accounts such as accounts receivable or property, plant, and equipment?

**18-10 (Objective 18-4)** Explain the relationship between accrued rent and substantive tests of transactions for the acquisition and payment cycle. Which aspects of accrued rent are not verified as a part of the substantive tests of transactions?

**18-11 (Objective 18-4)** In verifying accounts payable it is common to restrict the audit sample to a small portion of the population items, whereas in auditing accrued property taxes it is common to verify all transactions for the year. Explain the reason for the difference.

**18-12 (Objective 18-4)** Which documents will be used to verify accrued property taxes and the related expense accounts?

**18-13 (Objective 18-5)** List three expense accounts that are tested as part of the acquisition and payment cycle or the payroll and personnel cycle. List three expense accounts that are not directly verified as a part of either of these cycles.

**18-14 (Objective 18-5)** What is meant by the analysis of expense accounts? Explain how expense account analysis relates to the tests of controls and substantive tests of transactions that the auditor has already completed for the acquisition and payment cycle.

**18-15 (Objectives 18-2, 18-5)** How would the approach for verifying repair expense differ from that used to audit depreciation expense? Why would the approach be different?

**18-16 (Objective 18-5)** List the factors that should affect the auditor's decision whether or not to analyze an account balance. Considering these factors, list four expense accounts that are commonly analyzed in audit engagements.

**18-17 (Objective 18-5)** Explain how costs of goods sold for a wholesale company could in part be verified by each of the following types of tests:

a. Analytical procedures
b. Tests of controls and substantive tests of transactions
c. Analysis of account balances
d. Tests of details of balance sheet accounts
e. Tests of allocations

## MULTIPLE CHOICE QUESTIONS FROM CPA EXAMINATIONS

**18-18 (Objective 18-2)** The following questions concern internal controls in the acquisition and payment cycle. Choose the best response.

a. If preparation of a periodic scrap report is essential in order to maintain adequate control over the manufacturing process, the data for this report should be accumulated in the
   (1) accounting department.
   (2) production department.
   (3) warehousing department.
   (4) budget department.

b. Which of the following is not an internal control weakness related to factory equipment?
   (1) Checks issued in payment of acquisitions of equipment are *not* signed by the controller.
   (2) All acquisitions of factory equipment are required to be made by the department in need of the equipment.
   (3) Factory equipment replacements are generally made when estimated useful lives, as indicated in depreciation schedules, have expired.
   (4) Proceeds from sales of fully depreciated equipment are credited to other income.

c. With respect to an internal control measure that will assure accountability for fixed asset retirements, management should implement controls that include
   (1) continuous analysis of miscellaneous revenue to locate any cash proceeds from sale of plant assets.

(2) periodic inquiry of plant executives by internal auditors as to whether any plant assets have been retired.
(3) continuous use of serially numbered retirement work orders.
(4) periodic observation of plant assets by the internal auditors.

**18-19 (Objectives 18-2, 18-5)** The following questions concern analytical procedures in the acquisition and payment cycle. Choose the best response.

a. Which of the following comparisons would be most useful to an auditor in evaluating the results of an entity's operations?
(1) Prior year accounts payable to current year accounts payable.
(2) Prior year payroll expense to budgeted current year payroll expense.
(3) Current year revenue to budgeted current year revenue.
(4) Current year warranty expense to current year contingent liabilities.

b. The controller of Excello Manufacturing, Inc., wants to use ratio analysis to identify the possible existence of idle equipment or the possibility that equipment has been disposed of without having been written off. Which of the following ratios would best accomplish this objective?
(1) Depreciation expense/book value of manufacturing equipment.
(2) Accumulated depreciation/book value of manufacturing equipment.
(3) Repairs and maintenance cost/direct labor costs.
(4) Gross manufacturing equipment cost/units produced.

c. Which of the following analytical procedures should be applied to the income statement?
(1) Select sales and expense items and trace amounts to related supporting documents.
(2) Ascertain that the net income amount in the statement of cash flows agrees with the net income amount in the income statement.
(3) Obtain from the proper client representatives the beginning and ending inventory amounts that were used to determine costs of sales.
(4) Compare the actual revenues and expenses with the corresponding figures of the previous year and investigate significant differences.

**18-20 (Objective 18-2)** The following questions concern the audit of asset accounts in the acquisition and payment cycle. Choose the best response.

a. In testing for unrecorded retirements of equipment, an auditor most likely would
(1) select items of equipment from the accounting records and then locate them during the plant tour.
(2) compare depreciation journal entries with similar prior-year entries in search of fully depreciated equipment.
(3) inspect items of equipment observed during the plant tour and then trace them to the equipment master file.
(4) scan the general journal for unusual equipment additions and excessive debits to repairs and maintenance expense.

b. Which of the following is the *best* evidence of real estate ownership at the balance sheet date?
(1) Title insurance policy.
(2) Original deed held in the client's safe.
(3) Paid real estate tax bills.
(4) Closing statement.

**18-21 (Objectives 18-2, 18-4, 18-5)** The following questions concern the audit of liabilities or operations. Choose the best response.

a. Which of the following audit procedures is *least* likely to detect an unrecorded liability?
(1) Analysis and recomputation of interest expense.
(2) Analysis and recomputation of depreciation expense.
(3) Mailing of standard bank confirmation forms.
(4) Reading of the minutes of meetings of the board of directors.

b. Which of the following *best* describes the independent auditor's approach to obtaining satisfaction concerning depreciation expense in the income statement?
   (1) Verify the mathematical accuracy of the amounts charged to income as a result of depreciation expense.
   (2) Determine the method for computing depreciation expense and ascertain that it is in accordance with generally accepted accounting principles.
   (3) Reconcile the amount of depreciation expense to those amounts credited to accumulated depreciation accounts.
   (4) Establish the basis for depreciable assets and verify the depreciation expense.

c. Before expressing an opinion concerning the results of operations, the auditor would *best* proceed with the audit of the income statement by
   (1) applying a rigid measurement standard designed to test for understatement of net income.
   (2) analyzing the beginning and ending balance sheet inventory amounts.
   (3) making net income comparisons to published industry trends and ratios.
   (4) auditing income statement accounts concurrently with the related balance sheet accounts.

## DISCUSSION QUESTIONS AND PROBLEMS

**18-22 (Objective 18-2)** For each of the following misstatements in property, plant, and equipment accounts, state an internal control that the client could install to prevent the misstatement from occurring and a substantive audit procedure that the auditor could use to discover the misstatement.

1. The asset lives used to depreciate equipment are less than reasonable, expected useful lives.
2. Capitalizable assets are routinely expensed as repairs and maintenance, perishable tools, or supplies expense.
3. Construction equipment that is abandoned or traded for replacement equipment is not removed from the accounting records.
4. Depreciation expense for manufacturing operations is charged to administrative expenses.
5. Tools necessary for the maintenance of equipment are stolen by company employees for their personal use.
6. Acquisitions of property are recorded at an improper amount.
7. A loan against existing equipment is not recorded in the accounting records. The cash receipts from the loan never reached the company because they were used for the down payment on a piece of equipment now being used as an operating asset. The equipment is also not recorded in the records.

**18-23 (Objective 18-2)** The following types of internal controls are commonly employed by organizations for property, plant, and equipment:

1. A fixed asset master file is maintained with a separate record for each fixed asset.
2. Written policies exist and are known by accounting personnel to differentiate between capitalizable additions, freight, installation costs, replacements, and maintenance expenditures.
3. Acquisitions of fixed assets in excess of $20,000 are approved by the board of directors.
4. Whenever practical, equipment is labeled with metal tags and is inventoried on a systematic basis.
5. Depreciation charges for individual assets are calculated for each asset; recorded in a fixed asset master file that includes cost, depreciation, and accumulated depreciation for each asset; and verified periodically by an independent clerk.

## Required

a. State the purpose of each of the internal controls listed above. Your answer should be in the form of the type of misstatement that is likely to be reduced because of the control.

b. For each internal control, list one test of control the auditor can use to test for its existence.

c. List one substantive procedure for testing whether the control is actually preventing misstatements in property, plant, and equipment.

**18-24 (Objectives 18-1, 18-2, 18-3, 18-5)** The following audit procedures were planned by Linda King, CPA, in the audit of the acquisition and payment cycle for Cooley Products, Inc.

1. Review the acquisitions journal for large and unusual transactions.
2. Send letters to several vendors, including a few for which the recorded accounts payable balance is zero, requesting them to inform us of their balance due from Cooley. Ask the controller to sign the letter.
3. Examine a sample of receiving report numbers and determine whether each one has an initial indicating that it was recorded as an account payable.
4. Select a sample of equipment listed on fixed asset master files and inspect the asset to determine that it exists and its condition.
5. Refoot the acquisitions journal for one month and trace all totals to the general journal.
6. Calculate the ratio of equipment repairs and maintenance to total equipment, and compare with previous years.
7. Obtain from the client a written statement that all mortgages payable have been included in the current period financial statements and have been accurately recorded, and the collateral for each is included in the footnotes.
8. Select a sample of cancelled checks and trace each one to the cash disbursements journal, comparing the name, date, and amount.
9. For 20 nontangible acquisitions, select a sample of line items from the acquisitions journal and trace each to related vendors' invoices. Examine whether each transaction appears to be a legitimate expenditure for the client, and that each was approved and recorded at the correct amount and date in the journal and charged to the correct account per the chart of accounts.
10. Examine invoices and related shipping documents included in the client's unpaid invoice file at the audit report date to determine if they were recorded in the appropriate accounting period and at the correct amounts.
11. Recalculate the portion of insurance premiums on the client's prepaid insurance schedule that is applicable to future periods.
12. When the check signer's assistant writes "paid" on supporting documents, watch whether she does it after the documents are reviewed and the checks are signed.

## Required

a. For each procedure, identify the type of evidence being used.

b. For each procedure, identify whether it is an analytical procedure, a test of control, a substantive test of transactions, or a test of details of balances.

c. For each test of control or substantive test of transactions, identify the transaction-related audit objective(s) being met.

d. For each test of details of balances, identify the balance-related audit objective(s) being met.

**18-25 (Objective 18-2)** Hardware Manufacturing Company, a closely held corporation, has operated since 1993 but has not had its financial statements audited. The company now plans to issue additional capital stock to be sold to outsiders and wishes to engage you to audit its 1997 transactions and render an opinion on the financial statements for the year ended December 31, 1997.

The company has expanded from one plant to three and has frequently acquired, modified, and disposed of all types of equipment. Fixed assets have a net book value of 70 percent of total assets and consist of land and buildings, diversified machinery and equipment, and furniture and fixtures. Some property was acquired by donation from stockholders. Depreciation was recorded by several methods using various estimated lives.

## Required

a. May you confine your audit solely to 1997 transactions as requested by this prospective client whose financial statements have not previously been audited? Why?

b. Prepare an audit program for the January 1, 1997, opening balances of the land, building, and equipment and accumulated depreciation accounts of Hardware Manufacturing Company. You need not include tests of 1997 transactions in your program.*

**18-26 (Objective 18-4)** The following program has been prepared for the audit of accrued real estate taxes of a client that pays taxes on twenty-five different pieces of property, some of which have been acquired in the current year.

1. Obtain a schedule of accrued taxes from the client and tie the total to the general ledger.
2. Compare the charges for annual tax payments with property tax assessment bills.
3. Recompute accrued/prepaid amounts for all bills on the basis of the portion of the year expired.

## Required

a. State the purpose of each procedure.

b. Evaluate the adequacy of the audit program.

**18-27 (Objective 18-4)** As part of the audit of different audit areas, it is important to be alert for the possibility of unrecorded liabilities. For each of the following audit areas or accounts, describe a liability that could be uncovered and the audit procedures that could uncover it.

a. Minutes of the board of directors' meetings

b. Land and buildings

c. Rent expense

d. Interest expense

e. Cash surrender value of life insurance

f. Cash in the bank

g. Officers' travel and entertainment expense

**18-28 (Objective 18-5)** While you are having lunch with a banker friend, you become involved in explaining to him how your firm conducts an audit in a typical engagement. Much to your surprise, your friend is interested and is able to converse intelligently in discussing your philosophy of emphasizing the study of internal control, analytical procedures, tests of controls, substantive tests of transactions, and tests of details of balance sheet accounts. At the completion of your discussion, he says, "That all sounds great except for a couple of things. The point of view we take these days at our bank is the importance of a continuous earnings stream. You seem to be emphasizing fraud detection and a fairly stated balance sheet. We would rather see you put more emphasis than you apparently do on the income statement."

## Required

How would you respond to your friend's comments?

**18-29 (Objective 18-5)** Brian Day, a staff assistant, has been asked to analyze interest and legal expense as a part of the first-year audit of Rosow Manufacturing Company. In search-

*AICPA adapted

ing for a model to follow, Day looked at other completed working papers in the current audit file and concluded that the closest thing to what he was looking for was a working paper for repair and maintenance expense account analysis. Following the approach used in analyzing repairs and maintenance, all interest and legal expenses in excess of $500 were scheduled and verified by examining supporting documentation.

### Required

a. Evaluate Day's approach to verifying interest and legal expense.

b. Suggest a better approach to verifying these two account balances.

**18-30 (Objectives 18-1, 18-2, 18-5)** In performing tests of the acquisition and payment cycle for the Orlando Manufacturing Company, the staff assistant did a careful and complete job. Since internal controls were evaluated as excellent before tests of controls and substantive tests of transactions were performed and were determined to be operating effectively on the basis of the lack of exceptions in the tests of controls and substantive tests of transactions, the decision was made to significantly reduce the tests of expense account analysis. The in-charge auditor decided to reduce but not eliminate the acquisition-related expense account analysis for repair expense, legal and other professional expense, miscellaneous expense, and utilities expense on the grounds that they should always be verified more extensively than normal accounts. The decision was also made to eliminate any account analysis for the acquisition of raw materials, depreciation expense, supplies expense, insurance expense, and the current period additions to fixed assets.

### Required

a. List other considerations in the audit besides the quality of internal controls that should affect the auditor's decision as to which accounts to analyze.

b. Assuming that no significant problems were identified on the basis of the other considerations in part a, evaluate the auditor's decision of reducing but not eliminating expense account analysis for each account involved. Justify your conclusions.

c. Assuming that no significant problems were identified on the basis of the other considerations in part a, evaluate the auditor's decision to eliminate expense account analysis for each account involved. Justify your conclusions.

## CASES

### WARD PUBLISHING COMPANY—PART III (SEE CASE 17-33 FOR PARTS I AND II)

**18-31 (Objectives 18-1, 18-2, 18-5)** Examine the tests of controls and substantive tests of transactions results, including the sampling application in Case 17-33 for Ward Publishing Company. Assume that you have already reached several conclusions.

1. Your tests of details of balances for accounts payable are completed and you found no exceptions.
2. Acceptable audit risk for property, plant, and equipment and all expenses is high.
3. Inherent risk for property, plant, and equipment is high because in the current year the client has acquired a material amount of new and used printing equipment and has traded in older equipment. Some of the new equipment was ineffective and returned; an allowance was received on others. Inherent risk for expense accounts is low.
4. New computer equipment and some printing equipment are being leased. The client has never leased equipment before.
5. Analytical procedures for property, plant, and equipment are inconclusive because of the large increases in acquisition and disposal activity.
6. Analytical procedures show that repairs, maintenance, and small tools expenses have increased materially, both in absolute terms and as a percentage of sales. Two other expenses have also materially increased, and one has materially decreased.

7. In examining the sample for tests of controls and substantive tests of transactions, you observe that no sample items included any property, plant, and equipment or lease transactions.

## Required

a. Explain the relationship between the tests of controls and substantive tests of transactions results in Case 17-33 and the audit of property, plant, and equipment and leases.

b. How would the tests of controls and substantive tests of transactions results and your conclusions (1 through 7) affect your planned tests of details for property, plant, and equipment and leases? State your conclusions for each balance-related audit objective. Do not write an audit program.

c. Explain the relationship between the tests of controls and substantive tests of transactions results in Case 17-33 and the audit of expenses.

d. How would the tests of controls and substantive tests of transactions results and your conclusions (1 through 7) affect your planned tests of details of balances for expenses? Do not write an audit program.

**18-32 (Objective 18-2)** You are doing the audit of the Ute Corporation, for the year ended December 31, 1997. The following schedule for the property, plant, and equipment and related allowance for depreciation accounts has been prepared by the client. You have compared the opening balances with your prior year's audit working papers.

**Ute Corporation Analysis of Property, Plant, and Equipment and Related Allowance for Depreciation Accounts**
**Year Ended December 31, 1997**

| DESCRIPTION | FINAL 12/31/96 | ADDITIONS | RETIREMENTS | PER BOOKS 12/31/97 |
|---|---|---|---|---|
| **Assets** | | | | |
| Land | $ 22,500 | $ 5,000 | | $ 27,500 |
| Buildings | 120,000 | 17,500 | | 137,500 |
| Machinery and equipment | 385,000 | 40,400 | $26,000 | 399,400 |
| | $527,500 | $62,900 | $26,000 | $564,400 |
| **Allowance for Depreciation** | | | | |
| Building | $ 60,000 | $ 5,150 | | $ 65,150 |
| Machinery and equipment | 173,250 | 39,220 | | 212,470 |
| | $233,250 | $44,370 | | $277,620 |

The following information is found during your audit:

1. All equipment is depreciated on the straight-line basis (no salvage value taken into consideration) based on the following estimated lives: buildings, 25 years; all other items, 10 years. The corporation's policy is to take one-half year's depreciation on all asset acquisitions and disposals during the year.
2. On April 1, the corporation entered into a 10-year lease contract for a die-casting machine with annual rentals of $5,000, payable in advance every April 1. The lease is cancelable by either party (60 days' written notice is required), and there is no option to renew the lease or buy the equipment at the end of the lease. The estimated useful life of the machine is 10 years with no salvage value. The corporation recorded the die-casting machine in the machinery and equipment account at $40,400, the present value at the date of the lease, and $2,020, applicable to the machine, has been included in depreciation expense for the year.
3. The corporation completed the construction of a wing on the plant building on June 30. The useful life of the building was not extended by this addition. The lowest

construction bid received was $17,500, the amount recorded in the buildings account. Company personnel were used to construct the addition at a cost of $16,000 (materials, $7,500; labor, $5,500; and overhead, $3,000).

4. On August 18, $5,000 was paid for paving and fencing a portion of land owned by the corporation and used as a parking lot for employees. The expenditure was charged to the land account.
5. The amount shown in the machinery and equipment asset retirement column represents cash received on September 5, upon disposal of a machine acquired in July 1993 for $48,000. The bookkeeper recorded depreciation expense of $3,500 on this machine in 1997.
6. Crux City donated land and building appraised at $10,000 and $40,000, respectively, to the Ute Corporation for a plant. On September 1, the corporation began operating the plant. Since no costs were involved, the bookkeeper made no entry for the foregoing transaction.

**Required**

a. In addition to inquiry of the client, explain how you would have found each of the these six items during the audit.

b. Prepare the adjusting journal entries with supporting computations that you would suggest at December 31, 1997, to adjust the accounts for the above transactions. Disregard income tax implications.*

**18-33 (Objective 18-5)** You are the manager in the audit of Vernal Manufacturing Company and are turning your attention to the operations accounts. The in-charge auditor assessed control risk for all cycles as low, supported by tests of controls. There are no major inherent risks affecting operations. Accordingly, you decide that the major emphasis in auditing the operations accounts will be to use analytical procedures. The in-charge prepared a schedule of the key income statement accounts that compares the prior year totals to the current year's and includes explanations of variances obtained from discussions with client personnel. That schedule is included on page 640.

**Required**

a. Examine the schedule prepared by your staff and write a memorandum to the in-charge that includes criticisms and concerns about the audit work procedures performed and questions for the in-charge to resolve.

b. Evaluate the explanations for variances provided by client personnel. List any alternative explanation to those given.

c. Indicate which variances are of special significance to the audit and how you believe they should be responded to in terms of additional audit procedures.

*AICPA adapted.

## Vernal Manufacturing Co.
## Operations Accounts
## 12/31/97

| Account | Per G/L 12/31/96 | Per G/L 12/31/97 | Change Amount | Change Percent | Explanations by Client |
|---|---|---|---|---|---|
| Sales | $8,467,312 | $9,845,231 | $1,377,919 | 16.3 | Sales increase due to two new customers who account for 20% |
| Sales returns and allowances | (64,895) | (243,561) | (178,666) | 275.3 | of volume. Larger returns due to need to cement relations |
| Gain on sale of assets | 43,222 | (143,200) | (186,422) | -431.3 | with these customers. |
| Interest income | 243 | 223 | (20) | -8.2 | |
| Miscellaneous income | 6,365 | 25,478 | 19,113 | 300.3 | Trade-in of several sales cars that needed replacement. |
| | 8,452,247 | 9,484,171 | 1,031,924 | 12.2 | |
| Cost of goods sold: | | | | | |
| Beginning inventory | 1,487,666 | 1,389,034 | (98,632) | -6.6 | |
| Purchases | 2,564,451 | 3,430,865 | 866,414 | 33.8 | Increase in these accounts due to increased volume with new |
| Freight in | 45,332 | 65,782 | 20,450 | 45.1 | customers as indicated above. |
| Purchase returns | (76,310) | (57,643) | 18,667 | -24.5 | |
| Factory wages | 986,755 | 1,145,467 | 158,712 | 16.1 | |
| Factory benefits | 197,652 | 201,343 | 3,691 | 1.9 | |
| Factory overhead | 478,659 | 490,765 | 12,106 | 2.5 | |
| Factory depreciation | 344,112 | 314,553 | (29,559) | -8.6 | |
| Ending inventory | (1,389,034) | (2,156,003) | (766,969) | 55.2 | Inventory being held for new customers. |
| | 4,639,283 | 4,824,163 | 184,880 | 4.0 | |
| Selling, general and administrative: | | | | | |
| Executive salaries | 167,459 | 174,562 | 7,103 | 4.2 | Normal salary increases. |
| Executive benefits | 32,321 | 34,488 | 2,167 | 6.7 | |
| Office salaries | 95,675 | 98,540 | 2,865 | 3.0 | |
| Office benefits | 19,888 | 21,778 | 1,890 | 9.5 | |
| Travel and entertainment | 56,845 | 75,583 | 18,738 | 33.0 | Sales and promotional expenses increased in an attempt to |
| Advertising | 130,878 | 156,680 | 25,802 | 19.7 | obtain new major customers. Two obtained and program will |
| Other sales expense | 34,880 | 42,334 | 7,454 | 21.4 | continue. |
| Stationery and supplies | 38,221 | 21,554 | (16,667) | -43.6 | Probably a misclassification; will investigate. |
| Postage | 14,657 | 18,756 | 4,099 | 28.0 | Normal increase. |
| Telephone | 36,551 | 67,822 | 31,271 | 85.6 | Normal increase. |
| Dues and memberships | 3,644 | 4,522 | 878 | 24.1 | Normal increase. |
| Rent | 15,607 | 15,607 | 0 | 0.0 | |
| Legal fees | 14,154 | 35,460 | 21,306 | 150.5 | Timing of billing for fees. |
| Accounting fees | 16,700 | 18,650 | 1,950 | 11.7 | Normal increase. |
| Depreciation, SG&A | 73,450 | 69,500 | (3,950) | -5.4 | Normal change. |
| Bad debt expense | 166,454 | 143,871 | (22,583) | -13.6 | Haven't reviewed yet for the current year. |
| Insurance | 44,321 | 45,702 | 1,381 | 3.1 | Normal change. |
| Interest expense | 120,432 | 137,922 | 17,490 | 14.5 | Normal change. |
| Other expense | 5,455 | 28,762 | 23,307 | 427.3 | Amount not material. |
| | 1,087,592 | 1,212,093 | 124,501 | 11.4 | |
| | 5,726,875 | 6,036,256 | 309,381 | 5.4 | |
| Income before taxes | 2,725,372 | 3,447,915 | 722,543 | 26.5 | |
| Income taxes | 926,626 | 1,020,600 | 93,974 | 10.1 | Increase due to increased income before tax. |
| Net income | $1,798,746 | $2,427,315 | $ 628,569 | 34.9 | |

# 19

# AUDIT OF THE INVENTORY AND WAREHOUSING CYCLE

## LEARNING OBJECTIVES

Thorough study of this chapter will enable you to

**19-1** Describe the inventory and warehousing cycle and the pertinent functions, documents and records, and internal controls.

**19-2** Explain the significance of the five parts of the inventory and warehousing cycle to the auditor.

**19-3** Design and perform audit tests of cost accounting.

**19-4** Design and perform analytical procedures for the accounts in the inventory and warehousing cycle.

**19-5** Design and perform physical observation audit tests for inventory.

**19-6** Design and perform audit tests of pricing and compilation for inventory.

**19-7** Explain how the various parts of the audit of the inventory and warehousing cycle are integrated.

## DON'T IGNORE RED FLAGS

Packard, Packard and Dodge (PP&D) was a regional audit firm in the Midwest. As part of its quality control system, PP&D began using an Environmental Assessment Questionnaire on every audit. This questionnaire alerted the auditor about the existence of various possible "red flags" that could indicate the potential for material fraudulent financial reporting. The questionnaire was broken into several sections about the industry, management, and operations. At the end of each section and for the entire questionnaire, the auditor was to state his or her assessment of the risk of potential material fraudulent financial reporting based on any red flags indicated.

The first opportunity for PP&D to use the new questionnaire was on the Farago audit. Farago was a commercial finance company owned by a large Chicago heavy equipment dealer. When equipment was sold by the dealer on credit, the transaction was financed through Farago. Farago also made lending transactions on its own. PP&D had audited Farago for each of the seven years of Farago's existence. Each year Farago received an unqualified audit report.

Jerry Bliss had been the manager on the audit for the past seven years. He was like "family" at Farago's offices. The first year that the new questionnaire was used on the audit, Jerry asked the engagement senior, Rich Haney, to complete the form. Rich identified several red flags:

- The Company had a small accounting department, making segregation of duties difficult.
- Management's compensation depended significantly on financial results.
- Management was aggressive about the accounting policies used and seemed quite concerned about earnings.
- The commercial finance industry was undergoing some problems in recent years.

Rich discussed the questionnaire results with Jerry. Rich was concerned that maybe Farago was fairly risky, at least "medium" in his view. Jerry had a different opinion, "Look, Rich, I've been on this audit every year, and things are no different now than before. The only thing that's changed is that now we have to complete this form. Let's just state that risk is 'low' and stick it in the working papers."

The audit of Farago was done in essentially the same way as it had been done in the past. One of the areas in the audit was the valuation of repossessed equipment inventory. In determining the existence of repossessed equipment inventory, PP&D had always relied on internal reports from the branch managers who held the equipment. Based on the prior year's work, Rich concluded that physical inspection was not necessary. In determining the value of equipment inventory, Rich relied on discussions with management, the same as in the prior year. As in the past, management did not get appraisals of the equipment, stating that their familiarity with the industry allowed them to make reasonable estimates. The auditors accepted this without further challenge. Based on finding no significant exceptions, PP&D issued an unqualified report.

When PP&D conducted their audit of Farago the next year, Jerry Bliss had left the firm and a new manager was assigned. Conditions in the commercial finance industry had deteriorated even more during the year, and the amount of repossessed inventory had increased significantly. The listing of repossessed equipment included many large items that had been included in the previous year. The new audit manager insisted on physical inspection of larger repossessed items. The result of this procedure was the discovery that the items did not exist. Investigation revealed that they had been sold and the proceeds recorded against the allowance for uncollectible loans, which was also understated. It was also clear that these practices had existed for at least the past two or three years.

Inventory takes many different forms, depending on the nature of the business. For retail or wholesale businesses, the most important inventory is merchandise on hand, available for sale. For hospitals, it includes food, drugs, and medical supplies. A manufacturing company has raw materials, purchased parts, and supplies for use in production, goods in the process of being manufactured, and finished goods available for sale. We have selected manufacturing company inventories for presentation in this text. However, most of the principles discussed apply to other types of businesses as well.

For the reasons that follow, the audit of inventories is often the most complex and time-consuming part of the audit:

- Inventory is generally a major item on the balance sheet, and it is often the largest item making up the accounts included in working capital.
- The inventory is in different locations, which makes physical control and counting difficult. Companies must have their inventory accessible for the efficient manufacture and sale of the product, but this dispersal creates significant auditing problems.
- The diversity of the items in inventories creates difficulties for the auditor. Such items as jewels, chemicals, and electronic parts present problems of observation and valuation.
- The valuation of inventory is also difficult due to such factors as obsolescence and the need to allocate manufacturing costs to inventory.
- There are several acceptable inventory valuation methods, but any given client must apply a method consistently from year to year. Moreover, an organization may prefer to use different valuation methods for different parts of the inventory, which is acceptable under GAAP.

The trial balance for Hillsburg Hardware Co. on page 141 shows that only two accounts are affected by the inventory and warehousing cycle: inventory and cost of goods sold. However, both accounts are highly material. For a manufacturing company, far more accounts are affected because labor, acquisitions of raw materials, and all indirect manufacturing costs affect inventory.

The physical flow of goods and the flow of costs in the inventory and warehousing cycle for a manufacturing company are shown in Figure 19-1. The direct tie-in of the inventory and warehousing cycle to the acquisition and payment cycle and the payroll and personnel cycle can be seen by examining the debits to the raw materials, direct labor, and manufacturing overhead T-accounts. The direct tie-in to the sales and collection cycle occurs at the point where finished goods are relieved (credited) and a charge is made to cost

**FIGURE 19-1**

**Flow of Inventory and Costs**

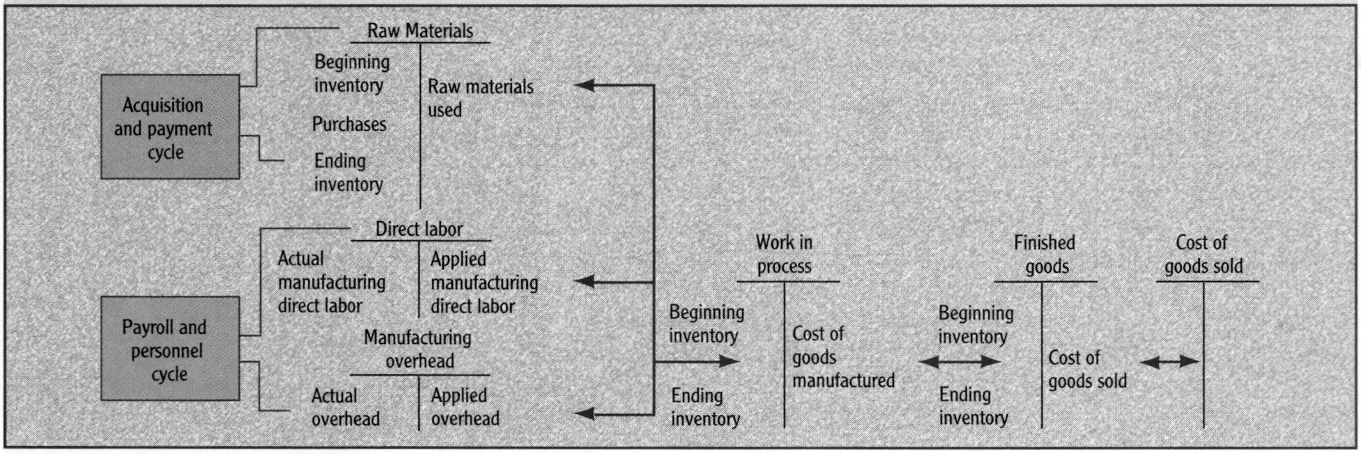

of goods sold. This close relationship to other transaction cycles in the organization is a fundamental characteristic of the audit of the inventory and warehousing cycle.

## FUNCTIONS IN THE CYCLE AND INTERNAL CONTROLS

**OBJECTIVE 19-1**
**Describe the inventory and warehousing cycle and the pertinent functions, documents and records, and internal controls.**

The inventory and warehousing cycle can be thought of as comprising two separate but closely related systems, one involving the actual *physical flow of goods,* and the other the *related costs.* As inventories move through the company, there must be adequate controls over both their physical movement and their related costs. A brief examination of the six functions making up the inventory and warehousing cycle will help students understand these controls and the audit evidence needed to test their effectiveness.

### Process Purchase Orders

*Purchase requisitions* are used to request the purchasing department to place orders for inventory items. Requisitions may be initiated by stockroom personnel or by computer when inventory reaches a predetermined level; orders may be placed for the materials required to produce a customer order; or orders may be initiated on the basis of a periodic inventory count by a responsible person. Regardless of the method followed, the controls over purchase requisitions and the related purchase orders are evaluated and tested as part of the acquisition and payment cycle.

### Receive New Materials

Receipt of the ordered materials is also part of the acquisition and payment cycle. Material received should be inspected for quantity and quality. The receiving department produces a *receiving report* that becomes a part of the necessary documentation before payment is made. After inspection, the material is sent to the storeroom and the receiving documents are typically sent to purchasing, the storeroom, and accounts payable. Control and accountability are necessary for all transfers.

### Store Raw Materials

When materials are received, they are stored in the stockroom until needed for production. Materials are issued out of stock to production upon presentation of a properly approved materials requisition, work order, or similar document that indicates the type and quantity of materials needed. This requisition document is used to update the perpetual inventory master files and to make book transfers from the raw materials to work-in-process accounts.

### Process the Goods

The processing portion of the inventory and warehousing cycle varies greatly from company to company. The determination of the items and quantities to be produced is generally based on specific orders from customers, sales forecasts, predetermined finished goods inventory levels, and economic production runs. Frequently, a separate production control department is responsible for the determination of the type and quantities of production. Within the various production departments, provision must be made to account for the quantities produced, control of scrap, quality controls, and physical protection of the material in process. The production department must generate production and scrap reports so that accounting can reflect the movement of materials in the books and determine accurate costs of production.

In any company involved in manufacturing, an adequate *cost accounting system* is an important part of the processing of goods function. The system is necessary to indicate the relative profitability of the various products for management planning and control and to value inventories for financial statement purposes. There are two types of cost systems, although many variations and combinations of these systems are employed: *job cost* and *process cost.* The main difference is whether costs are accumulated by individual jobs when material is issued and labor costs incurred (job cost), or whether they are accumulated by processes, with unit costs for each process assigned to the products passing through the process (process cost).

Cost accounting records consist of master files, worksheets, and reports that accumulate material, labor, and overhead costs by job or process as the costs are incurred. When jobs or products are completed, the related costs are transferred from work-in-process to finished goods on the basis of production department reports.

### Store Finished Goods

As finished goods are completed by the production department, they are placed in the stockroom awaiting shipment. In companies with good internal controls, finished goods are kept under physical control in a separate limited access area. The control of finished goods is often considered part of the sales and collection cycle.

### Ship Finished Goods

Shipping of completed goods is an integral part of the sales and collection cycle. Any shipment or transfer of finished goods must be authorized by a properly approved shipping document. The controls for shipment have already been studied in previous chapters.

### Perpetual Inventory Master Files

One of the records used for inventory that has not been previously discussed is a perpetual inventory master file. Separate perpetual records are normally kept for raw materials and finished goods. Most companies do not use perpetuals for work-in-process.

Perpetual inventory master files can include only information about the units of inventory acquired, sold, and on hand, or they can also include information about unit costs. The latter is more typical of well-designed computerized systems.

For acquisitions of raw materials, the perpetual inventory master file is updated automatically when acquisitions of inventory are processed as a part of recording acquisitions. For example, when the computer system enters the number of units and unit cost for each raw material acquisition, this information is used to update perpetual inventory master files along with the acquisitions journal and accounts payable master file. Chapter 17 described the recording of acquisition transactions.

Transfers of raw material from the storeroom must be separately entered into the computer to update the perpetual records. Typically, only the units transferred need to be entered because the computer can determine the unit costs from the master file. Raw material perpetual inventory master files that have unit costs include, for each raw material, beginning and ending units on hand and unit costs, units and unit cost of each acquisition, and units and unit cost of each transfer into production.

Finished goods perpetual inventory master files include the same type of information as raw materials perpetuals, but are considerably more complex if costs are included along with units. Finished goods costs include raw materials, direct labor, and manufacturing overhead, which often requires allocations and detailed record keeping. When finished goods perpetuals include unit costs, the cost accounting records must be integrated into the computer system.

### Summary of Inventory Documentation

The physical movement and related documentation in a typical inventory and warehousing cycle is shown in Figure 19-2. The figure reemphasizes the important point that the recording of costs and movement of inventory as shown in the books must correspond to the physical movements and processes.

## PARTS OF THE AUDIT OF INVENTORY

**OBJECTIVE 19-2**
**Explain the significance of the five parts of the inventory and warehousing cycle to the auditor.**

The overall objective in the audit of the inventory and warehousing cycle is to determine that raw materials, work-in-process, finished goods inventory, and cost of goods sold are fairly stated on the financial statements. The inventory and warehousing cycle can be divided into five distinct parts.

### Acquire and Record Raw Materials, Labor, and Overhead

This part of the inventory and warehousing cycle includes the first three functions in Figure 19-2: processing of purchase orders, receipt of raw materials, and storage of raw materials. The internal controls over these three functions are first understood, then tested as a

**FIGURE 19-2**

**Functions in the Inventory and Warehousing Cycle**

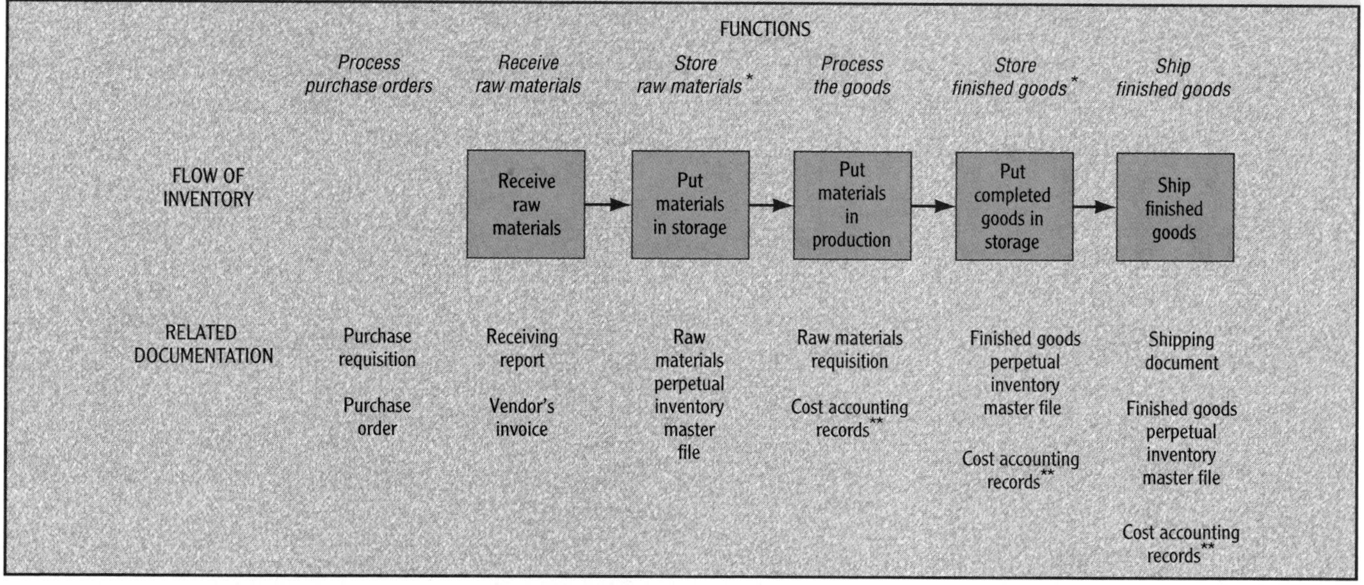


*Inventory counts are taken and compared with perpetual and book amounts at any stage of the cycle.The auditor must determine that cutoff for recording documents corresponds to the physical location of the items. A count must ordinarily be taken once a year. If the perpetual inventory system is operating well, this can be done on a cycle basis throughout the year.

**Includes cost information for materials, direct labor, and overhead.

part of performing tests of controls and substantive tests of transactions in the acquisition and payment cycle and the payroll and personnel cycle. At the completion of the acquisition and payment cycle, the auditor is likely to be satisfied that acquisitions of raw materials and manufacturing costs are correctly stated and samples should be designed to ensure that these systems are adequately tested. Similarly, when labor is a significant part of inventory, the payroll and personnel cycle tests should verify the proper accounting for these costs.

### Transfer Assets and Costs

Internal transfers include the fourth and fifth functions in Figure 19-2: processing the goods and storing finished goods. These two activities are not related to any other transaction cycles and therefore must be studied and tested as part of the inventory and warehousing cycle. The accounting records concerned with these functions are the cost accounting records.

### Ship Goods and Record Revenue and Costs

Recording of shipments and related costs, the last function in Figure 19-2, is part of the sales and collection cycle. Thus, internal controls over the function are understood and tested as a part of auditing the sales and collection cycle. Tests of controls and substantive tests of transactions should include procedures to verify the accuracy of the perpetual inventory master files.

### Physically Observe Inventory

Observing the client taking a physical inventory count is necessary to determine whether recorded inventory actually exists at the balance sheet date and is properly counted by the client. Inventory is the first audit area for which physical examination is an essential type of evidence used to verify the balance in an account. Physical observation is studied in this chapter.

### Price and Compile Inventory

Costs used to value the physical inventory must be tested to determine whether the client has correctly followed an inventory method that is in accordance with generally accepted accounting principles and is consistent with previous years. Audit procedures used to verify these costs are referred to as *price tests*. In addition, the auditor must verify whether the physical counts were correctly summarized, the inventory quantities and prices were correctly extended, and the extended inventory was correctly footed. These tests are called *compilation tests*.

Figure 19-3 summarizes the five parts of the audit of the inventory and warehousing cycle and shows the cycle in which each is audited. The first and third parts of the audit of the inventory and warehousing cycle have already been studied in connection with the other cycles. The importance of the tests of these other cycles should be kept in mind throughout the remaining sections of this chapter.

**FIGURE 19-3**

**Audit of Inventory**

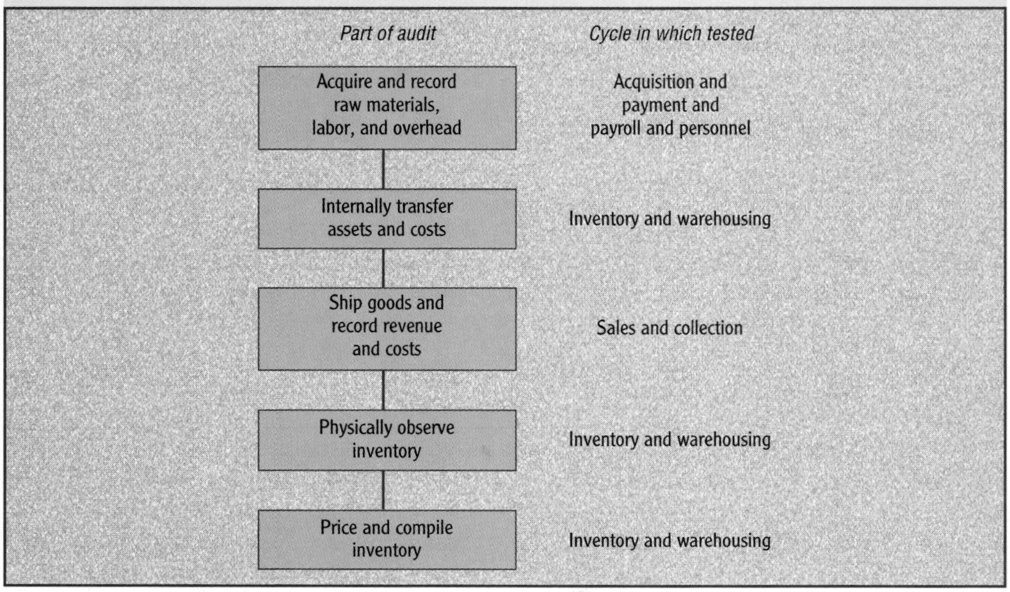


## AUDIT OF COST ACCOUNTING

**OBJECTIVE 19-3**
**Design and perform audit tests of cost accounting.**

Cost accounting systems and controls of different companies vary more than most other areas because of the wide variety of items of inventory and the level of sophistication desired by management. For example, a company that manufactures an entire line of farm machines will have a completely different kind of cost records and internal controls than a steel fabricating shop that makes and installs custom-made metal cabinets. It should also not be surprising that small companies whose owners are actively involved in the manufacturing process will need less sophisticated records than will large multiproduct companies.

### Cost Accounting Controls

*Cost accounting controls* are those related to the physical inventory and the related costs from the point at which raw materials are requisitioned to the point at which the manufactured product is completed and transferred to storage. It is convenient to divide these controls into two broad categories: (1) physical controls over raw materials, work-in-process, and finished goods inventory, and (2) controls over the related costs.

Almost all companies need physical controls over their assets to prevent loss from misuse and theft. The use of physically segregated, limited access storage areas for raw material, work-in-process, and finished goods is one major control to protect assets. In some instances the assignment of custody of inventory to specific responsible individuals may be necessary to protect the assets. Approved prenumbered documents for authorizing movement of inventory also protect the assets from improper use. Copies of these documents should be sent directly to accounting by the persons issuing them, bypassing people with custodial responsibilities. An example of an effective document of this type is an approved materials requisition for obtaining raw materials from the storeroom.

*Perpetual inventory master files* maintained by persons who do not have custody of or access to assets are another useful cost accounting control. Perpetual inventory master files are important for a number of reasons: they provide a record of items on hand, which is used to initiate production or acquisition of additional materials or goods; they provide a record of the use of raw materials and the sale of finished goods, which can be reviewed for obsolete or slow-moving items; and they provide a record that can be used to pinpoint responsibility for custody as a part of the investigation of differences between physical counts and the amount shown on the records.

Another important consideration in cost accounting is the existence of adequate internal controls that integrate production and accounting records for the purpose of obtaining accurate costs for all products. The existence of adequate cost records is important to management as an aid in pricing, controlling costs, and costing inventory.

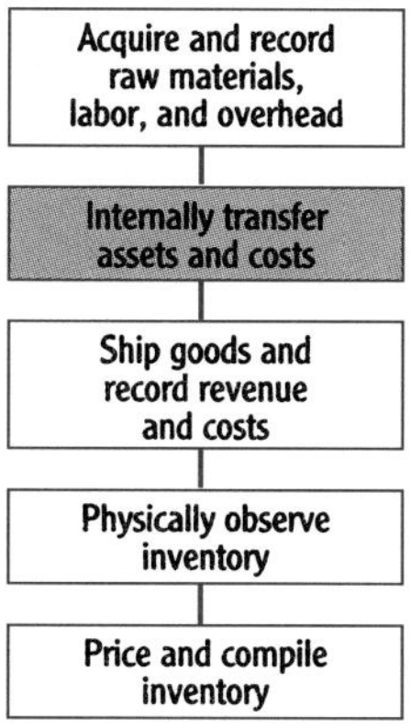


## Tests of Cost Accounting

The concepts in auditing cost accounting are no different from those discussed for any other transaction cycle. Figure 19-4 shows the methodology the auditor should follow in deciding which tests to perform. In auditing cost accounting, the auditor is concerned with four aspects: physical controls over inventory, documents and records for transferring inventory, perpetual inventory master files, and unit cost records.

**FIGURE 19-4**

**Methodology for Designing Tests of Controls and Substantive Tests of Transactions for Cost Accounting**

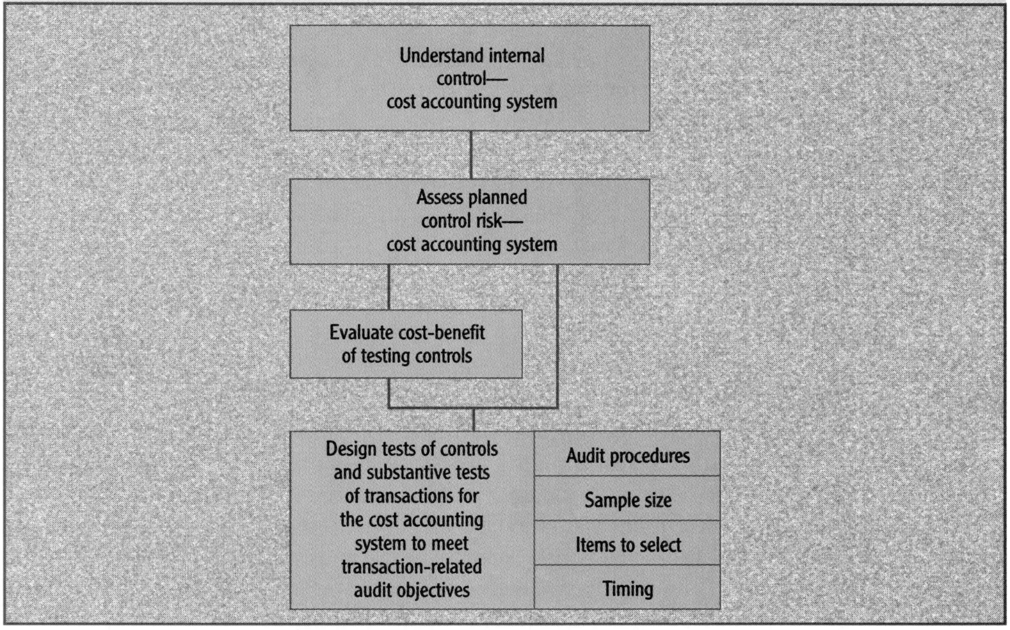


**Physical Controls** Auditor's tests of the adequacy of the physical controls over raw materials, work-in-process, and finished goods must be restricted to observation and inquiry. For example, the auditor can examine the raw materials storage area to determine whether the inventory is protected from theft and misuse by the existence of a locked storeroom. An adequate storeroom with a competent custodian in charge also ordinarily results in the orderly storage of inventory. If the auditor concludes that the physical controls are so inadequate that the inventory will be difficult to count, the auditor should expand his or her observation of physical inventory tests to make sure that an adequate count is carried out.

**Documents and Records for Transferring Inventory** The auditor's primary concerns in verifying the transfer of inventory from one location to another are that the recorded transfers exist, the transfers that have actually taken place are recorded, and the quantity, description, and date of all recorded transfers are accurate. First, it is necessary to understand the client's internal controls for recording transfers before relevant tests can be performed. Once the internal controls are understood, the tests can easily be performed by examining documents and records. For example, a procedure to test the existence and accuracy of the transfer of goods from the raw material storeroom to the manufacturing assembly line is to account for a sequence of raw material requisitions, examine the requisitions for proper approval, and compare the quantity, description, and date with the information on the raw material perpetual inventory master files. Similarly, completed production records can be compared with perpetual inventory master files to be sure that all manufactured goods were physically delivered to the finished goods storeroom.

**Perpetual Inventory Master Files** Adequate perpetual inventory master files have a major effect on the *timing and extent* of the auditor's physical examination of inventory. When there are accurate perpetual inventory master files, it is frequently possible to test the physical inventory prior to the balance sheet date. An interim physical inventory can result in significant cost savings for both the client and the auditor, and it enables the client to get the audited statements earlier. Perpetual inventory master files also enable the auditor to reduce the extent of the tests of physical inventory when the assessed control risk related to physical observation of inventory is low.

Tests of the perpetual inventory master files for the purpose of reducing tests of physical inventory or changing their timing are done through the use of documentation. Documents to verify the acquisition of raw materials can be examined when the auditor is verifying acquisitions as part of the tests of the acquisition and payment cycle. Documents supporting the reduction of raw material inventory for use in production and the increase in the quantity of finished goods inventory when goods have been manufactured are examined as part of the tests of the cost accounting records in the manner discussed in the preceding section. Support for the reduction in the finished goods inventory through the sale of goods to customers is ordinarily tested as part of the sales and collection cycle. Usually, it is relatively easy to test the accuracy of the perpetuals after the auditor determines how the internal controls are designed and decides to what degree assessed control risk should be reduced.

**Unit Cost Records** Obtaining accurate cost data for raw materials, direct labor, and manufacturing overhead is an essential part of cost accounting. Adequate cost accounting records must be integrated with production and other accounting records in order to produce accurate costs of all products. Cost accounting records are pertinent to the auditor in that the valuation of ending inventory depends on the proper design and use of these records.

In testing the inventory cost records, the auditor must first develop an understanding of internal control. This is frequently somewhat time consuming because the flow of costs is usually integrated with other accounting records, and it may not be obvious how the internal controls provide for the internal transfers of raw materials and for direct labor and manufacturing overhead as production is carried out.

Once the auditor understands internal control, the approach to internal verification involves the same concepts that were discussed in the verification of sales and acquisition transactions. Whenever possible, it is desirable to test cost accounting records as a part of the acquisition, payroll, and sales tests to avoid testing the records more than once. For example, when the auditor is testing acquisition transactions as a part of the acquisition and payment cycle, it is desirable to trace the units and unit costs of raw materials to the perpetual inventory master files and the total cost to cost accounting records. Similarly, when payroll costs data are maintained for different jobs, it is desirable to trace from the payroll summary directly to job cost records as a part of testing the payroll and personnel cycle.

A major difficulty in the verification of inventory cost records is determining the reasonableness of cost allocations. For example, the assignment of manufacturing overhead costs to individual products entails certain assumptions that can significantly affect the unit costs of inventory and therefore the fairness of the inventory valuation. In evaluating these allocations, the auditor must consider the reasonableness of both the numerator and the denominator that result in the unit costs. For example, in testing overhead applied to inventory on the basis of direct labor dollars, the overhead rate should approximate total actual manufacturing overhead divided by total actual direct labor dollars. Since total manufacturing overhead is tested as part of the tests of the acquisition and payment cycle and direct labor is tested as part of the payroll and personnel cycle, determining the reasonableness of the rate is not difficult. However, if manufacturing overhead is applied on the basis of machine hours, the auditor must verify the reasonableness of the machine hours by separate tests of the client's machine records. The major considerations in evaluating the reasonableness of all cost allocations, including manufacturing overhead, are compliance with generally accepted accounting principles and consistency with previous years.

## ANALYTICAL PROCEDURES

**OBJECTIVE 19-4**

**Design and perform analytical procedures for the accounts in the inventory and warehousing cycle.**

Analytical procedures are as important in auditing inventory and warehousing as any other cycle. Table 19-1 includes several common analytical procedures and possible misstatements that may be indicated when fluctuations exist. Several of those analytical procedures have also been included in other cycles. An example is the gross margin percent.

**TABLE 19-1**

**Analytical Procedures for the Inventory and Warehousing Cycle**

| Analytical Procedure | Possible Misstatement |
|---|---|
| Compare gross margin percentage with previous years. | Overstatement or understatement of inventory and cost of goods sold. |
| Compare inventory turnover (cost of goods sold divided by average inventory) with previous years. | Obsolete inventory which affects inventory and cost of goods sold.<br>Overstatement or understatement of inventory. |
| Compare unit costs of inventory with previous years. | Overstatement or understatement of unit costs which affect inventory and cost of goods sold. |
| Compare extended inventory value with previous years. | Misstatements in compilation, unit costs, or extensions which affect inventory and cost of goods sold. |
| Compare current-year manufacturing costs with previous years (variable costs should be adjusted for changes in volume). | Misstatement of unit costs of inventory, especially direct labor and manufacturing overhead, which affect inventory and cost of goods sold. |

## TESTS OF DETAILS FOR INVENTORY

The methodology for deciding which tests of details of balances to do for inventory and warehousing is essentially the same as that discussed for accounts receivable, accounts payable, and all other balance sheet accounts. It is shown in Figure 19-5 on page 650. Notice

**FIGURE 19-5**

**Methodology for Designing Tests of Details of Balances for Inventory**

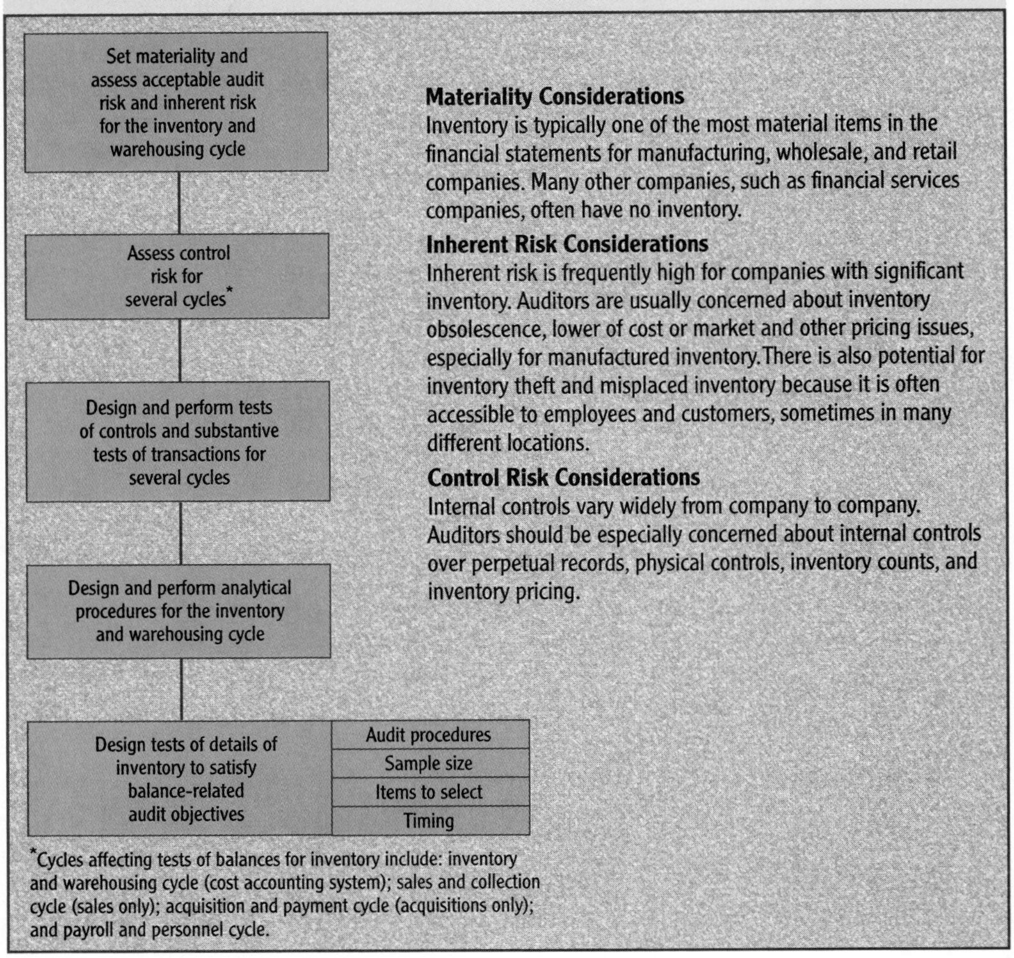


that test results of several other cycles besides inventory and warehousing affect tests of details of balances for inventory.

Because of the complexity of auditing inventory, two aspects of tests of details of balances are discussed separately: (1) physical observation and (2) pricing and compilation. These topics are studied in the next two sections.

## PHYSICAL OBSERVATION OF INVENTORY

**OBJECTIVE 19-5**
**Design and perform physical observation audit tests for inventory.**

Prior to the late 1930s, auditors generally avoided responsibility for determining either the physical existence or the accuracy of the count of inventory. Audit evidence for inventory quantities was usually restricted to obtaining a certification from management as to the correctness of the stated amount. In 1938, the discovery of major fraud in the McKesson & Robbins Company caused a reappraisal by the accounting profession of its responsibilities in auditing inventory. In brief, the financial statements for McKesson & Robbins at December 31, 1937, which were "certified to" by a major accounting firm, reported total consolidated assets of $87 million. Of this amount, approximately $19 million was subsequently determined to be nonexistent: $10 million in inventory and $9 million in receivables. Due primarily to their adherence to generally accepted auditing practice of that period, the auditing firm was not held directly at fault in the inventory area. However, it was noted that if certain procedures, such as observation of the physical inventory, had been carried out, the fraud would probably have been detected. SAS 1 (AU 331) states the following requirement exists for inventory observation:

- ...it is ordinarily necessary for the independent auditor to be present at the time of count and, by suitable observation, tests, and inquiries, satisfy himself respecting the effectiveness of the methods of inventory-taking and the measure of reliance which may be placed upon the client's representations about the quantities and physical condition of the inventories.

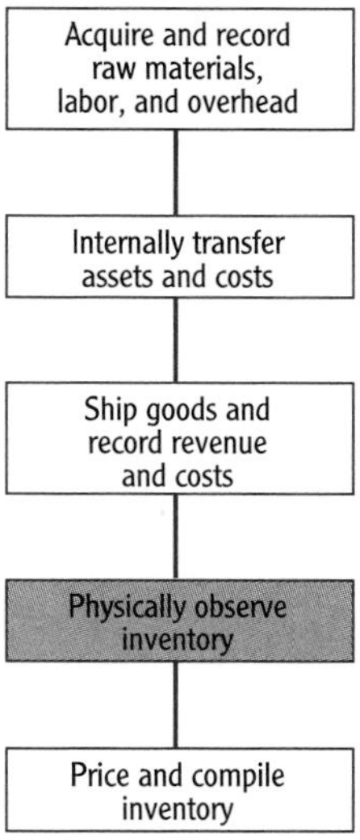


An essential point in the SAS 1 requirement is the distinction between the observation of the physical inventory count and the responsibility for taking the count. The client has responsibility for setting up the procedures for taking an accurate physical inventory and actually making and recording the counts. The auditor's responsibility is to evaluate and observe the client's physical procedures and draw conclusions about the adequacy of the physical inventory.

The requirement of physical examination of inventory is not applicable in the case of *inventory in a public warehouse.* The AICPA position on inventory stored in a public warehouse is summarized in the same section of the standard as follows:

- In the case of inventories which in the ordinary course of business are in the hands of public warehouses or other outside custodians, direct confirmation in writing from the custodians is acceptable provided that, where the amount involved represents a significant proportion of the current assets or the total assets, supplemental inquiries are made to satisfy the independent auditor as to the bona fides of the situation.

The SAS recommends that the supplemental inquiries include the following steps, to the extent that the auditor considers them necessary in the circumstances:

- Discussion with the owner as to the owner's controls in investigating the warehouseperson and tests of related evidential matter.
- Review of the owner's controls concerning performance of the warehouseperson and tests of related evidential matter.
- Observation of physical counts of the goods whenever practical and reasonable.
- Where warehouse receipts have been pledged as collateral, confirmation (on a test basis, where appropriate) from lenders as to pertinent details of the pledged receipts.

### Controls

Regardless of the client's inventory record-keeping method, there must be a periodic physical count of the inventory items on hand. The client can take the physical count at or near the balance sheet date, at a preliminary date, or on a cycle basis throughout the year. The last two approaches are appropriate only if there are adequate perpetual inventory master files.

In connection with the client's physical count of inventory, adequate controls include proper instructions for the physical count, supervision by responsible personnel, independent internal verification of the counts, independent reconciliations of the physical counts with perpetual inventory master files, and adequate control over count sheets or tags.

An important aspect of the auditor's understanding of the client's physical inventory controls is complete familiarity with them before the inventory begins. This is obviously necessary to evaluate the effectiveness of the client's procedures, but it also enables the auditor to make constructive suggestions beforehand. If the inventory instructions do not provide adequate controls, the auditor must spend more time making sure that the physical count is accurate.

### Audit Decisions

The auditor's decisions in the physical observation of inventory are of the same general nature as in any other audit area: selection of audit procedures, timing, determination of sample size, and selection of the items for testing. The selection of the audit procedures is discussed throughout the section; the other three decisions are discussed briefly at this time.

**Timing** The auditor decides whether the physical count can be taken prior to year-end primarily on the basis of the accuracy of the perpetual inventory master files. When an interim physical count is permitted, the auditor observes it at that time and also tests the perpetuals for transactions from the date of the count to year-end. When the perpetuals are accurate, it may be unnecessary for the client to count the inventory every year. Instead, the auditor can compare the perpetuals with the actual inventory on a sample basis at a convenient time. When there are no perpetuals and the inventory is material, a complete physical inventory must be taken by the client near the end of the accounting period and tested by the auditor at the same time.

**Sample Size** Sample size in physical observation is usually impossible to specify in terms of the number of items because the emphasis during the tests is on observing the client's procedures rather than on selecting items for testing. A convenient way to think of sample size in physical observation is in terms of the total number of hours spent rather than the number of inventory items counted. The most important determinants of the amount of time needed to test inventory are the adequacy of the internal controls over the physical counts, accuracy of the perpetual inventory master files, total dollar amount and type of inventory, number of different significant inventory locations, nature and extent of misstatements discovered in previous years, and other inherent risks. In some situations inventory is such a significant item that dozens of auditors are necessary to observe the physical count, whereas in other situations one person can complete the observation in a short time. Special care is warranted in the observation of inventory because of the difficulty of expanding sample sizes or reperforming tests after the physical inventory has been taken.

**Selection of Items** The selection of items for testing is an important part of the audit decision in inventory observation. Care should be taken to observe the counting of the most significant items and a representative sample of typical inventory items, to inquire about items that are likely to be obsolete or damaged, and to discuss with management the reasons for excluding any material items.

**THE CRAZY EDDIE, INC., FRAUD**

By 1970, Crazy Eddie, Inc., a consumer electronics retail company, had forty-three consumer sales outlets, sales of $350 million, reported net income before taxes of $21 million, and a market value of more than $500 million. By the end of 1989, the company had filed for bankruptcy, closed all stores, and liquidated all assets at a huge loss to investors.

Investigation by regulatory authorities found extensive financial fraud, the most important being a $65 million overstatement of inventory. There were extensive lawsuits against many parties, including the CEO, who was found guilty of fraud and sent to prison.

Naturally, the question arose as to why the auditors failed to uncover the fraud in their annual audit. The defense used by the auditor was the difficulty of uncovering the well-conceived fraud. The parties involved in or who knew of the fraud included the acting controller, the director of internal auditing, and the director of accounts payable. One example of fraud was the shipment of inventory from store to store immediately before the auditor arrived to count the inventory. Another was the destruction of documentation to conceal inventory shortages at various locations. The auditor argued that it is almost impossible to uncover fraud when there is extensive collusion. The suit against the CPA firm and other defendants was settled out of court in 1993.

*Source:* Michael C. Knapp, *Contemporary Auditing: Issues and Cases,* 2nd edition. West Publishing, 1996, pp. 69–78.

## Physical Observation Tests

The same balance-related audit objectives that have been used in previous sections for tests of details of balances provide the frame of reference for discussing the physical observation tests. However, before the objectives are discussed, some comments that apply to all the objectives are appropriate.

The most important part of the observation of inventory is determining whether the physical count is being taken in accordance with the client's instructions. To do this effectively, *it is essential that the auditor be present* while the physical count is taking place. When the client's employees are not following the inventory instructions, the auditor must either contact the supervisor to correct the problem or modify the physical observation procedures. For example, if the procedures require one team to count the inventory and a second team to recount it as a test of accuracy, the auditor should inform management if he or she observes both teams counting together.

Obtaining an adequate understanding of the client's business is even more important in physical observation of inventory than for most aspects of the audit because inventory varies so significantly for different companies. A proper understanding of the client's business and its industry enables the auditor to ask about and discuss such problems as inventory valuation, potential obsolescence, and existence of consignment inventory intermingled with owned inventory. A useful starting point for becoming familiar with the client's inventory is for the auditor to tour the client's facilities, including receiving, storage, production, planning, and record-keeping areas. The tour should be led by a supervisor who can answer questions about production, especially about any changes in the past year.

Common tests of details audit procedures for physical inventory observation are shown in Table 19-2 on page 654. Detail tie-in and presentation and disclosure are the only balance-related audit objectives not included in the table. These objectives are discussed under compilation of inventory. The assumption throughout is that the client records inventory on prenumbered tags on the balance sheet date.

In addition to the detailed procedures included in Table 19-2, the auditor should walk through all areas where inventory is warehoused to make sure that all inventory has been counted and properly tagged. When inventory is in boxes or other containers, these should be opened during test counts. It is desirable to compare high dollar value inventory to counts in the previous year and inventory master files as a test of reasonableness. These two procedures should not be done until the client has completed the physical counts.

## AUDIT OF PRICING AND COMPILATION

**OBJECTIVE 19-6**

**Design and perform audit tests of pricing and compilation for inventory.**

An important part of the audit of inventory is to perform all the procedures necessary to make certain that the physical counts or perpetual record quantities were properly priced and compiled. *Pricing* includes all the tests of the client's unit prices to determine whether they are correct. *Compilation* includes all the tests of the summarization of the physical quantities, the extension of price times quantity, footing the inventory summary, and tracing the totals to the general ledger.

### Pricing and Compilation Controls

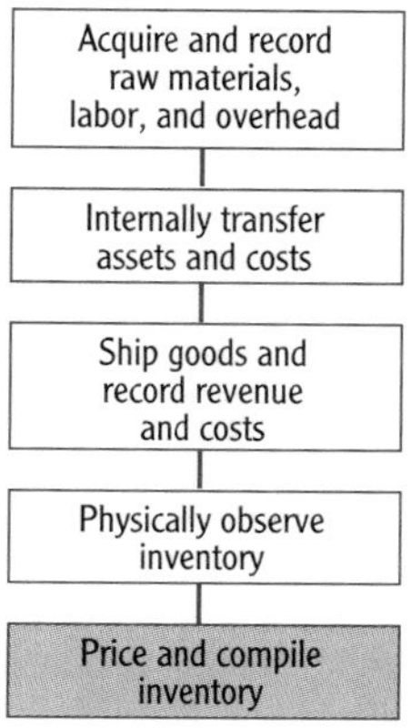


The existence of adequate internal controls for unit costs that are integrated with production and other accounting records is important to ensure that reasonable costs are used for valuing ending inventory. One important internal control is the use of *standard cost records* that indicate variances in material, labor, and overhead costs and can be used to evaluate production. When standard costs are used, procedures must be designed to keep the standards updated for changes in production processes and costs. The review of unit costs for reasonableness by someone independent of the department responsible for developing the costs is also a useful control over valuation.

An internal control designed to prevent the overstatement of inventory through the inclusion of obsolete inventory is a formal review and reporting of obsolete, slow-moving, damaged, and overstated inventory items. The review should be done by a competent employee by reviewing perpetual inventory master files for inventory turnover and holding discussions with engineering or production personnel.

*Compilation internal controls* are needed to provide a means of ensuring that the physical counts are properly summarized, priced at the same amount as the unit records, correctly extended and totaled, and included in the general ledger at the proper amount.

**TABLE 19-2**

**Balance-Related Audit Objectives and Tests of Details of Balances for Physical Inventory Observation**

| Balance-Related Audit Objective | Common Inventory Observation Procedures | Comments |
|---|---|---|
| Inventory as recorded on tags exists (existence). | Select a random sample of tag numbers and identify the tag with that number attached to the actual inventory.<br>Observe whether movement of inventory takes place during the count. | The purpose is to uncover the inclusion of nonexistent items as inventory. |
| Existing inventory is counted and tagged and tags are accounted for to make sure none are missing (completeness). | Examine inventory to make sure it is tagged.<br>Observe whether movement of inventory takes place during the count.<br>Inquire as to inventory in other locations.<br>Account for all used and unused tags to make sure none are lost or intentionally omitted.<br>Record the tag numbers for those used and unused for subsequent follow-up. | Special concern should be directed to omission of large sections of inventory.<br>This test should be done at the completion of the physical count.<br>This test should be done at the completion of the physical count. |
| Inventory is counted accurately (accuracy). | Recount client's counts to make sure the recorded counts are accurate on the tags (also check descriptions and unit of count, such as dozen or gross).<br>Compare physical counts with perpetual inventory master file.<br>Record client's counts for subsequent testing. | Recording client counts in the working papers on *inventory count sheets* is done for two reasons: to obtain documentation that an adequate physical examination was made, and to test for the possibility that the client might change the recorded counts after the auditor leaves the premises. |
| Inventory is classified correctly on the tags (classification). | Examine inventory descriptions on the tags and compare with the actual inventory for raw material, work-in-process, and finished goods.<br>Evaluate whether the percent of completion recorded on the tags for work-in-process is reasonable. | These tests would be done as a part of the first procedure in the accuracy objective. |
| Information is obtained to make sure sales and inventory purchases are recorded in the proper period (cutoff). | Record in the working papers for subsequent follow-up the last shipping document number used at year-end.<br>Make sure the inventory for the above item was excluded from the physical count.<br>Review shipping area for inventory set aside for shipment, but not counted.<br>Record in the working papers for subsequent follow-up the last receiving report number used at year-end.<br>Make sure the inventory for the above item was included in the physical count.<br>Review receiving area for inventory that should be included in the physical count. | Obtaining proper cutoff information for sales and purchases is an essential part of inventory observation. The appropriate tests during the field work were discussed for sales in Chapter 11 and acquisitions in Chapter 17. |
| Obsolete and unusable inventory items are excluded or noted (realizable value). | Test for obsolete inventory by inquiry of factory employees and management, and alertness for items that are damaged, rust- or dust-covered, or located in inappropriate places. | |
| The client has rights to inventory recorded on tags (rights). | Inquire as to consignment or customer inventory included on client's premises.<br>Be alert for inventory that is set aside or specially marked as indications of nonownership. | |

Important compilation internal controls are adequate documents and records for taking the physical count and proper internal verification. If the physical inventory is taken on prenumbered tags and carefully reviewed before the personnel are released from the physical examination of inventory, there should be little risk of misstatement in summarizing the tags. The most important internal control over accurate determination of prices, extensions, and footings is internal verification by a competent, independent person.

## Pricing and Compilation Procedures

Balance-related audit objectives for tests of details of balances are also useful in discussing pricing and compilation procedures. The objectives and related tests are shown in Table 19-3, except for the cutoff objective. Physical observation, which was previously discussed,

**TABLE 19-3**

**Balance-Related Audit Objectives and Tests of Details of Balances for Inventory Pricing and Compilation**

| Balance-Related Audit Objective | Common Tests of Details of Balances Procedures | Comments |
|---|---|---|
| Inventory in the inventory listing schedule agrees with the physical inventory counts, the extensions are correct, and the total is correctly added and agrees with the general ledger (detail tie-in). | Perform compilation tests (see existence, completeness, and accuracy objectives).<br>Foot the inventory listing schedules for raw materials, work-in-process, and finished goods.<br>Trace the totals to the general ledger.<br>Extend the quantity times the price on selected items. | Unless controls are weak, extending and footing tests should be limited. |
| Inventory items in the inventory listing schedule exist (existence). | Trace inventory listed in the schedule to inventory tags and auditor's recorded counts for existence and description. | The next six objectives are affected by the results of the physical inventory observation. The tag numbers and counts verified as a part of physical inventory observation are traced to the inventory listing schedule as a part of these tests. |
| Existing inventory items are included in the inventory listing schedule (completeness). | Account for unused tag numbers shown in the auditor's working papers to make sure no tags have been added.<br>Trace from inventory tags to the inventory listing schedules and make sure inventory on tags are included.<br>Account for tag numbers to make sure none have been deleted. | |
| Inventory items in the inventory listing schedule are accurate (accuracy). | Trace inventory listed in the schedule to inventory tags and auditor's recorded counts for quantity and description.<br>Perform price tests of inventory. For a discussion of price tests, see text material on pages 656–657. | |
| Inventory items in the inventory listing schedule are properly classified (classification). | Compare the classification into raw materials, work-in-process, and finished goods by comparing the descriptions on inventory tags and auditor's recorded test counts with the inventory listing schedule. | |
| Inventory items in the inventory listing are stated at realizable value (realizable value). | Perform test of lower of cost or market, selling price, and obsolescence. | |
| The client has rights to inventory items in the inventory listing schedule (rights). | Trace inventory tags identified as nonowned during the physical observation to the inventory listing schedule to make sure these have not been included.<br>Review contracts with suppliers and customers and inquire of management for the possibility of the inclusion of consigned or other nonowned inventory, or the exclusion of owned inventory that is not included. | |
| Inventory and related accounts in the inventory and warehousing cycle are properly presented and disclosed (presentation and disclosure). | Examine financial statements for proper presentation and disclosure, including:<br>Separate disclosure of raw materials, work-in-process, and finished goods.<br>Proper description of the inventory costing method.<br>Description of pledged inventory. Inclusion of significant sales and purchase commitments. | Pledging of inventory and sales and purchase commitments are usually uncovered as a part of other audit tests. |

is a major source of cutoff information for sales and purchases. Tests of the accounting records for cutoff are done as a part of sales (sales and collection cycle) and acquisitions (acquisition and payment cycle).

The frame of reference for applying the objectives is a listing of inventory obtained from the client that includes each inventory item's description, quantity, unit price, and extended value. The inventory listing is in inventory item description order with raw material, work-in-process, and finished goods separated. The total equals the general ledger balance.

## Valuation of Inventory

The proper valuation (pricing) of inventory is often one of the most important and time-consuming parts of the audit. In performing pricing tests, three things about the client's method of pricing are extremely important: the method must be in accordance with generally accepted accounting principles, the application of the method must be consistent from year to year, and cost versus market value (replacement cost or net realizable value) must be considered. Because the method of verifying the pricing of inventory depends on whether items are acquired or manufactured, these two categories are discussed separately.

**Pricing Purchased Inventory** The primary types of inventory included in this category are raw materials, purchased parts, and supplies. As a first step in verifying the valuation of purchased inventory, it is necessary to establish clearly whether LIFO, FIFO, weighted average, or some other valuation method is being used. It is also necessary to determine which costs should be included in the valuation of an item of inventory. For example, the auditor must find out whether freight, storage, discounts, and other costs are included and compare the findings with the preceding year's audit working papers to make sure that the methods are consistent.

In selecting specific inventory items for pricing, emphasis should be put on the larger dollar amounts and on products that are known to have wide fluctuations in price, but a representative sample of all types of inventory and departments should be included as well. Stratified variables or monetary unit sampling is commonly used in these tests.

The auditor should list the inventory items that he or she intends to verify for pricing and request the client to locate the appropriate vendors' invoices. It is important that sufficient invoices be examined to account for the entire quantity of inventory for the item being tested, especially for the FIFO valuation method. Examining sufficient invoices is useful to uncover situations in which clients value their inventory on the basis of the most recent invoice only and, in some cases, to discover obsolete inventory. As an illustration, assume that the client's valuation of an inventory item is $12.00 per unit for 1,000 units, using FIFO. The auditor should examine the most recent invoices for acquisitions of that inventory item made in the year under audit until the valuation of all of the 1,000 units is accounted for. If the most recent acquisition of the inventory item was for 700 units at $12.00 per unit and the immediately preceding acquisition was for 600 units at $11.30 per unit, the inventory item in question is overstated by $210.00 (300 × $.70).

When the client has perpetual inventory master files that include unit costs of acquisitions, it is usually desirable to test the pricing by tracing the unit costs to the perpetuals rather than to vendors' invoices. In most cases the effect is to reduce the cost of verifying inventory valuation significantly. Naturally, when the perpetuals are used to verify unit costs, it is essential to test the unit costs on the perpetuals to vendors' invoices as a part of the tests of the acquisition and payment cycle.

**Pricing Manufactured Inventory** The auditor must consider the cost of raw materials, direct labor, and manufacturing overhead in pricing work-in-process and finished goods. The need to verify each of these has the effect of making the audit of work-in-process and finished goods inventory more complex than the audit of purchased inventory. Nevertheless, such considerations as selecting the items to be tested, testing for whether cost or market value is lower, and evaluating the possibility of obsolescence also apply.

In pricing raw materials in manufactured products, it is necessary to consider both the unit cost of the raw materials and the number of units required to manufacture a unit of output. The unit cost can be verified in the same manner as that used for other purchased inventory—by examining vendors' invoices or perpetual inventory master files. Then it is necessary to examine engineering specifications, inspect the finished product, or find a similar method to determine the number of units it takes to manufacture a product.

Similarly, the hourly costs of direct labor and the number of hours it takes to manufacture a unit of output must be verified while testing direct labor. Hourly labor costs can be verified by comparison with labor payroll or union contracts. The number of hours needed to manufacture the product can be determined from engineering specifications or similar sources.

The proper manufacturing overhead in work-in-process and finished goods is dependent on the approach being used by the client. It is necessary to evaluate the method being used for consistency and reasonableness and to recompute the costs to determine whether the overhead is correct. For example, if the rate is based on direct labor dollars, the auditor can divide the total manufacturing overhead by the total direct labor dollars to determine the actual overhead rate. This rate can then be compared with the overhead rate used by the client to determine unit costs.

When the client has *standard costs records,* an efficient and useful method of determining valuation is by the review and analysis of variances. If the variances in material, labor, and manufacturing overhead are small, it is evidence of reliable cost records.

**Cost or Market** In pricing inventory, it is necessary to consider whether replacement cost or net realizable value is lower than historical cost. For purchased finished goods and raw materials, the most recent cost of an inventory item as indicated on a vendor's invoice of the subsequent period is a useful way to test for replacement cost. All manufacturing costs must be considered for work-in-process and finished goods for manufactured inventory. It is also necessary to consider the sales value of inventory items and the possible effect of rapid fluctuation of prices to determine net realizable value. Finally, it is necessary to consider the possibility of obsolescence in the evaluation process.

## INTEGRATION OF THE TESTS

**OBJECTIVE 19-7**
**Explain how the various parts of the audit of the inventory and warehousing cycle are integrated.**

The most difficult part of understanding the audit of the inventory and warehousing cycle is grasping the interrelationship of the many different tests the auditor makes to evaluate whether inventory and cost of goods sold are fairly stated. Figure 19-6 on page 658 and the discussions that follow are designed to aid the reader in perceiving the audit of the inventory and warehousing cycle as a series of integrated tests.

**Tests of the Acquisition and Payment Cycle** Whenever the auditor verifies acquisitions as part of the tests of the acquisition and payment cycle, evidence is being obtained about the accuracy of raw materials acquired and all manufacturing overhead costs except labor. These acquisition costs either flow directly into cost of goods sold or become the most significant part of the ending inventory of raw material, work-in-process, and finished goods. In audits involving perpetual inventory master files, it is common to test these as a part of tests of controls and substantive tests of transactions procedures in the acquisition and payment cycle. Similarly, if manufacturing costs are assigned to individual jobs or processes, they are usually tested as a part of the same cycle.

**Tests of the Payroll and Personnel Cycle** When the auditor verifies labor costs, the same comments apply as for acquisitions. In most cases, the cost accounting records for direct and indirect labor costs can be tested as part of the audit of the payroll and personnel cycle if there is adequate advance planning.

**FIGURE 19-6**

**Interrelationship of Various Audit Tests**

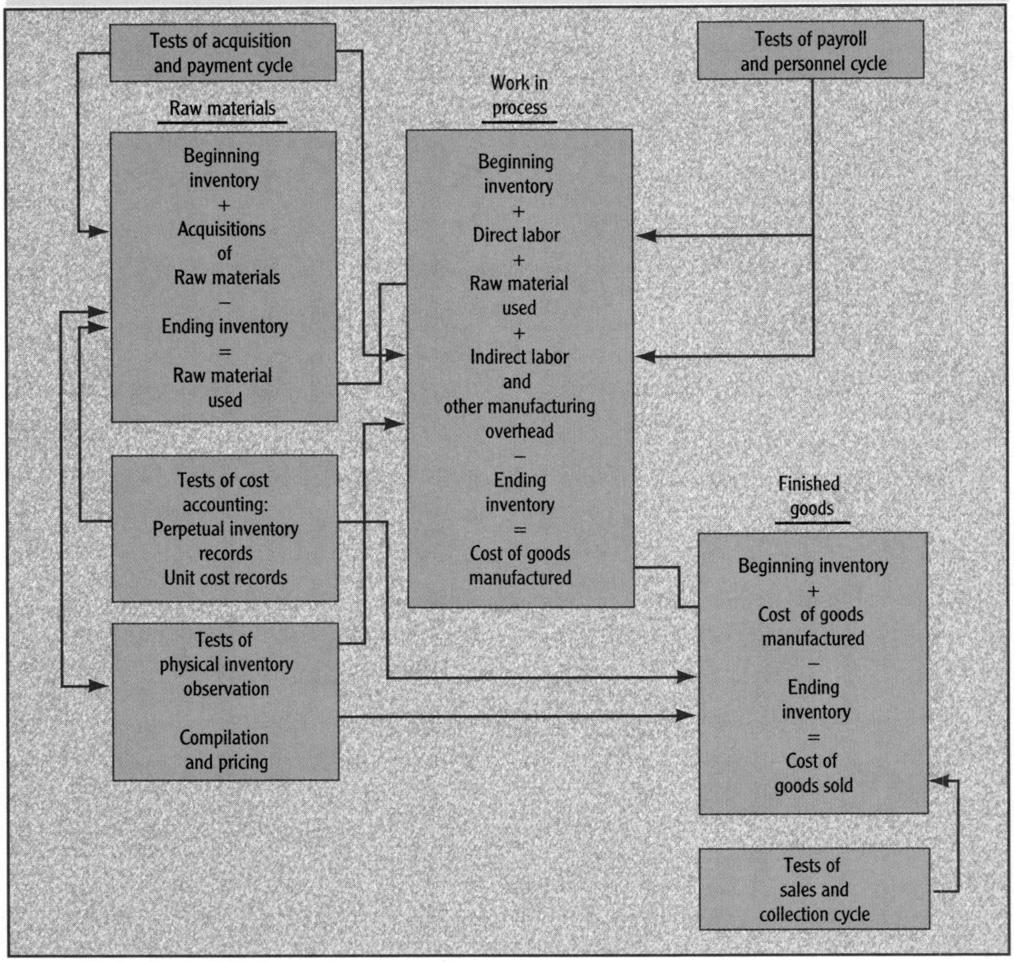


**Tests of the Sales and Collection Cycle** Although the relationship is less close between the sales and collection cycle and the inventory and warehousing cycle than between the two previously discussed, it is still important. Most of the audit testing in the storage of finished goods as well as the shipment and recording of sales takes place when the sales and collection cycle is tested. In addition, if standard cost records are used, it may be possible to test the standard cost of goods sold at the same time that sales tests are performed.

**Tests of Cost Accounting** Tests of cost accounting are meant to verify the controls affecting inventory that were not verified as part of the three previously discussed cycles. Tests are made of the physical controls, transfers of raw material costs to work-in-process, transfers of costs of completed goods to finished goods, perpetual inventory master files, and unit cost records.

**Physical Inventory, Compilation, and Pricing** In most audits the underlying assumption in testing the inventory and warehousing cycle is that cost of goods sold is a residual of beginning inventory plus acquisitions of raw materials, direct labor, and other manufacturing costs minus ending inventory. When the audit of inventory and cost of goods sold is approached with this idea in mind, the importance of ending inventory becomes obvious. Physical inventory, compilation, and pricing are each equally important in the audit because a misstatement in any one results in misstated inventory and cost of goods sold.

In testing the physical inventory, it is possible to rely heavily on the perpetual inventory master files if they have been tested as a part of one or more of the previously discussed tests. In fact, if the perpetual inventory master files are considered reliable, the auditor can observe and test the physical count at some time during the year and rely on the perpetuals to keep adequate records of the quantities.

When testing the unit costs, it is also possible to rely, to some degree, on the tests of the cost records made during the substantive tests of transactions. The existence of standard cost records is also useful for the purpose of comparison with the actual unit costs. If the standard costs are used to represent historical cost, they must be tested for reliability.

## ESSENTIAL TERMS

**Inventory compilation tests**—audit procedures used to verify whether physical counts of inventory were correctly summarized, inventory quantities and prices were correctly extended, and extended inventory was correctly footed

**Cost accounting controls**—controls over physical inventory and the related costs from the point at which raw materials are requisitioned to the point at which the manufactured product is completed and transferred to storage

**Cost accounting records**—the accounting records concerned with the manufacture and processing of the goods and storing finished goods

**Inventory and warehousing cycle**—the transaction cycle that involves the physical flow of goods through the organization, as well as related costs

**Job cost system**—the system of cost accounting in which costs are accumulated by individual jobs when material is used and labor costs are incurred

**Perpetual inventory master files**—continuously updated computerized records of inventory items purchased, used, sold, and on hand for merchandise, raw materials, and finished goods

**Inventory price tests**—audit procedures used to verify the costs used to value physical inventory

**Process cost system**—the system of cost accounting in which costs are accumulated for a process, with unit costs for each process assigned to the products passing through the process

**Standard cost records**—records that indicate variances between projected material, labor, and overhead costs, and the actual costs

## REVIEW QUESTIONS

**19-1 (Objective 19-1)** Give the reasons why inventory is often the most difficult and time-consuming part of many audit engagements.

**19-2 (Objectives 19-1, 19-7)** Explain the relationship between the acquisition and payment cycle and the inventory and warehousing cycle in the audit of a manufacturing company. List several audit procedures in the acquisition and payment cycle that support your explanation.

**19-3 (Objective 19-1)** State what is meant by cost accounting records and explain their importance in the conduct of an audit.

**19-4 (Objectives 19-2, 19-3)** Many auditors assert that certain audit tests can be significantly reduced for clients with adequate perpetual records that include both unit and cost data. What are the most important tests of the perpetual records that the auditor must make before he or she can reduce assessed control risk? Assuming the perpetuals are determined to be accurate, which tests can be reduced?

**19-5 (Objective 19-5)** Before the physical examination, the auditor obtains a copy of the client's inventory instructions and reviews them with the controller. In obtaining an understanding of inventory procedures for a small manufacturing company, these deficiencies are identified: shipping operations will not be completely halted during the physical examination, and there will be no independent verification of the original inventory count by a second counting team. Evaluate the importance of each of these deficiencies and state its effect on the auditor's observation of inventory.

**19-6 (Objective 19-5)** At the completion of an inventory observation, the controller requested the auditor to give him a copy of all recorded test counts to facilitate the correction of all discrepancies between the client's and the auditor's counts. Should the auditor comply with the request? Why?

**19-7 (Objective 19-5)** What major audit procedures are involved in testing for the ownership of inventory during the observation of the physical counts and as a part of subsequent valuation tests?

**19-8 (Objectives 19-4, 19-5, 19-6)** In the verification of the amount of the inventory, one of the auditor's concerns is that slow-moving and obsolete items be identified. List the auditing procedures that could be employed to determine whether slow-moving or obsolete items have been included in inventory.

**19-9 (Objective 19-5)** During the taking of physical inventory, the controller intentionally withheld several inventory tags from the employees responsible for the physical count. After the auditor left the client's premises at the completion of the inventory observation, the controller recorded nonexistent inventory on the tags and thereby significantly overstated earnings. How could the auditor have uncovered the misstatement, assuming that there are no perpetual records?

**19-10 (Objective 19-5)** Explain why a proper cutoff of purchases and sales is heavily dependent on the physical inventory observation. What information should be obtained during the physical count to make sure that cutoff is accurate?

**19-11 (Objective 19-6)** Define what is meant by compilation tests. List several examples of audit procedures to verify compilation.

**19-12 (Objective 19-4)** List the major analytical procedures for testing the overall reasonableness of inventory. For each test, explain the type of misstatement that could be identified.

**19-13 (Objective 19-6)** Included in the December 31, 1996 inventory of the Wholeridge Supply Company are 2,600 deluxe ring binders in the amount of $5,902. An examination of the most recent acquisitions of binders showed the following costs: January 26, 1997, 2,300 at $2.42 each; December 6, 1996, 1,900 at $2.28 each; November 26, 1996, 2,400 at $2.07 each. What is the misstatement in valuation of the December 31, 1996 inventory for deluxe ring binders, assuming FIFO inventory valuation? What would your answer be if the January 26, 1997 acquisition was for 2,300 binders at $2.12 each?

**19-14 (Objectives 19-6, 19-7)** The Ruswell Manufacturing Company applied manufacturing overhead to inventory at December 31, 1997 on the basis of $3.47 per direct labor hour. Explain how you would evaluate the reasonableness of total direct labor hours and manufacturing overhead in the ending inventory of finished goods.

**19-15 (Objective 19-7)** Each employee for the Gedding Manufacturing Co., a firm using a job-cost inventory costing method, must reconcile his or her total hours worked with the hours worked on individual jobs using a job time sheet at the time weekly payroll time cards are prepared. The job time sheet is then stapled to the time card. Explain how you could test the direct labor dollars included in inventory as a part of the payroll and personnel tests.

**19-16 (Objective 19-5)** Assuming that the auditor properly documents receiving report numbers as a part of the physical inventory observation procedures, explain how he or she should verify the proper cutoff of purchases, including tests for the possibility of raw materials in transit, later in the audit.

## MULTIPLE CHOICE QUESTIONS FROM CPA EXAMINATIONS

**19-17 (Objective 19-1)** The following questions concern internal controls in the inventory and warehousing cycle. Choose the best response.

a. In a company whose materials and supplies include a great number of items, a fundamental deficiency in control requirements would be indicated if

(1) a perpetual inventory master file is not maintained for items of small value.
(2) the storekeeping function were to be combined with production and record keeping.
(3) the cycle basis for physical inventory taking was to be used.
(4) minor supply items were to be expensed when acquired.

b. For control purposes, the quantities of materials ordered may be omitted from the copy of the purchase order that is
(1) forwarded to the accounting department.
(2) retained in the purchasing department's files.
(3) returned to the requisitioner.
(4) forwarded to the receiving department.

c. Which of the following procedures would *best* detect the theft of valuable items from an inventory that consists of hundreds of different items selling for $1 to $10 and a few items selling for hundreds of dollars?
(1) Maintain a perpetual inventory master file of only the more valuable items with frequent periodic verification of the validity of the perpetuals.
(2) Have an independent CPA firm prepare an internal control report on the effectiveness of the administrative and accounting controls over inventory.
(3) Have separate warehouse space for the more valuable items with sequentially numbered tags.
(4) Require an authorized officer's signature on all requisitions for the more valuable items.

**19-18 (Objectives 19-1, 19-3)** The following questions concern testing the client's internal controls for inventory and warehousing. Choose the best response.

a. When an auditor tests a client's cost accounting records, the auditor's tests are *primarily* designed to determine that
(1) quantities on hand have been computed based on acceptable cost accounting techniques that reasonably approximate actual quantities on hand.
(2) physical inventories are in substantial agreement with book inventories.
(3) the internal controls are in accordance with generally accepted accounting principles and are functioning as planned.
(4) costs have been properly assigned to finished goods, work-in-process, and cost of goods sold.

b. The accuracy of perpetual inventory master files may be established, in part, by comparing perpetual inventory records with
(1) purchase requisitions
(2) receiving reports.
(3) purchase orders.
(4) vendor payments.

c. When evaluating inventory controls with respect to segregation of duties, a CPA would be *least* likely to
(1) inspect documents.
(2) make inquiries
(3) observe procedures.
(4) consider policy and procedure manuals.

**19-19 (Objectives 19-1, 19-4, 19-5, 19-6)** The following questions deal with tests of details of balances and analytical procedures for inventory. Choose the best response.

a. An auditor would be *most* likely to learn of slow-moving inventory through
(1) inquiry of sales personnel.
(2) inquiry of store personnel.
(3) physical observation of inventory.
(4) review of perpetual inventory master files.

b. An inventory turnover analysis is useful to the auditor because it may detect
   (1) inadequacies in inventory pricing.
   (2) methods of avoiding cyclical holding costs.
   (3) the optimum automatic reorder points.
   (4) the existence of obsolete merchandise.

c. A CPA auditing inventory may appropriately apply attributes sampling in order to estimate the
   (1) average price of inventory items.
   (2) percentage of slow-moving inventory items.
   (3) dollar value of inventory.
   (4) physical quantity of inventory items.

## DISCUSSION QUESTIONS AND PROBLEMS

**19-20 (Objectives 19-1, 19-3, 19-4, 19-5, 19-6)** Items 1 through 8 are selected questions typically found in questionnaires used by auditors to obtain an understanding of internal control in the inventory and warehousing cycle. In using the questionnaire for a client, a "yes" response to a question indicates a possible internal control, whereas a "no" indicates a potential weakness.

1. Does the receiving department prepare prenumbered receiving reports and account for the numbers periodically for all inventory received, showing the description and quantity of materials?
2. Is all inventory stored under the control of a custodian in areas where access is limited?
3. Are all shipments to customers authorized by prenumbered shipping documents?
4. Is a detailed perpetual inventory master file maintained for raw materials inventory?
5. Are physical inventory counts made by someone other than storekeepers and those responsible for maintaining the perpetual inventory master file?
6. Are standard cost records used for raw materials, direct labor, and manufacturing overhead?
7. Is there a stated policy with specific criteria for writing off obsolete or slow-moving goods?
8. Is the clerical accuracy of the final inventory compilation checked by a person independent of those responsible for preparing it?

### Required

a. For each of the preceding questions, state the purpose of the internal control.
b. For each internal control, list a test of control to test its effectiveness.
c. For each of the preceding questions, identify the nature of the potential financial misstatement(s) if the control is not in effect.
d. For each of the potential misstatements in part c, list a substantive audit procedure to determine whether a material misstatement exists.

**19-21 (Objective 19-3)** The cost accounting records are often an essential area to audit in a manufacturing or construction company.

### Required

a. Why is it important to review the cost accounting records and test their accuracy?
b. For the audit of standard cost accounting records in which thirty-five parts are manufactured, explain how you would determine whether each of the following were reasonable for part no. 21.
   (1) Standard direct labor hours
   (2) Standard direct overhead rate
   (3) Standard overhead rate

(4) Standard units of raw materials
(5) Standard cost of a unit of raw materials
(6) Total standard cost

**19-22 (Objectives 19-1, 19-4, 19-5, 19-6)** Following are audit procedures frequently performed in the inventory and warehousing cycle for a manufacturing company.

1. Compare the client's count of physical inventory at an interim date with the perpetual inventory master file.
2. Trace the auditor's test counts recorded in the working papers to the final inventory compilation and compare the tag number, description, and quantity.
3. Compare the unit price on the final inventory summary with vendors' invoices.
4. Read the client's physical inventory instructions and observe whether they are being followed by those responsible for counting the inventory.
5. Account for a sequence of raw material requisitions and examine each requisition for an authorized approval.
6. Trace the recorded additions on the finished goods perpetual inventory master file to the records for completed production.
7. Account for a sequence of inventory tags and trace each tag to the physical inventory to make sure it actually exists.

## Required

a. Identify whether each of the procedures is primarily a test of control or a substantive test.

b. State the purpose(s) of each of the procedures.

**19-23 (Objectives 19-1, 19-5, 19-6)** The following misstatements are included in the inventory and related records of Westbox Manufacturing Company.

1. An inventory item was priced at $12 each instead of at the correct cost of $12 per dozen.
2. In taking the physical inventory, the last shipments for the day were excluded from inventory and were not included as a sale until the subsequent year.
3. The clerk in charge of the perpetual inventory master file altered the quantity on an inventory tag to cover up the shortage of inventory caused by its theft during the year.
4. After the auditor left the premises, several inventory tags were lost and were not included in the final inventory summary.
5. In recording raw material acquisitions, the improper unit price was included in the perpetual inventory master file. Therefore, the inventory valuation was misstated because the physical inventory was priced by referring to the perpetual records.
6. During the physical count, several obsolete inventory items were included.
7. Because of a significant increase in volume during the current year and excellent control over manufacturing overhead costs, the manufacturing overhead rate applied to inventory was far greater than actual cost.

## Required

a. For each misstatement, state an internal control that should have prevented it from occurring.

b. For each misstatement, state a substantive audit procedure that could be used to uncover it.

**19-24 (Objectives 19-5, 19-6)** Often an important aspect of a CPA's audit of financial statements is his or her observation of the taking of physical inventory.

## Required

a. What are the general objectives or purposes of the CPA's observation of the taking of the physical inventory? (Do not discuss the procedures or techniques involved in making the observation.)

b. For what purposes does the CPA make and record test counts of inventory quantities during his or her observation of the taking of the physical inventory? Discuss.

c. A number of companies employ outside service companies that specialize in counting, pricing, extending, and footing inventories. These service companies usually furnish a certificate attesting to the value of the inventory.

Assuming that the service company took the inventory on the balance sheet date:

(1) How much reliance, if any, can the CPA place on the inventory certificate of outside specialists? Discuss.

(2) What effect, if any, would the inventory certificate of outside specialists have upon the type of report the CPA would render? Discuss.

(3) What reference, if any, would the CPA make to the certificate of outside specialists in his short-form report?*

**19-25 (Objective 19-5)** You encountered the following situations during the December 31, 1997, physical inventory of Latner Shoe Distributor Company.

a. Latner maintains a large portion of the shoe merchandise in ten warehouses throughout the eastern United States. This ensures swift delivery service for its chain of stores. You are assigned alone to the Boston warehouse to observe the physical inventory process. During the inventory count, several express trucks pulled in for loading. Although infrequent, express shipments must be attended to immediately. As a result, the employees who were counting the inventory stopped to assist in loading the express trucks. What should you do?

b. (1) In one storeroom of 10,000 items, you have test-counted about 200 items of high value and a few items of low value. You found no misstatements. You also note that the employees are diligently following the inventory instructions. Do you think you have tested enough items? Explain.

(2) What would you do if you counted 150 items and found a substantial number of counting errors?

c. In observing an inventory of liquid shoe polish, you note that one lot is five years old. From inspection of some bottles in an open box, you find that the liquid has solidified in most of the bottles. What action should you take?

d. During your observation of the inventory count in the main warehouse, you found that most of the prenumbered tags that had been incorrectly filled out are being destroyed and thrown away. What is the significance of this procedure and what action should you take?

**19-26 (Objective 19-5)** In connection with his audit of the financial statements of Knutson Products Co., an assembler of home appliances, for the year ended May 31, 1997, Ray Abel, CPA, is reviewing with Knutson's controller the plans for a physical inventory at the company warehouse on May 31, 1997.

Finished appliances, unassembled parts, and supplies are stored in the warehouse, which is attached to Knutson's assembly plant. The plant will operate during the count. On May 30, the warehouse will deliver to the plant the estimated quantities of unassembled parts and supplies required for May 31 production, but there may be emergency requisitions on May 31. During the count, the warehouse will continue to receive parts and supplies and to ship finished appliances. However, appliances completed on May 31 will be held in the plant until after the physical inventory.

## Required

What procedures should the company establish to ensure that the inventory count includes all items that should be included and that nothing is counted twice?*

*AICPA adapted.

19-27 (Objective 19-4) The following are sales, cost of sales, and inventory data for Aladdin Products Supply Company, a wholesale distributor of cleaning supplies. Dollar amounts are in millions.

| | 1997 | 1996 | 1995 | 1994 |
|---|---|---|---|---|
| Sales | $23.2 | $21.7 | $19.6 | $17.4 |
| Cost of sales | 17.1 | 16.8 | 15.2 | 13.5 |
| Beginning inventory | 2.3 | 2.1 | 1.9 | 1.5 |
| Ending inventory | 2.9 | 2.3 | 2.1 | 1.9 |

## Required

a. Calculate the following ratios, using an electronic spreadsheet program (Instructor's option):
   1. Gross margin as a percentage of sales
   2. Inventory turnover

b. List several logical causes of the changes in the two ratios.

c. Assume that $500,000 is considered material for audit planning purposes for 1997. Could any of the fluctuations in the computed ratios indicate a possible material misstatement? Demonstrate this by using the spreadsheet program to perform a sensitivity analysis.

d. What should the auditor do to determine the actual cause of the changes?

19-28 (Objective 19-5) In an annual audit at December 31, 1996, you find the following transactions near the closing date:

1. Merchandise costing $1,822 was received on January 3, 1997, and the related acquisition invoice recorded January 5. The invoice showed the shipment was made on December 29, 1996, FOB destination.
2. Merchandise costing $625 was received on December 28, 1996, and the invoice was not recorded. You located it in the hands of the purchasing agent; it was marked "on consignment."
3. A packing case containing products costing $816 was standing in the shipping room when the physical inventory was taken. It was not included in the inventory because it was marked "Hold for shipping instructions." Your investigation revealed that the customer's order was dated December 18, 1996, but that the case was shipped and the customer billed on January 10, 1997. The product was a stock item of your client.
4. Merchandise received on January 6, 1997, costing $720 was entered in the acquisitions journal on January 7, 1997. The invoice showed shipment was made FOB supplier's warehouse on December 31, 1996. Since it was not on hand at December 31, it was not included in inventory.
5. A special machine, fabricated to order for a customer, was finished and in the shipping room on December 31, 1996. The customer was billed on that date and the machine excluded from inventory, although it was shipped on January 4, 1997.

Assume that each of the amounts is material.

## Required

a. State whether the merchandise should be included in the client's inventory.

b. Give your reason for your decision on each item.*

*AICPA adapted.

**19-29 (Objective 19-6)** As a part of your clerical tests of inventory for Martin Manufacturing, you have tested about 20 percent of the dollar items and have found the following exceptions:

1. Extension errors:

| Description | Quantity | | Price | Extension as Recorded |
|---|---|---|---|---|
| Wood | 465 | board feet | $ .12/board foot | $ 5.58 |
| Metal-cutting tools | 29 | units | 30.00 each | 670.00 |
| Cutting fluid | 16 | barrels | 40.00/barrel | 529.00 |
| Sandpaper | 300 | sheets | .95/hundred | 258.00 |

2. Differences located in comparing last year's costs with the current year's costs on the client's inventory lists:

| Description | Quantity | This Year's Cost | Preceding Year's Cost |
|---|---|---|---|
| TA-114 precision-cutting torches | 12 units | $500.00 each | Unable to locate |
| Aluminum scrap | 4,500 pounds | 5.00/ton | $65.00/ton |
| Lubricating oil | 400 gallons | 6.00/gallon | 4.50/barrel |

3. Test counts that you were unable to find when tracing from the test counts to the final inventory compilation:

| Tag No. | Quantity | Current-Year Cost | Description |
|---|---|---|---|
| 2958 | 15 tons | $75/ton | Cold-rolled bars |
| 0026 | 2,000 feet | 2.25/foot | 4-inch aluminum stripping |

4. Page total, footing errors:

| Page No. | Client Total | Correct Total |
|---|---|---|
| 14 | $1,375.12 | $1,375.08 |
| 82 | 8,721.18 | 8,521.18 |

## Required

a. State the amount of the actual misstatement in each of the four tests. For any item for which amount of the misstatement cannot be determined from the information given, state the considerations that would affect your estimate of the misstatement.

b. As a result of your findings, what would you do about clerical accuracy tests of the inventory in the current year?

c. What changes, if any, would you suggest in internal controls and procedures for Martin Manufacturing during the compilation of next year's inventory to prevent each type of misstatement?

**19-30 (Objective 19-5)** You have been engaged for the audit of the Y Company for the year ended December 31, 1997. The Y Company is in the wholesale chemical business and makes all sales at 25 percent over cost.

Following are portions of the client's sales and purchases accounts for the calendar year 1997.

SALES

| | | | Balance Forward | | |
|---|---|---|---|---|---|
| **Date** | **Reference** | **Amount** | **Date** | **Reference** | **Amount** |
| 12-31 | Closing entry | $699,860 | | | $658,320 |
| | | | 12-27 | *SI#965 | 5,195 |
| | | | 12-28 | SI#966 | 19,270 |
| | | | 12-28 | SI#967 | 1,302 |
| | | | 12-31 | SI#969 | 5,841 |
| | | | 12-31 | SI#970 | 7,922 |
| | | | 12-31 | SI#971 | 2,010 |
| | | $699,860 | | | $699,860 |

PURCHASES

| Balance Forward | | | | | |
|---|---|---|---|---|---|
| **Date** | **Reference** | **Amount** | **Date** | **Reference** | **Amount** |
| | | $360,300 | 12-31 | Closing entry | $385,346 |
| 12-28 | †RR#1059 | 3,100 | | | |
| 12-30 | RR#1061 | 8,965 | | | |
| 12-31 | RR#1062 | 4,861 | | | |
| 12-31 | RR#1063 | 8,120 | | | |
| | | $385,346 | | | $385,346 |

*SI, sales invoice.
†RR, receiving report.

You observed the physical inventory of goods in the warehouse on December 31, 1997 and were satisfied that it was properly taken.

When performing a sales and purchases cutoff test, you found that at December 31, 1997, the last receiving report that had been used was no. 1063 and that no shipments have been made on any sales invoices with numbers larger than no. 968. You also obtained the following additional information.

1. Included in the warehouse physical inventory at December 31, 1997, were chemicals that had been acquired and received on receiving report no. 1060 but for which an invoice was not received until 1998. Cost was $2,183.
2. In the warehouse at December 31, 1997, were goods that had been sold and paid for by the customer but which were not shipped out until 1998. They were all sold on sales invoice no. 965 and were not inventoried.
3. On the evening of December 31, 1997, there were two cars on the Y company siding:
   (a) Car AR38162 was unloaded on January 2, 1998, and received on receiving report no. 1063. The freight was paid by the vendor.
   (b) Car BAE74123 was loaded and sealed on December 31, 1997, and was switched off the company's siding on January 2, 1998. The sales price was $12,700 and the freight was paid by the customer. This order was sold on sales invoice no. 968.
4. Temporarily stranded at December 31, 1997, on a railroad siding were two cars of chemicals en route to the Z Pulp and Paper Co. They were sold on sales invoice no. 966 and the terms were FOB destination.

5. En route to the Y Company on December 31, 1997, was a truckload of material that was received on receiving report no. 1064. The material was shipped FOB destination and freight of $75 was paid by the Y Company. However, the freight was deducted from the purchase price of $975.
6. Included in the physical inventory were chemicals exposed to rain in transit and deemed unsalable. Their invoice cost was $1,250, and freight charges of $350 had been paid on the chemicals.

## Required

a. Compute the adjustments that should be made to the client's physical inventory at December 31, 1997.

b. Prepare a worksheet of adjusting entries that are required as of December 31, 1997.*

**19-31 (Objective 19-6)** You are testing the summarization and cost of raw materials and purchased part inventories as a part of the audit of Rubber Products and Supply Company. There are 2,000 inventory items with a total recorded value of $648,500.

Your audit tests are to compare recorded descriptions and counts with the final inventory listing, compare unit costs with vendors' invoices, and extend unit costs times quantity. A misstatement in any of those is defined as a difference. You plan to use difference estimation sampling.

You make the following decisions about the audit of inventory:

| | |
|---|---|
| Tolerable misstatement | $16,000 |
| Estimated point estimate | 4,000 |
| Acceptable risk of incorrect acceptance | 5% |
| Estimated standard deviation | 30 |
| (based on data contained in last year's working papers) | |

## Required

a. What would be the advantages of using difference estimation compared to nonstatistical sampling?

b. What is the sample size necessary to achieve your objectives using difference estimation.

c. Without regard to your answer to part b, assume that a sample of sixty items is selected and the following differences between book and audited values are identified (understatements are in parentheses).

| Item No. | Difference |
|---|---|
| 1 | $19 |
| 2 | 11 |
| 3 | (19) |
| 4 | 40 |
| 5 | 90 |
| 6 | 38 |
| 7 | (90) |
| 8 | 70 |
| 9 | (85) |
| Total | $74 |

*AICPA adapted.

For each of the other fifty-one items in the sample, there was no difference between the book and the audited values.

Based on this sample, calculate the upper confidence limit of the population misstatement amount at the acceptable risk of incorrect acceptance.

d. Given that actual sample size in part c was smaller than the required sample size in part b, explain why the confidence limits still fall within tolerable misstatement.

## CASES

**19-32 (Objective 19-6)** You are assigned to the December 31, 1996 audit of Sea Gull Airframes, Inc. The company designs and manufactures aircraft superstructures and airframe components. You observed the physical inventory at December 31 and are satisfied that it was properly taken. The inventory at December 31, 1996, has been priced, extended, and totaled by the client and is made up of about 5,000 inventory items with a total valuation of $8,275,000. In performing inventory price tests you have decided to stratify your tests, and you conclude that you should have two strata: items with a value over $5,000 and those with a value of less than $5,000. The book values are as follows:

| | No. of Items | Total Value |
|---|---|---|
| More than $5,000 | 500 | $4,150,000 |
| Less than $5,000 | 4,500 | 4,125,000 |
| | 5,000 | $8,275,000 |

In performing your pricing and extension tests, you have decided to test about fifty inventory items in detail. You selected forty of the over $5,000 items and ten of those under $5,000 at random from the population. You find all items to be correct except for items A through G at the bottom of this page, which you believe may be misstated. You have tested the following items, to this point, exclusive of A through G.

| | No. of Items | Total Value |
|---|---|---|
| More than $5,000 | 36 | $360,000 |
| Less than $5,000 | 7 | 2,600 |

Sea Gull Airframes uses a periodic inventory system and values its inventory at the lower of FIFO cost or market. You were able to locate all invoices needed for your examination. The seven inventory items in the sample you believe may be misstated, along with the relevant data for determining the proper valuation, are shown below and on page 670.

**INVENTORY ITEMS POSSIBLY MISSTATED**

| Description | Quantity | Price | Total* |
|---|---|---|---|
| A. L37 spars | 3,000 meters | $8.00/meter | $24,000 |
| B. B68 metal formers | 10,000 inches | 1.20/foot | 12,000 |
| C. R01 metal ribs | 1,500 yards | 10.00/yard | 15,000 |
| D. St26 struts | 1,000 feet | 8.00/foot | 8,000 |
| E. Industrial hand drills | 45 units | 20.00 each | 900 |
| F. L803 steel leaf springs | 40 pairs | 69.00 each spring | 276 |
| G. V16 fasteners | 5.50 dozen | 10.00/dozen | 55 |

*Note: Amounts are as stated on client's inventory.

INFORMATION FOR PRICING FROM INVOICES (SEA GULL AIRFRAMES)

| Voucher Number | Voucher Date | Date Paid | Terms | Receiving Report Date | Invoice Description |
|---|---|---|---|---|---|
| 7-68 | 8-01-91 | 8-21-91 | Net FOB destination | 8-01-91 | 77 V16 fasteners at $10 per dozen |
| 11-81 | 10-16-96 | 11-15-96 | Net FOB destination | 10-18-96 | 1,100 yards R01 metal ribs at $9.50 per yard; 2,000 feet St26 struts at $8.20 per foot |
| 12-06 | 12-08-96 | 12-30-96 | 2/10, n/30 FOB S.P. | 12-10-96 | 180 L803 steel leaf springs at $69 each |
| 12-09 | 12-10-96 | 12-18-96 | Net FOB destination | 12-11-96 | 45 industrial hand drills at $20 each; guaranteed for four years |
| 12-18 | 12-27-96 | 12-27-96 | 2/10, n/30 FOB S.P. | 12-21-96 | 4,200 meters L37 spars at $8 per meter |
| 12-23 | 12-24-96 | 1-03-97 | 2/10, n/30 FOB destination | 12-26-96 | 12,800 inches B68 metal formers at $1.20 per foot |
| 12-61 | 12-29-96 | 1-08-97 | Net FOB destination | 12-29-96 | 1,000 yards R01 metal ribs at $10 per yard; 800 feet St26 struts at $8 per foot |
| 12-81 | 12-31-96 | 1-20-97 | Net FOB destination | 1-06-97 | 2,000 meters L37 spars at $7.50 per meter; 2,000 yards R01 metal ribs at $10 per yard |

In addition, you noted a freight bill for voucher 12-23 in the amount of $200. This bill was entered in the freight-in account. Virtually all freight was for the metal formers.

This is the first time Sea Gull Airframes has been audited by your firm.

## Required

a. Review all information and determine the inventory misstatements of the seven items in question. State any assumptions you consider necessary to determine the amount of the misstatements.

b. Prepare a working paper schedule to summarize your findings. Use the microcomputer to prepare the schedule (Instructor option).

**19-33 (Objectives 19-5, 19-6)** You are observing inventory as a part of the August 31 year-end audit of Engine Warehouse Supply Company, a wholesale and retail engine parts company. Inventory includes a large number of diverse parts varying from small bolts to large engines for earth-moving equipment.

The company has ceased operation during the physical count except for receiving goods from suppliers and making shipments to essential wholesale customers. On the morning of the physical count, which is Saturday, September 2, you record in your working papers the last shipping document and receiving report number issued the previous day. They are 109,314 and 41,682 respectively.

You observe the client's counting procedures and test count selected inventory yourself. You conclude that the counts and descriptions are accurate. Before you leave the warehouse at the end of the day, after all counting is completed, you do several things:

1. Examine the receiving report book. The last number used was 41,685. The receiving clerk informs you that all goods received on September 2 were kept in the receiving department with other goods received during the past two or three days.
2. Examine the shipping document book. The last number used was 109,317. The shipping department informs you that three shipments were made before noon, two were made after noon, and one was still in the shipping department.
3. Ask the receiving department to identify all goods received September 1. He identifies receiving reports 41,680 through 41,682 as having been received September 1.
4. Ask the shipping department to identify all goods shipped or sold over the counter September 1. He informs you goods on shipping document 109,311 to 109,313 were shipped September 1. He shows you approximately 300 duplicate sales slips for September 1 over-the-counter sales. September 1 retail sales totaled $12,690, but they were not included in August sales.
5. Examine the client's inventory counts in the receiving department. Inventory had been counted only for receiving reports 41,674 to 41,684.

6. Examine the client's inventory counts in the shipping department. Inventory had been counted only for shipping documents 109,316 and 109,317. Further examination shows that inventory for all shipments made September 2 were included in the counts in the department from which the inventory was taken.

During the year-end audit work you obtain selling prices, costs, terms, and recording data for each receipt and shipment. They are as follows:

ACQUISITIONS OF INVENTORY

| Receiving Report No. | Date Shipped | Date Received | Dollar Amount of Acquisition | Included in or Excluded from August Acquisitions Journal | FOB Origin or Destination |
|---|---|---|---|---|---|
| 41,679 | 8-29 | 8-31 | $ 860 | I | Destination |
| 41,680 | 8-27 | 9-01 | 1,211 | I | Origin |
| 41,681 | 8-20 | 9-01 | 193 | I | Origin |
| 41,682 | 8-27 | 9-01 | 4,674 | I | Destination |
| 41,683 | 8-30 | 9-02 | 450 | E | Destination |
| 41,684 | 8-30 | 9-02 | 106 | E | Origin |
| 41,685 | 9-02 | 9-02 | 2,800 | E | Origin |
| 41,686 | 8-30 | 9-02 | 686 | E | Destination |

SHIPMENTS OF INVENTORY

| Shipping Document No. | Date Shipped | Dollar Amount of Sale | Included in or Excluded from August Sales Journal |
|---|---|---|---|
| 109,310 | 8-31 | $ 780 | I |
| 109,311 | 9-01 | 56 | I |
| 109,312 | 9-01 | 3,194 | I |
| 109,313 | 9-01 | 635 | I |
| 109,314 | 9-01 | 193 | I |
| 109,315 | 9-02 | 1,621 | E |
| 109,316 | 9-02 | 945 | E |
| 109,317 | 9-02 | 78 | E |
| 109,318 | 9-02 | 3,611 | E |

## Required

Assume that the information you have obtained from the receiving and shipping departments about the September 1 receipts and shipments is accurate.

a. Prepare all adjustments for cutoff misstatements in accounts payable, assuming that no acquisitions are made for cash.

b. Prepare all adjustments for misstatements in sales.

c. What is the amount of the client's misstatement in inventory, assuming a periodic inventory method, and no adjustments in part a or b affected inventory? For retail sales, assume that the gross margin percentage is approximately 30 percent.

d. How would you determine whether the receiving and shipping departments have given you accurate information about the September 1 receipts and shipments of goods?

# 20

# AUDIT OF THE CAPITAL ACQUISITION AND REPAYMENT CYCLE

## LEARNING OBJECTIVES

Thorough study of this chapter will enable you to

**20-1** Identify the accounts and the unique characteristics of the capital acquisition and repayment cycle.

**20-2** Design and perform audit tests of notes payable and related accounts and transactions.

**20-3** Describe the primary concerns in the design and performance of the audit of owners' equity transactions.

**20-4** Design and perform tests of controls, substantive tests of transactions, and tests of details of balances for capital stock and retained earnings.

## A DISHONEST CLIENT WILL GET THE BEST OF THE AUDITOR ALMOST EVERY TIME

Able Construction Company entered into long-term construction contracts, recognizing income using the percentage of completion method of accounting. This method requires, among other things, an agreement with well-defined, enforceable terms, a reliable method of estimating costs to complete the contracts, and recognition of losses at the time they become known. As part of the audit of Able, its auditors read the contracts for all projects in progress, test costs incurred to date, and assess the ultimate profitability of the contracts, including discussing them with management. A significant part of verifying income under percentage of completion is auditing costs incurred.

In the current year, management's records and schedules of projects indicate that all projects will result in a profit. For each project, there is a separate schedule showing estimated total revenue from the project, costs incurred in the current period, costs incurred to date, estimated total costs, percentage of completion, and profit recognized in the current period. The auditor discussed each project with management, performed audit tests to support the schedule, and concluded that the revenue, expenses, and profit were reasonably stated. Reported income allowed Able to meet its bonding requirements and obtain a large new project.

In fact, Able had incurred a significant loss on one of its major projects. Able engaged a subcontractor to do reconstructive work not anticipated in the original contract bid. In awarding the subcontract, Able entered into an agreement with the subcontractor that the work would not be paid for until after its audit was completed. Management hid the subcontractor's invoices from the auditors as they were received. During the next year, management recognized this loss, but doctored the invoices so that it appeared the "unexpected" additional cost was incurred during that year, and that the previous year's statements were correct.

The fraudulent misstatement was discovered several years later when Able went bankrupt and the CPA firm was sued for performing an inadequate audit. The firm was ultimately found not responsible, but only after spending extensive time and large amounts of money defending its audit.

**OBJECTIVE 20-1**
**Identify the accounts and the unique characteristics of the capital acquisition and repayment cycle.**

The final transaction cycle discussed in this text relates to the acquisition of capital resources in the form of interest-bearing debt and owners' equity and the repayment of the capital. The capital acquisition and repayment cycle also includes the payment of interest and dividends. The following are the major accounts in the cycle:

- Notes payable
- Contracts payable
- Mortgages payable
- Bonds payable
- Interest expense
- Accrued interest
- Cash in the bank
- Capital stock—common
- Capital stock—preferred
- Paid-in capital in excess of par
- Donated capital
- Retained earnings
- Appropriations of retained earnings
- Treasury stock
- Dividends declared
- Dividends payable
- Proprietorship—capital account
- Partnership—capital account

Four characteristics of the capital acquisition and repayment cycle significantly influence the audit of these accounts:

1. *Relatively few transactions affect the account balances, but each transaction is often highly material in amount.* For example, bonds are infrequently issued by most companies,

**FIGURE 20-1**
**Methodology for Designing Tests of Details of Balances for Notes Payable**

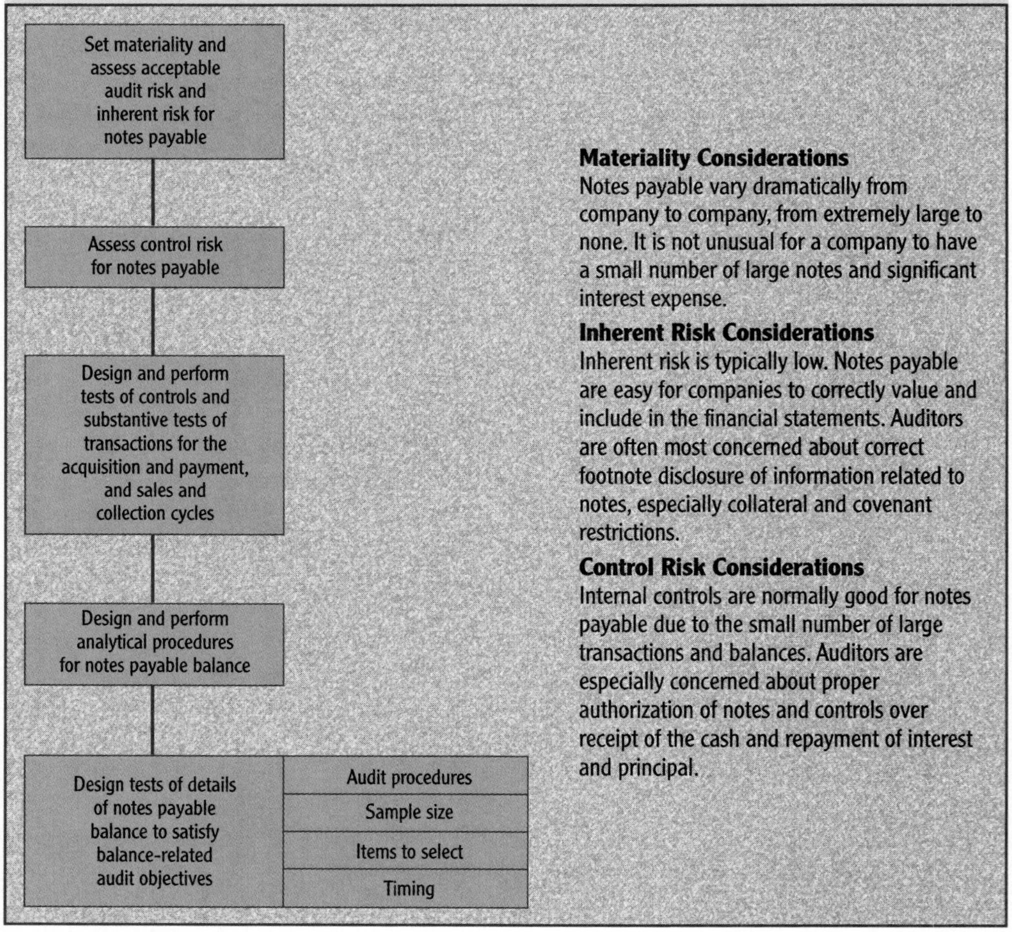

but the amount of a bond issue is normally large. Due to their size, it is common to verify each transaction taking place in the cycle for the entire year as a part of verifying the balance sheet accounts. It is not unusual to see audit working papers that include the beginning balance of every account in the capital acquisition and repayment cycle and documentation of every transaction that occurred during the year.

2. *The exclusion of a single transaction could be material in itself.* Considering the effect of understatements of liabilities and owners' equity, which was discussed in Chapter 17, omission is a major audit concern.

3. *There is a legal relationship between the client entity and the holder of the stock, bond, or similar ownership document.* In the audit of the transactions and amounts in the cycle, the auditor must take great care in making sure that the significant legal requirements affecting the financial statements have been properly fulfilled and adequately presented and disclosed in the statements.

4. *There is a direct relationship between the interest and dividends accounts and debt and equity.* In the audit of interest-bearing debt, it is desirable to simultaneously verify the related interest expense and interest payable. This holds true for owners' equity, dividends declared, and dividends payable.

The audit procedures for many of the accounts in the capital acquisition and repayment cycle can best be understood by selecting representative accounts for study. Therefore, this chapter discusses (1) the audit of notes payable and the related interest expense and interest payable to illustrate interest-bearing capital and (2) common stock, paid-in capital in excess of par, retained earnings, and dividends.

The methodology for determining tests of details of balances for capital acquisition accounts is the same as that followed for all other accounts. For example, the methodology for notes payable is shown in Figure 20-1 on page 674.

## NOTES PAYABLE

**OBJECTIVE 20-2**
**Design and perform audit tests of notes payable and related accounts and transactions.**

A *note payable* is a legal obligation to a creditor, which may be unsecured or secured by assets. Typically, a note is issued for a period somewhere between one month and one year, but there are also long-term notes of over a year. Notes are issued for many different purposes, and the pledged property includes a wide variety of assets, such as securities, inventory, and fixed assets. The principal and interest payments on the notes must be made in accordance with the terms of the loan agreement. For short-term loans, a principal and interest payment is usually required only when the loan becomes due; but for loans over 90 days, the note usually calls for monthly or quarterly interest payments.

### Overview of Accounts

The accounts used for notes payable and related interest are shown in Figure 20-2 on page 676. It is common to include tests of principal and interest payments as a part of the audit of the acquisition and payment cycle because the payments are recorded in the cash disbursements journal. But due to their relative infrequency, in many cases no capital transactions are included in the tests of controls and substantive tests of transactions sample. Therefore, it is also normal to test these transactions as a part of the capital acquisition and repayment cycle.

### Objectives

The objectives of the audit of notes payable are to determine whether:

- The internal controls over notes payable are adequate.
- Transactions for principal and interest involving notes payable are properly authorized and recorded as defined by the six transaction-related audit objectives.

**FIGURE 20-2**

**Notes Payable and the Related Interest Accounts**

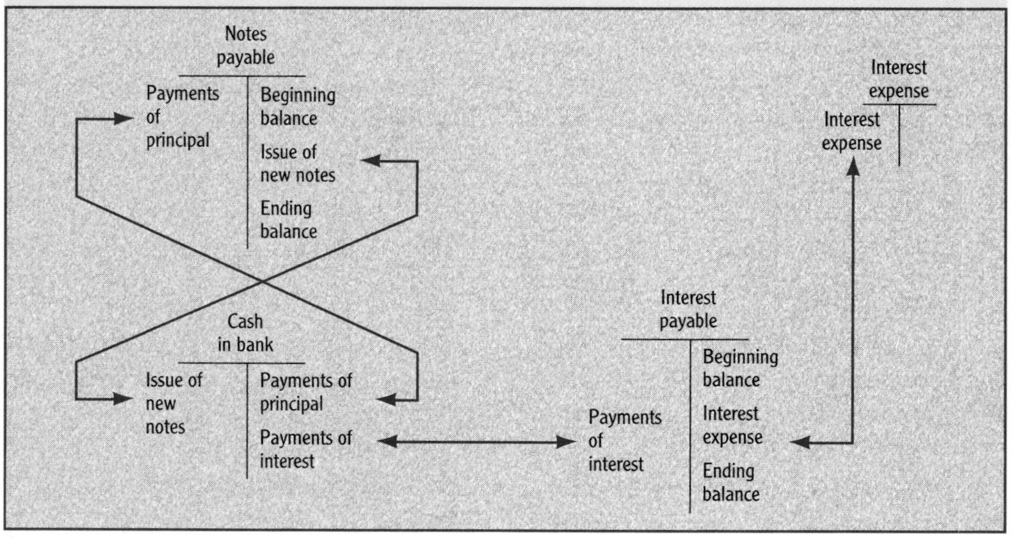


- The liability for notes payable and the related interest expense and accrued liability are properly stated as defined by eight of the nine balance-related audit objectives. (Realizable value is not applicable to liability accounts.)

## Internal Controls

There are four important controls over notes payable:

- *Proper authorization for the issue of new notes.* Responsibility for the issuance of new notes should be vested in the board of directors or high-level management personnel. Generally, two signatures of properly authorized officials are required for all loan agreements. The amount of the loan, the interest rate, the repayment terms, and the assets pledged are all part of the approved agreement. Whenever notes are renewed, it is important that they be subject to the same authorization procedures as those for the issuance of new notes.
- *Adequate controls over the repayment of principal and interest.* The periodic payments of interest and principal should be controlled as a part of the acquisition and payment cycle. At the time the note was issued, the accounting department should have received a copy in the same manner in which it receives vendors' invoices and receiving reports. The accounts payable department should automatically issue checks for the notes when they become due, again in the same manner in which it prepares checks for acquisitions of goods and services. The copy of the note is the supporting documentation for payment.
- *Proper documents and records.* These include the maintenance of subsidiary records and control over blank and paid notes by a responsible person. Paid notes should be cancelled and retained under the custody of an authorized official.
- *Periodic independent verification.* Periodically, the detailed note records should be reconciled with the general ledger and compared with the note holders' records by an employee who is not responsible for maintaining the detailed records. At the same time, an independent person should recompute the interest expense on notes to test the accuracy and propriety of the record keeping.

## Tests of Controls and Substantive Tests of Transactions

Tests of notes payable transactions involve the issue of notes and the repayment of principal and interest. These audit tests are a part of tests of controls and substantive tests of transactions for cash receipts (Chapter 11) and cash disbursements (Chapter 17). Additional tests of controls and substantive tests of transactions are often done as a part of tests of details of balances because of the materiality of individual transactions.

Tests of controls for notes payable and related interest should emphasize testing the four important internal controls discussed in the previous section. In addition, the accurate recording of receipts from note proceeds and payments of principal and interest is emphasized.

## Analytical Procedures

Analytical procedures are essential for notes payable because tests of details for interest expense and accrued interest can frequently be eliminated when results are favorable. Table 20-1 illustrates typical analytical procedures for notes payable and related interest accounts.

**TABLE 20-1**

**Analytical Procedures for Notes Payable**

| Analytical Procedure | Possible Misstatement |
|---|---|
| Recalculate approximate interest expense on the basis of average interest rates and overall monthly notes payable. | Misstatement of interest expense and accrued interest, or omission of an outstanding note payable. |
| Compare individual notes outstanding with the prior year. | Omission or misstatement of a note payable. |
| Compare total balance in notes payable, interest expense, and accrued interest with prior year. | Misstatement of interest expense and accrued interest or notes payable. |

The auditor's independent estimate of interest expense, using average notes payable outstanding and average interest rates, tests the reasonableness of interest expense, but also tests for omitted notes payable. An illustration of an auditor's working paper where such an analytical procedure has been performed is illustrated in Figure 6-3, page 197. If actual interest expense had been materially larger than the auditor's estimate, one possible cause would be interest payments on unrecorded notes payable.

## Tests of Details of Balances

The normal starting point for the audit of notes payable is a *schedule of notes payable and accrued interest* obtained from the client. A typical schedule is shown in Figure 20-3 on pages 678–679. The usual schedule includes detailed information of all transactions that took place during the entire year for principal and interest, the beginning and ending balances for notes and interest payable, and descriptive information about the notes, such as the due date, the interest rate, and the assets pledged as collateral.

When there are numerous transactions involving notes during the year, it may not be practical to obtain a schedule of the type shown in Figure 20-3. In that situation, the auditor is likely to request that the client prepare a schedule of only those notes with unpaid balances at the end of the year. This would show a description of each note, its ending balance, and the interest payable at the end of the year, including the collateral and interest rate.

The balance-related audit objectives and common audit procedures are summarized in Table 20-2 (pages 680–681). Realizable value is not included in the table because it is not applicable to notes payable. The schedule of notes payable is the frame of reference for the procedures. Again, the amount of testing depends heavily on materiality of notes payable and the effectiveness of internal controls.

The three most important balance-related audit objectives in notes payable are

- Existing notes payable are included (completeness).
- Notes payable in the schedule are accurately recorded (accuracy).
- Notes payable are properly presented and disclosed (presentation and disclosure).

**FIGURE 20-3**

**Schedule of Notes Payable and Accrued Interest**

PBC

ABC Company, Inc.
Notes Payable

12/31/96

Schedule AA-4 — Date
Prepared by DB — 1/12/97
Approved by JL — 1/16/97

| Payee | Date Made | Date Due | Face Amount of Note | Security Description | Security Valuation | Balance at Beginning of Period |
|---|---|---|---|---|---|---|
| First National Bank | 9/30/95 | 9/30/96 | 10000 | Investments | 15000 | 10000 |
| Second National Bank | 9/30/96 | 9/30/97 | 10000 | Investments | 16000 | |
| Third National Bank | 10/31/96 | 10/31/97 | 10000 | Fixed Assets | 22000 | |
| | | | 30000 | | 53000 | 10000 ① Λ |

① —Traced to prior year audit working papers.
② —Obtained copy of note included in permanent file.
③ —Examined cancelled note and/or check.
④ —Agreed to confirmation received from bank.
⑤ —Traced to general ledger.
⑥ —Recomputed expense; no differences noted.
Λ —Footed
X —Cross-footed

The first two objectives are important because a misstatement can be material if even one note is omitted or incorrect. Presentation and disclosure is important because generally accepted accounting principles require that the footnotes adequately describe the terms of notes payable outstanding and the assets pledged as collateral for the loans. If there are significant restrictions on the activities of the company required by the loans, such as compensating balance provisions or restrictions on the payment of dividends, these must also be disclosed in the footnotes.

**Summary**

Figure 20-5 (page 682) illustrates the major accounts related to notes payable in the capital acquisition and repayment cycle and the types of audit tests used to audit these accounts. This figure also shows how the audit risk model discussed in Chapter 8 relates to the audit of these accounts in the cycle.

## OWNERS' EQUITY

**OBJECTIVE 20-3**
**Describe the primary concerns in the design and performance of an audit of owners' equity transactions.**

A major distinction must be made in the audit of owners' equity between *publicly* and *closely held corporations.* In most closely held corporations there are few if any transactions during the year for capital stock accounts, and there are typically only a few shareholders. The only transactions entered in the owners' equity section are likely to be the change in owners' equity for the annual earnings or loss and the declaration of dividends, if any. Closely held corporations rarely pay dividends. The amount of time spent verifying owners' equity is frequently minimal for closely held corporations, even though the auditor must test the existing corporate records.

For publicly held corporations, the verification of owners' equity is more complex due to the larger numbers of shareholders and frequent changes in the individuals holding the stock. In this section the appropriate tests for verifying the major accounts—capital and

| Notes | | | | | Interest | | | |
| --- | --- | --- | --- | --- | --- | --- | --- | --- |
| Additions | Payments | Balance at End of Period | Rate | Paid to | Accrued at Beginning of Period | Expense | Paid | Accrued at End of Period |
| | 10000 (3) | -0- (4) | 9½% (4) | Maturity | 238 | 712 (6) | 950 (3) | -0- |
| 10000 (2) | | 10000 (4) | 10% (4) | Maturity | | 250 (6) | | 250 |
| 10000 (2) | | 10000 (4) | 10% (4) | Maturity | | 167 (6) | | 167 |
| 20000 | 10000 | 20000 (5) | | | 238 (7) | 1129 | 950 | 417 |
| ∧∧ | ∧∧ | ∧∧ x | | | ∧∧ | ∧∧ | | ∧∧ x |

common stock, paid-in capital in excess of par, retained earnings, and the related dividends—in a publicly held corporation are discussed. The other accounts in owners' equity are verified in much the same way as these.

## Overview of Accounts

An overview of the specific owners' equity accounts discussed in this section is given in Figure 20-6 on page 683.

## Objectives

The objectives of the audit of owners' equity are to determine whether:

- The internal controls over capital stock and related dividends are adequate.
- Owners' equity transactions are recorded properly, as defined by the six transaction-related audit objectives.
- Owners' equity balances are properly presented and disclosed as defined by the balance-related audit objectives for owners' equity accounts (rights/ obligations and realizable value are not applicable).

## Internal Controls

Several important internal controls are of concern to the independent auditor in owners' equity: proper authorization of transactions, proper record keeping, adequate segregation of duties between maintaining owners' equity records and handling cash and stock certificates, and the use of an independent registrar and stock transfer agent.

**Proper Authorization of Transactions** Since each owners' equity transaction is typically material, many of these transactions must be approved by the board of directors. The following types of owners' equity transactions usually require specific authorization.

***Issuance of Capital Stock*** The authorization includes the type of the equity to issue (such as preferred or common stock), number of shares to issue, par value of the stock, privileged condition for any stock other than common, and date of the issue.

**TABLE 20-2**

**Balance-Related Audit Objectives and Tests of Details of Balances for Notes Payable and Interest**

| **Balance-Related Audit Objective** | **Common Tests of Details of Balances Procedures** | **Comments** |
|---|---|---|
| Notes payable in the notes payable schedule agree with the client's notes payable register or master file, and the total is correctly added and agrees with the general ledger (detail tie-in). | Foot the notes payable list for notes payable and accrued interest.<br>Trace the totals to the general ledger.<br>Trace the individual notes payable to the master file. | Frequently, these are done on a 100 percent basis because of the small population size. |
| Notes payable in the schedule exist (existence). | Confirm notes payable.<br>Examine duplicate copy of notes for authorization.<br>Examine corporate minutes for loan approval. | The existence objective is not as important as completeness or accuracy. |
| Existing notes payable are included in the notes payable schedule (completeness). | Examine notes paid after year-end to determine whether they were liabilities at the balance sheet date.<br>Obtain a *standard bank confirmation* that includes specific reference to the existence of notes payable from all banks with which the client does business. (Bank confirmations are discussed more fully in Chapter 21.)<br>Review the *bank reconciliation* for new notes credited directly to the bank account by the bank. (Bank reconciliations are also discussed more fully in Chapter 21.)<br>Obtain confirmations from creditors who have held notes from the client in the past and are not currently included in the notes payable schedule. This is the same concept as a "zero balance" confirmation in accounts payable.<br>Obtain a standard confirmation for secured notes under the Uniform Commercial Code. Figure 20-4 (page 681) is an example of this type of confirmation.<br>Analyze interest expense to uncover a payment to a creditor who is not included in the notes payable schedule. This procedure is automatically done if the schedule is similar to the one in Figure 20-3 because all interest payments are reconciled with the general ledger.<br>Examine paid notes for cancellation to make sure they are not still outstanding. They should be maintained in the client's files.<br>Review the minutes of the board of directors' meetings for authorized but unrecorded notes. | This objective is important for uncovering both errors and fraud. The first three of these procedures are done on most audits. The others are frequently done only when internal controls are weak. |
| Notes payable and accrued interest on the schedule are accurate (accuracy). | Examine duplicate copies of notes for principal and interest rates.<br>Confirm notes payable, interest rates, and last date for which interest has been paid with holders of notes.<br>Recalculate accrued interest. | In some cases it may be necessary to calculate, using present-value techniques, the imputed interest rates, or the principal amount of the note. An example is when equipment is acquired for a note. |
| Notes payable in the schedule are properly classified (classification). | Examine due dates on duplicate copies of notes to determine whether all or part of the notes are a noncurrent liability.<br>Review notes to determine whether any are related party notes or accounts payable. | |

*[continued]*

**TABLE 20-2**

**Balance-Related Audit Objectives and Tests of Details of Balances for Notes Payable and Interest** *[continued]*

| Balance-Related Audit Objective | Common Tests of Details of Balances Procedures | Comments |
|---|---|---|
| Notes payable are included in the proper period (cutoff). | Examine duplicate copies of notes to determine whether notes were dated on or before the balance sheet date. | Notes should be included as current-period liabilities when dated on or before the balance sheet date. |
| The company has an obligation to pay the notes payable (obligations). | Examine notes to determine whether the company has obligations for payment. | |
| Notes payable, interest expense, and accrued interest are properly presented and disclosed (presentation and disclosure). | Examine duplicate copies of notes.<br>Confirm notes payable.<br>Examine notes, minutes, and bank confirmations for restrictions.<br>Examine balance sheet for proper presentation and disclosure of noncurrent portions, related parties, assets pledged as security for notes, and restrictions resulting from notes payable. | Proper financial statement presentation, including footnote disclosure, is an important consideration for notes payable. |

**FIGURE 20-4**

**Standard Confirmation**

Uniform Commercial Code - REQUEST FOR INFORMATION OR COPIES - Form UCC-11

IMPORTANT - Read instructions on back before filling out form

REQUEST FOR COPIES OR INFORMATION. Present in DUPLICATE to Filing Officer.

| 1 Debtor (Last Name First) and Address | Party requesting information or copies (Name and Address) | For Filing Officer, Date, Time, No.—Filing Office |
|---|---|---|
| | | |

☐ INFORMATION REQUEST ☐ COPY REQUEST

Filing officer please furnish certificate showing whether there is on file as of ________________, 19_____ at ________________ _____M., any presently effective financing statement naming the above debtor(s) and any statement of assignment thereof, and if there is, giving the date and hour of filing of each such statement and the name(s) and address(es) of each secured party(ies) therein. The statutory fee is enclosed.

Filing officer please furnish exact copies of each page of financing staements and statements of assignment listed below, which are on file with your office. Enclosed is $__________ fee for copies requested. In case any of said statements contain more than one page the undersigned agrees to pay the statutory fee for each additional page payable in advance.

DATE ____________________ (Signature of Requesting Party) ____________________

| File No. | Date and Hour of Filing. | Name(s) and Address(es) of Secured Party(ies) and Assignee(s), if any. |
|---|---|---|
| | | |
| | | |
| | | |
| | | |
| | | |

CERTIFICATE: The undersigned filing officer hereby certifies that:

☐ the above listing is a record of all presently effective financing statements and statements of assignment which name the above debtor(s) and which are on file in my office as of ________________________, 19_____ at ____________ M.

☐ the attached ____________ pages are true and exact copies of all available financing statements or statements of assignment listed in the above request.

Date ____________________ Signature of Filing Officer ____________________

COPY 1 STANDARD FORM NEW YORK STATE FORM UCC-11 Approved by New York Secretary of State

**FIGURE 20-5**

**Types of Audit Tests for the Capital Acquisition and Repayment Cycle—Notes Payable (See Figure 20-2 on page 676 for accounts)**

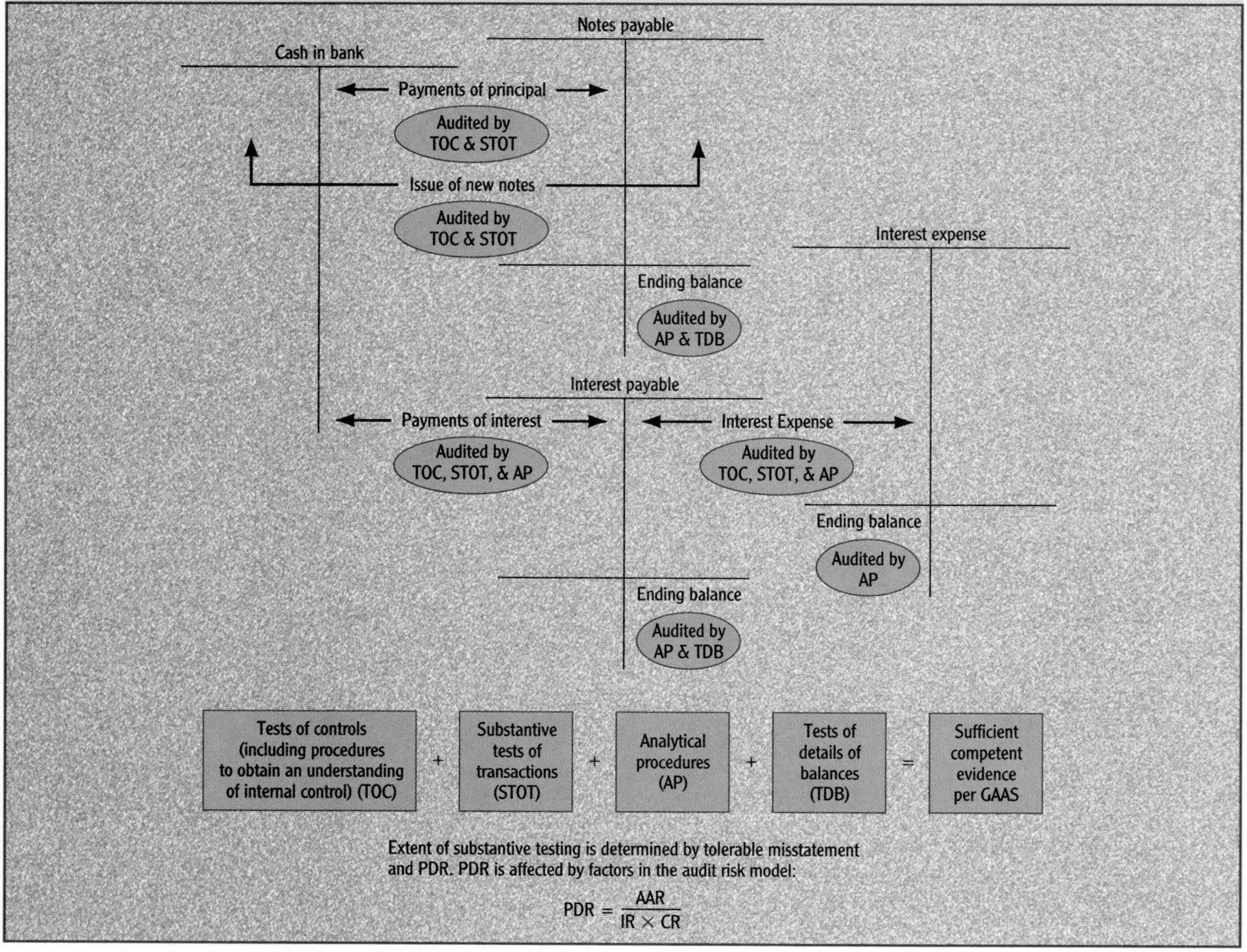


***Repurchase of Capital Stock*** The repurchase of common or preferred shares, the timing of the repurchase, and the amount to pay for the shares should all be approved by the board of directors.

***Declaration of Dividends*** The board of directors should authorize the form of the dividends (such as cash or stock), the amount of the dividend per share, and the record and payment dates of the dividends.

**Proper Record Keeping and Segregation of Duties** When a company maintains its own records of stock transactions and outstanding stock, the internal controls must be adequate to ensure that the actual owners of the stock are recognized in the corporate records, the correct amount of dividends is paid to the stockholders owning the stock as of the dividend record date, and the potential for misappropriation of assets is minimized. The proper assignment of personnel and adequate record-keeping procedures are useful controls for these purposes.

The most important procedures for preventing misstatements in owners' equity are (1) well-defined policies for preparing stock certificates and recording capital stock transactions and (2) independent internal verification of information in the records. The client must

**FIGURE 20-6**

**Owners' Equity and Dividend Accounts**

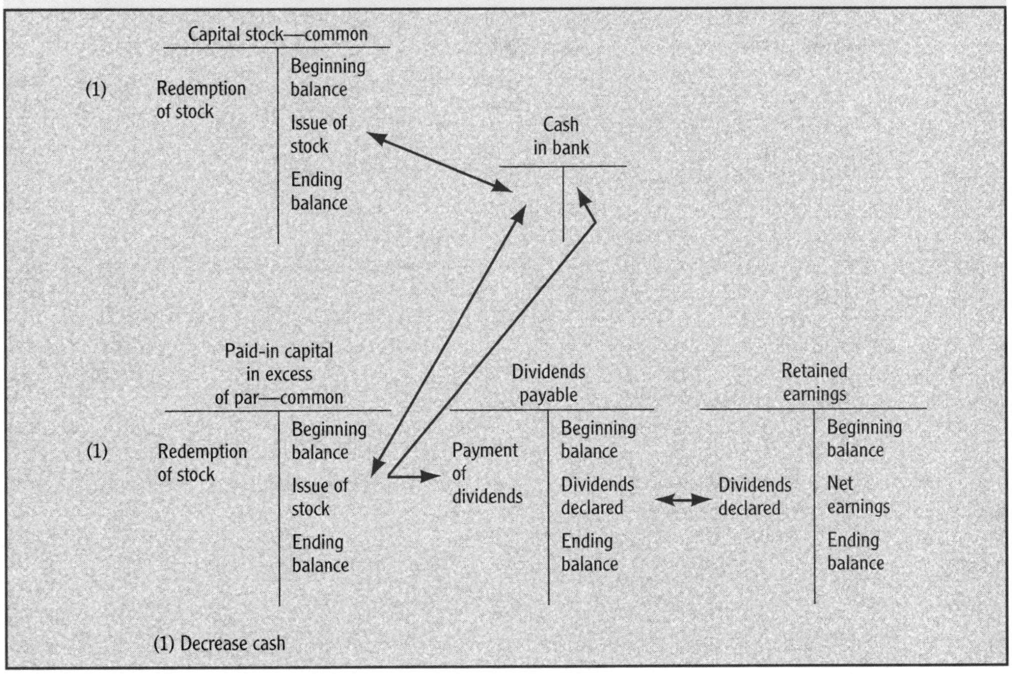


be certain when issuing and recording capital stock that both the state laws governing corporations and the requirements in the corporate charter are being complied with. For example, the par value of the stock, the number of shares the company is authorized to issue, and the existence of state taxes on the issue of capital stock all affect issuance and recording.

A control over capital stock used by most companies is the maintenance of stock certificate books and a shareholders' capital stock master file. A *capital stock certificate book* is a record of the issuance and repurchase of capital stock for the life of the corporation. The record for a capital stock transaction includes such information as the certificate number, the number of shares issued, the name of the person to whom it was issued, and the issue date. When shares are repurchased, the capital stock certificate book should include the cancelled certificates and the date of their cancellation. A *shareholders' capital stock master file* is the record of the outstanding shares at any given time. The master file acts as a check on the accuracy of the capital stock certificate book and the common stock balance in the general ledger. It is also used as the basis for the payment of dividends.

The disbursement of cash for the payment of dividends should be controlled in much the same manner as has been described in Chapter 16 for the preparation and payment of payroll. Dividend checks should be prepared from the capital stock certificate book by someone who is not responsible for maintaining the capital stock records. After the checks are prepared, it is desirable to have an independent verification of the stockholders' names and the amount of the checks and a reconciliation of the total amount of the dividend checks with the total dividends authorized in the minutes. The use of a separate *imprest dividend account* is desirable to prevent the payment of a larger amount of dividends than was authorized.

**Independent Registrar and Stock Transfer Agent** Any company whose stock is listed on a securities exchange is required to engage an *independent registrar* as a control to prevent the improper issue of stock certificates. The responsibility of an independent registrar is to make sure that stock is issued by a corporation in accordance with the capital stock provisions in the corporate charter and the authorization of the board of directors. The registrar is responsible for signing all newly issued stock certificates and making sure that old certificates are received and cancelled before a replacement certificate is issued when there is a change in the ownership of the stock.

Most large corporations also employ the services of a *stock transfer agent* for the purpose of maintaining the stockholder records, including those documenting transfers of stock ownership. The employment of a transfer agent not only serves as a control over the stock records by putting them in the hands of an independent organization but reduces the cost of record keeping by the use of a specialist. Many companies also have the transfer agent disburse cash dividends to shareholders, thereby further improving internal control.

## Audit of Capital Stock and Paid-in Capital

**OBJECTIVE 20-4**
**Design and perform tests of controls, substantive tests of transactions, and tests of details of balances for capital stock and retained earnings.**

There are four main concerns in auditing capital stock and paid-in capital in excess of par:

- Existing capital stock transactions are recorded (completeness).
- Recorded capital stock transactions exist and are accurately recorded (existence and accuracy).
- Capital stock is accurately recorded (accuracy).
- Capital stock is properly presented and disclosed (presentation and disclosure).

The first two concerns involve tests of controls and substantive tests of transactions, and the last two, tests of details of balances.

**Existing Capital Stock Transactions Are Recorded** This objective is easily satisfied when a registrar or transfer agent is used. The auditor can confirm with them whether any capital stock transactions occurred and the accuracy of existing transactions. Review of the minutes of the board of directors' meetings, especially near the balance sheet date, and examination of client-held stock record books are also useful to uncover issuances and repurchases of capital stock.

**Recorded Capital Stock Transactions Exist and Are Accurately Recorded** The issuance of new capital stock for cash, the merger with another company through an exchange of stock, donated shares, and the purchase of treasury shares each require extensive auditing. Regardless of the controls in existence, it is normal practice to verify all capital stock transactions because of their materiality and permanence in the records. Existence can ordinarily be tested by examining the minutes of the board of directors' meetings for proper authorization.

Accurate recording of capital stock transactions for cash can be readily verified by confirming the amount with the transfer agent and tracing the amount of the recorded capital stock transactions to cash receipts. (In the case of treasury stock, the amounts are traced to the cash disbursements journal.) In addition, the auditor must verify whether the correct amounts were credited to capital stock and paid-in capital in excess of par by referring to the corporate charter to determine the par or stated value of the capital stock.

When capital stock transactions involve stock dividends, acquisition of property for stock, mergers, or similar noncash transfers, the verification of amounts may be considerably more difficult. For these types of transactions, the auditor must be certain that the client has correctly computed the amount of the capital stock issue in accordance with generally accepted accounting principles. For example, in the audit of a major merger transaction, the auditor has to evaluate whether the transaction is a purchase or a pooling of interests. Frequently, considerable research is necessary to determine which accounting treatment is correct for the existing circumstances. After the auditor reaches a conclusion as to the appropriate method, it is necessary to verify that the amounts were correctly computed.

**Capital Stock Is Accurately Recorded** The ending balance in the capital stock account is verified by first determining the number of shares outstanding at the balance sheet date. A confirmation from the transfer agent is the simplest way to obtain this information. When no transfer agent exists, the auditor must rely on examining the stock records and accounting for all shares outstanding in the stock certificate books, examining all cancelled certificates, and accounting for blank certificates. After the auditor is satisfied that the number of shares outstanding is correct, the recorded par value in the capital account can be verified by multiplying the number of shares by the par value of the stock. The ending balance in the capital in excess of par account is a residual amount. It is audited by verifying the amount of recorded transactions during the year and adding them to or subtracting them from the beginning balance in the account.

A major consideration in the accuracy of capital stock is verifying whether the number of shares used in the calculation of earnings per share is accurate. It is easy to determine the correct number of shares to use in the calculation when there is only one class of stock and a small number of capital stock transactions. The problem becomes much more complex when there are convertible securities, stock options, or stock warrants outstanding. A thorough understanding of APB 15 is important before the number of primary and fully diluted shares can be verified.

**Capital Stock Is Properly Presented and Disclosed** The most important sources of information for determining proper presentation and disclosure are the corporate charter, the minutes of board of directors' meetings, and the auditors' analysis of capital stock transactions. The auditor should determine that there is a proper description of each class of stock, including such information as the number of shares issued and outstanding and any special rights of an individual class. The proper presentation and disclosure of stock options, stock warrants, and convertible securities should also be verified by examining legal documents or other evidence of the provisions of these agreements.

## Audit of Dividends

The emphasis in the audit of dividends is on the transactions rather than the ending balance. The exception is when there are dividends payable.

The six transaction-related audit objectives for transactions are relevant for dividends. But typically dividends are audited on a 100 percent basis and cause few problems. The following are the most important objectives, including those concerning dividends payable:

- Recorded dividends exist (existence).
- Existing dividends are recorded (completeness).
- Dividends are accurately recorded (accuracy).
- Dividends as paid to stockholders exist (existence).
- Dividends payable are recorded (completeness).
- Dividends payable are accurately recorded (accuracy).

Existence of recorded dividends can be checked by examining the minutes of board of directors' meetings for authorization of the amount of the dividend per share and the dividend date. When the auditor examines the board of directors' minutes for dividends declared, the auditor should be alert to the possibility of unrecorded dividends declared, particularly shortly before the balance sheet date. A closely related audit procedure is to review the permanent audit working paper file to determine if there are restrictions on the payment of dividends in bond indenture agreements or preferred stock provisions.

The accuracy of a dividend declaration can be audited by recomputing the amount on the basis of the dividend per share and the number of shares outstanding. If the client uses a transfer agent to disburse dividends, the total can be traced to a cash disbursement entry to the agent and also confirmed.

When a client keeps its own dividend records and pays the dividends itself, the auditor can verify the total amount of the dividend by recalculation and reference to cash disbursed. In addition, it is necessary to verify whether the payment was made to the stockholders who owned the stock as of the dividend record date. The auditor can test this by selecting a sample of recorded dividend payments and tracing the payee's name on the cancelled check to the dividend records to make sure that the payee was entitled to the dividend. At the same time, the amount and the authenticity of the dividend check can be verified.

Tests of dividends payable should be done in conjunction with declared dividends. Any unpaid dividend should be included as a liability.

## Audit of Retained Earnings

For most companies, the only transactions involving retained earnings are net earnings for the year and dividends declared. But there may also be corrections of prior-period earnings, prior-period adjustments charged or credited directly to retained earnings, and the setting up or elimination of appropriations of retained earnings.

The starting point for the audit of retained earnings is an analysis of retained earnings for the entire year. The audit schedule showing the analysis, which is usually a part of the permanent file, includes a description of every transaction affecting the account.

The audit of the credit to retained earnings for net income for the year (or the debit for a loss) is accomplished by simply tracing the entry in retained earnings to the net earnings figure on the income statement. The performance of this procedure must, of course, take place fairly late in the audit after all adjusting entries affecting net earnings have been completed.

An important consideration in auditing debits and credits to retained earnings other than net earnings and dividends is determining whether the transactions should have been included. For example, prior-period adjustments can be included in retained earnings only if they satisfy the requirements of APB opinions and FASB statements.

After the auditor is satisfied that the recorded transactions are appropriately classified as retained earnings transactions, the next step is to decide whether they are accurately recorded. The audit evidence necessary to determine accuracy depends on the nature of the transactions. If there is a requirement for an appropriation of retained earnings for a bond sinking fund, the correct amount of the appropriation can be determined by examining the bond indenture agreement. If there is a major loss charged to retained earnings because of a material nonrecurring abandonment of a plant, the evidence needed to determine the amount of the loss could include significant numbers of documents and records of the plant.

Another important consideration in the audit of retained earnings is evaluating whether there are any transactions that should have been included but were not. If a stock dividend was declared, for instance, the market value of the securities issued should be capitalized by a debit to retained earnings and a credit to capital stock. Similarly, if the financial statements include appropriations of retained earnings, the auditor should evaluate whether it is still necessary to have the appropriation as of the balance sheet date. As an example, an appropriation of retained earnings for a bond sinking fund should be eliminated by crediting retained earnings after the bond has been paid off.

The primary concern in determining whether retained earnings is correctly presented and disclosed in the financial statements is the existence of any restrictions on the payment of dividends. Frequently, agreements with bankers, stockholders, and other creditors prohibit or limit the amount of dividends the client can pay. These restrictions must be disclosed in the footnotes to the financial statements.

## Summary

Figure 20-7 illustrates the major accounts related to owners' equity in the capital acquisition and repayment cycle and the types of audit tests used to audit these accounts. This figure also shows how the audit risk model discussed in Chapter 8 relates to the audit of these accounts in the cycle.

**FIGURE 20-7**

**Types of Audit Tests for the Capital Acquisition and Repayment Cycle—Owners' Equity (See Figure 20-6 on page 683 for accounts)**

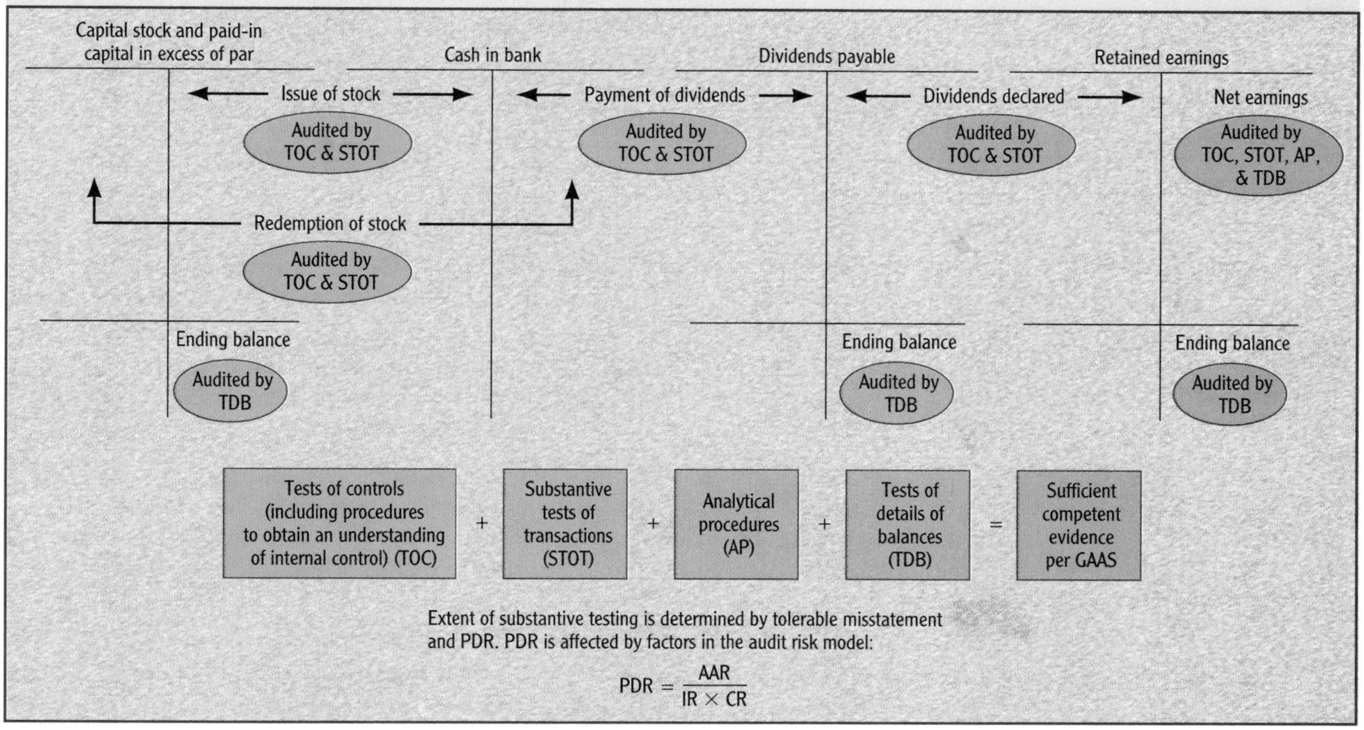


## ESSENTIAL TERMS

**Capital acquisition and repayment cycle**—the transaction cycle that involves the acquisition of capital resources in the form of interest-bearing debt and owners' equity, and the repayment of the capital

**Capital stock certificate book**—a record of the issuance and repurchase of capital stock for the life of the corporation

**Closely held corporation**—corporation whose stock is not publicly traded; typically, there are only a few shareholders and few, if any, capital stock account transactions during the year

**Independent registrar**—outside person engaged by a corporation to make sure that its stock is issued in accordance with capital stock provisions in the corporate charter and authorizations by the board of directors; required by the SEC for publicly held corporations

**Note payable**—a legal obligation to a creditor, which may be unsecured or secured by assets

**Publicly held corporation**—corporation whose stock is publicly traded; typically, there are many shareholders and frequent changes in the ownership of the stock

**Stock transfer agent**—outside person engaged by a corporation to maintain the stockholder records, and often to disburse cash dividends

## REVIEW QUESTIONS

**20-1 (Objective 20-1)** List four examples of interest-bearing liability accounts commonly found in balance sheets. What characteristics do these liabilities have in common? How do they differ?

**20-2 (Objectives 20-1, 20-2)** Why are liability accounts included in the capital acquisition and repayment cycle audited differently from accounts payable?

**20-3 (Objective 20-2)** It is common practice to audit the balance in notes payable in conjunction with the audit of interest expense and interest payable. Explain the advantages of this approach.

**20-4 (Objective 20-2)** Which internal controls should the auditor be most concerned about in the audit of notes payable? Explain the importance of each.

**20-5 (Objective 20-2)** Which analytical procedures are most important in verifying notes payable? Which types of misstatements can the auditor uncover by the use of these tests?

**20-6 (Objective 20-2)** Why is it more important to search for unrecorded notes payable than for unrecorded notes receivable? List several audit procedures that the auditor can use to uncover unrecorded notes payable.

**20-7 (Objective 20-2)** What is the primary purpose of analyzing interest expense? Given this purpose, what primary considerations should the auditor keep in mind when doing the analysis?

**20-8 (Objective 20-2)** Distinguish between the (a) tests of controls and substantive tests of transactions and (b) tests of details of balances for liability accounts in the capital acquisition and repayment cycle.

**20-9 (Objective 20-2)** List two types of restrictions long-term creditors often put on companies when granting them a loan. How can the auditor find out about these restrictions?

**20-10 (Objective 20-3)** What are the primary objectives in the audit of owners' equity accounts?

**20-11 (Objectives 20-3, 20-4)** Evaluate the following statement: "The corporate charter and the bylaws of a company are legal documents; therefore, they should not be examined by the auditors. If the auditor wants information about these documents, an attorney should be consulted."

**20-12 (Objective 20-3)** What are the major internal controls over owners' equity?

**20-13 (Objective 20-3)** How does the audit of owners' equity for a closely held corporation differ from that for a publicly held corporation? In what respects are there no significant differences?

**20-14 (Objective 20-3)** Describe the duties of a stock registrar and a transfer agent. How does the use of their services affect the client's internal controls?

**20-15 (Objective 20-3)** What kinds of information can be confirmed with a transfer agent?

**20-16 (Objective 20-4)** Evaluate the following statement: "The most important audit procedure to verify dividends for the year is a comparison of a random sample of cancelled dividend checks with a dividend list that has been prepared by management as of the dividend record date."

**20-17 (Objective 20-4)** If a transfer agent disburses dividends for a client, explain how the audit of dividends declared and paid is affected. What audit procedures are necessary to verify dividends paid when a transfer agent is used?

**20-18 (Objective 20-4)** What should be the major emphasis in auditing the retained earnings account? Explain your answer.

**20-19 (Objectives 20-3, 20-4)** Explain the relationship between the audit of owners' equity and the calculations of earnings per share. What are the main auditing considerations in verifying the earnings per share figure?

## MULTIPLE CHOICE QUESTIONS FROM CPA EXAMINATIONS

**20-20 (Objective 20-2)** The following multiple-choice questions concern interest-bearing liabilities. Choose the best response.

a. The audit program for long-term debt should include steps that require the
   (1) verification of the existence of the bondholders.
   (2) examination of any bond trust indenture.
   (3) inspection of the accounts payable master file.
   (4) investigation of credits to the bond interest income account.

b. During the year under audit, a company has completed a private placement of a substantial amount of bonds. Which of the following is the *most* important step in the auditor's program for the audit of bonds payable?
   (1) Confirming the amount issued with the bond trustee.
   (2) Tracing the cash received from the issue to the accounting records.
   (3) Examining the bond records maintained by the transfer agent.
   (4) Recomputing the annual interest cost and the effective yield.

c. Several years ago, Conway, Inc., secured a conventional real estate mortgage loan. Which of the following audit procedures would be *least* likely to be performed by an auditor auditing the mortgage balance?
   (1) Examine the current year's cancelled checks.
   (2) Review the mortgage amortization schedule.
   (3) Inspect public records of lien balances.
   (4) Recompute mortgage interest expense.

**20-21 (Objectives 20-2, 20-3, 20-4)** The following questions concern the audit of accounts in the capital acquisition and repayment cycle. Choose the best response.

a. During an audit of a publicly held company, the auditor should obtain written confirmation regarding debenture transactions from the
   (1) debenture holders.
   (2) client's attorney.
   (3) internal auditors.
   (4) trustee.

b. An audit program for the audit of the retained earnings account should include a step that requires verification of
   (1) market value used to charge retained earnings to account for a 2-for-1 stock split.
   (2) approval of the adjustment to the beginning balance as a result of a write-down of an account receivable.
   (3) authorization for both cash and stock dividends.
   (4) gain or loss resulting from disposition of treasury shares.

c. Where *no* independent stock transfer agents are employed and the corporation issues its own stocks and maintains stock records, cancelled stock certificates should
   (1) be defaced to prevent reissuance and attached to their corresponding stubs.
   (2) *not* be defaced, but segregated from other stock certificates and retained in a cancelled certificates file.
   (3) be destroyed to prevent fraudulent reissuance.
   (4) be defaced and sent to the secretary of state.

## DISCUSSION QUESTIONS AND PROBLEMS

**20-22 (Objective 20-2)** Items 1 through 6 are questions typically found in a standard internal control questionnaire used by auditors to obtain an understanding of internal control for notes payable. In using the questionnaire for a client, a "yes" response indicates a possible internal control, whereas a "no" indicates a potential weakness.

1. Are liabilities for notes payable incurred only after written authorization by a proper company official?
2. Is a notes payable master file maintained?
3. Is the individual who maintains the notes payable master file someone other than the person who approves the issue of new notes or handles cash?
4. Are paid notes cancelled and retained in the company files?
5. Is a periodic reconciliation made of the notes payable master file with the actual notes outstanding by an individual who does not maintain the master file?

6. Are interest expense and accrued interest recomputed periodically by an individual who does not record interest transactions?

### Required

a. For each of the preceding questions, state the purpose of the control.

b. For each of the preceding questions, identify the type of financial statement misstatement that could occur if the control were not in effect.

c. For each of the potential misstatements in part b, list an audit procedure that can be used to determine whether a material misstatement exists.

**20-23 (Objective 20-2)** The following are frequently performed audit procedures for the verification of bonds payable issued in previous years.

1. Obtain a copy of the bond indenture agreement and review its important provisions.
2. Determine that each of the bond indenture provisions has been met.
3. Analyze the general ledger account for bonds payable, interest expense, and unamortized bond discount or premium.
4. Test the client's calculations of interest expense, unamortized bond discount or premium, accrued interest, and bonds payable.
5. Obtain a confirmation from the bondholder.

### Required

a. State the purpose of each of the five audit procedures listed.

b. List the provisions for which the auditor should be alert in examining the bond indenture agreement.

c. For each provision listed in part b, explain how the auditor can determine whether its terms have been met.

d. Explain how the auditor should verify the unamortized bond discount or premium.

e. List the information that should be requested in the confirmation of bonds payable with the bondholder.

**20-24 (Objective 20-2)** In conducting an audit of a corporation that has a bond issue outstanding, the trust indenture is reviewed and a confirmation is obtained from the trustee.

### Required

List eight matters of importance to the auditor that might be found either in the indenture or in the confirmation obtained from the trustee. Explain briefly the reason for the auditor's interest in each of the items.*

**20-25 (Objective 20-2)** The Fox Company is a medium-sized industrial client that has been audited by your CPA firm for several years. The only interest-bearing debt owed by Fox Company is $200,000 in long-term notes payable held by the bank. The notes were issued three years previously and will mature in six more years. Fox Company is highly profitable, has no pressing needs for additional financing, and has excellent internal controls over the recording of loan transactions and related interest costs.

### Required

a. Describe the auditing that you think would be necessary for notes payable and related interest accounts in these circumstances.

b. How would your answer differ if Fox Company were unprofitable, had a need for additional financing, and had weak internal controls?

**20-26 (Objective 20-2)** The ending general ledger balance of $186,000 in notes payable for the Sterling Manufacturing Company is made up of twenty notes to eight different pay-

*AICPA adapted.

ees. The notes vary in duration anywhere from 30 days to 2 years, and in amount from $1,000 to $10,000. In some cases the notes were issued for cash loans; in other cases the notes were issued directly to vendors for the acquisition of inventory or equipment. The use of relatively short-term financing is necessary because all existing properties are pledged for mortgages. Nevertheless, there is still a serious cash shortage.

Record-keeping procedures for notes payable are not good, considering the large number of loan transactions. There is no notes payable master file or independent verification of ending balances; however, the notes payable records are maintained by a secretary who does not have access to cash.

The audit has been done by the same CPA firm for several years. In the current year, the following procedures were performed to verify notes payable:

1. Obtain a list of notes payable from the client, foot the notes payable balances on the list, and trace the total to the general ledger.
2. Examine duplicate copies of notes for all outstanding notes included on the listing. Compare the name of the lender, amount, and due date on the duplicate copy with the list.
3. Obtain a confirmation from lenders for all listed notes payable. The confirmation should include the due date of the loan, the amount, and interest payable at the balance sheet date.
4. Recompute accrued interest on the list for all notes. The information for determining the correct accrued interest is to be obtained from the duplicate copy of the note. Foot the accrued interest amounts and trace the balance to the general ledger.

## Required

a. What should be the emphasis in the verification of notes payable in this situation? Explain.

b. State the purpose of each of the four audit procedures listed.

c. Evaluate whether each of the four audit procedures was necessary. Evaluate the sample size for each procedure.

d. List other audit procedures that should be performed in the audit of notes payable in these circumstances.

**20-27 (Objective 20-2)** The following covenants are extracted from the indenture of a bond issue. The indenture provides that failure to comply with its terms in any respect automatically advances the due date of the loan to the date of noncompliance (the regular date is 20 years hence). List any audit steps or reporting requirements you feel should be taken or recognized in connection with each one of the following.

a. The debtor company shall endeavor to maintain a working capital ratio of 2 to 1 at all times, and, in any fiscal year following a failure to maintain said ratio, the company shall restrict compensation of officers to a total of $100,000. Officers for this purpose shall include chairman of the board of directors, president, all vice presidents, secretary, and treasurer.

b. The debtor company shall keep all property that is security for this debt insured against loss by fire to the extent of 100 percent of its actual value. Policies of insurance comprising this protection shall be filed with the trustee.

c. The debtor company shall pay all taxes legally assessed against property that is security for this debt within the time provided by law for payment without penalty, and shall deposit receipted tax bills or equally acceptable evidence of payment of same with the trustee.

d. A sinking fund shall be deposited with the trustee by semiannual payments of $300,000, from which the trustee shall, in his discretion, purchase bonds of this issue.*

*AICPA adapted.

**20-28 (Objective 20-2)** The Redford Corporation took out a 20-year mortgage on June 15, 1997, for $2,600,000 and pledged its only manufacturing building and the land on which the building stands as collateral. Each month subsequent to the issue of the mortgage, a payment of $20,000 was paid to the mortgagor. You are in charge of the current-year audit for Redford, which has a balance sheet date of December 31, 1997. The client has been audited previously by your CPA firm, but this is the first time Redford Corporation has had a mortgage.

### Required

a. Explain why it is desirable to prepare a working paper for the permanent file for the mortgage. What type of information should be included in the working paper?

b. Explain why the audit of mortgage payable, interest expense, and interest payable should all be done together.

c. List the audit procedures that should ordinarily be performed to verify the issue of the mortgage, the balance in the mortgage and interest payable accounts at December 31, 1997, and the balance in interest expense for the year 1997.

**20-29 (Objectives 20-3, 20-4)** Items 1 through 6 are common questions found in internal control questionnaires used by auditors to obtain an understanding of internal control for owners' equity. In using the questionnaire for a client, a "yes" response indicates a possible internal control, whereas a "no" indicates a potential weakness.

1. Does the company use the services of an independent registrar or transfer agent?
2. Are issues and retirements of stock authorized by the board of directors?
3. If an independent registrar and transfer agent are not used:
   (a) Are unissued certificates properly controlled?
   (b) Are cancelled certificates mutilated to prevent their reuse?
4. Are common stock master files and stock certificate books periodically reconciled with the general ledger by an independent person?
5. Is an independent transfer agent used for disbursing dividends? If not, is an imprest dividend account maintained?
6. Are all entries in the owners' equity accounts authorized at the proper level in the organization?

### Required

a. For each of the preceding questions, state the purpose of the control.

b. For each of the preceding questions, identify the type of potential financial statement misstatements if the control is not in effect.

c. For each of the potential misstatements in part b, list an audit procedure that the auditor can use to determine whether a material misstatement exists.

**20-30 (Objectives 20-3, 20-4)** The following audit procedures are frequently performed by auditors in the verification of owners' equity:

1. Review the articles of incorporation and bylaws for provisions about owners' equity.
2. Review the minutes of the board of directors' meetings for the year for approvals related to owners' equity.
3. Analyze all owners' equity accounts for the year and document the nature of any recorded change in each account.
4. Account for all certificate numbers in the capital stock book for all shares outstanding.
5. Examine the stock certificate book for any stock that was cancelled.
6. Recompute earnings per share.
7. Review debt provisions and senior securities with respect to liquidation preferences, dividends in arrears, and restrictions on the payment of dividends or the issue of stock.

## Required

a. State the purpose of each of these seven audit procedures.

b. List the type of misstatements the auditors could uncover by the use of each audit procedure.

**20-31 (Objectives 20-3, 20-4)** You are engaged in the audit of a corporation whose records have not previously been audited by you. The corporation has both an independent transfer agent and a registrar for its capital stock. The transfer agent maintains the record of stockholders and the registrar checks that there is no overissue of stock. Signatures of both are required to validate certificates.

It has been proposed that confirmations be obtained from both the transfer agent and the registrar as to the stock outstanding at the balance sheet date. If such confirmations agree with the books, no additional work is to be performed as to capital stock.

If you agree that obtaining the confirmations as suggested would be sufficient in this case, give the justification for your position. If you do not agree, state specifically all additional steps you would take and explain your reasons for taking them.*

**20-32 (Objective 20-4)** The Rico Corporation is a medium-sized wholesaler of grocery products with 4,000 shares of stock outstanding to approximately twenty-five stockholders. Because of the age of several retired stockholders and the success of the company, management has decided to pay dividends six times a year. The amount of the bimonthly dividend per share varies depending on the profits, but it is ordinarily between $5 and $7 per share. The chief accountant, who is also a stockholder, prepares the dividend checks, records the checks in the dividend journal, and reconciles the bank account. Important controls include manual check signing by the president and the use of an imprest dividend bank account.

The auditor verifies the dividends by maintaining a schedule of the total shares of stock issued and outstanding in the permanent working papers. The total amount of stock outstanding is multiplied by the dividends per share authorized in the minutes to arrive at the current total dividend. This total is compared with the deposit that has been made to the imprest dividend account. Since the transfer of stock is infrequent, it is possible to verify dividends paid for the entire year in a comparatively short time.

## Required

a. Evaluate the usefulness of the approach followed by the auditor in verifying dividends in this situation. Your evaluation should include both the strengths and the weaknesses of the approach.

b. List other audit procedures that should be performed in verifying dividends in this situation. Explain the purpose of each procedure.

**20-33 (Objective 20-4)** You are a CPA engaged in an audit of the financial statements of Pate Corporation for the year ended December 31, 1996. The financial statements and records of Pate Corporation have not been audited by a CPA in prior years.

The stockholders' equity section of Pate Corporation's balance sheet at December 31, 1996, follows:

| | |
|---|---|
| *Stockholders' equity:* | |
| Capital stock—10,000 shares of $10 par value authorized; 5,000 shares issued and outstanding | $ 50,000 |
| Capital contributed in excess of par value of capital stock | 32,580 |
| Retained earnings | 47,320 |
| Total stockholders' equity | $129,900 |

*AICPA adapted.

Pate Corporation was founded in 1988. The corporation has ten stockholders and serves as its own registrar and transfer agent. There are no capital stock subscription contracts in effect.

### Required

a. Prepare the detailed audit program for the audit of the three accounts comprising the stockholders' equity section of Pate Corporation's balance sheet. (Do not include in the audit program the verification of the results of the current year's operations.)

b. After every other figure on the balance sheet has been audited, it might appear that the retained earnings figure is a balancing figure and requires no further verification. Why does the CPA verify retained earnings as he or she does the other figures on the balance sheet? Discuss. *

*AICPA adapted.

# 21

# AUDIT OF CASH BALANCES

## LEARNING OBJECTIVES

Thorough study of this chapter will enable you to

- **21-1** Describe the major types of cash accounts maintained by business entities.
- **21-2** Describe the relationship of cash in the bank to the various transaction cycles.
- **21-3** Design and perform audit tests of the general cash account.
- **21-4** Recognize when to extend audit tests of the general cash account to test further for material fraud.
- **21-5** Design and perform audit tests of the payroll bank account.
- **21-6** Design and perform audit tests of petty cash.

## SOCIETY EXPECTS A LOT FROM AUDITORS

Bert Sampson was the controller of Pardoe Manufacturing Company. From 1989 through 1994, Bert paid himself an extra $2 million in "bonuses." He did this by transferring funds from the general account, writing checks to himself from the payroll account, destroying the checks when received from the bank, and making entries directly into the Company's computer files to disguise the theft. Bert was able to do this because he had almost complete control of the Company's accounting process.

Jack Baker of Tramenier and Baker, CPAs, had been the partner on the Pardoe audit since the Company was started. Although the Company was relatively small and had limited segregation of duties, Baker found a good control environment due to strong management, competent personnel, a good budgeting and reporting system, and a history of audits with few audit adjustments. Accordingly, Baker assessed control risk at maximum and used a "substantive" approach to the audit. Baker applied tests of details of balances and analytical procedures to the year-end financial statements. He did no tests of controls or substantive tests of transactions.

Because Sampson had lost all of the $2 million and Pardoe had no fidelity bond insurance, the company sued Tramenier and Baker, CPAs, for the loss, claiming breach of contract. Baker's defense was that he had done the audit in accordance with generally accepted auditing standards.

The trial revolved around the testimony of two expert witnesses. The witness for the Company argued that even though the auditors took a substantive approach to the audit, they should have seen that Sampson had the opportunity to commit the theft, extended their audit, and found it.

The expert for the defense argued that a substantive audit approach is allowed by generally accepted auditing standards. Sampson manipulated the records so carefully that the substantive procedures of the various payroll accounts did not indicate that the theft had occurred. Since there were no "red flags" evident that would have caused the auditors to extend their tests, the audit was clearly satisfactory.

Throughout the testimony, both experts quoted various sections of generally accepted auditing standards. In some cases, the experts quoted the same sentences in support of opposing arguments. In addition to expert witness testimony, several staff on the audit testified. They were all well-educated, bright, knowledgeable, and impressive.

The jury found against the auditors, and Tramenier and Baker, CPAs, was required to pay approximately $2.3 million in damages. When jury members were interviewed about their decision, they indicated that they didn't really understand the technical nature of the arguments made by the expert witnesses, but it was apparent to them that the people who did the audit were extremely bright and competent. Accordingly, the jury members felt that *the auditors certainly had the ability to find the theft* and the fact that they didn't meant that they didn't perform up to their potential.

The audit of cash balances is the last audit area studied because the evidence accumulated for cash balances depends heavily on the results of the tests in all transaction cycles. For example, if the understanding of internal control and tests of controls and substantive tests of transactions in the acquisition and payment cycle lead the auditor to believe that it is appropriate to reduce assessed control risk to low, the auditor can reduce detailed tests of the ending balance in cash. If, however, the auditor concludes that assessed control risk should be higher, extensive year-end testing may be necessary.

## TYPES OF CASH ACCOUNTS

It is important to understand the different types of cash accounts because the auditing approach to each varies. The following are the major types of cash accounts.

### General Cash Account

**OBJECTIVE 21-1**
**Describe the major types of cash accounts maintained by business entities.**

The general account is the focal point of cash for most organizations because virtually all cash receipts and disbursements flow through this account. The disbursements for the acquisition and payment cycle are normally paid from this account, and the receipts of cash in the sales and collection cycle are deposited in the account. In addition, the deposits and disbursements for all other cash accounts are normally made through the general account. Most small companies have only one bank account—the general cash account.

### Imprest Payroll Account

As a means of improving internal control, many companies establish a separate imprest bank account for making payroll payments to employees. In an imprest payroll account, a fixed balance, such as $1,000, is maintained in a separate bank account. Immediately before each pay period, one check is drawn on the general cash account to deposit the total amount of the net payroll into the payroll account. After all payroll checks have cleared the imprest payroll account, the bank account should have a $1,000 balance. The only deposits into the account are for the weekly and semimonthly payroll, and the only disbursements are paychecks to employees. For companies with many employees, the use of an imprest payroll account can improve internal control and reduce the time needed to reconcile bank accounts.

### Branch Bank Account

For a company operating in multiple locations, it is frequently desirable to have a separate bank balance at each location. Branch bank accounts are useful for building public relations in local communities and permitting the centralization of operations at the branch level.

In some companies, the deposits and disbursements for each branch are made to a separate bank account, and the excess cash is periodically sent to the main office general bank account. The branch account in this instance is much like a general account, but at the branch level.

A somewhat different type of branch account consists of one bank account for receipts and a separate one for disbursements. All receipts are deposited in the branch bank, and the total is transferred to the general account periodically. The disbursement account is set up on an *imprest basis,* but in a different manner than an imprest payroll account. A fixed balance is maintained in the imprest account, and the authorized branch personnel use these funds for disbursements at their own discretion as long as the payments are consistent with company policy. When the cash balance has been depleted, an accounting is made to the home office and a reimbursement is made to the branch account from the general account *after* the expenditures have been approved. The use of an imprest branch bank account improves controls over receipts and disbursements.

### Imprest Petty Cash Fund

A petty cash fund is actually not a bank account, but it is sufficiently similar to cash on deposit to merit inclusion. It is used for small cash acquisitions that can be paid more conveniently and quickly by cash than by check, or for the convenience of employees in cashing personal or payroll checks. An imprest cash account is set up on the same basis as an imprest branch bank account, but the expenditures are normally for a much smaller amount. Typical expenses include minor office supplies, stamps, and small contributions to local charities. Usually a petty cash account does not exceed a few hundred dollars and may not be reimbursed more than once or twice each month.

### Cash Equivalents

Excess cash accumulated during certain parts of the operating cycle that will be needed in the reasonably near future is often invested in short-term, highly liquid cash equivalents. Examples include time deposits, certificates of deposit, and money market funds. Cash equivalents, which can be highly material, are included in the financial statements as a part of the cash account only if they are short-term investments that are readily convertible to known amounts of cash within a short time and there is insignificant risk of a change of value from interest rate changes. Marketable securities and longer-term interest-bearing investments are not cash equivalents.

**Summary** Figure 21-1 shows the relationship of general cash to the other cash accounts. All cash either originates from or is deposited in general cash. This chapter focuses on three types of accounts: the general cash account, the imprest payroll bank account, and the imprest petty cash fund. The others are similar to these and need not be discussed.

**FIGURE 21-1**

**Relationship of General Cash to Other Cash Accounts**

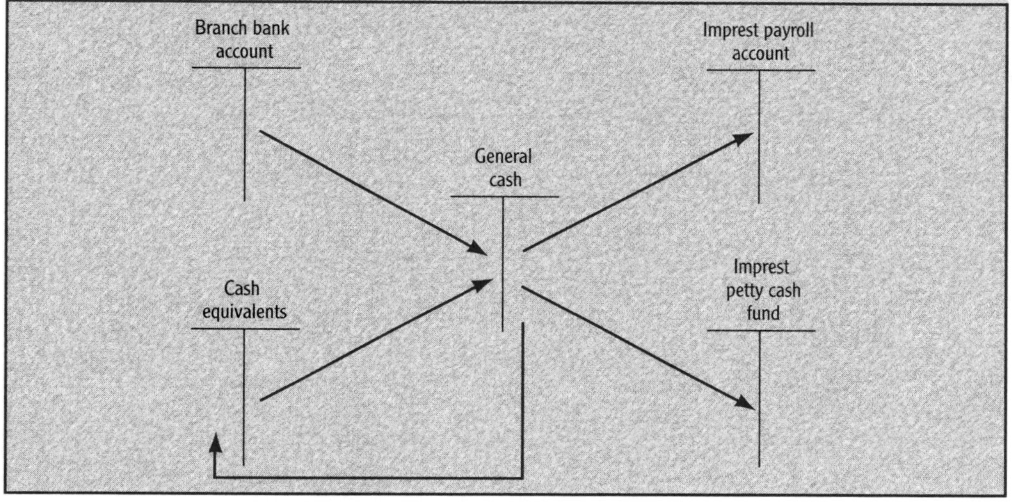


## CASH IN THE BANK AND TRANSACTION CYCLES

**OBJECTIVE 21-2**
**Describe the relationship of cash in the bank to the various transaction cycles.**

A brief discussion of the relationship between cash in the bank and the other transaction cycles serves a dual function: it clearly shows the importance of the tests of various transaction cycles to the audit of cash, and it aids in further understanding the integration of the different transaction cycles. Figure 21-2 on page 698 illustrates the relationships of the various transaction cycles, the focal point being the general cash account.

An examination of Figure 21-2 indicates why the general cash account is considered significant in almost all audits even when the ending balance is immaterial. The amount of cash *flowing* into and out of the cash account is frequently larger than for any other account in the financial statements. Furthermore, the susceptibility of cash to defalcation is greater than for other types of assets because most other assets must be converted to cash to make them usable.

**FIGURE 21-2**

**Relationships of Cash in the Bank and Transaction Cycles**

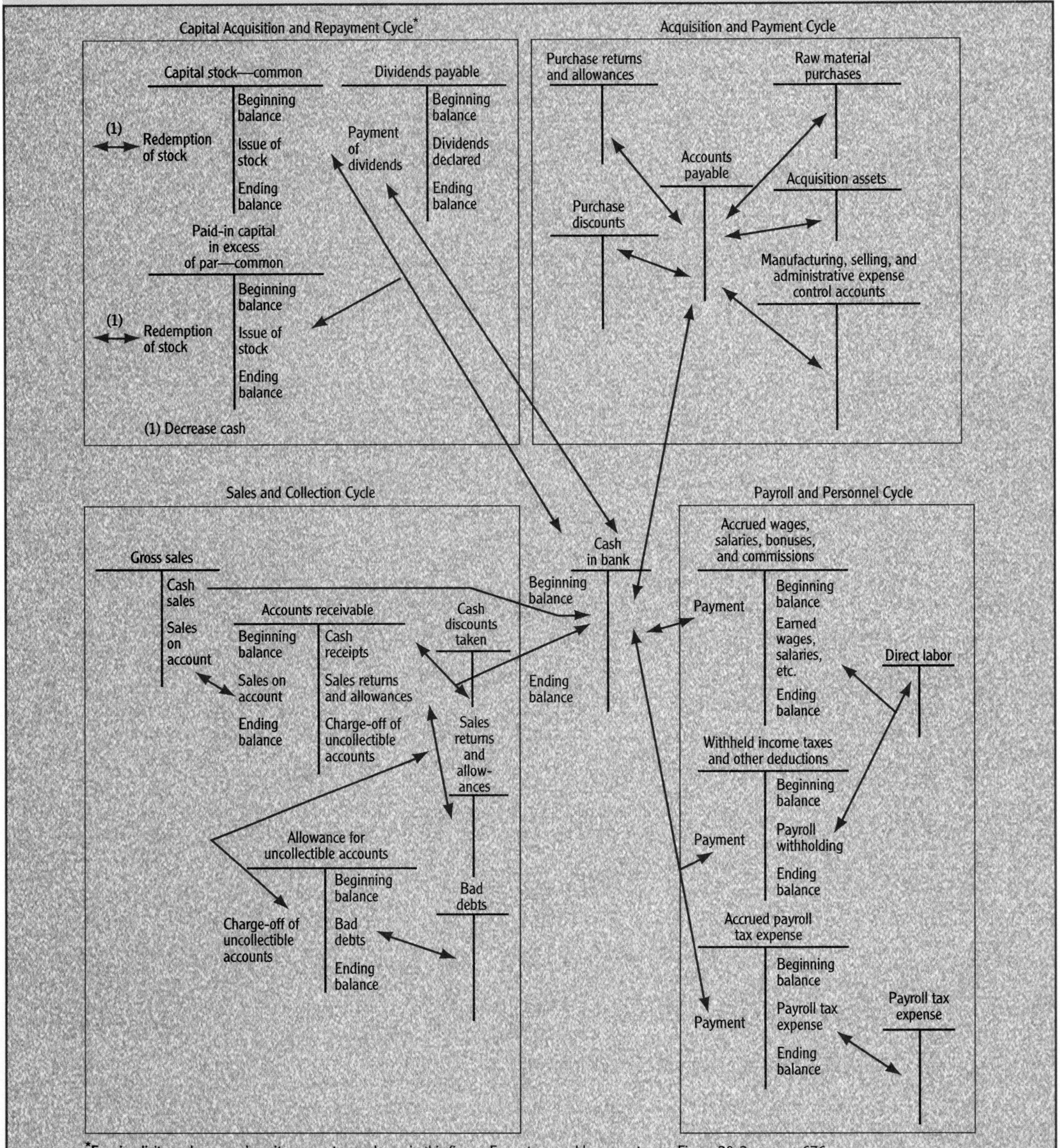


*For simplicity, only owners' equity accounts are shown in this figure. For notes payable accounts, see Figure 20-2 on page 676.

In the audit of cash, an important distinction should be made between verifying the client's reconciliation of the balance on the bank statement to the balance in the general ledger and verifying whether recorded cash in the general ledger correctly reflects all cash transactions that took place during the year. It is relatively easy to verify the client's reconciliation of the balance in the bank account to the general ledger, which is the primary subject of this chapter, but a significant part of the total audit of a company involves verifying whether cash transactions are properly recorded. For example, each of the following misstatements ultimately results in the improper payment of or the failure to receive cash, but none will normally be discovered as a part of the audit of the bank reconciliation:

- Failure to bill a customer
- Billing a customer at a lower price than called for by company policy
- A defalcation of cash by interception of cash receipts from customers before they are recorded; the account is charged off as a bad debt
- Duplicate payment of a vendor's invoice
- Improper payments of officers' personal expenditures
- Payment for raw materials that were not received
- Payment to an employee for more hours than he or she worked
- Payment of interest to a related party for an amount in excess of the going rate

If these misstatements are to be uncovered in the audit, their discovery must come about through the tests of controls and substantive tests of transactions that were discussed in the preceding chapters. The first three misstatements could be discovered as part of the audit of the sales and collection cycle, the next three in the audit of the acquisition and payment cycle, and the last two in the tests of the payroll and personnel cycle and the capital acquisition and repayment cycle, respectively.

Entirely different types of misstatements are normally discovered as a part of the tests of a bank reconciliation. For example,

- Failure to include a check that has not cleared the bank on the outstanding check list, even though it has been recorded in the cash disbursements journal
- Cash received by the client subsequent to the balance sheet date but recorded as cash receipts in the current year
- Deposits recorded as cash receipts near the end of the year, deposited in the bank in the same month, and included in the bank reconciliation as a deposit in transit
- Payments on notes payable debited directly to the bank balance by the bank but not entered in the client's records

The appropriate methods for discovering the preceding misstatements by testing the client's bank reconciliation will become apparent as we proceed. At this point it is important only that the reader distinguish between tests of controls and substantive tests of transactions that are related to the cash account and tests that determine whether the book balance reconciles to the bank balance.

## AUDIT OF THE GENERAL CASH ACCOUNT

**OBJECTIVE 21-3**
**Design and perform audit tests of the general cash account.**

On the trial balance of Hillsburg Hardware Co., on page 141, there is only one cash account. Notice, however, that all cycles, except inventory and warehousing, affect cash in the bank.

In testing the year-end balance in the general cash account, the auditor must accumulate sufficient evidence to evaluate whether cash, as stated on the balance sheet, is fairly stated and properly disclosed in accordance with six of the nine balance-related audit objectives used for all tests of details of balances. Rights to general cash, its classification on the balance sheet, and the realizable value of cash are not a problem.

The methodology for auditing year-end cash is essentially the same as for all other balance sheet accounts. The methodology is shown in Figure 21-3.

**FIGURE 21-3**

**Methodology for Designing Tests of Details of Balances for Cash in the Bank**

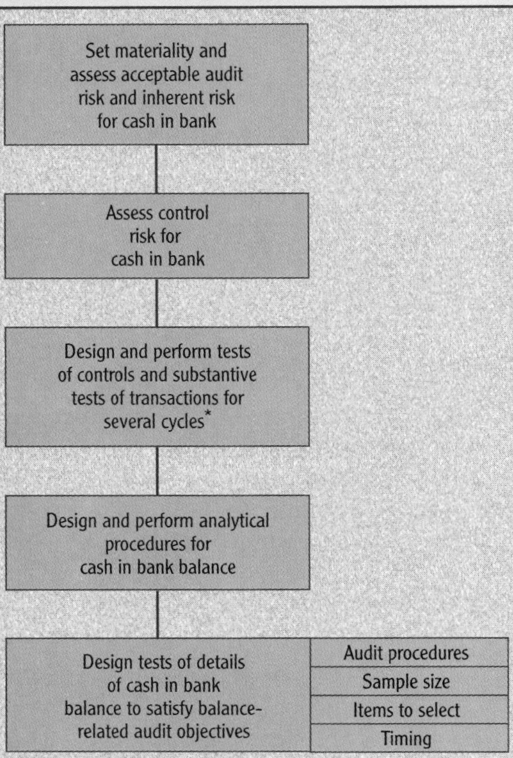


**Materiality Considerations**
The cash balance is immaterial on most audits, but the cash transactions affecting the balance are almost always extremely material. There is therefore often potential for material misstatement of cash.

**Inherent Risk Considerations**
Because cash is more susceptible to theft than other assets, there is high inherent risk for the existence objective. This objective is usually the focus in auditing cash balances. Typically, inherent risk is low for all other objectives.

**Control Risk Considerations**

- Internal control effectiveness over cash balances varies significantly for different companies. The most important internal control is independent bank reconciliations.
- Internal controls over cash receipts and disbursements are important considerations in the audit and were discussed in earlier chapters.

*Cycles affected include sales and collection, acquisition and payment, payroll and personnel, and capital acquisition and repayment.

## Internal Controls

Internal controls over year-end cash balances in the general account can be divided into two categories: *controls over the transaction cycles* affecting the recording of cash receipts and disbursements and *independent bank reconciliations.*

Controls affecting the recording of cash transactions have been discussed in preceding chapters. For example, in the acquisition and payment cycle, major controls include adequate segregation of duties between the check signing and accounts payable functions, signing of checks only by a properly authorized person, use of prenumbered checks printed on special paper, adequate control of blank and voided checks, careful review of supporting documentation by the check signer before checks are signed, and adequate internal verification. If controls affecting cash-related transactions are adequate, it is possible to reduce the audit tests for the year-end bank reconciliation.

A monthly *bank reconciliation* of the general bank account on a timely basis by someone independent of the handling or recording of cash receipts and disbursements is an essential control over the cash balance. The reconciliation is important to make sure that the books reflect the same cash balance as the actual amount of cash in the bank after considering reconciling items, but even more important, the *independent* reconciliation provides a unique opportunity for an internal verification of cash receipts and disbursements transactions. If the bank statements are received unopened by the reconciler and physical con-

**TABLE 21-1**

**Balance-Related Audit Objectives and Tests of Details of Balances for General Cash in the Bank**

| Balance-Related Audit Objective | Common Tests of Details of Balances Procedures | Comments |
|---|---|---|
| Cash in the bank as stated on the reconciliation foots correctly and agrees with the general ledger (detail tie-in). | Foot the outstanding check list and deposits in transit.<br>Prove the bank reconciliation as to additions and subtractions, including all reconciling items.<br>Trace the book balance on the reconciliation to the general ledger. | These tests are done entirely on the bank reconciliation, with no reference to documents or other records except the general ledger. |
| Cash in the bank as stated on the reconciliation exists (existence).<br>Existing cash in the bank is recorded (completeness).<br>Cash in the bank as stated on the reconciliation is accurate (accuracy). | *(See extended discussion for each of these.)*<br>Receipt and tests of a bank reconciliation.<br>Receipt and tests of a cutoff bank statement.<br>Tests of the bank reconciliation.<br>Extended tests of the bank reconciliation.<br>Proof of cash.<br>Tests for kiting. | These are the three most important objectives for cash in the bank. The procedures are combined because of their close interdependence. The last three procedures should be done only when there are internal control weaknesses. |
| Cash receipts and cash disbursements transactions are recorded in the proper period (cutoff). | *Cash receipts:*<br>Count the cash on hand on the first day of the year and subsequently trace to deposits in transit and the cash receipts journal.<br>Trace deposits in transit to subsequent period bank statement (cutoff bank statement).<br>*Cash disbursements:*<br>Record the last check number used on the last day of the year and subsequently trace to the outstanding checks and the cash disbursements journal.<br>Trace outstanding checks to subsequent period bank statement. | When cash receipts received after year-end are included in the journal, a better cash position than actually exists is shown. It is called "holding open" the cash receipts journal. Holding open the cash disbursements journal reduces accounts payable and usually overstates the current ratio.<br>The first procedure listed for receipts and disbursements cutoff tests requires the auditor's presence on the client's premises at the end of the last day of the year. |
| Cash in the bank is properly presented and disclosed (presentation and disclosure). | Examine minutes, loan agreements, and obtain confirmation for restrictions on the use of cash and compensating balances.<br>Review financial statements to make sure (a) material savings accounts and certificates of deposit are disclosed separately from cash in the bank, (b) cash restricted to certain uses and compensating balances are adequately disclosed, and (c) bank overdrafts are included as current liabilities. | An example of a restriction on the use of cash is cash deposited with a trustee for the payment of mortgage interest and taxes on the proceeds of a construction mortgage. A compensating balance is the client's agreement with a bank to maintain a specified minimum in its checking account. |

*mation with financial institutions.* This standard form has been agreed upon by the AICPA and the American Bankers Association.

The importance of bank confirmations in the audit extends beyond the verification of the actual cash balance. It is typical for the bank to confirm loan information and bank balances on the same form. The confirmation in Figure 21-5 includes three outstanding loans. Information on liabilities to the bank for notes, mortgages, or other debt typically includes the amount of the loan, the date of the loan, its due date, interest rate, and the existence of collateral.

Banks are *not responsible* to search their records for bank balances or loans beyond those included on the form by the CPA firm's client. A sentence near the bottom of the form obligates banks to inform the CPA firm of any loans not included on the confirmation *about which the bank has knowledge.* The effect of this limited responsibility is to require auditors to satisfy themselves about the completeness objective for unrecorded bank balances and loans from the bank in another manner. Similarly, banks are not expected to

**FIGURE 21-5**

**Standard Confirmation of Financial Institution Account Balance Information**

STANDARD FORM TO CONFIRM ACCOUNT
BALANCE INFORMATION WITH FINANCIAL INSTITUTIONS

*ABC Company Inc.*
CUSTOMER NAME

Financial Institution's Name and Address

[ *First National Bank*
*200 Oak Street*
*Midvale, Illinois 40093* ]

We have provided to our accountants the following information as of the close of business on ***December 31, 1996***, regarding our deposit and loan balances. Please confirm the accuracy of the information, noting any exceptions to the information provided. If the balances have been left blank, please complete this form by furnishing the balance in the appropriate space below.* Although we do not request nor expect you to conduct a comprehensive, detailed search of your records, if during the process of completing this confirmation additional information about other deposit and loan accounts we may have with you comes to your attention, please include such information below. Please use the enclosed envelope to return the form directly to our accountants.

1. At the close of business on the date listed above, our records indicated the following deposit balance(s):

| ACCOUNT NAME | ACCOUNT NUMBER | INTEREST RATE | BALANCE* |
|---|---|---|---|
| *General account* | *19751-974* | *None* | *109,713.11* |
| *Payroll account* | *19751-989* | *None* | *1,000.00* |

2. We were directly liable to the financial institution for loans at the close of business on the date listed above as follows:

| ACCOUNT NO./ DESCRIPTION | BALANCE* | DATE DUE | INTEREST RATE | DATE THROUGH WHICH INTEREST IS PAID | DESCRIPTION OF COLLATERAL |
|---|---|---|---|---|---|
| *N/A* | *50,000.00* | *1/9/97* | *10%* | *N/A* | *General* |
| *N/A* | *90,000.00* | *1/9/97* | *10%* | *N/A* | *Security* |
| *N/A* | *60,000.00* | *1/23/97* | *11%* | *N/A* | *Agreement* |

*A.L. Moore* — *January 1, 1997*
(Customer's Authorized Signature) (Date)

The information presented above by the customer is in agreement with our records. Although we have not conducted a comprehensive, detailed search of our records, no other deposit or loan accounts have come to our attention except as noted below.

*Margaret Davis* — *January 10, 1997*
(Financial Institution Authorized Signature) (Date)

*Vice President*
(Title)

| EXCEPTIONS AND/OR COMMENTS |
|---|
| ***None*** |

Please return this form directly to our accountants:

*Jones and Smith CPAs*
*2111 First Street*
*Detroit, Michigan 48711*

*Ordinarily, balances are intentionally left blank if they are not available at the time the form is prepared.
Approved 1990 by American Bankers Association, American Institute of Certified Public Accountants, and Bank Administration Institute. Additional forms available from: AICPA-Order Department, P.O. Box 1003, NY, NY 10108-1003

inform auditors of such things as open lines of credit, compensating balance requirements, or contingent liabilities for guaranteeing the loans of others. If the auditor wants confirmation of this type of information, a separate confirmation addressing the matters of concern should be obtained from the financial institution.

After the bank confirmation has been received, the balance in the bank account confirmed by the bank should be traced to the amount stated on the bank reconciliation. Similarly, all other information on the reconciliation should be traced to the relevant audit working papers. In any case, if the information is not in agreement, an investigation must be made of the difference.

**Receipt of a Cutoff Bank Statement** A *cutoff bank statement* is a partial-period bank statement and the related cancelled checks, duplicate deposit slips, and other documents included in bank statements, mailed by the bank directly to the CPA firm's office. The purpose of the cutoff bank statement is to verify the reconciling items on the client's year-end bank reconciliation with evidence that is inaccessible to the client. To fulfill this purpose, the auditor requests the client to have the bank send directly to the auditor the statement for 7 to 10 days subsequent to the balance sheet date.

Many auditors prove the subsequent period bank statement if a cutoff statement is not received directly from the bank. The purpose of this proof is to test whether the client's employees have omitted, added, or altered any of the documents accompanying the statement. It is obviously a test for intentional misstatements. The auditor performs the proof in the month subsequent to the balance sheet date by (1) footing all the cancelled checks, debit memos, deposits, and credit memos; (2) checking to see that the bank statement balances when the footed totals are used; and (3) reviewing the items included in the footings to make sure that they were cancelled by the bank in the proper period and do not include any erasures or alterations.

**Tests of the Bank Reconciliation** The reason for testing the bank reconciliation is to verify whether the client's recorded bank balance is the same amount as the actual cash in the bank except for deposits in transit, outstanding checks, and other reconciling items. In testing the reconciliation, the cutoff bank statement provides the information for conducting the tests. Several major procedures are involved:

- Verify that the client's bank reconciliation is mathematically accurate.
- Trace the balance on the cutoff statement (and/or bank confirmation) to the balance per bank on the bank reconciliation; a reconciliation cannot take place until these two are the same.
- Trace checks included with the cutoff bank statement to the list of outstanding checks on the bank reconciliation and to the cash disbursements journal. All checks that cleared the bank after the balance sheet date and were included in the cash disbursements journal should also be included on the outstanding check list. If a check was included in the cash disbursements journal, it should be included as an outstanding check if it did not clear before the balance sheet date. Similarly, if a check cleared the bank prior to the balance sheet date, it should not be on the bank reconciliation.
- Investigate all significant checks included on the outstanding check list that have not cleared the bank on the cutoff statement. The first step in the investigation should be to trace the amount of any items not clearing to the cash disbursements journal. The reason for the check not being cashed should be discussed with the client, and if the auditor is concerned about the possibility of fraud, the vendor's accounts payable balance should be confirmed to determine whether the vendor has recognized the receipt of the cash in its records. In addition, the cancelled check should be examined prior to the last day of the audit if it becomes available.
- Trace deposits in transit to the subsequent bank statement. All cash receipts not deposited in the bank at the end of the year should be traced to the cutoff bank statement to make sure that they were deposited shortly after the beginning of the new year.
- Account for other reconciling items on the bank statement and bank reconciliation. These include such items as bank service charges, bank errors and corrections, and unrecorded note transactions debited or credited directly to the bank account by the bank. These reconciling items should be carefully investigated to be sure that they have been treated properly by the client.

## Summary of Audit Tests for the General Cash Account

Figure 21-6 illustrates the types of audit tests used to audit the general cash account. This figure also shows how the audit risk model discussed in Chapter 8 relates to the audit of the general cash account.

**FIGURE 21-6**

**Types of Audit Tests Used for General Cash**

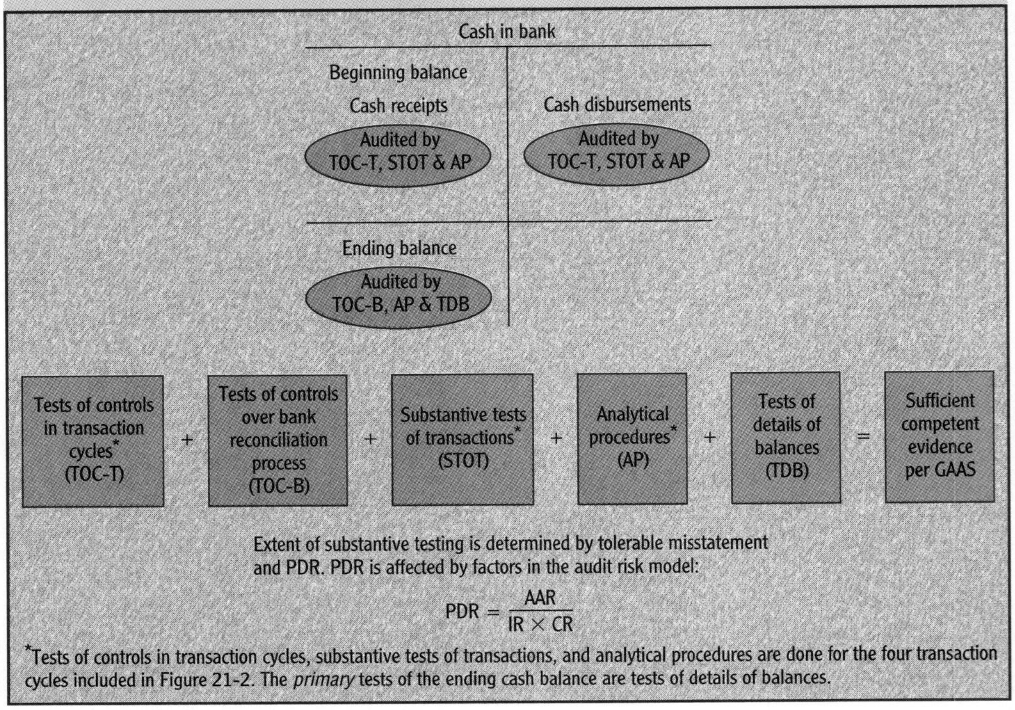


## Fraud-Oriented Procedures

**OBJECTIVE 21-4**

**Recognize when to extend audit tests of the general cash account to test further for material fraud.**

It is frequently necessary for auditors to extend their year-end audit procedures to test more extensively for the possibility of material fraud when there are material internal control weaknesses. Many fraudulent activities are difficult, if not impossible, to uncover; nevertheless, auditors are responsible for making a reasonable effort to detect fraud when they have reason to believe it may exist. The following procedures for uncovering fraud are discussed in this section: extended tests of the bank reconciliation, proofs of cash, and tests for kiting.

**Extended Tests of the Bank Reconciliation** When the auditor believes that the year-end bank reconciliation may be intentionally misstated, it is appropriate to perform extended tests of the year-end bank reconciliation. The purpose of the extended procedures is to verify whether all transactions included in the journals for the last month of the year were correctly included in or excluded from the bank reconciliation and to verify whether all items in the bank reconciliation were correctly included. Let us assume that there are material internal control weaknesses and the client's year-end is December 31. A common approach is to start with the bank reconciliation for November and compare all reconciling items with cancelled checks and other documents in the December bank statement. In addition, all remaining cancelled checks and deposit slips in the December bank statement should be compared with the December cash disbursements and receipts journals. All uncleared items in the November bank reconciliation and the December cash disbursements and receipts journals should be included in the client's December 31 bank reconciliation. Similarly, all reconciling items in the December 31 bank reconciliation should be items from the November bank reconciliation and December's journals that have not yet cleared the bank.

In addition to the tests just described, the auditor must also carry out procedures subsequent to the end of the year with the use of the bank cutoff statement. These tests would be performed in the same manner as previously discussed.

**Proof of Cash** Auditors sometimes prepare a proof of cash when the client has material internal control weaknesses in cash. A proof of cash includes the following:

- A reconciliation of the balance on the bank statement with the general ledger balance at the beginning of the proof-of-cash period
- A reconciliation of cash receipts deposited with the cash receipts journal for a given period
- A reconciliation of cancelled checks clearing the bank with the cash disbursements journal for a given period
- A reconciliation of the balance on the bank statement with the general ledger balance at the end of the proof-of-cash period

A proof of cash of this nature is commonly referred to as a four-column proof of cash—one column is used for each of the types of information listed above. A proof of cash can be performed for one or more interim months, the entire year, or the last month of the year. Figure 21-7 on page 708 shows a four-column proof of cash for an interim month.

The auditor uses a proof of cash to determine whether:

- All recorded cash receipts were deposited.
- All deposits in the bank were recorded in the accounting records.
- All recorded cash disbursements were paid by the bank.
- All amounts that were paid by the bank were recorded.

The concern in an interim-month proof of cash is not with adjusting account balances, but rather with reconciling the amounts per books and bank.

When the auditor does a proof of cash, he or she is combining substantive tests of transactions and tests of details of balances. For example, a proof of cash receipts is a test of recorded transactions, whereas a bank reconciliation is a test of the balance in cash at a point in time. A proof of cash is an excellent method of comparing recorded cash receipts and disbursements with the bank account and with bank reconciliation. However, the auditor must recognize that a proof of cash disbursements is not effective for discovering checks written for an improper amount, fraudulent checks, or other misstatements in which the dollar amount appearing on the cash disbursements records is incorrect. Similarly, proof-of-cash receipts is not useful for uncovering the theft of cash receipts or the recording and deposit of an improper amount of cash.

**Tests for Kiting** Embezzlers occasionally cover a defalcation of cash by a practice known as *kiting:* transferring money from one bank to another and improperly recording the transaction. Near the balance sheet date a check is drawn on one bank account and immediately deposited in a second account for credit before the end of the accounting period. In making this transfer, the embezzler is careful to make sure that the check is deposited at a late enough date so that it does not clear the first bank until after the end of the period. If the bank transfer is not recorded until after the balance sheet date, the amount of the transfer is recorded as an asset in both banks. Although there are other ways of perpetrating this fraud, each involves the device of increasing the bank balance to cover a shortage by the use of bank transfers.

A useful approach to test for kiting, as well as for unintentional errors in recording bank transfers, is to list all bank transfers made a few days before and after the balance sheet date and to trace each to the accounting records for proper recording. An example of a bank transfer schedule is included in Figure 21-8 on page 709. The working paper shows that there were four bank transfers shortly before and after the balance sheet date.

**FIGURE 21-7**
**Interim Proof of Cash**

ABC Company, Inc.
Interim Proof of Cash
12/31/96

Schedule A-5 | Date
Prepared by JG 7/15/96
Approved by RP 7/17/96

Acct. 101-General account, First National Bank

| | | 5/31/96 | Receipts | Disbursements | 6/30/96 |
|---|---|---|---|---|---|
| Balance per Bank | (1) | 121782.12 | 627895.20 | 631111.96 | 118565.36 |
| Deposits in transit | | | | | |
| 5/31 | (2) | 21720.00 | <21720.00> | | |
| 6/30 | (2) | | 16592.36 | | 16592.36 |
| Outstanding checks | | | | | |
| 5/31 | (3) | 36396.50 | | <36396.50> | |
| 6/30 | (3) | | | 14800.10 | <14800.10> |
| NSF checks | (4) | | <4560.00> | <4560.00> | |
| To allow for effect of a cash disbursement recorded as a credit item in Cash Receipts Journal | | | 8500.00 | 8500.00 | |
| Balance per bank, adjusted | | 107105.62 | 626707.56 | 613455.56 | 120357.62 |
| Balance per books, unadjusted | | 107105.62 | 626707.56 | 614957.04 | 118856.14 |
| Bank debit memos | (5) | | | 120.00 | <120.00> |
| Payroll checks erroneously entered in General Disbursements Journal | (6) | | | <1621.48> | 1621.48 |
| Balance per books, adjusted | | 107105.62 | 626707.56 | 613455.56 | 120357.62 |

(1) Per 6/30/96 bank statement
(2) Detailed listing filed below; traced to subsequent bank statements.
(3) Outstanding-check list filed below: examined cancelled checks.
(4) Detailed listing filed below; all NSF items were deposited and had cleared as of 7/15/96.
(5) Safety deposit rentals; traced to recording via journal entry.
Requested list of contents of safety deposit boxes.
(6) Traced to journal entry correcting error.

There are several things that should be audited on the bank transfer schedule.

- *The accuracy of the information on the bank transfer schedule should be verified.* The auditor should compare the disbursement and receipt information on the schedule to the cash disbursements and cash receipts journals to make sure that it is accurate. Similarly, the dates on the schedule for transfers that were received and disbursed should be compared to the bank statement. Finally, cash disbursements and receipts journals should be examined to make sure that all transfers a few days before and after the balance sheet date have been included on the schedule. The tick mark explanations on the working paper in Figure 21-8 indicate that these steps have been taken.
- *The bank transfers must be recorded in both the receiving and disbursing banks.* If, for example, there was a $10,000 transfer from Bank A to Bank B, but only the disbursement was recorded, this is evidence of an attempt to conceal a cash theft.
- *The date of the recording of the disbursements and receipts for each transfer must be in the same fiscal year.* In Figure 21-8 the dates in the two "date recorded in books" columns [columns (4) and (7)] are in the same period for each transfer, therefore, they are correct. If a cash disbursement was recorded in the current fiscal year and the receipt in the subsequent fiscal year, it may be an attempt to cover a cash shortage.

**FIGURE 21-8**

**Bank Transfer Working Paper**

ABC COMPANY, INC.
SCHEDULE OF BANK TRANSFERS
December 31, 1996

Schedule A-7
Prepared by Client/DED 1/10/97
Reviewed by SW 1/18/97

PBC

| | Disbursements | | | | Receipts | | |
|---|---|---|---|---|---|---|---|
| Check No. (1) | Bank (2) | Amount (3) | Date Recorded in Books (4) | Date Paid by Bank (5) | Bank (6) | Date Recorded in Books (7) | Date Received by Bank (8) |
| 2609 | National | 20,642 √ | 12-26-96 ⊗ | 12-28-96❐ | National Payroll | 12-28-96 Ⓥ | 12-28-96 ❐∅ |
| 2910 | National | 12,000 √ | 12-28-96 √̸ | 01-02-97❐ | Federal Charter | 12-30-96 Ⓥ | 12-31-96 ❐∅ |
| 2741 | National | 10,000 √ | 12-31-96 √̸ | 01-04-97❐ | Federal Charter | 12-31-96 Ⓥ | 01-02-97 ❐Ⓦ |
| 2762 | National | 23,721 √ | 01-03-97 ⊗ | 01-05-97❐ | National Payroll | 01-04-97 Ⓥ | 01-05-97 ❐∅ |

√ Traced to cash disbursements journal.
Ⓥ Traced to cash receipts journal.
√̸ Check included as outstanding on bank reconciliation.
⊗ Check not included as outstanding on bank reconciliation.
Ⓦ Receipt included as a deposit in transit.
❐ Traced to bank statement.
∅ Receipt not included as a deposit in transit.

Note: Examined cash disbursements and cash receipts journals for checks to and deposits from bank accounts. None included except those listed above.

- *Disbursements on the bank transfer schedule should be correctly included in or excluded from year-end bank reconciliations as outstanding checks.* In Figure 21-8, the 12-31-96 bank reconciliation should include outstanding checks for the second and third transfers but not the other two. [Compare the dates in columns (4) and (5).] Understating outstanding checks on the bank reconciliation indicates the possibility of kiting.
- *Receipts on the bank transfer schedule should be correctly included in or excluded from year-end bank reconciliations as deposits in transit.* In Figure 21-8, the 12-31-96 bank reconciliation should indicate a deposit in transit for the third transfer, but not for the other three. (Compare the dates for each transfer in the last two columns.) Overstating deposits in transit on the bank reconciliation indicates the possibility of kiting.

Even though audit tests of bank transfers are usually fraud oriented, they are often performed on audits in which there are numerous bank transfers, regardless of the internal control structure. When there are numerous intercompany transfers, it is difficult to be sure that each is correctly handled unless a schedule of transfers near the end of the year is prepared and each transfer is traced to the accounting records and bank statements. In addition to the possibility of kiting, inaccurate handling of transfers could result in a misclassification between cash and accounts payable. The materiality of transfers and the relative ease of performing the tests make many auditors believe they should always be performed.

**Summary of Fraud-Oriented Procedures** In designing audit procedures for uncovering fraud, careful consideration should be given to the nature of the weaknesses in internal control, the type of fraud that is likely to result from the weaknesses, the potential materiality of the fraud, and the audit procedures that are most effective in uncovering the misstatement. When auditors are specifically testing for fraud, they should keep in mind that audit procedures other than tests of details of cash balances can also be useful. Examples of procedures that may uncover fraud in the cash receipts area include the confirmation of accounts receivable, tests for lapping, reviewing the general ledger entries in the cash account for unusual items, tracing from customer orders to sales and subsequent cash receipts, and examining approvals and supporting documentation for bad debts and sales returns and allowances. Similar tests can be used for testing for the possibility of fraudulent cash disbursements.

**ELECTRONIC TRANSFER OF CASH**

Many organizations use electronic transfer when they are transferring cash among banks, collecting from customers, and paying vendors. Under these systems, cash is transferred instantly. For example, when Company A collects from Customer X, the cash is instantly transferred from Customer X's bank account to Company A's. There is no check.

Electronic transfers have the potential to improve internal controls in that no cash is handled by employees. However, there is also potential risk of cash thefts through inappropriate cash transfers. It is essential that excellent internal controls are in place for electronic transfers.

## AUDIT OF THE PAYROLL BANK ACCOUNT

**OBJECTIVE 21-5**
**Design and perform audit tests of the payroll bank account.**

Tests of the payroll bank reconciliation should take only a few minutes if there is an imprest payroll account and an independent reconciliation of the bank account such as that described for the general account. Typically, the only reconciling items are outstanding checks, and for most audits the great majority clear shortly after the checks are issued. In testing the payroll bank account balances, it is necessary to obtain a bank reconciliation, a bank confirmation, and a cutoff bank statement. The reconciliation procedures are performed in the same manner as those described for general cash. Naturally, extended procedures are necessary if the controls are inadequate or if the bank account does not reconcile with the general ledger imprest cash balance.

The discussion in the preceding paragraph should not be interpreted as implying that the audit of payroll is unimportant. A review of Chapter 16 should remind the reader that the most important audit procedures for verifying payroll are tests of controls and substantive tests of transactions. The most likely payroll misstatements will be discovered by those procedures rather than by checking the imprest bank account balance.

## AUDIT OF PETTY CASH

**OBJECTIVE 21-6**
**Design and perform audit tests of petty cash.**

Petty cash is a unique account because it is frequently immaterial in amount, yet it is verified on many audits. The account is verified primarily because of the potential for defalcation and the client's expectation of an audit review even when the amount is immaterial.

### Internal Controls Over Petty Cash

The most important internal control for petty cash is the use of an imprest fund that is the responsibility of *one individual.* In addition, petty cash funds should not be mingled with other receipts, and the fund should be kept separate from all other activities. There should also be limits on the amount of any expenditure from petty cash, as well as on the total amount of the fund. The type of expenditure that can be made from petty cash transactions should be well defined by company policy.

Whenever a disbursement is made from petty cash, adequate internal controls require a responsible official's approval on a prenumbered petty cash form. The total of the actual cash and checks in the fund plus the total unreimbursed petty cash forms that represent actual expenditures should equal the total amount of the petty cash fund stated in the general ledger. Periodically, surprise counts and a reconciliation of the petty cash fund should be made by the internal auditor or other responsible official.

When the petty cash balance runs low, a check payable to the petty cash custodian should be written on the general cash account for the reimbursement of petty cash. The check should be for the exact amount of the prenumbered vouchers that are submitted as evidence of actual expenditures. These vouchers should be verified by the accounts payable clerk and cancelled to prevent their reuse.

### Audit Tests for Petty Cash

The emphasis in verifying petty cash should be on testing controls over petty cash transactions rather than the ending balance in the account. Even if the amount of the petty cash fund is small, there is potential for numerous improper transactions if the fund is frequently reimbursed.

An important part of testing petty cash is first to determine the client's procedures for handling the fund by discussing internal controls with the custodian and examining the documentation of a few transactions. As a part of obtaining an understanding of internal control, it is necessary to identify internal controls and weaknesses. Even though most petty cash systems are not complex, it is often desirable to use a flowchart and an internal control questionnaire, primarily for documentation in subsequent audits.

Tests of controls and substantive tests of transactions depend on the number and size of the petty cash reimbursements and the auditor's assessed control risk. When control risk is assessed as low and there are few reimbursement payments during the year, it is common for auditors not to test any further for reasons of immateriality. When the auditor decides to test petty cash, the two most common procedures are to count the petty cash balance and to carry out detailed tests of one or two reimbursement transactions. In such a case, the primary procedures should include footing the petty cash vouchers supporting the amount of the reimbursement, accounting for a sequence of petty cash vouchers, examining the petty cash vouchers for authorization and cancellation, and examining the attached documentation for reasonableness. Typical supporting documentation includes cash register tapes, invoices, and receipts.

Petty cash tests can ordinarily be performed at any time during the year, but as a matter of convenience they are typically done on an interim date. If the balance in the petty cash fund is considered material, which is rarely the case, it should be counted at the end of the year. Unreimbursed expenditures should be examined as a part of the count to determine whether the amount of unrecorded expenses is material.

## ESSENTIAL TERMS

**Bank reconciliation**—the monthly reconciliation, usually prepared by client personnel, of the differences between the cash balance recorded in the general ledger and the amount in the bank account

**Branch bank account**—a separate bank account maintained at a local bank by a branch of a company

**Cash equivalents**—excess cash invested in short-term, highly liquid investments such as time deposits, certificates of deposit, and money market funds

**Cutoff bank statement**—a partial-period bank statement and the related cancelled checks, duplicate deposit slips, and other documents included in bank statements, mailed by the bank directly to the auditor. The auditor uses it to verify reconciling items on the client's year-end bank reconciliation.

**General cash account**—the primary bank account for most organizations; virtually all cash receipts and disbursements flow through this account at some time

**Imprest payroll account**—a bank account to which the exact amount of payroll for the pay period is transferred by check from the employer's general cash account

**Imprest petty cash fund**—a fund of cash maintained within the company for small cash acquisitions or to cash employees' checks; the fund's fixed balance is comparatively small, and is periodically reimbursed

**Kiting**—the transfer of money from one bank account to another and improperly recording the transfer so that the amount is recorded as an asset in both accounts; this practice is used by embezzlers to cover a defalcation of cash

**Proof of cash**—a four-column working paper prepared by the auditor to reconcile the bank's record of the client's beginning balance, cash deposits, cleared checks, and ending balance for the period, with the client's records

**Standard bank confirmation form**—a form approved by the AICPA and American Bankers Association through which the bank responds to the auditor about bank balance and loan information provided on the confirmation

## REVIEW QUESTIONS

**21-1 (Objectives 21-1, 21-2)** Explain the relationships among the initial assessed control risk, tests of controls and substantive tests of transactions for cash receipts, and the tests of details of cash balances.

**21-2 (Objectives 21-1, 21-2)** Explain the relationships among the initial assessed control risk, tests of controls and substantive tests of transactions for cash disbursements, and the tests of details of cash balances. Give one example in which the conclusions reached about internal controls in cash disbursements would affect the tests of cash balances.

**21-3 (Objective 21-3)** Why is the monthly reconciliation of bank accounts by an independent person an important internal control over cash balances? Which individuals would generally not be considered independent for this responsibility?

**21-4 (Objective 21-3)** Evaluate the effectiveness and state the shortcomings of the preparation of a bank reconciliation by the controller in the manner described in the following statement: "When I reconcile the bank account, the first thing I do is to sort the checks in numerical order and find which numbers are missing. Next I determine the amount of the uncleared checks by referring to the cash disbursements journal. If the bank account reconciles at that point, I am all finished with the reconciliation. If it does not, I search for deposits in transit, checks from the beginning outstanding check list that still have not cleared, other reconciling items, and bank errors until it reconciles. In most instances, I can do the reconciliation in 20 minutes."

**21-5 (Objective 21-3)** How do bank confirmations differ from positive confirmations of accounts receivable? Distinguish between them in terms of the nature of the information confirmed, the sample size, and the appropriate action when the confirmation is not returned after the second request. Explain the rationale for the differences between these two types of confirmations.

**21-6 (Objective 21-3)** Evaluate the necessity of following the practice described by an auditor: "In confirming bank accounts I insist upon a response from every bank the client has done business with in the past two years, even though the account may be closed at the balance sheet date."

**21-7 (Objective 21-3)** Describe what is meant by a *cutoff bank statement* and state its purpose.

**21-8 (Objective 21-3)** Why are auditors usually less concerned about the client's cash receipts cutoff than the cutoff for sales? Explain the procedure involved in testing for the cutoff for cash receipts.

**21-9 (Objective 21-1)** What is meant by an *imprest bank account* for a branch operation? Explain the purpose of using this type of bank account.

**21-10 (Objective 21-4)** Explain the purpose of a four-column proof of cash. List two types of misstatements it is meant to uncover.

**21-11 (Objective 21-3)** When the auditor fails to obtain a cutoff bank statement, it is common to "prove" the entire statement for the month subsequent to the balance sheet date. How is this done and what is its purpose?

**21-12 (Objective 21-4)** Distinguish between *lapping* and *kiting*. Describe audit procedures that can be used to uncover each.

**21-13 (Objective 21-5)** Assume that a client with excellent internal controls uses an imprest payroll bank account. Explain why the verification of the payroll bank reconciliation ordinarily takes less time than the tests of the general bank account, even if the number of checks exceeds those written on the general account.

**21-14 (Objective 21-6)** Distinguish between the verification of petty cash reimbursements and the verification of the balance in the fund. Explain how each is done. Which is more important?

**21-15 (Objectives 21-3, 21-4)** Why is there a greater emphasis on the detection of fraud in tests of details of cash balances than for other balance sheet accounts? Give two specific examples that demonstrate how this emphasis affects the auditor's evidence accumulation in auditing year-end cash.

**21-16 (Objective 21-3)** Explain why, in verifying bank reconciliations, most auditors emphasize the possibility of a nonexistent deposit in transit being included in the reconciliation and an outstanding check being omitted rather than the omission of a deposit in transit and the inclusion of a nonexistent outstanding check.

## MULTIPLE CHOICE QUESTIONS FROM CPA EXAMINATIONS

**21-17 (Objectives 21-3, 21-4)** The following questions deal with auditing year-end cash. Choose the best response.

a. A CPA obtains a January 10 cutoff bank statement for his client directly from the bank. Few of the outstanding checks listed on his client's December 31 bank reconciliation cleared during the cutoff period. A probable cause for this is that the client
   (1) is engaged in kiting.
   (2) is engaged in lapping.
   (3) transmitted the checks to the payees after year-end.
   (4) has overstated its year-end bank balance.

b. The auditor should ordinarily mail confirmation requests to all banks with which the client has conducted any business during the year, regardless of the year-end balance, since
   (1) the confirmation form also seeks information about indebtedness to the bank.
   (2) this procedure will detect kiting activities that would otherwise not be detected.
   (3) the mailing of confirmation forms to all such banks is required by generally accepted auditing standards.
   (4) this procedure relieves the auditor of any responsibility with respect to nondetection of forged checks.

c. On December 31, 1997, a company erroneously prepared an accounts payable transaction (debit cash, credit accounts payable) for a transfer of funds between banks. A check for the transfer was drawn January 3, 1998. This resulted in overstatements of cash and accounts payable at December 31, 1997. Of the following procedures, the least effective in disclosing this misstatement is review of the
   (1) December 31, 1997, bank reconciliation for the two banks.
   (2) December 1997 check register.
   (3) support for accounts payable at December 31, 1997.
   (4) schedule of interbank transfers.

**21-18 (Objective 21-4)** The following questions deal with discovering fraud in auditing year-end cash. Choose the best response.

a. Which of the following is one of the better auditing techniques to detect kiting?
   (1) Review composition of authenticated deposit slips.
   (2) Review subsequent bank statements and cancelled checks received directly from the banks.
   (3) Prepare a schedule of bank transfers from the client's books.
   (4) Prepare year-end bank reconciliations.

b. The cashier of Baker Company covered a shortage in his cash working fund with cash obtained on December 31 from a local bank by cashing an unrecorded check drawn on the company's New York bank. The auditor would discover this manipulation by
   (1) preparing independent bank reconciliations as of December 31.
   (2) counting the cash working fund at the close of business on December 31.

(3) investigating items returned with the bank cutoff statements.
(4) confirming the December 31 bank balances.

c. A cash shortage may be concealed by transporting funds from one location to another or by converting negotiable assets to cash. Because of this, which of the following is vital?
(1) Simultaneous confirmations.
(2) Simultaneous bank reconciliations.
(3) Simultaneous verification.
(4) Simultaneous surprise cash count.

## DISCUSSION QUESTIONS AND PROBLEMS

**21-19 (Objectives 21-3, 21-4)** The following are misstatements that might be found in the client's year-end cash balance (assume that the balance sheet date is June 30).

1. A check was omitted from the outstanding check list on the June 30 bank reconciliation. It cleared the bank July 7.
2. A check was omitted from the outstanding check list on the bank reconciliation. It cleared the bank September 6.
3. Cash receipts collected on accounts receivable from July 1 to July 5 were included as June 29 and 30 cash receipts.
4. A loan from the bank on June 26 was credited directly to the client's bank account. The loan was not entered as of June 30.
5. A check that was dated June 26 and disbursed in June was not recorded in the cash disbursements journal, but it was included as an outstanding check on June 30.
6. A bank transfer recorded in the accounting records on July 1 was included as a deposit in transit on June 30.
7. The outstanding checks on the June 30 bank reconciliation were underfooted by $2,000.

### Required

a. Assuming that each of these misstatements was intentional (fraud), state the most likely motivation of the person responsible.

b. What control could be instituted for each fraud to reduce the likelihood of occurrence?

c. List an audit procedure that could be used to discover each fraud.

**21-20 (Objectives 21-3, 21-4)** Following are misstatements that an auditor might find through substantive tests of transactions or by tests of details of cash balances:

1. The bookkeeper failed to record checks in the cash disbursements journal that were written and mailed during the first month of the year.
2. The bookkeeper failed to record or deposit a material amount of cash receipts during the last month of the year. Cash is prelisted by the president's secretary.
3. The cash disbursements journal was held open for two days after the end of the year.
4. A check was paid to a vendor for a carload of raw materials that was never received by the client.
5. A discount on an acquisition was not taken, even though the check was mailed before the discount period had expired.
6. Cash receipts for the last two days of the year were recorded in the cash receipts journal for the subsequent period and listed as deposits in transit on the bank reconciliation.
7. A check written to a vendor during the last month of the year was recorded in the cash disbursements journal twice to cover an existing fraud. The check cleared the bank and did not appear on the bank reconciliation.

## Required

a. List a substantive audit procedure to uncover each of the preceding misstatements.

b. For each procedure in part a, state whether it is a test of details of cash balances or a substantive test of transactions.

**21-21 (Objectives 21-3, 21-4)** The following audit procedures are concerned with tests of details of general cash balances.

1. Compare the bank cancellation date with the date on the cancelled check for checks dated on or shortly before the balance sheet date.
2. Trace deposits in transit on the bank reconciliation to the cutoff bank statement and the current year cash receipts journal.
3. Obtain a standard bank confirmation from each bank with which the client does business.
4. Compare the balance on the bank reconciliation obtained from the client with the bank confirmation.
5. Compare the checks returned along with the cutoff bank statement with the list of outstanding checks on the bank reconciliation.
6. List the check number, payee, and amount of all material checks not returned with the cutoff bank statement.
7. Review minutes of the board of directors' meetings, loan agreements, and bank confirmation for interest-bearing deposits, restrictions on the withdrawal of cash, and compensating balance agreements.
8. Prepare a four-column proof of cash.

## Required

Explain the objective of each.

**21-22 (Objectives 21-3, 21-4)** The Patrick Company had weak internal controls over its cash transactions. Facts about its cash position at November 30, 1996 were as follows:

The cash books showed a balance of $18,901.62, which included undeposited receipts. A credit of $100 on the bank's records did not appear on the books of the company. The balance per bank statement was $15,550. Outstanding checks were no. 62 for $116.25, no. 183 for $150.00, no. 284 for $253.25, no. 8621 for $190.71, no. 8623 for $206.80, and no. 8632 for $145.28.

The cashier stole all undeposited receipts in excess of $3,794.41 and prepared the following reconciliation:

| | | |
|---|---|---|
| Balance, per books, November 30, 1996 | | $18,901.62 |
| Add: Outstanding checks | | |
| 8621 | $190.71 | |
| 8623 | 206.80 | |
| 8632 | 145.28 | 442.79 |
| | | 19,344.41 |
| Less: Undeposited receipts | | (3,794.41) |
| Balance per bank, November 30, 1996 | | 15,550.00 |
| Deduct: Unrecorded credit | | (100.00) |
| True cash, November 30, 1996 | | $15,450.00 |

## Required

a. Prepare a supporting schedule showing how much the cashier stole.

b. How did he attempt to conceal his theft?

c. Taking only the information given, name two specific features of internal control that were apparently missing.*

*AICPA adapted.

**21-23 (Objective 21-3)** You are auditing general cash for the Pittsburg Supply Company for the fiscal year ended July 31, 1997. The client has not prepared the July 31 bank reconciliation. After a brief discussion with the owner you agree to prepare the reconciliation, with assistance from one of Pittsburg Supply's clerks. You obtain the following information:

| | General Ledger | Bank Statement |
|---|---|---|
| Beginning balance | $ 4,611 | $ 5,753 |
| Deposits | | 25,056 |
| Cash receipts journal | 25,456 | |
| Checks cleared | | (23,615) |
| Cash disbursements journal | (21,811) | |
| July bank service charge | | (87) |
| Note paid directly | | (6,100) |
| NSF check | | (311) |
| Ending balance | $ 8,256 | $ 696 |

**June 30 Bank Reconciliation**

| Information in General Ledger and Bank Statement | |
|---|---|
| Balance per bank | $5,753 |
| Deposits in transit | 600 |
| Outstanding checks | 1,742 |
| Balance per books | 4,611 |

Additional information obtained is:

1. Checks clearing that were outstanding on June 30 totaled $1,692.
2. Checks clearing that were recorded in the July disbursements journal totaled $20,467.
3. A check for $1,060 cleared the bank, but had not been recorded in the cash disbursements journal. It was for an acquisition of inventory. Pittsburg Supply uses the periodic-inventory method.
4. A check for $396 was charged to Pittsburg Supply but had been written on a different company's bank account.
5. Deposits included $600 from June and $24,456 for July.
6. The bank charged Pittsburg Supply's account for a nonsufficient check totaling $311. The credit manager concluded that the customer intentionally closed its account and the owner left the city. The check was turned over to a collection agency.
7. A note for $5,800, plus interest, was paid directly to the bank under an agreement signed four months ago. The note payable was recorded at $5,800 on Pittsburg Supply's books.

## Required

a. Prepare a bank reconciliation that shows both the unadjusted and adjusted balance per books.

b. Prepare all adjusting entries.

c. What audit procedures would you use to verify each item in the bank reconciliation?

**21-24 (Objectives 21-3, 21-4)** In the audit of the Regional Transport Company, a large branch that maintains its own bank account, cash is periodically transferred to the central account in Cedar Rapids. On the branch account's records, bank transfers are recorded as a debit to the home office clearing account and a credit to the branch bank account. Similarly, the home office account is recorded as a debit to the central bank account and a credit to the branch office clearing account. Gordon Light is the head bookkeeper for both the home office and the branch bank accounts. Since he also reconciles the bank account, the senior auditor, Cindy Marintette, is concerned about the internal control weakness.

As a part of the year-end audit of bank transfers, Marintette asks you to schedule the transfers for the last few days in 1996 and the first few days of 1997. You prepare the following list:

| Amount of Transfer | Date Recorded in the Home Office Cash Receipts Journal | Date Recorded in the Branch Office Cash Disbursements Journal | Date Deposited in the Home Office Bank Account | Date Cleared the Branch Bank Account |
|---|---|---|---|---|
| $12,000 | 12-27-96 | 12-29-96 | 12-26-96 | 12-27-96 |
| 26,000 | 12-28-96 | 01-02-97 | 12-28-96 | 12-29-96 |
| 14,000 | 01-02-97 | 12-30-96 | 12-28-96 | 12-29-96 |
| 11,000 | 12-26-96 | 12-26-96 | 12-28-96 | 01-03-97 |
| 15,000 | 01-02-97 | 01-02-97 | 12-28-96 | 12-31-96 |
| 28,000 | 01-07-97 | 01-05-97 | 12-28-96 | 01-03-97 |
| 37,000 | 01-04-97 | 01-06-97 | 01-03-97 | 01-05-97 |

## Required

a. In verifying each bank transfer, state the appropriate audit procedures you should perform.

b. Prepare any adjusting entries required in the home office records.

c. Prepare any adjusting entries required in the branch bank records.

d. State how each bank transfer should be included in the December 31, 1996, bank reconciliation for the home office account after your adjustments in part b.

e. State how each bank transfer should be included in the December 31, 1996 bank reconciliation of the branch bank account after your adjustments in part c.

**21-25 (Objective 21-3)** Toyco, a retail toy chain, honors two bank credit cards and makes daily deposits of credit card sales in two credit card bank accounts (Bank A and Bank B). Each day Toyco batches its credit card sales slips, bank deposits slips, and authorized sales return documents, and keypunches cards for processing by its electronic data processing department. Each week detailed computer printouts of the general ledger credit card cash accounts are prepared. Credit card banks have been instructed to make an automatic weekly transfer of cash to Toyco's general bank account. The credit card banks charge back deposits that include sales to holders of stolen or expired cards.

The auditor conducting the audit of the 1997 Toyco financial statements has obtained the following copies of the detailed general ledger cash account printouts, the manually prepared bank reconciliations, and a summary of the bank statements, all for the week ended December 31, 1997.

## Required

Based on a review of the December 31, 1997, bank reconciliations and the related information available in the printouts and the summary of bank statements, describe what action(s) the auditor should take to obtain audit satisfaction *for each item* on the bank reconciliations. Assume that all amounts are material and all computations are accurate. Organize your answer sheet as follows (see page 718), using the appropriate code number *for each item* on the bank reconciliations:*

*AICPA adapted.

| Code No. | Action(s) to Be Taken by the Auditor to Obtain Audit Satisfaction |
|---|---|
| 1. | |

**TOYCO—Detailed General Ledger Credit Card Cash Account Printouts**

| | Bank A Dr. or (Cr.) | Bank B Dr. or (Cr.) |
|---|---|---|
| Beginning balance, December 24, 1997 | $12,100 | $ 4,200 |
| Deposits | | |
| December 27, 1997 | 2,500 | 5,000 |
| December 28, 1997 | 3,000 | 7,000 |
| December 29, 1997 | 0 | 5,400 |
| December 30, 1997 | 1,900 | 4,000 |
| December 31, 1997 | 2,200 | 6,000 |
| Cash transfer, December 27, 1997 | (10,700) | 0 |
| Chargebacks, expired cards | (300) | (1,600) |
| Deposit errors (physically deposited in wrong account) | (1,400) | (1,000) |
| Redeposit of deposits made to wrong account | 1,000 | 1,400 |
| Sales returns for week ending December 31, 1997 | (600) | (1,200) |
| Ending balance, December 31, 1997 | $ 9,700 | $29,200 |

**TOYCO—Bank Reconciliations**

| | Add or (Deduct) | |
|---|---|---|
| **Code No.** | **Bank A** | **Bank B** |
| 1. Balance per bank statement, December 31, 1997 | $8,600 | $ 0 |
| 2. Deposits in transit, December 31, 1997 | 2,200 | 6,000 |
| 3. Redeposit of deposits made to wrong account | 1,000 | 1,400 |
| 4. Difference in deposits of December 29, 1997 | (2,000) | (100) |
| 5. Unexplained bank charge | 400 | 0 |
| 6. Bank cash transfer not yet recorded | 0 | 22,600 |
| 7. Bank service charges | 0 | 500 |
| 8. Chargebacks not recorded, stolen cards | 100 | 0 |
| 9. Sales returns recorded but not reported to the bank | (600) | (1,200) |
| 10. Balance per general ledger, December 31, 1997 | $9,700 | $29,200 |

**TOYCO—Summary of the Bank Statements**

| | (Charges) or Credits Bank A | Bank B |
|---|---|---|
| Beginning balance, December 24, 1997 | $10,000 | $ 0 |
| Deposits dated | | |
| December 24, 1997 | 2,100 | 4,200 |
| December 27, 1997 | 2,500 | 5,000 |
| December 28, 1997 | 3,000 | 7,000 |
| December 29, 1997 | 2,000 | 5,500 |
| December 30, 1997 | 1,900 | 4,000 |
| Cash transfers to general bank account | | |
| December 27, 1997 | (10,700) | 0 |
| December 31, 1997 | 0 | (22,600) |
| Chargebacks | | |
| Stolen cards | (100) | 0 |
| Expired cards | (300) | (1,600) |
| Deposit errors | (1,400) | (1,000) |
| Bank service charges | 0 | (500) |
| Bank charge (unexplained) | (400) | 0 |
| Ending balance, December 31, 1997 | $ 8,600 | $ 0 |

**21-26 (Objective 21-3)** In connection with an audit you are given the following worksheet (see below and on top of page 720):

**Bank Reconciliation, December 31, 1996**

| | | |
|---|---|---|
| Balance per ledger December 31, 1996 | | $17,174.86 |
| ***Add:*** | | |
| Cash receipts received on the last day of December and charged to "cash in bank" on books but not deposited | | 2,662.25 |
| Debit memo for customer's check returned unpaid (check is on hand but no entry has been made on the books) | | 200.00 |
| Debit memo for bank service charge for December | | 5.50 |
| | | $20,142.61 |
| ***Deduct:*** | | |
| Checks drawn but not paid by bank (see detailed list below) | $2,267.75 | |
| Credit memo for proceeds of a note receivable which had been left at the bank for collection but which has not been recorded as collected | 400.00 | |
| Check for an account payable entered on books as $240.90 but drawn and paid by bank as $419.00 | 178.10 | (2,945.85) |
| Computed balance | | 17,196.76 |
| Unlocated difference | | (200.00) |
| Balance per bank (checked to confirmation) | | $16,996.76 |

**Checks Drawn but Not Paid by Bank**

| No. | Amount |
|---|---|
| 573 | $ 67.27 |
| 724 | 9.90 |
| 903 | 456.67 |
| 907 | 305.50 |
| 911 | 482.75 |
| 913 | 550.00 |
| 914 | 366.76 |
| 916 | 10.00 |
| 917 | 218.90 |
| | $2,267.75 |

## Required

a. Prepare a corrected reconciliation.

b. Prepare journal entries for items that should be adjusted prior to closing the books.*

**21-27 (Objective 21-4)** You are doing the first-year audit of Sherman School District and have been assigned responsibility for doing a four-column proof of cash for the month of October 1996. You obtain the following information:

| | | | |
|---|---|---|---|
| 1. Balance per books | September | 30 | $8,106 |
| | October | 31 | 3,850 |
| 2. Balance per bank | September | 30 | 5,411 |
| | October | 31 | 6,730 |
| 3. Outstanding checks | September | 30 | 916 |
| | October | 31 | 1,278 |
| 4. Cash receipts for October | per bank | | 26,536 |
| | per books | | 19,711 |
| 5. Deposits in transit | September | 30 | 3,611 |
| | October | 31 | 693 |

6. Interest on a bank loan for the month of October, charged by the bank but not recorded, was $596.
7. Proceeds on a note of the Jones Company were collected by the bank on October 28, but were not entered on the books:

| | |
|---|---|
| Principal | $3,300 |
| Interest | 307 |
| | $3,607 |

8. On October 26, a $407 check of the Billings Company was charged to Sherman School District's account by the bank in error.
9. Dishonored checks are not recorded on the books unless they permanently fail to clear the bank. The bank treats them as disbursements when they are dishonored and deposits when they are redeposited. Checks totaling $609 were dishonored in October; $300 was redeposited in October and $309 in November.

## Required

a. Prepare a four-column proof of cash for the month ended October 31. It should show both adjusted and unadjusted cash.

b. Prepare all adjusting entries.

*AICPA adapted.

**21-28 (Objective 21-4)** The following information was obtained in an audit of the cash account of Tuck Company as of December 31, 1997. Assume that the CPA has satisfied himself as to the propriety of the cash book, the bank statements, and the returned checks, except as noted.

1. The bookkeeper's bank reconciliation at November 30, 1997.

| | | |
|---|---|---|
| Balance per bank statement | | $ 19,400 |
| Add: Deposit in transit | | 1,100 |
| Total | | $ 20,500 |
| Less: Outstanding checks | | |
| #2540 | $140 | |
| #1501 | 750 | |
| #1503 | 580 | |
| #1504 | 800 | |
| #1505 | 30 | (2,300) |
| Balance per books | | $ 18,200 |

2. A summary of the bank statement for December 1997.

| | |
|---|---|
| Balance brought forward | $ 19,400 |
| Deposits | 148,700 |
| | 168,100 |
| Charges | (132,500) |
| Balance, December 31, 1997 | $ 35,600 |

3. A summary of the cash book for December 1997 before adjustments.

| | |
|---|---|
| Balance brought forward | $ 18,200 |
| Receipts | 149,690 |
| | 167,890 |
| Disbursements | (124,885) |
| Balance, December 31, 1997 | $ 43,005 |

4. Included with cancelled checks returned with the December bank statement were the checks listed on page 722.
5. The Tuck Company discounted its own 60-day note for $9,000 with the bank on December 1, 1997. The discount rate was 6 percent. The accountant recorded the proceeds as a cash receipt at the face value of the note.
6. The accountant records customers' dishonored checks as a reduction of cash receipts. When the dishonored checks are redeposited they are recorded as a regular cash receipt. Two N.S.F. checks for $180 and $220 were returned by the bank during December. Both checks were redeposited and were recorded by the accountant.
7. Cancellations of Tuck Company checks are recorded by a reduction of cash disbursements.
8. December bank charges were $20. In addition, a $10 service charge was made in December for the collection of a foreign draft in November. These charges were not recorded on the books.
9. Check 2540 listed in the November outstanding checks was drawn in 1995. Since the payee cannot be located, the president of Tuck Company agreed to the CPA's suggestion that the check be written back into the accounts by a journal entry.
10. Outstanding checks at December 31, 1997, totaled $4,000, excluding checks 2540 and 1504.
11. The cutoff bank statement disclosed that the bank had recorded a deposit of $2,400 on January 2, 1998. The accountant had recorded this deposit on the books on December 31, 1997, and then mailed the deposit to the bank.

| Number | Date of Check | Amount of Check | Comment |
|---|---|---|---|
| 1501 | November 28, 1997 | $ 75 | This check was in payment of an invoice for $750 and was recorded in the cash book as $750. |
| 1503 | November 28, 1997 | $ 580 | This check was in payment of an invoice for $580 and was recorded in the cash book as $580. |
| 1523 | December 5, 1997 | $ 150 | Examination of this check revealed that it was unsigned. A discussion with the client disclosed that it had been mailed inadvertently before it was signed. The check was endorsed and deposited by the payee and processed by the bank even though it was a legal nullity. The check was recorded in the cash disbursements journal. |
| 1528 | December 12, 1997 | $ 800 | This check replaced 1504, which was returned by the payee because it was mutilated. Check 1504 was not cancelled on the books. |
| —— | December 19, 1997 | $ 200 | This was a counter check drawn at the bank by the president of the company as a cash advance for travel expense. The president overlooked informing the bookkeeper about the check. |
| —— | December 20, 1997 | $ 300 | The drawer of this check was the Tucker Company. |
| 1535 | December 20, 1997 | $ 350 | This check had been labeled N.S.F. and returned to the payee because the bank had erroneously believed that the check was drawn by the Luck Company. Subsequently, the payee was advised to redeposit the check. |
| 1575 | January 5, 1998 | $10,000 | This check was given to the payee on December 30, 1997, as a postdated check with the understanding that it would not be deposited until January 5. The check was not recorded on the books in December. |

## Required

Prepare a four-column proof of cash of the cash receipts and cash disbursements recorded on the bank statement and on the company's books for the month of December 1997. The reconciliation should agree with the cash figure that will appear in the company's financial statements.*

*AICPA adapted.

# 22

# COMPLETING THE AUDIT

## LEARNING OBJECTIVES

Thorough study of this chapter will enable you to

- 22-1 Conduct a review for contingent liabilities and commitments.
- 22-2 Obtain and evaluate letters from the client's attorneys.
- 22-3 Conduct a post-balance-sheet review for subsequent events.
- 22-4 Design and perform the final steps in the evidence-accumulation segment of the audit.
- 22-5 Integrate the audit evidence gathered, and evaluate the overall audit results.
- 22-6 Communicate effectively with the audit committee and management.
- 22-7 Identify the auditor's responsibilities when facts affecting the audit report are discovered after its issuance.

## GOOD REVIEW CAN NEVER ADEQUATELY COMPENSATE FOR BAD AUDIT PERFORMANCE

"The December 31, 1996 accounts payable were understated by $950,000! How can that be? I reviewed those working papers in detail myself." Larry Lenape's question literally bounced off the staff room walls, and everybody seemed to duck, afraid of what was coming. Lenape is the audit partner for Westside Industries, a large equipment manufacturer located just outside of Dallas, Texas. Lenape's firm, Santro, Best & Harmon, audited the Company for the year ended December 31, 1996. It is now the end of the first quarter of fiscal 1997, and a major "blow" in the 1996 financial statements had come to light.

Accounts payable is a major liability account for a manufacturing company, and testing accounts payable cutoff is an important audit area. Testing primarily involves reviewing the liability recorded by the client by examining subsequent payments to suppliers and other creditors to assure that they were properly recorded.

The person who did the detailed audit work for accounts payable was Clawson Little. Little worked for the firm for a short time, and then left after deciding that he had a better future with an investment firm as a broker. During the Westside Industries audit, Little had already made the decision to leave, and he spent a lot of his time on the phone working on his future plans.

In spite of Little's concentration on his personal affairs, he completed the audit work he was assigned within the time budget. His supervisor refrained from saying anything negative about Little to Lenape, but was glad that Little wouldn't be back next year.

Lenape came in to review the accounts payable working papers. He had another client who had problems in this area, so he wanted to make sure the Westside balance was reasonable. The schedules he saw were properly prepared, with tick marks entered and explained by Little indicating that he had made an extensive examination of underlying data and documents, and had found the client's balance to be adequate as stated. In particular, there were no payments subsequent to year-end for inventory purchases received during the audit period that had not been accrued by the Company.

When the problem of inadequacy with the accounts payable came to light, Santro, Best & Harmon agreed to do an investigation of the problem at their own expense. They went back and looked at all the documents Little had indicated on the working papers that he had inspected. It was quickly apparent that Little had either not looked at the documents or did not know what he was doing when he inspected them. There were almost a million dollars of documents that were applicable to the December 31, 1996 audit period that had not been included as liabilities. This was a major embarrassment to both Lenape and his firm and they lost Westside as a client. They agreed to refund 50 percent of the annual audit fee. From Lenape's point of view, the experience reinforced something he had known for a long time. All of the review in the world can't compensate for poor performance by staff.

After the auditor has completed the tests in specific audit areas, it is necessary to summarize the results and perform additional testing of a more general nature. This is the fourth and last phase of the audit, as shown in Figure 10-10 on page 348. The first four procedures for completing this audit phase are the major topics of this chapter. They are the following: review for contingent liabilities, review for subsequent events, accumulate final evidence, and evaluate results. In addition, communications with the audit committee and management and subsequent discovery of facts existing at the date of the auditor's report are discussed.

## REVIEW FOR CONTINGENT LIABILITIES AND COMMITMENTS

**OBJECTIVE 22-1**

**Conduct a review for contingent liabilities and commitments.**

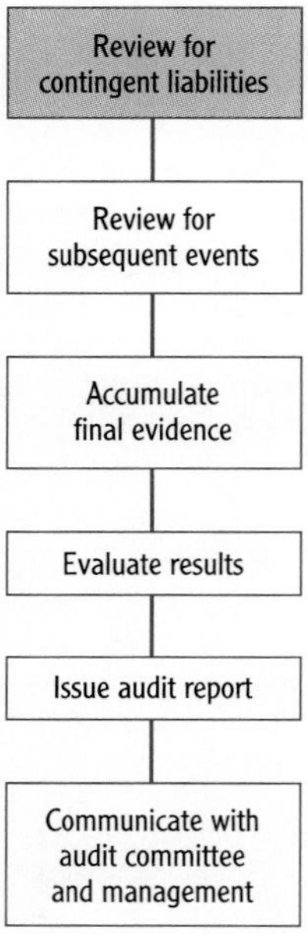


A *contingent liability* is a potential future obligation to an outside party for an unknown amount resulting from activities that have already taken place. Three conditions are required for a contingent liability to exist: (1) there is a potential future payment to an outside party or the impairment of some other asset that would result from an existing condition, (2) there is uncertainty about the amount of the future payment or impairment, and (3) the outcome will be resolved by some future event or events. For example, a lawsuit that has been filed but not yet resolved meets all three of these conditions.

This uncertainty of the future payment can vary from extremely likely to highly unlikely. SFAS 5 describes three levels of likelihood of occurrence and the appropriate financial statement treatment for each likelihood. These requirements are summarized in Table 22-1.

**TABLE 22-1**

**Likelihood of Occurrence and Financial Statement Treatment**

| Likelihood of Occurrence of Event | Financial Statement Treatment |
|---|---|
| Remote (slight chance) | No disclosure is necessary. |
| Reasonably possible (more than remote, but less than probable) | Footnote disclosure is necessary. |
| Probable (likely to occur) | • If the amount can be reasonably estimated, financial statement accounts are adjusted.<br>• If the amount cannot be reasonably estimated, note disclosure is necessary. |

The decision as to the appropriate treatment requires considerable professional judgment.

When the proper disclosure in the financial statements of a material contingency is through a footnote, the footnote should describe the nature of the contingency to the extent it is known and the opinion of legal counsel or management as to the expected outcome. The following is an illustration of a footnote for pending litigation and company guarantees of debt:

> There are various suits and claims pending against the company and its consolidated subsidiaries. It is the opinion of the company's management, based on current available information, that the ultimate liability, if any, resulting from such suits and claims will not materially affect the consolidated financial position or results of operations of the company and its consolidated subsidiaries.
>
> The company has agreed to guarantee the repayment of approximately $14,000,000 loaned by a bank to several affiliated corporations in which the company owns a minority interest.

Certain contingent liabilities are of considerable concern to the auditor:

- Pending litigation for patent infringement, product liability, or other actions
- Income tax disputes
- Product warranties

ment in SAS 12 (AU 337) has the effect of requiring management to give its attorneys permission to provide contingent liability information to auditors and to encourage attorneys to cooperate with auditors in obtaining information about contingencies.

## REVIEW FOR SUBSEQUENT EVENTS

**OBJECTIVE 22-3**
**Conduct a post-balance-sheet review for subsequent events.**

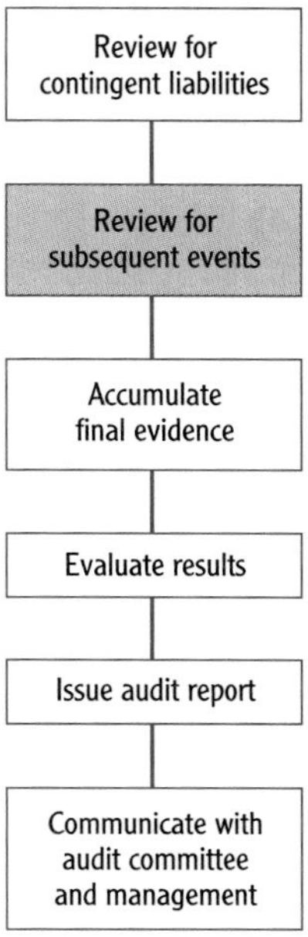


The auditor must review transactions and events occurring after the balance sheet date to determine whether anything occurred that might affect the fair presentation or disclosure of the current-period statements. The auditing procedures required by SAS 1 (AU 560) to verify these transactions and events are commonly referred to as the *review for subsequent events* or *post-balance-sheet review.*

The auditor's responsibility for reviewing for subsequent events is normally limited to the period beginning with the balance sheet date and ending with the date of the auditor's report. Since the date of the auditor's report corresponds to the completion of the important auditing procedures in the client's office, the subsequent events review should be completed near the end of the engagement.[1] Figure 22-2 shows the period covered by a subsequent events review and the timing of that review.

**FIGURE 22-2**

**Period Covered by Subsequent Events Review**

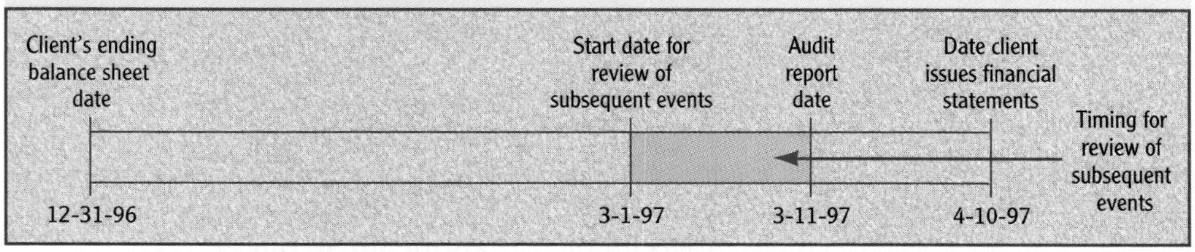


The auditor is responsible for reviewing for subsequent events occurring between 12-31-96 and 3-11-97, but not later than the audit report date. Most subsequent events audit procedures are performed between approximately 3-1-97 and 3-11-97.

### Types of Subsequent Events

Two types of subsequent events require consideration by management and evaluation by the auditor: those that have a direct effect on the financial statements and require adjustment, and those that have no direct effect on the financial statements but for which disclosure is advisable.

**Those That Have a Direct Effect on the Financial Statements and Require Adjustment** These events or transactions provide additional information to management in determining the fair presentation of account balances as of the balance sheet date and to auditors in verifying the balances. For example, if the auditor is having difficulty determining the correct valuation of inventory because of obsolescence, the sale of raw material inventory as scrap in the subsequent period would indicate the correct value of the inventory as of the balance sheet date.

Such subsequent period events as the following require an adjustment of account balances in the current year's financial statements if the amounts are material:

- Declaration of bankruptcy by a customer with an outstanding accounts receivable balance due to deteriorating financial condition

[1]When the auditor's name is associated with a registration statement under the Securities Act of 1933, his or her responsibility for reviewing subsequent events extends beyond the date of the auditor's report to the date the registration becomes effective.

- Settlement of a litigation at an amount different from the amount recorded on the books
- Disposal of equipment not being used in operations at a price below the current book value
- Sale of investments at a price below recorded cost

Whenever subsequent events are used to evaluate the amounts included in the statements, care must be taken to distinguish between conditions that existed at the balance sheet date and those that came into being after the end of the year. The subsequent information should not be incorporated directly into the statements if the conditions causing the change in valuation did not take place until after year-end. For example, the sale of scrap in the subsequent period would not be relevant in the valuation of inventory for obsolescence if the obsolescence took place after the end of the year.

**Those That Have No Direct Effect on the Financial Statements But for Which Disclosure Is Advisable** Subsequent events of this type provide evidence of conditions that did not exist at the date of the balance sheet being reported on but are so significant that they require disclosure even though they do not require adjustment. Ordinarily, these events can be adequately disclosed by the use of footnotes, but occasionally one may be so significant as to require *supplementing the historical statements* with statements that include the effect of the event as if it had occurred on the balance sheet date.

Following are examples of events or transactions occurring in the subsequent period that may require disclosure rather than an adjustment in the financial statements:

- Decline in the market value of securities held for temporary investment or resale
- Issuance of bonds or equity securities
- Decline in the market value of inventory as a consequence of government action barring further sale of a product
- Uninsured loss of inventories as a result of fire

## Audit Tests

Audit procedures for the subsequent events review can be conveniently divided into two categories: procedures normally integrated as a part of the verification of year-end account balances and those performed specifically for the purpose of discovering events or transactions that must be recognized as subsequent events.

The first category includes cutoff and valuation tests done as a part of the tests of details of balances. For example, subsequent period sales and acquisition transactions are examined to determine whether the cutoff is accurate. Similarly, many valuation tests involving subsequent events are also performed as a part of the verification of account balances. As an example, it is common to test the collectibility of accounts receivable by reviewing subsequent period cash receipts. It is also a normal audit procedure to compare the subsequent period purchase price of inventory with the recorded cost as a test of lower of cost or market valuation. The procedures for cutoff and valuation have been discussed sufficiently in preceding chapters and are not repeated here.

The second category of tests is performed specifically to obtain information to incorporate into the current year's account balances or footnotes. These tests include the following:

**Inquire of Management** Inquiries vary from client to client, but normally are about potential contingent liabilities or commitments, significant changes in the assets or capital structure of the company, the current status of items that were not completely resolved at the balance sheet date, and unusual adjustments made subsequent to the balance sheet date.

Inquiries of management about subsequent events must be held with the proper client personnel to obtain meaningful answers. For example, discussing tax or union matters with the accounts receivable supervisor would not be appropriate. Most inquiries should be held with the controller, the vice presidents, and the president, depending on the information desired.

**Correspond with Attorneys** Correspondence with attorneys, which was previously discussed, takes place as a part of the search for contingent liabilities. In obtaining letters from attorneys, the auditor must remember his or her responsibility for testing for subsequent events up to the date of the audit report. A common approach is to request the attorney to date and mail the letter as of the expected completion date for field work.

**Review Internal Statements Prepared Subsequent to the Balance Sheet Date** The emphasis in the review should be on (1) changes in the business relative to results for the same period in the year under audit and (2) changes after year-end. The auditor should pay careful attention to major changes in the business or environment in which the client is operating. The statements should be discussed with management to determine whether they are prepared on the same basis as the current period statements, and there should be inquiries about significant changes in the operating results.

**Review Records Prepared Subsequent to the Balance Sheet Date** Journals and ledgers should be reviewed to determine the existence and nature of significant transactions related to the current year. If the journals are not kept up to date, documents relating to the journals should be reviewed.

**Examine Minutes Issued Subsequent to the Balance Sheet Date** The minutes of stockholders' and directors' meetings subsequent to the balance sheet date must be examined for important subsequent events affecting the current period financial statements.

**Obtain a Letter of Representation** The letter of representation written by the client to the auditor formalizes statements that the client has made about different matters throughout the audit, including discussions about subsequent events.

### Dual Dating

Occasionally the auditor determines that an important subsequent event occurred after the field work was completed, but *before the audit report was issued.* The source of such information is typically management or the press. An example using the dates in Figure 22-2 on page 729 is the acquisition of another company by an audit client on March 23, when the last day of field work was March 11. In such a situation, SAS 1 (AU 530) requires the auditor to extend audit tests for the newly discovered subsequent event to make sure that it is correctly disclosed. The auditor has two equally acceptable options for expanding subsequent events tests: expand all subsequent events tests to the new date, or restrict the subsequent events review to matters related to the new subsequent event. For the first option, the audit report date is changed, whereas for the second, the audit report is *dual-dated.* In the example of the acquisition, assume that the auditor returned to the client's premises and completed audit tests on March 31 pertaining only to the acquisition. The audit report is dual-dated as follows: March 11, 1997, except for note 17, as to which the date is March 31, 1997.

## FINAL EVIDENCE ACCUMULATION

The auditor has several final accumulation responsibilities that apply to all cycles besides the search for contingent liabilities and the review for subsequent events. The four most important ones are discussed in this section. All four are done late in the engagement.

### Final Analytical Procedures

Analytical procedures were introduced in Chapter 6 and applied to specific cycles in several other chapters. As discussed in Chapter 6, analytical procedures are normally used as a part of planning the audit, during the performance of detailed tests in each cycle, and at the completion of the audit.

**OBJECTIVE 22-4**
**Design and perform the final steps in the evidence-accumulation segment of the audit.**

Analytical procedures done during the completion of the audit are useful as a final review for material misstatements or financial problems not noted during other testing, and to help the auditor take a final objective look at the financial statements. It is common for a partner to do the analytical procedures during the final review of working papers and financial statements. Typically, a partner has a good understanding of the client and its business because of ongoing relationships. Knowledge of the client's business combined with effective analytical procedures help identify possible oversights in an audit.

## Evaluate Going Concern Assumption

SAS 59 (AU 341) requires the auditor to evaluate whether there is a substantial doubt about a client's ability to continue as a going concern for at least one year beyond the balance sheet date. That assessment is initially made as a part of planning but is revised whenever significant new information is obtained. For example, if the auditor discovered during the audit that the company had defaulted on a loan, lost its primary customer, or decided to dispose of substantial assets to pay off loans, the initial assessment of going concern may need revision. A final assessment is desirable after all evidence has been accumulated and proposed audit adjustments have been incorporated into the financial statements.

Analytical procedures are one of the most important types of evidence to assess going concern. Discussions with management and a review of future plans are important considerations in evaluating analytical procedures. Knowledge of the client's business gained throughout the audit is important information used to assess the likelihood of financial failure within the next year.

## Client Representation Letter

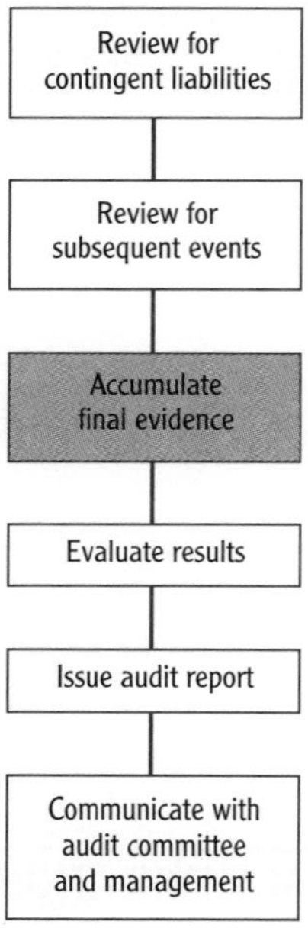


SAS 19 (AU 333) requires the auditor to obtain a *letter of representation* documenting management's most important oral representations during the audit. The client representation letter is prepared on the client's letterhead, addressed to the CPA firm, and signed by high-level corporate officials, usually the president and chief financial officer.

There are two purposes of the client letter of representation:

- *To impress upon management its responsibility for the assertions in the financial statements.* For example, if the letter of representation includes a reference to pledged assets and contingent liabilities, honest management may be reminded of its unintentional failure to disclose the information adequately. To fulfill this objective, the letter of representation should be sufficiently detailed to act as a reminder to management.
- *To document the responses from management to inquiries about various aspects of the audit.* This provides written documentation of client representations in the event of disagreement or a lawsuit between the auditor and client.

The letter should be dated as of the auditor's report date to make sure that there are representations related to the subsequent events review. The letter implies that it has originated with the client, but it is common practice for the auditor to prepare the letter and request the client to type it on the company's letterhead and sign it. Refusal by a client to prepare and sign the letter would require a qualified opinion or disclaimer of opinion.

SAS 19 suggests many specific matters that should be included, when applicable, in a client representation letter. A few of these are:

- Management's acknowledgment of its responsibility for the fair presentation in the statements of financial position, results of operations, and cash flows in conformity with generally accepted accounting principles or other comprehensive basis of accounting.
- Availability of all financial records and related data.
- Completeness and availability of all minutes of meetings of stockholders, directors, and committees of directors.
- Information concerning related party transactions and related amounts receivable or payable.
- Plans or intentions that may affect the carrying value or classification of assets or liabilities.
- Disclosure of compensating balances or other arrangements involving restrictions on cash balances, and disclosure of line-of-credit or similar arrangements.

A client representation letter is a written statement from a nonindependent source and therefore *cannot be regarded as reliable evidence.* The letter does provide documentation that management has been asked certain questions to make sure that management understands its responsibilities and to protect the auditor if there are claims against the auditor by management.

### Other Information in Annual Reports

SAS 8 (AU 550) requires the auditor to read information included in published annual reports pertaining directly to the financial statements. For example, assume that the president's letter in the annual report refers to an increase in earnings per share from $2.60 to $2.93. The auditor is required to compare that information with the financial statements to make sure it corresponds.

SAS 8 pertains only to information that is not a part of the financial statements but is published with them. Examples are the president's letter and explanations of company activities included in annual reports of nearly all publicly held companies. It usually takes the auditor only a few minutes to make sure that the nonfinancial statement information is consistent with the statements. If the auditor concludes that there is a material inconsistency, the client should be requested to change the information. If the client refuses, which would be unusual, the auditor should include an explanatory paragraph in the audit report or withdraw from the engagement.

## EVALUATE RESULTS

**OBJECTIVE 22-5**
**Integrate the audit evidence gathered, and evaluate the overall audit results.**

After performing all audit procedures in each audit area, the auditor must integrate the results into *one overall conclusion.* Ultimately, the auditor must decide whether sufficient audit evidence has been accumulated to warrant the conclusion that the financial statements are stated in accordance with generally accepted accounting principles, applied on a basis consistent with those of the preceding year.

Figure 22-3 on page 734 summarizes the parts of the audit that must be reviewed in the evaluation of results. The emphasis is on the conclusions reached through tests of controls, substantive tests of transactions, analytical procedures, and tests of details of balances for each of the five cycles shown in the figure. Five aspects of evaluating the results are discussed.

### Sufficiency of Evidence

The final evaluation of the adequacy of the evidence is a review by the auditor of the entire audit to determine whether all important aspects have been adequately tested, considering all circumstances of the engagement. A major step in this process is to review the entire audit program to make sure that all parts have been accurately completed and documented and that all audit objectives have been met. This review includes deciding whether the audit program is adequate, considering problem areas identified as the audit progressed. For example, if misstatements were discovered during tests of sales, the initial plans for tests of details of accounts receivable may have been insufficient. The final review should evaluate whether the revised audit program is adequate.

As an aid in drawing final conclusions about the adequacy of the audit evidence, auditors frequently use a *completing the engagement checklist.* Such a checklist is a reminder of aspects of the audit that must not be overlooked. An illustration of part of a completing the engagement checklist is given in Figure 22-4 on page 735.

If the auditor concludes that he or she has *not* obtained sufficient evidence to draw a conclusion about the fairness of the client's representations, there are two choices: additional evidence must be obtained, or either a qualified opinion or a disclaimer of opinion must be issued.

### Evidence Supports Auditor's Opinion

An important part of evaluating whether the financial statements are fairly stated is summarizing the misstatements uncovered in the audit. Whenever the auditor uncovers misstatements that are in themselves material, entries should be proposed to the client to correct the

**FIGURE 22-3**

**Evaluating Engagement Results**

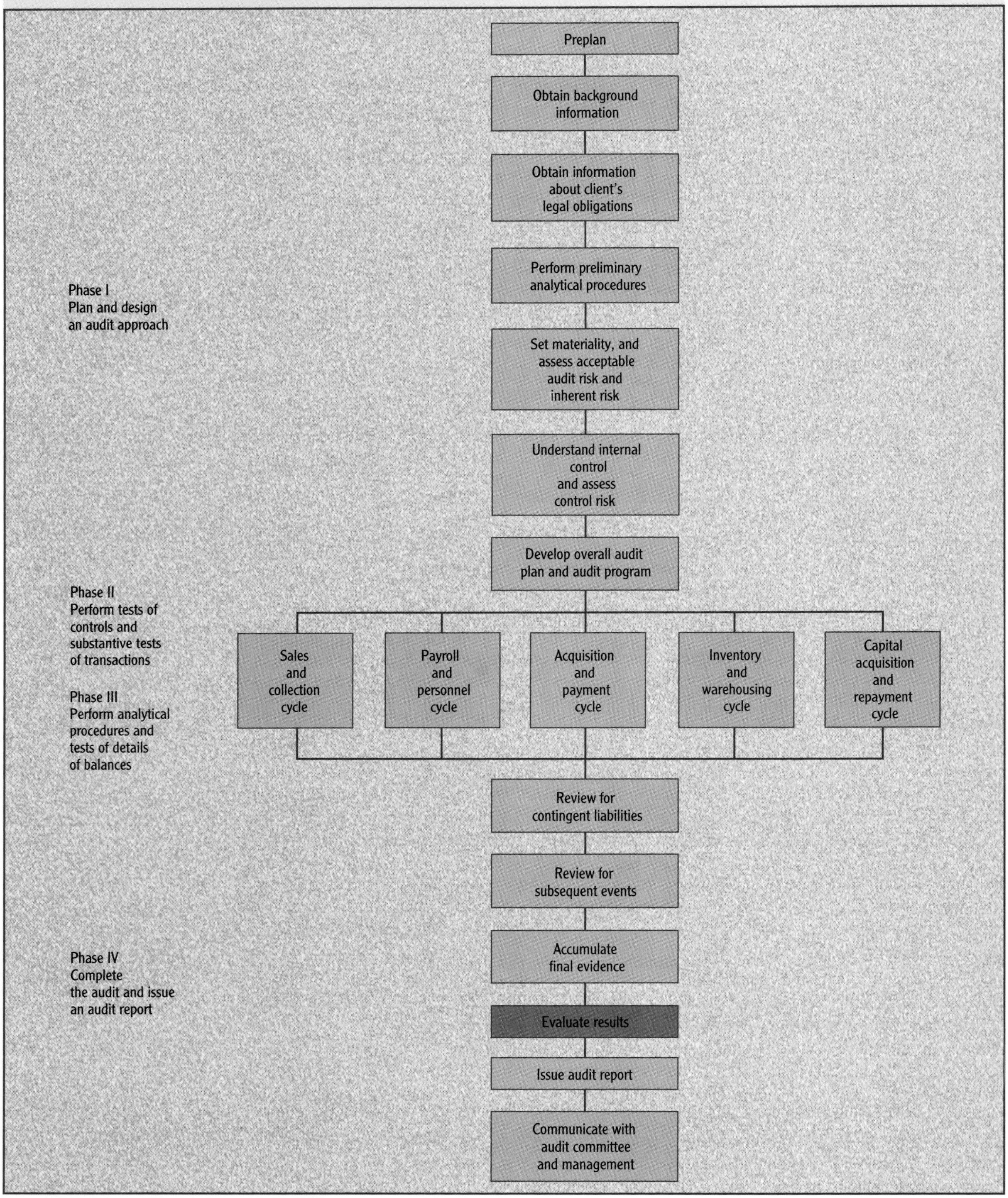

**FIGURE 22-4**

**Completing the Engagement Checklist**

| | YES | NO |
|---|---|---|
| **1. Examination of prior year's working papers** | | |
| **a.** Were last year's working papers and review notes examined for areas of emphasis in the current-year audit? | _____ | _____ |
| **b.** Was the permanent file reviewed for items that affect the current year? | _____ | _____ |
| **2. Internal control** | | |
| **a.** Has internal control been adequately understood? | _____ | _____ |
| **b.** Is the scope of the audit adequate in light of the assessed control risk? | _____ | _____ |
| **c.** Have all major weaknesses been included in a management letter and reportable conditions in a letter to the audit committee or to senior management? | _____ | _____ |
| **3. General documents** | | |
| **a.** Were all current-year minutes and resolutions reviewed, abstracted, and followed up? | _____ | _____ |
| **b.** Has the permanent file been updated? | _____ | _____ |
| **c.** Have all major contracts and agreements been reviewed and abstracted or copied to ascertain that the client complies with all existing legal requirements? | _____ | _____ |

statements. It may be difficult to determine the appropriate amount of adjustment because the true value of a misstatement may be unknown; nevertheless, it is the auditor's responsibility to decide on the required adjustment. In addition to the material misstatements, there are often a large number of immaterial misstatements discovered that are not adjusted at the time they are found. It is necessary to combine individually immaterial misstatements to evaluate whether the combined amount is material. The auditor can keep track of these misstatements and combine them in several different ways, but many auditors use a convenient method known as an *unadjusted misstatement worksheet* or *summary of possible adjustments.* It is relatively easy to evaluate the overall significance of several immaterial misstatements with this type of working paper. An example of an unadjusted misstatement worksheet is given in Figure 22-5 (page 736).

The schedule in Figure 22-5 includes both known misstatements that the client has decided not to adjust and projected misstatements, including sampling error. Observe that in the bottom left-hand portion of the working paper there is a comparison of possible adjustments to the preliminary judgment about materiality decided during planning.

If the auditor believes that he or she *has* sufficient evidence, but it does not warrant a conclusion of fairly presented financial statements, the auditor again has two choices: the statements must be revised to the auditor's satisfaction, or either a qualified or an adverse opinion must be issued. Notice that the options here are different from those in the case of insufficient evidence obtained.

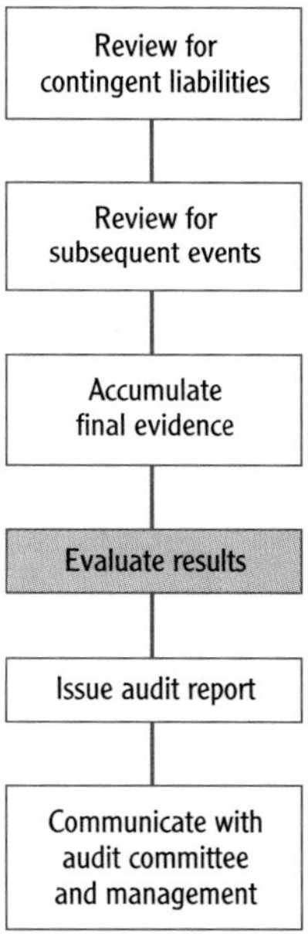


### Financial Statement Disclosures

A major consideration in completing the audit is to determine whether the disclosures in the financial statements are adequate. Throughout the audit, the emphasis is most often on verifying the accuracy of the balances in the general ledger by testing the most important accounts on the auditor's trial balance. Another important task is to make sure that the account balances on the trial balance are correctly aggregated and disclosed on the financial statements. Naturally, adequate disclosure includes consideration of all of the statements, including related footnotes.

The auditor actually prepares the financial statements from the trial balance in many small audits and submits them to the client for approval. Performing this function may seem to imply that the client has been relieved of responsibility for the fair representation in the statements, but that is not the case. The auditor acts in the role of advisor when preparing financial statements, but *management retains the final responsibility for approving the issuance of the statements.*

**FIGURE 22-5**

**Unadjusted Misstatement Worksheet**

ABC Company, Inc.
Summary of Possible Adjustments

12/31/96

Schedule A-3 Date
Prepared by PR 1/28/97
Approved by GS 1/31/97

| Workpaper Source | | Total Amount | Possible Adjustments-Dr <Cr> Current Assets | Non-current Assets | Current Liabilities | Non-current Liabilities | Sales and Revenues | Costs and Expenses | Federal Income Tax |
|---|---|---|---|---|---|---|---|---|---|
| B-32 | Unreimbursed petty cash vouchers | 480 | <480> | | 240 | | | 480 | <240> |
| C-4 | Possible underprovision in allowance for uncollectible accounts | 4000 | <4000> | | 2000 | | | 4000 | <2000> |
| C-8 | Accounts receivable/Sales cutoff misstatements | 600 | 600 | | <300> | | <600> | | 300 |
| D-2 | Difference between physical inventory and book figures | 5200 | 5200 | | <2600> | | | <5200> | 2600 |
| H-7/2 | Unrecorded liabilities | 4850 | 2000 | 1850 | <4350> | | | 1000 | <500> |
| V-10 | Repairs expense items which should be capitalized | 900 | | 900 | <450> | | | <900> | 450 |
| | Totals | | 3320 | 2750 | <5460> | | <600> | <620> | 610 |

Conclusions:

The net effects of the above items are as follows:

| | Possible Adjustments | Preliminary Judgment About Materiality |
|---|---|---|
| Working capital | $<2140> | $10,000 |
| Total assets | 6070 | 20,000 |
| Net income | <610> | 4,000 |

None of these aggregate effects or the individual items has a material effect on the financial statements in total or with respect to the components they pertain to. On this basis, adjustment of any or all of the items is passed.

Paul Roberts
1/28/97

Review for adequate disclosure in the financial statements at the completion of the audit is not the only time the auditor is interested in proper disclosure. Unless the auditor is constantly alert for disclosure problems, it is impossible to perform the final disclosure review adequately. For example, as part of the audit of accounts receivable, the auditor must be aware of the need to separate notes receivable and amounts due from affiliates and trade accounts due from customers. Similarly, there must be a segregation of current from noncurrent receivables and a disclosure of the factoring or discounting of notes receivable if such is the case. An important part of verifying all account balances is determining whether generally accepted accounting principles were properly applied on a basis consistent with that of the preceding year. The auditor must carefully document this information in the working papers to facilitate the final review.

As part of the final review for financial statement disclosure, many CPA firms require the completion of a *financial statement disclosure checklist* for every engagement. These questionnaires are designed to remind the auditor of common disclosure problems encountered on audits and also to facilitate the final review of the entire audit by an independent partner. An illustration of a partial financial statement disclosure checklist is given in Figure 22-6. Naturally, it is not sufficient to rely on a checklist to replace the auditor's own knowledge of gener-

**FIGURE 22-6**

**Financial Statement Disclosure Checklist: Property, Plant, and Equipment**

1. Are the following disclosures included in the financial statements or notes (APB 12, para. 5):
   a. Balances of major classes of depreciable assets (land, building, equipment, and so forth) at the balance sheet date?
   b. Allowances for depreciation, by class or in total, at the balance sheet date?
   c. General description of depreciation methods for major classes of PP&E (APB 22, para. 13)?
   d. Total amount of depreciation charged to expense for each income statement presented?
   e. Basis of evaluation (SAS 32, AU 431.02)?
2. Are carrying amounts of property mortgaged and encumbered by indebtedness disclosed (FASB 5, para. 18)?
3. Are details of sale and leaseback transactions during the period disclosed (FASB 13, para. 32–34)?
4. Is the carrying amount of property not a part of operating plant—for example, idle or held for investment or sale—segregated?
5. Has consideration been given to disclosure of fully depreciated capital assets still in use and capital assets not presently in use?

*Note:* Information in parentheses refers to authoritative professional literature.

ally accepted accounting principles. In any given audit, some aspects of the engagement require much greater expertise in accounting than can be obtained from such a checklist.

## Working Paper Review

There are three main reasons why it is essential that working papers be thoroughly reviewed by another member of the audit firm at the completion of the audit:

- *To evaluate the performance of inexperienced personnel.* A considerable portion of most audits is performed by audit personnel with less than four or five years of experience. These people may have sufficient technical training to conduct an adequate audit, but their lack of experience affects their ability to make sound professional judgments in complex situations.
- *To make sure that the audit meets the CPA firm's standard of performance.* Within any organization the performance quality of individuals varies considerably, but careful review by top-level personnel in the firm assists in maintaining a uniform quality of auditing.
- *To counteract the bias that frequently enters into the auditor's judgment.* Auditors must attempt to remain objective throughout the audit, but it is easy to lose proper perspective on a long audit when there are complex problems to solve.

Except for a final independent review, which is discussed shortly, the review of the working papers should be conducted by someone who is knowledgeable about the client and the unique circumstances in the audit. Therefore, the initial review of the working papers prepared by any given auditor is normally done by the auditor's immediate supervisor. For example, the least experienced auditor's work is ordinarily reviewed by the audit senior. The senior's immediate superior, who is normally a supervisor or manager, reviews the senior's work and also reviews less thoroughly the papers of the inexperienced auditor. Finally, the partner assigned to the audit must ultimately review all working papers, but the partner reviews those prepared by the supervisor or manager more thoroughly than the others. Except for the final independent review, most of the working paper review is done as each segment of the audit is completed.

## Independent Review

At the completion of larger audits, it is common to have the financial statements and the entire set of working papers reviewed by a completely independent reviewer who has not participated in the engagement. An independent review is required for SEC engagements. This reviewer frequently takes an adversary position to make sure that the conduct of the audit was adequate. The audit team must be able to justify the evidence they have accumulated and the conclusions they reached on the basis of the unique circumstances of the engagement.

## Summary of Evidence Evaluation

Figure 22-7 summarizes both the evaluation of the sufficiency of the evidence and deciding whether the evidence supports the opinion. The top portion of the figure shows the planning decisions that determine the planned audit evidence. It was taken from Figure 8-10 on page 271. The bottom portion shows how the auditor evaluates the sufficiency of actual evidence by first evaluating achieved audit risk, by account and by cycle, and then making the same evaluation for the overall financial statements. The auditor also evaluates whether the evidence supports the audit opinion by first estimating misstatements in each account and then for the overall financial statements. In practice, the evaluation of achieved audit risk and estimated misstatement are made at the same time. On the basis of these evaluations the audit report is issued for the financial statements.

**FIGURE 22-7**

**Evaluating Results and Reaching Conclusions on the Basis of Evidence**

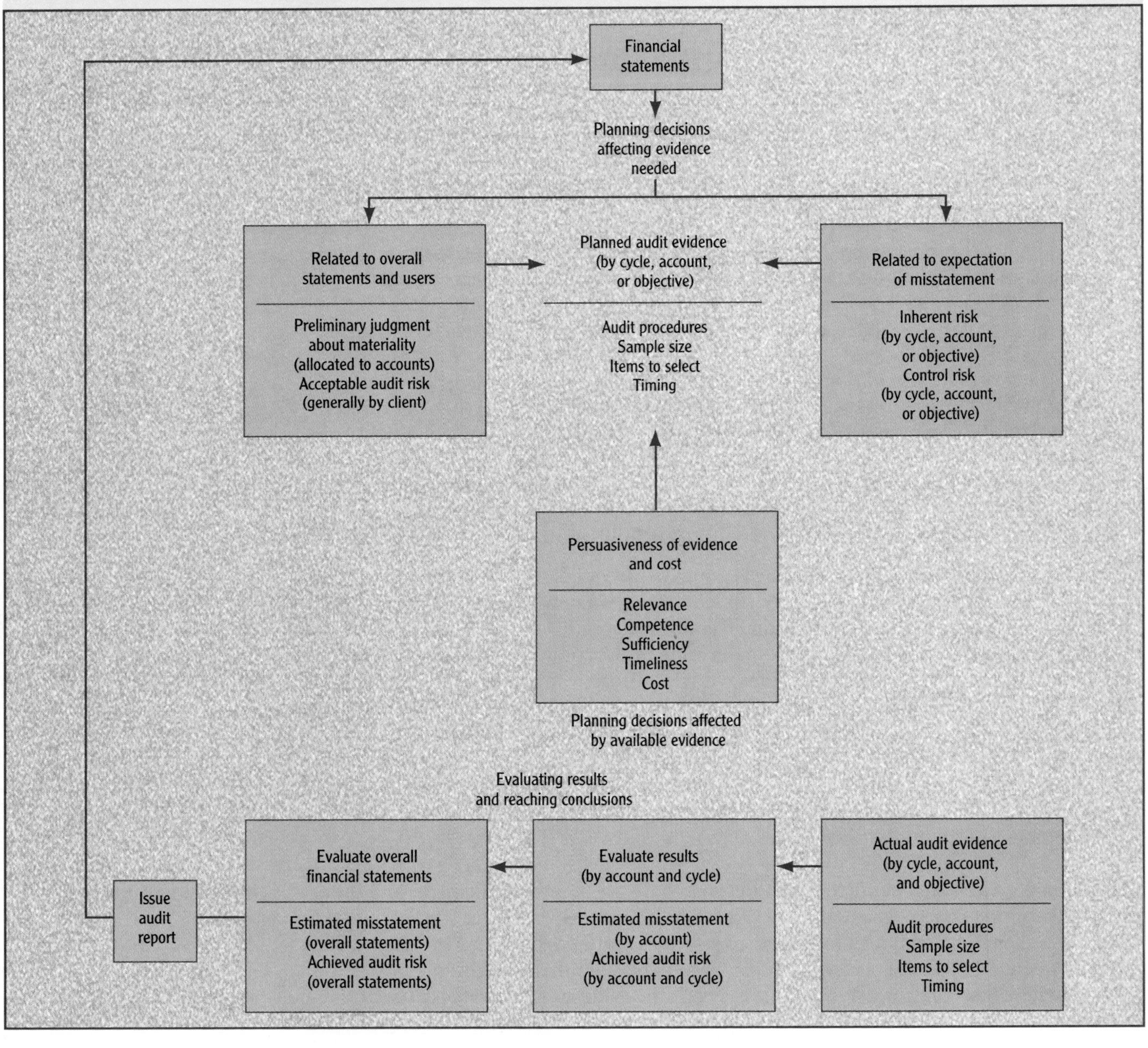

## COMMUNICATE WITH THE AUDIT COMMITTEE AND MANAGEMENT

**OBJECTIVE 22-6**
**Communicate effectively with the audit committee and management.**

After the audit is completed, there are several potential communications from the auditor to client personnel. Most of these are directed to the audit committee or senior management, but communications with operating management are also common.

### Communicate Fraud and Illegal Acts

SAS 82 (AU 316) and SAS 54 (317) require the auditor to communicate all fraud and illegal acts to the audit committee or similarly designated group, regardless of materiality. The purpose is to assist the audit committee in performing its supervisory role for reliable financial statements. This requirement indicates the increased concern of the profession over the auditors' responsibility for the detection and prevention of fraud.

### Communicate Reportable Conditions

As discussed in Chapter 9, the auditor must also communicate significant deficiencies in the design or operation of internal control. In larger companies this communication is made to the audit committee and in smaller companies to the owners or senior management. The nature and form of that communication were discussed in Chapter 9.

### Other Communication with Audit Committee

SAS 61 (AU 380) requires the auditor to communicate certain additional information obtained during the audit for all SEC engagements and other audits where there is an audit committee or similarly designated body. This communication is not required for most small nonpublic companies. Like all communications with the audit committee, the purpose is to keep the committee informed of auditing issues and findings that will assist them in performing their supervisory role for financial statements.

The following are major items that must be communicated to the audit committee or similarly designated body under SAS 61:

- Auditor's responsibilities under generally accepted auditing standards, including responsibility for evaluating internal control and the concept of reasonable rather than absolute assurance.
- Significant accounting policies selected and applied to the financial statements, including management's judgments and estimates of accounting-related issues.
- Significant financial statement adjustments found during the audit and the implications of both those that management has chosen to record and those proposed but not recorded.
- Disagreements with management about the scope of the audit, applicability of accounting principles, or wording of the audit report.
- Difficulties encountered in performing the audit, such as lack of availability of client personnel and failure to provide necessary information.

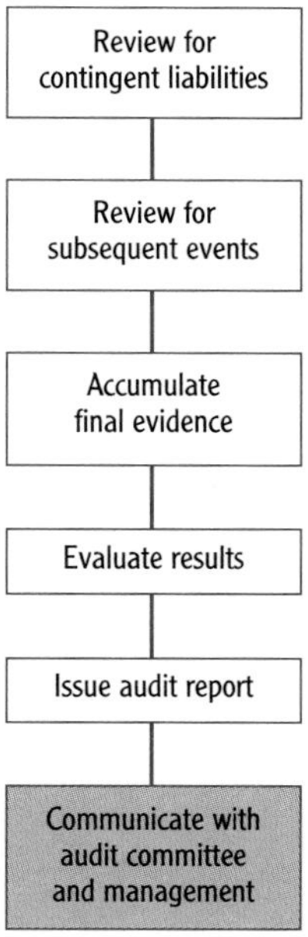


Communication with the audit committee normally takes place more than once during each audit and can be oral, written, or both. For example, issues dealing with the auditor's responsibilities and significant accounting policies are usually discussed early in the audit, preferably during the planning phase. Disagreements with management and difficulties encountered in performing the audit are communicated after the audit is completed, or earlier if the problems hinder the auditor's ability to complete the audit. The most important matters are communicated in writing to minimize misunderstanding and to provide documentation in the event of subsequent disagreement.

### Management Letters

The purpose of a management letter is to inform the client of the CPA's recommendations for improving the client's business. The recommendations focus on suggestions for more efficient operations. The combination of the auditor's experience in various businesses and a thorough understanding gained in conducting the audit place the auditor in a unique position to provide management with assistance.

A management letter is different from a reportable conditions letter discussed in Chapter 9. The latter is required by SAS 60 (AU 325) whenever there are reportable conditions.

It must follow a prescribed format and be sent in accordance with SAS requirements. A management letter is optional and is intended to help the client operate its business more effectively. Auditors write management letters for two reasons: to encourage a better relationship between the CPA firm and management, and to suggest additional tax and management services that the CPA firm can provide.

There is no standard format or approach for writing management letters. Each letter should be developed to meet the style of the auditor and the needs of the client, consistent with the CPA firm's concept of management letters. It should be noted that many auditors combine the management letter with the reportable conditions letter. On smaller audits it is common for the auditor to communicate operational suggestions orally rather than by letter.

## SUBSEQUENT DISCOVERY OF FACTS[2]

**OBJECTIVE 22-7**
**Identify the auditor's responsibilities when facts affecting the audit report are discovered after its issuance.**

If the auditor becomes aware *after the audited financial statements have been issued* that some information included in the statements is materially misleading, the auditor has an obligation to make certain that users who are relying on the financial statements are informed about the misstatements. The most likely case in which the auditor is faced with this problem occurs when the financial statements are determined to include a material misstatement subsequent to the issuance of an unqualified report. Some possible causes of misstatements are the inclusion of material nonexistent sales, the failure to write off obsolete inventory, or the omission of an essential footnote. Regardless of whether the failure to discover the misstatement was the fault of the auditor or the client, the auditor's responsibility remains the same.

The most desirable approach to follow if the auditor discovers that the statements are misleading after they have been issued is to request that the client issue an immediate revision of the financial statements containing an explanation of the reasons for the revision. If a subsequent period's financial statements are completed before the revised statements would be issued, it is acceptable to disclose the misstatements in the subsequent period's statements. Whenever it is pertinent, the client should inform the Securities and Exchange Commission and other regulatory agencies of the misleading financial statements. The auditor has the responsibility for making certain that the client has taken the appropriate steps in informing users of the misleading statements.

If the client refuses to cooperate in disclosing the misstated information, the auditor must inform the board of directors of this fact. The auditor must also notify regulatory agencies having jurisdiction over the client and, where practical, each person who relies on the financial statements, that the statements are no longer trustworthy. If the stock is publicly held, it is acceptable to request the Securities and Exchange Commission and the stock exchange to notify the stockholders.

It is important to understand that the subsequent discovery of facts requiring the recall or reissuance of financial statements *does not arise from business events occurring after the date of the auditor's report.* For example, if an account receivable is believed to be collectible after an adequate review of the facts at the date of the audit report, but the customer subsequently files bankruptcy, a revision of the financial statements is not required. The statements must be recalled or reissued only when information that would indicate that the statements were not fairly presented *already existed at the audit report date.* If, in the previous example, the customer had filed for bankruptcy before the audit report date, there is a subsequent discovery of facts.

In an earlier section it was shown that the auditor's responsibility for subsequent events review begins as of the balance sheet date and ends on the date of the completion of the field work. Any pertinent information discovered as a part of the review can be incorporated in the financial statements before they are issued. Note that the auditor has no responsibility to search for subsequent facts of the nature discussed in this section, but if the

[2]Subsequent discovery of facts is not a part of completing the audit. It is included in this chapter because the topic is easier to understand when it is compared to and contrasted with subsequent events.

auditor discovers that issued financial statements are improperly stated, he or she must take action to correct them. The auditor's responsibility for reporting on improperly issued financial statements does not start until the date of the audit report. Typically, an existing material misstatement is found as a part of the subsequent year's audit, or it may be reported to the auditor by the client.

Figure 22-8, which includes the same dates as Figure 22-2 on page 729, shows the difference in the period covered by the review for subsequent events and that for the discovery of facts after the audit report date. If the auditor discovers subsequent facts after the audit report date, but before the financial statements are issued, the auditor will require that the financial statements be revised before they are issued.

**FIGURE 22-8**

**Review for Subsequent Events and Subsequent Discovery of Facts**

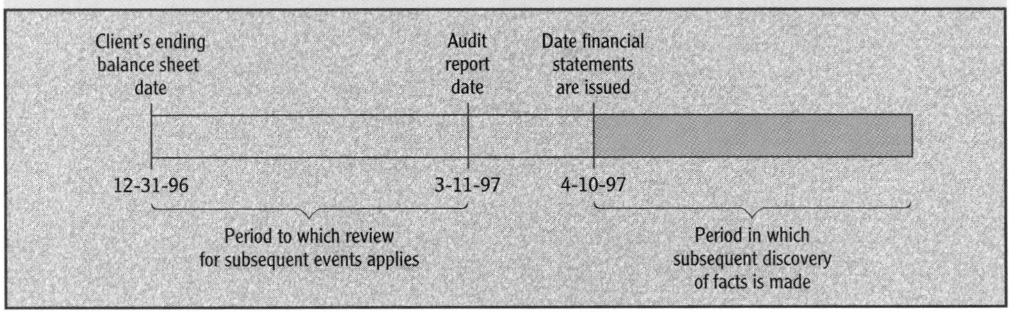


## ESSENTIAL TERMS

**Commitments**—agreements that the entity will hold to a fixed set of conditions, such as the purchase or sale of merchandise at a stated price, at a future date, regardless of what happens to profits or to the economy as a whole

**Completing the engagement checklist**—a reminder to the auditor of aspects of the audit that may have been overlooked

**Contingent liability**—a potential future obligation to an outside party for an unknown amount resulting from activities that have already taken place

**Dual-dated audit report**—the use of one audit report date for normal subsequent events and a later date for one or more subsequent events that come to the auditor's attention after the field work has been completed

**Financial statement disclosure checklist**—a questionnaire that reminds the auditor of disclosure problems commonly encountered in audits, and that facilitates final review of the entire audit by an independent partner

**Independent review**—a review of the financial statements and the entire set of working papers by a completely independent reviewer to whom the audit team must justify the evidence accumulated and the conclusions reached

**Inquiry of client's attorneys**—a letter from the client's legal counsel informing the auditor of pending litigation or any other information involving legal counsel that is relevant to financial statement disclosure

**Letter of representation**—a written communication from the client to the auditor formalizing statements that the client has made about matters pertinent to the audit

**Other information in annual reports**—information that is not a part of published financial statements, but is published with them. Auditors must read this information for inconsistencies with the financial statements.

**Review for subsequent events**—the auditing procedures performed by auditors to identify and evaluate subsequent events

**Subsequent events**—transactions and other pertinent events that occurred after the balance sheet date, which affect the fair presentation or disclosure of the statements being audited

**Unadjusted misstatement worksheet**—a summary of immaterial misstatements not adjusted at the time they were found, used to help the auditor assess whether the combined amount is material; also known as a *summary of possible adjustments*

**Unasserted claim**—a potential legal claim against a client where the condition for a claim exists but no claim has been filed

**Working paper review**—a review of the completed audit working papers by another member of the audit firm to ensure quality and counteract bias

## REVIEW QUESTIONS

**22-1 (Objective 22-1)** Distinguish between a contingent liability and an actual liability, and give three examples of each.

**22-2 (Objective 22-1)** In the audit of the James Mobley Company, you are concerned about the possibility of contingent liabilities resulting in income tax disputes. Discuss the procedures you could use for an extensive investigation in this area.

**22-3 (Objective 22-2)** Explain why the analysis of legal expense is an essential part of every audit engagement.

**22-4 (Objectives 22-1, 22-2)** During the audit of the Merrill Manufacturing Company, Ralph Pyson, CPA, has become aware of four lawsuits against the client through discussions with the client, reading corporate minutes, and reviewing correspondence files. How should Pyson determine the materiality of the lawsuits and the proper disclosure in the financial statements?

**22-5 (Objective 22-2)** Distinguish between an asserted and an unasserted claim. Explain why a client's attorney may not reveal an unasserted claim.

**22-6 (Objective 22-2)** Describe the action that an auditor should take if an attorney refuses to provide information that is within his or her jurisdiction and may directly affect the fair presentation of the financial statements.

**22-7 (Objective 22-3)** Distinguish between the two general types of subsequent events and explain how they differ. Give two examples of each type.

**22-8 (Objectives 22-2, 22-3)** In obtaining letters from attorneys, Bill Malano's aim is to receive the letters as early as possible after the balance sheet date. This provides him with a signed letter from every attorney in time to properly investigate any exceptions. It also eliminates the problem of a lot of unresolved loose ends near the end of the audit. Evaluate Malano's approach.

**22-9 (Objective 22-1)** Explain why an auditor would be interested in a client's future commitments to purchase raw materials at a fixed price.

**22-10 (Objective 22-3)** What major considerations should the auditor take into account in determining how extensive the review of subsequent events should be?

**22-11 (Objective 22-3)** Identify five audit procedures normally done as a part of the review for subsequent events.

**22-12 (Objectives 22-3, 22-7)** Distinguish between subsequent events occurring between the balance sheet date and the date of the auditor's report, and subsequent discovery of facts existing at the date of the auditor's report. Give two examples of each and explain the appropriate action by the auditor in each instance.

**22-13 (Objective 22-4)** Miles Lawson, CPA, believes that the final summarization is the easiest part of the audit if careful planning is followed throughout the engagement. He makes sure that each segment of the audit is completed before he goes on to the next. When the last segment of the engagement is completed, he is finished with the audit. He believes this may cause each part of the audit to take a little longer, but he makes up for it by not having to do the final summarization. Evaluate Lawson's approach.

**22-14 (Objectives 22-4, 22-5)** Compare and contrast the accumulation of audit evidence and the evaluation of the adequacy of the disclosures in the financial statements. Give two examples in which adequate disclosure could depend heavily on the accumulation of evidence and two others in which audit evidence does not normally significantly affect the adequacy of the disclosure.

**22-15 (Objectives 22-4, 22-6)** Distinguish between a client letter of representation and a management letter and state the primary purpose of each. List some items that might be included in each letter.

**22-16 (Objective 22-4)** What is meant by reading other financial information in annual reports? Give an example of the type of information the auditor is examining.

**22-17 (Objective 22-5)** Distinguish between regular working paper review and independent review and state the purpose of each. Give two examples of important potential findings in each of these two types of review.

## MULTIPLE CHOICE QUESTIONS FROM CPA EXAMINATIONS

**22-18 (Objective 22-1)** The following questions deal with contingent liabilities. Choose the best response.

a. The audit step most likely to reveal the existence of contingent liabilities is
   (1) a review of vouchers paid during the month following the year-end.
   (2) accounts payable confirmations.
   (3) an inquiry directed to legal counsel.
   (4) mortgage-note confirmation.

b. When obtaining evidence regarding litigation against a client, the CPA would be *least* interested in determining
   (1) an estimate of when the matter will be resolved.
   (2) the period in which the underlying cause of the litigation occurred.
   (3) the probability of an unfavorable outcome.
   (4) an estimate of the potential loss.

c. When a contingency is resolved immediately subsequent to the issuance of a report that was qualified with respect to the contingency, the auditor should
   (1) insist that the client issue revised financial statements.
   (2) inform the audit committee that the report cannot be relied upon.
   (3) take no action regarding the event.
   (4) inform the appropriate authorities that the report cannot be relied upon.

**22-19 (Objective 22-4)** The following questions concern letters of representation. Choose the best response.

a. A principal purpose of a letter of representation from management is to
   (1) serve as an introduction to company personnel and an authorization to examine the records.
   (2) discharge the auditor from legal liability for the audit.
   (3) confirm in writing management's approval of limitations on the scope of the audit.
   (4) remind management of its primary responsibility for financial statements.

b. A letter of representation issued by a client
   (1) is essential for the preparation of the audit program.
   (2) is a substitute for testing.
   (3) does not reduce the auditor's responsibility.
   (4) reduces the auditor's responsibility only to the extent that it is relied upon.

c. The date of the management representation letter should coincide with the
   (1) date of the auditor's report.
   (2) balance sheet date.
   (3) date of the latest subsequent event referred to in the notes to the financial statements.
   (4) date of the engagement agreement.

d. Management's refusal to furnish a written representation on a matter that the auditor considers essential constitutes
   (1) prima facie evidence that the financial statements are not presented fairly.
   (2) a violation of the Foreign Corrupt Practices Act.
   (3) an uncertainty sufficient to preclude an unqualified opinion.
   (4) a scope limitation sufficient to preclude an unqualified opinion.

**22-20 (Objective 22-3)** The following questions deal with review of subsequent events. Choose the best response.

a. Subsequent events for reporting purposes are defined as events that occur subsequent to the
   (1) balance sheet date.
   (2) date of the auditor's report.
   (3) balance sheet date but prior to the date of the auditor's report.
   (4) date of the auditor's report and concern contingencies that are not reflected in the financial statements.

b. A major customer of an audit client suffers a fire just prior to completion of year-end field work. The audit client believes that this event could have a significant direct effect on the financial statements. The auditor should
   (1) advise management to disclose the event in notes to the financial statements.
   (2) disclose the event in the auditor's report.
   (3) withhold submission of the auditor's report until the extent of the direct effect on the financial statements is known.
   (4) advise management to adjust the financial statements.

c. An example of an event occurring in the period of the auditor's field work subsequent to the end of the year being audited that normally would not require disclosure in the financial statements or auditor's report would be
   (1) decreased sales volume resulting from a general business recession.
   (2) serious damage to the company's plant from a widespread flood.
   (3) issuance of a widely advertised capital stock issue with restrictive covenants.
   (4) settlement of a large liability for considerably less than the amount recorded.

d. With respect to issuance of an audit report that is dual-dated for a subsequent event occurring after the completion of field work but before issuance of the auditor's report, the auditor's responsibility for events occurring subsequent to the completion of field work is
   (1) extended to include all events occurring until the date of the last subsequent event referred to.
   (2) limited to the specific event referred to.
   (3) limited to all events occurring through the date of issuance of the report.
   (4) extended to include all events occurring through the date of submission of the report to the client.

e. Karr has audited the financial statements of Lurch Corporation for the year ended December 31, 1996. Although Karr's field work was completed on February 27, 1997, Karr's auditor's report was dated February 28, 1997, and was received by the management of Lurch on March 5, 1997. On April 4, 1997, the management of Lurch asked that Karr approve inclusion of this report in their annual report to stockholders, which will include unaudited financial statements for the first quarter ended March 31, 1997. Karr approved the inclusion of this auditor's report in the annual report to stockholders. Under the circumstances Karr is responsible for inquiring as to subsequent events occurring through
   (1) February 27, 1997.
   (2) February 28, 1997.
   (3) March 31, 1997.
   (4) April 4, 1997.

## DISCUSSION QUESTIONS AND PROBLEMS

**22-21 (Objective 22-1)** Elizabeth Johnson, CPA, has completed the audit of notes payable and other liabilities for Valley River Electrical Services and now plans to audit contingent liabilities and commitments.

## Required

a. Distinguish between contingent liabilities and commitments and explain why both are important in an audit.

b. Identify three useful audit procedures for uncovering contingent liabilities that Johnson would likely perform in the normal conduct of the audit, even if she had no responsibility for uncovering contingencies.

c. Identify three other procedures Johnson is likely to perform specifically for the purpose of identifying undisclosed contingencies.

**22-22 (Objective 22-1)** In an audit of the Marco Corporation as of December 31, 1996, the following situations exist. No entries have been made in the accounting records in relation to these items.

1. The Marco Corporation has guaranteed the payment of interest on the 10-year, first mortgage bonds of the Newart Company, an affiliate. Outstanding bonds of the Newart Company amount to $150,000 with interest payable at 5 percent per annum, due June 1 and December 1 of each year. The bonds were issued by the Newart Company on December 1, 1994, and all interest payments have been met by that company with the exception of the payment due December 1, 1996. The Marco Corporation states that it will pay the defaulted interest to the bondholders on January 15, 1997.
2. During the year 1996, the Marco Corporation was named as a defendant in a suit for damages by the Dalton Company for breach of contract. An adverse decision to the Marco Corporation was rendered and the Dalton Company was awarded $40,000 damages. At the time of the audit, the case was under appeal to a higher court.
3. On December 23, 1996, the Marco Corporation declared a common stock dividend of 1,000 shares with a par value of $100,000 of its common stock, payable February 2, 1997, to the common stockholders of record December 30, 1996.

## Required

a. Define *contingent liability.*

b. Describe the audit procedures you would use to learn about each of the situations above.

c. Describe the nature of the adjusting entries or disclosure, if any, you would make for each of these situations.*

**22-23 (Objectives 22-3, 22-7)** The field work for the June 30, 1997, audit of Tracy Brewing Company was finished August 19, 1997, and the completed financial statements, accompanied by the signed audit reports, were mailed September 6, 1997. In each of the highly material independent events (a through i), state the appropriate action (1 through 4) for the situation and justify your response. The alternative actions are as follows:

1. Adjust the June 30, 1997, financial statements.
2. Disclose the information in a footnote in the June 30, 1997, financial statements.
3. Request the client to recall the June 30, 1997, statements for revision.
4. No action is required.

The events are as follows:

a. On December 14, 1997, the auditor discovered that a debtor of Tracy Brewing went bankrupt on October 2, 1997. The sale had taken place April 15, 1997, but the amount appeared collectible at June 30, 1997 and August 19, 1997.

b. On August 15, 1997, the auditor discovered that a debtor of Tracy Brewing went bankrupt on August 1, 1997. The most recent sale had taken place April 2, 1996, and no cash receipts had been received since that date.

c. On December 14, 1997, the auditor discovered that a debtor of Tracy Brewing went bankrupt on July 15, 1997, due to declining financial health. The sale had taken place January 15, 1997.

*AICPA adapted.

d. On August 6, 1997, the auditor discovered that a debtor of Tracy Brewing went bankrupt on July 30, 1997. The cause of the bankruptcy was an unexpected loss of a major lawsuit on July 15, 1997, resulting from a product deficiency suit by a different customer.

e. On August 6, 1997, the auditor discovered that a debtor of Tracy Brewing went bankrupt on July 30, 1997, for a sale that took place July 3, 1997. The cause of the bankruptcy was a major uninsured fire on July 20, 1997.

f. On May 31, 1997, the auditor discovered an uninsured lawsuit against Tracy Brewing that had originated on February 28, 1997.

g. On July 20, 1997, Tracy Brewing settled a lawsuit out of court that had originated in 1994 and is currently listed as a contingent liability.

h. On September 14, 1997, Tracy Brewing lost a court case that had originated in 1996 for an amount equal to the lawsuit. The June 30, 1997, footnotes state that in the opinion of legal counsel there will be a favorable settlement.

i. On July 20, 1997, a lawsuit was filed against Tracy Brewing for a patent infringement action that allegedly took place in early 1997. In the opinion of legal counsel, there is a danger of a significant loss to the client.

22-24 (**Objective 22-5**) Mel Adams, CPA, is a partner in a medium-sized CPA firm and takes an active part in the conduct of every audit he supervises. He follows the practice of reviewing all working papers of subordinates as soon as it is convenient, rather than waiting until the end of the audit. When the audit is nearly finished, Adams reviews the working papers again to make sure that he has not missed anything significant. Since he makes most of the major decisions on the audit, there is rarely anything that requires further investigation. When he completes the review, he prepares a pencil draft of the financial statements, gets them approved by management, and has them typed and assembled in his firm's office. No other partner reviews the working papers because Adams is responsible for signing the audit reports.

## Required

a. Evaluate the practice of reviewing the working papers of subordinates on a continuing basis rather than when the audit is completed.

b. Is it acceptable for Adams to prepare the financial statements rather than make the client assume the responsibility?

c. Evaluate the practice of not having a review of the working papers by another partner in the firm.

22-25 (**Objective 22-4**) Leslie Morgan, CPA, has prepared a letter of representation for the president and controller to sign. It contains references to the following items:

1. Inventory is fairly stated at the lower of cost or market and includes no obsolete items.
2. All actual and contingent liabilities are properly included in the financial statements.
3. All subsequent events of relevance to the financial statements have been disclosed.

## Required

a. Why is it desirable to have a letter of representation from the client concerning the above matters when the audit evidence accumulated during the course of the engagement is meant to verify the same information?

b. To what extent is the letter of representation useful as audit evidence? Explain.

c. List several other types of information commonly included in a letter of representation.

22-26 (**Objective 22-6**) In a management letter to the Cline Wholesale Company, Jerry Schwartz, CPA, informed management of its weaknesses in the control of inventory. He elaborated on how the weaknesses could result in a significant misstatement of inventory by the failure to recognize the existence of obsolete items. In addition, Schwartz made specific recommendations on how to improve internal control and save clerical time by installing a computer system for the company's perpetual records. Management accepted the recommendations and installed the system under Schwartz's direction. For several months the system worked beautifully, but unforeseen problems developed when a master file was erased. The cost of reproducing and processing the inventory records to correct the error was significant, and management decided to scrap the entire project. The company sued Schwartz for failure to use adequate professional judgment in making the recommendations.

## Required

a. What is Schwartz's legal and professional responsibility in the issuance of management letters?

b. Discuss the major considerations that will determine whether he is liable in this situation.

**22-27** **(Objective 22-3)** In connection with your audit of the financial statements of Olars Mfg. Corporation for the year ended December 31, 1996, your review of subsequent events disclosed the following items:

1. January 3, 1997: The state government approved a plan for the construction of an express highway. The plan will result in the expropriation of a portion of the land owned by Olars Mfg. Corporation. Construction will begin in late 1997. No estimate of the condemnation award is available.
2. January 4, 1997: The funds for a $25,000 loan to the corporation made by Mr. Olars on July 15, 1996, were obtained by him from a loan on his personal life insurance policy. The loan was recorded in the account "loan from officers." Mr. Olars' source of the funds was not disclosed in the company records. The corporation pays the premiums on the life insurance policy, and Mrs. Olars, wife of the president, is the beneficiary.
3. January 7, 1997: The mineral content of a shipment of ore enroute on December 31, 1996, was determined to be 72 percent. The shipment was recorded at year-end at an estimated content of 50 percent by a debit to raw material inventory and a credit to accounts payable in the amount of $20,600. The final liability to the vendor is based on the actual mineral content of the shipment.
4. January 15, 1997: Culminating a series of personal disagreements between Mr. Olars, the president, and his brother-in-law, the treasurer, the latter resigned, effective immediately, under an agreement whereby the corporation would purchase his 10 percent stock ownership at book value as of December 31, 1996. Payment is to be made in two equal amounts in cash on April 1, 1997 and October 1, 1997. In December, the treasurer has obtained a divorce from his wife, who was Mr. Olars' sister.
5. January 31, 1997: As a result of reduced sales, production was curtailed in mid-January and some workers were laid off. On February 5, 1997, all the remaining workers went on strike. To date the strike is unsettled.
6. February 10, 1997: A contract was signed whereby Mammoth Enterprises purchases from Olars Mfg. Corporation all of the latter's fixed assets (including rights to receive the proceeds of any property condemnation), inventories, and the right to conduct business under the name "Olars Mfg. Division." The effective date of the transfer will be March 1, 1997. The sale price was $500,000 subject to adjustment following the taking of a physical inventory. Important factors contributing to the decision to enter into the contract were the policy of the board of directors of Mammoth Industries to diversify the firm's activities and the report of a survey conducted by an independent market appraisal firm that revealed a declining market for Olars products.

## Required

Assume that the items described above came to your attention prior to completion of your audit work on February 15, 1997. For *each* item:

a. Give the audit procedures, if any, that would have brought the item to your attention. Indicate other sources of information that may have revealed the item.

b. Discuss the disclosure that you would recommend for the item, listing all details that you would suggest should be disclosed. Indicate those items or details, if any, that should not be disclosed. Give your reasons for recommending or not recommending disclosure of the items or details.*

**22-28 (Objective 22-3)** The following unrelated events occurred after the balance sheet date but before the audit report was prepared:

1. The granting of a retroactive pay increase
2. Determination by the federal government of additional income tax due for a prior year
3. Filing of an antitrust suit by the federal government
4. Declaration of a stock dividend
5. Sale of a fixed asset at a substantial profit

### Required

a. Explain how each of the items might have come to the auditor's attention.

b. Discuss the auditor's responsibility to recognize each of these in connection with his or her report.*

**22-29 (Objective 22-3)** The philosophy of Irene Hatton, CPA, is to intensively audit transactions taking place during the current audit period, but to ignore subsequent transactions. She believes that each year should stand on its own and be audited in the year in which the transactions take place. According to Hatton, "If a transaction recorded in the subsequent period is audited in the current period, it is verified twice—once this year and again in next year's audit. That is a duplication of effort and a waste of time."

### Required

a. Explain the fallacy in Hatton's argument.

b. Give six specific examples of information obtained by examining subsequent events that are essential to the current-period audit.

**22-30 (Objective 22-2)** In analyzing legal expense for the Boastman Bottle Company, Mary Little, CPA, observes that the company has paid legal fees to three different law firms during the current year. In accordance with her CPA firm's normal operating practice, Little requests standard attorney letters as of the balance sheet date from each of the three law firms.

On the last day of field work, Little notes that one of the attorney letters has not yet been received. The second request contains a statement to the effect that the law firm deals exclusively in registering patents and refuses to comment on any lawsuits or other legal affairs of the client. The third attorney's letter states that there is an outstanding unpaid bill due from the client and recognizes the existence of a potentially material lawsuit against the client but refuses to comment further to protect the legal rights of the client.

### Required

a. Evaluate Little's approach to sending the attorney letters and her follow-up on the responses.

b. What should Little do about each of the letters?

## CASES

**22–31 (Objective 22-5)** In your audit of Aviary Industries for calendar year 1996, you found a number of matters that you believe represent possible adjustments to the company's books. These matters are described on page 749. Management's attitude is that "once the books are closed, they're closed," and management does not want to make any adjustments. Planning materiality for the engagement was $100,000, determined by computing 5 percent of expected income before taxes. Actual income before taxes on the financial statements prior to any adjustments is $1,652,867.

*AICPA adapted.

Possible adjustments:

1. Several credit memos that were processed and recorded after year-end relate to sales and accounts receivable for 1996. These total $23,529. Similar unadjusted items existed at December 31, 1995, in the amount of $14,333.
2. Inventory cutoff tests indicate that $22,357 of inventory received on December 30, 1996, was recorded as purchases and accounts payable in 1997. These items were included in the inventory count at year-end, and therefore were included in ending inventory.
3. Inventory cutoff tests also indicate several sales invoices recorded in 1996 for goods that were shipped in early 1997. The goods were not included in inventory, but were set aside in a separate shipping area. The total amount of these shipments was $36,022. (Ignore cost of sales for this item.)
4. The company wrote several checks at the end of 1996 for accounts payable that were held and not mailed until January 15, 1997. These totaled $48,336. Recorded cash and accounts payable at December 31, 1996, are $2,356,553 and $2,666,290, respectively.
5. The company has not established a reserve for obsolescence of inventories. Your tests indicate that such a reserve is appropriate in an amount somewhere between $20,000 and $40,000.
6. Your review of the allowance for uncollectible accounts indicates that it may be understated by between $25,000 and $50,000.

## Required

a. Determine the adjustments that you believe must be made for Aviary's financial statements to be fairly presented. Include the amounts and accounts affected by each adjustment.

b. Why may Aviary Industries' management resist making these adjustments?

c. Explain what you consider the most positive way of approaching management personnel to convince them to make your proposed changes.

**22-32 (Objective 22-6)** You are the senior on the audit of Dahlstrom Manufacturing Company. Dahlstrom manufactures various sizes of cardboard boxes. These are customized both in terms of size and printing, and are used by producers of various types of retail food products. Your present task is to draft a reportable conditions letter and a management letter to the Company. Your firm prepares these letters using the following process:

1. As work is done, auditors who observe a possible reportable condition or management letter item fill out a form that shows a description of the item and a recommended solution.
2. The senior drafts both the reportable conditions letter and the management letter using word processing software and the firm's standard formats maintained on a computer file for firm use. The standard formats:

   a. Contain standard introduction and ending sections.

   b. Require three segments for each item: description of finding or observation, possible consequences if item is not resolved, and suggestion(s) for resolution.
3. The drafts are reviewed by the manager and discussed with appropriate client personnel. They are then finalized and delivered.

Following is a summary of the reportable conditions and management letter items being suggested by the audit team, in the order in which they were documented. Each item is stated and then followed by a suggested solution.

1. In sampling sales invoices, it was noted that in a sample of 60 items, 4 were recorded on a different date than the day the goods were shipped.

   The Company should batch invoices by the date of shipment, accounting for their numerical sequence, and ensure that the date of shipment is used when the invoices are input into the computer system.

2. While verifying prices on sales invoices, it was noticed that prices charged differed from catalog prices in a number of instances. These price differences were authorized by regional sales managers as per Company policy. However, we also received comments on our accounts receivable confirmation replies that some sales were in dispute, and the credit manager told us that there were some collection problems that arose from pricing differences.

   The Company should consider reviewing its pricing policies and related practices.

3. In conducting our inventory observation, we noted that there was a large buildup of work-in-process inventory between the cutting and printing operations. Workers in the folding/gluing operation were observed idle, waiting for output from printing to continue their work.

   The Company should consider reviewing the design of its production line, and specifically the printing operation, for a possible bottleneck problem.

4. When we conducted our inventory observation we noted a significant amount of cardboard stock [raw material to the production process] that had apparently not been used for some time. It was still bound by strapping and covered with dust.

   The client should determine whether this stock can be used in production, and if not, consider whether it can be sold.

5. In conducting our inventory observation, we observed several wall-hung fire extinguishers that were stamped with an expiration date prior to the date of our observation.

   All fire extinguishers should be kept in working condition.

6. When we counted petty cash at the Oakridge location, we found that the fund contained a personal check for $240 prepared by the fund custodian. The custodian told us it represented a "temporary loan." This is not in accordance with Company policy. We informed the Oakridge manager about this finding.

   The Oakridge manager should review the policy on petty cash funds with the custodian and ensure that the policy is adhered to in the future.

7. In reviewing the cash accounts, we noted that some payroll bank accounts had not been reconciled for more than 60 days.

   All bank accounts should be reconciled monthly.

8. In talking to the manager of the Oakridge location, he told us that he was having difficulty making production decisions because of constant changes in sales forecasts being issued by marketing. He said that if he could receive more stable sales forecast data, he could save significantly on set-up costs and also reduce both raw material and work-in-process inventories.

   The Company should consider reviewing its sales forecasting system with the objective of providing more stable information that is effectively integrated with production planning.

## Required

a. For each of the above eight items, decide whether the item belongs in a reportable conditions letter, a management letter, both, or neither. Document your decisions.

b. Prepare a draft of the reportable conditions letter for Dahlstrom Manufacturing Company using word processing software and the standard format provided on the diskette accompanying this text [instructor option]. The letter should be properly organized and effectively written. Feel free to make any assumptions you believe are reasonable and appropriate.

c. Prepare a draft of the management letter for Dahlstrom Manufacturing Company using word processing software and the standard format provided on the diskette accompanying this text [instructor option]. Note that the management letter can refer to items included in the reportable conditions letter without including details of these items. The letter should be properly organized and effectively written. Feel free to make any assumptions you believe are reasonable and appropriate.

# 23

# OTHER AUDIT, ATTESTATION SERVICES, AND COMPILATION ENGAGEMENTS

## LEARNING OBJECTIVES

Thorough study of this chapter will enable you to

- **23-1** Understand review and compilation services that may be offered to clients.
- **23-2** Describe special engagements to review interim financial information for public companies.
- **23-3** Describe audit or limited assurance engagements other than audits, reviews, or compilations of historical financial statements prepared in accordance with GAAP.
- **23-4** Understand the AICPA attestation standards, and the levels of assurance and types of engagements to which they apply.
- **23-5** Describe special engagements to attest to prospective financial statements.
- **23-6** Describe special engagements to attest to a client's internal control.
- **23-7** Describe special engagements to attest to a client's compliance with laws and regulations.
- **23-8** Describe agreed-upon procedures engagements.

## SKEPTICISM APPLIES TO ALL TYPES OF ENGAGEMENTS

Barnhart Construction Company was a contractor specializing in apartment complexes in the Southwest. The owner of the construction company, David Barnhart, met a promoter named Alton Leonard, who was selling limited partnerships for the development of apartment complexes. Limited partners invested cash up front and the partnerships borrowed additional funds to finance the construction of the projects.

Barnhart reached an agreement with Leonard to serve as contractor on the three projects Leonard was currently marketing. Barnhart would receive significant cash up front, construction costs during construction, and then a significant amount when the project was sold. Barnhart had serious cash flow problems at the time Leonard approached him and decided to contract with Leonard as a way of solving his cash problems. One problem was that the limited partnership offering periods were limited, and would be closed only if all partnership units were sold.

The first partnership offering was fully subscribed and Barnhart was paid. Unfortunately, the next two partnerships were not completely subscribed. To solve this problem, Barnhart loaned money to relatives and key employees who bought the necessary interests for the partnerships to close. Barnhart then got the money from the distribution.

When Barnhart Construction had a review service engagement performed by Renee Lathrup, CPA, a sole practitioner, the accounting records showed loans receivable from a number of individuals, noticeably people named Barnhart and known employees. She observed that the loans were made just before the second and third partnerships closed, and they were for amounts that were multiples of $15,000, the amount of each limited partnership unit subscription. Renee asked Barnhart to explain what happened. Barnhart told Renee, "When I received the money from the first partnership escrow, I wanted to do something nice for relatives and employees who had been loyal to me over the years." He told Renee, "This is just my way of sharing my good fortune with the ones I love. The equality of the amounts is just a coincidence."

When Renee considered the reasonableness of this scenario, she found it hard to believe. First, the timing was odd. Second, the amounts seemed to be an unusual coincidence. Third, if he really had wanted to do something special for these folks, why didn't he give them something, rather than loan them money? Renee asked that the promoter, Leonard, send her detailed information on the subscriptions for each partnership. Leonard refused, stating that he was under legal obligation to keep all information confidential. When Renee pressed Barnhart, he also refused further cooperation, although he did say he would "represent" to Renee that the loans had nothing to do with qualifying the partnerships so he could get his money. At this point, Renee withdrew from the engagement.

In addition to being involved with audits of historical financial statements prepared in accordance with generally accepted accounting principles, CPAs commonly deal with many situations involving other types of information, varying levels of assurance, and other types of reports. These are the subjects of this chapter and the following one.

Because the partners of many CPA firms believe there is relatively little growth potential for auditing in their practices, they are increasingly looking to other types of services to provide additional revenues. There are still opportunities for compilation and review services, but many practitioners believe nontraditional attestation services have even more potential. For example, forecasts and prospective financial statements are widely used by investors and other financial statement users, but these users prefer some type of assurance about the reliability of the information provided. Many CPA firms have the expertise to provide such assurance. Similarly, CPA firms are increasingly doing agreed-upon procedures engagements on a variety of information to provide some assurance about its reliability. One example is a CPA firm issuing an opinion on whether a chemical company has put the appropriate procedures into place to satisfy the requirements of the federal Environmental Protection Act. Even though such an engagement may not seem like auditing, many CPA firms now perform such attestation services.

Table 23-1 summarizes the six categories of engagements that will be discussed in this and the next chapter. The purpose of the discussion is to provide a general understanding of the nature of these engagements rather than detailed knowledge. Except for audits of historical financial statements in accordance with generally accepted accounting principles, they are discussed in the order listed.

**TABLE 23-1**

**Primary Categories of Audit, Other Attestation, and Compilation Engagements**

| Type of Engagement | Example | Source of Authoritative Support |
|---|---|---|
| Audits of historical financial statements prepared in accordance with generally accepted accounting principles | Audit of General Mills' financial statements | Auditing standards |
| Reviews or compilations of historical financial statements prepared in accordance with GAAP | Review of Ron's Shoe Store's quarterly financial statements | Accounting and review services standards for nonpublic companies; auditing standards for public companies |
| Audits or limited assurance engagements other than audits, reviews, or compilations of historical financial statements prepared in accordance with GAAP | Audit of Ron's Shoe Store's ending balance in inventory | Auditing standards |
| Attestation engagements under the attestation standards | Attestation of General Mills' forecasted financial statements | Attestation standards |
| Operational auditing | Operational audit of the effectiveness of General Mills' marketing department | None |
| Governmental auditing | Audit of Redwood City's financial statements | Auditing standards and governmental auditing standards |

## REVIEW AND COMPILATION SERVICES

**OBJECTIVE 23-1**
**Understand review and compilation services that may be offered to clients.**

Many CPAs are involved with nonpublic clients that do not have audits. A company may believe that an audit is unnecessary due to the active involvement of the owners in the business, lack of significant debt, or absence of regulations requiring the company to have one.

Common examples are smaller companies and professional corporations and partnerships of physicians and attorneys.

These organizations often engage a CPA to provide tax services and to assist in the preparation of accurate financial information without an audit. Providing these services is a significant part of the practice of many smaller CPA firms. When a CPA provides any services involving financial statements, certain requirements exist.

The financial statements resulting from accounting services provided to clients without audit have traditionally been called *unaudited financial statements.* Reporting and minimum standards of performance for unaudited financial statements were under the authority of the Auditing Standards Board until 1979. During the late 1960s and 1970s considerable controversy surrounded unaudited financial statements for two reasons. First, there were a significant number of lawsuits against CPAs involving unaudited financial statements. Second, there was considerable disagreement as to the "unaudited procedures" needed when a CPA firm was involved with unaudited financial statements.

In 1977, the AICPA established a new committee to develop standards for unaudited financial statements of nonpublic entities. The committee, which has authority equivalent to the Auditing Standards Board, is called the Accounting and Review Services Committee.

These standards, which became effective in 1979, are called *Statements on Standards for Accounting and Review Services* (SSARS). They govern the CPA's association with unaudited financial statements of nonpublic (private) companies. The two types of services provided in connection with these financial statements, covered by SSARS, are termed *reviews of financial statements* and *compilations of financial statements.*

The assurance provided by reviews and compilations is considerably below audits, and the practitioners' reports are intended to convey that difference. Similarly, the extent of evidence accumulation differs among the three types of engagements. Figure 23-1 illustrates the difference in both the evidence accumulation and the level of assurance provided. The amount of assurance and extent of evidence accumulation in Figure 23-1 are not well defined by the profession. This is because both evidence accumulation and assurance are subjective. Only a practitioner in the circumstances of an engagement can judge how much evidence is sufficient and what level of assurance has actually been attained.

**FIGURE 23-1**

**Relationship between Evidence Accumulation and Assurance Attained**

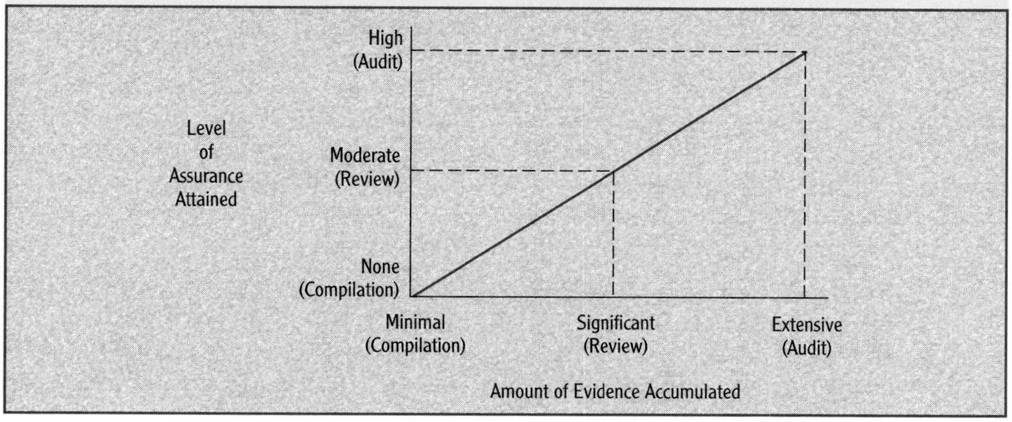


For public companies, unaudited financial statements are labeled as unaudited statements rather than reviews and they require a disclaimer of opinion in accordance with the fourth reporting standard. Interim statements of public companies can be reviewed by the accountant, as discussed in the next section of this chapter.

SSARS do not pertain to such services as preparing a working trial balance for a client, assisting in adjusting the client's accounts, preparing tax returns, or providing various manual or automated bookkeeping or data processing services *unless the output is financial statements.*

## Review

A review engagement requires the accountant to perform inquiry and analytical procedures that provide a reasonable basis for expressing limited assurance on the financial statements. It is notable that the SSARS standards refer to the practitioners performing reviews and compilations as accountants, never auditors. Reviews imply a level of assurance considerably less than an audit, but greater than a compilation.

**Procedures Suggested for Reviews** An SSARS review does not include obtaining an understanding of internal control, tests of controls, substantive tests of transactions, independent confirmations, or physical examinations. The emphasis in SSARS reviews is in four broad areas, plus a fifth specific requirement.

- Obtain knowledge of the accounting principles and practices of the client's industry. The accountant can study AICPA industry guides or other sources to obtain industry knowledge. The level of knowledge for reviews can be somewhat less than for an audit.
- Obtain knowledge of the client. The information should be about the nature of the client's business transactions, its accounting records and employees, and the basis, form, and content of the financial statements. The level of knowledge can be less than for an audit.
- Make inquiries of management. The objective of these inquiries is to determine whether the financial statements are fairly presented, assuming that management does not intend to deceive the accountant. Inquiry is the most important of the review procedures. The following are illustrative inquiries:

    1. Inquire as to the company's procedures for recording, classifying, and summarizing transactions, and disclosing information in the statements.
    2. Inquire into actions taken at meetings of stockholders and board of directors.
    3. Inquire of persons having responsibility for financial and accounting matters whether the financial statements have been prepared in conformity with generally accepted accounting principles consistently applied.

- Perform analytical procedures. These are meant to identify relationships and individual items that appear to be unusual. The appropriate analytical procedures are no different from the ones already studied in Chapter 6 and in those chapters dealing with tests of details of balances.
- The accountant is required to obtain a letter of representation from members of management who are knowledgeable about financial matters.

**Form of Report** There is only one form of review under SSARS—review of financial statements with full disclosure. The report in Figure 23-2 is appropriate when the accountant has made a proper review of the accounting records and the financial statements and has concluded that they appear reasonable.

There are three aspects of the report that are worth noting:

- The introductory paragraph is similar to an audit report except for its reference to a review service rather than an audit.
- The scope paragraph describes what the accountant has done, including an indication that a review consists primarily of inquiries and analytical procedures, and clearly states that no opinion is expressed.
- The last paragraph includes negative assurance by stating that "nothing came to the accountant's attention." This paragraph provides some assurance to users.

For the SSARS review report, the following are also required: The date of the accountant's report is the date of completion of the accountant's inquiry and analytical procedures, and each page of the financial statements reviewed by the accountant states "See accountant's review report."

**FIGURE 23-2**

**Example of Review Report**

> We have reviewed the accompanying balance sheet of XYZ Company as of December 31, 1997, and the related statements of income, retained earnings, and cash flows for the year then ended, in accordance with Statements on Standards for Accounting and Review Services issued by the American Institute of Certified Public Accountants. All information included in these financial statements is the representation of the management of XYZ Company.
>
> A review consists principally of inquiries of company personnel and analytical procedures applied to financial data. It is substantially less in scope than an audit in accordance with generally accepted auditing standards, the objective of which is the expression of an opinion regarding the financial statements taken as a whole. Accordingly, we do not express such an opinion.
>
> Based on our review, we are not aware of any material modifications that should be made to the accompanying financial statements in order for them to be in conformity with generally accepted accounting principles.

**Failure to Follow GAAP** If a client has failed to follow generally accepted accounting principles in a review engagement, a modification of the report is needed. The accountant is not required to determine the *effect of a departure* if management has not done so, but that fact must also be disclosed in the report. For example, the use of replacement cost rather than FIFO for inventory valuation would have to be disclosed, but the effect of the departure on net earnings would not.

The disclosure must be made in a *separate paragraph* in the report. The following are two examples of suggested wording:

- As disclosed in note X to the financial statements, generally accepted accounting principles require that land be stated at cost. Management has informed us that the company has stated its land at appraised value and that, if generally accepted accounting principles had been followed, the land account and stockholders' equity would have been decreased by $500,000.

or

- A statement of cash flows for the year ended December 31, 1996, has not been presented. Generally accepted accounting principles require that such a statement be presented when financial statements purport to present financial position and results of operations.

## Compilation

Compilation services are intended to enable a CPA firm to compete with bookkeeping firms. It is common for smaller CPA firms to own a computer and provide bookkeeping services, monthly or quarterly financial statements, and tax services for smaller clients. *Compilation* is defined in SSARS as presenting, in the form of financial statements, information that is the representation of management without undertaking to express any assurance on the statements.

**Requirements for Compilation** Compilation does not mean that the accountant has no responsibilities. The accountant is always responsible for exercising due care in performing all duties. Several things are required by SSARS for compilation. The preparer of the statements must

- Know something about the accounting principles and practices of the client's industry.
- Know the client, the nature of the client's business transactions, accounting records, and employees, and the basis, form, and content of the financial statements. The knowledge can be less than that for a review.
- Make inquiries to determine if the client's information is satisfactory.
- Read the compiled financial statements and be alert for any obvious omissions or errors in arithmetic and generally accepted accounting principles.

- Disclose in the report any omissions or departures from generally accepted accounting principles of which the accountant is aware. This requirement does not apply to a compilation that omits substantially all disclosures.

The accountant does not have to make other inquiries or perform other procedures to verify information supplied by the entity. But if the accountant becomes aware that the statements are not fairly presented, he or she should obtain additional information. If the client refuses to provide the information, the accountant should withdraw from the compilation engagement.

## Compilation Reports

One of three forms of compilation can be provided to clients.

**Compilation with Full Disclosure** Compilation of this type requires disclosures in accordance with generally accepted accounting principles, the same as for audited financial statements or reviews. Figure 23-3 shows the appropriate wording in such circumstances.

**FIGURE 23-3**

**Compilation Report with Full Disclosure**

We have compiled the accompanying balance sheet of XYZ Company as of December 31, 1997, and the related statements of income, retained earnings, and cash flows for the year then ended, in accordance with Statements on Standards for Accounting and Review Services issued by the American Institute of Certified Public Accountants.

A compilation is limited to presenting in the form of financial statements information that is the representation of management. We have not audited or reviewed the accompanying financial statements and, accordingly, do not express an opinion or any other form of assurance on them.

If the accountant uses a compilation with full disclosures report and the client fails to follow generally accepted accounting principles, the same report modification requirements exist that were discussed for reviews.

**Compilation That Omits Substantially All Disclosures** This type of compilation is acceptable *if the report indicates the lack of disclosures* and the absence of disclosures *is not,* to the CPA's knowledge, *undertaken with the intent to mislead users.* This type of statement is expected to be used primarily for management purposes only, but it affects all statements that will be shown to external users.

Figure 23-4 shows the appropriate wording when the accountant compiles statements without disclosures.

**FIGURE 23-4**

**Compilation That Omits Substantially All Disclosures**

We have compiled the accompanying balance sheet of XYZ Company as of December 31, 1997, and the related statements of income and retained earnings for the year then ended, in accordance with Statements on Standards for Accounting and Review Services issued by the American Institute of Certified Public Accountants.

A compilation is limited to presenting in the form of financial statements information that is the representation of management. We have not audited or reviewed the accompanying financial statements and, accordingly, do not express an opinion or any other form of assurance on them.

Management has elected to omit substantially all of the disclosures and the statement of cash flows required by generally accepted accounting principles. If the omitted disclosures were included in the financial statements, they might influence the user's conclusions about the company's financial position, results of operations, and cash flows. Accordingly, these financial statements are not designed for those who are not informed about such matters.

**Compilation Without Independence** A CPA firm can issue a compilation report even if it is not independent with respect to the client, as defined by the *Code of Professional Conduct.* When the accountant lacks independence, the following should be included as a separate last paragraph in either of the two previously discussed reports: "We are not independent with respect to XYZ Company."

For any of the three types of compilation reports, the following are also required: the date of the accountant's report is the date of completion of the compilation, and each page of the financial statements compiled by the accountant should state "See accountant's compilation report."

## REVIEW OF INTERIM FINANCIAL INFORMATION FOR PUBLIC COMPANIES

**OBJECTIVE 23-2**
**Describe special engagements to review interim financial information for public companies.**

Reviews of interim financial information are done to help management of public companies meet their reporting responsibilities to regulatory agencies. The Securities and Exchange Commission requires quarterly financial information as a part of quarterly 10-Q reports. The statements do not have to be audited, and the CPA firm's name need not be associated with the quarterly statements.

However, the SEC requires a footnote in the annual audited financial statements disclosing quarterly sales, gross profit, income, and earnings per share for the past two years. Typically, the footnote in the annual statements is labeled *unaudited,* but at a minimum the CPA firm must perform review procedures of the footnote information. There is no requirement that the review procedures be done on a quarterly basis. The review can be done as a part of the annual audit.

The disadvantage of doing the review procedures at the time of the annual audit is that potential discrepancies may arise between the quarterly information in the annual statement's footnote and the quarterly 10-Q reports. Management, therefore, frequently asks auditors to do quarterly reviews of financial statements to maximize the likelihood of consistency between the 10-Q reports and the footnotes to the annual statements.

### SAS 71 Reviews

The requirements for reviews of interim information for public companies are set forth by SAS 71 (AU 722). Even though they are issued by the Auditing Standards Board, the requirements are more closely related to unaudited review engagement requirements of SSARS than to audit requirements. The five requirements for review service engagements previously discussed are all applicable to both SSARS and SAS reviews.

Like reviews under SSARS, an SAS 71 review does not provide a basis for expressing a positive-form opinion. There are ordinarily no tests of the accounting records, independent confirmations, or physical examinations.

There are some differences, however, between the two types of reviews. First, because an annual audit is also performed for a client who has an SAS 71 review, the auditor must obtain sufficient information about the client's internal control for both annual and interim financial information. Similarly, since the client in an SAS 71 review is audited annually, the auditor's knowledge of the results of these audit procedures is used in considering the scope and results of SAS 71 inquiries and analytical procedures. Third, under SSARS, the auditor makes inquiries about actions of directors' and stockholders' meetings; under SAS 71, the auditor reads the minutes of those meetings.

The objective of an SAS 71 review is to provide the accountant with a basis for reporting to management, the board of directors, and the stockholders and others on significant matters found through inquiry and analytical procedures. The report on this review is made directly available to management and the directors; it is usually made available to stockholders and others by its inclusion in Form 10-Q, although this is required only when management states in the 10-Q that such a review has been made.

### Standard Interim Report

The standard report for interim financial statements that have been reviewed is recommended in SAS 71 (see Figure 23-5 on page 758).

**FIGURE 23-5**

**Example of a Report for Interim Financial Statements for a Public Company**

We have reviewed the consolidated balance sheet of Rainer Company and consolidated subsidiaries as of September 30, 1996, and the related statements of earnings, retained earnings, and cash flows for the three-month and nine-month periods then ended. These financial statements are the responsibility of the company's management.

We conducted our review in accordance with standards established by the American Institute of Certified Public Accountants. A review of interim financial information consists principally of applying analytical procedures to financial data and making inquiries of persons responsible for financial and accounting matters. It is substantially less in scope than an audit conducted in accordance with generally accepted auditing standards, the objective of which is the expression of an opinion regarding the financial statements taken as a whole. Accordingly, we do not express such an opinion.

Based on our review, we are not aware of any material modifications that should be made to the accompanying financial statements for them to be in conformity with generally accepted accounting principles.

The following comments refer to this report:

- The standards referred to in the second paragraph are those established in SAS 71.
- The second paragraph defines the nature of the work performed in more specific terms than does a standard unqualified opinion.
- The second paragraph states that an audit was not done and an opinion is not expressed.
- The final paragraph includes a *negative* assurance, which is the same wording used for an SSARS review report.

In addition, each page of the interim financial information should be clearly marked as "unaudited."

When interim information is included as a footnote in the annual audited statements and labeled "unaudited," it is unnecessary for the auditor to include a separate report. If the auditor has done the review procedures and if the information is fairly presented, the standard audit report is sufficient.

### Modification for Failure to Follow GAAP

When an SAS 71 review determines that there has been a material departure from generally accepted accounting principles or inadequate disclosure in the interim financial statements, a modification of the report in Figure 23-5 is required. This modification is similar to that used in an SSARS review, except that the added paragraph would state the effects of the departure on the interim information, if practicable. An example of the wording of such a modification is included in Figure 23-6.

**FIGURE 23-6**

**Example of SAS 71 Review Report Modified for Failure to Follow GAAP**

(separate third paragraph)
Based on information furnished to us by management, we believe that the company has excluded from property, plant, and equipment and debt in the accompanying balance sheet certain lease obligations that should be capitalized in order to conform with generally accepted accounting principles. This information indicates that if these lease obligations were capitalized at September 30, 1997, property, plant, and equipment would be increased by $1,070,000 and long-term debt by $1,100,000, and net income and earnings per share would be decreased by $10,000, $30,000, $.05, and $.15, respectively, for the three-month and nine-month periods then ended.

(concluding paragraph)

Based on our review, with the exception of the matter described in the preceding paragraph, we are not aware of any material modifications that should be made to the accompanying financial statements for them to be in conformity with generally accepted accounting principles.

## OTHER AUDITS OR LIMITED ASSURANCE ENGAGEMENTS

**OBJECTIVE 23-3**
**Describe audit or limited assurance engagements other than audits, reviews, or compilations of historical financial statements prepared in accordance with GAAP.**

Auditors are frequently engaged to provide assurance services that fall within the auditing standards but are not audits of historical financial statements in accordance with generally accepted accounting principles. The following are the most important of these:

- Other comprehensive basis of accounting
- Specified elements, accounts, or items
- Information accompanying basic financial statements
- Debt compliance letters and similar reports

### Other Comprehensive Basis of Accounting

Auditors frequently audit statements prepared on a basis other than GAAP. SAS 62 (AU 623) provides that generally accepted auditing standards apply to these audit engagements, but the reporting requirements differ somewhat from those described in Chapter 2. The following are common examples of bases other than generally accepted accounting principles:

- *Cash basis.* Only cash receipts and disbursements are recorded. There are no accruals. Typically, governmental agencies use this method.
- *Modified cash basis.* The cash basis is followed except for certain items, such as recording fixed assets and depreciation. Physicians and attorneys often follow this accounting method.
- *Basis used to comply with the requirements of a regulatory agency.* Common examples include the uniform system of accounts required of railroads, utilities, and some insurance companies.
- *Income tax basis.* The same measurement rules used for filing tax returns are often used for financial statement preparation, even though this is not in accordance with generally accepted accounting principles. Many small businesses use this method.

For the most part, these audits are done in the same way as those where generally accepted accounting principles are followed. Naturally, the auditor must fully understand the accounting basis that the client is required to follow. For example, in auditing a railroad, there are complex accounting requirements that require the auditor to have specialized accounting knowledge to conduct the audit.

A concern in reporting on a comprehensive basis is to make sure that the statements clearly indicate that they are prepared on a basis other than generally accepted accounting principles. If the statements imply that GAAP is followed, the reporting requirements of Chapter 2 apply. Consequently, terms such as *balance sheet* and *statement of operations* must be avoided by the client. Instead, a title such as "statement of assets and liabilities arising from cash transactions" would be appropriate for a cash basis statement.

Some other basis may qualify as comprehensive if it follows a definite set of criteria having substantial support and is applied to all material items in the financial statements. Examples would be current-cost and price-level bases.

The reporting requirements for audits of these comprehensive bases of accounting include the following:

**Introductory Paragraph** This paragraph is equivalent to the introductory paragraph of a report on statements that follow generally accepted accounting principles. The statements are identified, and the paragraph states that they were audited. The paragraph also states that the statements are the responsibility of management and that the auditor's responsibility is to express an opinion on them based on the audit.

**Scope Paragraph** This paragraph is equivalent to the scope paragraph in the ordinary report. It states that the audit was conducted in accordance with generally accepted auditing standards and describes the nature of the audit process.

**Middle Paragraph Stating the Accounting Basis** This paragraph is unique to this type of report. It states the basis of presentation and refers to a note to the financial statements that describes the basis of accounting followed. It states that such basis is a comprehensive basis of accounting other than generally accepted accounting principles. The note referred to will describe not only the basis followed but also how that basis differs from generally accepted accounting principles. It need not state the effects of the differences in quantitative terms. It is important for the auditor to consider whether the financial statements include all informative disclosures that are appropriate for the basis of accounting used.

**Opinion Paragraph** The opinion paragraph is comparable to that used in the standard report. It expresses the auditor's opinion with regard to conformity with the basis of accounting described.

**Restriction of Distribution Paragraph** If the financial statements are prepared in conformity with requirements of a governmental regulatory agency, a paragraph must be added that restricts the distribution of the report to those within the entity and for filing with the regulatory agency.

Figure 23-7 is a common example of a report prepared on an entity's income tax basis.

**FIGURE 23-7**

**Example of a Report on Income Tax Basis**

**Independent Auditor's Report**

We have audited the accompanying statements of assets, liabilities, and capital—income tax basis of ABC Partnership as of December 31, 1997 and 1996, and the related statements of revenue and expenses—income tax basis and of changes in partners' capital accounts—income tax basis for the years then ended. These financial statements are the responsibility of the Partnership's management. Our responsibility is to express an opinion on these financial statements based on our audits.

We conducted our audits in accordance with generally accepted auditing standards. Those standards require that we plan and perform the audit to obtain reasonable assurance about whether the financial statements are free of material misstatement. An audit includes examining, on a test basis, evidence supporting the amounts and disclosures in the financial statements. An audit also includes assessing the accounting principles used and significant estimates made by management, as well as evaluating the overall financial statement presentation. We believe that our audits provide a reasonable basis for our opinion.

As described in Note X, these financial statements were prepared on the basis of accounting the Partnership uses for income tax purposes, which is a comprehensive basis of accounting other than generally accepted accounting principles.

In our opinion, the financial statements referred to above present fairly, in all material respects, the assets, liabilities, and capital of ABC Partnership as of December 31, 1997 and 1996, and its revenue and expenses and changes in partners' capital accounts for the years then ended, on the basis of accounting described in Note X.

## Specified Elements, Accounts, or Items

Frequently, auditors are asked to issue reports on their audit of specific aspects of financial statements. A common example is a special report on the audit of sales of a retail store in a shopping center to be used as a basis for rental payments. Other common examples are reports on royalties, profit participation, and provision for income taxes. The authority for auditing specified elements, accounts, or items is SAS 62 (AU 623) Special Reports.

The type of engagement to be undertaken for specified elements, accounts, or items is usually an audit. Thus, it is typically like an ordinary audit but is applied to less than the full financial statements. There are two primary differences between audits of specified elements, accounts, or items, and audits of complete financial statements:

- Materiality is defined in terms of the elements, accounts, or items involved rather than in relation to the overall statements. The effect is to ordinarily require more evidence than would be needed if the item being verified were just one of many parts of the statements. For example, if the sales account is being reported on separately, a smaller

misstatement would be considered material than when sales is just one account of many being reported on as a part of a regular audit.
- The first standard of reporting under GAAS does not apply because the presentation of elements, accounts, or items is not a financial statement prepared in accordance with generally accepted accounting principles.

In addition, the auditor must be careful to extend his or her audit efforts to include other elements, accounts, or items that are interrelated with those that are the subject of the engagement. This will cause an increase in audit effort as well.

Figure 23-8 illustrates a report for royalties, which is a specified account. The format and contents of the report are similar to the standard audit report on the audit of financial statements in accordance with generally accepted accounting principles. However, it must also reflect the following requirements for reporting on specified elements, accounts, or items:

- The specified elements, accounts, or items must be identified.
- The basis on which the specified elements, accounts, or items are presented and the agreements specifying the basis must be described.
- The source of significant interpretations made by the client about the provisions of a relevant agreement must be indicated and described.
- If the specified element, account, or item is presented on a basis that is not in conformity with generally accepted accounting principles or another comprehensive basis of accounting, a paragraph that restricts the distribution of the report to those within the entity and the parties to the contract or agreement must be added.

**FIGURE 23-8**

**Example of a Report for Royalties**

**Independent Auditor's Report**

We have audited the accompanying schedule of royalties applicable to engine production of the Q Division of XYZ Corporation for the year ended December 31, 1996, under the terms of a license agreement dated May 14, 1994 between ABC Company and XYZ Corporation. This schedule is the responsibility of XYZ Corporation's management. Our responsibility is to express an opinion on this schedule based on our audit.

We conducted our audit in accordance with generally accepted auditing standards. Those standards require that we plan and perform the audit to obtain reasonable assurance about whether the schedule of royalties is free of material misstatement. An audit includes examining, on a test basis, evidence supporting the amounts and disclosures in the schedule. An audit also includes assessing the accounting principles used and significant estimates made by management, as well as evaluating the overall schedule presentation. We believe that our audit provides a reasonable basis for our opinion.

We have been informed that, under XYZ Corporation's interpretation of the agreement referred to in the first paragraph, royalties were based on the number of engines produced after giving effect to a reduction for production retirements that were scrapped, but without a reduction for field returns that were scrapped, even though the field returns were replaced with new engines without charge to customers.

In our opinion, the schedule of royalties referred to above presents fairly, in all material respects, the number of engines produced by the Q Division of XYZ Corporation during the year ended December 31, 1996, and the amount of royalties applicable thereto, under the license agreement referred to above.

This report is intended solely for the information and use of the boards of directors and managements of XYZ Corporation and ABC Company and should not be used for any other purpose.

**Report Modifications** It is important to realize that the circumstances and requirements that exist for modifying a report on an audit of GAAP financial statements also apply to special reports on both specific elements, accounts, or items and financial statements prepared on another comprehensive basis of accounting. These modifications would include not only departures from an unqualified opinion, but also an explanatory paragraph where appropriate. The form of the modifications would essentially be the same as discussed in Chapter 2.

**Information Accompanying Basic Financial Statements**

Frequently, clients request auditors to include additional information beyond the basic financial statements in the set of materials prepared for management or outside users. SAS 29 (AU 551) refers to this additional information as *information accompanying the basic financial statements in auditor-submitted documents.* In the past, the same information was called a *long-form report.* Figure 23-9 illustrates the basic financial statements and additional information.

**FIGURE 23-9**

**Information Accompanying Basic Financial Statements**

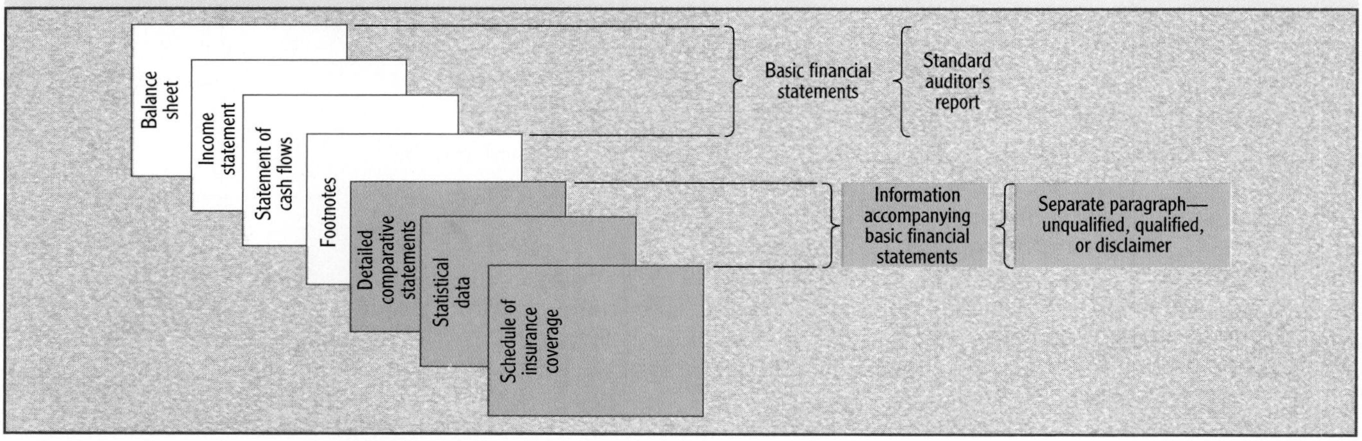


The profession has intentionally refrained from defining or restricting the appropriate supplementary information included to enable auditors to individualize the information to meet the needs of statement users. However, several types of information are commonly included in the additional information section:

- Detailed comparative statements supporting the control totals on the primary financial statements for accounts such as cost of goods sold, operating expenses, and miscellaneous assets
- Supplementary information required by the Financial Accounting Standards Board or Securities and Exchange Commission
- Statistical data for past years in the form of ratios and trends
- A schedule of insurance coverage
- Specific comments on the changes that have taken place in the statements

**Reporting Responsibilities** It is important that the auditor clearly distinguish between responsibility for the primary financial statements and for additional information. Usually, the auditor has not performed a sufficiently detailed audit to justify an opinion on the additional information, but in some instances the auditor may be confident that the information is fairly presented. The profession's reporting standards require the auditor to make a clear statement about the degree of responsibility he or she is taking for the additional information. At the present time, however, only two types of opinions are allowed: a positive opinion indicating a high level of assurance, or a disclaimer indicating no assurance. For example, if the auditor decided that sufficient evidence had *not* been accumulated for the additional data to justify an unqualified opinion, SAS 29 requires that a disclaimer paragraph such as the following be added to the standard audit report:

- Our audit was made for the purpose of forming an opinion on the basic financial statements taken as a whole. The accompanying information on pages x through y is presented for purposes of additional analysis and is not a required part of the basic financial statements. Such information has not been subjected to the auditing procedures applied in the audit of the basic financial statements, and, accordingly, we express no opinion on it.

When, on the same audit, the basic financial statements and accompanying additional information are issued to some users and only the basic statements are issued to others, the auditor should exercise special care to assure himself or herself that the additional information is not such that it would lend support to a claim that there is inadequate disclosure in the basic financial statements. For example, if the additional information contained exceptions, reservations, or material disclosures not appearing in the basic financial statements, there may be a basis for potential legal claims against the auditor for inadequate disclosure by users who received only the basic financial statements.

## Debt Compliance Letters and Similar Reports

Clients occasionally enter into loan agreements that require them to provide the lender with a report from a CPA as to the existence or nonexistence of some condition. For example, borrowing arrangements may require maintenance of a certain dollar amount of working capital at specified times and an independent accountant's report as to the compliance with the requirement.

These engagements are somewhat hard to define in terms of the attestation framework, but they might be described as a review of an item closely related to the financial statements. Reports on debt compliance and similar engagements are discussed in AU 623, paragraphs .19 through .21. These reports may be issued as separate reports or as part of a report that expresses the auditor's opinion on the financial statements by adding a paragraph after the opinion paragraph. In either case, the following matters are important for the auditor to observe in such engagements:

1. The engagement and report should be limited to compliance matters the auditor is qualified to evaluate. Some of the provisions of debt compliance agreements the auditor is normally in a position to verify are whether principal and interest payments were made when due, whether the proper limitations were maintained on dividends, working capital, and debt ratios, and whether the accounting records were adequate for conducting an ordinary audit. However, determining, for example, whether the client has properly restricted its business activities to the requirements of an agreement or if it has title to pledged property are legal questions that the CPA is not qualified to answer. Furthermore, the *Code of Professional Conduct* prohibits the auditor from practicing as an attorney in such circumstances.
2. The auditor should provide a debt compliance letter only for a client for whom he or she has done an audit of the overall financial statements. A debt compliance letter on a matter such as the existence of a current ratio of 2.5 or better would be difficult to do without having conducted a complete audit.
3. The auditor's opinion would be in the form of a *negative assurance,* stating that nothing came to the auditor's attention that would lead the auditor to believe there was noncompliance.

Figure 23-10 on page 764 is an example of a separate report on debt compliance. Note that this report does not accompany a separate set of assertions by the responsible party; those are implied. Note also that the final paragraph restricts distribution of the report to the directly affected parties.

## Other Compliance Presentations

Although debt compliance letters are common, they are only part of a broader set of special reports arising from contractual or regulatory requirements. These types of reports also include (1) presentations of financial statements that are in a form required by contract or regulation that are not in conformity with GAAP or another comprehensive basis of accounting and (2) presentations that are in conformity with one of those bases, but are incomplete. These situations are dealt with in AU 623 in a manner that is consistent with specific elements, accounts, or items; other comprehensive bases of accounting; and debt compliance letters as discussed.

**FIGURE 23-10**

**Example of Debt Compliance Report**

> **Independent Auditor's Report**
>
> We have audited, in accordance with generally accepted auditing standards, the balance sheet of XYZ Company as of December 31, 1996, and the related statements of income, retained earnings, and cash flows for the year then ended, and have issued our report thereon dated February 16, 1997.
>
> In connection with our audit, nothing came to our attention that caused us to believe that the Company failed to comply with the terms, covenants, provisions, or conditions of sections XX to XX, inclusive, of the Indenture dated July 21, 1994, with ABC Bank insofar as they relate to accounting matters. However, our audit was not directed primarily toward obtaining knowledge of such noncompliance.
>
> This report is intended solely for the information and use of the boards of directors and managements of XYZ Company and ABC Bank and should not be used for any other purpose.

## ATTESTATION ENGAGEMENTS

**OBJECTIVE 23-4**
**Understand the AICPA attestation standards, and the levels of assurance and types of engagements to which they apply.**

During the past 20 years, CPAs have increasingly been asked to perform a variety of audit-like, or *attest,* services for different purposes. An example is a bank that requests a CPA to state in writing whether an audit client has adhered to all requirements of a loan agreement. As specific types of requests became common, specific standards were issued to provide guidance. This guidance was usually in the form of an interpretation of generally accepted auditing standards. But since those standards relate primarily to historical financial statements prepared in accordance with generally accepted accounting principles, and the new services often dealt with other types of information, the guidance became difficult to formulate and communicate effectively without disrupting the cohesiveness of Statements on Auditing Standards.

This problem has been addressed by the profession through the issuance of *Statements on Standards for Attestation Engagements (SSAE).* The original purpose of the statement was to provide a general framework for and set reasonable boundaries around the attest function, including audits of historical financial statements.

In recent years, the Auditing Standards Board has attempted to distinguish between issues that should be addressed by auditing standards and others that should be addressed by attestation standards even though both are attestations. In general, attestations that deal with providing assurance on historical financial statements, including one or more parts of those statements, are addressed in auditing standards. Examples include audits of financial statements prepared in accordance with generally accepted accounting principles or some other comprehensive basis of accounting, audits of only a balance sheet, and audits of individual accounts. All other forms of attestation are addressed in the attestation standards (an exception is reviews of historical financial statements, which is addressed in SSARS). Attestation standards are established by the Auditing Standards Board following the same process used for auditing standards. Attestation standards are labeled as AT rather than AU. As of the date of publication of this text, standards through SSAE 6 have been issued.

### Attestation Standards

In 1986 the Auditing Standards Board issued eleven attestation standards that parallel the ten generally accepted auditing standards. They are included in Table 23-2 along with generally accepted auditing standards for comparison. The attestation standards are stated in sufficiently general terms to enable practitioners to apply them to any attestation engagement, including new types of engagements that may arise.

The most notable differences in the attestation and generally accepted auditing standards are in general attestation standards 2 and 3. Standard 2 requires the practitioner to have adequate knowledge of the subject matter over which there is attestation. For example, if a practitioner is to attest to a company's compliance with environmental protection

**TABLE 23-2**

**Comparison of Attestation Standards and Generally Accepted Auditing Standards**

| Attestation Standards | Generally Accepted Auditing Standards |
|---|---|
| **General Standards** | |
| 1. The engagement shall be performed by a practitioner or practitioners having adequate technical training and proficiency in the attest function. | 1. The audit is to be performed by a person or persons having adequate technical training and proficiency as an auditor. |
| 2. The engagement shall be performed by a practitioner or practitioners having adequate knowledge in the subject matter of the assertion. | |
| 3. The practitioner shall perform an engagement only if he or she has reason to believe that the following two conditions exist:<br>• The assertion is capable of evaluation against reasonable criteria that either have been established by a recognized body or are stated in the presentation of the assertion in a sufficiently clear and comprehensive manner for a knowledgeable reader to be able to understand them.<br>• The assertion is capable of reasonably consistent estimation or measurement using such criteria. | |
| 4. In all matters relating to the engagement, an independence in mental attitude shall be maintained by the practitioner or practitioners. | 2. In all matters relating to the assignment, an independence in mental attitude is to be maintained by the auditor or auditors. |
| 5. Due professional care shall be exercised in the performance of the engagement. | 3. Due professional care is to be exercised in the performance of the audit and the preparation of the report. |
| **Standards of Field Work** | |
| 1. The work shall be adequately planned and assistants, if any, shall be properly supervised. | 1. The work is to be adequately planned and assistants, if any, are to be properly supervised. |
| | 2. A sufficient understanding of internal control is to be obtained to plan the audit and to determine the nature, timing, and extent of tests to be performed. |
| 2. Sufficient evidence shall be obtained to provide a reasonable basis for the conclusion that is expressed in the report. | 3. Sufficient competent evidential matter is to be obtained through inspection, observation, inquiries, and confirmations to afford a reasonable basis for an opinion regarding the financial statements under audit. |
| **Standards of Reporting** | |
| 1. The report shall identify the assertion being reported on and state the character of the engagement. | |
| 2. The report shall state the practitioner's conclusion about whether the assertion is presented in conformity with the established or stated criteria against which it was measured. | 1. The report shall state whether the financial statements are presented in accordance with generally accepted accounting principles. |
| | 2. The report shall identify those circumstances in which such principles have not been consistently observed in the current period in relation to the preceding period. |
| | 3. Informative disclosures in the financial statements are to be regarded as reasonably adequate unless otherwise stated in the report. |
| 3. The report shall state all of the practitioner's significant reservations about the engagement and the presentation of the assertion.<br>4. The report on an engagement to evaluate an assertion that has been prepared in conformity with agreed-upon criteria or on an engagement to apply agreed-upon procedures should contain a statement limiting its use to the parties who have agreed upon such criteria or procedures. | 4. The report shall either contain an expression of opinion regarding the financial statements, taken as a whole, or an assertion to the effect that an opinion cannot be expressed. When an overall opinion cannot be expressed, the reasons therefor should be stated. In all cases where an auditor's name is associated with financial statements, the report should contain a clear-cut indication of the character of the auditor's work, if any, and the degree of responsibility the author is taking. |

laws, the practitioner needs a thorough knowledge of the laws and methods that companies use to assure compliance. Standard 3 requires any assertion about which the practitioner is asserting be capable of evaluation against reasonable criteria and be capable of reasonable estimation or measurement. Again, using the example of environmental protection laws, it may be difficult for the practitioner to conclude whether there is compliance because of measurement difficulties and the lack of specific criteria.

## Types of Attestation Engagements

The Auditing Standards Board has consciously made the decision to not attempt to define the potential boundaries of attestation engagements except in conceptual terms because new services are likely to arise. For example, Price Waterhouse & Co. has been attesting to the balloting for the Miss America contest for decades, but attesting to compliance with environmental protection laws started only in recent years.

Currently, specific attestation standards have been issued in only four areas: prospective financial statements, reports on internal control over financial reporting, compliance with laws and regulations, and agreed-upon procedures engagements. Standards have been developed for these types of engagements because practitioners are performing these services in sufficiently large numbers to need more specific guidance than is provided by the general attestation standards. These three standards are discussed shortly. The absence of specific standards for a type of service is not intended to imply that it is inappropriate to perform such a service.

## Levels of Service

The attestation standards define three levels of engagements and related forms of conclusions: examinations, reviews, and agreed-upon procedures.

An examination results in a conclusion that is in a *positive* form. In this type of report, the practitioner makes a direct statement as to whether the presentation of the assertions, taken as a whole, conforms with the applicable criteria. An example of an examination report written under the general guidance of the attestation standards, rather than more detailed standards, is shown in Figure 23-11. This is for an engagement to determine that the rate of return on a hypothetical portfolio, based on a brokerage firm's buy–sell recommendations, is correct as represented in the firm's promotional materials.

**FIGURE 23-11**

**Example of an Examination Report under the Attestation Standards**

*To Management*
*Akron Securities, Inc.*

We have examined the accompanying statement for investment performance statistics of the Akron Securities Model Portfolio for the year ended December 31, 1996. Our examination was made in accordance with standards established by the American Institute of Certified Public Accountants and, accordingly, included such procedures as we considered necessary in the circumstances.

In our opinion, the statement of investment performance statistics referred to above presents the investment performance of the Akron Securities Model Portfolio for the year ended December 31, 1996, in conformity with the actual results that would have been obtained if the buy–and–sell recommendations for the portfolio were followed as described in the buy–sell recommendations set forth in Note 1.

Farnsworth & Jackson, P.C.
Certified Public Accountants
Akron, Ohio
February 12, 1997

A report on an examination is unrestricted as to distribution by the client after it is issued. This means that a client can provide the information being examined and the related report to anyone.

In a *review*, the practitioner provides a conclusion in the form of a *negative assurance.* In this form, the practitioner's report states whether any information came to the practitioner's attention to indicate that the assertions are not presented in all material respects in conformity with the applicable criteria. A review report is also unrestricted in its distribution. It is interesting that review engagements are prohibited in all three types of engagements where specified attestation standards have been issued. The reason for the prohibition is the difficulty of setting standards for the limited assurance provided by reviews.

In an *agreed-upon procedures* engagement, the procedures to be performed are agreed upon by the practitioner, the responsible party making the assertions, and the specific persons who are the intended users of the practitioner's report. The degree of assurance being conveyed in such a report varies with the specific procedures agreed to and performed. Accordingly, such reports are limited in their distribution to only the involved parties, who would have the requisite knowledge about those procedures and the level of assurance resulting from them. The report should include a statement of what procedures management and the practitioner agreed to and what the practitioner found in performing the procedures.

Figure 23-12 summarizes the foregoing discussion.

**FIGURE 23-12**

**Types of Engagements and Related Reports**

| Type of Engagement | Amount of Evidence | Level of Assurance | Form of Conclusion | Distribution |
|---|---|---|---|---|
| Examination | Extensive | High | Positive | General |
| Review | Significant | Moderate | Negative | General |
| Agreed-upon procedures | Varying | Varying | Findings | Limited |

The remainder of this chapter discusses the four types of engagements for which detailed attestation standards have been issued.

## PROSPECTIVE FINANCIAL STATEMENTS

**OBJECTIVE 23-5**
**Describe special engagements to attest to prospective financial statements.**

As implied by the term, prospective financial statements refer to predicted or expected financial statements in some future period (income statement) or at some future date (balance sheet). An example is management's predictions of the income statement and balance sheet one year in the future.

Most practitioners believe that there are significant opportunities and potential risks for auditors to provide credibility to prospective financial information. It is well accepted that users want reliable prospective information to aid them in their decision making. If auditors can improve the reliability of the information, information risk is reduced in the same way as in audits of historical financial statements. The risks arise because prospective information is frequently different from the actual historical financial statements when they are compared at some future date. Regulators, users, and others may criticize and sue auditors, even if the prospective statements were fairly stated given the available information at the time they were prepared.

### Forecasts and Projections

There are two general types of prospective financial statements included in AT 2: *forecasts* and *projections. Forecasts* are prospective financial statements that present an entity's expected financial position, results of operations, and cash flows, to the *best* of the responsible party's knowledge and belief. These are commonly required by banks as a part of loan applications. *Projections* are prospective financial statements that present an entity's financial position, results of operations, and cash flows, to the best of the responsible party's knowledge and belief, given one or more *hypothetical assumptions.* An example is the preparation of projected financial statements assuming that the company is able to increase the price of its primary product by 10 percent with no reduction in units sold.

Both types of prospective financial statements are commonly prepared by management, but CPA firms have begun to associate their names with these statements only in recent years. A considerable body of literature has been developed to assist responsible parties in the preparation of both forecasts and projections. This guidance, along with guidance for independent accountants, is presented in the AICPA *Guide for Prospective Financial Statements* that was published concurrently with the AT. The guidance to preparers constitutes a set of established criteria against which an attestation engagement can be framed.

## Use of Prospective Financial Statements

Prospective financial statements are for either *general* or *limited* use. General use refers to use by any third party. An example of general use is the inclusion of a financial forecast in a prospectus for the sale of hospital bonds. Limited use refers to use by third parties with whom the responsible party is negotiating directly. An example of limited use is the inclusion of a financial projection in a bank loan application document.

Forecasts can be provided for both general and limited use, but projections are restricted to the latter. This is because limited users are in a position to obtain a better understanding of the prospective statements and related circumstances than are removed parties. For example, a limited user such as a potential venture capital investor can ask the responsible party about the hypothetical assumptions in a projection, whereas a removed user such as a reader of a prospectus cannot. Since users may have difficulty dealing with the meaning of hypothetical assumptions without obtaining additional information, the prospective standards in AT 1 prohibit their general use. An exception to this rule is that a projection may be issued as a supplement to a forecast for general use.

## Types of Engagements

AT 1 requires that one of the following types of engagements for prospective financial statements be undertaken: an examination, a compilation, or an agreed-upon procedures engagement. Only an examination, which is studied in the next section, is dealt with in this chapter.

An engagement to review a forecast or projection is prohibited. The reason is that a forecast or projection is essentially the result of mechanically applying a set of significant assumptions. It is relatively easy to define an examination as obtaining satisfaction as to the completeness and reasonableness of all the assumptions, and to define a compilation as primarily involving the computational accuracy of the statements, and not the reasonableness of the assumptions. It is difficult to define a meaningful middle ground. For example, none of the assumptions could be excluded because they are all significant. Therefore, being "moderately satisfied" about the assumptions, which is implied by a review service, is likely to confuse users. Rather than confuse users with this dilemma, the AICPA decided in AT 1 to allow only the clearer alternatives.

## Examination of Prospective Financial Statements

AT 1 makes it clear that the practitioner is not attesting to the accuracy of the prospective financial statements. Instead the focus is on examining the underlying assumptions and the preparation and presentation of the forecast or projection. Accordingly, the following are the four elements of an examination of forecasts and projections:

- Evaluating the preparation of the prospective financial statements.
- Evaluating the support underlying the assumptions.
- Evaluating the presentation of the prospective financial statements for conformity with AICPA presentation guidelines.
- Issuing an examination report.

These elements are based primarily on accumulating evidence about the completeness and reasonableness of the underlying assumptions as disclosed in the prospective financial statements. This requires the accountant to become familiar with the client's business and industry, to identify the significant matters on which the client's entity's future results are expected to depend ("key factors"), and to determine that appropriate assumptions have been included with respect to these.

The accountant's report on an examination of prospective financial statements should include:

- An identification of the prospective financial statements presented.
- A statement that the examination of the prospective financial statements was made in accordance with AICPA standards and a brief description of the nature of such an examination.
- The accountant's opinion that the prospective financial statements are presented in conformity with AICPA presentation guidelines and that the underlying assumptions provide a reasonable basis for the forecast or a reasonable basis for the projection, given the hypothetical assumptions.
- A caveat that the prospective results may not be achieved.
- A statement that the accountant assumes no responsibility to update the report for events and circumstances occurring after the date of the report.

Figure 23-13 is an example of a report on an examination of a forecast with an unqualified opinion. Note that the date of the forecasted balance sheet is more than a year later than the report date.

**FIGURE 23-13**

**Example of a Report on a Forecast**

We have examined the accompanying forecasted balance sheet, statements of income, retained earnings, and cash flows of Allstar, Inc., as of December 31, 1998, and for the year then ending. Our examination was made in accordance with standards for an examination of a forecast established by the American Institute of Certified Public Accountants and, accordingly, included such procedures as we considered necessary to evaluate both the assumptions used by management and the preparation and presentation of the forecast.

In our opinion, the accompanying forecast is presented in conformity with guidelines for presentation of a forecast established by the American Institute of Certified Public Accountants, and the underlying assumptions provide a reasonable basis for management's forecast. However, there will usually be differences between the forecasted and actual results, because events and circumstances frequently do not occur as expected, and those differences may be material. We have no responsibility to update this report for events and circumstances occurring after the date of this report.

*Manford & Brown*
*Certified Public Accountants*
*October 15, 1997*

**POTENTIAL LEGAL LIABILITY IN PROSPECTIVE FINANCIAL STATEMENTS**

A partner in one of the Big Six CPA firms stated recently in an informal meeting that his firm has decided not to do assurance engagements for prospective financial statements because of litigation costs. He reported that his firm calculated their total revenues (not profits) from all prospective financial statement engagements and also calculated all legal costs, including partner and staff time incurred to defend against lawsuits, involving these engagements. The firm calculated that legal costs exceeded revenues. The partner said, "You don't have to be a rocket scientist to conclude that if legal costs exceed revenues it's a bad business. Users sue when actual profits are less favorable than those projected regardless of what the CPA firm's report says."

## INTERNAL CONTROL OVER FINANCIAL REPORTING

**OBJECTIVE 23-6**
**Describe special engagements to attest to a client's internal control.**

A CPA firm may be engaged to report on an entity's internal control. This may be done for a regular audit client who wants such a report for internal use, for meeting the requirements of a regulatory agency, or for an entity such as an EDP service center for the use of its customers and their auditors. The report may cover all or part of internal control, and it may relate to the controls in effect as of a specified date or during a specified period. Reporting on internal control over financial reporting is the subject of AT 2.

A major reason for an attestation standard on internal control results from the emphasis on the importance of internal controls by Congress and regulatory agencies. For example, the Federal Deposit Insurance Corporation Improvement Act of 1991 requires management of federally insured depository institutions such as banks and thrifts to report on internal control effectiveness, and the act requires a CPA firm to attest to the report. Other legislative and regulatory proposals have included similar requirements.

## Comparison to Requirements for Audits

When auditors perform an audit of financial statements, they obtain an understanding of internal control in accordance with the second standard of field work. The scope of the study depends on the extent to which the auditor plans to reduce assessed control risk for the purpose of determining the nature, timing, and extent of related substantive tests. When reduced control risk is planned, the auditor considers the internal controls in effect for the entire audit period. Certain areas are *not* examined if reduced control risk in those areas is not planned.

When the practitioner is engaged to report on internal control under the attestation standards, however, all areas of internal control are included unless specifically excluded by agreement. Also, the time period covered is a matter of agreement. All agreements are made between the auditor and management, but regulatory agency requirements and customers' needs must be considered.

## Steps for Obtaining an Understanding and Testing Controls

Five steps, which are similar to those followed for an audit engagement, are followed when a CPA firm is engaged to report on internal control over financial reporting:

1. *Plan the scope of the engagement.* The practitioner, client, and others involved first agree on the areas to be covered and the timing of the study. The practitioner then obtains information about the client's business, industry and regulatory requirements, and the nature of accounting transactions and record-keeping system. This information provides a basis for planning the most effective approach to the remaining steps.

2. *Obtain an understanding of the design of internal control.* The practitioner obtains detailed information about the transactions, their flow through the system, transaction-related audit objectives, and control activities used to achieve control. A preliminary assessment is made to determine the apparent controls and weaknesses of internal control. The procedures for accomplishing this step are similar to those discussed in Chapter 9.

3. *Perform tests of controls to determine conformity with prescribed procedures.* Appropriate audit procedures must be performed to determine whether the controls needed to meet the transaction-related audit objectives were being followed. The methodology for these procedures is similar to that discussed in the chapters for each transaction cycle.

4. *Evaluate the results of the understanding and tests of controls.* A final evaluation of controls and weaknesses is now made. The primary criterion for the evaluation is whether there are material weaknesses either individually or in combination. A weakness is material if "the condition results in more than a relatively low risk of such misstatements in amounts that would be material in relation to financial statements."

5. *Prepare the appropriate report.* The type of report prepared depends on the purpose and scope of the engagement and the practitioner's findings. Different internal control reports are appropriate for different types of engagements and findings. Figure 23-14 shows a sample standard report prepared when the practitioner makes a study and evaluation of internal control at a given time and finds no material weaknesses.

As can be seen, Figure 23-14 contains a positive-form opinion of the type associated with an examination engagement.

**FIGURE 23-14**

**Example of Report on Internal Control**

We have obtained an understanding of internal control for XYZ Company in effect at September 30, 1996, and we have performed tests of the controls. Our understanding and testing was conducted in accordance with standards established by the American Institute of Certified Public Accountants.

The management of XYZ Company is responsible for establishing and maintaining internal control. In fulfilling this responsibility, estimates and judgments by management are required to assess the expected benefits and related costs of internal control.The objectives of internal control are to provide management with reasonable, but not absolute, assurance that assets are safeguarded against loss from unauthorized loss or disposition, and that transactions are executed in accordance with management's authorization and recorded properly to permit the preparation of financial statements in accordance with generally accepted accounting principles.

Because of inherent limitations in internal control, errors or fraud may occur and not be detected. Also, projection of any evaluation of internal control to future periods is subject to the risk that procedures may become inadequate because of changes in conditions or that the degree of adherence with the procedures may deteriorate.

In our opinion, the internal control of XYZ Company in effect at September 30, 1996, taken as a whole, was sufficient to meet the objectives stated above insofar as those objectives pertain to the prevention or detection of errors or fraud in accounts that would be material in relation to the financial statements.

## COMPLIANCE ATTESTATION

**OBJECTIVE 23-7**
**Describe special engagements to attest to a client's compliance with laws and regulations.**

The purpose of compliance attestation engagements is to determine and report on whether an entity has complied with specific laws, regulations, or other requirements. Standards for compliance attestation are included in AT 3.

There are a wide variety of potential compliance attestation engagements, varying from simple and straightforward to highly complex. An example of a simple compliance attestation engagement is to determine and report whether a client has met two provisions specified in a loan agreement as conditions for continuing the loan: the total debt to total equity ratio must not exceed 2.0 at the balance sheet date, and dividends declared for the year cannot exceed 50 percent of net income after taxes. Assuming that the CPA firm has either done the audit itself or is willing to rely on the audited financial statements provided by another CPA firm, this attestation engagement is simple to complete. At the other extreme, consider an attestation engagement where a client was successful on a bid for a federal government contract with the only remaining condition that management provides independent evidence of compliance with all applicable civil rights laws and the provisions of the Environmental Protection Act. Assume that the client asks a CPA firm to provide an opinion on the company's compliance. Should the CPA firm undertake such an engagement? Many practitioners are both willing and eager to do this type of attestation if the engagement can be structured to assure that everyone understands the CPA firm's responsibilities and the limitations implied in such an engagement.

### Comparison to Requirements for Audits

There are important distinctions between practitioners' requirements for determining compliance with laws and regulations under the auditing and attestation standards. In audits of historical financial statements, auditors have some responsibility to determine whether a client has complied with laws and regulations. These responsibilities were discussed in Chapter 5 as a part of the study of illegal acts. In these audits the purpose is to determine whether financial statements are presented fairly, and the only concern auditors have with violations of laws and regulations is when the fair presentation of financial statements is affected. In compliance auditing under the AT 3, the practitioner plans and performs the engagement for the purpose of issuing a report on compliance.

### Conditions for Compliance Attestation

Knowing the conditions required for performing a compliance attestation engagement is important for practitioners because many potential compliance engagements could lead to serious miscommunication between auditors and users. For example, if a client in the chemical industry requests an auditor to provide an opinion that the company has complied with the Environmental Protection Act requirements, it would probably be a disservice to society to provide such an opinion.

The following are the most important conditions required to accept a compliance attestation engagement:

- Management must provide a written assertion upon which the auditor provides assurance. The basis of the requirement is the belief that CPA firms should not be willing to provide assurances unless management is willing to state in writing that the entity has complied with specific laws and regulations.
- Management's assertion is capable of evaluation against reasonable criteria. Without reasonable criteria, it is questionable whether a relevant opinion can be provided.
- Management's assertion is capable of reasonably consistent estimation or measurement using such criteria.
- Management accepts responsibility for the entity's compliance with specified requirements.

### Engagement Performance

The only two types of engagements permitted by AT 3 are examinations and agreed-upon procedures. The standard encourages the use of agreed-upon procedures engagements whenever they meet users' needs because there is less likelihood of misunderstanding of the practitioner's opinion.

An important challenge in an agreed-upon procedures engagement is to gain agreement on the procedures the users want performed. The practitioner's agreed-upon procedures may be as limited or extensive as the users desire as long as the users participate in establishing the procedures to be performed and take responsibility for the adequacy. To gain agreement, the practitioner must know who the users are and either discuss the procedures with them or find other ways to agree upon the procedures. An example is to sign an engagement letter that the CPA firm will perform the procedures required in a federal regulation.

For examinations, practitioners must deal with materiality and attestation risk, inherent risk, control risk, and detection risk. Materiality and the four risks address the same concepts for compliance attestation engagements as for audits of financial statements, but they are more difficult to apply because compliance attestation engagements vary more than financial statement audits. Similarly, practitioners must plan a compliance engagement, obtain sufficient evidence, and form an opinion on management's assertion. These are all difficult challenges on complex compliance engagements if the auditor does not have considerable experience.

## AGREED-UPON PROCEDURES ENGAGEMENTS

**OBJECTIVE 23-8**
**Describe agreed-upon procedures engagements.**

When the auditor and management or a third-party user agree that the audit will be limited to certain specific audit procedures, it is referred to as an *agreed-upon procedures engagement.* Many practitioners refer to these as procedures and findings engagements because the report emphasizes the audit procedures performed and the findings when the procedures were completed.

The primary appeal to practitioners of agreed-upon procedures engagements is making management or a third–party user specify the procedures they want performed. Imagine the difficulty a CPA firm would face if it agreed to issue an opinion to a federal agency that a company complied with federal affirmative action laws for a two-year time period under compliance attestation SSAE 3. Now assume that the federal agency was willing to specify ten audit procedures the CPA firm was to perform, which would satisfy the agency. For example, one procedure is to determine that the standard company's employment application form had no reference to age, gender, or race. Assuming the CPA firm and federal agency could agree on the procedures, many CPA firms would be willing to perform the procedures and issue a report of its findings.

There are several professional standards that address agreed-upon procedures engagements, but the two primary ones are SAS 75 and SSAE 4. SAS 75 and SSAE 4 are referred to as mirror standards because of their similarity. The two primary differences are:

- the SASs deal with financial statement items, whereas the SSAEs deal with nonfinancial statement subject matter
- management must provide a written assertion for an SSAE engagement, but not for an SAS engagement. Written assertions were discussed under compliance attestation.

An example of an SAS 75 engagement is performing agreed-upon procedures on the gross sales account for a lease agreement. These engagements are commonly done for retail stores when the store leases from the building owner on the basis of a percent of gross sales. Figure 23-15 (below and on page 774) illustrates a report for such an engagement, including the three procedures agreed upon and the two findings when the procedures were completed.

Agreed-upon procedures engagements under the SSAEs have been permitted and frequently performed since the original issue of the attestation standards. SSAE 4 provides additional guidance to practitioners performing these engagements. An example of such an engagement is performing agreed-upon procedures for a mutual fund in calculating the internal rate of return, beta risk for measuring volatility, and other relevant information pertinent to investors.

**FIGURE 23-15**

**Example of an Agreed-Upon Procedures Report**

**Report of Independent Certified Public Accountants**

Board of Directors and Management of Morgil Company

We have performed the procedures enumerated below, which were agreed to by the Board of Directors and management of Morgil Company, solely to assist you in determining the amount of gross sales as defined in the lease agreement dated September 1, 1992, between Rocklin, Inc., lessor, and Morgil Company, lessee, for the year ended December 31, 1997. This engagement to apply agreed-upon procedures was performed in accordance with standards established by the American Institute of Certified Public Accountants. The sufficiency of these procedures is solely the responsibility of the Board of Directors and management of Morgil Company. Consequently, we make no representation regarding the sufficiency of the procedures described below either for the purpose for which this report has been requested or for any other purpose.

The procedures we performed are summarized as follows:

1. We obtained a schedule prepared by management, which reflected gross sales, as defined above, for the year ended December 31, 1997, of $35,675,000.
2. We obtained the weekly cash reports submitted by the store manager for the year. These reports show information on gross sales, cash register readings, sales taxes, returns, and allowances for discounts and other information.

*[continued]*

**FIGURE 23-15**

**Example of an Agreed-Upon Procedures Report** *[continued]*

3. We compared monthly summarizations of these reports with the schedule of gross sales and compared approximately 5 percent of the daily cash net receipts shown in the weekly cash reports with the bank statements.

Based solely on the foregoing procedures, we found:

1. The daily cash net receipts shown in the weekly cash reports that we compared with the bank statements to be in agreement.
2. The monthly summarizations to be in agreement with the schedule of gross sales we obtained from management.

These agreed-upon procedures do not constitute an audit or review of financial statements or any part thereof, the objective of which is the expression of an opinion or limited assurance on the financial statements or a part thereof. Accordingly, we do not express such an opinion. Had we performed additional procedures, other matters might have come to our attention that would have been reported to you.

This report is intended solely for the use of the specified users listed and should not be used by those who have not agreed to the procedures and taken responsibility for the sufficiency of the procedures for their purposes.

*Renfor, Malik and Co., CPAs LLP*

Chicago, Illinois

## ESSENTIAL TERMS

**Agreed-upon procedures engagement**—an engagement in which the procedures to be performed are agreed upon by the practitioner, the responsible party making the assertions, and the intended users of the practitioner's report; the practitioner's report is presented in the form of a negative assurance

**Assertion**—an explicit or implicit statement made by one party for use by another (third) party

**Assurance**—the practitioner's degree of certainty that the conclusions stated in his or her report are correct

**Attestation engagement**—one in which a practitioner is engaged to issue a written communication that expresses a conclusion with respect to the reliability of an assertion that is the responsibility of another party

**Compilation engagement**—a nonaudit engagement in which the accountant undertakes to present, in the form of financial statements, information that is the representation of management, without undertaking to express any assurance on the statements

**Examination**—an attest engagement that results in a positive assurance as to whether or not the assertions under examination conform with the applicable criteria

**Forecast**—a prospective financial statement that presents an entity's expected financial position, results of operations, and cash flows for future periods, to the best of the responsible party's knowledge and belief

**Projection**—a prospective financial statement that presents an entity's financial position and results of operations and cash flows for future periods, to the best of the responsible party's knowledge and belief, given one or more hypothetical assumptions

**Prospective financial statement**—a financial statement that deals with expected future data rather than with historical data

**Review**—an attestation engagement that results in a negative assurance as to the practitioner's awareness of any information indicating that the assertions are not presented in conformity with the applicable criteria

**SAS 71 review**—a review of interim, unaudited financial information performed to help public companies meet their reporting responsibilities to regulatory agencies

**SSARS review**—a review of unaudited financial statements designed to provide limited assurance that no material modifications need be made to the statements in order for them to be in conformity with generally accepted accounting principles or, if applicable, with another comprehensive basis of accounting

**Statement on Attestation Standards**—a statement issued by the AICPA to provide a conceptual framework for various types of attestation services

**Statements on Standards for Accounting and Review Services (SSARS)**—standards issued by the AICPA Accounting and Review Services Committee that govern the CPA's association with unaudited financial statements of nonpublic companies

## REVIEW QUESTIONS

**23-1 (Objective 23-1)** What is meant by the term *level of assurance?* How does the level of assurance differ for an audit of historical financial statements, a review, and a compilation?

**23-2 (Objective 23-1)** What is a negative assurance? Why is it used in a review engagement report?

**23-3 (Objective 23-1)** Distinguish between compilation and review of financial statements. What is the level of assurance for each?

**23-4 (Objective 23-1)** List and distinguish among the three forms of compilation that a CPA can provide to clients.

**23-5 (Objective 23-1)** List five things that are required of an auditor by SSARS for compilation.

**23-6 (Objective 23-1)** What steps should auditors take if during a compilation engagement they become aware that the financial statements are misleading?

**23-7 (Objective 23-1)** What procedures should the auditor use to obtain the information necessary to give the level of assurance required of reviews of financial statements?

**23-8 (Objective 23-1)** What should auditors do if during a review of financial statements they discover that generally accepted accounting principles are not being followed?

**23-9 (Objectives 23-1, 23-2)** What are the differences between the two types of reports covered by SSARS and SAS 71?

**23-10 (Objective 23-2)** Explain why a review of interim financial statements may provide a greater level of assurance than do SSARS reviews.

**23-11 (Objective 23-3)** What is the purpose of an engagement of specified elements, accounts, or items? List the four special requirements for reports on specified elements, accounts, or items.

**23-12 (Objective 23-3)** State the reporting requirements for statements prepared on a basis other than generally accepted accounting principles.

**23-13 (Objective 23-3)** The Absco Corporation has requested that Herb Germany, CPA, provide a report to the Northern State Bank as to the existence or nonexistence of certain loan conditions. The conditions to be reported on are the working capital ratio, dividends paid on preferred stock, aging of accounts receivable, and competency of management. This is Herb's first experience with Absco. Should Herb accept this engagement? Substantiate your answer.

**23-14 (Objective 23-3)** Explain what is meant by information accompanying basic financial statements. Provide two examples of such information.

**23-15 (Objective 23-4)** Define what is meant by *attestation standards.* Distinguish between attestation standards and generally accepted auditing standards.

**23-16 (Objective 23-5)** Explain what is meant by prospective financial statements and distinguish between forecasts and projections. What four things are involved in an examination of prospective financial statements?

**23-17 (Objective 23-6)** What is an engagement to report on internal control? Explain how the requirements differ from the responsibilities the auditor has for obtaining an understanding of internal control and tests of controls in an audit.

**23-18 (Objective 23-6)** Identify the five steps for obtaining an understanding of internal control and tests of controls.

**23-19 (Objective 23-7)** Contrast an auditor's responsibilities for determining compliance with laws and regulations under attestation standards and under auditing standards.

## MULTIPLE CHOICE QUESTIONS FROM CPA EXAMINATIONS

**23-20 (Objective 23-1)** The following are miscellaneous questions about compilation and review services. Choose the best response.

a. A CPA has been engaged to perform review services for a client. Identify which of the following is a correct statement.
   (1) The CPA must perform the basic audit procedures necessary to determine that the statements are in conformity with generally accepted accounting principles.
   (2) The financial statements are primarily representations of the CPA.
   (3) The CPA may prepare the statements from the books but may not assist in adjusting and closing the books.
   (4) The CPA is performing an accounting service rather than an audit of the financial statements.

b. It is acceptable for a CPA to be associated with financial statements when he or she is not independent with respect to the client and still issue a substantially unmodified report for which of the following:
   (1) Audits of companies following generally accepted accounting principles.
   (2) Audits of companies on a comprehensive basis of accounting other than generally accepted accounting principles.
   (3) Compilation of financial statements following generally accepted accounting principles.
   (4) Review of financial statements following generally accepted accounting principles.

c. A CPA is performing review services for a small, closely held manufacturing company. As a part of the follow-up of a significant decrease in the gross margin for the current year, the CPA discovers that there are no supporting documents for $40,000 of disbursements. The chief financial officer assures her that the disbursements are proper. What should the CPA do?
   (1) Include the unsupported disbursements without further work in the statements on the grounds that she is not doing an audit.
   (2) Modify the review opinion or withdraw from the engagement unless the unsupported disbursements are satisfactorily explained.
   (3) Exclude the unsupported disbursements from the statements.
   (4) Obtain a written representation from the chief financial officer that the disbursements are proper and should be included in the current financial statements.

d. Which of the following best describes the responsibility of the CPA in performing compilation services for a company?
   (1) The CPA must understand the client's business and accounting methods, and read the financial statements for reasonableness.
   (2) The CPA has only to satisfy himself or herself that the financial statements were prepared in conformity with generally accepted accounting principles.
   (3) The CPA should obtain an understanding of internal control and perform tests of controls.
   (4) The CPA is relieved of any responsibility to third parties.

e. Frank, CPA, performed compilation services omitting substantially all disclosures for a client and issued the appropriate report. Three months after the statements were issued, the client informed Frank that the statements had been given to a bank for a secured loan. Which of the following is appropriate under these circumstances?
   (1) Frank must revise the statements to include appropriate footnotes and attach a revised disclaimer of opinion.
   (2) The client may give the statements to the banker as long as Frank's disclaimer of opinion accompanies the statements.
   (3) The client should retype the statements on plain paper and send them to the banker without Frank's report.
   (4) The client may let the banker review the statements and take notes, but should not give the banker a copy of the statements.

f. In performing a compilation of financial statements of a nonpublic entity, the accountant decides that modification of the standard report is not adequate to indicate deficiencies in the financial statements taken as a whole, and the client is not willing to correct the deficiencies. The accountant should therefore
   (1) perform a review of the financial statements.
   (2) issue a special report.
   (3) withdraw from the engagement.
   (4) express an adverse audit opinion.

**23-21 (Objective 23-3)** The following questions concern reports issued by auditors, other than those on historical financial statements. Choose the best response.

a. Which of the generally accepted auditing standards of reporting would *not* normally apply to special reports such as cash basis statements?
   (1) First standard.
   (2) Second standard.
   (3) Third standard.
   (4) Fourth standard.

b. An auditor is reporting on cash basis financial statements. These statements are best referred to in his or her opinion by which of the following descriptions?
   (1) Cash receipts and disbursements and the assets and liabilities arising from cash transactions.
   (2) Financial position and results of operations arising from cash transactions.
   (3) Balance sheet and income statements resulting from cash transactions.
   (4) Cash balance sheet and the source and application of funds.

c. Which of the following statements with respect to an auditor's report expressing an opinion on a specific item on a financial statement is correct?
   (1) Materiality must be related to the specific item rather than to the financial statements taken as a whole.
   (2) Such a report can be expressed only if the auditor is also engaged to audit the entire set of financial statements.
   (3) The attention devoted to the specified item is usually less than it would be if the financial statements taken as a whole were being audited.
   (4) The auditor who has issued an adverse opinion on the financial statements taken as a whole can never express an opinion on a specified item in these financial statements.

d. When asked to perform an audit in order to express an opinion on one or more specified elements, accounts, or items of a financial statement, the auditor
   (1) may *not* describe auditing procedures applied.
   (2) should advise the client that the opinion can be issued only if the financial statements have been audited and found to be fairly presented.

(3) may assume that the first standard of reporting with respect to generally accepted accounting principles does *not* apply.
(4) should comply with the request only if they constitute a major portion of the financial statements on which an auditor has disclaimed an opinion based on an audit.

**23-22 (Objective 23-3)** The following questions concern information accompanying basic financial statements. Choose the best response.

a. Ansman, CPA, has been requested by a client, Rainco Corp., to prepare information in addition to the basic financial statements for this year's audit engagement. Which of the following is the best reason for Rainco's requesting the additional information?
   (1) To provide an opinion about the supplemental information when certain items are not in accordance with generally accepted accounting principles.
   (2) To provide Rainco's creditors a greater degree of assurance as to the financial soundness of the company.
   (3) To provide Rainco's management with information to supplement and analyze the basic financial statements.
   (4) To provide the documentation required by the Securities and Exchange Commission in anticipation of a public offering of Rainco's stock.

b. Ansman, CPA, has been requested by a client, Rainco Corp., to prepare additional information accompanying the basic financial statements for this year's audit engagement. In issuing the additional information, Ansman must be certain to
   (1) issue a standard short-form report on the same engagement.
   (2) include a description of the scope of the audit in more detail than the description in the usual short-form report.
   (3) state the source of any statistical data and that such data have not been subjected to the same auditing procedures as the basic financial statements.
   (4) maintain a clear-cut distinction between the management's representations and the auditor's representations.

c. Information accompanying basic financial statements should not include
   (1) exceptions or reservations to the standard short-form auditor's report.
   (2) details of items in basic financial statements.
   (3) statistical data.
   (4) explanatory comments.

d. Which of the following best describes the difference between information accompanying basic financial statements and the basic financial information?
   (1) The additional information may contain a more detailed description of the scope of the auditor's work.
   (2) The additional information permits the auditor to explain exceptions or reservations in a way that does not require an opinion qualification.
   (3) The auditor may make factual representations with a degree of certainty that would not be appropriate in a short-form report.
   (4) The use of additional information is limited to special situations, such as cash basis statements, modified accrual basis statements, or not-for-profit organization statements.

**23-23 (Objectives 23-4, 23-5, 23-6)** The following questions concern attestation engagements. Choose the best response.

a. Which of the following professional services would be considered an attestation engagement?
   (1) A management consulting engagement to provide EDP advice to a client.
   (2) An engagement to report on compliance with statutory requirements.
   (3) An income tax engagement to prepare federal and state tax returns.
   (4) A compilation of financial statements from a client's accounting records.

b. Which of the following statements concerning prospective financial statements is correct?
   (1) Only a financial forecast would normally be appropriate for limited use.
   (2) Only a financial projection would normally be appropriate for general use.
   (3) Any type of prospective financial statements would normally be appropriate for limited use.
   (4) Any type of prospective financial statement would normally be appropriate for general use.

c. Which of the following best describes a CPA's engagement to report on an entity's internal control?
   (1) An attestation engagement to examine and report on management's written assertions about the effectiveness of its internal control.
   (2) An audit engagement to render an opinion on the entity's internal control.
   (3) A prospective engagement to project, for a period of time not to exceed one year, and report on the expected benefits of the entity's internal control.
   (4) A consulting engagement to provide constructive advice to the entity on its internal control.

## DISCUSSION QUESTIONS AND PROBLEMS

**23-24 (Objective 23-3)** As a part of the audit of Ren Gold Manufacturing Company, management requests basic financial statements and, separately, the same basic financial statements accompanied by additional information. Management informs you that the intent is to use the basic financial statements for bankers, other creditors, and the two owners who are not involved in management. The basic financial statements accompanied by the additional information are to be used only by management. Management requests the inclusion of specific information, but asks that no audit work be done beyond what is needed for the basic financial statements. The following is requested:

1. A schedule of insurance in force.
2. The auditor's feelings about the adequacy of the insurance coverage.
3. A five-year summary of the most important company ratios. The appropriate ratios are to be determined at the auditor's discretion.
4. A schedule of notes payable accompanied by interest rates, collateral, and a payment schedule.
5. An aged trial balance of accounts receivable and evaluation of the adequacy of the allowance for uncollectible accounts.
6. A summary of fixed asset additions.
7. Material weaknesses in internal control and recommendations to improve internal control.

### Required

a. What is the difference between basic financial statements and additional information?

b. What are the purposes of additional information accompanying basic financial statements?

c. For the previously listed items (1 through 7), state which ones could appropriately be included as additional information. Give reasons for your answer.

d. Identify three other items that may appropriately be included as additional information.

e. Assume that an unqualified opinion is proper for the basic financial statements report, that no testing was done beyond that required for the basic financial statements report, and that only appropriate information is included in the additional information. Write the proper auditor's report.

**23-25 (Objective 23-3)** You have been requested by the management of J. L. Lockwood Co. to issue a debt compliance letter as a part of the audit of Taylor Fruit Farms, Inc. J. L. Lockwood Co. is a supplier of irrigation equipment. Much of the equipment, including that supplied to Taylor, is sold on a secured contract basis. Taylor Fruit Farms is an audit client of yours, but Lockwood is not. In addition to the present equipment, Lockwood informs you they are evaluating whether they should sell another $500,000 of equipment to Taylor Fruit Farms.

You have been requested to send Lockwood a debt compliance letter concerning the following matters:

1. The current ratio has exceeded 2.0 in each quarter of the unaudited statements prepared by management and the annual audited statements.
2. Total owners' equity is more than $800,000.
3. The company has not violated any of the legal requirements of California fruit-growing regulations.
4. Management is competent and has made reasonable business decisions in the past three years.
5. Management owns an option to buy additional fruit land adjacent to the company's present property.

### Required

a. Define the purpose of a debt compliance letter.

b. Why is it necessary to conduct an audit of a company before it is acceptable to issue a debt compliance letter?

c. For which of the five requested items is it acceptable for a CPA firm to issue a debt compliance letter? Give reasons for your answer.

**23-26 (Objective 23-3)** Independent certified public accountants customarily issue two types of auditor's reports in connection with an audit of financial statements: an *auditor's report* in connection with financial statements intended for publication, and a *report on additional information accompanying basic financial statements* for the purposes of management and other parties.

### Required

a. Outline in *general terms* the kinds of materials that are commonly included in the additional information other than those commonly included in basic financial statements.

b. Does the auditor assume the same degree of responsibility for additional information that he or she assumes for individual items in the customary basic financial statements (balance sheet and statements of income, retained earnings, and cash flows)? State the reasons for your answer.*

**23-27 (Objective 23-1)** Evaluate the following comments about compiled financial statements: "When a CPA associates his or her name with compiled financial statements, his or her only responsibility is to the client and that is limited to the proper summarization and presentation on the financial statements of information provided by the client. The opinion clearly states that the auditor has not conducted an audit and does not express an opinion on this fair presentation. If users rely on compiled financial statements, they do so at their own risk and should never be able to hold the CPA responsible for inadequate performance. Users should interpret the financial statements as if they had been prepared by management."

**23-28 (Objective 23-1)** You are doing review services and the related tax work for Regency Tools, Inc., a tool and die company with $2,000,000 in sales. Inventory is recorded at $125,000. Prior-year unaudited statements, presented by the company without assistance

*AICPA adapted.

from a CPA firm, disclose that the inventory is based on "historical cost estimated by management." You determine four facts:

1. The company has been growing steadily for the past five years.
2. The unit cost of the typical material used by Regency Tools has increased dramatically for several years.
3. The inventory cost has been approximately $125,000 for five years.
4. Management intends to use a value of $125,000 again for the current year.

When you discuss with management the need to get a physical count and an accurate inventory, the response is negative. Management is concerned about the effect on property and income taxes of a more realistic inventory. The company has never been audited and has followed this practice for years. You are convinced, based on inquiry and ratio analysis, that a conservative evaluation would be $500,000 at historical cost.

## Required

a. What are the generally accepted accounting principle requirements for valuation and disclosure of inventory for unaudited financial statements?

b. Identify the potential legal and professional problems that you face in this situation.

c. What procedures would you normally follow for review services when the inventory is a material amount? Be as specific as possible.

d. How should you resolve the problem in this situation? Identify alternatives and evaluate the costs and benefits of each.

**23-29 (Objective 23-1)** SSARS provide illustrative review procedures for accountants to use as a guideline for conducting reviews. The introduction to the illustrative inquiries states:

> • The inquiries to be made in a review of financial statements are a matter of the accountant's judgment. In determining his or her inquiries, an accountant may consider (a) the nature and materiality of the items, (b) the likelihood of misstatement, (c) knowledge obtained during current and previous engagements, (d) the stated qualifications of the entity's accounting personnel, (e) the extent to which a particular item is affected by management's judgment, and (f) inadequacies in the entity's underlying financial data. The following list of inquiries is for illustrative purposes only. The inquiries do not necessarily apply to every engagement, nor are they meant to be all-inclusive.

The inquiry procedures included in SSARS for the sales and collection cycle are:

**Revenue**

1. Are revenues from the sale of major products and services recognized in the appropriate period?

**Receivables**

1. Has an adequate allowance been made for doubtful accounts?
2. Have receivables considered uncollectible been written off?
3. If appropriate, has interest been reflected?
4. Has a proper cutoff of sales transactions been made?
5. Are there any receivables from employees and related parties?
6. Are any receivables pledged, discounted, or factored?
7. Have receivables been properly classified between current and noncurrent?

## Required

a. What other information about accounts receivable and revenue, besides the items listed, would the accountant have to obtain?

b. Compare the illustrative procedures for review services and those commonly performed for audits. What are the major differences?

c. Of whom should the accountant make inquiries in a small closely held company?

d. Under what circumstances would procedures beyond those illustrated likely be performed? Be specific.

e. Compare the levels of achieved assurance for review services and audits. Is the achieved level much higher for audits, somewhat higher, or approximately the same? Give reasons for your answer.

**23-30 (Objective 23-2)** Lucia Johnson, of Johnson and Lecy, CPAs, has completed the first-year audit of Tidwell Publishing Co., a publicly held company, for the year ended December 31, 1996. She has now been asked to do a review of interim financial statements under SAS 71 (AU 722) for the quarter ended March 31, 1997.

Johnson has never done an SAS 71 review, but her firm does extensive compilation and review work. She therefore has one of her most experienced assistants, Fred Blair, do the work. She instructs him to follow the firm's standard review services procedures for SSARS reviews and to do high-quality work because Tidwell is a high-risk client.

Blair completes the review of Tidwell's statements and Johnson carefully reviews Blair's work. No exceptions are found. Each page of the client's financial statements is marked "reviewed." The following report is issued.

SECURITIES AND EXCHANGE COMMISSION

We have reviewed the accompanying balance sheet of Tidwell Publishing Co. as of March 31, 1997, and the related statements of income, retained earnings, and changes in financial position for the year then ended, in accordance with standards established by the American Institute of Certified Public Accountants. All information included in these financial statements is the representation of the management of Tidwell Publishing Co.

A review consists principally of inquiries of company personnel and analytical procedures applied to financial data. It is substantially less in scope than an audit in accordance with generally accepted auditing standards, the objective of which is the expression of an opinion regarding the financial statements taken as a whole. Accordingly, we do not express such an opinion.

Based on our review, we are not aware of any material modifications that should be made to the accompanying financial statements in order for them to be in conformity with generally accepted accounting principles.

*Johnson & Levy, CPAs*
*March 31, 1997*

## Required

a. Is it appropriate to do a review service for a publicly held company? Explain.

b. Evaluate the approach taken by Johnson and Blair on the engagement.

c. Evaluate the report.

**23-31 (Objective 23-3)** Bengston, CPA, is conducting the ordinary audit of Pollution Control Devices, Inc. In addition, a supplemental negative assurance report is required to a major mortgage holder. The supplemental report concerns indenture agreements to keep the client from defaulting on the mortgage. Total assets are $14 million and the mortgage is for $4 million. The major provisions of the indentures are:

1. The current ratio must be maintained above 2.3 to 1.
2. The debt/equity ratio must be maintained below 3.0.
3. Net earnings after taxes must exceed dividends paid by at least $1,000,000.

## Required

a. Write the appropriate supplemental report if all three indenture agreement provisions have been satisfied.

b. How would the supplemental report change if net earnings after taxes were $1,010,000 and dividends paid were $60,000?

c. Assume the same situation as in part b and also assume that the client refuses to modify the financial statements or disclose the violation of the indenture agreement provisions on the grounds that the amount is immaterial. What is the nature of the appropriate auditor's report?

d. What is the nature of the appropriate supplemental report if all the indenture agreement provisions have been satisfied, but there is a lawsuit against the company that has resulted in disclosure of the lawsuit in a footnote to the financial statements?

**23-32 (Objective 23-3)** Quality CPA Review is the franchisor of a national CPA review course for candidates taking the CPA exam. Quality CPA Review is responsible for providing all materials, including cassettes and video material, doing all national and local advertising, and giving assistance in effectively organizing and operating local franchises. The fee to the participant is $700 for the full course if all parts of the exam are taken. There are lower rates for candidates taking selected parts of the exam. Quality CPA Review gets 50 percent of the total fee.

The materials for the review course are purchased by Quality CPA Review from Ronnie Johnson, CPA, a highly qualified writer of CPA review materials. Quality CPA Review receives one copy of those materials from Johnson and reproduces them for candidates. Quality CPA Review must pay Johnson a $60 royalty for each full set of materials used and 12 percent of the participant fee for partial candidates. The contract between Johnson and Quality CPA Review requires an audited report to be provided by Quality CPA Review on royalties due to Johnson. Recorded gross fees for the 1997 review course are $1,500,000.

Even before the audit is started, there is a dispute between Quality CPA Review and Johnson. Quality CPA Review does not intend to pay royalties on certain materials. Johnson disagrees with that conclusion but the contract does not specify anything about it. The following are the disputed sales on which Quality CPA Review refused to pay royalties:

| | |
|---|---|
| 1. Materials sent to instructors for promotion | $31,000 |
| 2. Uncollected fees due to bad debts | 6,000 |
| 3. Candidates who paid no fee because they performed administrative duties during the course | 16,000 |
| 4. Refunds to customers who were dissatisfied with the course | 22,000 |
| Total | $75,000 |

## Required

a. Assume that you are engaged to do the ordinary audit of Quality CPA Review and the special audit of royalties for Johnson. What additional audit testing beyond the normal tests of royalties is required because of the special audit?

b. Assume that the financial statements of Quality CPA Review are found to be fairly stated except for the unresolved dispute between Johnson and Quality CPA Review. Write the appropriate audit report.

c. Write the report for total royalties to Johnson, assuming that the information as stated in the case is all correct and the dispute is not resolved.

**23-33 (Objective 23-3)** Jones, CPA, has completed the audit of Sarack Lumber Supply Co. and has issued a standard unqualified report. In addition to a report on the overall financial statements, the company needs a special audited report on three specific accounts: sales, net fixed assets, and inventory valued at FIFO. The report is to be issued to Sarack's lessor, who bases annual rentals on these three accounts. Jones was not aware of the need for the report on the three specific accounts until after the overall audit was completed.

**Required**

a. Explain why Jones is unlikely to be able to issue the audit report on the three specific accounts without additional audit tests.

b. What additional tests are likely to be needed before the report on the three specific accounts can be issued?

c. Assuming that Jones is able to satisfy all the requirements needed to issue the report on the three specific accounts, write the report. Make any necessary assumptions.

23-34 **(Objective 23-5)** Carl Monson, the owner of Major Products Manufacturing Company, a small successful longtime audit client of your firm, has requested you to work with his company in preparing three-year forecasted information for the year ending December 31, 1996, and two subsequent years. Monson informs you that he intends to use the forecasts, together with the audited financial statements, to seek additional financing to expand the business. Monson has had little experience in formal forecast preparation and counts on you to assist him in any way possible. He wants the most supportive opinion possible from your firm to add to the credibility of the forecast. He informs you that he is willing to do anything necessary to help you prepare the forecast.

First, he wants projections of sales and revenues and earnings from the existing business, which he believes could continue to be financed from existing capital.

Second, he intends to buy a company in a closely related business that is currently operating unsuccessfully. Monson states that he wants to sell some of the operating assets of the business and replace them with others. He believes that the company can then be made highly successful. He has made an offer on the new business, subject to obtaining proper financing. He also informs you that he has received an offer on the assets he intends to sell.

**Required**

a. Explain circumstances under which it would and would not be acceptable to undertake the engagement.

b. Why is it important that Monson understand the nature of your reporting requirements before the engagement proceeds?

c. What information will Monson have to provide to you before you can complete the forecasted statements? Be as specific as possible.

d. Discuss, in as specific terms as possible, the nature of the report you will issue with the forecasts, assuming that you are able to properly complete them.

24

# INTERNAL AND GOVERNMENTAL FINANCIAL AUDITING AND OPERATIONAL AUDITING

## LEARNING OBJECTIVES

Thorough study of this chapter will enable you to

- **24-1** Understand the role of internal auditors in financial auditing.
- **24-2** Understand the nature of governmental financial auditing.
- **24-3** Distinguish operational auditing from financial auditing.
- **24-4** Give an overview of operational audits and operational auditors.
- **24-5** Plan and perform an operational audit.

## GOOD AUDITING OFTEN RESULTS IN IMPROVED CASH FLOWS

Sandy Previtz is a new internal audit staff person who has been with Erhardt Freight Company (EFC), a long-haul trucking company, only a year. Before being hired by EFC, she was an auditor for a CPA firm for five years. She is now doing internal audit work on the sales and receivables function.

The sales transaction document for a long-haul trucking company is a freight bill, evidencing a shipment for a customer. EFC has an extremely high growth rate, reaching a current volume of several thousand shipments a day. The accounting for all the freight bills, and the related receivables, is a massive accounting and systems problem. The problem is more complex because EFC is adding new customers and shipping agents daily. EFC's solution to this record-keeping problem has been to develop and implement a new state-of-the-art computerized information system. The parts of the system that have the biggest effect on the audit relate to the aging of accounts receivable and estimation of an appropriate allowance for uncollectible freight bills. By law, these bills must be paid within seven days.

Sandy decides to copy EFC's accounts receivable data file, take a statistical sample of outstanding freight bills, and estimate an aging from the bills. She gets approval from the head of internal auditing, Martha Harris, and makes arrangements with EFC's chief financial officer, Hal Stenson, to have the file copied and to proceed.

Sandy's initial sample consists of 300 items, selected at random from approximately 20,000 outstanding freight bills. She projects an aging from the sample and applies a formula to obtain a range estimate of the necessary allowance for uncollectible accounts. When she compares this to the Company's recorded allowance, it appears that the recorded amount may be understated by as much as $1 million, clearly a material amount.

When Sandy informs Harris of the situation, Harris calls a meeting with Stenson and asks Sandy to attend. At the meeting, Sandy explains that her findings are based on a statistical estimate, that the 95 percent confidence interval she obtained had an upper limit of $1 million and a lower limit of only $200,000, which is not a material amount. After some discussion of the meaning of the relevant statistical terms and procedures, Stenson states: "I certainly don't want to make an adjustment to the books based on this wide range estimate, and I hope you both agree with me."

Harris tells Stenson in no uncertain terms that as long as the confidence limit indicates that there *could* be a material misstatement, EFC must expand the sample until it is clear whether or not the allowance is materially misstated. After further discussion, Stenson finally agrees and tells Harris to go ahead.

Sandy's second sample increases the overall sample size to 600 items, and shows approximately the same results. However, at Harris's request, the items are analyzed from *both* a management and an accounting standpoint. When Harris and Sandy meet with Stenson to discuss the updated information, Harris points out that the real problem is not the allowance, but the fact that receivables are out of control and EFC faces a risk of a significant loss in cash flows if management does not do something about it. Stenson quickly agrees and responds by hiring a team of temporary workers to analyze the aging of all 20,000 freight bills and to institute a large-scale collection effort. He also decides to make an adjustment to the allowance account based on the results of the second sample. Not only does the Company's detailed analysis improve its cash flows, it also shows that Sandy's statistical estimate was right on target.

Internal and governmental auditors perform a significant amount of financial auditing similar to that done by CPA firms. CPA firms also do considerable financial auditing of governmental audits. The concepts and methodologies discussed throughout this book apply to audits by internal and governmental auditors and audits of governmental units by CPA firms or governmental auditors. The early part of this chapter focuses on the role of internal and governmental auditors and the unique consideration in auditing governmental units.

The last part of the chapter deals with operational auditing. In operational audits, the objectives relate to whether an organization's operating procedures and methods are efficient and effective. Operational audit engagements are in demand and represent a growing segment of CPAs' activities. They are also conducted extensively by other professionals, such as internal and governmental auditors. This portion of the chapter deals with differences between financial and operational auditing and provides an overview of performing these audits. A large number of examples are provided to assist in understanding the nature of these engagements.

## INTERNAL FINANCIAL AUDITING

**OBJECTIVE 24-1**
**Understand the role of internal auditors in financial auditing.**

As discussed in Chapter 1, internal auditors are employed by companies to do both financial and operational auditing. Their role in auditing has increased dramatically in the past two decades, primarily because of the increased size and complexity of many corporations.

In financial auditing, internal auditors are responsible for evaluating whether their company's internal controls are designed and operate effectively and whether the financial statements are fairly presented. Because internal auditors spend all of their time with one company, their knowledge about the company's operations and internal controls is much greater than the external auditors' knowledge.

Guidelines for performing internal audits for companies are not as well defined as for external audits. The reason is the lack of external users, who do not know what procedures the auditor performs, relying on the audit findings. Management of different companies may have widely varying expectations of the type and extent of financial auditing to be done by internal auditors. For example, management of one company may decide that internal auditors should evaluate the internal controls and financial statements of every division annually, whereas others may decide that a three-year rotation is sufficient.

### Institute of Internal Auditors

Instead of relying on the AICPA for professional guidance, internal auditors look to the Institute of Internal Auditors (IIA). The IIA is an organization similar to the AICPA that establishes ethical and practice standards, provides education, and encourages professionalism for its approximately 35,000 members. The IIA has played a major role in the increasing influence of internal auditing. For example, the IIA has established a highly regarded certification program resulting in the designation of Certified Internal Auditor (CIA) for those who meet the testing and experience requirements.

The IIA Practice Standards include five categories of guidance that encompass both financial and operational auditing: independence, professional proficiency, scope of work, performance of audit work, and management of the internal auditing department. The specific standards supporting these five categories are included in Figure 24-1. A comparison of these standards to the AICPA generally accepted auditing standards on page 18 shows both similarities and differences. Each of the standards in Figure 24-1 are also supported by more detailed guidance on how to meet the standard, similar to the AICPA's SASs.

### Relationship of Internal and External Auditors

There are both differences and similarities between the responsibilities and conduct of audits by internal and external auditors. The primary difference is whom each party is responsible to. The external auditor is responsible to financial statement users who rely on

**FIGURE 24-1**

**Institute of Internal Auditor Professional Practice Standards**

SUMMARY OF GENERAL AND SPECIFIC STANDARDS FOR THE PROFESSIONAL PRACTICE OF INTERNAL AUDITING

100 INDEPENDENCE. Internal auditors should be independent of the activities they audit.

110 *Organizational Status.* The organizational status of the internal auditing department should be sufficient to permit the accomplishment of its audit responsibilities.

120 *Objectivity.* Internal auditors should be objective in performing audits.

200 PROFESSIONAL PROFICIENCY. Internal audits should be performed with proficiency and due professional care.

**The Internal Auditing Department**

210 *Staffing.* The internal auditing department should provide assurance that the technical proficiency and educational background of internal auditors are appropriate for the audits to be performed.

220 *Knowledge, Skills, and Disciplines.* The internal auditing department should possess or should obtain the knowledge, skills, and disciplines needed to carry out its audit responsibilities.

230 *Supervision.* The internal auditing department should provide assurance that internal audits are properly supervised.

**The Internal Auditor**

240 *Compliance with Standards of Conduct.* Internal auditors should comply with professional standards of conduct.

250 *Knowledge, Skills, and Disciplines.* Internal auditors should possess the knowledge, skills, and disciplines essential to the performance of internal audits.

260 *Human Relations and Communications.* Internal auditors should be skilled in dealing with people and in communicating effectively.

270 *Continuing Education.* Internal auditors should maintain their technical competence through continuing education.

280 *Due Professional Care.* Internal auditors should exercise due professional care in performing internal audits.

300 SCOPE OF WORK. The scope of the internal audit should encompass the examination and evaluation of the adequacy and effectiveness of the organization's system of internal control and the quality of performance in carrying out assigned responsibilities.

310 *Reliability and Integrity of Information.* Internal auditors should review the reliability and integrity of financial and operating information and the means used to identify, measure, classify, and report such information.

320 *Compliance with Policies, Plans, Procedures, Laws, and Regulations.* Internal auditors should review the systems established to ensure compliance with those policies, plans, procedures, laws, and regulations that could have a significant impact on operations and reports and should determine whether the organization is in compliance.

330 *Safeguard of Assets.* Internal auditors should review the means of safeguarding assets and, as appropriate, verify the existence of such assets.

340 *Economical and Efficient Use of Resources.* Internal auditors should appraise the economy and efficiency with which resources are employed.

350 *Accomplishment of Established Objectives and Goals for Operations or Programs.* Internal auditors should review operations or programs to ascertain whether results are consistent with established objectives and goals and whether the operations or programs are being carried out as planned.

400 PERFORMANCE OF AUDIT WORK. Audit work should include planning the audit, examining and evaluating information, communicating results, and following up.

410 *Planning the Audit.* Internal auditors should plan each audit.

420 *Examining and Evaluating Information.* Internal auditors should collect, analyze, interpret, and document information to support audit results.

430 *Communicating Results.* Internal auditors should report the results of their audit work.

440 *Following Up.* Internal auditors should follow up to ascertain that appropriate action is taken on reported audit findings.

500 MANAGEMENT OF THE INTERNAL AUDITING DEPARTMENT. The director of internal auditing should properly manage the internal auditing department.

510 *Purpose, Authority, and Responsibility.* The director of internal auditing should have a statement of purpose, authority, and responsibility for the internal auditing department.

520 *Planning.* The director of internal auditing should establish plans to carry out responsibilities of the internal auditing department.

530 *Policies and Procedures.* The director of internal auditing should provide written policies and procedures to guide the audit staff.

540 *Personnel Management and Development.* The director of internal auditing should establish a program of selecting and developing the human resources of the internal auditing department.

550 *External Auditors.* The director of internal auditing should coordinate internal and external audit efforts.

560 *Quality Assurance.* The director of internal auditing should establish and maintain a quality assurance program to evaluate the operations of the internal auditing department.

*Source: Standards for the Professional Practice of Internal Auditing* (Altamonte Springs, Fla.: Institute of Internal Auditors, 1980), pp. 3–4.

the auditor to add credibility to the statements. The internal auditor is responsible to management. Even with this important difference, there are many similarities between the two groups. Both must be competent as auditors and remain objective in performing their work and reporting their results. They both, for example, follow a similar methodology in performing their audits, including planning and performing tests of controls and substantive tests. Similarly, they both use the audit risk model and materiality in deciding the extent of their tests and evaluating results. Their decisions about materiality and risks may differ, however, because external users may have different needs than management has.

External auditors rely on internal auditors through the use of the audit risk model. Auditors significantly reduce control risk and thereby reduce substantive testing if internal auditors are effective. The fee reduction of the external auditor is typically substantial when there is a highly regarded internal audit function. External auditors typically consider internal auditors effective if they are independent of the operating units being evaluated, competent and well trained, and have performed relevant audit tests of the internal controls and financial statements.

SAS 65 (AU 322) also permits the external auditor to use the internal auditor for direct assistance on the audit. This means that the external auditor is permitted to treat internal auditors much like his or her own audit staff. The incentive for management is a reduced audit fee, whereas the incentive for the CPA firm is retaining the client. The risk to the external auditor is the lack of competent and independent performance by the internal auditors. Before using internal auditors, the external auditor must be confident of their competence, independence, and objectivity. In addition, auditors typically reperform a sample of the internal auditor's work to make certain that it was done correctly.

## GOVERNMENTAL FINANCIAL AUDITING

**OBJECTIVE 24-2**
**Understand the nature of governmental financial auditing.**

The federal and state governments employ their own auditing staff to perform audits in much the same way as internal auditors. Chapter 1 briefly discussed the United States General Auditing Office (GAO). All states have their own audit agencies, similar to but smaller than the GAO. In addition, CPA firms do considerable financial auditing of governmental units. For example, some states require the audit of all city and school district financial statements by CPA firms.

The primary source of authoritative literature for performing governmental audits is a major publication of the GAO, *Government Auditing Standards.* It is a widely used reference by government auditors and CPAs who do governmental audit work. Because of the color of the cover, it is usually referred to as the "Yellow Book" rather than by its more formal name.

Financial auditing under the Yellow Book includes audits of financial statements of governmental units, government contracts and grants, internal control, fraud, and other noncompliance with laws and regulations. These categories of information are broader than audits under generally accepted auditing standards and encompass the types of attestation work discussed in Chapter 23 under the attestation standards. It is not surprising, however, that governmental units are as concerned with compliance with laws and regulations as with the reliability of financial statements.

### Single Audit Act

Prior to 1980, each federal financing agency had its own audit requirements. Consequently, recipients of federal funds received multiple audits. The same financial reports and underlying statements and transactions were audited numerous times, often simultaneously, by different auditors. This problem was remedied in 1984 with the passage of the Single Audit Act. The Single Audit Act provides for a single coordinated audit to satisfy the audit requirements of all federal funding agencies. The Single Audit Act and an accompanying publication, OMB Circular A-128, require that the Yellow Book standards be followed and specifies additional audit requirements.

Thus, when a state or local government agency receives federal financial assistance, it is subject to the audit requirements of the Yellow Book, the Single Audit Act, and OMB Circular A-128. These audit requirements also apply to subrecipients to whom state or local governments pass government assistance funds (this does not include individual recipients of the assistance). The audits can be performed by either external state or local government auditors or by CPAs, all of whom must meet the Yellow Book's independence and qualification standards.

## Audit and Reporting Requirements—Yellow Book

The auditing standards of the Yellow Book are consistent with the ten generally accepted auditing standards of the AICPA. There are, however, some important additions and modifications.

- *Materiality and significance.* The Yellow Book recognizes that in government audits the thresholds of acceptable audit risk and tolerable misstatement may be lower than in an audit of a commercial enterprise. This is because of the sensitivity of government activities and their public accountability.
- *Quality control.* CPA firms and other organizations that audit government entities in compliance with the Yellow Book must have an appropriate system of internal quality control and participate in an external quality control review program. The latter requirement exists for some CPAs, but only as a requirement for membership in the AICPA and/or the audit of public companies.
- *Legal and regulatory requirements.* The second supplemental planning field work standard in the Yellow Book states: "A test should be made of compliance with applicable laws and regulations." This is a compliance auditing requirement. The laws and regulations of primary concern are those that have a direct and material effect on the financial amounts. The Yellow Book states that the auditor should:

  1. Identify pertinent laws and regulations and determine which of those laws and regulations could, if not observed, have a direct and material effect on the financial statements or the results of a related financial audit.
  2. Assess, for each material requirement, the risks of material noncompliance. This includes consideration and assessment of the internal controls to assure compliance with laws and regulations.
  3. Design steps and procedures based on the assessment to test compliance with laws and regulations to provide reasonable assurance that both unintentional and intentional instances of material noncompliance are detected.

- *Working papers.* The Yellow Book contains a standard that is more specific and prescriptive about documentation of audit work.

These requirements are similar to generally accepted auditing standards pertaining to errors, fraud, and illegal acts. Under generally accepted auditing standards, the auditor should include a plan to detect material misstatements that arise from violations of laws and regulations. In fact, the objective of the Yellow Book standards is that these requirements can be met by performing a normal GAAS audit. However, Yellow Book requirements must relate to the expanded requirements of the Single Audit Act as summarized below.

The major difference between the Yellow Book and generally accepted auditing standards is in the reporting area. The auditor of a government entity issues a report on the audit of the financial statements in the normal manner, but includes several significant additional requirements. First, the report must state that the audit was done in accordance with both generally accepted auditing standards and government auditing standards.

Second, the auditor must issue a report on tests of compliance with applicable laws and regulations. This report may be separate or included in the report on the audit of the financial statements. The compliance report must give positive assurance on items tested for compliance, and negative assurance on those items not tested. All instances of noncompliance or indications of illegal acts, both of which could result in criminal prosecution, must be reported.

Third, the auditor must prepare a report on his or her understanding of the entity's internal control and assessment of control risk. This report may also be separate or included in the financial audit report. The report should include: (1) the scope of the auditor's work in obtaining an understanding of internal control and assessing control risk; (2) the entity's significant internal controls, including controls to ensure compliance with laws and regulations that have a material impact on the financial statements and results of the financial audit; and (3) the reportable conditions, including the identification of material weaknesses, that result from the auditor's work in understanding and assessing control risk.

This third requirement does not require the auditor to extend his or her work regarding internal control beyond that contemplated by generally accepted auditing standards. It does, however, formalize the reporting of the results. For example, generally accepted auditing standards *permit* identifying material weaknesses; the Yellow Book *requires* it.

## Audit and Reporting Requirements—Single Audit Act and OMB Circular A-128

The Single Audit Act and OMB Circular A-128 (referred to here collectively as the Act) require that an audit be conducted for recipients who receive total federal financial assistance of $100,000 or more in any fiscal year. If the recipient receives between $25,000 and $100,000, it may elect to implement the Act requirements in lieu of separate program requirements. If a government receives less than $25,000, it is exempt from federal audit requirements.

The Act expands the Yellow Book requirements in several ways. First, it identifies applicable laws and regulations as those that would have a material effect on *each major federal financial assistance program.* Major programs are those which are of a certain size in a given year, as defined in the Act. For example, $20 million is considered a major program when expenditures for all programs exceed $7 billion.

Second, the Act requires that the audit include the selection and testing of a representative number of charges from each major program for compliance. Yellow Book requirements are not as specific, asking only that tested items be identified. The design of the tests required by the Act is left to the auditor's judgment. They must, however, meet the following specific objectives:

- Whether the amounts reported as expenditures were for allowable services.
- Whether the records show that those who received services or benefits were eligible to receive them.
- Whether matching requirements (where the state matches federal funds), levels of effort, and earmarking limitations were met.
- Whether federal financial reports and claims for advances and reimbursements contain information that is supported by the books and records from which the basic financial statements have been prepared.
- Whether amounts claimed or used for matching were determined in accordance with OMB Circular A-87, *Cost Principles for State and Local Governments,* and OMB Circular A-102, *Uniform Requirements for Grants to State and Local Governments.*

Third, the Act, through the OMB *Compliance Supplement,* provides guidance on which laws and regulations should be covered by the compliance aspects of the audit. The *Compliance Supplement* identifies certain general compliance requirements and provides a list of specific requirements for various federal programs. The general requirements relate to political activity (Hatch Act and Intergovernmental Personnel Act), construction contracts (Davis–Bacon Act), civil rights, cash management, relocation assistance and real property acquisition, and federal financial reports. The *Compliance Supplement* also provides suggested audit procedures for these general compliance requirements.

Finally, the Act has its own reporting requirements. Required reports include:

1. A report on the audit of the financial statements. This would be the same as GAAS and the Yellow Book.
2. A report on the internal control of the entity as a whole, based solely on the work done as part of the audit of the financial statements. This would be the same as the Yellow Book report.

3. A report on compliance with laws and regulations that may have a material effect on the financial statements. This would be the same as the Yellow Book report.
4. A report on a supplementary schedule of the entity's federal financial assistance programs, showing total expenditures for each program. This is an additional requirement.
5. A report on compliance with laws and regulations identifying all findings of noncompliance and questioned costs. The Yellow Book requires reporting findings of noncompliance based on a less rigorous scope. Questioned costs are those expenditures examined by the auditor which he or she believes to be either unallowable, undocumented, unapproved, or unreasonable under the circumstances.
6. A report on internal controls (accounting and administrative) used in administering federal financial assistance programs. This is an additional requirement.
7. A report on fraud, abuse, or an illegal act, or indications of such acts, when discovered. This would be similar under GAAS or the Yellow Book, although the form under GAAS would probably differ.

### Guidance for Auditors

From the preceding discussion, one can see that entering the arena of government auditing is a complex undertaking. The auditor must be familiar with both generally accepted auditing standards and a series of government audit documents, laws, and regulations. Thus, the first step in preparing for such an engagement is extensive professional development. In fact, the Yellow Book requires that the auditor responsible for significant portions of the audit attend at least 24 hours of governmental audit education in the two-year period prior to the audit.

To assist auditors in this regard, the AICPA has issued some helpful documents. Foremost is SAS 74 (AU 801), *Compliance Auditing Considerations in Audits of Governmental Entities and Recipients of Governmental Financial Assistance.* The second is the *Audit and Accounting Guide for Audits of State and Local Governmental Units.* These two documents contain a great deal of useful background information. The *Guide,* for example, contains the entire Single Audit Act and OMB Circular A-128. They also provide guidance in planning a governmental audit, designing appropriate tests, and writing the required reports. Examples of many of the required reports are included in the *Guide.*

## OPERATIONAL AUDITING

Although *operational auditing* is generally understood to deal with efficiency and effectiveness, there is less agreement on the use of that term than one might expect. Many people prefer to use the terms *management auditing* or *performance auditing* instead of *operational auditing* to describe the review of organizations for efficiency and effectiveness. Those people typically describe operational auditing broadly and include evaluating internal controls and even testing those controls for effectiveness (tests of controls) as a part of operational auditing. Others do not distinguish among the terms *performance auditing, management auditing,* and *operational auditing.*

We prefer to use *operational auditing* broadly, as long as the purpose of the test is to determine the effectiveness or efficiency of any part of an organization. Testing the effectiveness of internal controls by an internal auditor is therefore a part of operational auditing if the purpose is to help an organization operate its business more effectively or efficiently. Similarly, the determination of whether a company has adequately trained assembly line personnel is also operational auditing if the purpose is to determine whether the company is effectively and efficiently producing products.

### Differences Between Operational and Financial Auditing

Three major differences exist between operational and financial auditing: purpose of the audit, distribution of the reports, and inclusion of nonfinancial areas in operational auditing.

**Purpose of the Audit** The major distinction between financial and operational auditing is the purpose of the tests. Financial auditing emphasizes whether historical information was

**OBJECTIVE 24-3**
**Distinguish operational auditing from financial auditing.**

correctly recorded. Operational auditing emphasizes effectiveness and efficiency. The financial audit is oriented to the past, whereas an operational audit concerns operating performance for the future. An operational auditor, for example, may evaluate whether a type of new material is being purchased at the lowest cost to save money on future raw material purchases.

**Distribution of the Reports** For financial auditing, the report typically goes to many users of financial statements, such as stockholders and bankers; whereas operational audit reports are intended primarily for management. As indicated in Chapter 2, well-defined wording is needed for financial auditing reports as a result of the widespread distribution of the reports. Because of the limited distribution of operational reports and the diverse nature of audits for efficiency and effectiveness, operational auditing reports vary considerably from audit to audit.

**Inclusion of Nonfinancial Areas** Operational audits cover any aspect of efficiency and effectiveness in an organization and can therefore involve a wide variety of activities. For example, the effectiveness of an advertising program or efficiency of factory employees would be part of an operational audit. Financial audits are limited to matters that directly affect the fairness of financial statement presentations.

## Effectiveness Versus Efficiency

Effectiveness refers to the accomplishment of objectives, whereas efficiency refers to the resources used to achieve those objectives. An example of effectiveness is the production of parts without defects. Efficiency concerns whether those parts are produced at minimum cost.

**OBJECTIVE 24-4**
**Give an overview of operational audits and operational auditors.**

**Effectiveness** Before an operational audit for effectiveness can be performed, there must be specific criteria for what is meant by *effectiveness.* An example of an operational audit for effectiveness would be to assess whether a governmental agency has met its assigned objective of achieving elevator safety in a city. Before the operational auditor can reach a conclusion about the agency's effectiveness, criteria for elevator safety must be set. For example, is the objective to see that all elevators in the city are inspected at least once a year? Is the objective to ensure that no fatalities occurred due to elevator breakdowns, or that no breakdowns occurred?

**Efficiency** Like effectiveness, there must be defined criteria for what is meant by doing things more efficiently before operational auditing can be meaningful. It is often easier to set efficiency than effectiveness criteria if *efficiency* is defined as reducing cost without reducing effectiveness. For example, if two different production processes manufacture a product of identical quality, the process with the lower cost is considered more efficient.

The following are several types of inefficiencies that frequently occur and often are uncovered through operational auditing.

| Types of Inefficiency | Example |
|---|---|
| • Acquisition of goods and services is excessively costly. | • Bids for purchases of materials are not required. |
| • Raw materials are not available for production when needed. | • An entire assembly line must be shut down because necessary materials were not ordered. |
| • There is duplication of effort by employees. | • Identical production records are kept by both the accounting and production departments because they are unaware of each other's activities. |
| • Work is done that serves no purpose. | • Copies of vendors' invoices and receiving reports are sent to the production department where they are filed without ever being used. |
| • There are too many employees. | • The office work could be done effectively with one less secretary. |

## Relationship Between Operational Auditing and Internal Controls

In Chapter 9, it was stated that management establishes internal controls to help it meet its own goals. The following three concerns in setting up good internal controls were identified and discussed in Chapter 9:

- Reliability of financial reporting
- Efficiency and effectiveness of operations
- Compliance with applicable laws and regulations

The second of these three client concerns is obviously directly related to operational auditing, but the other two also affect efficiency and effectiveness. For example, reliable cost accounting information is important to management in deciding such things as which products to continue and the billing price of products. Similarly, failure to comply with a law such as the Foreign Corrupt Practices Act could result in a large fine to the company.

There are two significant differences in internal control evaluation and testing for financial and operational auditing: the purpose of the evaluation and testing of internal controls, and the normal scope of internal control evaluation.

The primary purpose of internal control evaluation for financial auditing is to determine the extent of substantive audit testing required. The purpose of operational auditing is to evaluate efficiency and effectiveness of internal control and make recommendations to management. The control procedures might be evaluated in the same way for both financial and operational auditing, but the purpose is different. To illustrate, an operational auditor might determine if internal verification procedures for duplicate sales invoices are effective to ensure that the company does not offend customers but also receives all money owed. A financial auditor often does the same internal control evaluation, but the primary purpose is to reduce confirmation of accounts receivable or other substantive tests. A secondary purpose, however, of many financial audits is also to make operational recommendations to management.

The scope of internal control evaluation for financial audits is restricted to matters affecting fairly presented financial statements, whereas operational auditing concerns any control affecting efficiency or effectiveness. Therefore, for example, an operational audit could be concerned with policies and procedures established in the marketing department to determine the effectiveness of catalogs used to market products.

## Types of Operational Audits

There are three broad categories of operational audits: functional, organizational, and special assignments. In each case, part of the audit is likely to concern evaluating internal controls for efficiency and effectiveness.

**Functional** Functions are a means of categorizing the activities of a business, such as the billing function or production function. There are many different ways to categorize and subdivide functions. For example, there is an accounting function, but there are also cash disbursement, cash receipt, and payroll disbursement functions. There is a payroll function, but there are also hiring, timekeeping, and payroll disbursement functions.

As the name implies, a functional audit deals with one or more functions in an organization. It could concern, for example, the payroll function for a division or for the company as a whole.

A functional audit has the advantage of permitting specialization by auditors. Certain auditors within an internal audit staff can develop considerable expertise in an area, such as production engineering. They can more efficiently spend all their time auditing in that area. A disadvantage of functional auditing is the failure to evaluate interrelated functions. The production engineering function interacts with manufacturing and other functions in an organization.

**Organizational** An operational audit of an organization deals with an entire organizational unit, such as a department, branch, or subsidiary. The emphasis in an organizational audit is on how efficiently and effectively functions interact. The plan of organization and the methods to coordinate activities are especially important in this type of audit.

**Special Assignments** Special operational auditing assignments arise at the request of management. There are a wide variety of such audits. Examples include determining the cause of an ineffective EDP system, investigating the possibility of fraud in a division, and making recommendations for reducing the cost of a manufactured product.

## Who Performs Operational Audits

Operational audits are usually performed by one of three groups: internal auditors, government auditors, or CPA firms.

**Internal Auditors** Internal auditors are in such a unique position to perform operational audits that some people use *internal auditing* and *operational auditing* interchangeably. It is, however, inappropriate to conclude that all operational auditing is done by internal auditors or that internal auditors do only operational auditing. Many internal audit departments do both operational and financial audits. Often, they are done simultaneously. An advantage that internal auditors have in doing operational audits is that they spend all their time working for the company they are auditing. They thereby develop considerable knowledge about the company and its business, which is essential to effective operational auditing.

To maximize their effectiveness for both financial and operational auditing, the internal audit department should report to the board of directors or president. Internal auditors should also have access to and ongoing communications with the audit committee of the board of directors. This organizational structure helps internal auditors remain independent. For example, if internal auditors report to the controller, it is difficult for the internal auditor to evaluate independently and make recommendations to senior management about inefficiencies in the controller's operations.

---

**MAJOR CHANGES SEEN IN ROLE OF INTERNAL AUDITORS**

The control environment of major financial institutions has changed dramatically over the last five years in the face of shifting regulations, complex financial instruments, technological breakthroughs, and accelerating customer and stockholder demands. Crippling losses resulting from control failures are prompting far-reaching changes in the internal audit function. Some major changes:

**Tension Between Roles** Traditionally, internal auditors have been the "control conscience" of the organization, but they are now being asked to provide strategic and operational input. These conflicting roles of both creating and enforcing rules have resulted in tension that must be effectively managed. They also demand new types of skill sets, requiring that auditors have not only technical expertise, but also "live" skills such as communication, decision making, and business analysis.

**Risk Management** There are two major interrelated trends in the area of risk management: (1) the need for more audit attention to control the risks of derivative financial instruments, and (2) the movement toward integrated financial risk management, a central component of which is "value at risk"—the potential loss from adverse changes in market factors for a specified time period and confidence level.

**Electronic Commerce** Conducting financial activity in a "paperless" electronic environment poses a major concern. As reliance on computer networks increases, institutions must design and implement control systems that can adequately manage risk, particularly in areas such as data security and integrity, and vulnerability to viruses. Early involvement of internal audit is important in designing and developing new data systems and products, allowing institutions to build internal controls *into* new procedures and systems, as opposed to controlling them after the fact.

*Source:* "Major Changes Seen in Role of Internal Auditors," *Deloitte & Touche Review,* February 5, 1996, p. 2.

**Government Auditors** Different federal and state government auditors perform operational auditing, often as a part of doing financial audits. As already discussed, the most widely recognized government auditors group is the GAO, but there are also many state government auditors. Most of these auditors are concerned with both financial and operational audits.

The Yellow Book, which was discussed earlier, defines and sets standards for performance audits, which are essentially the same as operational audits. Performance audits include the following:

- *Economy and efficiency audits.* These have as their purpose determining (1) whether an entity is acquiring, protecting, and using its resources economically and efficiently; (2) the causes of inefficiencies or uneconomical practices; and (3) whether the entity has complied with laws and regulations concerning matters of economy and efficiency.
- *Program audits.* These have as their purpose determining (1) the extent to which the desired results or benefits established by the legislature or other authorizing body are being achieved; (2) the effectiveness of organizations, programs, activities, or functions; and (3) whether the entity has complied with laws and regulations applicable to the program.

The first two objectives of each of these types of performance audits are clearly operational in nature. The final objective in each is compliance in nature, and was discussed earlier.

To illustrate specific operational activities of a state governmental audit, the following three examples are taken from an article in the publication *Internal Auditor,* discussing auditing for economy and efficiency:

- A separate hospital with its own administrative staff occupied three buildings on the grounds of another state hospital. Our audit showed that the limited workload of the administrative activities of this separate hospital and its proximity to the offices of the main hospital would permit consolidation of the administrative functions of the two hospitals at a savings of $145,000 a year.
- A local school district exercised control over twenty-nine individual facilities. Our audit showed that the unused classroom facilities amounted to about 28 percent or the equivalent of eight schools and that enrollment was continuing to decline. We recommended consolidating and closing of individual facilities to the extent possible. Such action would not only reduce costs but also provide greater flexibility in class sizes and course offerings.
- The outstanding accounts receivable at a teaching hospital increased from $7 million to $11 million during a two-year period. An audit showed that this serious situation was caused, in part, by a lack of aggressive follow-up action, insufficient supervision, and insufficient staff to keep up with an increasing workload.[1]

**CPA Firms** When CPA firms do an audit of historical financial statements, part of the audit usually consists of identifying operational problems and making recommendations that may benefit the audit client. The recommendations can be made orally, but they are typically made by use of a *management letter.* Management letters were discussed in Chapter 22.

The background knowledge about a client's business that an external auditor must obtain in doing an audit often provides useful information for giving operational recommendations. For example, suppose that the auditor determined that inventory turnover for a client slowed considerably during the current year. The auditor is likely to determine the cause of the reduction to evaluate the possibility of obsolete inventory that would misstate the financial statements. In determining the cause of the reduced inventory turnover, the

[1]From *Round Table,* © 1982 by The Institute of Internal Auditors, Inc., 249 Maitland Avenue, Altamonte Springs, Fla. 32701. Reprinted with permission.

auditor may identify operational causes, such as ineffective inventory acquisition policies, that can be brought to the attention of management. An auditor who has a broad business background and experience with similar businesses is more likely to be effective at providing clients with relevant operational recommendations than a person who lacks those qualities.

It is also common for a client to engage a CPA firm to do operational auditing for one or more specific parts of its business. Usually, such an engagement would occur only if the company does not have an internal audit staff or if the internal audit staff lacks expertise in a certain area. In most cases, a management consulting staff of the CPA firm, rather than the auditing staff, performs these services. For example, a company can ask the CPA firm to evaluate the efficiency and effectiveness of its computer systems.

## Independence and Competence of Operational Auditors

The two most important qualities for an operational auditor are *independence* and *competence.*

Whom the auditor reports to is important to ensure that investigation and recommendations are made without bias. Independence is seldom a problem for CPA firm auditors because they are not employed by the company being audited. As stated earlier, independence of internal auditors is enhanced by having the internal audit department report to the board of directors or president. Similarly, government auditors should report to a level above the operating departments. The GAO, for example, reports directly to Congress as a means of enhancing independence.

The responsibilities of operational auditors can also affect their independence. The auditor should not be responsible for performing operating functions in a company or for correcting deficiencies when ineffective or inefficient operations are found. For example, it would negatively affect auditors' independence if they were responsible for designing an EDP system for acquisitions or for correcting it if deficiencies were found during an audit of the acquisitions system.

It is acceptable for auditors to recommend changes in operations, but operating personnel must have the authority to accept or reject the recommendations. If auditors had the authority to require implementation of their recommendations, the auditor would actually have the responsibility for auditing his or her own work the next time an audit was conducted. Independence would therefore be reduced.

The Institute of Internal Auditors considers independence of internal auditors critical. It has established in its *Statement of Responsibilities of Internal Auditing* a special requirement for independence, as follows:

- Internal auditors should be independent of the activities they audit. Internal auditors are independent when they can carry out their work freely and objectively. Independence permits internal auditors to render the impartial and unbiased judgments essential to the proper conduct of audits. It is achieved through organizational status and objectivity.

  Organizational status should be sufficient to assure a broad range of audit coverage, and adequate consideration of and effective action on audit findings and recommendations.

  Objectivity requires that internal auditors have an independent mental attitude, and an honest belief in their work product. Drafting procedures, and designing, installing, and operating systems are not audit functions. Performing such activities is presumed to impair audit objectivity.

Competence is, of course, necessary to determine the cause of operational problems and to make appropriate recommendations. Competence is a major problem when operational auditing deals with wide-ranging operating problems. For example, imagine the difficulties of finding qualified internal auditors who can evaluate both the effectiveness of an advertising program and the efficiency of a production assembly process. The internal audit staff doing that type of operational auditing would presumably have to include some personnel with backgrounds in marketing and others in production.

## Criteria for Evaluating Efficiency and Effectiveness

**OBJECTIVE 24-5**
**Plan and perform an operational audit.**

A major difficulty found in operational auditing is in deciding on specific criteria for evaluating whether efficiency and effectiveness have occurred. In auditing historical financial statements, GAAP are the broad criteria for evaluating fair presentation. Audit objectives are used to set more specific criteria in deciding whether GAAP have been followed. In operational auditing, no such well-defined criteria exist.

One approach to setting criteria for operational auditing is to state that the objectives are to determine whether some aspect of the entity could be made more effective or efficient and to recommend improvements. This approach may be adequate for experienced and well-trained auditors, but it would be difficult for most auditors to follow such a poorly defined approach.

**Specific Criteria** More specific criteria are usually desirable before operational auditing is started. For example, suppose that you are doing an operational audit of the equipment layout in plants for a company. The following are some specific criteria, stated in the form of questions, that might be used to evaluate plant layouts:

- Were all plant layouts approved by home office engineering at the time of original design?
- Has home office engineering done a reevaluation study of plant layout in the past five years?
- Is each piece of equipment operating at 60 percent of capacity or more for at least three months each year?
- Does layout facilitate the movement of new materials to the production floor?
- Does layout facilitate the production of finished goods?
- Does layout facilitate the movement of finished goods to distribution centers?
- Does the plant layout effectively use existing equipment?
- Is the safety of employees endangered by the plant layout?

**Sources of Criteria** There are several sources that the operational auditor can use in developing specific evaluation criteria. These include the following:

- *Historical performance.* A simple set of criteria can be based on actual results from prior periods (or audits). The idea behind using these criteria is to determine whether things have become "better" or "worse" in comparison. The advantage of these criteria is that they are easy to derive; however, they may not provide much insight into how well or poorly the audited entity is really doing.
- *Benchmarking.* Most entities subject to an operational audit are not unique; there are many similar entities within the overall organization or outside it. In those cases, the performance data of comparable entities are an excellent source for developing criteria for benchmarking. For internal comparable entities, the data are usually readily available. Where the comparable entities are outside the organization, they will often be willing to make such information available. It is also often available through industry groups and governmental regulatory agencies.
- *Engineered standards.* In many types of operational auditing engagements, it may be possible and appropriate to develop criteria based on engineered standards—for example, time and motion studies to determine production output rates. These criteria are often time consuming and costly to develop, as they require considerable expertise; however, they may be effective in solving a major operational problem and well worth the cost. It is also possible that some standards can be developed by industry groups for use by all their members, thereby spreading the cost and reducing it for each participant. These may be groups in the industry of the subject organization, or functional groups such as an EDP users' organization.
- *Discussion and agreement.* Sometimes objective criteria are difficult or costly to obtain, and criteria are developed through simple discussion and agreement. The parties involved in this process should include management of the entity to be audited, the operational auditor, and the entity or persons to whom the findings will be reported.

## Phases in Operational Auditing

There are three phases in an operational audit: planning, evidence accumulation and evaluation, and reporting and follow-up.

**Planning** The planning in an operational audit is similar to that discussed in earlier chapters for an audit of historical financial statements. Like audits of financial statements, the operational auditor must determine the scope of the engagement and communicate it to the organizational unit. It is also necessary to staff the engagement properly, obtain background information about the organizational unit, understand internal control, and decide on the appropriate evidence to accumulate.

The major difference between planning an operational audit and a financial audit is the extreme diversity in operational audits. Because of the diversity, it is often difficult to decide on specific objectives for an operational audit. The objectives will be based on the criteria developed for the engagement. As discussed in the preceding sections, these will depend on the specific circumstances at hand. For example, the objectives for an operational audit of the effectiveness of internal controls over petty cash would be dramatically different from those of an operational audit of the efficiency of a research and development department.

Another difference is that staffing is often more complicated in an operational audit than in a financial audit. This again is because of the breadth of the engagements. Not only are the areas diverse—for example, production control, advertising, and strategy planning—but the objectives within those areas often require special technical skills. For example, the auditor may need an engineering background to evaluate performance on a major construction project.

Finally, it is important to spend more time with the interested parties agreeing on the terms of the engagement and the criteria for evaluation in an operational audit than in a financial audit. This was alluded to in the preceding section for criteria developed through discussion. Regardless of the source of the criteria for evaluation, it is essential that the auditee, the auditor, and the sponsor of the engagement be in clear and complete agreement on the objectives and criteria involved. That agreement will facilitate effective and successful completion of the operational audit.

**Evidence Accumulation and Evaluation** The seven types of evidence studied in Chapter 6 and used throughout the book are equally applicable for operational auditing. Because internal controls and operating procedures are a critical part of operational auditing, it is common to extensively use documentation, client inquiry, and observation. Confirmation and reperformance are used less extensively for most operational audits than for financial audits because accuracy is not the purpose of most operational audits.

To illustrate evidence accumulation in operational auditing, we return to the example discussed earlier about evaluating the safety of elevators in a city. Assume there is agreement that the objective is to determine whether the inspection is made annually of each elevator in the city by a competent inspector. To satisfy the completeness objective, the auditor would, for example, examine blueprints of city buildings and elevator locations and trace them to the agency's list to ensure that all elevators are included in the population. Additional tests on newly constructed buildings would be appropriate to assess the timeliness with which the central listing is updated.

Assuming that the agency's list is determined to be complete, the auditor can select a sample of elevator locations and evidence can be collected as to the timing and frequency of inspections. The auditor may want to consider inherent risk by doing heavier sampling of older elevators or elevators with previous safety defects. The auditor may also want to examine evidence to determine whether the elevator inspectors were competent to evaluate elevator safety. The auditor may, for example, evaluate inspectors' qualifications by reviewing résumés, training programs, competency exams, and performance reports.

It is also likely that the auditor would want to reperform the inspection procedures for a sample of elevators to obtain evidence of inconsistencies in reported and actual conditions.

In the same manner as for financial audits, operational auditors must accumulate sufficient competent evidence to afford a reasonable basis for a conclusion about the objectives being tested. In the elevator example, the auditor must accumulate sufficient evidence about elevator safety inspections. After the evidence is accumulated, the auditor must decide whether it is reasonable to conclude that an inspection is made annually of each elevator in the city by a competent inspector.

**Reporting and Follow-up** Two major differences in operational and financial auditing reports affect operational auditing reports. First, in operational audits, the report is usually sent only to management, with a copy to the unit being audited. The lack of third-party users reduces the need for standardized wording in operational auditing reports. Second, the diversity of operational audits requires a tailoring of each report to address the scope of the audit, findings, and recommendations.

The combination of these two factors results in major differences in operational auditing reports. Report writing often takes a significant amount of time to clearly communicate audit findings and recommendations.

When reports are being rendered on performance audits in accordance with the Yellow Book, specific contents are required. The Yellow Book permits considerable freedom on the form of the report.

Follow-up is common in operational auditing when recommendations are made to management. The purpose is to determine whether the recommended changes were made, and if not, why.

## Examples of Operational Audit Findings

Each issue of the *Internal Auditor,* a bimonthly publication of the Institute of Internal Auditors, includes several internal operational audit findings submitted by practicing internal auditors. In reviewing a multitude of these reported findings, the authors concluded that almost all of them relate to efficiency rather than effectiveness. We believe the reason is that readers of the journal find efficiency findings more interesting reading than those related to effectiveness. If someone can state, for example, that an operational audit resulted in a savings of $68,000, it is likely to be more interesting than reporting on improved accuracy of financial reporting. The following examples from the *Internal Auditor* include two related to effectiveness and the rest to efficiency.

***Outside Janitorial Firm Saves $160,000***

- An internal auditor reviewed the efficiency and effectiveness of the janitorial services furnished by state employees for the buildings in the state capitol complex. The audit disclosed the costs of the janitorial services were excessive when compared to similar services performed by outside janitorial firms. In addition, the auditors found many janitorial tasks were not completed as required, resulting in unacceptable quality. A study of alternate janitorial services indicated equal or better service could be provided by an outside janitorial firm and at a saving of $137,000 a year. The auditor recommended the state seek competitive bids and contract with the janitorial firm submitting the lowest bid which meets the specifications. The resultant contract actually saved more than $160,000, and the quality of the cleaning improved noticeably.

***More Timely Credit Memo Processing***

- A frequent complaint heard by the internal auditor concerned the inordinate amount of time required to process customers' credit memos. The auditor found the complaint was justified because an average of 14 working days elapsed between the receipt of the request and the actual issuance of the memo. In some cases, as many as 21 working days elapsed before the memo was issued.

  Using a time-phased flowchart, the auditor determined the requests were not moving in an efficient linear flow. As a matter of fact, the time-phased flowchart looked like a zigzag with a bad case of hiccups. The requests moved from the originator for removal of the supporting documents. The request then went back again to one of the approving departments for sorting, coding, and batching. Finally, the request was transmitted to the computer to issue the memo. Each step required from one to five working days, depending on the workload and complexity of the request.

The auditor recommended each approving department perform all the required functions the first time it handled the request and substitute well-controlled procedures for after-the-fact approvals in place of the preapprovals. The recommendation was adopted, and credit memos are now being issued within five working days after the request is received. The auditor noted a higher degree of customers' satisfaction, and complaints have ceased.

***Legislative Auditors Detect $11 Million per Year Insurance Overcharge***

- Most states have insurance commissions to monitor and regulate the insurance industry, providing some assurance that insurance premiums are reasonable for the coverage received.

  Two legislative auditors, conducting a comparison with national loss ratios, found the state's property and liability policyholders, on average, had paid too much. In fact, the auditors determined policyholders within the state had overpaid approximately $55.1 million in premiums during the five years between 1974 and 1978 because:

  - Some of the insurance companies charged premium rates developed by regional rating bureaus that use regional—not state—loss statistics. The losses projected by this method were often higher than what actually occurred within the state.
  - In some lines of property and liability insurance, there was inadequate competition to force companies to adopt more competitive rates.
  - The rate increases requested by many insurance companies were not adequately analyzed. As a consequence, these rates were increased when the justification was questionable.

The auditors recommended the insurance commission regularly monitor the premium-to-loss ratios and implement a plan for each major line of property and liability insurance to get the state's loss ratios in line with the national average.

***Use the Right Tool***

- The company leased twenty-five heavy-duty trucks for use by service employees who installed and repaired about 20,000 vending machines in a large metropolitan area. All of the trucks were equipped with hydraulic lift-gates for loading and unloading vending machines.
- The internal auditor found that only a few of the trucks were actually delivering and picking up vending machines. The majority of the trucks were used for service calls which consisted of on-the-scene repair of coin boxes or other simple adjustments not requiring the hydraulic lift-gates.
- The auditor recommended most of the heavy-duty trucks be phased out and replaced by conventional light vans. Management agreed and the savings in lease rates and operating expenses were estimated at $25,000 a year.

***Computer Programs Save Manual Labor***

- ERISA requires an annual audit of profit-sharing plans. These internal auditors not only tested the finances, they also performed an operational review which provided a number of valuable recommendations to management.

  The EDP auditors devised a number of computer-assisted audit programs to test control over enrollment in and termination from the company's profit-sharing plan. The computer assistance saved much manual labor and detected a number of findings such as employees on the plan with less than the required one year of service and terminated employees still on the plan. The computer portion of the audit program also detected conflicting data between the payroll and profit-sharing plan master files.

When shown the results of the audit, management corrected all the problems and instituted additional controls to prevent the problems in the future. And the additional controls were . . . well, guess. Yep, they wanted the EDP auditors to leave their computer programs in the machine. The profit-sharing plan manager uses the programs periodically as a control to detect enrollment errors.

*Timely Depositing*

- During a cash review, the internal auditor found that bank deposits were not made until several days after the cash and checks were received. The cause was a complicated reconciliation/distribution process requiring three to fifteen days to complete.

  Management agreed to implement a direct-deposit or electronic-funds-transfer system and to perform the reconciliation/distribution process after the funds were deposited. The system's estimated additional interest is about $120,000 a year.[2]

## ESSENTIAL TERMS

**Compliance audit**—(1) a review of an organization's financial records performed to determine whether the organization is following specific procedures or rules set down by some higher authority; (2) an audit performed to determine whether an entity that receives financial assistance from the federal government has complied with specific laws and regulations

**Economy and efficiency audit**—a government audit to determine whether an entity is acquiring, protecting, and using its resources economically and efficiently, the causes of any inefficiencies or uneconomical practices, and whether the entity has complied with laws and regulations concerning matters of economy and efficiency

**Effectiveness**—the degree to which the organization's objectives are accomplished

**Efficiency**—the degree to which costs are reduced without reducing effectiveness

**Functional audit**—an operational audit that deals with one or more specific functions within an organization, such as the payroll function or the production engineering function

**Governmental Auditing Standards (GAS)**—see Yellow Book

**Government audit**—a financial or an operational audit of a government agency or a state-run institution

**Institute of Internal Auditors (IIA)**—organization for internal auditors that establishes ethical and practice standards, provides education and encourages professionalism for its members

**Operational auditing**—the review of an organization for efficiency and effectiveness. The terms *management auditing, performance auditing,* and *operational auditing* are often synonymous terms

**Organizational audit**—an operational audit that deals with an entire organizational unit, such as a department, branch, or subsidiary, to determine how efficiently and effectively functions interact

**Program audit**—a government audit to determine the extent to which the desired results or benefits established by the legislature or other authorizing body are being achieved, the effectiveness of organizations, programs, activities, or functions, and whether the entity has complied with laws and regulations applicable to the program

**Single Audit Act**—Federal legislation that provides for a single coordinated audit to satisfy the audit requirements of all federal funding agencies

**Special assignment**—a management request for an operational audit for a specific purpose, such as investigating the possibility of fraud in a division or making recommendations for reducing the cost of a manufactured product

**Standards for the Practice of Internal Auditing**—guidelines issued by the Institute of Internal Auditors, covering the activities and conduct of internal auditors

**Yellow Book**—a publication of the GAO that is widely used as a reference by government auditors and CPAs who do governmental audit work. The official title is *Governmental Auditing Standards.*

[2]Ibid.

## REVIEW QUESTIONS

**24-1 (Objective 24-1)** Explain the role of internal auditors for financial auditing. How is it similar to and different from the role of external auditors?

**24-2 (Objective 24-1)** What are the five parts of the scope of the internal auditor's work, according to the Institute of Internal Auditors' publication *Standards for the Practice of Internal Auditing?*

**24-3 (Objective 24-1)** Explain the difference in the independence of internal auditors and external auditors in the audit of historical financial statements. How can internal auditors best achieve independence?

**24-4 (Objective 24-2)** Explain how governmental financial auditing is similar to and different from audits of commercial companies. Who does governmental auditing?

**24-5 (Objective 24-2)** Explain what is meant by the Single Audit Act. What is its purpose?

**24-6 (Objective 24-2)** In what ways is the Yellow Book consistent with generally accepted auditing standards, and what are some additions and modifications?

**24-7 (Objective 24-2)** Identify the primary specific objectives that must be incorporated into the design of audit tests under the Single Audit Act.

**24-8 (Objective 24-2)** Identify the key required reports of the Single Audit Act.

**24-9 (Objective 24-3)** Describe what is meant by an operational audit.

**24-10 (Objective 24-3)** Identify the three major differences between financial and operational auditing.

**24-11 (Objective 24-4)** Distinguish between efficiency and effectiveness in operational audits. State one example of an operational audit explaining efficiency and another explaining effectiveness.

**24-12 (Objective 24-4)** Distinguish among the following types of operational audits: functional, organizational, and special assignment. State an example of each for a not-for-profit hospital.

**24-13 (Objective 24-4)** Explain why many people think of internal auditors as the primary group responsible for conducting operational audits.

**24-14 (Objective 24-4)** Explain the role of government auditors in operational auditing. How is this similar to and different from the role of internal auditors?

**24-15 (Objective 24-4)** Under what circumstances are external auditors likely to be involved in operational auditing? Give one example of operational auditing by a CPA firm.

**24-16 (Objective 24-5)** Explain what is meant by the criteria for evaluating efficiency and effectiveness. Provide five possible specific criteria for evaluating effectiveness of an EDP system for payroll.

**24-17 (Objective 24-5)** Identify the three phases of an operational audit.

**24-18 (Objective 24-5)** Explain how planning for operational auditing is similar to and different from financial auditing.

**24-19 (Objective 24-5)** What are the major differences between reporting for operational and financial auditing?

## MULTIPLE CHOICE QUESTIONS FROM CPA, IIA, AND CMA EXAMINATIONS

**24-20 (Objectives 24-1, 24-4)** The following questions deal with independence of auditors. Choose the best response.

a. The operational auditor's independence is most likely to be compromised when the internal audit department is responsible directly to the

(1) Vice president of finance.
(2) President.
(3) Controller.
(4) Executive vice president.
(5) Audit committee of the board of directors.

b. The independence of the internal audit department will most likely be assured if it reports to the
(1) President.
(2) Controller.
(3) Treasurer.
(4) Audit committee of the board of directors.
(5) Vice president of finance.

c. Which of the following may compromise the independence of an internal auditor?
(1) Reviewing EDP systems prior to implementation.
(2) Performing an audit where the auditor recently had operating responsibilities.
(3) Failing to review the audit report with the auditee prior to distribution.
(4) Following up on corrective action in response to audit findings.

d. Which of the following would contribute least to the independence of the internal auditing department?
(1) Having the director of internal auditing report directly to the chief operating officer of the organization.
(2) Requiring the internal auditing staff to possess collectively the knowledge and skills essential to the practice of professional internal auditing within the organization.
(3) Authorizing the director to meet directly and as needed with the audit committee of the board without the presence of management.
(4) Having both management and the board of directors review and approve a formal written charter for the internal auditing department.
(5) Requiring the director of internal auditing to submit to both management and the board periodic activity reports which highlight significant findings and recommendations as well as any significant deviations from approved audit schedules.

e. Internal auditors should be objective in performing audits. Which of the following situations violates standards concerning objectivity?
(1) The auditor who reviews accounts receivable worked in that department for three months as a trainee two years ago.
(2) The auditor reviews a department that continues to use procedures recommended by that auditor when the department was established.
(3) The auditor reviews the same department for two years in succession.
(4) The auditor reviews a department in which the auditor has the responsibility for cosigning checks.

**24-21 (Objectives 24-3, 24-4, 24-5)** The following questions deal with operational auditing. Choose the best response.

a. Which of the following best describes the operational audit?
(1) It requires constant review by internal auditors of the administrative controls as they relate to the operations of the company.
(2) It concentrates on implementing financial and accounting controls in a newly organized company.
(3) It attempts and is designed to verify the fair presentation of a company's results of operations.
(4) It concentrates on seeking out aspects of operations in which waste would be reduced by the introduction of controls.

b. The evaluation of audit field work of an operating unit should answer the following questions:
   **1.** What are the reasons for the results?
   **2.** How can performance be improved?
   **3.** What results are being achieved?
   What is the chronological order in which these questions should be answered?
   (1) 3—1—2. (4) 1—2—3.
   (2) 1—3—2. (5) 2—3—1.
   (3) 3—2—1.

c. The auditor is performing an operational audit of data processing's budgeting procedures. Which of the following procedures is least likely to be performed?
   (1) Review the extent to which the budget identifies controllable expenditures.
   (2) Review the total monetary budget and compare it with that of prior periods.
   (3) Compare billing rates charged to users with those approved for the specified level of service.
   (4) Reconcile depreciation on computer equipment to the property ledger.

d. Complaints from the public were received about processing automobile license applications in the state department of motor vehicles. You were assigned by the legislative auditor to review this operation. Which of the following should be your first audit step?
   (1) Send out questionnaires to recent licensees.
   (2) Test the system by licensing a vehicle.
   (3) Discuss the nature of the complaints with the chief of the licensing office.
   (4) Discuss the nature of the complaints with several licensing clerks.
   (5) Discuss the nature of the complaints with the director of the state department of motor vehicles.

e. The first step an operational auditor should take in performing a management study to help the director of marketing determine the optimum allocation of the advertising budget to company products is to
   (1) Analyze prior years' advertising costs.
   (2) Hold discussions with media personnel.
   (3) Establish and discuss with the director the key objectives of the study.
   (4) Determine the amount of projected sales for the purpose of establishing the proposed sales budget.
   (5) Do both (1) and (2).

f. A preliminary survey of the human resources in a data processing function includes a review of personnel records and practices. When the audit objective is to ascertain the economy of operation of the data processing function, the internal auditor would seek evidence with respect to
   (1) Procedures for rotation of job assignments.
   (2) Backup procedures relative to absenteeism, disability, and retirement.
   (3) Adequacy of the company's information dissemination procedures regarding personnel policies.
   (4) Assignment of personnel to tasks for which their education and training are appropriate.
   (5) Training programs that are in conformity with company policies and procedures.

**24-22 (Objectives 24-1, 24-4, 24-5)** The following questions deal with internal auditing departments and their responsibilities. Choose the best response.

a. Which of the following is generally considered to be a major reason for establishing an internal auditing function?
   (1) To relieve overburdened management of the responsibility for establishing effective systems of internal control.

(2) To ensure that operating activities comply with the policies, plans, and procedures established by management.
(3) To safeguard resources entrusted to the organization.
(4) To ensure the accuracy, reliability, and timeliness of financial and operating data used in management's decision making.
(5) To assist members of the organization in the measurement and evaluation of the effectiveness of established systems of internal control.

b. Which of the following is generally considered to be the primary purpose of an internal auditor's evaluation of the adequacy of internal control?
(1) To determine if the established internal controls are functioning as intended by management.
(2) To determine the extent of reliance the internal auditor can place on the established internal controls in the process of evaluating the financial statements prepared by the organization.
(3) To determine if all risks and exposures of the enterprise have been reduced or eliminated by the established internal controls.
(4) To determine if the established internal controls provide reasonable assurance that the objectives and goals of the organization will be met in an efficient and economical manner.

c. With regard to corrective action on audit results, which of the following is not the internal auditor's responsibility?
(1) Soliciting auditees' suggestions for corrective actions
(2) Recommending possible alternative corrective actions
(3) Directing the corrective actions
(4) Determining that the corrective actions are responsive to the audit results
(5) Evaluating new policy statements to determine whether they address the unsatisfactory conditions disclosed in the audit results

## CASES

**24-23 (Objectives 24-3, 24-4, 24-5)** Saint Gabriel Hospital, which is affiliated with a leading midwestern university, has an extremely reputable research department that employs several renowned scientists. The research department operates on a project basis. The department consists of a pool of scientists and technicians who can be called upon to participate in a given project. Assignments are made for the duration of the project, and a project manager is given responsibility for the work.

All major projects undertaken by the research department must be approved by the hospital's administrative board. Approval is obtained by submitting a proposal to the board outlining the project, the expected amount of time required to complete the work, and the anticipated benefits. The board also must be informed of major projects that are terminated because of potential failure or technological changes that have occurred since the time of project approval. An overall review of the status of open projects is submitted to the board annually.

In many respects, profit-making techniques used by business firms are applied to the management of the research department. For example, the department performs preliminary research work on potential major projects it has selected prior to requesting the board to approve the project and commit large amounts of time and money. The department also assesses the potential for grants and future revenues of the project. Financial reports for the department and each project are prepared periodically and reviewed with the administrative board.

Over 75 percent of the cost of operating the department is for labor. The remaining costs are for materials used during research. Materials used for experimentation are purchased by the hospital's central purchasing department. Once delivered, the research department is held accountable for storage, usage, and assignment of cost to the projects.

In order to protect the hospital's rights to discoveries made by the research department, staff members are required to sign waiver agreements at the time of hire, and at certain intervals thereafter. The agreements relinquish the employees' rights to patent and royalty fees for hospital work.

Saint Gabriel's excellent reputation is due in part to the success of the research department. The research department has produced high-quality research in the health care field and has always been able to generate revenues in excess of its costs. Saint Gabriel's administrative board believes that the hospital's continued reputation depends upon a strong research department, and therefore, the board has requested that the university's internal auditors perform an operational audit of the department. As a part of its request for the operational audit, the board presented the following set of objectives which the internal audit is to accomplish.

The operational audit to be conducted by the university's internal audit department should provide assurances that:

- the research department has assessed the revenues and cost aspects of each project to confirm that the revenue potential is equal to or greater than estimated costs.
- appropriate controls exist to provide a means to measure how projects are progressing and to identify if corrective actions are required.
- financial reports prepared by the research department for presentation to the administrative board properly reflect all revenues (both endowment and royalty sources and appropriated funding) and all costs.

### Required

a. Evaluate the objectives presented by the administrative board to the university's internal audit department in terms of their appropriateness as objectives for an operational audit. Discuss fully:
   (1) the strengths of the objectives
   (2) the modifications and/or additions needed to improve the set of objectives.

b. Outline, in general terms, the procedures that would be suitable for performing the audit of the research department.

c. Identify three documents that members of the university's internal auditing staff would be expected to review during the audit and describe the purpose that the review of each document serves in carrying out the audit.*

**24-24 (Objectives 24-1, 24-4)** Lajod Company has an internal audit department consisting of a manager and three staff auditors. The manager of internal audits, in turn, reports to the corporate controller. Copies of audit reports are routinely sent to the audit committee of the board of directors as well as the corporate controller and the individual responsible for the area or activity being audited.

The manager of internal audits is aware that the external auditors have relied on the internal audit function to a substantial degree in the past. However, in recent months, the external auditors have suggested there may be a problem related to the objectivity of the internal audit function. This objectivity problem may result in more extensive testing and analysis by the external auditors.

The external auditors are concerned about the amount of nonaudit work performed by the internal audit department. The percentage of nonaudit work performed by the internal auditors in recent years has increased to about 25 percent of their total hours worked. A sample of five recent nonaudit activities are as follows.

1. One of the internal auditors assisted in the preparation of policy statements on internal control. These statements included such things as policies regarding sensitive payments and standards of control for internal controls.

*CMA adapted.

2. The bank statements of the corporation are reconciled each month as a regular assignment for one of the internal auditors. The corporate controller believes this strengthens internal controls because the internal auditor is not involved in the receipt and disbursement of cash.
3. The internal auditors are asked to review the budget data in every area each year for relevance and reasonableness before the budget is approved. In addition, an internal auditor examines the variances each month, along with the associated explanations. These variance analyses are prepared by the corporate controller's staff after consultation with the individuals involved.
4. One of the internal auditors has recently been involved in the design, installation, and initial operation of a new computer system. The auditor was primarily concerned with the design and implementation of internal accounting controls and the computer application controls for the new system. The auditor also conducted the testing of the controls during the test runs.
5. The internal auditors are frequently asked to make accounting entries for complex transactions before the transactions are recorded. The employees in the accounting department are not adequately trained to handle such transactions. In addition, this serves as a means of maintaining internal control over complex transactions. The manager of internal audits has always made an effort to remain independent of the corporate controller's office and believes that the internal auditors are objective and independent in their audit and nonaudit activities.

### Required

a. Define *objectivity* as it relates to the internal audit function.

b. For each of the five situations outlined, explain whether the objectivity of Lajod Company's internal audit department has been materially impaired. Consider each situation independently.

c. The manager of audits reports to the corporate controller.
   (1) Does this reporting relationship result in a problem of objectivity? Explain your answer.
   (2) Would your answer to any of the five situations in requirement b above have changed if the manager of internal audits reported to the audit committee of the board of directors? Explain your answer.*

**24-25 (Objectives 24-1, 24-4, 24-5)** Lado Corporation has an internal audit department operating out of the corporate headquarters. Various types of audit assignments are performed by the department for the eight divisions of the company.

The following findings resulted from recent audits of Lado Corporation's White Division.

1. One of the departments in the division appeared to have an excessive turnover rate. Upon investigation, the personnel department seemed to be unable to find enough workers with the specified skills for this department. Some workers are trained on the job. The departmental supervisor is held accountable for labor efficiency variances but does not have qualified staff or sufficient time to train the workers properly. The supervisor holds individual workers responsible for meeting predetermined standards from the day they report to work. This has resulted in a rapid turnover of workers who are trainable but not yet able to meet standards.
2. The internal audit department recently participated in a computer feasibility study for this division. It advised and concurred on the purchase and installation of a specific computer system. While the system is up and operating, the results are less than desirable. Although the software and hardware meet the specifications of the feasibility study, there are several functions unique to this division that the system has been

*CMA adapted.

unable to accomplish. Linking of files has been a problem. For example, several vendors have been paid for materials not meeting company specifications. A revision of the existing software is probably not possible, and a permanent solution probably requires replacing the existing computer system with a new one.

3. One of the products manufactured by this division was recently redesigned to eliminate a potential safety defect. This defect was discovered after several users were injured. At present, there are no pending lawsuits because none of the injured parties have identified a defect in the product as a cause of their injury. There is insufficient information to determine whether the defect was a contributing factor.

The director of internal auditing and assistant controller is in charge of the internal audit department and reports to the controller in corporate headquarters. Copies of internal audit reports are sent routinely to Lado's board of directors.

## Required

a. Explain the additional steps in terms of field work, preparation of recommendations, and operating management review that ordinarily should be taken by Lado Corporation's internal auditors as a consequence of the audit findings in the first situation (excessive turnover).

b. Discuss whether there are any objectivity problems with Lado Corporation's internal audit department as revealed by the audit findings. Include in your discussion any recommendations to eliminate or reduce an objectivity problem, if one exists.

c. The internal audit department is part of the corporate controllership function, and copies of the internal audit reports are sent to the board of directors.
   (1) Evaluate the appropriateness of the location of the internal audit department within Lado's organizational structure.
   (2) Discuss who within Lado should receive the reports of the internal audit department.*

**24-26 (Objectives 24-4, 24-5)** Haskin Company was founded 40 years ago and now has several manufacturing plants in the Northeast and Midwest. The evaluation of proposed capital expenditures became increasingly difficult for management as the company became geographically dispersed and diversified its product line. Thus, the Capital Budgeting Group was organized in 1995 to review all capital expenditure proposals in excess of $50,000.

The Capital Budgeting Group conducts its annual planning and budget meeting each September for the upcoming calendar year. The group establishes a minimum return for investments (hurdle rate) and estimates a target level of capital expenditures for the next year based upon the expected available funds. The group then reviews the capital expenditure proposals that have been submitted by the various operating segments. Proposals that meet either the return on investment criterion or a critical need criterion are approved to the extent of available funds.

The Capital Budgeting Group also meets monthly, as necessary, to consider any projects of a critical nature that were not expected or requested in the annual budget review. These monthly meetings allow the Capital Budgeting Group to make adjustments during the year as new developments occur.

Haskin's profits have been decreasing slightly for the past two years in spite of a small but steady sales growth, a sales growth that is expected to continue through 1997. As a result of the profit stagnation, top management is emphasizing cost control, and all aspects of Haskin's operations are being reviewed for cost reduction opportunities.

Haskin's internal audit department has become involved in the company-wide cost reduction effort. The department has already identified several areas where cost reductions could be realized and has made recommendations to implement the necessary procedures

*CMA adapted.

to effect the cost savings. Tom Watson, internal audit director, is now focusing on the activities of the Capital Budgeting Group in an attempt to determine the efficiency and effectiveness of the capital budgeting process.

In an attempt to gain a better understanding of the capital budgeting process, Watson decided to examine the history of one capital project in detail. A capital expenditure proposal of Haskin's Burlington Plant that was approved by the Capital Budgeting Group in 1997 was selected randomly from a population of all proposals approved by the group at its 1996 and 1997 annual planning and budget meetings.

The Burlington proposal consisted of a request for five new machines to replace equipment that was 20 years old and for which preventive maintenance had become expensive. Four of the machines were for replacement purposes and the fifth was for planned growth in demand. Each of the four replacement machines was expected to result in annual maintenance cost savings of $10,000. The fifth machine was exactly like the other four and was expected to generate an annual contribution of $15,000 through increased output. Each machine had a cost of $50,000 and an estimated useful life of eight years.

## Required

a. Identify and discuss the issues that Haskin Company's internal audit department must address in its examination and evaluation of Burlington Plant's 1997 capital expenditure project.

b. Recommend procedures to be used by Haskin's internal audit department in the audit review of Burlington Plant's 1997 capital expenditure project.*

**24-27 (Objectives 24-4, 24-5)** Lecimore Company has a centralized purchasing department which is managed by Joan Jones. Jones has established policies and procedures to guide the clerical staff and purchasing agents in the day-to-day operation of the department. She is satisfied that these policies and procedures are in conformity with company objectives and believes there are no major problems in the regular operations of the purchasing department.

Lecimore's internal audit department was assigned to perform an operational audit of the purchasing function. Their first task was to review the specific policies and procedures established by Jones. The policies and procedures are as follows:

- All significant purchases are made on a competitive bid basis. The probability of timely delivery, reliability of vendor, and so forth, are taken into consideration on a subjective basis.
- Detailed specifications of the minimum acceptable quality for all goods purchased are provided to vendors.
- Vendors' adherence to the quality specifications is the responsibility of the materials manager of the inventory control department and not the purchasing department. The materials manager inspects the goods as they arrive to be sure that the quality meets the minimum standards and then sees that the goods are transferred from the receiving dock to the storeroom.
- All purchase requests are prepared by the materials manager based upon the production schedule for a four-month period.

The internal audit staff then observed the operations of the purchasing function and gathered the following findings:

- One vendor provides 90 percent of a critical raw material. This vendor has a good delivery record and is reliable. Furthermore, this vendor has been the low bidder over the past few years.
- As production plans change, rush and expedite orders are made by production directly to the purchasing department. Materials ordered for cancelled production runs

*CMA adapted.

are stored for future use. The costs of these special requests are borne by the purchasing department. Jones considers the additional costs associated with these special requests as "costs of being a good member of the corporate team."

- Materials to accomplish engineering changes are ordered by the purchasing department as soon as the changes are made by the engineering department. Jones is proud of the quick response by the purchasing staff to product changes. Materials on hand are not reviewed before any orders are placed.
- Partial shipments and advance shipments (that is, those received before the requested date of delivery) are accepted by the materials manager, who notifies the purchasing department of the receipt. The purchasing department is responsible for follow-up on partial shipments. No action is taken to discourage advance shipments.

### Required

Based upon the purchasing department's policies and procedures and the findings of Lecimore's internal audit staff,

1. Identify weaknesses and/or inefficiencies in Lecimore Company's purchasing function.
2. Make recommendations for those weaknesses/inefficiencies that you identify.*

Use the following format in preparing your response.

| Weaknesses/Inefficiencies | Recommendations |
|---|---|
| 1. | 1. |

**24-28 (Objectives 24-4, 24-5)** Superior Co. manufactures automobile parts for sale to the major U.S. automakers. Superior's internal audit staff is to review the internal controls over machinery and equipment and make recommendations for improvements where appropriate.

The internal auditors obtained the following information during the assignment:

- Requests for purchase of machinery and equipment are normally initiated by the supervisor in need of the asset. The supervisor discusses the proposed acquisition with the plant manager. A purchase requisition is submitted to the purchasing department when the plant manager is satisfied that the request is reasonable and that there is a remaining balance in the plant's share of the total corporate budget for capital acquisitions.
- Upon receiving a purchase requisition for machinery or equipment, the purchasing department manager looks through the records for an appropriate supplier. A formal purchase order is then completed and mailed. When the machine or equipment is received, it is immediately sent to the user department for installation. This allows the economic benefits from the acquisition to be realized at the earliest possible date.
- The property, plant, and equipment ledger control accounts are supported by lapse schedules organized by year of acquisition. These lapse schedules are used to compute depreciation as a unit for all assets of a given type which are acquired in the same year. Standard rates, depreciation methods, and salvage values are used for each major type of fixed asset. These rates, methods, and salvage values were set ten years ago during the company's initial year of operation.
- When machinery or equipment is retired, the plant manager notifies the accounting department so that the appropriate entries can be made in the accounting records.
- There has been no reconciliation since the company began operations between the accounting records and the machinery and equipment on hand.

*CMA adapted.

## Required

Identify the internal control weaknesses and recommend improvements that the internal audit staff of Superior Co. should include in its report regarding the internal controls employed for fixed assets. Use the following format in preparing your answer.*

| Weaknesses | Recommendations |
|---|---|
| 1. | 1. |

*CMA adapted.

# INDEX

Note: Essential Terms appear in boldface.


**Absence of causal connection,** 113
**Acceptable risk of incorrect acceptance (ARIA),** 486-88, 507, 509
**Acceptable risk of incorrect rejection (ARIR),** 508, 509
**Acceptable risk of assessing control risk too low (ARACR),** 413, 415-16
guidelines for establishing, 415-16
Access, unauthorized, 533
**Accounting**
**defined,** 4
distinction between auditing and, 4
Accounting Principles Board (APB), 25, 51, 686
opinion, 685
Accounting and Review Services Committee, 753
Accounting services, 13
Accounts payable
analytical procedures, 590-92
audit of, 590-97
balance-related audit objectives for, 591-92
confirmation, 594
cutoff tests, 594-95
internal controls in, 590
**master file,** 583
relationship of cutoff to inventory, 594-95
**trial balance,** 583
Accounts receivable
are accurate, 453
AICPA requirements, 456-57
audit of, 450-62
charging off uncollectible, 368
exist, 453
**lapping of,** 380
master file and general ledger, 452-53
Accounts receivable confirmation as evidence, 456-62
Accounts receivable master file, 367, 452-53
Accounts receivable trial balance, 367
Accrued liabilities
*see* Liabilities
Accumulated depreciation, verification of, 619-20
Accuracy, 154, 155
of accounts receivable, 453
of acquisitions, 588
of inventory, 648, 654
**Acquisition and payment cycle,** 579-610
accounts in, 580-81, 612
analytical procedures, 590-92
attributes sampling for tests of controls and substantive tests of transactions, 588-90
flow of accounting information in, 580-81
functions and internal controls in, 580-84
integrated tests of, 657
nature of the cycle, 580-84
tests of controls and substantive tests of transactions, 584-90
verification of selected accounts in, 611-40
Acquisitions
journal, 583
tests of, 586-88
verification of current year, 614-15
verifying, 586-88
Acts discreditable, 89-90
Additions, *see* Acquisitions
Adjusting entries in working papers, 233
**Adverse opinions** (report), 45
Advertising, 90-91
effect on profession, 91
**Aged trial balance,** 452
**Agreed-upon procedures engagement,** 772-74
AICPA, *see* American Institute of Certified Public Accountants
**Allocation**
of materiality, 252
**tests of,** 629-31
**Alternative procedures,** 460-61

**American Institute of Certified Public Accountants (AICPA),** 15-16
Auditing Standards Board, 16, 753
Code of Professional Conduct, *see Code of Professional Conduct*
CPA examination, 16
functions, 15-16
Generally Accepted Auditing Standards, 17-18
peer review in, 23-24
Private Companies Practice Section, 21-24
Professional Ethics Division, 93
Professional Oversight Board, 23
publications of, 16
rules of conduct and their application to members, 75-77
SEC Practice Section, 21-24
**Analysis,** 233
of exceptions, 418-19, 430, 433
of differences in accounts receivable confirmation, 461
**working papers,** 233
**Analytical procedures,** 159, 190-91, 333
as audit evidence, 187, 190-93
of cash balances, 701
computer software, 198
**defined,** 187, 190
final, 731-32
going concern, 191
of inventory and warehousing cycle, 649
of manufacturing equipment, 614
misstatements in financial statements, 191
for notes payable, 677
of operations audit, 628
of payroll and personnel cycle, 565
preliminary, 227
of prepaid insurance, 621
purposes of, 191-92
reduction of detailed audit tests, 191
relative cost of, 340-41
in sales and collection cycle, 449-50
statistical techniques, 196-97
timing, 192-93
types, 193-96
understanding client's industry and business, 191
APB, *see* Accounting Principles Board
**Application controls,** 533-34, 535
Application design, GAS, 541
ARACR, *see* Acceptable risk of assessing control risk too low
ARIA, *see* Acceptable risk of incorrect acceptance
ARIR, *see* Acceptable risk of incorrect rejection
ASB, *see* Auditing Standards Board
**Assertions,** 765
Assertions by management, 152-53
*see* Management assertions
Assets
manufacturing equipment audit and, 618-19
physical control over, 299
Assurance
engagements, 759
negative, 53-54
**Attestation,** 13
**engagements,** 764-67
level of service, 766-67
standards, 764-65
types of, engagements, 766
**Attribute,** 411
Attributes and exception conditions, 414
Attributes of interest, 428
**Attributes sampling,** 420
**defined,** 420
determination of sample size using, 422-24
evaluating results using, 424-26
professional judgment, 426
for tests of controls and substantive tests of transactions—acquisition and payment cycle, 588-90
use in auditing, 420-26
**Audit**
of capital stock and paid-in capital, 684-85
clients without, 752-53
completing the, 723-50
**compliance,** 5-6
of cost accounting, 646-49
by CPA firm, 13
dividends, 685
division of into cycles, 148-50
**failure,** 108
**of financial statements,** 4
of internal control, 769-71
**operational,** 4-5, 791-801
planning, 218-19, 227-28
planning and documentation, 217-46
types of, 4-6
**Audit assurance,** 259
*see also* Acceptable audit risk
**Audit committee,** 84, 739-40
**Auditing**
with computer, 537-40
**defined,** 2
distinction between accounting and, 4
economic demand for, 7-10
internal and governmental financial and operational, 785-811
internal financial, 786-88
nature of, 2
profession, 1-33
**Auditing around the computer,** 536-37
Auditing standards, 16, 17-20
*see also* Statements on Auditing Standards (SASs)
Auditing Standards Board (ASB), 16, 753
**Auditor**
communications between predecessor and successor, 220
defenses against client suits, 112
defenses against third-party suits, 115
**general accounting office,** 6
**independent,** 6
responsibility, 142-48
types of, 6-7
*see also* CPA
Audit plan, *see also* Audit program
**Audit procedures,** 179
appropriate as audit decision, 179
audit sampling, 417-18, 488-89, 510
for contingent liabilities, 725
in sales and collection cycle, 376-77
for subsequent events, 730-31
for testing contingencies, 725
terms, 189-90
timing of, as audit decision, 179-80
**Audit process,** 157-60, 346-50
phase I, plan and design approach, 158, 346-47
phase II, perform tests of controls and substantive tests of transactions, 159, 347
phase III, perform analytical procedures and tests of details of balances, 159-60, 349
phase IV, complete audit, issue a report, 160, 349-50
**Audit program,** 329-62
analytical procedures, 340-41
**defined,** 180
**design format,** 376-77, 386-88
design of, 339-46
illustrative, 344-46
**performance format,** 376-77, 389
tests of controls and substantive tests of transactions, 339-40
tests of details of balances, 341-43
**working papers** and, 229-36
**Audit reports,** 35-66
adverse opinion, 45
agreement with a departure, 42
auditor's decision process, 54-55
categories of, 39-40
conditions requiring a departure, 44, 48-52
disclaimer of opinion, 40, 45, 52
emphasis of a matter, 42
explanatory paragraph, 41-42
involving other auditors, 42-44
issuing, as CPA, 160
material uncertainties, 44
more than one condition requiring a departure or modification, 53
number of paragraphs, 53
other than unqualified, 45
parts of, 37-39
qualified, 45, 49, 50, 51
restricted scope, 49
**standard unqualified,** 37-39
subsequent discovery of facts existing at date of, 740-41
unqualified with explanatory paragraph or modified wording, 40-44
when departure required, 44
*see also* Reports

Audit responsibilities and objectives, 137-76
**Audit risk,** 108, 257
  **acceptable,** 218, 259
  changing acceptable risk to business risk, 259-61
  assessing, 261
  limitations, 266-67
  **model,** 257, 270-71
  for segments, 265-66
Audit sampling
  comparisons of, 484-85
  for tests of controls and substantive tests of transactions, 403-43
  for tests of details of balances, 483-525
*Audit Sampling Guide,* AICPA, 422
**Audit tests,** 330-35
  relative costs, 335-36
  *see also* Analytical procedures; Substantive tests of transactions; Tests of controls; Tests of details
Audit trail, *see* Transaction trail
Authoritative literature, 18-20
Authorization
  EDP systems, 531-32
  **general,** 298
  proper procedures for, as component of internal control, 298
  in sales, 371
  of uncollectible accounts, 380
  **specific,** 298

Background information, 223-25
Bad debts
  expense, 456
  providing for, 369
**Balance-related audit objectives,** 154-57
  for accounts payable, 591-92
  **for accounts receivable,** 447-49
  accuracy, 155
  classification, 156
  completeness, 155
  cutoff, 156
  detail tie-in, 156
  existence, 155
  **general,** 155
  for general cash in bank, 703
  for inventory observation, 653-54
  for manufacturing equipment, 615
  for notes payable, 677-78, 680
  meeting, 157-60
  for prepaid expenses, 621
  presentation and disclosure, 156
  for pricing and compilation of inventory, 655-56
  realizable value, 156
  relationship to management assertions, 157
  relationship of transaction-related objectives to, 346, 448-49
  rights and obligations, 156
  segmenting, 148-50
  setting, 151-52
  **specific,** 156-57
  tests of details to satisfy, 341-43
**Bank confirmation, standard,** 702-05
**Bank reconciliation,** 701-02, 705, 706-07
Bar Chris Construction Corp., 116-17
Bases for evaluating materiality, 250
Biases and motives of provider, 8
Big Six firms, 11-12
Billing customers, 367
Bill of lading, 366
Binomial distribution, 421
*Bily* v. *Arthur Young,* 115
Block sampling, 407
Bonuses, accrued, 567
Bookkeeping services, 13
**Branch bank account,** 696
Breach of contract, 110
**Budgets,** 196
**Business failure,** 108, 259
Business risk for customer, 7

**Capital acquisition and repayment cycle,** audit, 673-94
  accounts in, 674
**Capital stock certificate book,** 683
Capital stock and paid-in capital, audit of, 684-85
**Cash**
  balance in bank, audit of, 697-99
  **proof of,** 707-08
  *see also* Petty cash
**Cash accounts**
  audit of, 695-722
  **general,** 696
  types of, 696-97
Cash basis
  of accounting, 759
  modified, 759
Cash disbursements
  journal, 584
  procedures for verifying, 588
  processing and recording, 584
  subsequent, 593-94
**Cash equivalents,** 697
Cash receipts
  internal controls for, 378-80
  prelisting of, 368
  processing and recording, 367-68
  proper cutoff of, 454-55
  subsequent, 460
  testing for fraud, 378-80
  tests of controls and substantive tests transactions for, 378-80
Cash receipts journal, 368
*Cenco Incorporated* v. *Seidman & Seidman,* 112
**Certified Public Accountant** (CPA)
  **definition,** 10
  functions of, 10-11
  requirements, 10-11
  use of the title, 6
  ways encouraged to perform effectively, 17
  *see also* Auditor, CPA firms
**Chart of accounts,** 299
Check, 584
  payroll, 560
Classification
  of accounts receivable, 453
  of acquisitions, 588
Clients
  acceptance and continuance, 220
  correspondence with and accounts receivable, 460-61
  legal obligations, 225-27
  reasons for audit, 221
  scope of audit restricted by, 49-50
  understanding, 158, 224
**Closely held corporation,** 678
*Code of Professional Conduct,* 16, 19, 47, 51, 52, 68, 75-80, 123, 220, 236, 528
  applicability, 79
  bookkeeping services and audits for the same client, 83
  bylaws, 90
  defined, 75
  definitions, 79-80
  enforcement, 93
  engagement and payment of audit fees by management, 83
  ethical rulings, 79
  **financial interests,** 81-82
  interpretation of, 77-78
  litigation between CPA firms and client, 82-83
  maintaining independence, 84-86
  principles, 76-77
  rules of conduct and interpretations, 77-78
  *101,* 44, 78, 79, 80
  *102,* 78, 86
  *201,* 78, 86
  *202,* 78, 87
  *203,* 51, 78, 87
  *301,* 78, 87-88, 236
  *302,* 78, 89
  *501,* 78, 89-90
  *502,* 78, 90
  *503,* 78, 91-92
  *505,* 78, 92
Coding, generalized audit software, 543
**Collusion,** 293
Commissions
  accrued, 567
  expense, 567
  rules of conduct on, 91-92
  sales, 567
**Commitments,** 726
Common law, 107, 110
Communications systems, 529
Competence
  auditor's, 3
  of evidence, 180-81
Competent independent person, 3
Compliance presentations, other, 763-64
Compilation, audit of pricing and, 653-57
**Compilation of financial statements,** 755-57
  with full disclosure, 756
  omitting disclosures, 756
  requirements for, 755-56
  without independence, 757

Compilation and review standards, 16, 753
see also Statements on Standards for Accounting and Review Services (SSARSs)
Completeness, 453, 588
Complex exchange transactions, 8
Complex operating systems, 529
Compliance attestation, 771-72
comparison of requirements for audits, 771-72
conditions for, 772
engagement performance, 772
**Compliance audit,** 5-6, 789-91
OMB Circular A-128, 790-91
Single Audit Act, 788-89, 790-91
Yellow Book, 788-90
defined, 5
Comprehensive basis of accounting, other, 759-60
cash, 759
to comply with requirements of regulatory agency, 759
income tax, 759
modified cash, 759
reporting requirements for, 759-60
Computed precision interval, 512
**Computer upper exception rate (CUER),** 412, 413, 497
Computer
auditing around the, 536-37
auditing with use of the, 537-40
in auditing, 527-54
Computer selection of random numbers, 408-10
Computer service centers, audit of, 548
Computer software, auditor's, 198
Conduct, rules of, AICPA, 75-93
**Confidence level,** 406
Confidence intervals, 506
in statistical inference, 505-06
Confidence limits, 513
**Confidential client information,** 87-88, 109, 111, 125
Confidentiality
*Code of Profession Conduct*, 87
need for, 87-88
exceptions, 88
Confidentiality of working papers, 236
**Confirmation**
AICPA requirements, 456-57
of accounts payable, 594
of accounts receivable, 456-62
analysis of differences, 461
**as audit evidence,** 184
bank, 702-04
**blank form,** 457
control of, 460
decisions, 457-60
drawing conclusions, 462
information frequently confirmed, 185
**negative,** 457, 459
nonresponses, 460-61
**positive,** 457, 458
printing on computer, 544
sample size, 459
timing, 459
**timing differences,** 461
type of, 457-59
vendors' statements and, 594, 596
Continental Vending, 456
Contingent fees, 89
**Contingent liabilities,** 724-26
evaluation of, 626
Continuing education, 16, 21
Contract law, 110
Contracts, 226-27
**Control activities,** 296-300
adequate documents and records, 298-99
authorization, 298
independent checks on performance, 299-300
physical controls, 299
separation of duties, 297-98
**Control environment,** 294-96
assignment of authority and responsibility, 295-96
board of directors or audit committee, 295
commitment to competence, 295
human resource policies and practices, 296
integrity and ethical values, 295
management philosophy and operating style, 295
organizational structure, 295
**Control risk**
assess, 310-13
**assessed,** 305-06
communication of reportable conditions, 313
**defined,** 258
**management letters,** 313
**matrix,** 311
sales, 371-72
transaction-related audit objectives, 310
weaknesses, 310-11
**Controls, EDP,** 533-36
access, 534
**application,** 535
**general,** 533-35
**hardware,** 534
**processing,** 535
Control test deviation, 336
*Cooley on Torts*, 109
**Corporate bylaws,** 226
**Corporate charter,** 226
**Corporate minutes,** 226
**Cost accounting**
audit of, 646-49
**controls,** 646-47
integrated tests of, 658
**records,** 643-44
system, 643
tests of, 647-49
CPA, *see* Certified Public Accountant
CPA examination, 16
**CPA firms,** 11-13, 795-96
activities, 13-14
structure, 14-15
**division of,** 21-23
*CPA Newsletter*, 93
*Credit Alliance*, 114
Credit, granting, 366
Credit memo, 368
CUER, *see* Computed upper exception rate
Current files, 231-34
Customer order, 365
Customer order processing, 365-66
**Cutoff bank statement,** 705
**Cutoff misstatements**
in accounts payable, 594-95
in sales, sales returns and allowances, and cash receipts, 453-55
**Cycles**
**approach** to segmenting an audit, 148-49
relationship among, 149-51

Data
centralization, EDP systems, 531
loss of, 533
reliable, 290, 291
Data base management, 529
Data files, control over access to, 533
**Debit memo,** 583
Debt compliance letters, 763
negative assurance in, 763
Debt obligations and preferred dividends, 200
Debt–paying ability, 198-99
Decision rule
in difference estimation, 513-14
in monetary unit sampling, 500-01
Deduction authorization form, 558
Deeppocket concept of liability, 107
**Defalcation,** 111
in cash receipts, 378
Deloitte & Touche, 542, 543
Depreciation, accumulated, verification of, 619-20
Depreciation expense, verification of, 619
**Detection risk,** 257-58, 304, 307
**Difference estimation,** 506-07
illustration using, 508-14
Direct knowledge of evidence, 181
Disaggregation of planning, 343-44
Disagreements, reporting on, 23
**Disclaimer of opinion,** 45
Discreditable acts, 89-90
Disposals, verification of current year, 617-18
Distributed processing, 529
Dividends, audit of, 685
**Documentation**
**as audit evidence** and, 185-86
sample selection and need for adequate, 426
Documents and records
in acquisition and payment cycle, 581-84
adequate, as component of internal control, 298-99

Documents and records *(cont.)*
adequate, in sales and collection cycle, 371
examination of supporting, 615-17
**internal documents,** 186
in payroll and personnel cycle, 557-60
perpetual, in cost accounting system, 648
physical control over, 299, 534
prenumbered, 372
in sales and collection cycle, 365-69
sales tests of controls and adequate prenumbered, 371-72
shipping, 366
for transferring inventory, 648
unit cost, 648-49
**Dual dated audit report,** 731
Dun and Bradstreet, 193, 380

Economic demand for auditing, 7-10
EDP questionnaire, 536
EDP systems, *see* Electronic data processing systems
**Effectiveness,** 4
in operational auditing, 792
**Efficiency,** 4
in operational auditing, 792
of organization, 291
**Electronic data processing (EDP)** systems, 294, 527-54
complexity of, 528-30
effect on organizations, 531-33
extent of use, 529-30
improved controls, 533
noncomplex, 528-29
*1136 Tenants* v. *Max Rothenberg and Company,* 112
Employee
fraudulent, 562-65
**Engagement checklist, completing,** 733, 735
Engagement completion, 349-50, 723-50
**Engagement letters,** 221-22
Engagement staffing, 222
EPER, *see* Population, estimated exception rate
**Error,** 144
**Error listing,** 536
*Escott et al.* v. *Bar Chris Construction Corporation,* 117
**Ethics**
in business, 70
**defined,** 68-70
difference between CPA and other professionals, 74
ethical conduct in professions, 74
ethical conduct of CPAs, 75
**ethical dilemmas,** 71-73
ethical principles, 69
need for, 68
professional, 67-103
rationalizing unethical behavior, 71
six-step approach, 72-73
why people act unethically, 68
Evaluating results, 268-70
**Evidence,** 177-215
accumulating and evaluating, 3, 147-48, 268-70, 738
application to four evidence decisions, 189
combined effect, 182
**competence of,** 180-81
contrasted with legal and scientific evidence, 178
cost of types, 188-89
decisions, 179-80
**definition,** 3
final accumulation, 731-33
items to select, 179
**mix,** 337-38
nature of, 178-79
persuasiveness and cost, 183
**persuasiveness of,** 180-83
**planning worksheet,** 268, 434, 464
relationship of risk to, 256-57, 267-68
relationship between tests and, 335-337
**relevance of,** 180
reliability of in accounts payable, 595-97
supports auditor's opinion, 733-35
sufficiency of, 181-82, 733
**sufficient,** competent, 20
timeliness, 182
types of audit, 183
working papers, 229-36
Exception, 413
Exception analysis, 418-19, 433
Exception conditions, 414
**Exception rate,** 411
**estimated population,** 413, 416-17, 422
**sample,** 413, 418
**tolerable,** 413, 415, 418, 419
Exceptions
analysis, 418-19
analysis of, in payroll and personnel cycle, 561
analysis of, in sales and collection cycle, 381, 390
Exchange transactions, recording, 8
Existence, 453, 586-87
External auditors
relationship to internal, 786-88
**External documents,** 186
**Expense accounts**
**analysis** in operations audit, 629
tests of details of in payroll and personnel cycle, 567-68

Facilities for EDP systems, 531
Field work standards, 18
File controls, 534
Financial balances, tests of details of, 159-60, 333
Financial forecasts, *see* Forecasts
Financial interests and issues, 81-82
Financial ratios, 198-203
**Financial statement disclosure checklist,** 736-37
Financial statements
assertions by management, 152-53
audit of, 4, 9
compilation of, 755-57
cycles, 148-51
disclosures, 735-37
independent review, 737
information accompanying basic, 762-63
interim, 757-58
not GAAP, 44, 47, 50-52
objective of audit of, 142
prospective, 767-69
review of, 754-55
review of disclosures in, 735-37
and subsequent events, 729-31
Fixed assets, verification of, 613-14
**master file,** 613
**Flowchart,** 308
of sales and collection cycle, 369, 582, 583
**FOB destination,** 595
**FOB origin,** 595
**Forecasts,** 767
Foreign Corrupt Practices Act of 1977, 120-21, 293
Foreseeable users, 115
Foreseen users, 114-15
Form of organization and name, 92
**Fraud**
constructive, 110
**defined,** 110, 144
**fraudulent financial reporting,** 144
in general cash accounts, 706-09
**kiting** as, 707-09
**lapping** as, 380
**misappropriation of assets,** 144
Fraudulent hours, 565
Frequency distribution, 504
*Funds of Funds Limited, The,* v. *Arthur Andersen & Co.,* 111

GAAP, *see* Generally accepted accounting principles
GAAS, *see* Generally accepted auditing standards
GAO, *see* United States General Accounting Office
GAS, *see* Generalized audit software
General cash account, audit of, 699-709
**Generalized audit software (GAS),** 540-42
illustration for accounts receivable, 542-44
uses of, 544
Generally accepted accounting principles (GAAP)
basis other than, 759-60
failure to follow in compilation and review, 755, 756
financial statements not in accordance with, 44, 47-48, 50-52
inconsistent application of, 40-41
Generally accepted auditing standards (GAAS), 17-18
General standards, 18, 86

Going concern
assumption, 732
substantial doubt about, 41-42
Goods
finished, 644
flow in inventory and warehousing cycle, 643-44
process, 643-44
receipt of in acquisition and payment cycle, 582-83
shipping, 366, 645
**Governmental financial auditing,** 788-91
Government auditors, 795
*Government Securities* v. *Alexander Grand & Co.*, 121

Haphazard selection, 407-08
**Hardware controls,** 534
Hillsburg Hardware Company
attributes sampling, 427-34
attributes sampling data sheet, 429, 432
audit procedures, 427
audit program in cash receipts, 387-88
audit program in sales, 386-87
audit program for tests of controls and substantive tests of transactions, 389
comparative trial balance information, 463
computation of ratios for, 202-03
control risk matrix-cash receipts, 385
control risk matrix-sales, 384
cycle approach for, 148-49
design format, 386-88
engagement letter, 223
evidence planning worksheet for accounts receivable, 268, 434, 464
exception analysis, 430, 433
financial statements, 139-40
flowchart of sales and cash receipts, 383
generalize the population, 429-30
internal control questionnaire, 309
internal control system of, 382-90
management assertions and balance-related audit objectives, 157
organization chart, 382
overall test of interest expense, 197
performance format, 389
planning subparts, 228
random selection, 430
sales and collection cycle, 382-90, 462-66
setting preliminary judgment of materiality, 251-252
tolerable misstatement, 252-53
trial balance, 141
*Hochfelder* v. *Ernst & Ernst*, 118
Holding the cash receipts book open, 455
*Howard Sirota* v. *Solitron Devices, Inc.*, 119

**Illegal acts,** 147-48, 739
direct effect, 147
indirect effect, 147
**Imprest payroll account,** 560, 696
**Imprest petty cash fund,** 696-97
Income tax
basis of accounting, 759
**Independence**
aids to maintaining, 84-86
**in appearance,** 80, 84
and *Code of Professional Conduct*, 80-86, 220
of evidence provider, 181
**in fact,** 80, 84
lack of auditor, 52
in mental attitude, 3, 20
unpaid fees, 83
**Independent checks on performance,** 299-300
**Independent registrar,** 683-84
**Independent review,** 737
Information for CPA candidates, 10
**Information and communication,** 300
Information and established criteria, 2
**Information risk,** 7
causes of, 8
reducing, 8-10
shared with management, 9
**Inherent risk,** 219, 258, 261-65
assessing, 264
client motivation, 263
**defined,** 219
initial versus repeat engagement, 263
integrity of management, 263
judgment required, 264
makeup of the population, 264
nature of the client's business, 262
nonroutine transactions, 263
related parties, 263
results of previous audits, 263
susceptibility to defalcation, 264
**Input controls,** EDP, 535
**Inquiry of client as audit evidence,** 187
**Inquiry of client's attorneys,** 726-29
**Institute of Internal Auditors,** 786
Insurance, audit of prepaid, 620-24
**Insurance register,** 620
Integrity and *Code of Professional Conduct*, 69, 86
**Interim financial information, (SAS71) review of,** 757-58
Internal
ratios and percentages, 195, 231
Internal accounting control, *see* Internal control
**Internal auditors,** 7, 794
relationship to external, 786-88
**Internal control**
account balances, 380-81
of accounts payable, 590
in acquisition and payment cycle, 581-82, 583, 584, 617, 618, 620-21
and assessment of control risk, 289-327
assessments and decisions, 305-06
and auditor's concerns, 291-93
and audit tests for cash receipts, 378-80
and audit tests for sales, 369-73
and client's concerns, 290-91
comparison to requirements for audits, 770
components of, 294
control risk, 301-06
design and operation, 304-05
documentation of the understanding, 308-10
in EDP system, 536
effectiveness of control, 181
of general cash accounts, 700-01
inherent limitations in, 293-94
in inventory and warehousing cycle, 643-44, 651, 653-54
key concepts, 293-94
management's responsibility for, 293
of notes payable, 676
**obtaining an understanding,** 301-307, 330
operation of in meeting transaction-related audit objectives, 151-52
over financial reporting, 769-71
in owners' equity, 679, 682-84
of payroll and personnel cycle, 558, 559, 560
over petty cash, 710-11
of prepaid insurance, 620-21
**procedures to obtain an understanding,** 307-10
reasonable assurance, 293
report on, 769-71
size of business in relation to, 301
Study of, 289-328
understanding of, 20, 159, 301-10, 330, 369, 536, 770-71
**Internal control questionnaire,** 309-10
Internal documents, *see* Documents and records
Internal financial auditing, 786-88
standards, 787
**Internal Revenue Service (IRS) agents,** 6-7
Internal verification
as subcomponent of internal control, 299
procedures for sales, 372
International firms, 11-12
Introductory paragraph, 37-38
**Inventory**
**compilation tests,** 645-46, 653-54
coordination of cutoff tests, 594-95
cost allocation of, 649
documentation, 644
flow of, 643-44
integration of tests, 657-59
physical observation, 645, 650-52
**price tests,** 645-46, 653-57
transfer of assets, 645
in transit, 595
valuation, 562-63, 656-57
verification of transfer of, 645

Inventory pricing and compilation, 645-46, 653-56
**Inventory and warehousing cycle**
audit of, 641-71
functions in, 643-44
parts of, 644-46
relationship to other cycles, 594-95, 657-59
IRS, *see* Internal Revenue Service agents
Items to select
in accounts receivable confirmation, 459-60
as audit decision, 179
in inventory observation, 652

**Job cost system,** 643
Job time ticket, 558
*Journal of Accountancy, The,* 16, 19
**Judgmental sampling,** 406

Key controls, *see* Internal control
Key entry, GAS, 543
King Resources, *see Fund of Funds Limited, The,* v. *Arthur Andersen & Co.*

Labor
in inventory and warehousing cycle, 644-45
Lack of duty of perform, 113
**Lapping,** 380
Lead schedule, 232
Ledger, relationship to financial statements, 148-49
**Legal liability,** 106-136
changed environment, 106-07
Letters of recommendation, *see* Management letters
**Letter of representation,** 731, 732-33
**Liabilities**
audit of **accrued,** 624-26
out-of-period, 592-94
**Liability**
assessed proportion, 110
for acts of others, 109
to clients, 111-12
civil under Federal securities laws, 116-20
**contingent,** 724
**criminal,** 121-23
individual CPA's response to, 124-25
joint and several, 110
legal concepts affecting, 109
legal terms, 110
profession's response to, 123-24
recognizing, in acquisition and payment cycle, 583-84
separate and proportionate, 111
to third parties under common law, 113-15
Liability accounts, tests of details of balances
out-of-period, 592-94
payroll-related, 565
Limited and nonresponses for attorneys, 728-29
Liquidity, 199
Local and regional firms, 13
Lower misstatement bonds (LMB), *see* Misstatement bounds

Management
responsibility for financial statements, 142
**risk assessment,** 296
*see also* Fraud; Internal control
Management advisory services, 14
**Management assertions,** 152-53
completeness, 152
existence or occurrence, 152-53
presentation and disclosure, 153
relationship among management assertions and balance-related audit objectives, 157
rights and obligations, 153
valuation or allocation, 153
Management letters, 313, 739-40
when control system not effective, 419
Management representation letter *see* Letters of representation
Manufacturing equipment audit, 613-20
overview of accounts, 613
supporting documents, 615-17
**Materiality,** 45-48, 247-88
**allocation of preliminary estimate to segments,** 252-54
decisions, 47-48
**definition** of, 46, 248-49
effect on type of auditor's report, 45-48, 54-55, 248
evaluation of, 250
factors affecting, 250
guidelines for, 251
measurement limitations, 266-67
other considerations, 265-67
**preliminary judgment of,** 249-52
as relative not absolute concept, 250
**revised judgment of,** 250
in sales returns and allowances, 377
McKesson & Robbins Company, 456, 650-51
*McLean* v. *Alexander,* 119
**Mean-per-unit estimation,** 507
**Microcomputer aided auditing,** 545-47
problems, 537
quality control, 547
software, 545-46
uses, 546-47
Minutes of meetings, 226
**Misstatement**
assumption, 496
**bounds,** 496
errors, 144
EDP systems, 532-33
estimate, 254-55
fraud, 144, 739
material, 248
**projected,** 254-55
tolerable, 252-54, 448, 486
Monetary misstatements, 331
**Monetary unit sampling (MUS),** 492-503
audit uses, 502-03
differences between nonstatistical sampling and, 492-95
formulas for, 514-16
population, 493
sampling unit, 492
tolerable misstatement, 493
**Monitoring,** 300-01
internal audit function, 301
size of business and internal control, 301
Monthly statement, 367, 372
Morris, Robert Associates, 193

**Narrative,** 308
National firms, 12
Negative assurance
in debt compliance letters, 763
inappropriateness in standard short form audit report, 53-54
**Negligence,** 110
**contributory,** 113
gross, 110
ordinary, 110
Nonexistent employee, 564-65
**Nonnegligent performance,** 113
**Nonprobabilistic sample selection,** 407-08
Nonrepresentative sampling, 405
Nonresponses for attorneys, 728-29
Nonsampling error, 405
**Nonsampling risk,** 405
**Nonstatistical sampling,** 405-06
application, fourteen steps of, 412-20
steps for tests of details, 485, 485-92
summary of steps, 419-20
**Notes payable**
audit of, 675-78
**definition,** 675
objectives, 675-76
overview of accounts, 675

Obligations, client's legal, 225-27
**Objectivity,** 76, 78, 86, 181
*Code of Professional Conduct,* 86
**Observation,** 187
**Occurrence rate,** 411
Officers' compensation, 567
Offices, tour of, 224-25
OMB Circular A-128, 790-91
On-line processing, 529
Operating and performance ratios, 200-202
**Operational auditing,** 791-801
auditors, 794-96
competence, 796
economy and efficiency, 795
effectiveness vs efficiency, 792
**functional,** 793
versus fiancial, 791-92
findings, 799-801

**Operational auditing** *(cont.)*
independence, 796
relationship between internal control, 793
versus management, 791
**organizational,** 793
versus performance, 791
phases, 798-99
**program,** 795
**special assignment,** 794
types, 793-94
Operational audits
competence, 796
criteria for evaluating efficiency and effectiveness, 797
independence, 796
who performs, 794-96
Operations, audit of, 626-31
account balances, 629
Opinion paragraph, 39
Other audit, attestation services, and compilation engagements, 751-84
Other audit or limited assurance engagements, 759-64
**Other information in annual reports,** 733
**Output controls,** 535
Owner–manager controls, 301
Owners' equity
audit of, 678-79, 682-85
objectives, 679
overview of accounts, 679

**Parallel simulation,** 539-40
Partner rotation, 22
Payments, tests of, 585, 588, 589
Payroll
accrued taxes on, 567
electronic data processing techniques in, 561
**accrued expenses,** 565
payment of, 560
preparation, 558-59
preparation of tax forms, 560
reconciliation of total, 568
relationship between inventory valuation and, 562-64
summary report, 559
taxes withheld, 566
tax expenses, 568
**tax returns,** 560, 562
tests for nonexistent, 564-65
Payroll bank account, audit of, 710
Payroll check, 560
**Payroll imprest account,** 560
Payroll journal, 559
**Payroll master file,** 559
**Payroll and personnel cycle**
accounts in, 557
analytical procedures, 565
audit of, 555-78
flow of accounting information through, 556
functions in, 557-60
integrated tests of, 657
liability accounts in, 565-68
tests of details of balances, 565-68
tests of controls and substantive tests of transactions in, 560-65
**Peer review,** 23-24, 88
**Permanent files**
contents of, 224, 230-31
*see also* Documents and records
**Perpetual inventory master files,** 644, 647, 648
Personnel
audit of payroll and personnel cycle, 555-78
as subcomponent of internal control, 296
employment and, 557-58
**records,** 558
Petty cash, audit of, 710-11
Physical controls
of cost accounting system, 647-48
over assets and records, 299
**Physical examination** as audit evidence, 184
Physical observation tests, 650, 652-53
relationship of accounts payable cutoff, 594-95
Plan and design audit approach, 158-59
Planning and supervision, adequate, 20, 218
Planning and use of audit risk model, 257
Plants, tour of, 224-25
**Point estimate,** 489-90, 510, 512
Population
deciding on acceptability of, 419, 489-90, 500-01, 513
defining, 414-15, 486
**estimated exception rate,** (EPER), 413, 416-17
rejected, 491-92, 501
*see also* Sample size
Population distributions, 503-06
**Preliminary judgment about materiality,** 249-52
Prepaid expenses audit, 620-24
Prepaid insurance audit, 620-24
**Preplanning,** 220-23
Presentation and disclosure
of accounts receivable, 456
of capital stock, 685
in financial balance sheets, 729-30, 735-37
Pricing
manufactured inventory, 656-57
purchased inventory, 656
Pricing and compilation, audit of, 645-46, 653-57
Private Companies Practice Section, 23-24
Privileged communication, 109
**Privileged information,** 88
**Probabilistic sample selection,** 406, 408-11
**Probability proportion to size sample selection (PPS),** 411
Procedures, *see* Audit procedures
**Process cost system,** 643
Processing controls, 535
Process the goods, 643-44
Professional care, due, 20
Professional Conduct, Code of, *see Code of Professional Conduct*
Professional Oversight Board (AICPA), 23
Professional skepticism, 144
Program, *see* Audit program
**Projections,** 767-68
**Proof of cash,** 707-08
**Proof of cash receipts,** 378
Property taxes, audit of accrued, 624-26
**Prospective financial statements,** 767-69
**examination** of, 768-69
**forecasts** and **projections,** 767-68
types of engagements, 768
use of, 768
**Prudent person concept,** 109
Public accounting, 6, 80
**Publicly held corporation,** 678
**Purchase order,** 581
in inventory and warehousing cycle, 643
processing, 581-82, 643
**Purchase requisition,** 581, 643

Qualifications of evidence provider, 181
**Qualified opinion,** 45
**Quality control**
**defined,** 21-24
division of CPA firms, 21-23
elements of, 21-22
peer review, 23
as required by SAS, 18
Quality Control Standards Committee, 21
Questionnaire
EDP, 536
internal control, 309-10

**Racketeer Influenced and Corrupt Organization Act,** 120
*Random Decimal Digits, Table of 105,000,* 409
**Random number table,** 408-09, 467
documentation, 410
**Random sample**
**defined,** 408
for testing sales, 430
Random selection, 408
distinction between statistical measurement and, 426
by use of computer, 408
Rate authorization form, 558
**Ratio estimation,** 507
Ratios, financial, 198-203
Raw materials, 643, 644-45
Realizable value of accounts receivable, 455-56
Reasonableness test, 233
**Receiving report**
in acquisition and payment cycle, 582
Reclassification entries, 233

Recognition of liability, 583-84
**Reconciliation of amounts schedules,** 233
Recording cash disbursements, 584
Recording sales, 367
Record-keeping systems, 298-99
Records, *see* Documents and records
**Related party transaction,** 225, 263
  **defined,** 225
Reliability
  of types of evidence, 187
  of evidence in verifying accounts payable, 595-97
Remittance advice, 368
Remoteness of information, 8
**Reperformance,** 187-88
Replacement sampling, 409
Reporting standards, 18, 20
Reports
  **audit** 3
  compilation, 755-57
  debt compliance, 763-64
  forecasts, 767-69
  of GAS, 543
  on information accompanying financial statements, 762-63
  on internal control, 769-71
  other compliance presentations, 763
  on other comprehensive basis of accounting, 759-60
  under provisions of securities acts, 116-21
  review of interim financial information, 757-58
  of specified elements, accounts, or items, 760-61
  unaudited, 753
**Reportable conditions,** 313, 739
**Representative sample,** 404-05
Research
  by AICPA, 16
  in auditing, 123
Responsibilities
  to clients, 124
  for confidentiality, 87-88, 109, 111, 125
*Restatement of Torts,* 114
Retained earnings, audit of, 686
**Review**
  engagement, 754
  failure to follow GAAP, 755, 758
  of financial statements, 754-55
  form of report for, 754
  interim financial information, 757-58
  SAS 71 (AU 722), 757
  services, 13, 752-55
  **for subsequent events,** 729
  suggested procedures, 754
Rights to accounts receivable, 456
**Risk,** 247-88
  **acceptable audit,** 218, 259-61
  **assessment,** 296
  audit, 255-61
  business, 7, 259-60
  control, 258-59, 310-13
  **definition,** 255
  detection, 257-58
  factors affecting, 257-64
  of incorrect acceptance, 486-88, 507, 509
  information, 8-10
  inherent, 219, 258, 261-65
  revision, 270-71
  sampling, 405, 412, 507-08
  summary of, 264-65
Risk-free interest rate, 7
Rules of conduct, *see Code of Professional Conduct*
*Rusch Factors* v. *Levin,* 115

Salaries and wages, accrued, 566
**Sales and collection cycle,** 363-402
  accounts in, 364-65
  **business functions in,** 365-69
  **classes of transactions,** 366
  completing tests in, 445-81
  documents and records in, 365-69
  flow of accounting information in, 365-69
  integrated tests of, 658
  internal controls for, 369-72
  nature of, 365
  overview of, 364-65
Sales invoice, 367
Sales journal, 367
Sales order, 366
Sales returns and allowances, 368, 377
Sales returns and allowances journal, 368
Sample
  generalize to the population, 418, 489-90, 510-13
  generalizing when misstatements found, 496-500
  generalizing when no misstatements found, 495-96
  random, 408-10
  select, 417, 488
  *see also* Sample selection, Sample size, *and* Sampling
**Sample exception rate (SER),** 413, 418
**Sample selection**
  **block,** 407
  **directed,** 407
  **haphazard,** 407
  **judgmental,** 406
  nonprobabilistic, 407-08
  probabilistic, 408-11
  probability proportional to size (PPS), 411
  **random,** 408-10
  **representative,** 404-05
  **systematic,** 411
  using computer, 408-10, 544
Sample size
  audit decision, 179
  case illustrating determination of, 427-34
  confirmation of accounts receivable and, 459
  determination of, using attributes sampling, 422-24
  determination of, using difference estimation, 509-10
  determining initial, 417, 488, 501-02
  effect of changing factors on, 417
  for accounts payable, 597
  for monetary unit sampling, 501-02
  and physical observation of inventory, 652
  proper, as audit decision, 179
  *see also* Population size
Sampling
  attributes and exception conditions, 414
  define the population, 414-15, 486
  for exception rates, 411-12
  misstatement conditions, 486
  need for professional judgment, 426
  objectives of audit test, 413, 485
  random selection versus statistical measurement, 426
  replacement versus nonreplacement, 409
  sampling unit, 415, 486
  statistical versus nonstatistical, 405-06
  tolerable misstatement, 486
**Sampling distributions,** 421-22, 503-05
**Sampling error,** 254-55, 412
**Sampling risk,** 405, 412, 507-08
Sampling unit, defining, 415, 486
SASs
  SAS 1 (AU 110), 142
    (AU 220), 123
    (AU 331), 651
    (AU 530), 731
    (AU 560), 117, 729
    (AU 561), 88
  SAS 7 (AU 315), 84, 122, 220
  SAS 8 (AU 550), 733
  SAS 12 (AU 337), 729
  SAS 19 (AU 333), 123, 732
  SAS 21 (AU 435), 224
  SAS 22 (AU 311), 103, 158
  SAS 25 (AU 161), 21
  SAS 29 (AU 551), 762
  SAS 31 (AU 326), 152
  SAS 32 (AU 431.02), 737
  SAS 39 (AU 350), 252, 257, 404, 512
  SAS 41 (AU 339), 229
  SAS 45 (AU 334), 123, 225
  SAS 47 (AU 312), 113, 249, 257, 269
  SAS 50 (AU 625), 85
  SAS 54 (AU 317), 147, 739
  SAS 55 (AU 319), 290, 302
  SAS 56 (AU 329), 190
  SAS 58 (AU 508), 52
  SAS 59 (AU 341), 41-42, 732
  SAS 60 (AU 325), 313, 739
  SAS 61 (AU 380), 739
  SAS 62 (AU 623), 759, 760
  SAS 65 (AU 322), 301, 788
  SAS 67 (AU 330), 184, 457, 460
  SAS 71 (AU 722), 757-58
  SAS 73 (AU 336), 225
  SAS 74 (AU 801), 753

SASs *(cont.)*
SAS 75, 773
SAS 78 (AU 319), 290, 302
*see also* Statements on Auditing Standards
SAS 82 (AU 316), 113, 145, 144-47
Scope limitations, 44, 49-50
Scope paragraph, 38
SER, *see* Sample exception rate
SEC
Practice Section, 21, 123
*see also* Securities and Exchange Commission
**Securities Act of 1933,** 116
requirements of, 24-25
Securities Acts, Uniform, 121
**Securities Exchange Act of 1934,** 116-120, 291
auditor defenses, 120
**Securities and Exchange Commission (SEC),** 24-25, 107, 116-20, 291, 757, 762
*Accounting Series Releases*, 25
forms, 24
overall purposes, 24
*Regulation* S-X, 25
reports, 24, 116-17
Rule 2(e), 120
Rule 10(b)-5, 117-120
sanctions by, 120
Segmenting audit, 148-49
**Separation of duties,** 297-98
in EDP systems, 531
in sales, 371
SFAS, *see* Statements of Financial Accounting Standards
Shipping document, 366
Sick pay, accrued, 567
**Single Audit Act,** 788-89
audit and reporting requirements, 789-90
guidance for auditors, 791
OMB Circular 87, 790
OMB Circular 102, 790
OMB Circular A-128, 790-91
Solicitation, 90-91
*Solitron Devices* case, 119
Specialist, need for, 225
Specified elements, accounts, or items, 760-61
SSARS, *see* Statements on Standards for Accounting and Review Services
Staffing for EDP systems, 531
Standard Bank Confirmation Form, 702-05
**Standards for the Professional Practice of Internal Auditing,** 787
State Board of Accountancy, 93
**Standard cost records,** 657
Statements on Attestation Standards, 764
**Statements on Auditing Standards** (SASs), 18-20
Statements on Standards for Accounting and Review Services **(SSARSs),** 16, 753
Statistical techniques, 196-97
**Statistical inference,** 505-06
random selection distinguished from statistical measurement, 426
**Statistical sampling,** 405-06
Statistical tables
determining sample size, 422-23
use of, 422-23, 424-25
**Statutory law,** 110
**Stock transfer agent,** 684
Storage of finished goods, 644
Storage of raw materials, 643
**Stratified sampling,** 486, 507
Subsequent discovery of facts, 740-41
**Subsequent events,** 729-31
**Substantive tests**
reduction of detailed tests, 191-92
relationship between tests of controls and, 336
relative cost of, 335-36
**of transactions defined,** 331
Successor auditor, responsibilities of, 220
Summary acquisitions report, 583
Summary sales report, 367
Supporting schedules, 233-34
Systematic sampling, 411
Systems, EDP, 527-54

Tax services, 14
TER, *see* Tolerable exception rate
Technical standards, 86-87
Technical training and proficiency, adequate, 20
**Test data approach,** 538-39
Testing, *see specific tests*
**Tests of controls,** 306-07, 313-316, 331
**defined,** 306
extent of procedures, 315
procedures for, 314-15
relationship between substantive tests and, 336
relationship to procedures to obtain an understanding, 315-16
relative cost of, 372
**Tests of controls and substantive tests of transactions,** 159
for acquisition and payment cycle, 584-90
in audit program, 339-40, 396
for capital stock and paid-in capital, 684
for cash receipts, 378-80
four-step approach to design, 340
effect of results in sales and collection cycle, 381
for notes payable, 676-77
of operations audit, 628-29
for payroll and personnel cycle, 560-65
phase of audit, 346-50
relationship to evidence, 335-37
relationship between tests of controls and substantive tests, 336
for sales, 369-76
for sales and collection cycle, 449
trade-off between tests of controls and substantive tests, 336-37
**Tests of details**
audit sampling for, 483-525
**of balances,** 159-60, 333, 341-43
of balances in accounts payable, 592-97
of balances for accounts receivable, 446-62
of balances for capital stock and paid-in capital, 684-85
of balances in inventory, 649-50, 654-55
of balances for manufacturing equipment, 615
of balances in notes payable, 677-78
of balances in payroll and personnel cycle, 565-68
of balances worksheet, 267
for general cash in bank, 701-06
sample size, 488, 501-02
Third-party beneficiary, 110
**Time card,** 558
Timekeeping, 558-59
**Timeliness of evidence,** 182
Timing
as audit decision, 179, 192
confirmation of accounts receivable and, 459
and physical observation of inventory, 652
**Tolerable exception rate (TER),** 413, 415, 418, 419
guidelines for establishing, 415
revision of, 419
**Tolerable misstatement,** 252-54, 486
to balance-related audit objectives, 266
Transaction cycles, 148-51
relationship of cash to, 698
**Transaction-related audit objectives,** 153-54
accuracy, 154
for acquisition and payment cycle, 586-90
for acquisitions, 587
for cash disbursements, 589
for cash receipts, 379
classification, 154
completeness, 153
existence, 153
**general,** 153
meeting, 157-60
posting and summarization, 154
relationship to balance-related audit objectives, 449
**for sales,** 370, 373-76
segmenting, 148-51
setting, 151-52
**specific,** 154
timing, 154
Transaction trail
effect of EDP on, 532
visibility of, 532

Transaction walk-through, 304
**Trial balance (list),** 233
Trial balance
 working papers and, 233

*Ultramares Corporation* v. *Touche,* 113-14
***Ultramares* doctrine,** 113-14
**Unadjusted misstatement worksheet,** 735, 736
**Unasserted claim,** 726, 728
Unaudited financial statements, 753
Uncollectible account authorization form, 368
Uncollectible accounts, 368, 380, 455
Uniform Securities Acts, 121
Unit cost records, 648
United States General Accounting Office (GAO), 6
United States General Auditing Office, (GAO), 788
*United States* v. *Natelli,* 121
*United States* v. *Simon,* 122
*United States* v. *Weiner,* 121
**Unusual fluctuations,** 191
Upper misstatement bounds (UMB), *see* Misstatement bounds

Vacation pay, accrued, 567
**Variables sampling,** 503-08
 differences between nonstatistical sampling and, 503
**Vendor's invoice,** 583, 595
**Vendor's statement,** 584, 595-96
Verification
 of accrued liabilities, 624-26
 of asset balance, 618-19
 of current-year acquisitions, 614-15
 of current-year disposals, 617-18
 of prepaid expenses, 620-24
Visibility
 of input data, 532
 of processing, 532
 of transaction trail, 532
Voluminous data, 8
Voucher, 583
**Vouching,** *see* Documentation, 186

W2 form, 560
**Weaknesses, internal control,** 310
 fourstep identification method, 311
 identify and evaluate, 310-11
 required communication of material, 313
**Working paper review,** 737
**Working papers,** 229-36
 confidentiality of, 236
 contents and organization, 230
 **current files,** 231-34
 ownership of, 236
 **permanent files,** 224, 230-31
 preparation of, 234
 purposes, 229-30
**Working trial balance,** 232

Year-end cash, audit procedures, 701-706
***Yellow Book, (GAS),*** 788-91
 materiality and significance, 789
 quality control, 789
 legal and regulatory requirements, 789
 working papers, 789